BATAAN:
OUR LAST DITCH

BATAAN:
OUR LAST DITCH
The Bataan
Campaign, 1942

John W. Whitman

HIPPOCRENE BOOKS
New York

The views expressed in this book are those of the author and do not
reflect the official policy or position of the Department of the Army,
Department of Defense, or the U.S. Government.

For information, contact:
HIPPOCRENE BOOKS, INC.
171 Madison Avenue
New York, NY 10016

Library of Congress Cataloging-in-Publication Data

Whitman, John W.
    Bataan, our last ditch : the Bataan campaign, 1942 / John W.
Whitman.
        p.   cm.
    Includes bibliographical references and index.
    ISBN 0-87052-877-7
    1. World War, 1939–1945—Campaigns—Philippines—Bataan (Province)
2. Bataan (Philippines : Province)—History.   I. Title.
D767.4.W48   1991
940.54'25—dc20   90-42626
                                                         CIP

Printed in the United States of America

To
The Philippine Scouts
The finest soldiers in the Philippines

The author is grateful to the following publishers and companies for permission to reprint excerpts from material as noted below. Direct quotations retain the original grammer, spelling, and style.

Armor Magazine for "26th Cavalry (PS) Battles To Glory" by William E. Chandler, in *Armored Cavalry Journal*, copyright 1947, and "Rearguard in Luzon" by John Wheeler, in *The Cavalry Journal*, copyright 1943, both reprinted by permission of *Armor Magazine*.

Curtis Brown, Ltd., for *South From Corregidor* by John Morrill and Pete Martin, reprinted by permission of Curtis Brown, Ltd., Copyright 1943, 1971 by author.

Doubleday, for *General Wainwright's Story* by Jonathan M. Wainwright, copyright 1946 by Jonathan M. Wainwright. Used by permission of Doubleday, a division of Bantam, Doubleday, Dell Publishing Group, Inc.

E. P. Dutton, for *The Good Fight* by Manuel Luis Quezon. Copyright © 1974, 1946 by Aurora A. Quezon. A Hawthorn Book. Reprinted by permission of Dutton, an imprint of New American Library, a division of Penguin Books USA Inc.

Stanley L. Falk, for *Bataan. The March of Death* by Stanley L. Falk. Copyright © 1962, by Stanley L. Falk. Reprinted by permission of the author and his agent Blanche C. Gregory, Inc.

Houghton Mifflin Company, for excerpt from *The Years of MacArthur*, Vol. I, by D. Clayton James. Copyright © 1970 by D. Clayton James. Reprinted by permission of Houghton Mifflin Company.

Alfred A. Knopf, for *Men on Bataan* by John Hersey. Copyright 1942, used by permission of Alfred A. Knopf.

Macmillan Publishing Company, for *War to the Death. The Sieges of Saragossa, 1808–1809* by Raymond Rudorff. Copyright © 1974 by Raymond Rudorff. Reprinted by permission of Macmillan Publishing Company.

The Marine Corps Gazette, for "Naval Battalion at Mariveles" by William F. Prickett. Reprinted by permission of *The Marine Corps Gazette*.

McGraw-Hill Book Co., for *Reminiscences* by General of the Army Douglas MacArthur, McGraw-Hill Book Co., © 1964 Time Inc. Reprinted with permission.

Samuel B. Moody and Maury Allen, for *Reprieve from Hell*, copyright 1961 by Samuel B. Moody and Maury Allen. Reprinted by permission of the author.

W. W. Norton & Company, Inc., for *We Remained: Three Years Behind the Enemy Lines in the Philippines* by Russell W. Volckmann. Copyright 1954 by W. W. Norton & Company, Inc., copyright renewed 1982 by Colonel R. W. Volckmann. Reprinted with permission from the publisher.

Alvin C. Poweleit, for *USAFFE. A Saga of Atrocities Perpetrated During the Fall of the Philippines, the Bataan Death March, and Japanese Imprisonment and Survival* by Alvin C. Poweleit. Copyright 1975. Reprinted by permission of the author.

Presidio Press, for *The Naked Flagpole* by Richard C. Mallonee, II, editor. Copyright 1980. Reprinted by permission of Presidio Press.

The Putnam Publishing Group, for *The Dyess Story: The Eye-Witness Account of the DEATH MARCH FROM BATAAN and the Narrative of Experiences in Japanese Prison Camps and of Eventual Escape* by William E. Dyess. Copyright 1944 by Marajen Stevick Dyess. Reprinted by permission of the publisher.

Random House, Inc., for *The Rising Sun* by John Toland. Copyright © 1970 by John Toland. Reprinted by permission of Random House, Inc., and *But Not in Shame*, by John Toland. Copyright © 1961 by John Toland. Reprinted by permission of Random House, Inc.

Texas A & M University Press, for excerpts from *Bataan and Beyond: Memories of an American POW* by John S. Coleman, Jr. Copyright John S. Coleman, Jr., 1978, used by permission of Texas A & M University Press.

Contents

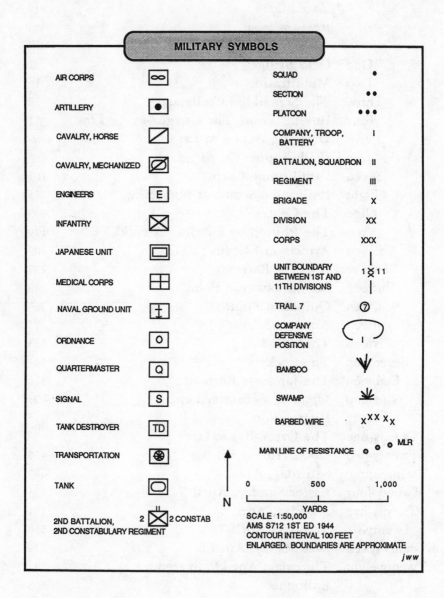

MILITARY SYMBOLS

AIR CORPS

ARTILLERY

CAVALRY, HORSE

CAVALRY, MECHANIZED

ENGINEERS

INFANTRY

JAPANESE UNIT

MEDICAL CORPS

NAVAL GROUND UNIT

ORDNANCE

QUARTERMASTER

SIGNAL

TANK DESTROYER

TRANSPORTATION

TANK

2ND BATTALION,
2ND CONSTABULARY REGIMENT

2 CONSTAB

SQUAD

SECTION

PLATOON

COMPANY, TROOP,
    BATTERY   I

BATTALION, SQUADRON   II

REGIMENT   III

BRIGADE   X

DIVISION   XX

CORPS   XXX

UNIT BOUNDARY
BETWEEN 1ST AND   1   11
11TH DIVISIONS

TRAIL 7

COMPANY
DEFENSIVE
POSITION

BAMBOO

SWAMP

BARBED WIRE

MAIN LINE OF RESISTANCE   MLR

N

0   500   1,000
                    YARDS
SCALE 1:50,000
AMS S712 1ST ED 1944
CONTOUR INTERVAL 100 FEET
ENLARGED. BOUNDARIES ARE APPROXIMATE
j w w

List of Maps

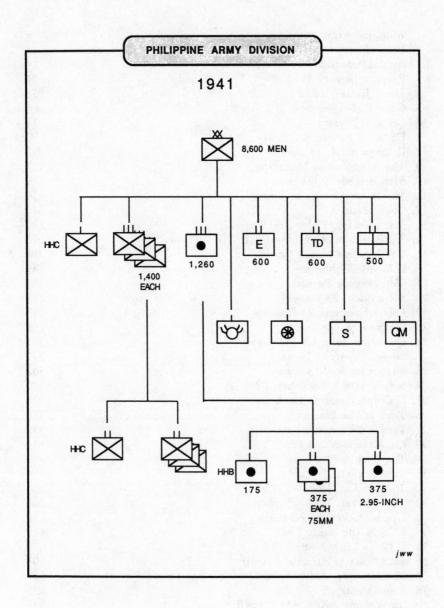

PHILIPPINE ARMY DIVISION

1941

8,600 MEN

HHC
1,400 EACH
1,260
E 600
TD 600
500

HHB 175
375 EACH 75MM
375 2.95-INCH

jww

Acknowledgments

The author owes his most heartfelt thanks first and foremost to the Bataan veterans who gave so freely of their time answering questions. Without their help this book could not have been written.

In particular, the assistance offered by Lieutenant Colonel Franklin O. Anders U.S. Army (retired), a veteran of the Scout 57th Infantry, is of the type researchers dream about but seldom receive. His help has been indisputably the most valuable, most voluminous, most interesting received during my eighteen years of research. Beginning in 1974 and concluding in 1989, Colonel Anders's correspondence has exceeded one thousand pages, single-spaced typed. His letters often ran twenty to thirty pages of detailed recollections that could inspire only awe at his memory and delight at his willingness to spend the time committing it to paper. I have found no more responsive, exact, and thorough contributor to this book. To him I offer my deep appreciation and sincere respect.

The number of other contributors precludes individual acknowledgments. More than three hundred Bataan veterans offered information that was used in preparing this history. Each is due my thanks, and I have mentioned as many names as the narrative could bear. It is my small thanks to the men who fought for us on an impossible battlefield. From unpublished manuscripts sent to me, to short letters answering specific questions, to the thousands of letters, cassette tapes, and interviews, these men and their experiences add life to this book. Interviewing and corresponding with these veterans was the most interesting and rewarding part of my research. These men were interested in telling their stories, and the sum of those stories is the history of the Bataan campaign.

My thanks also go to Dr. Richard J. Sommers, archivist-historian at the U.S. Army Military History Institute, Carlisle Barracks, Pennsylvania. From my first trip there to a funded two-week research period as an Advanced Research Fellow to several follow-up visits, Dr. Sommers has been a perfect host and gracious guide through the collection of Bataan documents. Frequent reference to his Civil War classic, *Richmond Redeemed*, also showed me how quality history is written.

I have had ample time to ensure the accuracy of this book; therefore, all errors are mine.

Preface

The battle for Bataan can be described as the last battle of World War I and the first battle of World War II. It used weapons only marginally improved from WWI and, therefore, tactics not unfamiliar to First War veterans. Yet the use of airpower, tanks, and mechanization placed Bataan in a newer time. For this reason, among many others, it is worthy of study. It was a "come-as-you-are" war, one that was fought with the men and materiel on hand, unreinforced (on the American side) by better-trained men with evolutionary or revolutionary new weapons. It was a battle that involved relatively few troops (when compared to later campaigns) and one that pitted untried soldiers of both nations against one another. Especially interesting was the employment of untrained Filipinos led by Americans.

It was America's first battle of World War II and because it ended in disaster, and because few men escaped to carry the tale to American citizens, it slipped into obscurity as better news of bigger battles drew the attention of correspondents, and later of historians. Surprisingly, there is not a single campaign study covering Bataan other than the Army's official history, *The Fall of the Philippines*. There are many books about specific units or people on Bataan but no true campaign study. This book is such a study, a history that covers ground, air, and sea action as well as command, supply, tactics, and doctrine as they pertained to Bataan.

Although a true study of the entire Philippine campaign would include actions on Luzon from the invasion through the battles on Bataan and into Corregidor, I have avoided the Luzon invasion and initial delaying actions as they would significantly increase the size of the book but not necessarily add to an understanding of the actions on Bataan. I have also avoided detailed discussion of the world situation, the political situation, and of activities related to, but not important to, the Bataan campaign.

xiii

Such information is available at the level where giants trod, with MacArthur, Marshall, Roosevelt, King, et al.

Each chapter of this book has a different flavor, often based on the availability of sources. In some chapters I have described the fighting at regimental and higher levels simply because there are few sources, especially individual recollections. In such cases the Army's official history was my guide. In other places I describe the fighting down to the individual soldier, mainly because I have found and interviewed participants. These are the most fascinating areas of the book, the portions where the average soldier provided the information.

In the public's eye there are only a few events worthy of note about the Philippines in World War II. There was MacArthur leaving the Philippines on a PT boat, there was the Death March, and there was Corregidor. Corregidor, in fact, stands for the entire campaign; few people know that Bataan preceded Corregidor. This book recounts the battle for Bataan and elevates that campaign into its rightful place in history.

CHAPTER ONE

Culo Bridge

A STIFLING HEAT COVERED THE BUS STOP AT LAYAC JUNCTION JUST north of the Culo River. The intersection of National Highways 7 and 110 held a tiny point on road maps between two small towns, Dinalupihan and Culis. On this warm evening Layac Junction was about to close its twenty-ninth day of war. Two days earlier, the first whispers of artillery had civilians looking north, and the unsettling noise became more audible as the days passed. Starting slowly, the flow of traffic rose day by day through Christmas Eve, into Christmas Day, and toward the new year.

For the past week Filipinos peering from their nipa and wooden huts along Highway 110 witnessed a sight never before seen in the Philippines. Mile-long columns of dust-covered, denim-clad, dull-eyed men filled the narrow road for hours at a time. Staff cars and scout cars, sedans and buses, trucks and ten-ton wreckers, tractors and tiny taxis, artillery prime movers and huge earthmoving equipment thundered their noxious way south toward Bataan. The din of engines, shrill shouts, and occasional bomb blasts numbed bystanders. Speed limits, stop signs, and ineffective efforts by a few military police to control the traffic were all ignored.

Through Layac Junction came Americans and Filipinos, khaki and blue denim, boots and tennis shoes, cavalry and tanks, infantry and artillery, airmen and supplymen, civilian refugees and military deserters, two-wheeled Filipino carts pulled by frothing ponies, and dusty-gray carabao loaded with family possessions. Dilapidated civilian trucks piled high with mattresses, cooped chickens, and trussed pigs dodged cannon-carrying half-tracks in the frantic drive south. Bumper to bumper, truck to

1

truck, it was a sight unmatched anywhere else that January 5 of 1942. Filipino recruits with two weeks' training who did not understand English, American officers who could not speak Tagalog, Filipino officers who could not talk to their sergeants, sergeants who could neither read nor write, and staunch Philippine Scouts—as well-trained and disciplined as any soldier in history—matched pace with light artillery obsolete in 1914. Three-quarter-ton trucks, lacking tow pintles and tie chains, jerked south pulling 75mm cannon tied with plaited straw or uniform belts, cannon which periodically broke loose and rolled into ditches. Modern General Stuart light tanks scarred the road trod only minutes before by barefoot draftees carrying broken bolt-action rifles.[1]

Failing to draw a single glance or a casual comment, abandoned gear—civilian and military—lay alongside the road. Empty rations cans with food residue drawing flies, worn-out tennis shoes, and cast-off clothing lay scattered alongside broken buses and overturned trucks. North of Layac Junction stood two yellow Pampanga Bus Company buses which from a distance seemed to hold sleeping Filipinos. Only upon closer examination did men note the soldiers were dead and the vehicles riddled from air attacks. Huge swarms of flies made the air around the buses shimmer. Occasional wisps of black smoke rose from smoldering sugar-cane fields and burning truck tires. Already, food was growing scarce as mango and papaya trees lost their fruit to the passing flood.[2]

Closer to Layac Junction six broken bodies in civilian clothes sprawled in a ditch. Earlier a Filipino refugee had stopped to tell Americans that Japanese carrying gunny sacks and wearing civilian clothes were coming to blow up the Culo Bridge. Waiting with the Americans, the Filipino pointed to six men. With raised Tommy guns, the Americans stopped the small group and asked about the bags. "Provisions," came the broken English reply, but when the bags were opened and disgorged sticks of dynamite the men then claimed to be Filipinos hoping to dynamite fish in the river. "They're Japs, not Filipinos," insisted the informant. The Americans held a quick discussion, turned back to the men, and killed them in a fast burst of fire.

Justice, if that word can be used, was equally swift at San Fernando. When an American military police detachment received word that Filipinos were trying to burn railroad cars containing ammunition and supplies, they hurried to the town and saw twenty men near an ammunition train and another twelve near some tank cars. The Filipinos scattered, but the MPs caught eleven. After searching the area, they found piles of kindling and dry grass under both the box and tank cars. The Filipinos admitted they were socialists but denied they had anything to do with the sabotage. The Americans turned the suspects over to a constabulary lieutenant. Barely a half-hour later the MPs heard shots from the vicinity of the railroad yards. The constabulary lieutenant had interrogated the men, lined them up against the wall of a coal shed, and had them shot.[3]

Scattered along roads running south into Bataan were lonely, forlorn pockets of American antiaircraft guns, 3-inch and 37mm guns too short-ranged to reach the high-flying Japanese bombers passing freely and contemptuously overhead. Range deficiencies really did not matter, for there were far too few guns to bother even low-flying strafers. Once night fell the gunners, generator operators, and rangefinders—mostly New Mexico State National Guardsmen—ate and slept. The Japanese did not fly at night so the men stood down.

Before 1942 Layac Junction had never been of any great importance. It had a small rain shelter for bus passengers and once had three road signs on cement posts, dismantled now to confuse enemy infiltrators. Insignificant as it had been, holding it now from the Japanese and keeping the river of men and equipment flowing south was the only way immediate and catastrophic defeat could be delayed, if not totally averted. There were thousands of men and hundreds of vehicles still miles north of the junction, while safety, transient as it might be, lay to the south. Ever since December 23, trucks from supply organizations and tactical units clogged the road going south and now, as the last flashes of the setting sun disappeared the flow peaked.[4]

Five hours before midnight of that twenty-ninth day of the war, glum civilians peered once more from grass-fringed windows and doorways. Their young men were in the Army and little had been heard from them. Rumors of Japanese successes shook morale and when MacArthur declared Manila an open city, the rumors of disaster were confirmed. The early evening had been free for a few moments of large numbers of vehicles, but just to the north two Philippine Army infantry divisions were nervously looking north and awaiting the concealing cloak of darkness. When the sky dimmed and enemy planes disappeared the roads north of Layac Junction filled with soldiers. Now could be heard the soft, muffled rustle of hundreds, then thousands of men, their bare or rubber-soled feet playing a background bass to the creak, clink, and clatter of canteens and cloth, leather and leggings. Those men who knew their location, and those who knew their destination, looked forward to one more long night's march to safety, sleep, and food. Most men cared little of their situation for they were too exhausted. "It was a tired mass of people," recalled Lieutenant Colonel Lee C. Vance, a veteran of the 1916 Mexico border incursion and service with the 1st Division in World War I, and now executive officer to the Philippine Scout 26th Cavalry. "They were just barely dragging along. They would stop and move, and stop again. We just herded them along as best we could. When they stopped, I had the scout cars fire a few shots in the air and they would move on."5

If nearby civilians had asked, they would have learned that this long column limping by, absolutely devoid of energy, belonged to the 11th Philippine Infantry Division, its combat history consisting of fifteen days of uninterrupted defeat and retreat. Only the night before a tank officer, Lieutenant Theodore I. Spaulding, found a huge 11th Division column "sound asleep from absolute exhaustion. I've never seen such a pitiful sight in my life. They had dead bodies tied on the back of their vehicles. They were all dirty, they hadn't eaten for many meals, and every single soul in that whole column was dead to the world."6 It took nearly two hours to wake everyone and send them on their way south, toward Bataan. They were beaten; they were hunted; they were dead on their feet and peered from drawn faces and sunken eyes; but they were still soldiers, and they were under control. Marching in the opposite direction, toward the Japanese, was a battalion of infantry from the 21st Division, hurrying to cover the 11th Division's withdrawal. If the men of the newly mobilized 11th Division had been alert, they would have seen shadowy figures sitting and sleeping on both sides of the road. Filipinos of the equally exhausted 21st Division sprawled at the junction of the two roads, waiting stoically for the 11th Division to clear the road.

Coming up from the south, 58-year-old Major General Jonathan M. Wainwright, North Luzon Force Commander, drove up to the Culo Bridge with his engineer officer, Colonel Harry A. Skerry. Wainwright, a tall, lean, hard-drinking cavalryman of the old school, an officer utterly without personal fear who could not tolerate mentally slow associates, dismounted and watched the 11th Division shuffle south. For ninety minutes three regiments of Filipino infantry, wearing a wild assortment of uniforms, plodded past the two officers. When the press of humanity diminished and finally stopped the 11th Division's chief of staff, Lieutenant Colonel Juan S. Moran, told Wainwright his division was clear of both Layac Junction and the Culo Bridge. The 11th Division was in Bataan!7

With that report, Colonel Ray M. O'Day, senior American instructor for Brigadier General Mateo M. Capinpin's 21st Division, found it was "now our turn to enter the promised land."8 O'Day gave the orders and just after 2030 hours, officers and sergeants shook their men awake and pushed them into march order. The division's vehicles roared to life and the milling crowd spilled onto the moonlit road. Drivers looked forward with slight enthusiasm to several more hours of blackout driving on ruined, potholed, bomb-racked roads. Joined by a dozen military command and staff cars, the collection of civilian vehicles pressed into service made the area look like "the parking lot of the Yale Bowl," and the roads were once more buried under heavy foot and motor traffic.[9] Men bunched in Napoleonic masses as if afraid they would be left behind, yet despite their obvious disorganization, they were quiet and orderly.

As the 21st Division passed through Layac Junction and reached the Culo River, the ground suddenly dropped away and the men found themselves walking on the heavy concrete flooring of a steel-truss-span highway bridge. Next to it stretched a smaller railroad trestle. Trucks shuttling infantry and towing artillery rolled across the short Culo Bridge, and minute after minute men and machines marched south. Proper distance between elements did not exist; platoons, companies, and battalions all pressed hard together. The last 75mm cannon of the 21st Division's artillery regiment cleared the bridge's south end at midnight.[10]

With the bridge now empty of vehicles, General Capinpin's infantry struggled into sight carrying loads of equipment and personal belongings. Some two-man teams shouldered clothes, shoes, and chickens slung from bamboo poles. The men had been on their feet and marching a long time, since dark the night before. Conflicting orders and inept commands kept the 21st Division surging forward and backward for nearly twenty-four continuous hours, and the effort had told. General Capinpin, a short, stout, long-term Philippine Scout officer who habitually told his soldiers he would shoot them if they did not do this thing or that thing, was beside himself with anger at the slow pace of his soldiers. He hurried along the column, kicking the men and urging haste. Wainwright, watching the procession stagger past with Capinpin nipping at its flanks, called jestingly, "How many men have you shot today, Matty?"[11]

At midnight, Wainwright and O'Day heard the distinctive sound of horses' hooves on pavement, the welcome sign that the rear guard 26th Cavalry was nearing the bridge. To Colonel O'Day, it also meant his men from the left were in, so he sent word to his units on the right to pull back to the bridge. But when Colonel Clinton A. Pierce's cavalrymen arrived, Pierce, a hard-riding, hard-hitting energetic officer, told O'Day he had passed two battalions of the 21st Division halted for a rest. Passing the infantry was against the cavalry's orders and left a route open to the enemy, and the two colonels argued until Wainwright interrupted. Wainwright was a decision maker, a man who did not hesitate or equivocate when called upon to take action. He had a mind like the proverbial steel trap and acted just as quickly. He had already decided in favor of O'Day and snapped, "I'll settle this matter. Pierce, you were wrong."[12] A tank platoon rumbled up the road to cover it until O'Day's two laggard battalions arrived.

At one o'clock the morning of January 6, the last foot soldiers of the 21st Division appeared out of the dark and crossed the bridge. "The engineers were hurrying us because they were going to blast the bridge," recalled Lieutenant Avelino J. Battad, heavy weapons company commander of the 2nd Battalion, 23rd Infantry. "So I told them no, not until all my men are accounted for. So I stood on the bridge and counted them."[13] As Battad's men passed by some tanks and half-tracks a few of the more enthusiastic Filipinos flashed the two-finger V sign and called to the tankers, "V for victory, Joe." The Americans, bemused by the constant retreats and unimpressed by Filipino military prowess, flashed the two-finger V and answered "V for vacate, Joe."[14]

A little before 0200 hours, the 48-year-old O'Day turned to Wainwright, raised his right hand in testimony, and formally reported, "To the best of my knowledge and belief all units of the 21st Division and tanks have cleared the Junction."[15] O'Day and Capinpin then walked across the short bridge, climbed into their car, and drove south. As they passed their marching infantry, Capinpin shouted, "The trucks will come back for you. You'll get your trucks." Following them across the bridge was the North Luzon Force rear guard, 13-ton Stuarts of Lieutenant Colonel Theodore F. Wickord's 192nd Tank Battalion, preceded by the gaunt horses and fatigued riders of the 26th Cavalry, the last Americans and Filipinos to reach the safety of northern Bataan.[16]

Some of the tanks almost did not make it. Each tank driver, National Guardsmen from Illinois, Ohio, and Wisconsin, sleepily watched for the tank in front to move, but the crew of the lead tank was asleep. "I waited by my tank for at least an hour before I realized I was the only man awake," remembered tank commander Sergeant Forrest K. Knox from Monroe, Wisconsin. "I ran the full length of the column and reached in and belted each driver on the head."[17] After the rear guard tanks crossed, Wainwright ordered Colonel Skerry to have Captain Antonio P. Chanco and his 91st Engineer Battalion destroy the Culo Bridge. Before touching off the charges, Captain Chanco asked a tank officer if all his men were south of the bridge. The tanker took "the usual position for a military oath," remembered the 53-year old Colonel Skerry, "and [swore] by all that was holy that all his tanks had crossed."[18] Even so, because no Japanese were in sight, Wainwright ordered a delay in demolition. A moment later, a lone American tank rumbled out of the darkness and crossed the bridge.

Waiting to detonate the charges, Captain Chanco's engineers felt confident with their day's work. Already to this engineer battalion's credit was the destruction of more than 150 wooden trestle, stone arch, and steel railroad and highway bridges. Chanco's experienced engineers had spent the day checking and double-checking their time fuses and explosives. They tied double charges along one side and set heavy dynamite charges in the unusually strong reinforced concrete flooring to shatter it as it fell. They hoped to drop the spans of the Culo Bridge in such a manner that the Japanese could use neither the spans nor the original abutments as a foundation for repairs. The engineers took similar precautions on the railroad trestle. Their work was supervised by Colonel Skerry who would remain at the bridges to ensure their destruction.[19]

With all preparations completed and the last tank in the fold, Wainwright turned to Skerry and ordered, "Blow It."[20] Captain Chanco's men lit the fuses. At 0205 hours, January 6, 1942, the well-placed charges detonated in a "roof-raising" explosion; steel blew apart, concrete flooring buckled, and the last two bridges between the Japanese and Americans collapsed into the river. Wainwright, packing his Colt 1873 single-action .45, purchased when he graduated from West Point, and Skerry, Wainwright's classmate at Fort Leavenworth, silently shook hands.

Slow in their pursuit, the Japanese were still far to the north. One of two approaching columns was more than fifteen miles away and the nearest was no closer than seven. As the clap of thunder signifying the destruction of the bridges rolled through deserted streets, Layac Junction began its thirtieth day of war.[21]

Thousands of miles from these milling columns of men, officers working in America's capital city searched desperately for some means to help the Philippines. In the old Munitions Building in Washington, D.C., Army Chief of Staff General George C. Marshall spent December watching his hopes for the Philippines fade in the smoke of burning planes at Clark and Iba Fields. With many personal friends there, and having served on Mindoro as a lieutenant in 1902, the threat to the garrison was a personal as well as a military challenge, and Marshall's chief efforts before Pearl Harbor were those made to strengthen the Philippine Islands. As the first days of war dragged by, more information, all bad, came into Washington. Marshall nurtured hopes of saving the men, but his hopes were not high.

As early as December 14, only seven days after Pearl Harbor, illusions of saving the Philippines sank even lower. Early on a Sunday morning an aide ushered in a newly arrived brigadier, 52-year-old Dwight D. Eisenhower, to see Marshall just hours after Eisenhower arrived by train at Union Station. This was only the fourth time Eisenhower had seen Marshall and the first time their conversation lasted for more than two minutes. Early this Sunday morning Marshall outlined the Pacific situation for Eisenhower. Although America's aircraft carriers escaped the fate of the Pacific Fleet's battleships, it would be months before an offensive action could be contemplated, and because Hawaii's garrison was weak, reinforcing its air and ground strength had priority over other Pacific efforts.[22]

After a twenty-minute monologue, Marshall abruptly asked Eisenhower, "What should be our general line of action?"[23]

"Give me a few hours," Eisenhower answered. He wanted to present a careful, reasoned reply.

Eisenhower left to develop his thoughts. He recognized that Marshall never once mentioned one of the most important factors in the Philippine problem, that of the psychological effects the battle would have on the American public and the peoples of the Pacific. "Clearly," recalled Eisenhower later, "[Marshall] felt that anyone stupid enough to overlook this consideration had no business wearing the star of a brigadier general." Eisenhower decided his answer would be short, emphatic, and based on reasoning in which he believed; oratory and generalities would not satisfy Marshall. He drafted his reply and typed it, triple-spaced on yellow paper, before going back into Marshall's office. His report was pessimistic, for Eisenhower realized reinforcements would depend on future rehabilitation of the Navy. It would take a long time to get help to the islands, "longer than the garrison can hold out with any driblet assistance, if the enemy commits major forces to their reduction." Eisenhower, a veteran of Philippine service and a colleague of MacArthur, stressed that everything humanly possible must be done to help the garrison. The populace of China, Dutch East Indies, and the Philippines would be watching.

General Marshall nodded his agreement. "Do your best to save them."

As Eisenhower recalled later, Marshall's tone "implied that I had been given the problem as a check to an answer he had already reached."

The Philippine situation improved neither with time nor the efforts of Eisenhower. In a War Department memorandum written for Marshall on January 3, planners estimated the Philippines could hold for three months, and they reached two conclusions at the end of the memorandum.

One, "That the forces required for the safety of the Philippines cannot be placed in the Far East area within the time available."[24] They estimated an army of several hundred thousand men was necessary.

Two, "That allocation to the Far East area of forces necessary to regain control of the Philippines would necessitate an entirely unjustified diversion of forces from the principal theater—the Atlantic."

The recommendation to Marshall was that full-scale operations to relieve the Philippines not be undertaken.

That same day, January 3, Marshall sent a message to MacArthur explaining his inability to send immediate aid:

> Previous losses in capital ships seriously reduce capacity of Navy to carry on indispensable tasks including convoys for heavy reinforcements for Far East and protection of vital supplies for six hundred thousand men in the Near East and to British Isles. Net result is a marked insufficiency of forces for any powerful naval concentration in the Western Pacific at this time.[25]

Unintentionally, the message also held an unwise and easily misunderstood promise of reinforcements.

> Our great hope is that the rapid development of an overwhelming air power on the Malay Barrier will cut the Japanese communications south of Borneo and permit an assault in the Southern Philippines. A stream of four-engine bombers, previously delayed by foul weather, is en route with the head of the column having crossed Africa. Another stream of similar bombers started today from Hawaii staging at new island fields. Two groups of powerful medium bombers of long range and heavy bomb-load capacity leave next week. Pursuit planes are coming on every ship we can use. Our definitely allocated air reinforcements together with British should give us an early superiority in the Southwestern Pacific. Our strength is to be concentrated and it should exert a decisive effect on Japanese shipping and force a withdrawal northward.[26]

Surely this message, and another received a week earlier, encouraged MacArthur, for it is easily read as promising immediate and massive help. But less than two days after this message reached the Philippines, Wainwright blew the bridges over the Culo River. The Filipinos were in their stronghold, ready to buy the time requested by Marshall, time "vital to the concentration of the overwhelming power necessary for our purpose."[27]

CHAPTER TWO

Mobilization

BATAAN, THE PLACE OF THE BATA, THE PLACE OF CHILDREN, THE place of the little men; named for the original Negritos who occupied the land. In the Tagalog dialect, pronounced in three syllables, Ba-ta'an, accent on the ta'. The peninsula with its mountain ranges was a beautiful sight to Manila's prewar tourists as the sun dipped into the sea. It was a wild land, a fourth-class province, very underdeveloped with few important towns, twenty-five miles long and twenty miles wide. Monkeys, wild pigs, pheasant and quail inhabited the jungle highlands, mountains blanketed with giant banyan trees, Philippine mahogany, snake-like vines, ferns, palms, brush and flowers. Bataan was actually a US military reservation, thereby subject to military rather than civilian control. The Philippine government considered it the worst malaria-infected region in the country, and a large lumber company with logging and milling operations on Bataan fled the peninsula in 1930 due to malaria. Ten thousand Filipinos lived in the capital, Balanga, and the entire peninsula provided a living for 20,000 more.[1]

With two large, almost alpine-like mountain ranges dominating the peninsula, one in the north and one in the south, the upper breakwater for Manila's great harbor was cut by numerous densely wooded ravines. Bataan was heavily vegetated, and only two roads suitable for modern traffic snaked their way along the lowland fringes of the twisted landscape. Yet for all its hostile exterior, Bataan was a godsend to Americans in early 1942. The Filamerican army, brushed aside by the Japanese at the Lingayen Gulf and Lamon Bay beaches, was staggering toward this haven. Here on Bataan the soldiers knew they could rest, draw on mountains of supplies, and bloody the Japanese until the Pacific Fleet steamed

11

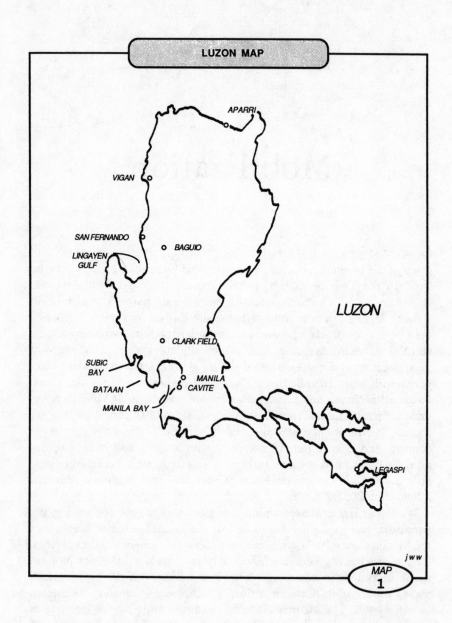

LUZON MAP

APARRI

VIGAN

SAN FERNANDO

LINGAYEN
GULF

BAGUIO

LUZON

CLARK FIELD

SUBIC
BAY

BATAAN

MANILA BAY

MANILA
CAVITE

LEGASPI

jww

MAP
1

into Manila Bay. No better terrain, considering the circumstances, could be found on which to make the final stand. On Bataan the terrain favored the defender, and in early 1942 there was no doubt who was defending. Military men considered large portions of the peninsula impassable to an invader. The steep impenetrable Mount Natib in the north with its tangled hills, rock ridges, and brush-choked valleys, combined with the relatively narrow defense line flanked on both sides by the sea, was to develop into the most critical piece of terrain on Bataan.[2]

Occasionally American officers drove through Bataan on weekend excursions, and the Army held exercises there to familiarize its leaders with the terrain, but such visits were not repeated often; there was not much to see. Another advantage to be reaped from the rugged peninsula was the concealment offered from an enemy with undisputed aerial supremacy. Although putatively a military reservation, heavy civilian encroachment on Bataan in 1940 began claiming giant hardwood trees for wood, other trees for charcoal, while jungle-covered slopes were stripped and planted with banana trees. Some military supply roads in the defensive network, heretofore concealed from view, were now alarmingly exposed. The Army had to station troops on Bataan to keep poachers from lumbering the land bare; logging was forbidden. Militarily, Bataan was of little importance except that, with the fortress island of Corregidor, it blocked the entrance to the great port of Manila. If American planes could reach it, and as long as Bataan held, it threatened the Japanese as an unsinkable aircraft carrier.[3]

The United States defended the Philippines using War Plan Orange 3. Ever since America conquered the islands, Joint Army-Navy Boards developed and updated plans to defend the Philippines against potential enemies. They completed the most recent revision, one covering war between America and Japan, only eight months before the war. Because no other enemies or allies were assumed, events proved the simple, two-sided war envisioned in WPO-3 obsolete, but tactically the plan was sound and adaptable to any number of circumstances. Two assumptions were that war would come with too little warning to reinforce the Philippines, and the blow would land during the dry season, after the rice crop was harvested, sometime in December or January. These assumptions held true.[4]

Under WPO-3, no attempt would be made to defend all the islands. Instead, planners bent all efforts toward holding central Luzon, and if the worst were to happen, the Army would hold Bataan to the last extremity. The key to the plan was to deny Manila Bay to the enemy. Philippine forces were expected to hold for six months by which time the Navy would have fought its way across the Pacific with massive reinforcements.

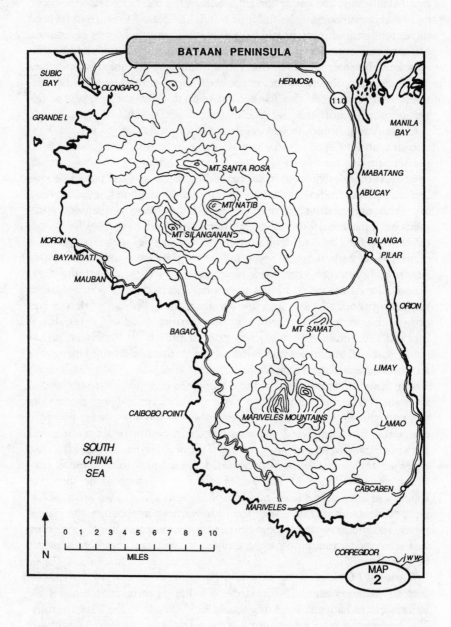

BATAAN PENINSULA

SUBIC
BAY

OLONGAPO

GRANDE I.

HERMOSA

110

MANILA
BAY

MT SANTA ROSA

MABATANG

ABUCAY

MT NATIB

MORON

MT SILANGANAN

BAYANDATI

MAUBAN

BALANGA

PILAR

ORION

BAGAC

MT SAMAT

LIMAY

CAIBOBO POINT

MARIVELES MOUNTAINS

LAMAO

SOUTH
CHINA
SEA

CABCABEN

MARIVELES

0 1 2 3 4 5 6 7 8 9 10

N

MILES

CORREGIDOR

jww

MAP
2

The strengthened Bataan garrison would sally forth and drive the isolated enemy into the sea. But no knowledgeable planner really believed the Navy could fight its way back to the Philippines in six months, and prewar plans were mute over what would happen if Bataan fell. No contingency plans existed for concentrating men and equipment on the American west coast for a relief effort. When the time came, planners hoped something could be done. Because there were not enough forces to defend successfully all the islands, or even Luzon, Washington faced two unenviable choices, either the humiliation of losing the islands and the garrison, or the decision to send an unprepared, under-equipped relief expedition.[5]

The planners almost realized the first half of their plan, that of holding Manila Bay for six months. Corregidor fell one day shy of five months, and armed resistance in the southern islands did not end until as late as June 9, six months and two days after war started. The second half of the plan, relief from the United States, failed.

As the world situation deteriorated in 1941, Douglas MacArthur was recalled to active duty as a major general in the United States Army on July 26 and was promoted to lieutenant general effective the next day. His status before the war had been unique. In 1935 he was about to retire as Army Chief of Staff when Philippine President-elect Manuel L. Quezon talked him into coming to the Philippines. MacArthur accepted and became the Military Advisor to the Commonwealth Government. In 1936 he was appointed to command the Philippine Army with the grade of Field Marshal. His job was to establish a program of national defense, and he hoped to build a force capable of defending the islands by the time independence was granted to the Philippines in 1946. To man his army, MacArthur trained two installments of Filipinos each year, five and a-half months of individual training that emphasized scouting and patrolling. Annual training of as few as 5,000 men proved a great drain on the Commonwealth's treasury, and more training was fiscally unpopular. Lacking cadre and equipment, MacArthur could do little in the area of field and weapons training. Unit training was first attempted in the summer of 1941 before the prewar call-up of reserves, and then it was restricted to small units for a period of two weeks. On the whole, premobilization training was not at all evident in the recruits drafted during the mobilization of late 1941.[6]

Rather than follow the "defeatist" WPO-3, MacArthur favored defending Luzon and the other major islands at the beaches. MacArthur's switch proved a major factor in the subsequent loss of huge quantities of supplies of all types, and most important, of food. But in the middle of 1941 the switch to a beach defense looked promising. In a letter dated

October 28, MacArthur optimistically outlined the Philippine military situation to Army Chief of Staff General Marshall. MacArthur pressed his plan for the defense of "all the land and sea areas necessary for the defense of the Philippine Archipelago," rather than just of Manila Bay.[7] In closing, MacArthur stressed his gratitude for the help he was receiving from Washington. "I wish to reiterate my appreciation of the splendid support you and the War Department are giving me. No field commander could ask more. Your attitude has been a marked factor in the building of morale here."

On November 21, responding to MacArthur's letter, Marshall concurred with the beach defense plan. Informal notice had come earlier, on November 3, and MacArthur started implementing his plans then. Little time remained to prepare the new strategy, nor was the recently recruited Philippine Army ready for the expanded mission, but if any cautions were raised, MacArthur ignored them. Under WPO-3, stocks of supplies were to be cached on Bataan but because of MacArthur's decision to fight at the beaches, these supplies were trucked to various camps and divisional areas so as to be readily available at the beaches. In this beach defense stance, the Filipinos received the Japanese December assault. MacArthur's army could do nothing but retreat.[8]

The subsequent siege of Bataan, starting on January 7, ended a disorderly delaying action during which time MacArthur's Filamerican Army beat a hurried and haphazard retreat from all corners of Luzon. In the north, Filipino forces ultimately occupied eight delay lines just long enough to force the Japanese to maneuver out of march formation for an attack. Then the Filipinos either withdrew, scattered, or deserted. Those collected by their officers repeated the process on the next line. The steadying presence of American light tanks, self-propelled artillery, and Philippine Scouts of the 26th Cavalry were barely sufficient to dignify the maneuver as a withdrawal rather than a rout. The simple fact that the retreat succeeded and the campaign did not end with a Japanese victory around Manila, as the Japanese planned, was a testimonial to the bravery of MacArthur's hurriedly recruited Filipinos, the small backbone of professional American and Scout cadre, and Japanese ineptness. In desperate circumstances and under constant enemy pressure, the untried Filamerican Army spread across north and south Luzon, withdrew in a dangerous double retrograde, joined safely, and retired into Bataan. The startling success of this twin retreat of forces separated by 200 miles, fighting an enemy with command of the air, can be appreciated only when the handicaps under which they operated are known.

The Philippine Army reaching Bataan dated its existence from just a few short months before the war began. In late 1941 the international situation was becoming bleaker. Although Philippine Army mobilization cantonments were not complete and could not accommodate full divisions, the most recent five-and-a-half month training period had just ended, freeing existing camps, and the camps would not be needed again until early 1942. MacArthur decided to mobilize increments of each reserve division in these camps. Engineer battalions were called immediately to prepare camps for each division. So in August of 1941, MacArthur issued orders calling ten infantry regiments into service by September 1, one regiment for each of the ten reserve infantry divisions. Upon mobilization, units and personnel were inducted into the armed forces of the United States. Cadres of other divisional elements were also called to the colors.[9]

MacArthur's orders affected ten divisions, the 11th, 21st, 31st, 41st, 51st, 61st, 71st, 81st, 91st, and 101st, of which all but the 61st, 81st, and 101st would fight on Bataan. The infantry regiments, unlike their American counterparts, had a standard numbering system. The 11th Division had the 11th, 12th, and 13th infantry regiments and was supported by the 11th Field Artillery Regiment, while the 41st Division had the 41st, 42nd, and 43rd infantry and was supported by the 41st Field Artillery Regiment. On December 18, ten days after hostilities started, MacArthur's headquarters, United States Army Forces in the Far East (USAFFE), ordered the induction of all Philippine Army units which had not yet been called. Reservists were called up and able-bodied men ages twenty to thirty were accepted as volunteers. The Philippine Army would total 120,000 men, but only 76,750 were on Luzon, the island fated to serve as the decisive theater.[10]

In bits and pieces the first regiments mobilized, and as soon as cantonment space became available, other regiments assembled and started training. The shortest period required to raise and train a division in the United States was about one year, and this assumed the necessary equipment, training areas, and instructors were available. But even in the States where mobilizing soldiers stood next door to factories and depots, assets were spread terribly thin. In the Philippines, infantry divisions were brought forth in haste, fielded in confusion, and sent into battle in less than four months. At best, the lucky units had three months of training before they were locked in a life and death struggle. When the Japanese struck on December 8, not one of the Philippine Army divisions was fully mobilized, and not one was at full strength. There was a shortage of antitank guns, a shortage of divisional artillery, and a shortage of engineers, medics, support and signal troops. Three divisions had to convert their artillery regiments to infantry after they failed to receive cannon.[11]

The job of organizing the Filipino recruits was difficult. "To put an unequipped, unorganized and untrained army into the field against a seasoned and trained up-to-the-minute enemy was something to make strong men quail," recalled Brigadier General Charles C. Drake, the Army's Quartermaster.[12] To staff these units with leaders, the Philippine government ordered Reserve Officer Training Corps cadets to report to their commandants to undergo cadre training. Schools were suspended and cadre in training sent back to their units where they tried to pick up the necessary technical, tactical, and administrative skills. Each division mobilization district established schools to train cadre as first-sergeants, staff officers, company commanders, platoon leaders, mess sergeants, supply sergeants, cooks, runners, clerks, and more. Filipino lieutenants with little experience commanded battalions and companies. The officer shortage was so serious that newly commissioned 3rd lieutenants commanded many of the battalions. Staff officers were new to their jobs, with most never before having held a staff position. Headquarters units, staffed by men expected to organize, equip, and train the new formations, were in no better shape than their subordinate units. Brigadier General George M. Parker, later commander of Bataan's II Corps, began training his South Luzon Force—equivalent to a corps—with five officers and two enlisted men. Parker formed a corps headquarters company out of some American military police, retired Philippine Scouts, civilian cooks, and houseboys. On the day war began, Parker's engineer staff consisted of one officer and two sergeants. Wainwright was no luckier. When he arrived on November 28 to take command of North Luzon Force, like Parker's South Luzon Force a corps organization, he found that his staff consisted of an adjutant, one supply man, and a surgeon, a total of three men for a corps staff, eleven days before war started.

Filipino division commanders and key staff members went to Baguio for the Command and Staff School in early October. Their six-week course at Camp Henry T. Allen, patterned after the American school at Fort Leavenworth, was designed to train these officers in procedures required for large units. "I ran the school from 8:00 in the morning until 11:30, and from 1:00 to 4:30 in the afternoon," recalled its commandant, Colonel Clifford Bluemel. "Then we all went out and walked for fifty minutes—everybody. The division staffs stayed together until they got to know each other. I also ran the school from 7:00 to 9:00 at night. They thought that was terrible, and that I was a rough S.O.B. But I had only six weeks to train them in. I even ran it all day on Saturday sometimes, and they didn't like that; they wanted their Saturday off. Sunday they had off. When I threatened to run it on Sunday, I almost had a riot one time."[13] Local politics played a part in selection of divisional staff officers. Although Filipino officers who had attended West Point and various American service schools were generally of a high caliber, the most deserving officers were not always picked for the most important assignments.[14]

The Philippine Army divisions were by necessity light divisions, never receiving the materiel and support standard to American divisions. As equipment became available from stocks in the United States, it was shipped to the islands. In this fashion, old equipment being used by the Filipinos would be replaced with more modern items. One hundred cargo ships with 875,000 tons of supplies and equipment were scheduled to arrive in the Philippines in the first ninety days of 1942. But time did not allow completion of this modernization, and never would a Philippine division reach half the strength of an American division. The Philippine Army retained its own national character, uniforms, pay scale, promotion lists, rations, and military law, but as the war progressed it took on the appearance of the American Army. Most significant was the influence exerted by the hundreds of American officers and enlisted men in Filipino ranks.[15]

But the most visible characteristic of the Philippine Army was its incompleteness. For example, prewar plans called for engineer mobilization to conclude in October 1942 with each divisional engineer battalion carrying 600 men. But as of December 1 not one had been completely equipped, and all were at about 80 percent strength. Even token organization of these divisional engineers was impractical, considering the untrained personnel and shortages of equipment. In November there were only two trained engineer units in the islands, and they were Scout and American units that existed before the mobilization. In addition to the single combat engineer battalion authorized each division, the master plan called for three combat engineer regiments, six separate battalions, two heavy pontoon battalions, and three topographic companies. They never saw the light of day.[16]

During mobilization the 11th Engineer Battalion's commander, Captain Amado N. Bautista, found many sergeants in his unit who could neither read nor write. Conversely, he discovered graduate physicians, lawyers, dentists, and ROTC graduates sent to him as privates. His requests to change the assignment of these highly-skilled privates went unanswered. Bautista's officers were reservists who had received five-and-a-half months' training between 1936 and 1939, and all had forgotten whatever they once knew about how to train men. Supplies could be obtained only through personal IOU's given to local civilians. The engineers of the battalion worked all day building barracks, roads, and water systems, leaving only two hours for basic training, one hour at reveille and one hour at retreat. On December 8, the battalion had only five rounds of ammunition per man borrowed from a nearby constabulary unit. "Previous requisitions for ammunition, explosive, leather shoes and additional clothing were not filled despite numerous follow-ups, tracers, telegrams and long-distance calls to both USAFFE and PA officers concerned," remembers Bautista.[17] On December 8, the military received permission to buy, rent, or seize all civilian supplies of dynamite, sandbags and sacks of all kinds, and every type of tool. Despite all efforts, equipment was scarce and consisted chiefly of hand tools; even shovels and axes were in short supply.

Corps, Army, and Communication Zone troops—support forces needed in modern armies—never mobilized; they were to have been formed in 1942. MacArthur had asked Washington for Army and Corps troops, for a field artillery brigade, a chemical company, three signal battalions, a medical supply depot, and a military police company. By mid-November Washington had approved the transfer to the Philippines of 19,359 officers and men belonging to specialized units and another 3,168 individual officers and enlisted specialists. But like the corps engineers, they did not arrive. They stacked up on the American west coast awaiting allocation of scarce shipping. By November, more than a million tons of materiel earmarked for MacArthur were backlogged in ports and depots, all awaiting space on seventy separate shipments. In late September, General Marshall found the shipping situation so alarming that he personally intervened with the Chief of Naval Operations, Admiral Harold R. Stark, to postpone conversion of three transports to small aircraft carriers. By keeping these ships as transports, Marshall hoped to move shipping dates from late February 1942 to December 1941. He succeeded and new shipping dates were set for the middle of December, but even that proved too late.[18]

It is a tribute to MacArthur that his ten-year plan for the defense of the Philippines was considered an important factor in Japan's decision to go to war. The Japanese were concerned over the menace MacArthur's preparations posed for their expansionist designs. Lieutenant General Akira Muto, Director of the Military Affairs Bureau of the War Ministry, claimed "if the Philippines were fortified and the defense strengthened by additional troops, Japan could not have undertaken war with the United States."[19] Lieutenant General Hikaru Haba, Intelligence Staff, 14th Army, echoed this by stating if there had been another 50,000 men in the Philippines, and if the defenses had been completed, Japan would have had to reconsider carefully the consequences of going to war, or war might have been delayed. Other Japanese studying the fledgling air force hatching in the islands held similar opinions. If more planes had been prepared to meet a Japanese attack, these men claim war could not have started successfully. This, in particular, had been General Marshall's hope. "If we could make the Philippines reasonably defensible," he testified, "particularly with heavy bombers in which the Air Corps at that time had great faith, we felt that we could block the Japanese advance and block their entry into war by their fear of what would happen if they couldn't take the Philippines, and we could maintain heavy bombers on that island."[20]

MacArthur's army was mobilizing to protect the Philippine Islands. From air bases on the islands, MacArthur would use his air force to prevent Japanese use of the seas. Unfortunately for Marshall's hopes, a balanced air force did not develop before the Japanese attacked. For nowhere outside the United States were American air forces strong enough to accomplish their missions. Nor could sufficient reinforcements be sent anywhere without severely affecting the training programs then developing in the States. The Philippine Islands shared this weakness, even though the Philippines had more B-17's than any other Army air force, either overseas or in the States. The air warning net was inadequate, fighter strength was inadequate, maintenance, communications, dispersal areas, tactics, and command were all inadequate. Without an approaching invasion fleet to attack, and without adequate fighter and antiaircraft gun protection, MacArthur's B-17 bombers were destroyed or driven south during the battle for air superiority.[21]

The Americans had not expected war to come as soon as it did. Colonel Constant L. Irwin, USAFFE Operations Officer, believed that "assuming we get no more than our share of bad breaks, the Philippine Army will become marginally combat effective by April 1942."[22] MacArthur was no better a forecaster. On November 25 he talked to Wainwright about the progress of North Luzon Force mobilization and told him that he would probably have until April to train his troops. Wainwright knew MacArthur was talking about war with Japan. If MacArthur had realized the gravity of the diplomatic situation, or if he had possessed more information, he certainly would have alerted his subordinates. MacArthur told High Commissioner Francis B. Sayre that Japanese troops and naval deployments convinced him there would not be an attack before spring. In his trips to various units, MacArthur assured the commanders there would be time for supplies and equipment to reach them before war began. As it was, very few people realized the terminal nature of the final prewar months.

One warning the Philippines received consisted of a November 27 notification that diplomatic relations with Japan were deteriorating.

Negotiations with Japan appear to be terminated to all practical purposes with only barest possibilities that Japanese government might come back and offer to continue. Japanese future action unpredictable but hostile action possible at any moment. If hostilities cannot, repeat cannot, be avoided the United States desires that Japan commit the first overt act. This policy should not, repeat not, be construed as restricting you to a course of action that might jeopardize the successful defense of the Philippines. Prior to hostile Japanese action you are directed to take such reconnaissance and other measures as you deem necessary. Report measures taken. Should hostilities occur you will carry out the tasks assigned in revised Rainbow Five which was delivered to you by General Brereton. Chief of Naval Operations concurs and request you notify Hart.[23]

USAFFE then sent a similar message to its commanders. Their subordinates, in turn, received repeats of this information over the next few days. After alerting his command, MacArthur assured General Marshall that:

Pursuant to instruction contained in your radio six two four air reconnaissance has been extended and intensified in conjunction with the Navy. Ground Security measures have been taken. Within the limitation imposed by the present state of deployment of this theater of operations everything is in readiness for the conduct of a successful defense. Intimate liaison and cooperation and cordial relations exist between Army and Navy.[24]

One small bright spot in the military situation was the elite, high-spirited 10,400-man Philippine Division. With its divisional insignia sporting a red carabao head on a blue background, it was a regular division stationed in the Philippines carried on the rolls of the United States Army. It had three well-trained and well-equipped infantry regiments: the 31st Infantry (US), composed exclusively of American officers and enlisted men; and the 45th and 57th Infantry (PS), officered by Americans and manned by Filipino enlisted men called Philippine Scouts. The enlisted men of the Scout regiments were fine fighters equipped with the same individual gear standard to American infantry and well known throughout the army for their superb marksmanship and their love of soldiering. Divisional artillery consisted of the two-battalion 24th Artillery, British truck-drawn 75mm guns and mule-packed 2.95-inch mountain howitzers, and the one-battalion 23rd Artillery with a single battery of 2.95-inch mountain howitzers and two batteries of 75mm guns.[25]

Before the war, plans were developed to deactivate the 45th Infantry in order to bring the 57th Infantry and other Scout units up to full strength. Rather than recruit additional Scouts, most of whom would have been the best of the Philippine Army or the civilian manpower pool, MacArthur asked instead for another American infantry regiment.

In preparation for deactivation of the 45th Infantry, officers from both Scout regiments went over unit rosters to determine where to place each soldier. The officers scheduled some men for other Scout units, some for headquarters positions, but most for infantry slots in the 57th Infantry. Some tentative decisions made then were later proved wrong. One idea was to take the older men out of the rifle companies and put them in less physically demanding jobs. But later, on Bataan, the older men were often the ". . . best in terms of physical staying power; best in terms of native cunning, best in terms of displaying initiative . . ." and the most courageous, most useful, and most determined at close combat. Many of the younger soldiers did not seem to have the heart for the hard service.[26]

To replace the 45th Infantry, a Montana National Guard regiment, the 161th Infantry, part of the 41st Division, was to be shipped to the Philippines and arrive on December 30, 1941. Another American regiment, the 34th Infantry, was scheduled to accompany the 161th Infantry to fill gaps in the 31st and 161st. MacArthur told Marshall that the entire plan would be put into effect when the new regiment arrived. To increase his artillery strength, MacArthur asked for two American field artillery battalions. In the States, staff officers collected the artillery and prepared it for shipment. In a letter prepared on December 5 but never sent, Marshall told MacArthur, "Not only will you receive soon all your supporting light artillery [130 75mm guns], but [also] 48 155mm howitzers and 24 155mm guns for corps and army artillery."[27] This reorganization did not come to pass, for war arrived before the reinforcement.

Earlier, on September 5, Marshall proposed sending a National Guard division to MacArthur, probably the 41st Division. But when Marshall warned that sending this division would cause severe strains on the already scarce shipping assets, MacArthur rejected the offer. He replied that he already had the Philippine Division, and that he was mobilizing ten reserve divisions. Therefore an American division would not be necessary. MacArthur did stress the necessity of equipping and supplying the forces he was then mobilizing. "I am confident if these steps are taken with sufficient speed that no further major reinforcement will be necessary for accomplishment of defense mission."[28] It is debatable whether a full American division would have affected the campaign's outcome. Most likely the division would simply have swelled the prisoner cages, for in the final analysis, Bataan fell from starvation.

If war had been delayed for just one more week, the Pensacola Convoy of four transports, the *Republic, Chaumont, Meigs,* and *Holbrook,* and three freighters, the *Admiral Halstead, Coast Farmer,* and *Bloemfontien,* then at sea and protected by the cruiser U.S.S. *Pensacola,* would have docked in the Philippines. The ships were carrying parts of three incomplete regiments of National Guard artillery, the 2nd Battalion, 131st Artillery, the 147th Artillery, and the 148th Artillery. Air and munition reinforcements consisting of 52 A-24 dive bombers, 18 P-40 fighters, 340 motor vehicles, antiaircraft ammunition, bombs, assorted supplies, and 4,600 men sailed in these ships. Hostilities rerouted them first toward Hawaii, and then on December 12 west to Brisbane, Australia, and they never reached the Philippines. As a result, the A-24 twin-seat dive bombers which might have hurt the Japanese invasion fleet did not arrive. Even if the planes had failed to stop the invasion, they would have been useful operating from Bataan's rude airstrips.[29]

The American regiment of the Philippine Division, the 31st Infantry, was celebrating its twenty-fifth anniversary in August 1941. Unfortunately, the regiment was badly under strength, especially in officers and sergeants, and fielded about 1,400 men, less than half the strength of a full stateside regiment. The 45th and 57th Infantry each carried about 2,000 men, but when detachments to the Philippine Army were considered, their true strength was closer to 1,750. There had been little combat training before the war in the American regiment, and two-thirds of the 31st Infantry were draftees rather than trained infantrymen. With hardly four months in the Army, they were simply processed through a reception station in the States and sent to the Philippines to be trained. Basic training took six weeks at a regimental training detachment. Then the men took advanced individual training at their companies and battalions.[30]

Private Raymond Knight was in the first group of recruits to arrive in the Philippines. He received no stateside training but was inducted, processed, and shipped overseas. He arrived in April 1941 and was sent to B-Range at Fort McKinley where he began his training. Living conditions were primitive and one-hundred degree weather normal. Their first task was to put up tents. Knight and his fellows received folding cots and two blankets and spent a few miserable weeks learning how to be infantrymen. After the men finished their training they found military life pleasant. There was plenty of night life in Manila, the people were nice to soldiers, and food was cheap. "The life of a soldier in the Philippines at this time was great," Knight recalled. "We always had training until noon. The afternoons were spent in the barracks with a quiet hour for siestas. A fifteen-mile forced march with full gear about one night each week was part of the training."[31] Regimental esprit was high. American money went a long way in the Philippines, far enough for soldiers to wear perfectly tailored uniforms. A bottle of gin cost thirty cents, and the men maintained a second set of mess gear, some chrome-plated, for display during inspections. Corporal William W. Wynn enlisted in 1940, trained at Fort Benning, and volunteered for the Philippines. Besides wearing tailored fatigues and dress uniforms, he bought handmade shoes and purchased a regimental insignia, a gold-plated polar bear with a small red ruby set in the bear's eye.

Before the September 1941 mobilization, Philippine service was languorous, torpid, flacid. The steamy days, unhurried pace, and "sluggish officialdom" wore down even the most ambitious and active men. Older officers nearing retirement came here to pass their final days in honorable quiet, a two-year vacation. Staffs came to work at eight o'clock, shuffled papers, and worked or socialized until one. Then it was siesta time, necessarily indoors until four because it was too hot outside. Even in the line units, there was little urgency in preparing the men for war. Corporal Burton Ellis remembered prewar training as going to the field in the mornings for a couple of hours and sitting under palm trees. Afternoons were free or were devoted to police of the post and athletics. Other soldiers received more useful training. The 31st Infantry's antitank company trained on their 37mm guns, using sub-caliber devices which fired .22-caliber bullets rather than the more expensive larger rounds. Unfortunately, there was little information about Japanese tanks, and field manuals had blank pages where photos should exist when describing enemy armor and even enemy uniforms. The antitank company ran numerous alerts and exercises, but with personnel strength at 50 percent, the effectiveness of this training was limited. But the Philippine Division's training tempo began to pick up in August and September, and by November one regimental newsletter noted that they were no longer a garrison and parade division. They had stopped parades, they were running maximum field training, and they even welcomed visiting dignitaries with field exercises instead of garrison ceremonies. The sparkle had definitely gone out of Island life, and most everyone realized war was threatening.[32]

Both the Americans and Scouts carried the new semiautomatic M-1 Garand rifle. Its eight-round clip and rapid fire—twenty to thirty aimed shots a minute—surprised the first Japanese to come up against it. The sights were designed to give good visibility at night, and it proved to be one of the most reliable and rugged rifles in military history. The M-1's replacement of the beloved 1903 Springfield did not sit well with all soldiers, especially with the older men who were proud of their careful trigger squeeze and marksmanship. The M-1 seemed to encourage volume of fire over accuracy, and when war started, some men went to the extreme of swapping their M-1's or buying an '03. Although the situation with rifles was good, there was a shortage of light machine guns, 60mm and 81mm mortars, .50-caliber machine guns, and the new 37mm anti-tank guns. Each rifle company had three 60mm mortars, and each heavy weapons company had one or two 81mm mortars. As a matter of comparison, a regiment in the United States was authorized eighteen of the new 81mm mortars.[33]

Because very few backpack SCR 195 voice-signal walkie-talkies were available, and because those in the hands of the soldiers did not have enough batteries to allow frequent operation, communication between companies and battalion was by runner. The regiment's vehicle park consisted of a conglomeration of military and civilian transport; taxicabs, privately owned vehicles, and buses from six major bus companies were on the rolls. Fuel varied from diesel to alcohol to gasoline. The polyglot transportation was not an oddity when the entire supply situation is examined. After requesting replacements for two inoperable machine guns, the regiment received two Navy Marlin machine guns wrapped in newspaper over Cosmoline. The newspapers were dated 1918.[34]

The Philippine Division's two Scout infantry regiments were famous for their soldierly qualities. Filipinos considered selection to the Philippine Scouts a great honor, and entry standards were strict. Long lists to enter Scout units were common, and instances of waiting ten years were not unknown. One American officer interviewed 1,500 candidates for 100 openings and was able to insist that each applicant be a college graduate. Athletes were always in demand, partly because they made excellent soldiers, but also to staff the regimental sports teams with quality contenders. Father-son combinations seldom drew comments. Although many Scouts were the sons of Aguinaldo's followers, they were now well trained, intensely loyal to the United States, and deeply proud of their regiments—the most important structure in their world, to which they devoted their lives. Scouts had served in America's armed forces all the way back to World War I, and no finer soldier could be found anywhere in the Philippines.[35]

The 3rd Battalion, 45th Infantry was a typical Scout unit and gave an excellent account of itself on Bataan. On December 8 it had ten American officers and about 520 enlisted Scouts. The enlisted men had between six months' and twenty years' service, while the average Scout had been in the army for seven-and-a-half years. "They had all signed up for life," remembered an American officer, "regardless of what the enlistment oath said."[36] Most were high school graduates, and all spoke a reasonable dialect of English, but not all were fluent with the English language. Reluctant to say no and admit they did not understand, their answers were sometimes suspect. Most men generally understood English, but to be sure, some American commanders gave their orders in

English and then let the Scout first sergeant give the order again in his version of English. Then everyone understood. They carried M-1 rifles and the new gas masks. For heavy weapons, the battalion deployed eighteen water-cooled .30-caliber machine guns, one 81mm mortar, and one .50-caliber machine gun. The Scouts had the latest infantry web gear, bed rolls, and unlimited small arms ammunition, and they wore fine leather shoes made specially for them in America, woolen olive drab clothing, and steel helmets. Their morale was excellent.

Scout units were as close as regular families. Their backgrounds were similar because they were often recruited from the same village, and the prospective Scout was always known to someone in the unit. There were few surprises or bad apples. Prospective recruits served an apprenticeship with the unit they wanted to join. They worked as houseboys, janitors, gardeners, painters, kitchen help, etc., and only after they had satisfied the unit's sergeants, and in particular the first sergeant, were their names put on the waiting list. Recruits were often weak and sickly, but with a few months of Scout routine and rations, they gained an excellent carriage and endurance. After just four months of training and discipline, it was hard to tell the long-service Scout from the new recruit. The new men were eager to learn and enthusiastic in their duties, for they knew there were highly qualified applicants ready to replace them if they faltered. With very few exceptions, Scouts were career soldiers. They enlisted for extended periods with pay and benefits similar to civilian scales, and when they retired, they settled in their native villages as honored men. They often became the police chief, fire chief, or similar official. A retired Scout's home was easy to spot. It was kempt, had a picket fence around the front, and exuded achievement.[37]

Rank was slow to attain and earned when achieved. Before prewar expansion, it could take a Scout twenty years to make private first class. During Scout expansion in early 1941, units took in many new recruits, oftentimes the sons of Scouts already in the unit. One American company commander, with a father and son in his unit, faced a real dilemma, the choice of promoting one of his veteran privates to corporal, or promoting a recruit who showed great potential. The recruit was the son of the veteran. Who to promote, the father or the son? After a long discussion among father, first sergeant, and company commander, the son received the promotion. The father left in tears, but they were from pride in seeing the great honor bestowed upon his son.[38]

One weakness of the Scouts was a general aversion to making decisions and accepting responsibility. "Wonderful peace-time soldiers as they were," wrote an officer who commanded Scouts, "typical response by a Filipino N.C.O. on being confronted with a charge of 'neglect of duty'

would be: 'Sir, I did nothing wrong. I did nothing at all.' "[39] The theory
was that if a soldier took action on his own initiative, he ran a serious risk
of taking the wrong action, and the loss of face would be humiliating. It
required constant pressure from the American leaders to develop initiative in their soldiers. Successes were limited but through no fault of
American or Filipino. Whatever faults the elite Scouts might have had,
they were still without peer in the world of soldiers. Colonel Ernest B.
Miller, commander of a battalion of light tanks during the campaign,
stated, "I have never seen, nor do I ever expect to see, any better or
braver soldiers than the Scouts. They were truly an inspiration."[40]

The Philippine Army soldiers, in contrast to their Scout brethren, were
quite another story. Language difficulties here were more acute with the
less highly educated and more diverse recruits. The languages of business
and society were English and Spanish, and of the hundreds of dialects in
the Philippines, only two were used extensively, Tagalog on Luzon and
Visayan in the southern islands. When first mobilized, other than some
regiments formed from Manila citizens, there was a language problem
that had to be experienced to be believed. The sergeant could not talk to
the corporal, and the corporal could neither talk to nor understand his
men. People and dialects were thrown together, and babel ensued. There
were twenty dialects within the 11th Infantry, and Lieutenant Wilbur J.
Lage from a machine gun company complained of having five dialects in
his company alone. It required several sessions with different interpreters
to address the entire regiment, and even then there was no assurance the
message reached all the men. Attention, forward march, and chow were
the only English words familiar to all. Training consisted of demonstration, application, and supervision. To add a touch of color, the 11th
Division contained men from nearly all the former headhunting tribes.[41]

Many Filipinos had trouble with new ideas, partly because they were
not familiar with the new English words. There was no Tagalog word
corresponding to the English word "trigger," so weapons instruction
stumbled over this minor point. Not understanding the reason for many
orders, Filipinos failed to respond. At unit messes, several large tubs of
water had to be kept boiling to sterilize mess gear. Mess kits and silver-
ware were dipped in the boiling water, and each man then received his
food. But time and again, Americans found the water cold just before
meal time. The Filipino mess officer, in answer to the angry American,
would patiently explain, "but sir, I have already boiled this water once
today."[42]

The Americans likewise learned new rules when working with Filipinos. "The Filipino way of attracting attention," remembered Lieutenant
John W. Fisher, "is by hissing. You can holler 'Hey' all day and get no

results. Just say 'Ssssssst' and 38 people will turn and look at you."[43] Americans in the Philippine Army also learned that the answer "yes" did not always mean yes. Normally it meant one of three things: Yes, I understand what you said and I will do it if it does not involve too much work; or yes, I have a hazy idea of what you want, but to be sure I will not do anything; or yes, I have not the remotest idea of what you have asked. Another problem affecting the pace of training was the Filipino level of physical endurance. Many Filipinos came from small barrios of mountain or jungle regions, and their lifelong diet had left them undersized, under-muscled, and without endurance. Americans set off on marches with the men, and by the end of the exercise, the Filipinos were worn out while the Americans were still relatively fresh. Longer legs, large size, and a better diet gave Americans a physical advantage over the smaller Filipinos.

Problems dogged the Filipinos at every step. Colonel Bluemel felt the Philippine Army soldier was proficient in just two things, "one, when an officer appeared, to yell attention in a loud voice, jump up and salute; the other, to demand 3 meals per day."[44] Extensive training was to have occurred during the five-and-one-half-month trainee instruction—before mobilization—and it should have included close and extended order drill, use of the bayonet, road marches with limited maneuvers, and training with rifles and machine guns. But in actuality, premobilization training had concentrated on close-order drill. Field and infantry work had been nonexistent. When a practice mobilization for several units was held in March 1941, the results were extremely unfavorable. "The training was just about the most horrible I could imagine," Bluemel recalled. "They were the people we had to take into battle."[45]

Considering how bad the Philippine Army was when compared to the Scouts, it is amazing how remarkably well they actually did. For although they had serious shortcomings in every area imaginable, they kept the more experienced and better-armed Japanese at bay for nearly one hundred days. The Philippine Army provided the vast majority of the soldiers on Bataan, occupied most of the fighting positions, were employed in the front lines longer than Americans or Scouts, and suffered the majority of combat and nonbattle casualties. Although performance during the first battles, especially before arriving in Bataan, was often disastrous, and although blind panic and refusal to obey orders were not uncommon, instances of entire battalions deserting their officers declined sharply as time passed. On Bataan the Filipinos were paragons of soldierly virtue when compared to their earlier performance. The Filipino soldier did stop the Japanese, did inflict staggering losses on him, and certainly delayed the complete and early conquest of Luzon. And considering the state of training, equipment, and the unqualified, poorly trained native leaders, these facts are astounding. The Filipinos were good material, but they needed training and leadership. With training and effective officers, they performed well. This is the recurring theme, the oft-repeated "if only" of Bataan veterans. If only there had been more time, if only the Philippine Army could have been trained to the level of the Scouts. If only! Untrained recruits of all nationalities will break and run with depressing regularity, and the Filipinos were no exception.[46]

So the question arises, why, with so many problems, did MacArthur decide to defend Luzon's beaches? How could he consider his army prepared? There was a great deal of propaganda and boasting in high places to justify and buttress the existence of the new army. Misleading progress reports so distorted the actual condition of the army that it was a tremendous shock to learn its true state. The most serious failing in this propaganda campaign was that the men grinding out the reports came to believe them. Even MacArthur looked on his new army as an effective fighting force able to defend the beaches.

A MacArthur biographer, D. Clayton James, gives an enlightening account of how this optimism affected the situation.

> Finally, MacArthur himself must bear a large share of the blame for the pitiful situation of the fall of 1941, which would soon lead to military disaster. He undoubtedly did his best with the men, materiel, and meager funds he was allocated from 1936 to 1941, and he was surely the most logical choice among American generals for the task of building a Filipino defense force. But his overconfidence and unjustified optimism as to the abilities of himself, his staff, and the untried Filipino soldiers unfortunately became a contagion which ultimately affected even the War Department and the Joint Army and Navy Board. As late as November 28, 1941, Marshall, in response to an enthusiastic message from MacArthur, replied with satisfaction: "The Secretary of War and I were highly pleased to receive your report that your command is ready for any eventuality."[47]

Unfortunately, the command was not ready.

The Filipino infantry divisions arriving on Bataan in January 1942 were hardly worthy of the title "division." A review of the 31st Division will serve to describe the condition of all reserve divisions. Its 56-year-old commander, Brigadier General Clifford Bluemel, West Point Class of 1909, carried the name "Blinkey" as a result of a facial tic. Bluemel had served with the 8th Infantry in the Philippines in 1913–1914, served in Panama, graduated from the Command and General Staff Course as the Distinguished Graduate, and returned to the Philippines to command the 45th Infantry on 21 July 1940 until 21 September 1941 when he became the commandant to the Command and Staff School at Baguio. Then, on

29 November 1941, he took command of the 31st Division with its all-Filipino staff.[48]

Bluemel had been a terror to his junior officers, using his caustic tongue and constant criticism to organize his division for the war he knew was coming. When commanding the 45th Infantry, he sent one of his battalions to Bataan for guard duty. Rather than being displeased at going to this remote and diseased land, the officers were overjoyed at being away from Bluemel's supervision. He was a perfectionist, very demanding, and not at all shy about making corrections. Lieutenant Matt Dobrinic formed a quick first impression of Bluemel; he felt Bluemel was the meanest man in the entire United States Army. Another officer recalled that Bluemel "raised hell with his untrained Philippine Army officers and soldiers, and, I guess, got them more scared of him than the enemy. Result—one of the finest Philippine Army performances in 1941–42."[49] Somewhat fatalistic, Bluemel feared neither man nor beast. He patterned himself after General Pershing and often commented that Pershing's soldiers were more afraid of him than the Germans, and this was the reason for Pershing's success in the war.

The 31st Division mobilized along Luzon's coastal plain west of the Zambales Mountains. Simply getting from the average town to the mobilization center could take a recruit nearly two weeks, and upon his arrival he hardly found a going concern. As late as November 18 the 31st Division cantonment was still under construction. The water system had not yet been installed. Each company purchased its own rations from the local economy, and because Zambales Province was not self-supporting in food, food became a problem as mobilization progressed and the division assembled. Gasoline had to be trucked into the camp with trips lasting five to seven hours one way. Rains from June through November delayed local construction. Roads and bridges washed out, foundations flooded, and everything rotted. The engineers hauled in thousands of cubic yards of crushed rock to surface roads, but under the punishment of 10-wheel ammunition trucks, every trace of hard surfacing sank into the sea of mud. The 31st Division's engineer battalion spent all its time building roads and received no other training.[50]

The division's artillery regiment, the 31st Artillery, did not finish organizing itself until it reached Bataan on December 26, and instead of six firing batteries, it had only two, each armed with four wooden-wheeled 1917 British 75mm guns, without sights and without fire control equipment. Whereas a battery normally had two battery commander telescopes, two aiming circles, one rangefinder, twenty field glasses, and several plotting boards, the issue to a Philippine Army battalion (not battery), when available, was one aiming circle, one BC scope, and maybe five field glasses. The guns were delivered to the artillerymen on December 7, many of whom had never seen a cannon fired. Lucky cannoneers were able to fire two rounds per gun. They owned nothing with which to tow the guns, no vehicles of any sort. Even after Bluemel commandeered fifty commercial trucks on the first day of war, the guns still could not be towed. The old, wooden wheels fell off if towed at normal truck speeds. The guns were therefore portaged, loaded onto truck beds.[51]

The 31st Division had three infantry regiments, the 31st, 32nd, and 33rd infantry. The 31st Infantry (PA), not to be confused with the all-American 31st Infantry (US), was the first of the division's regiments to mobilize. Using the Olongapo Naval Station rifle range, the soldiers fired their rifles for the first time on November 24; one battalion fired fifty rounds per man, another battalion fired twenty-five per man, while the last battalion did not get to fire at all. The 32nd and 33rd infantry were mobilized on November 1 and November 25 when it seemed there would be sufficient space to house them. Neither of the two regiments finished basic training. Fifteen of the division's twenty-seven rifle companies failed to conduct any known-distance rifle practice before entering combat. There was but a single Browning Automatic Rifle in each rifle company, only eight .30-caliber water-cooled machine guns for each machine gun company, and only two heavy .50-caliber machine guns in an entire regiment. Some of the machine gunners were lucky enough to fire a few rounds. None had fired the .50-caliber machine gun or the 3-inch mortar.[52]

One reason for the shortage of automatic weapons can be traced to the summer of 1940. The catastrophic defeat of French and British forces on the European continent resulted in America shipping to Britain 25,000 BAR's and 86,000 machine guns. Transfer of this equipment took a big bite out of the Army's small arms stocks. It was a critical bite as far as the Philippines were concerned. For high-angle fire, there was a pitiful total of six 3-inch mortars for each regiment (316 had gone to the British). The ammunition for the outdated 3-inch (75mm) Stokes mortar proved later to have a 70 percent dud rate. The ammunition so amused the Japanese that they yelled with laughter when it was fired at them. But no matter how bad this ammunition was, it was better than the up-to-date 60mm mortar ammunition, ammunition for the newest mortar in the American inventory. Ammunition for the 60mm mortar never arrived in the Philippines.[53]

The men of the 31st Division lacked entrenching tools and steel helmets. With only 20,000 helmets in Defense Reserve for all the Philippine Army, the Quartermaster Corps was mobbed by each division demanding its full issue. Even individual uniforms were hard to find and soon wore or rotted off the men. There was a crying need for clothing, shoes, and accoutrements. Because the division could not get enough standard khaki uniforms, the blue denim fatigue clothes became the daily dress. Shoes were shoddy, consisting of canvas tops and rubber soles, and lasted two weeks in hard service. Army quartermaster agents placed contracts in Manila for khaki uniforms, blue denim uniforms, canvas leggings, canvas and leather shoes. Open market purchases were made of underwear, socks, office equipment and supplies, cooking utensils, towels, blankets, sun helmets, and even athletic equipment.[54]

The Filipino infantrymen carried World War I .30-caliber Enfield and Springfield rifles with a stock too long for their short arms and shoulders. "That rifle stock we had was about three-quarters of an inch too long for a Filipino to get up and reach around and get hold of the trigger," remembered Lieutenant Colonel James V. Collier. "It was just murder when he fired that thing because it had a kick anyway. When I saw them on the range, their shoulders were black and blue in no time."[55] Filipinos also had trouble getting their eye close enough to the rear sight to use it effectively. The Enfield rifles were plagued by a weak extractor made brittle by age, and although the Ordnance Corps tried to re-temper the extractors so they would not break, success in this venture was not great.

The 31st Division's signal officer could not raise contact with units just a mile distant. He seemed to have learned nothing during his three months of training. Technically ignorant, he was no better at handling his men. The few radio sets were of limited range and reliability and untrained radio operators further reduced the effectiveness of the sets.[56]

In the 31st Division, as in the other reserve divisions, roughly forty American officers and twenty American or Scout sergeants served as instructors. The term "instructor" was something of a misnomer because the American high command held the American instructors responsible for each unit's success or failure. Except for the division and regimental commanders, the Americans did not command and could not officially issue orders. However, they were still responsible. If the Filipino commander was about to make a serious mistake, the instructor was required to step in and correct the problem, using his leadership qualities and great tact. Colonel William F. Maher told Lieutenant Colonel Richard C. Mallonee, instructor for the 21st Artillery, "It looks like a mess now, but it won't be if war comes. You won't have any trouble. I know these Filipino officers well. . . . There isn't one of them who won't be tickled pink to have the responsibility for decision taken out of his hands—they will be more than willing, they will be anxious."[57] Mallonee was not convinced, however, and he summed up everyone's concern over the instructor situation. "I cannot clearly visualize such a situation—a [Filipino] commander upon the battlefield, with an [American] advisor, instructor, inspector, call him what you want, camped on his tail, checking his every thought and action, interfering with the estimate of the situation, injecting his own personality into the deliberations and decisions. It sound[s] unworkable. It smacks of the soviet. I don't think it possible."

The officer instructors normally worked at division and regimental headquarters, and the sergeants served with battalions and companies. Platoon, company, and battalion commanders were all Filipinos, as were battalion, regiment, and division staff officers. Only the division and regimental commanders were Americans. The Filipinos had only the most rudimentary knowledge of their duties, and they knew even less about training troops. A few of the divisions were commanded by Filipino generals, but they were advised by Americans, the more senior of whom gloried in their troop-training nickname of the "hot sun and dust boys." Below regiments, Americans served as instructors. As the war progressed, necessity forced the replacement of many Filipino officers, especially battalion commanders, by Americans.[58]

During mobilization the crippling lack of leadership in the Philippine Army was partially resolved by the transfer of American officers and sergeants from American and Philippine Scout units, a transfer good for the Philippine Army but bad for the units which lost their experienced, long-service personnel. Too often the transfer meant the loss of a key sergeant from one unit and the assignment of a poor officer to another. Most American companies lost all but one officer and ten NCO's to instruct the new Philippine Army regiments and battalions, while American battalions and regiments lost their staff officers. The Philippine Division headquarters lost its commander, its division artillery officer, the G2, G3, Adjutant General, Quartermaster, Surgeon, Signal Officer, and several assistants. In addition to the Americans, approximately 2,300 Scouts had left their units by December 8 to cadre the reserve divisions. Once war began, some American enlisted men were given battlefield commissions and sent from American units to the Philippine Army. Most stayed with the Filipino units until killed or captured. For many, it was an unhappy experience. A few came wandering back to their old units after their Filipino units dissolved. Without a home, these newly commissioned lieutenants rejoined their old companies. Some American sergeants were offered commissions, but either recognizing their limitations or concerned over working with Filipinos, they refused.[59]

Experiences of these cadre varied, but all could claim they were not bored. An American artillery officer spread his Scout sergeants throughout a Filipino artillery battalion and told them to maintain order, using a pick handle if necessary. The Filipino officers did not like this, but the American told them that all they had to do was their duty, and no one would get hurt. Another officer's task was to replace the daily eight hours of close-order drill he found with some good, sound tactics. An American in Aparri, "the kingdom of ants, bugs, snakes, centipedes, and low-born fleas," was washed out to sea and spent ninety minutes swimming to shore through shark-infested waters. That evening he dined with his Filipinos on dried shrimp and roasted bat. Other instructors engaged strong-smelling mountain goats in hand-to-hand combat. One droll fellow claimed he was assigned to a new island which had just erupted from the sea. The island lay a couple of hundred miles south of Zamboanga, and he first needed to take an interisland steamer, change to a schooner, then to a fishing boat, and next to an outrigger canoe. Finally, claimed the man, he waded the last quarter mile to his new assignment.[60]

Eating with the Filipinos was an adventure. Sometimes the food was better than that available in Manila, but more often it was not. Coffee came in big brown crystals fortified with ants, spiders, and other creatures. Chicken was consumed in such quantities the Americans marveled that any birds survived to reproduce themselves. Boiled rice and fish was the Filipino's main fare. "The fish are served up in a most frank manner," one officer wrote his family. "When you look at them they look right back at you."[61] The Filipinos supplemented their mess with boiled vegetables and occasionally with beef or pork stew.

Attending a Filipino feast could be a trying experience for newly assigned Americans. "The main dish was the famous lechon, or pig roasted whole on a stick," recalled Lieutenant Fisher. "The meat was not cooked quite enough for me so I didn't any more than just taste it, and the sample didn't particularly overwhelm me. They had some fancy kind of sauce to put on it. Then there was a sweet sticky mess of rice with peppers, chicken, and a lot of other stuff in it—it tasted something like Spanish rice. Plenty of the inevitable 'manook' (chicken) was served up, cooked in several different ways. I was also given a couple of great big shrimps with the eyes and feelers still present and accounted for. Then they passed a bowl of stuff that raised a slight doubt in my mind which was confirmed when they told me that it was the blood of the pig—curdled and turned brown somehow, and full of some stuff that was probably tripe. Needless to say, I didn't fill up on that particular course."[62]

The Philippine Military Academy at Baguio graduated its first four-year class in 1939, but with a total enrollment of only 400 cadets in all four classes, annual officer production was insignificant. Another home-grown source of officers for the Philippine Army was the semiannual class of reservists. Twice a year, men inducted for their five-and-a-half months of training were screened and the most promising were selected for another six months of training as sergeants. Then the best from the NCO course went into Officer Candidate School and received commissions as third lieutenants. More officers came from ROTC units at colleges and universities. Politics proved a problem in developing effective leaders, and a large number of newly appointed officers owed their commissions to political patronage. This proved to be one of the greatest stumbling blocks in training the army. These officers were completely untrained, yet the Americans could not relieve them and replace them with competent personnel. USAFFE stopped anyone from making or breaking NCO's or removing unfit officers, apparently on the grounds that there would be sufficient time to evaluate them and then make changes. An interesting sidelight on these Philippine Army officers is that the proud Philippine Scouts, trained by and serving under competent American officers, often refused to salute Philippine Army officers. The Scouts felt that the Philippine Army officers were not real officers like their American leaders, they were just Filipinos, and the Scouts wanted nothing to do with them. This attitude caused "lots of trouble." Even within the Philippine Army officer corps, there was marked antagonism between former Scout and Constabulary officers.[63]

Another source of leaders was the influx of American officers from the United States. In August the War Department was preparing to ship 500 reserve officers to the Philippines and took under consideration a request for 246 regular officers. There were only 101 regulars in the grades desired available to fill this request, so the War Department had to substitute 145 reservists, often captains instead of the more senior officers requested. MacArthur also received permission to retain officers in the Philippines past their normal two-year tour until replacements arrived. These new officers normally spent a week or two in Manila where they received briefings before being assigned to Filipino units as instructors. Brigadier General Edward P. King, Jr., briefed some newly arrived colonels and told them that there was no such thing as racial superiority. The Americans would have to demonstrate any superiority they desired to claim. King explained that Filipinos were extremely proud and sensitive. Many of their reactions had their roots in real or perceived racial slights. The Filipino people had demonstrated personal bravery and individual fighting ability throughout history, and it was the job of the Americans to train and weld that individual fighting ability into an army. General King cautioned the Americans not to judge the Filipinos by American standards, they were not immoral but amoral, not lazy but lacking an American's stamina, not liars unless it was essential to avoid embarrassment or disgrace.[64]

But efficient handling and dispatch of these newly arrived officers did not always receive a high priority. Lieutenant Fisher arrived on the SS *President Coolidge* and was met by officers from the Philippine Department while the ship was still in the middle of Manila Bay. The officers brought assignment orders and passed out information about quarters, uniforms, and administrative details. They went into even more detail about bars and nightclubs. Fisher was then trucked to Fort McKinley where he waited for the next two weeks with nothing to do except obtain things he needed for service with the Philippine Army. Fisher and the other lieutenants spent their time visiting Manila and generally enjoying themselves. "It was a life of luxury," Fisher recalled. "I felt like a rich planter, dressed in crisp white, eating fine food and well served in every way by the little Filipinos."[65] The faster paced activity common to the temperate zone was officially discouraged in the Philippines. "Slow down, boys, you're in the tropics now," was the refrain greeting anyone who questioned the leisurely pace.[66]

Until the day after Christmas, the 31st Division averaged between half and three-quarters strength. On December 26, the assignment of recently recruited Filipinos, whose training varied between little and absolutely none, brought the division to full strength. Bluemel arrived on Bataan with about 7,000 men and agreed to take another 800 new recruits. As an unexpected bonus he had dumped on him another 1,500. Bluemel's immediate problem was to feed the men. He brought his artillery regiment up to strength by accepting this collection of civilians. But without a full complement of artillery equipment, most of these men were organized as provisional infantry and never saw a cannon. For the division's campaign on Bataan, a full quarter of the men were recently drafted civilians with no idea of how to fight. Even the men who joined the division early received only rudimentary basic training. There was no chance for battalion, regimental, or division training exercises.[67]

The problems experienced by the 31st Division were similar to those faced by all the reserve divisions. Each unit was desperately short of qualified officers and enlisted men, while logistically even the most basic of equipment was in critically short supply. Most serious, and unknown to the men bustling about their bivouacs, they were short of the most precious item necessary for their survival. Time. Supply and training problems could have been solved in six months to a year, but nowhere was there a supply of time. And although the hasty and confused mobilization may seem to show an absence of good planning, this was not the case. It was probably the best that could have been done under the circumstances. If the Philippines had waited until adequate supplies were present before mobilizing, there would have been no hope of delaying the Japanese at the beaches or fighting them on Bataan.[68]

CHAPTER THREE

The Scramble into Bataan

AFTER THEIR SUCCESSFUL LANDINGS ON LUZON'S BEACHES, THE Japanese 14th Army closed in on MacArthur's Filamerican army from both the north and the south. Lieutenant General Masaharu Homma commanded nine regiments organized into two divisions, the 16th and 48th. From the north came four infantry regiments, two tank regiments, and a reconnaissance regiment, while from the south pushed two infantry regiments. Two regiments of medium artillery, three regiments of engineers, and five battalions of antiaircraft guns supported Homma's infantry. With these forces—tactical formations filled with men who could maneuver under fire—the Japanese evicted the more numerous defenders from one position after another. But MacArthur was buying time, trading the large spaces of Luzon for the hours needed to enter Bataan.[1]

As Wainwright's North Luzon Force struggled toward Bataan from Lingayen's beaches, the Philippine Scout 14th Engineer Battalion was marking defensive positions along the Bataan defense line. When Filipino units staggered into the peninsula, some of them were able to dig in along surveyed lines, but others found only the most dense jungle imaginable. Air Corps engineers, augmented by civilians, built four gravel-surfaced airstrips: Pilar, Bataan, Cabcaben, and Mariveles. Before the war there was a single airstrip on Bataan, a 2,000-foot strip cut from the jungle where Bataan Field would later be built. The airfield was named "Richard's Folly," satirizing the officer responsible for its construction. Although it was used to evacuate sick soldiers to Manila before the war, few people believed it would ever be used during a war. This field, now named Bataan Field, was only 68 percent complete the first week of December, but it was handling P-40's by early January. After December 8 engineers started work on three more fields. The American 803rd Engineer Aviation Battalion took over construction and maintenance of the four fields and made considerable improvements. Hard work turned Cabcaben into a field big enough to handle B-17 bombers. Engineers even strung landing lights to allow night landing of the large aircraft. But the work was in vain; the four-engined fortresses never arrived.[2]

Work on the four airfields was continual, because anything that looked like an airfield drew enemy attention. Cabcaben barrio next to Cabcaben Field was destroyed save for a half-dozen stilted nipa houses. The natives were gone, and a fine gray ash marked where their houses had stood. At Bataan's southern tip, Mariveles Field required round-the-clock work because a high water table and enemy bombing ravaged the runway. At Bataan Field, dust on the runway became a problem, and without equipment or materiel with which to lay a permanent surface, the men looked for an unconventional solution. Major Wendell W. Fertig, a mining engineer and a graduate of Colorado University, remembered his tennis playing days in Colorado when water and sugar-beet syrup dampened dust on clay courts. The ingredients were available, so workers applied water and waste molasses to Bataan Field. It worked.[3]

Even though the number of friendly planes diminished with discouraging rapidity, engineers kept the airfields operating so as to receive the aerial reinforcements expected from the United States. Japanese planes bombed the fields during the day, and American construction crews repaired them at night. Often, big tractors were pushing dirt back into bomb holes, graders were scraping the ground smooth, and tampers were at work almost before the enemy planes were out of sight. Because the ground was solid, the raids did little more than put the field out of action for an hour or so. Because the engineers working on the big machines could not hear enemy planes approach, a detail of men acted as lookouts. They blew whistles and fired rifles—three shots in succession—at which the equipment operators stopped work and ran to foxholes spaced along both sides of the runway. The engineers succeeded in driving their equipment into the concealing jungle more often than not.[4]

Preceding MacArthur's ground forces, his badly reduced Air Force flew into its new airstrips. Aerial combat, bombings while immobile on their fields, and frequent accidents—including destruction by friendly antiaircraft fire—reduced MacArthur's fighter strength to where P-40's operated only for reconnaissance and harassing missions. The P-40 was the best American fighter available in the Philippines. Manufactured by

Curtis-Wright, this single-seat plane was originally designed for ground support and coastal defense of the American continent. Best known for its subsequent service with the Flying Tigers in Burma and China, it could absorb punishment and come home. The P-40's took off on mid-morning reconnaissance missions which hardly lasted thirty minutes. Then the P-40 would reappear, land, and hurry back into the jungle. More inhibiting than bombing to American use of its airfields was the patrol of Japanese Type-97 dive bombers established over each field. Oftentimes, P-40's had to dodge these strafers when they desired to take off or land. From time to time, P-40's surprised and destroyed the rigid-landing gear Japanese, but P-40's were also lost. Although the Japanese could maintain the rate of exchange, the Americans could not. American combat patrols were not much more impressive than their reconnaissance missions; they could not control the air over friendly lines. All they could do was hit and run. Trouble plagued American pilots even when the skies were clear of Japanese. When three P-35's tried to land at Pilar, little more than a dirt strip cut from dry rice paddies, nervous antiaircraft gunners shot down the first plane and killed the pilot. The second pilot was so unnerved he overshot the runway and stood the plane on its nose. Later, when a P-40 landed, it ground looped and lost its propeller and one wing.[5]

On Christmas Day, American air strength consisted of sixteen P-40's and four P-35's. On January 4, the Americans launched a concerted interception effort against a flight of Japanese bombers headed for Corregidor. Colonel Harold H. George told his air staff that when the Japanese came that day, the P-40's would attack. Known as "Pursuit George" so as not to confuse him with another Harold George known as "Bomber George," Colonel George had his staff analyze Japanese tactics and habits and develop an interception plan. Although all Bataan's P-40's would participate, one squadron would refuel and fly south to Mindanao after the interception, leaving nine planes on Bataan; the P-40's were too concentrated and to vulnerable to leave all sixteen in place. So on January 4, plane-weary men moving about Bataan heard a new sound, the strong, high-pitched buzz of sixteen P-40's circling for altitude. The planes disappeared into clouds and headed for the high-flying twin-engined Japanese. But the P-40's failed to overtake the bombers, and when the squadron detailed to fly to Mindanao left, only nine P-40's remained to support MacArthur's army.[6]

When MacArthur ordered his Far East Air Force headquarters to redeploy to bases farther south from which American air could protect the lines of communication into Luzon, General Lewis H. Brereton alerted his staff, issued orders on December 24 for all elements to move to

Bataan, and placed Colonel George in charge of those elements which would remain on Luzon. Brereton's headquarters then left Luzon without leaving anyone in charge to coordinate the moves or answer questions. As a result the subsequent movement of Air Corps ground echelons from central Luzon into Bataan was a confused, uncoordinated event which, to the amazement of many, somehow succeeded. Most squadrons received no more than a hurried telephone call, telling them to move immediately. Because Colonel George was then making a reconnaissance for possible air fields, no one remained at Fort McKinley to oversee the evacuation of the numerous squadrons. Consequently, specific orders did not exist and units hit the road in mild panic. Great haste was urged, but no instructions as to what to do or how to travel were issued. Throughout the daylight hours of December 24, Air Corps formations streamed out of Fort McKinley, Nichols Field, Nielson Field, and Clark Field, all headed for Bataan.[7]

Captain Maurice G. Hughett, acting commander of the 17th Pursuit at Nichols, succeeded in contacting Colonel George's headquarters and asked what he should do with all the field's spare parts, oil, gas, ammunition, and supplies—should he try to evacuate them, was the road to Bataan still open? Hughett was told to evacuate as much as possible by convoy, so he gathered all the trucks he could find. He even filled empty ones with food taken from the Quartermaster Docks and its regulation-bound Quartermaster captain who had to be encouraged by a .45-caliber pistol. The 17th Pursuit reached their new home, Pilar Field, the afternoon of Christmas Day.[8]

The 27th Materiel Squadron was also at Nichols when orders to move arrived, and its commander grabbed a large moving van with its civilian driver, collected his scattered elements, and headed for Manila's Pier Five. The airmen started loading into a large interisland ship and by dark they had loaded 1,500 men and some equipment on the ship. The ship was so crowded that the men could not lie down. The ship anchored off Bataan the next morning, and all 1,500 men climbed into barges and shuttled ashore. After the last soldiers disembarked, enemy planes attacked and sank the ship.[9]

Only a handful of airmen were still at Nielson Field when the withdrawal order arrived, and they had to get to Manila's docks by 1900 hours. Three second lieutenant pilots, each fresh from flying school, flew three reconnaissance planes to Corregidor where they damaged two on landing. The Nielson Field garrison boarded a ship and sailed to Mariveles. The 91st Bomb Squadron made such a hurried departure from San Marcelino that they literally did not finish lunch. They left almost all their equipment behind.[10]

At Clark Field, Major Andrews of the Philippine Air Corps received orders to burn everything, including twelve basic-training planes and six P-26's. Technical equipment, photographic laboratory supplies, aviation gas, and airfield hangers were all torched. Fearing the Japanese were only hours away, men frantically raced back and forth, destroying materiel and installations in a haphazard sequence. They stripped .50-caliber machine guns out of wrecked planes and packed every type of portable equipment onto trucks. The 27th Bomb Group started rolling just after the noon meal, and forty-two trucks were on the road before nightfall. The Group ordered its widely dispersed squadrons to meet at the Manila Docks where the first 300 men crammed aboard a boat build for 100 and sailed to Bataan.[11]

Destruction of bombs and gasoline at Clark fell to seventeen men of the 698th Ordnance Company who began their task on Christmas Day. "We had no experience with a job of this sort nor [did] anyone tell us how it was to be accomplished," recalled Private Millard Hileman.[12] They entered the five large igloo-type magazines—some holding up to 5,000 tons of bombs—as well as piles dispersed in the jungle, placed sticks of dynamite with blasting caps into fuse wells of 500-pound bombs, and attached fifteen-foot long fuses. Upon hearing one rifle shot, the men lit the fuses and jumped aboard two vehicles for a dash out of Clark Field. As they passed the gasoline dumps, the airmen fired tracers into the piles of 55-gallon drums and set them afire. The Japanese did not reach Clark Field until January 2, eight days after the start of the Air Corps evacuation.

Although American air power was not covering itself with glory, Japanese air was likewise surprisingly inefficient. Time and again, Japanese aircraft crossed appalling traffic jams and tangled roadways, but they droned blindly away to bomb their assigned targets, usually Manila or Corregidor. Americans on the ground found it inconceivable that the Japanese did not deem the choked roads a suitable target. The spectacle of roads clogged with military and civilian vehicles and thousands of soldiers—the refugees fleeing to Bataan—could not help but draw an aviator's excited gaze. "There were stretches of two to three miles where the interval between vehicles was three to five yards," recalled Colonel Collier. "A winding cloud of dust, ever reaching higher and higher, followed the curves and turns of the road. Hostile bombers with the rising sun glistening on wing tips, flying at low and high altitudes, crossed and recrossed the road."[13] The mess on the ground was a lucrative target, but the Japanese never hit the roads on an organized, sustained basis.

Even a halfhearted Japanese effort against the roads would have caused chaos and destruction completely out of proportion to the resources expended. Hours would have been spent clearing wreckage and filling craters, and the less stouthearted soldiers would have found it convenient to shed their uniforms and return home. The Filipinos were completely untrained in march formations and dispersion, and even loading vehicles could be a chaotic experience. "As each bus moved into place," remembered Colonel Mallonee as he loaded his 21st Artillery, "all men in its vicinity swarmed over it and fought each other for seats, then had to be forced out to load equipment. The officers had great difficulty getting the men to obey; [Lieutenant] Hendry, the mildest-mannered and most even-tempered of the American officers, had to use a flailing piece of bamboo on one occasion."[14]

Once the Filipinos were aboard, they proved easy targets for Japanese planes. Lieutenant Wayne Liles, a graduate of Oklahoma State University, was withdrawing with his Filipino 12th Infantry in a column of bumper-to-bumper buses. He found it almost impossible to get the Filipinos to keep distance between them, and he never understood why they did not get strafed and bombed when caught on the roads. So the flow of traffic continued, and the men on the ground shook their heads in collective disbelief.[15]

Nor did the Japanese give the railroads any special attention. Despite Japanese disinterest in Filipino trains, the Manila Railroad, the main artery of supply for MacArthur's army, went out of control on December 15 and collapsed on Christmas Day when the crews deserted their engines. The Japanese also ignored critical bridges over wide rivers. They did hold some heated discussions as to whether or not to hit the bridges, especially the Calumpit Bridges. The Japanese 48th Division, watching the Filipinos slip away, wanted the bridges hit, but the opinion of Colonel Monjiro Akiyama, 14th Army air officer, prevailed. For some reason he believed destruction of the bridges would accomplish little. Even when the 14th Army approved a watered-down version of a bridge-destroying mission, Japanese air made only insignificant efforts. A vigorous campaign against the vulnerable lines of communications would have fatally crippled MacArthur's army, and there would have been no battle for Bataan.[16]

It should not have taken any real talent for the Japanese to spot these convoys, for the civilian buses still sported their prewar orange and yellow paint jobs. Buses had fancy names printed all over them, "Henrietta," "Amelia," the name of the driver's favorite girlfriend. Painted all the colors of the rainbow, with bright advertisements bedecking the sides, each convoy gave the appearance of a huge civilian picnic, an outdoor party by the whole of Luzon. "Units were pouring into Bataan," remembered Captain Clarence R. Bess, a two-year veteran of the Philippines and service company commander to the American 31st Infantry. "Organizations were intermixed with other organizations and separate supply trucks which were hauling supplies from Manila. It was evident that either higher headquarters had failed to provide a movement schedule, or that it was being entirely disregarded. The long tightly jammed column turned south at the Layac Junction, and crawled down the only road into the Bataan Peninsula. Two large formations of Japanese heavy bombers . . . roared overhead. They were not interested."[17] The men in the columns were actually worried that soldiers manning antiaircraft guns might shoot and attract Japanese attention, but the gunners did not fire and the planes did not attack. There is no doubt that if the Japanese had initiated an aerial campaign, they would have destroyed most of the army's vehicles and equipment. MacArthur had neither sufficient aerial nor antiaircraft assets to offer even the most rudimentary protection to the miles of roads. And more critical than the loss of equipment would have been the loss of time. The Japanese failure to exploit their air arm was the most significant and far-reaching tactical mistake they made during the entire Philippine campaign.

Almost as if trying to offset Japanese errors, the Americans lost incredible quantities of supplies just north of Bataan. War Plan Orange 3 called for a six-month supply of food, materiel, and ammunition for Bataan, but a series of decisions combined to frustrate prewar plans. The first slip was MacArthur's decision to store supplies at depots across Luzon to support the forces defending the beaches. "Upon this decision," wrote Brigadier General Charles C. Drake, MacArthur's Quartermaster, "our Quartermaster people had used a large amount of the defense supplies for stocking our depots behind the troops at these beaches instead of shipping it to Bataan as contemplated in our defense plans. . . . Now with a change in the plans we were faced with the rather difficult task of getting these supplies back from the depots to Bataan. . . ."[18] Had supplies been moved to Bataan beginning on December 8, Quartermaster officers were confident they would have been fully prepared to meet obligations by January 3. General Drake figured it would take two weeks to stock Bataan once the order was given. When the Japanese landed, their control of the air and the defender's pressing need for troop transport left the prestocked and dispersed depots immobile, and when Drake received the order to stock Bataan, he had only seven days to do so.

Reflecting the haste and frenzy of rear-echelon evacuation, the Americans received orders to abandon Fort Stotsenburg on December 24, a week before the Japanese arrived. After the hospital was evacuated by train, other rail cars were filled with artillery ammunition, bombs, and food and sent south. Depending upon the unit, its leaders, and its state of discipline, some units arrived on Bataan with all equipment, some with none. Some evacuations were so disorganized that Lieutenant Colonel Collier at USAFFE headquarters reported the abandonment of several serviceable planes. "Air Corps officers say the planes were obsolete," Collier remembered, "but never-the-less, they could have been used on much needed reconnaissance and observation missions and were so used by the enemy. One Air Corps Lieutenant (story not verified) did go back and fly a plane out. Another Lieutenant made minor repairs on two planes at Nichols Field between 25 December and 1 January and flew the planes to Bataan, one of which was a P-40."[19] After shipping 50,000 gallons of gasoline to Guagua, and after issuing as much as possible to nearby units, supply personnel had to destroy another 250,000 gallons because they could not evacuate it. Each afternoon from December 25–29, crews returned to Fort Stotsenburg and worked all night loading twenty-five railroad cars nightly with food, gas, and ammunition. Another twenty trucks carried materiel to Porac. Because of the hurried evacuation, there are wildly conflicting reports as to whether or not all supplies were removed from Fort Stotsenburg.

Even the equipment salvaged from Fort Stotsenburg by round-the-clock work stopped at rail terminals just north of Bataan. At San Fernando, Lubao, and Guagua, 308 railroad boxcars crammed with vitally needed supplies sat on sidings. Those supplies included six cannon, ten carloads of 155mm shells, and sixty carloads of supplies, all removed from Fort Stotsenburg. By December 30, no Army railroad personnel could be found to move the cars, nor did Filipino dispatchers know what to do with the tons of gasoline, food, and ammunition. It sat waiting for someone to organize its movement into Bataan, all the time prey to enemy aircraft. On December 31, Japanese planes bombed the San Fernando station, destroying dozens of freight cars. Then, when MacArthur's army withdrew past the rail terminals on January 1 and 2, the supplies were lost.[20]

The Philippine Government Rice Central at Cabanatuan held 10,000,000 pounds of rice and was abandoned partly because Commonwealth regulations forbade transfer of rice from one province to another. Although permission to move the rice was requested, authority to do so did not arrive in time, and enough rice to feed Bataan's garrison for a year was lost. Whether sufficient transportation existed to move the rice if permission had been received is a moot point. Equally incredible was the loss of 2,000 cases of canned fish and corned beef and a stock of clothing at Tarlac, seventy road miles from Bataan. Japanese wholesalers owned the items, and when the American commander of the advance quartermaster depot there tried to confiscate these supplies, USAFFE issued specific orders forbidding his action. Because the materiel was considered private property, USAFFE warned Lieutenant Colonel Charles S. Lawrence that if the stocks were disturbed, he would face a court-martial. Those supplies at Tarlac under Lawrence's direct control were placed in dumps in the area of Wainwright's North Luzon Force in hopes the Filipinos would pick them up as they retreated. Enough food for five days was left for each division and separate unit.[21]

Just before the Americans abandoned Manila, quartermaster troops opened the huge commissary there to anyone who would come by. Even so, little of the canned goods were moved to Bataan because transportation could not be found; all the vehicles were committed to moving tactical units or had been stolen by pistol-waving soldiers. Although the Motor Transport Service had collected over 1,000 civilian vehicles with their drivers, had centralized them, and was running a dispatch service, these convoys were commandeered by officers needing transport, or officers kept the vehicles after they had delivered their loads. Because commanders did not understand the system, and because they feared they would be left without transportation, they grabbed everything in sight. Armed guards had to be placed on vehicles to prevent their theft. "Informal measures were taken to coordinate the movement of supplies to the rear," recalled Brigadier General Allan C. McBride, Deputy Commander of the Philippine Department. "Each unit and service had its own motor transport and each was busy moving its own supplies, regardless of the requirements of other services for transportation and labor."[22] In short, it was every unit for itself and damned be anyone who spared his transportation to move food for the good of the army. It is possible that only the Air Corps took serious advantage of Manila's open warehouses. Their vehicles were observed loaded to the axles with food. USAFFE had told its units to forage extensively and turn in whatever they had collected when they reached Bataan. But although many units arrived with ten to twenty-five days' rations, not an ounce was turned over to the Quartermaster dumps.

After the Manila Railroad and the Motor Transport Service collapsed, the only asset General Drake had to evacuate supplies was the Water Transport Service. Drake, a six-foot-tall, 54-year-old, 200-pound West Pointer, dispatched Army officers to take possession of all water transport in Manila Bay and the Pasig River, and he ordered useless small craft destroyed. Drake hoped to collect enough tugs, barges, and boats to move the food out of Manila. The first boats sailed to Corregidor to complete stockage of the island. This took only one day because rations for 10,000 men were already stored there. Then Drake routed the shipping to Bataan. Without any vehicles to move his equipment, engineer Major Arnold A. Boettcher trucked his supplies in civilian vehicles to docks on the Pasig River, loaded them into lighters, and had them towed to Mariveles. Bombings of the loading sites drove off many of the stevedores and slowed the loading, but manpower in the form of 200 American and British civilian volunteers kept the supplies flowing. The unwieldy barges could be towed at only three miles per hour, and the round trip between Manila and Bataan was sixty miles. Strong winds on Manila Bay slowed passage even more and delayed unloading at Bataan's three small piers. In good weather it took four hours to unload one barge.[23]

About 300 bargeloads slipped out of Manila, and by the time the city fell, 150 barges and five small ocean-going freighters were anchored in the North Channel and along Bataan's lower shore. Service Command soldiers unloaded the barges at night, and their efforts were so successful that 140 of the barges were brought in and all materiel hustled ashore and into the jungle. As long as the barges were returned to the same anchorage before first light the next morning, the Japanese seldom bombed them; they believed the craft were derelicts. The Americans lost ten barges to bombings and dragged anchors. Larger vessels, not surprisingly, suffered the attention of Japanese planes. The *Si-Kiang,* originally destined for Indochina with 2,500 tons of flour and large stocks of fuel, was bombed and sunk.[24]

One success story resulted from an officer disobeying orders. Captain Richard W. Fellows received an order on December 24 to evacuate the Philippine Air Corps repair parts depot to Bataan by midnight. Unable to leave by that time, the 27-year-old West Pointer was equally unwilling to abandon the airplane parts. Fellows and his men stayed near Manila for three days, loading parts into trucks and repairing four P-40's. On the night of December 27, the 200-ton coaster *Dos Hermanos* carried eighteen P-40 Allison engines and seven B-17 Wright engines to Bataan. Also stuffed aboard were seventy tons of tools, parts, and sheet metal. Three planes flew out using the city streets as runways, trucks shuttled between Bataan and Manila, and the last trucks and the fourth P-40 departed Manila the day the Japanese occupied the city, January 1.[25]

Despite movement of supplies to Bataan by land and sea, initial inventories showed about twenty-five days of food for the number of soldiers and civilians estimated to be on Bataan. General Drake called the inventory "heart breaking." Instead of the planned 180-day supply of rations, the inventory turned up, at normal rates of consumption, 59 days of canned meat and fish, 40 days of canned milk, 39 days of canned vegetables and flour, and a 20-day supply of rice. There were 500,000 C rations for emergency use. The Quartermaster Corps counted 10,000 trousers and 10,000 shirts, 50,000 shoes, 50,000 issue socks, 75,000 commercial socks, 20,000 issue underwear, 50,000 commercial undershirts, and 25,000 commercial drawers. Supply personnel expected to get only four million rounds of .30-caliber ammunition to Bataan, but they succeeded in bringing in nearly sixteen million. This accomplishment is attributable to the fact that two-thirds of the ammunition reserves, 15,000 tons, were already in Bataan when the war started. Another 15,000 tons were shipped in by the new year. Most of the munitions were stored in 137 magazines that had been constructed in southern Bataan before the war. Forward ammunition supply points would be resupplied nightly from these magazines.[26]

Prewar plans called for a defense force of 43,000 men to fight on Bataan for six months. Instead, there were now 15,000 Americans, 65,000 Filipinos, and 26,000 refugees. General Drake headed to Corregidor to tell General Richard K. Sutherland, MacArthur's chief of staff, this surprising news. "He was not willing to believe the strength report," recalled Drake. "He figured that there were not altogether 75,000 to 80,000 persons on Bataan and that the organizations were undoubtedly padding their reports in order to get more rations. I was very willing to accept that view as I believed the same thing, but I said that the only thing the Quartermaster could and would do, was to supply the food as called for. I stated also that putting the whole thing together the food would last only for about 20 days and recommended that we go on half rations at once . . . 30 ounces of 2,000 calories per day per man."[27]

There were problems also with fuel. Trucks arrived on Bataan with drums of gasoline and did not know where to go, so the drivers simply drove down the East Road, rolling the 55-gallon drums into ditches alongside the road. Whoever needed gas drove up to a drum and filled up. Even stocks of fuel already centralized in Bataan at Limay in prewar bodegas—300,000 gallons of gas and oil brought in during the summer of 1941—were dispersed for fear of air attacks. In mid-December, the 55-gallon drums were dumped in ditches where a considerable amount was stolen. During the first week of January, officers discovered gasoline consumption was exceeding 14,000 gallons a day. A similar situation existed with food; drivers dumped their loads under trees, and units then plundered the supplies as they marched past.[28]

One of the first officers to recognize the trouble with vehicles and gasoline was Colonel Hugh H. Casey, USAFFE's Engineer Officer. In a January 2 letter, he reported the traffic situation was out of hand with heavy congestion, numerous wrecked trucks on the road, and poor road discipline. Roads were not marked, command posts were hidden where even friendly forces could not find them, and military police could not accomplish their mission because they were frequently overruled by officers. Drivers bunched together on the road, refueled in plain sight of enemy aircraft, and if they ran out of fuel, they pushed their vehicles into ditches and walked away. An American officer dispersing fuel at Lamao found numerous vehicles running up and down the peninsula on nothing more than social calls. He cut off fuel supplies, and gradually the stream of vehicles thinned to those on official business. Harsh orders had to be issued concerning looting of supply dumps. One order stated that anyone caught looting or hoarding supplies would be either court-martialed or shot. Guards received orders to shoot anyone caught near a supply dump without proper reason or authority.[29]

With all these grim supply reports, MacArthur's generals still had to think about building a defense on Bataan. The Japanese were coming.

CHAPTER FOUR

Buying Time, The Guagua-Porac Line

ON JANUARY 2 MACARTHUR WAS DEPLOYING HIS FILIPINOS ALONG the two roads leading to the neck of the Bataan peninsula. Ten days of fighting placed the Japanese at the gates to Bataan, and a front of more than ten miles was in hasty organization. Fifteen miles from the entrance to Bataan the 21st and 11th infantry divisions, supported by the 26th Cavalry and two American light tank battalions, prepared to buy some time. The South Luzon Force had reached safety and the withdrawals for the purpose of concentrating on Bataan were complete. The longer Wainwright's North Luzon Force could hold the Japanese, the more time MacArthur's soldiers would have to construct defenses in Bataan itself.[1]

With the Zambales Mountains to the left and the Pampangan tidal swamps to the right the two most battle-tested Filipino divisions nervously awaited what they believed to be the entire Japanese 14th Army, an army rumored to be 120,000 strong. Actually, Japanese strength on Luzon was about 60,000 and, even then, only two reinforced regiments were poised to strike at Bataan. But at MacArthur's headquarters, Colonel Charles A. Willoughby estimated the enemy had about three divisions, or 45,000 men, aimed at the entrance to Bataan. What the Americans did not know was that the main body of Homma's 14th Army was marching toward Manila. For despite years in which to ferret out the secrets of War Plan Orange 3, MacArthur's movement into Bataan surprised the Japanese. The Japanese considered Manila the core of American ground, air, and naval strength in the Philippines, the capture of which would achieve the aim of invading the islands. Because they expected the Americans to make their last stand around Manila, most Japanese believed the columns winding into Bataan were no more than insignificant forces, remnants of the routed beach defenders.[2]

There was ample Japanese discussion about the troops entering Bataan. One group of officers believed Bataan should be besieged immediately, besieged but not attacked. They felt that because the Americans had originally intended Bataan as the main battlefield, and because there could not be less than 50,000 soldiers there, the Americans would offer considerable resistance across very difficult terrain. It would be foolish to launch an assault against a deeply entrenched enemy who could more easily be starved into submission. The second group of officers argued for an immediate attack. They believed only remnants of the Philippine Army survived to reach the peninsula. These remnants would be in poor shape with low morale. The 10,000 to 30,000 troops estimated to have survived the beach debacle could easily be overwhelmed. Experience during the march across Luzon seemed to support those who believed the Filipinos were beaten. All that was needed was just one more hard push.[3]

General Homma's chief of staff, Lieutenant General Masami Maeda, understood MacArthur's move, but his counsel was ignored. Everyone's sights were set on Manila, always considered the principal objective, and little could distract or interest anyone in Bataan. So the Japanese dispatched minor forces toward the peninsula. General Maeda did not feel he learned too late about the Filipino movement to Bataan, nor did he feel the army staff was taken by surprise. Rather, he claimed the Filipinos began their movement away from the beaches sooner than expected; the beach defense forces fled before the main body of the 14th Army could land and start the pursuit. "I must confess too," Maeda wrote, "that the destruction of all bridges by the American forces delayed our advance."[4] General Wainwright's North Luzon Force had ravaged the country's bridges, railroad equipment and rolling stock, telegraph stations and centrals, surplus supplies, gasoline storage tanks, and piers. The Japanese were very impressed by American use of "unimaginably great quantities of dynamite," 230 tons of which had been supplied by civilian mining companies. Heavily supported by artillery, the Japanese advancing against Bataan were deployed in two large columns with the mission of pushing down both main roads. They were not overly concerned about the upcoming action, for they expected to make quick work of the Filipinos and had every confidence in their ability to rout them.[5]

General Mateo Capinpin's 21st Division held the west road leading into Bataan. As was common in all the reserve divisions, the 21st Division was filled with recruits, although some of the enlisted men had attended the premobilization training period. Capinpin and his staff took command of the division on November 18 after completing the command and staff course at Camp Henry T. Allen. The senior officers of the division spent only three weeks at their new duties before the war began. Most of the junior officers were reservists called to active duty in September, and although they were sharp and could understand the theoretical aspects of their duties, they were generally unable to apply the "book" to actual situations in the field. Far too often these officers evidenced little interest in anything other than their own well-being.[6]

On the left of the line General Capinpin deployed Lieutenant Colonel Valentin Valasco's 21st Infantry on flat open sugarcane fields from the mountains to Route 74. Most of the Filipinos of the 21st Infantry had joined the regiment later than General Capinpin and received only marginal training. The regiment was tired and "used up" from several hard days of fighting, and now hardly 100 riflemen held each kilometer of the long front. G Troop, 26th Cavalry, using a pack radio and mounted messengers for communication, tied the 21st Infantry's left flank into the Zambales Mountains. On the right of the division's front, Major Joaquin D. Esperitu's 22nd Infantry dug in behind the Porac-Guagua Road. The 22nd Infantry was the strongest and best trained of the division's three regiments but training had progressed slowly because of the time spent constructing beach defenses in December. Except for the 22nd Infantry, which was fortunate enough to receive eight weeks training, training throughout the division was "terribly inadequate."[7] Five miles to the rear in division reserve was the most recently mobilized regiment, Major Liberato Littaua's 23rd Infantry which had received practically no training at all. In fact the first time the men ever practiced firing their rifles was on December 12. Lieutenant Colonel Nemisio Catalan's 21st Artillery—three battalions of 75mm cannon—deployed in support of the division on cane fields as flat as a billiard table.

Equipment in the 21st Division was inadequate with the exception of rifles. Spare parts could not be obtained in acceptable quantities for any piece of equipment. Tactical transportation did not exist, and even shoes were scarce in the 23rd Infantry. Although Philippine Army infantry divisions did not normally have the new 81mm mortar, the 21st Division learned of some at Camp Del Pilar, the field artillery school. During the retreat they broke into the storeroom and picked up nineteen of the valuable mortars, but when supply personnel requisitioned ammunition, the Ordnance Department investigated and reclaimed all but six tubes. Even then, no ammunition was supplied until late March when some rounds were received by submarine from Australia.[8]

On the afternoon of January 2 lead elements of the Japanese 9th Infan-

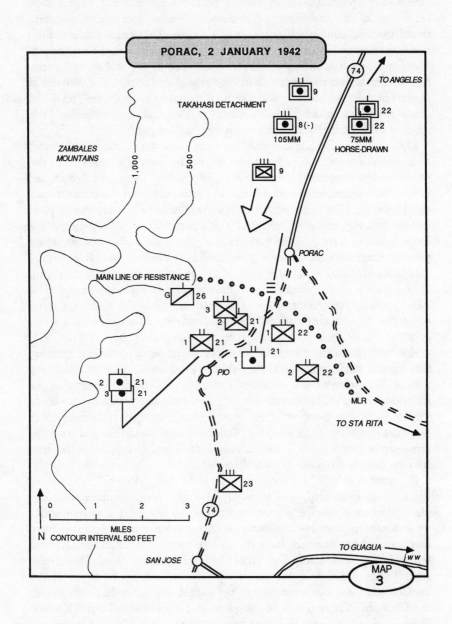

PORAC, 2 JANUARY 1942

TO ANGELES

TAKAHASI DETACHMENT

ZAMBALES
MOUNTAINS

1,000

500

9

8(-)

105MM

22

22

75MM
HORSE-DRAWN

9

PORAC

MAIN LINE OF RESISTANCE

G   26

3

2   21

1   21

22

1

1   21

PIO

2   21

3   21

2   22

MLR

TO STA RITA

23

0   1   2   3

MILES

N   CONTOUR INTERVAL 500 FEET

74

TO GUAGUA

SAN JOSE

MAP
3

try rolled down Route 74 and hit the Filipinos at Porac. The 9th Infantry formed the infantry component of the Takahashi Detachment, named for Lieutenant Colonel Katsumi Takahashi. Colonel Takahashi was actually the commander of the detachment's artillery but he rose to command everything after the death of Colonel Kamijima three days earlier. Supporting the 9th Infantry were two batteries of the 22nd Field Artillery—horse-drawn 75mm's—and most of the 8th Field Heavy Artillery Regiment's 105mm guns. The 9th Independent Field Heavy Artillery Battalion, then near Tarlac, advanced toward Porac to support the attack. Colonel Takahashi's mission was to drive down Route 74, break the Filipino line, and seize Dinalupihan. To soften the defenses, heavy Japanese mortar and artillery fire walked across the line, and a disproportionate number of Filipinos suffered head wounds because the men did not have helmets. Small as the Japanese force was, it pushed the stubborn 21st Infantry back 2,000 yards into its reserve.[9]

Just short of the regimental reserve line near the town of Pio the 21st Infantry rallied and, supported by division artillery firing at ranges of less than 600 yards, held the Japanese. The enemy came so close to the Filipino guns that they were "about as far from the muzzles as outfielders would play for Babe Ruth if there were no fences."[10] Artillery officers detailed spare men to fire small arms while the remainder serviced the guns. The Filipino infantry held to their positions through the night without further enemy attacks but the artillery prudently withdrew to better positions southwest of Pio. Using the night to conceal the move, the 21st Division headquarters ordered an infantry battalion from the reserve 23rd Infantry up to the 21st infantry for a dawn counterattack.

When there was enough light to see on the morning of January 3—around 0630 hours—it seemed the Japanese had pulled back, and a possibility existed the original line could be restored. Filipino patrols moved forward without opposition, then the reinforced 21st Infantry walked north across the fields, spread out in open formation. But the Japanese had other ideas. During the night the main body of Japanese infantry joined what until then had been just an advance guard. Additional artillery pulled into position during the night and prepared to shoot at first light. The advancing Filipinos ran smack into the Japanese. Small arms fire laced the slow-reacting recruits and men fell, including the commander of the recently arrived 2nd Battalion, 23rd Infantry. Never having practiced offensive maneuvers, the Filipinos were virtually helpless once they dove for cover. Some of the newly enlisted Filipinos panicked and fled into barren cane fields only to flee again when the cane prunings and mulch caught fire. One man exited the burning cane wearing only a pink girdle with garters. Behind the Japanese 9th Infantry their 8th Field

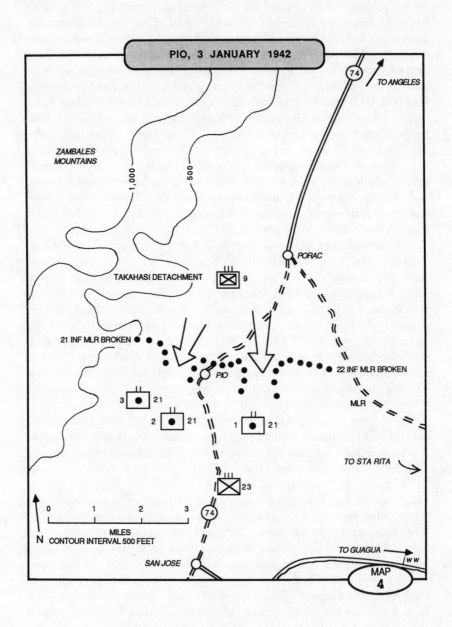

PIO, 3 JANUARY 1942

ZAMBALES
MOUNTAINS

1,000

500

74

TO ANGELES

PORAC

TAKAHASI DETACHMENT

9

21 INF MLR BROKEN

PIO

22 INF MLR BROKEN

MLR

3 21

2 21

1 21

TO STA RITA

23

74

0   1   2   3

MILES

N   CONTOUR INTERVAL 500 FEET

TO GUAGUA

jww

SAN JOSE

MAP
4

Heavy Artillery Regiment went into action. "We had our first taste of the muchly heralded Japanese 105," recalled 45-year-old Colonel Richard C. Mallonee, a veteran of Philippine service as a battery commander between 1926 and 1929, "and I will say I do not like the receiving end one damn bit."[11] The 105mm shells, combined with three Japanese planes strafing the disorganized Filipinos, chased the defenders south past the town of Pio. Here, the forward rush of the Japanese stopped. Colonel William A. Wappenstein, regimental senior instructor, held a glum conference with his tired, hungry, and dejected 21st Infantry instructors; several were wounded and all were concerned about their decimated battalions. When the conference ended each officer grimly returned to his unit.

When the Japanese started firing their artillery that morning General Capinpin dispatched a message to North Luzon Force reporting the fact. The return message read, "Re message 9 a. m. Instructions of yesterday stand. Hold line or die where you are."[12] The message irritated Capinpin, for it was obvious North Luzon Force believed his earlier report was an attempt to justify a withdrawal when all Capinpin meant it to be was information. The difficulty over this one message is not surprising. Communications were bad and terrible bottlenecks formed at each switchboard. Filipino operators, speaking different dialects, could not understand each other's English, let alone the Americans shouting into the lines. Under increasing pressure, operators froze and stopped answering calls. And when operators did understand each other, the innate politeness of the Filipinos slowed calls; it was considered rude to end a conversation without discussing each other's health, and general situation, and the latest rumors. Wainwright's North Luzon Force headquarters carried just two radios in a single scout car as its sole mobile communications center, one radio borrowed from the 200th Artillery, and the second radio and the car borrowed from the 26th Cavalry.

The lull in the Japanese advance was only a respite. At 1100 hours, they reformed and once again hit the 21st Infantry. Filipino artillery observers reported the Japanese were buzzing out of recently captured Pio "like bees out of a swarm."[13] They pushed the left flank 3rd Battalion out of position and captured all but one of its water-cooled machine guns. Then the Japanese assaulted and captured the 2nd Battalion's command post. By noon, hardly an hour after they started, the Japanese broke the 21st Infantry's reserve line. The staff of the 21st Infantry almost fell into enemy hands when the Japanese, moving down a sunken road, broke through to the regiment's command post. As the Filamerican staff scattered, Colonel Wappenstein's new command post was "in his hat." The regiment's 1st Battalion withdrew to keep from being outflanked. The Japanese pushed between the 21st and 22nd Infantry, and the battle dissolved into a confused melee. "Shelling and bombing by the enemy continued incessantly," recalled Major Esperitu, commanding the 22nd Infantry. "It was a bloody battle. The left flank of the 1st Battalion was engaged in hand-to-hand fight."[14] Black smoke and cane-field fires fragmented all attempts at rallying the troops. Men whose only desire was to avoid the violent activities swirling about them used the concealment of the smoke to drift away.

Lieutenant Grover C. Richards, one of the American instructors, headed for the crumbling front. Before he reached the front he met Filipinos running to the rear. An American corporal threatened to shoot them, but they just bowed their necks and kept moving. Richards continued forward to a hill where he saw the Japanese and came under enemy fire. He guided some American light tanks into positions but they fired only a few rounds before they withdrew. After being coaxed up once more, a tank fired its 37mm gun with its muzzle cover still on and split the barrel. The tankers backed out, thinking they had been hit by an antitank gun. The tanks came forward a third time when Richards offered to walk in front of the vehicles. A tank sergeant joined Richards and the small column moved forward.[15]

Only the artillery prevented complete disaster. The 21st Artillery had three under-strength battalions commanded by Philippine Army second lieutenants, men who had never before commanded even a battery, with American artillery lieutenants, all ROTC graduates, as instructors. The young American reservists were fine, bright, intelligent fellows, but they had only limited training and experience. The most senior Filipino battalion commander had five years' service while the other two were 1940 graduates of the Philippine Military Academy. The Filipino regimental commander, Lieutenant Colonel Nemisio Catalan, had left the army as a captain for health reasons but later joined the Philippine Army and served in junior staff jobs. Although he had attended the Command and General Staff School, he had never commanded a unit of any size. Catalan's units lacked sufficient panoramic sights, aiming circles, binoculars, quadrants, fuse setters, sponges, rammers, staff, picks, shovels, aiming stakes, fuse wrenches, and numerous other gun tools. The Filipino gunners had trained on bamboo mock-ups until they received real cannon in December. To tow their pieces—one-third of which were wooden-wheeled 75mm guns from horse artillery days—the regiment started the war with two trucks. Later the artillerymen acquired four Canadian trucks and numerous civilian vehicles. Now, as the Filipino infantry dissolved in front of each artillery battalion, the gunners, 80 percent of whom had been trained before the war as infantry, did not in turn limber up their cannon and take to their heels. It would have been difficult to stop firing, hitch the guns to trucks, and try to drive away, all in open terrain under small arms fire. Instead, the Filipinos—Pangasanans, Illocanos, Pampangans, and Bontocs—fired point-blank direct fire for six long hours and serviced the guns as cooly as if it were a peacetime practice. "As attack after attack came on, broke, and went back," remembered Colonel Mallonee, "I knew what Cushing's artillerymen must have felt with the muzzles of their guns in the front line as the Confederate wave came on and broke on the high water mark at Gettysburg."[16]

Standing fast and firing at visible enemy required tremendous courage from the gunners and strong, steady leadership from the officers. For six hours the artillerymen were the most advanced elements of the entire division, "the bones of a meatless skeleton," and throughout the afternoon the gunners neither saw nor heard any of their own infantry. Lieutenant Valdez's 1st Battalion, 21st Artillery, east of the north-south road, swung its eight British model-1917 75mm guns to the left front and fired shrapnel shells at targets less than eight hundred yards away, stopping a Japanese penetration in the center of the division. West of the road, Lieutenant Mercado's wooden-wheeled 2nd Battalion and Lieutenant Acosta's 3rd Battalion fired high explosive up the Pio Ravine into an assembly area holding Japanese tanks. The two artillery battalions fired eight rounds per minute from each of sixteen cannon and turned the assembly area into a smoking cauldron. The tanks did not attack.[17]

At 21st Division headquarters General Capinpin finally decided to commit the remaining two battalions of his reserve 23rd Infantry. When this news reached the artillerymen—still firing and breaking apart one Japanese attack after another—the gunners cheered. But getting the 23rd Infantry in motion was not easy. As delays lengthened, Capinpin lost his temper, and his headquarters "spewed staff officers out . . . to build a fire under the 23rd."[18] The 23rd Infantry, now properly motivated, approached the thin line of artillerymen at the same time the Japanese launched their most violent attack of the day. The telephone line between the guns and Capinpin's headquarters went silent; the line was not dead, but the men with the guns were so busy fighting they could not spare time to talk. After a terrible fifteen-minute wait, Lieutenant Carl J. Savoie, the red-headed, volatile Louisianian instructor to the 3rd Battalion's guns, came on the phone and jubilantly reported the enemy's defeat. For the last time that day Japanese infantry faltered and withdrew under galling, point-blank artillery fire. The entire battle provided one of the finest artillery actions of World War II.

At a few points, however, Japanese infiltrated Filipino lines and created chaos in rear areas. "The situation was so confused," recorded the 21st

Division, "that there were instances when the enemy was occupying the 21st Division kitchens and the 21st Division troops were north and in the rear of the Japanese lines."[19] Then fire from a Japanese heavy artillery piece along the division's left flank nearly paralyzed both foot and motor traffic across rear areas. As night fell the Japanese reorganized and evacuated their dead and wounded from the line of fire of the deadly artillery. The numerous small villages through which they had to fight and a stubborn artillery left them with costly, limited gains. The 21st Artillery defended the division so well that the Japanese made no efforts against the line the next day. Civilian operatives, working behind Japanese lines, reported heavy enemy casualties from the day-long battle. A large number of trucks hauled Japanese dead to be cremated, and civilians in Porac said it took many days for the Japanese to finish the job. USAFFE, out of touch with reality but pleased that the Filipinos had held, estimated the Japanese had attacked with three or four infantry regiments.[20]

The 21st Division broke contact with the enemy and withdrew the night of January 4 to their next delay position. Lacking the expertise to properly form a covering shell, the division pulled out without any protection. The 22nd Infantry assembled in a parade-ground formation just behind their empty foxholes to count noses before moving south. The Japanese failure to press the Filipinos was a blessing, for when the Filipinos reached their new line they did little work toward preparing it. There was considerable confusion as the division spread out behind the Gumain River; the men went to sleep and junior Filipino officers submitted false reports and proved completely unwilling to accept or assume responsibility. In disgust, Colonel Mallonee characterized these officers as "children in men's clothes—high school cadets playing at war."[21] His artillery, without the spur of Japanese assaulting them, sank into apathy and set their guns so close together they were almost in a bivouac formation. Trucks clustered around each gun like newborn puppies around their mother. No one dug foxholes, trenches, or revetments to protect the men, guns, and fire-direction centers. And worse, as Colonel Mallonee recalled, ". . . no one seemed to give a damn and no one was doing anything. . . . We had no [Japanese] pressure on our front—thank God, because the infantry, as far as I could see, and certainly the artillery, were incapable of offering even feeble resistance."[22] The Japanese, failing to probe or pursue, left the 21st Division strictly alone.

The fighting in front of General Capinpin's 21st Division was only half the story. Holding the road running through Wainwright's right flank was General William E. Brougher's 11th Division. It too was short all types of equipment. In the 11th Infantry alone 556 rifles had broken extractors. The Filipinos carried a split piece of bamboo and used it like a ramrod, pushing it down the barrel after each shot to knock out the expended casing. The similarity to ancient muskets would have been funny if it had not been such a serious problem. Machine gun companies were armed with .30-caliber water-cooled Brownings whose serial numbers never exceeded four digits, a demoralizing indication of their antiquity. The barrels all had a minimum of 15,000 rounds fired through them.[23]

The 11th Infantry owned one radio with which the regiment hoped to talk to division headquarters, but traffic was not possible because they did not have a trained operator. There were only six 3-inch Stokes mortars, and only two .50-caliber machine guns, twenty-four .30-calibers, and thirty-six BARs in the entire 11th Infantry. No typewriters were ever issued so all correspondence was accomplished in longhand. Each infantry company owned one axe, one shovel, and one pick. Individual training had been spotty, especially in rifle marksmanship, scouting, and patrolling. Only one of the division's three regiments trained in units larger than company level.[24]

In the 11th Infantry, the senior instructor and acting executive officer was 30-year old Major Russell W. Volckmann, a West Pointer, class of '34. He arrived in the Philippines in 1940 and was assigned to the American 31st Infantry. In late 1941 he was transferred to the Philippine Army. He found his Filipino recruits had excellent memories, were sharp, attentive, and quick to learn, but one problem Volckmann could not solve was the language difficulty. The regiment was filled with north Luzon lowlanders called Ilocanos and Cagayanos and some mountain tribesmen from northern Luzon called Igorots, tough men with broad flat faces. The Igorots differed from the average Filipino, being shorter and squat with powerful legs and bodies. Half the regiment were Christian Filipinos and the other half pagan Igorots; the 1st Battalion was entirely Christian, the 2nd Battalion almost exclusively pagan, and the 3rd Battalion a mixture of both.[25]

Initially, no single camp was large enough to hold the full regiment, so the 11th Infantry started training in eight different camps. For the regimental commander to spend a few hours at each station required a trip of seven to ten days. Considerable distances and poor roads slowed travel. Rivers were crossed using primitive ferries that ceased operation whenever the water rose. It was not until October 10 that the regiment received orders to assemble, and assembly was completed on October 16. The 12th Infantry did not mobilize and assemble until the first week of November.[26]

There were problems with the inexperienced Filipino officers. Colonel Glen R. Townsend, the 11th Infantry's commander, found that the officers, often being political appointees, had less training than their men. But Townsend found the Filipino enlisted man to be in good physical shape, sturdy, independent in character, with no disciplinary problems, and the best he had seen outside the Scout regiments. They were eager and willing to learn. All it took was a reasonable amount of rice, a small portion of fish or meat, and fair and considerate treatment. Because the war interrupted the training of officers and men, Filipino officers incapable of commanding their units were replaced by Americans. "To the credit of the Filipino officers concerned," Townsend recalled, "they accepted the situation in good spirit and, without exception, gave their full support to the arrangement."[27]

The Americans had willing, if admittedly very raw, material with which to work. Captain Lage found that "they had practically no knowledge of fundamentals and basic techniques. In addition, the little they did know was in most cases wrong."[28] It was easy to teach the men something new, but trouble occurred when instructors tried to change incorrect procedures learned earlier. Colonel Townsend had ten American officers and seven sergeants to train and lead the men. All but one of the officers were recently arrived reservists with limited experience. Six of the seven sergeants received commissions after the war began while the seventh was killed before his commission came through. Of the sixteen Americans who entered the war with the 11th Infantry, only three survived both the war and prison camps.

Although the 11th Division was unmolested through January 2, during which time the 21st Division to the west was under attack, the men were busy. "Again the same old routine," recalled Major Volckmann in the 11th Infantry. "Reconnoiter the sector, issue orders to the battalion commanders, inspect the positions, establish contact and tie in with the units on our flanks, work out plans for counterattacks and plans for the next withdrawal."[29] The 13th Infantry held the right of the division line and straddled the road to San Fernando, while on the left, the 11th Infantry held the Guagua-Porac road as far north as Santa Rita. The 11th Infantry put its three battalions on line and, for the first time in the war, found itself with friendly artillery support. Japanese artillery fired on the 11th Infantry's command post and caused some losses. Lieutenant Eric F. Davis had printed a Christmas card before the war showing him reclining on a luxurious couch, drinking a beer, and fanned by a native girl. Printed on the card were the words, "Sherman might have been wrong." While emplacing machine guns of his 11th Infantry north of Guagua, Lieutenant Davis was killed by an enemy shell. Filipino artillery replied and the infantrymen took great comfort in the presence of their own guns. The division was able to give as well as receive. "Its fire was possibly not highly effective as the 11th Field Artillery had been organized and equipped only after the war began," remembered Colonel Townsend. "However the sound of its guns contributed greatly to the morale of the soldiers in the foxholes."[30]

First ground contact came on January 3 when a cautious Japanese advance guard appeared. This was part of the Tanaka Detachment, three battalions of the 2nd Formosa Infantry, one battalion from the 47th Infantry, a company of tanks, and three battalions of artillery. After American tanks took the Japanese under fire the Tanaka Detachment's advance guard spent five and a half hours advancing six miles. Because of the marshy terrain flanking the single road, the Japanese could not deploy so they waited for the main body to come up in support. Around noon, the Japanese built up enough strength to force tanks from C Company, 194th Tank Battalion, to withdraw. Even then, the Japanese were slowed by bad terrain, numerous small barrios, and punishing 37mm tank fire. The American tankers were veterans now, familiar with the art of delay and withdrawal. Taking advantage of every turn in the road, ducking into concealment offered by huts and vegetation, and using their speed, the Americans flayed the Japanese as they doggedly pushed south. When the Japanese switched their attacks to the foxhole line of the 11th Division, they fared no better.[31]

The next day, gaining some maneuver room and exploiting the value of their armor, the Japanese 7th Tank Regiment, supported by a battalion of 150mm howitzers, penetrated the 13th Infantry's line and occupied Guagua early in the afternoon. American tankers hunkered down under heavy mortar fire while large numbers of Filipinos headed south out of the town. Self-propelled mounts from Captain Gordon H. Peck's provisional battalion supported the tankers as they withdrew from Guagua and Sexmoan. Next, the Japanese hit the right of the 11th Infantry and badly manhandled Captain Antonio Alejandro's part Christian-part pagan 3rd Battalion. In a short time the 3rd Battalion suffered 150 men killed and wounded. Despite their losses the 11th Infantry and elements of the 13th fought long enough and well enough to allow both regiments to withdraw.[32]

Hoping to relieve pressure on the main line, the men from Janesville, Wisconsin's A Company, 192nd Tank Battalion and elements of the 11th Division attacked the flank of the Japanese line pressing Guagua, but the attempt miscarried. Filipino infantry mistook American tanks for Japanese, fired mortars at them, and almost hit Brigadier General James R. N. Weaver who was trying to coordinate the attack from an open jeep. Once the mortars were stopped—happily before they inflicted any friendly casualties—the men involved in this impromptu rear guard ac-

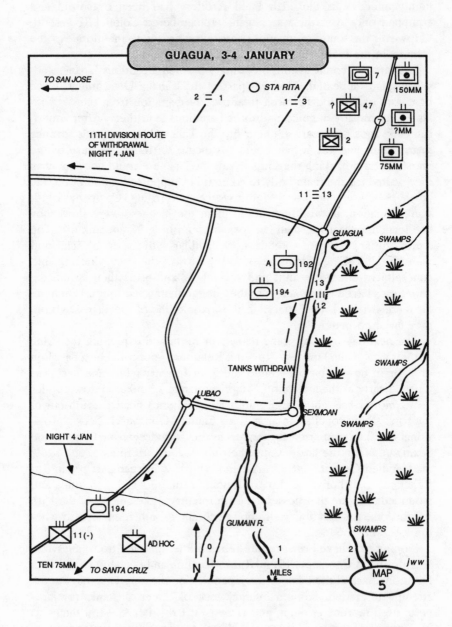

GUAGUA, 3-4 JANUARY

TO SAN JOSE

STA RITA

2 = 1

1 = 3

7

150MM

? 47

?MM

2

75MM

11TH DIVISION ROUTE
OF WITHDRAWAL
NIGHT 4 JAN

11 = 13

GUAGUA

SWAMPS

A 192

13

194

12

SWAMPS

TANKS WITHDRAW

SWAMPS

LUBAO

SEXMOAN

SWAMPS

NIGHT 4 JAN

194

GUMAIN R.

SWAMPS

11(-)

AD HOC

0   1   2

TEN 75MM   TO SANTA CRUZ

N   MILES

MAP
5

jww

tion successfully broke contact and withdrew. At 1600 hours, and as the tanks withdrew toward Lubao, the Americans observed Japanese in battalion strength coming down the road toward Sexmoan. Leading the Japanese were three Filipinos carrying white flags. Disregarding the hostages, American tanks and four self-propelled 75mm guns cut the enemy column to pieces. The Americans then left Lubao in shambles with the hotel in flames and the entire area under enemy mortar and artillery fire. The Americans assumed new positions a mile or two above Santa Cruz.[33]

The successes achieved by Japanese tanks convinced Wainwright it was time to pull his entire line back and that evening his two divisions withdrew. The movement, however, was not accomplished according to plan. The Japanese capture of Guagua and their rapid advance toward Lubao cut off the 11th Infantry from its planned route of withdrawal, but since the 11th Infantry had been cut off before and had survived, the men accepted the situation calmly. Hasty reconnaissances for secondary roads failed to find any feasible routes. The only remaining choice was a long twenty-five mile march west through the 21st Division areas, then south, and then back north into new positions. The 11th Infantry started its move at 1600 hours accompanied by a tank company and several hundred stragglers. Eight hours later the column reached San Jose where they boarded trucks and buses, drove south to Layac, and then rolled northeast to Santa Cruz. They took up positions at dawn on January 5 to the rattle of Japanese small arms. The arrival of the 11th Infantry was a great relief to the thin line of 200 Americans and Filipinos who, until the 11th Infantry arrived, believed themselves the only force in position.[34]

After withdrawing first from Guagua and then Lubao, lead elements of Colonel Miller's 194th Tank Battalion occupied new positions at 1430 hours. The last of the battalion closed at 1930 hours and deployed astride the highway along a creek bed, probably the Gumain River. Tanks, half-tracks, and Bren gun carriers settled into the line, and small parties of men emplaced outposts to the front and flanks. As the men dug in, Japanese aircraft bombed Culis, wounding a few tankers.[35]

When the full moon appeared a little after sunset the tankers saw they possessed excellent visibility across incredibly flat turnip fields. At 0150 hours, Americans on an outpost challenged someone walking toward them. Voices sounding like Filipinos answered but Master Sergeant William Boyd, a soldier possessing leadership and judgment, was not fooled. He fired. Now Japanese voices were clearly audible. "We are the peepul," one shouted, "who are not afraid to die by boolets."[36] Guiding on the road and clearly visible in the bright moonlight, the Japanese attacked. West of the road they deployed reasonably well, but east of the road they came at the Americans in column. Infantry, unassisted by their own tanks and artillery, have absolutely no business attacking tanks across open ground. Possibly the Japanese believed only Filipino infantry opposed them. Whatever the reason, it was stupid as well as costly. Dozens of machine guns carried by the armored force fired, and a battery of 75mm SPM's laid down deadly artillery fire. Again and again Japanese infantry tried to cross the terribly open fields, and with them came what appeared to be gas but was actually only smoke. A breeze blew the smoke back into enemy lines.

Inside his light tank, 29-year-old Private William N. Kinler and his National Guard comrades from Minnesota saw the Japanese approaching. "There was a moon, and the Japs attacked," he recalls. "Some were wearing white shirts and they came across the field shouting. They were clearly visible and we inflicted a lot of damage."[37] As Kinler worked his .30-caliber machine gun back and forth across the Japanese, hot brass piled up around his feet. Missourians from B Company and Californians in C Company joined Kinler's A Company in erecting a deadly steel curtain. For three hours the Japanese suffered without penetrating the line of vehicles. Colonel Miller believed there was no way the Japanese could make it across the field, but he was concerned about his flanks because of a lack of friendly infantry. However, the Japanese made no attempt against the flanks and broke off the attacks at the approach of daylight. Colonel Miller's tanks had been well-peppered by enemy small-arms fire and looked like well-fed birds had roosted on them.

Colonel Miller did not know it but he did have some infantry support that night. After being kicked out of Guagua, General Brougher of the 11th Division found Captain John W. Primrose south of the town and told him to stop everyone he could and form a temporary line. Captain Primrose and another officer stopped all vehicles going south and unloaded everybody with a rifle whether he was in the infantry or not. The two Americans pulled Filipino officers off buses and placed them in charge of positions along the line. Riflemen were mainly from the 11th Division, but unit designations were unimportant now. It took until midnight, but they built a line of 600 men that formed concurrently with Miller's tank battalion. General Brougher also gathered ten cannon from the 11th Artillery and several self-propelled mounts.[38]

After dark, Lieutenant Wayne C. Liles finished checking his men and went to his car to sleep. As he was about to drop off, firing began and Liles heard the same screaming heard by the tankers, a yell that sounded like a Comanche Indian charge in the movies. "I have never heard anything to equal it in real life," recalled Liles. "Someone said they were yelling in Tagalog. We asked a Filipino in one of the tanks, who had lived in the States, what they were saying. He said, 'We are about to die.' "[39]

The Filipinos joined the firing and, with the tankers, stopped the Japanese. The combined fire of the tanks and infantry was devastating. A few Americans and Filipinos were wounded, some severely, but the line did not budge. As dawn broke on January 5 the Japanese lay exhausted. Those fighting Colonel Miller's tanks and the 11th Division since January 2 suffered so badly they were withdrawn and replaced by the 1st Formosa Infantry.

On the morning of January 5 the Filipinos found themselves in yet another delay position. The 21st Division was still on the left just south of the Gumain River. Establishment of a new line and extension of the right flank toward the 11th Division was progressing so slowly that Colonel O'Day went forward to discover the problem. He found that some units had stopped marching and were eating a leisurely meal. O'Day had to give firm orders to push units out to the east to contact the 11th Division. Despite O'Day's efforts the 21st Division line never did get organized. No sooner were "firm orders" given the troops to dig in than they received orders pulling them back five kilometers. Once the withdrawal began, an order from North Luzon Force headquarters told the 21st Division to stop its withdrawal and hold the Gumain River line until further orders, so the soldiers turned about and marched north. All this marching, countermarching, and confusion was accomplished without the slightest interference from the Japanese, doubtless because of caution, infantry losses, and a sudden respect for Filipino firepower. One final hurdle remained for the army before reaching Bataan, and this obstacle was the funneling of the 21st and 11th Divisions across the Culo Bridge. The move succeeded.[40]

Passing through Layac on January 5 and January 6 and through a fresh covering force, Wainwright's North Luzon Force relaxed as it left the Japanese north of the Culo River. Americans who believed Bataan was well stocked with food and honeycombed with fighting positions entered Bataan with a feeling of complacency and smug satisfaction. They had survived the withdrawal and they could now fight the Japanese from surveyed, established positions. Colonel O'Day was as relieved as everyone else at reaching Bataan, for there were times when the odds of reaching the peninsula seemed mighty long. As Colonel Townsend marched into Bataan with his 11th Infantry he saw that "The towns along the road—Hermosa, Orani, Abucay and Balanga—had been bombed during the day. Fires were still blazing and the horrid smell of burning human flesh filled the night."[41] The 11th Infantry found the roads relatively clear but when the head of the column reached Balanga they found one poor MP trying vainly to untangle a massive traffic jam, and the guides that were to lead the men to their destination were missing. Colonel Townsend halted his infantrymen and reconnoitered the town in hopes of finding the guides. Finally Townsend found General Brougher, who ordered the unit to move through Balanga and then west on a side road. But before the regiment could start its march a II Corps staff officer countermanded the division order and told the 11th Infantry to move instead by a more northern route to the barrio of Guitol.

When the 11th Infantry tried to march along the road designated by II Corps they found it jammed with other units and vehicles in the same predicament as the 11th Infantry. They did not know where to go so they stopped. Colonel Townsend's men progressed only with the greatest of difficulty, and a three-hour effort gained a mile of road. Then a courier arrived with a message from General Brougher. The regiment was on the wrong road. Brougher ordered Townsend to retrace his steps to Balanga and then move south, but such a maneuver was easier ordered than executed. The head of the column was just approaching Guitol and by the time orders to turn about reached it lead elements were going into bivouac. The battalions turned about and hobbled back through Balanga and toward a new destination.[42]

But stop! The next night they countermarched again through Balanga and back to Guitol.

MacArthur, writing about the withdrawals to Bataan, remembered the events as he would have like them to have occurred, not as they actually unfolded. "No trained veteran divisions," he wrote, "could have executed the withdrawal movement more admirably than did the heterogeneous force of Filipinos and Americans."[43] Regardless of how the withdrawal was executed, MacArthur's army was finally in Bataan.

CHAPTER FIVE

Delaying Action at Layac

AFTER DESTRUCTION OF THE CULO BRIDGE ONE LAST POSITION
remained between the Japanese and the main American line at Abucay.
The Americans wanted to hold this delaying position, just south of Layac
and the small Culo River, long enough to stop the forward elements of
the Japanese army. By fighting here the Americans would deny the Japanese Route 110 leading south into the Bataan peninsula and deceive the
enemy as to the location of the main line. USAFFE considered it of the
utmost importance to delay the Japanese and give the Filamerican forces
more time to entrench along the main battle position. South of the Layac
covering force, I and II Philippine corps were working along the main
battle position trying to settle units into place and prepare for the Japanese. After the Japanese deployed for a full-dress attack, USAFFE hoped
the covering force could withdraw without serious casualties and even
fight a delay south toward the main battle position. The origins of the
Layac delaying position lay in WPO-3, so there was little surprise when
orders came for its occupation. On January 2, MacArthur ordered Wainwright to organize a covering force before turning it over to Major General George M. Parker, the commanding general, Bataan Defense Force.
In turn, Parker was told that Layac would be given to him and held until
a coordinated attack forced a withdrawal.[1]

Brigadier General Clyde A. Selleck, commander of the 71st Division,
received actual responsibility for establishing the Layac Line. Born in
1888 at Brandon, Vermont, "Pappy" Selleck, an artilleryman, was a West

Pointer, class of 1910, had commanded a battalion of the 21st Field Artillery, and had served as chief of staff to both VII Corps Artillery and to First Army Artillery in World War I. He graduated from the Command and General Staff School in 1927 and the Army War College in 1935. Wainwright alerted Selleck on January 2 and instructed him to hold the position for several days. He would thereby cover the withdrawal of the 11th and 21st Divisions and gain time to prepare the Abucay Line. Although the plan for occupying the Layac Line was known to seemingly all senior officers in the Philippines, it was not known to Selleck. His short time in the islands—he arrived in the Philippines on October 23, 1941—few briefings on war plans, and an absence of information about the position itself resulted in one of the least knowledgeable officers on Luzon commanding the line.[2]

To accomplish the tasks assigned him, Selleck had four regiments, the American 31st Infantry, the Scout 26th Cavalry, and two Philippine Army infantry regiments. Selleck deployed the two infantry regiments of his 71st Division on the right. As he positioned his men on January 3 and 4, Selleck found more to worry about than simple unfamiliarity with defense plans; his men were causing him great concern. Combat elements of the entire division were desperately short of experienced officers, and although American colonels commanded the 71st and 72nd infantry and American captains served as regimental staff officers, Filipino lieutenants commanded the battalions. Selleck's Filipinos wore blue denim trousers without leggings, short-sleeve shirts, and lacked steel helmets, mosquito nets, and blankets. The soldiers were wearing their only set of clothes when they marched into Bataan. As headgear, they wore shellacked canvas or coconut pulp helmets. These hats glistened in the sun until the first battle, after which they were hastily "unglistened."[3] In the short time available, some dog tags were cut and fashioned from metal ammunition cans, and a few standard aluminum disks with holes for strings were procured, but most Filipinos who died on Bataan were buried unidentified.

On the right of the line, Selleck placed Lieutenant Colonel Donald Van N. Bonnett's 71st Infantry. The 71st Infantry's right was partially protected by marshy tidal streams and water-covered ground, while the remainder of the ground was monotonously flat. Action between Lingayen Gulf and Bataan had reduced the 71st Infantry to 1,200 men, and Selleck now considered the 71st Infantry as "far from being a trained regiment because of inability of officers, NCOs, and shortage of equipment and facilities."[4] The regiment had just completed thirteen weeks of training but was still weak in range firing, field work, and communications training. Colonel Bonnett was 46 years old and had first served as a private with the Ohio National Guard from 1916-1917. The Ohioan had put his heart into building his regiment, and he was especially good at keeping his men calm and confident in a crisis. Despite all Bonnett's work, however, his Filipino staff officers were still inexperienced and his men untrained for combat.

To the left of the 71st Infantry stood Lieutenant Colonel Irwin Compton's 72nd Infantry, two battalions on line and one in reserve. Having mobilized at its Negros mobilization station in November, it was in even worse shape than its sister 71st Infantry. The regiment's defeat at Sison on December 23 and its subsequent forced marches cut unit strength to 1,300 weary, demoralized survivors. Leadership was poor at all levels, and the regiment was still badly disorganized. Selleck considered the 72nd Infantry thoroughly unfit, and junior officers agreed with the judgment of their general; to wit, the regiment fell apart when routed from Sison. Combat losses were light, but desertions were heavy.[5]

The 71st Division owned only a third of its authorized automatic weapons. There were no mortars or any .50-caliber machine guns, no flares, inadequate transportation, no entrenching tools, only 100 hand grenades for the entire division, and mess equipment of the rudest nature; cooks transported food and water in open five-gallon tin cans. The 71st Infantry's headquarters received part of its communications equipment, but its battalions received none. The 72nd Infantry had no communications equipment at all. Just before the war, division headquarters received several radio sets with which the men were completely unfamiliar. Several large switchboards were also received, but they were so heavy they required motor transportation. Telephone wire was so limited that only the simplest single-line hookup was possible, and General Selleck's headquarters had to set its command post at Culis in front of its own artillery simply so it could talk to its regiments. When the division signal officer asked II Corps for more telephones, he was told, "No, you have lost too many already."[6] Finally, a covering force should be mobile and consist of cavalry, mechanized, and motorized troops; Selleck's Filipinos were foot mobile. With all these problems on his mind, Selleck moved the bulk of his force into position.

The backbone of Selleck's force was Colonel Charles L. Steel's 1,600-man American 31st Infantry which arrived at Layac late on January 4. The men arrived after dark and did not deploy until the morning of the fifth. The regiment occupied the center of the covering force line, left and west of the 71st Division, and commanded the most likely enemy avenue of approach, Route 110 that runs down the east coast of Bataan. Colonel Steel had graduated from Pennsylvania State College in 1914, joined the Maryland National Guard, and was commissioned in 1916.

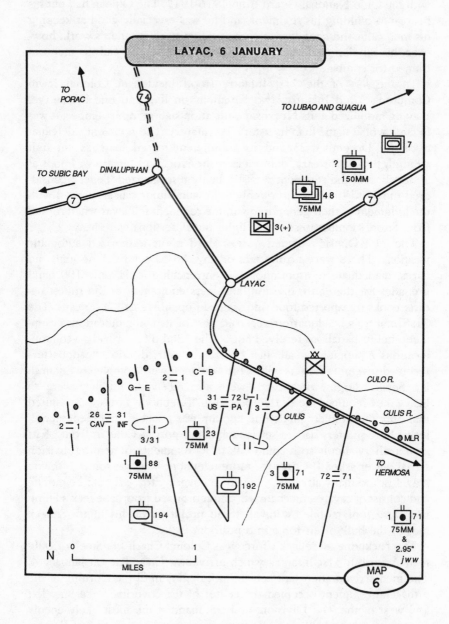

LAYAC, 6 JANUARY

TO PORAC

74

TO LUBAO AND GUAGUA

TO SUBIC BAY

DINALUPIHAN

7

7

7

? 1
150MM

4 8
75MM

3(+)

LAYAC

CULO R.

C - B

2 1

G - E

31
INF

26
CAV

2 1

3/31

31
US

72
PA

I

3

CULIS

CULIS R.

MLR

1 23
75MM

1 88
75MM

192

3 71
75MM

72 71

TO HERMOSA

194

1 71
75MM
&
2.95"
jww

N

0   1

MILES

MAP
6

His highest schooling saw him graduate from Fort Leavenworth's Command and General Staff School in 1937. Although his regiment was unique in not yet having seen any action, and although morale was high, the regiment's strength was low. Many of the most experienced men had been pulled from their units and sent to instruct or command the new Filipino formations. C Company lost eight of its sergeants to the Philippine Army. G Company sent ten experienced NCOs and all but one of its officers to fill Filipino units. Two officers and seventeen sergeants left L Company. All across the regiment new men were holding new jobs, and the lack of experience would tell.[7]

Colonel Clinton A. Pierce's reduced 26th Cavalry Regiment with 657 men reached Selleck late the night of January 5 and extended his line west to the foothills of the Zambales Mountains. They began reconnaissances the morning of January 6, but even then the 2nd Squadron on the extreme left did not get into position until 1400 hours, well after the fight started. Colonel Pierce had joined the regiment in February 1940 as a squadron commander, later became regimental executive officer, and then commander in October 1941. He now decided to establish a standing screen of patrols from the mountains on the left to the American regiment on the right; the bulk of the regiment would mass and be ready to react to enemy penetrations. Pierce and his executive officer rode their horses along the screen, insuring their men were properly placed.[8]

Selleck's divisional artillery consisted of two two-gun 75mm batteries and one four-gun 2.95-inch pack howitzer battery, a total of eight guns in his 71st Artillery. The artillery staff, battery commanders, and battalion commanders were all Filipino—the only Americans were the regimental commander, Lieutenant Colonel Halstead C. Fowler, and three assistants. The Scout 1st Battalion, 23rd Artillery was in direct support of the 31st Infantry with two batteries of 75mm's. Both batteries were relatively new to the Army, having been activated only nine months before the war. In general support of Selleck's line were two batteries from the Scout 1st Battalion, 88th Artillery armed with 75mm guns. They too had existed as a unit for only nine months. For some reason, maybe because of an oversight, no one gave Selleck any long-range 155mm support. This could hardly have been Selleck's fault, for he was graduate of the Field Artillery School Advanced Course and had taught at the Field Artillery School, so he knew how to employ cannon.[9]

The fault seemed to lie with II Corps. Lieutenant Colonel Arthur L. Shreve, assigned as II Corps' chief of artillery the afternoon of January 5, had his first look at II Corps' disposition of artillery mid-afternoon on January 6. He was surprised when he found there were no 155mm's supporting Selleck. Some of the Corps' 155mm's could have been positioned either close to or well behind the line to cope with either enemy artillery or enemy infantry. With a range of over fourteen kilometers, Corps 155mm's were the only guns capable of firing deep enough to reach Japanese 150mm's. A major concern about emplacing 155mm's with Selleck had to be the severe mobility restrictions facing the towed pieces. The guns were hauled by big prime movers, 10-ten caterpillar tractors, that had been in service since World War I and that were now in poor mechanical shape. USAFFE had experienced great difficulty in pulling six of the heavy guns out of South Luzon during the withdrawal to Bataan, so a legitimate fear for their loss at Layac existed. Regardless of the reason, however, the absence of the big guns would prove a major error.[10]

The Provisional Tank Group was also in support with eighty light tanks, forty-two half-tracks, and fifteen Bren gun carriers. Brigadier General James R. N. Weaver—late of the 68th Armored Regiment, 2nd Armored Division—commanded the two-battalion group. A West Pointer, class of 1911, the 61-year-old Weaver had served with the 8th and 9th Infantry in the Philippines from 1911 to 1913 and had fought the Moros in 1912. His tank group had been scheduled to receive two medium tank battalions to add punch to the light tanks already in the Philippines, but the heavier tanks never arrived. Now Weaver's light tanks were at Layac, well dispersed so as to offer enemy artillery a limited target. However, in a serious failure, no arrangements were ever made allowing Selleck to give the tankers orders. Nor, it seems, did USAFFE give the Tank Group orders either to support the Layac position or to cover its withdrawal. Finally, it seems Selleck never asked the Tank Group for tank support. The tanks were there, but they were responsible solely to their own commanders. In fact, the Tank Group commander, General Weaver, considered his presence at Layac a "gratuitous mission," above and beyond any orders given him.[11]

Two battalions of 75mm self-propelled artillery covered tank approaches. In a pinch they could act as antitank artillery as well as normal field artillery. The self-propelled mounts had been built in the United States as tank destroyers and were shipped to the Philippines in response to an urgent USAFFE request for 37mm antitank guns, a request Washington could not fill. But their usefulness to Selleck, like the tanks, was limited by their instructions. "I was ordered to stay under cover no matter what happened," remembered Captain Ivan W. Weikel, an ROTC graduate from Oregon State University who commanded the two-gun C Battery. "I was to go into action only if tanks came through our lines and down the road."[12] The only fire control equipment Weikel had was a pair of field glasses and a pocket compass.

Occupation of the line had begun on January 3, but without engineer support—Selleck's battalion of divisional engineers was working for North Luzon Force—progress was slow. Higher engineer priorities had drawn the few USAFFE-level engineer assets deeper into Bataan, leaving Selleck with nothing. Additionally, the construction effort at Layac was the first time the 71st Division had ever tried to string barbed wire or build obstacles. With few exceptions, the tired and dispirited Filipinos made very little progress organizing the ground and entrenching. A visiting American engineer found little desire on the part of the 71st Division to hold their positions for even a short time.[13]

Lieutenant Colonel James V. Collier, USAFFE assistant operations officer G3 at Corregidor, was a tall, handsome, courteous man and was described as remarkably efficient. Collier felt that the Layac position was a strong line held by a fair-sized force. General Parker was also comfortable with the ground and fields of fire. From Selleck's much more intimate position, however, and especially from his firsthand knowledge of the qualities of his 71st Division, the Layac position was weak. The right of the line faced east and could be enfiladed from the west, while the center of the line faced north and could be enfiladed from the east. The low rolling hills were hardly more than bumps in the uniformly flat ground. The tiny Culis River itself did not provide an obstacle, and even the larger Culo River was fordable to dismounted troops. The Culo's steep, almost vertical banks made vehicular traffic difficult, but an engineer effort could cut approaches for a crossing. The best Selleck could organize was a series of mutually supporting strong points entrenched and wired as much as time and materiel would permit. For some reason, Selleck did not push forward his own outposts. Undoubtedly, his two Philippine Army regiments were not well enough trained to hazard men forward of the main line, but the Americans of the 31st Infantry were properly trained and had sufficient vehicles to deploy outposts well forward. Surprisingly, they failed to do so.[14]

Selleck's higher headquarters, first North Luzon Force (Wainwright) and then II Corps (Parker), did not help him much during his preparation of the line. North Luzon Force originally told him to put the American 31st Infantry on the Olongapo Road well to the west, then they told him to use the regiment at Layac. This order required a change of plans and a shifting of frontages, and the American 2nd and 3rd battalions did not return to Layac until 1630 hours on January 4. Finally, a battalion of the 21st Infantry that Selleck planned to use as a reserve was taken away, requiring yet another redeployment. Most distressing to Selleck was that no one told him he would lose that battalion. He learned that their orders had been changed only after the unit failed to arrive. Transfering

Selleck from Wainwright's North Luzon Force to Parker's II Corps on January 6 did not help Selleck at all. II Corps was still setting up shop, having expanded from its division-sized South Luzon Force configuration to a four-division corps. Its priority was to build a main line of resistance farther south, not bother with a division-level delay. II Corps' glaring failure to give Selleck 155mm artillery, and USAFFE's failure to arrange some useful command relationship between Selleck and the Provisional Tank Group showed all too well that Selleck's bosses were attending to other matters.[15]

Despite shifts in frontages, the American 31st Infantry organized their positions in a much better fashion than did the 71st Division, partly because the Americans had their normally attached company of Scout engineers, C Company, 14th Engineers. Both the 1st and 2nd battalions put two rifle companies on line, and the reserve 3rd Battalion spent its time digging into reverse slope positions and making extensive reconnaissances to insure smooth forward movement should the battalion be needed. Trucks brought supplies forward, including a forced issue of 60,000 rounds of small arms ammunition for each rifle company. On the left flank of the regiment in the 2nd Battalion, Sergeant Earl F. Walk set his .50-caliber machine gun next to a trail under a clump of bushes and put his two mortars on a hill. The ground was so hard it was like digging in rock. Mighty swings of a pick broke the earth into pieces of reddish clay no larger than a man's thumb, and a few men poured water from canteens and even urinated on the ground trying to soften it. Despite difficulties, the Americans worked through the hot afternoon and into the evening, chipping shallow foxholes and gun positions out of the unyielding ground.[16]

Although the Americans entrenched better than the Filipinos, there were exceptions. The 1st Battalion's B Company on the right of the regiment's line did a poor job. "It was like a picnic," remembered Private Paul Kerchum. "No barbed wire and very few foxholes. Tools were there but nobody enforced digging. There was a definite lack of leadership."[17] Two Filipinos carried a washtub of ice and San Miguel beer through B Company, selling the beer for one peso per bottle. In other places the Americans set a better example. Digging in behind the Americans were Scout gunners from the 23rd Artillery, artillerymen who had been well trained and who knew their job, but who were reluctant to entrench. Only after Lieutenant William Miller pointed down the slope to the 31st Infantry, which was hard at work, did the Scout artillerymen decide to follow their example. "If Americans were sweating away," recalled Miller, "maybe they had better get busy too, and digging went on well after dark."[18]

The covering force line was almost fully occupied when the sun rose at 0722 hours on January 6. That morning Wainwright visited Selleck's command post, a six-foot square by four-foot deep foxhole at the town of Culis, and told Selleck the sector was now under the control of General Parker's newly activated II Corps. Selleck would therefore report to Parker. Then a liaison officer from II Corps arrived and was followed by a communication truck with a radio. Selleck's signalmen tied into the old North Luzon Force wire net. Unfortunately, Selleck did not have any information about the enemy. After the rear guard of North Luzon Force had begun its march to the Culo Bridge the previous evening, all contact with the Japanese had been lost. As far as Selleck knew, there might be a regiment or there might be two divisions heading for him. Although MacArthur's G2 estimated the Japanese Lingayen force at 45,000 men, this information did not reach Selleck. Selleck's observation posts collected only meager information, and officer patrols found forward areas eerie and depopulated. Filipino civilians had fled their huts and farms, leaving the countryside empty. Lieutenant Fisher recalled that "we passed a number of miserable nipa houses including one which was mysteriously on fire, but we found only one living soul, an old man who gave us some fruit."[19]

Watching from camouflaged positions, American forward observers had the area to the north under good observation, and they spotted the Japanese at 1000 hours. Coming down the road from San Fernando was a regiment of infantry, soldiers with puttee-wrapped legs carrying long, ten-pound bolt-action Model 38 Arisaka 6.5mm rifles first issued in 1905. Spaced through the columns were men toting twenty-pound Model 99 light machine guns. These soldiers were part of Colonel Hifumi Imai's "Imai Detachment" built around the 1st Formosa Infantry, a company of the 7th Tank Regiment, two battalions of 75mm guns from the 48th Mountain Artillery, and eight big 150mm howitzers from the 1st Field Artillery Regiment. The Americans and Japanese were each hauling twenty-four cannon into the fight, but the Japanese held an advantage in size and range. Observers reported these sightings to Selleck and requested permission to fire when the enemy came into range. Selleck agreed, and the Scout artillerymen prepared for their moment.[20]

A half hour later the Japanese were close enough. At 1030 hours, two batteries of 75mm guns, portee, from Lieutenant Colonel Hanford N. Lockwood's 23rd Artillery, opened the action and were followed by eight 75mm guns of the 88th Artillery. The first rounds impacted squarely on the road, an admirable reflection of Scout training. The guns immediately changed to rapid volley fire and walked bursting projectiles up and down the road, scattering several Japanese horse-drawn mountain guns with attendant animals, caissons, and gear. This was the first time the Japanese had experienced the effects of Scout artillery, and they were obviously unprepared for it. In B Battery, 23rd Artillery, the officers alternated in yelling fire commands to the five gunners on each piece, gunners who themselves kept up exhortations to one another in their Tagalog and Pamamgo dialects. "We got hoarse from hollering at those guys," recalled Lieutenant Miller, "and we would take turns shouting at them."[21] Standing between the number two and three guns, each gun fifty yards apart, the two officers passed corrections in elevation and deflection and kept the shells on target. The B Battery commander, perched in a tree spotting the fall of his shells, telephoned his officers and reported the destruction of the lead enemy artillery. "I saw the wheels go up," he yelled as pieces of Japanese guns went flying.[22] Joined by the eight guns of the 71st Artillery, Selleck's twenty-four cannon forced the Japanese to deploy about two and a third miles north of the lines occupied by his American and Filipino infantry. For just under thirty minutes, Selleck's guns fired without any Japanese reply.

Japanese artillery not caught in the initial rain of shells hustled forward and quickly rolled into action. Drivers angled off roads, bounced over small earthen dikes, and swung onto hard, flat rice paddies. Gunners unhitched their cannon, observers climbed trees, and crewmen laid their guns. Looking southwest, the Japanese saw the slight rise marking Filipino positions—the first tentative foothills reaching down from Mount Natib. When they fired their first rounds to determine the range, they hit the bivouac of the 26th Cavalry, killing eight horses and wounding three Scouts. Japanese 75mm and 150mm shells, directed and corrected by aerial spotters, who dropped as low as 2,000 feet in their search for targets, began to fall near the defending artillery and infantry. Peering from their circling aircraft, pilots easily pinpointed Selleck's artillery and infantry works. American antiaircraft guns which earlier covered this area had moved farther south the night of January 3, so enemy aircraft were not bothered by ground fire. Little escaped their attention, and Japanese artillery grew more and more accurate. Because the Model-4 150mm howitzers firing 10,500 yards outranged the smaller Filipino 75mm's, they were untouched by Filipino counterbattery fire. II Corps' failure to place any 155mm's near Layac for counterbattery proved to be the most significant mistake made by American artillery in the entire campaign.[23]

As the hours passed, Japanese fire began to hurt the 71st Division. Shells hit Selleck's command post, wounded some men, sent others running into the hills, scared away the American crew operating the radio truck, destroyed several vehicles, and badly disrupted communications.

Selleck cooly directed the evacuation of the wounded, placed a doctor who tried to flee under arrest, and set such an example of personal courage that those around him had no choice but to emulate him. Lieutenant Hilarion Sarcepuedes and a comrade laid a new wire line from Selleck's command post to the 71st Artillery and reopened communications with the guns. Behind Selleck, Filipino artillery was severely shelled and took several direct hits. By mid-afternoon, every gun in the 71st Artillery had been hit at least once, and four were damaged beyond repair and abandoned. Changes in gun positions made little difference because of Japanese aerial observation, for no sooner were the guns in a new location than they were once again under fire. Concealment was scarce and cover nonexistent, and the old artillery maxim "a battery seen is a battery lost" held true. Under galling fire, the Filipinos from the 1st Battalion, 71st Artillery abandoned their guns, carrying away the firing pins and keys to the prime movers. The guns were later rescued and pulled to safety.[24]

Equally relentlessly, the Japanese concentrated on the Scout 23rd Artillery. The Scout guns were in defilade behind a hill, but Japanese planes spotted them. When the first shells exploded nearly, Lieutenant Miller, having left his job as traffic manager of the Pampanga Bus Company for active duty only seven days before, was shocked. "Those son of a bitches are trying to kill us!"[25] Communications with battalion headquarters were soon lost, and when B Battery tried using the radio, it did not work well. Lieutenant Miller switched again to telephones, but both wires were soon cut. In hopes of repairing the wire, Captain Samuel Llewellyn Barbour Jr. organized a four-man detail and began a harrowing walk along the telephone wire looking for breaks. For most of the distance the men jumped up and down as they avoided bursting artillery. Despite the bravery of Barbour's crew, their work was futile. As soon as they patched one break, artillery ripped open another.

As Japanese artillery steadied on Lieutenant Miller's position, one shell burst directly on a Scout emplacement, putting the gun out of action and severely wounding four gunners. The Scout gunners knew their jobs, were intensely loyal, and obeyed orders from their American officers without question. So despite losses, and despite the alarming sight of an American infantryman in full flight, the Scouts steadfastly serviced their guns. Miller remembered that the American deserter caused a disgusting scene, "falling flat on the ground and crying out the Japs are coming. He was in a pure funk. We barely had time to look at him but told him to get out of our way, and he ran off to the rear."[26] Nearby, American medics treating the wounded Scout artillerymen, watched enemy fire impact around the Scouts. "They were exchanging shell for shell with the Japanese," remembered 18-year-old Kansas medic John G. Lally. "It was the bravest thing I ever saw."[27]

Bamboo thickets surrounding the cannon of the 23rd Artillery caught fire and threatened the guns more than the enemy shelling. Some poor planning now intervened to insure the destruction of B Battery's guns. The evening before, the prime movers were collected at battalion headquarters where they would be safe. So as the bamboo fire approached the immobile guns, there was no way to move the pieces out of danger. And because telephone lines were cut, B Battery could not tell battalion headquarters to send the vehicles forward. Finally, when the fire leaped into the pits with the gunners, the men jumped out, and the guns were lost. Although the Scouts saved only one of the battalion's eight guns, this single piece continued the fight, firing and moving, then firing and moving again. Because the 1st Battalion, 88th Artillery was shooting from better protected terrain than the 23rd, it did not suffer as badly. Even so, the ammunition train was hit, several prime movers were disabled by enemy fire, and personnel losses were heavy. Japanese fire drove the crew of an A Battery gun to cover, dragging their wounded with them. When Sergeant Jose Calugas, a mess sergeant from another battery and a native of the island of Panay, saw the crew leave the gun, he ran across shell-swept ground to the idle piece, organized a pick-up crew, and put the gun back into action despite continued enemy shelling. His reward was the Medal of Honor.[28]

Large clouds of dust rose off plowed fields as Japanese artillery reached toward the front of the 3rd Battalion, 72nd Infantry, but with their overhead cover the Filipinos clung to their lines with only minor losses. To the left of the 72nd Infantry the Americans of the 31st Infantry were likewise hit by enemy guns. "The shelling was deadly accurate," remembered Private William J. Garleb from H Company.[29] He was crouching in his foxhole when a round burst only six inches from the edge, exploding up and out, leaving him unhurt. This was the first time the Americans had heard enemy artillery explode, and it was disconcertingly loud. Under this fire Sergeant Walk's H Company machine gunners burrowed into their eighteen-inch deep holes. For five minutes all Walk could see was dust and he was sure he had lost the whole squad. But when the fire stopped, Walk found that not one man was scratched. Each man, however, was furiously engaged in deepening his foxhole.

G Company also took a pounding but lost only a few men wounded. Captain John I. Pray, the company's six foot two, 171-pound, serious-minded commander, crouched in his command post foxhole and peered at a little red bird five feet away. The bird was singing its heart out as howitzer shells crashed all around it. During lulls, Pray crawled along his line encouraging his men who, seeing him disappear in shell bursts and smoke, reported him killed three times. Japanese fire was heaviest in the 1st Battalion area. Twenty-seven-year-old Private James C. Spencer remembered that he spent most of the day in a deep foxhole listening to the shells exploding and the whirring of fragments. Spencer raised his head from time to time and saw two young Americans running from the front lines until a captain, waving a drawn revolver, ordered them back to their duty.[30]

These two men were probably from Lieutenant Lloyd G. Murphy's B Company. The terrain upon which B Company built their line was rolling and sloped gradually toward the river, offering good fields of fire. At 1400 hours the Japanese organized themselves well enough to put several infantry units across the small Culo River, and at 1600 hours their patrols probed the junction between the 31st Infantry and the 72nd Infantry. In so doing they bumped into B Company. "I looked out over the front," remembers Private Harold J. Garrett, "and it seemed that whole field got up and moved."[31] Garrett aimed his rifle and started firing. Corporal Milton G. Alexander and two members of his squad raked the enemy with their air-cooled .30-caliber machine gun and when two BAR's joined Alexander's gun, Japanese fire momentarily slowed. But then enemy bullets washed over B Company's line. "It seemed like a bunch of bees hit our position, the snap, crackle, and pop of small arms and machine gun fire," recalled Private Kerchum, a four-year Army veteran. "Five minutes later, B Company panicked. The whole company took off up the hill towards our artillery."[32]

They finally stopped 800 yards behind the main line, and some stopped near the battalion headquarters, but their flight could not be tolerated if the Layac position was to delay the Japanese. Lieutenant Robert K. Carnahan's C Company, on line to the left of B Company's now abandoned foxholes, held firm. As C Company waited for the Japanese to close to within 300 yards, 20-year-old Private George Uzelac watched the enemy approaching with fixed bayonets, bayonets that seemed small when they were 500 yards away but that looked twice as long as they got closer. Uzelac, dirty, hungry, and convinced he was too young to die, was shaking badly until he started firing his BAR, then he calmed down and helped stop the Japanese. The Americans stopped firing when Japanese aid men appeared to collect their casualties. After talking with regimental headquarters, the 1st Battalion commander, Lieutenant Colonel Edward H. Bowes, West Point class of 1918, ordered his reserve company to counterattack and restore the line. But when local efforts with Captain Cecil R. Welchko's A Company failed to close the hole, Colonel Steel called on his reserve 3rd Battalion to plug the gap. Because the battalion was also General Selleck's reserve, Steel asked permission to use it, and Selleck agreed.[33]

A little after 1600 hours Lieutenant Donald G. Thompson of L Company and Captain Ray Stroud of I Company received orders to report to their battalion commander. When they arrived, Lieutenant Colonel Jasper E. Brady told his officers that parts of B Company were passing through regimental headquarters after leaving their positions. "I and L Companies will immediately move forward from their present positions to the front-line sector formerly occupied by B Company," Brady said. "Report by runner to me as soon as you have your companies in position. K Company will remain in reserve prepared to move up into the lines on my order."[34]

Lieutenant Thompson, commissioned in 1940 at the University of Nebraska, called his L Company platoon leaders together. Thompson decided on a reconnaissance, and he ordered his platoons to an assembly area. The platoon leaders, all sergeants, made their small squads ready for movement. The attached platoon of machine guns from the heavy weapons company also prepared for movement. Then Thompson made his reconnaissance. When First Sergeant J. P. Flynn returned he told Thompson he failed to find any officers in the left flank company of the 72nd Infantry, but he did find numerous Filipinos wandering aimlessly across the battlefield. Flynn, a veteran of fifteen years' service in the Philippines, talked to them and got them back in their foxholes. The Filipinos gained confidence once they knew that American troops were going into position on their left flank. Thompson sent Flynn back to the Filipinos with orders to keep them in their trenches.[35]

Thompson told his 1st Platoon to follow the left flank of the 72nd Infantry, using a concealed route along a dry stream bed. The other two platoons fixed bayonets and formed into platoons abreast. Two I Company squads were attached to Thompson and served as his reserve. The 3rd Platoon with attached machine guns moved to the right, and the 2nd Platoon worked its way forward with orders to reestablish the line to the right of C Company which was still in place on the main line. Captain James J. O'Donovan, battalion executive officer, walked with L Company and lent his colorful presence to the attack. He waved a .45 caliber pistol in the air, carried a Smith & Wesson .38 on one hip, and sported another .45 in the center of his back.[36]

From the start of Thompson's advance a battery of Japanese guns on the Guagua Road 7,000 yards away tracked L Company's progress. As the platoons crossed the ridges the enemy artillery fired. The Americans laid down upon hearing the reports of the guns, ran forward after the shells landed, reformed in the gullies, and started out again. The advance was rapid and the company well under control as the men covered the one kilometer toward their objective. The enemy's artillery was consistently either over or short, and some shells that were on target failed to detonate.[37]

Japanese artillery fire was more effective against Captain Stroud's I Company than it was against Thompson's L. Bursting shells badly disorganized the men as they prepared for the counterattack. "In the distance we could hear a salvo of four guns," recalls Private Grant E. Workman, "then another and still another. After the shells started landing on our outfit, it was havoc. Soldiers were hit, bushes and hard clay flying all over the place."[38] Like B Company, I Company broke, and like B Company, they broke more from disorganization and shock than from actual casualties. Captain Stroud was at his advanced command post, did not hear an order given by one of his sergeants to withdraw, and was left there as his men decamped. Some of the men dodged from one shell hole to the next, figuring the Japanese gunners would correct after each shot and aim at another spot. Movement was all to the rear.

When lead elements of L Company entered a big cane field, Japanese infantry spotted them, took them under fire and slightly wounded one American. Thompson's point squad, with attached BARs, returned the fire and dispersed the enemy. L Company advanced through the brutally hot cane field and into the positions lost by B Company. Two of Captain Thomas P. Bell's M Company water-cooled machine guns, positioned in sight defilade and well to Thompson's rear, lofted streams of bullets into Japanese occupying papaya trees off to Thompson's right and bowled off the road as their first victim a Japanese motorcycle messenger. On their objective, Thompson's men found two heavy machine guns and several BARs abandoned by their former American owners, and they used them to support the advance. Thompson's men distinguished themselves by their quick action, confidence, and aggressive movement. "There wasn't any doubt in our minds that we could whip the Japs," recalled 18-year-old Private Wilburn L. Snyder, a medic with L Company. "We accomplished what we set out to do, push the Japs back."[39]

When the platoons reported they were in position, Thompson confirmed the reports by a personal check and tied his left flank into Captain Welchko's A Company. Looking across the front, Thompson saw several Japanese patrols still looking for a soft spot; they never realized the damage they had done to the 1st Battalion's line. Thompson dispatched a runner to battalion, reporting his situation—the gap was closed, he had contact with elements to the right and left, he was receiving small arms and mortar fire, and Japanese were still crossing the river in front of the 72nd Infantry. Colonel Brady then sent Captain Coral M. Talbott's K

Company up to support Thompson, initially to the right of Thompson to support the Filipinos. "We advanced 300 yards through fierce shelling, dashing thirty or forty paces, going down, then running again," remembered 22-year-old Private Mondell White from West Virginia.[40] K Company entered the line after dark and spotted Japanese with green flashlights moving in some cane 200 yards away. Captain Talbott, a West Pointer with three years' service, deployed his machine guns and shot up the enemy. Then he moved his company into B Company's old positions to the left of Thompson.

Although the 31st Infantry had now restored its line, the situation still looked bad. The Japanese had bombed the town of Hermosa, exploded an ammunition dump there, set the town afire, blocked the East Road with rubble, and cut all communications with the right flank 71st Infantry. Most of Selleck's artillery was out of action, enemy planes left him without concealment, and all his infantry reserves were committed. If the Japanese broke through the 71st Division, they would cut the only road leading south and trap the entire Layac force. Light firing was continuing along the American regiment's front into the early evening, still more Japanese were seen arriving at Layac, and Japanese movements forward of the 72nd Infantry were increasing. With no accurate information on enemy strengths or dispositions, Selleck was forced to assume the bulk of General Homma's 14th Army faced him. Selleck's mission was to defend the position until a coordinated attack forced a withdrawal, not to fight a pitched battle. He had already lost the two-battery 23rd Artillery and the 1st Battalion, 71st Artillery. Two American rifle companies had run and were out of the fight, his reserve battalion was committed, and the Filipinos along the 71st Division's front—even though they had not been seriously pressured—were shaky and ready to bolt.[41]

At 2000 hours Colonel Steel explained the 31st Infantry's situation to Selleck, but Selleck refused permission to withdraw. A second report by Steel to Selleck stressed the possibility of a disastrous daylight withdrawal the next day if the men did not get out that night. This time Selleck agreed and asked II Corps for permission to withdraw to an assembly area behind the Abucay Line. When General Parker received Selleck's request he initially considered reinforcing Selleck and counterattacking at dawn, but he dropped the idea after his artillery staff told him it was impossible to position cannon at night and shoot at dawn without a daylight reconnaissance. So at 2200 hours II Corps reluctantly ordered Selleck to conduct a night withdrawal. Some nervous shuffling was already evident. The Tank Group commander, General Weaver, considered that it was "idle to remain," but he issued orders to stay until dark, then withdraw. But at 1830 hours American tanks had started toward the East

Road after it appeared the Japanese might cut the route. This move, ordered by Lieutenant Colonel Miller, was in direct disobedience of orders given him by General Weaver. One company of Miller's tanks was supposed to stay in position and cover any withdrawals, yet they began their move well before Selleck even asked permission to withdraw.[42]

In the 31st Infantry, Colonel Steel dispatched warning orders to his three battalions, and company commanders felt their way along their dark lines, telling their men about the upcoming movement. It took time, but a little after midnight everyone was ready. Kitchen and supply vehicles rolled south, while behind them guides waited at creek beds and trails to keep the main body of infantry on course. Most units had enough time to plan for the move, but without the means to evacuate it they had to abandon the small arms ammunition delivered two days before in 60,000 round lots. The 31st Infantry positioned three rifle companies as a covering shell and pulled the bulk of the regiment out at 0130 hours. "Some guys from E Company came over woke us up, and told us they were relieving us," remembered Private Paul C. Gilmore who had enlisted only five months before.[43] E Company covered the 2nd Battalion as F and G companies pulled south. Light from a half-moon filtered through a slight overcast and helped the soldiers pick their way along trails and roads. Then at 0230 hours, at the moment the covering shell itself started to pull out, the Japanese launched a night attack. Intense small arms fire erupted, and Captain Robert S. Sauer's E Company was destroyed as a tactical entity. Survivors wandered into friendly lines for the next four days. F Company halted, deployed, and repulsed the enemy.

The Filipino 71st Infantry withdrew by the book and in massed parade-ground formations. In the 72nd Infantry the covering shell withdrew too soon and allowed Japanese to infiltrate the line of withdrawal, requiring part of the 31st Infantry to leave the planned route and march cross country to reach the East Road. Once again, as happened during the withdrawal to Bataan, the lack of equipment and transportation actually aided the Filipinos. Although the Japanese got behind the Filipinos, the lightly-equipped native infantrymen simply flowed around the roadblocks.[44]

The 26th Cavalry on the extreme left of the line had been the last unit to move into the Layac line on January 6, and it was now the last unit to hear of the withdrawal. The cavalrymen's only motorized route of egress was over a trail covered by the Americans to their right, so at 2030 hours Colonel Pierce asked the 31st Infantry to keep him informed of the situation, especially concerning the road. The Americans said the trail would probably remain open until daylight. But for some reason, warning came too late. At 0130 hours, the moment the right flank cavalrymen noticed the 31st Infantry was pulling out, B Troop radioed regiment, "Believe road closed by 3:30 A.M. Am moving out."[45] The startled headquarters tried to contact both Selleck and the American regiment, but to no avail. About 0230 hours the 26th Cavalry received an undecodeable radio message from the 31st Infantry, undecodeable because the code had been changed without the cavalrymen's knowledge. Mounted patrols dispatched to the right drew fire. On the heels of this message came a call from the Scout 2nd Squadron that a withdrawal had been ordered and the 1st Squadron with the scout car platoon was about to move. Colonel Pierce told the 1st Squadron to move as planned. The scout cars were dispatched at 0400 hours but ran into Japanese near Culis a half hour later. Three cars were lost, Lieutenants Graves, Chandler, and Cahoon were killed, Franz Weisblatt (a United Press correspondent, an old Manila hand and a veteran of Manchuria and Japan) was wounded and captured, eighteen cavalrymen were killed or captured, and the regiment's colors were lost. One scout car escaped and returned to regimental headquarters with word the road was cut. The regimental headquarters and 2nd Squadron stayed put until daylight, then spent January 7 marching along the foothills of Mount Natib behind Japanese lines trying to find a safe trail south.

Despite local confusion, the withdrawal succeeded, and Selleck's force broke contact with the Japanese who, now unopposed, occupied Hermosa in the dark. All things considered, the delay force was lucky—the Japanese failed to pursue, and the defenders once again traded space for time. But this one-day delay did prove costly, especially since USAFFE had expected more than a single day's delay out of Selleck's men. At least one officer at USAFFE recorded the mission as a failure. Although Selleck's guns did land the first blows, his artillery regiments lost eleven of twenty-four guns. There was a lack of determination in several 31st Infantry units; two company commanders, B Company's Lieutenant Murphy and I Company's Captain Stroud, were relieved of command. The 31st Infantry reported only three killed, eighteen wounded, and one hundred missing, with most of the missing from E Company. These casualties indicate a feeble fight, especially when the Japanese were able to work their way into the main line and scatter two companies. The severity of Japanese artillery shook officers and men alike. All things considered, the kudos must go to the Japanese. The battle was a nice example of a numerically inferior, better trained force evicting a larger, less well-trained force.[46]

Although a covering force should avoid decisive engagements with the enemy, it should dispute their advance and make it as difficult as possible.

But once Selleck retreated and was clear of his covering force positions along the Culo River, he headed directly south for friendly lines. He made no effort to maintain contact with the Japanese. Whether or not he had a formal delay mission from II Corps or USAFFE is unknown. Regardless, MacArthur's headquarters or II Corps should have made arrangements to maintain contact with the enemy and to fight short, sharp actions as the Japanese approached the main line of resistance at the main battle position. The American command was admittedly in a defensive and almost defeatist mood, so it is possible no one thought to continue the delay. If so, the responsibility for failing to maintain a covering force to further delay the Japanese must rest with II Corps unless Selleck had that mission and simply abandoned it. From the early morning hours of January 7 until moderate contact was regained at the outpost line of resistance on January 10—at Japanese initiative—the Japanese were unopposed by anything other than artillery, big 155mm's that kept the East Road from Hermosa south under fire day and night.[47]

When the last of Selleck's units left Layac it was with a sigh of relief and a feeling of determination. The newly formed Filipino units felt they had not been given a fair chance to show their abilities. Now, as the Japanese closed off the neck of the peninsula, the Filipinos knew they were in the final stage of the game. It was here they would prove themselves to MacArthur, a leader in whom they had complete and adoring confidence. Hope was not yet dead, partly because only MacArthur and a few of his staff knew how disastrous the situation actually was. "Our only contact with the outside world, our world, was by radio," recalled Colonel Collier. "We had had no word from families or friends, and could see no chance of receiving any. But the morale was good. The general feeling seemed to be, 'We have run far enough. We'll stand now and take 'em on.' "[48]

CHAPTER SIX

II Philippine Corps

ON BATAAN, MACARTHUR DIVIDED HIS FILAMERICAN ARMY INTO
two infantry corps, a physical necessity posed by a precipitous geographi-
cal makeup of Mount Natib and Mount Silanganan, 4,222 and 3,620
feet, respectively, above the sea. A rough north-south line drawn down
the center of the peninsula formed the boundary between the two corps.
Planners placed Bataan's first line of defense as far forward as possible to
permit dispersion and flexibility in the conduct of the defense and to gain
time to prepare the reserve line. The reserve battle position, considered
the main line before the war, lay about eight miles south of the new main
battle line. South of the reserve battle position, and delineating the
southern one-third of the peninsula, was an east-west corps boundary,
this one containing Service Command.[1]

Major General George M. Parker's II Corps consisted of 25,000
Americans and Filipinos who protected the eastern portion of the penin-
sula, an east-west line of about 15,000 yards called the Abucay Line.
Parker, a slender, gray-haired, 52-year-old Iowan, was not new to the
Philippines, for he had served there with the American 21st Infantry
from 1911-1912. Parker completed the Command and General Staff
School in 1923 as an honor graduate and two years later attended the
War College. He knew his tactics and was strong on details. Promoted to
brigadier general only nine months earlier, he had been catapulted by
the war one more grade into a corps commander. On December 24
Parker was relieved of command of the South Luzon Force and ordered
to take part of his staff into Bataan to command the Bataan Defense
Force. II Corps was officially constituted on January 7, and Parker established his headquarters two miles west of Limay close to Manila Bay.

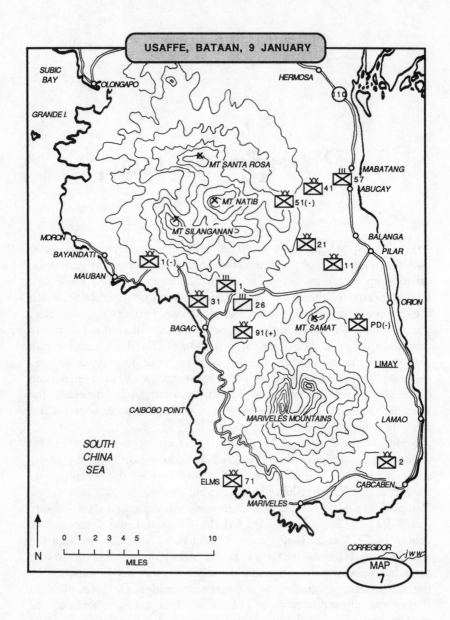

USAFFE, BATAAN, 9 JANUARY

SUBIC
BAY

GRANDE I.

OLONGAPO

HERMOSA

110

MT SANTA ROSA

MT NATIB

MT SILANGANAN

III   MABATANG
57   ABUCAY

XX
41

XX
51(-)

MORON

BAYANDATI

MAUBAN

XX
1 (-)

XX
21

BALANGA
PILAR

XX
11

III   1

III   26

XX
31

ORION

BAGAC

XX
91(+)

MT SAMAT

XX
PD(-)

LIMAY

CAIBOBO POINT

MARIVELES MOUNTAINS

LAMAO

SOUTH
CHINA
SEA

XX
2

ELMS

XX
71

CABCABEN

MARIVELES

CORREGIDOR   j w w

N

0 1 2 3 4 5   10

MILES

MAP
7

Parker would prove less competent a corps commander than Wainwright. Parker was in poor health, lacked the vigor needed to animate soldiers in a desperate situation, and never visited his front lines.[2]

The newly created II Corps found a much flatter and more developed area than did I Corps along the uninhabited and heavily wooded western coastline. Prosperous small communities lined the east coast, and numerous fish ponds, rice paddies, and nipa swamps extended inland from Manila Bay for about two miles until reaching the gradually rising hills and cane fields of Bataan's lowlands. This rolling hilly area ran for another five miles before it hit the steep slopes of Mount Natib. Because of the relatively open terrain here, II Corps undertook significant defensive preparations, especially along the East Road, the obvious focal point of any Japanese effort. The East Road was flat and sandy bordered by coconut and sugarcane plantations. The Japanese described II Corps line as well constructed with "covered rifle pits and machine gun emplacements . . . ; between them were placed foxholes . . . ; The fields of fire had been cleared of cover; camouflage was thorough; the rear communications network had been carefully and thoroughly laid."[3]

Although somewhat embellished, the Japanese report was correct except for the spiny, tangled slopes of Mount Natib where construction of a line proved impossible with the troops and equipment then available. Even small patrols operated there only with the utmost difficulty, and never did the two corps establish physical contact. In early January few officers considered the huge gap terribly important. In fact there was a feeling of smug complacency in the Corps headquarters about the security of the Corps left flank. The officers believed the steep slopes were impassable to military formations, and no one seemed alarmed that there was no contact with I Corps to their left. The Americans were not stupid, nor were they inattentive. It happens, however, even among professional, well-schooled soldiers, that impassable terrain is often more a state of mind than a state of nature. The terrain did, in fact, prevent large numbers of Japanese from operating and sustaining themselves there. But the numbers that did maneuver there, even without sustainment, would prove decisive.[4]

On the far right of the II Corps line, the eastern portion and acting as the right flank anchor of the Bataan defenses, stood the fresh 57th Infantry (PS), one of the three infantry regiments of the elite Philippine Division. The Scout regiment straddled the only road running north and south along the east coast. To the left of the 57th Infantry stood the Philippine Army 41st Division. The American officers and enlisted men assigned there were instructors, not commanders. In late August Colonel Malcolm V. Fortier became the senior instructor to the 41st Infantry

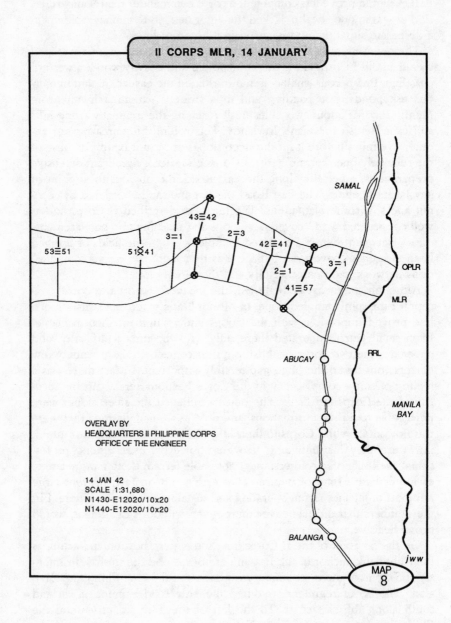

II CORPS MLR, 14 JANUARY

SAMAL

43≡42

3≡1   2≡3

53≡51   51✕41   42≡41   3≡1

OPLR

2≡1

41≡57

MLR

RRL

ABUCAY

MANILA
BAY

OVERLAY BY
HEADQUARTERS II PHILIPPINE CORPS
    OFFICE OF THE ENGINEER

14 JAN 42
SCALE 1:31,680
N1430-E12020/10x20
N1440-E12020/10x20

BALANGA

jww

MAP
8

Regiment and on November 11 became the senior instructor to the division when Brigadier General Vicente Lim became its commander. General Parker told Fortier that, as the division's senior instructor, he was to offer advice to General Lim. If Lim refused to accept the advice, Fortier was authorized to give the advice as an order from the corps commander. "General Lim was well aware of this arrangement and willing to abide by it," recalled Fortier.[5] Fortier never took unfair advantage of this strange relationship. He always talked things over with Lim, but it was Fortier who gave the orders and accepted responsibility for them. The two officers worked well throughout the campaign.

Similar command arrangements existed at lower levels. In the 1st Battalion, 41st Infantry, Captain John J. Martin arrived in the Philippines in October, went to the mobilizing Philippine Army, and became the instructor to Filipino Captain Jacobo Zobel's 1st Battalion. Captain Zobel was a graduate of Notre Dame, a wealthy polo-playing playboy with a palatial home in Manila, and a political appointee from a rich, land-owning family. General Lim came down and told Zobel, "Now you listen to this man here," pointing to Martin. "He has been to the Infantry School and knows what he is doing."[6] Zobel accepted the advice graciously, and he and Martin worked well together and developed an excellent rapport. But being an American instructor did not guarantee competence. Colonel Fortier quickly realized that many of his American instructors, who were often reserve captains and lieutenants just called to active duty, should have been receiving training, not giving it. Sadly, they were in charge of training units as large as battalions.

The 41st Division never reached full strength. It began its mobilization with eleven American officers and seventeen American enlisted men, all drawn from the American 31st Infantry. Filipino workmen built camps of nipa barracks to house the Filipino infantrymen, but only 60 percent of the new soldiers reported on time. The remainder straggled in for several weeks after the initial notice. Fortier found that there was a thirteen-week mobilization training program available, but no time had been added for receiving the new soldiers and arranging their camps. Two of the biggest problems the trainers were to face was the lack of training manuals and an absence of rifle ranges. Many camps did not have rifle ranges even though marksmanship was one of the first items on training schedules. Only three Browning Automatic Rifles (BARs) were issued to each company, and the only antitank armament available to the 41st Division were vintage .50-caliber water-cooled Colt machine guns of a model so dated that none of the American officers or sergeants were familiar with them. Each machine gun took six men to operate it, including a man in an adjacent foxhole who cranked a water pump to cool the barrel. The water hoses were worn out and unreplaceable. There were problems even with the water-cooled .30-caliber machine guns. The barrels were old and badly worn, making overhead fire dangerous, inaccurate, and impractical. No steel helmets or pistols were ever procured. There were only seventeen government-supplied vehicles in the entire division. But through all these hardships the Filipinos remained cheerful and morale was excellent.[7]

When lead elements of the 41st Division arrived on Bataan on Christmas Day, General Parker gave it a front of 15,000 yards, virtually everything in II Corps line except for the East Road. This incredibly wide front was completely inappropriate for a single division, and Parker later reduced it by half when the 51st Division arrived and occupied the left portion. Even with the line cut to about 7,000 yards, it still required emplacement of all three regiments abreast on the hills above the shallow Balantay River. This deployment gave each regiment a front of about 2,300 yards, well within doctrinal limits, but large for the small, poorly equipped Filipino units. Although the Balantay River provided little in the way of a defensive obstacle, the deep gorge cut by the easily fordable river was of significance.[8]

The 41st Division's front consisted of slowly rising abandoned rice and sugarcane fields partially reverted to brush land. Along this line "not a blade of grass nor a shovelful of earth had been turned" until the Division arrived.[9] Leaders initiated extensive reconnaissance and drove their soldiers into their first efforts at digging foxholes, establishing communications, and clearing fields of fire. Actually sitting the lines and positioning weapons proved to be a tremendous task, made more onerous because the line seemed to have been selected from a trail map rather than from a terrain reconnaissance. Because of these difficulties, Colonel Fortier had to make a careful study of the planned line to see exactly where to set units and where to place unit boundaries. Considerable confusion existed when units arrived to occupy their lines. The presence of abandoned alcohol-burning vehicles, former division transport, in front of the main line caused problems until they were removed and fields of fire assigned. As work progressed, long truck and troop columns snaked up and down the line, yet Japanese air failed to attack.

None of the 41st Division's men had individual entrenching tools, and because there were only fifty picks and shovels and just a few axes in the engineer battalion, the job of digging required improvision. Without tools, the Filipinos substituted bayonets and bolos, and some men resorted to meat-can lids to dig foxholes. Yet even with limited tools, they turned with a will to the task of building a formidable defense. The men pitched in and worked hard, but the lack of training was immediately apparent: they piled fresh dirt in front of foxholes instead of carrying it out of sight, they cleared fields of fire so enthusiastically they looked like mowed lawns, and they placed their foxholes in straight lines resulting in some fields of fire running no longer than twenty-five yards. The soldiers failed to clear vegetation from the far side of barbed wire, and few wire entanglements were covered by machine guns or automatic weapons. The Filipinos had received so little training that setting up a simple guard rotation required a ridiculous effort followed by close supervision. Only three months before finding themselves in foxholes, these men, mainly agricultural workers from the huge sugar and rice haciendas, had been growing crops and caring for carabao. Now they were expected to face a modern, twentieth-century army bent on their destruction.[10]

The 41st Division's engineer battalion worked all across the division area, but inexperience and haste often ruined an entire day's work. One group would drain water from a rice paddy to build a road only to have another group with different orders flood the area to construct an obstacle. Traditional disagreements between infantry and engineers began when the first shovelful of earth was turned. Infantrymen often refused to cooperate with the engineers or give them help, claiming it was the infantry's job to fight. Engineer officers felt that if the infantry had their way, the engineers would end up digging individual foxholes for the infantry. The reluctance of untrained infantry to construct fortifications when engineers were handy caused countless arguments and appeals to higher headquarters.[11]

Division and nondivisional engineers found themselves short of all types of equipment. The most serious shortages were barbed wire, burlap bags, axes, bolos, picks, and shovels. It was amazing that in the Philippines, where the bolo is a common tool, there was a severe shortage of the large jungle-cutting knives. In construction equipment, bitumen, cement, steel pipe, acetylene, and oxygen were the critically short items. To augment their meager supplies, engineers scoured Bataan stripping fences of their barbed wire and nails and salvaging roofing and lumber from destroyed buildings. They collected all manner of materiel, repaired it, and used it again. One operation raised 100 tons of barbed wire from a ship sunk off Cabcaben. In place of sandbags, engineers rolled mats three feet wide and five to twelve feet long—woven from wire, bamboo, and vines—filled them with dirt, and used them as revetments.[12]

The shortage of trained engineers and qualified officers reduced the effectiveness of the new engineer units. Because building military fortifications required more from soldiers than raw labor, the shortage of trained men at all levels was serious; the necessary manpower was available, but the technical skill was not. There were so few trained engineer officers that a civilian served for a time as an engineer battalion commander. When war broke out the army appealed to civilian engineers to help defend Luzon. Many volunteered—some brought their civilian crews with them—and were soon known as Casey's dynamiters in honor of USAFFE's engineer officer. "These men, although they in general knew little of the military, were ideally qualified to perform all phases of engineer operations," recalled Colonel Casey. "They were of a pioneer type accustomed to doing crude engineer[ing] under great difficulties . . . and capable of improvising and getting the work done."[13] To insure their protection under the laws of war, the civilian engineers were commissioned. Depending upon experience, previous status, and duties to be performed, the army commissioned men twenty-five to twenty-eight as second lieutenants, those from thirty to thirty-five as first lieutenants, and those older than thirty-five as captains. Only a few specially qualified men were commissioned as majors. All these men were admittedly splendid technicians, but they knew little of the military. As a result, they were often either overly familiar with their men, thereby losing the men's respect, or they were too distant, setting themselves up as martinets.

The 41st Field Artillery Regiment supported the 41st Division with sixteen light 75mm guns, eight 2.95-inch howitzers, a forward observer at each line battalion, and artillery liaison officers at regimental command posts. The 41st Artillery also had the mission of supporting the 51st Division and received a battalion of the 21st Artillery as an attachment. By January 8 construction in the 41st Division was nearing completion, and "confidence was beginning to creep into the hearts of the personnel."[14]

Anchoring the II Corps left flank on the rugged base of Mount Natib were two regiments of Brigadier General Albert M. Jones's 51st Division, the 51st and 53rd Infantry. Jones's division had a front of 5,000 yards. Although the 51st Division, riding in buses from the Batangas, Tayabas, and Laguna bus companies from South Luzon, began arriving on Bataan the night of December 31, it did not bus to the Abucay Line until January 4, leaving the men little time to dig in and prepare for the Japanese. Jones's third regiment, Colonel Virgil N. Cordero's 52nd Infantry, considered by Jones as the only regiment capable of offering effective resistance, was then on beach defense along Manila Bay. Jones's right flank regiment was Colonel Loren P. Stewart's 51st Infantry, and it covered 2,000 meters and tied in with the left of the 41st Division. To insure coordination with adjacent units, the 51st Infantry sent men to each flank with instructions to report developments.[15]

The 51st Division's left flank regiment, Lieutenant Colonel John R. Boatwright's 53rd Infantry, occupied 3,000 meters of line that petered out as single foxholes on the extreme left where they encroached into nearly impassable mountains. When this regiment mobilized in the last week of November, no training of any note took place. Only the officers and sergeants received training; as a result, the men were realistically civilians in uniform. It was the worst-prepared regiment in the 51st Division and the worst trained in the entire II Corps line. The small Filipino infantrymen were afraid of the kick of their rifles. Rifle ranges had to be improvised. Because there was little rifle ammunition available for practice, results of the hurried rifle marksmanship training were bad. Small arms ammunition was of First World War vintage and misfires were frequent. Many of its soldiers went into action without ever having fired on a rifle range.[16]

The regiment's World War I machine guns had elevation wheels but no traversing mechanisms, so the gunners had to slap the gun left and right to change the direction of fire. The heavy water-cooled .50-calibers were cumbersome and awkward to use in the thick vegetation. Most of the water pumps were missing and could not be requisitioned or replaced. The Filipinos performed well with machine guns, so the best rifle shooters were assigned to the automatic weapons. The Filipino officers came from the Manila area and spoke Tagalog, but the troops came from the Bicol Peninsula and spoke the Bicol dialect. Despite all these difficulties, morale was high because, as Sergeant Romualdo C. Din remembered, "We heard from the Voice of Freedom that US planes and aid were coming. We heard that Filipino soldiers would receive the same pay as the Americans. General Douglas MacArthur promised us that in equal risk there must be equal pay."[17]

The 51st Division's artillery consisted of eight wooden-wheeled British 75mm guns organized into two batteries. The batteries were mobilized after December 8 and lacked sights and fire control equipment. Efforts were made to arrange artillery support by laying as many telephone lines as the limited supply of wire allowed. But the guns did not always respond as requested, and in one instance they virtually shelled a friendly battalion out of position before the gunners discovered their mistake.[18]

In II Corps reserve waited Brigadier General Mateo Capinpin's 21st Division. It arrived on Bataan quite exhausted after twenty-four hours of solid marching, and it spent its time trying to reorganize and make good the loss of 600 men. Just before reaching Bataan, the division's headquarters and signal company were both hit by Japanese air near Hermosa, suffered twenty men killed or wounded, and lost much of their equipment including civilian telephone wire and phones salvaged from the Del Carmen Plantation. The loss of this equipment was particularly unfortunate, because signal gear was soon in very short supply. Upon their arrival on Bataan, division officers immediately undertook reconnaissances of the Abucay Line.[19]

The last division to be mentioned in II Corps is the 11th Division. It was mobilized on September 1, yet by December the three infantry regiments were scarcely at two-thirds strength. The division artillery was still mobilizing and had not yet arrived, and training in support of the infantry was not attempted by the artillerymen until the division actually deployed for battle. Service elements joined the division when war started, but they had not been organized or trained as units. Transportation was almost nonexistent, and there was a serious shortage of all types of equipment. When Lieutenant Donald Blackburn joined the 12th Infantry as the headquarters battalion instructor in communications and transportation, he found there were no trucks, no radios, and only one field telephone. His men were housed in temporary bamboo barracks with thatch roofs, bamboo strip bunks, and sod floors. He was not at all impressed with the quality and competence of the Ilocano officers. They had failed to require their men to use the latrines—a shortcoming found in almost all Filipino units—and some Filipino officers ruined their status by gambling with their men. Blackburn and his fellow Americans often despaired of teaching the Filipinos the intricacies of modern equipment. Blackburn believed a platoon of Igorots—hardy mountain headhunters—armed with spears would be more formidable than a battalion of lowland Ilocanos armed with Enfields.[20]

A 52-year-old southerner from Jackson, Mississippi, Brigadier General William E. Brougher commanded the 11th Division. Before September 1941, Brougher had commanded the elite 57th Infantry, but when the Philippine reserves were mobilized he was assigned to command the 11th Division. A full colonel before the war, he was promoted to brigadier general on December 18, the same day he was sending his units north to slow the Japanese advance. Brougher and his officers instilled a high sense of belonging, a high esprit, in the men in part through spirited athletic competition. Group singing died quickly because of the numerous dialects. Brougher tried to create a feeling of unity among his men, something that would bind them, and he succeeded in teaching that in unity there is strength. He wanted them to realize that the worst thing that could happen was for them to become separated or lost from their unit. The men had to be convinced that in order to be fed, sheltered, and cared for, they must stay with their units and retain their weapons and equipment. "One of the most forlorn sights of the war," Brougher remembered, "were the large numbers of aimless stragglers, lost from their units—hungry, hopeless, pathetic, usually without arms or equipment, frequently without uniform."[21]

Desperately in need of vehicles, Brougher requisitioned all the civilian trucks, buses, and cars he could find—with their drivers. On December 8 one of his regiments commandeered thirty-five vehicles to augment their six military vehicles. The difficulty with pressed civilian drivers was obvious but unavoidable. The drivers and mechanics were sometimes unreliable and, not surprisingly, abandoned their vehicles at the first sign of danger. Very few spoke English.[22]

The 11th Division suffered heavily during its retreat from the north. The 3rd Battalion, 11th Infantry alone lost 394 killed or wounded during a disastrous retreat across a forty-foot wide stream with the Japanese in happy pursuit. The 12th Infantry lost heavily in the mountains near the summer capital of Baguio when the men were trapped by terrain and the Japanese. Once on Bataan, a reorganization proved necessary. The 13th Infantry was disbanded and the survivors transfered to the 12th Infantry. From then on, the 11th Division fought with just two regiments, the 11th and the 12th. Despite these problems, General Brougher felt he had a good division, and he told the men exactly that by means of a general order.[23]

> In the opinion of the Division Commander, no more difficult and exhausting operation was ever attempted by such a poorly prepared unit. It was only by superhuman effort on the part of key officers and non-commissioned officers in one critical situation after another that complete disaster was averted. For those pathetic figures who proved unequal to the task of facing danger and making their contribution to the bulwark of fire with which the invading foe must be resisted to the last we can now feel only contempt, tempered with pity. And now, in the face of future dangers, all officers and men are called upon to unite themselves in the common cause of making the maximum effort of which the 11th Division is still capable in any mission to which we may be assigned.[24]

Once on Bataan, the 11th Division was assigned the defense of Bataan's east coast. In addition to its organic artillery regiment, the 11th Division was supported by most of the 21st Artillery, temporarily detached from the 21st Division. On the night of January 9 the 11th Infantry took up positions on a line from Abucay to Orion fronting Manila Bay, while the 12th Infantry extended the division's sector south to Limay. Because the East Road had to be protected and because the road was so close to the beach, defenses could not be organized in too great a depth. So automatic weapons were positioned to provide interlocking bands of fire, and entrenched riflemen lined the coast. Although MacArthur's orders forbade demolition of numerous huts that lined the beach and blocked fields of fire, the coast was at least screened.[25]

As with many units, the 11th Division's arrival on Bataan ended the mental and physical strain of the long retreat, and the men now had some reason to hope. They had survived the worst the Japanese had to offer— the 11th Infantry losing one in every five men—and they now felt they could await relief from the United States. "At least there would be no more of this withdrawing business," remembered Major Volckmann. "We were at the end of the line. It was now fight and hold, or else."[26] Some of the happiest troops on Bataan were the 11th Engineers. They were assigned a beach defense sector, and although they had a long sector to fortify, they also found a chance to augment their rations by a liberal fishing policy.

Two regiments provided antiaircraft protection for Bataan. On December 9 Colonel Charles G. Sage's 1,800-man 200th Coast Artillery (AA) sent 500 men to cadre a second regiment. Each battery, section, and squad was split so that a complete new formation was established. Originally named the 200th Provisional Coast Artillery Regiment, it received its official title eleven days later, the 515th Coast Artillery. Lieutenant Colonel Harry M. Peck assumed command and at 2300 hours battery commanders set out to collect their men. By 0200 hours on the ninth the artillerymen began receiving their 3-inch guns, 37mm guns, directors, range finders, and vehicles from reserve stocks at Fort Santiago. Some gun parts were missing or broken, so machinists fabricated new parts by hand. The first unit, F Battery, was ready to shoot at 1000 hours, and the remaining batteries were on line by 1600 hours. By midmorning the next day the 515th Artillery was firing at Japanese planes near Manila's docks.[27]

Both the 200th and 515th were equipped and organized much the same. A Battery contained searchlights, B, C, and D batteries owned 3-inch guns, E Battery had .50-caliber machine guns, and F, G, and H batteries operated 37mm guns. The only difference between the two regiments was that the 515th did not have an E Battery; their .50-calibers were divided among the other batteries. The 515th ended up with twelve 3-inch guns, twenty-three 37mm guns, and fifteen searchlights. Because both regiments were understrength they received Philippine Army recruits. The Filipinos were untrained in the technical aspects known to the Americans and were therefore used as a labor force. They carried ammunition, dug emplacements, and filled sandbags. In the first two weeks of January the two antiaircraft regiments took up defensive positions around airfields and rear areas on Bataan.[28]

For armored support, MacArthur's army had two battalions of tanks. The 192nd and 194th tank battalions played a critical role in delaying the Japanese during the long withdrawal from the beaches. The first use of armor took place under conditions extremely inimical to successful armored warfare. Tanks are offensive weapons, and the doctrine of mass, mobility, penetration, firepower, and exploitation was difficult to apply with just two light battalions whose mission was defensive. Even so, their presence was critical to hopes of a prolonged defense. Both battalions entered the war with fifty-four M-3 light tanks each, a total of 108 tanks controlled by the Provisional Tank Group.[29]

The M-3 General Stuart light tank weighed just under thirteen tons, stood seven feet tall, mounted a 37mm main gun, one coaxial .30-caliber, two or three .30-calibers mounted in the hull, and one .30-caliber antiaircraft gun atop the turret. The tank carried a crew of four: tank commander, gunner, driver, and assistant driver. There were some glaring deficiencies in the tank's design: the fuel cap could not be locked, which allowed enemy infantry to drop in grenades; the sponson-mounted machine gun required a circus acrobat to reload it; and the absence of a bottom escape hatch led to the death of crewmen forced to bail out through exposed topside hatches. Engine noise was so loud that commands were passed by hand and foot signals. Tank commanders used foot pressure on the driver's shoulders and head when standing in the turret, and used their hands when the tank was buttoned up. The tanks had radios, but sending was restricted to the use of a "key" set using morse code. Not all tanks had transmitters—only the leaders did—although all had receivers. Moving formations were guided by arm signals and flags pushed through openings in turrets. Seeing these signals was difficult, for dust would cover the bullet-proof vision slits until the tanks were nearly blind; unless the crew was alert for signals, a maneuver ordered by a leader could become very messy. The tanks were not comfortable, but they had plenty of power and armor thick enough to stop most enemy shells. On the whole, the crewmen liked them.[30]

The 192nd Tank Battalion was organized from four separate National Guard companies in 1940 and worked with the 1st Armored Division during the Louisiana maneuvers of 1941. The battalion arrived in the Philippines only two weeks before the war, offloading their tanks in Manila on November 20. After a trip to Fort Stotsenburg, the tankers settled down to cleaning their gear and learning about their new half-tracks. The men had operated with scout cars in the States, so it took them time to learn how to handle the new vehicles. Mechanics worked to get vehicles into shape, and crewmen "de-Cosmolined" machine guns. Barracks were not ready, so the soldiers lived in pyramidal tents. Because the 192nd arrived in the Philippines with four companies, and because the 194th had only two, D Company, 192nd was transfered to the 194th.[31]

The 194th Tank Battalion had more time than its sister 192nd to become acclimated and organized. The battalion arrived in the Philippines on September 26, carrying new equipment picked up on the docks at San Francisco, equipment so new the men were unfamiliar with it. About 35 percent of the men were recent draftees and new to any kind of tank. More than half the company commanders were lieutenants rather than captains. Once in the Philippines, there were restrictions on gas and ammunition, and few range facilities existed. Even after war started the battalion received orders not to expend a single round of ammunition in practice; everything had to be saved to repulse the Japanese landings. Some tankers fired their weapons for the first time at the Japanese. Efforts to familiarize the Philippine Army with the sight of American tanks met with limited success. On one occasion an American officer approached a Japanese tank, thinking it was American.[32]

Tank losses were very heavy during the withdrawal from the beaches. The 194th lost twenty-four tanks before reaching Bataan. Some tanks were lost from a combination of a too-hasty retreat, poor communications, and a failure of command mixed with a liberal portion of bad luck. Most of the twenty-four tanks were stranded on the wrong side of a river after a bridge was blown, and by failing to look for a fording site, the company commander lost the opportunity to get his vehicles across. Just a half mile away was a shallow stretch of water where tanks could have crossed. That there was a ford nearby was logical, for before bridges were built in the Philippines, roads and trails ran across rivers at shallow points, and bridges were normally built on or near traditional roads. Consequently, fords were nearby.[33]

The arrival of the tanks on Bataan provided them with their first chance to reorganize since the war began. At a bivouac south of Pilar the men undertook overhauls of engines, communications, and weapons. The 17th Ordnance Company set up their ten-ton wreckers, shop trucks, welding and machine shops, and supply bins. Spare parts were in good supply. The men made some tank repairs at the unit level, while heavy wreckers towed other tanks to the ordnance bivouac. Long-awaited spare parts, batteries, and radios replaced worn ones. For the first time tank crews were able to eat from their field kitchens. Both battalions reorganized, and companies were reduced to just ten tanks each with each platoon having just three tanks.[34]

For mobile artillery support fifty self-propelled 75mm guns arrived in September and were formed into a Provisional Self-Propelled Artillery Group. The guns normally operated with the tanks giving the tanks uniquely mobile artillery support. The self-propelled mount (SPM) (a combination WWI French 75mm field piece mounted on an American half-track) was actually the result of a mid-1941 attempt by the Army to field a mobile antitank gun. Successful tests were held during the Louisiana Maneuvers, and of the first eighty-six M-3 tank destroyers built, fifty went to MacArthur. The gun had a good traverse and a good field of fire. To bring the SPM units up to strength and to augment their mobility, ninety-six trucks with drivers from the 200th Artillery were assigned. Battalion and battery commanders were American, gun commanders were poorly-trained Philippine Army soldiers, half-track drivers were Scouts from the 14th Engineer Battalion, and truck drivers were Americans from the 200th Artillery. There were originally enough guns to form three battalions with four, four-gun batteries in each battalion, but because of combat losses—seventeen guns—one battalion was inactivated, and the guns were distributed throughout the other two battalions.[35]

One more addition to the mobility of the tank battalions came when the Canadian SS *Don Jose* slipped into Manila Bay eight days after the war started. Originally destined for Hong Kong, the freighter held sixty Bren gun carriers minus the guns. The vehicles were meant to equip two Canadian motorized infantry battalions. The Canadian government raised no objections to MacArthur's use of the vehicles if they could not reach either Hong Kong or Singapore. American tankers armed some of the carriers with .30-caliber machine guns. The *Don Jose* also carried seventy five General Motors Corporation trucks which proved an especially valuable addition to the army's mobility, withstanding the vigors of the campaign very well.[36]

CHAPTER SEVEN

I Philippine Corps

OCCUPYING THE LEFT OF BATAAN'S DEFENSES WAS THE I PHILIPPINE Infantry Corps commanded by Major General Jonathan M. Wainwright, IV. Wainwright came from a long line of military men; his grandfather, a member of the first class to graduate from the Naval Academy in the 1840's, lost his life on January 1, 1863, while commanding the USS *Harriet Lane* at Galveston Harbor. An uncle, an ensign, was killed in 1870 off Mexico's west coast on board the USS *Mohican* during an engagement with a pirate vessel. Wainwright's father entered West Point by 1871.[1]

After graduating from West Point, Jonathan Wainwright served as a second lieutenant for six years and as a first lieutenant for another four. The Philippines were not new to Wainwright for he served there in 1909–1910 in a campaign against the Moros. As a major in the 82nd Division he participated in the St. Mihiel and Meuse-Argonne offensives in World War I. A brigadier general in 1938, his drinking problem in the late 1930s became too obvious to ignore, so the War Department put him out to pasture, sent him to finish his career quietly in the Philippines. Assigned to the Philippines in November 1940 and then promoted to major general enroute, Wainwright assumed command of the elite Philippine Division, the most important post he ever held and the realization of a considerable personal goal. Command of the Philippine division was welcomed, but this was not the end of advancement. He selected his next assignment when in September 1941 MacArthur offered him his choice of forces. "Which do you consider the most important point on the Philippines to defend?" he asked MacArthur. "Where do you think the main danger is—the place where some distinction can be gained?"[2]

"The North Luzon Force, by all means," answered MacArthur. This corps-equivalent force guarded the area in which a Japanese invasion could most likely be expected. Wainwright became its commander with three words. "I'd like that."

So on November 28 during the great mobilization of the Philippine Army MacArthur placed him in command of the ground forces protecting northern Luzon. In Wainwright's command were the Scout cavalry regiment and four Philippine Army reserve infantry divisions, the 11th, 21st, 71st, and 91st. Wainwright's infantry divisions, as part of MacArthur's concept for defending Luzon, were to destroy enemy landings and protect friendly airfields. When it became apparent the beaches were lost, Wainwright's men were ordered to conduct a series of delaying actions on successive lines south, down Luzon's Central Plain. While Wainwright delayed the enemy, MacArthur would collect his forces from the south and slip into Bataan. There, in the rugged Bataan hills, MacArthur planned to use his intimate knowledge of the terrain and his secure flanks to offset the enemy's superiority in tanks, planes, and quality of fighting men.[3]

Five delay lines were selected and reconnoitered during peace time. Each line was about ten to fifteen miles distant from the previous, or about the distance that could be covered easily in a single night's march. Each line was anchored on the flanks by mountains, and the center took advantage of rivers, swamps, and high ground. Of the five lines, only the last, the one closest to Bataan, was expected to hold for long, just long enough for the South Luzon force to come up from below Manila and march into Bataan. Because each line was too wide to be held by the forces involved, the commanders placed their men along the most likely avenues of approach. The Filipinos were supposed to fight and force the Japanese to halt for a full-dress attack. The Filipinos would then withdraw at night to the next line. Wainwright's mission was not to inflict serious casualties on the enemy, rather, he was to delay them as long as possible without becoming decisively engaged.[4]

Wainwright's North Luzon Force gave a desperate example of a tactically inferior force delaying a tactically, if not numerically, superior enemy. Wainwright was successful enough for the operation to be better than a rout but still less than a professional operation. Over a period of ten days Wainwright's men withdrew from the Lingayen beaches until on January 2, they covered the two roads leading into Bataan. Wainwright surprised the Japanese from time to time with sharp, local actions, and these unexpected stands were followed by the roar of blown bridges. His engineers gave the weary troops the obstacles needed to make the Japanese stumble. Most of the demolitions "called for engineer support of a type that bore no resemblance to long-established military doctrine," recalled one man. "Especially with respect to their demolitions, the engineers with their makeshift equipment and field expedients may be said to have been literally blazing new trails."[5] As a result, the Japanese became cautious, much too cautious for the circumstances. They had it in their power to turn the withdrawal into rout, but they repeatedly failed to seize glittering opportunities.

The North Luzon Force accomplished two missions during this time: It delayed the enemy long enough to permit Brigadier General Albert M. Jones's South Luzon Force to enter Bataan, and it allowed time for some defenses to be constructed on Bataan. Without the successful withdrawal from the north, Jones's South Luzon Force would not have reached the Bataan peninsula. And without Jones's men MacArthur could not have properly manned the Bataan defenses. The tactical competence shown by the defenders under severe restrictions of training, language, and supplies should be recognized. The withdrawal was not without cost however, for losses were heavy and many Filipinos deserted as they passed their homes. Desertions stripped Wainwright's North Luzon Force from 28,000 men to only 16,000 by the time it entered Bataan. Only a small number of the missing 12,000 men were killed or wounded.[6]

USAFFE constituted I Corps on January 7, 1942, and tasked it to defend Bataan's western half and prevent hostile landings along the west coast. Wainwright's I Corps, now reinforced to 22,500 men, was generally from the same organizations as those that comprised his North Luzon Force: the 26th Cavalry, the 1st Regular Division, the 31st Division, the 91st Division, and the badly battered elements of the 71st Division. Both the 71st and 91st Divisions arrived on Bataan on January 2; the 91st went into reserve because of its disorganized condition, but the 71st Division fought once more at Layac before going into I Corps. Wainwright's 11th and 21st Divisions were both transferred to II Corps.[7]

The most effective unit available to Wainwright was the 26th Cavalry, a Philippine Scout unit thoroughly imbued an offensive spirit, a spirit traditional to American cavalry. Mounted both on horses and vehicles, they went into reserve after a gallant delaying action in northern Luzon. Their first combat had occurred at the town of Damortis on the Lingayen beaches. Receiving orders to hold the town, the cavalry regiment began an operation of which history is made. The regimental commander and his staff overlooked the Japanese invasion fleet as the cavalry squadrons trotted up. The squadron commanders rode up, received their orders, and returned to their men. As each cavalry troop arrived, the men galloped into the hills in the most perfect hasty occupation of a defensive position that could be imagined. When the Japanese attacked, the Scouts lay quietly behind their rifles and flayed the enemy with galling, accurate fire. "It was a wonderful thing," recalled Major William E. Chandler, "to watch these little brown soldiers, who had never before seen a gun fired in anger, calmly choosing their positions, adjusting their rifle slings, and proceeding to pick off Japs as though they were silhouette targets on the rifle range. 'Why not,' they would have said, 'this is what we were trained for, and this is what you have ordered us to do.' "[8] The battle was the first of many as the cavalrymen covered one withdrawal after another. Organized with two squadrons of three troops each, the cavalry's delaying actions reduced their original strength from over 800 officers and men to less than 650. Although an American stateside cavalry regiment had an authorized 1,251 officers and men, the 26th Cavalry peaked at 843. After a punishing and dangerous cross-country retreat at the approaches to Bataan, during which time everyone but Wainwright, an old cavalryman himself, had written them off as lost, the regiment joined I Corps on January 9.

When MacArthur visited I Corps on January 10 he talked with Wainwright. "Jonathan, I'm glad to see you back from the north. The execution of your withdrawal and of your mission in covering the withdrawal of the South Luzon force were as fine as anything in history."[9] Such praise pleased Wainwright, but he took into consideration MacArthur's expansiveness in speaking and wondered if he really deserved the praise. MacArthur's words were doubly pleasing to Wainwright because MacArthur spoke in front of Wainwright's subordinate generals. More substantial than vocal plaudits were MacArthur's next words, for MacArthur promised to make Wainwright a permanent major general of the Regular Army. Addressing the I Corps staff, MacArthur told them that "the enemy's temporary superiority of the air would soon be a thing of the past."[10] No doubt MacArthur was thinking of Marshall's message, received a week earlier, about streams of planes headed for the Philippines. He also hinted of a counterattack by II Corps and by 20,000 Philippine Army soldiers on Mindanao who could reinforce Bataan. MacArthur then talked about reoccupying Manila in the near future and concluded by telling the I Corps officers how their gallant fighting had caught the imagination of the American people.

MacArthur turned back to Wainwright. "Where are your 155mm guns?"

Wainwright told him there were six fairly close by and suggested they walk over to see them.

"Jonathan, I don't want to see them. I want to hear them!"[11] Before leaving, MacArthur and Sutherland had a long, private talk with Wainwright, trying to get a feel of I Corps status, both physical and mental.

Wainwright answered all their questions and explained his deployment. MacArthur's visit cheered the I Corps officers, but to some enlisted men the visitors from Corregidor were overdressed, wearing ties and pressed uniforms. They contrasted sharply with Wainwright wearing tired, dirt and sweat-stained khakis. The men agreed that Wainwright was the more impressive of the two commanding generals.

Spread about 8,000 yards from the South China Sea toward Bataan's interior, I Corps held the coastal strip with the 3rd Infantry of the 1st Regular Division. The 1st Regular Division—commanded by Brigadier General Fidel V. Segundo, a 1917 West Point graduate—was the Philippine Army's oldest division, activated in 1936 as the nucleus of the standing army of the Commonwealth of the Philippines. Upon its induction into USAFFE on December 19, 1941, it was filled with recently recruited trainees, ROTC cadets, and civilian volunteers; the majority of its trained regular army enlisted personnel had been transferred to the newly activated reserve divisions as cadre. There was little optimism in the 1st Division. "The utter unpreparedness and lack of arms, ammunition, equipment and supplies contributed much to the difficulties of the situation," recalled Captain Alfredo M. Santos, the 1st Infantry Regiment's commander. "The division suffered scores of casualties, both officers and men, as a result of enemy bombing and strafing while still reorganizing in Camp Murphy, Quezon City, its home station."[12] At the outbreak of war, the 1st Division had but two regiments, the 1st and the 3rd; the missing 2nd Infantry was on Mindanao. The division had an engineer and a medical battalion, but both were at reduced strength; there was no artillery. Companies and platoons were officered by newly commissioned 1st and 2nd Class cadets, recent graduates of the Philippine Military Academy. The other officers were reservists and a sprinkling of professors from the Academy.

The Division's 1st Infantry arrived on Bataan on December 29 and having suffered during its retreat to Bataan went into reserve. Its strength had increased significantly when more than 375 old Philippine Scouts from the Fort McKinley Post Service Detachment, led by Major Montgomery McKee, joined the 1st Infantry on December 26 in a hurriedly assembled fleet of taxicabs. Trained and disciplined by a lifetime in the Scouts and having long since served their time, these retired soldiers arrived to stiffen the green regiment. Their presence was a most welcome addition to the shaky unit. The 3rd Infantry followed the 1st Infantry into Bataan two days later and went into the I Corps front line. The regiment had not seen any action up to this point and was still a cohesive force, but it too was filled with untrained recruits.[13]

In I Corps reserve and beach defense was Brigadier General Clyde A.

Selleck's badly mauled 71st Division. The division's appearance was now quite different from the first time Selleck saw it. When he joined the division in mid-November Selleck wanted to look at his men and let them look at him so he held a formation. His soldiers were wearing short-sleeved khaki shirts, short khaki trousers, and rubber-soled canvas shoes. His officers and men were young, of medium size, lean and attentive. Selleck remembered that they looked quite smart. Selleck talked briefly, but it proved necessary to translate his words into two dialects before everyone understood. Less than two months had passed since that talk and the 71st Division was now in very bad shape. War had seemed far away during mobilization, and training had proceeded at a stately pace on the southern island of Negros. Selleck did not arrive at the division's Luzon training camp, Camp O'Donnell, until November 18. The day after his arrival Selleck drove to Fort McKinley to visit South Luzon Force headquarters. "I was given an elaborate training directive while there," he recalled. "It sounded as if we were an organized, going outfit with no end of equipment and facilities."[14]

But he knew differently after he saw the division's camp. The area was littered with building materials, and although directed not to take time building training areas and base camps, Selleck found it absolutely necessary to spend precious days simply clearing a space to live and arranging for sanitation. Even moving into finished buildings proved difficult. The 71st Division had to clean up after native laborers who had lived in the barracks during construction with their families, chickens, and pigs without sanitary supervision. Despite frantic construction work, nearly everything was unfinished when the 72nd Infantry arrived on December 7. The newly arrived regiment overtaxed the inadequate water system and the regiment had to move out of camp to a nearby village where a river provided the needed water. The medical battalion arrived in camp only four days before the war without any equipment and with practically no individual or organizational training. Headquarters personnel had no special qualifications and had been assigned by lot; a large percentage were illiterate. The division had twenty-three vehicles from an authorized level of 369. Tactical training in the infantry regiments had hardly begun and was handicapped by a shortage of rifle ranges and transportation. Leadership abilities and the absence of trained personnel were ghastly; several infantry battalions were commanded by Filipino third lieutenants.[15]

Training for the 71st and 72nd infantry followed the same pattern. American instructors travelled to a cadre center where they organized and taught the Filipinos who would in turn train and instruct the recruits as each regiment mobilized. Only the most rudimentary of military skills could be taught. Living conditions were spartan in the extreme and in many camps a fifteen-minute warning was adequate to alert everyone to leave with all personal and military gear. The Filipinos were willing but had so much to learn that the American instructors almost despaired. The recruits had to learn about wearing shoes, proper sanitation, and handling weapons, all with inadequate supplies of clothing, equipment, and weapons.[16]

During mobilization each infantry battalion received two American officers and two enlisted men to train the unit. The 72nd Infantry staff consisted of five Americans, with the other positions filled by Filipinos. Lieutenant John W. Fisher was typical of the newly arrived American reserve lieutenants. A graduate of Montana State University, Fisher entered active duty on June 9, 1941. He was assigned to Fort Lewis and the 3rd Division, but looking for more excitement he volunteered for the Philippines. He received orders and departed San Francisco on the SS *President Coolidge*. Despite numerous arrivals such as Fisher, there still were not enough officers. Once war began, American enlisted men assigned to Filipino units were promoted to second lieutenant and assigned as company commanders, but these junior officers often needed training as badly as the units they were to instruct. Despite every measure USAFFE took to provide leaders, the Philippine Army regiments remained far short of qualified leaders.[17]

The 71st Division staff was entirely Filipino. Filipino officers had more training than their men, but it still seemed a pale reflection of what the Americans considered a minimum. Key Filipino officers of the 71st Division staff went to the Command and Staff School at Baguio for a six-week course and were then expected to handle division level training and administration. General Selleck's chief of staff was a Filipino West Point graduate of long service but without staff experience. Nor was Selleck impressed with the quality of his officers, for he had received the leftovers after more senior American and Filipinos had made their choices. The 71st Division received those no one else desired, so the poor performance of the 71st Division once it faced the Japanese was not hard to explain.[18] As Selleck wrote later:

> The shortage and inadequacy of equipment were most serious handicaps. Detaching one infantry regiment, 71st, one half of the infantry strength in numbers and about 100% with reference to training the day before our first contact with the veteran enemy and later detaching all combat troops to reinforce the 91st Division disorganized and demoralized the division. These circumstances coupled with an almost complete lack of enemy information, practically no advice or assistance from higher headquarters, and a very brief acquaintance of the Division Commander with the country, the

people or any war plans, may permit of a better understanding of the operation of the 71st Division. The division was never organized, was never adequately equipped, and the training was so meager that when attacked by veteran troops, bombed and confronted by tanks it had a minimum of stability.[19]

Although much can be said in criticism of the quality of the junior officers, being a senior officer did not guarantee competence. Throughout the entire campaign, from mobilization to capitulation, numerous American colonels failed to handle the pressure and were relieved. Outside of service in World War I, these officers had risen in rank in a peacetime army. A large number failed to perform well during the prewar Louisiana maneuvers, so these physically and psychologically burned-out field grade officers were shipped to the Philippines to end their careers honorably in this quiet backwater. When faced with the harsh conditions of war where results rather than procedures measured success, many failed. A few reliefs were disguised as matters of health and some honor saved, but other reliefs were not disguised and the officer's career was ruined.[20]

North of Selleck's 71st Division stood Brigadier General Luther Stevens's 91st Division. Both the 71st and 91st divisions were filled with men from Samar and Leyte and came to Wainwright each minus one infantry regiment. The missing regiments, the 73rd and 93rd, remained on the island of Negros because of a shortage of water transportation. Both divisions were badly understrength when they arrived on Bataan, and there was such a dearth of American officers in the 92nd Infantry that orders were passed directly from regimental headquarters to the companies, bypassing the understrength battalion headquarters that operated solely in an administrative role. The soldiers of Colonel John H. Rodman's 92nd Infantry were recruited from the Visayas: Samar, Negros, Panay, Leyte, Cebu, and other islands. They spoke Hurai-Hurai or Ceuano, and their Filipino officers from the politically dominant island of Luzon spoke Tagalog or a Luzon dialect. The Americans, of course, spoke neither. When one American desperately asked his boss what to do about the language problem, the answer was "try Esperanto."[21]

In place of steel helmets the Filipinos wore headgear made from well-shellacked coconut palm fiber. The men carried their individual equipment in light canvas packs. Things were rough for the division at the start. The 92nd Infantry arrived on Luzon six days after the war started and was bombed while unloading in Manila. The regiment lost its commanding officer and four other Americans even before arriving in Bataan. To make up for losses suffered during the retreat from Lingayen, the 91st Division received cannon-less artillerymen, medics, ROTC cadets, and civilians. A reorganization on January 3 brought the companies to about 80 percent strength, but despite the reorganization, the 91st Infantry had been so badly damaged in December that once on Bataan only one battalion could be reorganized. So the 91st Division began the Bataan campaign with but four infantry battalions instead of the normal nine. Cannon in the 91st Artillery consisted of eight 2.95-inch howitzers, portee, organized into two batteries.[22]

Another infantry division in I Corps was the 31st Division, now defending the west coast. USAFFE sent orders to the 31st Division which were received at noon on December 24, ordering General Bluemel's men to Bataan. Bluemel's division left the Luzon beach defenses and shuttled in buses to Bataan. The buses, from the Trytran Company, were under the management of a future president of the Philippines, Ramon Magsaysay. The last elements of the division arrived the evening of December 26. One regiment held the Mauban-Mount Natib Line until relieved by elements of the 1st Regular Division, then the 31st Division took up beach defenses from the rear of the I Corps regimental reserve line south to Saysayan Point.[23]

Through luck, Japanese failures, and some hard-fought delays, MacArthur's army had assembled on Bataan and had occupied its main line of resistance. Japanese chances for a quick victory had disappeared, although neither the Japanese nor the Americans knew it. The resulting battles would comprise the Bataan campaign, three months of savage fighting that even then was overlooked by the world.

CHAPTER EIGHT

Philippine Scouts at Mabatang

THE FIRST BATTLE IN BATAAN WOULD BE FOUGHT ON THE MAIN battle position commonly known as the Abucay Line, pierced by the north-south East Road. The 57th Infantry, ordered to Bataan on December 30 as part of the withdrawal then occurring across Luzon, was one of two Scout infantry regiments in the elite Philippine Division. Despite the reassignment of more than half the officers, nearly all the veteran company commanders, and a third of the sergeants as cadre to the mobilizing Philippine Army, the staunch Philippine Scouts were still an effective force. But loss of seasoned leaders did leave the line companies short of practical experience, and teamwork was especially hurt after nearly all the veteran company commanders went to the Philippine Army as cadre. The two-year Philippine tour for American officers insured rotation of half the officers each year, and officer losses due to mobilization were so great that only forty-eight of the original pre-mobilization complement of 120 remained.[1]

Organized with an authorized strength of 114 officers and 2,162 enlisted men, the 57th Infantry actually fielded nearly 200 fewer when they occupied positions along the main line of resistance at the little barrio of Mabatang. Young American reserve officers with six to eighteen months service and little practical experience commanded the rifle companies. Fortunately, the regimental commander and two of the battalion commanders were soldiers with experience dating from World War I. But the two battalion commanders were unfamiliar with their men, having joined

115

their units on December 8. The enlisted men, the Scouts themselves, were without peer. Their enthusiastic and immediate obedience to orders inspired their American officers. Everyone who was to serve with the well-disciplined Scouts felt themselves privileged.[2]

Each rifle company had 130 men on its rolls and included an organic weapons platoon of four .30-caliber air-cooled machine guns and three 60mm mortars. The mortars were so new to the Philippines that ammunition had not yet arrived when hostilities commenced. Ammunition never arrived, and none could be improvised, so the mortars were stored in the battalion trains and the crews assigned elsewhere. A heavy weapons company of two officers and 151 enlisted men supported each battalion with three machine gun platoons of four heavy .30-caliber water-cooled machine guns each and a mortar platoon of two 81mm mortars and two .50-caliber machine guns. Because of a lack of 81mm ammunition (none arrived in the Philippines until well after the war started) the mortars fired old 3-inch (75mm) Stokes projectiles with a resulting loss of range and accuracy, and a high number of duds.[3]

The 57th Infantry's line ran from the waters of Manila Bay west across some fish ponds, crossed over the well-gravelled East Road just south of the stone and wood-plank bridge over Mabatang Creek, then continued along the south bank of the Mabatang Creek (north) and up a gentle rise to the right flank of the 41st Division, terminating at the eastern fence of the Mabatang cemetery. The regiment put two battalions on line and held one in reserve. On the regiment's right the 1st Battalion's front consisted of large fish ponds divided by banks three feet wide and six feet tall. The water was so deep and the mud so thick that Japanese tanks could not operate here, and even infantry would face the unenviable task of advancing single file along the dikes or swimming through the ponds. Cover and concealment for an attacker simply did not exist along the 1st Battalion's 1,300 yards of front split by the East Road. Even inexperienced soldiers would have little difficulty in stopping attacks here. The Japanese knew of this barrier and concluded that passage was impossible.[4]

The 1st Battalion's commanding officer, Major Royal Reynolds, born in California in 1910 and a 1933 graduate of the Military Academy, assumed command as a captain in October 1941. His experience with the 57th Infantry spanned the previous two years, during which time he served first as regimental communications officer and then as headquarters commandant. A 1938 graduate of the Infantry School Regular Course at Fort Benning, Reynolds, a deliberate, well-trained officer put his schooling to good use when he occupied his line. "I followed all the principles and instruction I had learned at the Infantry School," he re-

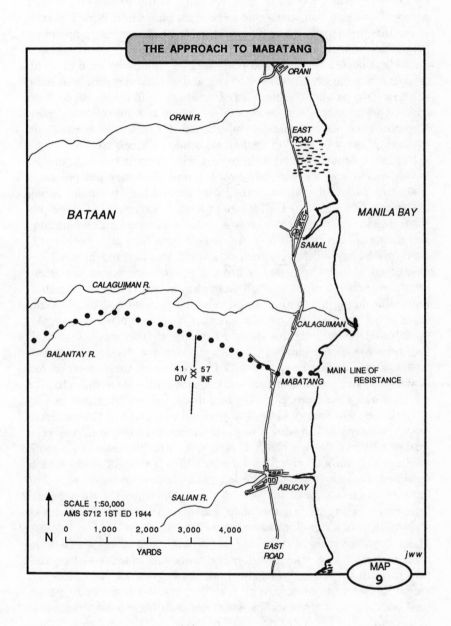

THE APPROACH TO MABATANG

ORANI

ORANI R.

EAST ROAD

BATAAN

MANILA BAY

SAMAL

CALAGUIMAN R.

CALAGUIMAN

BALANTAY R.

41 DIV $\times\times$ 57 INF

MABATANG

MAIN LINE OF RESISTANCE

ABUCAY

SALIAN R.

SCALE 1:50,000
AMS S712 1ST ED 1944

N

0   1,000   2,000   3,000   4,000

YARDS

EAST ROAD

jww

MAP 9

membered. "I adapted all of their teaching to the particular terrain I occupied—village, fish ponds, and some sugar cane fields. What I learned at the Infantry School paid off immeasurably."5 To prevent pinpointing his positions during night fighting, Reynolds withdrew all tracer ammunition. He occupied his command post—a large hole in the ground—with an operations officer, an artillery officer, and a signal sergeant with some runners. Two parallel double rows of sandbags, with dirt between them covered with timbers and corrugated tin, protected the command post. Reynolds gave the structure the appearance of a collapsed, burned ruin by placing torn and bent tin roofing alongside an access trench.

Reynold's Scouts erected little barbed wire to their front because of limited stocks and the naturally strong terrain, but they did put some concertina and double apron barbed wire around their positions. Along the front of Captain Loyd Mills's right flank C Company all three platoons dug in on line. The company's weapons platoon sent one machine gun squad to each rifle platoon. A few heavy machine guns bolstered C Company's line, and "every inch of ground was covered by fire," remembered Mills.6 The company had the new 60mm mortar, a tremendously important weapon in small unit fights, but, of course, no ammunition. Mills dug in his command post behind a rice paddy dike 200 yards south of his platoons, and he used a runner from each platoon to supplement his telephone lines. An artillery forward observer was ready to call fires on anyone rash enough to attack through the flooded ponds and nipa swamps. A few crews from D Company dug their water-cooled heavies into the junction of paddy dikes, albeit with some difficulty, for the high water table prevented digging more than two or three feet.

To the left and west of C Company waited the Scouts of Captain Frederick J. Yeager's A Company, two platoons forward and one in reserve, a total of 129 men. Yeager had full responsibility for the main north-south road running through the 57th Infantry's line. The right flank platoon straddled the East Road, and the left flank platoon extended westward until thirty yards west of the last fish pond. On January 7 these Scouts levelled Mabatang barrio, a wooded, park-like collection of nipa shacks on both sides of a tree-lined east-west trail, to clear fields of fire. Because Major Reynolds realized that if the barrio caught fire flames would drive his A Company from their positions, he requested and received permission to burn the village. He also burned off grass and placed debris around his lines to camouflage his foxholes, but he left the huge mango tress standing so their branches would conceal the ground from aerial observation. The hard, dry rice fields to the left of A Company left little protection for an attacker, while fish ponds protected the center and right of the company. With A Company were three of the regiment's new M-3 anti-tank guns positioned to cover the East Road. In 1st Battalion reserve was Captain Eugene H. Anthony's B Company.[7]

As a final precaution, Scout engineers destroyed bridges over the rivers and creeks north of the main line. They blew a small vaulted stone culvert just south of Samal, dropped the stone and concrete-piered Calaguiman bridge with its steel girders and wooden planking, blew another stone culvert, and destroyed a stone, concrete, and wooden bridge over the south fork of the Calaguiman. Blowing these bridges should not have been particularly significant, for now, during the dry season, these rivers were easily forded by moving several hundred yards inland. The Japanese, however, found that bridge destruction south of Hermosa caused them tremendous difficulties in communication and supply. They had to assign a large force led by an infantry battalion commander to repair duty. On January 11, the Japanese 16th Engineer Regiment assembled at Dinalupihan, took control of two companies of the 122nd Infantry, and began repairing the structures so that heavy vehicles could use them.[8]

The left flank battalion of the 57th Infantry, Lieutenant Colonel Philip T. Fry's 3rd Battalion, lay west of the East Road. When Fry, a pleasant, sociable, capable officer who had started his service with the North Carolina National Guard in 1917, met his officers on December 8 he was amazed at their youth; "they all seemed so young," the World War I veteran recalled.[9] But Fry was pleased with them and considered them a great bunch, so good they were "idolized" by the enlisted men. The right flank of the 3rd Battalion was defended by 119 men of Captain Charles W. Haas's K Company, two platoons on line supported by a section of heavy machine guns from M Company. Haas had joined K Company in August, so he was a "veteran" company commander of five months compared to his peers. Haas's right flank platoon dug in under the concealment of Mabatang's woods, and the left flank platoon entrenched in open country facing a clear, uncultivated strip of land. Haas set his command post thirty yards behind his platoons and placed his reserve platoon slightly behind his command post. The 3rd Battalion's left consisted of Lieutenant Herman F. Gerth's 123-man strong I Company. Behind his lines ran several shallow draws formed by small ridges running off Mount Natib, which offered the defenders covered lateral movement. In battalion reserve 600 yards to the rear was Captain Ernest Brown's L Company with 128 Scouts.

Preparations to receive the Japanese were impressive considering the limited means at hand. "[We] drove these Scouts like slaves," remembered Colonel Fry. "They liked it though, because we told them that the big battle for the Philippines would begin at this point."[10] The 3rd Battalion Scouts erected double apron barbed wire, using wooden pickets in lieu of the scarce metal ones. A platoon of Scout engineers from A Company, 14th Engineers, cheerfully helped prepare defensive works. Because the most probable enemy avenue of approach ran into the 3rd Battalion's sector, engineers placed more than 2,000 mines here, and they laid a smaller number of antitank mines—actually cases of TNT—to stop enemy armor. As a final touch, antitank guns covered the East Road. With one officer and 142 men the antitank company's platoon of three new M-3 guns sat behind a destroyed bridge and covered egress from Calaguiman barrio across fields as flat as a pool table. A platoon of older 1916 guns was dug in north of Abucay to defend against a sudden breakthrough.

In an unorthodox move a battery of the 24th Artillery entrenched on the firing line with the riflemen to cover the two best routes into the 3rd Battalion's sector, one running down the East Road and the other, actually the best of the routes, leading directly in west of the road. C Battery burrowed its four 75mm cannon into dugout emplacements next to large mango trees and prepared to fire against both tanks and infantry. The remainder of Lieutenant Colonel Charles B. Lienbach's 1st Battalion, 24th Artillery, was farther to the rear in direct support. Additional artillery came from a battery of 75mm self-propelled mounts on the north edge of the town of Abucay, four 75mms south of Abucay, and a battery of 2.95-inch howitzers dating from the turn of the century 500 yards northwest of Abucay. Another two-battery battalion, the 2nd Battalion, 88th Artillery, was in a reinforcing role supporting the Scout infantry. These artillerymen, like their brethren in the 57th Infantry, were Scouts. This battalion had moved into the Abucay area on Christmas Day, and the men busied themselves digging in the guns and trucks, selecting alternate firing positions, building dummy positions, duplicating telephone lines, and surveying critical points. Each gun had 400 rounds and enough transport to carry it if the guns displaced. Individual shelters, revetted gun emplacements, protected ammunition dumps, vigorous camouflage discipline, and the effective use of dummy positions all played a large part in the extreme effectiveness of the defending guns. II Corps engineers were under 27-year-old Illinois Captain William C. Chenoweth, a conscientious officer with common sense as well as book knowledge, not a common pairing in an engineer according to one infantryman. His men built fifty dummy guns from stove pipe and bamboo and exploded small dynamite charges to simulate cannon fire.[11]

Long-range heavy artillery support came from Lieutenant Colonel Winfield Scott's 86th Artillery (PS) and its twelve 155mm guns. The 86th was a separate Scout 155mm GPF (Grande Puissance Filloux) battalion, a veteran unit in that it had been activated on 19 April 1941, organized with three four-gun batteries. Sixteen more 155mm guns and two 155mm howitzers came from Colonel Alexander S. Quintard's 301st Artillery using the guns originally shipped to the Philippines to defend the straits leading into the inland seas. Excluding Corregidor's seacoast artillery, Bataan's 155mm wooden-wheeled, slow-speed First World War cannon were the biggest pieces in the Philippines. These guns were durable and simple and had an efficient recoil system and a wide traverse, but they could not be towed faster than five miles an hour. Even then, artillerymen needed to stop hourly to grease and cool the wheel bearings. Colonel Quintard's regiment was much, much newer than Scott's 86th Artillery. Cadre from the 301st Artillery were those men originally selected to lead the 101st Artillery on Mindanao (war prevented the cadre from sailing to Mindanao), while the bulk of the gunners consisted of enlisted men from the 92nd Coast Artillery and Philippine Army soldiers. The regiment filled itself with two groups of volunteers totalling 700 men, half of whom joined as late as December 20. Dug in west of Abucay, these guns covered all of the main line as well as the East Road.[12]

Well to the front of the 1st and 3rd battalions were elements of the 57th Infantry's 2nd Battalion occupying the regimental outpost line of resistance. The 2nd Battalion had been away from the regiment until January 6 and therefore had six days fewer in which to prepare its line. Time was short, and planning for the outposts was not as complete as it could have been. The remainder of the 2nd Battalion garrisoned the regimental reserve line. Behind this line was the town of Abucay where the regiment's aid station was established in three classrooms on the ground floor of the Convento, immediately north of the massive 400-year-old Spanish stone church. Dark, weathered, heavy rock walls and a five-tiered steeple gave the grounds a look of time-defying permanence. Heavy stone walls protected the patients. Medical support was inadequate, but a program to train riflemen as medics helped alleviate the shortage. Members of the regimental band augmented the medics as stretcher bearers, but most medical support came from C Company, 12th Medical Battalion, organized as a unit on December 9.[13]

The entire Mabatang Line was relatively strong, but trouble would come from a sugarcane field growing across the front of Fry's 3rd Battalion. The field ran from as far out as 400 yards to as close as 150 yards from the main line. Japanese could enter the cane field from the edge of Calaguiman barrio via a dry stream bed and move safely and secretly right up to the Scout main line. Ignorance did not leave the cane intact; there were too many professional soldiers present simply to forget. Colonel Fry, his company commanders, and the regimental operations officer all agreed the cane should be cleared; reconnaissances as far north as the main branch of the Calaguiman River convinced them the field was a serious threat. But Colonel George S. Clarke, the regimental commander, a veteran of World War I with the 1st Division, forbade any cutting. He believed the newly cut cane would show on aerial photos and indicate the presence of major defensive positions. Even after Colonel Fry asked that the "no cut" order be reconsidered, Colonel Clarke believed Scout artillery could deny use of the cane field as an assembly area. Unfortunately for the Scouts, his hope proved painfully unfulfilled.[14]

On January 10, just a day before the first heavy attacks on the 57th Infantry, General MacArthur arrived at the Scout's command post. As early as January 6 MacArthur had decided to visit his army, but when Philippine President Quezon heard about the plan he protested. "With great diffidence and as much diplomacy as I was capable of, I voiced the general feeling among Americans and Filipinos in Corregidor that General MacArthur should not take any chances and risk his life, for if he were lost the consequences to the morale of the fighting men would be incalculable. . . ."[15] Conversely, MacArthur's appearance would be very beneficial for morale. His timing was also important, for he knew from intelligence reports that a major Japanese attack could be expected on January 11. Realizing he was about to be hit, MacArthur messaged Washington, complaining about the passive American naval stance:

> The lack of any naval menace on our part is beginning to threaten failure in this entire theatre. Even if no great naval concentration can be expected in the near future some naval demonstration tending to deceive the enemy should be attempted. Ground and air cannot win alone here against ground and air and naval strength. Complete unity of effort must be obtained before it is too late.[16]

With this message dispatched, MacArthur told his chief of staff, Major General Richard K. Sutherland, what he wanted. Sutherland—commissioned a lieutenant of infantry after graduation from Yale in 1916, having served in France, and promoted to major general in December 1941 —arranged for the two corps commanders to assemble their general officers for a conference. Traveling by PT boat, MacArthur crossed from Corregidor the morning of January 10 to see the layout and boost "sagging" morale. Landing at Mariveles, MacArthur and Sutherland first visited the field hospitals and rear command posts. He stopped at the Headquarters, Philippine Department where soldiers regarded his presence as simply a morale visit. MacArthur told everyone that help was definitely on the way and that they must hold out until it arrived. His party drove to Hospital Number 1 at Limay, and MacArthur strode through the compound, entered one of the wards, and stopped and asked a wounded man, "How are you, son?" Then MacArthur collected some of the officers and asked, "Does anybody here want to bet me fifty dollars we'll be back in Manila by Easter?"[17] Few thought this would happen, but none dared challenge MacArthur. The visit failed to awe one of the doctors, Lieutenant Jack D. Gordon. "He seemed overbearing and uncaring. His ego showed very distinctly. I did not like him." MacArthur then drove north along the East Road in a Ford sedan until he met the II Corps commander at Balanga. Here MacArthur assured General Parker and his officers that reinforcements were coming from the United States.

The next leg of the journey was up to Abucay to the 57th Infantry's command post where the regiment's command element occupied a bunker and various staff sections spilled into nearby ditches and foxholes. Bamboo poles, palm trunks, and hardwood planks overlaid with sandbags provided protection from all but direct hits. Colonel Clarke, attired in helmet, cased gas mask, and pistol belt, was effusive in his conversation with MacArthur, referring to him as "My General." Standing near the old Abucay churchyard, Clarke presented his staff, "my boys, my dear, dear boys," and assured MacArthur that the Scouts would defend their positions to the last man. The meeting was an emotional rededication to the defense of Bataan and lacked any true communication. Major Harold K. Johnson, the regiment's operations officer, considered it a morale building visit, and in that vein it succeeded. Johnson recalled that when the Scouts arrived at Abucay, the USAFFE G2 had come up to visit. Colonel Willoughby, an old friend of Colonel Clarke, painted a very dark picture to Johnson and Clarke. His assessment was one of a quick surrender. MacArthur's visit dispelled some of that gloom, but his promise that the sky would be black with American planes soon proved hollow.[18]

MacArthur next went up to the 1st Battalion's command post where he talked with Major Reynolds. Here too, MacArthur's presence and comments lifted the spirits of officers and men alike. The fact that the commanding general was on the front line told the men three things; MacArthur was not afraid, he was interested in his soldiers, and the position was an important one. Colonel Clarke had made a single perfunctory visit to his front lines, so MacArthur's appearance was a delightful surprise.[19]

North of Abucay's churchyard stood the Japanese of the approaching 65th Brigade, reinforced from its normal 6,500 men to nearly 13,000. Total Japanese strength on Bataan would soon reach 23,222. Lieutenant General Akira Nara, commander of the three infantry regiments which made up the "Summer Brigade," held few illusions about the prospects facing him. Nara had attended Amherst College as a classmate of President Coolidge's son and furthered his education while in America by graduating from the Infantry School at Fort Benning. A stocky, middle-aged man, he was a well-known administrator and tactician. One reason he was picked to command the Philippine occupation force was because of his many years in the United States and his knowledge of Americans. Nara considered his brigade completely unprepared and unequipped for front line duty. His regiments, the 122nd, 141st, and 142nd, had not yet seen combat so this would be their first taste of battle. Organized in 1941 as a garrison unit—there were but two instead of three infantry battalions in each regiment—Nara's men were conscripts. What training they accomplished was limited, and unit training progressed only so far as company level. Although the men put forth an "unstinted effort," the brigade had difficulty working itself into a smoothly functioning team.[20]

The 65th Brigade landed at Lingayen Gulf on January 1 and it started south the next day across roads now in terrible shape, the direct result of 184 bridges blown by Colonel Skerry and his engineers. In addition to being delayed by demolitions, Nara's unconditioned men struggled south in the unaccustomed tropical heat with stragglers stretching half-way back to Lingayen. Soldiers sickened from the exertion. Colonel Takeo Imai had special difficulty keeping his overheated 141st Infantry on their feet, and the brigade was in a state of physical collapse when it reached the gates of Bataan on January 7. "They had made their march," recorded the 65th Brigade's history, "but were footsore and exhausted."[21]

January 7 found General Nara sitting at his desk in the town of Angeles twenty miles north of Bataan working on his operations order. "It seems," he wrote in an estimate of the situation, "that a part of the strength of the enemy immediately confronting us will withdraw to the Olongapo sector, and the main strength of force will withdraw to the vicinity of the Balanga sector."[22] He then issued instructions for movement of various 65th Brigade elements into Bataan. Nara finished and distributed the order which would bring the 65th Brigade against the Scouts of the 57th Infantry.

However unsure Nara was of the prospects facing his brigade, his superior, General Masaharu Homma, commander of the Philippine invasion force, left no doubt in Nara's mind as to what he must do. Attack! The 53-year-old Homma—peacetime commander of Japan's Formosa Army—was a wordly, well-travelled officer, a distinguished general who had served his country in England in World War I, in India after the war, and then in London as a military attache. Now, besides Homma's normal desire to conclude the campaign, an additional spur came from the Japanese throne. The Emperor desired to issue an Imperial Rescript commemorating war dead, and Homma was told that Bataan should be taken as soon as possible to allow issue of the Rescript.[23]

Homma told Nara that only 25,000 disorganized, demoralized enemy soldiers faced him, and the 14th Army operations order given to Nara on January 11 stated that the 65th Brigade would annihilate the routed enemy on Bataan. The Japanese believed that Manila's fall considerably weakened the strength and spirit of the Filamerican forces. Colonel Motoo Nakayama from 14th Army headquarters visited Nara's headquarters to discuss the upcoming operation and, just before leaving, turned to Nara and said, "At any rate, please carry out the pursuit. The enemy force is only 20,000 strong or so. As soon as you get there, start fighting immediately. Dilly-dallying serves only to give the enemy time for preparing."[24]

Aerial reconnaissance gave the Japanese no reason to believe the Filipinos were constructing strong defenses. In fact, aerial photos indicated the Filipinos were retreating toward Bataan's southern tip. Actually, the Japanese would encounter 15,000 Americans and 65,000 Filipinos. Even had the Japanese known this, they still would not have been too upset, for they were unimpressed with the abilities of their enemy. The Japanese believed that the slack living habits of the tropics and the intermingling of races had developed both a laziness and a feeling of unease in the American army. "It is difficult to perceive any good qualities in general in the enemy," wrote one staff officer.[25] Many frustrated Americans serving with Filipino units would have voiced a hearty amen! The Japanese were specially disgusted over American reluctance to launch banzai-type charges, feeling their reluctance to do so reflected poorly on American courage. The Japanese held the will of the Filamerican army in low esteem.

Japanese strategic planning called for the reduction of Luzon within fifty days from the outbreak of war and the subsequent transfer of the 48th Division and the 5th Air Group—the backbone of General Homma's invasion force—out of the Philippines for operations elsewhere. Imperial General Headquarters realized the withdrawal of these forces ahead of schedule might affect operations in the Philippines but they considered the early conquest of Java critical to their plans. The desire to maintain their momentum in the Pacific was irresistible, and Homma's easy march to Manila convinced the planners that the campaign could be concluded without the 48th Division. "Difficulties would undoubtedly arise in the future in the Philippines," concluded the Japanese, "but the Southern Army thought that the Philippines could be taken care of after the conclusion of the campaign in Java."[26] In short, they were willing to take a calculated risk in order to secure Java early. Estimates as to the time required to finish the Philippines remained at one to two months from the time of the first landings. There were hopes the campaign could be ended on schedule, but no one expected real problems if subjugation took a little longer.

Homma learned he was to lose the veteran 48th Division on January 2, the very day he triumphantly occupied Manila. Although the message arrived on January 1, transmission difficulties rendered it unreadable, so 14th Army asked Southern Army for a repeat and received it the night of January 2. The bulk of Homma's air power was to go to Burma—leaving him with only sixty-eight fighters, bombers, and reconnaissance aircraft— while the 48th Division would sail for the Dutch East Indies. Homma protested this order and asked to keep the division for just one more month, but to no avail. There is no doubt the campaign would have ended in January or early February had the 48th Division remained. The 65th Brigade alone was enough to keep the Americans on the brink of disaster, and the 48th Division—one of Japan's most experienced divisions—would have been decisive. One factor that allowed the early release of the 48th Division was the early departure of the 65th Brigade from Formosa. Nara's brigade was scheduled to arrive in the Philippines on the forty-fifth day of war, January 22, but their early departure now made them available on the twenty-fifth day of war.[27]

Homma had just ordered the bulk of the 48th Division to Bataan when he received the order to release it. He therefore turned to the 65th Brigade, even though it was a garrison unit, and ordered it to deploy for active combat. At noon on January 4, Homma sent Nara an order. "The 65th Brigade will immediately advance southward on the Angeles-Dinalupihan Road. After reaching the 1st line it will take over command of and combine with the Takahashi Detachment and the 9th Independent Field Heavy Artillery Battalion to destroy the enemy on the immediate front."[28] There would be other Japanese units involved in the fighting, both infantry and support troops, but the backbone of the attack would be the 65th Brigade. Nara's men hastened to relieve the 48th Division which was pressing Homma for immediate relief. Scheduled to be aboard ship by February 1, the commander was anxious to begin preparations.

Nara's orders were to pursue the enemy in column down the East Road, but these orders sat uncomfortably with him. For six years Nara had been a professor at the Japanese War College and he had taught his students never to attack without accurate maps or proper preparations. He now found himself without accurate maps, and he had just been advised not to "dilly-dally." There was no time to acclimate his men or properly organize them, and he could not even collect all his supplies which had been off-loaded at Lingayen. Nara was most unhappy about the entire situation. "When we got there," he recorded, "we could not even obtain maps . . . there were two or three 300,000 or 500,000 scale maps. But there were no detailed maps. How could we fight the battle?"[29] He found American 1:200,000 topographic maps inaccurate, and although he asked for and received aerial photo missions over Bataan, the supply of photos was limited. Nor could cameras see under thick jungle canopy.

Homma's intelligence service also failed Nara by suggesting Filamerican strength on Bataan was 25,000 men with forty tanks. They believed the defenders were in poor physical shape and that the Americans were taking strong action to stop Filipino desertions. Nor did the Japanese have much of an idea where Filipino lines began. Believing them four miles north of their actual location, the Japanese plotted their initial artillery fires well short of any real targets.[30]

Nara was happy about one thing, and that was the attachment to his brigade of the veteran 9th Infantry, a battalion of field artillery, and an engineer regiment, all from the 16th Division. The 9th Infantry had seen action in China, and it was part of the first Lingayen landings executed on December 22. And even though General Homma thought that "it did not have a very good reputation [for its] fighting qualities," Nara was delighted to have it.[31] Its commander, Colonel Susumu Takechi, was an old friend of Nara's from the Academy. The 65th Brigade itself possessed only a platoon of two guns while each regiment had but a battery, so the guns brought in with the 9th Infantry were welcomed. Although Nara knew his men were exhausted and in no condition to attack, he realized that in order to take advantage of his enemy's obvious disorganization, he could not wait long. But he was having trouble integrating the newly assigned units into the brigade's command and control net. So although he did not want to wait, circumstances forced a two-day delay in his attack.

On the morning of January 8 Nara established his headquarters at Floridablanca. That afternoon he issued another order which would bring his brigade into contact with the Scouts on the East Road. "The enemy immediately confronting us," Nara told his units, "has a portion of his strength on a line from the hills south of Dinalupihan to the hills south of Hermosa and with his main body has occupied positions on the line from the Mt. Santa Rosa area to Abucay. He is constructing positions in the intervening sectors as if planning to offer successive resistance in this sector."[32]

As Nara's elements prepared for the attack, rear echelons were making enormous efforts to get the East Road back into shape to carry supplies.

Because the roadbed averaged only three feet above the mean water level of Manila Bay, the East Road with its heavy stone fill and gravel sand surface was the only route along the coast that heavy vehicles could use. Unfortunately for the Japanese, the road and the bridges needing repair were under American artillery interdiction, thus exposing repair crews to serious danger. Communications personnel were also having troubles. Each time signal crews tried to lay their single-strand light yellow wire, artillery fire cut it. Fearing the East Road would be under artillery fire for some time, Nara ordered his engineers to construct another road from Culis, near the entrance to Bataan, along the eastern edge of Mount Natib.[33]

For his attack against II Corps, Nara organized two forces. The eastern wing consisted of the 141st Infantry, the 3rd Battalion, 48th Mountain Artillery Regiment (75mm pack), a battery of antitank guns, and supporting engineers and signalmen. The 141st Infantry would attack the 57th Infantry. Designated as the 65th Brigade's left flank unit, the 141st Infantry was ordered to "deploy in general on the line of the road from Dinalupihan to Hermosa. They will take the enemy positions confronting them and advance to the line of the Calaguiman River."[34] Nara ordered the 7th Tank Regiment to reinforce the 141st Infantry, but because of the bad road it did not get into the fight in time to be of service. Japanese engineers were busy repairing bridges and removing roadblocks but they had not yet finished.

Nara planned his main effort on his right, on the west flank. Here he pinned his hopes for a quick victory on the experienced and veteran 9th Infantry reinforced by the 2nd Battalion, 48th Mountain Artillery Regiment (75mm pack), a battery of antitank guns, and normal support troops. Colonel Takechi's men were to overwhelm the II Corps left flank, move against the flank and rear of the Filipinos, and turn toward Manila Bay to meet the 141st Infantry which by then should have broken through any resistance encountered on the East Road. To exploit the breakthrough in the west, Nara placed his reserve, the 142nd Infantry, behind the 9th Infantry. Colonel Gen Irie's 14th Army Artillery, consisting of the 1st and 8th Field Heavy Artillery Regiments and the 9th Independent Heavy Artillery Battalion, would support the attack across the entire front. In anticipation of supply problems, each unit received three extra days' ration.[35]

So with little time for planning and with grossly incomplete reconnaissance of Filipino lines, Nara attacked at 1500 hours on January 9. Heavy artillery fire from about seventy cannon preceded his infantry and shook the northern reaches of Bataan. Although the rumble of Japanese artillery was impressive, its accuracy and effectiveness was not. Lead elements

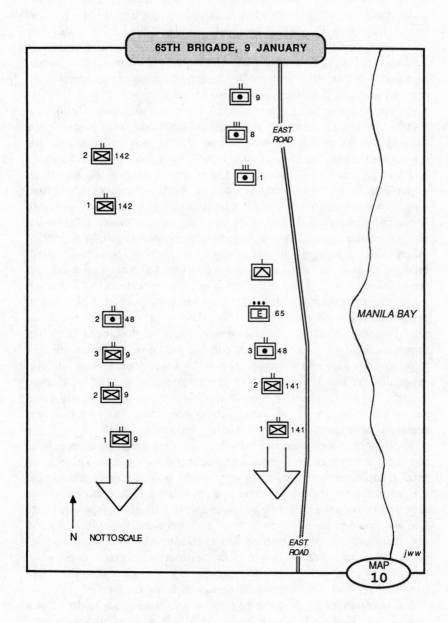

65TH BRIGADE, 9 JANUARY

EAST ROAD

142
142

48
9
9
9

65

48
141

141

EAST ROAD

MANILA BAY

N NOT TO SCALE

jww

MAP
10

of the 141st Infantry waited tensely to launch their attack, and when the order came they confidently stepped out along the East Road with flags flying. Expecting to pursue defeated and demoralized Filipinos, they were unexpectedly stopped and disorganized by heavy and extremely accurate artillery fire coming from II Corps. A 155mm shell slammed into the 65th Brigade's artillery headquarters, killing the greater part of the staff and badly disrupting Japanese artillery support.[36]

As the Japanese tried to press forward in the afternoon, Scout and Filipino 155mm cannoneers worked over their World War I pieces. Their mission was to interdict hostile routes of approach and dislocate the enemy's command and fire control system with long range destruction and interdiction fires. Following II Corps orders to keep the East Road under fire day and night, Scouts from the 86th Artillery (twelve guns) and Filipinos from the 301st Artillery (sixteen guns) ran forward with shells and powder, loaded the guns, and ran back for more. They landed the 100-pound projectiles with thundering devastation among enemy infantry until the Japanese, fifteen minutes after the first round had landed, finally dispersed and abandoned the road. This fire was so effective and the Japanese miscalculated the location of Filipino lines so badly that not a single infantry skirmish resulted from what was supposed to be a major, brigade-strength attack. Not only did defending artillery disperse the lead Japanese infantry, it also blocked supply organizations trying to move south to support the attack and backed them up along the East Road and for four miles along Route 7. As a result, defending artillery, especially the big 155mm's, soon became a prime target for Japanese aircraft. Air attacks, however, were terribly inaccurate. The small number of planes also reduced their effectiveness—only thirty-six bombers remained after the bulk of the 5th Air Group departed.[37]

The Japanese had great difficulty locating defending guns because of the vigor with which artillerymen camouflaged their pieces. This was no small compliment to the gunners, for in the tropical heat, vegetation cut for camouflage withered and died in a short time. A constant effort was required to keep the concealing foliage green. Part of the Japanese problem was that they held the low ground and therefore possessed few good observation posts. More trouble was encountered when stringing telephone wire over difficult jungle trails to observation posts. Even when Japanese infantry were close enough to see Filipino guns shooting, Japanese artillery had trouble locating them and firing on them.[38]

Nara desired to see how the battle was progressing, so he drove to a hill just south of Culis where all he could see was the furious enemy barrage. Bamboo, mango trees, cane fields, and coconut palms crisscrossed agricultural lands and prevented him from seeing anything more.

Attempts to secure information from the 14th Army Flying Unit met with limited success. When information from planes did arrive, it could not be plotted on a map. Radio was the only means of communication, and with the 65th Brigade's command post located in the jungle, radio effectiveness declined dramatically.[39]

Because he expected to hit the main Filipino line on the first day of his attack, Nara was falsely encouraged by reports from his units. The absence of opposition allowed the Japanese to advance unhindered by anything but artillery. The push was going so well that Nara considered it a hasty pursuit rather than an attack. He concluded, happily and incorrectly, that the Filipinos had withdrawn and fled into the jungle without a fight. He was, admittedly, surprised by the heavy artillery fire flaying his men. The Japanese advanced their own artillery in hopes of coping with the fire falling on them, but they could not locate the defending batteries. When the Japanese tried to establish installations in the towns they occupied, they were shot out of them by Scout and Filipino artillery. The Japanese complained that "The [enemy] took a great liking to shelling and firing incendiaries at them [houses]. We finally could not use them, as fires broke out at the provision dump, and the ammunition dump exploded."[40]

One of Nara's officers was also having trouble. Colonel Imai was forced to move the bulk of his 141st Infantry away from the East Road because of the intense artillery fire. He kept his 2nd Battalion near the road and told them to continue south using a wide cane field for concealment. The remainder of the regiment approached the Philippine 41st Division. Movement away from the East Road reduced casualties, but when signal units tried to follow to string telephone wire, they either ran out of wire on the winding trails or got lost. Rice harvesting had just finished and the rice paddies were firm and dry for infantrymen. But the ground underneath was wet and trucks broke through the crust and bogged down. So vehicles still needed to use the road, and traffic control squads wearing white arm bands struggled with traffic and bursting shells. Despite all these difficulties, Nara was pleased with the progress of his attack. He believed the defenders were evacuating all positions directly to his front and were falling back to the town of Balanga. Japanese planes spotted heavy motor traffic, an indication of a possible withdrawal. But long before Nara was to enter Balanga where he expected the Filipinos to make a stand, he hit the Scouts of the 57th Infantry.[41]

General Selleck's withdrawal of his covering force from the Layac delay position on the night of January 6 was so quick that he lost touch with the Japanese, so to reestablish contact the Scouts began patrolling with the regimental reconnaissance section. At first light on January 9 two six-man patrols left Scout lines and headed north, carrying two days' rations and a single radio. One patrol spotted Japanese just south of Hermosa, seven miles north of the Scout main line. From noon on January 9 through the upcoming attacks, reconnaissance patrols kept an eye on the Japanese.[42]

Lieutenant Harry Stempin's G Company held the 57th Infantry's outpost line of resistance with two platoons and a section of machine guns. Commanded by Lieutenant Paul Shure, the men dug shallow individual and two-man foxholes. Observation to the north was good, and the first Japanese column was plainly visible as it approached on January 9. It provided an appealing aerial target, but too few American planes remained to attempt a strike. As the Japanese came in range the Scouts directed a devastating blanket of artillery on the snake-like column. Corporal Eliseo Prado was with A Battery, 24th Artillery, when the call for fire arrived, and he helped lay their 1903-vintage 2.95-inch howitzers on target. "After breakfast," Prado recalled, "Battery A was ordered to fire the first gun section. The first round was followed by a second. After that, the Battery's first, second, third, and fourth gun sections fired simultaneously."[43]

As the Japanese started to recover from the artillery strikes every move they made was under observation from a Scout patrol hiding 500 yards northeast of Hermosa, now eight miles behind Japanese lines. From his small post Sergeant Crisogono Maquiraya and five Scout riflemen observed a stream of heavy trucks enter Hermosa and watched men construct large supply dumps around the town. A thousand yards south a battalion of Japanese infantry bivouacked for the evening. Just before dark the patrol saw large artillery pieces towed into the town and an ammunition dump in the process of construction. The Japanese felt so secure they established a lighted vehicle park powered by a generator.[44]

At midnight Sergeant Maquiraya extracted his patrol and started back to Scout lines where he briefed the regiment's intelligence officer on his observations. At dawn on January 10 a second Scout patrol saw truck convoys rolling into Orani and soldiers marching to assembly areas south of the town. Orani's silver-domed white-walled church built in 1714 received another coat of gray dust as two battalions marched by with several hand-pulled, iron-wheeled, short-barreled mountain guns. Orani turned into a beehive of activity and the patrol identified two large heavy artillery parks, supply trains, frequent movements of command vehicles, and activities indicating the town was a major command center.[45]

The south reconnaissance patrol reported these movements to the outpost line for relay to regiment. So close to the Japanese that they might hear the whine of the radio's generator, the patrol went on radio silence as Japanese columns marched past, then runners carried the information to the outpost line. Although there was some doubt among the American officers as to the accuracy of the patrol's reports, the information was uncannily accurate. The marching columns were the two battalions of the 141st Infantry, and the artillery parks were portions of the 65th Brigade's artillery. "The heavy concentrations of both marching columns and the build up of motor traffic in Orani alerted [us] that contact was imminent," remembered Captain Franklin O. Anders. "II Corps responded with raking and ranging artillery concentrations on the national highway, the areas east and west of it, and from Samal north beyond Orani toward Hermosa."[46] The artillery fired so many rounds on January 10 that MacArthur's staff chided II Corps about excessive expenditures. II Corps calmed USAFFE by explaining that even at this "excessive" rate, ammunition would last longer than the barrels of the cannon. In short, the guns would wear out before the shells ran out. There is no doubt the fire was effective, for the Japanese complained that "The barrage on the coastal road on the 10th was more intense than that on the 9th. The area around Hermosa and the village north of it was left burning."[47]

The Japanese did not have much experience fighting an enemy that used artillery. They did not know how to conceal their guns, nor did they show much expertise in maneuvering infantry when within range of enemy artillery. They had received a small lesson in the handling of artillery just north of Bataan, and they were now about to enter graduate school. But artillery alone is seldom enough to stop a determined enemy, and this case was no exception. By the afternoon of January 10 the 141st Infantry deployed a sizable force against Lieutenant Shure's outposts and began to pressure them. At 1600 hours three widely spaced platoons were advancing against Shure. A half hour later, Shure, after suffering twenty wounded, prematurely withdrew without receiving permission.[48]

The 57th Infantry realized it would lose observation and early warning if the outpost line was not replaced. Major Johnson, the S3—a West Pointer class of '33, a 1938 graduate of the Infantry School Regular Course, and a veteran of eighteen months in the Philippines—decided to place the outposts a little farther south this time. After first light on January 11 a platoon of fresh Scouts supported by a platoon of machine guns from H Company moved through the main line at Mabatang, spread out behind the Calaguiman River, and at 0730 hours began digging in. But the outposts were not fated to remain there long. Only hours later the Japanese pushed and Lieutenant Stempin reported he would have to pull out if he was to save any of the force. The Japanese were so close Stempin was afraid to use his radio. Late in the afternoon, with permission, the men easily broke contact with the enemy and with-drew.[49]

The main line of resistance was the next obstacle to face the Japanese. Captain Ernest Brown was in 3rd Battalion reserve with his L Company. "11 January found us resting contentedly behind our barb wire and mines," he recalled, but their rest was soon to be disturbed.[50] At the same time the physical security of the Scouts was about to be tested, the mental attitude and morale of the regimental headquarters had already suffered. The focus of the trouble was the regimental commander, Colo-nel Clarke. Clarke had come to the regiment as its executive officer in July of 1940, then assumed command in September 1941. He loved his Scouts, knew all the senior Scout NCO's, and was godfather to many of their families and grandchildren. Clarke spoke impeccable Tagalog and had numerous friends in the Filipino military and civilian communities. Despite long service—he was commissioned in 1916 in the Philippine Constabulary—and despite extensive schooling (Honor Graduate of the Philippine Constabulary Officer School in 1913, attendance at the Infan-try School Company Officers' Course in 1925, Advanced Course in 1930, both the Chemical Warfare School Field Officers' Course and Marine Corps Field Officers' School in 1931, and Army Industrial Col-lege in 1932), he was not ready for war. Since December the 51-year-old Clarke had developed a crippling preoccupation for his personal safety. He believed airplanes had so changed the nature of warfare that foot soldiers had no hope of survival at all. His fears developed into a deadly fixation, and simply the sound of an airplane would drive him to a fox-hole. He believed enemy planes were aloft solely to locate and destroy his headquarters. On the Mabatang Line his physical and mental bearing deteriorated sharply, and his activities developed combat fatigue in his officers even before they contacted the Japanese. Blowing a whistle and shouting, he personally forced vehicles away from his command post and kept everyone wearing a helmet, side arm, and cased gas mask regardless of the situation.

Colonel Clarke required his staff to stay near him and refused to allow his operations officer to perform his normal duties—inspect positions, travel to subordinate units, and the like. "Everytime I did go out of the hole the few of us occupied," Major Johnson remembered, "within thirty seconds to a minute his head would be out, 'Want to see you for a minute.' I'd go back. He really didn't want to see me, he just didn't want to be alone."[51] Staff officers tried to sneak away to perform the necessary functions of command and control. The junior officers found their frus-tration growing into exasperation and then to anger. The 57th Infantry, normally in the highest of spirits, awaited the Japanese with a battle fatigue casualty as its commander.

The Japanese launched their first probes against the regiment's right flank, against the 1st Battalion. Options as to avenues of approach were limited, and the Japanese were under constant Scout observation. When defensive artillery dispersed the probes, the Japanese slid to the west, away from the coast and toward the 3rd Battalion. They were quick to learn they faced a resolute defense. "A report came in from the front-line units," recorded the 65th Brigade, "that the enemy positions, which took advantage of the jungle and were prepared in depth, were impregnable and that the enemy was determined to resist."[52] The Japanese spent the afternoon of January 11th preparing for a night attack.

Either because their artillery had not caught up with the infantry, or because they decided surprise was more important than fire support, Japanese artillery did not play an important role in the upcoming action. The Japanese knew that defending artillery would be a real threat to their communications and they resolved to destroy the Filipino guns as quickly as possible, but resolutions were easier than action. When Japanese artillery did come into action, it concerned itself with counterbattery fire. However, even counterbattery fire faced problems. Although the Japanese pushed their guns forward, they could not neutralize defending artillery because the guns were so difficult to locate. They tried to establish a signal network to improve observation, but they failed because of the terrain, vegetation, and lack of knowledge of the location of their own units.[53]

When night fell on January 11 the Japanese advanced and massed in the uncut cane field a scant 150 yards from Colonel Fry's 3rd Battalion. From a point just south of Samal a line of mature cane 350 to 500 yards wide reached to the south bank of the Calaguiman River, and after the Japanese drove in the Scout outposts, large numbers of soldiers from the 141st Infantry assembled here. Using gullies, covered approaches, and concealment offered by the cane, the Japanese worked their way close to the Scouts. The men from the 2nd Battalion, 141st Infantry were keyed up, confident, and ready to go. Their comrades from other units had chased the Filipinos out of each position they dared occupy, and it would be no different now—or so they believed. Despite the concealed routes, the Japanese failed to move in completely undetected. Scout listening posts heard noises and sounds of significant movement, but they could not see anything because the moon had not yet risen, although it would very soon. Their reports were relayed to artillery fire direction centers, and a call for fire went to the guns of the 24th Artillery.[54]

At this very moment, when calls for fire were reaching the artillery and

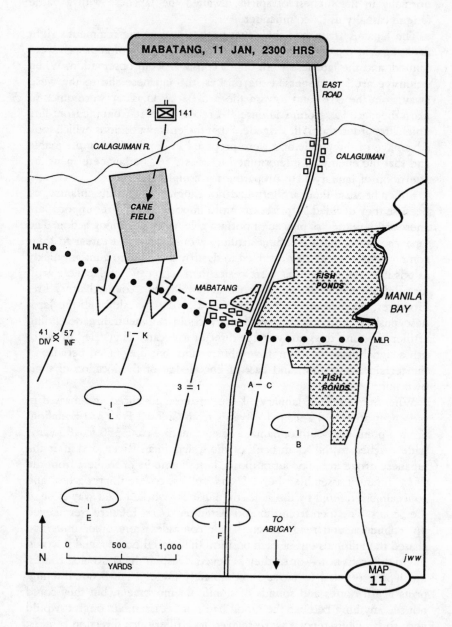

MABATANG, 11 JAN, 2300 HRS

EAST ROAD

2 ⊠ 141

CALAGUIMAN R.

CALAGUIMAN

CANE FIELD

MLR

MABATANG

FISH PONDS

MANILA BAY

41 DIV ✕✕ 57 INF

I – K

MLR

3 = 1

A – C

FISH PONDS

I L

I B

I E

I F

TO ABUCAY

jww

N

0   500   1,000

YARDS

MAP 11

the 75mm cannon were being laid, the Japanese were creeping to the south edge of the cane. They began firing long-range small arms and some light mortars at Scout lines. Then they increased the tempo of their machine guns. As Colonel Fry and several men headed up to the 3rd Battalion observation post, a bullet hit a runner in the arm. Despite the runner's pleas to continue, Fry ordered him to the rear. Requests for artillery fire on the cane field reached the gunners an hour before midnight, and Scout artillerymen began their well-drilled routine. They put range and deflection on the guns, pushed rounds into breeches, and stepped clear. Battery officers yelled, "Fire!" Just as the first 75mm projectiles exploded in the tall stalks of sugar, "the cane field seemed to vomit Japanese in great numbers screaming, howling, yelling 'Banzai' as they charged."[55]

Quickly, the fortuitously placed C Battery, straddling the K and A company boundary, beautifully camouflaged and silent until now, adjusted gun trails, leveled its 75mm's at the inviting target, and fired point-blank over open sights into the mass of charging Japanese. The guns bounced from the recoil, and explosions tore holes in the assault formation, knocking men down with each round. Scout gunners worked furiously over their pieces as enemy infantry dodged past clumps of bamboo and uncut brush. Japanese bullets banged against the small gun shields and forged dozens of indentations. A few rounds found resting places in Scout gunners. Captain David J. Barry hastily organized his artillerymen for defense against infantry, yet kept men on the guns to maintain a hot fire. Japanese infantry, sighting on the guns, picked off cannoneers, but the Scouts ignored their losses and sent round after round into the charging riflemen. Joining the fires of C Battery were the other two batteries of the battalion.[56]

Despite the appalling effects of massed artillery and small-arms fire, the Japanese continued across the open fields carried by their own momentum. Departing the cane field, they ran downhill, crossed a small creek, then pushed uphill across moderately vegetated ground, through dry rice paddies, and into Scout barbed wire. Watching the Japanese from his L Company command post, Captain Brown was amazed at the speed of the attack. "It seemed they were acrobats in the manner they crossed the moonlit stretch of ground between the cane field and our position."[57] In contrast to the 1st Battalion on the right, Colonel Fry's 3rd Battalion was firing tracers mixed with the ball ammunition, and the streams of bullets gave the Japanese a good idea of the battalion's line, especially the location of machine guns and automatic rifles.

As Captain Brown watched, the Japanese from Fukuyama threw themselves on the barbed wire and succeeding squads climbed over the bodies

pinned to the wire. Lieutenant John M. Compton from the heavy weapons company watched the action near I Company and begged Colonel
Fry to let him join the fight. Fry agreed, for he knew Compton was a born
fighter and just what I Company needed. Several sections of heavy water-
cooled machine guns were supporting I and K companies, so Compton
went forward to check his guns. Battle noise indicated the Japanese thrust
was centered against I Company, so Compton headed for the firing.[58]

One of the machine guns he checked was manned by Private First
Class Narcisco Ortilano. Ortilano was with his water-cooled .30-caliber
when eleven Japanese came into his line of fire. He killed four before the
gun jammed, then he felled five more at close range with a pistol. When
that weapon emptied, the two remaining Japanese charged with leveled
bayonets. Ortilano grabbed a bare blade, lost a thumb, wrenched the rifle
away, and bayoneted the Japanese. The second man stabbed Ortilano in
the arms and legs. Turning, Ortilano fired the rifle and killed the last
enemy. Badly wounded in the legs, back, chest, arms, neck, and head,
Ortilano returned to his machine gun where he was found the next morning. He was evacuated to a hospital and when asked what had happened,
all he could remember was that eleven Japanese had tried to scare him.
He was awarded the Distinguished Service Cross. Caught up in this fighting, Lieutenant Compton crawled to where the Japanese were swamping
the wire and threw hand grenades into dozens of the enemy. Shrugging
off the grenade attack, the Japanese crossed the wire and killed Compton.[59]

Once over the wire the Japanese pushed into the Scout foxhole line.
The excited yelling ceased, and only Japanese officers and sergeants
shouted orders and encouragement. These leaders did not last long, for
their drawn swords and loud voices made them conspicuous targets. The
Scouts fired at everything, and the Japanese lost their cohesion. Despite
the incredible confusion and the close proximity of the Japanese, the
Scouts calmly held their ground. Tracers darted about from all directions,
fitfully lighting the body-strewn ground. But the Japanese were as determined as the Scouts, and they worked their way from foxhole to foxhole.
Some Scouts were physically manhandled out of position with the men
on both flanks suffering the most. I Company's commander, Lieutenant
Gerth, telephoned Fry and asked for help, and Captain Brown, the reserve commander, pleaded with Fry to let him counterattack. But Fry was
unwilling to commit his reserve this early. Sometime after 0200 hours
Lieutenant Gerth started an inspection of his lines with his first sergeant
and two riflemen. At 0315 hours Gerth's party came upon Japanese occupying three foxholes in the center of the line, and a quick fight ensued.

Five Japanese died, but rifle fire also shattered Gerth's hip. He could not walk, so his soldiers dragged him back to his command post.[60]

To the right of I Company were the soldiers of K Company, and the Japanese attack lapped into K Company's left flank. At midnight the heavy pressure caused Captain Haas to reinforce his left with two squads from his reserve platoon. One squad bolstered the front and the second faced west to refuse the company's left flank. At 0130 hours the Japanese formed a casualty bridge over the barbed wire and swamped I Company immediately adjacent to K Company. Private Valentin Baldonado, a K Company Scout, volunteered to stem the flow of Japanese crossing the wire. He filled a sack with hand grenades, crawled near the break, tossed them, and crawled back for more. He made three round trips, pulling a sack as heavy as he could manage. Even more effective than the exploding grenades was the courageous example he set for the rest of the men. Realizing he would lose his entire left if it remained in place, Captain Haas moved a section of machine guns behind his left flank and began a careful withdrawal of the left flank platoon and the two reserve squads. Lieutenant David W. Maynard's presence on the vulnerable flank steadied the Scouts and controlled the limited withdrawal. Luckily, previous construction left ready-made works into which the Scouts safely settled. The move was beautifully executed.[61]

Captain Anders, the regiment's intelligence officer, made three circuits across the 3rd Battalion's front, visiting both I and K companies to learn what was happening. Reaching the heavily engaged I Company about 0300 hours, Anders entered the command post and found Lieutenant Green on the phone to the 3rd Battalion. While Green was talking to Major Paul D. Wood, the battalion executive officer, two enlisted men carried the badly wounded Gerth into the CP. There was no way to evacuate Gerth, but even had there been, it would not have mattered. Gerth refused to leave his men, and Lieutenant Arthur W. Green, the company executive officer, started collecting data on which Gerth could act. When Captain Anders returned to the regiment's command post he gave Major Johnson firsthand information on how the men were doing. Johnson received the news appreciatively, for, as he recalled, "with my inability to leave the command post, I had to depend on Anders being our eyes and ears."[62]

In the regiment's command post a strange sight awaited Anders. Against one wall of the dugout lay the regimental commander with a blanket covering his head and shoulders. Colonel Clarke was completely out of the picture. He believed friendly outgoing artillery was enemy incoming, and even after he was assured it was friendly he tried to stop the guns lest their muzzle flashes draw Japanese fire on his command post. When some 75mm self-propelled mounts fired from directly behind the dugout, Colonel Clarke collapsed and left Major Johnson to run the battle. No one knew what to do with Clarke; even the regimental executive officer had never heard of a procedure to use in this case.[63]

From his talk with the wounded Lieutenant Gerth, Anders told Johnson that I Company still held two-thirds of the original line but that nearly thirty men were casualties, both flanks of the company were gone, and there was a small penetration in the center. Working in the miniature command bunker which was crowded when more than four people stood around the lone field table, Major Johnson phoned II Corps headquarters, telephone code name ASTOR. His first effort was to argue more guns from the II Corps artillery officer. II Corps gave Johnson two more batteries of 155mm's, another battery of 75mm towed, and a battery of 75mm self-propelled mounts. Happily for the 57th Infantry, there were no competing demands for artillery from other infantry units, so II Corps could afford to mass what totalled eleven batteries of artillery in support of a single infantry battalion. Johnson's next request was for more ammunition. Within two hours of the Japanese attack the 3rd Battalion had burned up a day's supply of small arms ammunition and was drawing on its reserve load. As morning crept closer the Scouts were firing the reserve load of the regiment's reserve battalion. When ordnance personnel said it would take twenty-four hours before more ammunition could be made available, Johnson broke through the bureaucrats, and shortly thereafter transport was hauling two days of ammunition to the anxious regiment.[64]

The same trouble occurred with artillery ammunition. On the evening of January 11 artillery units supporting the 57th Infantry carried three days' fire at battery level and in the battalion trains. But such was the rate of fire that by 0900 hours the next morning the artillery had run through a three-day stock of projectiles. In the 88th Artillery one battery arrived near Abucay late on January 11 and unlimbered their guns on the north edge of a line of woods. The 75mm guns opened fire just before midnight and kept up the action for six hours. The gunnery officer, Lieutenant Robert Fugate, lost his voice from shouting fire commands. In six hours Fugate expended two-and-a-half days of fire, his voice, and an eardrum.[65]

Artillery commanders urgently requested resupply, but they were told they had plenty and that more would come up in two days. Major Johnson tried to convince II Corps ordnance personnel that not only could he not successfully counterattack without continued overexpenditure, the regiment would not be able to defend itself. When Johnson failed to convince II Corps of his need, he phoned General Sutherland on Corregidor, who issued orders to the Chief of Ordnance to replace each day's fire as it was expended and not according to the calendar.[66]

As Major Johnson argued with various officers at higher headquarters, confused fighting raged across the dark battlefield. Just before dawn Lieutenant Green set out to tour his I Company platoons. Both the right and left flanks were destroyed or dispersed, but the center and the command post still remained, all now well forward of Japanese on either flank. The Scouts, seriously short of rifle ammunition, crawled from foxhole to foxhole collecting rounds from the dead and wounded. Returning to the command post, Green reached the parapet of I Company's dugout when Japanese machine gun fire from the cane field hit and killed him. Scouts dragged Green's body to cover and laid him against sandbags at the entrance to the command post. Lieutenant Gerth, still badly wounded, was buoyed up on adrenalin and continued to command the company. He used his first sergeant, clerk, and several runners to gather and pass information. He found the telephone line dead when he tried to phone battalion headquarters to ask for help, so he dispatched a runner to request another officer to replace Green. The runner also carried the news that 40 percent of the company line was lost and over a third of the men killed or seriously wounded. Another ten Scouts were wounded but refused to leave; they continued to fight. After the runner departed, I Company's reserve platoon advanced and tied in with the bent flanks, forming an all-around defense. I Company now looked like "the circling of covered wagons when a band of wild and wooly Indians hove into sight."[67]

At the same time as Lieutenant Green's death, the K Company executive officer, Lieutenant Kenneth L. Wilson, a tall, lanky, strong-faced man, crawled forward of friendly lines to retrieve Lieutenant Compton's body where he lay after trying to stop the Japanese thrust. Wilson and Compton were close friends, and Wilson was emotionally upset over Compton's death. "He was my friend," he told another officer, "I have to bring him back."[68] At 0600 hours sporadic but heavy small arms fire still pinned Wilson to a sunken carabao track. Awaiting a lull in the fire, Wilson carefully crawled toward the body. Equally carefully, he began dragging Compton back. Halfway to safety, Japanese spotted Wilson, fired at him, and killed him, just after dawn. Three Scouts saw Wilson get hit, and without orders, Sergeant Escolastico Collado, Corporal Tranquilino Sudaria, and Private Fernando Tan ran across the open area, placed Wilson on a stretcher, and carried him uphill through 100 yards of enemy fire. For their extreme courage, each man received the DSC.

It had been obvious for some time that the 3rd Battalion's line was badly disorganized and that the two front line companies needed help.

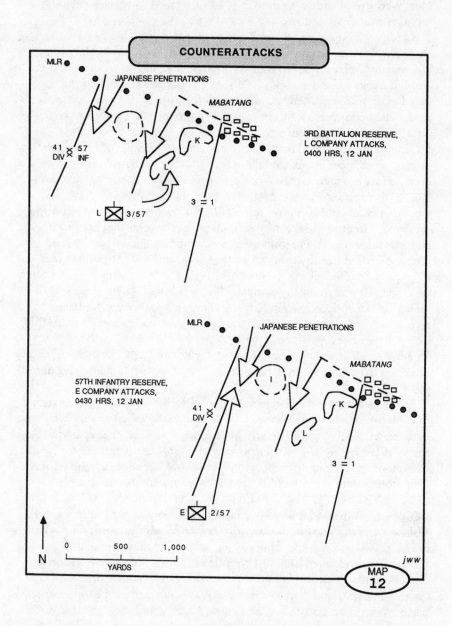

COUNTERATTACKS

MLR

JAPANESE PENETRATIONS

MABATANG

I

K

41 DIV ✕ 57 INF

L

L ⊠ 3/57

3 = 1

3RD BATTALION RESERVE,
L COMPANY ATTACKS,
0400 HRS, 12 JAN

MLR

JAPANESE PENETRATIONS

MABATANG

I

K

57TH INFANTRY RESERVE,
E COMPANY ATTACKS,
0430 HRS, 12 JAN

41 DIV ✕✕

L

3 = 1

E ⊠ 2/57

N

0   500   1,000

YARDS

jww

MAP
12

Colonel Fry alerted his reserve, L Company, for a counterattack. Major Wood ordered Captain Brown to prepare his men to reestablish the main line. Led by Brown, a gay, flamboyant bachelor, impetuous and aggressive, a man who a hundred years before would have led charges waving a saber, L Company's Scouts formed at 0400 hours and advanced to stop the Japanese. The minute they appeared, the open rice paddies were criss-crossed by enemy machine gun fire that hit several Scouts. In the dark, Brown's L Company mixed with Captain Haas' K Company and foundered. Despite happy shouts of greeting from K Company, it was nearly impossible to tell friend from foe and extremely dangerous to approach any foxhole, so L Company's arrival created terrific confusion. K Company had taken considerable mortar and rifle fire during the Japanese attack and then received machine gun fire as I Company's lines were penetrated. K Company was not prepared to have a friendly company climb up its back.[69]

With L Company cluttering his line, Captain Haas reorganized his left flank platoon once more and reestablished it facing northwest at the center of his original line. He acted so decisively and with so little concern for his own safety that he won the DSC. Captain Brown likewise recovered from the confusion, extricated his men from K Company, tied his right flank to Haas, and extended K Company's line running to the southwest. The entire action cost Brown five of his men. Unfortunately, the counterattack only contained the Japanese and did little more than extend K Company's flank southwest to the battalion reserve line. A big hole still existed.[70]

With the failure of the 3rd Battalion's counterattack, only the regimental reserve remained to stop the Japanese. At 0430 hours Major Johnson ordered the 2nd Battalion's E Company into action. When preparing their defenses in early January, Lieutenant Colonel Frank E. Brokaw and his 2nd Battalion officers conducted terrain walks over areas across which they might counterattack. Then they held several night exercises to familiarize key leaders with the terrain. Brokaw was following the 3rd Battalion's difficulties, and shortly after 0300 hours had alerted Captain Donald T. Childers and his E Company for possible commitment to the left flank of the battered I Company. Major Johnson's subsequent orders, therefore, came as no surprise—the 2nd Battalion was ready. Captain Childers, a husky, happy-go-lucky hard worker, met with Major Wood and received his orders. E Company followed recognizable terrain features along the regiment's left boundary and attacked without error into I Company's sector. Captain Childers advanced with two platoons forward, right platoon echeloned to the right rear in anticipation of meeting the left of L Company, and filled the gap remaining between the left of L Company and the right flank of the 41st Division.[71]

Childers's advance overran and killed five small teams of Japanese, but he stopped when it became apparent there was still vigorous M-1 rifle fire coming from I Company's area. Childers was certain he would kill more I Company Scouts than Japanese if he continued in the dark. So E Company went to ground and dug in between the battalion reserve line and the center of I Company still on the main line. E Company's effort, although not reaching the main line, stalled the Japanese and contained the penetration.[72]

As decisive as E Company's attack was, the tremendous weight of Scout artillery falling all night in front of the line, on the cane field, and on avenues of approach was even more important. The Japanese suffered over 200 killed or wounded, losses that included the battalion commander. However much they tried, substantial Japanese reinforcements could not push through the curtain of fire as long as enough of the 3rd Battalion remained to keep heavy small arms fire lacing across the defensive wire. The combination of small arms fire and artillery concentrations completely frustrated Japanese attempts to exploit their initial successes. Although the Japanese were strong enough to contain the counterattack of two Scout companies, they were trapped in Scout lines and were slowly dying; reinforcements could not reach them. The Japanese report of this attack reads as if it were a completely different battle:

> The Hattori Battalion [2nd Battalion, 141st Infantry] which had lost communication with the main force, re-formed its ranks and waited until preparations were completed. At dawn on the 12th, the Battalion suddenly penetrated a section of the enemy's main positions in defiance of strong resistance and vigorously exploited the success, without suffering a single casualty. While repulsing the enemy's persistent counterattacks, the Battalion held fast to the drainage ditch on the south side of the highway in the sector . . . although isolated by the enemy.[73]

In the next sentence of the Japanese report, the author becomes more accurate. He admits the battalion stayed in place because it was pinned and unable to move, a rather sudden reversal of the successful attack without a single casualty.

As morning dawned the Scouts saw the results of their night-long battle. "We were a little awed by the great number of [Japanese] dead in our position," recalled Captain Brown. "They were everywhere, in our gun positions and trenches, in the open ground to our front, and hanging on our barbed wire."[74] Japanese officer losses were so heavy that two days later a staff captain came up to assume command of the battalion. Captain

Anders tried to count the enemy bodies and came up with sixty-two definite and another fourteen possible, but he had trouble where the bodies were clumped together. He tried counting legs and arms and dividing by four but decided that was impossible. He tried counting heads, but that too failed.

With the slow coming of light, the tough Scouts began straightening their lines and winkling out isolated Japanese. The most serious effort was in front of K and L companies where Captain Brown and others led BAR and grenade teams against enemy positions. Captain Haas pushed back to his original left flank positions while L Company maneuvered with two platoons to keep in touch with Haas' men. "As we closed in," recalled Brown, "four [Japanese] threw down their arms as we approached and ran under a bridge in a futile attempt to hide. As I drew near them, they threw themselves down on the ground and made gestures of surrender."[75] Scouts grabbed the four and hustled them to the rear. Although Scouts counted another thirty Japanese dead after retaking this ground, live Japanese still held a thin salient. During the early morning mop-up Major Wood told his men to give first aid to a wounded Japanese. After the wounded man was bandaged, another Japanese, presumed dead by the Scouts, grabbed a rifle and killed a Scout. A more serious situation was discovered after the Scouts reclaimed most of the area lost the night before. Scouts found two of their comrades who had been on the outposts when the Japanese attacked. A sergeant was found with his hands tied behind his back, gagged, and lying face down in a small stream. A second man had his elbows bound behind him, hands cut off, and bayonet wounds in the body.

The officers in the 57th Infantry's command post were concerned with three things during the daylight hours of the twelfth. The first was to restore the original main line of resistance, and throughout the day Scouts cleared small pockets of enemy infantry. A new officer was found and sent up to I Company to relieve the wounded Gerth. Gerth spent fifteen minutes briefing the captain but he wasted his time. The new captain abruptly stated that he did not like war and that this was no place for him. He deserted his post and returned to southern Bataan. Only after a second captain was found and sent to I Company did Gerth consent to be evacuated, just before noon. Second on the regiment's list was its desire to burn the offending cane field under the protection of tanks, but the armored vehicles could not be obtained. Among other reasons, the Tank Group hoped to save the tanks for a breakout from Bataan.[76]

Last, the Scouts initiated action against Japanese snipers. There were two distinct groups; first were regular Japanese infantrymen who cut through Scout lines during the assault. They were not specially trained, only average soldiers now isolated and run to ground. The second and more disruptive group consisted of less than a dozen men, either trained specialists or unusually good marksmen. They separated themselves from the regular infantry and infiltrated into rear areas. Some carried binoculars, scope-mounted rifles, concentrated dry rations, and light, strong rope used to climb trees and tie themselves to branches. When both the 1st and 3rd battalions phoned regiment asking for help in removing the snipers, Major Johnson told them the problem was solely theirs; the Japanese were in the sectors of the two battalions and they should evict them. The 1st Battalion was quite capable of doing this, for the night attack hardly touched them and their communications net was still intact. The 3rd Battalion would find the task more difficult.[77]

The 1st Battalion detailed one officer and some Scouts from A Company to take care of the snipers. A Company was suffering the most from sniper fire so A Company provided the antisniper party. Much of the fire was coming from behind K Company's line, so the 1st Battalion actually hunted the enemy behind the 3rd Battalion. The first Medal of Honor (the second won but the first awarded) in World War II went to Second Lieutenant Alexander R. Nininger for his actions in clearing the snipers. Hailing from Gainesville, Georgia, and a 1941 graduate of West Point, the 23-year-old Nininger commanded A Company's 1st Platoon. Nininger was a quiet, studious, reflective man, not the typical warrior type. But he had a persistent, stubborn streak that drove him to become one of America's bravest soldiers this January 12. At 0830 hours he collected some wandering 3rd Battalion Scouts and, with his own men, passed the left limit of his battalion into the 3rd Battalion's area and twice pushed into Japanese-infested trees. When he was wounded, he refused medical aid. Now enraged, he attacked once more, this time alone. Hit once again, he grenaded an enemy position and killed several Japanese. Then he collapsed and died a little before noon. The rest of A Company's patrol killed a dozen Japanese, mostly survivors of the attack on I Company.[78]

Efforts by the 3rd Battalion to clear the enemy from behind K Company failed. Despite several Scouts killed and several more wounded in these efforts, confirmed kills of Japanese were depressingly small. The snipers seldom fired at patrols but allowed them to pass and then concentrated on officers, sergeants, and messengers. Snipers harassed ration and ammunition parties all through the morning, and front-line companies ducked similar fire. Major Reynolds remembered the snipers "were bothersome, to put it mildly."[79] When friendly casualties from sniper hunts became too numerous, a different approach was tried, but it had to wait until the next day.

Neutralizing small pockets of Japanese regular infantry proved less difficult than combating the snipers. K Company emplaced a section of machine guns on its left flank and spent the day firing short bursts over Japanese foxholes. The Japanese were content to lay low. When the Scouts brought mortars to bear on the Japanese, the old 3-inch Stokes ammunition fired from 81mm tubes proved so unreliable in both range and deflection that the Scouts were in as much danger from the infrequent bursts as the Japanese. More aggressive Scout action was handicapped by a shortage of hand grenades. The night battle exhausted the Scout supply, and company commanders begged for more before night fell again.[80]

At the 65th Brigade headquarters in Hermosa, General Nara was unaware of the specifics of the night's fighting at Mabatang. The day before, he realized his 141st Infantry was badly overextended, so he ordered his reserve into action. "142 Inf Reg Commander and subordinate forces will form the new left-flank unit. They will deploy immediately on the left flank of the 141 Inf. Regt., which is now the new right flank unit."[81] So Nara's January 11 order started the movement of two fresh infantry battalions toward the Abucay Line. By midmorning of January 12 the 142nd Infantry and two companies of the 122nd Infantry were probing the lines of the 41st Division just to the west of Mabatang.

At II Corps headquarters General Parker was concerned about the fighting in front of his Scout regiment, and Corregidor also was receiving pessimistic reports about the battle. Major General Sutherland came to Bataan, picked up the Provisional Tank Group executive officer, Lieutenant Colonel Thaddeus E. Smyth, whose tanks were in direct support of II Corps, and drove north to visit the 57th Infantry. The 48-year-old Sutherland was a well-schooled officer, Command and General Staff School in 1923, the French Ecole Superieure de Guerre in 1930 and the Army War College in 1933. At Abucay, Sutherland found Major Johnson in charge and learned of Colonel Clarke's condition. Standing in front of the bunker containing Clarke, Sutherland talked with Johnson and the 57th Infantry's executive officer, Lieutenant Colonel Edmund J. Lilly. They then climbed the bell tower of the Abucay church and studied the terrain to the north. Johnson requested tanks to drive out pockets of Japanese and run the enemy out of the cane field but Colonel Smyth declared the ground unsuitable for tanks. "This, of course, was absurd," recalled the regiment's adjutant Captain John E. Olson who was also in the tower and who felt the terrain was fine.[82]

Sutherland and Smyth returned to II Corps where Sutherland told Parker about Clarke's condition and recommended Clarke's relief. Parker set about finding a replacement and, more to the point, started

looking for reinforcements to send to help the Scouts. Parker knew that
if the Japanese broke through the Scouts, his entire center and left, consisting of two divisions, could be bypassed and trapped in the mountains.
So he had good reason to send the Scouts some help. Late in the afternoon of January 12 he released from II Corps reserve the two-battalion
21st Infantry (minus the regimental headquarters) and gave it to the 57th
Infantry.[83]

The 21st Infantry had been reorganized in Bataan with only two battalions because of heavy casualties while defending the Vilasis Bridge on
Christmas Eve. Now only the 2nd and 3rd battalions remained, and after
dark on January 12, the two American battalion senior instructors reported to the Scout command post. Major Johnson had developed written plans for their deployment, and he spent the evening giving the two
officers—both slightly apprehensive about entering the confusing battle
—a very thorough briefing. Advance parties of both battalions filtered
into the Abucay area early the morning of January 13. After receiving
their orders for an early morning counterattack, the two battalions
marched independently of each other into assembly areas behind the
Scout regimental reserve line. The 3rd Battalion bivouacked next to Manila Bay while the 2nd Battalion moved close behind the Scouts. But
before the scheduled 0600 hour counterattack could begin the Japanese
attacked again.[84]

Despite their failure during the all-night fight, the Japanese tried once
more to push the Scouts off the East Road. Inept coordination, however,
insured they would fail. General Nara issued another order at 1600
hours on January 12 and made a reasonable estimate of the forces opposing him.

> The enemy, in strength of approximately one division, consisting mainly
> of US troops, is occupying positions in depth in the sector between the
> Calaguiman and the Salian Rivers. He has utilized the jungle on his left
> flank ingeniously to resist every step. He plans to check our advance on his
> right flank to the best of his ability with prepared artillery fire.[85]

Nara then told his commanders to resume the attack the next day, at dusk
on January 13. But the battalion facing the Scouts attacked a day ahead of
Nara's schedule, either because they did not receive the order or because
they believed another effort would succeed.

An hour before midnight of January 12, the 2nd Battalion, 141st Infantry launched another charge from the cane field, but this time the
attack withered and died a quick death beneath the thunder of Scout
artillery. Philippine Army 2.95-inch pack howitzers from the 41st Divi-

sion speeded the breakup of the assault formations. Scout machine gun fire, the presence of a new I Company commander, Captain Carl V. Schermmerhorn, and the company's first sergeant all steadied the line. The Japanese recoiled before reaching the defensive wire. But this repulse did not discourage the Japanese, for they mounted a quick second effort. As the Japanese crossed the mine fields they drove carabao before them which tripped mines and absorbed some of the Scout fire. Using what little protection the ground afforded, the Japanese swept into I Company's line, killed Lieutenant Maynard and First Sergeant Domingo Quiaoit. The Scouts fell into utter confusion. After losing a quarter of their comrades and half their original line the night before, after losing one company commander seriously wounded, and another through desertion, hungry and separated from the rest of the 3rd Battalion, some Scouts withdrew. Into their positions came the Japanese. Off to I Company's right, K Company lost First Sergeant Cirilo Rios killed, and a mortar burst wounded Captain Haas. Private Fernando Tan, the man who won a DSC just the day before, was hit numerous times, overwhelmed, and killed. The 3rd Battalion was again badly disorganized.[86]

Pressing their advantage, the Japanese infiltrated around and behind the 3rd Battalion's command post. Talking to regiment by telephone, Colonel Fry—at times something of an alarmist—was so sure he would not survive the fighting that he dictated several detailed messages for his "widow." While Fry was on the phone, Captain Brown in L Company adjusted artillery across the battalion's front. Once more, Scout cannon were decisive to the survival of the Scouts. When not firing on observed enemy, the artillery hit the cane field and the concealed approaches leading to Scout lines. The explosions prevented the Japanese from reorganizing, consolidating, or reinforcing.[87]

Evacuation of Scout wounded proceeded smoothly. The medics were determined to do everything possible to get the men out quickly and safely. The regimental surgeon, 35-year-old Major Edward R. Wernitznig, commissioned in 1934, and his assistant, Captain Garnet P. Francis, ran an efficient operation. Medics stabilized the wounded and sent them to the better-equipped hospitals. After being bandaged, some of the walking wounded insisted on returning to the fight and they reported back to their units. C Company (Collecting), 12th Medical Battalion supported the 57th Infantry by evacuating wounded from the regiment's aid stations. Ambulances evacuated seriously wounded men to Hospital Number 1 in the town of Limay lying between the East Road and Manila Bay. Although built as a battalion post for soldiers guarding Bataan's prewar supplies, farsighted planners had included utility connections for operating rooms, laboratories, and other hospital services. On

December 23, 321 hospital personnel occupied the barracks area containing twenty-nine long, narrow buildings with mahogany floors, woven split bamboo walls, and roofs of thatched nipa grass. Six large bodegas sheeted with galvanized and corregated tin housed the quartermaster, utilities, and medical supply depots. A Red Cross flag flew over the compound, which was surrounded by lofty mango trees heavy with unripe fruit, and a huge red cross was painted on sheets and spread across the center of the hospital.[88]

Hospital personnel barely opened a new building before it filled with wounded. A receiving station accepted Scouts from ambulances, and doctors sorted through the casualties, worked on minor wounds, and sent the others to the operating room. "We couldn't spend too much time on the hopeless cases, so we were very stringent in the triage," recalled Sergeant Daniel N. Weitzner, a surgical technician.[89] On January 8, even before the fight for Bataan proper had begun, fifteen wards of fifty beds each were crammed. Orderlies had to empty warehouses and fill them with beds, and still more wounded arrived. Because front line medical officers begged Limay to take more of their sick and wounded, Hospital Number 1 roofed over spaces between wards to make more room. The operating ward with its seven tables was busy day and night. There were normally twelve to eighteen patients lying on stretchers awaiting the surgeons, and the four-man surgical teams vied with one another in informal competition to see which team could handle the largest number of patients. In a single thirty-six hour period, the hospital performed 420 operations, and the surgical teams lived on coffee until all the wounded were handled. Despite the best efforts of the doctors, a burial squad stayed busy.

Back at Mabatang, Scout units could no longer maneuver, but enough 3rd Battalion soldiers stayed in position to stop the Japanese attack. Behind the crooked line of tired E, I, L, and K company Scouts waited two fresh rifle companies of the 2nd Battalion. And behind them, two Philippine Army battalions spent the night and early morning assembling for a counterattack. The Filipinos arrived late on January 12 and ate a hot meal. Major Bob Scholes left the Scout 2nd Battalion and prepared to guide the Filipinos through his lines. Scholes placed guides at twenty-five yard intervals behind his deployed F and G companies to collect stragglers and then waited to lead Captain Philip A. Meier's 2nd Battalion, 21st Infantry through the Scout reserves. Carrying parties placed extra rifle ammunition and heavy weapons ammunition along Scholes's picket line for pickup by the Filipinos. Captain Meier's men departed their assembly area before midnight, met the first set of guides, marched for thirty minutes, and came to Major Scholes's guides. Here sergeants inspected the Filipino soldiers, passed out extra ammunition, and secured and muffled equipment. Carrying parties were organized for the weapons and ammunition of the heavy weapons company. After a final check the men filed past the reserve line without incident and approached their line of departure. All this was accomplished in the dark under sporadic firing. Two rifle companies deployed abreast, the third was fifty yards to the rear, and the heavy weapons company followed the reserve. At 0330 hours, as a waning moon rose, the Filipinos reached their line of departure, the 3rd Battalion's reserve line, where Captain Meier made a final check of his men. Meier then relaxed to await the fire of three battalions of artillery which would start his attack.[90]

At 0600 hours on January 13 Meier's Filipino infantry advanced vigorously behind a rolling cloud of impacting artillery until halfway to their objective, the old main line. Here Meier found both his flanks completely open, so he shifted eastward until he contacted and replaced K Company, which still held a portion of the original line. All this movement bothered the Japanese. The Japanese 2nd Battalion, 141st Infantry sent a message to General Nara at his Hermosa church command post which Nara received at noon. "The enemy has launched an offensive against 2nd Battalion in the immediate front of the left-flank unit. A battle is now raging."[91] Not knowing if this battalion had reached Abucay or just Mabatang, Nara sent air elements to reconnoiter Abucay, and Japanese artillery increased its fire into the area they believed the Scouts occupied. The 142nd Infantry sent one of its rifle companies toward Mabatang to help the 141st Infantry. Japanese planes bombed the Scout 86th Artillery, destroyed ninety rounds of ammunition, killed one man, and destroyed a truck. But the planes could not stop the guns from firing.

Although Captain Meier's battalion made some progress, it did nothing more than relieve Scouts from the main line of resistance. This is not surprising considering Meier's Filipinos had engaged in some severe fights north of Bataan just a week before, and their state of training placed them at a level just above that of an organized mob. The Scout 2nd Battalion commander uncharitably, and not completely accurately, described them as being as capable as Boy Scouts on their first overnight hike. Lieutenant Colonel Brokaw was certain they would run that night if the Japanese fired at them. So early in the afternoon Captain Robert Pennell's 3rd Battalion, 21st Infantry arrived to help. Captain Pennell was relatively junior, having graduated from the Military Academy in 1939, but he had a bulldog nature and was tenacious. He had been a private in the 15th Artillery from 1933 to 1934 and he had served with the 57th Infantry for two years until sent to the Philippine Army. As a result, the 27-year-old Oklahoman, son of a West Pointer, was mature and known as a good soldier.[92]

At 1300 hours Pennell's men advanced to relieve the Scouts remaining on the main line west of Meier's 2nd Battalion, but Japanese artillery that was shooting at Scout artillery temporarily stopped the Filipinos. Finally realizing they were not suffering casualties, the blue-clad Filipino infantry stood up and advanced. "At about 1500 hours," recalled Lieutenant Grover C. Richards, "we are strung, platoons echeloned to the right, and are moving to the front. . . . The Jap's continue to shell, but we move on with no losses."[93] Pennell's men spent the early evening linking with the 41st Division, but a few soldiers lost contact with their units and headed to the rear. Small groups passed through the Scouts of G Company who were preparing for their own attack and created no little disgust among the Scouts and Americans. The Filipinos remaining on the front line were so tired by the day's activities that they all went to sleep and used men from the 41st division to stand guard.

Although conditions were now stabilized in the 3rd Battalion's area, an enemy pocket just in front of, and snipers behind, the 1st Battalion still remained. Efforts to evict them on January 12 failed. On the following day a scout combat patrol advanced into no-man's-land to destroy the enemy pocket and blow down concealing vegetation. Covered by fire, Scouts from Captain Charlie M. Dempwolf's A Company, 14th Engineers moved in to place charges and blow down likely trees. Private Francisco T. Respicio strapped TNT to his back and crawled through enemy fire to reach the trees that needed removal. After much work, the Japanese forward of the 1st Battalion were removed. Next, Second Lieutenant Ira B. Cheaney, Jr., initiated local actions behind the 1st Battalion. The California native, a West Pointer, led Scouts in repeated efforts behind A Company and ultimately silenced the enemy. That same day First Lieutenant Arthur Wermuth received permission to specially arm a party of men for sniper hunting. Wermuth collected BARs for two visiting Marines and four Scouts from D Company, while he himself carried a Thompson sub-machine gun with a circular ammunition feed tray. Wermuth's party liberally sprayed each tree thought to contain an enemy from left to right, top to bottom, until no person could possibly remain alive. Then Scout engineers belted the trees with explosives and blew them down. It took all day, but seven Japanese died, and peace returned to the rear areas.[94]

That same day II Corps relieved Colonel Clarke of command of the 57th Infantry. Colonel Arnold J. Funk, a tall, trim officer from USAFFE G-3 assumed command. The forty-six-year-old Funk—commissioned a lieutenant of infantry from Oregon State Agriculture College in 1917, a graduate of the Infantry School Company Officer Course in 1924, the Advanced Course in 1934, and the Command and General Staff School in 1939—had worked with the Scout 45th Infantry before the war and knew what Scouts could do. Funk looked a little like a young Pershing. Brusque, honest, and outspoken, he was one of those few men everyone respects, a very capable leader, and an officer who inspired confidence wherever he went. He had been given the prewar mission of planning, locating, and constructing the ten Philippine Army division cantonments, and he had done an outstanding job considering the difficulties. Now he would get a chance to prove himself as a combat leader. His arrival at the 57th Infantry's command post relieved the heavy burden which had fallen on the operations officer. "It is utterly impossible," Major Johnson wrote in his diary, "to describe the relief I felt when Colonel Funk appeared on the scene."[95] Funk immediately held a meeting, familiarized himself with the situation, and took firm control. He moved the command post from its small dugout into the Abucay church. His aggressive, brisk, outspoken but honest personality heartened the staff and morale soared. Within an hour of his arrival, the headquarters was once again a smoothly functioning team. Funk visited the three front-line battalions and reported the shaky condition of the 21st Infantry to II Corps. II Corps immediately alerted the 22nd Infantry for movement toward Abucay.

By the close of January 13 the Japanese were decisively repulsed and retained only a meager portion of the Scout line, small reward for two days of costly fighting. Scout casualties were heavy, especially in officers. In the 3rd Battalion forty men were killed and sixty wounded. The other two battalions suffered fourteen killed and twenty-four wounded. Although fighting continued for several more days, there were no significant changes. The Filipino 22nd Infantry moved to the Bani-Balanga Road on the thirteenth, and after night fell, moved up to Abucay. The evening of January 13 there were eight battalions of infantry where once only three stood. On January 15 the three battalions of the 22nd Infantry began relieving the two battalions of the 21st Infantry. Efforts by the 22nd Infantry to straighten the line cost them dearly in men killed and wounded. "This was one of the bloodiest battles of the 22nd Infantry," remembered its commander, whose description of his regiment's activities here was more colorful than accurate. "[We were] ordered to attack despite enemy air superiority and the terrain was very much unfavorable. Enemy artillery pieces made frantic efforts to halt our advance, but our boys courageously advanced to about 50 yards from the enemy position."[96] Covered by artillery and mortar fire, Lieutenant Wermuth led his reinforced antisniper platoon across their own wire, through the mine field, and into the cane field fronting the old 3rd Battalion lines. They tried to burn the field, but the stalks were too green.

The effective American counterattacks during each phase of the battle and the timely reinforcement of the 57th Infantry by five Philippine Army battalions were excellent reactions to the Japanese attacks. Instead of a passive defense, II Corps showed itself capable of managing an active, aggressive battle. The two-day battle along the East Road and the actions of the 57th and 21st infantry brought out the best in the American-led, Filipino-manned battalions. The counterattacks were pushed vigorously, commanders acted quickly and correctly, and soldiers executed orders well under enemy artillery and against determined infantry. Japanese hopes were dashed and led them to complain that "the attack failed to develop according to plan."[97] Although the battle at Mabatang was an encouraging example of what the entire Philippine Army might have done with a few more months' training, it must be remembered that a single battalion of Japanese infantry caused the commitment of eight battalions of II Corps infantry.

MacArthur reported the results of this fighting to Washington. "The enemy is now attempting general infiltration. Two determined enemy thrusts in force strongly supported by mobile artillery and aircraft were repulsed. Enemy losses severe. Our losses medium."[98]

CHAPTER NINE

The Center

JAPANESE OF THE 141ST INFANTRY OPPOSITE THE CENTER OF THE II
Corps line were no more successful in budging the Filipinos than were
their comrades along the coast. Brigadier General Vicente Lim's 41st
Division held the sector to the left of the Scout 57th Infantry. Lim, an
American of part Chinese ancestry, was a Philippine Army general and
had the distinction of being the first Filipino graduate of West Point,
Class of 1914. He retired from the US Army in 1936 as a lieutenant
colonel for medical reasons—a weak heart—but immediately joined the
Philippine Army as a brigadier general. He served until the war as the
Philippine Army's Assistant Chief of Staff, Chief War Plans Division, and
as Deputy Chief of Staff. Just before the war, Lim had attended the
Baguio Command and Staff School until November 15 when he went to
the 41st Division, probably the best of the reserve divisions. Unfortunately, Lim's health problems—his heart and an infected tooth—kept him
in his command post and he never visited his front lines. Lim's fate was
tragic, for he was executed while a captive of General Yamashita.[1]

At the start of the Bataan campaign Lim's division had not yet seen any
action and was one of the first divisions to reach Bataan, its lead elements
arriving on Christmas morning. The regiments deployed along the II
Corps main line starting the night of December 26. The division was
intact and did not have the severe losses and disorganization common to
the other divisions. From right to left, the 41st Division deployed the
41st Infantry (five weeks of training), the 42nd Infantry (thirteen weeks
of training), and the 43rd Infantry (no training).[2]

Using whatever engineer support it could find, the right flank 41st
Infantry spent the first week of January entrenching. The Filipino com-

mander was Major Fidel N. Cruz, and the American senior instructor was Colonel Loren A. Wetherby. Each of the three battalions had one American officer and two to four American enlisted assistants. These Americans worked out detailed plans as to routes, unit boundaries, gaps, fire plans, and final protective lines. Artillery units distributed artillery concentration sheets, and signalmen laid telephone lines between regimental headquarters and artillery fire direction centers. The Filipinos strung double apron barbed wire in front of the 41st Infantry's main line, then strung all the wire they could find until units down to platoon level were protected.[3]

First blood was drawn on January 8 at 1600 hours on the right of the division's line; an officer and several men were killed on the 41st Infantry's outpost line. Heavy Japanese air activity and infantry probes against the outpost line were followed by artillery on the main line of resistance. The 41st Infantry's outposts, about a mile forward of the main line, then withdrew under the command of its American instructor, drawing the ire of the regimental commander for not fighting hard enough. The 42nd Infantry's outposts then withdrew, probably because the 41st fell back, and finally the 43rd Infantry's outpost line of resistance was ordered back because the 42nd had pulled back.[4]

The 41st Artillery, four batteries of old British 75mm's and two batteries of even older 2.95-inch pack howitzers, fired its first counterbattery missions in response to the enemy's fires. The guns also turned on Japanese infantry marching down the East Road, but their effectiveness was suspect. When the artillery regiment had mobilized on November 20 there was not even a written training program they could follow, and the regiment's cannon did not arrive until December 8. Each gun had fired just five rounds for training while on beach defense. The regimental commander, 50-year-old Lieutenant Colonel Arthur P. Moore, a 1916 graduate from Virginia Polytechnic Institute and a First War veteran, did the best he could to train his artillerymen, but training of gun crews and fire direction centers had not progressed sufficiently for them to shoot indirect fire missions. As a result the guns were now located fairly close to the front lines, only 1,800 yards back, to allow them to shoot direct fire missions. Even as they deployed and prepared to fight, the Americans were giving the Filipino artillerymen at least four hours of training a day in service of the piece.[5]

The 1st Battalion, 88th Artillery—a Scout unit—also provided support, and it carried two days' ammunition with more farther to the rear in service and ammunition batteries. When the Japanese attacked the Philippines this battalion did not have an S&A Battery, so artillerymen commandeered eighteen trucks and five cars straight off the highways, along with their unenthusiastic drivers. Lieutenant John J. Morrett, a 25-year-old ROTC graduate from Ohio State University, recalled how strange and unmilitary the S&A Battery looked when it drove from one point to another. Even so, the civilian drivers executed their duties in an honorable fashion. With but few exceptions, the Filipino drivers stayed with their units, delivered ammunition to the firing batteries, and drove through artillery barrages and aerial bombings. Many of them were never paid, and if they were paid, they could not get the money to their families.[6]

On January 9, the second day of live-fire warfare for the 41st Division, Japanese planes strafed several Filipino command posts, artillery fell into the division area, and small arms and automatic weapons fire made life on the front lines dangerous. Just before dark, three low-flying planes passed parallel to and slightly behind the 41st Division's front. They did not attack, but when darkness fell, heavy firing broke out in the rear, creating alarm everywhere. Before long, everyone was firing madly and the lack of fire discipline gave Japanese scouts an excellent picture of Filipino strong points and automatic weapons positions. The inexperienced Filipinos became confused and frightened at the thought that Japanese were behind them. Leaders spent nearly an hour quieting the semihysterical soldiers and calming them enough to restore peace. After an investigation the division discovered the firing had been caused by delayed-action firecrackers dropped by the Japanese planes.[7]

That night some Japanese slipped in between the Filipino outpost line and the main line of resistance of the 41st Infantry, then fired in all directions to spook the Filipinos. Captain John J. Martin, a reservist who had turned down a proffered tour in Panama only to be sent instead to the Philippines, received a call from his outposts, reporting they were being fired upon from the rear. The Filipino officer in charge of the outposts requested permission to withdraw.

"How many men have you lost?" asked Martin in his deep southern accent.

"Oh, we haven't lost any men yet," was the reply.

"Well," Martin answered, "you're winning the war. You stay right where you are."[8] Despite these orders, the Filipino bypassed Martin without his knowledge, and received permission from division headquarters to withdraw. The men were loyal and brave, but they just did not know how to fight. With time, they would have become excellent soldiers, nearly as good as the Scouts; but there was not enough time.

Japanese artillery fire increased as morning dawned on January 10, then more ground contact occurred as the Japanese drove in the remainder of the outposts and laid heavy artillery fire on the main line. At the peak of the bombardment, fifty rounds were falling every minute. Men in the most forward foxholes, until now established along the south side of the Calaguiman River, were forced back into the main line, and although the withdrawal of the outpost line was considered premature, it was not totally unexpected from green troops. Some Filipinos set outstanding examples of bravery, if not of common sense. One Filipino lieutenant heard incoming artillery, ordered his men to the ground, and then continued walking unconcerned as four rounds burst nearby. He was upset when an American captain berated him for recklessly exposing himself. "I'm not afraid," answered the lieutenant in astonishment.[9] Others were not as calm or as brave. The heavy enemy fire began to tell and caused confusion in the 41st Infantry's sector; some soldiers abandoned their foxholes and, as a result, what had been the company support line soon became the new main line of resistance.

When the Japanese 141st Infantry swept out of the cane field into the 57th Infantry the night of January 11, the 41st Infantry, on the edge of the fight, laid some heavy fire into the Japanese flank. This was the first close infantry fighting experienced by the 41st Infantry and they put on a heartening performance. To cover the regiment's exposed right flank, C Company moved into a position facing the 57th Infantry. After the Japanese attack collapsed in the early morning hours of January 12, other Japanese spent the daylight hours placing 47mm, machine gun, and small arms fire on the forward positions of the 41st Infantry. The enemy fire was especially frustrating because the Filipinos could not reply; the galling punishment continued all day, destroying several Filipino machine guns and mortars. Covered by this devastating fire, a large Japanese patrol probed the junction between the 1st and 2nd battalions, 41st Infantry. Sergeant Joaquin Magpantay saw confusion building to the left of his 1st Battalion, and despite direct fire pinning his men and the loss of two of his machine gun crew, Sergeant Magpantay singlehandedly shifted a heavy water-cooled machine gun to an exposed position where he could fire better. He maintained this fire until running out of ammunition, and the enemy attack collapsed.[10]

When the Japanese stormed the 57th Infantry for a second time the morning of January 13, the 41st Infantry once more bolstered its right flank, collected twenty I Company Scouts, and slowly developed an idea of what was happening. In a surprisingly efficient operation, the 41st Infantry's American instructor arranged for an immediate ammunition resupply for the Scouts closest to the 41st Infantry. Before the battle, wiremen had laid a lateral telephone line between the commanders of the 41st Infantry and the 3rd Battalion, 57th Infantry. Cut off from news of his I Company, Colonel Fry discussed the situation with the 41st Infan-

try's Colonel Wetherby, and both agreed that quick action was imperative. When Fry mentioned that Japanese were on both sides of his command post, Wetherby assured Fry he would send a rifle company and any
Scouts he could find. The 50-year-old Washington State native had
learned his trade during the long, slow, peacetime years, and he was
comfortable with making decisions. So Wetherby decided to launch an
immediate attack with his Filipinos to stabilize the situation long enough
for more help to arrive. There was not time for the 41st Infantry to clear
this action with division headquarters so, as Wetherby recalls, "I decided
to do it and tell Hq. 41st division . . . about it after daylight."
Wetherby knew he was sticking his neck out by committing his men
outside the division sector, but he felt it had to be done at once.[11]

In the 41st Infantry's 1st Battalion, Captain William E. Webb collected
a force composed of his C Company and survivors from the Scout I
Company and deployed them behind a four-foot high rice paddy dike.
Platoon leaders and company commanders briefed each man on what he
was to do, then gave their men a final check. The Filipinos had never
even seen what a company in the attack looked like, so this would be
their first experience in offensive tactics. Just before they started, a platoon of heavy machine guns from the 57th Infantry arrived and inte-
grated themselves into the attack. At 0550 hours Scout machine guns
reached out to suppress enemy positions, and Webb's small force climbed
the dike only to take ten killed and wounded in the first few seconds. The
Filipinos cautiously cleared some woods as they advanced and after finishing their work stopped at a creek just south of the main line where
they were relieved by the counterattack organized by the Scouts. The
Scouts were surprised when the Filipinos appeared in their area; at first
glance, the Scouts thought the Filipinos, dressed in blue denim uniforms,
were Japanese.[12]

On January 13 and 14 the Japanese applied steady, painful pressure to
the 41st Division. On the division's left, Japanese drove the 43rd Infantry's outposts across the Balantay River and into the main line where the
1st and 3rd battalions guarded the steep-fingered, wooded slopes with
nothing more than strong points. This regiment was the least trained of
the three, its three battalions filled with men from three different islands:
1st Battalion with Batangas and Laguna men from Luzon, 2nd Battalion
filled by men from the island of Palawan, and the 3rd Battalion hailing
from Mindoro. Mobilized on December 1, the 43rd Infantry never fired
a round before it found itself in battle, and the only tactical training the
men ever received took place on beach defense while awaiting the main
Japanese landings.[13]

The 43rd Infantry had two battalions on line, the 3rd on the left, and the 1st on the right, both backed by the reserve 2nd Battalion. Their defensive efforts, however, were severely hampered by bad mortar ammunition. Their 3-inch Stokes mortars fired ammunition so old that only three in every ten rounds exploded. Much to the surprise of the mortarmen, ammunition manufactured in 1917 detonated more often than rounds produced in 1933. Because the Japanese burrowed into holes and creek beds, flat trajectory weapons were of limited value. Without mortars, only close fighting was effective, but the Filipinos, without training in close combat, were at a decided disadvantage and the close fighting proved costly. The 43rd Infantry received heavy artillery fires beginning on January 12 and the next day the left flank 3rd Battalion was so badly shelled that the battalion commander asked Colonel Lewis for permission to withdraw. Lewis told him to hold for twenty more minutes—until dark —because the Japanese usually stopped their artillery at dark. Lewis was correct, the fire stopped. On January 14 Colonel Lewis counterattacked with the newly attached 2nd Battalion, 23rd Infantry, but could only hold to the center of his reserve line.[14]

Along the 41st Division's center in the sector of the 42nd Infantry the American senior instructor, Colonel E. C. Atkinson—a physically weak man who could not check his lines as often as he should—made repeated efforts to keep his 42nd Infantry's outposts in position, but as quickly as he reestablished them, the men fell back to the main line. Things were so bad on his left at the junction with Colonel Lewis's 43rd Infantry that Atkinson committed his reserve 1st Battalion facing west.[15]

To Atkinson's right, Japanese artillery savaged the 41st Infantry and blasted its command post; over four hundred 105mm shells fell within four hundred yards of the command post. Carrying parties could not distribute rations and water, and all activity ceased until dark. Filipino and American forward observers ducked hostile artillery fire, located Japanese guns, and prepared to retaliate with their own cannon once darkness allowed them to shoot. The 41st Division appealed to II Corps for help in silencing the Japanese fire, so the 301st Artillery's eleven and a half ton 155mm's swung into action. "We had the Japanese pretty well located on that front, so we let them have it," wrote Lieutenant Colonel Arthur L. Shreve at II Corps Artillery. "As [our] fire increased, I could hear the Jap art[illery] die out. Nice feeling." That the 301st could fire that well was amazing. The regiment had not even received sights for the guns until December 23. And because the sights were panoramic sights set on a bolted metal arms welded to the gun, instead of regulation quadrant sights, there was more than average trouble in shooting straight. The regiment was formed and its men assigned by verbal orders;

no written orders were ever received. Its transportation consisted of twenty-four civilian trucks of every make and state of repair.[16]

Despite placing heavy pressure on the 41st Division, the Japanese did not have everything their own way. General Homma's 14th Army headquarters decided that because of the rough terrain on Bataan, the 65th Brigade should rely solely on infantry to accomplish its mission. "It is no exaggeration to say that the Army estimate of the enemy situation at that time was wrong," admitted the 14th Army later, "and the army was completely ignorant concerning the terrain on the Bataan peninsula."[17]

The 14th Army frequently cautioned General Nara to conserve ammunition for the upcoming assault on Corregidor, and even when the 65th Brigade was finally forced to use artillery, 14th Army placed severe restrictions on the number of artillery pieces and the quantity of ammunition it gave to Nara. It became obvious to experienced Americans that the Japanese had an ammunition shortage, for after their guns zeroed in on a target and fired for effect once or twice, they stopped. As the Japanese recalled,

> The [65th] Brigade, which did not have the proper artillery support aside from the Regimental Infantry Gun Company, suffered greatly, as two battalions of the currently attached 48th Mountain Artillery Regiment were detached, and the tanks and the main body of the artillery were kept in reserve in preparation for future operations. The enemy artillery to the immediate front of the Brigade had kept up a ferocious barrage day after day. Since this enemy artillery was not neutralized, it was difficult to achieve our purpose.[18]

Imperial General Headquarters and Southern Army did not expect prolonged resistance on Bataan, and although the delays north of Abucay were annoying, few Japanese were yet pessimistic enough to think that Bataan, and not Corregidor, was the decision objective. The artillery which was available fired various missions, but Japanese guns had trouble accomplishing anything useful because of difficulties in finding targets in the thick vegetation. Aside from receiving considerable Filipino artillery fire themselves, they found it difficult to learn the location of their own infantry. Artillery fired against the Filipinos under these conditions stood as much chance of hitting Japanese as it did of hitting Filipinos.

Japanese infantry was not having much more success than the artillery. The 9th Infantry was trudging heavily through thick jungle in its encircling movement, and at the close of January 10 had not yet made contact with their target, the Philippine 51st Division. The Japanese were surprised by the extreme ruggedness of the hills, the thick woods, and the deep gullies; fighting in the central plain of Luzon had not prepared them for Bataan. To compound their troubles, the majority of the 9th Infantry became lost and marched the wrong way, to the east, and found themselves behind the 141st Infantry instead of far to its right. The 65th Brigade headquarters admitted, in an understatement, that the 9th Infantry "misjudged the lay of the terrain, thus slowing down the advance."[19]

Imperfect small-scale maps, communication failures, and the well-handled Filipino artillery were turning Nara's attack into a shambles. Nara's inexperienced signal unit was so hapless that an hour's worth of radio traffic a day was considered good, but even that small amount was not achieved often. Radio operators in the front lines were equally inexperienced. Communications wire in the 65th Brigade was so scarce—only sixty spools of small insulated wire—that signal men tapped into civilian telephone lines to stretch their limited supply. "The wire signal communication could not keep up during this period because the Signal Unit was small and the front line advanced very quickly," read their history. "The signal men often wandered in the jungle looking for their units. Since the front-line units were not skilled in operating the wireless, they experienced great difficulty and lacked smoothness. Time after time a fierce concentration of enemy shells would fall on the radio station as soon as transmission started. Telephone lines were cut to pieces by enemy shells."[20]

On the evening of January 11 General Nara realized he needed to do something to reorganize his faltering attack, so he decided to assemble his commanders for a meeting at his headquarters in Dinalupihan. The next morning he dispatched messengers to notify the necessary people. At 1600 hours infantry representatives met with artillery, tank, and air units. After each officer presented the situation of his unit, Nara explained his plan. Attacks would begin the evening of January 13, thereby allowing each unit a full day to prepare. The 141st Infantry was to continue its slippage to the west and become the 65th Brigade's right flank. The reserve unit, the 142nd Infantry, would advance out of reserve and move down the east coast to become the brigade's left flank. The 9th Infantry was designated the encircling unit and told to strike the Filipino left and take General Parker's II Corps in the rear. In short, everyone would move to the right while the 142nd Infantry took position on the left.[21]

But even before this reorganization took place, Japanese fortunes improved opposite the Filipino 51st Infantry. The terrain here was extremely rough, covered by underbrush and cut by many small streams. Effective organization of the ground proved impossible. There were no real roads here, only carabao cart trails used to connect the sugar cane fields to the barrios housing the cane workers and their families. On

January 12, the day of Nara's meeting, Japanese infantry tore a hole in the right flank of the 51st Division's right flank regiment, the 51st Infantry. Filipino counterattacks employed reserves from both the 51st Infantry and a battalion from the recently arrived 52nd Infantry. Additionally, the 2.95-inch howitzer battalion from the 41st Artillery displaced to firing positions southeast of the Abucay Hacienda where their mobile, high-angle howitzers could help the 51st Division. At the 51st Division's command post Brigadier General Albert M. Jones called Colonel Virgil N. Cordero, commander of the two-battalion 52nd Infantry, "Bicol's Own," to his command post and told him a gap had opened in the 51st Infantry's front. Most of Cordero's regiment was still marching up from its beach defenses, but his 3rd Battalion, with Major Babcock as its senior instructor, was available. Cordero, born in the Philippines in 1893 and a graduate of Pennsylvania State College, the Field Artillery Battery and Infantry School Company Officer Courses, returned to his command post and called the 3rd Battalion officers back from a reconnaissance. He set 1730 hours as the line of departure time and formed the battalion into march order while waiting for the officers to return.[22]

The Filipinos reached the line of departure on time but hardly advanced thirty yards before the Japanese opened a heavy fire. "At first I doubted very much that these scarcely-trained Filipino boys were going to stand the terrific amount of fire the enemy was concentrating upon them," remembered Cordero, "but honor and praise is due them—they did."[23] The Filipinos made slow progress and regained part of the lost ground by the time night fell. The 51st Infantry's commander, Colonel Loren P. Stewart, and the instructor to the 1st Battalion, Captain Wilbur M. Kreuse, were both killed by machine gun fire while on a reconnaissance in support of Cordero's attack, and the loss of these two key officers at a critical point in the battle was disastrous. Without the steady hand of the two American leaders, regimental headquarters fell into a dazed state of confusion, and the Filipino commander of the 1st Battalion ordered a night withdrawal, without permission. The battalion pulled out and the men scattered across Bataan. At 2300 hours, after Colonel Cordero phoned General Jones and told him of the death of Stewart and Kreuse, Jones placed Cordero in charge of the 51st Infantry pending arrival of a replacement. Cordero and his operations officer remained on the firing line for the night.

On January 13 the 52nd Infantry's two battalions continued their counterattack with hopes of closing the hole left by the routed 1st Battalion, and although they succeeded in recovering a little more of the ground lost the night before, success was not total. The 51st and 52nd infantry were by now so mixed that no one knew who was in command of whom, and it proved practically impossible to maneuver the units. Unable to evict the Japanese, the two remaining battalions of the 51st Infantry, this time under orders, withdrew to a more easily defended line south of the Balantay River and tied in with the 43rd Infantry to their right. Up to this point, General Jones had found it very difficult to maintain contact with the 41st Division.[24]

At II Corps headquarters General Parker realized his front line needed help, so he ordered the 23rd Infantry's three battalions closer to the main line to have them handy if help was needed suddenly. Once in place, the regiment could march into action without resorting to vehicles. On the night of January 13 the 23rd Infantry reacted to Parker's orders and bused to a bivouac just behind the 41st Division's command post. The harassed officers struggled from dusk until one o'clock the next morning to get the untrained men loaded and moving. Much of the regiment's baggage was stashed in some woods and never seen again.[25]

On the morning of January 14 the Japanese 141st Infantry again pushed against the right flank of the 51st Infantry, drove in the outposts, and forced the Filipinos back to their main line. When the Japanese also pushed the 43rd Infantry's outposts into the main line, they incorrectly interpreted their successes as the destruction of the Filipino defenses. As a result, Japanese front line commanders received orders that night to closely pursue the Filipinos and drive them toward the distant town of Orion.[26]

Because the 43rd Infantry had to curl its left backwards in response to attacks on the 51st Infantry, and because its right flank was also under heavy pressure, the junction between the 43rd and 42nd Infantry became badly strained. Colonel Atkinson considered the situation of his 42nd Infantry very critical. To strengthen the junction, reinforcements in the form of an infantry battalion were sent forward in the dark. Unfortunately, Japanese artillery scored one of its greatest successes at that moment. Lieutenant H. E. Wandell's 3rd Battalion, 23rd Infantry, having moved close to the fighting just the night before under General Parker's orders, was caught by a single volley of artillery while moving out of its bivouac and suffered numerous casualties. Originally reported destroyed, the battalion lost seventy-five men killed while the remainder stampeded. Less than a company actually arrived at the objective. But even without the routed battalion, the center of the 41st Division held.[27]

By the close of January 14, with the total loss of both the 41st and 51st division outposts, a real threat was developing. But help was on the way —reinforcements above and beyond the 23rd Infantry—for from Wainwright's I Corps came the entire 31st Division. On the evening of January 14, I Corps sent the 31st Division a warning order of a possible move to the east, and because telephone lines were believed tapped by the Japanese and thereby insecure, I Corps called General Bluemel to its headquarters around midnight to receive the order in person. Because the 32nd Infantry had one battalion in division reserve and would be the easiest to move, Bluemel warned them they would receive orders when he returned from the meeting. The 32nd Infantry was to prepare to move on an hour's notice. Other division elements were also alerted, but they were scattered along Bataan's west coast and would require time to assemble.[28]

At Wainwright's headquarters Bluemel learned that his division was being moved to the Manila Bay sector, and he was given just twelve hours in which to complete the march. No destination was specified nor was any mission or proposed mission assigned, although I Corps did order him to insure at least two of his three infantry regiments were settled into II Corps by noon the next day. These orders caught him by surprise. All his reconnaissance had been in I Corps and along the Zambales coast. Bluemel got on the phone and asked General Parker how he could find his way to II Corps.[29]

"Well," answered Parker, "you just follow the road. There is a wire that leads up there. All you have to do is follow the wire."[30] But there were dozens of telephone wires running in all directions. It is not difficult to imagine the frantic planning, the hasty orders dashed off by messenger, and the absolute uncomprehending confusion that resulted from the midnight order to move. Only the hour warning given to the 32nd Infantry when Bluemel went to receive the order allowed the move to succeed. In a near-miracle of staff work, the first buses were rolling toward II Corps by 0230 hours. The lead regiment arrived in II Corps the morning of January 15 and, at the junction of the Pilar-Bagac Road and the Back Road, military police directed it to turn left on the Back Road. "Go as far north as you can," was the only guidance, and the regiment was expected to do this without guides and without route markings.[31]

While his division snaked across Bataan's narrow roads, Bluemel drove to Parker's headquarters, two and a half miles west of Limay, where he finally received a mission and a destination. Heading north, he caught up with Colonel Edwin H. Johnson's 32nd Infantry. The regiment had been forced out of its transport and was seeking cover from low-flying aircraft, but the Filipinos had not suffered any losses. For the first time, Colonel Johnson, a 1916 enlistee in the D. C. National Guard and a veteran of both the 1916 Mexican border campaign and World War I, learned his destination, the town of Guitol, and his mission, prepare to relieve the Philippine Division after its counterattack. Having covered the width of Bataan through half the night without knowing where he was going, the 45-year-old Johnson welcomed this information. But his relief was short-lived. No one knew where Guitol was. Even Filipinos living in the area were unfamiliar with the town or roads leading to it, so Bluemel began a reconnaissance to find it. After inquiring of everyone he met as to Guitol's location, Bluemel finally found a Filipino officer from the 51st Division who guided him there. Guitol turned out to be two small nipa shacks in the middle of a large forested area mixed with sugar cane fields. Quickly, the 32nd Infantry bused into an assembly area, and Bluemel established a division command post. No sooner did Colonel Johnson's 32nd Infantry arrive at Guitol than it moved once more, under II Corps orders, this time to back-stop the 41st Division.[32]

The 31st Division's arrival in II Corps did not make an immediate impression on the Japanese. On January 15 the Japanese 141st Infantry exploited their initial successes with a strong attack at the junction of the 41st and 51st Divisions. The reinforced 41st Division fought gamely and held its ground despite very heavy pressure on its left flank regiment; that regiment's 3rd Battalion was badly disorganized and driven off its main line. Officers collected the men and placed them on the division's left flank facing west. At midnight Colonel Johnson's 32nd Infantry moved even closer to the immediate rear of the 41st Division to act as the reserve for the fully committed division.[33]

To the 41st Division's left the 51st Division committed all its reserves, including service troops, simply to maintain its precarious hold on the Balantay River. Through a stifling hot day of hard fighting, the Filipinos made determined efforts to hold the Japanese, but late in the afternoon the dusty, sweat-stained 141st Infantry crawled, rushed, and fought their way across the river and secured a foothold on the south bank. Once again the Japanese felt they had broken the main line and were in a position to assault the reserve positions. This achievement split the two Filipino divisions and left prospects for the next day decidedly unpleasant. "51st Infantry very perceptibly weakening," wrote Colonel Stuart C. MacDonald, the division chief of staff, as he watched the division disintegrate. "II Corps notified as to seriousness of situation and urgently requested to send help."[34]

In an effort to aid General Jones, the 21st Division's engineer battalion assembled from work projects and moved north. This battalion had no combat training, having spent its prewar time on camp construction. The commander, Captain Louis Bartholomees, was a newly commissioned civilian engineer with no Army experience, and the only two engineer-qualified personnel in the battalion were two Philippine Scout sergeants assigned to each company. The officers of the battalion had great difficulty moving the engineers toward the fighting because the men scrambled for cover whenever aircraft appeared. They felt they had good cause to fear airplanes. Their original commander, Captain Atilano F. Montesa, had been killed and the American instructor seriously wounded by a bombing only two weeks earlier. Colonel O'Day from the 21st Division started up the trail toward Jones's command post, only to find 51st Division stragglers hiking away from the fighting. O'Day drew his pistol for whatever psychological effect it might have, and he turned the stragglers around and sent them back up the trail. He also dragged his engineers out of hiding places and pushed them forward. Despite his efforts, it was not until the next day that the men closed on the front line, and by the time the 21st Engineers joined Jones's 51st Division, the battalion was neither cohesive nor useful.[35]

Although the means to resist were declining, the will still remained. In an order issued to his command on January 15 MacArthur exhorted his soldiers:

> Help is on the way from the United States, thousands of troops and hundreds of planes are being dispatched. The exact time of arrival of reinforcements is unknown as they will have to fight their way through Japanese attempts against them. It is imperative that our troops hold until these reinforcements arrive. No further retreat is possible. We have more troops on Bataan than the Japanese have thrown against us; our supplies are ample; a determined defense will defeat the enemy's attack. It is a question now of courage and determination. Men who run will merely be destroyed but men who fight will save themselves and their country. I call upon every soldier in Bataan to fight in his assigned position resisting every attack. This is the only road to salvation. If we fight we will win; if we retreat we will be destroyed.[36]

The next day MacArthur sent a message to his officers calling for them to display "that demeanor of confidence, self-reliance, and assurance which is the birthright of all cultured gentlemen and the special trademark of the army officer."[37]

MacArthur also updated Washington on the situation:

> Enemy infiltration methods producing general fighting all along the line. He is using specialized shock battalions with intensive support from the air. His air strafing of front lines and artillery positions with dive bombers is incessant. His troops are systematically looting and devastating the entire countryside.[38]

To meet the mounting Japanese pressure, General Parker, having committed most of the 21st and 31st Divisions, asked MacArthur's headquarters for even more reinforcements. The request came as no surprise, for

their own evaluation of the situation was similar to Parker's, and
USAFFE was in the process of ordering reserves into II Corps. When the
army occupied the Bataan peninsula in early January an advance echelon
from USAFFE headquarters placed a forward command post on Signal
Hill about four kilometers southwest of Mariveles Mountain. Represen-
tatives from each of the general staff sections established themselves
there to provide close cooperation between USAFFE on Corregidor and
I Corps, II Corps, and Service Command on Bataan. MacArthur placed
Brigadier General Richard J. Marshall in charge as his Deputy Chief of
Staff. A VMI graduate, Marshall had fought with the 1st Division in
France as an artilleryman. After the war he switched to the Quartermaster
Corps and graduated from the Quartermaster School, the Command and
General Staff School, the Army Industrial College, and the Army War
College. Known as an unusually good administrator, he was an excellent
choice to represent USAFFE on Bataan. From this forward headquarters
Marshall made an inspection of Bataan's fighting lines on January 12 and
became concerned over the large gap imposed by Mount Natib. "I don't
believe we can over-estimate the importance of denying observation of
both our battle positions which would be available to the enemy were he
in possession of Mt. Natib," he wrote the next day.[39] Now, with enemy
pressure building along the lower slopes of the mountain, USAFFE decided to buttress the front by committing the two remaining regiments of
the elite Philippine Division, the Scout 45th Infantry and the American
31st Infantry.

On the evening of January 15, after learning of the two Philippine
Division regiments coming to him, General Parker decided to counterattack the next morning, using the 51st Division. Parker would reinforce
the 51st Division with the 3rd Battalion, 21st Infantry, a unit that had
fought alongside the Scouts of the 57th Infantry just two days before.
Following the 51st Division counterattack, Parker planned to attack with
the two Philippine Division regiments. Bluemel's 31st Division would
act as corps reserve and would relieve the Philippine Division after it
restored the line. Parker could not expect to keep these two regiments,
for they were the only units on Bataan capable of fighting offensively,
and they had to reassemble as army mobile reserve.[40]

When at about midnight General Jones received Parker's order to
counterattack at daybreak with his 51st Division, Jones protested vigorously, arguing that the recently lost line was a bad position, that his
troops were exhausted, and that he was just barely holding while fighting
defensively. The terrain north of the Balantay River was less easily defended and had fewer natural obstacles than present positions, and to
reestablish the old main line would be tactically unsound. The weakened

condition of his soldiers from days of fighting and heavy losses made any sort of attack hazardous. Finally, the 51st Division was entirely committed and had no reserves; even Jones's service troops were fighting. Jones presented some good points. Organizing a counterattack with poorly trained troops is difficult, and it was made even more so in this case by Japanese pressure and the disorganization of the division. The competence of Jones' Filipino staff officers left much to be desired. In Jones's view, practically no Filipino, captain or above, could function properly as a staff officer. In a less than perfect fix, he had to replace them with young, inexperienced American reserve officers and sergeants when fighting began. At the company level some Filipino officers proved capable and brave, but the majority lacked experience and failed to win the confidence of their men. The average Filipino had more confidence in an American officer than in a Filipino.[41]

Understanding all these difficulties better than II Corps, Jones bluntly told corps headquarters that the attack was extremely hazardous. Somewhat bitterly, Jones recalled that the corps operations officer, Lieutenant Colonel Howard D. Johnston, West Point 1918, would "not listen to reason."[42] II Corps should have listened to Jones; he was one of the coolest, toughest officers on Bataan, a 1924 honor graduate from the Command and General Staff School and a 1933 War College graduate. Disappointments and setbacks did not affect him—so he was not crying wolf. His father and both grandfathers had fought in the Civil War, one brother had fought in the Spanish-American War and World War I, another brother in World War I, and Jones's four sons were to fight in World War II. Unfortunately, General Parker had visited the Abucay Line only once, and his G-2 and G-3 had never visited the line. Although II Corps sent several assistants forward on inspections, these officers were "youngsters" who lacked experience and judgment. Jones demanded the matter be presented to General Parker, but the order to attack was not rescinded. Although II Corps promised Jones the 3rd Battalion, 21st Infantry as reinforcements, buses to transport the men were late, and then a broken bus blocked the narrow trail. Leaving the blocked vehicles, the battalion then marched the remainder of the distance, but it arrived forty-five minutes too late to participate in the counterattack.

Overruled by higher headquarters, Jones considered prospects for a successful conclusion of the battle most inauspicious. He prepared for the next day's effort with little hope for success. Jones's divisional general staff officers had completed the six week course at the Command and Staff School on November 15, but these officers still lacked practical training in staff work. His technical and administrative staffs were in the same shape. Lacking trained staff officers, he tried to arrange the attack.

When Jones's weary Filipinos rose from foxholes and trenches the morning of January 16, they immediately hit strong resistance. The Japanese were planning a breakthrough here and were expecting a Filipino attempt to stop them. Surprisingly, the 51st Infantry on the right of the division's attack succeeded in advancing against the enemy and aggressively beat back the Japanese facing them. But the Filipinos proved too successful, for as they advanced they pulled ahead of elements to both their left and right. By 0900 hours they had exposed both flanks badly.[43]

Fortune now favored the Japanese. The 51st Infantry's unsupported advance presented the Japanese with a glittering opportunity, and they seized it. Between noon and one o'clock, the Japanese 141st Infantry moved against the gap opening between right of the 51st Infantry and the 43rd Infantry, and the lost 9th Infantry, completely unplanned and completely without warning, burst from the woods and hit the Filipino's left flank. "We were surprised when they attacked us from the rear," remembered Sergeant Romualdo C. Din, a platoon leader in F Company. "We were disorganized and had to retreat."[44] Officers found it impossible to untangle the troops, and the Filipinos fled in disorder leaving their dead and wounded behind. Even the most veteran unit would be severely shaken if suddenly assaulted on both flanks while itself in the process of attacking. Under this unexpected double onslaught the 51st Infantry collapsed and became badly mixed with the men of the 52nd. Even though Colonel Cordero used all the odds and ends of troops he could scrape together, he could not stop the Japanese. General Jones issued orders for the 51st Infantry to fall back by phase lines but the men could not be rallied, and Jones's hopes for an orderly withdrawal faded. The long-awaited hole in the Abucay Line was now open.

Although the hole beckoned, Colonel Imai hesitated to push his 141st Infantry into the gap for fear he, in turn, would be hit as his flanks were exposed. It was not unreasonable for him to assume Filipino reserves awaited his pursuit. So while maintaining pressure on the battered 43rd Infantry, Colonel Imai shunned the empty positions of the 51st Infantry and sidestepped eastward to attack the center of the 41st Division. As badly placed as they were, Imai's attacks still threatened to split the 41st Division in two. The 42nd Infantry held its ground, but the regimental instructor became concerned over the condition of both his flanks. The 41st Infantry on the right was fighting hard to recapture its main line, but without much success. The 43rd Infantry on the left was getting in trouble now that its left flank had lost touch with the broken 51st Infantry.[45]

The Japanese 9th Infantry, after hitting the 51st Infantry from the west, was equally reluctant to attempt an exploitation. They believed the Filipinos were present in large numbers, so they spent a great deal of time reducing the few Filipinos who remained. When Colonel Takechi met with General Nara after his surprise attack on the Filipino 51st Infantry, Takechi explained that his 9th Infantry had become lost on Mount Natib. Nara was sympathetic and ordered Takechi to take his regiment into reserve. But because Nara's order seemed like punishment for getting lost, Colonel Takechi once again led his men up Mount Natib, this time determined to cross the daunting mountain in direct disobedience of Nara's orders. Nara's 65th Brigade headquarters was astonished by Takechi's move and, lacking something better to call it, christened it a reconnaissance in force around the Filipino flank to avoid the heavier defenses they believed faced them directly to the south. Reports as to what the 9th Infantry was doing and where it was going were contradictory. "We were at a loss to decide what report to believe," recorded the 65th Brigade.[46] So both Japanese regiments, the 141st and 9th Infantry, literally sitting atop II Corps's weakest point, decided to go elsewhere.

When the Japanese routed the 51st Infantry the Filipinos of the 43rd Infantry refused their left flank and curled back to the regimental reserve line. The terrain here was steep with many ridges running off the slopes of Mount Natib. Under heavy pressure the 43rd Infantry fought a slow withdrawal and gave up their strong points one by one. The regiment had suffered 300 killed or wounded up to this point. The dead could not be buried, and the stench was brutal. With the 43rd Infantry in trouble, and with the entire line under heavy enemy pressure, the division formed a provisional battalion to meet the crisis on the left flank. The division headquarters grabbed the 41st Engineer Battalion, men from the signal company, the quartermaster detachment, and stragglers and formed a new battalion. The 450-man Provisional Battalion first saw action the evening of January 16, arriving on the 43rd Infantry's line in the early evening and going into position with the mission of holding at all costs. By dark, the 43rd Infantry's lines had retreated to within 100 yards of the regimental command post. Despite the threatening situation, Lieutenant Colonel Eugene T. Lewis refused to move. The 37-year-old West Pointer's steadfast and courageous leadership stopped the enemy advance and held the division's flank until the arrival of the counterattacking Philippine Division the next day.[47]

The events of January 16 were mirrored farther to the rear at artillery positions. "Hell of a day," wrote Colonel Quintard in his diary, "bombing—planes overhead 8 hours—all installations got it. Line out but we did get to fire on 4 battery targets. How[itzer] platoon shelled, 2 killed and 4 wounded. Shelled from close range! and men and officers became panic stricken and took to the brush. . . . Rumor: our left flank has been turned."[48] As the Japanese pushed deeper and deeper into II

Corps's left flank, the Scout 1st Battalion, 88th Artillery, found itself firing farther and farther to the left until they were firing at a 90-degree angle to their original direction of fire. Japanese artillery hit this battalion, killing and wounding a dozen officers and men. Even so, the morale of the Scout artillerymen remained high. In the 2nd Battalion, 88th Artillery, the two firing batteries scheduled their shoots around the snooping of enemy aerial observers. Battery executive officers set all the necessary firing data on the guns and raised their arms. Then, as enemy observation planes flew by and faced away from the gunners, arms dropped and guns fired. In this sporadic manner, artillery support for the 41st Division continued.

Now the fog of war rolled over the Filipinos and hastened the collapse of the 51st Division elements still on the extreme left of the line. The commander of the left flank regiment, Colonel John R. Boatwright, had begun his military service in 1916 as a private in the 1st Infantry, Virginia National Guard. Now the 45-year-old infantryman was feeling badly, for he believed his 53rd Infantry was isolated, realized he could not maintain contact with the routed 51st Infantry on his right, and felt the newly arrived Japanese 9th Infantry would turn on him at any moment. Boatwright pulled his right flank back in an effort to maintain contact with anyone to his east, but he failed; there was no one there, and bad terrain prevented patrols from finding friendly elements. His right flank soon lost its cohesiveness and continued its rearward displacement. Boatwright called the 51st Division chief of staff, Colonel Stuart C. MacDonald, and explained the 53rd Infantry's precarious situation.[49]

Although the situation looked bleak, it was not hopeless. The Japanese 9th Infantry had halted to reorganize and reconnoiter after hitting the 51st Infantry and was not an immediate threat, so although Nara's men had beaten the Filipinos out of their defensive positions, they did not quite realize it. More important, most of the Japanese were now committed against the 41st Division farther east. But Boatwright did not know this, nor did he know he had a reserve. The 3rd Battalion, 21st Infantry had arrived the morning of the sixteenth, too late to join the 51st Division's counterattack, but they did take position behind the most critical point in the line. Unfortunately for Boatwright, he never learned of their presence. Equally unaware of the 53rd Infantry's predicament, this battalion accepted orders to move farther south and by late afternoon was out of the battle area.[50]

Fearing disaster if the 53rd Infantry remained in place, Colonel MacDonald at division headquarters got on the phone and, in the absence of General Jones who was then forward, ordered the 53rd Infantry to withdraw to the southwest and establish contact with I Corps. But he did not specify to what line the regiment was to withdraw; Colonel Boatwright was expected to take whatever position the situation might dictate. Upon receipt of this order, the regiment started an exhausting and demoralizing retreat, and the entire left flank of the 51st Division crumbled into isolated groups of men—often without equipment—trying to reach safety to the south and west. Units became separated in the thick jungle. Without supplies, soldiers ate boiled snails, leaves, and roots to survive. All one officer had to eat for three days was a single can of pineapple which he shared with several others. Colonel Boatwright reached friendly lines after a four-day march with just seventy-five men. No more than a battalion was ever assembled in I Corps, and they played no further part in the Abucay fight.[51]

Now that all three 51st Division regiments were out of action, Japanese patrols overran the 51st Division's command post and forced a hurried displacement. In the process, the headquarters had to destroy all its irreplaceable communications equipment. During the late afternoon the appearance of enemy troops again forced the headquarters to move, and with the hasty displacement of the command post and the breakup of the 53rd Infantry, the 51st Division was destroyed. At the close of January 16 the division headquarters controlled only 100 men. Many more survived the debacle, but they were not under control, and as General Jones organized a weak covering force with these 100 men, he had the ironic thought that he now commanded the smallest division in the world. During the night, as Jones slept, forward observers along the lines of the 43rd Infantry sent firing data to their guns. At midnight the entire 41st Artillery, reinforced, fired into the gap left by the 51st Division. How effective the fire was is not known, but the Japanese did not advance.[52]

On January 17, the day after the disastrous counterattack, Jones collected and assembled survivors in rear areas near Guitol. His small screen regained contact with the Japanese, and the Filipinos fended off a few minor Japanese probes. Luckily for Jones and his men, the Japanese had shifted the emphasis of their attacks to the 41st Division. Most of the men Jones placed astride the Guitol-Natib Trail were from the 52nd Infantry, and they were replaced the next day by remnants of the 51st Infantry and the haggard 21st Division engineers. Contact patrols tried to cover the great gap between the right flank of the 51st Division and the newly arrived Philippine Division. The left flank of Jones's screen flapped in the wind and could not do anything about Japanese forces moving down the Abo Abo River Valley. General Parker had attached the 21st Division staff to Jones and at dusk General Capinpin and his senior advisor started up on foot to see if they could help. Colonel O'Day arrived first and learned from an officer that Jones did not desire any help. When Capinpin arrived, the two officers decided to talk to Jones anyway and made their way down to his tent next to a stream. After a short talk, Jones stated he would "wash his own dirty linen," and that Capinpin and O'Day should return to Guitol to reorganize 51st Division stragglers and return them to the front.[53]

In addition to the hole left by the 51st Division's collapse, there already existed a significant penetration in the main line of the 41st Infantry. On January 14 the Japanese 9th Independent Antitank Company, now working for the 142nd Infantry, dragged its 47mm guns forward and placed direct, observed fire on Filipino foxholes. Using periscopic binoculars to locate individual positions, Japanese gunners methodically walked their rounds into one foxhole after another, and Filipino after Filipino died as prewar deficiencies came home to roost. Badly cleared fields of fire, fresh earth in front of uncamouflaged foxholes, and regular, easily identified lines presented the Japanese with obvious targets. The fire became so murderous that the 2nd Battalion's line companies suffered 50 percent casualties and withdrew late in the afternoon. Somewhat later the 1st Battalion likewise withdrew from the galling punishment. Casualties in the regiment were heavy, 550 killed and wounded, and the Japanese realized they were succeeding. "At 1440 hours," reads their report, "the [142nd Infantry] crossed the deep ravine of the south tributary of the Kabiawan River under powerful artillery support and commenced assault. The left front line battalion reduced the enemy's strong resistance in the immediate front and flanks after being exposed to furious enemy rifle and artillery fire for two desperate hours while getting past the irregular barbed wire network around the position."[54] Once darkness fell, Filipino artillery fired at the enemy gun positions, but the damage had already been done. During the evening, the regiment's reserve 3rd Battalion replaced the chopped-up 2nd Battalion, and men spent the night carrying food, water, and machine gun ammunition into position to face the next day's attacks.

Filipino efforts at daylight on January 15, supported by artillery, to recapture the terrain lost the day before, failed. The 41st Infantry's attack on the right of the line with Captain Jacobo Zobel's 1st Battalion gained ground, but the 3rd Battalion on the left was stopped with heavy casualties. The 1st Battalion made the only progress of the day, but because both flanks were exposed, they retired into friendly lines after dark. Because of the losses involved in the day's fighting, the remnants of the 2nd Battalion combined with the survivors of the 3rd. During this reorganization, the 2nd Battalion commander, Lieutenant Constancio de Zosa, was mortally wounded in Colonel Wetherby's command post only 150 yards from the front lines. His successor, Lieutenant Villafuerte, was killed in the same spot thirty minutes later. In the absence of competent Filipino replacements, Wetherby placed American Major Lee A. Lauderback in charge of the composite 2nd-3rd Battalion, and because of a fatal absence of security, Wetherby moved his command post that night to a safer position. When the 41st Engineer Battalion joined the 41st Infantry and occupied the regiment's reserve line, they were so confused and frightened by Japanese firecrackers that they fired into the rear of their own main line.[55]

At 1700 hours on January 15, with the attachment of most of the 3rd Battalion, 32nd Infantry, enough men became available to the 41st Infantry for it to try another attack the next day. The entire 32nd Infantry was a II Corps asset and its units could not be committed without permission from General Parker's headquarters. The 41st Division was not able to contact II Corps either by wire or radio. But the situation was so critical in the 41st Infantry's sector that the battalion was ordered into action without Corps approval. It deployed near the rear of the reserve line now occupied by division engineers, but because of straggling, lack of guides, and the dark, only 180 men arrived.[56]

At 0615 hours on January 16 the 41st Infantry attacked under the cover of a fifteen-minute artillery preparation. Again the 1st Battalion pushed into the old main line, but Japanese were dug in to their left along a creek bed completely immune to direct fire weapons. Again, the advance was costly; two companies of the fresh 3rd Battalion, 32nd Infantry, failed to make any progress partly because thirty-two Filipinos deserted. Several more were killed or wounded, including the battalion executive officer, 3rd Lieutenant Bell, who died from a stomach wound. Even though the Japanese were within three hundred yards of Filipino infantry, Filipino artillerymen would not fire on targets closer than four hundred yards from Filipino lines for fear of hitting their own men. The attack died four hours after it began. Once more, officers started preparations for an effort the next day. After dark, Lieutenant N. L. Matthews reported to the 41st Infantry with his 2nd Battalion, 43rd Infantry, sent by division headquarters to help restore the original line. The shot-up 3rd Battalion, 32nd Infantry settled into the reserve line with but fifty men still under control.[57]

The January 17 attack was scheduled to start later than normal to allow officers of newly arrived units to study the ground. The third attempt began at 0830 hours, and for the third time the 1st Battalion, 41st Infantry, pushed into its old positions. The newly arrived Lieutenant Matthews was killed leading his battalion, and his men stopped after an advance of just a few yards. Friendly artillery could not reach into the ravine from which the Japanese were stopping each attack, and when patrols tried to clear the thickly vegetated area, they were only partially successful. By the end of the day, six of every ten soldiers in the 41st Infantry were dead, wounded, or missing.[58]

At an evening conference, officers planned a major effort for the next day. The 41st Artillery emplaced a battalion of 75mm guns to fire directly at the Japanese, and all six mortars of the 41st Division were collected and sited to fire together. A forward observer was detailed to advance with the assault troops and keep friendly artillery fire within 100 yards of the attacking line. The 42nd Infantry would support the attack by fire and subsequently advance with two provisional companies improvised from spare parts and regimental headquarters personnel. The assault formations were the 1st Battalion, the composite 2nd-3rd Battalions, and the 2nd Battalion, 43rd Infantry. The 3rd Battalion, 32nd Infantry, would stay on the regimental reserve line. Enemy bombing had destroyed the 41st Infantry's service area, so there was no food that night for the men scheduled to attack the next day.[59]

Hungry and tired, the Filipinos climbed from foxholes at 0625 hours and pushed smoothly forward. A forward observer spotting from an exposed position sent artillery fire crashing into the Japanese 2nd Battalion, 142nd Infantry. Five minutes later, flanking parties and the assault force all dashed forward. Leading the 42nd Infantry's advance, Corporal Andes Baldimas's squad worked its way through enemy fire until only fifty yards from a strong point. There, Baldimas ordered a bayonet charge, but enemy fire hit his rifle, broke it, and drove everyone to cover. Even so, Baldimas crawled alone and weaponless to the Japanese gunner, leaped on him, wrestled the machine gun from him, and fired and wounded the man. As they struggled, an exploding artillery round killed them both. The rest of Baldimas's squad rushed up and took the position.[60]

Elsewhere, assault parties were equally violent and equally successful. They drove the Japanese out of the main line and in the process wounded the Japanese officer in charge of the fight. The Filipinos reestablished their original positions by 0800 hours. The success of the Filipino attacks can be laid at the door of the artillery; the guns were so close to the enemy they could not miss. The commander of the Japanese 142nd Infantry now decided that "the menace of enemy flanking fire from the right flank precluded further developing the attack, and consequently the attack operations in that area were immediately suspended."[61] The 41st Infantry claimed they found three hundred enemy dead in the recaptured area, but this count is much too high. Whatever Japanese losses actually were, they again failed to pierce the tough 41st Division. General Parker was effusive in his praise of General Lim and the division's senior instructor, Colonel Malcolm V. Fortier. Fortier's performance during the critical days of heavy pressure were worthy of the highest praise, and the 41st Infantry later received the Presidential Unit Citation for its defense of the Abucay Line. The remainder of January 18 was spent evacuating dead and wounded, reorganizing, and burying enemy dead. Many Filipinos killed early in the fighting and abandoned in their foxholes could not be identified because of advanced decomposition.

Despite relatively good news from the 41st Division, the Japanese had won the battle in the 51st Division's area. But instead of pushing through the hole left by the 51st Division's collapse, they repeatedly attacked the left and center of the 41st Division, gaining little beyond bloody noses. "It is tragic," recorded the Japanese, "that the attack could not succeed even though the Brigade Reserve Unit was thrown into the front."[62] On January 18 the 65th Brigade began losing its artillery and tanks to 14th Army; the 7th Tank Regiment was removed from Nara's control; and 14th Army withdrew two battalions of 150mm guns, one battalion of 100mm guns, and one independent mortar battalion, a total of four desperately needed battalions of artillery.

When Nara's headquarters moved south to a new location, it was struck by American planes. Two American flyers were involved in that attack, Lieutenant Marshall J. Anderson from the 20th Pursuit and Lieutenant Jack W. Hall from the 34th Pursuit. They had orders to take off, strike quickly, and return before the Japanese could respond. They took off just after daylight and shot down an observation plane near the Abucay Line. Then they attacked three dive bombers and shot down one. Next they scattered nine bombers and forced them to drop their bombs into Manila Bay. As they returned to Bataan they spotted a truck column moving into Bataan and strafed it. As the 65th Brigade recalled, "Enemy P-40's came down several times, strafing with machine guns (machine cannons). Also the enemy's long-range artillery opened concentrated fire, destroying a portion of an ammunition dump."[63] It had been a bad day.

MacArthur was not any happier than the Japanese. He radioed his assessment of the fighting to Washington:

> The food situation here is becoming serious. For some time I have been on half rations and the result will soon become evident in the exhausted condition of the men. The limited geographical area which I occupy offers no food resources. I am entirely dependent upon a line of sea communications the responsibility for which has not been under my control. In my radio nine of January four I asked for blockade running ships. No reply has been received except to that feature dealing with a submarine carrying

antiaircraft ammunition. The strategic problem involving an advance from the south will not relieve the food situation here in time. The rations necessary to supply this command measured in ships capacity are small indeed. Many medium sized or small ships should be loaded with rations and dispatched along various routes. The enemy bomber formations are no longer here but have moved south. Unquestionably ships can get through but no attempt yet seems to have been made along this line. This seems incredible to me and I am having increasing difficulty in appeasing Philippine thought along this line. They cannot understand the apparent lack of effort to bring something in. I cannot over emphasize the psychological reaction that will take place unless something tangible is done in this direction. A revulsion of feeling of tremendous proportions against America can be expected. They can understand failure but cannot understand why no attempt is being made at relief through the forwarding of supplies. They contrast the lack of effort here to the concentrated and successful efforts against a stronger blockage line in the Atlantic. This reaction may eventually appear among the troops. Hungry men are hard to handle. Recommend that the question be immediately taken up with General Wavell and that simultaneous efforts be made from the NEI and the United States to get in the small amount of food that would see me through. The repeated statements from the United States that Hitler is to be destroyed before an effort is made here is causing dismay. The Japanese forces-air-sea-and ground-are much overextended. His success to date does not measure his own strength but the weakness of his opposition. A blow or even a threatened blow against him will almost certainly be attended with some success. I am professionally certain that his so called blockade can easily be pierced. The only thing that can make it really effective is our own passive acceptance of it as a fact. I repeat that if something is not done to meet the general situation which is developing the disastrous results will be monumental. The problems cannot be measured or solved by mere Army and Navy strategic formulas. They involve the comprehensiveness of the entire Oriental problems.[64]

As MacArthur's message left Corregidor, the American 31st Infantry was in the process of fighting its way through a storm of small-arms fire. The Philippine Division had attacked.

CHAPTER TEN

The Philippine Division Attacks

WITH THE CENTER OF HIS II CORPS LINE TEMPORARILY STABILIZED by General Lim's hard-fighting 41st Division, General Parker decided to counterattack with the newly arrived Philippine Division, the only division the Americans considered able to maneuver offensively. Parker knew that the counterattack was the decisive element of defensive doctrine, and he also knew that he could not hold his line solely by passive resistance. Parker was not happy about how he was going to use the Philippine Division. He had been hoping to use the entire division in an offensive counterblow (details of which are unknown), but the Japanese were preempting him. The 57th Infantry had not yet untangled itself from the Mabatang fight, and it was dangerous to leave that avenue of approach solely in the hands of the Philippine Army. So at best, Parker would have only two regiments with which to attack. Using the 31st and 45th infantry, Parker hoped to restore the original 51st Division line the morning of January 17 for, as he concluded after a careful study of his options, "Unless the 51st Division sector could be regained, it was evident that my left flank would be enveloped and the position would be lost."[1]

But Parker was a relatively timid general, not a man to gamble all on one throw. He had, as one close observer believed, a constitutional aversion to the risks required in war. Parker had reacted to each Japanese thrust, and even now he was reacting once again, trying to plug a hole rather than seizing the initiative. He was attacking Japanese strength, in

179

bad terrain, with no hope or intention of doing anything more than holding his main line of resistance.

Receiving II Corps's counterattack orders sometime after noon on the sixteenth, Brigadier General Maxon S. Lough led two of his three regiments toward the battle, and the move extended into the moonless evening. General Lough, a 55-year-old North Dakotan, had served with the Philippine Constabulary from 1908 until 1911 when he was commissioned as a second lieutenant. He fought in France as a captain where he won a Distinguished Service Cross and was wounded twice. He graduated as an Honor Graduate from the Command and General Staff School in 1924, and graduated from the Army War College in 1928. Lough planned for his two-regiment attack, his all-American 31st Infantry and the Scouts of the 45th Infantry, to kick off the morning of January 17. Colonel Charles L. Steel's 31st Infantry—the Polar Bears—was a proud outfit that boasted the only Army battle award ever earned during a time of peace, the Yangtze Service Medal, received for action during the Shanghai Incident of 1932. In honor of that service, the regiment cast a piece of silver known as the Shanghai Bowl, a large punch bowl and drinking cups made from 1,500 Chinese silver dollars. The 31st Infantry, activated in Manila in 1916 with men from four other infantry regiments, was known as America's Foreign Legion, for the regiment never served in the continental United States. Its first service was in Siberia from 1918 to 1920, where it suffered nearly one hundred men killed and wounded and scores more frost-bitten. The men to this day wear a small polar bear insignia affixed to the front of their caps in honor of that cold campaign.[2]

The morning of January 17 dawned as another in which the fortunes of war could swing dramatically in favor of the Japanese. General Nara began to realize he held a potential winning hand. If he could complete the turning of the American left flank—a likely prospect following the destruction of the 51st Division—then the Abucay Line would become untenable for the hard-pressed defenders. II Corps would be forced to retreat, leaving the field to the Japanese. American hopes now depended upon the performance of the 31st Infantry. The only white infantry regiment in all the Philippines was about to attack.

As early as the afternoon of January 15 the 31st Infantry had received a warning order to move to the Philippine Army Cadre Barracks west of Balanga to back up the 51st Division, which at that time was still fighting. The warning order found the Americans preparing defensive positions astride the East Road across from Mount Samat. They had been digging there for a week and had constructed an excellent line with good fields of fire and excellent obstacles. It was the second time the 31st Infantry had built defensive positions that they left to another unit. In preparation for the motor march, each man picked up an extra bandolier of M-1 rifle ammunition containing clips of eight rounds, stuffed what food he could find into his gas-mask carrier, and threw the gas mask into the brush. Following an afternoon of preparation, orders to move were received after 2000 hours, and the men filled canteens from a water trailer. Around midnight the regiment began its move to an assembly area just west of Balanga. The infantrymen completed the trip in buses, disembarked at 0300 hours on January 16, and found a hot meal waiting for them. In the confusion and nervousness of occupying new positions at night, Americans mistook Philippine Army stragglers as Japanese and fired at them. Some of the Filipinos wore only white undershorts, having abandoned their uniforms and rifles. When questioned, they would not identify their units, saying only that their officers and sergeants had left, so they too decided to leave.[3]

At noon on January 16 the regiment was ordered to move directly to the main line of resistance, and the infantrymen started the march fifteen minutes after being alerted. The 2nd Battalion formed the regiment's advance guard. Its commander, Major Lloyd C. Moffitt, a short, roly-poly officer from Denver, assembled his executive officer, company commanders, adjutant, medical and communications officers, then explained the situation and issued an order for the march. He said the 51st Division had broken, that the 41st Division had successfully refused its left flank, and that the 31st Infantry would counterattack to restore the old main line. Once the main line was restored, the 11th Division would march up and relieve the 31st Infantry, making the Americans available for more counterattacks. Moffitt ordered G Company forward as the battalion's advance guard. They were to march up the Hacienda Road until they made contact with the 43rd Infantry. After Major Moffitt's conference ended, the company commanders hurried to their units, passed on what little information they had, and prepared for the march. There would not be any trucks this time, nor would there be the concealment of night. Officers warned their men to keep a sharp eye toward Japanese controlled skies. G Company stood up, shouldered their gear, and stepped out, picking up the proper interval once they were on the road. Then F, E, and H companies followed.[4]

The 31st Infantry approached the Abucay Line with the 2nd, 1st, and 3rd battalions in line of march. The antitank company, engineers, and the self-propelled 75mm artillery from Major Babcock's battalion, followed the 3rd Battalion. Leaders urged everyone to hurry. Information reached the troops in fragments with promises of more to come later. Sharing the trail were numerous Filipinos moving south. "They were all smiles and wished us good luck," recalled Private Tillman J. Rutledge, an underaged Texan so determined to join the Army he talked his father into signing a statement he was eighteen years old.[5] Japanese planes were active and dove occasionally at the column, but because the Americans dispersed well, little damage was done. The Americans had received so many low-level bombings since the war began that they could predict where the bombs would land and had time to run from one foxhole to a safer one. Many of the bombs were of a very low order, some hardly more than iron pipe filled with explosives and scrap-iron farm machinery, clock, and automobile parts. Most of the Japanese planes ignored the infantrymen and flew toward Corregidor.

The regiment marched for two solid hours before the first halt. It was a hot, hard, tiring uphill march of thirteen miles. The physical exertion was tough for the riflemen; their eyes, ears, and hair became coated with dust. But it was even more difficult for the heavy weapons personnel. Machine guns and mortars were portable after being broken down into several parts, but the most annoying piece of equipment was the forty-five pound mortar base plate. The unfortunate men carrying that load struggled to keep up with the marching files of men. The infantrymen plodded along, cursing the nine-and-a-half pounds of their M-1 rifles, while steel helmets dug into heads, and shoes and canvas leggings blistered feet and legs. Bulky loads of ammunition chafed hips and shoulders, and clips of M-1 ammo perversely worked their way out of their cloth bandoleers and clattered onto the road. Some men sickened in the brutal, dusty heat and fell out of the line of march.[6]

The regiment reached the left of the 43rd Infantry at 1900 hours, well after sunset but with a little light in the sky. During the last hours of daylight, Japanese observation planes watched the regiment, but they refrained from launching any attacks. The Americans made the march with only two ten-minute rest breaks. They thankfully bivouacked about 2,000 yards east of the Abucay Hacienda, and leaders rushed to get in a quick reconnaissance. Disorganized groups of Filipinos trickled to the rear crying, "The Japs are coming."[7] The Americans were pretty tired by then, so they were not terribly concerned if the Japanese were, in fact, coming. The regiment established local security, soldiers paired off, and everyone tried to get comfortable. The Americans had outmarched their support, and they went to sleep hungry.

The arrival of the 31st Infantry was a big boost for the morale of the hard-pressed 43rd Infantry. The Filipinos had suffered over 450 men killed, wounded, or missing, and the situation had been deteriorating ever since the rout of the 51st Division. An American company commander talked to two sergeant-instructors from the 43rd Infantry and learned from them that the situation was pretty fluid. The Filipinos had fought back to their present location, and the American instructors hoped the men would hold, but they could not guarantee it. Major Moffitt went to see Lieutenant Colonel Lewis at his 43rd Infantry command post, a dug-out in the side of a ravine and, by this time, part of the front line. It was so close to the battle that the next day, when the 31st Infantry's 2nd Battalion attacked, wounded Americans rolled down the ravine into Lewis's headquarters. Lewis was tired, having slept only in snatches over the past five days. He knew little of the enemy or friendly situation and could not give Moffitt any details. There was no actual enemy contact at the moment, but patrols were active. Lewis assured the Americans their right flank would be secure.[8]

It was past midnight when the battalion commanders of the 31st Infantry met with Colonel Steel at his regimental command post. Steel had already met 41st Division commander General Lim and the senior instructor, Colonel Fortier, and had discussed the situation with them. Steel received little information about enemy strengths or locations, but he now passed on what he had. His briefing was followed by orders for the next day's attack. Sunrise was at 0724 hours, and the attack would start at 0800 hours with the 1st Battalion on the left, west, and the 2nd Battalion straddling Trail 12 on the right, east. The 3rd Battalion was in reserve. Direction of attack was north. The officers returned to their battalions an hour after midnight.[9]

At the 3rd Battalion, company commanders met to receive the attack order. Lieutenant Colonel Jasper E. Brady opened his one and only map, a small-scale Caltex road map, showed his officers their general location, where unit boundaries would be, and gave them their orders. Brady had begun his military service as an enlisted man in 1917 and was wounded in France. The 44-year-old Brady covered matters such as ammunition, food, medical evacuation, and the location of the battalion aid station. He pointed out the location of the regimental aid station, a spot on the reverse slope of a hill with access to a road for ambulance service. Brady told his commanders to move at once farther west along the Hacienda Road. Upon being dismissed, company commanders groped back to their companies, assembled their platoon leaders, and issued their own instructions. The companies then picked up their gear and moved to their assembly positions. "Our artillery was firing, their artillery was coming in, we'd get the command to hit the dirt and then move on," remembered medic John G. Lally. "It was just like a movie from the First World War."[10] Once at the assigned position, a mango grove, the battalion tried to snatch a few hours sleep.

In the 2nd Battalion, Major Moffitt called his officers together at his command post, a shallow, wooded ravine, and gave them their orders.

G Company would attack on the left astride Trail 12, E Company would attack on the right, and F Company would follow in battalion reserve. Moffitt told his company commanders to move farther west along the Hacienda Road to Trail 12. After answering questions, Moffitt sent his officers back to their companies where they briefed their men. Private Richard M. Gordon, F Company, was an oldtimer, having arrived in the Philippines in 1940. He met with his company commander, Lieutenant Eugene B. Conrad, a "great big rascal," while it was still dark. Conrad told his men of the counterattack and stressed the need to recover the lost ground.[11]

In the 1st Battalion Lieutenant Colonel Bowes briefed his officers. Bowes had significant foreign service under his belt—service in the Panama Canal Zone and then with the Tacna-Arica Plebiscite Commission on Chile. He had arrived in the Philippines only five weeks before the war started. In Bowes's D Company, the D Company commander gave his men a pep talk and concluded by saying he hoped this would be the start of the drive back to Manila. In B Company, the order was simple. Captain John W. Thompson told his men, "Fix bayonets and let's get 'em."[12] Some of the B Company soldiers believed they were picked as the assault company as punishment for their flight from the Layac Line on January 6. The regiment's riflemen spent the waning hours of darkness wondering, as all men do before battle, what they might be doing at that time the next day. The Americans collected straggling Filipinos and gave several to each company to carry machine gun ammunition. Hands ran over gear, fingered ammunition, and adjusted loads. Officers watched their wristwatches and looked toward Manila for the first indications of dawn. As the sun crept across the Pacific, the 31st Infantry made its final preparations. But while plans were proceeding according to expectations at lower levels, there was trouble at higher echelons.

As originally planned, both the 31st and 45th infantry were to have attacked, but Colonel Thomas W. Doyle's 45th Infantry, coming out of a reserve position in I Corps, lost its way during the night approach march and was not in position when morning dawned. Doyle was a long-service soldier—he first served as a private with G Company, 6th Massachusetts Infantry, National Guard, in 1898, then became a lieutenant in 1916. He attended the Infantry School's Company Officers' Course in 1923 and the Advanced Course in 1932. Like the 31st Infantry, Doyle's 45th Infantry filed out of bivouacs and marched toward the Abucay Line the afternoon of January 15, through the evening, and into the morning of January 16. After leaving the Pilar-Bagac Road and entering the rough trail leading north to Bani, the march slowed. Weapons trucks repeatedly sank into mud holes created by preceding vehicles. The infantrymen nearly exhausted themselves pushing and pulling the stuck vehicles out of the mud. Moving by bus, then truck, and finally on foot, the Scouts took six hours to close into a bivouac. Once they reached the bivouac, information as to what was happening was sketchy; the 51st Division was reported to have run, and the rest of the line was in danger of being turned. One lieutenant heard that the 57th Infantry had lost nine officers while defending Mabatang, so he felt glum about the upcoming counterattack. The officers spent the daylight hours of the sixteenth reconnoitering northward, trying to get an idea of the ground. But no troop movements were made; the concealment of darkness was desired for two reasons—secrecy and protection from enemy planes.[13]

At 1700 hours II Corps headquarters telephoned the 45th Infantry's operations officer and directed the regiment move to an area southwest of the Balantay River northwest of the Capitangan Valley to back up the 31st Infantry. With a minimum of time, without any II Corps guides, and with little chance for a detailed reconnaissance, the Scouts marched up the Back Road and at 2300 hours became lost in a maze of small trails. The commander of I Company, Captain George B. Moore, a good, steady Chicagoan, had reconnoitered the route during the day but despite this precaution, the column became hopelessly lost. The collection of trails offered an infinite number of routes. The night was completely black, no stars, no moon, and no guides or signs to indicate the proper direction. Cursing inaccurate maps, pressured for time, with no liaison and no assurance of friendly forces nearby, columns of Scout infantry wound blindly through tall grass, across rocky creeks, and over steep trails. At times even the trails disappeared. The 1st Battalion drifted off during the march, ending somewhere to the west. "It was a horror of hardship in canyon-cut terrain," recalled Major Adrianus J. Van Oosten, a naturalized American born in the Netherlands.[14] The 3rd Battalion's weapons trucks stuck fast in a ford and were left behind. To the north, artillery banged away, lighting the sky for fleeting seconds and reminding the officers they were needed elsewhere.

"That night was like something out of a movie," recalled platoon leader Lieutenant Anthony Ulrich. "The sky to our front was splashed with red from the burning sugar cane fields while the big artillery guns punctuated the silence. Occasionally the sputter of machine guns and small arms fire could be heard."[15] To the 2nd Battalion's surgeon, Lieutenant Basil Dulin, called to active duty in 1941 from his internship in Indiana, the flashes of artillery reminded him of summer sheet lightning. Moving to their first combat, the men retained vivid memories of that night march. The thick vegetation and broken terrain, which until now had so frustrated the Japanese, had turned with a vengeance upon the defenders. Sufficient time had existed to rendezvous with the 31st Infantry had the regiment marched during the day, but they tried to move only at night. So instead of two regiments abreast, only one would be in position to attack. There was not time now to wait for the 45th Infantry and a cardinal error was about to be committed. The counterattack became a piecemeal commitment of the best troops on Bataan.

Everything now depended on the Polar Bears of the American 31st Infantry. If their attack succeeded, II Corps's line could hold for some time to come. The Japanese did not have unlimited power, and if stopped here, they would need to reorganize before mounting another effort. But if the Americans failed, and especially if they were routed, the entire Filamerican line would have to retreat, probably under heavy Japanese pressure. Even Wainwright's I Corps would be forced to retreat to conform to II Corps's movement. And if the Americans broke, as B and I companies did at Layac, what hope could be placed in the less well-trained Filipinos?

Earning the nickname "the Thirsty-First" in honor of their Manila drinking bouts, the 31st Infantry attacked at 0815 hours with two battalions abreast. Jumping off from their line of departure, the men initially encountered little resistance. On the left, following trails in the thick jungle, "Eddie" Bowes's 1st Battalion drove ahead even after encountering substantial resistance. Part of this drive dissolved into hand-to-hand fighting. Corporal Jim Laird, a young BAR man from Missouri, had joined the Army in 1939 and sailed to the Philippines in November 1941. Fighting beside the men in Captain John W. Thompson's B Company, he was grazed in the leg by an enemy rifleman only thirty feet away. The Japanese soldier was shot out of his tree, but rather than dying, he attacked Laird with a bayonet. It was an unequal struggle, for the Japanese had a bayonet but Laird did not. Struggling to parry the long bayonet with his heavy BAR, Laird was cut three times in the face and then slashed in his hand as he threw up his arm. The fight ended when Laird's platoon sergeant arrived and killed the Japanese. The Americans met more resistance at a sugar cane field bordered by a ditch and a road, a cane field "absolutely full of Japs," where close combat was the rule because of the thick vegetation and broken ground.[16]

Japanese fire knocked down one B Company infantryman, and after Private Harold J. Garrett spotted the gun, he crawled under the machine gun fire until within hand grenade range. Timing his effort, he jumped up and threw a grenade into the enemy crew. The instant he released the grenade, two machine gun bullets ripped through both his legs, and a mortar shell burst ten feet behind him, knocking him forward and blowing the stock off his rifle. Garrett's squad leader was shot through the

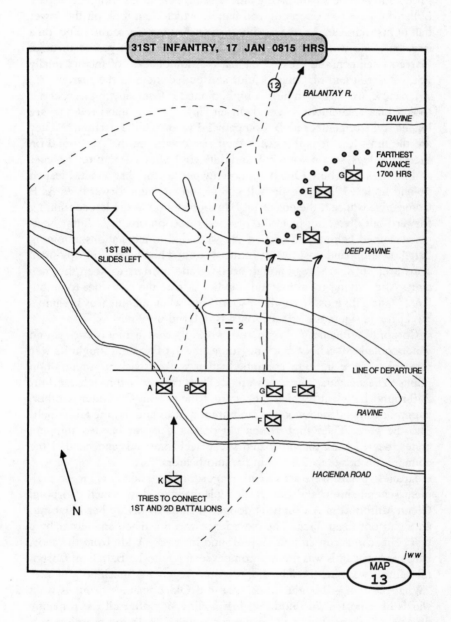

31ST INFANTRY, 17 JAN 0815 HRS

BALANTAY R.

RAVINE

FARTHEST
ADVANCE
1700 HRS

G

E

F

DEEP RAVINE

1ST BN
SLIDES LEFT

1 = 2

LINE OF DEPARTURE

A   B   G   E

F

RAVINE

HACIENDA ROAD

K

TRIES TO CONNECT
1ST AND 2D BATTALIONS

N

jww

MAP
13

groin, and another man, taking aim with his M-1 at his shoulder, took a bullet on the rifle's operating rod handle which then took off the lower half of his right ear. As two medics started carrying Garrett to safety on a stretcher, one was shot through the leg while a bullet passed through Garrett's canteen and creased his back. Another team of medics finally got to Garrett and his squad leader and pulled them to the rear.[17]

Japanese fire, although mostly high, pinned B Company in place, and it took a bizarre incident to get them moving. "The Filipino red ants are legendary," remembered B Company's Private Paul Kerchum. "They are the most ferocious things for their size on this earth. They stand on their hind legs, spit in your eye, and defy you! They got into my britches and bit me in the butt. One bit me on my pecker and that was it. I leaped up and hollered 'lets get the hell going' and we went forward!"[18] As B Company advanced, the entire 1st Battalion slid off to the left continuing forward but diverging from the planned direction of attack. Litter bearers remained behind and carried the wounded to aid stations adjoining battalion command posts. Most of the wounded had been struck by small arms fire, but there was enough artillery and mortars to keep the men alert. After giving them first aid, medics carried the casualties to ambulances, and Filipinos drove them south. But when ambulances became a target for Japanese air, evacuation was delayed until dark.

Corporal William W. Wynn was working with a ninety-two pound water-cooled .30-caliber machine gun as the 1st Battalion fought its way forward. As the fighting continued, men walked back to ammunition points. The machine gunners were well on their way through the four 250-round belts with which they started the action. One after another, ammo bearers opened wooden ammunition cases and fed the fabric belts into the guns. Then supply men cut open the larger banded shipping crates, peeled back the tin-coated sheet-steel inner lid, and handed the ammunition boxes to the waiting ammo bearers.[19]

Japanese planes were active and dangerous. Dive bombers hit the regiment several times, and observation planes kept close watch. Corporal Glenn Milton from A Company dodged a plane by diving head first into an eight-foot deep ditch. The experience was not made any easier by a belt of machine gun ammunition around his neck. Aside from the short battle at Layac, this was the first combat seen by the 1st Battalion. Corporal Milton was surprised by his reactions to enemy machine gun fire. "What the hell," thought the 27-year-old Oklahoman, "so this is what war is like; no fear, no nothing. Just feeling silly after all the romantic dreams I had about activity on the battle-field."[20] As the morning progressed, most of the soldiers discarded their light packs and gas masks. Prewar field packs consisted of a blanket roll, shelter half, tent poles, tent pegs, raincoat, and socks, but this collection hardly lasted the first few days. The weather was hot so the men did not need a blanket, and no one liked the leggings so the men just threw them away. They stuffed anything important in the gas-mask carrier and slung it over the shoulder or around the waist. Other men found the carrier to be an excellent hand-grenade container and packed them full of the small bombs.

Major Moffitt's 2nd Battalion was on the right of the regiment's attack. As the men walked 800 yards up the Hacienda Road early on January 17 they passed through a mango grove containing some wounded Filipinos, filled canteens from a water pipe near the Hacienda, and when dawn broke, made a 90-degree right turn up to their line of departure. The 2nd Battalion attacked with G and E companies abreast and a machine gun platoon attached to each. After crossing the line of departure, the Americans received mortar and small arms fire interspersed with a terrific cracking and banging of Japanese firecrackers.[21]

In G Company, Captain John I. Pray's left flank platoon pushed forward 400 yards until stopped by automatic weapons firing down lanes cut in a sugar cane field. The cane field was badly tangled with strong vines that the Americans had to hack clear before they could advance. When enemy fire lifted for a moment, Sergeant George Hasson led his squad into the cane but stopped after hearing soft voices and machete noises on bamboo. Hasson, believing the voices might be from Filipinos, challenged them only to receive a prolonged burst of machine gun fire. Private Paul C. Gilmore, in the Army for only six months, threw a hand grenade which failed to explode. The Japanese had better munitions, and fragments hit Gilmore in the left leg. Next to Gilmore, Private Salvatore Puzzanghera sat bolt upright in surprise and said he was hit in the shoulder. Gilmore also saw a hole right through the middle of Puzzanghera's helmet with blood trickling from the wound. Gilmore threw another grenade, one that worked, and the squad pulled out of the enemy's fire. Left behind was a dead American no one in Gilmore's squad knew, a small man wearing a fresh, neatly pressed shirt, the three military creases up the back still crisp, spoiled only by a bullet hole.[22]

Then G Company's right flank platoon stumbled into an unexpected seventy-five foot deep ravine. The battalion executive officer led some of G Company's men up the ravine and to within thirty feet of the enemy. The six Americans spread into line and prepared to throw grenades. They tossed the grenades, "and then we all started firing," recalled Private First Class Albert Taylor. "I couldn't see the enemy but I could hear them."[23] The Japanese responded with their own grenades, wounding Taylor, Major O'Donovan, and three others. The small party of Americans withdrew, most heading toward the aid station. Captain Ralph E.

Hibbs, the 2nd Battalion's surgeon, was at the aid station when the casualties started arriving, "and it was pretty hot and heavy," remembered Hibbs. "There were calls for litter teams. Most wounds were from small arms, little from fragmentation."[24] Captain Hibbs, a graduate of medical school at the University of Ohio, handled arm and leg wounds without too much difficulty, but several stomach wounds worried him. He could do nothing about them there, for he was very close to the front lines, and it was a matter of not getting shot himself.

In an unusual move, Major Moffitt withdrew his left flank company and switched it to the battalion's right. He then pushed Lieutenant Eugene B. Conrad's F Company, the battalion's reserve, into the hole left by G Company's departure. Unhappily for Moffitt's plan, F Company was hardly more successful than G. Enemy machine gun fire was so intense here that it cut swaths of cane and stacked it on the ground as if ready for harvesting. As Japanese fire swept over F Company, Private William Garleb dove into an abandoned 51st Division foxhole. Another American tumbled in on top of Garleb shaking uncontrollably, tossed his rifle to Garleb, and cried that he could not stand the pressure. Garleb got so mad he forgot his own fear. Despite individual terrors, F Company started a slow advance, and as they crawled forward several men passed a wounded comrade. His hand was badly mangled and his face scarred, but as he lay there, he was singing, "God Bless America."[25]

A few men from F Company, bellies hugging the ground, crept forward and used hand grenades to reduce the closer gun positions. Private Garleb worked his way into a shallow hole with a BAR man to his right. Telling the soldier to lay down a base of fire, Garleb brought his left leg up under his body, sprang up, tossed a grenade, and fell back into his little hole. He used fourteen grenades, but only seven exploded, and he was bitter about the duds. "When the Japs are within throwing distance and the hand grenades don't go off, you can get pretty sore about it."[26] The BAR man was equally frustrated, and he stood up and fired a roaring twenty-round burst from his automatic rifle. When the advance resumed, F Company found an abandoned enemy position heaped with empty cartridges, but no machine gun and no bodies. A dead American lay nearby, and big ants were already eating holes in the body.

When the 2nd Battalion called a halt for mortars to work over the Japanese, the infantrymen refilled empty canteens from a small spring bubbling into the creek running through the deep ravine. The 2nd Battalion's weapons company had two mortars, one new 81mm and one old WWI Stokes 3-incher. The crews had only thirty-one rounds of the 81mm ammunition, so they fired the more numerous but less accurate 3-inch rounds. Sergeant Earl F. Walk, the mortar platoon leader, did not have much faith in the old rounds. "When we assembled the rounds," he recalled, "the insert that went into the body of the shell was red at one end and yellow at the other. If the colors were faded, generally the shell would not go off when it hit the ground, but we always hoped it would hit a Jap on the head. I believe one on the head would put anyone out of action."[27]

Company weapons trucks carried the men to within 1,000 yards of the fight, then crewmen continued forward on foot carrying tubes, bipods, baseplates, and ammunition. Japanese bullets cracked and popped just over their heads, and a few artillery rounds exploded nearby, mortally wounding one crewman. An infantryman showed Sergeant Walk where three Americans had just been killed at the far edge of a cane field. Walk positioned his two mortars on the near edge of the field hardly seventy-five yards from a Japanese machine gun. Walk's mortarmen opened wooden ammunition boxes and screwed together the head, body, and tail of each round. Twenty Stokes rounds were sent tumbling end over end at the Japanese. As explosions shook the tree line, an enemy helmet bounced down the ravine, and fragments reached as far back as the mortars. One round hit the edge of the enemy machine gun emplacement, and when the Americans overran the position, they found the foxhole splashed with blood. But not all the rounds reached the enemy. One projectile rose a drunken twenty feet into the air, wobbled over, and headed back at the crew. When it hit the ground, it failed to explode.[28]

After the mortars stopped, it was the infantry's turn again. As the 2nd Battalion's three companies worked their way across the deep ravine, they ran into even heavier fire. The rifle company commanders, Sauer, Conrad, and Pray, met and voted, two to one, to make a concerted effort. As soon as heavy machine guns were carried into position, each company would attack. But before the attack was launched, a runner from battalion arrived and ordered the three companies back to the south side of the ravine. The time was now 1730 hours, and it was debatable if further progress could be made that day. The rifle companies, exhausted by the day's fighting, made their way across the big ravine, G Company swung back to the battalion's left flank, and the three companies set up for the night.[29]

The performance of the 2nd Battalion was characterized by valor at the individual level, but it was crippled by an absence of leadership from the battalion. Major Moffitt was isolated from events occurring along the front line and could not influence the action. As a result, the company commanders found themselves developing their own plans after several hours of stalemate. The officers did not know the terrain and their maps were nearly useless. The lack of radios and the difficulty in using telephones in the attack was part of the problem, and use of messengers was just too slow. Neither the 1st nor the 2nd Battalion had eaten a solid meal since 0400 hours on the sixteenth, and now, on the seventeenth, the men tired quickly.[30]

When the 2nd Battalion hit resistance, and when the 1st Battalion shied to the left, a gap developed between the two battalions, so regiment tapped the reserve battalion for one company to fill the hole. K Company moved into position between B and G companies. The terrain over which K Company moved was wooded and broken, and they had difficulty establishing contact with B and G companies and then had even more difficulty maintaining contact. Men disappeared into gullies or vanished behind thick vegetation. All things considered, the day's progress would have been much more agreeable had the Scout regiment been there to help. Only on the left, in the 1st Battalion, did the Americans reach their objective, the Balantay River. "We accounted for quite a few enemy here," recalled Private Kerchum. "Private First Class Morrison picked off a whole squad that was trying to sneak up on us. They were below us and never knew what hit them."[31]

With the coming of enough light to lead them out of the trail maze, the 45th Infantry spent January 17 trying to get into position. As was the case in its sister regiments, the 45th Infantry was understrength. It had lost three of every four officers and two of every five sergeants as cadre to the Philippine Army, and war arrived before new leaders could be trained. The regiment marched most of the day through tall grass across rugged ground where every ridge line seemed to run perpendicular to the line of march. In one instance the 3rd Battalion spent two hours crossing the steep gorge cut by the Capitangan River. The 2nd Battalion lost contact with the 3rd, and the 3rd Battalion lost, for a time, its medical section, M Company, and all heavy weapons. One officer remembered the march as "cross country on foot, dragging machine guns, mortars and a 37mm gun for miles through jungle, up and down ravines up to 30 feet deep using ropes and vines."[32] The soldiers were hot, hungry, and tired. The Scouts liked to sing Filipino rice-planting songs during marches, but the heat, large loads—ammunition for one day—and terrible terrain left them with hardly enough breath to walk. The only good thing anyone recalled was the sight of two American P-40's that bounced three Japanese planes and downed one of them. This was the first time the infantry had seen friendly planes in action and it was a cheering sight.

Two hours after midnight guides from the 21st Engineer Battalion met and escorted 45th Infantry officers to the command post of the 41st Division, where the senior instructor, 41st Division, and commanders, Philippine Division, 31st and 45th Infantry, were meeting. They hashed out events for the next day, the eighteenth. The predawn conference resulted in agreement to continue the attack. The 45th Infantry would attack any Japanese found between the Americans and the left of the Philippine Army 43rd Infantry. The Scouts would provide the main effort with battalions echeloned to the right. The American regiment would launch a holding attack. Unfortunately, the plan miscarried almost immediately.[33]

The Scout 3rd Battalion missed the 45th Infantry's assembly area, continued marching to the west, and finally stopped next to the left flank of the 31st Infantry facing the Hacienda. Here the Scouts pulled out knives and machetes and cut sugar cane to relieve their thirst. Making a virtue of necessity, the 3rd Battalion was allowed to attack from its present location. It would relieve some of the pressure building to the left of the American 31st Infantry. The battalion commander called his officers together. Major Dudley G. Strickler told his leaders that the line had been broken but that it had been reestablished during the night. He explained that the battalion would counterattack with the 31st Infantry on the right.[34]

The officers returned to their men, the battalion deployed, companies in column, L, I, and K with M dispersed in the rifle companies. At 1200 hours, as the point squad approached the sugar plantation, a shot rang out and the lead Scout fell dead, shot between the eyes. The other Scouts quickly fanned out and advanced through the area without meeting resistance. They passed through what may have been the 51st Infantry's command post where a large quantity of small arms ammunition lay scattered about. The Scouts found a wounded Filipino belonging to the 51st Division and carried him to safety. The man had lain there since the sixteenth without help.[35]

The 3rd Battalion reformed just south of the seven one-story buildings. Major Strickler, a 39-year-old West Pointer, class of 1927 and captain of the Academy's basketball team, called his commanders together and gave his attack order. West Point had been difficult for Strickler—he was sent down from the class of '26 to '27 due to problems in English analysis and composition—and even the peacetime army had proved dull. With an unhurried, lackadaisical personality, he had some noticeable shortcomings; in particular, he had gotten drunk before the war and told off a full colonel. Charges were going to be preferred but were dropped when war broke out. Strickler may never even have known the trouble he faced. War had invigorated him and turned him into one of the finest battalion commanders in the Philippines. A natural, magnificent leader, Strickler had served with troops all but three years of his fourteen-year career. Strickler now made a risky decision and placed all three compa-

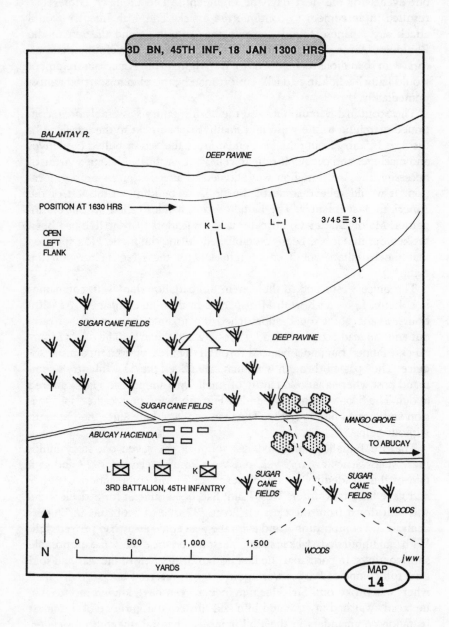

3D BN, 45TH INF, 18 JAN 1300 HRS

BALANTAY R.

DEEP RAVINE

POSITION AT 1630 HRS

OPEN
LEFT
FLANK

K — L   L — I   3/45 ☰ 31

SUGAR CANE FIELDS

DEEP RAVINE

SUGAR CANE FIELDS

MANGO GROVE

ABUCAY HACIENDA

TO ABUCAY

L   I   K

3RD BATTALION, 45TH INFANTRY

SUGAR
CANE
FIELDS

SUGAR
CANE
FIELDS

WOODS

N

0   500   1,000   1,500

YARDS

WOODS

jww

MAP
14

nies on line, leaving none in reserve. It was to prove a wise move. Time was short, too short to allow for a reconnaissance. Just before giving the order to attack, Strickler moved past each officer, offering words of encouragement. Stopping with Lieutenant Ulrich, Strickler asked if Ulrich knew what his job was.[36]

"Yes sir," replied Ulrich, "to keep contact between L and I Companies and keep the men moving forward."

"That's right, and be sure you don't take any unnecessary risks."

The two men sat for a moment in silence. "Well," concluded Strickler, "good luck to you and I'll see you sometime this evening after we halt." They shook hands and Strickler went off to the next officer.

With platoons in column, companies on line, L, I, and K from left to right, the 3rd Battalion crossed the Hacienda at 1300 hours and pushed north. The machine gun platoons, with four .30-caliber water-cooled guns each, were attached one platoon to each company. The battalion's single .50-caliber and lone 81mm mortar were set on the line of departure in support of the battalion. The left flank company advanced in squad column, three platoons on line with scouts forward. The machine guns stayed just in sight of the lead platoons but out of any immediate brawl. Pushing their way through sugar cane with visibility limited to a few feet, the men hiked forward for 250 yards before coming out of the uncut cane into a burned area. Here, Japanese automatic weapons cut accurately through L Company. As the Scouts threw themselves to the ground, the attached machine guns doubled into action and returned a hot fire. The remainder of Captain Pierce's L Company deployed on the skirmish line formed by the foremost men. An officer went to the rear to request mortar fire, but when he tried to locate the enemy on a map, the map was so different from the actual terrain that he could not pinpoint the spot. The mortar fired some rounds in the general direction but none came close. The Japanese gun was finally destroyed by rifle fire.[37]

As L Company continued forward, Japanese fire increased, all of it coming from the left flank. A large draw, covered by enemy fire, delayed the Scouts but they crossed the obstacle without too much trouble. North of the ravine, enemy fire peaked. The Scouts returned the fire and subdued the enemy's initial enthusiasm, but not before L Company and attached machine gunners suffered thirty men killed or wounded. Some of the unhurt men were in shock at seeing the terrible wounds inflicted on their comrades. But the obvious necessity for action forced them to move. The direction of attack was running the men laterally across the front of the Japanese machine guns. The Japanese, not unnaturally, lost little time in taking advantage of the targets. Helping them in their firing was an east-west trail that provided an excellent field of fire. When the

Scouts were within 100 yards of their objective—the abandoned foxholes of the 51st Division—the companies received an order from battalion headquarters to return to the line of departure. This they accomplished but not before L Company suffered more men killed and wounded as they again passed in front of the Japanese. The order to withdraw may have come from the 45th Infantry headquarters, possibly an attempt to correct confusion resulting from the 3rd Battalion's attack. The 3rd Battalion's right flank overlapped and ran up the back of the American's left. Whatever the reason, the order to withdraw was shortsighted in the extreme.[38]

When II Corps heard of the halt they countermanded the order and told the badly used battalion to advance again. Major Strickler shuffled his companies and put K Company on the exposed left flank. Once again the men rose from the protection of the ground and walked forward. Once again the Japanese cut up the left flank company. But this time, by a quick rush across some open ground, the 3rd Battalion reached its objective. The soldiers closed on the scrub-lined ravine overlooking the Balantay River and contacted the Polar Bears to their right. The time was 1630 hours, three and a half hours after the attack started. The battalion's front was 1,400 yards wide with a completely exposed left flank. There was a definite feeling of loneliness way out there on II Corps's left flank. The men lost little time in improving their positions. The Scouts took casualties from Japanese in a mango grove to their front. Scout losses should have been lighter than they were but the men had not yet learned to look into trees for the enemy. Scout machine gunners worked the grove over and shot a few Japanese.[39]

During the night the Japanese infiltrated between the overextended line companies and the battalion command post. Headquarters personnel occupied one-man foxholes ringing their battalion commander. Carrying parties tried to bring up a hot meal, but Japanese ambushed the men in a deep draw. The Japanese used firecrackers to confuse the Scouts, keep them awake, and keep them nervous. The firecrackers also concealed the more deadly crack of real rifles. Because of enemy activity, the companies could not evacuate their dead and had to bury them in their foxholes. When Scouts attempted to move wounded and dead to the rear, more men were hit. The next day at 1700 hours the first food and water seen by the men for two days arrived.[40]

The Japanese, for their part, were surprised by the casual attitude taken by the Scouts when threatened from the flank and rear. "It seems," reads the 65th Brigade report, "that the native Army thinks very little of the threats from the rear. Even though elements of our Army advance close to the rear of the main enemy position, the enemy at the flanks remains and continues firing. Many of them stay hidden, and although they depend on leadership from the rear, they hold their positions even when the surrounding situation is unknown. This is worth studying."[41] Considering the general sensitivity of Filamerican forces to threats from the flank and rear, the Japanese report is surprising. But in this case the Japanese were facing Scouts, and the Scouts were exceptionally capable and courageous soldiers. They would not move from their positions unless physically dragged from them.

The problems encountered by Major Strickler's Scout battalion were only part of a larger picture. To the right of the 31st Infantry waited the 1st and 2nd battalions, 45th Infantry. They remained in contact with regimental headquarters after arriving near the 41st Division and were able to comply with the original attack order. At 1600 hours they attacked north between the 31st and 43rd infantry against very little opposition. The Japanese did not have enough men to press the entire Abucay Line and a thin screen was the best they could manage here. The 1st Battalion advanced followed by the 2nd in reserve. As the Scouts approached their line of departure—a road running east and west along which friendly artillery was firing—a Japanese counterbattery round landed in the middle of Filipino gunners. Expecting a gruesome clean-up job, everyone was relieved to see the only damage was the battery commander's trousers. The round blew the seat off his pants without scratching him or any or the men around him.[42]

The 1st Battalion advanced in columns of platoons, each company 300 yards apart. Despite rolling, semicultivated hills offering good visibility, contact with the trailing 2nd Battalion was lost. About a mile from their start point a sniper killed a man in C Company and wounded two more Scouts in quick succession. Carrying parties evacuated the wounded to the battalion aid station. In some cases the terrain was so bad that wounded men on stretchers had to be lowered from cliffs overlooking deep ravines. The men had to improvise ropes from jungle vines in order to accomplish this. At the aid station medics applied bandages, often while lying in a shallow depression to avoid enemy fire, and took action to stabilize the wounded man's condition. Compresses, bandages, and morphine were normally the only aid available until the patients reached the general hospitals.[43]

Despite losses, the Scouts pressed forward. At the objective the Scouts found a few foxholes and some uncut barbed wire, all once part of the 51st Division's line. Off to the west the Scouts heard heavy firing. The 1st Battalion sent patrols to the east and north but they could not find any friendly troops. To the west, in the direction of the firing, Scout patrols ran into Japanese. By now it was obvious something was wrong. The battalion was no longer intact and the rest of the regiment was nowhere in sight. Once night fell, artillery and small arms rattled and flashed to the east and west. To the rear popped sporadic small arms fire. The next morning the men withdrew and rejoined the rest of the battalion. Messengers had been sent forward the day before to recall the 300 men but the messengers could not find them. The 2nd Battalion's activities on January 18 was likewise unexciting. Two companies went on line with the third in reserve. They received light artillery and mortar fire but nothing severe enough to stop them. Because there were no enemy in sight the attack sailed through the air.[44]

The 45th Infantry's effort accomplished little beyond occupying some ground the Japanese either did not want or could not control. The complete absence of information as to enemy dispositions and intentions lost the Americans a chance to make better use of the 45th Infantry. Less well-trained Philippine Army troops could have moved into this empty area. II Corps was using two Philippine Army divisions—the 21st and 31st—as fire brigades behind the 41st Division. A regiment or more of these units could have replaced the Scouts along the main line. Then the entire 45th Infantry could have switched to the left flank of the 31st Infantry where the Scout 3rd Battalion was already heavily engaged. But not knowing the enemy's intentions, the two battalions of the 45th Infantry remained in a quiet sector. An even greater tactical error was II Corps's failure to order the 57th Infantry into the fight. Over the past four days that regiment had been replaced at Mabatang by Filipinos and the Scouts were available. Admittedly, the Japanese continued to pressure the Philippine Army at Mabatang, but this activity ceased after January 16. Had II Corps been bolder, the 57th Infantry's presence at the Hacienda could have been decisive.[45]

The 31st Infantry on January 18 achieved some local successes but the overall situation did not improve. When enemy machine gun fire stopped the advance of E Company, Private First Class James H. Cody and Private Albert F. Tresch volunteered to go after the weapon. Carrying automatic rifles and hand grenades, Cody and Tresch crawled under the enemy fire to a point close to the gun. Measuring the distance, both men threw grenades and then fired their BAR's. Not only did they destroy the gun and its crew, but their fire silenced another gun long enough to allow the Americans to advance. Both men received the Silver Star.[46]

Although the situation looked bleak to the Americans, the Japanese were also reaching a crisis. Every time they made some progress the defenders rushed up reinforcements and launched a strong counterattack. First their attacks against the 57th Infantry on the East Road were repulsed after the arrival of substantial Filipino reinforcements. Then their attacks against the 41st Division failed when that unit received help from the 31st and 21st divisions. Now their successes against the 51st Division were threatened by counterattacks from the Philippine Division. "The enemy," the Japanese recorded, "who had once started to retreat to the south and east, seemed to have received reinforcements. His flank and rear fire inflicted incalculable casualties. During the afternoon of the 18th, the enemy resistance suddenly became a powerful and stubborn counterattack and eventually stalled our advance . . . the combat situation stagnated."[47] Another Japanese report described units as "battered by fierce enemy resistance and fire power." Both reports refer to the attacks of the 3rd Battalion, 45th Infantry, and the continuing push by the entire 31st Infantry. The Japanese staff officer representing General Nara in this action was wounded during the counterattack.

To get things rolling the Americans attempted a coordinated attack on January 19. The 3rd Battalion was to attack east against the right flank of the enemy, the 2nd Battalion would push north along Trail 12, and the two 45th Infantry battalions were to attack the Japanese left. In the battalions, officers gathered at their command posts, no more than a spot on the ground where they dropped their bedrolls and unfolded their maps. Nearby, battalion surgeons readied their small aid stations for casualties. The 41st Artillery provided some artillery fire in support of the effort but artillery support was limited. It was difficult to get cannon far enough west into the rough terrain where they could shoot effectively. Those guns in range could do little because of dense forests, bad maps, and inadequate communications. When Lieutenant Heintzleman, an intrepid forward observer, tried to move his telephone forward to call fires, Japanese shot and killed him. Lieutenant Colonel Lester J. Tacy, another artilleryman, was wounded as he tried to rescue Heintzleman. More serious was the absence of large quantities of mortar fire. The 2nd Battalion deployed F, G, and E companies from left to right. After a few rounds of artillery the men entered the big ravine but fragmented in the thick underbrush. "The ravine was very deep," recalled Private Garleb, "the sides were perpendicular, and we climbed down on vines. We crossed a knee-deep creek and climbed the other side with our machine gun. At the top, I heard Japanese sergeants yelling fire commands to their men."[48] Men became lost, leaders disappeared when they went scouting, and confusion prevailed.

When Major O'Donovan arrived at G Company at 1730 hours, he gave the order "attack at once," and some progress was made. Crawling up a dry waterfall using rifles to hoist and pull each other up, one rifle and one weapons platoon worked their way out of the ravine. But it was dark when they reached the top. Behind them, another platoon reached the top and engaged a group of Japanese. In the dark no one could tell what was happening, and a coordinated effort was impossible. Corporal Stanley P. Nogacek was accidently killed by his own men as he came back from a reconnaissance. Both platoons received orders to return to their start point. Groping through the pitch-dark ravine, the men felt their way across the rocky creek and pulled themselves up the cliff. "The attack started about 1600 and ended at 1900 in much confusion," recalled Lieutenant Conrad in F Company. "The objective was not taken. I am not sure to this day just what the objective was except the enemy."[49] Similar troubles were experienced by all units. A full battalion effort might see one or two platoons actually fighting while the remainder stumbled about looking for the enemy.

The Air Corps launched a strike on January 19 in an effort to improve the lot of the men on the ground. Four P-40's bounced two dive bombers and shot them down. But this time a P-40 was also lost. First Lieutenant Marshall J. Anderson, a veteran of the successful strike two days earlier, bailed out of his damaged P-40 only to have Japanese pilots shoot at his parachute, collapse it, and drop him to his death.[50]

At the Hacienda faulty hand grenades proved fatal to one man. When machine gun fire hit B Company, 31st Infantry, Private First Class Ronald T. Wangberg volunteered to destroy the weapon. Crawling close to the enemy position, he threw one grenade which exploded but he missed the gun. So he crawled even farther forward and threw a second grenade, but this one was a dud. The Japanese saw Wangberg, fired, and killed him. When reports of bad ammunition filtered into D Company, supply sergeant Michael Gilewitch checked his company's ammunition. Some grenades contained very little powder while others held none at all. Other men unscrewed the grenade's cap, emptied the bad explosives, cleaned the detonator by soaking it in gasoline, dried it, coated it with oil, added dry rifle powder, and reassembled it. The Japanese were similarly troubled with poor ammunition. Although their hand grenades functioned well and the burst was loud, the fragmentation effect was slight. Japanese rifle grenades were corrugated to increase fragmentation effects, but many were duds.[51]

The only progress made on January 19 was in the 45th Infantry's sector. There the Scouts followed the same axis used the day before by the 1st Battalion and reached the Balantay River. The regiment now held a low hill line overlooking a mile-wide valley. Well covered and concealed draws led into Scout positions, giving Japanese the opportunity to slip close undetected. But little activity ensued. The Scouts removed and buried dead Filipinos found in their foxholes. These were some of the casualties suffered by the 51st Division, men who had not run but had fought to the death. The Scouts also collected numerous automatic weapons and a large amount of ammunition.[52]

In a frustrating stalemate the Americans and Scouts launched attack after attack on January 20 and 21 while their higher headquarters watched the Japanese increase their pressure on the far left battalions. The 3rd Battalion's effort on January 20 to reduce Japanese positions dug into a mango grove fared poorly. Shortly after 0800 hours mortarmen fired eighty rounds of the new 81mm mortar ammunition. The fire was accurate and all rounds detonated. The battalion crossed a deep ravine and cleared the other side by 1100 hours. Then I and L companies moved through a cornfield and into a canefield where they were stopped. A Japanese machine gun sprayed Corporal Burton C. Ellis and another man as they scouted in front of I Company. Bullets hit Ellis in both legs and tumbled him to the ground. Other Americans could not reach him, and he lay in the blazing sun all day. The tight leggings covering his legs and ankles served as pressure bandages and kept him from bleeding to death. That evening a Filipino doctor carrying a small lantern found Ellis, and aided by a helper carried him to safety. It was a strange experience for Ellis, lightheaded from loss of blood and a bad case of sunburn, to see the doctor and his lantern.[53]

To the right of Ellis, L Company was ordered to attack the grove. Two patrols led the way. Skirmishes broke out and several Japanese were killed. Then another patrol led by Sergeant C. E. Clegg spotted some Japanese sitting in a grove, apparently without security. Private P. J. Chamonte climbed a tree and counted seventy enemy. Platoon leaders moved the Americans into position, using hand and arm signals, positioned some to fire into the grove and placed others to watch for Japanese in trees. On order, the entire company fired. Several Japanese were hit but the survivors reacted quickly, laid down heavy automatic weapons fire, and immediately wounded seven Americans. First aid dressings were placed on the wounded and medics evacuated them to the 2nd Battalion aid station. Medic John Lally carried several casualties to safety and was wounded in the process. Later, a mortar shell blew Lally into the air and partially blinded him. No advance was possible against this fire and the Americans scrambled back to the cover of the big ravine. Lieutenant Thompson requested mortars be fired at the Japanese position but the request was denied.[54]

Just before noon Captain Pray from the 2nd Battalion became impatient, for the three rifle companies of the 2nd Battalion were supposed to follow the 3rd Battalion and exploit their successes. Pray waited for thirty minutes and then went forward to see what was happening. He did not know what the 3rd Battalion plan was, nor was he able to find anyone who did. Pray decided to do something. By 1730 hours he had maneuvered his company, now reduced to just fifty-five men, around and behind the mango grove. "That's when everything turned loose," recalled Private Taylor. "There was Jap rifle and machine gun fire from everywhere in front of us."[55] Two men were killed and eight wounded. Sergeant Heimie Bograd, a long-service soldier, emplaced his water-cooled .30-caliber and started firing. A mortar shell exploded under the barrel and rolled the heavy gun on top of the crew, but miraculously no one was hurt and the crew righted the gun and continued firing. Captain Pray's effort stalled when reinforcements failed to arrive. As the Americans pulled back, one man averted a small disaster. Machine guns from M Company were supporting I Company but in the confusion a crew set its sights on an I Company light machine gun. Sergeant George F. Braga saw the danger but realized his voice would not carry over the noise of battle. He made a frantic dash to M Company and arrived just in time to stop the gun from firing. For his presence of mind Braga received the DSC. Four days later he received an Oak Leaf Cluster to the DSC for another heroic act.

Nothing was going right. Frustration stole over the American officers and men. Patrols tried to develop the situation. K Company dispatched some men to find the enemy, and "not long after, what was left of the patrol came back," remembered Private Kerchum. "One guy kept saying 'watch my thumb' which was half shot off, but he didn't realize half of his leg was gone. I asked him what happened. 'The grenades we threw at the machine gun position didn't go off.' "[56] There was an absolute absence of information on the enemy despite having fought him for several days. Nor was information about friendly locations much more complete. Many units operated without maps, and overlays and rough terrain sketches were crude and limited in value. Communications between battalions and companies were more often out than in. Two Americans were killed while laying telephone wire a quarter of a mile from the regiment's command post. The lush vegetation was blasted from the earth and the hills became a wasteland. A single Scout artillery battery received seventy-two 12-round salvos from Japanese artillery in a space of six hours. Casualties everywhere were severe. L Company, 45th Infantry, arrived at the Hacienda on January 18 with 131 officers and men. When they finally withdrew, they walked out with 79. Food carriers had to operate at night, for movement during the day was fatal.

Daily reports of the fighting reached MacArthur and he relayed them to Washington. "In Luzon, heavy fighting on the center where enemy infiltrators were thrown back and all lines restored. Fighting was of a peculiarly savage character and losses heavy."[57] Between January 20 and

24 the 31st Infantry repulsed ten enemy attacks. The Americans halted the Japanese each time, but each attack was more difficult to stop than the last. Along K Company's front one Japanese attack was repulsed only after the Japanese came very close indeed. An American picked up a shoe poking from a bush. Inside the shoe was a foot, and the foot was still attached to a Japanese killed only a yard from the foxhole line. Enemy soldiers came so close that Americans still retain a vivid memory of hearing Japanese sergeants shouting to their men barely thirty yards away. One Japanese party attacked a machine gun and all but one were gunned down. The surviving soldier continued his one-man charge until the machine gunner, his weapon now empty, drew his pistol, took careful aim, and felled him. "There were so many Japanese killed," remembered Private Wilburn Snyder, "that machine gun fields of fire were blocked by the bodies. The stench and the flies got real bad."[58]

Private Forrest F. Dreger, K Company, was dodging from one point to another when enemy machine gun fire found him. He dropped to the ground, supporting himself slightly by one arm. As he watched, a burst passed between his arm and the ground, failing to hit him, but the bullets kicked up a clod of dirt which hit his thumb so hard he thought it was broken. During this close combat, ammunition resupply by ordinary means was impractical. Private Dreger went to the rear and loaded himself with several dozen bandoliers of M-1 ammunition. The men threw the cloth bandoliers from one foxhole to the next. Dead Japanese became a major resupply point. Americans took rations from Japanese bodies to supplement their meager fare, and it seemed that every dead Japanese carried American money. Some men collected thousands of dollars but then had no place to spend it. Sixteen-year-old Grant Workman helped repulse the Japanese attacks. He lied about his age when he enlisted at South Bend, Indiana, at the tender age of fifteen. In Indiana, Workman had used his grandfather's shotgun to shoot rabbits, but the rabbits never shot back. "So my first experience at shooting Japs was quite different," Workman recalls. "I recall looking down my M-1 rifle sights at the first Jap I shot at, but soon realized that I was in a position of shoot or get shot. After the first shot it came easier, then developed into eagerness to kill every Jap that I could."[59]

Although Japanese attacks were steadily weakening American and Scout units, losses were also mounting in Japanese units. By the close of January 22 the 65th Brigade recorded losses of 342 men killed and 777 wounded, losses completely unacceptable if a quick result could not be obtained. Despite all they could do to force the issue, the Japanese admitted that "the enemy, showing no signs of retreating, was resisting with increased tenacity."[60]

Gloom was equally thick in Filamerican units. Ominous reports were reaching II Corps headquarters of Japanese moving south along the slopes of Mount Natib. On January 19 a three-man Scout patrol hiding on Mount Natib watched the Japanese 9th Infantry walk by just yards from their position. The 9th Infantry's march through the jungle clinging to the side of Mount Natib was horrible. This was the same terrain that the Americans had considered impassible. Now, the Japanese would certainly have agreed. Countless ravines and valleys, cut by heavy water flows, ran across their line of march and slowed the column to a crawl. Some gullies were absolutely impossible to climb and utterly defeated the tired infantrymen until they strung climbing ropes or cut zig-zag trails by hand. Trails along the mountain wandered aimlessly or came to abrupt halts. Even pack horses could not keep up with the men, and they had to be hauled up and down cliffs with ropes. The effort expended in moving the regiment's heavy weapons was enormous. When elements broke contact they found it virtually impossible to find one another again. Although practically all Japanese supplies were wrapped securely in heavy, tightly-woven straw bags and matting and were easily carried by man, cart, or pack animals, the soldiers ran out of food on January 23. They found and killed a few carabao, dug and ate grass roots, and resorted to every field expedient possible to gather food. Resupply from their own lines this far south was impossible, and air drops were unreliable. The 9th Infantry needed to link with other Japanese units, and the only way to do that was to drive out the Filipinos.[61]

At noon on January 19 civilians reported that Japanese were descending the mountain toward the little barrio of Guitol, well behind II Corps's main line. The only units available to meet this threat were remnants of the 51st Division, a single battalion of the 21st Division, and parts of the 31st Division. When Colonel O'Day heard about the Japanese he told General Capinpin, using the byword so popular at division headquarters, "Sir, we are surrounded."[62] Capinpin smiled as he recognized the division's unofficial motto, but O'Day continued, "No, this is true this time. An enemy patrol is down on the river and the 21st Infantry has sent a patrol to investigate." The patrol from the 3rd Battalion, 21st Infantry, soon returned with the battalion commander, Captain Pennell—veteran of the Mabatang fight—wounded from a bullet that struck his submachine gun and smashed his right hand. The incident spurred the 31st Division into action.

Elements deployed to the north and west, and soon a full-fledged fight was in progress. The Filipinos fired madly but were unable to see or hit any Japanese. Japanese machine guns and light mortars searched the thin Filipino line. The 21st Division headquarters, whose job was to collect and organize 51st Division stragglers, felt to do so in the middle of a battle was impossible. Japanese .25-caliber bullets were cutting through trees, bringing down branches, and mortar fire was falling into bivouac areas. Colonel O'Day phoned II Corps and requested permission to move. "Johns[t]on [the operations officer] could hear the firing, bullets hitting the limbs of the trees above my head as I phoned," recalled O'Day, "and it convinced him my idea, approved by General Capinpin, was well founded."[63]

When General Bluemel arrived at Guitol he found everything in consternation and excitement; no one could tell him anything definite except that Colonel Louis D. Hutson, commanding the 33rd Infantry, had been severely wounded by a bullet through the hip. Bullets cracked through the CP every few minutes, and because it was about to get dark, Bluemel took his soldiers in hand, formed an all-around defense with the men elbow to elbow, and ordered fixed bayonets and absolutely no firing. If the Japanese attacked, the men were to use the bayonet. The minute the Filipinos stopped shooting, friendly casualties ceased. By the time a counterattack could be launched the next day, the Japanese had voluntarily departed for quieter quarters with only minimal losses.[64]

During the next two days, January 20 and 21, the Japanese facing II Corps completed preparations for what they hoped would be the final attack of the Abucay fight. Colonel Imai was gradually shifting the bulk of his 141st Infantry westward, around the open left flank of the Scout 3rd Battalion. Despite extensive use of Scout mortars to break up enemy movements, the high proportion of dud rounds in the 3-inch rounds rendered the mortars relatively impotent. At noon on January 22, after several days of preparation, the Japanese launched another effort. They massed large air and artillery forces and the bombardment fell most heavily on the American 1st Battalion. All available Japanese bombers and fighters swept in to help their infantry. Japanese pilots amused themselves by diving low across the battlefield, grinning and waving at the frustrated Americans. Knee mortars added to the pounding. So many rounds impacted that dust and smoke hid the advancing Japanese. Brush fires burst out in dry cane fields and raised curtains of smoke. With visibility disappearing, the Americans became disorganized. On the heels of the Japanese air and artillery came the infantry. Grudgingly, out of touch with friends on both flanks, the 31st Infantry recoiled. "I was standing up getting ready to withdraw," remembered Private Kerchum, "when a mortar blast knocked me out. When I came to, my helmet was destroyed and two palm trees were completely cut down."[65]

Seeing this movement, the Scout battalion on the far left spent a nervous hour before it received orders to withdraw south of the Hacienda to act as a reserve for the Americans. Under orders, the Scouts broke contact. Two squads of riflemen and a machine gun crew from the left flank company were sent back to dig in and form a base on which the remainder of the men could rally. Beginning at 1400 hours, the 3rd Battalion withdrew under the cover of four machine guns, a squad of riflemen, and the battalion executive officer. An officer noted with pride that the battalion brought out all its own ammunition and equipment as well as machine gun belts, mortar rounds, grenades, and rifle ammunition abandoned earlier by other units. The 3rd Battalion, 31st Infantry, now exposed on both flanks, also withdrew. Despite forcing the Americans backwards, the Japanese did not feel they were making any progress. Their slight advances were accomplished only after extreme efforts against a cohesive defense. The Americans were massed, and their firepower was impressive. Against this resistance the Japanese entertained little hope for a sudden breakthrough. The battle was boiling down to who would last the longest—whoever lost heart first would lose.[66]

By late afternoon of January 22 the Philippine Division was back to its January 19 positions. The Americans had suffered heavily in men and equipment. Some companies lost 60 percent of their strength. Especially galling was the complete air superiority enjoyed by the Japanese. Scout and Filipino artillery were finding it increasingly difficult to fire without being smothered by enemy counter-battery fire directed by aerial spotters. Japanese planes started dropping tin cans and rocks with their bombs, or sometimes only cans and rocks and no bombs. The odd-shaped missiles made a terrible racket. Americans crouched in foxholes wondered if there were bombs mixed with the noisy trash. After enemy planes disappeared the men were still reluctant to leave cover. Even inoffensive observation planes took shots at the defenders. The Japanese had welded fins on captured American artillery shells and would chuck them out open cockpits at the infantrymen. The Americans were especially nervous about the reconnaissance aircraft, for the men felt the planes could see every individual, regardless of his camouflage.[67]

On the afternoon of January 23 the Japanese continued their flanking movement and drove between the outposts of the small 51st Division screen, shot up Colonel Boatwright's regimental command post, and routed the personnel. The next day two flights of nine and eleven planes worked over the center of the American 31st Infantry. A bomb landed next to a machine gunner and the concussion exploded a grenade carried in his gas mask carrier, mortally wounding him. Another bomb passed through the limbs of a huge tree covering a two-man foxhole and exploded between two soldiers. There was little left to bury. When these planes finished they were followed by seven more groups of dive bombers which kept the area under attack all afternoon.[68]

Conflicting conclusions were drawn by Generals Parker and Nara at the close of January 22. General Parker surveyed his II Corps and realized that "it was now evident that the MLR in the 51st Division sector could not be restored by the Philippine Division."[69] The counterattack which might have saved the Abucay Line had failed. The situation was now so bad the Japanese might drive all of II Corps against Manila Bay and end the Bataan defense. The biggest threat was the emergence of the Japanese 9th Infantry after its trek along the "impenetrable" slopes of Mount Natib. Only its continuing difficulty with the terrain kept it from sweeping through II Corps's rear.

Despite his relatively advantageous position, General Nara was displeased with the progress of his 65th Brigade. Indications were that all his efforts had been in vain. Nara saw no end to the punishing fighting and the terrible attrition of his units. The volume of Filipino artillery fire was increasing again and he was worried about another counterattack, while restrictions placed on Japanese artillery prevented them from doing all they could. Numerous targets were sighted, but they were not allowed to engage them. If this bloody fighting continued Nara felt sure he would run out of soldiers. Every time it seemed he might break through, he was hit by a vicious counterattack. "Indignant in a towering rage," Nara could see no hope of victory.[70] Even so, he pushed his men forward day after day. As serious as the loss of personnel was the decline in spirit.

Both sides were ready to quit.

CHAPTER ELEVEN

Attack on I Corps

BEFORE REVIEWING II CORPS'S RETREAT AND THE JAPANESE REAC-
tion, the situation on Bataan's west coast must be examined. When the
Japanese began planning for the reduction of Bataan, they decided that
prospects for success were more favorable on the east coast than on the
west. They therefore assigned relatively minor forces for a subsidiary
effort in the west. To operate along the west coast, General Nara organized a force around the 122nd Infantry, a battalion of field artillery, a
platoon of engineers, and miscellaneous support troops. Led by Colonel
Yunosuke Watanabe, their objective was the town of Bagac.[1]

The Japanese occupied the port of Olongapo on January 10, and two
days later they seized Grande Island at the entrance to Subic Bay. Then
they assembled barges, boats, and sundry floating craft in Subic Bay. On
the same day, General Homma decided to reinforce the 65th Brigade
elements facing Wainwright. Homma's reinforcements came from the
16th Division's 20th Infantry. The 20th Infantry arrived with only two of
its three battalions; the third would join later. Artillery support was provided by half the regimental gun battery of the 33rd Infantry and an
antitank battery. These men departed Manila for Bataan on January 15.
Although Homma believed success would come from operations along
the Manila Bay coast, he now hoped to overwhelm both corps at the
same time. If he could keep pressure on both corps, he could prevent the
defenders from switching forces from one side of the peninsula to the
other to meet the more serious threat. Such a movement had already
occurred when the 31st Division marched from I to II Corps and prevented disaster there by the narrowest of margins. On the evening of
January 15 Homma made some command changes. He relieved Nara of

209

responsibility for Bataan's western side and created the Kimura Detachment, named for Major General Naoki Kimura, commander of the 16th Division's Infantry Group. With attachments, Kimura's force numbered 5,000 men, which he organized into two wings. The 3rd Battalion, 20th Infantry, was to hit the Filipinos on their inland flank. The 122nd Infantry would attack along the West Road. Kimura kept the 2nd Battalion, 20th Infantry, in reserve.[2]

Japanese preparations were still well north of Wainwright's I Corps, but Japanese occupation of Olongapo was countered by a brief Filipino occupation of Moron, a small fishing barrio of thirty to forty huts three miles north of the most advanced Filipino outposts. MacArthur's staff had considered Moron as a site to anchor I Corps's left flank, but a long sandy beach south of the town offered too good an opportunity for a Japanese amphibious landing. The Filipino occupation of Moron was short-lived, partially because of the absence of suitable fields of fire and an overly exposed supply line. Wainwright withdrew the soldiers from Moron two days later when there was no further southward movement of the Japanese. I Corps's left flank ended up on Mauban covered by a steep ridge.[3]

The terrain in I Corps was extremely rugged, almost completely wooded and virtually uninhabited. Wainwright's engineer officer was Colonel Harry A. Skerry, an exuberant, energetic Brooklyn native who graduated from the University of California in 1912 with an engineering degree, and was commissioned in 1917. Known to some as "Pat" in honor of his Irish background and to others as "Hurry" Skerry, he was technically qualified from attendance at both the Infantry and Engineer School Company Officers' courses as well as the Command and General Staff School. He had been the commander of the 14th Engineer Regiment (PS) until December 4 when he was assigned as the North Luzon Force Engineer. He described the ground occupied by I Corps as presenting "a most formidable appearance of very high timbered banks with a solid mass of woods stretching east to a high mountain range, heavily timbered throughout, except for a break at Bagac and Moron."[4] The area was so heavily cloaked in dense, luxuriant tropical undergrowth that travel, even in the dry season, required a map, compass, and a sharp bolo. Mountains reared up from the west coast and formed the western half of the twin Mount Silanganan-Mount Natib. The giant volcano cone rose abruptly from the shore, and the years had carved deep ravines now filled with swift streams. Mount Silanganan shades Moron until the sun clears the mountain's crest, therefore Silanganan, "where the sun rises."[5] Communications—radio, wire, and messenger—were poor. The all-weather road running from Moron to Bagac was surfaced with crushed rock.

To add strength to the natural advantages offered by the terrain, Filipino labor and combat engineer battalions developed defensive positions during the first week in January. They bent their efforts to building roads and trails, laying mines, building gun emplacements, clearing fields of fire, digging foxholes, and stringing barbed wire. Colonel Skerry inspected progress and found the work to be half completed. The outpost line had good fields of fire, but too much of the scarce barbed wire was used there, leaving the regimental reserve line short of wire. On the main line the Filipinos dug their foxholes too close to the wire, a shortcoming which subsequently allowed the Japanese to throw hand grenades into defensive positions from just outside the entanglements.[6]

Along I Corps's outpost line of resistance stretched a screen of 26th Cavalrymen, positioned there late on January 10. G Troop was small, only three officers and seventy-five Scouts, and they were tired. Two platoons of two squads each, a corporal and seven men in each squad, could cover only so much ground. The commander, Captain John M. Fowler, had vigorously trained his men before the war in withdrawals, delaying actions, counterattacks, cover and concealment. Partly as a result, his troop suffered the fewest casualties in the regiment during the withdrawal from the north. The entire 26th Cavalry was equally well trained. Although the regiment was small and under-equipped, regimental officers believed there was not another regiment in the entire US Army with better morale, better training, or more ready for a fight than the 26th Cavalry. Captain Fowler's mission was to provide early warning of Japanese attacks and confuse the enemy as to location of the main line. Fowler dispatched two-man patrols on horseback to establish contact with the Japanese. His men sighted Japanese patrols, and some contact resulted; one officer and two Scouts were killed.[7]

Behind the outpost line, the 3rd Infantry held the main line from the coast part way up Mount Silanganan. The 3rd Infantry and the 1st Engineer Battalion worked tirelessly to construct trenches, wire entanglements, and mine fields. The 3rd Infantry strung double-apron barbed wire, but the rest of I Corps had to settle for whatever obstacles the jungle and naturally rough terrain provided. A battalion of the sister 1st Infantry occupied a regimental reserve line which straddled the West Road, while the remainder of the 1st Infantry sat in 1st Division reserve. The 1st Battalion, 92nd Infantry, was attached to Brigadier General Fidel V. Segundo's 1st Division and added a little depth to the line.[8]

Stretched to the right of the 1st Division was the 2nd Battalion, 31st Artillery, a three-battery unit formed, lightly equipped, and deployed to fight as infantry because they had no cannon. On the extreme right of Wainwright's line, and with the impossible mission of establishing contact with II Corps's left flank, was K Company, 1st Infantry. On January 11

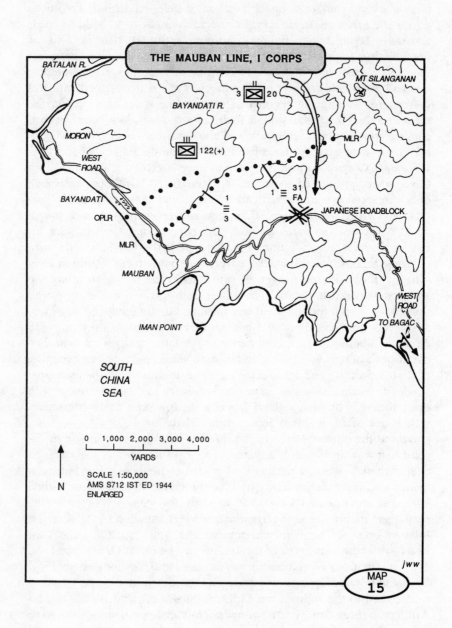

THE MAUBAN LINE, I CORPS

BATALAN R.

MT SILANGANAN

3 ⊠ 20

BAYANDATI R.

MORON

122(+)

MLR

WEST ROAD

BAYANDATI

1 ≡ 31 FA

1 ≡ 3

OPLR

JAPANESE ROADBLOCK

MLR

MAUBAN

WEST ROAD

TO BAGAC

IMAN POINT

SOUTH CHINA SEA

0   1,000 2,000 3,000 4,000

YARDS

N

SCALE 1:50,000
AMS S712 IST ED 1944
ENLARGED

jww

MAP
15

USAFFE ordered that contact between the two corps be "actual and physical," and that all avenues of hostile approach be defended, to include the rough areas in the center of the peninsula. The message was a result of MacArthur's visit to Bataan the day before. General Sutherland had told both corps commanders to shift troops into the unoccupied areas on Mount Natib-Silanganan. Wainwright did not believe the Japanese could maneuver there, nor did he have sufficient men to occupy the ground. But Sutherland was adamant that the area had to be covered. A visit on January 12 from USAFFE's forward headquarters by the quiet, professorial-looking Brigadier General Marshall raised again the problem over the hole between the corps. Wainwright again said the terrain was too rugged for the enemy to use. It was I Corps's mission to maintain contact with II Corps, but a 1st Division patrol dispatched to establish contact with II Corps could not get past the western slopes of Mount Silanganan. Another patrol led by Major Salvador T. Villa confirmed that the 1st Division was occupying positions along the mountain's slopes, but even Major Villa's men could not push their way through the impossible terrain. The four-man patrol was gone three days, traversed razor-sharp ridges, climbed down deep gorges and up vertical ravines, and crept through wild tropical growth, but still failed to find the left flank of II Corps. When they reported back to I Corps they were in a terribly dilapidated state.[9]

Artillery along the Mauban Line consisted of an odd collection of cannon. Lieutenant Colonel Halstead C. Fowler had his 71st Artillery staff and the 2nd and 3rd battalions, 71st Artillery, with seven 75mm's and eight Vickers 2.95-inch mountain howitzers respectively. These Filipino artillerymen were veterans of the artillery duel at Layac on January 6. Twelve more mountain howitzers came from A Battery, 23rd Artillery (four tubes), and from the 1st Battalion, 91st Artillery (eight tubes). A four-gun 75mm SPM battery and two 155mm's rounded out the thirty-three gun "Groupment Fowler." Most of the cannon were sited along Mauban Ridge and on the high ground to the northeast.[10]

On January 14 the Japanese gathered their gear and marched toward Moron. Part of the 122nd Infantry embarked in boats and sailed for Moron, but because of poor maps and unfamiliar terrain they landed north of the town. After linking with foot elements marching south along the coast, the Japanese closed to within a mile of Moron by the morning of January 16. Their approach did not go undetected. The 1st Division's intelligence officer was receiving accurate reports about the advance and, the day before, General Segundo ordered the 1st Infantry (-) and his engineer battalion back to Moron. The cannon of two artillery battalions, carried by light trucks, displaced forward to give support. When the

Japanese crossed the Batalan River the morning of January 16 they hit 3rd Lieutenant Daniel L. Ledda's I Company and pushed through the burned-out town toward the waiting 1st Infantry. A general engagement ensued, casualties mounted, and the Japanese stalled. Major Osa S. Mc-Collum, commanding the 1st Infantry, was shot in the head, but his helmet prevented a fatal wound. Colonel Kearie L. Berry, a brave, energetic, resourceful officer, took command of the 1st Infantry pending a replacement for McCollum. Wainwright, reasonably certain his inland flank was too rugged for an enemy advance, had always believed the main enemy attack would come along the coast, so the enemy's effort at Moron seemed to confirm his belief. Wainwright drove to Mauban Ridge and placed Captain John Z. Wheeler's combined Troop E-F, consolidated earlier because of losses north of Bataan, at the disposal of the 1st Infantry. Wainwright also called up a company of tanks, C Company, 194th Tank Battalion, but when a reconnaissance spotted at least one enemy antitank gun, the tank attack was abandoned.[11]

General Segundo, a Scout officer who had once commanded a cavalry troop himself, welcomed the horsemen. Segundo was a 1917 Military Academy graduate and had served with both artillery and cavalry. From 1929 to 1940 service as Assistant and then Commandant of Cadets at the University of the Philippines for seven years and then as a staff officer at Philippine Army level took him away from real soldiering for eleven years. He rejoined troops in mid-1940, but his experiences left him ill-prepared to be a division commander. His leadership technique seemed to be to swear fluently in several languages, and he spent much of his time swearing at his soldiers and his staff for their stupidity. Segundo decided to counterattack, and he gathered a composite force of cavalrymen, engineers, and infantry. Colonel Fowler's guns preceded the attack with a half-hour artillery preparation, no doubt something of a shock to the Japanese. Under the reassuring sound of Fowler's cannon, American officers led the rested Scouts of Troop E-F at a trot through rice paddies into a wooded area surrounding Moron. Lieutenant Ramsey pushed a small advance guard into the town. "As we neared the town," remembers Captain Wheeler, "our artillery barrage lifted and left an unearthly quiet. Riding in between the houses with pistols raised, we did not know what was going to hit us, but knew something would."[12] Halfway to the town square, Wheeler's point received Japanese machine gun fire, an easily identified snapping sound. In the advance guard was 19-year-old Private First Class Pedro Euperio. He spotted three men in Philippine Army uniforms and galloped forward to investigate. When the three men fired at him and hit him several times in the upper body, Euperio dismounted, returned the fire with his pistol, and chased the

Japanese. The other Scout skirmishers deployed and rode through the town in groups of four abreast, yelling and firing, turning into side streets and charging surprised Japanese. Under heavy fire the exposed Scouts took cover after suffering one killed and three wounded.

Farther back, Captain Wheeler's main body went into dismounted action. They tied their mounts between some nipa huts and started crawling down the road along two gutters. They cautiously crept up to Lieutenant Ramsey's point, and the first thing Captain Wheeler saw was Private Euperio. Euperio was drenched in blood, propped against a house. Holding a pistol in his one good hand, he directed Wheeler's men how to advance, warning about spots under enemy fire. The Scouts shot at noises and the sounds of enemy firing, and when they swept through the town they found many Japanese sprawled in death. The cavalrymen reached the beach, turned, and attacked back through the woods, sweeping south and killing Japanese under houses, in trees, and under bushes. When twenty Japanese broke and threw their equipment into the high grass, Captain Wheeler walked along grabbing maps and compasses. Then the reinforced Japanese swarmed against Wheeler's men, cut off twenty-five horses, and forced the Scouts out of Moron. The Scouts fought hard, and their only concern was for the safety of their American officers. "Don't go there, sir, I will go," was a constant refrain.[13]

In an effort to support Captain Wheeler's action, Major Alva R. Fitch, a 1930 graduate of West Point from Nebraska and one-time aide to Army Chief of Staff Leslie J. McNair, advanced a battery of 2.95-inch howitzers. Fitch's own four guns, part of Colonel Fowler's artillery groupment, hurried into position only 500 yards from the fighting. These were British mountain howitzers, Vickers, made late in the nineteenth century with a range of about 5,000 yards. The cannon had no recoil mechanism, so the gunners ran ropes through the wheels and staked them to the ground to absorb the recoil. Because Fitch's men had not seen action before, and because of the unclear conditions forward of the guns, Fitch walked forward to reconnoiter. As he approached the front, Fitch met Major McCollum coming out. A Japanese soldier had bounced a bullet off his head.[14]

Fitch tried to find the command post but ran into some snipers. They had infiltrated into all parts of the position so that when Fitch found the cavalry horses and tried to approach them, he drew so much fire that he retreated. Major Fitch put his liaison section in a ditch and continued forward to find a spot from which he could observe the fall of shot. As he rounded a turn in the trail, he spotted an enemy machine gun about fifty feet away. Fitch and his enemy saw each other at the same time, and Fitch dove quickly back around the corner, so quickly that he lost two hand grenades that were clipped to his belt. Fitch landed on his face with machine gun bullets buzzing past his ears like flights of bees. Fitch, sans grenades, thought it impractical to attack the machine gun with a pistol, so he went back to collect some Filipino riflemen and a machine gun of his own. When he tried to adjust some artillery on the enemy position, he nearly landed two rounds on his own men. Deciding to charge with his squad of infantry, Fitch and his men overran the enemy position only to find the Japanese gone. Fitch's infantry career ended when his colonel radioed him and ordered he stop playing corporal. Encouraged by the artillery fire and the cavalry attack, the 1st Infantry drove the Japanese against the Batalan River and then across it out of Moron.[15]

But the next morning the Japanese received reinforcements, attacked the Filipinos, penetrated the town, and secured the ruins. Three cavalry Scouts had remained near Moron, protecting the twenty-five horses cut off the day before. In the morning a detail led by two American officers tried to recover the horses. Major C. A. Thorpe, I Corps's provost marshal, was wounded, and Lieutenant Hardewicke killed, but the patrol reached First Sergeant Belhara and his two troopers and guided them to safety. Farther inland, Japanese patrols were active. A "rather incredible report" arrived in the 1st Division's headquarters about a large Japanese force moving toward Mount Silanganan. The report was more true than incredible. One Japanese patrol penetrated the 1st Infantry and fired on divisional engineers 400 yards behind the front line. The engineers stopped working, took up their rifles, and returned the fire. Later in the day a depleted Filipino infantry company arrived and drove the Japanese back to their own lines. Just before dark Wainwright's men at Moron withdrew, in good order and according to plan, through their outposts to a commanding ridge a mile and a half to the south.[16]

The 1st Infantry took position to the right of the 3rd Infantry, but attempts to extend the 1st Infantry's line up Mount Silanganan failed. Colonel Berry, now commanding both the 1st and 3rd infantry, was a veteran soldier who began his service in 1917 as a private with the Texas National Guard. Promotion in the post-World War I Army was slow, and it took him fifteen years to advance from captain to major, a common occurrence. The 48-year-old infantryman now sent a rifle company to extend the flank, but the untrained Filipinos stopped at the first line of bamboo. A few intrepid souls ventured to the next woodline, but within minutes all returned to their start point. Colonel Berry gave them hell and sent them forward again, but with the same results. Berry was never able to get them into position.[17]

Despite a seemingly good day of battle, not all was well with Wainwright's new line. Several days earlier Wainwright had lost the 31st Division to II Corps, and because the division had defended I Corps's beaches, he was forced to replace them with the four-battalion 91st Division. Although the 91st Division took over the 31st Division's lines, the newcomers were not as powerful or efficient as the men they replaced. The 91st Division was especially short of automatic weapons. It had stocks of .50-caliber ammunition but no .50-caliber machine guns. To cover his inland flank and create some depth, Wainwright removed the 72nd Infantry from beach defense and placed it astride the Pilar-Bagac Road seven miles south of the main line. Artillerymen dug gun positions along Mauban Ridge and on high ground northeast of the coast. Artillerymen placed a battery of guns along a second ridge about 300 yards farther south, a job involving exhausting work. Battery personnel cut trails from virgin jungle while keeping an eye open for Japanese planes.[18]

The Japanese launched an attack on January 18 and drove in Wainwright's outpost line with little difficulty. Wainwright now knew he was in for a fight. The Japanese advanced a company near the coast directly onto an artillery registration point. An American forward observer called in the sighting, and three Filipino batteries laid a heavy concentration into the area, driving the Japanese into a swamp. Although the Japanese were now out of sight, the artillery fired into the swamp "just to worry them."[19]

Three disjointed events highlighted the day of confused fighting. When a canoe approached the shore behind Filipino lines, Filipinos ran to the beach to help the refugees ashore. But the occupants turned out to be Japanese. The Japanese jumped back into their canoe and the Filipinos ran for safety. Nearby, someone retained enough presence of mind to fire a machine gun. Everyone within range joined in and riddled the boat and its occupants. Five hundred yards north a Filipino company commander heard the unexpected firing and, thinking himself surrounded and cut off, set fire to the barrio he occupied and pulled his men south. It took three hours, an artillery preparation, and an American lieutenant to get the men back to their positions in the flattened barrio. Later in the day the outpost line and the main line got into a fight with one another and kept shooting until dark. Because everyone fired high, few men were hit. The last event of this strange day involved four Japanese ships trying to land supplies for their men just north of Moron. Scout 155mm guns from B Battery, 92nd Artillery, sited on Mauban Point, engaged the ships. Fortunately for the Japanese the shooting was excited and inaccurate. "This action was at fairly long range," recalled Lieutenant Edwin Kalbfleish, Jr., a graduate of Washington University in St. Louis, "about 15,000 yards. Due to our sea-level location we could not ascertain if any hits were made; however, the ships did turn off course and headed west instead of south."[20]

On the morning of January 19 a Japanese force came into full view of the 3rd Infantry's main line and started cutting the barbed wire. Not a shot was fired as the Japanese cut one strand after another. Finally, an American lieutenant cut loose with rifle fire and single-handedly drove the unenthusiastic Japanese away from the wire. Artillery duels took up most of the afternoon. The Japanese placed a battery of 75mm guns on an open beach near Moron and their fire outranged the nearby Filipino 2.95-inch battery, which broke and ran. The Japanese were subdued only when a Filipino 75mm battery came into action and shelled the Japanese out of position.[21]

As Japanese probes moved inland, and after visits by General Marshall and Colonel Funk to see how I Corps was guarding its right flank, Wainwright expressed concern as to whether or not General Segundo's 1st Division actually had men on Mount Silanganan's slopes. Earlier, an American officer found that the troops that were supposed to be on the right flank were not there. General Segundo "poo-pooed" the report and "proved" it wrong by pointing to a map and declaring the men were there. Major Houston P. Houser, G1 to I Corps, volunteered to reconnoiter and see if troops were actually there. Promoted to major just a month before, this ex-platoon leader and company commander from the 45th Infantry, for a time commander and then executive officer to the 32nd Infantry, ten years out of West Point, had been up Silanganan once before so the terrain was somewhat familiar to him. Early on January 20 Houser checked in at the 1st Division's command post, talked with General Segundo, and picked up a mounted patrol. The patrol followed a trail 500 yards behind and parallel to the main line. After riding less than 1,000 yards they received small arms fire. Houser did not believe he had been fired upon by the enemy so he did not report it. The patrol continued and found a Filipino trail guard. Half a mile beyond this man, fifteen Japanese, most in trees, ambushed Houser's horsemen on a narrow jungle trail. The Filipinos retreated. They then tried another trail to the southeast but met similar resistance. Realizing he could not continue with just six men, Houser returned to the 1st division and reported his contacts to General Segundo.[22]

On January 20 the Japanese attack rolled into high gear. The 122nd Infantry put pressure on the 1st Division's main line, and the 3rd Battalion, 20th Infantry, started slipping through holes in the Filipino line. Some who slipped through were those who stopped Major Houser's patrol. The holes used by the Japanese were created when riflemen of the 31st Artillery withdrew to the main line. An engineer company and an infantry company replaced them, but the commanders of both these companies also withdrew their men. Learning from Major Houser that Japanese were well to his rear, General Segundo pulled B Company, 92nd Infantry, from its bivouac and ordered it up the trails to drive the enemy to the northeast. The Filipino infantrymen deployed on both sides of the trail and quickly bogged down against stiff resistance. Two hours later, at 1800 hours, C Company arrived and Major Houser took it up another trail until it met resistance. Both companies held their ground, but they were not able to accomplish their mission of driving the Japanese back up the mountain. By late afternoon it was apparent that if there were Filipinos on Mount Silanganan, they were cut off, and the main body of the 1st Division was also in danger of being isolated.[23]

The next day, January 21, Segundo committed the last rifle company belonging to the 1st Battalion, 92nd Infantry, to help B and C companies. After blunting the final Filipino reaction, other Japanese continued their march. Hardly a half hour after A Company joined the fight the Filipinos heard enemy machine gun fire on the West Road, a clear signal the Japanese had cut past Segundo's blocking force. After three days of marching, Lieutenant Colonel Hiroshi Nakanishi's 3rd Battalion, 20th Infantry, built a roadblock across the vital West Road. Nakanishi's coup was the first demonstration on Bataan of the Japanese Army's ability to infiltrate large formations through defended, inhospitable terrain. In this case the Japanese had placed I Corps in a dangerous position, for Nakanishi's men sat astride the only road suitable for use by heavy vehicles and the only road capable of supplying Filipino front lines. Lieutenant Colonel Fowler, a solidly-built extrovert and a splendid leader, a twenty-one year veteran out of West Point, was the first to hear about the block and went forward with an automatic rifle to evict the Japanese. Fowler was an experienced leader and had served before in the Philippines from 1923 to 1927. He was also a horseman and was the polo coach while serving at Ohio State University just before coming to the Philippines again in 1940. Not realizing the strength of the enemy force, Fowler attacked and was shot through the chest and lung. The bullet cut through a lung, disappeared somewhere in his torso, but did not exit his body. Medics from B Collecting Company reached Fowler and rushed him to an aid station. Later Colonel Jonas Haskins, commanding I Corps Artillery, was killed at the block while driving to the front lines.[24]

Upon discovering the roadblock, the Americans and Filipinos attacked with everything they could find. Wainwright heard the firing, gathered men from the 92nd Infantry's Headquarters Company, and at 1100 hours led a Filipino officer and twenty men against the Japanese. From the north, Captain Leitner led a platoon of D Company and a section of headquarters company into the fight, but they were as unsuccessful as Wainwright. Colonel John H. Rodman, commander of the 92nd Infantry, ordered Major J. B. Crow to establish a line north of the block with the few personnel remaining to the regiment's headquarters. The first forces used to attack the Japanese were small only because Wainwright had nothing stronger. Elements of the 71st Division and parts of the 26th Cavalry were already committed to the defense of the Pilar-Bagac Road as a reaction to the difficulties in II Corps. After two hours of fighting in bad terrain packed with trees and broken by deep gorges, Wainwright realized he needed more men than the few he had. Wainwright himself missed death when his orderly pulled him to cover just as Japanese bullets zipped by and killed two Filipinos standing next to him.[25]

Wainwright put a Scout in charge of the twenty men south of the roadblock and then headed for his corps command post. En route he ran into an artilleryman, Major Bell, and ordered him to take charge of the roadblock effort and assemble as many men as possible. Wainwright promised to send help as quickly as he could. Major Bell energetically gathered engineers from road repair, a few pack-train Scouts, and some artillerymen. With 100 soldiers, Bell reinforced the original group of twenty. After Wainwright reached his command post he issued orders to the 1st Battalion, 91st Infantry, and the 2nd Battalion, 92nd Infantry, to assemble. He likewise ordered the 2nd Squadron, 26th Cavalry, north to reinforce Major Bell.[26]

On the morning of January 22 some of the forces alerted the day before arrived. The 1st Battalion, 91st Infantry, marched in and was fighting by 1000 hours. Fifteen minutes later a platoon of C Company, 194th Tank Battalion, drove up and reported to Colonel Rodman. Rodman ordered them to break through the roadblock. The tank commander, Captain Fred Moffitt, pointed out the absolute necessity of close infantry support and stressed that the Japanese carried pie-pan mines, mines strong enough to blow off a tank's track. But Moffitt argued in vain. The best he could get was a skirmish line to lead the tanks, but no one was assigned to stay with the vehicles. When three of the tanks attacked, they ran into log obstacles, and after Filipinos cleared the logs, the tanks roared forward only to run into antitank mines which blew the tracks off the two lead vehicles. Crewmen from the damaged tanks got out, hooked cables to tanks farther back, and pulled the crippled vehicles to safety.[27]

North of the roadblock, Scout cavalrymen from B Troop and two companies of the 91st Infantry fought the Japanese over command of an important ridge. The terrain was so bad and troop locations so uncertain that indirect artillery support was impractical. Major Fitch sent some pack howitzers in to put direct fire on the area, but they drew such heavy fire from snipers that Fitch had to withdraw them and felt lucky to get them out. Even when self-propelled mounts arrived, the semi-armored vehicles had to withdraw under heavy Japanese rifle and mortar fire. Erroneous information that the roadblock was cleared resulted in the dispatch rearward of a truck packed with fourteen wounded. The truck, marked with a large red cross, was ambushed. Only two men escaped, one of whom was the 42-year-old Colonel Fowler still badly wounded from the day before. He was sitting at the rear of the truck and jumped out at the first burst, ran along the edge of the jungle, and walked back to his headquarters. A man who saw Fowler noted that he "was a little worn down by this time, but still very much alive."[28]

At noon, the 3rd Battalion, 72nd Infantry, joined the fight south of the block to the left of the cavalrymen. The main Japanese position lay just east of the road, and enemy supply lines ran north through the jungle. The 3rd Battalion was ordered to move to the west side of the road and outflank the main enemy resistance. When the attack started at 1500 hours, Scouts of the 2nd Squadron pushed up the south side of a cleared ridge and denied the Japanese an important position with good fields of fire. Soon after, the 2nd Battalion, 92nd Infantry, arrived and went on various security, reserve, and patrolling missions. Then the 1st Battalion, 2nd Constabulary, arrived and went into bivouac. Attempts to reinforce the attacks were slowed by Japanese aircraft, and one column of Filipinos riding civilian buses was totally destroyed by air attacks.[29]

On the morning of January 23 the Constabulary began a march southwest around the enemy-held ridge while other units maneuvered in support. C Company remained as a blocking force just below the roadblock. As the battalion turned north, the Japanese attacked it. Major Jose A. Arambulo dropped D Company off to insure containment of the enemy and continued toward the lines of the 1st Regular Division. Arambulo's men reached the hill held by elements of Troop E-F just as the Scouts were pushed out by the Japanese. All along the line the Japanese were unexpectedly counterattacking to regain the ridge lost the day before. Major Arambulo maneuvered his two companies into line and started up the hill. In a unique passage of lines the two Constabulary companies rushed the crest and cleared it before the Japanese could consolidate their gains. The Constabulary continued the fight until they opened the westernmost part of a trail until then under enemy control. Several trucks heavily loaded with 1st Division wounded then moved farther to the rear, but the West Road itself remained closed. Then the Japanese pushed into the fragmented Constabulary battalion, forcing them away from the ground they had won during the day. As night fell, Major Arambulo set up defensively in hopes of keeping the Japanese from reaching the sea. The underfed and poorly supplied Filipinos proved unequal to evicting the equally underfed and poorly supplied Japanese.[30]

Frontal attacks and local flanking efforts were doing little to reduce the roadblock. So Colonel Rodman tried a new approach the morning of January 24. He picked Major Arambulo's Constabulary battalion to climb well up Mount Silanganan, turn north to a ridge on the east flank of the Japanese, and then attack downhill into the left rear of the roadblock. The Constabulary ate a good meal, and C Company, 92nd Infantry, joined the battalion. As morning dawned on the twenty-fourth, Arambulo's men snaked their way up the hill with orders to be in position by 1200 hours. But they found the terrain so rugged they could not get to their line of departure until three hours later than planned. When they did attack, they were opposed first by Japanese on horses and then by infantry. The Filipinos made some gains, but heavy mortar fire reduced their progress to a crawl. When the Japanese counterattacked at 1700 hours, all Filipino attacks ceased.[31]

Not all the action centered around the roadblock. Wainwright's main line was north of the block, and by the evening of the twenty-fourth, enemy pressure against the main line combined with the isolation created by the roadblock had placed the defenders in untenable straits. The Japanese were pressuring both the 3rd Infantry and the left of the 1st Infantry so badly that the situation was desperate. Food was almost gone and rifle ammunition was running short. "Our artillery ammunition was exhausted," remembered Colonel Fowler, "and Colonel Berry's [infantrymen] had only a few hours rifle and machine gun fire left. Word from I Corps indicated that their attempt to relieve us had failed."[32] On the afternoon of the twenty-fourth, Major Alva Fitch had conferred with his artillery commanders and ordered them to destroy their cannon if the defenses suddenly failed. Other than Colonel Berry, who now commanded all the men north of the roadblock, Major Fitch was the only regular officer in the fight. Colonel Berry decided to assemble the men that night and fight his way south to safety. He was issuing orders for the move when a runner arrived with a message from Wainwright. "Hold your position," the runner told them. "Plenty of help is on the way. Food will reach you tomorrow."[33] Berry complied. He repositioned his soldiers and did what he could to consolidate the ground he still held.

By now there certainly should have been enough Filipinos at the roadblock to handle the situation. There were six battalions of infantry and some artillery. But with the exception of the Scout cavalry, none of the units had machine guns. The infantrymen carried only their single-shot bolt-action rifles while the Japanese employed their normal complement of automatic weapons. Although six battalions of infantry may seem to be an imposing force, these units had marched into battle from beach defense across difficult terrain and were committed to an offensive action for which none had been trained. Then it took from two to three days before food was rerouted to their new locations. Under these circumstances the Filipinos did not accomplish much.[34]

On the front line the 1st Division was short rations when the roadblock was established, and now the shortage was severe. Because this was I Corps's first combat, enemy ruses proved very effective. The Japanese used fire crackers to cover the sound of their light machine guns, and patrols fired Roman candles at night. The untrained Filipinos responded by rifle and machine gun fire thereby revealing their own positions. Later in the battle, ruses were less successful, but at the moment they were effective. But it was not ruses that were winning the battle for the Japanese; rather it was training, determination, and leadership.[35]

It was impossible for the Filipinos north of the roadblock to stay any longer in their precarious positions. For two straight days the men in the foxholes fought without food or ammunition resupplies. The sudden collapse of the Filipino battalion north of the roadblock decided the situation for Colonel Berry. He learned of the battalion's collapse when Japanese arrived near his command post riding buses belonging to his rear echelon. The Filipinos who lost their line filtered around the roadblock and headed south. By now all wire communications to Wainwright were cut, and only a single radio remained. Berry sent a message describing his plight to Wainwright and, in return, Berry received a coded message which his signal men could not decode. Berry was the senior officer with both the 1st and 3rd infantry, and he decided to withdraw. He made the decision on his own authority without receiving permission from Wainwright. Berry had some uncertain moments wondering how Wainwright would react to the unauthorized withdrawal. It was the proper decision. USAFFE had ordered I Corps to withdraw beginning January 25, and the outcome of Berry's decision was a recommendation for the DSC. With their line of retreat cut along the West Road, the only route remaining for Berry's withdrawal ran along the narrow beach washed by the South China Sea. Although Berry realized this route would require abandonment of all vehicles and artillery north of the roadblock, he gave the order.[36]

By this time, although Berry did not know it, no hope remained of staying in position even if the roadblock were reduced. II Corps was withdrawing to the Pilar-Bagac Road, and I Corps would have to conform to II Corps's movements. On the morning of January 25, I Corps's retreat began. It started on the right flank with each unit moving along the battalion support line under the concealment of trees and vegetation. When the men reached the 3rd Infantry's command post, they followed trails to the sea. Guides then fed them along the boulder-strewn coast until they reached Bagac. Captain Santos's 1st Battalion, 1st Infantry, was first to act as rear guard, and they passed that duty to Captain Algas's 1st Battalion, 3rd Infantry. Twice the Japanese attacked the men holding the line of withdrawal, but each time the Filipinos held their ground. When the last Filipino battalion reached the beach, the Japanese woke up and pressed their attack. But Major Arambulo's Constabulary battalion, positioned along the regimental reserve line, stopped them. The rear guard fought off the enemy with a minimum of friendly casualties.[37]

Because of II Corps's withdrawal, Wainwright had suspended attempts to reduce the roadblock, so Berry's men were on their own during their march south. The most serious loss caused by Berry's withdrawal was the destruction of all supplies, trucks, and most significant, the precious artillery that could not be moved along the beach. The trail over which Berry's men marched was narrow and difficult even for men on foot, so saving the guns was out of the question. Lost were a battery of 155mm guns from the 92nd Artillery just south of Moron; A Battery, 23rd Artillery; four SPMs from I Battery; all the 71st Artillery; and all the 1st Division's artillery. "My officers and myself destroyed the guns with tears in our eyes," remembered Colonel Fowler.[38] Gunners removed breach blocks and carried out other hasty destruction. Crewmen put long fuses on shells, pushed them head first into cannon muzzles, loaded the guns, and fired them. At least one attempt was made to save some of the trapped guns. First Lieutenant Olin G. King tried to build a raft to float his disassembled 2.95-inch howitzers to safety. His men completed a difficult three-hour trek to water and assembled some bancas, but a Japanese patrol surprised his work party and killed King.

Keeping the men together and moving in the right direction was difficult. Japanese were all over the area and firing at small groups of Filipinos. The men stayed as near to the shore as the trails and cliffs would allow, but regardless of the route, movement was extremely difficult. Not even a mule could have made it. Fortunately for the Filipinos, they did not encounter any Japanese. Colonel Fowler, wounded in the chest, survivor of the ambushed ambulance, had eight stretcher bearers detailed to carry him. His party kept up with the column for the first several miles, but a steep trail left them trailing the faster walkers. So Fowler climbed off his stretcher and hiked the fifteen kilometers to safety.[39]

The withdrawal continued into the evening of January 25. "The first few kilometers were easy," recalled Lieutenant Victor J. Sevilla commanding A Company, 3rd Infantry. "We encountered no enemy troops, not even the sound of rifle fire or machine gun. But as we plunged deep into the night, and moved further from Moron, the road by the sea became increasingly difficult."[40] Struggling men stumbled and picked their painful way over defenses built by other Filipinos. Sevilla's column was soon disorganized and scattered as the stronger men pushed steadily south while weaker men fell behind. Rallying or organizing the men was impossible. There was much confusion, which approached flight. A cavalry officer watched the Filipinos stumble past and recorded, "Rout of 1st Division continues. All guns lost and most of small arms discarded, its personnel streaming down the beach in a mob."[41]

Behind the rear guard and under its protection, the retreat along the beaches cut apart the sneakers worn by the soldiers, and most men ended the march barefoot. Morning of January 26 found many Filipinos still on the open beach. Japanese planes attacked these men who, without much cover, were badly mauled. The retreat became harder on the men as the sun rose higher in the eastern sky. Without shade or relief from the heat, Filipinos discarded their individual gear as personal survival superseded property accountability. The men had to cross cliffs and deep watery inlets, and some fell to their death or drowned. Litter bearers struggled with the wounded, and the stronger men carried weaker ones on their backs. One in every four came out along the beach wearing only his underwear after discarding weapon, equipment, and uniform to speed his flight.[42]

As the men straggled into Bagac, Colonel Berry walked in and was met by Wainwright. "Berry," he called, "I'm damned glad to see you."[43] Berry explained where his men were and asked for instructions. Wainwright pointed south. "Keep going down the road to Trail 9. You'll take up position in there." Then with a smile, Wainwright, a gentleman "to his fingertips" and a kind person, added, "I'll see that you're mentioned in orders."

Wainwright's forces just south of the roadblock now pulled out and headed for Bagac. I Corps ordered the 91st Division to withdraw under the concealment of darkness, and Colonel Lee C. Vance received telephoned orders to cover the withdrawal. I Corps's orders were very general, usually boiling down to "take whatever action is necessary." I Corps gave Vance the 1st Battalion, 1st Constabulary, and the 2nd Battalion, 2nd Constabulary, which he put on line straddling the West Road. Promoted to Colonel and now commanding the 26th Cavalry, Vance placed his 1st Squadron behind the Constabulary as a mobile reserve. "The plan clicked like clockwork," remembered Major Chandler, S3 of the cavalry regiment. "Each unit, as it was outflanked by Japanese units toiling through the jungles on each side of the Moron road, moved through the already prepared line of the troop to the rear and moved southward to the assembly and bivouac area."[44] The withdrawal went as planned, and with the exception of a few 91st Division units that had to fight to break away, all units pulled out without incident.

Although I Corps had slipped away from the enemy, reorganization on Trail 9 proved difficult. Wainwright's entire corps now owned but four 75mm and two 155mm guns. MacArthur's headquarters viewed the artillery's loss as a catastrophe. I Corps Artillery, weak at the start of the fight, was now so pitiful that USAFFE had to move three artillery battalions from II Corps to I Corps. At Trail 9, officers tried to sort out the debris remaining to them. "After daylight, we began sorting, assembling, and reorganizing," recalled Major Fitch. "We found oil drums and cooked them some rice. We obtained rifles for those who had thrown theirs away. We made rosters and lists of missing. I stole some medical supplies and set up an aid station, dug latrines, stole a truck and hauled water—Lord! There was a lot to do with a mob of almost 1,000 men, disorganized, demoralized, hungry, exhausted. . . ."[45] A Company, 3rd Infantry, for instance, lost a quarter of its men, and it took them several days to reorganize while waiting for stragglers to rejoin.

But the men were still alive, and they formed the backbone for I Corps's new line.

CHAPTER TWELVE

II Corps Retreats

ON JANUARY 22 MACARTHUR SENT HIS CHIEF OF STAFF TO BATAAN to visit both corps headquarters and get a clear picture of the situation. After talking to Parker at II Corps headquarters at Limay, Sutherland went to talk with Wainwright on the west coast. But even before he arrived in I Corps, Sutherland was convinced a retreat of the entire army to the reserve battle position was an immediate necessity, and he decided that "a withdrawal from the Abucay-Mt Natib position was essential."[1] The enemy was driving a wedge between the two corps, most particularly the turning movement made by the relatively small 9th Infantry, only two battalions strong at the moment. Without doubt, this threat was more apparent than real, but the Americans had little idea of the enemy's strength and could only assume they had been outnumbered as well as outmaneuvered.

In the west, I Corps's very existence was in jeopardy because of the Japanese roadblock on the West Road. And because USAFFE had committed all of its reserves, that headquarters was left with little choice in the matter. Before leaving Bataan for Corregidor, Sutherland gave Parker and Wainwright verbal warning orders to prepare for a withdrawal to the vicinity of the Pilar-Bagac Road. After hearing Sutherland's report, MacArthur decided to withdraw. Detailed orders already existed in draft, so finalizing them took only a matter of hours. Beginning with the words, "Hostile penetration through the center of the Main Battle Position makes the further defense of this position inadvisable," USAFFE issued Field Order Number 9 the night of January 22 to both corps headquarters.[2]

Although Parker did not recommend to Sutherland that a withdrawal be undertaken, he did consider the decision sound. Not everyone, however, favored retreating. Brigadier General Hugh J. Casey, the USAFFE Engineer, believed movement to a new line would cause many problems. Much effort had gone into constructing the Abucay Line, which possessed better fields of fire and was better wired than the new line. Friendly artillery had much better firing sites here than would be found along the reserve battle position. It would be impossible to recover the bulk of the precious barbed wire strung over hill and dale. Once on the reserve battle position, the defenders would be crowded into a corner of Luzon only fifteen miles square, and Bataan Air Field would be vulnerable to long-range artillery fire. More important, almost nothing had been done to prepare the new line for occupation. At the beginning of January the reserve battle position was scarcely more than a line sketched on a map, and by January 22, when MacArthur decided to occupy it—even though two companies from the 301st Engineer Combat Regiment (PA) and 600 other soldiers rushed to work on the line—it was not much better. The 14th Engineer Battalion had been the only unit working full time on emplacements since late December.[3]

But all arguments against a withdrawal were academic; the Japanese had already overrun the left of II Corps, and Filamerican counterattacks had failed to restore the line, so the decision to withdraw was "timely and necessary even if more than regrettable."[4] Retreating to the reserve battle position along the Pilar-Bagac Road was not entirely an admission of defeat because the defense of Bataan was always envisioned as a defense in depth. Whereas the reserve battle position was to be held at all costs, the northern Abucay Line was never meant to be the location of a last-ditch stand. The Mauban-Abucay Line was to be held as long as possible for two reasons: to keep the Pilar-Bagac Road, valuable for its lateral communications, in friendly hands, and to enable the reserve battle position to be prepared. After USAFFE issued the necessary orders and set the plan in motion, MacArthur radioed the War Department with news of the upcoming maneuver:

In Luzon: Heavy fighting has been raging all day. The enemy has been repulsed every where. He seems to have finally adopted a policy of attrition as his unopposed command of the sea enables him to replace at will. My losses during the campaign have been very heavy and are mounting. They now approximate thirty-five percent of my entire force and some divisions have registered as high as sixty percent. My diminishing strength will soon force me to a shortened line on which I shall make my final stand. I have personally selected and prepared this position and it is strong. With its occupation all manuevering possibilities will cease. I intend to fight it to complete destruction. This will still leave Corregidor. I wish to take this opportunity while the army still exists and I am in command to pay my tribute to the magnificent service it has rendered. No troops have ever done so much with so little. I bequeath to you the charge that their fame and glory be duly recorded by their countrymen.[5]

MacArthur also recommended that, in case of his death, General Sutherland be appointed to succeed him. Of all his officers, MacArthur felt that Sutherland had the best grasp of the situation. With those rather pessimistic lines, the army prepared to move. USAFFE's order was simple and left most of the execution to the corps commanders. USAFFE expected little difficulty in I Corps. The real problems were in the east with II Corps, for if the withdrawal of Parker's men was seriously disrupted, the entire force might be destroyed before it reached the relative safety of the new line.[6]

II Corps held a meeting at 1000 hours on January 23 to alert commanders about the move. General Parker's staff published II Corps Field Order Number 2 and distributed it the next day to confirm instructions issued on the twenty-third. The first units to move in II Corps would be the hard-firing heavy artillery. Corps Artillery needed as much time as possible to displace. It could take twelve hours to move a single 155mm gun, and in the 301st Artillery there were only eight tractors to pull sixteen cannon, and only twelve draw bars that attached the guns to the prime mover. The cannon of II Corps Artillery would have priority on the roads and would begin their move south the night of January 23 and be repositioned by the morning of January 25 ready to support the withdrawing infantry. Cannoneers broke down their ammunition dumps, loaded them into vehicles for the trip south, then unloaded them at their new installations. Some light pieces would stay in place until the last moment; each division's artillery regiment would leave one 75mm battery for each infantry regiment of the covering shell. Some infantry would start moving on the twenty-third; General Brougher's 11th Division, less its artillery, would depart II Corps for reassignment to I Corps, one-third of its men the night of the twenty-third and the remainder, minus a few beach defense companies, the night of the twenty-fourth. General Parker would also lose a Scout regiment to Wainwright, and he picked the 45th Infantry to go west.[7]

Service and support units would displace south with the artillery. Truck convoys ran day and night hauling supplies south out of harm's way. USAFFE, in a move justified by their fear of a sudden collapse during the withdrawal, spirited 25,000 cases of meat and C rations from the peninsula to Corregidor. Two rice mills operating in Pilar and Orion were dismantled for shipment south. General Hospital Number 1 at

Limay was now untenable, so medical personnel began the transfer of men and equipment to new positions at Little Baguio. On the evening of January 23 the hospital transferred 682 patients to Hospital Number 2 near Cabcaben. Sixty-four white crosses remained in the Limay Cemetery. Orderlies ripped up water pipe and electrical wire and loaded it into trucks. Between January 23 and 25 the entire hospital, with all equipment—fifteen wards, operating room, minor surgery, dental clinic, laboratory, bakery and messes—with its hospital personnel and 500 patients, trucked and bused at night to a semipermanent site on the southern slopes of Mariveles Mountain. The trip was too rough for twenty badly wounded patients; they died during the move or upon reaching the new hospital. The day after the buildings at Limay were emptied and the red crosses removed, the Japanese bombed and shelled them.[8]

Withdrawal of II Corps's tactical elements would commence at dark on January 24 and continue through the night into the next day in three phases. The first phase would start at 1900 hours when a covering force, commanded by Brigadier General Maxon S. Lough, would extricate itself from the main line, march south, and establish a line from Balanga west to Guitol, through which both II Corps's main body and its covering shell could withdraw. General Lough's covering force consisted of the remnants of the 51st Division, one-third of the American 31st Infantry, a third of the 57th Infantry, all the 33rd Infantry, and the 1st Battalion, 31st Infantry (PA). Tanks and self-propelled 75mm's would support Lough's covering force. The tracked vehicles left their reserve positions during daylight hours on January 24 and occupied their covering force positions. Lough's men, supported by four 155mm guns, would stay in position through January 25. After the main body and covering shell passed through Lough, he would withdraw his men the night of January 25.[9]

The second phase of the plan was the march of II Corps's main body. It would pull out at 2100 hours and march through Lough's covering force to new positions along the Orion-Bagac Road. There, on the new line, it would deploy and prepare to repulse the Japanese after the covering force withdrew. For their part, the Japanese would have to uproot every logistical and combat support activity they had in order to resume their assaults, now nine miles further south.[10]

The third phase of the withdrawal placed a thin shell of men to cover the main line of resistance. Each unit on the Abucay Line was tasked to provide its own shell, normally a third of the infantry bolstered by machine guns. The shell's mission was to prevent the Japanese from overrunning the vulnerable main body as it marched south. The shell would hold until 0300 hours on the twenty-fifth and then pull south.[11]

Initial withdrawal of artillery and support troops the night of January 23 proceeded without alerting the Japanese, a real surprise considering Japanese command of the air. But the Japanese were not flying at night, and their artillery practically never fired at night, so the blacked-out convoys rolled south unmolested. At midnight on January 23 the Japanese launched infantry attacks against the main line near the Abucay Hacienda, but the defenders stopped them about dawn. Along the sector held by the 41st Division's Provisional Battalion, the Japanese almost forced a local withdrawal ahead of schedule, but the Filipinos rallied and broke the assault just short of the foxhole line by heavy, if admittedly inaccurate, rifle fire. A half hour after the sun set the next day, at 1900 hours, the elements assigned to General Lough's covering force quietly left the main line and marched toward Balanga. Then covering shell personnel crept into the abandoned positions and hoped the main body could depart without alerting the Japanese. Two hours after the covering force disappeared, the main body walked away from their fighting positions, and the covering shell filtered into those empty holes.[12]

Now, all along the Abucay Line, Filipinos and Americans assembled for the long march south behind the covering shell. The 41st Division had learned of the move on January 23 when General Lim was called to II Corps headquarters. Colonel Fortier issued a warning order to the regiments after Lim returned from the briefing. Written orders and their supporting plans were in the hands of regimental commanders by 1600 hours on January 24. Movement of divisional elements would begin at 1900 hours; order of march was from right to left, 41st, 42nd, and 43rd infantry followed by the 22nd, 45th, and American 31st. Reconnaissance parties were dispatched, and heavy baggage, ammunition, and rations were collected at dumps for movement by truck. Each regiment was to leave a battalion in position as its covering shell, and D Battery, 41st Artillery, was tasked to remain behind to support the shell. The withdrawal began at 1930 hours—a half hour late—and the 41st Division closed its command post at 2100 hours, after the main body of the division was well past. Some of the soldiers on the front line were resentful of the withdrawal order; they had honorably held their positions against heavy attacks, and because they did not know about the 51st Division's collapse, they were disturbed over the requirement to give up the ground they had defended so well.[13]

Captain John J. Martin, a University of Alabama ROTC graduate, commanded the shell left behind by the 41st Infantry, and the men of his 1st Battalion tried to maintain a normal volume of fire and the normal activity expected from a regiment. Extra machine guns made it seem the line was still occupied, and the Japanese did not bother Martin's men. The

Filipinos, not really understanding what was going on and not sure what a shell was supposed to do, were told that when 2300 hours arrived, they were to cease firing, grab everything, and take off for the rear. "When eleven o'clock came, everybody turned loose and ran," Martin recalled.[14] As he hastened south Martin felt if he were to survive this night, he would survive the war.

At the American 31st Infantry's command post orders were issued to destroy two radio trucks and three wire vehicles. The danger of alerting the Japanese to the withdrawal by allowing noisy movement of the trucks was too great. The drivers poured sugar into the gas tanks, partially dismantled the engines, and placed primed hand grenades on drive shafts as booby traps. Regimental headquarters personnel marched away shortly after dark with leaders repeatedly stressing the need for absolute silence. Everything was orderly; the men filed from the south side of a draw past large trees and bamboo, which had helped conceal them. Some men caught rides after reaching major roads, and one who did, Private Spencer, considered himself lucky until he realized he was sitting on a sack of hand grenades.[15]

Across the entire II Corps front the night began badly and degenerated to chaotic. Planning for the withdrawal was incomplete, and execution of the planning that had been accomplished was poor. Road nets and trails, in particular, made the withdrawal difficult. As early as 1600 hours the East Road running through Balanga was a bottleneck, jammed with buses going south or trying to turn around. But the greatest confusion developed along the left and center of the corps's line. As the front line infantry, except for the small covering shell, withdrew, they jammed onto the one road leading to safety, and at the intersection of the Back Road and the Abucay Hacienda Road was "the worst traffic jam imaginable."[16] The mass of six regiments of infantry concentrated here, and military police were not present to control traffic. "It was confusion and chaos like you never saw in your life," recalled Lieutenant Spaulding who watched from his half-track. "Units did not come out as companies, or battalions, or regiments. They came out as hordes of men with their commanders and advisors trying to gather together something that resembled an organization to move south."[17]

Soldiers were badly packed on roads and trails, and if the Japanese had fired their artillery seriously that night, the withdrawal would have turned to rout. Either the Japanese did not know a withdrawal was in progress, or they did not trust their artillery and air at night. Whatever the reason, II Corps was fortunate, for as one officer recalled, "had the Japanese fired artillery on the roads, particularly in the town of Balanga, our losses would have been very severe—in fact, mass slaughter."[18] Just

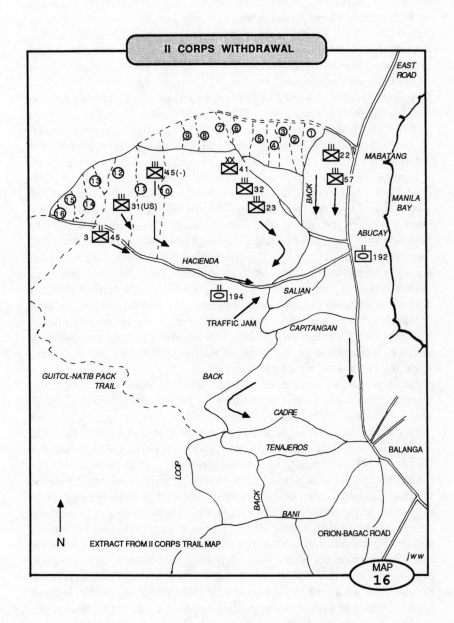

II CORPS WITHDRAWAL

EAST ROAD

⑨ ⑧ ⑦ ⑥ ③ ①
⑤ ② ①
④ ②

22 MABATANG

57

XX 45(-) 41

⑬ ⑫ MANILA BAY
⑪ ⑩ 32

⑮ ⑭ 31(US) 23
⑯
3 45 BACK

HACIENDA ABUCAY

194 SALIAN 192

TRAFFIC JAM CAPITANGAN

GUITOL-NATIB PACK TRAIL BACK

CADRE

LOOP TENAJEROS BALANGA

BACK

N BANI

ORION-BAGAC ROAD

EXTRACT FROM II CORPS TRAIL MAP jww

MAP
16

before the withdrawal reached its critical stage, the unlucky Japanese 65th Brigade artillery headquarters received another concentrated artillery strike. The artillery headquarters was marching just behind the 65th Brigade headquarters as both elements moved south when a thousand (Japanese count) rounds of artillery burst about their ears. Materiel and personnel were badly shot apart, and the ability of the Japanese to coordinate their cannon was disrupted. Here might be an explanation for the withdrawal avoiding Japanese artillery interdiction.

When the 41st Infantry, five battalions strong at the moment, marched up to the junction of the Back Road and Hacienda Road, they found it jammed even though they should have been the first unit to arrive there. When the senior instructor, Colonel Wetherby, and the commander, Colonel Cruz could not find anyone to give them orders, they pushed the 41st Infantry column right through the stalled formations and thereby started some of the others. The 22nd Infantry joined the mess at 2200 hours—a full hour ahead of schedule—and blocked motor movement to the east. Next, the American 31st Infantry trying to reach the East Road, arrived earlier than planned and ran into the 22nd Infantry, and both units claimed the single road. Then the 45th Infantry arrived and demanded priority on the Back Road because they had the longest distance to travel. Without anyone to regulate the traffic, soldiers poured uncontrollably into the intersection, but few departed despite the pressure added by each new unit. The press of humanity threatened to choke the route into complete immobility.[19]

As the situation became increasingly difficult, more and more commanders left their units and waded into the press to direct traffic. Colonel Doyle from the 45th Infantry found vehicles bumper to bumper and "not a wheel turning," so he tried to send them east along the Hacienda Road while directing foot troops south along the Back Road. Colonel Fortier, the 41st Division's 51-year-old senior instructor, stepped into the crossroads to take charge and sent two 41st Division staff officers down the Back Road. The two officers pushed their way through the mob until they came to the cause of the block. At a stream just a half mile south of the intersection, at the Silian River, Filipinos were trying to keep their feet dry by picking their way across the water on rocks. Colonel Fortier's two officers found the water only ankle deep, yet because of an absence of supervision at this critical point, disaster threatened. The two officers ran the Filipinos across the stream at a double time—wet feet be damned —and the jammed column sluggishly started moving. Fortier frantically worked in the center of the junction from 2115 until 0015 hours and, slowly, the combined efforts of officers like Fortier told.[20]

Only vaguely understanding the shouted commands, the untrained Filipinos tried to make up in speed what they did not know in technique. Instead of remaining dispersed and in their separate organizations, they jammed together, becoming disorganized and even less responsive to commands. "It was impossible to do anything but keep the mass moving to the rear," recalled tanker Colonel Miller, "praying—hoping—talking to yourself out loud—gesticulating—and trying to make yourself understood. It was a nightmare."[21] On the East Road the hundreds of vehicles and the pounding of thousands of feet raised choking clouds of fine, white, powdery dust that filled eyes and lungs. Packing the road were vehicles crammed to overflowing with exhausted soldiers, while on both sides of the road trudged men unlucky enough to be without a ride. Traffic slowed, stopped, and then advanced at a good clip, only to slow again for no apparent reason. Units blended into one another, parted, and mingled again. Men walking with comrades suddenly found themselves marching with strangers. Officers lost what little control they possessed at the start of the march, and the only effect they had on their men was dependent upon their physical presence and hardly reached beyond their arms or their voices. "It was complete bedlam," remembered Captain Ralph Hibbs, surgeon to an American unit. He got out of his command car, laid stretchers across it, and started picking wounded Filipinos out of ditches. "If this is an organized military force," he mused, "I'd like to see what a rabble looks like."[22] Yet somehow the flow of men and machines continued south.

Luckily, the moon was already up when the sun went down, and the waxing globe lit the road for the struggling drivers. Slowly, traffic jams cleared and units hastened south. Visibility was good, and men recalled seeing the outlines of Manila far across the bay. By midnight the immediate danger to the bulk of II Corps had passed.[23]

As all this marching south was in progress, Japanese pressure reached its greatest intensity on the thin covering shell. Enemy artillery hit the main line at 1800 hours, and Japanese infantry launched probes a half hour later. In front of I Company, 31st Infantry, Japanese soldiers rushed forward through burning cane fields. "The flames were shooting 20 feet in the air," remembered Private Grant Workman. "It lit up the sky like daylight and in front of it came screaming Japs like you wouldn't believe."[24] The Americans fired and fired, but they too fell as enemy rounds took affect. Workman held the head of a fatally wounded sergeant as the man pulled a gold watch from his shirt and gave it to Workman, asking that it be returned to the sergeant's father. Then Private Wyatt H. Irvine screamed for help, his assistant machine gunner had been hit and he needed another crewman. Private Workman scrambled to Irvine's position and fed belts of .30-caliber ammunition into the air-cooled gun.

When it overheated the two men found a water-cooled gun and hosed the advancing enemy until that gun also jammed. They then fired their M-1 rifles, and those weapons performed faithfully.

On the left of the 31st Infantry's sector were the troops of the 1st Battalion's covering shell. A and B companies marched away just before dark; then, just after dark, D Company gathered its men and heavy weapons and followed the route taken by the two rifle companies. Lieutenant Robert K. Carnahan's C Company positioned itself to cover the withdrawal and deployed as the left flank of the 31st Infantry's covering shell. It was clear, hot, and muggy when the Japanese started crossing a ravine in front of C Company. "We had this gully lined with machine guns," remembers Corporal Milton, "a self-propelled 75mm was firing point blank into the Japs, yet they would come right back into the area. It was foolhardy, but I guess they were doing it their way. The artillery was firing over our heads, which wasn't helping my headache."[25]

A week earlier Milton had acquired an abandoned BAR, one of more than twenty automatic weapons lost by the 51st Division and recovered by the Americans. He covered the withdrawal as did machine gunners, all firing at full blast. Milton watched the Americans pull out, some with blistered shoulders from carrying the boiling hot-water-jacketed machine guns. As the covering shell gave ground, Milton disassembled his BAR, bent the operating rod, and tossed the pieces into the jungle. Then he picked up his M-1 and slipped down a gully. Just as he reached the bottom, he heard a man crying for help and identifying himself as an American. It turned out to be Private Hill from A Company. Milton and another man turned to help, and they continued their withdrawal with one man carrying Hill and Milton carrying two rifles. Nearby, Private Charles Bell engaged the Japanese with his BAR. Although wounded, Bell refused evacuation, dressed his own wound, and continued to fight. As his comrades withdrew, Bell stayed in place and covered them while they worked their way past enemy fire. Only then did Bell leave.[26]

Numb from their exertions, the 1st Battalion's covering shell passed through the left flank of the 3rd Battalion's shell, elements of L Company. As the last of the 1st Battalion plodded past and faded into the dark, L Company, in the center of the regiment's line, began its fight to hold the Hacienda Road. Orders had been issued orally to the 3rd Battalion's company commanders. First, the battalion commander summarized what had to be done, then Major O'Donovan, the executive officer, gave routes, times, and other details. O'Donovan, still packing three pistols, was the battalion's covering shell commander.[27]

Now the 3rd Battalion's plan was in operation. When I and K companies passed through L Company, the men bantered with those staying behind; "Keep 'em flying," "To Hell with the Mikado," and the quiet, sincere "good luck" marked their departure. Lieutenant Thompson had already issued orders to his platoon sergeants—he had no officers—and watched the last of the battalion file by. His men were deployed across a canefield in one- and two-man foxholes. On the heels of C Company's withdrawal came the Japanese, and with their arrival all hell seemed to break out. Thompson worked his way up to one of his .30-caliber light machine guns where he could see what looked like hundreds of Japanese forming for an attack down the Hacienda Road. Although the enemy were using a drainage ditch for cover, they had to expose themselves at a bend in the road in order to cross. At the bend Thompson could see a stack of dead Japanese.[28]

Thompson decided he needed some help so he sent a messenger to ask the heavy weapons company for any fires he could get. The 1st Battalion, 41st Artillery, was supporting the 31st Infantry's shell, so some 75mm support was also available. Then Thompson moved his exposed machine gunners away from friendly mortar bursts and repositioned them to fire on Japanese assembly areas. "The artillery was a life saver," recalled Private Wilburn Snyder. "They were dropping the shells so close to us it was frightening even to us. But they had to do it because the enemy was so close."[29] Without radios or telephones, Thompson's only means of communication was personal contact, so he coordinated his requests for fire and moved his platoons from one place to another by juggling his small command group, sending a runner in one direction and making personal contact in another direction. Messengers, stumbling about in the dark, trusted to God and poor marksmanship to get where they were going. Cane fields in front of and behind Thompson's men were afire, silhouetting both friendly and enemy troops. For an hour Thompson's men fought a confusing battle. Suddenly a mass of Filipinos and Americans poured onto the Hacienda Road, all heading in Thompson's direction. A serious problem Thompson's men faced was the similarity in height between Japanese and Filipinos, and in the dark, identification was nearly impossible. The identity of the approaching mob was solved by loud, booming cursing coming from Captain John Ellis, an friend of Thompson's from the University of Nebraska.

After Captain Ellis passed, Thompson spotted his battalion commander in the road directing traffic. Lieutenant Colonel Brady ordered Thompson to gather as many men as he could and reassemble 2,000 yards to the rear. Thompson collected his company and wasted little time putting distance between his men and the Japanese. But unknown to Thompson, one of his soldiers, Private Stanley R. Monroe, was still on the firing line. Just as L Company pulled out, Monroe learned that a friend was lost forward of the line. In the dark, Monroe walked toward the Japanese, searching the ground. Miraculously, he found the badly wounded and partially paralyzed man. Monroe destroyed the man's automatic rifle, and then, with the Japanese only yards away, picked him up and ran to safety.[30]

To the right of Thompson's company the regiment's 2nd Battalion, withdrawing up a hill through a forest fire, was faced with the prospect of running through the fire and providing perfect targets in the glare of the flames. The Americans picked their way through the fire, chased by the pop-pop-pop of Japanese rifle fire. The sky was filled with tracers, and the Americans ran as fast as they could through the burning trees. Exhilarated by his escape, one man started singing, "Give me some men who are stout-hearted men who will fight for the rights they adore," and soon the entire column was roaring the song in a release of nervous tension. Keeping the Japanese in check was the 2nd Battalion's covering shell, the men of G Company. Once the main body was clear, G Company began a withdrawal over the burning hill. "It was what we had been trained not to do," remembered Private Taylor, "but it was the only way out."[31] They pulled to safety through heavy but ineffective Japanese fire. When the American covering shell withdrew, they passed through Scouts of the 3rd Battalion, 45th Infantry, who were still attached to the American regiment.

The covering shell Scouts had orders to fight a delaying action and then pass through a screen of tanks about 3,000 yards to their rear. With one rifle company on each side of the Hacienda Road, Major Strickler's men prepared for the Japanese. The Scouts were in good spirits for they had just eaten a hot meal of rice fed to them in their positions. The delay force's right flank company, two thirty-five man platoons from L Company, was hit first. L Company had arrived at Abucay with 131 officers and men, and they were now down to less than eighty. Major Strickler, wearing an old khaki hat and carrying a pistol, spent the evening walking his line completely unconcerned over the dangers facing him, and he kept his two companies under firm control. After considerable close action and hand-to-hand fighting, the Japanese faded into the dark. Fighting slowed after 2000 hours and allowed the two rear-most companies of II Corps to continue their withdrawal.[32]

After making the Japanese cautious by their spirited resistance, the Scouts left their fighting positions and joined the Americans in the next delay line. At 0300 hours the Polar Bears of the 31st Infantry, covered by 37mm tank fire, completed their withdrawal from the Abucay Line. During prewar maneuvers in Louisiana, the 192nd Tank Battalion developed the habit of hailing columns of men and asking them their identity.

As Sergeant Forrest Knox watched this line of men walk wearily by, he called, "What outfit?" Despite their exhaustion, the Americans proudly answered, "31st Infantry."[33] Behind the tanks, fifteen trucks and Major Everett V. Mead, the regiment's S4, waited to carry the covering shell to safety. The soldiers struck Mead as looking like walking dead men. "They had a blank stare in their eyes, and their faces, covered with beards, lack[ed] any semblance of expression . . . they looked like anything but an efficient fighting force."[34] The infantrymen thankfully climbed into the service company's trucks and drove south. Behind them came the Japanese.

A column of Japanese infantry, part of Colonel Imai's 141st Infantry, marched down the Hacienda Road into the guns of five American light tanks. It was very dark now—the moon had set at 0123 hours—and the tankers and self-propelled mounts simply guessed at the range, added a small safety factor, and fired. The Japanese scattered. Not expecting tanks, confused, and thinking he had surprised an artillery position, Colonel Imai organized his men for an attack. But then groups of Filipino and American stragglers, still withdrawing from the front, bumped into Imai's rear and flanks. Confusion prevailed, and Imai and his headquarters went to ground. The Japanese were sufficiently discouraged that the remainder of the withdrawal went undisturbed; Imai delayed further pursuit until daylight.[35]

It is quite possible that Imai had been hit in his rear by F Company, 45th Infantry, for F Company was then in the process of trying to extricate itself from a bad situation. Captain Ralph Amato's Scouts had fulfilled their mission of covering the withdrawal of the 2nd Battalion and, in accordance with orders, pulled out at 0300 hours. But by then the other shells to their left had already passed behind them closely pursued by the Japanese. When Amato's men marched east along the Hacienda Road—2nd Platoon, company headquarters, 3rd and 1st platoons—Japanese opened fire on the point. Lieutenant William B. Davis, company executive officer and commanding the point, deployed his men and scattered the enemy, all in perfect darkness. The Scouts resumed the advance until again hit by rifle and machine gun fire. After Davis deployed to the left of the road and the 3rd Platoon went on line to the right, the two platoons drove the enemy eastward. When the Scouts ran into even heavier resistance for a third time, it was clear that the enemy was across the line of withdrawal in force. After failing to budge the Japanese in a thirty-minute fight, Amato decided to circle behind, north of, the Japanese. He succeeded, but in the dark his platoons lost contact with one another, and it took six days for some of them to reach friendly lines.[36]

South of F Company's brawl with Colonel Imai's men, and south of the

American tanks, trails were still full of troops. To the men involved in that night's movement, it was utter confusion; units broke apart, distant firing added to everyone's apprehension, and it was easy to believe everything had gone wrong. But regardless of the confusion at the individual level, the withdrawal was proceeding according to plan. The 65th Brigade reported their troops conducted "a whole hearted, vigorous pursuit and engaged in a succession of moonlight skirmishes. Enemy corpses, abandoned ammunition, material and signal wire were scattered about. It looked as if the enemy had been routed."[37] That analysis was not completely accurate, for they made only limited efforts to pursue. It was not until the morning of January 25 that the Japanese finally realized a major withdrawal was in progress. They reformed their infantry and hurried south to regain contact. The main strength of Japanese artillery pulled up from firing positions, displaced toward Abucay, and threw a few rounds at the Filipinos, but they stopped their fire when ammunition ran low. Japanese engineers halted routine rear area construction and started rebuilding bridges along the East Road.

Japanese air now became devastatingly effective. Fighters and bombers climbed from captured American fields and headed for the smoke rising from Bataan. "It was about noon that clear day that out of the blue sky appeared several Zeros," remembers Corporal Eliseo Prado, a Scout with the 24th Artillery. "They dropped their eggs and strafed at the same time. Vehicles here and there are on fire. Some with ammunition exploded. Everybody is on his own either running to the left or right to get away from the planes."[38] Throughout the long day Japanese planes in formations of threes strafed and bombed the retreating columns. American infantry, trained to scatter and take cover at the approach of aircraft, suffered only minor hurts; L Company, 31st Infantry, was hit by three planes, but the soldiers were atuned to air attacks and ran into ditches and full-grown cane fields. Scouts from the Philippine Division infantry regiments were equally agile.

But the Philippine Army was not as proficient as either the Americans or the Scouts. Nowhere in their limited training did they learn how to react to aircraft, and they now milled about, suffering more and more casualties on each attack. Bunched together in a futile search for safety, the Filipinos were driven from one inadequate piece of cover to another. After each attack, survivors looted wrecked vehicles, dragged dead men to the side of the road, and aided the wounded. Drivers climbed back into vehicles and rolled south until the next attack. The East Road had assumed an appearance all its own by now. The rutted road wore an ankle-deep blanket of dust; the steady pounding of feet raised swirling storms around each man and painted the grass and jungle a dull, dusty gray. Drivers, intent on saving themselves and their loads, drove with little thought to the infantrymen they buried under clouds of dust. American khaki and Filipino denim took on the same shade of dull white. The Filipinos, peering from under coconut fiber helmets, wound for miles through small barrios, splashed across shallow creeks, and panted past heat-shimmering valleys.[39]

Offering futile resistance to air attacks were American antiaircraft batteries, men and guns firing ammunition that often did not explode. Fuses to 3-inch rounds were badly corroded, and sometimes only one in every six shells burst. Antiaircraft shells were of two types, the first being the powder-train fused ammunition which exploded after burning through a coil of powder. The newest rounds were dated 1932. One man took fuses out of a box that had stencilled across it, CONDEMNED, MAY 1923. The brass fuses were green from oxidation. The artillerymen cleaned them, put them on the antiaircraft shells, and fired them. "And once and awhile, one would go off," recalled Captain Garry Anloff.[40] In one instance, gunners saw a shell pass through the wing of a Japanese plane without exploding. The plane, losing fuel through the hole, casually turned and flew safely home. The second type of shell was the mechanically fused ammunition which worked like a set of clockworks, exploding at a certain time and reaching 30,000 feet. Although better than the powder-train fuses, there were not many of the mechanically fused shells in the Philippines. And even with good shells, antiaircraft effectiveness would have been sharply limited because there were but two regiments of guns on Bataan.

Not convinced all friendly troops had withdrawn through his covering force tank screen, Lieutenant Colonel Smyth, the Tank Group Executive Officer and former instructor in chassis and engines at the Tank School, made "memorable solitary checks" after everyone was supposed to have been south of him, and he found numerous groups, one numbering 200 men, lost and leaderless, and quickly guided them south to safety. He did not find them all, for the Japanese reported annihilating groups of Filipinos and Americans who had lost their way. One unit was, in fact, forgotten in the haste and disorganization of the withdrawal. The 2nd Battalion, Provisional Air Corps Regiment, was in position near Guitol. Somehow, orders to withdraw failed to reach them, and to their surprise the constant concussions rolling over them from the Abucay Hacienda ceased the morning of January 25. Even the blowflies and mosquitos, which until then had plagued them, were gone. When a reconnaissance to the rear found the regimental command post empty, the officers decided it was time to leave. The airmen assembled at the base of their hill and made a long hike to safety. When they reached friendly lines, they were asked, "Where have you been?"[41]

Another man who did not hear about the withdrawal was Sergeant Gilewitch, and as he drove toward his unit's old positions, he ran into Japanese. He slouched down in his vehicle, turned it around slowly, and started back. "The Japs glanced at the truck and went about their business. I kept going real slow until almost back on the road, then gave it all it had!"[42] Gilewitch bounced through a big ditch, lost most of the ammunition he was carrying, and reached the road amid a hail of small arms fire. There was another close call in the 11th Infantry. The regimental signal officer remained in his old position salvaging as much telephone wire as he could. When he dashed toward I Corps, he reached the Pantingan River bridge after the fuses to demolition charges had been lit. Realizing the value of the signal equipment he was carrying, he ordered the driver to cross; his vehicle cleared the west side just before the charges exploded.

As these close calls continued, General Nara arrived at his 142nd Infantry to personally direct the pursuit. He had already published his operations order for the day. He wanted to pursue the Filipinos swiftly and prevent them from occupying prepared positions further south. He made several small changes to the brigade's organization, gave his units their objectives, and coordinated for artillery, air, engineer, signal, medical, and road construction support. The left flank element of his 65th Brigade—a combat team built around the 1st Battalion, 142nd Infantry —arrived in Abucay the morning of January 25. When their lead infantry marched south out of the town, observers from Major Joseph Ganahl's self-propelled artillery spotted them. Ganahl's 75mm cannon were backed under nipa shacks on the south side of the Pilar-Bagac Road, and the thirty-eight-year-old West Point artilleryman, a prewar polo-playing friend of Wainwright, had established an observation post in Balanga's church tower. "He gave me a shift and called for a volley," recalled Captain Ivan W. Weikel with C Battery. "The first salvo struck in the middle of the Japanese. They ran into a large bamboo thicket. My next volley struck in the middle of it. They scattered in all directions. After I had fired 120 rounds, the Japanese troops were so scattered that further action was useless."[43] A dive bomber hunted Weikel's guns, but Weikel only fired when the plane was flying away and then ducked back under the nipa shacks.

Nara and his infantry advanced under this artillery fire until reaching a position two kilometers west of Capitangan, a short distance south of Abucay, where they stopped for the night. The Japanese were elated at their advance, and although the brutal Abucay fighting left them "burn-

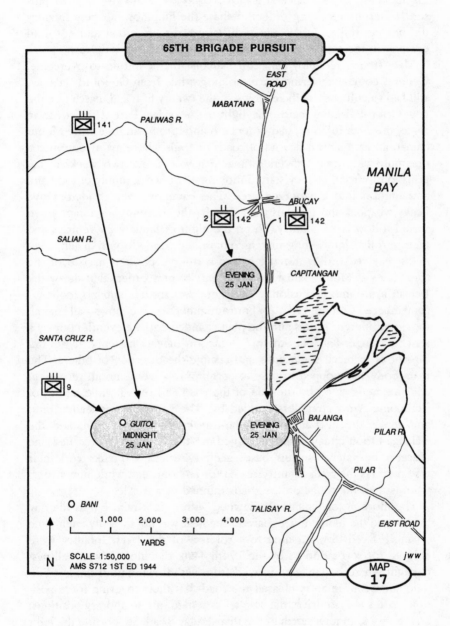

65TH BRIGADE PURSUIT

EAST ROAD

MABATANG

PALIWAS R.

141

MANILA BAY

SALIAN R.

2 142   ABUCAY   1 142

EVENING 25 JAN

CAPITANGAN

SANTA CRUZ R.

9

O GUITOL MIDNIGHT 25 JAN

EVENING 25 JAN   BALANGA

PILAR R.

PILAR

O BANI   TALISAY R.

EAST ROAD

0   1,000   2,000   3,000   4,000

YARDS

jww

SCALE 1:50,000
AMS S712 1ST ED 1944

N

MAP
17

ing to smash all resistance at a blow," they were sluggish in their pursuit.[44] Despite receiving orders to chase the Filipinos, Japanese infantry did not get rolling in the east until late in the afternoon and not until evening in the center, almost a full day after II Corps withdrew.

MacArthur's redeployment still had one major hurdle to overcome. General Lough's covering force, holding a line from Guitol to Balanga, still had to pull out late the evening of the twenty-fifth and march into the new Orion-Balac line before daylight the next day. Part of the covering force, the 57th Infantry, had orders moving it to positions astride Mount Samat, an area almost devoid of roads or trails whose main route was a one-mule-wide trail. Officers estimated it would take two weeks to cut trails to the front, so they started moving a two-week supply of food and ammunition into the rugged area. The battalions were told to move heavy weapons and supplies immediately; the more mobile infantrymen would follow cross country. So on the night of January 25 vehicles and men unrolled into a long march column and headed south. Then, regiment received orders moving it into a reserve position instead of the front lines at Mount Samat, just one part of new orders that threw the Bataan army into confusion. "Well here was trouble and no fooling," remembered Colonel Fry. "An entire regiment on the move—all [battalions] on different routes and the plan changed at the eleventh hour by a staff messenger [no one knew]."[45] Liaison officers hastened in several directions to recall some units and change the direction of others. The main body was stopped in time to permit a relatively smooth rerouting, and the men waited by the side of the road and rested while masses of Philippine Army stragglers shuffled by. The various roads leading into and across the new line—the Pilar-Bagac, the Capot-Orion, and the Balanga-Orion-Limay—were "clogged most to a standstill," recalled one officer as he watched sedans, buses, artillery, trucks, and tanks work their way past. As the 57th Infantry rested for an hour, and while new orders were issued, the traffic on the roads thinned to a trickle.

The morning of January 26 dawned with a light rain, but as the day progressed the temperature soared. The heat was not the only enemy the Japanese faced, for pursuing foot soldiers of the 141st Infantry were delayed for several hours by the 194th Tank Battalion. It was well past daylight when the tankers, delayed from withdrawing until the last Filipino and Scout infantry cleared the road, left their covering force positions. After a short drive, the M-3 tanks settled into temporary positions, now only a kilometer north of the Pilar-Bagac Road. Supporting the light tanks were four self-propelled 75mm mounts from Major Ganahl's battalion. Tank Group's orders to the 194th were to delay the Japanese, and using a well-worn routine developed during the Luzon delaying actions, commanders issued their orders.[46]

> Tanks will execute maximum delay, staying in position and firing at visible enemy until further delay will jeopardize withdrawal. If a tank is immobilized, it will be fought until the close approach of the enemy, then destroyed; the crew previously taking positions outside and continuing the fight with the salvaged and personal weapons. Considerations of personal safety or expediency will not interfere with accomplishing the greatest possible delay.[47]

A Filipino civilian running down the road warned the tankers that Japanese were approaching in several columns. Thoroughly alerted, the armored force waited for the Japanese. The Americans were about to eat breakfast when the Japanese, marching in formation without security, came into sight. The tankers immediately took them under fire. The self-propelled guns were in excellent positions and fired everywhere the Japanese jumped for cover. Each exploding round drove them from safety and into tank machine gun fire. The battalion's half-tracks were interspersed among the tanks, and their .30-caliber and .50-caliber machine guns added to the carnage. Colonel Miller walked up and down his line of vehicles directing their fire, spitting tobacco juice out of both sides of his mouth, and cautioning his machine gunners not to fire too fast or they would burn out their barrels. "It was quite a sight, and frankly, quite an inspiration to the rest of us," remembers Lieutenant Theodore I. Spaulding, the reconnaissance platoon leader.[48] Japanese aircraft came into play with their usual lack of skill and dropped their bombs utterly without effect. Bomb fragments ripped a fender off a tank and peppered a half track; in exchange, the tankers shot down one plane.

The fight started at 1030 hours, but it was not until nearly noon that the Japanese finally unlimbered some artillery and fired at the tanks. For half an hour their fire was inaccurate, but by noon it had become a threat. Two friendly tanks which had run off the road had to be abandoned after extensive efforts to extract them failed, and the Japanese subsequently reported capturing them. Colonel Miller turned his battalion south, broke off the action, and retired behind the new main line of resistance without losing a single man.[49]

The withdrawal was now complete, and MacArthur reported his actions to Washington in two messages, neither of which bear too great a resemblance to fact. On January 25, the first day of the withdrawal, he radioed,

> Our counterattack on the right was a smashing success. Our powerful artillery concentrations of one five fives was deadly. Our infantry found the

enemy completely disorganized in this area; he left hundreds of dead on
the field and quantities of supplies and equipment.[50]

The counterattack MacArthur mentions may be his way of alluding to
breaking contact. Nor were there hundreds of enemy dead left on the
field! Two days later, after the withdrawal was complete, and one day
after his 62nd birthday, he reported again.

> In Luzon: Under the cover of darkness I broke contact with the enemy
> and without the loss of a man or an ounce of material am now firmly
> established on my main battle position. The execution of the movement
> would have done credit to the best troops in the world.[51]

It is easy to become annoyed with MacArthur's messages. If poetic
license were not allowed—and it should not be in military communications—the two messages could, at best, be classified as self-serving, de-
ceitful oration. What MacArthur said was untrue, false, a lie. Many men
were killed and captured during the withdrawal, tons of valuable equipment were lost or destroyed, and execution of the movement bordered
on chaotic. Much engineer equipment was lost; the 41st Engineer Battalion alone lost 1,700 shovels and 140 rolls of barbed wire, and almost all
of the barbed wire and engineer equipment expended on the Abucay
Line was abandoned.[52]

Nor, as MacArthur asserted before the withdrawal, was the new position strong. Neither was it "firmly established." The first problem the
engineers faced was to cut a five-foot-wide path just to mark the location
of the main line. An engineer officer and a light crawler tractor went to
each corps to do this. The next problem was to cut an adequate trail
network south of the main line to supply units, evacuate wounded, and to
move artillery into position. In some cases the best the engineers could
do was pick the most heavily traveled goat trail and widen it enough to
accommodate pack mules. Because of these priorities, the engineers
could do little on the main line itself. In most places the line was the
rawest jungle imaginable. Construction along the new line had to be
accomplished with bayonets, mess kits, and tin cans.[53]

Once on the new Orion-Bagac Line, the soldiers discovered it was
similar to the Abucay Line when they occupied it in early January; little
or no work had been done, and it would fall to the infantry to dig their
own positions. "Again," complained the 41st Division, "not a scratch
had been done in the way of organization, and we were really now in a
bad way for organizing material, also we were badly short of wire and
communications equipment."[54] Constant enemy shelling at Abucay had
repeatedly cut telephone lines, and even more wire was abandoned dur-

ing the withdrawal. Because fewer trucks arrived to carry equipment than expected, much of the division's gear, including some weapons and ammunition, was left to the Japanese. Even the soldiers' individual equipment in their barracks bags was lost. The arrival of the 41st Division on the new line paralleled events in the other divisions. The Filipinos were exhausted, having started the march heavily burdened and having hiked twenty four kilometers. They dropped gas masks, mosquito nets, and blankets alongside the road as they tired. Arriving at the new line, they established an outpost line about a mile north of the Pilar-Bagac Road. One hundred eighty engineers from the 51st Division worked from January 26 until February 8 on the 41st Division's outpost line, helped repulse three Japanese attacks, and lost forty-five men killed or wounded.

American instructors began the difficult job of preparing a new line from scratch, and everyone worked desperately to dig new holes before the Japanese regained solid contact. But once again, the Filipinos dug their foxholes too close together—so close they could reach across and shake hands—and foxholes were poorly camouflaged and terribly conspicuous. Almost no work could be accomplished on alternate and supplementary positions. Many of the American officers instructing the Filipinos, mostly the reservists, were untrained in organizing ground. Colonel Quintard, finding his 301st Artillery too close to the front, travelled to II Corps headquarters to persuade them not to use his big cannon as machine guns. Another reason for his visit was to find out where the front lines actually were.[55]

Before the Japanese could organize themselves for a formal attack on MacArthur's new line, they were surprised and hurt in an astonishing fashion. For several days, reconnaissance reports coming into American headquarters described a large concentration of Japanese aircraft at Nichols and Nielson fields near Manila and seaplanes anchored near the Yacht Club off Manila Boulevard. The commander of Bataan's air force, Brigadier General George, had standing permission to launch an attack whenever conditions looked favorable, and on January 27 conditions looked favorable indeed; there would be a full moon, and visibility was expected to be good. The Japanese certainly were not expecting air action to erupt out of Bataan. On Bataan only the necessary people were briefed on the attack, for too many times Filipino agents had signalled the departure of American planes. Once night fell, airmen started preparing the seven remaining P-40's. Trucks hauled bombs out of ammunition dumps, and small tractors towed the planes from their camouflaged revetments. General George alerted Corregidor that American planes would be overhead at 2000 hours as they climbed for altitude. Seven pilots, Lieutenants

Woolery, Stinson, Hall, Obert, Baker, Ibold, and Brown, climbed into the cockpits of their planes. Then the command, "All clear!"[56]

The improvised field lights were kept dark while engines turned over and advanced to full power without a warmup. No one had wanted to tip off the enemy by taking special antidust measures on Bataan Field, so as the planes bumped down the field toward Manila Bay, dust and sand obscured the vision of one pilot, Lieutenant Ibold. His wheel ran off the strip into the rough, a wing dipped violently, and three bombs exploded. Emergency vehicles raced to the plane and pulled the badly burned pilot from the wreckage. The remaining six P-40's climbed for altitude above Corregidor, causing consternation among the antiaircraft gunners there who had not heard about the operation. But they held their fire, and the planes finished their climb and headed for their targets. Manila was in plain view with the lights of the city showing Japanese contempt for possible air attacks. But as the American pilots peered toward Nichols and Nielson fields, they noticed lights were blurred and diffused. A ground mist covered the low, swampy area.

The six planes separated for their runs on the two fields. The ground fog forced them low, and without warning they roared over the astonished Japanese. Enemy planes were lined up neatly at both fields, and the Americans returned some of the damage they had received on December 8. Fragmentation bombs fell first, and then the P-40's arched across the fields, chopping at the immobile aircraft with heavy .50-caliber machine guns. Zeros and Type-97 dive bombers smoked and burst into flames. A newly constructed building on Nichols Field, lights showing from open windows, was bombed and shattered. With ammunition expended, the Americans, unpursued, turned their unscratched ships back toward Bataan. Not a single Japanese plane gained the air. At Cabcaben two P-40's refueled, rearmed, and flew back toward Manila, but the Japanese installations were so covered by smoke that hitting specific targets was impossible.

The results of the raid were impressive: between fourteen and thirty-seven planes hit and burned, fuel and oil storage burned, and three hundred Japanese killed or wounded. The Japanese were sufficiently impressed to begin a dispersal of their air assets.

CHAPTER THIRTEEN

Longoskawayan Point

AS THE FIGHTING CONTINUED ALONG THE ABUCAY LINE THROUGH mid-January, the Japanese decided to make an amphibious landing along the left flank of the Filamerican lines, along Bataan's west coast. During a meeting at San Fernando on January 14 General Homma told Major General Naoki Kimura, the Infantry Group commander of the 16th Division and then commanding Japanese forces along the west coast, that he was concerned over the slow progress Nara's 65th Brigade was making on the east coast. The stalemate on the west coast was equally unacceptable. Major Shoji Ohta, a staff officer in the 16th Division, was present during the meeting and recalled that "[Homma] expressed his earnest desire to General Kimura to break the stalemate on the west coast and instructed him to attack the enemy from land and also carry out a landing operation on the enemy's rear area in order to insure rapid success."[1]

Homma pointed out that similar amphibious operations had proved their worth against the British in Malaya where General Yamashita continually cut behind defending lines, forcing the British to withdraw, thereby avoiding costly frontal attacks. Late the evening of January 15 Homma published an operations order putting Kimura in charge of the west coast effort and transferring Nara's men there to Kimura. Homma went so far as to order landing craft moved from Lingayen to Olongapo. Planners ultimately set Caibobo Point as the operation's beachhead and the West Road as the objective, an objective to be seized at all costs. In response to Homma's suggestions, General Kimura selected Lieutenant Colonel Nariyoshi Tsunehiro's 2nd Battalion, 20th Infantry, to make the watery end run. Ever since landing at Mauban on Luzon's southeast coast on December 24, the 2nd Battalion had been in reserve. Tsunehiro's men had run into some trouble at Mauban when they hit the Filipinos of the 2nd Battalion, 1st Infantry, but aside from that one action, the Japanese had suffered few casualties, and the men were fresh. Tsunehiro's amphibious operation was not to be an independent affair. At the time Homma made his decision to flank I Corps by sea, Japanese infantry had penetrated Wainwright's main line, so the amphibious operation would support Kimura's overland thrust after he defeated I Corps and turned against II Corps. If the Japanese succeeded, and if they could reinforce their landing, they could destroy all of Wainwright's I Corps by cutting off its line of retreat. With I Corps gone, there would not be much hope for prolonged resistance from II Corps.[2]

The amphibious attack would land on the Bataan Service Command. In addition to the two infantry corps on the main line of resistance, a third corps area, the Service Command, administered and defended the southern third of the peninsula. Service Command was constituted on December 25 when selected personnel from the Philippine Department were ordered into Bataan to develop a support base for the incoming army. Originally responsible for all coastal defense, the Service Command now held the beaches generally south of Mariveles Mountain, but even with its reduced responsibility, it had to cover forty miles of rugged terrain. Brigadier General Allan C. McBride commanded Service Command and had three major organizations with which to accomplish his mission. On January 7 the 1st Philippine Constabulary Regiment defended the west coast down to Mariveles, the 4th Constabulary guarded the coast between Mariveles and Cabcaben, and the 2nd Constabulary held the area from Cabcaben north to Limay. These three regiments were collected under the headquarters of the recently constituted 2nd Regular Division. Supporting the 2nd Division was an engineer battalion and a "heavy weapons" battalion.[3]

Assigned the mission of guarding the southwest sector of the Bataan coast was Brigadier General Clyde A. Selleck. He was now missing the combat elements of his 71st Division—his two infantry regiments were attached to the 1st and 91st divisions—and retained only his 71st Division headquarters, service troops, and a reduced battalion of artillery. In return for his detached infantry regiments, USAFFE gave him a mixed bag of sailors, Marines, airmen, Constabulary, and Philippine Army troops. USAFFE's directive to Selleck ordered that he defend his sector against amphibious operations, and if the Japanese succeeded in establishing a foothold, he was to isolate them and drive them back into the sea. With this diverse force, Selleck had to construct obstacles, position his men along the beaches most suitable for landings, maintain observation posts, and insure that a battalion size reserve was ready to move by bus on thirty-minutes notice. As it developed, the men had two weeks to prepare themselves before the Japanese stepped ashore, and they put their time to good use. Selleck's men began cutting and improving trails to the more important peninsulas along the coast. The grounded American airmen were so intent on learning their duties and on improving their positions that there were marked improvements in the defenses every day.[4]

The Americans considered the Agloloma Bay region the most critical of the numerous sites because of its deep water approaches and good trails leading to the West Road. If the Japanese landed here and exploited the landing, they could interdict road-bound supplies to I Corps. Using the meager resources left to him, Selleck strung barbed wire, established a network of lookouts, and connected his units by wire and radio. Four 6-inch naval guns became available but he could mount only two before the Japanese landed. A third gun was scheduled for Quinauan Point, but the cement was still wet when the Japanese overran the position. American airmen salvaged heavy machine guns from wrecked airplanes, fitted them with improvised firing mechanisms, and positioned them along the coast. Antiaircraft artillerymen selected locations for searchlights, but the lights arrived too late to be of use. After much effort, Selleck had on beach defense by January 22 the 17th Pursuit Squadron; the 3rd Battalion, 1st Constabulary; the 34th Pursuit Squadron; the 2nd Battalion, 1st Constabulary; the 3rd Pursuit Squadron; and the Naval Battalion. In reserve were the 1st Battalion, 1st Constabulary, and the 20th and 21st pursuit squadrons.[5]

Luckily for Selleck, the Japanese were as unprepared for the venture as he. Because of a lack of time, the Japanese omitted the detailed preparations and planning so necessary to amphibious operations. The only map they could find was a 1:200,000 scale map, completely useless in locating landing beaches on a rugged coast. As a result, they had to send several planes a day roaring along the coast hardly 100 yards from the shore to take pictures. They produced an aerial photograph on which the planners sketched a route from Moron south to Caibobo Point, and an offshoot of another route to Quinauan Point and Agloloma Bay. To add to navigational difficulties, the coast along the west side of Bataan blended into Mariveles Mountain so well that it was difficult to distinguish headland from cove even in the day. From the sea, the coast presented a formidable appearance with very high timbered banks rising to tall mountains. At night, distinguishing headland from cove proved impossible.[6]

Embarking from Mayagao Point north of Moron the night of January 22, Colonel Tsunehiro's 900-man 2nd Battalion, 20th Infantry (rein-

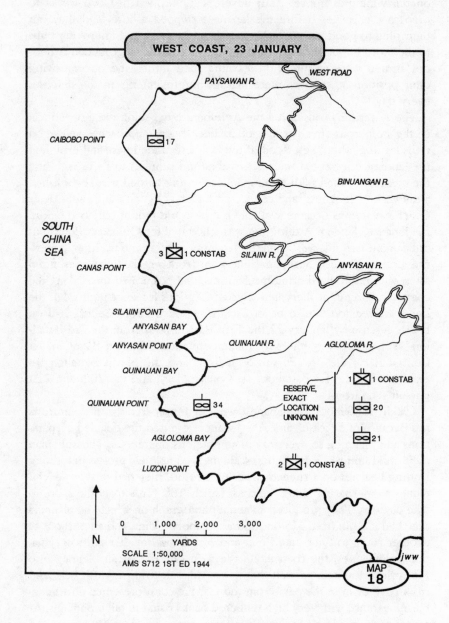

WEST COAST, 23 JANUARY

WEST ROAD

PAYSAWAN R.

CAIBOBO POINT ▭ 17

BINUANGAN R.

SOUTH
CHINA
SEA

3 ⊠ 1 CONSTAB

CANAS POINT SILAIIN R.

ANYASAN R.

SILAIIN POINT

ANYASAN BAY

ANYASAN POINT QUINAUAN R. AGLOLOMA R.

QUINAUAN BAY

1 ⊠ 1 CONSTAB

QUINAUAN POINT ▭ 34

RESERVE,
EXACT
LOCATION
UNKNOWN

▭ 20

▭ 21

AGLOLOMA BAY

LUZON POINT 2 ⊠ 1 CONSTAB

N

0   1,000   2,000   3,000

YARDS

SCALE 1:50,000
AMS S712 1ST ED 1944

jww

MAP
18

forced), immediately sailed into trouble. Encountering strong tides, pitch-black skies, and rough seas, the soldiers jammed aboard the landing craft were further plagued by motor torpedo boat 34 commanded by Ensign Barron W. Chandler. Chandler's boat—seventy feet long, twenty feet wide, and powered by three Packard engines—mounted torpedo tubes and four .50-caliber machine guns in two twin mounts. Finishing a routine patrol off Subic Bay, Ensign Chandler was coming home when he sighted an unidentified craft off Canas Point. As the two boats converged, the unknown craft blinked a dim, unintelligible series of white dots and dashes. Chandler changed course, increased speed, and closed on the vessel. Closer observation revealed a small launch two miles off shore heading down the coast. Still unsure of what it was, Lieutenant John D. Bulkeley, the squadron commander, yelled "Boat ahoy."[7] The answer was immediate, Japanese machine gun fire from twenty-five yards, which ripped through the boat fourteen times and hit Ensign Chandler in both ankles.

At 0442 hours, the four American .50-caliber machine guns rattled into action and were joined by automatic rifle fire from engine room personnel firing over the sides. The Japanese increased speed to eighteen knots and headed for Bagac Bay. PT 34 circled the launch three times, firing into the vulnerable flank of the 47-foot Japanese landing boat, and under this pounding, the boat sank lower and lower and finally disappeared. Sixteen minutes after the first shot, only Chandler's boat remained. It was too dark to look for survivors, but PT 34 stayed in the area for the next ninety minutes searching for more Japanese boats, but they did not see any. When PT 34 moved closer to shore in its search, friendly machine gun and 3-inch shore battery fire forced the boat out to sea.[8]

Almost at dawn, at 0610 hours, Lieutenant Bulkeley sighted a second landing barge three miles off shore, and PT 34 went to full speed to investigate. The enemy craft increased its speed to fifteen knots and pushed north. PT 34 overtook the Japanese and opened fire from 400 yards, certainly a more prudent distance than the previous engagement. When a tracer round hit the Japanese vessel's fuel tank, the boat started burning and drifting. As PT 34 closed the distance, the barge tried to ram Bulkeley. A couple of well-thrown hand grenades took the fight out of the Japanese, and Bulkeley boarded the enemy. The barge was empty except for one dead and two wounded Japanese, one of whom was an officer. Bulkeley was collecting the muster record of the landing party and the operation plan when the holed barge sank. He tread water and kept his two prisoners afloat until the sailors on PT 34 fished them out.[9]

Because of the tide, heavy seas, and disrupting influence of PT 34, the

Japanese, relying on inadequate maps and now badly separated from one another, came ashore at two different points, neither of which was the one called for in the plan. Disorganized and lost, the only advantage the Japanese held was that of complete surprise. One group of 300 men landed at Longoskawayan Point, ten miles south of the intended landing point on a ridge running off the hill mass of Mariveles Mountain. Only 300 to 400 yards wide and 700 yards long, Longoskawayan Point lay 3,000 yards from Mariveles harbor. Japanese control of the key terrain here—617-foot tall Mount Pucot—would enable them to block the main road along the west coast, dominate Mariveles Harbor, and control the road going out of Mariveles with light artillery. Mount Pucot sat on Lapiay Point, a piece of ground just north of Longoskawayan and only 1,000 yards from the critical West Road.[10]

Although the Japanese landed at Longoskawayan without alerting the beach defenses, it had been a near thing. On another finger of land jutting into the water barely 2,000 yards north of Longoskawayan, the 60th Coast Artillery's E Battery maintained a watch with searchlight section number one and a primitive radar apparatus, an ECR 268. The radar was a large science-fiction shaped cross, forty feet wide and fifteen feet tall, operated by fourteen men. It had been held on Corregidor through most of December, but then regimental headquarters called E Battery's commander, Captain William Massello, and told him he could have it. "The scuttlebutt was," Massello recalls, "that they had not been able to make any use of it themselves. The two vans were sent to us during the night in a barge. The E Battery men managed, by sheer determination and muscle power, to unload those two monsters off the barge in the dark and onto a stone pier at Mariveles. I honestly don't know how in hell we ever did it. [We] had it functioning within a couple of days, much to the astonishment of the boys back on Corregidor."[11] E Battery laboriously hauled the radar into position on December 20 in two huge, unwieldly vans over a road cut expressly for that purpose and positioned it 300 yards from the shoreline in the center of a large clearing. Although his unit was primarily intended for air defense, whenever Captain Massello emplaced any of his ten searchlights, he tried to position them to do double duty by pointing out to sea. The searchlight section next to the west coast was nicknamed the "suicide squad" because the men did not think they would survive if the Japanese landed. Although isolated, the artillerymen found the duty easier than recent prewar life. The 34-year-old Captain Massello had been a "slave driver" before the war, "a physical fitness nut," an officer who would ship his nonperforming soldiers off to the 31st Infantry. Massello had found Corregidor loaded with sunshiners, career soldiers who knew what a soft assignment "The Rock"

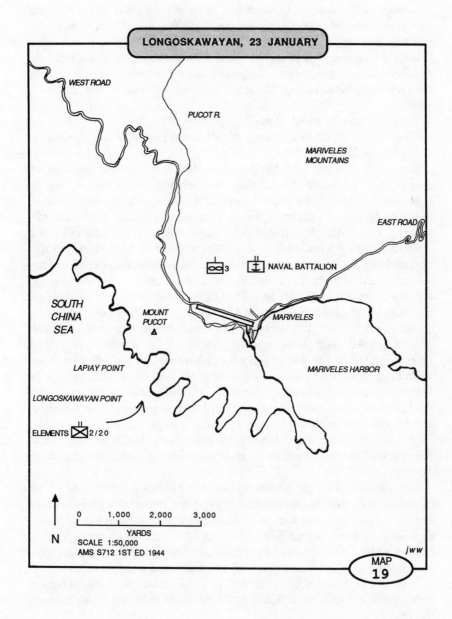

LONGOSKAWAYAN, 23 JANUARY

WEST ROAD

PUCOT R.

MARIVELES
MOUNTAINS

EAST ROAD

∞3   NAVAL BATTALION

SOUTH
CHINA
SEA

MOUNT
PUCOT
▲

MARIVELES

LAPIAY POINT

MARIVELES HARBOR

LONGOSKAWAYAN POINT

ELEMENTS ⊠2/20

N

0   1,000   2,000   3,000

YARDS

SCALE 1:50,000
AMS S712 1ST ED 1944

jww

MAP
19

was. These men kept reenlisting for the Coast Artillery, and with each reenlistment their paunches increased. With Massello, however, training on Corregidor had become so vigorous that a few men honestly believed Massello was trying to kill them.

On the evening of January 22 Captain Massello received a telephone call from his radar operator, Sergeant Joseph Messery. Reporting from the radar site, Messery told Massello there was a "bounce" on the radar screen.

"Are you sure?" asked Massello.

"Yes, it's no cloud or anything, it's a bounce at a very low altitude. It might be on the ocean."[12]

Massello contacted a USAFFE representative on Bataan, told him of the sighting, and headed for his radar. Lieutenant Colonel Guy H. Stubbs immediately phoned the more powerful Air Corps radar, told them of the sighting and approximate location, and asked them to confirm the spotting. After Massello arrived at his radar site, he received a call from Colonel Stubbs who told him the Air Corps radar had failed to spot the object. Even so, Massello's men were positive there was something on their screen despite lack of confirmation, and the crew continued to track the object lingering off the coast. Hoping to see the source of the elusive pip, Captain Massello ordered his Number 5 searchlight pointed out to sea and switched on. Results were inconclusive; the men thought there was a slight reflection as the beam hit something, but it was too far out to be certain. The big 60-inch Sperry-Rand light was turned off after more frustrating uncertainty. Barely was it off when a telephone call came into Massello from his regimental commander demanding an explanation why the light was on at such a low elevation. Massello explained the situation and his attempts to spot whatever his radar had shown.

"Whatever is out there is none of your damn business," came the retort from Colonel Theodore Chase, "you turn that light off right away. You are air defense."

Massello kept the light off but had trouble believing it was none of his business. Although he no doubt believed his regiment's motto, *Coelis Imperamus*—we rule the heavens—Massello was now on lower ground, and the blip was offshore from him, maybe a landing attempt. After a little thought, he ordered the light back on. Again his phone buzzed with an order to turn it off, but this time Massello tried a different answer.

"Oh, that isn't our light out there," he answered confidently. "That's a light from the 200th Coast Artillery. They have a light just a little way up the road here."

"Well, all right," came the answer from Corregidor.

E Battery continued tracking until the early hours of January 23 when they finally decided to quit. They just could not get a positive reading. Bataan fell dark until the sun rose. After the light went out, the illusive bounce—Japanese barges—turned toward shore and the barges landed their occupants, more than 300 well-trained infantrymen of the 20th Infantry.

The first confirmed sighting of Japanese came when a naval lookout spotted them at 0840 hours. Mount Pucot was crowded with men whose mission was to spot enemy landings; four men from the 60th Artillery were charged with observing and reporting all land and sea activity to Corregidor, and a seacoast observing and spotting detail of ten men with observation gear from the 59th Coast Artillery shared the hill with a Navy detail of eight men. But it was well past sunrise before anyone noticed anything, and then it did not require great powers of observation. An American, descending from a watchtower on Mount Pucot, saw movement in the brush. He yelled a challenge and was answered by rifle fire, then a small Japanese patrol sprayed the American camp with small arms fire. The Americans scrambled off the steep hill leaving rifles, two walkie-talkies, a radio, and an operations chart. The breathless men sounded the alarm. Three Marine air warning lookouts atop nearby Mount Mauankis also spotted the Japanese, telephoned their boss, and then scurried off the mountain.[13]

The first friendly forces to confront the Japanese were part of Commander Francis J. Bridget's Naval Battalion. Bridget, a ramrod-straight naval aviator with a waxed mustache, picked up the nickname "Fidgety Frank" when he told his men before the war to "get war conscious."[14] The Naval Battalion itself was created by a memorandum written by Rear Admiral Francis W. Rockwell on January 9 in which he directed that men be collected and trained for the defense of naval installations in and around Mariveles. Bridget assembled 150 naval aviators from the planeless Patrol Wing Ten, 130 sailors from the USS *Canopus*, 80 men from the Cavite Naval Ammunition Depot, 120 general duty men from various bases, and 120 Marine antiaircraft artillerymen. During the planning for Bataan's coastal defense, the Navy agreed to move against a landing if the Army had not already occupied the area. Bridget's sailors —clerks, welders, steamfitters, machinists, repairmen, torpedo men, storekeepers—were dressed in a yellow, mustard-like uniform, so colored by an unsuccessful attempt to dye Navy uniforms khaki by soaking them in coffee. "Perhaps two-thirds of the sailors knew which end of the rifle should be presented to the enemy," recalled one man.[15] The Naval Battalion counted 602 members, but with many duties over a large area, no more than 200 ever faced the Japanese at any one time.

When Comander Bridget learned about the Japanese, he alerted his battalion. Ensign Grundels from C Battery, 3rd Battalion, 4th Marines, took a platoon toward Mount Pucot while the battery's commander, Marine Lieutenant Wilfred D. Holdridge, took another part of the battery toward Longoskawayan Point. Marine Lieutenant William F. Hogaboom took a platoon of A Battery into the hills while Lieutenant (j.g.) Leslie J. Pew, a naval aviator, headed for Mount Pucot with the battery's other platoon. The area was soon boiling with small detachments looking for Japanese or simply trying to discover what was happening. Lieutenant Colonel Howard E. C. Breitung and Captain Calloway, commanders of the 2nd Battalion, 60th Artillery, and its Headquarters Battery, collected thirty men and made a hasty reconnaissance to determine what had happened to their detail on Mount Pucot, and whether or not E Battery's Number 2 searchlight was in danger.[16]

When General Selleck learned of the landing, he dispatched a Philippine Army pack howitzer and Captain Henry G. Thorne's 3rd Pursuit Squadron, Air Corps mechanics and armament specialists carrying a variety of cast-off weapons. Some airmen sported .50-caliber machine guns rigged with bamboo mounts and fitted with pull wires in place of missing triggers. A few composite Marlin machine guns were constructed from inoperable guns by canabalizing parts. About half the men had received some infantry training before entering the Air Corps, but once in the flying business, they were reluctant to learn about rifles or other "non-Air Corps matters." Now the cry was, "Hey, Sarge, you know about bayonet drill and rifles, how about teaching us."[17] Some drill was taught, but without bayonets, for none were available.

By the time General Selleck had alerted his Army forces, the Japanese main body was off the shoreline and climbing the lower slopes of the mountain. Even so, only small Japanese patrols had neared the top and it was a race to see who could put the most men on Mount Pucot the soonest. First blood went to the Japanese during a meeting engagement on Mount Pucot's southeastern slopes—they wounded Ensign Grundels and his senior sergeant and disorganized and demoralized the collection of Marine artillerymen and sailors. But the firing attracted three more Naval Battalion platoons that marched to the sound of the guns, and as a Japanese point element reached the top of Mount Pucot, Lieutenant Pew's platoon climbed the hill, deployed near the top, and attacked through sporadic small arms fire. Pew's bluejackets took the summit without trouble, and the Japanese fled. Pew's men then joined the other three platoons and busied themselves removing enemy from Pucot's lower slopes. The expertise of the Navy infantrymen, or rather the lack thereof, startled and frightened the Japanese. "Today we have encountered a new kind of enemy," read a diary taken from a dead Japanese.

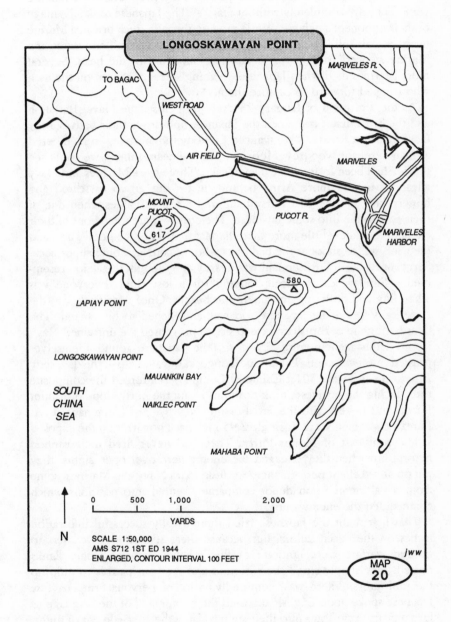

LONGOSKAWAYAN POINT

TO BAGAC

WEST ROAD

MARIVELES R.

AIR FIELD

MARIVELES

MOUNT
PUCOT.
△
617

PUCOT R.

MARIVELES
HARBOR

580
△

LAPIAY POINT

LONGOSKAWAYAN POINT

MAUANKIN BAY

SOUTH
CHINA
SEA

NAIKLEC POINT

MAHABA POINT

N

| 0 | 500 | 1,000 | | 2,000 |

YARDS

SCALE 1:50,000
AMS S712 1ST ED 1944
ENLARGED, CONTOUR INTERVAL 100 FEET

jww

MAP
20

"They come walking into the front yelling 'Hey, Mac, where the hell are you?' They are completely without fear."[18] The Japanese took advantage of their opponent's naivete. While moving through thick brush, a Marine heard a man call, "Don't shoot, soldier, we're friends," and when the Marine stepped from cover, a Japanese shot him in the head. Several more Marines died when Japanese, feigning surrender, fired on the men who stepped forward to capture them.

As the afternoon of January 23 drew to a close, the Naval Battalion and the 3rd Pursuit contained the Japanese and drove their patrols away from the West Road. "We advanced Cowboy-Indian style," remembered airman Sergeant Woodrow McBride. "As we neared them, we could see that we had been formed like a layer cake. There were Marines and Navy ahead of us and more Army behind, just a big group of scared and hungry kids."[19] The 3rd Pursuit suffered a few casualties when one of their patrols ran into some Japanese. The airmen were totally out of their element and knew little more than the fact they were the good guys, and their job was to shoot at the bad guys who, of course, would shoot back. Sergeant Robert D. Rosendahl was nearby and thought the action resembled a Sunday school picnic looking for a lost child. Everyone was whooping and hollering and poking in bushes. Once near the coast, the Americans found the Japanese too well-entrenched to be evicted. The dense, tough underbrush and steep slopes prevented the untrained Navy troops from maneuvering. Even so, the Japanese found themselves pressed into two points, Lapiay and Longoskawayan. Late in the day, sixty Americans from the 301st Chemical Company reinforced the composite force facing the Japanese, took positions along the north slope of Mount Pucot, and linked with the 3rd Pursuit. Nearby, 3rd Lieutenant A. A. Perez's eight men set their single 2.95-inch pack howitzer on the exposed saddle southeast of Mount Pucot. They had never fired their cannon before, but when they engaged the enemy here over open sights, they put on an excellent performance. At dusk, extra Navy and Marines, some from naval ammunition depot companies, settled into positions which commanded the enemy's line.

That first night the Japanese tried their usually successful infiltration tactics on the beach sailors, but because these seafaring newcomers to ground warfare were ignorant of the lethality of having ones flanks turned, they simply stood their ground and sent out patrols to mop up the infiltrators. There was, admittedly, a lot of nervous firing. A few Japanese spoke good English and used their command of the language to lure unwary Americans into their sights. Using the concealment of night, some Japanese established themselves in positions on the west and south slopes of Mount Pucot.[20]

On January 24, the second day of the landing, the Americans drove the Japanese back to Lapiay and Longoskawayan Points for the second time. A patrol led by Lieutenant Holdridge accidently penetrated the enemy's line and found itself overlooking a couple of small Japanese cannon, probably antitank guns. Holdridge placed his men in position and ripped the enemy apart. Taking the advice of his BAR gunner who yelled, "Let's get the hell out of here! This will really make them mad," Holdridge extracted his men.[21] Naval Battalion efforts at fire and maneuver were uncoordinated and of a level expected from sailors and airmen. Captain Massello was passing Navy lines when a redheaded Navy lieutenant hailed him and invited him to the fight. Massello watched them move forward with caution and considerable courage, for their ignorance of jungle warfare was obvious. After advancing about 200 yards, the sailors were stopped by enemy automatic weapons fire which hit a few men. After medics dragged the wounded to safety, the rest of the men decided to entrench and sit out the rest of the day. Japanese machine guns and mortars kept everyone low and honest. At Mariveles, word of the landing and the fighting spread, and sailors asked the wounded where the fighting was, then drew rifles, cartridge belts, and headed for the coast. "They said it would just be a matter of a couple hours," recalled a Marine, "and we'd be back for supper."[22]

During the night, Lieutenant M. E. Peshek from Corregidor's 4th Marines joined Commander Bridget's battalion with two 81mm mortars and took up defilade firing positions in a saddle low on the northwest slopes of Mount Pucot. Peshek and his Marines set an observation post atop the hill and at dawn lobbed their Stokes shells into both Lapiay and Longoskawayan Points. Peshek's Marine machine gun platoon sprayed bullets into suspected enemy positions and covered the advance of patrols toward both points. Bridget's men found Lapiay abandoned, but the Japanese repulsed the advance against Longoskawayan. When Lieutenant Holdredge pressed onto Longoskawayan, his men unwittingly passed some Japanese who shot up Holdredge's men from the rear. The subsequent report to Corregidor had the task of explaining that the wounded had not been running away but were hit in the back as they faced the enemy.[23]

After some discussion, the American command decided to swing the big guns of Corregidor on the enemy. Washington had earlier radioed Corregidor about the possibility of using the island's cannon against enemy troops.

Records of War Department indicate several hundred Mark VI A 700-pound high explosive gun projectiles—1,890 with bands modified for use

in mortars are on hand at Corregidor. These shells were specially designed
for obtaining extreme effects against troops and personnel in the open by
using Mark III Super Quick fuse or—46 Super Quick fuse. These projectiles may be used in either Battery Smith or Hearn as well as in mortars.
The above information is furnished because of uncertainty here that the
feasibility of using these highly effective projectiles in the rifle batteries is
known at your headquarters.[24]

These heavy projectiles with their point-detonating fuses were deadly
to exposed personnel within the bursting radius of 500 yards. Alerted for
possible fire missions since the morning of January 25, the men at Battery
Geary with their eight huge 12-inch mortars spent the day impatiently
awaiting orders to shoot. Their disappointment at not receiving orders
disappeared late in the day when Major General Edward P. King,
USAFFE Artillery Officer, gave the word to shoot. Commander Bridget
spent the evening on Longoskawayan clearing his men away from the
target area. At 0011 hours on January 26 Battery Geary fired its first 670-
pound round, then its second, and then its third. "About the 3rd or 4th
shot landed on a ridge in my field of view," recalled Colonel Paul D.
Bunker, a big, burly, all-American type, watching from Corregidor, "and
I could see the grand explosion and the swirling smoke of the fire."[25]
After the fourth round burst on Longoskawayan, Lieutenant Richard P.
Fulmer, a 1941 graduate of UCLA and now the forward observer on
Mount Pucot, reported that big fires prevented him from spotting the
bursts, and he had to change his target in order to see the rounds burst.
Fulmer's makeshift telephone line ran through three switchboards, and
Corregidor could not hear Fulmer's corrections. Another officer, midway
between Mount Pucot and Corregidor, screamed Fulmer's corrections
into the phone so Corregidor could hear them.

Gunners shifted their deflection 200 yards left and fired five more 12-
inch shells. But trouble plagued the artillerymen; several lanyards broke,
and primer misfires slowed the shoot. Because the mortars were firing at
their extreme range, Zone 10, the powder completely filled the cham-
bers. On one occasion the gunners could not force the powder far
enough into the chamber to shoot. The final two rounds were fired together, but a one-degree error in deflection landed the big shells close to
Bridget's men. Bridget called "cease fire" and refused to let Battery
Geary fire any more that morning. "For speed and efficiency it was a
terribly humiliating experience," remembered Colonel Bunker, but to
the men at Longoskawayan, the shoot was extremely impressive.[26] The
Americans had been warned to stay in their foxholes, and to Private
Orville D. Roland, "The shells sounded like freight trains coming down
from the sky. There wasn't a twig over two inches tall left standing."[27]

Results within Japanese lines were devastating. "We were terrified," one wounded Japanese later told his captors. "We could not know where the big shells or bombs were coming from; they seemed to be falling from the sky. Before I was wounded, my head was going round and round, and I did not know what to do. Some of my companions jumped off the cliff to escape the terrible fire."[28] A few Japanese tried to swim away, but their progress was poor. At dawn Sergeant Rosendahl from the 3rd Pursuit saw a man swimming weakly, using just one arm, directly in front of his position. The man was not armed, so Rosendahl went down to the beach, pulled him in, and captured him. Hard on the heels of Corregidor's barrage, the Naval Battalion attacked, but the Japanese repulsed them and strongly counterattacked.

The Americans planned another try for the next day. At 0700 hours on January 27 they brought all available artillery to bear on the Japanese. A 75mm battery from the 88th Artillery, two 81mm mortars from the 4th Marines, Lieutenant Perez's lone 2.95-inch pack howitzer, and the big, vintage 1908 12-inchers from Battery Geary fired. Battery Geary fired four rounds of high explosive, fuse super quick, and then six rounds of deck-piercing, fuse delay of 0.05 seconds. The next fourteen rounds were a mixture of HE and DP, and the Scout coast artillerymen stopped firing only after the telephone line to the forward observer went dead. The results of the shoot were so impressive, especially the twenty-four rounds of 12-inch, that the ground soldiers asked that the fires be moved even closer to their own positions. When a request to shoot at enemy positions only 200 yards in front of friendly lines reached Corregidor, Colonel Bunker wrote in his diary, "Suicidal for, at 14,000 yards, we can't place shots as accurately as that and, besides, the destructive radius is well over 500 yards. Very flattering request but impossible."[29]

However difficult it may have been to survive this pounding, the Japanese not only weathered the steel storm, they also almost cut off an element of the attacking Naval Battalion. The reason for the enemy's near success was the surprising failure of two 4th Marine rifle platoons sent to Bataan from Corregidor. The two platoons, for whatever reason, withdrew when the Japanese advanced and caused the difficulty. At 1800 hours Commander Bridget collected the Marines on the West Road and tried to bully them back into the line, telling them they had disgraced the Marine Corps and the Navy, and had let down their shipmates in the Naval Battalion. Only excellent mortar and artillery support called in during this period allowed Bridget's sailors to withdraw without heavier losses. The naval amateurs were having real problems against the regular Japanese infantry.[30]

Finally, trained soldiers were alerted to move to Longoskawayan. The

Navy and Air Corps had held the enemy when there were no regulars available, and now the veterans of Mabatang were at hand. A command change made on January 25 deactivated General McBride's Service Command and relieved him of the responsibility of fighting a war as well as supplying the Bataan army. The boundary between I and II corps was extended south until it hit the coast just east of Mariveles. Wainwright therefore picked up responsibility for the Longoskawayan fight. On January 26 USAFFE released two Scout infantry battalions to Wainwright, and Wainwright sent one to Longoskawayan. At dusk on January 27, 475 Scouts from Lieutenant Colonel Hal C. Granberry's 2nd Battalion, 57th Infantry, arrived at Longoskawayan. Granberry's battalion had left the last delay position during the Abucay withdrawal the morning of the twenty-sixth and received a day's rest before being alerted and sent to Longoskawayan. Some of the Scouts were smarting from having to leave Mabatang before really getting into the fight, and they were anxious to vent their frustration on the Japanese.[31]

The 2nd Battalion, 57th Infantry, had both a tremendously talented commander and an executive officer who functioned beautifully together; neither were book soldiers, and both were impetuous and fearless, a bit on the daring side. They took turns manning the command post, and whoever was on the phone was in command. Granberry, a quiet Mississippian, a thinker who graduated from West Point in 1923, had started the war as the South Luzon Force Signal Officer and came to the 57th Infantry around January 19. He was completely comfortable with soldiers, for he had spent three years with the 38th Infantry in Colorado, a year in the Canal Zone, two years in the Philippines from 1934–36 (he liked warm weather), two years with the 3rd Infantry, and two with the 25th Infantry. Granberry now spent half of his time with the front line companies, and when he was in the command post, Major Robert D. Scholes, an aggressive hard-charger, was out with the companies. Colonel Granberry and Major Scholes spent the afternoon reconnoitering the enemy's most advanced positions and picked a big gap in the Naval Battalion's line as their line of departure. Granberry planned to attack southeast, parallel to the Pucot River, to clean out the most-easterly Japanese, then swing 90-degrees to his right and seize the high ground fronting Longoskawayan Point.[32]

The Scout's arrival at Longoskawayan was most welcome. Marine Lieutenant Hogaboom met the Scouts and passed them several maps and sketches of the area to include, as best could be pinpointed, enemy strong points. "I was thoroughly impressed by the efficiency, discipline, and precision of their occupation of the area," remembers Hogaboom. "They were every inch first-class fighting men going in to take over a situation they knew how to handle."³³ Scouts tied in with tired Naval Battalion sailors, and a hand on the shoulder and a whispered, "Oke, Joe, you go now, I take over," was the first many of the sailors knew of their relief.

After completing his reconnaissance and talking to Major Scholes, Colonel Granberry put his two most experienced company commanders on line, Captain Donald T. Childers with his E Company on the left and Captain William C. Anderson, a strong, quiet, level-headed leader, with F Company on the right. Working in the dark, Childers and Anderson each deployed a single platoon on line with the remaining platoons following closely behind the deployed formations. Fighting was serious, but the disciplined Scouts drove the Japanese through tangled second growth and the more open virgin jungle, made their 90-degree right turn, and took the high ground that overlooked Longoskawayan. Here, Captain Thomas F. Chilcote, a policeman in Portland, Oregon, before being called to active duty, led his G Company in to relieve Anderson's F, leaving G and E in place. Both companies then put a second platoon on line, giving the battalion a four-platoon front. Then the men settled down to wait for daylight.³⁴

Preparation for the upcoming day's work was thorough. Scout mortars registered and machine guns dug in to cover the advance. Covered by small arms fire and artillery support, Granberry's Scouts attacked at 0600 hours and made steady progress the morning of the twenty-eighth until their supporting weapons were masked by Mount Pucot. After a platoon of machine guns shifted to cover the immediate area and a platoon of D Battery, 88th Artillery moved so it could once again cover the advance, and while Bridget's sailors held firmly to Mount Pucot, the Scout infantrymen resumed their attack and forced the Japanese to the lower third of the small peninsula. In hopes of keeping friendly losses to a minimum—the Scouts were literally irreplaceable—Granberry planned extensive artillery fires for the next day's attack.³⁵

At 0630 hours the next morning the Scouts pulled out of the way of the scheduled artillery preparation. At 0659 hours, with Lieutenant Commander John H. Morrill's 185-foot long minesweeper U.S.S. *Quail* standing offshore to adjust fire, Scout 75mm cannon fired, and a minute later Battery Geary's 12-inch mortars burst into action. The first four 12-inch rounds lifted tall, majestic water spouts just off the point, but corrections walked the projectiles onto the jut of land. "The shells sound like freight trains in the sky," reported an American forward observer. "I can see them high in the air and follow them to the ground. The armor-piercing shells cause minor earthquakes that drive the Japs out of their caves. The anti-personnel ones flatten all vegetation at ground level. Many men are jumping off the cliff—and no wonder, it's hell down there."[36] Commander Morrill's minesweeper stood offshore and fired its 3-inch guns. The ship's gunners fired their first rounds at a range of 2,200 yards at the western edge of the beach and one salvo landed in the middle of a Japanese mortar crew. After the *Quail* closed to within 1,300 yards of the beach, crewmen sniped with their 3-inchers at individual Japanese and sent ninety-five rounds of high explosive into every cave and clump of vegetation in sight. Japanese dive bombers were operating nearby, but they did not take any interest in the *Quail.*

Despite the 12-inch shells falling on the top of Longoskawayan, not all the Japanese jumped to the beaches to avoid the fires. Some followed the morning withdrawal of the Scouts and reoccupied the positions lost the day before. A Scout machine gun crew tried to stop the Japanese, but the Japanese took them under fire and forced the crew, one by one, out of position until only Private Raymundo Legaspi remained. In a final effort the Japanese killed Legaspi, but their advance likewise died. After stopping the Japanese the Scouts spent four hours evicting them from the same ground won the day before. In the short time remaining to him, the Japanese commander ordered several light field pieces and crew-served weapons, for which he now had no ammunition, buried. Subsequently, Scouts found a 70mm antitank gun partially buried, wrapped in heavy oiled paper. Upon close examination, ordnance personnel noticed that the small parts of these guns were not interchangeable with others of the same make. When Colonel Granberry committed his reserve—Captain Anderson's F Company—it took only three more hours to finish the job. By 1900 hours the Scouts stood triumphant on Longoskawayan.[37]

Small skirmishes continued along the rough shoreline for the next three days. On January 30 Scout patrols hunted Japanese across steep cliffs littered with fallen logs and huge, fan-like rooted trees sprouting from rocky crevices. Major Scholes of the Scout battalion and Lieutenant Hogaboom from the Naval Battalion led a patrol that killed seven Japanese. When Lieutenant James C. Brokaw took an E Company platoon along the beach to flush die-hard Japanese, he lost two Scouts killed—one from a premature explosion from his own dynamite hand grenade—and five wounded. Hoping to husband their Scouts, the 2nd Battalion coordinated support with Commander Goodall from an armored launch. Navy machinists had converted a 40-foot motor launch into a "Mickey Mouse battleship" by adding armor plate, a 37mm light field piece, two .50-caliber machine guns in the bow, and two .30-calibers in the waist. The machinists installed 3/8-inch shields of boiler plate in front of the engine and the bow and placed sandbags to protect the gasoline tank. Now this launch bobbed offshore looking for a target, so Lieutenant Brokaw planted a pole with a white flag at the base of the cave he wanted hit. After the launch made three firing passes, Brokaw dashed at the cave and threw a dynamite hand grenade, but he took an enemy bullet across his face. The .25-caliber round penetrated Brokaw's left upper cheek bone, both lower nasal sinuses and the nasal passage, and exited the right side of the face, but it missed the optic nerves and everything else important and required only minor surgery to repair.[38]

On January 31 an armored launch searched Lapiay Point, killing one Japanese and capturing another, while along Longoskawayan's rocky beaches four more enemy were killed and three captured. Finally, on February 1, the last four Japanese died. The fight here cost the Japanese dearly, for nearly three hundred infantrymen perished; the landing force's muster, captured after the battle, listed 294 men and 7 officers as coming ashore. Japanese 14th Army headquarters were completely unaware of the landing at Longoskawayan, and some officers could not believe their troops had landed so far south until shown the Japanese cemetery after Bataan fell. So even if Colonel Tsunehiro's assault troops had seized the West Road or captured some important terrain, they could not have exploited their success. No one except the Americans knew they were there.[39]

American and Scout losses were twenty-two killed and sixty-six wounded, not at all excessive for the results achieved. Of the twenty-two killed, eleven were Scouts and eleven Navy or Marine, while two men from the Naval Battalion were missing and thirty wounded. Commander Bridget was so pleased over the help the Scout battalion gave his Naval Battalion at Longoskawayan that he dug into Navy food stocks and sent the Scouts two truckloads of canned fruits, vegetables, salmon, corned beef, meats, soups, and jams and jellies. Each succeeding Sunday a Navy truck, protected by armed guards, delivered cigarettes, cigars, bottles of rum, scotch, bourbon, and a five-gallon can of freshly frozen ice cream. The Navy knew how to live![40]

One sharp naval action must be mentioned before turning to the second group of Japanese which landed the morning of January 23. After Lieutenant Bulkeley's adventure the morning of January 23, Lieutenant George Cox's PT 41 departed its anchorage the night of January 24 and cruised north along Bataan's west coast. Nearing Subic Bay, PT 41 slowed to idling and crept into the bay on one engine. A half mile from shore the boat's lookouts spotted a 4,000- to 6,000-ton Japanese freighter of new construction with streamlined bridge and small stack, sitting low in the water, still heavily laden. On a course of 320 degrees, PT 41 worked up to full speed and drove to the attack. At 800 yards Cox fired the starboard torpedo, which ran hot, straight, and normal, struck the ship, and exploded. Wreckage fell about the fast-moving PT boat. At 500 yards Cox fired the second torpedo, but the tail struck the boat's deck as it was launched. The Japanese aboard the stricken freighter were now firing at the boat, and as the second torpedo bounced errantly into the sea, a shore battery started firing.[41]

PT 41 turned hard to port and machine gunned the Japanese ship. As Lieutenant Cox dashed for safer water, the crew saw a torpedo boat obstruction net. There was time to turn, and the boat cleared the net by twenty yards. Splashes from the shore battery surrounded the small boat as it made its escape in a vigorous zigzag. Both crew and boat departed Subic Bay untouched, leaving the wreckage of the Japanese ship to mark their visit.

CHAPTER FOURTEEN

Quinauan Point

THE SECOND AND LARGER PART OF LIEUTENANT COLONEL Tsunehiro's battalion came ashore at Quinauan Point, a timbered peninsula where the Cadwallader Company of Manila had done some lumbering before the war. Quinauan Point formed the north shore of Agloloma Bay, a bay considered by far the best landing site along the west coast. Two trails, capable of carrying tanks, led from the beach to the West Road. Late on the night of January 22 disquieting reports filtered into several Filipino command posts. Listening posts heard boat engines off Quinauan and Agloloma. The moon had set at 2347 hours, and even though a Filipino lieutenant heard boats barely 200 yards out to sea, it was so dark the listeners could not see a thing.[1]

Barges carrying a portion of Tsunehiro's invasion force tried to land at the proper location, Caibobo Point, considered by the Americans as one of the three most probable landing sites and selected by the Japanese as their amphibious beachhead. Several craft that stood in close to the shore sailed into Air Corps .50-caliber machine guns. The American crews fired, and the barges tried to turn away but only succeeded in presenting their vulnerable sides to the heavy guns. Barrels of the 17th Pursuit Squadron's machine guns glowed cherry red as thousands of rounds arched over the water at the packed boats. The large .50-caliber rounds chewed through the nearest barges, scything across the hapless Japanese infantrymen. A battery of 75mm guns ranged the boats and then fired for effect. Abandoning the doomed craft, survivors swam to barges standing farther offshore. Rescuing the bedraggled swimmers, the little flotilla sailed south. By now the navigators were badly confused and the boats scattered.[2]

Some time after the Japanese were driven away from Caibobo Point, Sergeant Larry H. Cohen, farther south of Caibobo Point on Quinauan Point, told his buddies he saw lights flashing out to sea. But no one else could confirm his report. When an officer from the 34th Pursuit arrived, he likewise failed to see the dim, flickering lights. Something was off the coast, however. Using hooded lights to count heads and reorganize after the Caibobo repulse, the Japanese turned toward Quinauan. Edging east, they found this piece of terrain more hospitable than Caibobo. Still having no idea where they were, the Japanese, big men and well equipped, splashed over the rocky, ankle-turning beach without opposition.[3]

Reports from different American listening posts soon indicated the Japanese were coming ashore, but the airmen could not determine specific landing sites or enemy strengths. Nor were any Americans especially inclined to stumble around in the dark to find them. The beach defenders reported the enemy's general location to General Selleck at 0230 hours on January 23, six hours sooner than he learned about the Japanese who landed farther south at Longoskawayan. At Quinauan Point, 600 wet-booted Japanese were climbing near-vertical dirt cliffs. General Selleck knew the 34th Pursuit was not strong enough to stop them, so he alerted his reserve and told Lieutenant Colonel Irvin E. Alexander, the American senior instructor to the 1st Constabulary, to execute Plan Four and counterattack with his 1st Battalion. "Sammy" Alexander had been an infantry officer detailed to the Quartermaster Corps when he arrived on Bataan, and in January he requested a combat assignment and was sent to the 1st Constabulary. As senior instructor to the 1st Constabulary, and as infantry advisor to General Selleck, Alexander helped plan the defense of the west coast. He had recommended that the American Air Corps squadrons be placed at the most likely invasion beaches; as a result, the 34th Pursuit found itself confronting the landing. Until the Constabulary arrived, the 34th Pursuit had to fight alone.[4]

The 34th Pursuit Squadron, 260 men and two .50-caliber machine guns salvaged from wrecked aircraft, defended Quinauan's lovely, white, sandy beaches. Each .50-caliber sat on a homemade four-legged mount with a sandbag hung over the barrel to hold it down when firing. One Browning automatic rifle and one .30-caliber machine gun rounded out the squadron's firepower. The airmen's infantry training consisted of being handed a rifle and a cloth bandoleer of ammunition and receiving one hour of instruction on how to form a skirmish line. Some of the men never found a chance to fire their newly acquired rifles. When posted at Quinauan the airmen scraped shallow foxholes from the rocky sides and inlets of the coast and planted sharp bamboo stakes and barbed wire on the beach, but there was no real construction on Quinauan Point itself.

Everyone assumed the boulder-strewn shore and daunting cliffs would deter the most determined and reckless of amphibious planners. But the Japanese, bobbing offshore in leaking landing craft, were not picky.[5]

Sounds carried clearly across the water that night, and nearby Americans heard the Japanese coming ashore, the boats rattling and banging against rocks, and Japanese shouting and singing. One outpost, nervously watching the Japanese climb the steep slopes, telephoned a warning to squadron headquarters. But the rest of the men could not react to the warning; they were in the wrong spot and their weapons faced the wrong way. Within minutes, the first Japanese infantrymen scrambled over the cliff's edge and completely avoided the beach defenses. As the night's concealment lifted and dawn broke, an American in the northernmost outpost of the 34th Pursuit, a small rock fort, mistook some Japanese for Filipinos. The Japanese, walking close and shouting "Hi, Joe," a common Filipino greeting, shot Private Richard L. Morrell in the stomach and killed him. A second American, Private Stanley Felsher, drove the Japanese to cover with his Lewis machine gun—badly burning his hand on the hot gun in the process—and then escaped to raise the alarm.[6]

Unsure as to the enemy's location or intentions, the squadron organized a five-man patrol that carefully walked along the base of Quinauan's cliffs looking for the Japanese. The patrol found the landing site, identifiable from the erosion of the cliff where the 600 Japanese had scaled the heights. The patrol could hear the Japanese digging in with considerable energy. As the Americans listened, rocks and dirt from the enemy's construction effort slid down the cliff.[7]

In the afternoon, with this confirmation of the enemy's presence, First Lieutenant Jack H. Jennings, an ex-Marine, placed the squadron's platoons into a skirmish line, but the men bunched much too close together because of the jungle's thickness. Three Filipinos with an automatic rifle materialized and joined the line. As the men advanced through the woods, a corporal's rifle accidently discharged, and everyone hit the ground in panic. "We didn't have the least idea of what to expect," remembered aircraft mechanic Private Loren G. Pierce. "We didn't even have the advantage of having seen newsreels of infantry fighting. It was like taking untrained men off the streets, giving them guns and sending them into combat against trained, experienced enemy troops that were dug in and well supplied. It was just no contest."[8] Still not sure of the enemy's location or their size, Lieutenant Jennings ordered a reconnaissance by fire to draw an enemy reaction. Return fire showed the Japanese were still some distance away, so the airmen moved forward until they received effective automatic weapons and mortar fire. Here the Americans dove for cover under a hail of machine gun and rifle fire, fire that hit a sergeant in the jaw and clipped branches off trees just above the prone airmen. As the Japanese warmed to their task, they hit a second airman in the upper thigh. Jennings moved from man to man, encouraged them, and directed their fire until enemy bullets shattered his leg. Medics crawled forward and pulled him to the rear, but Jennings would not leave until he assured himself the other wounded were safe and the squadron under control.

"When the firing slackened," remembered Private Pierce, "I looked around and the only ones in sight were a wounded man about 15 feet from me and a buck sergeant about 30 feet behind us. Everybody had disappeared including the Filipinos with their automatic rifle."⁹ As Pierce looked around he tried to figure out where everyone had gone. He crawled to Sergeant Paul H. Duncan, whose leg was twisted and the bone broken. Duncan asked Pierce to straighten his leg, but Pierce hesitated; the wound was not bleeding badly and Pierce did not want to make things worse. He called for a medic and then fired a few rounds in the general direction of the Japanese, feeling he should be doing something other than just wait. But after a wait and no medic, he crawled back and fetched one personally. The two men succeeded in getting Sergeant Duncan to safety, but the wound was fatal.

The heavy Japanese fire had stopped the airmen cold. Realizing their inadequacy as infantrymen, the Americans discontinued active efforts to dislodge the Japanese. Sergeant James O. Bass took charge of the squadron and ordered the men to go easy on the ammunition. Although no further movement was possible, the 34th Pursuit's fumbling efforts were enough. The Japanese, concerned over the noisy reaction to their landing and missing a full third of their force—lost somewhere at sea that confusing night—looked for a place to dig in. Without his missing 300 men, now fighting at Longoskawayan, Colonel Tsunehiro felt too weak to press on toward the West Road. No doubt he was surprised to find Americans fighting him. He could only assume they were from the 31st Infantry, whereas he had no reason to suspect they were untrained airmen. Unfortunately for the Japanese, Tsunehiro's decision to halt was a serious mistake, for the 600 infantrymen then ashore could have scattered the airmen by simply advancing. By hesitating, the Japanese lost their best chance to cut the road; the 34th Pursuit certainly could not have withstood even a mild ground attack. As Sergeant Thomas E. Gage, an Oklahoman, recalled, "if they had come out in force on the 23rd they could have walked right through us."¹⁰

Using the time purchased by the airmen, Filipino reserves were assembling. After being alerted early that morning, Captain Jose Tando's 1st Battalion, 1st Constabulary, received movement orders and sent A Com-

pany, reinforced by a machine gun platoon, to help the hard-pressed 34th
Pursuit. A dirt road runs west off the West Road, and 1,700 yards toward
the coast splits in two, one branch running along the north side of
Quinauan and the other leading to the south side. At 1000 hours Lieutenant Ramon Delfin, a dentist before the war, led A Company west on
the northern trail. The company was still marching when hidden Japanese riflemen laced the Filipinos with small arms fire. Bullets shattered
Lieutenant Delfin's left arm, cut down two of his men, and drove the rest
to the cover of trees, rocks, and the good earth. Although the Filipinos
deployed and returned a hot fire—as hot as could be maintained with
bolt-action rifles—they could not advance. Most of the Constabulary had
some background in police work, but their time had been spent in garrison on administrative duties. Some were veterans of fights with Moros or
skirmishes with bandits and criminals, but like the Americans, the Constabulary were not good enough to face trained Japanese. Japanese fire,
some from automatic rifles that chattered like angry squirrels, pinned
them in place. Filipino efforts to push west along the trail stalled, two
more officers and several men were hit, and casualties mounted.[11]

The Constabulary's A Company was not left unsupported for long, for
the remainder of the battalion was aboard buses rolling toward
Quinauan. After the Constabulary left their vehicles to the sound of distant rifle fire, Captain Tando, a seasoned soldier with Mindanao Moro
campaign experience, collected his company commanders and issued his
attack order. Companies B and C deployed on the southern trail and
headed west toward the ocean. Lieutenant T. Caguioa's C Company ran
into Japanese after moving but a short distance. Not only did rifle fire
greet them, but the executive officer, Lieutenant Guillermo Angeles, lost
an eye and another man was killed by the explosion of a booby trap.
Heavy fighting here forced the commitment of the reserve, Lieutenant
Jesus L. Gonzales's B Company, which slipped between the stalled A
Company on the north and C Company on the south. While trying to get
part of the line moving, Alexander was fired on by an unseen Japanese.
Only an instant before his head hit the ground, a bullet smacked the same
spot. The close call so scared Alexander that he lay there mesmerized
until someone said in a dry, lugubrious voice, "That guy was sort of
shooting at you, wasn't he?" The words snapped Alexander out of his
daze. Nearby, a Filipino corporal jumped up, kicked his men to their
feet, and started a small advance until a machine gun killed the intrepid
corporal and stopped the attack. As daylight faded, the Constabulary
reinforced their line, and A Company stretched north until their right
flank rested on the Quinauan River. With his attack stymied, Colonel
Alexander requested help.[12]

General Allan C. McBride, commanding Bataan's coastal defenses, was in General Selleck's headquarters when Alexander's request for reinforcements arrived. The two officers discussed various ways to strengthen the attack. McBride turned to MacArthur's deputy chief of staff, the quiet, pleasant Brigadier General Richard J. Marshall, and asked for tanks. But the plea could not be honored; the tanks were already committed to cover II Corps's Abucay withdrawal scheduled to begin that very night. After dark, two Bren gun carriers roared and bucked their way close to the front and provided the noise, if not the cannon or armor, of tanks. While at Selleck's headquarters, General Marshall, a 1915 VMI graduate, an artillery battery commander in World War I, and now a quartermaster officer, concluded that Selleck's actions in dealing with the Japanese landing were unsatisfactory. Marshall felt that Selleck had not conducted, nor could conduct, the aggressive offense necessary to destroy the enemy. Selleck was not calling for the help he needed nor did he go to the front to see what was wrong. Marshall erroneously believed only a few Japanese were ashore, and he felt Selleck was not displaying enough aggressiveness to destroy them. Marshall talked with MacArthur's chief of staff, General Sutherland, and voiced his concern. Satisfied he had done all he could, Marshall phoned Selleck late that night and told him to personally push the next morning's attack; those were MacArthur's orders.[13]

Sutherland was receiving similar, and worse, reports about Selleck from people besides Marshall. Although a fine officer, Selleck just could not seem to cope with the actual business of fighting. So on the night of January 23 USAFFE decided to relieve Selleck of his command and replace him with 47-year-old Colonel Clinton A. Pierce, a wild Irish type who had built an excellent reputation and won a DSC while commanding the 26th Cavalry. A native of Brooklyn, Pierce had left the University of Illinois in 1916 to serve as a corporal with the 1st Field Artillery, Illinois National Guard, during the Mexican border crisis and was commissioned a second lieutenant of cavalry in 1917. His cavalry experience had been extensive. He had served with the 2nd, 8th, 12th, and 14th cavalry regiments, had developed a reputation as a hard-riding, hard-hitting, energetic officer of great promise, and had instructed at the Cavalry School before taking command of the 26th Cavalry. A motorcycle messenger reached Pierce at 2330 hours, presented Wainwright's compliments, and gave Pierce orders relieving him of command of the 26th Cavalry and ordering him to report to USAFFE Forward for extended duty. At about midnight Pierce arrived at I Corps headquarters—newly occupied by the corps staff and consisting of a few tents and a small house-trailer for

Wainwright—where Wainwright woke up, rubbed his eyes, and walked out of his quarters to greet Pierce.[14]

"Colonel," Wainwright said, "when I was promoted to be a brigadier general, the information was given me by General Malin Craig. He not only gave me the information but he reached up and detached two stars from the stars he wore on his shoulder. I now wish to inform you that you are from this moment a brigadier general."[15] Wainwright then opened his clenched right hand. "These are the stars that Malin Craig gave me. I want you to have them and wear them always—no matter how many more stars you get. Also, I want you to proceed to the west coast and kick hell out of the Nips who have landed there."

Wainwright then sent Pierce to USAFFE Forward where Pierce reported to the duty officer, Colonel Hirsh. General Marshall relayed an order through Hirsh for Pierce to relieve Selleck and assume command of the 71st Division. At 0230 hours on the 24th, Pierce arrived at the 71st Division where he found Selleck in conference with his officers. Pierce shocked Selleck when he explained why he was there; it was the first Selleck heard of his relief! When Pierce asked for a resume of the situation, Selleck turned to a map and told Pierce that he was planning an attack for early that morning. Selleck explained that the Japanese had come ashore at two places, Longoskawayan and Quinauan. Although Selleck was no longer in command, Pierce, in a considerate gesture, asked Selleck to accompany him to observe the morning attack. Considering that 600 well-trained Japanese were ashore at Quinauan and opposed solely by a Constabulary battalion and an Air Corps pursuit squadron, the failure to evict the enemy in one day cannot reasonably be attributed to Selleck. Despite limited time, the Japanese had constructed their defenses in depth so that any Filipino advance overrunning the first line would come under fire from the second. Even after strong reinforcements were sent to Pierce, long days of bitter fighting remained. But Selleck had used up his good will at higher headquarters. His 71st Division had performed poorly during the withdrawals from Lingayen, and Selleck's one-day fight at Layac gained him few admirers. So when he ran into trouble again at Quinauan Point, it was once too often, and he had to go.[16]

After an early breakfast Pierce and Selleck drove to a spot just behind the front lines. The two officers walked over a rough jungle trail for 500 yards until they found Colonel Alexander's 1st Constabulary Regiment command post, where preparations for the day's attack were in progress. Selleck asked Alexander if he needed anything. "I need some trained soldiers," Alexander answered, "but since I know they aren't available, I need wire communications with division headquarters."[17] All around

Alexander the Constabulary were finishing a cold breakfast and distributing ammunition. After an hour or so Selleck left to pack his gear and report to General McBride. Selleck was reduced to colonel one day later, on January 25. Colonel Charles A. Willoughby, MacArthur's mercurial intelligence officer, returning from a visit with Wainwright, arrived and asked that some prisoners be taken. Born in Germany in 1892, Willoughby started his career in 1910 as an enlisted man with the 5th Infantry, was commissioned in 1916, and graduated from both the Command and General Staff School and the War College. While Willoughby and Alexander walked toward the front line, they turned back many Filipinos trying to leave. The two tried to get Filipino officers out from behind trees to control their men but the men would not budge. After much confusion, the attack started at 0900 hours. Alexander and the Filipino regimental commander, Colonel Mariano Castaneda, a muscular, tennis-playing weight lifter destined to be Chief of Staff of the Philippine Army from 1948–1949, had to lead their men physically to insure they advanced. The soldiers were neither enthusiastic nor aggressive, and it was obvious they did not know combat procedures. More and better trained men were obviously needed, but until some could be found a fresh squadron of American Air Corps was all that Alexander would get.

As a stop-gap measure, a platoon of the 21st Pursuit Squadron bused from Mariveles to Quinauan. They carried a variety of weapons: Navy Marlin machine guns, Air Corps .50-caliber machine guns salvaged from P-40's, Browning water-cooled heavies, Lewis .30-calibers, and a few automatic rifles. The squadron, actually a small company, had only three bayonets, but this was all right, "because only three of our 220 air force men know anything about using them . . . ." recalled the squadron commander.[18] Despite having taken some hurried infantry training, the airmen were still unskilled. They found it impossible to form a line, and when someone yelled, "Maintain your interval," another airman yelled back, "Let the son-of-a-bitch who gave that order try to maintain it!"[19] "All we lacked was training and equipment," recalled 19-year-old mechanic Ray C. Hunt. "Fear we possessed. There was not a single entrenching tool among us. Many gas masks were thrown away and the containers used to carry ammunition. A rifle to me was no more than a stick."[20] With time and experience, however, the Springfield became Hunt's best friend. But inexperience seemed to help. When the Americans entered the fight next to the Constabulary, they made so much noise yelling, shooting, and crashing through the jungle that the Japanese believed major forces were deploying against them. The 21st Pursuit pushed around the jungle looking for Japanese, but the Japanese simply avoided them. The airmen stopped looking for the enemy when shadows lengthened and the light failed, and they were soon holding to each other's belts to avoid losing contact.

In the Constabulary's area the Japanese were less loathe to show themselves. The driver and gunner of a Bren gun carrier decided to attack a Japanese machine gun. After scouting the enemy position, the two men agreed to drive at the enemy with their small vehicle and shoot it out using their heavy .50-caliber. The driver gunned the engine, the tracks dug into the ground, and as the vehicle rounded a turn, the American gunner opened fire. He was immediately greeted by an antitank gun. The first round hit the heavy steel bumping bar in front of the carrier and bounced off, but the next shot penetrated the thin armor, exploded, and seriously wounded the gunner. The driver hastily backed to safety before another round arrived. By noon the Constabulary's attack had bogged down. Wounded staggered to the rear assisted by men trying to avoid the fight, and carrying parties wandered about looking for the midday rice. General Pierce and Colonel Alexander hauled Constabulary out from under trees and bushes, ignoring their claims of hunger and serious foot troubles. The Filipinos returned to the fight "most reluctantly."[21]

As the hours passed, both the Filipinos and Americans took casualties, thinning an already weak line. The Constabulary lost their battalion commander, Captain Tando, wounded in the right arm by fragments. Four men from the 34th Pursuit were shot, one of whom, when hit in the shoulder, grabbed his arm only to have another bullet shoot off a finger. The men could not see what they were shooting at, so they would fire, crawl a bit, and fire again when their officers told them to. Luckily, reinforcements in the form of a Philippine Army Air Corps provisional infantry battalion, Major Pelagio Cruz commanding, and Americans from A Company, 803rd Aviation Engineer Battalion, First Lieutenant Edmund P. Zbikowski commanding, arrived and went into line on the south and north ends of the Constabulary.[22]

At 1630 hours, when General Pierce left Alexander's command post for the 71st Division headquarters, a Japanese rifleman shot him in the foot. When Pierce fell, the two Constabulary with him fled. "After several minutes of quiet," Pierce remembered, "I crawled behind some trees, examined my left foot, found much blood but no broken bones, replaced my footgear and crawled to the rear."[23] It seemed to be a good day for shooting senior American officers, and the Japanese did not stop with Pierce.

As the long day drew to a close, Colonel Alexander crawled forward in one last attempt to advance, turned, and waved and yelled for everyone to follow. The Filipinos responded and drew abreast of Alexander. He repeated the process several times: crawling forward, stopping, and calling for the Constabulary. This continued for a few minutes until a man yelled a warning. As Alexander looked up, his rifle was shot from his hand, phosphorous from a tracer bullet burned into his skin, and his right thumb was hit. Then he noticed one finger from his left hand was gone and another considerably mangled. He dodged to another position and threw up. Colonel Willoughby led Alexander, suffering from exhaustion and shock, out of the fight to an aid station. There a doctor found a small piece of metal stuck in his breastbone after having penetrated fifty-four folds of thick paper of a map tucked in his shirt. At the aid station Alexander estimated he was facing an enemy battalion of 700 men. With a feeling of relief and thankfulness at leaving the fight for a place of safety, Alexander was driven to Hospital Number 2.[24]

Alexander's report, with many others, filtered up to Corregidor where MacArthur was analyzing the battle. MacArthur's report to Washington of the Japanese landing showed his deep concern.

> In Luzon, the enemy has landed fresh troops in the Subic Bay area and is attacking in force along my left and along the coast at many points. His coastal thrusts are covered by Navy warships and air force. I am counterattacking these landings on my right to relieve the pressure by diversion but the worn condition of my troops pitted against the fresh units of the enemy makes the result hazardous. There is little that I can do except to try to stabilize the situation by the ferocity of my fighting. I am doing everything possible along this line.[25]

Fighting continued without pause the third day, January 25, but faulty munitions slowed Filipino progress. One Constabulary company commander threw a hand grenade at a Japanese position but when it failed to explode, the Japanese tossed it back. It still did not explode. Only after a man threw it at a rock did it finally detonate. When mortarmen fired a Stokes 3-inch projectile, the round hit an overhanging tree limb and fell back on the gunners. It too failed to explode. The jungle was so dense that Filipinos and Japanese physically bumped into each other, and with no room to fire a rifle, they punched, kicked, and used pistols and knives. The lines became so intermixed that both Japanese and Filipinos slandered each other only a dozen yards apart. Captain Wayne C. Liles, an Oklahoman who had worked before the war with the U. S. Department of Agriculture, was eating when he heard a noise, looked up, and saw three Japanese standing before him. The Japanese frantically tried to get their rifles off their shoulders while Liles grabbed at his rifle and tried to get the safety off. Both Liles and the Japanese jumped to opposite sides of the same big tree. Liles poked his rifle over the tree's wide roots and fired. The Japanese did the same, firing from two sides. When the Japanese stopped to reload, Liles dashed to a safer tree.[26]

The use of American and Filipino airmen as infantry was a desperate attempt to stop the Japanese until stronger forces could be deployed, and as is common with desperate ventures, casualties were heavy and malingering common. The Philippine Army Air Corps battalion took exceptionally heavy losses. "The Filipinos didn't want to be there any more than I did," remembered airman Tom Blaylock. "They made every excuse to leave. There was one Filipino with a bullet in his arm, and one Filipino was carrying his helmet, one was carrying his rifle, one was carrying his ammunition bag, one was carrying his gas mask, and one was carrying his mess kit."[27] As frequent as casualties was heroism. Captain Pedro Q. Molina spotted a wounded officer lying twenty yards to his front. The wounded man was bleeding badly and could not live long unattended. Although the entire unit was pinned by Japanese fire, Molina ran forward, grabbed the man, and sprinted to cover. The wounded man survived, and Molina received the DSC.

Another noninfantry unit to suffer badly was First Lieutenant Zbikowski's A Company, 803rd Engineers, an Air Corps unit created at Westover Field, Massachusetts, hardly six months earlier and which arrived in the Philippines on October 23. On January 24 the ninety-man company was working on the West Road and coastal gun emplacements when an early morning phone call alerted the engineers and put them on the road. Leaving their heavy earth-moving equipment behind, the Americans picked up their two machine guns, a few automatic rifles, and numerous Springfields and pistols. Arriving at Quinauan that afternoon, they unloaded and milled about in confusion. An Air Corps major told Lieutenant Zbikowski that there were about forty Japanese there, and the airmen should evict them.[28]

But the engineers did not know how to do that. They had no idea what they were doing. The Americans were treated to the sight of several dead Japanese—big men despite the bloating caused by two days in the sun—and a badly damaged Bren gun carrier. The engineers spent the remainder of the day looking for phantom snipers. "The jungle was so thick, and we made so much noise I guess we scared the Japs off," recalled Sergeant Floyd T. Niday.[29] When night fell the engineers tried to establish a guard but, one by one, everybody fell asleep. Sergeant Gilbert B. Soifer was certain that had a Japanese patrol found them, "they would have killed every one of us."[30]

After breakfast the next morning the engineer company went on line and with 30-year-old Lieutenant Zbikowski in the lead began a slow sweep. Imaginations were rampant, and the men envisioned Japanese behind every tree. Airmen were firing their pistols, rifles, and BAR's, and it seemed a major battle was in progress. But to Sergeant Soifer the most miraculous thing was that no one had been shot. It seemed like Cowboys and Indians, and Soifer started thinking that things were not so tough after all. Events soon took a more serious turn. Slightly forward of Soifer was Private Raymond T. Goldbach from Connecticut, and as the airmen pushed through the jungle, Goldbach shouted, "Sarge, I'm hit." Soifer heard the cry and bulled his way through some vicious thorn bushes directly into the sights of a Japanese rifleman. A bullet entered Soifer's left side, broke the two bottom ribs, and exited just under his chest leaving a big, ugly hole. Soifer felt a tremendous pain, fell to the ground, and muttered, "What a lousy way to die."[31]

But when Soifer realized he was still alive, he used his first aid kit to cover the large hole left by the bullet's exit. As he fumbled with the bandage, he watched a big Kansan, Private Elmer C. Yochum, pick up a water-cooled .30-caliber machine gun and spray a long burst into the trees. An instant later, Yochum's head snapped back from the impact of a bullet, and he fell to the ground dead. Yochum's assistant gunner, Sergeant Paul Gellert from Flushing, New York, was hit and killed, and another two-man gun crew to the left died. A skinny kid from Brooklyn was badly wounded and called for his mother in Italian. When other engineers tried to rescue him, they, in turn, were killed or wounded. Engineers continued to drop, Filipino ammunition bearers refused to move forward, and medics hid in the rear to avoid exposing themselves to the fire. The engineers, many slipping into shock from their experiences, threw dozens of hand grenades, but only a few exploded. One man rose to toss a grenade and took a bullet through his shoulder. As he fell prone, another machine gun traversed over him. Bullets creased him lightly on the heels and legs, cut deeper across his buttocks, shallow across the small of his back, and deeper again across his shoulders. When someone tried to bandage his wounds, the large-size bandage disappeared into a gaping hole.[32]

BAR-man Private John J. Mackowski, a big 25-year-old from Brooklyn, had just shifted his position from the left of the line toward the center in a scared, wiggling, sweating dash when he saw the sun glint off a cartridge falling from a tree. Mackowski took a half crouch and emptied his BAR's twenty rounds into the tree, only to find the ground around him jump and jerk as Japanese bullets slapped in. "I got the hell out of there in a hurry," he recalled.[33] But his fire had been effective, for the tree "ran red." Nearby, Sergeant Soifer continued to patch his wound. Although his ribs hurt, he wandered away from the enemy fire until he found another man who took him to a jungle aid station. As Soifer left the fight, all he could think of was how badly his unit had been handled, like little leaguers playing the Yankees.

Captain Liles was following the engineers with his Filipinos of the 1st Battalion, 12th Infantry, listening to the sporadic shooting as the Americans pressed forward. At 1600 hours machine gun fire stopped the engineers. Liles realized the engineers had hit the main Japanese line. "The engineers got tired of the slow progress they were making," Liles recalled, "so they decided to rush the Japs. This was a fatal mistake, in a few minutes after the rush started, five of them had been killed and fifteen wounded out of the platoon immediately to our front."[34] An engineer officer asked Liles for help in removing the casualties. Liles agreed, but he found it difficult to get the Filipinos forward while the firing was in progress. After much work, the dead and wounded were removed.

Still trying to evict the Japanese with only airmen and Constabulary, the American command planned an attack for the afternoon of January 26. In order to surprise the enemy, the Constabulary battalion decided to launch their attack without first building up a base of fire. The men started a slow crawl to get as close to the Japanese as possible and this time, without the noise of a preparation to signal their intention, the Filipinos caught the Japanese unaware. Constabulary jumped into the closest enemy foxholes and trenches before the alarm was sounded. Hand-to-hand fighting cleared the enemy, but before the Filipinos could exploit their success, they were pinned from positions hidden to the flanks and rear of those just captured. The net result of four days of heavy fighting was a gain of just 100 yards. In preparation for yet another effort, a Scout 75mm battery from the 2nd Battalion, 88th Artillery, arrived at Quinauan.[35]

The lines holding the Japanese were now manned by an ad hoc force from the Air Corps V Interceptor Command; the 21st and 34th pursuit squadrons; some Philippine Army Air Corps; headquarters personnel from the 71st Division; the 1st Battalion, 1st Constabulary; and A Company, 803rd Engineers. Despite the wide assortment of units, there were only 500 men facing the 600 Japanese. Day by day they learned a little more about jungle combat, but always at a cost. Some men died while trying to retrieve the bodies of their comrades and it soon became difficult to recover even the wounded. The Japanese took special pains to watch for evacuation attempts. Riflemen in trees proved an invisible and deadly foe. So many Filipinos and Americans were shot from above that they fired thousands of rounds into trees, trying to neutralize the threat. As the situation worsened, pressure brought out the true nature of the soldiers. Peacetime loudmouths had trouble living up to their prewar images. Some of the strongest men did only what was asked, while quiet, unassuming men rose to the occasion and performed heroically.[36]

The morning of January 27 saw the Constabulary battalion, still the major force facing the Japanese, attack and fail. After resting and receiving a resupply of ammunition, they tried again. At the cost of numerous casualties—Major Sam Jones from the American advisory group died, and First Sergeant Camilo Sindion of A Company met his death in a Japanese foxhole—they pushed into the second line of Japanese. But no matter what their success, it was apparent they would never generate the power necessary to destroy the Japanese. The American high command had finally realized this, and help was on the way. And this time it was regular, trained infantry.[37]

When the first reports of the Japanese landing reached Major Dudley G. Strickler's 3rd Battalion, 45th Infantry, at 1000 hours on January 27, Strickler was told only twenty-five to fifty Japanese needed to be evicted. The battalion was into only its second day off after a thirty-two mile march out of the Abucay Hacienda and one of those days off included another march and foxhole digging. When the order arrived, the Scouts were still resting and cleaning equipment but Strickler wasted no time in ordering his men to assemble. Being suspicious as to the number of Japanese he would face, Strickler requested he be allowed to take his entire battalion to Quinauan, not just a reinforced company as originally ordered. His Scouts assembled so quickly that one company commander, Captain Henry J. Pierce, made the march in the only uniform he had, a wet one he had been washing.[38]

Major Strickler contacted the commander of the forces containing the Japanese and after a reconnaissance decided to bed his Scouts down for the night and begin the relief the next morning. The Scouts were still arriving after dark and a night relief would create terrible confusion. The Scouts ate supper and went to bed early. At daylight the Scouts prepared to relieve the Filipinos and the American airmen. All three Scout rifle companies went on line, K, I, and L from left to right, covering a front of 900 yards with a machine gun platoon attached to each company placed where resistance was expected to be the strongest. The men moved up to within twenty five yards of the front line and prepared to attack, while the Constabulary and airmen prepared to withdraw once the Scouts reached them.[39]

Beginning at 0830 hours on January 28 the Scouts attacked through the thick jungle, but despite their best efforts the veterans of the Abucay Hacienda battle were held to surprisingly small gains. Captain Louis Besbeck, commanding M Company, was seriously wounded while reconnoitering enemy lines. The bamboo here was so thick that even heavy

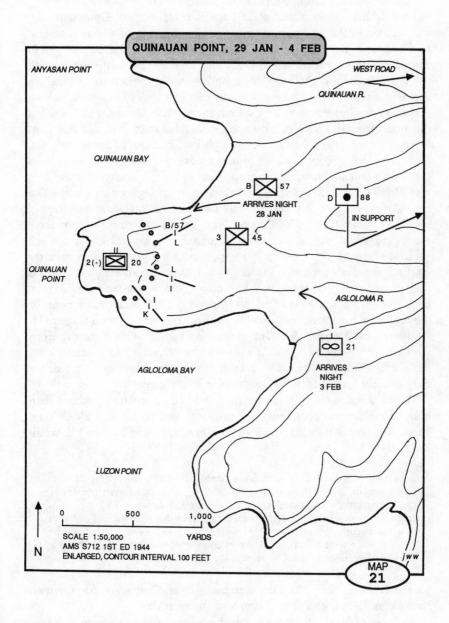

QUINAUAN POINT, 29 JAN - 4 FEB

ANYASAN POINT

WEST ROAD

QUINAUAN R.

QUINAUAN BAY

B ⊠ 57

ARRIVES NIGHT
28 JAN

D ● 88

IN SUPPORT

B/57

L

3 ⊠ 45

2(-) ⊠ 20

L

I

QUINAUAN
POINT

K

AGLOLOMA R.

∞ 21

ARRIVES
NIGHT
3 FEB

AGLOLOMA BAY

LUZON POINT

0   500   1,000

N

SCALE 1:50,000   YARDS
AMS S712 1ST ED 1944
ENLARGED, CONTOUR INTERVAL 100 FEET

jww

MAP
21

.30-caliber rounds glanced off the tough wood. The most effective weapons would have been 60mm and 81mm mortars, but no 60mm ammunition existed in the Philippines, and a severe shortage of 81mm ammunition reduced the effectiveness of that weapon. In place of the 81mm round, mortarmen used inaccurate 3-inch (75mm) projectiles. Although the Japanese held slightly lower ground than did the Scouts, normally a disadvantage, this positioning seemed to favor them because attacking Scouts were silhouetted when they advanced. The advantages of holding the high ground, those of observation and fields of fire, did not exist because of the vegetation and close fighting. Because of Japanese firing from atop trees, Scout machine gunners were tasked to shoot apart trees that might contain Japanese—a mission of no little difficulty—for the area was heavily forested with trees climbing sixty to eighty feet high. "The enemy never made any movements or signs of attacking our force," recalled Captain Clifford A. Croom, "but just lay in wait for us to make a move and when we did casualties occurred and we still could not see even one enemy."[40] Despite the expertise the Scouts held in infantry fighting, the day's progress was less than 100 yards, while at some points they gained only ten. Major Strickler now knew he was facing more than fifty Japanese, so once the battalion stopped at 1700 hours to prepare for the night, he requested reinforcements. That evening Captain Eugene H. Anthony's B Company, 57th Infantry, was attached to his battalion. Even with the extra riflemen, and even with the arrival of D Battery, 88th Artillery, Strickler's attack the next day failed to make any progress, for the Japanese fought furiously, especially in the center.

The Japanese were not any happier about their isolated position than Major Strickler was about his slow progress, and on January 29 Colonel Tsunehiro sent a message to General Kimura, telling him of his battalion's plight.

> Various units, which landed, have been surrounded by enemy of superior strength, and it is becoming doubtful whether our forces can collect enough strength to hold out. . . . the unit has suffered 152 casualties, reducing our fighting strength to such an extent that maintaining our position has become precarious. Our ammunition and food supplies have become low. In spite of this, our officers and men are fighting well. We pray for your Excellency's success. Banzai for the Emperor.[41]

This may have been the last message out of Quinauan, for General Kimura lost all contact with Tsunehiro the next day.

On January 30 the Scouts fired an hour-long mortar barrage in hopes of softening the Japanese. The vegetation was too dense to observe the fall of the shells, so men on the front lines listened to the bursts and fed information to mortar crews over telephone lines. They achieved some surprising control with rounds landing as close as twenty-five yards from friendly lines. When the mortars stopped firing an hour before noon, the Scout riflemen built up a tremendous volume of fire with M-1 rifles, machine guns, and even pistols until it was impossible to hear anything but the roar of the guns, the short, flat snap of the Japanese .25-calibers, the staccato crack of American .30-calibers, the arresting booming of the big .50's, and the background pounding of mortars "beating the temp for death's dance."[42] Bullets splatted into tree trunks, leaves fell, and dust rose as machine guns tore the earth. Then the infantry advanced. Lieutenant Anthony Ulrich from L Company stood up and moved about to encourage his men when a bullet popped past his ear. Scout infantry pressed themselves as close to the protecting ground as possible as they inched forward. At the rate of one round a minute, friendly howitzer shells thumped into the Japanese, heard by the Scouts but not seen. After an effort lasting forty-five minutes—fighting in tight jungle and a deafening world of noise—L Company Scouts gained only twenty yards at the cost of eleven men killed and wounded. The Japanese were well entrenched, and even the most sharp-eyed Scouts could not spot their positions until within a few feet. The Scouts gained so little ground that Major Strickler ordered everyone to return to the foxholes dug the previous day; it was easier for the men to spend the night there than expend the energy in building a new line.

The next day, January 31, events paralleled those of the previous day —terrific firing, an attempt to advance, and fourteen Scouts from L Company carried to the rear. At the close of the effort the frustrated Scouts reoccupied their old foxhole line. The high point of the day occurred at dusk when Sergeant Cabiles and three men from I Company made a dash into enemy lines, killed and wounded several Japanese, and returned with three rifles, a helmet, and several flags. Because of their complete failure to evict the Japanese, the Scouts fully expected the Japanese to mount their own attack that evening and simply run over them. Consequently, it was a nervous night. Every fifteen minutes someone fired a round and he was joined by everyone else. The Japanese, also fearing a night attack, returned a heavy fire. Oceans of sound rose, peaked, and receded, leaving everyone wondering why they were shooting. The Japanese did not attack; they spent the night low in their foxholes as the ground around them was cut apart by Scout fire.[43]

On February 1 General Pierce arrived at Major Strickler's command post and asked why so little progress was being made and why Strickler wanted help. Strickler tried to explain the situation. "I can't state with any degree of accuracy," he told Pierce, "but there are a hell of a lot more than fifty Japs."[44] Strickler handed Pierce an aerial photo, taken from a dead Japanese, covered with Japanese writing and arrows. To all Strickler's requests for aid, Pierce, a short, stocky, pugnacious cavalryman, said no; Strickler would have to fight with what he had. Pierce was not being hardheaded. He knew these Japanese were not garrison troops or poorly trained youngsters, they were "real, seasoned fighters," but Pierce just did not have many men. There were still Japanese resisting at Longoskawayan, another small force had landed just that night north of Quinauan, the Japanese were playing hell with Wainwright's main line of resistance, and Nara's 65th Brigade was flinging itself against II Corps at the entrance to Trail 2.

After Pierce left around noon Strickler walked forward to observe the effects of his mortar fire. When he arrived, his adjutant, Captain Croom, spotted him and called with his foghorn voice, "You'd better get down, Major, the fragments come flying through here like rain."[45] Just then, a round burst and blew pieces of metal and hunks of jungle through the underbrush. Croom coaxed Strickler down behind a log.

"This is a hell of a place to invite anyone to," answered Strickler. "I'm going over to B Company. Keep that mortar going and if I'm not back, start the attack at noon."

As he left, Lieutenant Ulrich called out, "Be careful, Major." Ulrich watched him go, the seat of Strickler's torn trousers flapping as he moved toward B Company. But the 39-year-old Strickler, a veteran of five year's China service, never reached his destination. At the junction between L and B companies, he walked out from between friendly lines into a Japanese machine gun. When he had not been seen for some time, his men launched a search, but they failed to find him. Captain Croom, a burly ex-football player from North Carolina State, assumed command of the battalion until the regiment's executive officer, Lieutenant Colonel Donald B. Hilton, took charge the next day.[46]

When the mortar fire ended the two center rifle companies made a quick dash forward, but aside from the initial burst of speed they failed to make further progress. These Scouts had fought at the Abucay Hacienda for seven straight days and had now been at Quinauan for five more hard days without relief. Those still alive had watched one of every two men carried to the rear, dead or wounded. After a conference the morning of February 2 the American officers planned another attack for that afternoon. At 1400 hours the men began their painful crawl toward the enemy under the ear-splitting roar of rifle fire. Scout machine guns fired and moved, fired and moved, and howitzer shells crashed down through the trees with dull booms that made shirts flap from the concussion. "All along our line, officers and men could be heard urging the men forward," recalled Lieutenant Ulrich.[47] Captain Croom stood up and led the men until a bullet hit his arm. His men forced him to an aid station, but he was quickly back urging his Scouts forward. The men hoped they would find Major Strickler alive if they could just go far enough forward. Slowly the Scouts gained ground.

At 1600 hours Captain Croom called General Pierce and asked for some tank support. In a surprisingly short time—seventy-five minutes—three tanks arrived. But even the addition of three tanks from the 192nd Tank Battalion to the Scout attack had little impact on the enemy's powers of resistance. Fallen trees impeded the tanks, thick vegetation reduced their fields of fire, and the tanks operated hesitantly. When the tanks spotted an antitank gun, the vehicles beat a hurried retreat. After "quite a discussion" with infantry officers, the tankers were convinced to try again the next day. But of the twenty-three tanks in I Corps, only three operated here, and they spent most of their time making short rushes into the jungle clearing a path for the infantry. The same three tanks were used continuously, and the tankers neared exhaustion in their oven-like vehicles.[48]

Lieutenant Ulrich discussed the slow progress with his company commander, Captain Pierce, a slender, wiry officer. "What the hell's the matter with our men out there?" asked Pierce as he pointed to some prone figures.[49] Lieutenant Ulrich crawled over only to find they were dead. Hearing the news, Pierce yelled to some other Scouts to use hand grenades against an enemy machine gun. The Scouts tried, but they were not successful. Pierce then called Sergeant Zacharais and Private Ablanto to his tree. He promised them both Distinguished Service Crosses if they knocked out the machine gun. Without saying a word, the two soldiers started out on opposite sides of the tree. Ulrich started to tell Zacharais to stay low when the cloth on Zacharais' shirt gave two little jumps, and Zacharais's crumbled to the ground dead. The two officers then looked at Private Ablanto who was also on the ground. When Pierce ordered him forward, Ablanto lifted his head to look back, gave the two officers a pitiful, futile look—only a second's worth—and dropped his head to the ground, dead.

Men were hit all across the line. Sergeant Fernandez had fought the Moros during that rebellion and had served the United States for twenty-nine years, first in the Constabulary, and then in the Scouts. Now he had been hit in the right side, losing most of his hip and a great deal of blood. Evacuation to the rude hospitals offered no surcease, for he died of his wounds. The net result of L Company's attack, just one of four rifle companies taking part in the February 2 effort, was seventeen killed and wounded, leaving but two officers and twenty-seven men alive. The next day two more Scouts died and two disappeared somewhere along the front line. Then on February 4 five more men were lost. The fighting was savage and unending, and to the few survivors it seemed only death would grant them rest.[50]

The tanks returned to the front the morning of February 3 and attacked after a thorough reconnaissance. Despite their presence, losses in the rifle companies continued to rise with some, like L Company, suffering horrendous casualties until everyone was worn down both physically and mentally. To put some fresh blood into the line, seventy Americans from the 21st Pursuit Squadron entered the line late the evening of the third and paired one by one with the Scouts. "On our return," remembered Captain William E. Dyess, a big, good-looking, blond-haired Texan deeply respected by his men, "we found that the scouts had occupied fifty yards more of the high jungle above the bay—at terrible cost to themselves. Their casualties had run about fifty percent. The sight and stench of death were everywhere. The jungle, droning with insects, was almost unbearably hot."[51]

Finally, on February 4, a coordinated attack using five tanks and close radio control forced the faltering Japanese into a shrinking perimeter only fifty yards from the cliffs at the very edge of Quinauan Point. Airmen of the 21st Pursuit, festooned with bandoleers of ammunition, heavy hand grenades, and various weapons, participated in the slow advance, fighting an enemy hardly more distant than the width of a small city street. Hand grenades, so heavy they had to be thrown side-arm, were unreliable and did better on the second or third toss than on the first. In fact, one Japanese wrote in his diary that he was more afraid of being hit by the heavy piece of metal than by it exploding. One American, recalling prewar movies where the heroes pulled grenade pins with their teeth, tried to do the same but ended with sore teeth and an unpulled pin. The ground was pitted with foxholes, scarred with forty-foot long trenches, and carpeted with toppled trees, uprooted brush, and shattered vegetation. Just before they advanced, Lieutenant Golden called to Sergeant Robert L. Miller, the chief clerk of the squadron, "Come on sarge, let's go."[52]

"Well, lieutenant, you're in charge, you lead," Miller responded.

"But I'm only a pilot. I don't know a damn thing about this business. You're the sergeant, you've been here a few days, you know what to do." The two men finally agreed to go forward at the same time. When the airmen advanced in company with a light tank, the tank stopped directly over a Japanese, straddling his foxhole. Undaunted, the soldier poked his rifle between the tank's road-wheels and shot Lieutenant James E. May as he ran past. May gave a single cry and fell dead. Nearby a tracer bullet barely cleared Sergeant Hunt's head and so shocked him that he did not know whether to be afraid or relieved. Another man took a bullet from the side across both upper legs, a bullet that should have hit, but somehow missed, his genitals. The squadron's flight surgeon jokingly accused the man of playing with himself when he was shot.[53]

The airmen, who suffered five killed and twenty-seven wounded on this day, learned not to assume an enemy was dead despite physical evidence seeming to confirm that state. Live Japanese pulled the bodies of their dead comrades over themselves and waited for the Americans to pass. As Corporal J. W. Bohner recalled, "You would come up to a foxhole with two dead Japanese in it, and the one on the bottom would have maggots all over his face and the one on top would be bloated and we would pass it on by and then this man who was supposed to be dead would rise up with hand grenades and get half a dozen people."[54] So the Americans carefully uncovered the numerous camouflaged foxholes and even more carefully tried to insure all the Japanese were dead.

Corporal Bohner, six and a half feet tall, weighing 220 pounds, and with the inevitable nickname "Shorty," was rear security when the 21st Pursuit advanced and he followed the line by a few yards, crawfishing forward while looking to the rear. The airmen, yelling and shouting to one another to maintain contact, crawled within twenty feet of a hidden machine gun that popped from a foxhole and fired. Bohner, watching to the rear, was hit in the left forearm, almost losing his hand, and another bullet dug into his hip. The remaining rounds moved away as the gunner traversed, hitting nine more airmen. The surviving Americans pinned the enemy with fire and killed him. Bohner crawled to the protection of a huge tree and slowly worked his way to the rear where he met four Filipino stretcher bearers. Bleeding badly, and very worried about his hand, Bohner was carried back to the squadron's doctor. The doctor said the hand could be saved if the surgeons at one of the base hospitals could spend four hours on their task. When Bohner arrived at the hospital, he was relieved to see the operating ward empty and the doctors looking for something to do. They saved his hand.[55]

In front of the Scout L Company, progress was now a little easier. The tanks, numbered one through five, were given a magnetic azimuth to follow, a radio-laden half-track from the Tank Group helped control the vehicles, and infantrymen guided the tanks with walkie-talkies. The Japanese took great interest in the radio antennas poking into view above the shattered terrain, and they concentrated their fire on them. The tanks, their sirens wailing, were the deciding factor now. The once-thick concealing vegetation had been shot away, allowing the tanks to see and maneuver. Guided by radio, they moved forward firing at targets spotted by nearby infantrymen. They shot apart Japanese positions or crushed them with their 13-ton weight. Three infantrymen followed each tank, one covering the right side, one the left, and one the center. When Japanese ducked into their foxholes to avoid the tanks, the following infantry shot or bayonetted them before they could recover. Surviving Japanese retreated until they occupied a perimeter slightly larger than a football field. Completely frustrated in their inability to stop the American armor, two Japanese took off their shoes and hurled them at a tank. The Americans shouted at the Japanese to surrender, but the two continued to fight. The tankers finally ran over them.[56]

Then an astonishing event occurred. Pushed past human endurance from thirteen days of vicious fighting without relief or resupply and facing tanks they could not destroy, the remaining Japanese jumped up shrieking and yelling, ripped off their uniforms, leaped off the cliff, and scrambled down the crumbling ledges. Captain Dyess watched the strange behavior. "I'll never forget the little Filipino who had set up an air-cooled machine gun at the brink and was peppering the crowded beach far below. At each burst he shrieked with laughter, beat his helmet against the ground, lay back to whoop with glee, then sat up to get in another burst."[57] Exultant Scouts and Americans fired machine guns and rifles into the beach and surf, killing scores of Japanese. About twenty Japanese tried to swim away, but they only provided the poor-shooting Americans with tremendous sport and marksmanship practice. The few good shooters among the airmen dropped into the prone position, wrapped their arms around hasty slings, and commenced a slow, deliberate, deadly fire. Indications of hits came first from the sound the bullets made when hitting a swimmer, then from the spreading blood.

In the area captured by the 21st Pursuit, the airmen picked their way through piles of dead Japanese enveloped by a stench so bad they stuffed cotton into their noses. One dying Japanese, his open wound crawling with maggots, lay partially concealed under two dead comrades. Although it was a terrible sight, a medic said that the maggots helped the man's wound by eating away all the dead flesh. Sergeant Hunt saw a single Japanese dart from a cave, run across the rocky beach, and dive into the water. "Japan is a hell of a long way," thought Hunt.[58] Nearby, a Scout machine gunner saw the man, slowly set his mess kit on the ground, settled behind his weapon, and fired. Spouts of red foam marked the strike of the bullets.

Yet this slaughter did not end the fighting, for it took another four days to kill the last of the Japanese. The remnants of Colonel Tsunehiro's battalion dug themselves into caves along the shore, and American and Scout patrols that climbed down the ravines or moved along the beach only succeeded in losing men. Although now starving and low on ammunition, the Japanese grimly held off all attempts at eviction. With help from a platoon of 71st Division engineers supervised by officers from the I Corps staff, the Scouts drove the largest enemy group into a single cave. The Scouts called upon the enemy to surrender, and the Americans used loudspeakers to entice the Japanese from the cave, but not a single man accepted the offer. Instead, they fired upon the men calling for their surrender. So in a move inspired by the American Civil War Petersburg mine, Scouts crawled from the landward side and destroyed the caves with 50-pound boxes of dynamite. The ground shook when the roof of the largest cave fell in on the fifty Japanese sheltering there.[59]

When the Scouts ran into trouble with smaller caves, caves facing the ocean, two motor launches and two whaleboats from the U.S.S. *Canopus* were again active. The launches shoved off from Mariveles at 0600 hours on February 8 towing the whaleboats and came into sight of the caves after a two-hour cruise. Lieutenant Commander Henry W. Goodall scanned the beach and cliff with 7×50 binoculars. Under a clear and cloudless sky and atop an almost motionless sea, Goodall saw a very shallow shoreline and a small beach with shrubs and rocks covering the cliff. Goodall's launch carried an antitank gun, two .50-caliber machine guns, and two .30-caliber machine guns. Both launches fired at targets marked by bed sheets hung from the top of the cliff.[60]

"On the left was a large and deep cave on which I opened fire with the 37mm gun," Goodall recalled, "and on the second shot at about 300 yards or less, the whole cave collapsed. We continued firing the 37mm at selected areas until about 175 yards from the beach when we shifted to the synchronized .30-caliber MG."[61] After almost running aground, the boat withdrew and repeated the process. After the second run, the whaleboats carrying airmen from the 21st Pursuit were called in. Simultaneously, three Japanese dive bombers pounced on the craft with 100-pound fragmentation bombs. Two boats with twenty airmen landed, grounding about 200 yards apart.

As the first boat banged into a rock, the airmen splashed into the blood-warm, crystal-clear water. Sergeant Cecil Ammons scrambled ashore with Captain Dyess. Looking up, Ammons saw the Japanese gunners leaning out of their rear cockpits looking down on the Americans. The men in the second boat—the party commanded by Lieutenant I. E. "Jack" Donalson—jumped into the water and splashed for shore even before the boat grounded. The coxswain steering the boat gunned it backwards, looked up at the diving planes, and jumped overboard as the first bullets impacted around the landing force. Despite one man killed, the airmen worked their way to the peninsula's tip and the Scout battal-

ion on top slowly advanced down the steep ravines. The Scouts captured
one Japanese who was fleeing from the airmen. The airmen, unable to
get an unwounded Japanese to stop feigning death and stand up, shot
him in the head. On his body was a letter, in English, written to him from
his sister attending a university in Oregon. In a ravine, Americans found
the remains of a command post with Japanese still seated as if going about
their work, except they were all dead.[62]

Commander Goodall and his boats began their trip back to the *Canopus.* But after thirty minutes of sailing, four Japanese planes joined an
observation plane that had been keeping the boats under surveillance.
The planes were high and seemingly not anxious to attack. Then a lookout's warning brought Goodall's attention to a plane diving out of the
sun. Goodall ordered right full rudder and was halfway through the turn
when a small bomb hit alongside, perforating the hull, wounding the
boat's engineer in the stomach and carrying away part of Goodall's left
foot. Gunner's mate Kramb shot down one Japanese plane but died at his
guns under the fire of his victim. Although badly hurt, Goodall beached
the boats and ordered the men to care for the wounded. All four boats
were chased ashore and lost, and three sailors were killed. The survivors
improvised crude stretcher and cut their way through the jungle to the
West Road.[63]

The battle for Quinauan was over. The Japanese 2nd Battalion, 20th
Infantry, was destroyed, its 900 men dead. To General Homma, the
battalion had been lost "without a trace."[64] The battles along the small
line had been unusually bitter. Lieutenant John R. Pugh, Wainwright's
aide, found a Japanese officer and a Filipino sergeant lying next to each
other. The Japanese had cut off the Filipino's right hand, but the Filipino
had killed his enemy with a pistol fired from his left hand. Every depression and foxhole was filled with Japanese dead, and pictures of wives and
children fluttered over the bodies. Having looted American and Filipino
dead, the Japanese, some wearing four wristwatches on their arms, were
now fair game.

Friendly losses at Quinauan were five times those suffered at Longoskawayan, nearly 500 Filipinos and Americans killed or wounded. More
than fifty Filipinos from the 1st Constabulary were lost, and of four
American instructors assigned, one was killed and two wounded. Scouts
of the 3rd Battalion, 45th Infantry, had carried the brunt of the battle.
They entered the fight on January 27 with 500 officers and men. Just
twelve days later only 212 men remained. Major Strickler was found
lying on his stomach, still wearing a helmet, carrying a long bolo on his
back, and identifiable only by the tear in his trousers. His death wound
was behind his left ear. The two Scout runners who had accompanied

him were also found next to him. Most impressive was the fact that every man in the battalion was accounted for as either present for duty, buried, or evacuated as wounded; there were no stragglers or deserters. On the battlefield not a tree, bush, or piece of vegetation had escaped the fighting. Large trees had been chopped in half and then chewed to pieces on the ground. Dud artillery and mortar rounds made the area hazardous even after the fighting ended.[65]

Before the Americans could consider the west coast secure, however, the results of two more landings had to be countered. In another effort to outflank I Corps from the sea, one company of Japanese from the 1st Battalion, 20th Infantry landed on January 27 and the remainder of the battalion came ashore the first night of February.

CHAPTER FIFTEEN

Anyasan-Silaiim

ALTHOUGH THE JAPANESE KNEW THEIR BATTALION AT QUINAUAN
Point was in trouble, they still hoped to achieve decisive results there.
And although Homma was not ready to give the Quinauan landing his
full support, he was interested in maintaining pressure against I Corps. So
on January 25 Homma ordered the 16th Division commander, Lieutenant General Susumu Morioka, to leave Manila with two of his infantry
battalions and the 21st Independent Engineer Regiment headquarters
and assume command of the operations against Wainwright's corps.
When General Morioka received orders to go to Bataan, he had limited
forces at his disposal; his 9th Infantry was working for General Nara on
Bataan's east side, his 33rd Infantry was spread across the Philippines and
completely unavailable for employment on Bataan, and Nara's 122nd
Infantry was tied down in front of Wainwright's main line of resistance.
Morioka decided to reinforce the Quinauan landings with one company
from his 1st Battalion, 20th Infantry.[1]

Reinforced with two small artillery pieces, this company assembled in
Manila and trucked quickly to Olongapo. The soldiers reached the town
after dark on January 26, picked up their supplies, and boarded their
landing craft. They also loaded extra food and ammunition for their
comrades at Quinauan. Under the light of a disappearing first quarter
moon they shoved off from Olongapo's docks at midnight, cruised out of
Subic Bay, and made the thirty-mile trip in three hours. But once again,
poor seamanship, a dark night, and difficulty in spotting landmarks along
Bataan's coast brought the Japanese 2,000 yards short of their objective.
From offshore the points and bays so easily identified on maps merge into
a solid mass of woods and appear as an unbroken curved shoreline. Some

Filipino artillery splashed near the Japanese, a few boats ran aground on reefs, and when the bulk of the ammunition could not be landed, it was returned to Subic Bay. Although the spot at which the Japanese came ashore looked much like Quinauan Point, the 200 Japanese actually landed between the Anyasan and Silaiim rivers, just north of Quinauan Point. The terrain here was covered with thick jungle growth cut by dry streambeds branching off from the two main rivers. Only one trail led in the proper direction, east, toward the critical West Road. Even though the Japanese encountered no resistance, they were slow in moving inland.[2]

There were men along the coast who might have made a fight of it, but elements of Captain Apolinar G. Fajardo's 3rd Battalion, 1st Constabulary fled, and no one reported the landing until an L Company platoon leader and some American airmen wandered into various headquarters. Not unusual in men involved in dishonorable flight, they reported that their units had been overwhelmed. When this news reached Brigadier General Pierce, the Sector commander, he ordered the 17th Pursuit Squadron—one of his reserves—to advance to the beach. The 17th Pursuit consisted of about 170 men armed with rifles and pistols scrounged in early December. The airmen had pulled many of the weapons straight out of shipping cases still heavily coated with Cosmoline. Other men had lifted corroded small arms ammunition from ammunition cans of World War I vintage. The airmen had four .50-caliber machine guns salvaged from wrecked P-40's, and using homemade sights, locally fabricated ammunition racks, and jerry-built mounts, the gunners could hold short bursts fairly close to targets.[3]

The 17th Pursuit had recently occupied a bivouac to train and serve as a reserve company, and the men were sleeping when the squadron commander, Captain Raymond Sloan, received orders to proceed immediately to the area of the landing. Sloan woke Lieutenant Stephen H. Crosby and said, "We're not going to train, we're going to fight!"[4] The officers told their men they were going to repel a landing by fifty Japanese. The airmen hastily ate breakfast, boarded cutaway buses, and convoyed up the West Road. When the squadron arrived—now only ninety men after clerks, pilots at Bataan Field, and the sick, lame, and lazy had been left behind—neither guides nor orders awaited them, but because the leaders had some knowledge of the area, they found the nearest trail and headed for the sea. Getting the airmen moving was simple; "Follow me," Lieutenant Crosby ordered, and they started down the three-foot-wide trail.

With their point element out—men with a .30-caliber air-cooled machine gun—the airmen walked 100 yards and entered the abandoned

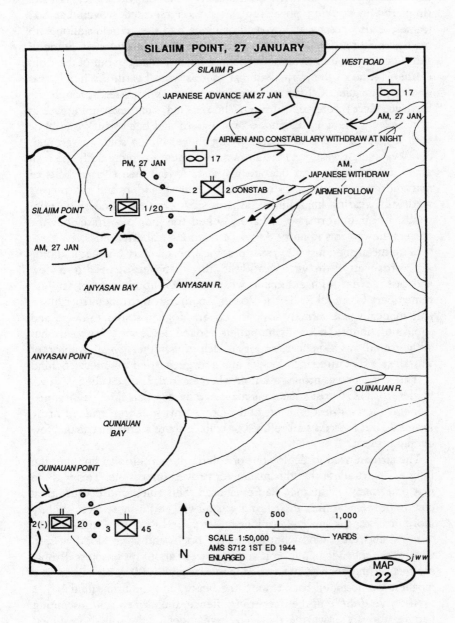

SILAIIM POINT, 27 JANUARY

SILAIIM R.

WEST ROAD

JAPANESE ADVANCE AM 27 JAN

∞ 17

AM, 27 JAN

AIRMEN AND CONSTABULARY WITHDRAW AT NIGHT

PM, 27 JAN

∞ 17

AM,
JAPANESE WITHDRAW

2 ⊠ 2 CONSTAB

AIRMEN FOLLOW

SILAIIM POINT

? ⊠ 1/20

AM, 27 JAN

ANYASAN BAY

ANYASAN R.

ANYASAN POINT

QUINAUAN R.

QUINAUAN
BAY

QUINAUAN POINT

2(-) ⊠ 20   3 ⊠ 45

N

0   500   1,000

YARDS

SCALE 1:50,000
AMS S712 1ST ED 1944
ENLARGED

jww

MAP
22

headquarters of the panicked Constabulary battalion where breakfast still simmered in cooking pots. Tents stood on elevated woven bamboo frames, trails were cut and marked by vines, and the unit aid station with medicine sitting on rocks and folded stretchers lay abandoned. Some of the Americans found clean uniforms and quickly changed out of their old clothes. None of the normal animal sounds were heard; the jungle was unnaturally quiet. Crosby was with the point as it passed through the bivouac. "Fires were still burning," he recalled, "and everything was in order except the field telephone switchboard had been struck one blow with a hand axe and it was still lying there. Not a soul was around. Spooky—man it was!"[5] As the airmen continued down the trail, one man asked an officer how to operate his rifle. A few men carried belts of machine gun ammunition draped over their shoulder, and the officers were still wearing khaki uniforms, low quarters shoes, and shiny pilot wings. Their uniforms were hardly suited for jungle warfare, but the officers viewed this infantry duty as a temporary aberration.

With the airmen just 300 yards past the Constabulary bivouac and only 400 yards west of the vital West Road, three Japanese stepped into view and opened fire with automatic weapons. "We about died of fright," remembers Corporal Robert J. Vogler, an aircraft instrument specialist.[6] Automatically, the airmen dove for cover. Vogler, scared to death and squirming under the low-flying bullets, looked desperately for cover, but all he found was a small tree root an inch in diameter. Small as the root was, the six foot three inch Vogler and a sergeant tried to squeeze behind it. The sergeant was prone to stutter when excited, and he yelled, "Va-va-vogler, for C-C-Christ's sake, ma-ma-move over." Captain Sloan phoned General Pierce's headquarters and reported his squadron had hit many Japanese, but Pierce's staff refused to believe there were more than a few enemy present.

The airmen tried to deploy out of column into a skirmish line, but the jungle was so dense that this maneuver proved impossible. This was the first time many of the men had ever fired their rifles, and because they could not see anything, their firing was high. The Japanese were slightly more proficient; a small .25-caliber bullet passed through Crosby's right arm just above the elbow but missed the bones and large blood vessels. Crosby had a bandage put on it and then went about his business. Probably feeling they had too few men, and already 1,000 yards inland, the Japanese outposts fell back toward the beach, and the firing died.[7]

After lying there in the deepening silence, the airmen sent a scouting party cautiously down the trail. The remainder of the squadron joined the point element and, fulfilling their mission as a pursuit squadron, pursued the Japanese down a slight slope until within a thousand yards of the coast. The Americans stumbled through the vegetation, skirted huge trees, and crossed rocky creeks hollering "Where's the left flank?" "Bring up the right flank," "Where the hell is chow?"[8] Officers and sergeants yelled orders trying to put the airmen on line, and the men cursed and screamed at each other trying to maintain contact. Listening to all this noise with astonishment, the Japanese halted, deployed, and stopped the airmen cold. Although no one was hit by the fire, the 17th Pursuit was decidedly stopped.

Earlier that day at 1100 hours the 2nd Battalion, 2nd Constabulary, received orders to join the fight. Major Diogracias U. Tenasas's battalion moved from its reserve location and joined the 17th Pursuit that night. When the Constabulary arrived, Captain Sloan confered with Major Tenasas, and the two decided to attack. Although the resulting fire fight was loud, the Filipinos and Americans found themselves fighting thick jungle creepers, vines, and underbrush as much as the Japanese. Lieutenant Jerry O. Brezina, leading some Constabulary against a machine gun, exploded a booby trap that killed him. Then the Japanese put on a burst of fire. "We never saw a thing," Crosby recalled, "and I think most of it was firecrackers, but my god, in that jungle, it sounded as if we were being attacked by an army. The green troops broke and move back up the trail."[9] The Americans stopped in the vicinity of the abandoned bivouac, and there they dug in for the night clustered in small groups. During the night another heavy fire fight spread across the line. The Americans fired as fast as possible drowning their fears in noise, and this time their bullets found a target. The Americans shot a Japanese scout in half, not a difficult feat since everyone was firing. Further to the rear, General Pierce heard the roar and thought a major engagement was in progress.

At I Corps, Wainwright was becoming more and more concerned over the safety of his corps as one Japanese landing after another splashed ashore behind his main line. On the afternoon of January 27 he sent a memorandum to MacArthur recommending consideration, and consideration only, of moving both corps farther south to shorten both the front and the coastal flanks. Wainwright stressed that his memorandum was a suggestion only and not a recommendation.

> My coastal flank is very lightly held, so lightly that the Japs appear to infiltrate through it at night at points selected by them. If I take troops off my front to thicken the Coast Defense, they will certainly crash through the front. They already attacked there today with infantry and artillery and have tanks in position.[10]

Wainwright was also concerned over his right flank units, his 11th Division and 2nd Philippine Constabulary. Without roads upon which to move—only narrow foot trails—they stood in serious danger of being cut off if the Japanese broke through to the West Road. When Wainwright wrote his memorandum, he was faced with a penetration of his front and the beginning of a pocket similar to the one that forced him from his original position. When he looked seaward, all he could see were Japanese coming ashore and threatening his lines of communications. Even his retreat could be endangered, so he had reason to be concerned. But MacArthur refused to order further withdrawals, and rightly so. General Sutherland considered the withdrawal idea bad, and he recalled that Mac-Arthur replied in "one of the most blistering letters" he had ever seen.[11] Maybe Sutherland considered the response blistering, but it does not now seem to merit that adjective. It took only a day for MacArthur to reply.

> There is no position that we can take that will shorten your line except the mere beach-head. Were we to withdraw to such a line now it would not only invite immediate overwhelming enemy attack but would completely collapse the morale of our own force. Sooner or later we must fight to the finish. Heretofore we have been maneuvering, falling back from position to position until we have now reached our last ditch. Our only safety is to fight the enemy off. He is not in great strength and if you can once really repulse him you will obtain relief from his pressure. He will continue to apply pressure, however, just so long as we continue to yield to it. If you clear him out on the coast his threats there will always be small. You must, however, hold on your front and there is no better place we can find than the one you are now on. Strengthen your position constantly. Organize your defensive groups in depth and prepare each one then to attack either to the right or to the left. Cover each beach and trail and do not let the enemy penetrate your main line of resistance. . . . Explain constantly to your officers and men if they run they will be doomed but that if they fight they will save themselves. The few days which we will have now before the enemy can make a serious attack, if vigorously employed by all officers, may spell the difference between victory and defeat. Drive everything hard in this period of lull. Make maximum use of artillery; it is your most reliable arm and its efficient use saved the II Corps on the original battle position. Every available resource at the disposal of the Headquarters has been committed and you must depend largely upon what you have.
>
> Once again, I am aware of the enormous difficulties that face you. Am proud, indeed, of the magnificent efforts you have made. There is nothing finer in history. Let's continue and preserve the fair name that we have so fairly won.[12]

The day after the landing, January 28, the 2nd Battalion, 2nd Constabulary, and the 17th Pursuit launched another attack. The previous day's combat had not taught the airmen any fine points of jungle warfare. The airmen had visions of masses of enemy facing them. Corporal Vogler recalled that they "hollered, screamed, moaned. Somebody would see something in a tree and they'd pot at it. I guess we shot at every monkey around. The Japanese must have thought there were thousands of us."[13]

It was only after a battalion of Scouts from the 45th Infantry arrived the next day that any progress was made and the situation considered under control. The 2nd Battalion, 45th Infantry, arrived on January 29 just in time to prevent a Japanese sortie from succeeding. The battalion's executive officer, Captain Arthur C. Biedenstein, commanding in the absence of Lieutenant Colonel Ross B. Smith who was reported missing during the II Corps withdrawal, led a reconnaissance party into Japanese fire. He returned with the information he needed and with one Scout casualty. A few airmen walked over to meet the Scouts—hard, tough-looking men, generally much older than the American or Filipino soldiers. The Scouts were friendly however, and joked, "What's the matter, Joe, got some problems? We'll take care of it."[14]

After the Scouts organized themselves, the officers planned an attack for January 30 but the effort proved premature. Planning was quick, and not everyone knew where everyone else was positioned. Registration by D Battery, 88th Artillery, began. When the first shell dropped on a slope up from the sea, Lieutenant Crosby called on a phone, "Bedy, where was that from you?"[15] Biedenstein answered that it was just off his point and "damn near got one of my men." Although the range was raised and corrections sent to the artillerymen, somewhere a mistake was made. When the Scout infantry attacked, their effort was shot apart by tree bursts from friendly artillery that killed four Scouts, including G Company's first sergeant, and wounded sixteen more. "Biedenstein was just madder than a hornet, Ol' Bedy was madder than hell," remembered Crosby, and Biedenstein came back to General Pierce's headquarters to report the short rounds.[16] The artillerymen investigated and found they had fired some very old rounds with powder that reduced the normal range.

As the units facing the Japanese collected their wits, General Pierce looked for someone to command the diverse forces collecting at Any-asan; Pierce wanted an infantryman. Major Harold K. Johnson, then unemployed, volunteered and reported to Pierce at his command post, a large tent fly attached to a small tent. Johnson met the chief signal officer of the Philippine Department and a host of people who offered him equipment and advice. Johnson rejected their offers telling them, "The first thing I have to do is to find out what the situation is there."[17]

Johnson made a reconnaissance and found "about as complete a lack of

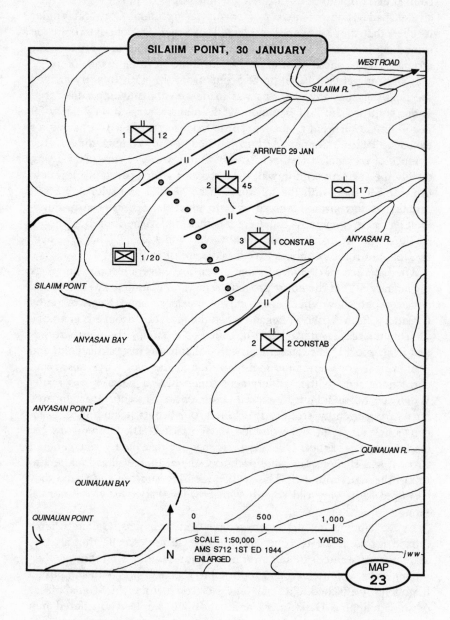

SILAIIM POINT, 30 JANUARY

WEST ROAD

SILAIIM R.

1 ☒ 12

ARRIVED 29 JAN

2 ☒ 45

∞ 17

3 ☒ 1 CONSTAB

ANYASAN R.

☒ 1/20

SILAIIM POINT

ANYASAN BAY

2 ☒ 2 CONSTAB

ANYASAN POINT

QUINAUAN R.

QUINAUAN BAY

QUINAUAN POINT

0   500   1,000

SCALE 1:50,000   YARDS
AMS S712 1ST ED 1944
ENLARGED

N

j w w

MAP
23

knowledge of conditions on the coast along which the Japanese had landed as could be imagined."[18] A confused collection of units cluttered the area and made control difficult. Trying to operate together were a battalion of Philippine Army, a battalion of Scouts, two battalions of Constabulary, and an Air Corps pursuit squadron. Johnson was concerned about the quality of his force. Johnson's hasty estimate indicated that there was little hope of destroying the Japanese with the forces at hand. F company of the 2nd Battalion, 45th Infantry, had been hurt in the withdrawal from Abucay a few days before, having been cut off while acting as the battalion's covering shell. It lost twenty-nine men killed, wounded, or missing, while another forty evaded the enemy for six days before reentering friendly lines. So when Johnson arrived, the company was combat ineffective and had been attached to H Company. A second company, G Company, had just been hit by its own artillery, and the rest of the battalion was still tired from its long march. The one company Johnson sent toward Anyasan Point made only slow progress even though unopposed, and it was too small by itself to advance if the Japanese fought. The 17th Pursuit was already disorganized from its introduction to land warfare and would not be particularly helpful in an assault. Johnson held the Constabulary in low esteem. Not the least of Johnson's worries was the obvious desire of the Sector commander to see some results. General Selleck had been relieved and reduced to colonel for his failure at Quinauan, and the newly promoted General Pierce could hardly help but think of this.

But before Johnson's forces could take action, the Japanese launched a desperate attempt to save the forces being destroyed at Quinauan and Silaiim Points. On January 27 General Homma ordered General Morioka to reinforce Quinauan Point and seize Mariveles Mountain. Assigned this huge task was the rest of the 1st Battalion, 20th Infantry, also known as the Kimura battalion after its commander, Major Mitsuo Kimura. Like its lead company, the 1st Battalion moved to the coastal town of Olongapo and embarked for the trip to Quinauan to reinforce the stranded 2nd Battalion. There was little time to plan and rehearse, for Major Kimura received his orders on January 31 and had to sail the next evening.[19]

The 500-man battalion was in trouble even before it left friendly shores the first night of February. On January 28 a Filipino patrol on Bataan's east coast found a mimeographed order on the body of a dead Japanese officer. A Filipino from the 31st Division killed the officer coming out of a sugar cane field and secured his dispatch case. In the case, General Bluemel found a notebook and what appeared to be diagrams showing a loading plan for a ship along with an operations order.

Bluemel looked it over and then sent it to II Corps, for he realized it was important and that it should be immediately translated. The order revealed Japanese intentions of reinforcing the western landings and driving to Mariveles Mountain. The decision to reinforce the Quinauan effort had been made only the day before so the capture of the order a day later set a record for speed of transfer. Confirmation of Japanese intentions came on January 30 when Scouts captured a Japanese aerial mosaic of the west coast. The mosaic indicated the enemy's ultimate objective was the capture of the West Road.[20]

There were also signs of pending reinforcements at Quinauan Point itself. At dusk on the February 1 a Japanese ship drew very close to Quinauan as if to draw fire. People on shore thought it was a minelayer or minesweeper, and the Americans could see the Japanese using binoculars to reconnoiter the coast. The Americans took immediate action to counter the expected landings. Staff officers alerted observers along the west coast and dispatched one of the two American tank battalions to the threatened area. The 3rd Battalion, 45th Infantry, on Quinauan placed heavy and light machine guns on both the north and south shore of the peninsula. The 2nd Battalion, 45th Infantry, collected twelve .30-caliber machine guns and placed them to cover Silaiim Bay and the sea.[21]

Just after dark General George's fighter aircraft went on strip alert. Ground crews moved around ten-foot-tall revetments to reach their aircraft, and the last of the Air Corps's precious P-40's were fueled, armed with three 100-pound antipersonnel bombs under each wing, and loaded with .50-caliber machine gun ammunition. Chicken wire on bamboo poles held foliage over each plane, and huge trees seventy-five feet tall supported jungle vines that completely covered work areas making aerial detection impossible. Under this canopy mechanics rolled the planes from their protective revetments along jungle paths to the airfields. Once in place, they stood ready for immediate take-off. Trucks crept along the runway laying a string of landing lights. Here was a chance to take the initiative, lash out and claw at the Japanese before they could land. Everyone waited in tense anticipation; the weather was good and the sky clear, moonlit, and cloudless.[22]

With his plan already compromised, Major Kimura encountered a second serious problem soon after his boats sailed. Three US Navy signalmen perched in an observation post atop a tree spotted his flotilla in the light of a full moon, a moon that rose at 1801 hours and would not set until nearly sunrise the next day. Using a direct line to Wainwright's I Corps command post, the signalmen sounded the alarm, and the carefully laid defense plan—the first coordinated air-sea-land action of the campaign—slipped into gear. Navy PT boats sped into the area, and the 26th

Cavalry left I Corps's reserve for Caibobo Point riding Bren-gun carriers and buses. Pilots of the 17th Pursuit Squadron had just gone to bed when they were alerted. Four P-40's roared from their dirt strips, climbed over Mariveles Mountain, and dropped toward the sea to attack the twelve or more enemy barges. Working in the coastal defense role for which they were originally conceived, the first P-40 swept over the trees—Allison engine screaming—flashed over the water, and dropped six fragmentation bombs squarely amidst the slowly sailing, troop-laden barges. "Oh, it was a wonderful sight," enthused Private Henry S. Winslow, a 21-year-old Iowan, "we knew we were really giving it to them. It was a wonderful feeling."[23]

On the second pass the low-flying pilots, two of whom were veterans of the strikes against Nichols and Nielson Fields five days earlier, subjected the barges to murderous .50-caliber fire from six wing-mounted heavies, a noisy procedure watched by Americans peering up from the coast. Five barges sank carrying the equipment and ammunition-encumbered Japanese with them. The P-40 blitz was a shock for the Japanese, until then confident in their undisputed aerial superiority. A Japanese plane flew into the area and was shot down by the P-40's. It was a grand and glorious night. The American planes returned to base, made a night landing without loss, and quickly rearmed for another strike. Ground personnel worked nearly all night servicing the P-40's, preparing them for sortie after sortie. Ground crews were amazed to see the planes encrusted with salt spray kicked up from the sea, and excited pilots regaled the mechanics with stories about the bright moon lighting the sea as if it were day; they could not miss. After eight sorties—flown individually as soon as a plane was rearmed—four fresh pilots replaced the original fliers and took off for yet another strike.[24]

The slaughter continued. After heavy 155mm guns of E Battery, 301st Artillery, and then light 75mm cannons of D Battery, 88th Artillery, found the range, they were joined by the unmistakable rapid booming of heavy .50-caliber ground-mounted machine guns from Scout and Air Corps units. The rain of big shells and heavy machine-gun fire cut into Japanese infantry crowding the tightly packed barges. As the Japanese drew closer to land, Scount infantry fired their shorter range weapons; their light machine guns and rifle fire chopped into the water. When soldiers of the Filipino 12th Infantry joined the Americans and Scouts with a stream of fire skipping over the water, tracers jumped and bounced in every direction as bullets glanced off barges, boats, and the sea. Captain Liles was busy controlling a battalion of the 12th Infantry while Japanese fired mortars at positions occupied by his men earlier that day. Liles watched as the barges came into view. "We ordered our troops to fire," Liles recalled. "I had a rifle company, four machine guns, the 45th Infantry had six machine guns and two companies of riflemen, the ground troops of the Air Corps had three .50-caliber machine guns. They all opened up at the same time firing tracers."[25]

Corporal Vogler was second gunner on a .50-caliber, one of three collected by the 17th Pursuit and now dug in on the beach barely eighteen inches above the high-water mark. Vogler could hear the barges coming in toward the beach. "They brought in the barges with a launch and then threw them sideways and we opened up on them," Vogler recalls. "It was shooting at less than a hundred yards. Beautiful!"[26] Tracers punched in at water level and exploded out the other side. The gunners had earlier changed the ratio of ball to tracer and were now shooting one tracer to every three ball; the heavy slugs, capable of piercing steel, wreaked havoc in the wooden-sided barges. Fifteen airmen made repeated trips from an ammunition point to the gun, lugging seven-foot belts of the heavy rounds over an uneven trail.

To the south, lying low in their foxholes on rocky Quinauan Point— the objective of the Japanese attempt—Lieutenant Ulrich and his Scouts were awakened by the battle noise, in particular by the Japanese facing them who were trying to support the landing. Several shells fired from the sea hit the 3rd Battalion but failed to injure anyone. Ulrich realized that the Japanese were trying to land, and he prayed something favorable would happen; his few men could not stop an attack once they landed, even though his line was being reinforced by battalion headquarters personnel and unit cooks. "All of our guns were pouring forth as fast as men could fire," he remembered, "then we heard the most welcomed sound . . . into the jungle night came the unmistakable deep-throated roar of our planes. One, two, three, four . . . we counted as they dove across our point. Bombs dropped, their machine guns rattled death, and excited cries could be heard from B Company's areas."[27] Ulrich was so happy and relieved he wept for joy.

Finally, Lieutenant Vincent E. Schumacher's PT boat dashed about firing machine guns and two torpedoes at the Japanese minelayer *Yaeyama,* which was supporting the attack. PT 32 had seen gun flashes along the coast, and despite a hull jury-rigged with wires and braces to hold it together, Schumacher headed for the fight. The *Yaeyama* pinned PT 32 with a bright searchlight and began firing two-gun salvos. PT 32 launched its starboard torpedo at 4,000 yards and its port torpedo at 3,000 yards. "At this time there was an explosion below the searchlight, definitely not gunfire, and debris came up into the searchlight beam," Schumacher reported.[28] Actually, the minelayer dodged the torpedoes but took a direct hit on her bow from shore-based artillery. After losing half their force before even touching shore, the thoroughly battered Japanese turned about and limped north. The air, sea, and land battle was a spectacular sight for the Americans and Filipinos. Shortly after midnight men able to see the barges watched them turn north away from Quinauan. But either because of his tenacity of because his damaged boats could not make the return trip to Moron—the closest safe harbor—Major Kimura beached the survivors at Silaiim Point and joined his one company already there. When General Pierce heard they had landed, he angrily shouted, "God damn it! they can't do that to me."[29] Pierce set Colonel Lilly and Major Johnson to work moving units against the Japanese.

Filipinos and Americans spent the next morning running down the few isolated Japanese who survived the sinking of their barges. Americans called upon several to surrender, but they tried to flee and were killed. One Japanese, floundering in waist-deep water, laid his head back and drowned himself rather than surrender. One barefoot, shirtless dead soldier who washed ashore had a handkerchief with the words "Me and Herman" and "The hair of the dog." Captain Liles's men buried him. Liles "wondered what his home was like, if his folks would find out where he died and what would be their reaction."[30]

But all was not well. The Japanese who landed with their equipment at Silaiim were full of fight. Some supplies were lost, some men were dead, and some equipment was missing, but fighting spirit remained. To keep the Japanese off balance, two batteries of Filipino and Scout artillery poured a thousand rounds of 75mm and 155mm high explosive into the beach head in the first twenty-four hours after the landing. At least now there did not have to be haphazard improvisation, no juggling of Constabulary, Air Corps, Philippine Army, and Scouts, for sufficient forces were on hand. Two battalions of the 57th Infantry, the 1st and 3rd, had arrived. The regimental colors carried its motto "Anywhere-Anytime" written on a ribbon held by an eagle's beak. The time was the night of January 30, and the "where" was the South Sub-sector. Both battalions moved into the South Sub-sector that night and next to the points the following night. As was the case whenever Scouts entered battle, there was an immediate lift of morale. "Make way, make way, the Scouts are moving in," an anonymous poet would one day write. To Major Johnson, the presence of the 57th Infantry "was [a] decided comfort believe you me," for his attempts to lead his muddled force against the Japanese had failed.[31] First he had ordered some airmen and 45th Infantry Scouts down a trail, but they stopped after fifty yards without coming under fire. Then Johnson stepped in front, called out "Follow me," and walked forward before realizing no one was following him.

The 57th Infantry brought friendly forces to three battalions of Scouts, a battalion from both the Constabulary and Philippine Army, and a pursuit squadron. The Scouts would be the main maneuver force while the airmen, Constabulary, and Philippine Army would protect the flanks and patrol rear areas. Lieutenant Colonel Edmund J. Lilly, a 47-year-old North Carolinian and the fourth commanding officer of the 57th Infantry in three weeks, assumed command of all the forces in the area on February 1, replacing Colonel Fry who suffered a heart attack. Lilly, a 1915 graduate of the University of North Carolina at Chapel Hill and the Infantry School Company Officers' Course, had arrived in the Philippines in February 1941 but did not reach the 57th Infantry until six months later; a chance encounter with Wainwright led to the assignment, much to Lilly's delight. Lilly served as executive officer to the 3rd Battalion, then commanded that battalion, and was regimental executive officer at Mabatang. Lilly was a quiet, self-effacing man whose rapport and empathy with his officers made him a respected father figure. He encouraged his men to use their initiative. Major Johnson had worked with Lilly at Mabatang and now became his operations officer. By now, fighting along Bataan's west coast had sucked up five of the six Scout infantry battalions on Bataan, and it was imperative that Lilly finish the fighting quickly so as to return these elite troopers to reserve. Until they were again free, a Japanese breakthrough would face only the American 31st Infantry as a mobile reserve.[32]

Discussions by Scout officers with units in contact disclosed that unit leaders knew they were in contact, but nothing more; no enemy locations, no enemy strengths, no number and type of enemy weapons. Because of the almost complete absence of firm information upon which to base a plan, Lilly decided to spend February 1 making a very thorough reconnaissance. Lilly took A Company off road security and sent it to check Anyasan Point, for until then no friendly troops were in position to offer resistance there. The signal people did not have enough telephone wire for A Company, so regiment gave them an SCR 131 Morse code radio. But because the radio was too large to carry through the jungle, it stayed on the road while runners carried messages between company and radio. One squad wormed its way down the Anyasan River bed to the coast without encountering any Japanese. This suggested the enemy were concentrated along trails. Elsewhere, the day's reconnaissance revealed the Japanese were establishing a perimeter from Silaiim River to Quinauan River, roughly two miles in length and 2,300 yards deep. This was large for the small force there—less than 450 men—but the line indicated the enemy's outer shell only, not where they would stand and fight.[33]

At the 57th Infantry's command post, conferences and briefings extended late into the night, but precious little additional information was uncovered. Patrols proved largely unsuccessful in locating the enemy and determining his strength, but they did reduce by 75 percent the area thought to be occupied by the enemy. Briefings were vague. The company commanders received very little information as to enemy strength or their location. All the officers learned was that the enemy had landed in considerable strength and was occupying several points. The staff finalized preparations for the next day, and because they now knew the enemy's general trace, they could assign specific objectives for each battalion. As there was no one spot from which Colonel Lilly could easily control all his units, signalmen laid eleven miles of telephone wire to tie everyone together.[34]

Major Reynolds's 1st Battalion received the mission of taking the southern-most objective, Anyasan Point, while Major Paul D. Wood's 3rd Battalion, north of Reynolds, was assigned Silaiim Point and the mouth of the Anyasan River. Lieutenant Colonel Ross B. Smith's 2nd Battalion, 45th Infantry, was to take the mouth of the Silaiim River and the north side of the point. Philippine Army, Constabulary, and Air Corps units were kept in reserve against a sudden Japanese breakthrough toward the West Road. Lilly's 2nd Battalion, 57th Infantry, rejoined the regiment from Longoskawayan on February 1 and went into reserve. Breakfast was fed in an assembly area, and each Scout picked up six hand grenades, one belt of machine gun ammunition, and an extra bandoleer of rifle ammunition; a limited number of 3-inch and 81mm mortar rounds were to be hand carried. Extra rations were not available.[35]

In the predawn darkness of February 2 the two 57th Infantry battalions departed their West Road assembly areas, 1st Battalion on the left and 3rd Battalion on the right. The 3rd Battalion, still weak from losses at Mabatang, filed out of its assembly area at 0445 hours and spent twenty-five minutes moving to its line of departure where it executed a passage of lines with the Constabulary battalion. The 1st Battalion, missing its B Company then attached to the 45th Infantry at Quinauan, had a shorter distance to march and moved out at 0515 hours. It was still dark on the jungle floor at 0600 hours when the men crossed the line of departure, but rather than providing surprise and concealment for the Scouts, the darkness only hampered the attack. Not needing light, the Japanese simply fired their prearranged fires and forced the Scouts off the trails into the jungle. Formations mixed, and leaders fought a losing battle to find and control their men. It quickly became apparent nothing could be done until the sun rose, so the Scouts went to ground and waited for daylight.[36]

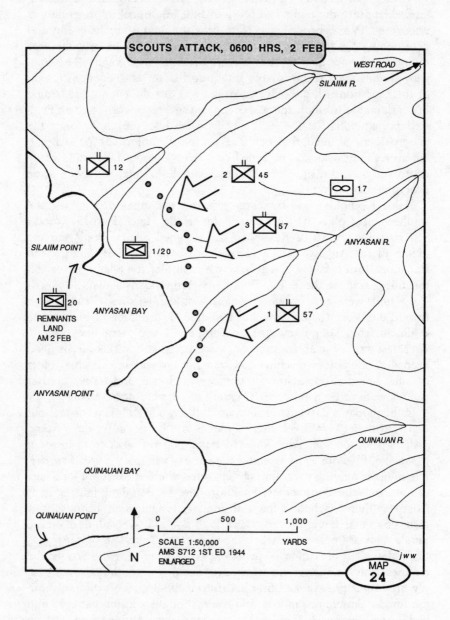

SCOUTS ATTACK, 0600 HRS, 2 FEB

WEST ROAD

SILAIIM R.

1 ⊠ 12

2 ⊠ 45

∞ 17

3 ⊠ 57

SILAIIM POINT

1/20

ANYASAN R.

1 ⊠ 20

ANYASAN BAY

REMNANTS
LAND
AM 2 FEB

1 ⊠ 57

ANYASAN POINT

QUINAUAN R.

QUINAUAN BAY

QUINAUAN POINT

0   500   1,000

N

SCALE 1:50,000
AMS S712 1ST ED 1944
ENLARGED

YARDS

j w w

MAP
24

When it was light enough to start again, progress was still slow and fighting at close quarters. The Japanese were dug into a series of well-organized self-contained strong points, each prepared for all-around defense, connected by communication trenches and possessing good fields of fire. They employed their light machine guns in pairs. When one ran out of ammunition, the other took up the fire as the first reloaded. The Scouts quickly found they were facing a better trained enemy here than they had faced at Mabatang. These Japanese were regulars whereas those at Mabatang were 65th Brigade soldiers with no combat experience. Luckily, the Scouts kept their casualties low partly because the small caliber Japanese bullet inflicted few mortal wounds; the bullets frequently skidded around bones rather than breaking them. Even men with complete punctures of the head or neck often survived with little damage. Even so, the advance was slow and cautious. Line of sight was five to ten yards, and runners were hindered by an absence of lateral trails. Movement perpendicular to the line of advance was almost impossible. Resupply of food, water, and ammunition depended on physical endurance, and manhandling bulky containers between close-spaced trees, over huge rocks, and through narrow machete-cleared trails proved as important a task as the actual fighting.[37]

Japanese riflemen maintained excellent camouflage and fire discipline shooting only when Scout rifle fire covered the noise of their own weapons. Enemy soldiers fired with the purpose of drawing Scout fire and then, having located the Scout line, Japanese riflemen had a confirmed target. By the end of the first day Scout gains were negligible. The 1st Battalion spent the day pushing its way through amazingly thick vegetation along the only two trails in the area. A Company was on the right and C on the left, and they lost contact as they tried to cut paths into the jungle. C Company chopped its way toward the sea, and it was not until late afternoon that the Scouts bumped into some Japanese who shot and killed the lead Scout in Lieutenant Paula's 1st Platoon. Paula deployed his men, returned the fire, and sent a runner to his company commander. "It was getting dark," recalled Captain Mills, "and because of the heavy jungle undergrowth, I felt it would not be wise to bring the other platoons into contact without knowing what we were running into."[38]

That evening the Japanese counterattacked and regained all the ground lost earlier that day. Japanese counterattacks were launched with individuals, small elements, and on occasion, large formations, and became a daily routine. Working independently, they tried to find an unprotected flank through which they could slip. But after the surprise of the first counterattacks, the Scouts dug in each afternoon and held the

enemy. At times, however, the expenditure of ammunition to stop the
Japanese was huge when compared to the damage inflicted.[39]

On February 3 the infantry received some support from nine light
tanks from Captain Harold W. Collins's C Company, 192nd Tank Battalion. The west coast was bad for armor everywhere and completely impossible in the 1st Battalion's area. The only place they could operate was
opposite Silaiim Point, and even here they were restricted to a single
narrow trail walled in by trees. "The hardest thing our men had to learn
was not to fire when going single file," recalled tanker Forrest Knox. "If
the first tank started firing, the file behind him would start sweeping the
area with machine gun fire. The first day I think they killed more Scouts
than Japs."[40] Mines posed the greatest danger to the tanks. Japanese
either pulled them across the tank's path with ropes or dashed from
concealment and attached them magnetically. There were real problems
the first day tanks were employed. Scout infantry operated under what
they considered doctrine, that of following the tanks by 150 yards. But
doctrine did not apply to the jungles of Bataan, and when the lead tank
lost a track to an enemy mine, it lay isolated from friendly support.
"Nobody could believe what happened next," recalled one man. "A Jap
rushed from the jungle, leaped upon the tank, lifted the hatch, and
dropped a grenade inside."[41]

The next day four infantrymen followed each tank and killed the Japanese who ducked into their foxholes. "I didn't have to say one word to
the Scouts," recalls Lieutenant Claude N. Kline in I Company, "it was as
though they had received training for this. The tanks blew the enemy to
bits."[42] Scout infantry guided the tanks forward and the tankers found
the close support most welcome. The tankers took signals from the
Scouts, and the Americans quickly formed a strong bond with the Scouts.
The longer the tankers worked with the Scouts, the better they liked
them. On some days each tank machine gun burned up 10,000 rounds,
machine gun barrels wore out, and supply officers screamed about expenditures. But the tank crews could not believe anyone would deny them
ammunition when they were in action, so they continued to shoot. Very
few bullets found a mark, but the huge volume of fire prevented the
Japanese from shooting back, and Scout infantry could crawl forward
with minimal losses. The tankers knew most of the fire was wasted, but it
allowed the Scouts to kill the pinned enemy, "and that was the name of
the game."[43]

Despite the tanks, it was still an infantryman's battle, and the foot
soldiers relied on rifles, bayonets, and untrustworthy hand grenades. Too
often a Scout pulled the pin and threw the grenade, but then nothing
happened except that the Japanese threw it back. "So we snatched it up

and tossed it back again," recalled Knox. "A silly game of hot potato. The damn things were duds, the detonator springs had rusted. So finally we would toss that one away and put a fresh one in play. Same thing."[44] Days of combat taught both sides small tricks. Japanese infantry dug inverted bell-shaped foxholes, and when a grenade rolled in, they curled back against the wider top and allowed the grenade to explode harmlessly below. As soon as this practice proved its value, the Scouts ran out of grenades and began tossing sticks of dynamite. The resulting blast was fatal to foxhole occupants wherever they were.

Because of thick vegetation and small fields of fire, the Scouts attached their heavy machine gun platoons to the rifle companies. The heavy weapons company of the 3rd Battalion had, since the start of the war, collected machine guns abandoned by Philippine Army units and now sported thirty water-cooled .30-calibers. The battalion was therefore able to maintain an incredible volume of fire, and the massed guns literally cut the jungle apart. One infantryman recalled that his unit suffered few casualties, "maybe because we fired up one hell of a lot of ammo. The jungle began to look less and less like a jungle."[45] But as the 3rd Battalion advanced away from the West Road, and as fields of fire and visibility both declined, the effectiveness of machine guns diminished. More important, the problems of bringing adequate ammunition over the rough terrain resulted in machine gunners being used as ammunition bearers for the riflemen. Light machine guns and automatic rifles proved the most useful weapons, for those weapons could bring enemy positions under heavy fire while riflemen crawled close enough to use hand grenades.

Artillery, although adequate in the number of pieces, was severely handicapped by the terrain. Despite many hours of reconnaissance, no one spot was ever found where more than two guns could be placed together. With the guns at an elevation of 800 feet, with the Japanese under trees sixty to eighty feet tall standing 100 feet above sea level only 4,000 yards from the guns, the problem of hitting the enemy without hitting friendlies was never solved. Treetops were regularly blown off, but the rounds could not reach the ground. The 2nd Battalion, 88th Artillery, firing British 3-inch and American 75mm guns laid over thirty-eight miles of telephone wire trying to coordinate fires, and the supported infantry gave the gunners priority use of their nets, but the guns never lived up to their capabilities despite firing 5,000 rounds. The single battery of high-angle 155mm howitzers did not have fire control equipment and could not be used for close infantry support. Even using mortars was difficult, for the thick vegetation seldom provided overhead clearance through which the rounds could be fired. Manhandling the mortars and ammunition over difficult terrain wore out crews at a fantastic rate. Yet despite all these difficulties, the Japanese found enemy artillery galling. They dispatched patrols deep into Scout lines to fire into battery positions, cut telephone wires, and shoot at small groups of men. Scout riflemen had to escort wire teams when they searched for cuts in the lines.[46]

The advance on February 4 disclosed a grisly scene. Scouts found Private Hilario Bernades of L Company hanged from a tree, and physical mutilation showed the Japanese had used him as a bayonet dummy. When the 3rd Battalion heard this news the next morning, their slow advance turned to a rush as they drove 200 yards into enemy lines. As the Scouts advanced and the situation cleared, Colonel Lilly committed his Constabulary and Air Corps reserves to link the 57th Infantry with the 3rd Battalion, 45th Infantry, further south at Quinauan. There were also gaps in the center of Lilly's line, for as the 1st Battalion advanced it opened a hole between itself and the 3rd Battalion to the north. General Pierce's Sector headquarters ordered the 1st Constabulary to send its reserve battalion to the Silaiim area, so the 1st Battalion, 1st Constabulary, veterans of the earlier Quinauan battles, loaded onto buses and bumped to the points.[47]

After dark on February 5 Captain Tando reported to Colonel Lilly, and Lilly showed Tando his sector and told Tando not to cross the Anyasan River because the other side was controlled by the 3rd Battalion. "Your mission is to plug the gap between the 3d on your right and the 1st Battalion on your left," Lilly told Tando. "Destroy the enemy as you push toward the cliff and beach."[48] Tando left Lilly, rejoined his battalion at 2000 hours, and led his men down a trail toward the coast. They groped along for twenty minutes until challenged by Scout sentries. A guide took Tando to Major Reynolds's command post where Reynolds explained the local situation and showed Tando where to place his men. By 0400 hours the Constabulary had two rifle companies north of Reynolds and one to the south. American Air Corps troops were placed to the left of the southernmost Constabulary company with the task of linking the line to Quinauan Point.

By now the month-long semistarvation diet was making itself felt. A day's ration was a slice of bread, two to eight ounces of rice, and an ounce or two of tinned sardines with a touch of evaporated milk. Men were listless and less eager to fight than before. In this terrain injured men could be moved only by litter, and litter bearers were now too weak to do a quick job. Considering the terrain, roads, and means of evacuation, transport to a general hospital was relatively speedy, taking two to four hours. Even so, some men died solely because they could not be evacuated quickly enough. Effects of the bad diet were cumulative, and even when extra rations were made available, the spirit of the troops did not noticeably rise. The Scouts had salvaged some C rations during the retreat to Bataan, and now one can was issued each day to each man actually fighting. Morale was good, but the men were suffering from prolonged starvation exacerbated by extensive mental and physical demands. Getting the food to the front lines could take up to four hours at night and two during the day. The few instances of chiseling by kitchen personnel were quickly eliminated, and because the Scouts realized they were getting all the food available, they doggedly persisted.[49]

The 2nd Battalion 57th Infantry—having destroyed the Japanese landing at Longoskawayan—relieved the tired 3rd Battalion on a moonlit night and pushed the Japanese closer to the sea. Tanks from A Company, 192nd Tank Battalion, often stood hull to hull with less than ten feet between vehicles as they flayed the Japanese. "The combined fire of all machine guns and tank cannons was fierce," remembered Sergeant Knox. "The infantry followed right behind the tanks as we fired and crept forward. Everything was killed in the spider holes and foxholes as we passed over them with grenade and rifle fire."[50] The Japanese in Major Kimura's 1st Battalion, 20th Infantry, were now in desperate straits. Unless help arrived, he was doomed. Kimura messaged General Morioka of his plight. "I am unable to make contact with the Tsunehiro Battalion [2nd Battalion, 20th Infantry]. The battalion is being attacked by superior enemy tanks and artillery, and we are fighting a bitter battle. The battalion is about to die gloriously."[51]

But rather than let Major Kimura's battalion die, gloriously or otherwise, Morioka ordered the 21st Independent Engineer Regiment to rescue the trapped men. With an odd collection of craft—one armored boat, eight motor boats, and twenty-one collapsible boats—the engineers departed Olongapo and sailed down the west coast the night of February 7. Peering from their tossing transportation, the Japanese failed to locate any of their troops, and when they approached the shore for a better look, they ran into two Bataan-based P-40's, artillery, and numerous machine guns.[52]

Corporal Leo Arhutick from the 17th Pursuit had a ringside seat overlooking the action. "From midnight till 3 a.m.," he wrote in his diary, "they tried to land but we held them off. We had help from the artillery, and also two P-40's from my own Sq'dn, bombed, and straffed [sic] the landing barges."[53] From shore, two self-propelled 75mm guns banged away at the Japanese while forward observers called corrections to a phone near the guns. Within a short time telephone corrections were no longed needed; the gun crews brought the barges under observed, direct fire. The next morning abandoned boats floated offshore. In one boat Americans found some maritime lifesaving equipment marked "U.S.A.T. *Merrit*," part of relief supplies sent from the Philippines to Japan on the Army transport *Merrit* after the bad earthquake and fire there in 1923. The next night the Japanese engineers succeeded in getting thirty-four of their wounded to safety by small boat, but they were the last Japanese to escape. Another twenty almost made it, but their boat engine failed. Before dawn, Scouts and airmen quietly positioned machine guns and riflemen on a cliff above the boat. Three Japanese were feverishly working on the engine as the first hint of dawn lit their plywood boat. The machine guns roared to life, and a Scout yelled at the American airmen, "Shoot them, shoot them, shoot them."[54] The boat flew to pieces beneath the floundering Japanese, and every man died.

About this time USAFFE tried its hand at psychological warfare and dispatched a sound truck to the coast with two Japanese-Americans who spoke fluent Japanese. But the attempt was handled badly. There was not a prepared script so the 57th Infantry had to write one, and it also became the responsibility of the regiment to emplace the truck and protect the two interpreters. The 57th Infantry had had some unpleasant experiences with Japanese prisoners. One had tried to blow up himself and a battalion headquarters with a hand grenade. Several of the regiment's men had been found on an earlier position with their hands wired behind them, bayonet wounds in their backs, and face down in a stream. As a result the Scouts had no desire to take prisoners. Enough passive resistance developed against the sound truck that it was not used. And although neither the Scouts nor the Japanese were interested in taking prisoners, it did happen. Scouts carried a wounded, completely helpless Japanese into the command post of the 1st Battalion. Lying on a stretcher, he looked up at his captors and drew his hand across his throat in a slicing motion, asking to be killed. Although the Scouts would have happily obliged, the Americans sent him to a hospital.[55]

For two days, February 7 and 8, the 1st Battalion, 1st Constabulary, sandwiched between two Scout battalions, made steady progress through relatively empty jungle delayed only by the slower progress of Scouts on each flank. The men were confident and anxious to move against what they felt were weak points. On the ninth, however, machine gun fire stopped the Constabulary. The enemy was in such a newly dug position that the fresh earth had not been carried away. Captain Tando directed Lieutenant Tinio, a machine gun platoon leader, to bring the enemy under fire, then Tando crawled toward the fresh mound of earth. Only twelve yards distant he threw a grenade that exploded in the entrenchment. One burly Japanese who survived the blast charged Tando, but

Lieutenant Tinio was still at his machine gun and chopped the enemy down. With this position reduced, the Constabulary rushed some supporting entrenchments so swiftly that the Filipinos were in the enemy foxholes before the Japanese could react. The Constabulary pushed completely through the enemy's line, captured a mountain gun, and advanced to within sight of the South China Sea.[56]

With the latest seaborne rescue attempt thwarted, General Morioka relieved Major Kimura from his original mission of linking with the Quinauan force and ordered him to evacuate his men using whatever materials were available. On the afternoon of February 9, as Captain Tando's Constabulary neared the sea, Japanese planes dropped bamboo message tubes to Kimura's men, but many of the tubes fell into Filipino hands. The tubes held instructions to withdraw, the time of the tides, hour of moonrise, and various methods of constructing rafts. "At 2200 every night," the message concluded, "barges will stand by about one-half kilometer from the shore to pick up those who will be found nearby."[57] American interpreters translated the message, and couriers passed the information to the Filipinos along the west coast. That night, soldiers with vantage points fired at swimming Japanese and shattered the escape attempt. The 21st Pursuit, having received only infrequent marksmanship practice, especially profited from the firing. Artillery observers spotted a tug towing five barges a mile offshore. Their guns engaged the tug and sank it, then turned on the unpowered barges sinking three and capsizing two. That night there was nothing to which intrepid swimmers could swim.

On February 10 the Japanese continued to retreat before the Scouts and Constabulary. When Captain Tando's battalion reached the coast the day before, Tando and his American instructor took great glee in reporting this fact to the Scouts. Captain George Manneschmidt was so delighted over the success of his much-maligned Constabulary that he taunted 1st Battalion Scouts about "streamlining" their foxholes rather than attacking. Spurred by hearing that Constabulary had advanced more quickly, albeit against much lighter resistance, the Scouts pushed steadily through minor opposition and neared the coast by late morning. At noon they ran into the final enemy positions and engaged in some close combat. In front of E Company the Japanese massed their fire on a particularly bothersome Scout machine gun, killing the gunner and driving the crew to cover. Private Bibiano Dapulang crawled through the fire, retrieved the gun, and dragged it to safety. E Company continued its attack, but the jungle and heavy enemy fire made any advance extremely dangerous. Only with effective suppressive fire could the Scouts hope to succeed. Sergeant Antonio Ocinar advanced his section of machine guns to a vantage point to cover the crawling infantry and kept up an effective fire from both his guns until he was killed. Private Bernardo De la Paz stayed with his gun when it jammed, and despite enemy rounds ripping into the dirt around him, he tried repeatedly to repair it. He stayed too long, and enemy rifle fire killed him. Through efforts such as these, the Scouts finally shoved the Japanese onto Silaiim Point itself and both sides could see the end approaching.[58]

A few Japanese broke away, crossed the Anyasan River, and prepared for a last stand on a small, wooded islet protected by a narrow but deep marsh. They killed three Constabulary and wounded several more. Covered by heavy machine gun fire, twenty picked Constabulary with fixed bayonets waded across the marsh onto the islet, worked their way through the trees, and shot or bayoneted the exhausted, emaciated Japanese. As a last effort, some Japanese tried to swim away, but it was like shooting sitting ducks. Airmen of the 17th Pursuit, 600 yards away, saw the swimmers and placed cigarette bets on each other's marksmanship. "I was always a pretty good shot," remembered Corporal Vogler, "and we would have 'call shots.' We'd pick out a Jap in the water, just like in a shooting gallery. I could generally shoot one round high, one low, and then drop him. You could tell when you had a score."[59]

During the morning of February 11 the Japanese strongly attacked the junction of the 2nd Battalion, 45th Infantry, and the 2nd Battalion, 57th Infantry, looking for a way out of the shrinking beachhead. That afternoon, Japanese combat patrols attacked E and G companies, 45th Infantry, but were no more successful than that morning. They must have found a weak spot, however, for in a final effort to escape the tightening ring of Scouts, 200 Japanese launched a desperation drive out of Silaiim Point at dawn on February 12. The assault drove through the junction between E and F companies, 45th Infantry, and ran into two H Company water-cooled .30-caliber machine guns. The Scout platoon leader, Sergeant Edrozo, joined Corporal Oxonian's gun crew. The men put up a gallant fight, temporarily stopping the enemy until running low on ammunition. A Scout went for more and stopped at nearby Air Corps positions asking for belted .30-caliber ammunition, but the airmen were armed only with rifles. The man ran on to a machine gun post, but while he was gone, the Japanese assaulted Corporal Oxonian's position. Edrozo fired his pistol until it emptied, then, with six other Scouts, died under Japanese rifle fire and grenades. The second Scout gun also ran out of ammunition, but this crew withdrew to safety. Captain Louis F. Murphy reached the right flank of his battered E Company and, hardly fifty yards from the Japanese, crawled from position to position reorganizing his Scouts, putting them into firing positions, and refusing his right flank.[60]

Losing about thirty men, the Japanese broke free, turned north, and ran into the command posts of the 17th Pursuit and F Company, 45th Infantry. Captain Raymond Sloan was trapped in his squadron headquarters, and when he tried to find a way out, he was shot in the stomach by a machine gun and died in a hospital. The Japanese surged forward and overran both command posts. Lieutenant Colonel Ross B. Smith, having rejoined his battalion a week earlier much the worse for wear after being cut off during the Abucay withdrawal, hurriedly called the 57th Infantry at 0700 hours and told them his command post was coming under fire. Three hours later, just as the Japanese hit the command post's security, and just as they started firing into the Scouts with machine guns, the 3rd Battalion, 57th Infantry, arrived. Leaders held a quick reconnaissance to determine how to attack.[61]

The 3rd Battalion's reconnaissance almost ended in disaster. Battalion officers were 200 yards west of the West Road quietly discussing what to do. While talking, they walked into a Japanese machine gun. Bullets zipped just over their prone bodies, and only a shallow depression saved them after they hit the ground. Captain Otis E. Saalman rolled toward a slight dip in the ground thinking it might offer better shelter, but as he rolled over he noticed weeds next to his nose being clipped by bullets hardly five inches away. He rolled back to his original position. Pinned and unable to move, the officers lay there worrying about enemy hand grenades and listening to the Japanese yelling to one another. A platoon of I Company Scouts heard the firing and crawled up to the officers. The platoon sergeant spotted his company commander and asked permission to use one of his two hand grenades against the Japanese. "Hell, yes," answered Captain Carl V. Schermmerhorn, "use both of them."[62] The sergeant crawled forward, threw both grenades, and was rewarded by two explosions. The platoon rushed the gun and found nine dead Japanese lying in a circle like spokes on a wagon wheel.

At noon, with the command group rescued, the 3rd Battalion formed a skirmish line with K and L companies and stabilized the situation. As L Company pushed against light resistance, Corporal Pablo Bayangos spotted some Japanese hiding in dense foliage. Bayangos tossed hand grenades and killed most of them, but not before he was hit in the shoulder by return fire. Even then, he charged the last Japanese, a man armed with a sword and pistol. Bayangos shot the sword from the man's hand, and then both men fired simultaneously, and both died.[63]

Hardly had K and L companies gone on line than twenty-five Japanese swamped an L Company machine gun losing twenty of their own men in the process. Captain Brown was elated over the enemy's losses, losses which included a beautiful Samurai sword that Brown showed to everyone in sight. Not so fortunate in this fight was the commander of K Company. A Japanese had grievously wounded Captain Charles Haas, so Lieutenant Claude N. Kline came over from I Company to take command. Kline, a sergeant until commissioned a second lieutenant two weeks earlier, found the Scouts gone to ground, some behind a fallen thirty-foot-long tree. He ran to the tree, crawled to its edge, and peeked around the corner in time to see a Japanese grab a Scout hand grenade and toss it toward the log. "Luckily, the Jap didn't have enough strength to thrown the grenade over the log," Kline recalled.[64] When another Scout grenade landed next to an enemy foxhole and rolled in, Kline ducked back behind the log. He did not hear the usual noise of a grenade exploding in the open. Instead, it was a dull thud, and Kline looked just in time to see dirt and flesh fly from the hole. The Scouts lept over the log, rushed past the dead Japanese, and pushed the exhausted enemy back toward the sea. When the Scouts overran an enemy command post, they found an officer's body next to a broken radio with four dead Japanese scattered around maps. In his diary the officer recorded he would soon be killed because every Scout seemed to be armed with a machine gun. Although the Japanese fought hard and skillfully, they were not in prepared positions. Their attack was broken, momentum was lost, and when the 3rd Battalion hit them, the survivors scattered.

By 1500 hours the next day the Scouts reached the beach. Nine Japanese piled into a small native banca and paddled furiously for open water. An Air Corps unit set up a .50-caliber on a point further north and played with the Japanese, firing in front of the banca forcing it left, then changing aim and forcing it right. Finally, the gunner laid a long burst directly on the boat killing all aboard. Along the shore, Scout patrols cautiously checked for hidden Japanese. Corporal Vogler was with a Scout patrol when they heard another group coming. The Scout in charge had everyone get down on each side of the trail and used hand signals to show where to heave a grenade. Then the Scouts heard the other group stop and deploy. After a few challenges in Tagalog, the newcomers were identified as Scouts from the other side of Silaiim. Vogler wanted to kiss every Filipino in sight. "We hugged right out in the middle of nowhere."[65]

The entire coast was covered with Japanese dead. Quartermaster troops were detailed to clean the area, but they just dumped Japanese in foxholes and threw a little dirt on them. Bodies were sticking out of the ground, and the smell was terrible. Emergency burial teams from Graves Registration Service Company No. 1 came into the area. They supervised Filipino laborers hired daily, workers who required the utmost supervision. The ground was carpeted with mortar duds, and men had to walk carefully to avoid stepping on them. The beach was littered with clothing, weapons, and all the trash of defeated men. When Major Johnson went through the area, he found it a regular slaughterhouse. Dead Japanese filled every foxhole, and the shore was covered by bloated bodies of the men who had tried to swim to safety. Another American saw a Scout sitting at the edge of a stream washing his clothes. Within arm's reach was a dead Japanese lying in the stream half submerged, his bare stomach protruding above the water. The Scout soaped his clothes, casually set the bar of soap on the dead man's stomach, then vigorously scrubbed his gear.[66]

Of the 200 Japanese who tried to break out from Silaiim, more than eighty managed to slip through. Travelling only at night, they marched to within a mile of I Corps's main line. On February 16 they ran through the 1st Division's motor pool and lost ten men to Filipino rifle fire. The early morning shooting woke the nearby 26th Cavalry, but it was not until 1730 hours that a troop was alerted to chase the Japanese. Major James C. Blanning, West Point class of '31 and Wainwright's headquarters commandant until February 2, assembled Troop E-F and marched after the Japanese. Blanning caught them and settled into position for the night.[67]

With his men on line, Blanning attacked at daylight, but he hit only light resistance, for the main body of the Japanese had moved west during the night. Two Scout patrols moved southwest and a third moved east. When one patrol reported some Japanese were surrounded on the west end of Trail 5 near the West Road, Blanning collected his men, distributed his machine guns to his riflemen, and sent an advance guard 100 yards forward of his main body. As they approached the Japanese, heavy fire hit the Scouts from both flanks. Crawling back to the main body, Blanning ordered four light machine guns forward to build a base of fire. Using fire and movement, the cavalrymen forced the Japanese from their position and found several enemy dead. Farther west they discovered even more enemy dead. The Japanese were in bad shape, caught on a ridge with barbed wire from the Filipino main line to the north and Filipinos and Scouts to the west, south, and east. Blanning used all his automatic weapons to place heavy fire on the Japanese for about ten minutes, then his men moved slowly forward against sporadic firing.

The Scouts overran the enemy and counted seventy-four dead, the last survivors of the Japanese 1st Battalion, 20th Infantry.[68]

Friendly casualties at Silaiim and Anyasan were estimated at 70 killed and 100 wounded, an unusually high proportion of killed to wounded. Most of the losses were from the 2nd Battalion, 45th Infantry, which was in the fight from the start; they lost 26 killed and 42 wounded. Noteworthy was the performance of the hard-fighting 1st Battalion, 1st Constabulary.[69]

At Longoskawayan and Quinauan, Wainwright's men wiped an infantry battalion from the Japanese order of battle. Now at Silaiim and Anyasan, they destroyed a second battalion, half of it at sea. USAFFE sent a photographer into the area and Lieutenant Stempin escorted him. "The most unforgettable thing was the stench of the dead bodies in the tropical heat," he recalled.[70] One ravine literally overflowed with Japanese dead; the Japanese had pulled their bodies back with them as they retreated and piled them in this cut. A few had been run over so often by tanks that they had disappeared into the ground. The incredible stench and choking reek remained the most memorable experience of Americans and Filipinos alike.

Now only a single battalion remained to the ill-starred 20th Japanese Infantry, and its time would come in the Battle of the Pockets. General Morioka's attempt to flank I Corps and force a speedy end to the campaign had ended in unmitigated disaster. Without adequate reconnaissance, committed piecemeal in different locations on different days, harassed before landing and contained after stepping ashore, everything that could go wrong for the Japanese did. The concept was good, and if things had gone well the landings would have posed a real threat to MacArthur's army. Even as poorly as the maneuver was executed, the landings caused considerable concern and forced the committment of five Scout infantry battalions, but the net accomplishment of three weeks of bitter fighting was the complete destruction of the 1st and 2nd battalions, 20th Infantry. By mid-February the threat to I Corps from the sea was eliminated. "Raiding areas on west coast of Bataan now completely mopped up," MacArthur radioed Washington. "Enemy counted dead number more than eighteen hundred. Estimated losses over three thousand. Own own losses very small."[71]

In early March the War Department recognized the part played by I Corps during this fighting.

The I Philippine Corps, United States Army Forces in the Far East is cited for outstanding performance of duty in action. Attacked on January 21 [sic], 1942, in the Bataan peninsula by Japanese forces that were superior in numbers, training, and equipment, and with complete superiority in the air, its units maintained position through sheer tenacity despite penetrations in its front and left rear. Skillfully executed counterattacks driven home with magnificent courage on the part of the troops resulted in the isolation of four hostile elements and their subsequent complete annihilation, thus restoring on February 14, 1942, the integrity of the corps front.[72]

CHAPTER SIXTEEN

Trail 2

AFTER FORCING THE AMERICANS OUT OF THE ABUCAY LINE, AND during the battles that raged along the west coast, General Nara launched his 65th Brigade against the newly established reserve battle position known as the Orion-Bagac Line. Three major battles were being fought during this period: the Points just mentioned, Trail 2 at the Orion-Bagac Line, and the Pockets behind I Corps's main line of resistance. Basing his plans on an American map found in an underground storeroom in Manila—a map that portrayed the American defenses across the center of Bataan as two lines—Nara now made the opposite mistake he had made earlier when facing the Abucay Line. Homma's intelligence officer believed the first line showed outposts and the second line the main line of resistance, so Nara thought the forces to his immediate front were there simply to delay him. The main strength, he believed, lay farther south where the Filipinos would make a final stand along a line running from Limay across Mount Limay to Mariveles Mountain.[1]

At Abucay, Nara believed the Filipino line was north of its actual location and now, in front of Trail 2, he thought it was south of its action position. Once again without proper planning and without artillery support, he launched his infantry regiments against what he believed was the Filipino outpost line, only to stumble into the main line of resistance. Part of Nara's difficulty in determining exactly what forces opposed him was due to the terrain; his men found the jungle in front of Mount Samat choked with shrubs six- to nine-feet tall. Aerial observation was next to impossible considering the concealment offered by the vegetation. Progress was impossible without the laborious task of cutting trails. Although there were some trails wide enough for one man at a time, they

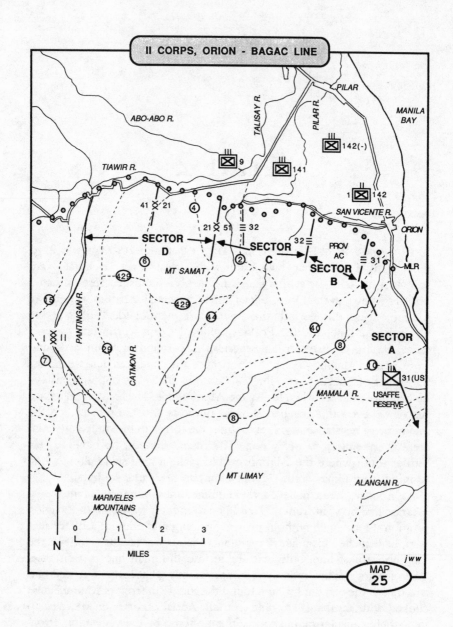

II CORPS, ORION - BAGAC LINE

PILAR

MANILA BAY

ABO-ABO R.

TALISAY R.

PILAR R.

142(-)

TIAWIR R.

9

141

1 142

41 21

4

21 51

32

SAN VICENTE R.

ORION

SECTOR D

SECTOR C

32

PROV AC

SECTOR B

31

MLR

MT SAMAT

2

6

42

5

42

44

40

29

46

8

7

8

SECTOR A

10

31(US

MAMALA R.

USAFFE RESERVE

8

MT LIMAY

ALANGAN R.

PANTINGAN R.

CATMON R.

MARIVELES MOUNTAINS

0   1   2   3

N

MILES

jww

MAP 25

ran in a confusing maze. The Japanese lacked trail maps and were daunted by the winding paths, fearing if patrols were sent into the tangle, they would never find their way out. Without aggressive patrolling, the Japanese could not locate Filipino lines.[2]

Nara was not confident about his upcoming offensive. He knew his brigade had suffered badly at Abucay with front-line units dropping to one-third of their previous strength and officer losses especially staggering. Second lieutenants commanded companies composed of only a dozen men, and dysentery plagued the soldiers who remained. Supply lines had not caught up with units after the sudden advance from Abucay, nor was artillery far enough forward to support a new attack. In fact, a 14th Army operations order issued on the afternoon of January 26 directed the 65th Brigade to pursue the Filipinos "without waiting for the artillery to catch up. . . ."[3] Although Nara had doubts, he did not hesitate. He wanted to take advantage of Filipino disorganization, a confusion he believed was so great that the Filipinos had merely fled into their new defenses. For some reason Nara believed the Americans would only fight a delay and then surrender.

In contrast to Nara's problems, the Orion-Bagac Line offered MacArthur's army numerous advantages. For the first time since the Philippine Army arrived on Bataan, I and II corps were in physical contact with one another. Moreover, the length of the line was only a little more than half the distance held at Abucay-Mauban, and the amount of beach needing protection declined by more than a third. But command problems within MacArthur's headquarters temporarily surrendered the advantages offered by the ground. While planning for the withdrawal from Abucay, MacArthur's staff visualized the three Philippine Division infantry regiments as an army-level reserve. USAFFE considered them the only units capable of maneuvering against the enemy under fire. But using these regiments as an army reserve was overruled by MacArthur's chief of staff, General Sutherland; Sutherland felt the new Orion-Bagac Line needed all the experienced units it could get. Experience had so far proved Sutherland correct. The 57th Infantry successfully defended the East Road in early January, and the 31st and 45th infantry fought the Japanese to a stalemate at Abucay Hacienda. Without the three regiments spread between the less-staunch Philippine Army divisions, disaster might send the new line back in rout. Sutherland therefore decided to commit the Philippine Division regiments to the new line and not hold them in reserve. The 45th Infantry was to go to I Corps, and the 31st and 57th would go to II Corps, all "without any strings attached."[4] Because these regiments were the best available, each corps commander put them along the most dangerous avenues of approach. USAFFE made no provision for an army reserve, figuring that "after the withdrawal was accomplished an Army Reserve could be formed."[5]

So during the Abucay withdrawal and occupation of the Orion-Bagac Line, both corps commanders had every right to assume the Philippine Division regiments would be available for employment along critical sectors of their line. But on January 25, the day of the withdrawal from Abucay and with the occupation of the new line in full swing, USAFFE decided to collect the entire Philippine Division and use it as an army reserve. The two Japanese landings at Quinauan and Longoskawayan were looking dangerous, especially since local counterattacks were failing to evict them, so USAFFE told the Philippine Division to withdraw from the main line on January 26. When the order arrived at I and II corps, hand carried by an officer from USAFFE G3, the three regiments were in the process of occupying their positions on the new main line of resistance. With barely twenty-four hours to release these forces, both corps were thrown into confusion. Staffs undertook frantic efforts to switch assets back and forth to cover the holes.[6]

In I Corps the removal of the 45th Infantry required premature commitment of two badly disorganized battalions from the 1st Infantry. These two battalions faced the task of holding the main line until the remainder of the 1st Division could come forward. Although II Corps objected strongly to the order, that corps nevertheless lost the 57th Infantry from the left of its line and the 31st Infantry (US) from the right. The Filipino 31st Infantry was nearby and reasonably available and marched up to take the American's sector, but a solution for the 57th Infantry was not as easy. The 57th Infantry was moving into the new line when it received the new orders and was split in two by the sudden change in orders, losing for a time two heavy weapons companies and most of the regimental supply train. Because the units affected were on a new, unfamiliar line, and because communications were not completely established, some people failed to get the word. II Corps grabbed the 33rd Infantry from General Bluemel to replace the 57th Infantry, but they forgot to tell Bluemel they were taking the regiment.[7]

General Bluemel faced the worst experiences. At daybreak on January 24, II Corps had ordered him to come to a meeting at Pilar at the corps advance command post. Realizing the summons was probably going to result in withdrawal orders, Bluemel told his chief of staff to round up regimental representatives to meet with him when he returned. When Bluemel arrived at Pilar, the II Corps operations officer issued orders to withdraw from the Abucay Line, withdrawal to begin at dark that night. Bluemel's 33rd Infantry and the 1st Battalion, 31st Infantry (PA), would be part of II Corps's covering force. They would withdraw from their

covering force positions the night of January 25 and occupy new positions the morning of January 26. II Corps gave Bluemel the shattered
51st Division and told him to use it and his 31st Division to defend
Sector C, a 4,500-yard wide sector covering Trail 2 where it ran south
into friendly lines.[8]

After receiving his orders, Bluemel drove to the new main line. There,
with his chief of staff, G2, G3, and regimental representatives, he reconnoitered the line and assigned each regiment its boundaries. A 51st Division representative had not yet arrived so coordination with that element
was delayed. Bluemel found that some engineer work had been accomplished along the line; foxholes existed for 600 yards on both sides of
Trail 2, and barbed-wire entanglements ran in front of the foxholes east
of the trail. Bluemel established his division command post and spent the
day checking the area. As the infantry regiments began planning for the
move, the division artillery commander, Lieutenant Colonel Harry J.
Harper, West Point class of '25, started looking for gun positions for two
battalions of artillery, one each from the 31st and 51st divisions, a total of
four firing batteries and sixteen 75mm guns.[9]

Now Bluemel's troubles really began. At the end of the day he learned
his 31st Infantry (PA) would be detached from him to defend the
beaches along Manila Bay—only the regiment's 1st Battalion would stay
with him. At dark the 31st Division began its withdrawal: the 31st Infantry headed for the beaches, the 33rd to its covering force positions, and
the 32nd toward the new main line of resistance. A 51st Division representative arrived and was shown where to place his men.[10]

As morning dawned on January 25 Bluemel's soldiers began to arrive
at the new line. Division headquarters personnel drove in and occupied
the command post, and the 32nd Infantry filed into its area and settled
into assigned boundaries. Sixty headquarters personnel from the can-
nonless 3rd Battalion, 31st Artillery, occupied the foxholes running east
from Trail 2. The artillerymen were to work here temporarily until the
51st Division and 33rd Infantry arrived, so Bluemel ordered them to
clear a sugar cane field to its front north of the Pilar River. As January 25
drew to a close, Bluemel sent his driver and car to II Corps to tell them
his progress and bring back any changes to his orders.[11]

During the night men from the 51st Infantry arrived. The units were
still disorganized from the beating received at Abucay where the 1,500
Filipinos lost all their .50-cal machine guns, all their mortars, and most of
their light machine guns and automatic weapons. But the energetic Colonel Adlai C. Young, their new commander, drove his Filipinos into their
lines west of Trail 2. Young had joined H Company, 3rd Infantry, Wisconsin National Guard, in 1916 as a Quartermaster and Mess Sergeant

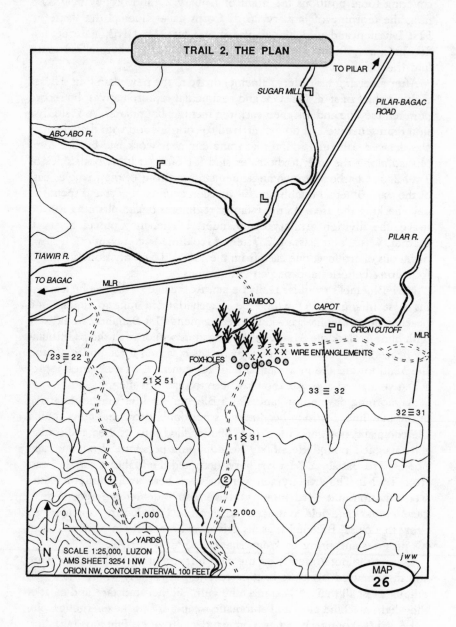

TRAIL 2, THE PLAN

TO PILAR

SUGAR MILL

PILAR-BAGAC
ROAD

ABO-ABO R.

PILAR R.

TIAWIR R.

TO BAGAC

MLR

BAMBOO

CAPOT

ORION CUTOFF

MLR

FOXHOLES

X X X X X   WIRE ENTANGLEMENTS

23 ≡ 22

21 ✕ 51

33 ≡ 32

32 ≡ 31

51 ✕ 31

④

②

0   1,000   2,000

YARDS

N

SCALE 1:25,000, LUZON
AMS SHEET 3254 I NW
ORION NW, CONTOUR INTERVAL 100 FEET

jww

MAP
26

and was commissioned in 1917 when 26 years old. Young was a veteran, having already escaped one tight spot in south Luzon on Christmas Eve. His battalion headquarters had been severely bombed, then attacked by Japanese tanks, armored cars, and infantry. His battalion was overwhelmed, and Young evaded capture by walking through swamps to friendly lines. Now safely on Bataan, and now owning minimal communications equipment, Colonel Young relied on personal contact to put his men into position along the foothills of Mount Samat. "The terrain was thickly forested and the canyons were steep," remembered Sergeant Romualdo C. Din in F Company, 51st Infantry, "and we were not able to do much except to dig our individual foxholes."[12]

As Young's men tried to arrange themselves before morning, artillerymen of the Sector artillery readied their guns, but putting the guns where they would be most useful and well protected would have required a logging operation "on the scale of a large lumber company."[13] So the men had to squeeze the guns into awkward, cramped positions until engineers could scratch clearings out of the virgin forest. No suitable firing positions could be found within the assigned area, so the guns were positioned east of the right flank boundary.

Expecting to find things in some order of acceptability, Bluemel set out on the morning of January 26 to check his lines. His first jolt came when he found his 1st Battalion, 31st Infantry, marching away from their assigned positions.

"Where the hell are you going?" Bluemel demanded of the battalion commander.[14]

"We're looking for Colonel Irwin, sir. We've been ordered to join him."

"Irwin's not commanding this damn division," Bluemel lashed back. "You're not going to take those goddam troops out of the line." Then the battalion commander said his orders came from the corps commander, General Parker. This infuriated Bluemel.

"Listen, I'm the commanding general of this division, and no one else can give you an order. You put that battalion back in the line where I told you, and you keep it there till I tell you you can move it. I don't care if Jesus Christ tells you to move it. You keep it there until I tell you to move it."[15] Realizing it was safer to face the Japanese than their own general, the battalion faced about and returned to the front line. A more serious shock was still to come. At 1000 hours, after putting the 1st Battalion back where it belonged, Bluemel had hardly resumed his inspection when he found an entire regiment, his 33rd Infantry, missing. It was to have occupied the line just to the right of Trail 2, but it was not there. Except for the sixty artillerymen, there was not a single soldier

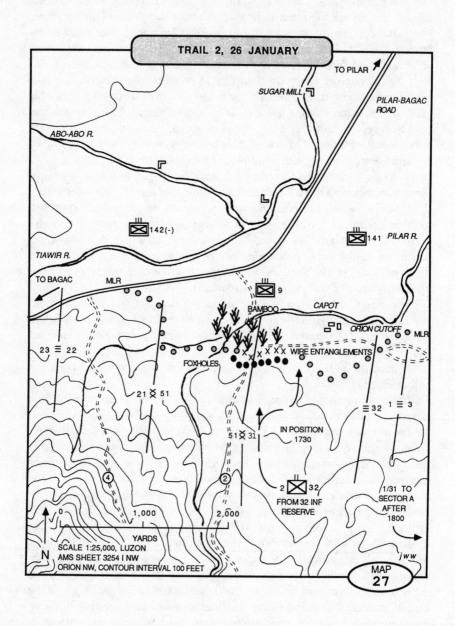

TRAIL 2, 26 JANUARY

TO PILAR

SUGAR MILL

PILAR-BAGAC ROAD

ABO-ABO R.

142(-)

141   PILAR R.

TIAWIR R.

TO BAGAC   MLR

9

BAMBOO   CAPOT

ORION CUTOFF   MLR

23 ≡ 22

FOXHOLES   X X X X X   WIRE ENTANGLEMENTS

21 ⊠ 51

≡ 32   1 ≡ 3

51 ⊠ 31

IN POSITION 1730

④

②

2 ⊠ 32

1/31 TO SECTOR A AFTER 1800

FROM 32 INF RESERVE

N

0   1,000   2,000

YARDS
SCALE 1:25,000, LUZON
AMS SHEET 3254 I NW
ORION NW, CONTOUR INTERVAL 100 FEET

jww

MAP
27

along a front of 1,500 yards, the most critical 1,500 yards of the entire II Corps line!

Standing in the gaping hole left by the missing 33rd Infantry, Bluemel turned to his intelligence officer, Major Salvador T. Villa, a fiery resourceful Filipino, and said, "Now listen, Villa. You see all these foxholes? I want you to see a soldier in each foxhole before you get back to my headquarters, even if you're there til the day after tomorrow. I want that done!"[16] Bluemel knew his 32nd Infantry had one battalion in reserve, so he scribbled a quick message for Villa to give to Colonel Johnson. "You will have your reserve battalion occupy sector assigned to 33rd Infantry. That regiment has been taken away. They will move immediately."[17] He sent Villa to fetch them and put them in place. By 1730 hours, Villa had completed his mission, and the men of the 2nd Battalion, 32nd Infantry, were in place.

Still looking for his lost regiment, Bluemel was getting madder by the minute. Trailed in his search by his all-Filipino staff, he turned on them. "Listen," he demanded, "the general has a staff to help him and take care of him. You people are no God damned good. I have to take care of you. What the hell good are you?" After some more fruitless searching, he faced his staff and implored them, "Show me you're some good, any of you. Where's the 33rd Infantry?"[18] No one knew. In a quest lasting four hours, Bluemel sent messengers to every conceivable place. The II Corps covering force had withdrawn, the tanks that had covered the withdrawal were leaving, and because there were no prepared positions behind the line manned by the sixty artillerymen, any Japanese penetration could easily break the defenses and roll into II Corps's rear area.

Finally, Bluemel learned what happened to his regiment. A staff officer told Bluemel he found an enlisted man who overheard the 33rd Infantry's supply officer tell another officer the regiment would be with the Philippine Division in army reserve, not with Bluemel. But this word never reached Bluemel, at least not officially. Even this information was partially wrong, the regiment was actually on the left of the corps line, replacing the 57th Infantry. Regardless of how the regiment was lost, Bluemel had now done everything within his power to plug the gap. Even so, instead of three regiments holding his front, he had only four battalions and a weak reserve. And yet another blow was about to fall. When Bluemel telephoned II Corps to complain about the loss of the 33rd Infantry, he was ordered to send the 1st Battalion, 31st Infantry, to Sector A to join the rest of the regiment. Bluemel was now down to three battalions with an uncertain reserve of an engineer battalion, and the Japanese were finally knocking at the door to Trail 2. The Japanese arrived with their advanced elements at 1900 hours, but the reserve battalion of the 32nd Infantry, placed there by Major Villa a nervous ninety minutes before the Japanese attacked, stopped the Japanese. Filipino cannon firing from the southeast played a major role in sending the Japanese stumbling back.[19]

Belatedly realizing the danger posed by the thin line along Trail 2, II Corps gave Bluemel two battalions of the 41st Infantry, and Bluemel immediately dispatched a staff officer to Sector D to pick them up. The 2nd and 3rd battalions, 41st Infantry, began their hike the evening of January 26 toward Trail 2. There were only 947 men in the regiment, and they came to Bluemel without a single machine gun. The regiment's 1st Battalion was then acting as the outpost line for the entire 41st Division, and General Lim decided to keep all the regiment's machine guns with the one battalion remaining to him. Lim even relieved the regiment of all its telephone wire before releasing the men. The withdrawal of these two battalions caused a great deal of unhappiness in the 41st Division. It made no sense to send a regiment to support the 31st Division when the 31st Division itself had lost the 33rd infantry to the immediate left of the 41st Division.[20]

It was now night and regimental officers had trouble assembling the men in the dark. The march started about 0130 hours. "Movement was very slow," recalled Colonel Wetherby, the senior instructor, "as the trail led up a river bottom across fords and up onto Mt. Samat's northern slopes. Single file was required and rests had to be made every few minutes."[21] Everything was hand carried, and the fourteen-kilometer march was made along a newly cut pack trail following a compass and trail map. No one in the regiment had ever seen the trail before, and even the guide was unsure as to the proper route. At the 21st Division, Colonel O'Day watched the men pass and spotted Wetherby and noticed how wet with sweat and worn out he was. At 1600 hours on the twenty-seventh, after a 19-hour march, the regiment's commander, Lieutenant Colonel Fidel N. Cruz, moved the men into a bivouac on Bluemel's reserve line. F Company immediately pushed forward to add depth to Trail 2 and act as a reserve for the units already on the main line, while the rest of the 41st Infantry sprawled in exhausted sleep.

The point the Japanese chose for their next attack proved to be the weakest in II Corps's line because of the switching of units, conflicting orders, and march and countermarch. The Japanese objective lay south of Trail 2 where the trail cuts through the Pilar River, and their plan was relatively simple. The Japanese recorded that their patrols had located Filipino lines astride Trail 2 on "a plateau covered with low jungle, with enemy positions on the lowest foothills. This was overlooked by the eastern base of Mount Samat, so that not only was a close-up attack by us difficult, but owing to the unfavorability of observation from the north, it was also most difficult to develop the power of the artillery."[22]

Initial probes with forces hardly stronger than reconnaissance patrols were repulsed. At midnight on the twenty-sixth, the 9th Infantry reached the north bank of the Pilar River, while farther east the 141st Infantry moved close to Filipino lines. Nara ordered his most easterly unit, the 1st Battalion, 142nd Infantry, to investigate Filipino strength near Orion. On January 26 these Japanese departed Balanga at 1400 hours and marched south along the East Road until reaching Santo Domingo, barely a mile north of Orion. Then they found Orion abandoned. The Filipinos waited about a mile south behind flooded rice paddies. The remainder of the 142nd Infantry departed their bivouac west of Balanga at 1900 hours and walked into Filipino artillery that delayed their movement until midnight. By the early morning hours of January 27 the Japanese were in position to attack.[23]

In planning for the new offensive, Nara was concerned over what he believed were strong fortifications near Orion. "Enemy positions around Orion along the Bagac-Pilar Road had been prepared for a considerable time, the terrain being skillfully used and strong constructions made. The area from directly in front of them to their rear was swept by a fire net, especially by the artillery, thus making the position seem impregnable. Moreover, the positions were joined with the fortress of Corregidor, where it was reported that provisions for two years were stored."[24] The Japanese had little hope for success along the coast but they could not completely ignore the area. So Nara decided to have one battalion feint along the East Road, and the remainder of the 65th Brigade would make the main attack down Trail 2. The Japanese realized there were gaps in the Filipino line but they were wrong about which area was weak. Major Tadaji Tanabe, commanding the left flank pursuit unit—the 1st Battalion, 142nd Infantry—saw some gaps during a reconnaissance. "There are enemy forces of considerable strength near Capot, occupying positions facing northeast but apparently there are none in the Mount Samat region. Strong enemy forces are also in occupation of the uplands west of Orion but their main positions are apparently unoccupied. There are also reports from air units to the effect that the enemy are still continuing their retreat toward Limay and that their main strength has advanced to the mountainous area west of that locality."[25]

Nara issued his attack order at 1100 hours on January 27 and selected two regiments, the 9th and 141st, to make the main attack. They would be supported by the 142nd Infantry (-) which was to move to their right. The brigade's mission was to capture the northeast slopes of the dominating terrain, Mount Samat. Because Nara still believed he was only facing an outpost line, he did not expect serious resistance until he arrived in the vicinity of Limay, about six miles southeast of Mount Samat. He believed the Filipinos were disorganized and that gaps existed through which he could drive his men. Nara was correct about the gaps and disorganization, but his analysis of the situation was one day too late.[26]

A little after noon on January 27 Major Tanabe's 1st Battalion, 142nd Infantry, began its approach march and contacted the Filipinos holding the East Road. Tanabe's mission was to divert and tie down any Filipinos he met and prevent them from reacting to Nara's main attack. But Tanabe did not push his feint aggressively even though he reported meeting fierce resistance. The lack of enthusiasm by these men is not surprising considering the losses they had incurred at Abucay and that their mission now was simply a feint. The Filipinos manning this portion of the line did not even know they were being attacked.[27]

Slightly to the west of Trail 2 the bulk of Colonel Masataro Yoshizawa's 142nd Infantry completed their march and became the brigade's new right flank unit (it was designated the enveloping unit), and at 1600 hours bumped into the Filipinos of the 22nd Infantry. A few small elements succeeded in seizing the outpost line but after that the 22nd Infantry pinned the Japanese against the Tiawir River. Colonel Grattan H. McCafferty asked for artillery fire beyond his 22nd Infantry's outposts, but because Filipino guns had not yet registered here, the artillerymen were reluctant to shoot. McCafferty repeated the request and the guns fired. "To our ghastly sorrow," O'Day remembered, "it was short and it took hours to get it stopped owing to lack of communications. I sweated blood with every round that I heard fired. We suffered a number of casualties and would have had more if our troops had been occupying the OPLR in the position intended, but it developed . . . the OPLR was nearly 1,000 yards short of where it was meant to be."[28] Consequently, most rounds accidentally fell on the Japanese.

The 142nd Infantry's pressure was more serious against the 51st Infantry's line, but although the Japanese increased their effort during some brisk evening fighting, they failed to make progress. In front of one Filipino foxhole a pile of empty cartridges grew until it was thirty-six inches wide and eight inches high. With both left and right flank attacks stopped cold, Nara now hit the Filipinos with his main strength, the 9th and 141st infantry. Considering the size of the assault force, it should not have been too difficult to evict the Filipinos, but the Japanese failed miserably. With the exception of one battalion of Colonel Takechi's veteran 9th Infantry which pushed into several lines of barbed wire entanglements at midnight, no Japanese crossed the Pilar River. As January 27 closed, and after an effort involving three regiments, Nara could claim the capture of a short section of barbed wire.[29]

One reason for the weak Japanese attack was that both the 141st and 142nd infantry had lost almost all their officers as battle casualties, and most units were at half to one-third strength. The 9th Infantry, the strongest of Nara's regiments, was reporting an average of sixty men in each rifle company. Adding to Japanese troubles was the difficulty in moving supplies forward to front line troops. Roads were under American observation from Mount Samat and therefore under artillery fire. Because of the hot, dry weather, each vehicle threw up a cloud of dust and signalled its position. The Japanese finally restricted daylight use of roads to single, fast trips. Convoys and major movements tooks place at night. The situation was no better farther east along the more developed East Road. There the road was so badly wrecked that, until repaired, it was almost completely useless to the Japanese. Without their usual supplies, the Japanese infantrymen scoured the country for water buffalos and plant roots. Success was limited, for the Filipinos had been on half ration for a month, and their foraging had already culled the unwary animals and nearby vegetation. "It was unpleasant," the Japanese reported, "but starvation was prevented."[30]

Almost every man in the 65th Brigade had diarrhea from drinking bad water, and those who escaped the sickness were considered unusually lucky. Filipino artillery fire covered obvious watering holes, and the Japanese had to dodge high explosives to quench their thirst. The weather also played a part in tiring the Japanese. In direct sunlight, heat was extreme, and movement in the enervating heat was hard. Japanese soldiers experienced great difficulty in even the lightest activity and sweat ran off them in streams. At night the sudden drop in temperature left the soaked men shivering in thin blankets. Crossing the various streams and rivers running from the center of the peninsula to the east coast was difficult—not because of the water's depth—but because of the sheer cliffs that sometimes rose more than sixty feet above the riverbeds. Moving vehicles and supplies across rivers required considerable engineering efforts. The only good point to these cliffs was the protection they offered from Filipino artillery fire. Even then, concussion from exploding shells loosened the dirt, and no little danger existed that men sheltering there would be buried alive if the bank collapsed.[31]

On the morning of January 28, Filipinos of the 41st Infantry (-) marched out of their bivouac and occupied positions east of Trail 2. The 3rd Battalion relieved the single battalion of the 32nd Infantry then in position, and the 2nd Battalion occupied the partially constructed regimental reserve line. When the relief was completed by mid-afternoon, a fresh force was in place to defend a critical 1,200 yards of Bluemel's line. H Company, 32nd Infantry, remained to provide the 41st Infantry (-) with automatic weapons support.[32]

The Japanese spent the daylight hours of January 28 reorganizing. Nara ordered the attack shifted westward, and he moved the 141st Infantry, then east of the 9th Infantry, to a position west of that regiment. A few shells splashed into Nara's headquarters and killed some headquarters personnel, and because of the danger from Filipino artillery, Nara ordered the 141st Infantry's move to take place after dusk. Nara hoped the realignment would put some pressure on the Philippine 21st Division. But even as he regrouped his forces, Nara still believed he faced an outpost line; in his uncertainty as to the actual situation, Nara continued to mount pursuit operations against a solid, unbroken line. As a result, the Japanese were dramatically unsuccessful. It took some time, but Nara finally realized his original estimate was wrong. "Thus," he concluded, "enemy resistance was extremely tough, and it was impossible not to suspect that, after all, enemy positions in this sector were the advanced positions of the enemy's main positions near Limay."[33] Although finally acknowledging there was something more substantial than an outpost line in front of him, Nara still believed the main line was at Limay. Regardless of where the main line was, he realized the Filipinos along Mount Samat's northeast slopes had to be reduced. Nara estimated two to three Philippine Army divisions faced him here.

One by one, the Japanese solved some of the problems facing them. Artillery became available although still in limited numbers. Guns from two artillery regiments advanced but had trouble shooting because of Filipino counterbattery fire. Although the 1st and 8th Heavy Field Artillery Regiments arrived west of Balanga on January 27, it was not until the evening of the twenty-ninth that they occupied positions from which they could shoot. Then they were so badly harassed by Filipino guns that the Japanese were convinced they had occupied an old artillery moving target range—thus the extremely accurate fires. Nara then formed a provisional artillery unit by combining the artillery companies belonging to the 141st and 142nd infantry and positioned them to provide close support to his attacks, but they were still a long way from silencing the defending artillery. Colonel Quintard's 301st Artillery fired on a Japanese truck concentration the morning of January 29, after which he switched his fire to Nara's artillery and silenced four batteries. The 86th Artillery joined Quintard and silenced four more. Filipino cannon fired at everything "that stuck up its head—patrols, machine guns, moving truck columns—and anything which would fulfill our role of infantry support."[34] Artillery so demoralized the Japanese that one unit declined to rush forward but instead dug trenches toward Filipino lines. By slow work the Japanese were at the outer edge of Bluemel's positions that evening.

Despite reorganizing his forces, Nara did not give them enough time to reach their new positions. What he had planned as a coordinated attack stumbled toward a piecemeal beginning. The 142nd Infantry waded the Tiawir River at 1830 hours and attacked the 22nd Infantry only to be unceremoniously stopped. The Japanese reported that the Filipinos counterattacked and threw their units into confusion. The 141st Infantry, because it failed to reach its line of departure until midnight, was too late to join the attack. All things considered, the effort against the 21st Division was a miserable failure.[35]

That same evening, Colonel Takechi's 9th Infantry continued its advance against the rude entanglements of the recently arrived 41st Infantry (-) and the reconstructed combat team of the 51st Division. An hour's artillery preparation roared across Filipino lines on both sides of Trail 2, reached as far back as the regimental reserve line, and ripped up most of Sector C's telephone net. With his telephone lines cut, Bluemel sent his G4, Major Napoleon D. Valleriano, in the only jeep he owned to his artillery commander, asking for defensive fires on the ford over the Pilar River. The request was honored, and Colonel Harper's guns covered the ford and trail with exploding 75mm projectiles. As quickly as Filipino 155mm guns could get the range, they fired counterbattery and reduced the enemy's guns to a mere annoyance. But still the Japanese came. Starting at 1900 hours, and preceded by sapper operations and concealed by bamboo thickets, the 9th Infantry spent forty minutes forcing their way up to Filipino positions. West of Trail 2, the 51st Combat Team found itself in trouble when some of its men fled, but a platoon from F Company, 41st Infantry, steadied the line. At the 301st Artillery's headquarters the fire direction center received a request for fire which, when plotted, lay well behind the 51st Combat Team's outpost line. But the 301st fired, and the 51st reported the rounds were fine.[36]

East of Trail 2, K Company, 41st Infantry, staying low in their foxholes and supported by machine guns from Bluemel's H Company, repulsed all attempts against its positions. At a spot 200 yards east of Trail 2, Filipino foxholes lay behind a very low dirt embankment and two strands of barbed wire stretched along a row of trees. Some intrepid Japanese crawled to the north side only a yard or two short of the Filipinos, but those who reached the trees and tried to crawl through the wire were bayoneted by Filipinos from their foxholes. Captain Kuntz, an American in the 41st Infantry, watched the Japanese attack and die in such numbers that their bodies stacked up along the final protective line of the machine guns. K Company killed thirty Japanese in the tactical wire just north of the Orion cut-off and counted ninety-seven dead along a front of 150 yards, a score of whom died within ten yards of the Filipinos. For two days this spot had been the most vulnerable in the entire II Corps line, but Bluemel found just enough time to repair his line, and the 41st Infantry once again proved itself a veteran, unshakeable outfit. As Bluemel recalled, "They bombed hell out of us and shelled us with artillery all the way back to my command post. But we held."[37] Japanese units reported "considerable" casualties and survivors of the encounter with K Company said their attack was stopped by an artillery barrage and by "furious, devastating and concentrated small arms fire."[38] Filipino casualties, in contrast, were light.

Confused, indecisive fighting continued for the next few days. Nara needed more strength at the center of his attack, so he withdrew the 1st Battalion, 142nd Infantry, from its feint position near the East Road and moved it to his headquarters. The weary, discouraged Japanese attacked again and again only to be repeatedly repulsed after leaving more and more dead on the field. Two of Nara's three regiments had scarcely any company grade officers left on their feet. Because Nara was having difficulties communicating with his units, he moved his headquarters to within several hundred yards of the fighting. Despite constant breaking of his telephone lines, he could now at least use messengers with some hope of success. The Japanese believed their radio transmissions were picked up by the Americans, plotted, and artillery fired at the radio's position. Ground-cloth panels laid out to identify Japanese lines to their aircraft were spotted by American observers high atop Mount Samat and taken under fire. To compound Nara's difficulties, the Filipinos captured an order signed by Nara which stated his headquarters was at "the Sugar Mill." So Bluemel "shelled hell out of every sugar mill in the neighborhood" and forced Nara to move.[39]

Nara certainly cannot be faulted for his persistency. At 2200 hours on January 29 General Homma issued orders for the return of the 9th Infantry to its parent 16th Division, the return to be completed by 1800 hours two days later. Either Nara did not immediately receive the order, or he tried to get additional combat time out of the regiment, for he continued to employ them. Determined to get to Limay where he believed the main line lay, he planned yet another attack against these surprisingly strong advance positions. But bowing to the inevitable, Nara finally issued orders at 1100 hours on January 31 for the 9th Infantry to return to the 16th Division.[40]

On the early evening of the thirty-first, Japanese artillery laid down a two and a half-hour barrage along trails reaching into Filipino reserve positions, and Japanese aircraft bombed II Corps's artillery positions hoping to provide some relief to their infantry. Positions along the Pandan River were especially hard hit. "At the same time," wrote Nara, "the artillery opened a bombardment of the enemy front line positions at 1800 hours until the Bataan Peninsula shook with the thunderous din of guns and all gunfire in the enemy's front line ceased."[41] Next to Trail 2, the focus of the attack, there was only one casualty. Major Lee A. Lauderback, the American instructor to the 2nd Battalion, 41st Infantry, was killed.

Just as the barrage lifted at 1930 hours and Japanese infantry formed for the assault, Filipino artillery opened up against the ford over the river. Simultaneously, "a tornado of concentrated machine-gun fire" hit the assembling Japanese. Unable even to leave their assembly areas, the Japanese quickly conceded defeat. The attack, Nara mourned, "was frustrated."[42] The effectiveness of Filipino machine gun fire was such that the Japanese infantry did not attack or attempt to advance. This was a rather extraordinary event. The Japanese, supported by air and artillery, launched a full-dress attack, killed one American, but failed to get beyond their assembly areas. Not a single Japanese soldier closed with the Filipinos. Even as Nara mourned over his frustrated attack, he was having some bad moments from another direction. He was receiving unsettling reports of powerful forces massing behind Filipino lines. Aerial surveillance noted troops moving north of the Pandan River and numerous vehicles moving toward Mount Samat. Some of this activity was Bluemel's preparation for a counterattack, ordered by General Parker, to remove the too-intimate 9th Infantry from its positions just forward of his main line.

Concurrent with Bluemel's counterattack plans, the 9th Infantry received orders to rejoin the 16th Division, and it started to withdraw from its trenches the night of January 31. Despite the aid of an all-night full moon, the large number of wounded slowed the movement and disrupted the time schedule. So badly did the wounded hamper travel that by morning only one battalion of the regiment had broken contact and moved out of the area. The next night, February 1, a second battalion extricated itself. But before the last battalion could get free, the Filipinos started applying pressure. As early as January 30 the 51st Combat Team on the left pushed its outposts far enough forward to tie in with the 21st Division, and on the far right the 32nd Infantry pushed its outpost line right up to the Pilar River. In the center, however, the Japanese temporarily held their ground.[43]

Bluemel's attack planned here for February 1 aborted. II Corps attached a 2.95-inch howitzer battery to Bluemel, and Bluemel wanted it to support his attack from as close to his line of departure as possible. The American battery instructor declined to use direct fire and spent the day looking for a position from which he could shoot indirect fire. Finally Bluemel ordered the howitzers placed with the assault echelon. With his local planning completed, Bluemel attacked on February 2 with the two 2.95-inch howitzers only 300 yards from the Japanese-held bamboo thicket. Colonel Young's 51st Combat Team sponsored the day's events, and adjacent Filipino units provided support with rifle and machine gun fire. The main maneuver element would be the 31st Engineer Battalion, drawn from Sub-sector reserve. These men were very lightly armed. They carried Enfields and three BAR's in each platoon. The three companies could count about ninety-four men each, giving the battalion a strength of about three hundred engineers. Major Mirasol deployed three companies on line, A, C, and B from left to right, A and B to fire while C Company would crawl to within hand grenade range. The 31st Engineers—now really only C Company since it was the force selected to advance—crossed its line of departure at 0800 hours and hit stiff resistance from the one battalion of Japanese still in the bamboo. Progress was slow, for the Filipinos were as reluctant to walk into heavy fire as had been the Japanese. When elements of the 41st Infantry joined the attack, they reached the thicket. The engineers and infantry between them lost twenty killed or wounded in the process. Here they halted for the night.[44]

In the bamboo, the Japanese were pinned by Filipino artillery fire, and night did not provide any relief. "Their guns," the Japanese reported "amounted to well over 120 and their bombardment was extremely furious. During the daytime they surmised where our troops were located and conducted unaimed fire at this region. Movements were made by a number of our personnel to the rear of the front line, but enemy fire immediately became concentrated and continued without intermission from evening to midnight, bombarding our front line and the whole rear zone, using the orientation which they had determined during the day. They fired at least 10,000 rounds during the day."[45]

The next day, February 3, the Filipinos girded themselves for a resumption of the attack. They expected rugged resistance, but after a cautious approach that failed to draw fire, the Filipinos were pleasantly surprised to find the last of the 9th Infantry gone. They found many dead enemy, considerable equipment, and an elaborate defensive position. The bamboo was now theirs for the taking, so Bluemel quickly advanced his Sector C outpost line to within 150 yards of the Pilar-Bagac Road. Not content to simply maintain this line, Bluemel pushed his outposts deeper and deeper into Japanese territory, attacking and harassing them

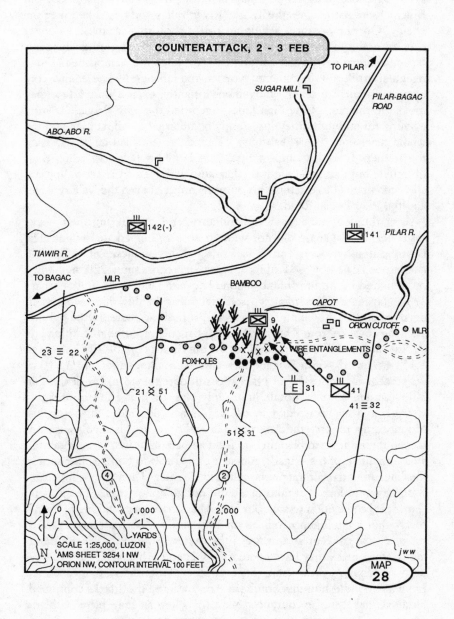

COUNTERATTACK, 2 - 3 FEB

TO PILAR

SUGAR MILL

PILAR-BAGAC
ROAD

ABO-ABO R.

142(-)

141   PILAR R.

TIAWIR R.

TO BAGAC   MLR   BAMBOO

CAPOT

9

ORION CUTOFF   MLR

23 ≡ 22   WIRE ENTANGLEMENTS

X X X X X

FOXHOLES

E 31

21 ⊠ 51   41

41 ≡ 32

51 ⊠ 31

4

2

0   1,000   2,000

YARDS
SCALE 1:25,000, LUZON
AMS SHEET 3254 I NW
ORION NW, CONTOUR INTERVAL 100 FEET

N

jww

MAP
28

as he advanced. The outpost line halted at the Pilar-Bagac Road, but Bluemel sent patrols into the Talisay River Valley and raised hell with the enemy. On one occasion a Filipino patrol shot up a Japanese engineer platoon going to the front to lay antitank mines, and in other incidents Japanese signal personnel working on wire lines were ambushed. Using irregular artillery fire, Bluemel worried the Japanese. "The enemy concentrated their fire on any movement instantly, even if only a few men moved in the rear of the First Line," recorded the 65th Brigade. "From evening till midnight, they incessantly bombarded our First Line and the whole rear zone."[46] On February 21 Bluemel launched an attack using the soldiers from his outpost line. The Filipinos failed to reach their objective, but that same night the Japanese withdrew from the valley and allowed Bluemel to establish his outposts north of both the Talisay River and the Pilar-Bagac Road.

After the departure of the 9th Infantry, and considering their heavy casualties, the Japanese did not seem to pose an immediate danger. The fighting in and around Trail 2 had savaged the Japanese. They left 240 dead to be buried by the Filipinos. Japanese records show 220 men killed or wounded in the 9th Infantry alone between January 27 and February 1. The Japanese 141st Infantry also fought near the thicket, so when their dead are added, the Filipino count is surprisingly accurate. In the fighting after the advance from Abucay, the 65th Brigade reported 441 killed and 817 wounded. Added to the figures for the Abucay fight—701 killed and 1,151 wounded—65th Brigade losses were crippling, a total of 3,110 or 46 percent of the total. Yet Nara was still determined to break the Filipino line. He felt that morale in his units was still high (he was probably wrong), and all he needed to do was launch one more attack against Mount Samat to force the Americans to withdraw. As his supply echelons turned their efforts to bringing up food and ammunition, he reorganized what remained of his brigade and sent out patrols to find a softer spot in the line. Infantry commanders rested their men. Then they slipped toward new positions, but their move did not go undetected. "The general [Japanese] conception to split our forces has not been abandoned," wrote MacArthur's intelligence officer on February 5. "The message pattern shows a slow concentration toward the center."[47] Some of Nara's determination to attack may have come from General Homma. On February 4 or 5 Colonel Masami Ishii, Staff Officer of Southern Army, visited Homma and told him that Southern Army wanted the attacks continued. Homma may have encouraged Nara, or Homma may have withheld orders to suspend attacks based on Southern Army's desires, but Homma's better judgment soon prevailed.

On February 8 Nara was in the process of assembling his commanders to issue a new attack order when he received a telephone call from 14th Army headquarters, telling him to stop all attacks. An hour before midnight he received another call directing him to withdraw north of the Pilar-Bagac Road to await further orders. There is little doubt Homma's orders prevented another disastrous failure on the part of the 65th Brigade.[48]

So as Nara withdrew, fighting at Trail 2 ceased. The immediate threat to II Corps ended.

CHAPTER SEVENTEEN

The Pockets

EVERYTHING WAS TURNING TO DUST FOR THE JAPANESE. THE 65TH Brigade had heavy losses at Trail 2 without even denting the defenses, the landings along the west coast were either destroyed or in the process of being destroyed, and the upcoming overland attempt against I Corps was heading toward disaster. Lieutenant Colonel Hiroshi Nakanishi's 3rd Battalion, 20th Infantry, attacking on January 26 and 27, hit the left and center of the 91st Division's new line, but met "bloody and decisive repulses."[1] The Japanese had hit the best prepared sector of I Corps's line, for despite having only two officers available to reconnoiter the area before occupying it, the 91st Division was more fortunate than either the 11th or the 1st divisions and thus withstood the enemy attacks.

Conversely, when the 11th Division arrived in I Corps after the Abucay withdrawal, General Brougher was appalled by his sector. "The defensive positions finally occupied had not even been located, much less prepared," Brougher recalled. ". . . not a stick of brush had been cut. No lines had been located or laid out. Complete, continuous, and coordinated positions across the entire front should have been laid out by trained officers, in advance."[2] When the 11th Infantry filed into the new line on January 26, the staff officer showing Major Volckmann his position stopped in the middle of Trail 7. Surrounded by dense jungle, the officer faced west and told Volckmann his sector ran for 500 yards in that direction. Turning about, he pointed and said the line ran for another 2,000 yards to the east. But because of the dense jungle, Volckmann could see only ten yards in any direction along his 2,500-yard front. Volckmann tried to reconnoiter the area, but he wasted his time; the mile and a-half piece of ground was solid jungle. As he returned from his

347

reconnaissance, Volckmann recalled his days as student at the Infantry School where "The problems and instruction had never covered a situation like this."[3] The men would need to work hard to prepare a line here, so General Brougher issued vigorous guidance and put them to work.

> All officers and men must be impressed with the fact that this is our last stand. *HERE IS WHERE WE WIN THE WAR.* Get rid of the cowardly fool idea that a small group of infiltrating Japs can "cut off" any important element of this command. Reverse the viewpoint and consider any infiltrating group as easy victims to be immediately surrounded and captured or destroyed. The 11th Division front has never been cracked yet. *We are going to hold on this line.*[4]

Besides the normal effort necessary to prepare any new area for occupation, I Corps encountered other problems as it tried to entrench before the Japanese arrived. The main line of resistance ran through thick, dense forests and over steep, rugged, broken ground. None of the line had been adequately plotted, and because the Japanese landings along the west coast had drawn off I Corps's reserves, I Corps's front had little depth. When a few reinforcements did arrive, they were incomplete, tired, and missing organic elements. The 11th Division entered its new lines without its 12th Infantry. The 45th Infantry arrived in an exhausted condition and within twenty-four hours was snatched away by USAFFE headquarters. The unexpected requirement to replace the 45th Infantry with the disorganized 1st Regular Division—a division without artillery and automatic weapons—capped Wainwright's woes.[5]

The 1st Division had lost much of its materiel around Mauban and was still considerably disorganized when it assumed the mission of the departed 45th Infantry. Two hastily reorganized battalions from the 1st Infantry and one from the 3rd moved into the line late on January 26. The Filipinos began entrenching the next day but they were slow in organizing the line. Without shovels, they dug shallow foxholes using mess kits and bayonets. Later that day another battalion arrived and tried to find its sector. Each battalion had to post strong covering forces forward of the front lines to allow their engineers to work unmolested in the line itself. Engineers worked around the clock. "The problem we had," recalled the I Corps Engineer, Colonel Skerry, "was to stave off pursuit by the enemy after the crushing of the main battle position and to organize and occupy the reserve battle position. . . . I doubt if . . . any staff engineer in the I Philippine Corps got over two hours sleep a night. Some nights none."[6] Efforts to establish the artillery were equally strenuous and equally difficult. Many guns were poorly emplaced, few had effective camouflage, and observation posts were not yet built. Firing data was often badly misplotted and of little use, nor was there enough telephone wire to establish the necessary communication links.

Into all this confusion marched the last battalion of Colonel Yorimasa Yoshioka's 20th Infantry. On January 28 Yoshioka's regimental head-quarters and Nakanishi's 3rd Battalion moved east along I Corps's line, probing the defenses. They quickly discovered a weak spot when they found the area where the 1st Division was still entrenching. The terrain here was higher on the Japanese side, allowing them to dominate the lower Filipino lines. Untrained Filipino officers erroneously placed the main line on the low ground to comply exactly with what was only meant to be a general trace drawn hastily on a map, and by following the map trace they surrendered better defense terrain which lay nearby. The Japanese hit the 2nd Battalion, 1st Infantry, ruptured the outpost line late in the day, and then drove a rifle company off the main line. With no barbed wire to slow their charge, the Japanese walked in with 1,000 men. The Filipinos failed miserably to halt or even delay the Japanese advance. In the confusion of the moment, no one believed many Japanese were involved in the penetration, so when the firing stopped, the Filipinos reoccupied the main line and went back to digging foxholes.[7]

The Japanese continued their advance, now uphill, along the steep-banked Tuol River through jungle so thick that they moved unnoticed through the 1st Division's rear, cutting telephone wire and harassing the defenders. In this extremely tangled growth, with visibility limited to fifteen yards, the Japanese themselves became separated. Unsure as to their location, two forces curled around small pieces of ground. Less than one Japanese company held the Little Pocket atop a bamboo-covered hill only 400 yards behind the main line, while the remainder of the 1,000 Japanese settled into position about a mile south of the front line and formed the Big Pocket.[8]

The first indication of the enemy's presence came early on January 28 from a Filipino patrol. While moving along the Pilar-Bagac Road west of Trail 7, the patrol came across Japanese telephone wire that crossed the road running south. The Filipinos cut and collected several yards of the yellow wire and returned to friendly lines. Upon hearing about the wire, the 11th Division strengthened the patrol and sent it out with orders to follow the wire to its southern terminus. Concern mounted when information came into the 11th Infantry reporting that no friendly troops were in position to the 11th Division's left, the area assigned to the 1st Division. As a precaution, the 11th Division placed a company of infantry along its left flank. The 1st Division, also worried about infiltration

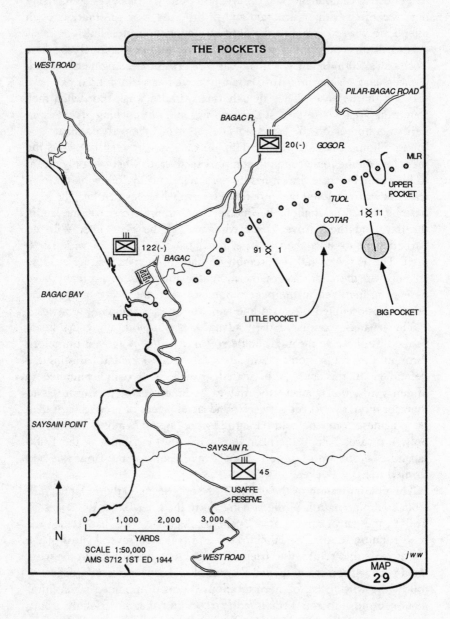

THE POCKETS

WEST ROAD

PILAR-BAGAC ROAD

BAGAC R.

20(-)   GOGO R.

MLR

UPPER
POCKET

TUOL

COTAR   1 ⊠ 11

122(-)

BAGAC

91 ⊠ 1

BAGAC BAY

MLR

LITTLE POCKET

BIG POCKET

SAYSAIN POINT

SAYSAIN R.

45

USAFFE
RESERVE

N

0   1,000   2,000   3,000

YARDS

SCALE 1:50,000
AMS S712 1ST ED 1944

WEST ROAD

jww

MAP
29

and unsure as to what was happening on the main line, placed a provisional battalion, composed of remnants of the 51st Division, to the right rear of their lines. The next morning Japanese, wielding long bayonets, attacked this battalion. Some of the Filipinos panicked and scattered, but the remainder rallied and stopped the attack. Properly motivated now, the Filipinos dug in and built a line south of Trail 5, on the left of the 11th Infantry soldiers already straddling Trail 7.[9]

Additional notice that the Japanese were behind the main line came at 0800 hours on January 29. About 200 yards north of Trail 5 on Trail 7, Japanese fired upon an 11th Infantry staff car carrying Second Lieutenant T. B. Shone. Rifle rounds punctured the car but not the occupants. Trail 7 was carrying a fair amount of traffic and the next car was not as lucky. The 2nd Battalion, 11th Infantry's medical officer and his driver were ambushed, the driver was killed, and no trace was ever found of the medical officer. Noise of this firing was heard at the 11th Infantry's command post and Sergeant Guy Murthy, a 31st Infantryman on duty with the Filipinos, collected several soldiers and walked north to investigate. The Japanese ambushed the patrol and killed Sergeant Murthy as he tried to crawl off the trail. The Filipinos broke contact and brought Murthy's body back to the regimental command post. North of this skirmish, at the regiment's 2nd Battalion headquarters, Sergeant William S. Satterlee received permission to drive a Bren gun carrier along the trail to determine the location and strength of what they believed was just an enemy patrol. As he drove down the trail, Satterlee was hit in the head by rifle fire. His Filipino gunner returned the fire, and the seriously wounded Satterlee drove completely through the Japanese position.[10]

At the 11th Infantry's command post Colonel Townsend hastily placed clerks and supplymen across Trail 7 just south of the junction with Trail 5; then Townsend ordered the reserve rifle companies from his two front line battalions to his headquarters. Townsend hoped to stop the Japanese from marching farther south toward division headquarters and supply facilities. Because he believed the Japanese force was no more than a strong patrol, Townsend wanted to catch them before they could split into small, harder-to-find sniper teams.[11]

Roughly three hours after Lieutenant Shone discovered the Japanese, C and G companies completed their move south from reserve positions. Townsend told C Company to attack west across Trail 7, and he sent G Company north of the trail junction to support C Company by fire and to prevent the Japanese from escaping north. Townsend dispatched a section of machine guns to help the small group of supply and clerical personnel guarding Trail 7. Because personal contact was the only means of communication other than runner, organizing the attack took time. Cap-

tain Winfield N. Robinson, a forester in civilian life who now commanded the 1st Battalion, led C Company when they attacked, but the
Japanese drove the Filipinos to cover with a storm of fire. The Filipinos
quickly discovered the Japanese were on both sides of Trail 7. Captain
Robinson's men cautiously advanced by crawling along the jungle floor,
but when within a few yards of enemy lines they found themselves helpless. They had no hand grenades to toss at the Japanese, nor did they
have mortars to provide indirect fire support. G Company tried to help
by attacking what they believed was the rear of the enemy, but the Japanese stopped them by fire from well-concealed positions. After the two
companies stalled, the Filipinos dug in for the night—a difficult task—for
none of the men carried entrenching tools. They scraped small holes
from the jungle floor with bolos and knives. The day's fighting proved
the enemy was in force, considerably stronger than the "strong sniper
patrol visualized at the beginning of the day's fighting."[12]

Because the Japanese were still pressuring the Filipino lines along the
main line of resistance, and because 11th Division reserves were fully
committed, General Brougher asked I Corps to send a battalion of the
45th Infantry to help. The Scouts of the 1st Battalion, 45th Infantry,
were bivouaced in I Corps reserve on Trail 9, bathing, cleaning equipment, and recovering from the fighting at Abucay. An I Corps messenger
arrived at 1600 hours and handed Lieutenant Colonel Leslie T. Lathrop a
yellow sheet of ruled tablet paper. Written in pencil was a mission. "Send
a platoon immediately to CP, 11th Infantry, at Trails 5 and 7 to clean out
seventeen snipers there. J. M. Wainwright."[13]

Colonel Lathrop was a kind, soft-spoken officer, but he could make his
men jump when necessary. Born in Iowa in 1891, Lathrop graduated
from the University of Minnesota in 1916, was commissioned in 1917,
and completed the Infantry School Company Officers' Course in 1927
and the Tank School in 1932. Lathrop acknowledged the order, said he
would move in half an hour, and alerted his entire battalion for immediate departure. He called his officers together and gave them a route,
order of march, and time of movement. He told them some snipers had
closed a trail and the battalion was needed to clean them out. Lathrop
ordered First Lieutenant Robert K. Roberts and his B Company to board
trucks and move immediately, then Lathrop, his executive officer, communications officer, chaplain, and two medical officers departed for the
11th Infantry's command post. The supply and ammunition officers remained behind to shuttle the rest of the battalion to the fight. Each rifleman carried 160 rounds of M-1 ammunition, and the machine gunners
carried 1,000. Although rifle ammunition was in adequate supply, there
was a shortage of M-1 clips, which reduced the Scouts to stripping the

.30-caliber rounds from five-round Springfield clips and putting them into eight-round M-1 clips. But morale was high. A third of the troopers had between eight and thirty years' service, and even the newest recruit had at least nine months. All were excellent marksmen. Dressed in khaki trousers, leggings, wool shirts, and steel helmets, the Scouts rolled their packs and shouted, *"Petay si la,"* "They shall die."[14]

Colonel Lathrop and his party drove over a good trail and reached Trail Junction 5 and 7 at 2000 hours, where Colonel Townsend met them. Townsend told the Scout officers about the ambush of his medical officer from the 2nd Battalion. Townsend gave Lathrop information on the actions he took to seal off the enemy and prevent further advances. Lathrop had orders from Wainwright not to commit more than one company to the reduction of the Japanese position for, at the time, one company was believed sufficient. When B Company arrived, the Scouts unloaded and formed on both sides of Trail 7 facing north. As the rest of the battalion arrived, Lathrop sent his company commanders on a hasty reconnaissance. The company commanders found rolling ground covered with thick clumps of bamboo, vines, and large full-rooted banyan trees. When the officers returned, B Company moved north a short distance. The lead platoon was commanded by Sergeant Fernandez, an Olympic athlete with twenty-six years service in the Scouts. But B Company was effectively stopped after receiving Japanese fire. Lathrop sent a section of machine guns forward but even then the Scouts could not budge the Japanese. Lathrop decided to halt the attack and organize a formal effort the next morning.[15]

In the early morning hours of January 30 Lathrop called his commanders together and gave his order. "A small force, probably an enemy squad, is across Trail 7 severing communications. Our mission will be to attack and drive the enemy back across Trail 7, and then reorganize on the west side of Trail 7 and continue the attack. A Company will attack on the left and Company C will attack on the right. . . . There shouldn't be much resistance, and we are supposed to have Trail 7 open today and should have the resistance wiped out in a day or so. The battalion headquarters will be along the trail where you see it here. Any questions? Move out."[16] C Company, 11th Infantry, would assist and maintain contact as the Scouts advanced, and G Company would support by fire.

At 0800 hours, A and C companies, 45th Infantry, and C and G, 11th Infantry, began their attacks supported by 37mm fire, the only cannon support then available. Captain Archie L. McMasters, commanding C Company, put Lieutenant Edward W. Stewart on the right flank of the company while he took the left. McMasters hoped that with an officer at each end of his company, he would get better control. McMasters cau-

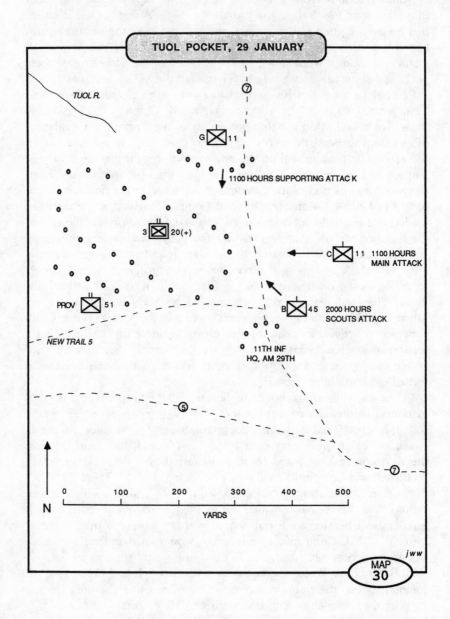

TUOL POCKET, 29 JANUARY

TUOL R.

G ☒ 11

↓ 1100 HOURS SUPPORTING ATTACK

3 ☒ 20(+)

C ☒ 11   1100 HOURS
MAIN ATTACK

PROV ☒ 51

B ☒ 45   2000 HOURS
SCOUTS ATTACK

NEW TRAIL 5

11TH INF
HQ, AM 29TH

⑦

⑤

⑦

N

| 0 | 100 | 200 | 300 | 400 | 500 |

YARDS

jww

MAP
30

tioned his men to keep contact with their comrades on the right and left.
He then sent a runner to the left flank to keep in touch with A Company
to his left. The first attempt to advance resulted in the discovery that the
compass azimuth did not agree with the direction of the trail. McMasters
called his soldiers back and explained the correct direction.[17]

On the right, Lieutenant Stewart, on active duty for barely eight
months and still not fully recovered from a wound received at Abucay,
organized his platoon into a tight skirmish line with three to five feet
between each man. The Scouts walked forward for twenty yards, scan-
ning trees, bushes, and folds in the ground, straining to see the enemy.
After twenty yards they came to a small clearing. Peering into the jungle
on the other side, Stewart saw a face under a Japanese helmet staring
back at him. "Hit the deck," Stewart yelled.[18] He fired his pistol and
dove for cover. Heavy fire exploded over the heads of the Scouts and
they squirmed for cover. Try as they might, the Scouts could not distinguish enemy positions from surrounding foliage. Stewart called for a
runner. "Tell Captain McMasters there is dug-in enemy at least platoon
size. I'll attempt to dislodge them." Stewart then ordered one squad to
advance around the clearing on the left and one to do the same on the
right. He reinforced his third squad with one water-cooled and one air-
cooled machine gun to build a base of fire. "Neither squad went more
than 20–25 feet forward in the most intense fire fight I have ever heard,"
recalls Stewart. "No single round could be distinguished in the roar for
about 10–15 minutes." One Scout squad leader was killed and two other
Scouts wounded. Unable to make any progress with a single platoon, the
rest of C Company moved up and linked with the stalled men. During
the short but fierce fight the Scouts lost four men killed and six wounded.
The estimate of enemy strength was raised to a reinforced company.

The failure of Colonel Lathrop's attack induced Wainwright to order
commitment of the entire battalion. Personally observing the fighting,
Wainwright promised to send up some tanks. Wainwright, one of whose
greatest assets was his willingness to make personal reconnaissances,
watched the afternoon's efforts from the Scout's command post no more
than seventy-five feet from the lead elements. They were so close that
Major Edgar Wright was hit on the eyebrow by a Japanese bullet, and a
Scout soldier was wounded twenty yards behind the battalion command
post. Officers accompanying Wainwright prevailed upon him not to be
foolish and to move to safer ground. Recalled Major Van Oosten, "You'd
have thought he was walking to the Club for a Scotch."[19] Some heavy
firing into surrounding trees finally accounted for the persistent sniper—
clad in a green uniform, rubber-soled shoes, and using a sniper rifle with
telescope. Scouts dropped the green-faced soldier only ten yards from

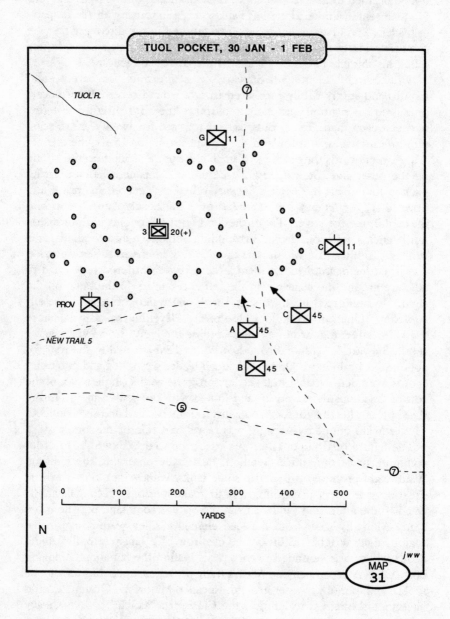

TUOL POCKET, 30 JAN - 1 FEB

TUOL R.

G ⊠ 11

3 ⊠ 20(+)

C ⊠ 11

PROV ⊠ 51

NEW TRAIL 5

C ⊠ 45

A ⊠ 45

B ⊠ 45

⑤

⑦

N

0   100   200   300   400   500

YARDS

jww

MAP
31

the command post. Lathrop's men launched five more assaults, but each attack only produced more friendly casualties. The fighting did identify part of the enemy line, and the Scout battalion could now identify a stretch of 400 yards.

A few attempts by the Japanese that night to break Scout lines were checked with little difficulty. The heavy volume of fire produced by massed M-1 rifles had a mental as well as physical effect on the Japanese. This rifle fire was dangerous only to Japanese who left their entrenchments, and because few did, few were hit. The Japanese knew now they were facing Scouts and not Philippine Army. Under serious pressure, the Japanese of the 20th Infantry worked hard to improve their positions. They entrenched themselves deep in a network of connecting tunnels and dugouts. Each man skillfully developed his position and even disposed of the freshly turned dirt to prevent detection. Their efforts were successful, for when the Scouts attacked on January 31, they failed to advance. Four attacks launched on February 1 were likewise futile and gained not a foot of ground despite Scout antitank guns firing at Japanese hardly fifty yards distant. By the end of the day, C Company, 45th Infantry, alone had suffered twelve killed and twenty wounded out of 120 men committed.[20]

Around noon on February 2 one platoon of four tanks from A Company, 192nd Tank Battalion, reported for duty. One tank had a sticky accelerator that prevented the driver from controlling the vehicle, so only three tanks could be used. The tank commander discussed the situation with Lathrop, and both agreed that the tanks could not attack through the jungle. They would be utterly blind and might fall off the steep slopes or jam themselves in the vegetation. The tanks would have to stay on the trail where a platoon of infantry could protect them. At 1500 hours, three tanks, their noise covered by heavy rifle fire, moved north along the trail. The driver of the second tank, Private Daniel N. Stoudt, was fighting the jungle as much as the Japanese. "God, you couldn't see," he recalls. "Half the time I was driving I couldn't see. I actually didn't see a thing as far as Japs. All I did was drive and shoot both .30's just to make noise more than anything."[21] With Japanese fire rattling off the armor, the tankers passed completely through the enemy position, but the supporting infantry was stopped cold. A second sortie was even less rewarding. A mine blew through the belly of a tank up into the tank commander who received a right leg full of fragments. Despite the explosion and lost track, the tank struggled into friendly lines.

As night fell, the Japanese took the initiative. At 2200 hours Scouts of C Company spotted Japanese approaching their lines. Captain McMasters was with his men when the Japanese appeared. "[We] had 2 heavy and 2 light machine guns and a platoon of D Co. with 4 heavy machine guns attached in the line. As the enemy attack was in darkness, the firing line let go with everything it had."[22] Finding their progress challenged by eight machine guns, not to mention scores of M-1 rifles, the Japanese recoiled. Filipino machine gunners from the nearby 11th Infantry also fired, and they fired so vigorously they ran out of ammunition. Even the Scouts fired too liberally. Colonel Lathrop called McMasters and demanded better fire control, especially from the machine guns.

On February 3 a light tank commanded by Sergeant Leroy C. Anderson, supported by Scout infantry, ran into heavy Japanese fire. Sergeant Satterlee, badly wounded only six days before, was serving as the tank's gunner. One particularly bothersome Japanese position was dug into the large flanged roots of a huge banyan tree, and the roots kept the tank from crushing the defenders. Inside the tank, Sergeant Anderson reached down to the shoulder of the driver to guide him. A squeeze on his right shoulder swung the tank to the right. Nearing the enemy position, Anderson placed his hand on the driver's head, the signal to stop. Satterlee tried to depress the 37mm cannon to get at the machine gun, but the tank was too close.[23]

Lieutenant Willibald C. Bianchi, a Scout battalion staff officer, accompanied Lieutenant Roberts's infantry platoon, which was supporting the tanks. Bianchi was firing an M-1 rifle from behind Anderson's tank when two bullets hit him in the left hand. Unable to hold his rifle, he drew a pistol and continued to shoot. Bianchi then spotted a Japanese machine gun and silenced it with a hand grenade. Seeing the tank could not depress its main gun enough to hit the Japanese under the banyan tree's roots, Bianchi climbed onto the tank, laid the antiaircraft machine gun on target, and fired. He continued to fire even after being hit in the arm and chest by two machine gun bullets. Then an antitank gun hit Anderson's tank, blew Bianchi off, and wounded him a third time. The crew bailed out with their hair on fire and crawled away under the protection of Lieutenant Roberts's riflemen.[24]

Another tank became stuck on a tree stump near the same large tree. Firing machine guns, the crew neutralized enemy fire long enough for two Scouts to crawl within range. Both Scouts tossed hand grenades and destroyed the last enemy gun. The tankers abandoned their immobile vehicle and returned to friendly lines. As Lieutenant Bianchi was carried out, he spoke a few words to Colonel Lathrop and then asked Major Van Oosten to take care of his camera. Bianchi survived and returned to duty a few weeks later. Lathrop and Van Oosten both saw part of Bianchi's exploit, and after hearing reports from others on the action, Lathrop said, "That deserves the DSC."[25] Van Oosten wrote up the award and submitted it. The citation made such an impression at higher headquarters that they upgraded the award, and Lieutenant Bianchi received the Medal of Honor. Bianchi lived until January 15, 1945, when he and hundreds more were killed on a Japanese prison ship at Takao, Formosa. Sergeants Anderson and Satterlee each received the Distinguished Service Cross.

At the end of the day artillerymen brought up a 75mm gun and tried to destroy Anderson's immobile tank. Firing from 100 yards, the gun failed to burn the tank, but explosions threw up a wall of broken bamboo nine feet tall. Additional Philippine Army units arrived and extended the encirclement of the Japanese until, on February 3 and 4, they cut the 20th Infantry's communications with the north. When Scouts discovered Japanese light artillery in the pocket, they raised their estimate of the forces there to a reinforced battalion.[26]

The close fighting was unbelievable. Junior officers carrying sacks of grenades rode up to enemy foxholes on the front of tanks. When enemy fire was too intense for this, volunteers from the 11th Division were solicited. Only dangerous tactics could overcome one disadvantage of the American light tanks, that of their limited field of vision. Someone was required outside the tank to observe and direct the tank's fire. Third Lieutenant Auero Capili won the DSC doing just that. Lieutenant Capili led a tank into enemy fire and directed the tank's guns by waving a white handkerchief attached to a stick. He guided the tank while sheltering behind the same tree where another officer had been wounded the day before. The tank's fire was effective and the Japanese position destroyed.[27]

By February 4 three of A Company's tanks had been destroyed, so B Company entered the fight as replacements. B Company's first attack found the 11th Division Igorotes providing close support to each tank, but this procedure did not work. When tankers spotted Japanese soldiers moving toward the lead tanks, machine gunners in the following vehicles fired, and the fire often hit the accompanying Filipinos. A solution was finally adopted. If the Filipinos would ride the tanks, both they and the tanks could fire freely into the surrounding area. There, then, was the answer. In the next attacks they tested the procedure and found that it worked. The Igorotes rode the tanks and pounded on one side of the tank and then the other to guide it right and left. Visibility from inside the dust-enveloped tanks was poor, and the drivers had to be careful which way they went. When one driver misjudged the size of a tree and hit it dead center, the tank commander broke his nose and the rest of the crew were bruised and bumped. Tank-infantry coordination improved with experience. After a tank ran over an enemy position, the Igorotes shot down into the foxhole or dismounted and went after the Japanese with knives and hand grenades. Igorotes fighting alongside the tanks had a fine time once they found that killing Japanese did not put them in jail. Their former headhunting activities had been suppressed before the war, and they now found a new and lawful release to their pent-up spirit.[28]

The Japanese resisted these tank attacks fiercely, but they seemed to be short armor-piercing rounds. Enemy shells exploded against the tanks, orange flames squirted through a few cracks, and dust rose, but the rounds did not penetrate the armor. If hit just right, tank rivets popped out and zipped around inside the tank until running out of momentum or hitting a tanker. The effects of enemy fire and jungle vegetation was such that the outsides of some tanks were entirely stripped of headlights, sirens, and fenders. Inside the tanks, it was so hot some men wore only boots and a pair of shorts. Crews closed hatches and buttoned up at the last possible moment. Open hatches any other time were a necessity. Wearing little clothing was only a partial solution to the heat, for it also created problems. Hot cannon and machine gun cartridges bounced off bare skin and raised blisters. After a time it was easy to identify a veteran tanker. He was the one with bruised and burned skin.[29]

The Japanese were not alone with ammunition problems. "All we had was armor piercing, and they were not very effective against personnel unless you wanted to be a sharpshooter." recalled Sergeant Zenon R. Bardowski, a race-car driver before the war and with one enemy plane to his credit. "I liked aiming with the four-power telescope and see a Jap and press the trigger and watch that 37mm with a tracer go through him. That was good hunting."[30] The tankers developed a technique with the supporting Filipino infantry that supplemented their meager rations. As the tanks probed into Japanese positions, the Filipinos cut field packs off dead Japanese, tossed the packs on the tanks, and continued the attack. When the fighting stopped for the day, the men opened the packs and divided the Japanese rations of hardtack, sweet corned beef, and sweet fried meats.

On February 4 Captain George Crane's F Battery, 24th Artillery, brought their 2.95-inch mountain howitzers into action. The battery pulled into position at night and set to work chopping down trees to open a spot to emplace and fire the howitzers. Gunners unloaded ammunition, emplaced machine guns for local security, and dragged the cannon into the thick trees with only the muzzle showing. Axemen felled only a few trees because the tubes were on a forward slope. But there were problems from the start. The battery's communication sergeant was killed as he tried to lay wire to the forward observers. The guns were on a ridge 2,000 yards to the rear of the fighting, and without accurate maps, fire was sure to fall on the wrong spot. Short rounds and tree bursts were common, and one forward observer in a tree was wounded twice by the shells he was adjusting. Another forward observer dragged a telephone to the base of a tree, climbed the tree to spot fire, crawled over several branches, but could not see anything because of the thick vegetation. After dark he climbed down but could not find his telephone. "I sat there all night afraid to move because of rifle fire," recalled Lieutenant Fred Wildish from Downers Grove, Illinois. "The next morning I found that I came down a different tree about ten yards from the one I went up."[31] The artillerymen were forced to make the best of a bad situation. They had to shoot and then make corrections after friendly casualties were reported. The Japanese further confused the issue by firing at the same time to hamper corrections.

Indirect fire was slowed by poor visibility, small-scale inaccurate maps, and the absence of high-angle guns. When the fighting began there were only 150 mortar rounds available for the Filipino units initially committed. The high ratio of duds in the Stokes ammunition seriously reduced the effectiveness of the mortar fire, and Captain Crane's 2.95-inch howitzers provided little beyond some friendly casualties and mountains of broken bamboo. There was some discussion of bringing the cannon right up to the front lines to fire, but they would have been so close as to be endangered by their own exploding shells. "All the artillery would do," recalled Lieutenant Wildish, "was shatter the bamboo and improve [enemy] protection. They were beautifully dug in."[32]

On February 5 Lieutenant Reed from the 11th Division staff was selected to call upon the Japanese to surrender. He threw a note tied to a stone into their lines. The only answer was continued machine gun fire. By now, the forces surrounding the Japanese consisted of five 1st Division companies, two 92nd Infantry battalions, two 11th Infantry companies, one Scout battalion, one Constabulary battalion, some tanks and artillery. This mass of men shot at every movement, every sound, and at every suspicious occurrence. The constant fire took a toll of the Japanese as well as the vegetation. But the Japanese proved equally effective in their return fire. Casualties were heavy among Filipino BAR men, for they were a high priority target. After lightweight Filipinos wrestled their twenty-pound weapons into position, the distinctive noise of the automatic weapon drew enemy fire. The Japanese killed and wounded so many gunners that Filipinos picked to be BAR men felt themselves doomed. Losses declined somewhat when BAR gunners stayed a little to the rear of the riflemen during each movement forward. Incidents of self-inflicted wounds rose as the strain of the fighting increased. Opposing lines were so close together and fluctuated so often that the Japanese were soon firing American weapons and the Filipinos banged away with an assortment of Japanese rifles and machine guns. Lines were too close for normal ration resupply. Soldiers pushed cans of food with sticks from one foxhole to the next, and even then the cans were sometimes hit.[33]

Several factors steadied the Philippine Army's morale. Knowledge that Scouts were in action nearby had a good effect. The presence of American officers of all ranks in the front lines was another significant factor, and their appearance under heavy small-arms fire was beneficial. General Jones accidently stumbled his way right up to the front lines looking for the Scout command post. He was set straight just before he walked into the Japanese. Wainwright's appearance at forward positions, where he would spend three to six hours each day, set the tone for other officers. Lieutenant Stewart was walking to battalion headquarters for a briefing when Wainwright called him over to compliment him on his performance. Leaning on his command car, Wainwright pointed to a case of Scotch with five full fifths. "This is the last of it," Wainwright told Stewart.[34]

"We both took drinks," Stewart remembers, "out of the bottle—no chaser. I thanked him and staggered on to the CP area."

Filipino morale needed all the help it could get. The fighting was rugged. It was extremely difficult to evacuate the wounded and took so long that by the time casualties reached a hospital, their wounds were already rotting and crawled with fat maggots. Doctors were reluctant to operate immediately, because it was more important to give them a transfusion and load them up with fluids and feed them just to ward off shock and death. A patient's first request was always for food. Dead men were buried in their foxholes. Constant firing cut the bamboo into mounds that covered the ground. Filipinos found themselves falling through the bamboo into Japanese foxholes, resulting in serious disputes as to ownership of that piece of ground. All movement was fair game after dark. Although it was difficult to locate enemy positions, a liberal use of hand grenades tossed at suspected Japanese positions began a slow, steady attrition of enemy riflemen.[35]

The ground was soon thickly littered with every variety of dud ammunition. American and Japanese hand grenades, mortar rounds, and artillery projectiles lay in profusion about the battlefield. Both sides began booby-trapping hand grenades and mortar rounds. Objects other than dud ammunition impeded progress. American tankers had the disagreeable job of scraping pieces of Japanese out of their tank treads, wheels, and sprockets. In desperation, they threw sand against tank hulls to reduce the stench. American tankers did not have everything their own way. On February 6 Second Lieutenant Edward G. Winger's tank attacked Japanese machine guns and flame throwers. The tankers reduced several positions, but Winger's tank stalled, and he and his crew evacuated the vehicle. As Winger scrambled toward friendly lines, Filipinos mistook him for an enemy and shot him in the stomach and legs. In the time it took to evacuate Winger, gas gangrene set in, and he died during surgery.[36]

By now the Japanese were cut off from supplies and could not get out, and the Filipinos could not get in or evict them. A few Filipinos, taken prisoner by the Japanese, escaped and reported the Japanese were thirsty and hungry, so hungry they were killing their horses for food. They also reported that the Japanese were tying prisoner's arms behind their backs and then bayoneting them. One Filipino from the 11th Infantry crawled out of Japanese lines with nine bayonet wounds. He reported that others in his platoon were bayoneted and tortured to death.[37]

The Japanese tried to drop supplies to their men, but most of the bundles fell into Filipino hands and proved a welcome addition to the slim rations. A bad supply drop on February 6 followed a Japanese bombing strike. The bombs all fell squarely on the Japanese in the pocket itself. Japanese pilots then had less luck with the supply bundles. They dropped twelve, and eleven floated to Filipino lines. The single bundle that stayed within the pocket snagged a tree and remained out of reach. Besides ammunition, the containers were packed with cigarettes, emergency biscuit rations, and sugar candies.[38]

The Japanese realized they had to do something if they were to save the trapped men. Desperate efforts were then in progress to break through to the surrounded 20th Infantry. But all attempts by the Japanese 122nd Infantry and the 2nd Battalion, 33rd Infantry, to penetrate Wainwright's main line and relieve their comrades failed. Undaunted, the Japanese girded themselves for another try. The 2nd Battalion, 33rd Infantry, began a late night attack on February 6. Until this evening, the 1st and 2nd battalions of the 11th Infantry had been successful in holding the Japanese. Christian Filipinos from Iloces Province and Igorotes from the mountain provinces of Luzon had held firmly to their lines. But now, as the Japanese attack gained momentum in the early morning hours of the seventh, they overran the 2nd Platoon of F Company, killing eighteen of the twenty-nine men in their foxholes. Major Helmert J. Duisterhof, commanding the 2nd Battalion, organized a force of headquarters personnel, service units, and stragglers and held the Japanese 800 yards short of the Big Pocket. The Filipinos fought steadily and did not run.[39]

To the 11th Infantry's left was the 1st Division. When the Japanese broke through the 11th Infantry, Lieutenant Roland "Frenchy" Saulnier, a private before the war, and Lieutenant Napoleon Mangonon, commanding the 1st Division's right flank battalion and company respectively, rallied some of the troops and reformed the right flank in an inward facing fish-hook formation. The Japanese put three Filipino machine guns out of action and captured a fourth after the crew died, but a Filipino counterattack recaptured all four guns. Although attacked from three sides, the 1st Division held.[40]

All 11th Infantry reserves were now committed. Service units had already left their normal support functions and were carrying rifles, so Colonel Townsend needed to look elsewhere for help. He called 11th Division headquarters and briefed General Brougher on the situation. Brougher promised to find something as quickly as he could, and he did. Major Tenasas's 2nd Battalion, 2nd Constabulary, arrived and reported to Townsend. In the fading light of February 7 the Constabulary struggled through thick jungle, trying to stretch a line across the Japanese salient before dark. When night ended their efforts, there still were some gaps, but the Japanese did not find them. After a 600-yard advance, the shoulders of the penetration held and the Americans named the unsuccessful breakthrough the Upper Pocket. Although unable to link with the 20th Infantry, the Japanese continued their efforts to deepen the hole. But when additional reinforcements bolstered the Filipino line on February 8, the Japanese stalled.[41]

It was only after repeated failures against the two pockets that the American command finally drew up a coordinated plan for their reduction. At 1000 hours on February 5 General Wainwright, his chief of staff Colonel William F. Maher, and Generals Jones, Brougher, and Segundo sat down at the 1st Infantry's command post to decide the best way to finish the weary business. One problem plaguing all efforts was the divided command. The battle included elements from two divisions and numerous smaller units, yet no one man was in charge of the entire operation. General Jones offered his solution. "They have to be pinched out. First, I'd isolate the pockets and throw a cordon around each one."[42] The pockets would be attacked simultaneously in order to contain both and prevent shifting of forces between the pockets. Jones would reduce the Little Pocket first and then the Big Pocket. Wainwright agreed, solved the command problem by putting Jones in charge of the operation, and ordered Jones to put his operation into high gear as soon as possible but not later than February 7. Jones remained in charge until the eleventh when a acute attack of dysentery forced him to a hospital.

On February 7 the 1st Division surrounded the Little Pocket, drew its cordon tight, and pushed. The attack started at 1500 hours and progress was slow. The Filipinos carried Enfield rifles, a few Browning automatic rifles, and a few machine guns. Filipino artillery was impotent in such close quarters. "Our only hand grenades were made by stuffing a piece of dynamite with a [fuse] attached, into a stem of bamboo," recalled Colonel Townsend. "The [fuse] had to be lighted with a match. If too short, it exploded before it could be thrown; if too long, the Japs promptly tossed it back. . . . More than anything, we needed mortars. Even the old Stokes mortar with good ammo would have been of great value. But the only ammo available had been stored in the islands since World War I and had greatly deteriorated. . . . On one occasion in the Tuol Pocket we fired 70 rounds and got only 14 bursts. . . . [Later] we used up our last 22 rounds and got 5 bursts. No wonder the Japs once set up a captured Stokes mortar between the lines and scoffingly draped it with flowers."[43]

More to the point, the Filipinos were inexperienced in offensive operations. They were timid in their movements and failed to build an adequate base of fire to cover their advance. Nor were the Japanese ready to quit. They set one tank on fire with a hand grenade, and only quick action by Sergeant John O. Hopple with a fire extinguisher saved the tank and crew. Results of the first day's operation were so disappointing that General Jones directed Colonel Berry to take personal command and, so far as possible, place American officers in charge of the attacking units. Officers discussed the plan for the next day in detail. To overcome the fire power problem, a minimum of one machine gun platoon was to be used to build a base of fire. Because of this detailed planning and reorganization, the attack on February 8 went well. But on the night of the eighth, the Japanese slipped out of the Little Pocket with the last of their forces. Their trip was brief, however, for the surviving Japanese stumbled into the entrenched Filipinos of Lieutenant Saulnier's battalion on the main line and were destroyed to the last man.[44]

On February 9 and 10 the Filipinos at the Little Pocket redeployed to the Big Pocket and sped their preparations for the next attack. Reduction of the Little Pocket proved their jungle tactics worked. Filipinos pressed in from all sides until fire from one side was endangering friendlies on the opposite side. The Scout battalion worked over the enemy with its single 81mm mortar, using telephone lines to adjust the fire. Although Philippine Army Stokes shells were now falling exclusively on the enemy, only a few exploded. Lieutenant Colonel Lincoln Pebbles, I Corps Ordnance Officer, brought forward a supply of Stokes rounds that his technicians stripped, checked, and reassembled. Then the ordnance personnel checked the ammunition on hand, removed each nose and cleaned and replaced each fuse. Finally, the battalion's weapons company commander personally conducted the fire. Despite this effort, only twelve of seventy-two rounds exploded. After the battle Filipinos found

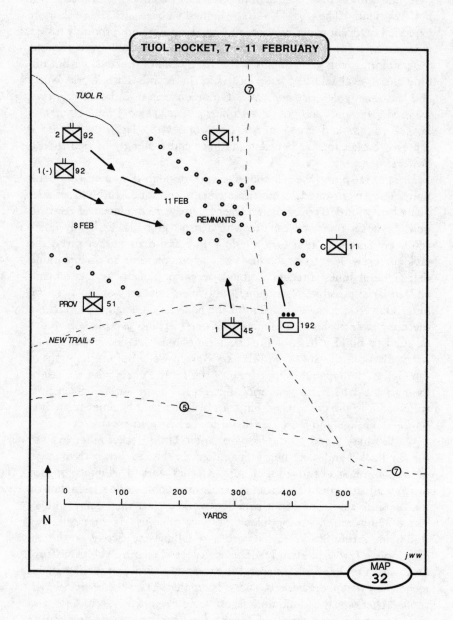

TUOL POCKET, 7 - 11 FEBRUARY

TUOL R.

2 ⊠ 92

1(-) ⊠ 92

G ⊠ 11

11 FEB

REMNANTS

8 FEB

C ⊠ 11

PROV ⊠ 51

1 ⊠ 45

192

NEW TRAIL 5

0   100   200   300   400   500

N   YARDS

jww

MAP
32

numerous unexploded mortar rounds lying within a yard or two of enemy machine gun emplacements. Unexploded shells were found in Japanese foxholes and trenches. When the round did occasionally explode, it was devastating.[45]

The Filipinos made slight gains from time to time but always at a cost. Although there were no spectacular victories, it was apparent the Japanese were losing strength. Filipino morale climbed as they saw their gains increase each day. The Philippine Army was learning the art of the offense. Continuous pressure squeezed the Japanese closer and closer together and pushed them away from their only source of water, the Tuol River. On February 10 the Filipinos finally secured Trail 7. It had taken them twelve days to push the Japanese 150 yards.[46]

On February 11 the Filipinos overran the 20th Infantry's command post and captured the regimental colors. One of the tanks lost earlier was recaptured. The guns still worked, so some Filipinos manned them and used the tank as a stationary pill box. Scout infantry found they could not occupy one area they captured because of the terrible odor of dead bodies. Huge swarms of blue bottle flies "sent out an unbelievably strange noise. . . ."[47] By evening of the best day yet in the Big Pocket, it was apparent that the end was in sight. But the Japanese refused to collapse. Instead, they started slipping away.

With Filipino pressure becoming more serious each day, the 20th Infantry's commanding officer, Colonel Yoshioka, realized his position was critical. On February 9, as a result of a conference held at 14th Army that decided upon a general withdrawal all across Bataan, Yoshioka received orders dropped by plane to fight his way back to friendly lines. But to do so with his severely weakened men in the face of converging Filipino attacks would be difficult in the extreme. Of his original 1,000 men, 400 were now dead and another 100 badly wounded. But he had to break out, for nothing would ever get to him. He sent patrols to probe Filipino lines cautiously and look for any sort of gap. On the evening of February 10 the Japanese made a strenuous effort to break out, but they hit stiff resistance and recoiled. On February 11 Colonel Yoshioka ordered his mountain guns and heavy items buried. At each spot where equipment was interred, the Japanese set a piece of wood like a small tombstone listing the items left there. Then Yoshioka's men began a dangerous withdrawal. They cut through the jungle northward to a gap where Filipino forces had not linked and made a slow, painful trek out of the pocket. Amazingly, hundreds of Japanese passed through the Filipino cordon without detection. Most of the regiment's officers were dead, and controlling the men was difficult. Carrying the wounded required much time and labor, and the column halted frequently to regain contact between elements. Utilizing a rear guard, the last living Japanese departed the pocket on February 12.[48]

The sudden end of resistance surprised everyone. "We jumped from one cover to another but encountered no Japanese troops," recalled Lieutenant Sevilla. "We closed in more cautiously till we reached the Japanese stronghold. The sight that met us was appalling. Cornered and with no place to go, the Japanese troops had made a last heroic defense in a 20 meter diameter and a meter deep hole. Sprawled all over the place were hundreds of the Japanese fallen dead, piled up on top of each other like sardines."[49] The Filipinos found a small aid station and took three wounded Japanese prisoner. At this point, officers had trouble keeping their men advancing, not because of enemy fire, but because the soldiers were reluctant to pass the enemy dead without looting them. The front-line Filipinos knew their comrades following them would reap the booty unless they took immediate action. They had done the fighting, they reasoned, and should receive the spoils. When Sevilla's men departed, they were laden with Japanese watches, flags, swords, pistols, and rifles.

Japanese survivors of the Big Pocket continued their dangerous march northward in search of friendly lines. They were soon reduced to subsisting on tree sap and horseflesh. When they finally reached their own lines and met a friendly officer patrol on February 15, only 377 exhausted men remained. The rest of the original 1,000 soldiers lay dead behind Filipino lines. Unburied in the Big Pocket were 300 Japanese and another 150 or more in graves, over which blue bottle flies swarmed in dense clouds. American estimates of enemy losses ran as high as 2,400 dead. No one knew about the escape of the regimental commander and a third of his men. The Americans believed, not illogically, that they had destroyed the entire 20th Infantry at the Tuol River. Even the most modest estimates ran well over a thousand dead enemy too many.[50]

Regardless of the number of Japanese dead, the battle was a tremendous victory for Wainwright's men. The Filipinos captured a large quantity of weapons and equipment, including an antitank gun which they put back into action against its former owners. It is difficult to give an exact accounting of enemy dead and materiel losses. The most accurate list was prepared by Major Arthur K. Noble, 11th Division Intelligence Officer, who recorded 300 bodies and 150 graves in the Big Pocket. The Japanese buried from three to six dead in some of their graves. Lieutenant Anderson, 11th Engineers, helped bury the enemy dead and conservatively estimated 450 dead in the Big Pocket alone. At the Little Pocket, eighty enemy bodies and forty-five graves were discovered. Flame throwers, light and heavy machine guns, mortars, artillery pieces, rifles, pistols, bayonets, bugles, sabers, and officer briefcases were found. Much of the

Japanese equipment was looted by the first troops to enter the area and
was never officially recorded. An incomplete listing of friendly casualties
carried two Scout officers and sixty-four enlisted men killed or wounded.
Three hundred Philippine Army soldiers were killed or wounded in the
11th Infantry alone.[51]

After cleaning up the Big Pocket, the victorious Filipinos marched
north to the main line of resistance. Beginning on February 12, units of
the 1st Division moved up to the west boundary of the Upper Pocket.
Two light tanks drove up Trail 7 to lend some help, but here, as at the
Big Pocket, bad terrain almost precluded their use. Only with close infantry aid could the tanks operate. Igorot soldiers, singly and in pairs,
climbed atop the tanks and cut away creepers and vines to give the drivers a clear view of the area ahead. When an Igorot saw an enemy, he
tapped the turret with the dull edge of his bolo, and the tankers zeroed in
and eliminated the target.[52]

On February 14 the Filipinos reduced the salient by half. The Japanese
were reluctant to lose this ground, and they liberally sprayed the area
with automatic weapons and searched reverse slopes with light mortars.
The next day Filipinos again halved the penetration to an area 100 by 75
yards. On the morning of the seventeenth, Igorotes, supported by tanks,
attacked again. "Every detail was worked out with minute precision,"
reads the 2nd Division's history. "Only 75 yards of the troublesome
Upper Pocket remained, while at the MLR the gap that remained to be
sealed was barely fifty yards . . . a barrage of incredible intensity was
laid down . . . turning the battleground into a veritable inferno as the
shells descended on the giant leafless trees and scarred rocks with deafening, crushing blows."[53]

There was a moment of silence when the barrage lifted, but it was
quickly drowned out as the lead infantry elements came under fire. Attempts to neutralize enemy positions by return fire proved unsuccessful.
Sergeant Aubrocio Lappay, a Constabulary soldier on duty with the 11th
Infantry, and four of his men attacked an enemy gun. When his attempts
to eliminate the position with grenades failed, and when several of his
men were hit, Sergeant Lappay rushed forward with a fixed bayonet. He
shot or stabbed the Japanese gun crew and, without a pause, charged a
second position and killed everyone in sight. Reacting to his example,
Filipinos moved quickly over the enemy. Japanese fast enough to hop out
of their foxholes were killed by rifle fire. Those who stayed succumbed to
hand grenades. The relative ease with which the Filipinos advanced was
due, in part, to the fact the Japanese no longer needed this ground. The
survivors of the 20th Infantry were now safe, so there was little reason to
hold the Upper Pocket. As the Japanese abandoned the salient, the Filipi-

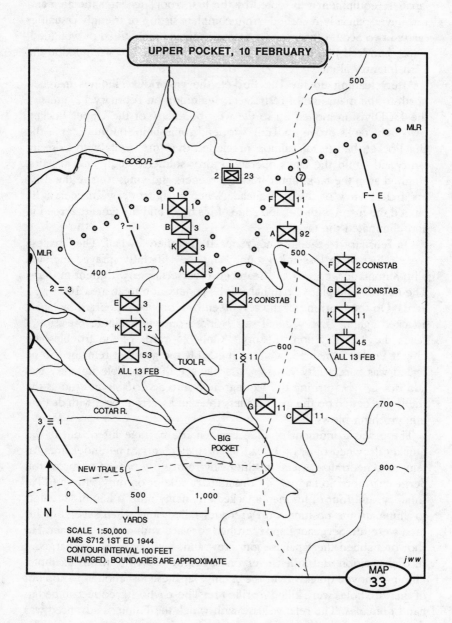

UPPER POCKET, 10 FEBRUARY

500

MLR

GOGO R.

2 ⊠ 23

⑦

F — E

F ⊠ 11

I ⊠ 1

? — I

B ⊠ 3

K ⊠ 3

A ⊠ 92

MLR

A ⊠ 3

400

500

F ⊠ 2 CONSTAB

2 ≡ 3

E ⊠ 3

2 ⊠ 2 CONSTAB

G ⊠ 2 CONSTAB

K ⊠ 12

K ⊠ 11

53

1 ⊠ 45

ALL 13 FEB

TUOL R.

1 ⊠ 11

600

ALL 13 FEB

700

COTAR R.

3 ≡ 1

G ⊠ 11

C ⊠ 11

BIG
POCKET

800

NEW TRAIL 5

0   500   1,000

N

YARDS

SCALE 1:50,000
AMS S712 1ST ED 1944
CONTOUR INTERVAL 100 FEET
ENLARGED. BOUNDARIES ARE APPROXIMATE

jww

MAP
33

Troops arriving in Manilla on November 20, 1941 aboard the S.S. *President Coolidge. Courtesy of Casimir T. Bobulski.*

An M-3 Stuart light tank on Luzon. *Courtesy of Albert L. Allen, Jr.*

An M-3 Stuart tank and motorcycle on Luzon. *Courtesy of Albert L. Allen, Jr.*

75mm Self-Propelled Mount (SPM) manned by Philippine Army soldiers. *Courtesy of Albert L. Allen.*

Above: 12th Infantry Regiment, Philippine Army, at marksmanship practice during mobilization. *Courtesy of Wayne C. Liles.*

Left: Half-track with .50-caliber machine gun. *Courtesy of Albert L. Allen, Jr.*

Below: 11th Infantry Regiment nipa barracks near Dagupan during mobilization. *Courtesy of Wayne C. Liles.*

Philippine Army troops in Aparri on Commonwealth Day. *Courtesy of Wayne C. Liles.*

American 31st Infantry Regiment soldiers, 23 September 1941. *Courtesy of Donald G. Thompson.*

Philippine Army soldiers during mobilization. *U.S. Army Signal Corps.*

2nd Battalion, 72nd Infantry Regiment, inspection in khakis, November 1941. *Courtesy of John W. Fisher.*

2nd Battalion, 72nd Infantry Regiment on the march in blue denim, November 1941. *Courtesy of John W. Fisher.*

2nd Battalion, 72nd Infantry Regiment in training camp, November 1941.
Courtesy of John W. Fisher.

H Company, 2nd Battalion, 72nd Infantry Regiment during .30-caliber machine gun instruction, November 1941. *Courtesy of John W. Fisher.*

Hospital on Bataan, 1942. *U.S. Army Signal Corps.*

Bomb damage on Bataan. *Courtesy of William A. Marrocco.*

The last P-40 on Bataan. *Courtesy of Ralph Levenberg.*

Major General Edward P. King at the surrender, April 9. *U.S. Army Signal Corps.*

nos reoccupied the original line where they found 200 enemy bodies in the Upper Pocket.[54]

The hard battles along the Tuol River produced many heroic actions. Lieutenant Bianchi won the Medal of Honor. Of sixteen American officers in the 11th Infantry, five won Distinguished Service Crosses, four won Bronze Stars, three received Silver Stars, and two were awarded the Legion of Merit. General Brougher received the DSC and later the Philippine Distinguished Service Star. Filipinos were likewise heavily decorated. The 11th Division received its second Presidential Unit Citation. The men earned "Purple Hearts galore."[55] I Corps's morale peaked at the end of the Tuol fight. It was the first time Filipinos defeated a sizable Japanese force on ground of its own choosing by offensive action. This was not a defensive battle where the Japanese threw themselves upon entrenched Filipinos. Rather, it was the offensive spirit, fire power, and ability of the Filipinos which destroyed the Japanese.

Having begun the Bataan campaign with 2,690 men, all three battalions of the Japanese 20th Infantry were now gone. No more than 650 wounded and diseased survivors remained. The 20th Infantry was elevated to the status of national heroes for their valiant fight and subsequent destruction. Reports available to the Americans indicated the Japanese 122nd Infantry was in disgrace for its failure to relieve the trapped 20th Infantry. By February 26 the I Corps's line was restored and the Battle of the Pockets concluded. Wainwright, well known for praising and taking care of his people, published General Order Number 16 thanking his corps.[56]

> It is with a sense of profound gratitude for their splendid accomplishment of a difficult task that the Corps Commander extends to all officers and men of the First Philippine Corps, the 45th Infantry (less 2nd and 3rd Battalions), 2nd Battalion, 2nd Regiment (PC), and Company "C" 192nd Tank Battalion his sincere congratulations and high commendation for the part taken by every officer and soldier during the operations near the TUOL River and along Trail Seven south of the main line of resistance from February 7th to 17th, 1942.[57]

Despite the temptation, it was not possible for the Filipinos to rest on their laurels. After the fighting ended the men turned to rebuilding the main line. Of necessity, construction had been delayed while efforts were directed at the Japanese penetration. Now the work picked up again. Much of the early work did not fit into the overall plan. Change after change wasted labor, time, and materiel. Soldiers went through the laborious process of taking down barbed wire so as to string it again in a better spot. Concurrent with construction requirements, the soldiers started showing the effects of malnutrition, malaria, dysentery, and other tropical diseases. Hookworm was a problem, and a medical study determined that because of the poor physical condition of the troops, it was too dangerous to use a vermifuge. Although conditions under which the line was built were poor, the Filipinos were now veteran enough to realize the need to strengthen the line. They worked as hard as their poor diet and failing strength allowed. Although Japanese attacks ceased, Colonel MacDonald, chief of staff, Left Sub-sector, realized more were to come. "We all felt that this respite was not forever and did what could be done, under the poor supply conditions, to place all in readiness for [the] storm that the future would bring."[58]

CHAPTER EIGHTEEN

The Japanese Retreat

BLOODIED AND REALIZING IT WAS FUTILE TO CONTINUE THE OFFEN-
sive, General Homma prepared to withdraw his 14th Army from the
entire front up to as much as ten kilometers. Commanders and staffs
huddled over maps and climbed hills searching for good defensive terrain. The Japanese were concerned that a Filamerican offensive might
push out of Bataan into Luzon's central plains, and to those who knew
the true state of the Japanese army, even the loss of Manila seemed
possible. But before the withdrawal was undertaken—admittedly a dras-
tic course of action—there was heated debate within 14th Army headquarters. On February 8, a muggy day with temperature standing at a
humid and enervating 95 degrees, General Homma called a meeting of
his staff at his San Fernando headquarters. The question he posed was,
how were they to continue the campaign most economically and, simultaneously, most expeditiously? The word "expeditiously" was the key.
Southern Army Headquarters as well as Imperial General Headquarters
were urging Homma to conclude the campaign, and the pressure was
making him uncomfortable.[1]

At San Fernando, General Maeda, chief of staff to the 14th Army and
presiding as chairman of the meeting, called the assembled officers to
order. He opened with a description of the Japanese Army's plight. No
word was then available from the two infantry battalions fighting near
Quinauan Point. The third battalion that had disappeared behind Wainwright's main line was dying in the Tuol Pockets. General Nara's repeated attempts to break the new Filamerican line at Trail 2 had collapsed in bloody ruins. To the experienced eyes of the Japanese staff the
situation was not merely desperate, it was catastrophic. A huge, un-

friendly Filipino population lived behind their lines and had the potential of disrupting their supply lines and of overwhelming small pockets of isolated Japanese. Although this threat was not terribly significant, Homma's men could not ignore it. Maeda's talk convinced everyone of the gravity of the situation and the pressing need for decisions. When Maeda stated that effective Japanese strength on Bataan consisted of only three infantry battalions, consternation spread through the room. Then the other officers started talking.[2]

The senior operations officer of the 14th Army, Colonel Motoo Nakayama, argued that the offensive should be pushed aggressively. But instead of attacking I Corps, the main attacks should be launched against the eastern portion of the line, against II Corps. There the ground was better and the Japanese would not have to fight the hills and jungle as well as the Filipinos.[3]

General Maeda believed otherwise. The offensive should be discontinued. The best course of action, he insisted, would be to completely isolate the peninsula from supplies and starve the defenders into submission. The remaining and as yet unconquered islands of the archipelago could be captured during the blockade. Maeda's opinion carried weight with Homma, for Maeda had been the first and most vocal of Homma's staff to predict the main Filipino stand would be on Bataan rather than around Manila. As a captain and graduate of the Imperial War College, Maeda had posed as a traveling merchant and, starting in 1925, criss-crossed the Philippines gathering the information he now used to sway Homma.[4]

Homma's decision was something of a compromise. He would stop the attacks, but rather than wait passively for the Americans to starve, a rather inglorious manner in which to conquer, Homma would call Southern Army, and through it Imperial General Headquarters, and request more troops. Homma's decision to ask for help was not easy, for he and Prime Minister Tojo nursed something of a personality conflict dating to when Tojo trained in Germany and Homma in England. Homma had studied in England during WWI, served in India and London, and had visited the United States, Canada, and the Middle East. Back in Japan both officers became leading spokesmen of the divergent philosophies of the German and British schools. By 1942 the two were established enemies, and Homma's appeal to Tokyo for reinforcements was a terribly bitter pill for him to swallow. Homma had failed to accomplish his mission with the forces given him in the prescribed time.[5]

Homma planned to rest his men, train, and await the reinforcements with which he would launch a final attack. The campaign could no longer be waged on a shoestring. Concurrent with the request for more men, Homma ordered all commands to tighten the blockade around Bataan.

The Japanese knew some supplies were running their cordon, and they set out to stop them. The 14th Army staff drafted an operations order, had it approved at 1900 hours, and dispatched it to the field. The 16th Division, then opposite I Corps, was ordered to the northern heights of the Bagac River and told to prepare for enemy attacks. Nara's 65th Brigade was ordered to defend the mountains north of the Talisay River. Telephone calls to Nara that evening stopped his imminent attack. Even though Maeda's arguments carried the conference, and even though his ideas were accepted and put into action, his days as Homma's chief of staff were numbered.[6]

At the end of this depressing conference, Homma's staff filed out of the room. Then an aide handed him a telegram from Imperial General Headquarters. The message said that victory had been achieved in several theaters of war; General Tomoyuki Yamashita's 25th Army was about to achieve a stupendous feat by reducing the great base of Singapore. There was, however, a lack of satisfaction about the extended campaign in the Philippines. No doubt Homma would have understood the cry of French soldiers in 1809 at the second siege of Spanish Saragossa. "Has anyone ever heard of an army of 20,000 men besieging another of 50,000? We are barely masters of one quarter of this city and already we are exhausted. We must wait for reinforcements, otherwise we shall all perish and these cursed ruins will become our tombs before we have forced the last of these fanatics out of their final stronghold."[7] Substitute peninsula for city and jungle for ruins and you have a perfect description of Homma's plight.

Although Homma was, for the moment, stalled, his situation was not nearly as bad as announced by the Americans. USAFFE received several reports claiming Homma had committed suicide over his disgraceful failure to conquer Bataan. Homma had reportedly picked General MacArthur's apartment in the Manila Hotel for his gory departure, and his funeral was held in Manila in the presence of representatives from the Emperor, after which his ashes were flown to Japan. USAFFE heard that General Yamashita had replaced Homma. "I suggest you initiate publicity in this matter," MacArthur requested of Washington. "It will have a greater psychological effect if announced by Washington rather than by me."[8] Yamashita did assume command of the Philippines, but not until October 1944 when he was faced with defending the islands from MacArthur. So despite the delight with which the Filamerican force received the news of Homma's death, he remained alive.

The day after Homma's conference the news coming into 14th Army Headquarters had not improved. His staff reported a cutting defeat for his air force, an event triggered by Japanese successes against Corregidor.

The Japanese had emplaced their big guns in the hills along the southern entrance to Manila Bay, and heavy artillery fires were falling on Corregidor and the fortified islands. American counterbattery fire was limited in its effectiveness because of the difficulty in spotting the well-camouflaged Japanese. So, on February 9 the American air force received orders to fly a reconnaissance mission to find the guns. Because the bulky camera could not fit in a P-40, mechanics took an old Curtis 0-1 biplane, cut a hole in its belly, and installed the camera. Captain Jesus A. Villamor, a Philippine Army Air Corps pilot, taxied his unarmed plane onto Bataan Field and lifted into the air.[9]

Captain Villamor was a veteran pilot with over 2,000 flying hours. He was the son of the first president of the University of the Philippines, and he always had the ambition to fly, going so far as taking lessons in Dallas, Texas. He and two other PAAC pilots had downed two Japanese planes on the first day of the war, and MacArthur had personally decorated Villamor with the Distinguished Service Cross. From Bataan and Cabcaben Fields six P-40's rose to escort the camera plane. Lieutenant Ben S. Brown led the flight, flying at 17,000 feet with the photo plane at 15,000 feet. Over the mountains near Ternate, Villamor spotted the guns, and his photographer, Master Sergeant Juan V. Abanes, took the necessary pictures. There were no enemy planes to bother Villamor, so he flew over his target several times and took 110 pictures before he banked his slow plane back toward Bataan. But Bataan called the pilots and told them that six Japanese Zeros were waiting for them at 8,000 feet. The P-40's went under the Zeros so as to protect Villamor, then tried to climb up to fight the Japanese.[10]

Because the Americans were lower, the Japanese attacked but overshot and flew past the P-40's. On the ground everyone with an unrestricted view looked skyward. "We stood and watched," recalled Jesse White, a crew chief to one of the P-40's, "as the photo plane dived straight toward Bataan Field and landed safely while the P-40's tore into the Zeros and climbed straight up after exchanging fire. Over Manila Bay the sky was filled with swarming planes in a dogfight as chilling as a John Wayne movie. Oblivious to the danger of spent bullets, we watched in awe as Zero after Zero plunged into the bay. The maneuverability of the Zeros outclassed the P-40's, but our superior pilots made the difference. They literally wrung out the P-40's in maneuvers thought to be impossible, rolling, looping in and out in precision to find their targets."[11]

During the fight, Lieutenant Earl R. Stone, a veteran of the attacks against enemy barges off the west coast, dove his plane into a cloud to escape a Zero, but the cloud he picked shrouded a large mountain. His plane crashed and Stone died. Another P-40 was presumed lost over the bay, but it miraculously returned from the dead the next day. The pilot was afraid his damaged plane would block a runway, so he flew south to Mindanao where he safely landed, was repaired, and returned to Bataan. Five Japanese planes were shot out of the sky and the sixth badly damaged. The surviving Zero fluttered down to the Pilar Air Field behind Japanese lines only to be promptly destroyed by American artillery. Even the Japanese reconnaissance plane "Photo Joe" that innocently wandered by found itself caught in the battle and hastily flew into cloud cover to elude a P-40.[12]

The loss of six Zero's was no more than irritating to the Japanese but it carried a deeper meaning that the Japanese were beginning to understand, the effect the successful and prolonged resistance was having throughout the world. Lieutenant Colonel Yoshio Nakajima, 14th Army intelligence staff, believed that "there was an influence, a spiritual influence, exerted by the American resistance on Bataan. Not only did the Japanese at home worry about the length of the period of American resistance on Bataan, but it served as a symbol to the Filipinos that the Americans had not deserted them and would continue to assist them."[13]

The Filamerican resistance was proving costly to the Japanese. Since early January, Homma's 14th Army recorded 2,725 men killed in action, 4,049 wounded, and 250 missing. In addition to battle casualties, 10,000 to 12,000 soldiers were sick with malaria, beriberi, and dysentery. The 14th Army had ceased to exist as a fighting force. Homma's two combat units, the 16th Division and the 65th Brigade, had been ground to impotence. The 16th Division's effective infantry strength on February 24 was 712 men. One entire regiment of the division, the 20th Infantry, was totally destroyed and gained the unusual distinction of having 1,700 men killed and only a few wounded. The 16th Division's 9th Infantry suffered 750 killed or wounded in a month of fighting with Nara's 65th Brigade. The one battalion of the 33rd Infantry that fought on Bataan was badly bruised in the Upper Tuol Pocket.[14]

From January 9 to January 24, 65th Brigade losses were as follows: In the 141st Infantry, 335 were killed and 364 wounded from an initial strength of 1,919 officers and men; the 142nd Infantry entered Bataan with the same strength and sustained 226 killed and 387 wounded; other Brigade elements suffered 140 killed and 400 wounded; in just sixteen days of combat the 65th Brigade lost 701 killed and 1,151 wounded, 27 percent of the force, more than one man in four; then, from January 25 to February 15, the brigade suffered 441 more killed and 817 wounded bringing the losses to 46 percent of the total force, almost every other man killed or wounded. These figures do not include ineffectives due to illness. In a month of fighting on Bataan the Japanese lost four times the number of men they lost killed or wounded during their invasion and conquest of the rest of Luzon. The Japanese realized their losses were extreme. "The fighting strength of the various Brigade units became quite low about this time," recorded the 65th Brigade. "This was especially true of the infantry, which was in direct contact with the enemy at all times and was engaged in combat day and night. Its casualties were exceedingly heavy. The fighting strength of one company became lower than one peacetime platoon. The greater part of company officers and central staff officers who led in action were lost and finally there were many cases in which NCO's took over company command. The unit reached the extreme stages of exhaustion."[15]

During his postwar war-crimes trial, Homma declared that if MacArthur had counterattacked at this time, the Filamerican force could have walked to Manila "without encountering much resistance on our part."[16] Although the 14th Army was truly "in very bad shape," Homma's claim is extreme. But his statement does show the appalling condition to which the Japanese had been reduced.

In compliance with Homma's orders to occupy good defensive terrain and blockade Bataan, General Nara made plans to launch a feint to cover his withdrawal. On February 15 Nara's air support attacked Filipino front lines, and an hour later, at 1800 hours, he initiated an artillery bombardment. "Japs started shelling at 6:00 P.M." wrote Colonel Quintard in his diary, "Seven batteries reported at same time, also they kept planes up all the time so we accomplished very little. "B" shelled, our lines to OP out. Brigade's line to their OP also out."[17] Japanese planes also worked over the 41st Division. The Japanese used fifty vehicles to simulate heavy troop movements, and infantry units advanced at dusk, deployed, and opened fire but then remained in position. They made no attempt to close with the Filipinos, for their detailed orders were clear. None of their formations was to exceed six men, and distance between groups was to be at least 50 meters. They had orders to conceal themselves when defending artillery fired.

The Japanese considered these sham battles so successful that they continued them for three days. Defending Filipino artillery was a high-priority target. B Battery, 301st Artillery was shelled on February 16 and early on February 17. "B shelled again," wrote Colonel Quintard in his diary. "2 men wounded. Will move them tonight. Japs seem to have spotted "A" and "C". While returning from reconnaissance, we could see shells falling in vicinity of A, C, and D batteries. We had to go too close to "D" on the way back to suit me! A small shift would have gotten us. When we reached the CP we found fragments falling in and around it."[18]

Both sides traded small arms and artillery fire until, in the words of the Japanese, "the base of Mt. Samat shook with the din of the bombardment on both sides and the position seemed exactly like a real attack."[19] The activity worried some men. Lieutenant William H. Montgomery viewed the increased firing with misgivings, for he felt that the Japanese would not receive much opposition if they attacked. Montgomery noticed that one group of Filipinos might be fighting tooth and nail, all weapons firing and raising a terrific din, but a hundred yards away another outfit would be placidly pounding corn and cooking their supper. The problem, of course, was the scanty training they had received. Nor was the outlook bright for the Japanese. Their infantrymen were cautious about putting their lives on the line for a feint, and no one pushed forward hard enough to upset the defenders. Even so, the Japanese felt these attacks succeeded in drawing Filipinos from the western side of Bataan to the east, thereby allowing Japanese forces to withdraw unhindered. Actually, the sham battles made little impression on the American command, and no troop movements were made in response to the feints.

Before leaving the front of the Philippine 41st Division, a Japanese lieutenant pinned a note to a tree saying they were withdrawing to Olongapo but that they would be back and fight more fiercely than before. The Japanese officer asked the Filipinos why they were fighting America's war and advised them to kill their American officers, to surrender their arms, and go home to their loved ones. After the Japanese withdrew it took some time for the Filipinos and Americans to understand the move. "The Nips have gotten us crossed up again," wrote Lieutenant Montgomery in his diary. "Their lines have pulled back for a considerable distance. They have left prepared positions and gun emplacements. Our patrols are out looking for a reason. They contact enemy patrols every day but as yet have been unable to ascertain the real reason for withdrawal."[20]

Heavy fighting ended after the Japanese withdrew. Between February 21 and 23 the II Corps's 155mm cannons had but a single fire mission. Japanese activity was so minor that American forward observers could not spot targets. "Feb. 24," wrote Colonel Quintard, "went to Corps. Col Dougherty gave me a bottle of Scotch! Not a round fired. This has nothing to do with the Scotch."[21] That same day USAFFE's intelligence summary of the enemy situation reported that the enemy's performance was so passive as to discount any immediate threat of attack. Colonel Willoughby, MacArthur's intelligence officer, felt the circumstances lent themselves to limited objective attacks by the American command.

Filipino successes in holding and then defeating the Japanese provided a terrific boost to morale. After the fighting along the west coast, Trail 2, and at the Tuol Pockets, morale reached its highest peak. A favorable reaction was setting in on soldiers and commanders alike. Through December and January the Japanese had harassed and harried the Americans and Filipinos across the length and width of Luzon, then battered the army out of the northern half of Bataan. Now the Japanese had pulled up exhausted. The instinctive desire for revenge, to strike out and retaliate for all the previous hurts, swept over the Filamericans. A member of MacArthur's staff noted that morale was high and the army wanted to take the offensive. There appeared to be no enemy opposition along the east coast except dead Japanese and tons of abandoned equipment. Japanese prisoners gave the impression that morale was low.[22]

But although morale was climbing along the front lines, there were disturbing waverings at higher levels. In late January Philippine President Manuel Quezon wrote a long message to MacArthur, which MacArthur passed to Washington. Beginning with an assertion of continued loyalty and belief in the ultimate successful outcome of the war, President Quezon voiced his strong concern over United States failures to take effective relief action.

> My loyalty and the loyalty of the Filipino people to America have been proven beyond question. Now we are fighting by her side under your command despite overwhelming odds. But, it seems to me questionable whether any government has the right to demand loyalty from its citizens beyond its willingness or ability to render actual protection. . . . We decided to fight by your side and we have done the best we could and we are still doing as much as could be expected from us under the circumstances. But how long are we going to be left alone? Has it already been decided in Washington that the Philippine front is of no importance as far as the final result of the war is concerned and that, therefore, no help can be expected here in the immediate future, or at least before our power of resistance is exhausted. If so, I want to know it, because I have my own responsibility to my countrymen whom, as President of the Commonwealth, I have led into a complete war effort. I am greatly concerned as well regarding the soldiers I have called to the colors and who are now manning the firing line. I want to decide in my own mind whether there is justification in allowing all these men to be killed, when for the final outcome of the war the shedding of their blood may be wholly unnecessary. It seems that Washington does not fully realize our situation nor the feelings which the apparent neglect of our safety and welfare have engendered in the hearts of the people here.[23]

MacArthur understood the importance of Quezon's letter. At the same time, the letter suited his purposes. He too was urging that reinforcements be sent to the Philippines, he too was urging a more active strategy, and he constantly urged Washington not to abandon the Philippines for other theaters. In President Quezon's letter MacArthur found additional ammunition for his arguments with Washington. He felt that the letter was of such a nature that it could only be answered by the president. President Quezon's concerns rose as the days passed, and his next message was addressed directly to President Roosevelt. Sent under MacArthur's comment, "The following message has just been received by me from President Quezon for President Roosevelt," it reached Washington on February 8.

The situation of my country has become so desperate that I feel that positive action is demanded. Militarily it is evident that no help will reach us from the United States in time either to rescue the beleaguered garrison now fighting so gallantly or to prevent the complete overrunning of the entire Philippine Archipelago.

My people entered the war with the confidence that the United States would bring such assistance to us as would make it possible to sustain the conflict with some chance of success. All our soldiers in the field were animated by the belief that help would be forthcoming. This help has not and evidently will not be realized. Our people have suffered death, misery, devastation. After two months of war not the slightest assistance has been forthcoming from the United States. Aid and succour have been dispatched to other warring nations such as England, Ireland, Australia, the N.E.I. and perhaps others, but not only has nothing come here, but apparently no effort has been made to bring anything here. The American Fleet and the British Fleet, the two most powerful navies in the world, have apparently adopted an attitude which precludes any effort to reach these islands with assistance.

As a result, while enjoying security itself, the United States has in effect condemned the sixteen millions of Filipinos to practical destruction in order to effect a certain delay. You have promised redemption, but what we need is immediate assistance and protection. We are concerned with what is to transpire during the next few months and years as well as with our ultimate destiny. There is not the slightest doubt in our minds that victory will rest with the United States, but the question before us now is: Shall we further sacrifice our country and our people in a hopeless fight? I voice the unanimous opinion of my War Cabinet and I am sure the unanimous opinion of all Filipinos that under the circumstances we should take steps to preserve the Philippines and the Filipinos from further destruction.

Thanks to wise generalship two thirds of my country is as yet untouched. We do not propose to do this by a betrayal of the United States. It appears to us that our mission is only to fight as a sacrifice force here as long as possible in order to help the defense of the Dutch and British in this area of the world. But you do not need to sacrifice the people of the Philippines to win this war. Members of your Government have repeatedly said that the action against Hitler would determine the outcome of the entire war.

I feel at this moment that our military resistance here can no longer hold the enemy when he sees fit to launch a serious attack. I feel that the elements of the situation here can be composed into a solution that will not reduce the delaying effect of our resistance here but which will save my country from further devastation as the battle ground of two great powers.

I deem it my duty to propose my solution. The Government of the United States under the McDuffie Tydings law is committed to grant independence to the Philippines in 1946, and the same law authorized the President to open negotiations for the neutralization of the Philippines. On the other hand, the Japanese government has publicly announced its willingness to grant the Philippines her independence. In view of the foregoing I propose the following:

That the United States immediately grant the Philippines complete and absolute independence;

That the Philippines be at once neutralized;

That all occupying troops, both American and Japanese, be withdrawn by mutual agreement with the Philippine Government within a reasonable length of time;

That the Philippine Army be immediately disbanded, the only armed forces being maintained here to be a constabulary of modest size;

That immediately upon granting independence the trade relations of the Philippines with foreign countries be a matter to be determined entirely by the Philippines and the foreign countries concerned;

That American and Japanese civilians who so desire be withdrawn with their respective troops under mutual and proper safeguards. It is my proposal to make this suggestion publicly to you and to the Japanese authorities without delay and upon acceptance in general principle by those two countries that an immediate armistice be entered into here pending the withdrawal of their respective garrisons.[24]

Before MacArthur sent this message to Washington, he appended his thoughts.

My estimate of the military situation here is as follows: The troops have sustained practically 50% casualties from their original strength. Divisions are reduced to the size of regiments, regiments to battalions, battalions to companies. Some units have entirely disappeared. The men have been in constant action and are badly battle worn. They are desperately in need of rest and refitting. Their spirit is good but they are capable now of nothing but fighting in place on a fixed position. All our supplies are scant and the command has been on half rations for the past month.

It is possible for the time being that the present enemy force might temporarily be held, but any addition to his present strength will insure the destruction of our entire force. We have pulled through a number of menacing situations but there is no denying the fact that we are near done. Corregidor itself is extremely vulnerable. This type of fortress, built prior to the days of air power, when isolated is impossible of prolonged defense. Any heavy air bombardment or the location of siege guns on Bataan or even on the Cavite [side] is extremely vulnerable and may go at any time. Every other vital installation can be readily taken out.

Since I have no air or sea protection, you must be prepared at any time to figure on the complete destruction of this command. You must determine whether the mission of delay would be better furthered by the temporizing plan of Quezon or by my continued battle effort. The temper of the Filipinos is one of almost violent resentment against the United States. Every one of them expected help and when it has not been forthcoming they believe they have been betrayed in favor of others. It must be remembered they are hostile to Great Britain on account of the latter's colonial policy. In spite of my great prestige with them, I have had the utmost difficulty during the last few days in keeping them in line. If help does not arrive shortly nothing, in my opinion, can prevent their utter collapse and their complete absorption by the enemy. The Japanese made a powerful impression upon the Philippine public imagination in promising independence.

So far as the military angle is concerned, the problem presents itself as to whether the plan of President Quezon might offer the best possible solution of what is about to be a disastrous debacle. It would not affect the ultimate situation in the Philippines for that would be determined by the results of other theaters. If the Japanese Government rejects President Quezon's proposition it would psychologically strengthen our hold because of their Prime Minister's public statement offering independence. If it accepts it, we lose no military advantage because we would still secure at least equal delay. Please instruct me.[25]

MacArthur obviously pulled out every stop in his desire to wake Washington. His message is virtually a backhanded indorsement, for shock value, of Quezon's proposal. He drew the picture as bleak as possible to draw a reaction. MacArthur was blunt, but he was soon to find that Roosevelt was equally blunt and even more able to pen a wilful message. Roosevelt immediately answered Quezon's first message, but before it reached the Philippines, Quezon sent Roosevelt his proposed announcement of neutralization. Concerned over the prospect of Quezon taking unilateral action, Roosevelt answered again, this time with a measure of iron in his reply.

Your message of February 10th evidently crossed mine to you of February 9th. Under our constitutional authority the President of the United States is not empowered to cede or alienate any territory to another nation. Furthermore, the United States has just bound itself in agreement with 24 other nations to united action in dealing with the Axis powers and has specifically engaged itself not to enter into any negotiations for a separate peace.

You have no authority to communicate with the Japanese government without the express permission of the United States Government.

I will make no further comments regarding your last message dated February 10th pending your acknowledgment of mine to you of February 9th through General MacArthur.[26]

The February 9 message to which Roosevelt referred then reached Quezon and read as follows:

I have just received your message sent through General MacArthur. From my message to you of January 30, you must realize that I am not lacking in understanding of or sympathy with the situation of yourself and the Commonwealth Government today. The immediate crisis certainly seems desperate but such crises and their treatment must be judged by a more accurate measure than the anxieties and sufferings of the present, however acute. For over forty years the American Government has been carrying out to the people of the Philippines a pledge to help them success- fully, however long it might take, in their aspirations to become a self- governing and independent people, with the individual freedom and eco- nomic strength which that lofty aim makes requisite. You yourself have participated in and are familiar with the many carefully planned steps by which that pledge of self-government has been carried out and also the steps by which the economic independence of your Islands is to be made effective. May I remind you now that in the loftiness of its aim and the fidelity with which it has been executed, this program of the United States towards another people has been unique in the history of the family of nations. In the Tydings-McDuffie Act of 1934, to which you refer, the Congress of the United States finally fixed the year 1946 as the date in which the Commonwealth of the Philippine Islands established by that Act should finally reach the goal of its hopes for political and economic inde- pendence.

By a malign conspiracy of a few depraved but powerful governments, this hope is now being frustrated and delayed. An organized attack upon individual freedom and governmental independence throughout the entire world, beginning in Europe, has now spread and been carried to the South- western Pacific by Japan. The basic principles which have guided the United States in its conduct toward the Philippines have been violated in the rape of Czechoslovakia, Poland, Holland, Belgium, Luxembourg, Den- mark, Norway, Albania, Greece, Yugoslavia, Manchukuo, China, Thai- land, and finally the Philippines. Could the people of any of these nations honestly look forward to a true restoration of their independent sover- eignty under the dominance of Germany, Italy, or Japan?

You refer in your telegram to the announcement by the Japanese Prime Minister of Japan's willingness to grant to the Philippines her indepen- dence. I only have to refer you to the present condition of Korea, Manchu- kuo, North China, Indo-China, and all other countries which have fallen under the brutal sway of the Japanese Government, to point out the hollow duplicity of such an announcement. The present sufferings of the Filipino people, cruel as they may be, are infinitely less than the sufferings and permanent enslavement which will inevitably follow acceptance of Japa- nese promises. In any event is it longer possible for any reasonable person to rely upon Japanese offer or promise?

The United States today is engaged with all its resources and in company with the governments of 26 other nations in an effort to defeat the aggres- sion of Japan and its Axis partners. This effort will never be abandoned until the complete and thorough overthrow of the entire Axis system and the governments which maintain it. We are engaged now in laying the foundations in the Southwest Pacific of a development in air, naval and military power which shall become sufficient to meet and overthrow the widely extended and arrogant attempts of the Japanese. Military and naval operations call for recognition of realities. What we are doing there constitutes the best and surest help that we can render to the Philippines at this time.

By the terms of our pledge to the Philippines, implicit is our forty years of conduct towards your people and expressly recognized in the terms of the Tydings-McDuffie Act, we have undertaken to protect you to the uttermost of our power until the time of your ultimate independence had arrived. Our soldiers in the Philippines are now engaged in fulfilling that purpose. The honor of the United States is pledged to its fulfillment. We propose that it be carried out regardless of its cost. Those Americans who are fighting now will continue to fight until the bitter end. Filipino soldiers have been rendering voluntary and gallant service in defense of their own homeland.

So long as the flag of the United States flies on Filipino soil as a pledge of our duty to your people, it will be defended by our own men to the death. Whatever happens to the present American garrison we shall not relax our efforts until the forces which we are now marshalling outside the Philippine Islands return to the Philippines and drive the last remnant of the invaders from your soil.[27]

Roosevelt passed this long message through MacArthur, and Roosevelt appended a section specifically for MacArthur's eyes.

My reply [to Quezon] must emphatically deny the possibility of this government's agreeing to the political aspects of President Quezon's proposal. I authorize you to arrange for the capitulation of the Filipino elements of the defending forces, when and if in your opinion that course appears necessary and always having in mind that the Filipino troops are in the service of the United States.

For this purpose the Filipino troops could be placed by you under the command of a Filipino officer who would conduct actual negotiations with the enemy whereas such negotiations must involve military matters exclusively.

Details of all necessary arrangements will be left in your hands, including plans for segregation of forces and the withdrawal, if your judgment so dictates, of American elements to Fort Mills. The timing will also be left to you.

America forces will continue to keep our flag flying in the Philippines so long as there remains any possibility of resistance. I have made these decisions in complete understanding of your military estimate that accompanied President Quezon's message to me. The duty and the necessity of resisting Japanese aggression to the last transcends in importance any other obligation facing us in the Philippines.

There has gradually been welded into a common front a globe-encircling opposition to the predatory powers that are seeking the destruction of individual liberty and freedom of Government. We cannot afford to have this line broken in any particular theater. As the most powerful member of this coalition we cannot display weakness in fact or in spirit anywhere.

I therefore give you this most difficult mission in full understanding of the desperate situation to which you may shortly be reduced. The service that you and the American members of your command can render to your country in the titanic struggle now developing is beyond all possibility of appraisement. I particularly request that you proceed rapidly to the organization of your forces and your defenses so as to make your resistance as effective as circumstances will permit and as prolonged as humanly possible.[28]

Roosevelt's messages to both Quezon and MacArthur succeeded in their intent. Quezon, in his book *The Good Fight,* says he was especially moved by Roosevelt's pledge to defend the Philippines with Americans alone if the Filipinos wanted to quit. "When I realized that he [Roosevelt] was big enough to assume and place the burden of the defense of my country upon the sacrifice and heroism of his own people alone, I swore to myself and to the God of my ancestors that as long as I lived I would stand by America regardless of the consequences to my people and to myself."[29] Quezon sent a message to Roosevelt thanking him for his message and agreeing to abide by Roosevelt's decision as to neutralization. An eyewitness, however, recalled that Quezon flew into a violent rage upon reading Roosevelt's message. Quezon felt himself better positioned to judge what was best for the Philippines.

Despite MacArthur's and Quezon's feelings of abandonment, the fact is that by March 1942 four times as many troops had departed the United States for the Pacific as had departed for Europe, a total of 79,000 men. The majority of the available airplanes were also Pacific bound. And despite MacArthur's belief the blockade could be pierced if only the Navy would act, one only need look at the fighting that resulted off Guadalcanal six months later to realize the American Navy was not capable of confronting the Japanese in February. The final message that closed the neutralization and surrender discussions was sent by MacArthur. He was shocked by Roosevelt's answer; Roosevelt's unambiguous handling of possible Filipino surrender called MacArthur's bluff. MacArthur had overstated his case, and now he had to climb down.

I have not the slightest intention in the world of surrendering or capitulating the Filipino elements of my command. Apparently my message gave a false impression or was garbled with reference to Filipinos. My statements regarding collapse applied only to the civilian population including Commonwealth officials the puppet government and the general populace.

There has never been the slightest wavering among the troops. I count upon them equally with the Americans to hold steadfast to the end."[30]

Happily for the men on the front lines, they knew nothing about the messages flowing between Corregidor and Washington, and they had other things to consider anyway. They were offensive-minded and confident. Patrolling, always a dangerous job, became more aggressive, and one patrol from General Bluemel's 31st Division penetrated to the old Abucay Line. Patrols from General Lim's 41st Division followed the Japanese retreat, and they too reached the Abucay positions. Bluemel proposed to General Parker at II Corps that a reconnaisance in force be launched preparatory to a general advance to restore the Abucay Line.[31]

On February 28 USAFFE Headquarters issued a press release that read in part, "The enemy has adopted a defensive attitude. There is definite indication that his heavy losses have shaken him. He begins to show signs of exhaustion. We are probably entering upon a phase of positional warfare of indecisive character."[32] Although the Filamerican army remained in place, local probes by happy Filipinos collected large stocks of rice abandoned by the Japanese. A naval intelligence officer on Corregidor radioed his superiors in Washington that "Army morale on Bataan is higher in the past ten days than at any other time since the beginning of the war. . . . The opinion here is that the Army has improved by many discharges and thousands of desertions, by the realization that it has to fight its own battles with little if any substantial aid. . . . Lastly, fighting qualities have improved by experience."[33] The Filipinos were turning into soldiers.

During this period USAFFE requested a change be made to the nature of the Stateside press releases beamed to the Philippines. The glibly optimistic tone was unwelcome. Morale was good enough that bald propaganda was not needed, and the ultimate retention of Bataan rested on aid from the outside, not press releases. Morale was hurt by long, detailed radio announcements from San Francisco describing appropriations of billions of dollars and the production of war material. Bataan's soldiers had no interest in the production of 120,000 airplanes in 1943, but they were interested in a modest number of planes over Bataan in February 1942. The optimistic talk from the States about arms production hurt Filamerican morale. "Heard President Roosevelt talk on what our production will be in 1943–44," wrote Major Tisdelle in his diary on February 23. "The President means to cheer us up. Actually, his talk tends to weaken morale. We are not interested in what production will be in 1943–44 and 45. All we want are two things, but we need them right now. Unless supplies arrive soon we will be finished by the later part of March."[34]

Although success in stopping the Japanese lifted the spirits of the combat troops, morale in Manila and occupied areas soared even higher. To the Filipinos, it seemed that the Japanese with their planes, tanks, and well-fed and well-equipped men had failed miserably to conquer the tiny province of Bataan, and the Filipinos attributed their army's success to the brilliance of General MacArthur. A story circulated that General Yamashita promised MacArthur safe passage to the United States if he would surrender. "If I could silence the guns of Singapore," the Filipinos quoted Yamashita, who actually was not even in the Philippines, as bragging, "there is no reason why I couldn't do the same thing with the obscure defenses of Bataan and Corregidor." MacArthur reportedly answered, "Singapore fell because I wasn't there."[35] Filipinos made bets on the date MacArthur would return to Manila in a triumphant march. The American air attacks on Nichols and Nielson Fields drew unfeigned enthusiasm from civilians. An American doctor talked with civilians coming into American lines from north of Bataan, and they told him the same story about endless lines of trucks leaving Bataan each night, carrying dead Japanese.

Naughty smiles, winks of the eye, and spreading two fingers to form the "V" sign displayed Manila's optimism. The favorite topic of conversation was the terrible beating MacArthur's army was giving the Japanese. "Before Christmas" was the most common prediction of Japanese defeat. Pronouncements from Corregidor's radio "The Voice of Freedom" about mile-long convoys and reinforcements of planes and ships kept hopes high. There were rumors, eagerly received and repeated, that Japanese soldiers were refusing to go to Bataan. Outrageous stories circulated. Bombs rolled off hills by MacArthur's men killed hundreds of Japanese. Secret electromagnetic forces drew Japanese to their deaths and plucked enemy planes from the sky. Knowledgeable people described the miles of underground tunnels linking the Bataan defenses. Huge areas were charged with electricity until the trees, waters, and the very ground boiled. Filipinos living near Japanese cantonments knew when the enemy received orders to go to Bataan, for the Japanese infantrymen would cry. Other more desperate Japanese would, claimed the civilians, kill their officers, change into civilian clothes, and run away. Some chose firing squads over service on Bataan. These rumors were so pervasive they even reached General Homma's ears. "According to what prisoners have told us," Homma wrote, "the enemy seems to be using electric-wire entanglements, but I wonder how? From where can 2,000 volts be supplied? At any rate this can be easily recognized by its insulators."[36]

The first press dispatches sent to the United States from the Philippines portrayed the Japanese in an undeserved and inaccurate light. Sent by Associated Press correspondent Clark Lee, they were the result of four days of hectic interviews. "The Japanese Army," Lee reported, "is an ill-uniformed, untrained mass of young boys between fifteen and eighteen years old, equipped with small-caliber guns and driven forward by a desperate determination to advance or die."[37] The .25-caliber bullets fired by Japanese rifles and light machine guns did not impress Lee. "Unless they strike a vital spot, these .25-caliber bullets will not kill a man. I have talked to many of the defenders who had been wounded three and four times with these bullets and were still walking about." Because of reports such as these, there were many people, even some on Bataan, who still believed their own propaganda, but their numbers were declining. An especially shocking revelation was the quality of Japanese airplanes and pilots, a matter of considerable levity before the war. Some Americans had a feeling that it was distinctly unfair for the Japanese to have all the materiel they did. "They're no damned good on the ground," an American cavalry colonel told Lee. "We licked the pants off them three times and were beaten only by their tanks and planes. When our tanks and planes go into action we'll chase them back to the sea."

Dispatches similar to those mentioned put the campaign in a rosy light, and the mood of the United States public was one of confidence. Although misleading newscasts might have helped homefront morale, the announcements played havoc on Bataan. Radio broadcasts reaching Bataan were cheerful and utterly without foundation. To be fighting a desperate battle thousands of miles from home, without adequate supplies or hope of relief, was bad enough. But then to hear from radio announcers sitting safely in their chairs that everything was fine and that the Japanese were doomed was too much to swallow. The last thing a P-40 pilot wanted to hear was a civilian in San Francisco boasting about the American aviation industry when his battered P-40 was not fast enough to catch the Japanese twin-engine craft that bombed him daily. Of infamous fame was the San Francisco announcer who dared the Japanese to bomb Corregidor.[38]

The optimism of radio announcers was not matched by the soldiers facing the Japanese. Short of food, living in primitive conditions, and often sick, the soldiers were not too hopeful. "Dugout Doug may be a big shot to the outside world," wrote an American in his diary, "but he is taking a verbal beating here. The Filipinos are getting very discouraged at waiting. The Americans are getting very fed up with poor food and very tough conditions. They are losing faith in their leadership."[39] MacArthur's promise of thousands of troops and hundreds of planes made

him few friends when the promise evaporated. As active as some Manila
civilians were in passing rumors about Japanese failures, there were some
Americans on Bataan who were equally active in spreading tales of
gloom. These men were arch pessimists from the start, and they took
strange delight in spreading rumors about defeats and the awful things
about to happen. They succeeded in creating a gloomy, miserable atmosphere.

Regardless of the Japanese withdrawal and the increase in Filipino
morale, the Bataan army did not try to break out of the peninsula, simply
because the situation had not changed. Although a breakout may have
been physically possible, its purpose would have had to be for escape or
guerrilla operations. The Japanese were better at open warfare than the
Filipinos, and faced with Japanese aerial supremacy, marching columns of
Filipinos would have been very, very vulnerable. Even more important,
it must be remembered that the Philippine Army was operating under
the most rudimentary and haphazard of communications systems. Although it was a twentieth century army, its command and control were
reminiscent of the American Civil War. During the retreat from Lingayen
Gulf, North Luzon Force headquarters used the civil telephone network
as its primary means of communication. Only tank battalion radio nets
worked with any degree of consistency, and even these were few in
number. Messengers and conferences were often the only reliable means
of passing information.

Unlike a Civil War battle, any advance from Bataan would spread
across an area scores of miles in length and width. No single commander
could mount a hill and direct the fight, and staffs at all levels were poorly
trained and understrength. The passage of an order from a corps headquarters to a division, the analysis of that order by the division, and the
subsequent passage of the order to regiments and battalions might easily
take more than a day if the units were advancing or widely separated.
The Americans had little information about the Japanese and their
strength and disposition, and they did not have aerial observation or the
means to pass information up to command levels while it was still useful.
Even the smallest of Japanese elements could stop and disorganize the
unwieldy Philippine Army units. Without the training necessary to reduce a simple roadblock, and without communications to artillery units, a
600-man Filipino infantry battalion would be almost powerless to evict a
determined Japanese platoon. Considering the fanatical determination
shown by the Japanese in defensive positions, there was no reason to
believe they would collapse or run away.

Of course, the Philippine Division's three infantry regiments, the
Scout cavalry regiment, and the two American tank battalions supported

by selected Philippine Army units and mobile artillery would have fielded a formidable force. But small Japanese units could cut roads at will, destroy bridges, and prevent the movement of supplies from Luzon back into Bataan. Although a mobile Filamerican force might have maneuvered freely for a time, all too soon it would have found itself fighting defensively. Local tactical victories did not change the strategic picture, that of a besieged garrison. The Japanese could reinforce their army at will, and that is exactly what they did. And if MacArthur's army did break into central Luzon in search of food, their front line would have become extended and their flanks thinned, making the entire force vulnerable to Japanese reactions. Finally, Bataan's human and materiel resources had to be conserved. An offensive would consume the limited stocks of gasoline, trucks, and ammunition, thereby jeopardizing MacArthur's mission, that of holding the entrance to Manila Bay. Certainly, to have launched an attack and recover lost ground would have given the public a tremendous lift and would have boosted the morale of the army itself. But although an offensive would have been useful tactically and for morale purposes, it would have been counterproductive strategically. Whether or not the army could have again retreated into Bataan after Japanese reinforcements arrived is also open to question.[40]

A lull now descended on Bataan as both Japanese and Filipinos tried to recover from the hard fighting. The defenders had only a small pool of men to replace numerous battle casualties, one source being the Army Air Corps, which entered Bataan with about 7,000 Americans. As planes were destroyed, pilots and ground personnel were reassigned to Air Corps infantry units and to Philippine Army units. These airmen, with few exceptions, were untrained and unfamiliar with infantry weapons and tactics and were of limited value. One Air Corps sergeant was given an hour to decide whether or not to become an officer. A staff officer from Corregidor told Master Sergeant William Montgomery he had been recommended for a commission, and if he accepted he would go to the front to lead Filipino troops. Montgomery realized it would be the hardest decision he would ever make. It meant leaving the work he knew and liked to one filled with dangers he could not anticipate. But he also knew that Singapore had fallen and that their chances of receiving replacement aircraft were remote. He had come into the Army to become a soldier, and he realized that fighting was part of soldiering. Sergeant Montgomery accepted the commission and celebrated his promotion with a little "medicinal alcohol" mixed with raspberry juice. He went to bed a second lieutenant of infantry, without a uniform, rank insignia, or even a piece of paper certifying his promotion. He knew a little about close order drill and had the hazy feeling that infantrymen divided their time between crawling around and charging wildly at the enemy. "I discounted my knowledge of close order drill," he recalled, "and the hills were too steep for much running even without fixed bayonets, so I concluded, with some despair, that I would have to content myself with crawling through the mud and dust."[41]

Montgomery was impressed with the 41st Division's headquarters, the first stop en route to his unit. Lush trees covered a beautiful area cut by two small streams. A neat bamboo bridge spanned one small creek, well-camouflaged bamboo huts blended into the hillside, and sprouting like plants along the stream banks were elements of supply, engineers, and artillery. The area seemed cool and secure. Montgomery marvelled that while the Filipinos might not be winning, they had picked a lovely setting in which to lose. Other airmen who had received commissions with him, a mechanic and a parachute rigger, were as inexperienced as Montgomery, but they soon learned one of their principal functions was simply to be present physically. Montgomery's first night on the outpost line was a nervous one, for the Filipinos with him thought they were surrounded. They wanted to withdraw, but a veteran American officer sharing duty with Montgomery kept them in place. The night passed without incident.[42]

Various support personnel were assigned to the American 31st Infantry to replace casualties but because they were not properly trained, they were often of little use in a fight. Strength in some rifle companies, even after receipt of these men, seldom rose above 60 percent of their authorized level. The 4th Chemical Company was stripped of its men to replace 31st Infantry losses. Although three or four men went to each company, the 31st Infantry's strength barely increased by fifty men. The chemical newcomers had received some training in riflery before joining the Polar Bears, but they were most familiar with pistols and mortars and most often went to the weapons companies. Private Walter Bell, assigned to the Philippines since 1939, was given an hour's worth of target practice with an M-1 rifle and sent to I Company as a qualified rifleman. A total of 375 men went to the 31st Infantry, 200 from military police companies and 175 from the Chemical Warfare Service.[43]

To replace losses in the two Philippine Scout regiments, specially selected Philippine Army soldiers went to each regiment in early March on a probationary basis. The 45th Infantry received 298 men and the 57th Infantry 252 men. Even then there were problems in finding enough M-1 rifles for the new soldiers. These men proved to be the only replacements received by the Scouts during the war. On the whole, they were acceptable and responded well to training but it was difficult to require a starving man to undergo strenuous tactical training. Although helpful to the Scout regiments, the loss of 550 of the best Philippine Army soldiers from their units was just another drain on their already inadequate resources. Attempts were also made to recruit American enlisted men as officers to lead the depleted units of the 45th Infantry. An officer came to the 31st Infantry and offered the sergeants commissions if they would join the 45th Infantry. None of the sergeants accepted, and when the officer reduced the grade requirement to private first class, there were still no takers.[44]

The poverty of supplies on Bataan resulted in much improvisation. The soldiers built command posts, living quarters, and all manner of structures from bamboo and banana leaves. The constant use of bamboo for every type of construction earned the Philippine Army the nickname "the bamboo army." Whenever something was requisitioned, harassed supply clerks responded that nothing was on hand and could not bamboo be used? To help the construction effort, engineers requisitioned an easily portable saw mill and reassembled it at Mariveles. They started a logging operation, and the mill turned out 25,000 board-feet of lumber a day. The paucity in communication equipment and signal supplies was severe. There were only a few small items such as batteries and tape. An issue of these items from to a signal officer was so small that a division's supply could be carried in a man's pocket.[45]

Before the war a shortage of antitank guns resulted in a call to Corregidor where supply officers turned over their entire stock of 75mm subcaliber devices for modification into antitank guns. These devices fit inside the tubes of the big coastal guns and allowed the crews to fire smaller caliber ammunition without the expense and wear of firing the standard shells. At the small arms level, fabric machine gun belts frayed and tore from heavy use. When supplies started to fail, gunners collected and patched together bits and pieces of old belts and launched raids into old positions in hopes of finding complete belts.[46]

Construction of defensive positions proceeded with as much vigor as could be mustered by men on a starvation diet. At company level, American officers struggled with their Filipino charges. The work was repetitious, seeing that weapons were cleaned, latrines dug, cans buried, and fighting positions sand-bagged. Sanitation was always a big problem. A battalion instructor, Major John Martin, was constantly frustrated at enforcing sanitation discipline. His men looked at him in honest confusion whenever he stressed the need to boil drinking water.

"But, sir," the Filipinos answered, "we have lived next to creeks like this all our life."

"Yes," answered Martin in despair, "but you didn't have a cavalry regiment just upstream washing their horses."[47] It seemed to Martin that nothing he said was of any lasting use.

Flies were ever present, and the biggest cause of flies was human waste. Unit latrines had to be properly constructed and then correctly closed to stop flies from breeding. Trench latrines had to be deep and narrow. Crude oil, when available, was sprayed into latrines daily, or a strong disinfectant if oil was not available. Because of the breeding period of flies, a trench latrine could not be used longer than six days. Fly larvae were so strong they could push out of closed latrines unless burlap, soaked with oil, was placed over the waste and covered with dirt. Sanitation problems were not necessarily solved even when units dug proper latrines. "A life long characteristic of many of the barrio Filipinos," recalled Colonel Skerry, "seemed to be to relieve his bowels when and where he chose. To scramble out of a foxhole at night and run for the platoon latrine in the inky jungle darkness with dysentery or diarrhoea dogging at his heels required a lot more training in field discipline than the average Filipino was granted the time to acquire."[48] As a result, the main line of resistance was often located by odor alone. The absence of facilities to clean mess kits posed more problems. Men cleaned their gear locally rather than in messing areas, and this resulted in pieces of food scattered over wide areas. Empty food cans, thrown into the brush rather than buried in a pit, provided perfect breeding sites for flies.

Because the Pilar-Bagac road running across the middle of Bataan now lay in enemy hands or under his guns, a new route paralleling the old one was necessary. Wainwright needed this road to link I with II Corps. The Scout 14th Engineer Battalion collected five bulldozers, a tractor, and two graders, and on February 5 started working on the route. About half the battalion was filled by veteran construction men from the Baguio gold mining area and the men knew what they were doing. Two weeks later the road was finished, one day ahead of schedule. It ran behind the regimental reserve lines and allowed quick lateral movement of reserves. The road cut through the jungled northern slopes of Mariveles Mountain and across river valleys with vertical drops of 2,000 feet. It was truly a remarkable feat of engineering.[49]

After stringing barbed wire and connecting foxholes with trenches, I Corps engineers planted three large minefields along likely enemy avenues of approach. They laid 1,400 improvised box mines, rectangular wooden boxes 9×9×11 inches that would explode under a weight of 500 pounds. They were filled with dynamite at engineer depots just before installation in mine fields. Once in place, flashlight batteries were inserted and the mines were armed. A singular disadvantage with these mines was that warping of the wooden boxes sometimes caused them to explode prematurely, an event especially inconvenient if friendly troops were nearby. Another thirty-five 300-pound submarine depth charges, set to explode on contact or by command, were borrowed from Corregidor and planted. Engineers laid them in the Tiis River area, near Bagac, and forward of the 1st Division near Trail 7. Antitank defenses on the Tiis River were strengthened by modifying Navy 3-inch guns for use in a ground role. Rice paddies were flooded in front of Filipino positions; the Rivers Bagac, Tuol, and Tiis were partially dammed; and the jungle along the west coast was cleared by civilian laborers to open fields of fire. Officers along the coast were "working like [beavers], inspecting new beach defenses, correcting gun positions, pushing the engineer to salvage wire, reorganizing the wire placement and in general doing a bang-up job."[50]

In March, General Brougher made a determined effort to strengthen the main line of his 11th Division. His men had moved into new positions after the retreat from Abucay, had fought at the Tuol Pocket, and then carved defenses from untouched jungle. Working in necessary haste, the first work was done poorly or even entirely wrong, and correction took backbreaking labor by the undernourished men. Appealing to the men's pride, Brougher announced the division's nickname would be "Trailblazers," with a motto of "work and fight." In a general order Brougher told his men, "Everyone works without limit until the Division sector is prepared to maximum strength. When the Japs come, everybody fights with maximum courage and determination. There must be a continuous impassable obstacle across the entire front of the 11th Division on the Main Line of Resistance. . . . All officers and men must be impressed with the fact that this is our last stand. . . . The 11th Division has never been cracked yet. We are going to hold on this line!"[51]

Using salvaged telephone wire from a depot at Guagua, the division signal unit laid thirty miles of wire and even loaned wire to neighboring units which had none. Crews strung wire from division headquarters to all regiments, from regiments to battalions, and from battalions to rifle companies. Regiments and battalions were connected laterally with one another, and enough wire remained to allow the division artillery to lay its own net directly to all front-line units. Crews ran wire lines over different routes to prevent them from being destroyed by one shell. Forward switching controls and check stations for trouble shooting were established and actively employed. The 11th Engineer Battalion developed Trail 7 into a two-lane road with good bridges, feeder trails, and bypasses and turn-outs that allowed passage of two-way traffic. Workers cut branch trails to regimental and battalion command posts as well as to artillery positions. These trails were then turned into motor roads, a most difficult and remarkable undertaking considering the mountainous, jungle-covered terrain. In preparation for the rainy season, engineers reinforced the trail with drainage ditches, culverts, and bridges. During all this work, leaders needed to keep a constant watch to insure the men were getting the small issue of food due them. "Any plan, no matter how perfect, that does not insure the feeding of the men, will fail," recalled General Brougher. "With Filipino troops, just as soon as they miss a meal they will quit work or stop fighting and begin to look for food."[52]

In addition to working on trails, Brougher's engineers dug trenches and tunnels along the main line. Communication trenches linked everyone, and automatic weapons poked from well-protected emplacements. Forward of these positions, Filipinos dug traps and emplaced punji pits, contact mines, and other obstacles common to men short of conventional materiel. Skillful handling of bamboo and giant jungle vines provided a substitute for barbed wire. Headquarters personnel constructed bombproof dugouts at the division command post. Because of these shelters, the headquarters did not suffer a single casualty from enemy bombs or artillery. In anticipation of the rainy season, the men built so many rainproof huts and shelters from salvaged bus-tops that the command post became known as the bus-top bungalow village. Using Filipinos familiar with native bamboo huts, Brougher turned the division's headquarters into a model village with an aid station, a hospital with several buildings, quarters for officers, a conference room, a mess hall, and a guard house for off-duty guards.[53]

I Corps was not alone in construction work. In II Corps, engineers dammed the Pilar River, making a stretch of 500 yards impassable to enemy tanks. They mined roads leading to major crossroads and dynamited or cut extensive bamboo thickets to open fields of fire. Engineers emplaced over 1,500 yards of double-apron barbed wire and burned houses near Limay along the Manila Bay coast to clear fields of fire. The 21st Division used the February lull to settle into their positions. They set their command post near the junction of Trails 4 and 429 in an area providing defilade from enemy artillery and offering good concealment from aerial observation. Monkeys, birds with unusual chirps, screeches, and calls, the buzzing of locusts, beautifully colored butterflies, and numerous flowers painted the scene. The men placed their cots close to the buttresses of the huge belote trees averaging 125 feet tall, trees so luxuriant that sunlight seldom penetrated to the ground. Engineers developed Trail 429 into a motor road, a road safe from prying eyes because of the thick overhanging tree limbs. Although there had been no rain of note up to March, work details covered trails with rock and gravel to provide all-weather use, and the men built little huts as protection against the expected rains.[54]

The 21st Medical Battalion surveyed, planned, and constructed a 400-bed hospital. The battalion established a collecting station 1,500 yards south of the main line and a clearing station on Trail 429 near the division command post using only hand tools and construction materiel portable over steep, narrow trails. Colonel Wibb E. Cooper, surgeon for USAFFE's successor, United States Forces in the Philippines (USFIP), recalled that "the Filipino soldier displayed unbelievable ingenuity and skill in the construction of these clearing stations. After the dense jungle undergrowth had been cleared away, bamboo frames were erected, on which patients were placed. These were covered in order to give protection from the weather. No tentage was available."[55] An overriding consideration in the planning and construction of these hospitals and clearing stations was concealment from enemy air. Concealment became so good that low-flying planes could not detect these field hospitals, and a man on foot could pass within a few yards without seeing them.

Besides constructing the division field hospital, the 21st Medical Battalion cared for division casualties for three weeks until a trail could be cut to allow their evacuation. The 21st Division's one clearing station filled to overflowing and forced the three medical collecting companies to establish 150-bed installations close to the front lines. Even these forward aid stations were soon swamped with sick. Besides being overcrowded, aid stations and even the base hospitals were short of recuperative-type foods. "It was quite a site [sic]," recalled a doctor at Hospital Number 2, "to see post-operative cases and those who should receive adequate soft and liquid diet trying to eat a gob of sticky, gummy half-cooked rice. It was ordinarily a fight between individual and flies as to who got the rice."[56] In the 41st Division medics tried using carabao and native ponies to move the sick and wounded, but when both animals proved unsuitable, the burden of evacuation returned to human stretcher-bearers. Litter routes were long and tedious, wound up and down hills and along trails obstructed by big stones and thick vines. The physical effort in carrying a litter and patient was enormous, and as the soldiers received less and less food, their ability to carry the heavy loads declined.

In early March the sick rate increased, due in part to the starvation diet. The nature of the Bataan terrain and the conditions under which the defenders lived required an energy output of 3,500 to 4,000 calories per man per day. In January the average ration was 2,000 calories; in February 1,500; and by March 1, with caloric intake at 1,000, serious muscle-wasting was evident. As the official ration dropped, foraging increased.

The men occasionally confiscated a carabao from a Filipino—perhaps his only farm power and transportation. The increasing number of sick filled division hospitals, but even then they could not be evacuated to the two general hospitals. The evacuation policy was strictly limited to several narrow categories: the first were patients requiring medical or surgical procedures not available at the divisions; second, those cases where the expected length of disability would exceed twenty-one days; and third, all cases of psychosis and men requiring mental observation. Medical personnel realized that these policies were contrary to standard medical tactics and could be justified only by the tactical situation and by the limited evacuation facilities. Everyone hoped that ample warning and enough transport could be provided so that medical stations could be quickly emptied when the tactical situation dictated.[57]

Those patients evacuated to General Hospitals Number 1 and 2 in southern Bataan found rude facilities. When Doctor Walter H. Waterous had first arrived at Cabcaben where Hospital Number 2 was to be built, he found nothing but uncut jungle along the banks of the Real River, one and a half kilometers above Cabcaben. There were no buildings, no installations, and only a few dusty trails winding through the woods. Filipino civilians cleared brush, leveled ground, and erected medium hospital tents over plank floors. Eighteen wards, each holding up to 200 men, were finally built. A water purification system and an automatic chlorinating plant prepared water, incinerators burned refuse, and GI garbage cans over fires heated water to sterilize mess kits. But some efforts at sanitation were futile. Straddle trenches seethed with maggots and the entire hospital swarmed with flies. Efforts to build straddle trenches with toilet seats, periodic burning of the pits, and all attempts to screen the latrines failed to reduce the plague of flies. Dysentery ran rampant along all ranks, and the hospital's lab equipment was not adequate to determine the type of germs responsible. The doctors tried to segregate surgical patients from diseased patients, but overcrowding outpaced good intentions. Ninety-five percent of admissions developed malaria by cross infection before they left the wards. Other segregation efforts were even less effective. A half hour was set aside each day for female nurses to bathe in a nearby stream. Guards were posted to provide privacy and burlap was strung around a pool, but these precautions were not always adequate.[58]

Work at Hospital Number 2 was accomplished under primitive conditions. Surgical Technician Alvin L. Fry recalled that they had neither buildings nor tents. There were mainly just hundreds of beds out under trees in the jungle. The operating room was a frame building with sackcloth walls and a corrugated metal roof covered with tar paper. "We had no schedule of hours to work, we just kept going till there were no more patients to care for. Some times it seemed that we could go no longer, then more patients would come in and we just had to keep going."[59] Ward space expanded under the influx, and it took an hour just to walk from the first to the last. Men died unattended at night and were found and tagged for removal the next morning. Some patients were killed from antiaircraft shell residue falling from the guns defending Cabcaben airfield.

There were two general hospitals on Bataan, and the second, named Hospital Number 1, was located at Little Baguio. The climate here was similar to Luzon's mountain town of Baguio where people flocked during Manila's fetid summers. The high, dry ground here, unlike the river ground near Hospital Number 2, reduced mosquito breeding and kept malaria low. Cool winds swept through huge hardwood groves shading the two-acre site. As quickly as workmen erected wards, casualties filled them. Most patients arrived at night because Japanese planes made special efforts to disrupt daylight motor traffic. Heavy fighting at the Points, Pockets, and Trail 2 added new wards to the original 500 beds. Workmen built bamboo beds, or medics stacked the regulation white iron beds two and three deep, set mattresses on the bare ground, and laid blankets over bare bed springs. When beds and mattresses became scarce, the hospitals asked Corregidor for help. Salvage sections combed through Corregidor's bombed barracks and other buildings and shipped 2,000 beds and mattresses to Bataan. Linen was scarce and hardly would recently washed sheets be dry before they were used again. All too soon the hospital held 1,600 patients. Medical service was greatly handicapped by reliance on old, revamped 1917-type medical chests. For some reason, case after case of Kotex showed up in hospital stocks, which initially seemed ridiculous but which made excellent abdominal packs for stomach wounds. Yet despite these shortcomings, Hospital Number 1 was a smooth-running operation with a General Medical Ward, Orthopedic Ward, Surgery Ward, Head-Eyes-Ears-Nose-Throat Ward, and Abdominal Ward. As the fighting progressed, a ward was set aside for thirty-three wounded Japanese.[60]

The March lull did not see an end to fighting. Filipino attempts to push the outpost line north beyond the Abo Abo River met with varied success. The 23rd Infantry advanced but had trouble tying in with the unit to its left, and sharp actions erupted as the Filipinos tried to claim their new territory. When a patrol from E Company, 23rd Infantry, ran into enemy infantry supported by machine guns and mortars, Private First Class Emilio Somera ran to the front of his patrol to lay down a base of fire with his BAR. His example, and the large volume of fire, allowed the patrol to accomplish its mission, but Private Somera was killed. The 22nd Infantry was not as successful as the 23rd, for it could not get beyond the Talisay River. Yet just to the west the Filipinos could move into rice fields and gather pilay in full view of the Japanese. However, any attack against these same Japanese was met with determined resistance.[61]

Two entries in Lieutenant Montgomery's diary describe the routine on the 41st Infantry's outpost line: "We toured the OPLR this A.M. My company is in not such good shape. They need constant supervision. I go out every day for several hours. The Philippine officers are very lax in instructions and the NCO is very poor in carrying out orders. They all are fine at pounding rice."[62] And the next day: "A trip to the OPLR and dodged a Jap strafer for an hour or more. He was cruising at 1,000 feet or so circling over our position. I crouched by a banana tree and did my best to look like a banana." Constant exposure to danger developed a certain calm in the men. "If you have 15 minutes free, you lie down, close your eyes, and are asleep. It does not matter whether someone is shelling you or some other outfit is having a scrap with a Japanese patrol off to your left. That is their business. If you get the chance to sleep, you sleep. [Once] the 22nd Infantry was fending off an attack by a well-muscled Japanese patrol some 100 yards to our left. They were going at the business hammer and tongs. From time to time, we could see men running, firing and maneuvering for a better position. All this time, our boys, some chewing sugar cane, were stolidly pounding rice for their evening meal. They had no more interest in a fight outside their sector than the 22nd would have had for a fight that did not threaten them. Our only concern was that the 22nd Infantry would muster enough strength to push the Japs into our sector. Toward that eventuality we set up a perimeter guard. Our code of ethics called for pushing the Japs back toward their own lines, not to the flank into another outfit's sector. This rule, while not always honored, did work pretty well."

During the lull, artillerymen made efforts to improve the fires of their guns. Forward observers built observation posts, and communications personnel laid wire lines to the guns of adjacent units. Artillery from the 31st, 41st, and 51st artillery were coordinated to support most of II Corps's line. There was one problem the artillerymen never solved, the demoralizing frequency of short rounds. Front-line units often reported rounds falling short and hitting friendly troops. Single guns were carefully laid and fired in an effort to spot the errant piece, but the short gun was never found. It is possible the Japanese were firing in concert with the defending artillery, but pieces of American shells, not Japanese, were found when the rounds fell short. It is also possible the Japanese were firing captured American cannon. Despite such difficulties, Filipino artillery was effective, especially in the woods surrounding the Talisay River. "When we called for fire," remembered Lieutenant Montgomery, "either by runner bearing a map with the coordinates or by telephone, we could hear the heavy 90-pound slugs whistle overhead. If the target was really inviting, we would call for four shots to the right, four to the left, four long and four short. Then with the surrounding bamboo and brush cut down, the gun would be directed to lay four right on dead center. With each shell having a bursting radius of some 30 yards, the whole area would be cleared of brush and enemy."[63]

In late February a 21st Division patrol discovered a dump of 75mm shells stashed forward of their lines, ammunition abandoned during the withdrawal from Abucay. Work details collected 1,064 rounds and carried them to friendly artillerymen. It was a day's worth of fire, and it was not long before it was returned to the enemy. The Filamerican army's use of artillery was so effective that commanders everywhere wanted their services, but not their presence because they attracted bombers and shellfire. The big 155mm's were active but results were sometimes suspect. Observers often reported hits on enemy targets, but the enemy would have run out of artillery if every report had been true.[64]

To gather information on the Japanese, there was no one better than the tiny black aborigines, the original Bata, little men, driven into the hills by the Japanese. They were specially effective in capturing stray Japanese. The Bata toted the Japanese into Filipino lines trussed up in bamboo cages like chickens. Sometimes the only means of reconnaissance were the northern Igorotes who somehow knew their way around Bataan's rough terrain even though they hailed from the mountain provinces of northern Luzon. General Sutherland was concerned that any long inactivity and absence from the front would make the American 31st Infantrymen reluctant to fight, so he used patrols to keep the regiment active and offensive minded. On several occasions 31st Infantry patrols went out to grab prisoners, a mission not considered especially difficult or dangerous. The patrol would scout around until it found a two- or three-man Japanese outpost, crawl as close as possible, and then rush the Japanese. After killing one or two, the Americans captured the last man and calmly carried him home. It was considered all in a day's work. Not all attempts to secure prisoners ended in success, however. A fifty-man patrol from a Philippine Army division captured a group of sleeping Japanese, but a Japanese patrol pursued them and forced them away from friendly lines into the hills. The Filipino patrol was running low on food and water and was slowed by the blindfolded and gagged Japanese. On the second night of the chase the American officers realized they were not going to survive if they were slowed any more by their captives. So that night the prisoners were disposed of with knives.[65]

The 41st Division organized a special, heavily-armed, deep-penetration patrol and supplied it with M-1 rifles, helmets, and everything necessary to outfight the enemy. On their first mission they were ambushed within 200 yards of friendly lines and had several men killed. After that poor showing the division returned to their bare-footed, torn-trouser, unorthodox Filipinos. Although the information they brought back was not always trustworthy, the men and information did come back. Some Filipinos went north in civilian clothes. Unarmed, they could circulate freely but they could not fight if cornered. The American command placed great reliance on civilians who shuttled between Japanese-held areas and Bataan. Much of their information was confused and exaggerated, but with prudent analysis intelligence personnel collected a great deal of useful data.[66]

Japanese teams, in turn, infiltrated Filipino lines and tied themselves to trees. Snipers wore hoods of green cloth and mosquito netting to cover their helmets and used rope to climb trees, tie themselves in, and form boxes 200 yards on each side. They carried rations for five days, water, quinine, a first-aid kit, gas mask, a can of chlorine or similar substances to purify water, extra socks, a toothbrush, and gloves. Rations consisted of a five-inch sack of rice, a small bag of hardtack, a half pound of rock candy, food concentrates, and vitamin pills. The first indication of a sniper's presence was often a single shot that would fatally drop an officer or sergeant. It was not long before American officers removed their rank insignia and, when on patrol, darkened their faces mahogany color. But after deducing the repetitious placement of Japanese snipers, sniper-hunting parties became quite successful. Hunting the Japanese, when approached with the proper degree of caution, became a favorite off-duty sport for the bold. To aid in sniper-hunting, men with bows and arrows shot sticks of dynamite into trees suspected of containing Japanese. To counter infiltration, American and Filipino patrols constantly swept rear areas. In the Philippine Army inexperienced sentries began to learn their jobs. Now they remained concealed when challenging a suspected enemy and then moved so as to avoid shots aimed at their voices.[67]

Enemy probes helped develop a degree of combat effectiveness in the Filipinos. On the 41st Infantry's outpost line Lieutenant Montgomery watched a Japanese patrol rush his line. "They were close before we could spot them. Our machine guns and rifles opened up. There must have been 30 well-trained Nips in that patrol and they were determined to silence that machine gun. In a sort of skirmish line they charged the gun, walking doggedly into its lethal fire. As one after another of them was dropped, another took his place. Before they withdrew, they had lost some twelve killed and several others wounded. They got their wounded away with them. In another ten minutes the machine gun would have blown up from the heat of firing. The Filipinos could never quite appreciate the limits of a piece of machinery. Instead of firing in short bursts and allowing the gun to cool in between, they would depress the trigger and hold until they had run through a belt or got a jam. This quirk the Japanese knew quite well and that is why they kept coming. We had more than one gun captured that way. Those Japanese were brave and even foolhardy men. Their discipline was iron clad and their physical condition was good. We buried many Japs on that outpost line and took many trophies."[68]

In short, the Philippine Army was standing up under the strain of combat. On February 22 MacArthur, considering the similar conditions under which Filipinos and Americans were serving, recommended paying Philippine Army personnel the same as Americans. MacArthur believed that both nationalities should receive the same pay. "The equalization of battle on soldiery," he announced in a general order, "needs no further elaboration of argument to support such action."[69] MacArthur's second recommendation on March 9 received General Marshall's concurrence. The US House of Representatives introduced implementing legislation at the end of March, but with Corregidor's surrender in May the bill died. Before their hasty withdrawal into Bataan, Philippine Army personnel had not received any advance pay. During their three months on Bataan their families suffered from the absence of the breadwinner, and even when President Quezon advanced his soldiers three months' pay in February, the men were unable to get the money to their families.

Despite pay problems, and even though quartermasters doled out supplies in smaller and smaller quantities, morale remained high for some time. Most Americans and Filipinos could not believe Washington would abandon them. "MacArthur had sent out a message," recalled airman George Koury, "and he said we had more troops than the enemy, and we had this, that, and the other, and all this kind of stuff, and what we could do, and that we had to hold. We believed that. We really did up until they said surrender. We believed it!"[70] Even when the bad news overwhelmed the most optimistic, morale did not drop immediately. Full understanding of the situation seemed to help morale. The men became more determined. The defenders knew they had given the Japanese a terrific licking, man to man, with all the advantages on the enemy's side.

Some men reacted with rough humor to rumors of relief. After hopes were repeatedly raised and dashed, a cynical attitude appeared. Someone tacked a picture to a tree showing a sailing ship loafing along before a

gentle breeze and wrote on it, "We told you so. Help IS on the way."[71]
The Japanese did their best to lower morale by dropping large quantities
of propaganda leaflets, none of which were very effective. "I must have
collected 100 different ones," recalled Colonel Fortier, "varying in ten-
ure from home, wives, sweethearts to sex and every imaginable form of
lie, pictures of Nips and Filipinos fraternizing—one of these was tennis
matches in Manila several years before the war."[72]

Despite the bleak outlook, USAFFE did not passively accept the terrible supply situation. Although many MacArthurphiles and enemies of
Roosevelt claim the Philippines were deliberately abandoned to spite
MacArthur, the bulk of American troops and supplies that left the United
States went to the Pacific in early 1942. Although once the supplies
sailed they faced a Japanese blockade, not everyone was willing to accept
the enemy's blockade effort. MacArthur was certain that the enemy's
blockade could easily be pierced. He felt that only by passively accepting
it could it be effective. But it took some time before any effort worthy of
the name was mounted. The American military presence in Australia was
still embryonic and lacked the organization to gather the resources,
which did not exist anyway, necessary to penetrate the blockade.[73]

Marshall pressured and flooded officers in Australia with guidance.

> Use your funds without stint. Call for more if required. [There is] a
> credit of ten million dollars of Chief of Staff fund which can be spent in
> whatever manner [deemed] advisable. I direct its use for this purpose.
> Arrange for advance payment, partial payments for unsuccessful efforts,
> and large bonus for actual delivery. Your judgment must get results. Orga-
> nize groups of bold and resourceful men, dispatch them with funds by
> planes to islands in possession of our associates, there to buy food and
> charter vessels for service. Rewards for actual delivery Bataan or Corregi-
> dor must be fixed at level to insure utmost energy and daring on part of
> masters.[74]

Concluding his message, Marshall stressed that "only indomitable determination and pertinacity will succeed and success must be ours. Risks
will be great. Rewards must be proportional." Similar orders were
radioed to Australian-British-Dutch-American commanders, but despite
the orders and money, insurmountable difficulties remained.

Blockade runners had to be big enough to carry a worthwhile cargo,
fast enough to survive, and with the necessary fuel capacity and range.
Once supplies reached the southern islands, they had to be offloaded
onto smaller trans-island steamers capable of unloading at Corregidor in
one night. Sufficient barges to form floating docks for two large ships
were hidden in Bataan's Sisiman Bay to take any ships Corregidor could

not handle. Despite vigorous efforts, it was exceedingly difficult to char-
ter or assign a ship for the Philippine run. Such an assignment was considered the ship's death warrant. The Dutch and British refused to release their ships for the dangerous run. When ships did become available,
crews were extremely reluctant to sign on even when offered large bo-
nuses, and a few crews actually mutinied or sabotaged their vessels.[75]

The S.S. *Florence D* and the *Don Isidro* were among the first to attempt
the run. The crew of the *Florence D,* after being strafed, voted to abandon
the run and head for Darwin. The ship was sailing south on February 19
when they spotted a US Navy PBY on patrol out of Darwin. As the men
watched, Japanese fighters attacked the flying boat and sent it crashing
into the sea. The ship altered course, picked up the Navy crew, and
continued south. But then twenty-seven enemy planes from an aircraft
carrier struck the *Florence D,* sending bombs through hatches 1 and 2,
into the bridge, and into the engine room. The ship settled onto the
shallow sea bottom with decks awash. Lost were a quarter of a million
rations, a million and a half .30-caliber rounds, over 5,000 3-inch antiaircraft shells, and 125,000 .50-caliber rounds. The *Don Isidro,* also fleeing
Japanese pursuit, was beached and lost the next day with 550 tons of
food, 853,000 rounds of .30-caliber, and 75,000 rounds of .50-caliber.
The *Cia de Filipinas,* carrying 300 tons of corn and rice, was bombed and
sunk off Mindoro on February 21. The Texas Oil tanker *Estrella,* loaded
with 500 tons of gasoline and oil for Mariveles, was caught off Lubang
Island the next day and sunk. Two Chinese ships under British contract,
the *Hanyang* and the *Yuchow,* carrying 2,400 and 2,900 tons of rations,
were at sea on February 19 when the crews learned of a heavy Japanese
air attack on Darwin. The crews refused to proceed, and both ships
returned to Darwin where they unloaded.[76]

A Dutch freighter attempted the run in late February with 720,000
rations and was never heard from again. A Chinese ship chartered by the
British, the *Taiyan,* sailed for Cebu on February 26 with 1,250 tons of
food and 10,000 3-inch antiaircraft rounds and disappeared without a
trace. The 10-knot *Coast Farmer,* a luckier ship, departed Brisbane on
February 10 and successfully unloaded on the nineteenth at Mindanao.
The ship's Merchant Marine crew attributed their luck to the Chief Engineer's Angora rabbit. MacArthur jumped on the ship's safe arrival and
fired off a message to Washington.

The Coast Farmer, first surface vessel dispatched to run blockade from
Australia, arrived safely in Mindanao February 19. Cargo twenty-five hundred tons balanced rations, two thousand rounds eight-one mm mortar
ammunition, eight hundred thousand caliber thirty and thirty thousand

rounds caliber fifty. She had no difficulty in getting through. The thinness of the enemy's coverage is such that it can readily be pierced along many routes including direct westward passage from Honolulu. I have secure bases for reception in Mindanao and the Visayas. I suggest that the problem of supplying me should be revised in the above circumstances.[77]

But the *Coast Farmer*'s supplies were still a long way from Bataan. Four smaller vessels were sent from Cebu to take on the *Coast Farmer*'s cargo. There was no trouble loading the supplies, but the Japanese heard about the operation. Japanese warships caught and sank three of the four vessels. The fourth ship, the *Elcano,* reached Corregidor on February 26 with 1,100 tons of balanced rations. Two ships trailed the *Coast Farmer* out of Australia. On March 10 the *Dona Nati,* a large passenger and commercial freighter, arrived at Cebu City and unloaded 5,000 tons of food, one and a half million rounds of .30-caliber, 4,000 81mm mortar rounds, 5,000 rifle grenades, and assorted medical, engineer, and signal supplies. This materiel was to have been loaded into three smaller vessels for the run to Corregidor, but misfortune dogged the smaller ships. The *Venus* and the *Kanloan II* were both sunk the same day the *Dona Nati* had docked at Cebu. The *Bolinao,* the third of the three vessels, was lost five days later.[78]

The next ship to reach Cebu was the Chinese *Anhui,* carrying 2,500 tons of food, 2,008 81mm mortar rounds, one million rounds of .30-caliber, three crated P-40's, and limited medical, engineer, and signal supplies. At Cebu her supplies, including 400 pounds of propaganda leaflets MacArthur wanted, were unloaded and packed aboard smaller craft for the dash to Corregidor. But it was all in vain. The *Regulus,* with 500 tons of food, was captured off Mindoro on March 7, and the *Govenor Smith* was bombed off Coron Island and sunk the same day. Some ships sailed as close as one night's dash from Corregidor, and one was as close at fifteen miles from its goal, before being sunk. In early March the American command in Australia decided the sea lanes to the Philippines were too dangerous to risk ships and cargoes, especially when it seemed Australia was Japan's next target. Shipments by surface craft ceased.[79]

When it became apparent there would be a food shortage on Bataan, the Americans tried interisland supply runs. The island of Panay lay one fast night's run south of Corregidor. Panay raised some of the finest rice in the Philippines and there was an abundance waiting there, along with dried meats, fish, beans, and vegetables, fruits, coffee, sugar and salt, enough to supply the entire army's needs. Three days' sail away was the Cebu Quartermaster Depot, also with everything Bataan needed. The trouble was the distance involved and the requirement for fast boats. But if secrecy could be maintained, and if loyal captains and fearless crews could be found, it might be possible to slip past the Japanese on a nightly basis. General Drake knew that running in supplies through a blockade to a beleaguered garrison was not impossible. History has shown that it has been done before, and Drake knew that it could be done again, provided certain precautions were taken.[80]

Planners first considered a well-armed Coast Guard cutter, but she burned coal and could be spotted too easily from smoke and sparks. They next considered the steamer *Legaspi,* belonging to the Inter-Island Steamship Company of Manila. The *Legaspi* mounted diesel engines, the crew was available, and the ship was lying off Corregidor in the North Channel. President Quezon asked the crew if they would undertake the hazardous trip. "Mr. President," replied Captain Lino Conejero, the ship's skipper, "all you have to do is give the order and I will leave as soon as I can."[81] His crew volunteered to a man, and MacArthur thanked them in a "most complimentary talk."

President Quezon ordered the governors of Iloilo and Capiz to assemble as much rice and other food as time allowed for delivery to the *Legaspi.* In great secrecy Corregidor worked out details with Brigadier General Bradford G. Chynoweth at Panay and with the governor of the province. On Panay, workers arranged food in 500-ton lots. All communications between Corregidor and Panay were kept to a minimum. Radio messages would contain only the ship's name and the time of sailing, both in code. Even then the messages would be sent sometime after the vessel sailed to avoid alerting the Japanese an important event was beginning. All cruising was planned for times of absolute dark, and isolated coves and bays were selected for hideouts. The run would take a full night each way.[82]

The *Legaspi* sailed on her first voyage on January 20 and after making two successful round trips, there were hopes for more. On February 20 a newcomer, the *Princesa de Cebu,* arrived at Corregidor with 700 tons of food. But after returning to her starting point at Cebu, she was sunk to prevent capture in mid-March. So Bataan was back to the *Legaspi.* Everyone looked forward to the next docking of the veteran, but here was a problem. Seemingly everyone knew about the vessel and her trips. Whether this leaked to the Japanese is not known, but on March 1, after the *Legaspi* departed from the town of Capiz, Panay, on her third trip, a Japanese gunboat overhauled her off the north coast of Mindoro and forced her to scuttle. The crew beached the ship, the captain set her afire, and all hands took to the hills.[83]

With the longer trips now too dangerous, supply officers prepared smaller vessels for quick sorties to the provinces immediately south of

Corregidor, provinces under Japanese control. Filipino agents went ashore and arranged for purchase and assembly of rice, bananas, coconuts, and livestock. The fifteen-mile run to Looc Cove meant that blockade runners had to leave Corregidor after dark, sail through the mine fields, and move out to sea. Once at Looc Cove, the sailors had to load the small cargoes, then sail to Corregidor and reenter the minefield before daylight. Corregidor chartered two small motor vessels of 500-ton capacity, the *Bohol II* and the *Kolambugan.* They each made two successful trips and many more unsuccessful ones where the presence of Japanese prevented loading. Despite all these efforts, despite ships from Australia, from Panay, and from Cebu, all that reached the Bataan army was a four-day supply of food. Trouble did not end once the food was offloaded at Corregidor, for much of the food had broken from containers, leaving piles of mixed, unidentified canned goods. Flour and sugar sacks often broke and mixed with the cans. Most distressing, onions and potatoes that were piled high as deck cargo rotted under the fierce tropical sun and had to be destroyed.[84]

Most of the food went to the bottom of the ocean. On one disastrous day, February 28, no fewer than six ships totalling 3,450 tons of cargo were sunk, captured, or scuttled while forcing the blockade. *Lepus,* 1,100 tons of food, was bombed and captured off Palawan; *Estrella,* 500 tons; *Mayon,* 800 tons; *Don Esteban,* a new ship carrying 500 tons; *Augustina,* 300 tons; and *Emelia,* 250 tons, were all lost that day. All told, nearly two months' rations for Bataan's garrison were lost at sea during the two months of effort.[85]

Because it was deemed possible to slip blockade runners into the Philippines from the wide reaches of the Pacific east of the Islands, plans were begun in early January to ship supplies directly to the Philippines from the United States. Seven converted World War I destroyers used by the United Fruit Company as banana carriers were to be loaded with food, medicine, ammunition, and signal supplies and sent from New Orleans, through the Panama Canal, to Hawaii. Then they would speed west to the Philippines. By February 5 the *Masaya, Matagalpa,* and *Teapa,* with speeds of 14-1/2 knots, cargo capacities of 1,500 tons, and cruising radius of 10,000 miles, were delivered to the War Department.[86]

The first destroyer-transport, the *Masaya,* was scheduled to sail from New Orleans on February 28, but she did not leave until March 2. The *Matagalpa* and *Teapa* sailed on March 11 and 18, and as they departed, three more ships were undergoing conversion. Each ship took aboard a 4-inch or 37mm gun in the bow, a 3-inch .50-caliber in the stern, and four Army .50-caliber machine guns. With these modifications, cargo capacity dropped to 1,000 tons. The Navy could not provide gun crews, so Army personnel came aboard. Delays haunted the entire program. The first three ships passed through the Panama Canal but put in at Los Angeles for repairs and reloading. Three other ships finally left San Francisco, the *Margaret Schafer* on March 16, the *Mount Baker* on March 28, and the *Texada* on April 11. By the time they reached Hawaii, the situation on Corregidor was so desperate it was obvious they would arrive too late. With MacArthur's concurrence, the *Masaya* and *Matagalpa* were diverted to Melbourne and Sydney respectively. The *Matagalpa* burned and sank in the harbor four days after arrival. The *Teapa* returned to San Francisco. The *Margaret Schafer, Mount Baker,* and *Texada* went to Seattle where they entered Alaskan service.[87]

The last effort to pierce the blockade directly from the east came when the Hawaiian Department procured the Navy-chartered freighter *Thomas Jefferson,* a big, slow ship. She sailed for the Philippines in early April, was diverted in mid-ocean to New Caledonia, and finally turned around and steamed back to Honolulu. MacArthur agreed with Marshall that it was now, on April 11, virtually impossible for surface ships to reach Corregidor, so all ships then enroute were diverted.[88]

Although surface vessels were suffering prohibitively high losses, another means of supply did exist. Submarines. Despite the need for submarines to operate against Japanese shipping, the benefits to be gained by containing enemy troops in the Philippines by prolonged resistance, tying enemy shipping to the islands, and in terms of morale, all argued for cargo trips by submarines. Four boats succeeded in unloading at least part of their cargoes totalling twenty-seven tons of food and some antiaircraft and small arms ammunition. The first mission involved the U.S.S. *Seawolf* sailing from Darwin. The crew removed sixteen of *Seawolf's* torpedoes, rounded up all the ammunition they could find in Darwin, and loaded it into the boat. The *Seawolf* left Darwin on January 16 for the ten-day, 1,800 mile trip, carrying a pitiful total of seventy-five 3-inch antiaircraft shells and 675 boxes of .50-caliber machine gun ammunition. "The way they were expending ammo up there," recalled the *Seawolf's* skipper Fred Warder, "it amounted to about one day's supply."[89] The Army welcomed the .50-caliber but was disappointed with the 3-inch; sufficient quantities were on hand, and one shell in three was a dud anyway. The crew took aboard sixteen torpedoes for the trip home. When she left Corregidor, the *Seawolf* also carried submarine spare parts and twenty-five personnel: a British intelligence officer, twelve Army pilots, eleven Navy pilots, and one Navy yeoman.

The second cargo submarine surfaced at Corregidor the night of February 3 with 3,517 rounds of 3-inch. In return, the U.S.S. *Trout* took on ten torpedoes and 27,000 gallons of fuel oil. But the *Trout* needed additional ballast, and the captain asked for twenty-five tons of filled sandbags. Instead, the *Trout* was selected to carry twenty tons of gold and silver removed from Manila's banks. One by one, 583 gold bars were passed aboard, then eighteen tons of silver coins were carried into the boat. The bullion safely reached Pearl Harbor.[90]

Another submarine, the U.S.S. *Seadragon,* sank the fully loaded 6,441-ton troop transport *Tamagawa Maru* on February 2 outside Lingayen Gulf. She was then ordered to Corregidor to take off the codebreaking personnel stationed there. Two nights later seventeen American codebreakers from the Cast Unit (Cast originally meant Cavite and then meant Corregidor) were embarked along with 1-1/2 tons of gear, their RED (Japanese naval attache traffic) and PURPLE (Japanese diplomatic traffic) radios, and codebooks. Work parties were bothered by Japanese artillery fire, but they succeeded in stuffing the *Seadragon* with two tons of submarine spare parts and twenty-three torpedoes. Eleven days later, another thirty-six dangerously knowledgeable codebreakers were evacuated by the U.S.S. *Permit.* On February 14 the U.S.S. *Sargo* delivered a million rounds of .30-caliber to western Mindanao.[91]

Attempts to fly supplies into the Philippines were limited to small, light items. Medicine such as morphine and quinine were priority items, and one B-24 actually made it to Mindanao. But the supplies came only as far forward as Mindanao. They remained there because of the difficulty in flying them to Corregidor. Airmen on Bataan raised a Navy Amphibian, a "Duck," from the waters off Mariveles and repaired it. It then flew in supplies, medicine, official mail, and candy, earning it the name of the candy clipper. "The candy was manna," remembered Captain Dyess. "Our food situation was growing rapidly worse. We were eating lizards, monkeys, and anything else that came under our guns. We set off dynamite in the water in the hope of getting fish, but the blasts usually burst the fishes' floats and they sank. The life expectancy of anything that walked, crawled, or flew on lower Bataan was practically nil."[92] Pioneering trips were soon made by men flying a Beechcraft, Bellanca, and other rattletraps to Cebu, Del Monte, or Mindanao. The planes were packed with quinine, blood plasma, gas gangrene serum, and as much food as could be shoved into odd corners. The bamboo airfleet carried in twenty tons of medicines, foodstuffs, cigarettes, and candy while evacuating 100 men to the southern Philippines.

Without supplies from outside Bataan, the men on the fighting line were in difficult straits. But the rice crop along Manila Bay was ripe. It was harvest season and the grain lay stacked and unthreshed. In mid-January, the Quartermaster Corps built two mills that operated continuously until they exhausted the rice supply in mid-February. The mills produced 30,000 pounds of rice each day for a month, but because consumption at half ration was 50,000 pounds a day, this was only a temporary aid. Had modern farm equipment been available, the Quartermaster might have recovered ten times the amount actually reclaimed by their necessarily primitive methods. Much of the unthreshed rice lay close to or behind Japanese lines in northeast Bataan. Some foraging parties penetrated Japanese lines at night to collect the valuable food. Local Filipinos were asked to turn in their stores of rice for which they were paid a fair price. The Quartermaster Corps established a fishery at Lamao and sent local fishermen out on nightly expeditions; these men were soon netting 12,000 pounds of fish each night. But the Japanese learned about the fishing and started killing any fishermen they found on the water. When shelling from both enemy and from nervous friendly guns fell among the small boats on their nightly errands, and when friendly troops pillaged the catches once they were landed, the fishermen called it quits and refused to fish. Unfortunately for the defenders, this very valuable supplement to the half ration ended at a time when the need for extra rations was increasing.[93]

Cooks erected six antiquated bake ovens to handle the available flour, but this operation was so noisy the officer in charge plastered mud and straw over the ovens and turned them into Dutch ovens. With other ovens, this equipment produced 25,000 pounds of bread a day until the supply of flour ran out at the end of February. To supply salt for the diet, seawater was boiled in large cauldrons. Four hundred pounds of salt were produced each day, covering a fourth of the daily requirement. There was not enough salt to issue to the soldiers, but there was enough to give to the bakery operation and to a few of the messes for cooking.[94]

The Quartermaster issued fresh meat at regular intervals as long as it lasted. Between thirty and forty animals were slaughtered and dressed each day, and 3,880 carabao, 326 horses, 200 beef cattle, 100 pigs, and 87 mules met their fate at the Lamao abattoir. Carabao, the normal meat issue, were killed at a small slaughterhouse and quickly sent to the units. If the meat stood unprotected in the sun, heat and maggots spoiled it within thirty minutes. Despite these meat issues, Bataan always needed help from Corregidor. Bataan was entirely dependent upon salmon from Corregidor because it was impossible to slaughter sufficient carabao for all units. The men on Bataan believed this salmon was left over from the First World War, allegedly cost three cents a can, and was undoubtedly the world's worst.[95]

A further difficulty in supplying the fighting men with food was the necessity of diverting food to civilians. Up to 26,000 civilians, mostly refugees, crowded the rear areas. In late January, Service Command set up the first camp for displaced Filipinos a half mile west of Cabcaben, and by late February there were four camps in existence housing 11,000 people. Most every occupant was destitute, and the conditions under which they existed were worse than the conditions endured by the front-line soldiers. The camps were self-governing and local officials handled the administration. The Filipinos did odd jobs for the military, washed clothes, aided in construction efforts, and hunted food to eat and sell. "These civilians were hard pressed to find anything to eat," remembered an American infantryman, "and so a lot of times we sent our laundry out. They'd go down and wash your laundry in a creek. While you are living in a foxhole it's something to be able to send your laundry out!"[96] When the Army could afford it, they gave the refugees inferior rice and cheap salmon. When no food was available, the refugees boiled bark and leaves. One American officer worked at each camp to advise officials, insure proper sanitation, distribute food, and collect work details, but nothing these officers could do could help the sick and dying Filipinos. Sanitary conditions were the most deplorable of any on Bataan, and by late March the death rate was appalling. The refugees lived, drank, and bathed along the Real River, a river so contaminated it was beyond description. Flies covered the area in clouds, and the camps were riddled with dysentery, typhoid, and innumerable intestinal diseases. A final agony occurred on February 13 when enemy planes hit the Cabcaben camp with phosphorous bombs. Among the wounded were seventy-five badly burned children.

The supply situation along the front varied from one division to the next depending on location, transportation, and the aggressiveness with which officers and men pursued their logistical duties. Terrain often dictated if the men were fed, for if the ground was difficult, it was hard to carry the rations forward. For a long time, the 41st Division was forced to bring all its food in by pack animal. It was the division farthest inland, and General Lim's men had the most difficult time of any unit getting their food to the front. "We were given an allowance of 2 gals. of gas per vehicle at our headquarters," remembered Colonel Fortier at the division's command post. "It took 10–12 gals. in the jeep to make a trip to Corps CP. The jeep was out of order most of the time. Very soon they cut out all gasoline allowance. We were the farthest left unit of II Corps. Hell of a trip back for supplies."[97] Fortier found the quantity of food diminished as time went by, and his attempt to get C-rations because of the division's isolated position failed.

The 31st Division received bags of rice recorded as weighing 100 pounds each. But when General Bluemel and his men weighed the bags, they varied from sixty to eighty-five pounds each. At the conclusion of one day's issue, the men were shortchanged over 2,000 pounds of rice. Enemy action also destroyed food. On March 26 a Japanese bomb destroyed a refrigeration plant on Corregidor holding 24,000 pounds of carabao quarters, almost a full day's supply of meat. The bomb had hit the same hole opened by a previous bomb, passed through the rubble, and exploded. Quartermaster personnel immediately prepared some of the meat for movement to Bataan, but five more air raids delayed loading, and the meat sat in barges through the entire day. By evening it was unfit to eat.[98]

Attempting to increase their meager ration allotment, line divisions padded their strength reports. At one time, figures showed 122,000 rations being issued daily on Bataan. A warning brought the figure down to 94,000, but this was still 20 percent above the actual figure. The 31st Division, with two of its three regiments detached and on the ration strength of other divisions, drew 11,000 rations on one day, yet at full strength the division would not have exceeded 8,200 men. Investigating this incident, Lieutenant Colonel Nicoll F. Galbraith wrote his superiors, "Have just talked to II Corps G4 who is here and the 11,000 ration drawing on February 6th by the 31st Div has already started an investigation by them. This was one of the most glaring discrepancies. . . . It is also a 'boner' on the QM to make such an issue. Maybe we will have a couple of scalps for you."[99]

When food became scarce, Wainwright ordered all cavalry horses and mules slaughtered. The last of the 26th Cavalry's mounts and pack mules were eaten on March 15. The cavalry horses had served nobly, first as transportation and then as food. In what surely was the worst pun from Bataan, Colonel Townsend wrote, "So you might say we had eaten our cavalry and had it, too."[100] Unusual dishes developed and drew comparisons. "I can recommend mule," wrote one man. "It is tasty, succulent and tender—all being phrases of comparison, of course. There is little to choose between calesa pony and carabao. The pony is tougher but better flavor than the carabao. Iguana is fair. Monkey I do not recommend. I never had a snake."[101] The acceptance of mule depended upon the part received. One unit received a mule's head for eighty-seven men. The head was hanging from a bamboo pole, ears sticking up, without even a neck. Colonel Quintard watched the lack of food affect his artillerymen. There was much sickness among all ranks. The men were getting very weak, and battery commanders noticed that their men could not put in a full day's work. His artillerymen used leaves and roots to add bulk to the food they did receive.

Adding some relief to a few lucky people was the U.S.S. *Canopus,* an idyllic throwback to prewar days. The *Canopus,* "Submarine Tender No.

9—named for the star of the same name—the first vessel so called," remained in Manila Bay after the December evacuation of the more valuable ships. Built in 1921 as a combination freighter-passenger carrier, the Navy acquired the ship and gave her extensive machine shops, foundries, and storerooms. She had just received an overhaul at Cavite Navy Yard when war began, and she stayed in Manila Bay to provision submarines that sneaked in and out of the harbor. In the first weeks of war the ship was tied up against Manila's docks camouflaged to look like part of the dock complex. The crew rigged nets over the ship, emptied exposed fuel tanks, and filled them with water. Then the ship moved to Mariveles Bay, and the crew worked to make the ship look like part of the jungle. The sailors achieved some success by using a mottled green paint and tree branches.[102]

But on December 29, an armor-piercing bomb crashed through every deck and detonated on the ship's propeller shaft. The explosion started fires and blasted open the ship's magazines full of explosives and torpedo warheads. Some powder charges were crushed and a few exploded. The bomb's explosion fortuitously cut some steam lines that wet down the powder bags and helped extinguish the fires. Further attempts to camouflage the ship were futile, for a week later a fragmentation bomb hit the ship's smokestack and sprayed the upper decks with fragments. Gun crews that ducked behind their small gun shields were unprotected against the shower of overhead fragments and three-quarters of the men present, fifteen, were hit. More bombs near-missed, causing even more damage, springing plates, and causing the *Canopus* to take on a serious list. Sailors stopped the worst holes by some fast action.[103]

"The next morning," recalled the ship's skipper, Commander E. L. Sackett, "when 'Photo Joe' in his scouting plane came over, his pictures showed what looked like an abandoned hulk, listing over on her side, with cargo booms flapping askew, and with large blackened areas around the bomb holes from which wisps of smoke floated up for two or three days. What he did not know was that the smoke came from oily rags in strategically placed smudge pots, and that every night the 'abandoned hulk' hummed with activity, forging new weapons and patching up old weapons for the beleagured [sic] forces of Bataan."[104]

Besides the work that went on inside the ship, the *Canopus* also offered some luxuries. Nearly every evening Army officers and nurses who were able to slip from their duties gathered on the ship. "We had refrigeration, excellent cooking facilities, and decent living quarters, which seemed heaven to them compared to their hardships in the field. To enjoy a real shower bath, cold drinking water, well-cooked meals served on white linen with civilized tableware, and the greatest luxury of all, *real butter,* seemed almost too much for them to believe. When these favored ones returned to their primitive surroundings and described these 'feasts' topped off with ice cream and chocolate sauce, they were often put in the same 'dog house' with the optimists who claimed to have seen a fleet of transports steaming in."[105]

Captain Mills and several other 57th Infantry officers were invited to dine on the *Canopus* as a Navy thank-you for Scout help rendered the Naval Battalion at Longoskawayan. "I will never forget that dinner on the *Canopus*," recalled Mills. "Waiters in white jackets, a beautiful table cloth, real silver, wine goblets filled with wine, the whole works. The menu—Roast Turkey, Ham, mixed vegetables, salad, white bread, butter, and the dessert of all things, ice cream. After dinner came after dinner drinks and fine cigars. I felt at the time I was surely in the wrong branch of the service. I stuffed myself so much that I was sick for three days."[106] But most men never saw such meals. In the 41st Infantry one can of salmon, one can of evaporated milk, and seven-and-a-half pounds of rice constituted the daily issue of food for twenty Americans and Scouts of the advisory group.

When the Tuol Pocket fighting ended, even though the tactical situation had never looked better, no one believed that Bataan could hold longer than a few more months. First to leave Corregidor was Philippine President Quezon. MacArthur had raised the subject of Quezon's possible evacuation in a message to General Marshall on February 2. MacArthur felt that with the possible loss of Bataan and a subsequent siege of Corregidor, Quezon's presence would be inappropriate.

> I have no means of evacuating him and his physical condition precludes use of air transportation. It is possible he could sustain a submarine trip. Can any plans be arranged from Washington for his possible evacuation thereto? Under the contingency I have described he wishes to take advantage of the previous suggestion that he be evacuated to the United States.[107]

Washington's answer arrived the next day.

> The President and his advisors feel that if and when the military considerations no longer call for continued presence of President Quezon and other Philippine officials the evacuation of Quezon and family, of Osmena and of other such officials will become desirable.
>
> The question whether any of those persons and whether any other persons including Mr. Sayre and family, Mrs. MacArthur and son, and other Americans, shall at any time be evacuated will be for your decision in the light of the military situation, the feasibility and hazard of operations of evacuation and wishes of individuals concerned.

Oportunities [sic] for such evacuation should occur shortly with arrival
of a submarine from the south carrying 3-inch AA ammunition to you and
another from Hawaii also carrying 3-inch ammunition.

Steps will be taken to provide for reception of those evacuated at whatever places they may be taken while enroute to this Country and upon their
arrival in the United States.[108]

President Quezon was in agreement with the evacuation proposal. He
concluded that if the fight was to be continued, his place was not on
Corregidor. The U.S.S. *Swordfish* surfaced off Corregidor on February
19, refueled, and took on thirteen torpedoes. The next day the submarine took aboard the president and a party of nine: Quezon's wife, two
daughters and a son, Vice-President Osmena, Chief Justice Santos, and
three Philippine Army officers. "Quezon was in ill health," remembered
the *Swordfish*'s skipper Chester C. Smith, "suffering from tuberculosis,
which was aggravated by the dust generated by the bombs falling on
Corregidor. He wore pajamas the whole trip. Quezon's two little girls
and Mrs. Quezon were seasick and miserable. But the son, Manuel, had a
ball."[109] The passengers disembarked on the island of Panay.

After Quezon's departure the next most prominent figure whose fate
needed fixing was MacArthur. At first, Washington made only oblique
mention of his possible departure. But in early February General Marshall broached the subject. In a secret message to MacArthur—a message
hand-carried to the encoding room by Brigadier General Eisenhower
and seen only by Marshall, Eisenhower, and the encoder—Marshall
messaged, "The most important question concerns your possible movements should your forces be unable longer to sustain themselves in Bataan and there should remain nothing but the fortress defense of Corregidor. Under these conditions the need for your services there might be
less pressing than at other points in the Far East."[110]

Marshall then presented two courses of action. One was to proceed to
Mindanao and organize guerrilla operations in the Visayas and on Mindanao. Then MacArthur could continue south to resume command of the
United States forces in the Far East. The alternative was to go south
without pausing at Mindanao. "The purpose of this message is to secure
from you a highly confidential statement of your own views. It is to be
understood that in case your withdrawal from immediate leadership of
your beleaguered forces is to be carried out it will be by direct order of
the President to you. What I want are your views in advance of a decision."[111] Marshall also asked about capitulation of that portion of the
army that should not or could not be evacuated to Corregidor. Marshall
asked if the senior Philippine Army officer should be authorized to surrender with the assurance that surrender would not imply unsoldierly

conduct. Marshall assured MacArthur that no record of MacArthur's answer would be made within the War Department and that handling would be limited to two people, the decoding clerk and Marshall. MacArthur did not answer immediately, and when he did he announced that he and his family would share the fate of the garrison.

MacArthur's pronouncement was unacceptable to Washington. In a message sent on February 22, Marshall wrote in part:

> The President directs that you make arrangements to leave Fort Mills and proceed to Mindanao. You are directed to make this change as quickly as possible. The President desires that in Mindanao you take such measures as will insure a prolonged defense of that region—this especially in view of the transfer of President Quezon and his government to the southern Philippines and the great importance the President attaches to the future of the Philippines by prolonging in every way possible the continuance of defense by United States troops and retention of the active support of the Philippine government and people. From Mindanao you will proceed to Australia where you will assume command of all United States troops.[112]

MacArthur's initial reaction to the order was to refuse to obey it, and he went so far as to draft a blunt note of refusal. He called in his staff and told them of his decision, only to have them argue in favor of his accepting the order. A major concern for MacArthur was Marshall's phrase "as quickly as possible." MacArthur radioed Marshall that his abrupt departure could adversely affect morale.

> I know the situation here in the Philippines and unless the right moment is chosen for this delicate operation, a sudden collapse might occur which would carry with it not only the people but the government. Rightly or wrongly these people are depending upon me now not only militarily but civically and any idea that might develop in their minds that I was being withdrawn for any other purpose than to bring them immediate relief could not be explained to their simple intelligence. At the right time I believe they will understand it but if done too soon and too abruptly it may result in a sudden major collapse. Please be guided by me in this matter.[113]

Marshall then left the timing to MacArthur's discretion.

As MacArthur prepared for departure, he also prepared the necessary command changes. General Sutherland phoned Wainwright the evening of March 9 and told him to come to Corregidor the next day at noon. Wainwright did not know the reason for the summons, but with his aides Major Pugh and Captain Dooley, he crossed the stretch of water in the paint-chipped motor launch that ferried personnel back and forth between Bataan and Corregidor. Once he arrived, Sutherland told him MacArthur was leaving for Mindanao by PT boat and then by B-17 to

Australia. "The President has been trying to get him to leave Corregidor for days," explained Sutherland, "but until yesterday the general kept refusing."[114] Sutherland then took Wainwright to see MacArthur.

"Jonathan," MacArthur began, "I want you to understand my position very plainly. I'm leaving for Australia pursuant to repeated orders of the President. Things have gotten to such a point that I must comply with these orders or get out of the Army. I want you to make it known throughout all elements of your command that I'm leaving over my repeated protests."

"Of course I will, Douglas," Wainwright replied warmly.

MacArthur repeated the information already mentioned by Sutherland. Wainwright would take command of all forces on Luzon, General Jones would receive another star and assume command of I Corps, and General Parker would retain command of II Corps.

"If I get through to Australia you know I'll come back as soon as I can with as much as I can. In the meantime you've got to hold." MacArthur stressed the need of defending Bataan in depth. "You're an old cavalryman, Jonathan, and your training has been along thin, light, quick hitting lines. The defense of Bataan must be deep. For any prolonged defense you must have depth."

"I know that. I'm deploying my troops in as great depth as the terrain and number of troops permit."

"Good! And be sure to give them everything you've got with your artillery. That's the best arm you have."

After a pause, Wainwright asserted, "You'll get through."

"And back," MacArthur agreed with determination. He gave Wainwright a box of cigars and two large jars of shaving cream. The talk continued as MacArthur again explained his reasons for leaving, why he was taking certain officers and leaving others.

"Good-by, Jonathan. When I get back, if you're still on Bataan I'll make you a lieutenant general."

"I'll be on Bataan if I'm alive."

The same launch carried Wainwright back to I Corps. He wondered how to tell his men their top commander was leaving, and how they would react to the news. MacArthur's departure by PT boat is well known and will not be described here. It is enough to say that the later spectacular successes in the Pacific were due, in part, to his successful escape. MacArthur stood as the one great personality in the Philippine campaign, but he did have detractors. A personality so dominant is a target for abuse. One comic situation had an airman imitating a San Francisco broadcast. "Ladies and Gents, KGEI now brings you fifteen minutes of the latest war news from the Pacific. MacArthur, MacArthur,

MacArthur, MacArthur, etc. And now to repeat the headline news—MacArthur, MacArthur, MacArthur. Ladies and Gentlemen, for the past fifteen minutes you have been listening to news from the war in the Pacific. KGEI now sings off."[115] While facetious, it had, like most humor, elements of truth. Nor did MacArthur's statement "I shall return" escape the knives of local wits. One standard joke was, "I'm going to the latrine. But I shall return!"[116]

Many men took MacArthur's departure philosophically. "This morning we learned that General MacArthur had left Corregidor via PT boat," wrote Captain Alvin C. Poweleit in his diary. "Several men were upset by this. However, most of them felt he could do a better job in another area, like Australia. I remembered reading . . . that Napoleon took leave of his army on two occasions, when he felt that he could recruit another army and bring success to an earlier defeat."[117] But reaction was serious among the Filipinos, not outwardly as one man remembered, but as expected. "They gave lip service to our lip service—but the heart went out of them."[118] Filipinos realized that it was a great honor for "their" MacArthur to assume command of all US troops in Australia and for all that such command implied, but the men on Bataan also realized that MacArthur's departure was their own death sentence.

After MacArthur departed the army was reorganized. Wainwright's army, the men in Bataan and those forces holding out in Luzon's mountains, was named Luzon Force. Brigadier General Funk left II Corps to become Luzon Force's chief of staff. Other staff officers came from USAFFE's advance headquarters on Bataan. General Jones, 51-years-old and having served in places as diverse as Alaska, the Mexican border, and Panama, took command of I Corps. A graduate of the Army War College, Jones had received command of the 51st Division on November 15, 1941. He commanded the successful retreat of the South Luzon Force into Bataan, but it was his division that collapsed at Abucay. So it was a measure of trust that he was placed in charge of a corps. Because MacArthur insisted on retaining control of Philippine operations from Australia, Wainwright remained under his command.[119]

Surprisingly, MacArthur did not notify Washington of the new command structure. In honest ignorance, Washington addressed Wainwright as commander of all the Philippines when, in MacArthur's view, he commanded only Luzon. MacArthur wanted separate commands throughout the Philippines to preclude one local surrender from ending resistance in unaffected areas. He planned to retain control of the Philippines through a deputy chief of staff left on Corregidor, Brigadier General Lewis C. Beebe. When Marshall learned of this, he talked Roosevelt into agreeing that divided command in the Philippines was impractical, and Roosevelt agreed to accept whatever the War Department arranged.[120]

On March 17 Washington told Wainwright of MacArthur's safe arrival in the Philippines.

> General MacArthur has arrived in Australia and has been assigned to supreme command. The President and the War Department felt justified in agreeing to his new assignment because of confidence in your leadership and the demonstrated fighting morale of your Army. The prestige of the white man in the Orient, particularly in China, has rested on the gallantry and determination of the fight in Bataan and the loyalty of the Filipino soldier and people. Your task is therefore one of vast importance and, we recognize, of exceeding difficulty. We hope to relieve pressure on you by a series of determined naval and air attacks against the Japanese left flank.
>
> I assume that you are fully acquainted with the various measures that have been instituted for running the blockade and keeping our forces partially supplied with critical items. In an effort to provide you with some air assistance we are placing one or two crated P-40s on each blockade runner, including six converted destroyers of which the leading vessels are now enroute via Hawaii. Any questions on these and similar matters will be promptly answered.
>
> The area of General MacArthur's responsibility extends northward to include the Philippines and consequently you remain under his supervisory control. Because of the isolation of your command you are instructed to maintain direct communication with the War Department and submit daily reports as has been the practice in the past. These instructions will not be construed as interference with your subordination to General MacArthur. A paraphrase copy of this radiogram is being repeated to him.[121]

After several days of confused messages among Australia, the Philippines, and Washington, Wainwright was elevated one more level of command into control of all the forces in the Philippines, but he was still subordinate to MacArthur. Wainwright left Bataan on March 21 and took up his duties on Corregidor. His command was named United States Forces in the Philippines (USFIP), and he received another star on March 22, making him lieutenant general. Wainwright delivered a message to his Army.

> Acting under the instructions of the President of the United States, I have assumed command of the United States Army forces in the Philippines. I am proud to have been given this opportunity to lead you, whose gallantry and heroism have been demonstrated on the field of battle and who have won the admiration of the world. We are fighting for a just cause and victory shall be ours. I pledge the best that is in me to the defense of the Philippines. Assisted by your courage and by your loyalty we shall expel the invader from Philippine soil.[122]

After taking command, Wainwright told his aides, "Lee marched on Gettysburg with less men than I have here. We're not licked by a damn sight."[123] To fill the slot left vacant by Wainwright's assumption of Philippine command, Wainwright selected a new Luzon Force commander, Major General Edward P. King, Jr., an artilleryman. Born in Atlanta on July 4, 1884, he had served in the Philippines with the 2nd Field Artillery in 1915–1917. King assumed command of Luzon Force on March 21.

CHAPTER NINETEEN

Japanese Reinforcements

FOLLOWING THE JAPANESE WITHDRAWAL IN FEBRUARY UNTIL THEIR final effort in April, both armies prepared for the next round of fighting. The Japanese began receiving reinforcements after General Sugiyama, Chief of Staff of Imperial General Headquarters, visited Bataan in mid-February. Originally unconcerned with the slow progress in the Philippines, Imperial General Headquarters was now irked by the embarrassingly tenacious defense, and they now considered it essential to the success of Southern Army's operations to gain complete victory in the Philippines before the end of March. For as small as were the forces assigned here, still they were required in more vital areas.[1]

Because General Homma's badly reduced army was too weak to reduce Bataan, an order for assistance went out and Japanese reinforcements flowed into the Philippines. Southern Army and 14th Army staff officers shuttled between Manila, Saigon, and Tokyo, working on plans to bring additional forces to Luzon. The first significant changes occurred in Homma's staff. Inspecting officers from Tokyo found 14th Army staff officers living in comfortable conditions in Manila while heavy fighting raged in Bataan, and the inspectors did not overlook the contrast between Manila's luxury and Bataan's disasters. If the fighting on Bataan had gone well, the relative luxury of Homma's staff would not have been noticed. But now someone had to pay. Lieutenant General Maeda, the man who predicted MacArthur's withdrawal to Bataan, and the man whose arguments carried the February 8 conference, was fired on February 23. Also summarily dismissed were the 14th Army's operations and supply officers.[2]

Lieutenant General Takaji Wachi, then Chief of Staff of the Taiwan

Army and Homma's chief of staff when the 14th Army was activated, was ordered to Saigon. Wachi arrived there on February 25 and reported to Marshal Count Terauchi, commander of the South East Asia Theater of operations. After being briefed, Wachi flew to Manila and reported to Homma at San Fernando on March 1. Wachi was not impressed by what he saw when he visited the units. "The morale of the troops has been completely broken down," he noted, "and they confined themselves to the bottom of the ravines or the canyons because they had fought to no avail. Battle after battle they failed successively and in the face of too many defeats their morale could not be sustained. They could not penetrate into the thick forest and their only want at the time was aerial attack. . . . The Japanese Army was severely beaten by the Philippine Army. [Enemy] artillery was so accurate and powerful that the Japanese Army feared this most."[3]

In addition to a new chief of staff, a flood of soldiers poured into Olongapo. The decimated 16th Division and the ruined 65th Brigade each received 3,500 men. From Shanghai came the 11,000 men of Lieutenant General Kenzo Kitano's 4th Infantry Division, an Imperial General Headquarters reserve unit. General Kitano had served as a regimental commander under Homma in 1935–1936 when Homma commanded a brigade of the 4th Division, so the two officers knew one another. Kitano's division was alerted to the possibility of a move as early as February 4, and Kitano received firm orders a week later. The first convoy with headquarters elements and one regiment reached Lingayen Gulf on February 27, and by the middle of March the bulk of the division was ashore.[4]

Many Japanese, however, considered this division to be the worst equipped in the entire army. Although the 4th Division contained three infantry regiments (the 8th, 37th, and 61st) and a cavalry regiment, an artillery regiment, and normal support forces, each infantry battalion had only three of the normal four rifle companies, and the battalions lacked antitank guns. To care for its wounded, the division had only two of its four field hospitals. General Homma held such a low opinion of the 4th Division that if he had not received other reinforcements besides Kitano's men, Homma claimed he could not have attacked. But the 4th Division was not the end of reinforcements, for 3,939 men from the 21st Division led by Major General Kameichiro Nagano, commander of the infantry group of that division, bolstered the 14th Army. Working under Nagano's infantry group headquarters were the 62nd Infantry Regiment, a battalion of mountain artillery, and a company of engineers. General Nagano had been sailing from North China to French Indo-China with the 21st Division when events in the Philippines necessitated his diversion. His convoy arrived off Luzon on February 26. Another five independent infantry battalions grouped under the 10th Independent Garrison arrived from Japan too late to be used in the April fighting.[5]

Of particular importance was the arrival of large numbers of heavy artillery. Realizing that a shortage of heavy artillery had contributed materially to earlier failures to breach enemy lines, the Japanese made plans to insure an adequate number of the big guns for the next battle, and Japanese staff officers concluded that sufficient big guns could be moved into position by early April. Heavy artillery reinforcements, in the form of the Kitajima Artillery Group, previously stationed in Hong Kong, arrived in the first part of March. They included the 1st Field Heavy Artillery Regiment (240mm howitzers) from Hong Kong, the 2nd Independent Heavy Artillery Battery (240mm) from Japan, the 2nd Independent Mortar Battalion (150mm mortars) from Malaya, the 3rd Independent Mountain Artillery Regiment (75mm mountain guns) from Central China, the 3rd Mortar Battalion from Central China, the 14th Independent Mortar Battalion (300mm mortars) from Malaya, the 20th Independent Mountain Artillery Battalion (75mm mountain guns) from South China, and one company of the 21st Field Heavy Artillery Battalion (150mm) howitzers from Malaya. A balloon company from Malaya and an artillery intelligence regiment from Hong Kong accompanied the artillery. To control this mass of cannon, Lieutenant General Kishio Kitajima, after whom the force was named, commanded the 1st Artillery Headquarters. Kitajima's guns would win the next battle even before Japanese infantry started their advance. Although most of these newcomers to the Philippines were already acclimated, they underwent three weeks of jungle training before being positioned for the April offensive. Rumors were rife among the Americans that the new Japanese were veterans of the Malaya and Singapore campaigns, but of the Japanese infantry which arrived on Luzon, none came from the south.[6]

Japanese air reinforcements, collected by pulling back army and navy air units from throughout the southern area, consisted of two heavy bombardment regiments, the 60th and 62nd, with three heavy bombardment squadrons each. The sixty twin-engine bombers landed at Clark Field on March 16 after a flight up from Malaya and Southern French Indo-China, and they were placed under a headquarters, the 22nd Air Brigade commanded by Major General Kizo Mikami. General Homma also received two squadrons of Betties (24 land-based, twin-engine bombers) one squadron of Zekes (fighters) and one squadron of carrier-based bombers. A squadron of reconnaissance seaplanes was based farther south at Davao on Mindanao.[7]

Critiques, terrain studies, and reconnaissance of Filipino positions convinced Homma that a lack of suitable combat training was one cause for earlier Japanese failures. The units selected to participate in the April offensive were therefore withdrawn, one at a time, to undergo extensive training. By using abandoned American and Filipino positions along the Abucay-Mauban line, veteran officers gave their soldiers an intense course of training in attacking fortified areas, following artillery barrages, and close combat in jungles and gullies. At night they attacked old enemy positions protected by barbed wire emplaced across precipitous terrain. The Japanese discovered that their hand grenades did not damage Filipino emplacements, so instructors told their students to close to within ten to twenty yards of the Filipinos so their hand grenades could get into the entrenchments. The Japanese stepped up their training for open warfare, for bayonet charges against artillery at close quarters, and for meeting engagements in ravines and jungle. Units trained hard. They learned to reduce the equipment they carried, and they left behind the gear not specifically needed for the coming action. The leaders toughened their men and smoothed combat procedures.[8]

In the 65th Brigade General Nara felt that he and his officers had a grave responsibility to learn from their mistakes of January and February, so he held critiques for his officers. He encouraged his subordinates to recall their experiences and circulate the results so everyone could learn from each other's mistakes and successes. Nara had found himself in an information vacuum during the fight at Abucay, and submission of reports from subordinates had been so poor that he complained that it was not being done at all. Many of the reports received were of poor quality. Comparatively, losses among staff officers who tried to find out what was happening were greater than among any other group. Nara believed there was no single cause, rather, "in the great majority of the cases it is because the Staff Officers present themselves in dangerous positions and lead their men at the head of the units. This is indeed a good custom and a glory to our army and should be furthered."[9] Nara was a realist, however, and qualified his statement by explaining that the loss of experienced officers crippled the experience level of an entire unit. Nara stressed ways to reduce casualties without losing the effect of personal leadership.

First, it was unsuitable for an officer to be the first man in a column. Instead, a scout or patrol should lead and be ready for the sudden appearance of the enemy. This was especially true in the case of patrol leaders. A second cause of numerous casualties was the Japanese officer's affinity for observing the enemy or giving orders from the standing position. It was imperative, Nara lectured, to lead from a low position. Nara believed that an officer who could not lead his men unless he was standing was a fool, not a hero. Personal protection for officers should not be slighted. Trenches and shelters had to be prepared for officers as well as the front-line soldiers.[10]

Nara's men learned from hard experience that it was dangerous to advance on the roads. It was better to move a little distance off the road. The desire to cluster together is the bane of all armies, and Nara mentioned two instances in which his officers gathered together at the head of their men to give orders. In the first case, the company commander and all his platoon leaders were killed, and in the second case, the platoon leader and all his squad leaders were killed. As Americans learned, wearing rank insignia or clothing different from the private soldier was not conducive to longevity. The Japanese were very concerned about Filipino snipers and impressed with Filipino marksmanship. They were stung most frequently when facing the sharpshooting Scouts.[11]

The Japanese discovered they were failing to build up sufficient fire superiority before a charge. They did not have enough heavy weapons to support their attacks without using infantry rifles, but because many soldiers felt it was the job of machine guns to fire on the enemy during attacks, the soldiers were slow to shoot their rifles. Consequently, when the Japanese formed for an assault, their fire power was relatively weak. Without a large volume of fire to suppress the defenders, the Filipinos "calmly increase their firepower so as not to let our men get near a position for a charge and thus made it seem as though we were overpowered. . . ."[12] Because the Japanese were convinced they were superior to their opponents in all other areas, they made significant efforts to equal the enemy's level of fire power. When fire power became equal, the natural ability of the Japanese soldier would then overwhelm the Filipinos. Nara ordered his officers to train their men in the proper use of all infantry weapons to prevent the Filipinos from thinking the Japanese army could be "easily handled."

The favorite Japanese tactic, extolled to no end, was the assault. But the Japanese were greatly disappointed that so few charges succeeded. Nara was upset over instances where officers initiated charges only to be left helpless when the men did not follow. It was of vital importance that all men understand that if a charge was to succeed, it was everyone's duty to charge directly into the enemy's position. Failures resulted when men stopped under fierce Filipino fire and lost the momentum of the attack. Commanding officers and a few steadfast men then found themselves isolated, ahead of their troops, and were killed. For a charge to succeed against heavy fire, a close and detailed reconnaissance was necessary. Patrols needed to locate obstacles such as barbed wire, and then plans were needed to destroy them. The remedy to unsuccessful assaults was detailed planning. In one case, before Lieutenant Hara led his 2nd Company, 1st Battalion, 141st Infantry against a position on the Abucay Line, he called his officers and men together and ordered them to follow him regardless of the resistance they might meet. He launched his assault, his men obeyed orders, "and not only made a successful assault with relatively light losses but also led up to the destruction of the enemy along the entire front."[13] The lesson was simple. Although closing with the enemy might seem dangerous, the safest place was right next to him and out of his deadly small-arms crossfire.

At Abucay the Japanese experienced a large number of stragglers, and as losses mounted, so did straggling. When questioned, the men claimed they had just delivered casualties or had been sent to the rear for supplies. Although true in some instances, the men roamed around for a few days, trying to stay away from the battle. A 65th Brigade order warned against this practice. Officers were to insure that detailed orders were given men sent to the rear. Nara hoped his officers would instill in their men "the pride to be in the front lines."[14]

Concurrent with tactical training, Nara made efforts toward improving the condition of equipment. The wear and tear of active field service was hard on equipment, so Nara ordered his officers to supervise their men carefully and insure that weapons were cared for and properly used. Too many rifles and machine guns had been abandoned by wounded men, nor were crew-served weapons being picked up and carried forward after the original crews were killed. "When the gunner of a light machine gun is killed after making a charge into the enemy's position and the ammunition carrier disregards the danger and brings back the gun after spending a whole night under cover of darkness, it is a true expression of the love and respect of weapons."[15] Mundane items, such as how to fasten ammunition pouches to prevent losing ammunition, occupied the time of leaders and soldiers alike. Proper placing of ammunition dumps to save them from enemy artillery was a subject of command emphasis, for the terrible force of Scout and Filipino artillery impressed all Japanese. Homma was amazed at the amount of ammunition thrown at his men. "Occupying vantage points and having an almost inexhaustable supply of ammunition," he recalled, "they were in a position to shower thousands of shells upon us to a point where they were practically wasting them. Under ordinary circumstances artillery units hardly ever shell at night, whereas our enemy at Bataan shelled us at night. By far the greatest number of our wounded were hit by shrapnel, testifying to the fierceness of the enemy bombardment."[16]

Fortifications became vitally important after the Japanese were forced onto the defensive. The difficulty all armies have in making their soldiers dig in was experienced by both sides on Bataan. "Putting this matter in a nutshell," wrote Nara, "our Army in general is grossly neglecting the work of construction."[17] Because the Japanese believed they were on the offensive, little thought or energy was expended on constructing defensive works. But Japanese manpower was too limited to defend a large front, and the only solution was to stretch the combat power by protecting it with well-constructed fortifications. When in China, Nara had seen how effective fortifications could be if only the officers would push and supervise the men.

Nara was seriously concerned over the decline in competent officers and sergeants. He received officer replacements from Japan, but they were young and inexperienced. He realized it was impossible to expect them immediately to lead their men in active combat, so he told his regimental and battalion commanders to see that the new officers were properly received and quickly oriented. At the conclusion of his long critique, Nara explained the reasons for the numerous criticisms and summarized the problems he and his men faced. "I have no doubt that I need not have expressed these facts if the operation had progressed favorably, instead of having the fighting strength of the Force destroyed with the majority of the officers being killed in the early stages of the battle."[18]

There were problems in the newly arrived 4th Division as well. General Kitano knew that for the first time his division would face artillery and tanks, something they had never encountered in China. He requested flame throwers and antitank guns, but he received only two of each. The 4th Division spent three weeks training along Bataan's east coast, utilizing captured American positions. After hearing that the decision for the final offensive had been made, Kitano recorded his thoughts in his diary. "Though I know not the manner of the fight hitherto, I shall go with the determination such as Masashige Kusunoki had in 1331 when he went to the battle front, Minatagawa Hyogo, expecting to sacrifice his life for the sake of the Emperor Godaigo."[19]

Because the campaign had by now assumed great significance for the Japanese, unit commanders were ordered to plan their attacks with skill and in great detail. Homma cautioned them to be conservative in their progress. Small, limited attacks were to be planned and objectives overrun one at a time. Commanders were warned against accepting needless losses or throwing the plan off schedule by staging reckless attacks. At 14th Army headquarters Homma analyzed General King's army and came to the following conclusions. "It seems that the enemy soldiers have had about the same amount of training as our trained men, and low-classed officers who were trained at Universities. They may be very efficient in combat. Filipino officers who have devoted their lives to America have great fighting spirit."[20] The Japanese did not especially fear the composite Filamerican force, especially the infantry, but they knew the artillery was of a high order. The hard fighting did impress some Japanese. "We considered the average American soldier to be a coward," recalled one colonel, "[but] after the defense of Mt. Natib on Bataan, we changed our minds about him, and respected his courage and tenacity."[21]

While preparing for the final offensive, the Japanese spent some time attacking the defender's morale. Besides showering the peninsula with numerous leaflets, they beamed a radio program to the Americans that seemed to have some impact. "The damned Nips have got a new propaganda program that does not help our morale any," wrote Major Tisdelle in his diary. "The men joke happily but underneath they are disquieted. KZRH in Manila plays American songs to American soldiers on Bataan and Corregidor at 2145 hours every night. Theme song 'Ships that never come in' followed by popular records."[22] Other inducements to surrender came in the form of leaflets, thousands of which were dropped showing nude women, pictures of fruit markets, and happy prisoners of war eating big meals.

Although the arrival of fresh forces did much to swing the balance of power back to the Japanese, their lot was not an especially happy one. Japanese supplies, like those of the Filipinos, were critically low. A breakdown in their logistical system resulted in the normal ration of sixty-two ounces a day being cut to twenty-three. Added to this ration was whatever the Japanese could buy or steal from the generally uncooperative Filipino populace. From the middle of February until the end of March the Japanese subsisted on this reduced ration, a ration about three ounces more than that being received by the Filipinos in late March. Nor was sickness just a bane of the defenders. Medical support for the Japanese was as insignificant as that received by the Filipinos. Quinine exports from Java to Japan had been embargoed for about a year before war started, and there was an acute shortage of the drug even in the military. The 14th Army landed on Luzon with a single month's supply of quinine. Because of the shortage, preventive doses of quinine were discontinued in mid-January for all except the front-line soldiers. On March 10 preventive quinine was cut off for all Japanese except those seriously ill already in hospitals. As a result, front-line strength declined. "Only about one half of the artillery pieces," a senior officer in the 1st Artillery Headquarters reported, "of any given artillery unit were employed in an operation because of 50 percent loss of able gunners through malaria. The number of batteries remained constant, but the fire power of a four-gun battery was usually down to less than three guns, and the fire power of a two-gun battery was usually down to one."[23]

Between January 1 and March 31, 13,000 Japanese were hospitalized as nonbattle casualties. Hospital space could accommodate only 5,000; Filipino hospitals in Manila were overcrowded and poorly equipped; and field hospitals were in even worse shape. One ill Japanese wrote that the field hospital where he lay consisted of "just a shack with straw floors, built in tiers on a hill."[24] Men who could not be admitted were treated "in tents by their respective units, in the mountains, under trees or by the rivers." Nutrition was a problem to recovery. The normal ration consisted of rice, fish, vegetables, soup, and pickled plums or radishes. Meat, fruit, and sweets were issued on special occasions. With the breakdown in the Japanese supply system, the soldiers lived on significantly less than that prescribed in the manual.

CHAPTER TWENTY

Preparation

DESPITE THE LULL IN THE GROUND ACTION, THE AIR CORPS WAS busy. At 1125 hours on March 2 Bataan Air Control learned that two large Japanese tankers and three supply ships were entering Subic Bay. After capturing Subic and the town of Olongapo, the Japanese had developed them into significant supply terminals; materiel and personnel arriving there were only a short truck ride from the front lines. With this opportunity beckoning, American flyers decided to try their makeshift 500-pound bomb release for the first time. The bomb release was a collection of valve springs, steel valve rods, and parts salvaged from vehicles and airplanes. If all went well, it would drop a 500-pound bomb from under the belly of a P-40 at the correct moment, without pitching it through the plane's propeller. The device made the P-40 into an ersatz dive-bomber. The new rig had not been tested, and there was concern as to whether or not the plane could even take off.[1]

Brigadier General George, commanding the last pursuit elements on Bataan, ordered his remaining P-40's to load with fragmentation and high explosive. George called Captain William E. Dyess and asked, "Do you think that your homemade rig for releasing the heavy egg is ready for a practical test?"[2]

"There never was a better day, General. I am sure it will work."

"All right. Load up and stand by for final orders."

Two P-40's were just returning from a reconnaissance to the south after searching for the missing blockade runner *Don Esteban*. The ship had reported itself under air attack on February 28. The planes spotted her just off the northwest tip of Mindoro, but not before Japanese destroyers had attacked and burned her, a complete loss. Once these two

433

P-40's were loaded, George would have a total of five planes, but they were not all immediately available. Planes three and four were being loaded at Mariveles Field and would soon follow. Once loaded, a single bomb-laden plane rose from Bataan field, and in it Lieutenant John Posten—the first man to reach Subic Bay—held the element of surprise. He laid his six fragmentation bombs squarely on Olongapo's crowded docks and returned to Bataan Field as Captain Dyess climbed into his aircraft. The 25-year-old Dyess was a tremendously talented pilot, and General George once stated that Dyess did not fly airplanes, he wore them. Dyess had graduated from both the Air Corps Primary Flying School and the Advanced School's Pursuit Course in 1937. Dyess took off at 1230 hours, and a P-40 from Mariveles joined him as rear guard. The two planes climbed to 10,000 feet and turned north toward Subic. No Japanese planes were aloft to interfere and the short flight was uneventful.[3]

As Dyess flew over Subic Bay he noticed the ships were concentrated at Grande Island at the mouth of the bay rather than at Olongapo as originally reported. Two transports were unloading on the north side of Grande Island, two more were inside Subic Bay, and a large transport was steaming into the bay. "Ten thousand feet below me Subic bay lay smooth as a floor except for the feathery wakes of Japanese transports and warships," recalled Dyess. "It was a beautiful, cloudless flying day. The scene below me was like a brilliant lithograph, the colors almost too real. At 5,000 feet, with the throttle wide open, I saw that I was to receive a big-time reception. Antiaircraft batteries opened up from the island and most of the ships."[4] Dyess picked the transport steaming into the bay along the west side of Grande island. His first strike with a green 500-pound bomb missed the ship by forty feet, but the blast sprung plates on the ship's hull and holed the superstructure.

Dyess was angry at his miss, so he pulled around and strafed the ship three times. Dyess then turned toward a 100-ton motor vessel. "I caught one of them well out in the open and concentrated on its two forward guns, then started firing amidships into the hull, hoping to get the engine room. By this time I was just above the water and coming in fast. The Japs aboard her were putting on quite an act. Those astern were running forward and those forward were rushing astern. They couldn't have done better for my purpose. They met amidships where my bullets were striking."[5] A second pass tore the sides out of the vessel and sank it. As Dyess flew back to Battan, two more P-40's lifted from Mariveles Field with fragmentation bombs, and both planes attacked the docks. But when the lead pilot pulled out of his dive, his wingman was missing, probably a victim of antiaircraft fire. As Lieutenant White returned without his wingman, Lieutenant Sam Grashio dived in the Grande Island docks only to have his bomb-release jam. Grashio made a tricky landing at Mariveles Field without blowing up.

Captain Dyess's plane was once again ready and he and another pilot headed back to Subic. The situation was unchanged and Dyess picked two freighters as his target. His bomb passed just over the outer freighter and landed in a cluster of barges and lighters receiving cargo from the ships. As Dyess pulled up, he saw large numbers of Japanese leaving the ships and running along the dock toward shore. He pulled around and drove the Japanese off the dock. Finally, Dyess went after another 100-ton motor vessel, set it afire, and sank it. He punched the last of his .50-caliber rounds into a tanker with no apparent damage, but under the pounding of Dyess and the other pilots, ship's holds were springing open, spaces flooding, and rivets buckling. The ships frantically got underway and headed for the open sea.[6]

Back on Bataan another hasty rearm sent two P-40's back for a third strike, this time from a darkening sky. Incredibly, there were still no Japanese planes aloft to contest the Americans. At 10,000 feet Captain Dyess and Lieutenant Burns went into a dive at supply dumps clustered along the north shore of Grande Island. One terrific explosion scattered burning debris across the island, and the wreckage burned through the night. Dyess then turned back to strafe a freighter trying to slip out of the bay. He silhouetted the ship against the glow of a disappearing sun, and his six .50-calibers delivered converging streams of bullets that started fires on the after deck. Dyess's second pass concentrated on the bow and the bridge. With Dyess at 1,800 feet diving at forty-five degrees, the ship exploded and threw Dyess's plane to 4,000 feet before he regained control. He then headed for another vessel, set it afire, but could not make it explode. The ship beached itself and burned through the next day.[7]

As the planes headed for home, reports filtered into General George's headquarters. Observers reported that an 8,000-ton heavily laden transport or cargo vessel burned and blew up with a tremendous explosion. Another ship of 14,000 tons also burst into flames and beached itself. Large fires burned all across Grande Island. General George sent two P-40's into the air from Mariveles Field to cover the landing of Dyess and Burns. Dyess landed safely, but now the price for the day's successes was about to be paid. Each airfield reported to General George when its aircraft returned. Cabcaben reported that Lieutenant Burns landed with a strong tail wind and ground-looped. When the two rear guard P-40's came in to land, a bad wind caught both planes. Lieutenants Fosse and Stenson both overshot the runway and cracked up at the far end.[8]

The gloom lightened when all three pilots emerged unhurt. General George recovered first. "Forget it. We couldn't have done better and this

was bound to happen sooner or later."[9] Before this day's activities, airfields housing the American aircraft had been bombed twenty-seven
times in thirty-one days. Luck, excellent camouflage, and sturdy revetments had prevented damage to the planes. In celebration, General
George pulled out a quart of whiskey and lightened the gloom even
more. But the planes were now gone. The old motto "Keep Them Flying" now became "Keep it Flying." The Air Corps on Bataan now possessed one serviceable P-40. A prank note written several days earlier
was unearthed. Addressed to President Roosevelt, it read, "Dear Mr.
President: Please send us another P-40. The one we have is all shot
up."[10] Along more practical lines, mechanics built an entire P-40 from
parts of all the wrecked, crashed, and cannibalized P-40's on the peninsula and christened it "P-40 Something." Another group of men began a
donation drive to collect money for a "Bomber for Bataan" fund.

It was unfortunate the Americans did not have planes more suitable for
ground attack missions. At the end of January MacArthur had requested
that an attempt be made to fly A-24 dive bombers into Bataan, a trip
possible with attachment of auxiliary gas tanks. The A-24's were much
better than modified P-40's for ground missions. These planes would
have kept the Japanese a little more honest, and irregular raids on Japanese fields would have reduced enemy air operations against Bataan.
Although the planes would ultimately have been destroyed, they would
have been of great help tactically and for morale purposes. But MacArthur's request could not be honored, for when the Japanese captured
Tarakan, Borneo, they cut the proposed ferry route.[11]

The day after the raid the Japanese indirectly complimented the Americans in a Tokyo broadcast by claiming that fifty-four heavy bombers,
mostly four-engined, had attacked their shipping in Subic Bay. The
broadcast reported that at least four of the bombers were shot down. The
Americans likewise reported the action. MacArthur radioed Washington,
"We made a surprise attack on Olongapo and Subic Bay destroying the
following vessels: one of twelve thousand tons one of ten thousand tons
one of eight thousand tons and two motor launches. Inflicted much damage on smaller craft. Large fires were started at shore installations on
Grande Island and Olongapo."[12]

In return, compliments crossed the Pacific from the United States.
"The Air Force congratulates you and your depleted Air Force on your
raid on Subic Bay shipping," read a message from Major General Henry
H. Arnold, Chief of the Army Air Forces. "It sounds like the rabbit and
hat trick of a master magician. The marvelous initiative of yourself and
your small Air Force in piecing together enough equipment to carry out
this attack is an example of spirit and resourcefulness of all ranks of your

command."[13] But messages were all the Bataan army received. The only reinforcements for MacArthur's fighter command were two tired P-35's that flew in from Mindanao. Air Corps armorers attached bomb racks and christened them dive bombers.

On the ground the Philippine Army 51st Infantry got in a few licks. The Abucay fight had reduced the regiment to only 640 men, well below the 1,752 with which they started the war, and the reorganized 51st Combat Team now consisted of three infantry battalions and a provisional battalion similar to a prewar heavy weapons battalion. In late February constant Japanese mortar fire and machine gun harassment of F Company's lines became too much for its commander, Captain Brice J. Martin, and an artillery officer, Lieutenant Dobson. From an observation post Martin and Dobson made a detailed examination of Japanese positions. Martin found some spots where he could place his machine guns to cover enemy open areas. He then set his mortars in defilade and arranged for a battery of 75mm guns to support him. If Martin could drive the Japanese from their forward positions, they would have to cross a large open area between the Pilar-Bagac Road and their prepared positions on the Talisay River. Martin decided to attack at noon on February 28. His 3-inch mortars would fire on the ditch north of the road, his machine guns would hit the open areas, and the 75mm guns would fire on the prepared positions along the Talisay River. He did not contemplate a foot advance, only an attack by fire.[14]

At noon mortarmen lofted their first round into the air. A quick adjustment brought the second round squarely on target, and the crews fired for effect. The Japanese returned the fire, but an increase in volume by the Filipinos drove the enemy out of action, out of their ditch, and into Martin's machine guns. The .30-caliber rounds chased the Japanese until they reached the Talisay River. Then the 75mm cannon fired, the rounds and the Japanese reaching the same spot at the same time. "By this time," recalled Martin, "the area of the 51st Infantry took on the life of a movie-set battle. The whole front began to blaze from both sides and amid all this confusion the Japanese continued to move from Ditch to River, River to Ditch and back again."[15] No one counted the number of trips the Japanese made, but the fight lasted ten minutes before ammunition and targets were exhausted. Everyone involved in the day's work felt fat, dumb, and happy. During mutual congratulations, Martin received orders that indicated the entire II Corps's line was making a general advance to secure better terrain. The 51st Combat Team would attack the next day.

When Captain Martin's F Company jumped off, they encountered no resistance whatsoever. The Japanese may have believed the previous day's fight was a preparation for a large scale attack, and thereby abandoned their forward strong points and withdrew. "We just walked up," remembered Martin, "and occupied our new position, about 900 yards in advance of our old OPLR South of the Pilar-Bagac Road."[16] Martin told his officers to place their men into position, and then he returned to the rear to report and check on further developments. After reaching the Pilar-Bagac Road, the first officer Martin saw was the Sector commander, General Bluemel. Martin walked up to the general, saluted, and reported, "Captain Martin, Company F, right flank, 51st Infantry, reporting Sir. My company is now on the North bank of the Talisay. Any further instructions?"

Bluemel looked at him for a moment, blinked, and said, "Yes. Push on to the Abo Abo River."

Not having a map and not knowing where that river was, Martin asked how he would know he reached it.

"Oh, you'll know it Martin. It is about six or eight kilometers to your front; it isn't as wide as Manila Bay but you can't step over it either."[17] Bluemel told Martin that units on his right and left would also advance. After returning to his company and issuing orders, Martin and his Filipinos advanced, scouts out, flank patrols out, and the main body in squad columns, a total of 110 officers and men. They walked north at a slow pace for four hours without seeing anything of the units that were supposed to be on their flanks. Captain Martin began to imagine scenes from Custer's Last Stand as it became more and more obvious that something was wrong. He had no doubt as to what he was to do. His orders were clear yet there he was, all alone with his company and the Japanese Army. The fact that he was unsupported and deep in enemy territory deserved serious thought. There were numerous signs of an enemy force having passed in haste shortly before; water in Japanese canteens was still cool despite lying in direct sunlight. While discussing this predicament, a lone Filipino was seen running as fast as possible toward the company. When he arrived, he was so winded he could not talk, so he simply handed Captain Martin a field message from his commanding officer, Major Cory. It read, "Come on back, Junior," and was signed, "Cory." Martin's men returned to the Talisay in splendid time and spent the remainder of the day entrenching.

To the left of the 51st Combat Team stood the 21st Division. On the day of F Company's attack Colonel O'Day arrived at the 22nd Infantry's command post and found everyone highly excited about the advance, for only scattered enemy patrols had offered resistance. O'Day continued forward to the main line, crossed the Talisay River, and looked at abandoned Japanese trenches, dugouts, and some dried out enemy dead still along the road where they had fallen in late January. No one knew how far the Japanese had withdrawn, but the Filipinos quickly established their new outpost line beyond the Abo Abo River, dug positions, and wired the area. The 21st Infantry's outpost line ended up so far north of the main line that they organized two intermediate positions for security purposes.[18]

Filipino artillery was as active as conditions permitted and still the most effective arm available to the defenders but profligate spraying of shells, which marked procedures in January, had given way to conservation. Now observers had to locate targets accurately. No longer could they throw dozens of shells into a several hundred square yard area in hopes of hitting the enemy. One observation post spotted sixty Japanese gathering for lunch, and gunners fired a single 155mm round which burst squarely on the group. On the same day Colonel Quintard's 301st Artillery ranged in on a bumper-to-bumper enemy truck column. The big guns fired four rounds; the first shell hit the tail of the convoy while the other three walked the length of the vehicles, scattering men and pieces of equipment. After several disastrous attempts to use this road, the Japanese changed their route sharply to the west in the vicinity of Abucay. This new line was out of range of American guns.[19]

Front-line soldiers gleefully showed their dangerous positions to better-protected rear echelon officers. "On one occasion," recalled Major Fitch, an artilleryman, "I took [two colonels] to one of my OPs that had to be entered by walking through no-man's land, parallel to our front lines for about 100 yards. We usually went in and out at night. On this occasion, I took them in in broad daylight, without explaining the situation. After we were safely in, I stirred up the Japs with a little well placed artillery fire. They responded with a pair of machine guns about 200 yards to our direct front. An infantry lieutenant explained the situation to my charges. I had a hell of a time getting them back. They never came to see me again."[20]

Although the campaign's outcome began to look more and more hopeless, the men on Bataan kept fighting. Units started schools and training programs to increase the proficiency of the poorly trained Philippine Army soldier. Success in jungle fighting depended more than ever before on the individual soldier. Limited visibility in jungle terrain required initiative from each man. Because platoon leaders could not see or be seen in the dense foliage, small parties of men under local leaders had to carry the battle to the enemy. The men learned hard lessons. The soldier must carry an absolute minimum of gear; his primary weapon, ammunition, hand grenades, entrenching tool, and first aid packet. Anything else which might impede his progress had to be discarded. Officers warned their soldiers to keep under cover at all times and beware examining "dead" Japanese, for the enemy had developed the ruse of shamming death to lure forward the unwary. The safest solution was to treat each Japanese as dangerous unless he had surrendered or was confirmed dead.[21]

The American command learned many lessons from the battles around the Tuol Pocket. The first objective in containing a pocket was to put reserve forces in front of the penetration and stop its forward movement. Then both flanks of the penetration had to be enclosed. Finally, the rear would be cut to prevent resupply of food, water, and men. In subsequent operations it was best to attack from two adjacent sides at the same time. The other sides remained under cover, firing only at enemy who exposed themselves. Extreme caution had to be taken to prevent a gap from developing, especially at boundaries between advancing units and stationary units. The Japanese proved time and again they could slip through the smallest of openings. Reserves had to plug these gaps when they developed. Basic tactical doctrine had proved sound, but more stress was needed on reconnaissance and on vigorous patrolling. The army established a school for scouting and patrolling to train Filipinos in fundamentals. Instructors taught soldiers to advance slowly through the jungle and halt two hours before dark to dig in for the night. The best time to cook the one hot meal of the day was just before nightfall.[22]

One hard lesson, never fully learned, was the proper employment of tanks in jungle warfare. Like the French in 1940 and the British during the early North African battles, the Americans dispatched their tanks in penny packets, a company here, a platoon there, several tanks somewhere else. They guarded airfields and patrolled likely invasion beaches. When the Japanese launched their final offensive there was no strong, massed formation of tanks available to meet the blow. Admittedly, even had the tanks been massed, their usefulness would still have been severely limited. There simply were not many places on the jungle-covered peninsula where tanks could spread out and maneuver. Nor was infantry or artillery trained to provide the close, mobile support needed to protect tanks from enemy antitank guns and determined foot soldiers.

For their part, infantrymen considered tanks indestructible and a fine substitute for their own easily-punctured bodies. After all, reasoned the infantry, tankers rode wherever they went, and they were protected by all that armor, so it was only fair that they be placed where the fire was the hottest. Most infantry commanders were unhappy with the support they received, or failed to receive, from tank units. Part of the problem stemmed from the newness of tanks to warfare and misunderstanding as to the best method of employment. The men in the tanks felt they were committed whenever the infantry hit even slight resistance. Once in the fight, tankers felt they were poorly supported by the foot soldiers. "The tanks were mistakenly considered invulnerable, self-sustaining fortresses;" the Tank Group commander complained, "capable of going anywhere, surmounting extraordinary obstacles; and performing prodigies such as operations against snipers, flushing enemy out of cane fields, patrolling against infiltration—operations stymied by the inherrent blindness of the tank, the noise of its operation, and its considerable dead space. . . ."[23] Officers tried to institute a policy that utilized the strong points of both tanks and infantry. Tanks would advance and fire on enemy strong points while infantry would follow closely to stop Japanese who attacked with satchel charges and magnetic mines. Tanks were best suited for employment against limited objectives, always within range of the infantry. Never were tanks to be employed as pillboxes or left forward of front lines without infantry protection. To instruct line units in these procedures, tank units rotated through infantry battalions, giving classes on the fundamentals of tank-infantry coordination.

Defensive training, however, took priority over tank-infantry practice. The 14th Engineer Battalion established training teams to give classes and assist the infantry in field fortification training. The biggest problem was the failure of the inexperienced chain of command to force the men to do the work. Without close and unrelenting pressure by officers and sergeants, the men left the difficult task of digging until the next day. But much work was done despite leadership and materiel problems. To supplement the value of the scarce barbed wire, the Filipinos developed all types of field expedients. They hung chicken wire in front of their foxholes as protection from enemy hand grenades. When they could not find chicken wire, they used loosely woven bamboo. Narrow trenches in front of foxholes caught hand grenades as they rolled off the bamboo where they could safely detonate. The Filipinos turned their few hand grenades into booby traps and command-detonated mines. Pits lined with sharpened stakes in dead space caused enemy soldiers to hesitate before throwing themselves to the ground. Some units used contact mines and remote controlled electric-detonated bombs. Filipino patrols slipped behind Japanese lines to salvage barbed wire, and even though only limited quantities could be snatched out from under the Japanese, just a single strand strung across a rice paddy slowed a charge long enough to bring weapons to bear.[24]

But there was not enough time or enough energy for the Filipinos to do all they should have done. Trenches were sometimes so close to the defensive barbed wire that Japanese could lie outside the wire and lob grenades onto the Filipino defenders. Most Filipinos did not appreciate the value of grazing fire. Foxholes were frequently dug behind a mound of earth which gave fine protection but prevented the soldier from firing at the enemy. Defensive lines were constructed along the top of ridge lines rather than at the base or along the military crest, because inexperienced commanders believed it was easier to retreat from the top of a hill than from the forward slope. Junior officers often positioned wire entanglements with little regard to the positions they were meant to protect. It then became necessary for the American instructors to locate and trace the line where barbed wire should go. There was simply too little of the valuable barbed wire to string it in the wrong place. Inspectors found several instances where beach defense troops emplaced wire to follow the contour of the beach with no regard to the positioning of machine guns. Wire not covered by observation and fire was worthless. The effort involved in incorrectly stringing, then recovering, and finally resisting the wire was extravagant.[25]

Fields of fire and proper camouflage needed continuous attention, for the men lacked the necessary experience and training required to clear proper fields of fire. The correct procedure was to thin the vegetation rather than cut great swaths out of the jungle. By thinning rather than clearing, detection by ground and aerial observation became more difficult. Additional efforts were needed to cut and clear any trees or brush that, when cut by bullets, might fall and obscure the defender's vision. Camouflage consisted of more than hacking down the nearest vegetation and piling it atop a foxhole. Enemy tracers would set the dead brush on fire and displace the foxhole occupant. Growing vines should not be cut at all, for after a few days the vine in the tree above the cut died and indicated activity in the area. Dirt dug from entrenchments needed to be carefully collected, carried away, and spread under trees and bushes.[26]

Working with the Filipinos to improve their positions was a difficult job. The first time Lieutenant Montgomery checked the 41st Infantry's outpost line, he expected to find men crouched in foxholes with rifles and machine guns poised for action. Instead, he found his men pounding rice, sleeping in the open and under bushes, and singing and chatting. Some were tending small fires and stirring rice that cooked in small pots over the flame. Their rifles leaned against the bushes or lay longside the men in the dirt. The men had been given orders to dig deep, small foxholes, but Montgomery found that most of the holes were long and shallow so that the soldiers could sleep comfortably. As Montgomery recalled, "We left instructions that the men were to sleep as much as possible during the day and stand guard at night. The noncommissioned officers would listen to our instructions, nod somewhat understandingly and smile appreciatively. In all my time on the outpost line, though, I never knew of any changes in the type of foxholes or of any great attempt to stand formal guard at night. There were areas in the line where the undergrowth was thick. We left orders that it was to be cut back to allow a field of fire. In subsequent days, we repeated the orders. As far as I could determine, no attempt was ever made to comply with the order. Each time we called the corporal's attention to the oversight, he would grin, say that he would have it done 'only this afternoon, sir' and go on to his complaints about the poor rations."[27]

In late February USAFFE issued formal orders to strengthen the defenses. "Organization of positions must be continued beyond the foxhole stage;" wrote General Sutherland, "reserve and support positions prepared; trenches dug; drainage allowed for; camouflage improved; clearing of fields of fire extended to the front to include all foliage and cover afforded the enemy within small arms range. . . . Commanders and staffs of all echelons must not only supervise the execution of orders but continually check to see that orders are being complied with."[28] The Americans started a training program for Filipino battalions and divisional engineers. Officers from the Scout 14th Engineer Battalion and American 803rd Engineer Battalion were assigned to Filipino engineer battalions. These officers stressed the basics, how to use tools, prepare foxholes, and emplace machine guns to take advantage of grazing fire. As the tactical situation worsened, engineer battalions started training to fight as infantry.

In the first week of March the Luzon Force Engineer, Brigadier General Casey, made a coast to coast, foot by foot inspection of the entire line. "There is a strong tendency," Casey began in his six-page report, a report that was Casey's swan song, for he would leave with MacArthur just three days later, "particularly in the lower units, to be concerned solely with its own unit and front, without recourse to mutual supporting actions or adjacent guns or units. In numerous cases unit commanders did not know and had not consulted with commanders of adjacent units. There are many cases where a unit can do its most effective defense by covering by enfilade fire the front of an adjacent unit rather than its own, securing similar coverage of its own front from the adjacent units. In some cases the defensive strength can be increased many fold by such action."[29] After inspectors identified technical difficulties, most commanders willingly corrected them.

Casey found that unit commanders unduly lengthened their lines by following every twist and turn in a river or a mountain contour. Lines could be shortened and men massed by cutting across such features. Positions had to be closer together in jungle warfare than specified in training manuals because of the restricted visibility. Senior officers learned that the regimental reserve line had to be closer to the main line than usual, again because of the thick jungle growth. Casey was concerned over the need to develop a defense in depth and the need for a reserve. Neither could be accomplished if the men were scattered over a snakelike main line. But although an elastic, deep defense was a good idea, it was impossible to achieve. With the exception of the Philippine Division, Filipino units were neither trained, nor properly armed, nor properly led for the counterattacks necessary for a defense in depth. Japanese command of the air would subject vehicle-mounted reserves to significant losses and delays as they moved from reserve positions to the fighting. Finally, the communications net of the Bataan army could not provide the necessary control for a large counterattack. The Filamerican line was fated to fight where it stood. Maneuver, while desirable, did not offer any real hope.[30]

General Casey discovered that some division commanders did not know how to employ their engineer battalions properly, and a few commanders even refused to allow their engineer officers to report problems through engineer channels. In the 41st Division an American engineer reported that "General Lim is determined that no report of deficiencies in his division will get to higher headquarters but he does not take steps to correct his deficiencies. He considers his division his kingdom and does not intend for anyone to interfere with him."[31]

General Casey's recommendations, combined with repeated inspections by army and corps engineers, additional training of engineer troops, and better understanding by commanders of engineering operations resulted in a slow, steady improvement of defensive works. The soldiers constructed effective tank and infantry obstacles in front of most positions. On March 9 USAFFE issued its last barbed wire to I Corps, a total of fifteen tons. In turn, I Corps issued seven tons to the divisions on the main line, five tons to beach defense units, and kept three tons in corps reserve. With this issue, wire defenses were materially improved. Work continued in converting principal roads to all-weather operations. The wet season would begin in late May or early June, and although only the most optimistic of soldiers really expected to use the roads in June, work commenced. Skerry and his officers avoided criticizing the men on the front lines, for they knew that the will to fight it out was as important as any construction effort.[32]

Rear areas received as much engineer work as did the front lines. Luzon Force headquarters was sited in a dense forest concealed by huge trees. Military police took extreme care to insure that the well-traveled roads and trails leading in and out of the headquarters were invisible from the air. Headquarters personnel lined the operations-intelligence building with black paper to prevent light from showing at night. The men lived in small wall tents, and a portable generator provided electricity for the area. Despite precautions, enemy activity became so intense in March that the men were jumping into shelters several times a day during air raids aimed at adjacent installations. One Japanese bomb landed squarely in the middle of the compound but failed to explode. Experience taught the men to build foot-thick overhead cover on their foxholes to protect against tree bursts. Deciding that camouflage was only half the answer to safety from enemy air, Luzon Force built a dummy headquarters. They towed wrecked cars into place and erected false installations. The men built bamboo huts and conference rooms, dug foxholes, and cut roads into the jungle. Work crews moved the cars daily to simulate activity, especially the coming and going of messengers. As a result, the Japanese heavily bombed the dummy headquarters but did not touch the real installation.[33]

For the few regular army units, transportation before the war had been adequate. They owned military vehicles and did not have to fight as vigorously as reserve units for civilian transport. Conversely, reserve divisions, although authorized 867 vehicles, found themselves with inadequate transportation. The 41st Division grabbed everything in sight when war began, but because they were garrisoned far from busy roads they did not get their fair share. Before MacArthur evacuated Manila, car thefts by men in uniform were so common they excited no interest. Once in Bataan, vehicle use was curtailed; even then, there was still too much unauthorized travel. The large pool of vehicles collected by USAFFE in December had dropped from more than 1,000 to 18 upon arrival in Bataan. Cars and trucks had been hijacked off the roads by desperate men, became lost and attached themselves to the nearest unit, or drivers simply drove home and let the war swirl by. Units kept vehicles after they unloaded supplies, and other units grabbed empty trucks when they headed back to reload. "Under the circumstances," General Beebe wrote Brigadier General Marshall on February 7, "it appears that further reduction in the number of cars and trucks allocated to the corps will be necessary. . . . Obviously it is better to reduce the number of passengers and cargo vehicles at this time and require people to do more walking than it would be to use all the available gasoline and have nothing left with which to make distribution of essential supplies."[34]

In mid-March transportation officers took steps to improve the general mobility of the army. Military police stopped and searched vehicles. If not on a legitimate mission, they were sent to an army motor pool. Some units found there was nowhere to drive anyway, so they surrendered their vehicles. On March 14 USFIP published a general order that col-

lected all nonorganic transportation into a Motor Transport Service.
Then, on March 21, the remaining 1,200 trucks, buses, and cars were
grouped under the control of this headquarters and its four Motor Transport Service Regiments. In the four regiments were twenty-four truck
companies and a car battalion. Only 200 were of military manufacture;
the remainder were civilian models driven by civilians.[35]

Vehicles were serviced by 1,500 civilians, by enlisted men from the
12th Quartermaster Regiment, and by men from the 19th Truck Company (Air Corps). Truck companies were assigned to Motor Transport
Centers and distributed to pools within these centers. Motor pools furnished on-call vehicle support for the movement of troops and supplies.
Within limits imposed by gasoline and equipment shortages, the Motor
Transport Service met the critical transportation needs of the army. "The
loyalty of the officers and men . . . was without exception of the highest
order," remembered Colonel M. A. Quinn, the Luzon Force Transportation Officer. "Although [men were] in bad shape physically from starvation, dysentary [sic], and malaria, at no time did a vehicle fail to leave
when ordered. At one time it was necessary to render Pool 4 at
Mariveles nonoperative due to an epidemic of malaria. Men with raging
fevers drove vehicles and on several occasions became unconscious behind the steering wheel. Hence it became absolutely necessary to take
them off driving status. No quinine was available."[36] Although performance of these civilian drivers varied, most did all that could be asked of
them. They subsisted on the same meager fare as the soldiers. Over
twenty-five were killed in action, and Purple Hearts were awarded to
another seventy-five. Later in the campaign USFIP issued an order that
authorized civilian drivers to enlist in the army. The order regularized
the status of the drivers under the Geneva Convention, and it allowed
compensation and recognition of those men who served so well under
such difficult circumstances.

The remaining stocks of gasoline were issued on a controlled basis.
Daily issues were first decreased to 8,000 gallons, then to 3,000 gallons,
and once again, until the supply became so low it precluded quick vehicle
evacuation of sick and wounded soldiers. Captain Paul Ashton wrote to
his commander about the difficulties he was having evacuating his
wounded. "[I have] at present several serious battle casualties, bilateral
femoral compound fractures, pericardial wounds, etc., of several days
duration which I have been unable to evacuate. Furthermore my gasoline
supply has been cut off as you'll note by the appended letter from my
transportation officer."[37] During a period of seventeen days Captain Ashton received ten gallons of gas with which to evacuate patients. In one
division a round trip to Hospital Number 1 consumed twelve gallons of

gas, so most wounded had to be treated in the division area. Many men died who otherwise would have been saved at the larger hospitals.

As an expedient, quartermaster personnel mixed surplus high octane aviation gasoline with kerosene and low octane gasoline for use in tanks and other vehicles. Each tank battalion received a daily issue of fifteen gallons, and their issue was later cut to a ridiculous ten gallons a day per battalion. In the 515th Artillery each antiaircraft battery found itself with a daily issue of three gallons. The three gallons was divided in half, one-half going to the battery power plants which were started just before enemy planes appeared, and the remainder for the ration and water trucks. Because of the fuel shortage, no battery could displace without approval of Luzon Force headquarters and an issue of gasoline for the move. In the 2nd Battalion, 88th Artillery, the Scouts had to manage on eighteen gallons a day. They used the fuel to pick up rations, maintain communications wire, and conduct reconnaissances. The 21st Artillery placed some of the guns in dead storage; they were not manned or moved, but they were available in case of an emergency.[38]

The Bataan army met other shortages by field expedient methods. Tires of 37mm antiaircraft gun carriages proved fine on good roads, but they wore out quickly on the unimproved roads criss-crossing Bataan. Tires became so scarce that some batteries could not displace. Finally, out-sized tires from canabalized 1-1/2 ton trucks were installed backwards on carriage axles, and they gave excellent service. When distilled water for vehicle batteries ran out, the Chemical Warfare Section supplied the need through use of their equipment, and when battery electrolite ran out, chemical personnel manufactured an acid substitute.[39]

All equipment was in short supply and nothing could be wasted. A light tank, disabled, burned, and its crew entombed with dirt, underwent a major overhaul. A wrecker hauled it in from the west coast, turned it upside down, and maintenance men washed out the stinking interior with hoses. But the work succeeded, for the tank was soon back in operation. The 17th Ordnance Company was so short of spare tank parts that the mechanics used pieces of engines from old, salvaged buses. Any vehicle mechanics despaired of fixing they stripped for parts. Clothing and accoutrements were also wearing thin. When Colonel Townsend inspected his 11th Infantry, he found 90 percent of the uniforms unserviceable. Only one man in four owned either a blanket, raincoat, or shelter half. One man in four had no shoes, and the shoes still in existence were in poor condition.[40]

With medicine nearly exhausted, the inability to treat the sick was a major reason for low strength in front-line units. On March 21 USFIP Surgeon Colonel Wibb E. Cooper toured Bataan and found some 3,000 active cases of malaria. There were many reasons for the malaria epidemic: lack of prophylactic quinine, absence of mosquito headnets, gloves, and protective clothing for the men on duty at night, cross infection from the inability to isolate malaria patients, and premature release of patients from hospitals before arresting the infection. The small doses of prophylactic quinine that had held the malaria rate below epidemic proportions gave out, and by the end of March the 25 percent sick rate jumped to 75 percent. Commanders reported hundreds of new cases each day. In a letter to General King, Luzon Force Surgeon Colonel Harold W. Glattly outlined the seriousness of the medical situation. The admission rate for malaria was averaging 600 men a day, and the relapse rate of the men treated and released was high. "When the present stock of quinine has been exhausted," Glattly warned on March 23, "a mortality rate in untreated cases of 7 to 10% can be expected. Those who do not succumb to the disease can be classified as non-effective from a military standpoint due to their weakened and anemic condition. Blood-building food and drugs are not available. The gravity of this situation superimposed upon the present state of malnutrition that exists generally among the troops of the Luzon Force cannot be overestimated. The rising curve of non-effectives can be expected soon to destroy the combat potentialities of this force."[41]

General Wainwright sent messages to Washington on March 20 and 23 stressing the urgent need for quinine. It would take 100,000 quinine tablets a day to resume the prophylactic issue to Bataan's army, and although there were three million five-grain quinine tablets at sea en route to the Philippines, none were available on Bataan. The recuperative powers of the men had vanished. Many deaths occurred from the absence of intravenous quinine. Doctors tried putting quinine in a syrup form to disguise the taste, but the average patient was already sick as a dog when he entered the hospital, so when he received his dose of powdered quinine in syrup or water, too often he vomitted the concoction. "It's terrible stuff to take," remembered Corporal Read. "Oh, it's terrible, it's horrible. Even in taking the tablet you taste the bitterness. First, they ran out of the tablets, and then when you went through the chow line, they made everybody take a spoonful of liquid quinine, and that ruined the whole meal."[42] A doctor, Ralph Hibbs, remembered it as "absolutely the most bitter, paralyzing mouthful of junk you have ever tried."[43]

Even the most minor of ailments became medical disasters when they went untreated. Doctor Alvin Poweleit worked in Hospital Number 1 and noted that although many operations succeeded, the patients might still die. Simply starting a general anesthetic would sometimes be enough to collapse the remaining resistance in an undernourished soldier. As many operations as possible were therefore done under local anesthesia. As Dr. Poweleit recalled,

> [One] afternoon we received many casualties. Many had to have their legs and arms amputated. We also had men with jaws, ears and noses blown off. Our casualties were in very distressing conditions. Many looked like skeletons. Men who had weighed 175–185 pounds were brought in weighing about 120–125 pounds, with arms or legs off and abdominal wounds. Many died during surgery—death resulting, not from the operation, but from malnutrition and physical exhaustion. It is difficult to comprehend unless you were there.[44]

Many casualties developed gas gangrene. Because the germs could not live in the presence of oxygen, doctors split the skin to allow the gas to escape, irrigated the wound with large amounts of hydrogen peroxide, and packed it with a chlorine-producing chemical in gauze. Response to the treatment was normally excellent, but if the surrounding tissue became swollen and blanched, and if thin, dirty, bubbly fluids escaped from the wound, then the patient died in two or three days. There were numerous cases of tetanus among the Filipinos who had not received tetanus injections. These patients died of respiratory failure regardless of treatment.[45]

By the opening days of April the Filamerican line was staggering from weakness. The American ration, figured with either fresh or canned meat, was 19.32 or 14.54 ounces respectively. The Filipino ration was almost identical in weight. Prewar rations had been 70.9 ounces for Americans and 63.67 for Filipinos. By agreeing to a starvation date of April 15, instead of later as originally planned, Wainwright increased supplies slightly in mid-March. If bulk food requiring transport in large ships could not break the blockade, Wainwright hoped that vitamins could be brought in to alleviate the suffering from vitamin deficiency. The absence of Vitamin B in the diet caused beri-beri and serious degeneration of the heart muscles, while lack of Vitamin C caused scurvy. By this time the entire peninsula was picked clean of fruits and edible vegetation, so there was no possible treatment for scurvy. A hundred pounds of vitamin concentrates daily would have gone a long way toward restoring the health of the Bataan army. On March 31 Wainwright sent a request to Washington for ten million vitamin concentrates. They never arrived.[46]

One select group of men received almost normal prewar rations. In mid-March, pilots were becoming too worn out to fly the four remaining planes, two P-40's and two P-35's. Flight Surgeon Lieutenant Colonel William Keppard convinced General King that if additional food was not forthcoming, flying would stop. King arranged for extra rations for twenty-five pilots for ten days. Before the food was issued, Captain Dyess, commanding the squadron doing the flying, wanted to insure there would be no hard feelings on the part of the enlisted men. "The men think it's wonderful you're going to get extra grub," answered the squadron's first sergeant. "They said that if the new stuff isn't enough they'll give you theirs!"[47] Although there was not a balanced meal available anywhere at any price, the extra food worked a miracle for the fortunate flyers. Ham, bread, peas, pineapple, juice, sugar, coffee, canned corned beef hash, and vitamin tablets kept the pilots fit to fly.

But for the men required to live on the field ration, results were often fatal. A 45th Infantry surgeon watched Scouts brought into the battalion aid stations die of dysentery or malaria before they could be tagged and classified for evacuation. The number of sick reached 50 percent in nearly all units. Small aid stations and clearing stations overflowed, and evacuation of these patients was impossible; there was no place to send them. Men with malaria and temperatures of 102 and 103 degrees lay beside their foxholes because they could not be moved to the rear. Procedures for handling the sick varied from unit to unit depending on trail networks, transportation, local supplies, and density of sick in areas farther to the rear. Only men seriously sick or wounded who required elaborate aid were evacuated to the two base hospitals.[48]

With the steady drop in food and the climb in sickness came a corresponding drop in morale. "One hundred days, Tuesday March 17th," wrote Lieutenant Montgomery in his diary. "Things are tightening up. Tojo seems to get a bit more boisterous each night and food seems some scarcer. Our rations are so small we can't stretch them without some supplementary food. We're not always lucky enough to scare up that extra bit. I hiked over the hill this AM to scout around division headquarters but was met by the same old story. Everybody in the same fix."[49] But once in a while a surprise ration became available. "We really hit it lucky," recalled Private Joe F. Svrcek. "A quartermaster mule strayed into our position unattended. That night and for breakfast each of us had all the Irish stew we cared to eat. The meat tasted sweet, was dark and very gristly, but who cared?"[50]

In the final weeks before capitulation the efficiency of the Bataan army was reduced more than 75 percent from malnutrition, disease, and fatigue. Because there were no quiet areas on Bataan, it was impossible to relieve front-line troops and send them to the rear for a rest. Individual battalions were rotated off the outpost line to the reserve line, but even here they received daily bombings and artillery attacks. The steady, month-by-month accumulation of nervous tension lowered each man's ability to withstand an attack. "By March 12th," read an I Corps report, "offensive action on a large scale by this command was impracticable, due to exhausted conditions of troops, as well as lack of transportation and supplies."[51] At one time Bataan's antiaircraft defenses were reduced by crew sickness to a single battery of 37mm guns. In B Battery, 515th Artillery, only nineteen officers and men were available from an assigned strength of 100. Colonel Chenoweth, II Corps engineer officer, estimated that a job normally requiring a day to accomplish, using one man, now took ten days or required ten men. The soldiers were incapable of physical efforts for any duration.

By April 1 the combat efficiency of the army continued its steady decline and rapidly approached zero. The lack of food was on everybody's mind. Generally, the Filipinos did not complain, but as the American soldiers grew hungrier, they complained loudly and looked for someone to blame. They did not know where to place the blame, so they naturally picked the Quartermaster Corps. The Americans bitterly accused the quartermaster troops of living off the fat of the land while the front-line soldiers went hungry. Sometimes the quartermaster was at fault. When Major Walter H. Waterous, Ward Surgeon for Hospital Number 2, went to investigate the small quantities of food coming to his hospital, he discovered a shocking situation. Waterous learned that the quartermaster officer supporting Hospital Number 2 was delivering only 50 percent of the authorized supplies. He would draw the day's ration, but if the supplies did not fit in one truck, the officer did not bother to return for the remainder.[52]

Part of the reason for feeling abandoned by supply personnel was a result of poor discipline and poor inspection procedures in line units. Food stocks disappeared through theft and hijacking as they neared the front lines. Military police were incapable of controlling traffic, and orders from higher headquarters were often either disregarded or obeyed in a halfhearted fashion. Theft of supplies was common. "There were a few times," remembered an American tanker, "that I was with a group that hijacked our own supplies from trucks headed for Mariveles, presumably to ship the food to Corregidor. We had heard there was plenty of food on the 'Rock' and we couldn't figure out why rations were so short on Bataan while supplies were being shipped out."[53]

The movement of food to Corregidor was difficult for the soldiers to understand, but there was a reason. Entitled the "Bataan Reserve," food stored on the island was safer from enemy action and spoilage, and the food was still earmarked for distribution to Bataan's soldiers. Corregidor and the fortified islands were the actual installations that denied Manila Bay to the Japanese, so if Bataan were lost, as little food as possible should be lost with it. A large reserve, enough for 20,000 men to last until 30 June 1942, was created on Corregidor. Twenty thousand men was 8,000 more than the present garrison, but Wainwright expected major elements of the Philippine Division to reinforce Corregidor before Bataan fell. The backbone of the reserve was 10,000 cases of C rations (80,000 rations), and 3,705 tons of miscellaneous foodstuffs. Any difference in food between the planned 20,000 men on Corregidor and the actual 12,000 was issued to Bataan. Every ten days about 100,000 half rations became available and went to Bataan. Finally, however inequitable it may have seemed for Corregidor's garrison to eat better than Bataan's soldiers, to have distributed Corregidor's "excess" to Bataan would have made but a tiny impact on Bataan and might have starved Corregidor before the Japanese landed. Ultimately, all but 5,000 cases of C rations returned to Bataan and were consumed there.[54]

Although the food situation worsened with each passing day, the soldiers did survive. "It was surprising," wrote Major Bautista about his engineer battalion, "how the boys could still keep their morale, in spite of our dwindling food supplies and apparent hopelessness of the whole situation. Day after day, the boys would scan the skies for the long awaited Allied planes that would allow us to win over the enemy; lookouts never tired of watching for the convoy of ships that would bring us supplies and reinforcements. We busied ourselves making our positions more impregnable."[55]

CHAPTER TWENTY-ONE

The Orion-Bagac Line

THE OFFICER COMMANDING LUZON FORCE WITH ITS TWO CORPS WAS Major General Edward P. King, and he was destined to be the forgotten general of Bataan. A Georgian, a kind and thorough gentleman, King had served his country for thirty-six of his fifty-seven years. He had commanded a battalion of artillery, had served three times in the Office of the Chief of Field Artillery, was an honor graduate in 1923 from the Command and General Staff School, and had graduated from both the Army and Navy War Colleges. King was a veteran of the Philippines, for he had served there from 1915 to 1917, and upon his return in 1940, had supervised the artillery training of the new Philippine Army divisions until he became USAFFE Artillery Officer. But now, serving in the shadows of MacArthur and Wainwright left King in obscurity. Despite his low profile, he, not MacArthur or Wainwright, was the commander on Bataan. As of April 3, King's Luzon Force had, on paper, 79,000 soldiers, 6,000 civilian employees, and about 20,000 refugees. Of the soldiers, approximately 11,796 were Americans, 8,270 were Philippine Scouts, and 59,000 were Philippine Army. Not one of the divisions was near its authorized strength, and each division now contained personnel untrained to fight as riflemen, men from cannibalized administrative and service units. Even those men considered as trained infantry included thousands of civilians whose first military service came after their induction on Bataan.[1]

Because of the small size of surviving units and difficulties in communicating, the Orion-Bagac Line had been divided into subsectors in late January, and each subsector commander reported directly to his respective corps. A sector headquarters might control up to six regiments, or as

in the case with Sector B, control a single regiment. Although this practice divided some divisions and made command responsibilities hard to
follow, it was beneficial. Battle experience in January proved the value of
having Americans well forward with Filipino combat troops. But after
the withdrawal from Abucay to the Orion-Bagac Line, large staffs started
forming at division and sector level. Empire building was discouraged by
a letter from USAFFE headquarters that reminded everyone that creation
of the sector organization was "for the purpose of decreasing rather than
increasing overhead."[2] USAFFE did not contemplate or desire sector
staffs to be comparable in size to either division or corps staffs. In particular, the practice of assigning experienced American officers as assistants to
principal staff jobs was forbidden. They were to work on the front lines
while less experienced American and Filipino officers would serve as staff
assistants. Concurrent with USAFFE's February 3 order, corps commanders were given authority to break up any units too small to be
effective and give the men and equipment to other units to increase their
fighting ability. By reducing the number of units, more American officers
would be available for the units remaining.

Along II Corps's 15,000-yard-long line stood the men upon whom the
greatest weight of the enemy attack would fall. The relatively open, rolling terrain offered the Japanese their best opportunity for maneuver, and
the trail network here allowed more avenues of approach than did the I
Corps's line. The steep mountains and dense jungle in I Corps, combined
with bad memories of losing an entire regiment there, deterred the Japanese from making any serious efforts in the west. General Parker's
28,000-man II Corps, entrenched in field fortifications, would be the
target. Command arrangements in II Corps divided the line into four
sectors (A–D) defending the land approaches, and one sector (E) defending the Manila Bay coast. Guarding the Manila Bay flank and about
2,500 yards of II Corps's front was Colonel John W. Irwin's Sector A
composed of Irwin's Philippine Army 31st Infantry. Part of the twenty-
four-gun 21st Artillery supported Irwin.[3]

Sector B, Colonel Irvin E. Doane's two-battalion Provisional Air Corps
Regiment, covered another 2,000 yards of the front and extended
Parker's line to the west. The airmen had dug in behind the San Vicente
River, a river big enough, with its deep channel and steep sides, to
constitute an antitank obstacle across most of Sector B. The airmen
bunkered machine gun positions with palm-tree trunks to overwatch
flooded rice paddies. Eight 75mm and four 2.95-inch guns from the
Scout 1st Battalion, 24th Artillery, supported the Air Corps Regiment.
On March 31 the regiment carried 90 officers, 1,408 enlisted men, and
17 Scouts on its rolls. The old squadrons were now designated as infantry

companies. Each company averaged 100 men on the front line with another 20 or more scattered across the rear pulling various support functions. A few of these men stayed at the airfields where their mechanical
skills were in demand.[4]

The airmen had been on Bataan about a week when each man received
an Enfield or Springfield rifle and fired some rounds into a hill. The
airmen were then baptized as combat infantrymen. Their infantry training consisted of extended order drill, some bayonet work, some scouting
and patrolling. It was unusual for these thirty to thirty-five year old technicians to be involved in such training, but they understood there was no
choice. There were several accidental shootings before the men learned
how to handle their new weapons. They carried machine guns salvaged
from wrecked airplanes, and a few armorers developed some weird con-
coctions in their quest for fire power. One mount held triple Lewis machine guns mounted abreast with a metal bar running in front of all three
triggers for simultaneous firing. Their advanced individual training, as
well as most of their basic training, took place under combat conditions
with trained infantrymen from the American 31st Infantry attached as
instructors. Some of the 31st Infantrymen were old soldiers with more
than ten years service at exotic stations such as China and Panama. The
classroom consisted of actual patrols.[5]

More than an average number of men were wounded during this training because they did not know yet how to crawl or dive for cover.
Wounds of the buttocks were common until experience taught the men
to keep the entire body low. "Its hard to imagine just how difficult it is to
go into combat with men who had been trained in everything except
combat," remembered Sergeant Jack D. Bradley. "Some of them had
never fired a gun. Sometimes when I took twenty men on a night combat
patrol, I was more afraid of the probable accidents with our own men
than I was of the Japs."[6] Every few days, under the concealment of night,
intelligence patrols waded the San Vicente River and sneaked into rice
paddies next to the main road. There they laid all day in the searing sun
counting enemy vehicles, men, and weapons. Then, after it was dark, the
patrols crossed carefully back into friendly lines.

From late January through March the airmen concerned themselves
with patrolling, food, and construction of better positions. With the moti-
vation provided by the enemy, digging holes became second nature to
the Americans, but the limited number of men and their weakened physical condition prevented speedy work even on the main line. Although
they built a regimental reserve line, they could not effectively use it
because there was no third battalion in the regiment to man it. Units
rotated their platoons from the main line to the outpost line, and from

the outpost line to the reserve line. This rotation kept them relatively fresh and alert when forward, yet allowed regular rests when in the rearmost position. Footgear and leather deteriorated rapidly in jungle use. To replace worn shoes, airmen collected moldy, cast-off Navy footgear and thoroughly washed them with sand and water. Most men wore their shoes without socks after their only pair rotted off. To keep uniforms in shape, patient men pulled thread from work clothing and used it to patch what remained.[7]

For food, it was not unusual for two one-pound cans of salmon to be issued to 100 men. As a result, volunteers for patrols were easy to find. The incidental food obtained by foraging was well worth the risk of getting shot. Food served in unit messes was mainly canned fish and rice, and then there were but two meals each day. One mess sergeant was a cook in World War I, so when horse meat was issued, he made an acceptable stew. Even with less-experienced cooks, few men turned down their meager portions of meat. Soldiers constantly stalked unwary animals, including insects the size of large grasshoppers. Patrols returned with peanuts, sugar cane, roots, native sweet potatoes, and everything remotely palatable. Men manning night listening posts chewed on sugar cane, making a racket loud enough to cover the approach of an enemy. But despite eating everything in sight, it still was not enough. The airmen developed mild scurvy with bleeding from the bowel, symptoms promptly cured by fresh fruit or vegetables. "The fact that one had malaria or legs swollen out of shape by beri-beri meant nothing," recalled Lieutenant George Kane. "There was no place to go and everyone stayed at the MLR and carried on as best he could. He was exempt from patrols and OPLR duty but that's all. Physical condition from lack of food was worse than from lack of medicine. Unless one was there, he could not visualize how gaunt the men were."[8]

To the left—west—of the airmen stood the 4,500-yard-wide Sector C and the fiery Brigadier General Clifford Bluemel. He commanded the reinforced 32nd Infantry from his own 31st Division and the reconstituted 3,500-man 51st Combat Team now organized with four infantry battalions and two field artillery batteries. The 31st Artillery—eight 75mm guns—and the eight 75mm cannon belonging to the 51st Combat Team gave Bluemel sixteen guns.[9]

Next, in Sector D, covering the most likely enemy avenue of approach, was the 5,500-man 21st Division—all three regiments on line—and the three regiments of the 5,900-man 41st Division also all abreast on the main line. Brigadier General Maxon S. Lough commanded this large force, almost a corps in itself, and he used his Philippine Division staff to control the sector. The 41st Division had received its 41st Infantry back from Bluemel in early March in exchange for the 33rd Infantry, until then under 41st Division control. When the 41st Infantry took up the 33rd Infantry's old positions, they were dismayed at the condition of the line. The 33rd Infantry had been badly overextended, and their work on the line was only half finished. Cleared areas around foxholes were too conspicuous, the line was constructed on the topographical crest rather than on the military crest, and little work had been done on the battalion support line. The regimental reserve line was hardly 30 percent complete. Correcting all these deficiencies demoralized and exhausted the men of the 41st Infantry, for this was the third time they had been required to dig in on the Orion-Bagac Line. But at least they were now back with their division.[10]

Clustered around the dominant terrain in Sector D's line, Mount Samat, stood General Lough's sector artillery: sixteen 75mm guns and eight 2.95-inch mountain howitzers, all from the 41st Artillery, and all clinging to Mount Samat's slopes. Every effort was made to protect the guns from Japanese observation and fire. They were located deep in woods and on precipitous slopes, and some gunners roped their cannon to trees to keep them from rolling down the steep hills. The final sector of II Corps lay along the Manila Bay shore, Sector E. Parts of General Guillermo B. Francisco's 2nd Regular Division, a company of tanks, and a battery of self-propelled artillery protected the area.[11]

To give general support artillery to II Corps's line, General Parker's Corps Artillery consisted of the sixteen-gun 301st Artillery and the four-gun B Battery, 86th Artillery, both with 155mm's, both in general support near Limay. In all of II Corps there were seventy-two 75mm guns (towed), twelve 2.95-inch howitzers, and twenty 155mm's. Artillery continued to play an important role in defending the main line, but Bataan's cannon were still hampered by a lack of fire control equipment and aerial observation, inadequate communications equipment, and a shortage of motor vehicles and fuel to displace from one location to another. The success of the guns now depended on the number and location of alternate firing positions, protected ammunition sites, bunkers for personnel, roads, observation posts, cleared fields of fire, and weeks of labor. As the physical condition of the men deteriorated, they made fewer and fewer improvements. Infantry reserves in II Corps consisted of the 33rd Infantry (minus 1st Battalion) located southeast of Mount Samat, and the 201st and 202nd engineer battalions (PA).[12]

At Luzon Force, General King controlled the Provisional Tank Group and twenty-seven 75mm self-propelled artillery pieces of the Provisional Artillery Brigade. The 200th and 515th antiaircraft artillery protected airfields and rear installations and in a pinch could be used, with greatly reduced effectiveness, for ground defense. Quantities of artillery ammunition were still adequate. On April 2 there were 50,905 rounds of 75mm and 4,338 rounds of 155mm. For the infantrymen there still existed 5,745,098 rounds of .30-caliber, roughly one-third of the amount with which they began the campaign. King's army-level reserve consisted of the American 31st Infantry bivouacked on the Alangan River and the 57th Infantry farther south on Signal Hill. King's staff collected buses and trucks, gassed them, and pooled them next to the two regiments to give them the mobility required to move quickly to any part of the line. The 14th and 803rd engineer battalions were ordered to make plans for assembly and possible commitment as infantry.[13]

Both corps staffs made plans for the relief from beach defense of the 1st and 4th constabulary regiments for possible deployment. As replacements for beach defense troops, primarily for the 2nd Division in II Corps, commanders of service, quartermaster, depot, dump, chemical, and motor park units were required to prepare to take over beach defenses at a moment's notice. Officers and sergeants reconnoitered routes both at day and night and on March 28 made a trial run under the concealment of darkness. Each unit occupied its position with all its men except for a few left behind to guard equipment. Trucks and buses were pooled and gassed in reserve areas to move these forces.[14]

In the 32,600-man I Corps, General Jones's front undulated across 13,000 yards of ridges and ravines. He held his line with the 6,400-man 91st Division, two regiments strong, reinforced by 3,500 men from the attached 71st and 72nd infantry. General Luther Stevens's 91st Division held part of the west coast and ran inland until meeting the 1st Division. When Colonel Cordero came to I Corps on March 13 to command the 72nd Infantry, he found the front line very formidable. "Our position was impregnable; it had a very elaborate system of field fortifications, and the open field to our front was all mined as was the highway running through my sector."[15] Both the 91st and the 1st divisions were grouped under General Stevens' Left Sector. Supporting Stevens were eight 75mm guns from the 91st Artillery.

I Corps's 5,000-yard Right Sector, commanded by Brigadier General Brougher, consisted of the 4,500-man 11th Division, the 2,200-man 2nd Constabulary, and ten 75mm guns. The 11th Division was a two-regiment unit, the 13th Infantry having been absorbed by the 12th after the retreat from Abucay. In front of the 11th Division a twelve-foot high bamboo wall screened the front from enemy observation. The wall had originated with a young Filipino captain who built a screen across the front of his company. Other units liked the idea and built their own walls until a continuous barrier stretched across the 11th Division's front. It

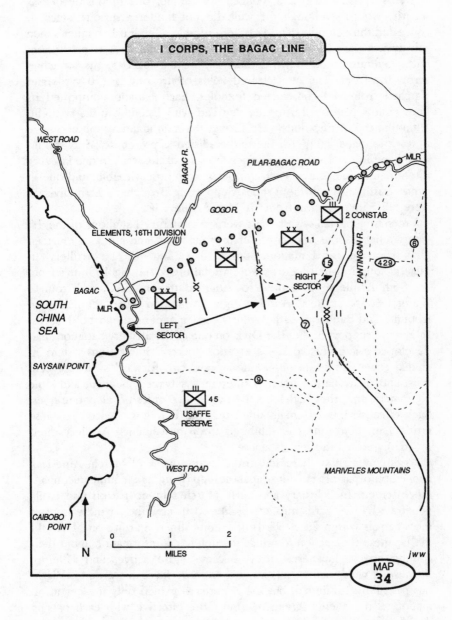

I CORPS, THE BAGAC LINE

WEST ROAD

BAGAC R.

PILAR-BAGAC ROAD

MLR

GOGO R.

2 CONSTAB

ELEMENTS, 16TH DIVISION

XX 11

XX 1

PANTINGAN R.

6

15

429

XX

RIGHT SECTOR

BAGAC

SOUTH CHINA SEA

MLR

XX 91

LEFT SECTOR

7

I XX II

SAYSAIN POINT

9

III 45

USAFFE RESERVE

WEST ROAD

MARIVELES MOUNTAINS

CAIBOBO POINT

N

0   1   2

MILES

jww

MAP
34

slowed surprise attacks and reduced the number of Filipinos needed as security troops. Although the wall did not hinder a serious attack, it concealed the defenders and bolstered morale. General Brougher's men substituted giant bejuco vines for scarce barbed wire. A trench system with communication trenches and automatic weapons pits stretched across the front. The men cleared fields of fire out to 250 yards and watched from well-constructed foxholes. Each battalion outposted its lines with a platoon during the day and with listening posts at night. Although the fortifications were strong, the men manning the line were in terrible shape. Fully half the soldiers listed as present for duty should have been in a hospital. Losses since the start of the war ran one in every three men. Nine of every ten uniforms were unserviceable, and one in every four men was without shoes. Supporting Brougher's 11th Division were ten 75mm cannon from his 11th Artillery.[16]

Protecting Bataan's west coast were the infantry battalions of the 1st Constabulary, some Air Corps pursuit squadrons, and a mix of fourteen guns from the 2nd Battalion, 88th Artillery and the 71st Artillery. In general support of all I Corps were a total of sixteen big 155mm's from the 86th Artillery, from the Provisional Battalion, CAC, and from G Battery, 301st Artillery. Another eight 75mm and four 2.95-inch came from the 2nd Battalion, 24th Artillery, also in general support of I Corps. In general support of the 91st Division one of the artillery battalions had developed a good network. Observation and communications system included seven front-line observation posts, two forward switching centrals, and many liaison lines. Artillerymen salvaged, begged, and stole equipment until they had collected twenty-five miles of telephone lines. Such effective fire was maintained that the Filipinos silenced Japanese artillery in their zone and inhibited troop movements. Artillery duels invariably ended in silent Japanese.[17]

As enemy activity increased in the second week of March, American and Filipino patrols ran into Japanese deploying as a counterreconnaissance screen. In February and early March Filipino patrols had easily penetrated 4,000 yards into enemy lines. But now the Japanese stopped most patrols within 2,000 yards of Filipino lines. Starting on March 11 the Japanese took action to refuse the defenders information about their coming attack. Japanese patrols became more active, and Filipinos skirmished with enemy units moving to more favorable ground. Vigorous patrolling continued, but the Americans gained only meager information as the enemy screen became more effective with each passing day.[18]

Japanese patrols were now composed of more experienced soldiers than those which began the Bataan campaign, and the Americans believed that the veterans of Singapore had arrived. They carried new equipment and wore new, clean uniforms. As Japanese preparations matured, their patrols crept to within 1,000 yards of the Orion-Bagan Line. Japanese tanks even launched a halfhearted probe, dodging in and out of bamboo thickets. In response, the 31st Infantry Anti-Tank Company took the Japanese under fire, and after getting the range, hit a few tanks and destroyed at least one. Then the Japanese withdrew. Next it was the turn of the infantry. Just after dark on March 10 Japanese in front of the 21st Division sortied, and in the yelling, shooting, and confusion, drove the Filipinos from their outposts. The next day the Filipinos counterattacked and pushed the enemy out of all but a few of the original foxholes. One Japanese patrol crawled through a drainage ditch the night of March 21 and hit a battery of rifle-carrying 31st Division artillerymen. The Filipinos drove the Japanese off, and outposts reported that as the enemy withdrew, the Japanese were dragging three of their comrades by their feet. Six days later the Japanese raided the same battery and again were repulsed. But when the Japanese hit the Filipinos for a third time, the Filipinos broke. The Japanese did not pursue, and a strong Filipino patrol, commanded by an American lieutenant, counterattacked and filled the hole.[19]

Reports of increased patrol activity reached General Wainwright on Corregidor and he passed the information to Washington. "During the past twenty-four hours," he reported on March 21, "enemy patrolling has been more active along the front of the Luzon Force. Continued activity indicates that enemy is building up strength for a possible renewed assault of the Bataan position."[20] Enemy air, seen only infrequently after early February, returned to the skies, diligently searching for Filipino artillery positions, supply dumps, and vital installations.

But before committing their forces to an actual assault, the Japanese called for the Americans to surrender. They dropped messages in beer cans addressed to Wainwright.

To his Excellency Major General Jonathan Wainwright, Commander-in-Chief of the United States in the Philippines. Anyone who gets this letter is requested to send it to the Commander-in-Chief of the United States Forces in the Philippines.

YOUR EXCELLENCY: We have the honor to address you in accordance with the humanitarian principles of "Bushido" the code of the Japanese warrior. It will be recalled that, sometime ago, a note advising honorable surrender was sent to the Commander-in-Chief of your fighting forces, to this, no reply has, as yet, been received. Since our arrival in the Philippines with the Imperial Japanese Expeditionary Forces, already three months have elapsed, during which, despite the defeat of your allies, Britain and the Netherland East Indies, and the face of innumerable difficulties, the

American and Philippine forces under your command have fought with such gallantry. We are, however, now in a position to state that with men and supplies which surpass, both numerically and qualitatively, those under your leadership, we are entirely free, either to attack and put to rout your forces or to wait for the inevitable starvation of your troops within the narrow confines of the Bataan Peninsula. Your Excellency must be well aware of the future prospects of the Filipino-American forces under your command. To waste the valuable lives of these men in a utterly meaningless and and hopeless struggle would be directly opposed to the principles of humanity and, furthermore, such a course would sully the honor of a fighting man.

Your Excellency, you have already fought to the best of your ability. What dishonor is there in avoiding needless bloodshed? What disgrace is there in following the defenders of Hong Kong, Singapore and the Netherlands East Indies in the acceptance of an honorable defeat? Your Excellency, your duty has been performed. Accept our sincere advice and save the lives of those officers and men under your command. The International Law will be strictly adhered to by the Imperial Japanese Forces and your Excellency and those under your command will be treated accordingly. The joy and happiness of those whose lives will be saved and the delight and relief of their dear ones and families would be beyond the expression of words. We call upon you to reconsider this proposition with due thought. If a reply to the advisory note is not received from Your Excellency through a special Messenger by noon of March 22nd, 1942, we shall consider ourselves at liberty to take any action whatsoever.

Signed——Commander-in-Chief of the Imperial Japanese Army & Navy.[21]

In his headquarters at Luzon Force, General King read the ultimatum. Then he looked at his staff and smiled. "You know, gentlemen, I have been both a student and an instructor at the Command and General Staff school and the War College and neither has ever taught surrender. I don't think we'll accommodate Mr. Moto!"[22] Wainwright told Washington about the manifesto and said that no reply was necessary.

Word of the surrender message did reach the men of King's army. On March 22 Lieutenant Montgomery wrote in his diary, "Tojo issued an ultimatum yesterday. If we don't surrender by noon of the 22nd we are to be starved and annihilated. It is now afternoon and the die is cast. We may see activity this evening."[23] Activity picked up the next day.

Japanese artillery batteries, mortars, and heavy infantry guns massed in an area five kilometers wide and four kilometers deep. They reached far into the defenses. Firing from positions west of Balanga, most of the shells were aimed at putting the Filipino guns out of action. The Japanese 1st Balloon Company emplaced their equipment on high ground west of Abucay with excellent observation of Filipino positions. The 5th Artillery Intelligence Regiment deployed its sound, flash, and visual observers across the peninsula to locate the well-hidden Filipino cannon. In January, Filipino artillery could shoot, move, shoot and shift again to avoid Japanese fire. Now, with the severe cuts in gasoline, the gunners were pinned to one spot, and the Japanese started finding them. Japanese 75mm, 105mm, and 150mm guns searched the most likely positions for Filipino artillery and, with their balloon observation, began hitting some of the guns. Although the Japanese effort to silence the defending artillery failed, Filipino fire was degraded by the severe disruption of communications and observation. The destruction of materiel was not too great, but the effect on the weakened and famished troops was serious. Jumping into foxholes when Japanese artillery crashed in, then running back to fire a few rounds, tired the gunners. Now and then an artilleryman fell from a bomb or shell fragment, but the survivors maintained their fire.[24]

The first appearance of the 1st Balloon Company's finned, gondola-carrying captive balloon meant trouble. But the Americans were unwilling to allow the Japanese unimpeded observation without a struggle. For the first three days the balloon was used every American and Filipino observer in II Corps took compass readings on the point the balloon landed. At II Corps Artillery headquarters the Americans plotted each azimuth until they reduced the location of the balloon to a small area. When the Japanese lowered the balloon at the close of the fourth day, every 155mm gun in II Corps within range fired at the plotted grid. It was five days before the Japanese once again raised the balloon, and this time they positioned it farther north, out of range of the 155mm's.[25]

Japanese air was dangerous, but the planes usually knocked off for three hours after lunch, and knowledgeable drivers crammed their daylight driving into those three hours. By 1500 hours most traffic was once again off the road. Unofficial antiair ambushes collected, from time to time, a toll of Japanese planes. Tankers from the 192nd Tank Battalion noticed the Japanese made a habit of attacking American PT boats near the east coast each morning, so American half-tracks and tanks assembled where their fire could link with that of the PT boats. Each PT boat's four .50-caliber and the .50-calibers on the half-tracks managed to put up a large volume of fire, and on one occasion the gunners claimed to have downed nine of the twelve attacking planes. The remaining American P-40's destroyed a few enemy planes in unusual ways. Pilots from Cabcaben often flew into enemy formations, gathered a few pursuers, and then dove for Manila Bay. A P-40 could outdive a Zero, and when the P-40 pulled up just over the water and dashed for the airstrip, the Zero plunged into the bay or became an easy target for Bataan's antiaircraft guns.[26]

Corresponding with the March increase of Japanese artillery and aerial activity, II Corps artillery observers spotted large enemy truck and mate-

riel movement travelling from Layac Junction south into Bataan and then
west from Abucay. Up to 600 trucks entered and departed Bataan daily.
The Japanese built a new road that paralleled the American-dominated
Pilar-Bagac Road, and they funneled their supplies over this route. This
buildup continued for twelve days. Luzon Force Intelligence Officer,
Lieutenant Colonel Frank L. Holland, believed the convoys were part of
a preparation for a large offensive against II Corps, and Holland figured I
Corps would receive only diversionary assaults. Civilian refugees reported buildups and troop concentrations. The Japanese warned civilians
to evacuate certain areas, explaining that the areas might be involved in
military activity. Filipino patrols from the 11th Division, probing north
of the Pilar-Bagac Road, observed the Japanese building trails and supply
dumps. Despite heavy Japanese activity, the Filipino patrols were so ob-
sessed with the desire to gather food they actually slipped into enemy
supply dumps and stole small amounts of rice and sugar.[27]

On March 23 the Japanese launched fifty-four Betties against the defenders. Twin-engine bombers had not been seen since the January battles, and bombings in the rear areas now became extremely heavy with
defending artillery a prime target. The next day nine twin-engine bombers hit Mariveles and Cabcaben. The high-level bombers worried Colonel Quintard. "You never know when they are going to unload, and the
waiting gets hard; when they do unload any place near, it sounds like an
express train bearing down on you for a few seconds before they hit."[28]
As March waned, aerial activity waxed along the main line of King's two
corps and over the immobile facilities clustered throughout rear areas.

As Japanese air and artillery activity increased, life on the receiving
end became more and more difficult. "March 25–26," wrote Lieutenant
Montgomery in his diary, "More bombing in the past two days. Airplanes over all the time and they do keep us on edge. Many desertions
from the Philippine Army. Tojo is dropping much effective propaganda.
Pictures of laughing Filipinos and much food along with glowing accounts of good treatment. It may all be so and many of these boys believe
it. Our chow goes from bad to worse."[29]

On March 25 the Japanese 16th Air Regiment sent its light bombers in
fifty-seven attacks against front-line positions and defending artillery. The
next day planes concentrated on the Filipinos of the 41st Division. Under
this constant fire, personnel developed a marked reluctance to move
from cover. Enemy planes seemed to drop down every few minutes to
attack vehicles, wire-laying details, machine guns, food-carrying parties,
smoke from cooking fires, and even individuals in the open. One exception to the reluctance to move around was the constant search for food.
Patrols scoured the area between the two lines. General Bluemel was

bothered by large and increasing numbers of men from the 21st Division moving along his outpost line heading east to Pilar. There the Filipinos could buy food and cigarettes at high prices. On their return trip they insisted on passing through Bluemel's outposts. To stop this practice and prevent his own men from joining, Bluemel stopped all infiltrating Filipinos, questioned and searched them, confiscated the food purchased at Pilar, and divided the food among his men on the outposts. But even this failed to slow the traffic. In another attempt to dissuade foragers from moving through his lines, Bluemel required each man to dig a foxhole before he was released.[30]

Even when Japanese planes came into range, antiaircraft gunners were restricted by the rules of engagement. Because of ammunition shortages, no more than six rounds could be fired at any one plane. This restriction made the normal correction of fire impossible, because by the time the first round exploded, at least five of the six allotted shells had been fired. If the plane returned, it could be re-engaged. Single planes were not to be shot at unless they actually attacked. When fired, the 3-inch ammunition showed a 30 percent malfunction rate, and seven percent of the 37mm rounds were duds. The 3-inch ammunition consisted of leftover World War I shells dated 1917 and 1918. The shells had received repeated coats of paint during their long lives, and the thicker shells caused dangerously long recoils of the guns. Cracked projectiles frequently burst in the barrel and scattered pellets all over the place like a huge shotgun. Other projectiles malfunctioned in more fatal ways. C Battery, 91st Artillery, was defending Cabcaben airfield against a Japanese attack when a faulty fuse detonated a 3-inch shell just as it cleared the muzzle. It killed two American officers, wounded two more, and killed several Scouts. C Battery was out of action for several days.[31]

Despite losses from both enemy and friendly fire, the gunners were not shy. They fired their guns until bombs fell or machine gun bullets hit their positions. Everyone then sprinted for trenches, waited out the attack, and then ran back to the guns. Morale soared when Japanese attacks failed to produce casualties, a failure attributable to hard work. The guns and fire control equipment were dug in and then sandbagged for protection against planes and bomb fragments. Communication trenches connected each gun, linked range section units to each gun, and burrowed to perimeter machine guns.[32]

The Japanese picked the key piece of terrain in II Corps as their initial objective for the April attack. Mount Samat, covered with heavy hardwood trees six feet in diameter and 100 feet tall, rises gently at first, especially in the east, then juts suddenly to almost 2,000 feet. The mountain was blanketed by dense foliage, and large thorns guarded rugged ground cut by numerous streams. It was difficult to move across the mountain, and only the lower eastern slopes offered ground flat and open enough for fields of fire. Movement was limited to pack trails. But the view from Mount Samat is breathtaking and ideal for spotting the fall of artillery, and the mountain was infested with observation posts.[33]

The Japanese plan to seize Mount Samat envisioned the destruction of II Corps's left flank. After capturing Mount Samat the Japanese would drive southeast to Manila Bay. Their plan was based on the incorrect belief that the Filipinos were deployed in depth with three separate lines; the first in front of Mount Samat, the second along Mount Limay, and the last near Mariveles. Cautious from his earlier repulses, and now nursing a healthy respect for the capabilities of his foe, General Homma covered all bases when he analyzed the forthcoming battle. "I do not know whether the enemy on Bataan will try to fight to the end at their first and second line, whether they will retreat back to Corregidor and fight, escape to Australia, the Visayas or Mindanao, or give up at the right time, but I still propose to prepare for the worst."[34] Homma believed it would take a month to finish the job on Bataan.

Homma's new chief of staff was more optimistic. "We had no secondary plan if we failed in our attack," recalled General Wachi. "We were confident we would not fail because our preparation was thorough. Besides, we got reinforcements from China, Japan and the southern regions. With this preparation backed by fresh troops, we believed we could take Bataan in one month."[35] Even more confident was the commander of the assault division, General Kitano of the 4th Division. He believed that once Mount Samat was taken, all that would remain would be pursuit. During planning, General Homma's intelligence officer, Lieutenant Colonel Hikaru Haba, presented his estimate of enemy strength as 25,000 men. Homma left no doubt in Haba's mind that he considered this figure too low. "Go back and estimate again," Homma told him. Properly chastised, the officer returned with a second figure of 40,000. Still not convinced, Homma developed his own figure of 60,000.[36]

To break the Filipino line, Homma planned a strong attack against Mount Samat, and he issued orders to his major commanders on March 23 during a meeting at San Fernando. For his main effort Homma detailed the newly arrived 4th Division and the reconstituted 65th Brigade. General Nara's 65th Brigade, now about up to strength, would operate west of Mount Samat. The arrival of 3,500 replacements left Nara with over 7,500 men with which to accomplish his task. The main Japanese blow would be launched at Mount Samat with two columns, both from the 4th Division. The Right Wing consisted of the 7th Tank Regiment and the 61st Infantry plus an infantry battalion from the 8th Infantry.

Homma detailed the Right Wing to seize the western half of Mount Samat. The Japanese Left Wing, composed of the 8th Infantry (-), would attack the right of Sector D held by the Philippine 21st Division. The 4th Division, with the two wings and the reserve, totalled 11,076 officers and men.[37]

Elements of the Japanese 21st Division opposite II Corps, as well as the 16th Division facing I Corps, were to launch diversionary attacks to draw forces away from the Filipino center. On March 24 General Mikami's 22nd Air Brigade would begin an intensive air attack to isolate forward units, destroy communications and command posts, and silence artillery positions. The 16th Division would begin its diversionary attacks on March 31 to pin I Corps to its fortifications and prevent dispatch of reinforcements to the center.[38]

The Japanese found no difficulty in setting the date of the attack, April 3, but H-hour posed a problem. General Kitano and his 4th Division staff argued that the attack should start before noon, for if the troops waited in assembly areas any longer than that, they would be vulnerable to artillery. General Nara, on the other hand, knew how effective Filipino artillery could be, and he wanted to avoid observed fire by attacking at dusk under the concealment offered by darkness. Both officers had good points, but when neither would budge from his position, 14th Army set 1500 hours as a compromise.[39]

After issuing the order Homma asked his chief of staff to further explain the plan. General Wachi launched into a discussion of the significance of Bataan to the war effort. Bataan was not just a local action in the larger Pacific-wide war. Rather, the three-month delay here contrasted vividly with successes in Malaya and the Dutch East Indies. The anti-Axis powers were calling world attention to this uniquely hopeful battle as the first step toward eventual victory. So for the Japanese, conquest of the Philippines would affect the attitude of American and British resistance elsewhere, especially in Australia. Victory in Bataan would play a part in evicting the enemy from all Southeast Asia. But General Wachi warned his audience that although the Filipinos lacked discipline and equipment, they hid easily and took advantage of the terrain and their artillery. Under no circumstances should Japanese commanders take reckless action when confronted by unexpected defeats. There were enough men, ammunition, and supplies to do the job.[40]

Homma now had, from east to west, the single-regiment infantry group of the 21st Division (62nd Infantry), three regiments of the 4th Division (61st, 8th, 37th), the 65th Brigade with three regiments (122nd, 141st, 142nd), and the 16th Division. "Our four [infantry] groups," reported Homma, "have been brought into line and on a front of twenty-five kilometers, ten [regimental] flags are lined up. Artillery is plentiful. There are also more than enough special guns, and supply arrangements have been prepared. Methods of penetrating the dense forests have been considered. There is no reason this attack should not succeed."[41]

As the date of the attack approached, ground activity increased. On the night of March 24 a Filipino patrol from the 41st Division took a detailed Japanese order for a reconnaissance in force in the Mount Samat area from the body of a dead Japanese officer. The American command already believed the Japanese would concentrate their efforts here, and the capture of the reconnaissance order seemed to confirm their belief. The order went into great detail about the coming attack and indicated with considerable exactitude the probable enemy plan for attack. The 21st Division had captured another document earlier in mid-March. After destroying a twelve-man Japanese patrol the Filipinos found a document that carried orders for that patrol to check the nearby Abo-Abo River, scout for possible tank approaches, check for fords, and measure the depth of the water and the slope of the banks. The enemy document followed a regular form and included a description of the terrain, report of defending forces, and the direction of the prevailing wind. Japanese interest in the direction of the wind caused consternation at American headquarters, because the Filamerican forces were extremely susceptible to a gas attack.[42]

By March 27 American intelligence officers estimated enemy forces in front of Parker's II Corps at a division. That same day Wainwright travelled to Bataan for a meeting with the principal commanders there, King, Parker and Jones, and the division commanders. The meeting was held to coordinate action to be taken when the Japanese finally attacked. The next day enemy forces had increased to four regiments supported by tanks, and by March 29 Luzon Force estimated there were five Japanese regiments in position. All this information was interesting, but its usefulness was limited. The stalwart Philippine Scouts, as well as the Americans, had lost weight down to two-thirds of normal. Although not everyone had malaria, it seemed everyone had dysentery and, without a doubt, everyone was weak. The ration was down to one-fifth, and a man could almost hold his day's food in the palm of his hand. Quinine was gone, and nothing else for malaria was available.[43]

At the end of March a desperate tone appeared in Wainwright's messages to Washington. Wainwright again emphasized his precarious supply situation; he had enough food to feed Corregidor until June 1, but he warned Marshall that Bataan's food would last only until April 15, and at that time Bataan would be starved into submission; the most critical needs were food and quinine sulfate. Soldiers were down to 1,000 calories a day, a level barely sufficient to sustain life without physical activity. Every attempt to run the blockade from Cebu for the past three weeks had failed, the last stocks of burlap had been issued for use as blankets, and spare parts for every piece of equipment could be obtained only from items turned in for salvage. Soldiers entering the hospital were discouraged and tired. Ominously, very few hesitated to surrender their weapons upon admission. Instead, they threw them in a large pile at the receiving ward. The number of patients diagnosed as not needing medical attention, diagnosed as malingerers, rose to as high as 25 percent.[44]

On March 30, in response to a message from General Marshall, Wainwright messaged Washington:

> Manila Bay approaches [are] effectively blockaded by enemy surface vessels preventing entrance our supply vessels from southern islands. Food, antiaircraft ammunition with mechanical fuse, fuel oil and gasoline situation requires emergency measures. Request assignment of at least two submarines adaptable to cargo carrying operations (Argonaut or Narwhal class) to bring the above supplies from Hawaii and remain this area to bring in food and fuel from southern islands. I make this seemingly extravagant request in view of your invitation to tell you frankly what my requirements are.[45]

Surprisingly, this was the first time the War Department received a firm count of the number of soldiers on Bataan and Corregidor. The War Department believed there was something more than 7,000 white combat troops, exclusive of airmen, and 30,000 Filipinos, figures presented to Marshall on January 3 in a memorandum concerning the fate of the garrison. But Wainwright had reported 90,000 people on Bataan alone. Washington's surprise was so great that Marshall asked for specific figures, adding that 90,000 men was greatly in excess of what Washington understood was there. Wainwright's answer to Marshall was even more surprising than his earlier message, for when all military, to include civilians and Navy personnel being fed by the Army, were totalled, the figure was 110,000 on Bataan and Corregidor.[46]

While Wainwright and Marshall exchanged messages as to the size of the garrison, the men composing that garrison began to see their fate. Hints as to the outcome filtered down the chain of command. A week before the final Japanese offensive, General Parker arrived at Sector C to brief the officers there on the situation. After a short talk Parker called General Bluemel and Captain Dobrinic aside and told them to ease up and not be so rough on their Filipino troops. Parker did not want the the Filipinos to turn on the Americans in an emergency. This was a shock to

Bluemel, for he could read between the lines. After Parker departed, Bluemel turned to Dobrinic. "It looks like the jig is up. He knows something we don't."[47]

Officers with line units could see the approaching end even easier. "I hate to get despondent over the situation," wrote Lieutenant Montgomery in his diary, "but these ill trained [men] have shot their wad. They have been on the line too long. They sneak off for days at a time. Some return and some don't. They think nothing of it."[48] The men were so weak that it now took ten days to do construction work that the Engineer Tables said should take half a day. Among the Americans a fatalistic, what-the-hell attitude developed; they shook their heads and laughed at one another in disgust. The stronger men did not feel sorry for themselves—although they did agree they had had tough luck. For the Regulars, the only bitterness came from the knowledge that the Japanese victory would be a defeat for American arms, a defeat an unknowing world would lay to the Regular Army and the Regular officers and sergeants.

By the end of March the Japanese had pushed their counter-reconnaissance screen to within a mile of Filipino lines. When Filipino observers spotted many small boats and native craft on the north shore of Manila Bay, fears grew over possible Japanese amphibious landings along the east coast. Japanese 75mm guns mounted on barges shelled the shoreline, and the amphibious threat tied up a substantial part of the American tank force. On March 28 General Homma issued his final orders, and his units started moving to attack positions. His troop movements were covered by artillery and air attacks. Thirty-nine sorties of light bombers sought targets up and down the peninsula that day. One of the installations to feel the weight of the Japanese air offensive was General Hospital Number 1, located at the old engineer camp at Little Baguio after its withdrawal from Limay in January. The location was not especially good except for cool, high ground, excellent water and electrical facilities, and some semipermanent buildings. Its most singular disadvantage was that it stood in the middle of legitimate military targets: ordnance shops, huge ammunition dumps, an antiaircraft unit, engineer headquarters, and quartermaster dumps. Doctors were worried that while aiming at these targets, Japanese pilots might miss and hit the hospital despite Red Cross flags and signs painted on roofs. It would take exceptionally fine bombing to miss the wards.[49]

On March 27 near misses by incendiaries had partially burned the enlisted men's barracks. A little after 0700 hours on March 30 the throb of approaching airplane engines swept over the wards. "The noise became louder and louder," recalled Captain Poweleit. "Just as I remarked to Captain Weinstein, 'I'll bet those S.O.B.'s drop them on the hospital', I heard the shriek of falling bombs."[50] Poweleit dropped to the floor as the bombs exploded. Lysol spilled over Poweleit and he thought it was blood. Concussion shattered practically all the windows in the operating room, and bomb fragments splintered the walls. Wards containing the patients were spared on the first pass, but fourteen Filipino orderlies died. One bomb landed near the doctors' hut and took half the house apart, a second bomb narrowly missed surgery, and the receiving ward took a near miss. Hospital personnel and walking wounded worked wildly, throwing buckets of dirt on fires.

The planes made a second pass and hit the mess, doctors' and nurses' quarters, and sundry outlying areas. In the orthopedic ward nurses cut traction ropes, and orderlies helped the patients to roll out of their beds to seek cover. Flying debris, clouds of dust, and pieces of huts sailed through the air. A third pass scored a direct hit on the patient-packed wards, and one large bomb smashed bamboo sheds, hurled tin roofs through the air, and buckled beds. Bodies and pieces of bodies lay strewn all over the area, some hanging from trees. The attack finally ended, but it was just the beginning of efforts to rescue survivors from the ruins. Blankets, mattresses, and hospital paraphernalia littered the ground and hung in shattered trees. Twenty-three men were killed and seventy-eight wounded. One bomb landed near the ward occupied by wounded Japanese prisoners but caused no losses there.[51]

When news of the bombing reached Wainwright, he messaged Washington:

> The hostile air force continues to bomb front lines and rear areas in Bataan. Base Hospital Number One in Bataan was bombed at noon today and numerous casualties resulted. This hospital is plainly marked and has been studiously avoided by the enemy air force until today. There is no question but that the attack was deliberate.[52]

For whatever comfort it may have provided, the Japanese promptly apologized over Manila Radio for the bombing, stating it had been unintentional.[53]

As early as the night of March 27 both the Filipino 21st and 41st divisions found their outposts under heavy attack. The 21st Division's outpost line was driven back into the main line, but they restored their advanced positions the next day after heavy fighting. In front of the 42nd Infantry a Japanese push the afternoon of March 28 dislodged the Filipinos, and a hastily organized counterattack using the regiment's reserve battalion failed to get off before dark. An attempt to regain the original outposts on the following day failed despite using every man available, so the outposts stabilized 300 yards forward of the main line. Wainwright realized this steady probing of his outposts was a standard indication of a coming attack, and on March 29 he alerted Washington.

> Enemy launched infantry attack against right center of our lines at 6:30 PM in Bataan accompanied by artillery shelling, bombing and strafing. Outpost line driven back. Prompt and vigorous counterattack restored the OPLR by daylight. Air raids continue against front lines and rear areas. Active patrolling in other sectors of front.[54]

Two days later Wainwright reported once more.

> Enemy again launched an attack against the right center of our front in Bataan at 7:55 PM yesterday. By repeated charges with bayonets supported by heavy mortar fire he succeeded in breaking through the OPLR. Our determined stand resulted in hand to hand fighting which blocked the hostile advance before it reached the main line of resistance.[55]

Japanese bombing continued and it made an impression. "Terrific bombing all day," wrote Major Tisdelle in his diary on March 31. "Food situation critical. Malaria cannot be controlled. Front of 42nd Infantry evacuated. OPLR pushed back and not restored."[56] And still the Japanese pressed. Sixteen bombers from the 60th Air Regiment hit artillery positions on Mount Orion, and twenty-one bombers from the 16th Air Regiment hit the 41st and 21st divisions. Spotter planes directed artillery, and reconnaissance planes snapped scores of photographs of Filipino lines. The observation balloon was active again, and American artillerymen seethed over their inability to reach it. On the night of April 1 Japanese infantry from the 65th Brigade drove most of the 41st Division's outposts all the way into the main line. Tank engines were clearly audible that evening in front of the 21st Division, and listeners also detected the noise of tractors towing heavy artillery into position. General King ordered both corps to send strong combat patrols forward to pierce the enemy screen, but the patrols were unable to force their way through.

Early the morning of April 2 heavy artillery fires fell on the remaining outposts of the 41st Division. Bamboo thickets caught fire and sent clouds of black smoke rolling around the base of Mount Samat. Most outposts fell back to the main line, and only the 41st Infantry retained its picket line. Then eighty-two Japanese light and heavy bombers planted rows of bombs amidst the Filipino infantry in front of and on Mount Samat. Both the 42nd Infantry's outpost and main lines of resistance broke and were restored only just before dark. In the early afternoon the outposts of the 41st Infantry, composed of the 2nd Battalion, were also hit and the Filipinos lost an officer and several men in the skirmish. Because the outposts were soon isolated, they received orders to withdraw. From new lines the Filipinos sniped at Japanese who showed themselves, but after just a short delay the Filipinos received additional withdrawal orders. Covered by overhead fire from the main line, they pulled back. By evening all 41st Infantry outposts were at the main line, and the Filipinos lay exhausted. "It's to be quite a push from the looks of things," Lieutenant Montgomery guessed. "We're hanging on by the skin of our teeth. A penetration has been made on our left. We'll be next I suppose."[57]

At 1900 hours the Japanese crashed into the 43rd Infantry's outpost line. Attacking behind a short mortar preparation, the first line of Japanese took casualties and went to cover under Filipino fire, but after a short respite they came again, now with their long bayonets fixed. In perfect Tagalog, the Japanese yelled to the Filipinos to stay in their foxholes where they would not be harmed. After the Japanese made two small penetrations, another line of infantrymen appeared. This group got among the Filipinos and bayoneted them as they fought from their foxholes. At 2200 hours the Japanese made a third breach and deepened the original two. After conferring with division headquarters, Colonel Salgado, Filipino commander of the 43rd Infantry, authorized a withdrawal to the main line. Telephone lines were still working, and the outposts withdrew in good order, bringing men and equipment back intact. Initial reports showed half the Filipinos as dead or missing, but by morning many stragglers filtered back to their units.[58]

The last outposts were now gone and the Japanese were in their attack positions. April 3 was about to dawn.

CHAPTER TWENTY-TWO

Good Friday, April 3

THE MORNING OF APRIL 3 SAW GENERAL NARA LOOKING SOUTH UN-
der a cloudless sky at the most important terrain in his path, the natural
corridor leading into Filipino lines cut and bordered by the Catmon and
Pantingan Rivers. His mission was to support the 4th Division's attack
and to cover its right flank. As to most Japanese who had come to Bataan,
the Philippines had taken a toll on Nara; his face was gaunt, and his
weight had dropped from a normal 150 to 110 pounds. More than half
his men were replacements new to the islands, and the remainder were
veterans wary of Filipino firepower. As Nara contemplated launching his
men at the Filipinos he felt that if he were lucky he would be controlling
his initial objective, the area west of Mount Samat, within one week. He
had more artillery than ever before, more tanks, more air, and more time
to reconnoiter and plan—time he did not have at Abucay and Trail 2.
Nara also realized the Filipinos were on their last legs physically, mentally, and materially. Despite these auspicious conditions he believed that
if his much-battered 65th Brigade hit resistance similar to earlier battles,
his three regiments would probably collapse. Nor was General Homma
especially optimistic. Even though he now had over 67,000 soldiers on
Bataan, he expected his 14th Army would need three to four weeks to
overwhelm General King's army, and he hoped to conclude the campaign before April 29, Emperor Hirohito's birthday.[1]

The Filipinos straddling General Nara's route west of Mount Samat—
the excellent north-south Trail 29 that led five miles deep into Filipino
territory and linked with several east-west trails—were part of Brigadier
General Vicente Lim's 41st Division. The commanders of the opposing
units, Nara and Lim, had been classmates at the Fort Benning Infantry

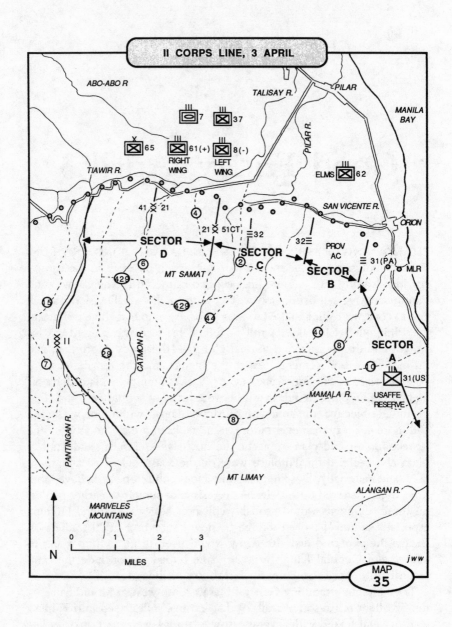

II CORPS LINE, 3 APRIL

ABO-ABO R.

TALISAY R.

PILAR

MANILA BAY

7   37

65   61(+)   8(-)
RIGHT WING   LEFT WING

PILAR R.

ELMS   62

TIAWIR R.

SAN VICENTE R.

ORION

41   21

4   21   51CT   32   32   PROV AC   31(PA)   MLR

SECTOR D   SECTOR C   SECTOR B

6   2

429

429

44   41

15   8   SECTOR A

I   II

26

7   8   31(US) USAFFE RESERVE

PANTINGAN R.

CATMON R.

MT SAMAT

MAMALA R.

MT LIMAY

ALANGAN R.

N

MARIVELES MOUNTAINS

0   1   2   3
MILES

jww

MAP 35

School in 1928; Nara remembered Lim and liked him. General Lim was sick, suffering from fevers each afternoon caused by malaria. He was also enduring a bad tooth and he refused to go to the rear to have pulled; he was afraid his men would think he was deserting them. Along the lines fronting Lim's division Japanese infantry waited in trenches or moved forward to their attack positions. Large stocks of ammunition were dug in next to each Japanese battery and artillerymen, working in un-camouflaged gun pits just out of range of the defending 75mm guns, carefully sighted their pieces on Filipino positions. The Japanese were plainly visible to American observers as they prepared for their bombard-ment, and before the view was obscured two American observers atop Mount Samat counted nineteen batteries of Japanese artillery and ten batteries of mortars. Farther east, Filipino and American observers saw additional artillery massed in support of the Japanese infantry. One hun-dred ninety-six Japanese guns were ready to shoot, of which one hundred were field or mountain artillery of not less than 75mm, and ninety-six were 120mm or larger.[2]

Lieutenant General Kishio Kitajima's artillery started registering their fires at 0900 hours and continued for sixty minutes, methodically walking their impacting shells onto target, each gun making final adjustments. Fire for effect started at 1000 hours. Opening with a barrage of World War I intensity, Japanese artillery and air plowed into outpost lines, main lines, and battalion support lines and devastated the months of painstak-ing construction work. The miles of barbed wire, trenches, foxholes, dugouts, telephone wire, artillery positions, assembly areas, supply dumps, command posts, obstacles—all so laboriously constructed—were churned and deposited in a confused and broken heap. Protective camou-flage was shredded and stripped from front line positions, trails, and motor parks.[3]

Japanese fire concentrated on a very narrow sector of II Corps's line—the heaviest against General Lough's Sector D with the 41st and 21st divisions—and shells showered down faster than they could be counted. American veterans of World War I said it was worse than anything they had ever received from the Germans, and a few artillerymen said it was heavier per yard than the American barrages of St. Mihiel and the Ar-gonne. Its severity was due in part to the narrow front at which the shells were aimed. The Japanese hoped to blow open II Corps's line with artil-lery rather than fight through it with infantry. Between 1000 hours and 1330 hours the storm of incoming artillery and aerial fires completely staggered the defenders. The noise, concussion, and emotional exhaus-tion produced by hours of fearful waiting drew the last physical reserves from the Filipino riflemen crouched in their foxholes. At 1330 hours

Japanese gunners took a half-hour break and then, upon hearing a 150mm signal gun fire at 1400 hours, resumed firing for another hour.[4]

Aircraft from Major General Kizo Mikami's 22nd Air Brigade climbed from their fields—heavy bombers from Clark, light bombers from Nichols, fighters from Zablan, reconnaissance craft from Nielson—and began dropping what would, by the end of the day, total sixty tons of bombs. From dawn to dusk an air blanket of 150 sorties immobilized defending infantry and inhibited defensive artillery with big bombs, small antipersonnel fragmentation bombs, and white phosphorous. Nimble Japanese Zeros swept down to strafe troop concentrations, while fighters and bombers concentrated on Filipino artillery which dared to reply to the overwhelming Japanese preparation. A flight of Japanese planes hovered over the location of Sector C's artillery, sixteen cannon belonging to the 31st and 51st artillery. Whenever the defending artillery fired, enemy planes immediately bombed the suspect gun position. This persistent overwatch materially inhibited counterbattery fire. Fragmentation slashing through gun positions drove cannoneers to cover, and repeated explosions cut telephone lines running from the guns to forward observers. Despite a Japanese report of intense antiaircraft fire, American 37mm and 3-inch resistance was ineffective. The gunners watched in frustration as the Japanese sailed serenely over them, just above their maximum range. The light guns picked at low-flying Japanese, but there were not enough antiaircraft batteries to discourage even faint-hearted fliers.[5]

Because of these aerial inhibitions, Filipino counterbattery fire was sporadic and light. "Hell broke loose this AM," Colonel Quintard, whose big 155mm's were outranged by the smaller Japanese 105mm's, wrote in his diary. "6 batteries opened up at 9:05 AM. Two of our batteries and OP heavily shelled, all lines to the front out, observation planes up all the time, 5 waves of bombers dropped their loads forward. It kept up all day. 'C' had over 130 rounds fall just over their position. We fired when we could but planes up from 9:00 AM until 6:00 PM and the lines out most of the time. 1 killed and 7 wounded in 'B' 86. Our OP #1 shelled and hilltop burned, at least a mile of wire burned with it and none to replace it."[6] The 41st Artillery managed to silence two batteries of enemy pack howitzers and a propaganda loudspeaker, but this was a minor achievement. Without effective counterbattery fire to distract them, Japanese artillerymen spent the day unhindered in their work.

There was no doubt in anyone's mind this was a major Japanese effort. Lieutenant Montgomery from the 1st Battalion, 41st Infantry, was on the regiment's battalion support line when the shelling started at 0900 hours, so he settled into his foxhole to wait out the attack. But instead of moderating, the barrage intensified, and Montgomery could pick out the different sounds made by mortars, artillery, and antitank rounds as they impacted nearby. "The firing would rise to a crescendo of blasting, tearing, ripping metal punctuated by the distant detonations of whole batteries firing simultaneously," Montgomery recalled. "It was like the beating of huge drums with the answering clash of cymbals."[7] By midmorning all communications forward of 41st Division regimental command posts were cut. Periodically Japanese artillery lifted to allow flights of dive bombers to come in and work, and after the planes left the artillery resumed their fire. Montgomery and his men knew they were beaten, both physically and mentally. The Filipinos were swollen from nutritional edema, and a large number were pale and anemic from repeated attacks of malaria or dysentery. Seventy-five percent of the men had been stricken by malaria, flu, or dysentery over the past month. "We had shot our wad and we knew it," Montgomery remembered. "We knew our boys could not put up much of a real fight against well-fed troops. We ourselves [Americans] were almost too weak from lack of food, constant fatigue and utter despondency to resist much longer. We had lost the will to fight."

Japanese artillery was so heavy and covered Filipino lines so completely that the natural foliage caught fire. When incendiary bombs dropped on Sector D by the 22nd Air Brigade burst in the dry leaves and bamboo, fires spread even more rapidly. Green bamboo had been lying in front of the 42nd Infantry in March and Filipino efforts to burn it to clear fields of fire had always failed. But now it caught fire. Unable to fight the raging blaze because of exploding shells, some units fled the intense heat and choking smoke. When Major Regoberto Atienza's 42nd Infantry reported they had withdrawn because of the heat, the 41st Division answered that if it was that hot, the Japanese could not advance up the hill. Division ordered the regiment to reoccupy their line when it cooled.[8]

So much red dust and grey-black smoke rose into the air that American artillery observers on Mount Samat could not see to adjust or direct defending artillery fires onto the Japanese. "We had the only point of observation that was useful, and they bombed that place," recalled Corporal Read about Mount Samat. "That mountain rocked!"[9] As the Japanese artillery preparation slammed into the main line of resistance, fragmentation cut telephone wires time and again, and wire crews trying to effect repairs were killed, driven to cover, or prevented from even starting to work. Flames ate through the rubber insulation on telephone wires, knocking out command and control nets and rendering forward observers impotent. All communications forward of 41st Division regimental command posts were cut early in the morning. Leaders resorted to messengers, but messengers used considerable time going from one point to another and had the bad habit of getting killed. So without target data coming into Filipino guns, the cannon remained mute while lucrative targets swarmed about the front lines.

In the five hours Japanese artillery and air pounded the area the Philippine 41st Division was shattered, two of its three regiments obliterated. Captain Carlos Quirino remembered these Japanese fires as the most devastating of the entire campaign. The lines of the 41st Division "resembled no man's land, for the former green vegetation and trees of the jungle had been burned to [a] crisp and only the charred stumps and trunks of trees remained in mute testimony to the severity of the barrage."[10] The short-ranged 2.95-inch howitzers of the 3rd Battalion, 41st Artillery, were neutralized in their forward positions before they could fire. Formerly well-concealed positions now lay terribly exposed and vulnerable.

Waiting for the artillery to finish, General Nara's entire 65th Brigade (minus a reinforced battalion on his right that was to pin the right of I Corps) finished massing in front of the solitary 42nd Infantry. The 42nd Infantry was physically in ruins from disease and starvation. Its 1st Battalion had only 399 men on the rolls, and of these, 125 were sick in the battalion aid station, 150 were sick but had to remain on the front line, and only 17 were fit for duty. North of the Filipinos weeks of hard tropical training in the 65th Brigade had produced competent, confident Japanese infantrymen, well-armed and by this time, well-supplied. Their confidence grew as they listened to the lengthening artillery barrage and watched walls of smoke climb over Filipino lines. The center of Nara's thrust was targeted against the junction of Trail 29 and the Pilar-Bagac Road. If Nara succeeded, Trail 29 would take his men south up one of the large ridges running north off Mariveles Mountain, the ridge bordered on the west by the Pantingan River and on the east by the Catmon River. Five miles south, Trail 29 connected with the critical east-west Trail 8, the main lateral route in II Corps's rear. Nara's men now waited patiently to enter Trail 29, and when the artillery shifted south at 1500 hours, light tanks from the 7th Tank Regiment led them men against the 42nd Infantry.[11]

The 42nd Infantry's main line of resistance lay behind the steep banks of the Tiawir River and was considered by the Filipinos as impregnable. Even the Japanese planned to halt after reaching the junction because they expected to encounter stiff resistance here. But the results of the tremendous artillery barrage and aerial bombing were soon obvious; both the 42nd and 43rd infantry, in most part, had dissolved, and Nara's 65th Brigade was so unopposed that they continued south. By nightfall the Japanese were 1,000 yards deep in the defensive works. The 42nd Infantry's American senior instructor, Colonel Ronald G. MacDonald, assigned to the regiment just two days earlier as a replacement for Colonel Atkinson who was evacuated to the hospital with dysentery, lay dead with many of his men, and the regiment he had just joined was shattered and in flight. Some soldiers of the 42nd Infantry had eyes so coated with dirt they could not see, and as they retreated, they walked off trails and bumped into trees. By overrunning the 42nd Infantry's abandoned main line, the Japanese gained entrance to the first of three excellent north-south trails, Trail 29.[12]

Nara's accomplishment, although spectacular, was not the major Japanese effort of April 3. Only one mile east of Nara's 65th Brigade was the Right Wing of Lieutenant General Kenzo Kitano's 4th Division, the division tasked with the major ground effort of the offensive. The Right Wing, led by the 4th Division's Infantry Group commander, Major General Kureo Taniguchi, and composed of the reinforced 61st Infantry and tanks, was targeted against Trail 6—the second of the three north-south trails. General Taniguchi hoped to cut into the junction between the 41st and 21st divisions. The Right Wing was expected to rupture the Filipino main line and gain access to Trail 6 over which it could exploit the rupture. After the artillery lifted off the main line at 1500 hours and shifted south, the 61st Infantry, reinforced by a battalion from the 8th Infantry and spearheaded by twenty-five tanks from the 7th Tank Regiment, passed over the largely abandoned main line of resistance of the 43rd Infantry. A few surviving Filipino machine gunners from the 43rd Infantry, stunned by the shelling and showing their inexperience, rattled away at the tanks, but the tanks took the Filipino strong points apart with deliberate, well-aimed 47mm cannon fire, projectiles that burst on Filipino positions before the cannon's report arrived.[13]

Machine guns alone had not been expected to fight tanks here, but the two American antitank guns placed on the line the night of April 2 to cover Trail 6 had long since been reduced by Japanese artillery. Private Leon O. Beck from the 31st Infantry was in the crew that dug in one 37mm gun, sandbagged it, and concealed it, but to no avail. Japanese artillery drove the gunners to cover, destroyed both guns, and smashed trucks and kitchen vehicles farther to the rear and presumably in defilade. By mid-afternoon the Americans were in retreat without having had a chance to fire a single round. Nowhere in the 43rd Infantry's sector did the Japanese receive anything more than sporadic fire. The line broke before 1530 hours and by 1700 hours the last of the 43rd Infantry, with losses approaching 500 men and the survivors completely shell-shocked, had cleared the area. Japanese tanks that passed over the empty positions of the 43rd Infantry and the shattered left flank battalion of the 21st Division were taken under fire by Filipino artillery directed from observers on Mount Samat's western slopes. The guns scored several hits but the fire did not stop the tanks. Showing little concern, the tanks continued on their way.[14]

With the 42nd Infantry destroyed and the 43rd Infantry routed, the 41st Division command post pulled up and retreated. Colonel Fortier and his headquarters personnel found Mt. Samat's trails filled with the most hopelessly shocked personnel they had ever seen. Whenever a 41st Division officer tried to stop and reorganize the fleeing men, he was met with blank stares and complete apathy. Two of Lim's regiments were now destroyed, and the only one to survive, the 800-man 41st Infantry on the division's left, began the evening by marching away from the battle because of misunderstood orders.[15]

The 41st Infantry had missed the brunt of Japanese fires, but there were still plenty of problems. Wire lines to the 2nd Battalion of the 42nd Infantry to the right went out at 1030 hours, and runners sent from the regiment's command post to that battalion failed to return. Wire lines to the 2nd Philippine Constabulary to the left were cut at 1430 hours, repaired under heavy fire, and cut again. About 1400 hours the 41st Infantry received word from the 42nd Infantry that division headquarters had ordered all regiments to retire "to the rear." Although this order was not valid, it was in line with earlier discussions between Colonels Wetherby and Fortier, that is, the 41st Infantry should withdraw south on Trail 29 to rejoin the division if the regiment ever got cut off and had to retreat. But that was not what Colonel Fortier wanted. He had sent a message by two runners, ten minutes apart, to the 41st Infantry, telling them that the rest of the Division was withdrawing on Limay and for them to attach themselves to the right flank of the 11th Division and protect it. Fortier did not want the 41st Infantry to leave the main line, he only wanted them to understand they were now to protect the 11th Division's right flank, but Fortier's runners apparently never reached Colonel Wetherby. The only information Wetherby received was unofficial and garbled, and that information indicated all regiments should withdraw.[16]

By this time Wetherby's right flank units were pinned down by Japanese fire, and he could not raise the 42nd Infantry by either wire, radio, or runners. Enemy air was prowling overhead, enemy tanks were active off to the right, and Filipino losses were high all across the regiment's front. Then at 1630 hours, as disorganized elements of the 42nd Infantry passed through Wetherby's rear areas, local security near the regiment's command post reported Japanese advancing only a quarter of a mile away to the right rear. At 1730 hours Wetherby sent runners to the battalions with orders to withdraw just before sunset to the regimental reserve line; he hoped to get there before the Japanese arrived in force. There, strong bunkers had been prepared for machine guns, and the regiment could make a stand. Covered by a thin line of skirmishers thrown out to the north and east, the regiment picked its way back to the reserve line.[17]

It was getting dark as the men filed into their new positions. "I showed them their places and collared several who tried to keep on toward the rear," recalled Lieutenant Montgomery from the 1st Battalion. "While I stayed close to the phone, [Captain] Sparks got them into position, supervised the handling of ammo boxes and showed them where to set the machine guns. There was an air of frantic haste, some confusion and a babble of frightened conversation."[18] Barely had Montgomery's men settled into the reserve line than they received Wetherby's orders to withdraw at once along the Pantingan Corridor. Montgomery asked for some verification that the message was authentic, and the telephone caller identified himself as being from regimental headquarters. Montgomery refused to accept the order, for not only was he a very junior officer, he considered the order insane. His men had a good position, and although they were in no condition to fight, they were at least in position and there was no one else available to take their place. Montgomery called another officer to the phone who recognized the caller's voice and accepted the order.

But the early evening march of the regiment away from Trail 29-429 was a mistake. "We just walked off and left the whole front line for the Nips to swallow up without a shot," Montgomery lamented. "No sooner did we arrive at the proper place about 3 AM than a courier in a command car came racing down the road and ordered us back into our positions."[19] The regiment milled in confusion after first meeting Colonel Juan Moran from the 11th Division who told them they were now attached to his division. Then, shortly after 0330 hours, Colonel Robert J. Hoffman, G3 for Section D, found the 41st Infantry, stated that previous withdrawal orders were wrong, and ordered the regiment back to its reserve line. But it was too late, for the Japanese had partially occupied those positions.

Through the efforts of Nara's 65th Brigade, the 42nd Infantry had been destroyed and the 41st Infantry pried off the main and reserve lines. Through the efforts of the 4th Division's Right Wing, the 43rd Infantry had been routed. But the day's damage was not confined to the 41st Division. East of the 41st Division the left flank of Brigadier General Mateo Capinpin's 21st Division also felt the weight of Japanese artillery and subsequently the Right Wing. Communications within the division's left flank two-battalion 21st Infantry—with less than 1,000 men at the start of the day—were disrupted within an hour of the start of the artillery barrage. Bombing and shelling shattered the 21st Infantry's left flank battalion. The American officers could not keep their Filipinos in place, and starting about 1330 hours, still under artillery fire, the men scrambled from their positions and headed for the rear. After a great deal of persuasion, most of them stopped at the regimental reserve line.[20]

When Lieutenant Colonel Velasco at the 21st Infantry's command post learned at 1600 hours of the rout of the 41st Division, he passed this information to his division headquarters. Division ordered the 21st Infantry to remain in place and promised a counterattack would recover the lost ground. But despite the order to hold and the promise of a counterattack, the regiment's right flank battalion, watching disaster overtake its sister battalion just to the west, had to refuse its left flank by pulling those men west of the Catmon River off the main line and repositioning them on the east bank of the river facing northwest. Disorganized parties from the 43rd Infantry stumbled into 21st Infantry lines, but once there were of little use. The regimental senior instructor, Colonel William A. Wappenstein, succeeded in collecting part of his left flank battalion and placed them behind the Catmon River after tying them to his right flank battalion.[21]

Despite efforts by men such as Colonel Wappenstein, the Japanese Right Wing was now on Trail 6, the second of three north-south trails leading into the heart of II Corps and toward the important east-west Trail 8. Trail 6 ran just west of Mount Samat, and if II Corps failed to block the route, the Japanese could simply march past the most important piece of terrain in the area. All across the front Japanese successes exceeded their most optimistic expectations. With recent memories of stubborn resistance at Abucay, Trail 2, the Pockets and the Points, Japanese officers found it almost inconceivable for the advance to have proceeded so smoothly. The Japanese can thank the weight of their artillery and air for this auspicious beginning. After five hours of cannonading, bombing, and strafing, and after being burned out of their positions by brush fires, the starved and sick soldiers of the 42nd and 43rd infantry broke and fled in absolute disorder. In January and February stragglers had kept their arms and equipment and could be rallied and returned to the front. But on April 3 stragglers kept neither arms nor equipment, and only force could return them to their units; the men were surly and physically exhausted.[22]

When General Parker at II Corps learned of the rout of the 41st Division and the big break in his left flank late in the afternoon, he committed his corps reserve, Major Stanley "Stan-the-Man" Holmes's 33rd Infantry (less the 1st Battalion). Parker sent the Filipinos to his battered Sector D, and at dusk General Lough led them out of reserve, west along Trail 429, and onto Trail 6 where they marched north. Because the two-battalion 33rd Infantry counted hardly more than 600 men—all mentally drained and physically exhausted even though they avoided the day's artillery bombardment—Major Holmes ordered his two battalion commanders to bring every man strong enough to walk; he needed everyone he could muster. Lieutenant Robert M. Chapin's 3rd Battalion had 300 soldiers, of which 100 were about to be left behind, until Chapin received the order to bring everyone who could get out of bed. Captain Lloyd M. Buchel's 2nd Battalion was in similar shape. The night was quite dark but it quickly became apparent that there were large numbers of men going south. The 33rd Infantry thought these men were part of the counterattack. But as more and more men, leaderless, without weapons, and unresponsive to questions, jammed the trail, they slowed the march of the 33rd Infantry. With difficulty, the 33rd Infantry shouldered its way through these stragglers until reaching Trail 6. Here the flow of leaderless men suddenly stopped. After marching north for another mile, Major Holmes found a platoon of 41st Division engineers constructing tank obstacles, so he deployed his men in depth, one battalion behind the other, and waited for dawn. For the moment, Trail 6 was corked.[23]

In the 21st Division a five-party phone call between regimental commanders and division staff resulted in the designation of new lines. Division warned the 23rd Infantry to watch for Japanese from the west. General Lough arrived at the 21st Division where he found General Lim and Colonel Fortier. Lim felt there was a chance to salvage the 43rd Infantry and use it the next day, so Lough ordered Fortier to find and reorganize the regiment, an attempt Fortier knew was doomed. Colonels Fortier and Lewis worked all night collecting survivors of both the 42nd and 43rd infantry, assembled some of the men, and tried to calm them. By 0430 hours they had gathered several hundred Filipinos and gave them hot coffee before trying to move them back to the front. But suddenly a Japanese artillery concentration rained down about their ears and scattered the demoralized men to the four winds. To Fortier and Lewis it was a crushing end to a night of sleepless labor.[24]

General Lough had a good idea of the disaster overtaking the 41st Division, and on the night of April 3 he told II Corps that the 42nd and 43rd infantry had disintegrated, that the 41st Infantry had withdrawn, that the 33rd Infantry was digging in, and that the Japanese would probably attack to the southeast the next day to roll up the defenders. II Corps, however, discounted Lough's report, feeling that the 41st Division had safely reached its regimental reserve line with all three regiments.[25]

Although American spirits were low, the Japanese were exhilarated by the first day's progress. "The troops made slow, hazardous, but steady progress through the enemy's brilliantly organized maze of field fortifications, wire, minefields, and obstacles constituting the main line of resistance. Mutually supporting strong points covered the steep jungle hills, each point organized to take maximum advantage of the terrain. Flanks were cleverly bent back along natural obstacles and there were many alternate positions to lend fluidity to the defense. But the weeks of training in the rear had benefited the troops, and on the first day the enemy was driven from the forward part of the main line of resistance."[26] The toll exacted from the Japanese by the Filipinos on the first day was minimal, and losses never caused the Japanese even the slightest concern.

Wainwright likewise reviewed the progress of the day's fight in his first report to Washington on April 3.

> Bombing and strafing of front line troops and rear areas in Bataan continues with unabated fury. In addition enemy artillery put down what appeared to be heavy preparatory fire for a period of over three hours. The degree and intensity of the artillery fire indicated that an attack would follow but none has developed.[27]

As the afternoon progressed and more information became available, Wainwright realized that the enemy was seriously pressing his line.

> Enemy launched attack late afternoon 3d April against right center of front lines. Enemy succeeded in forcing our troops back to regimental reserve line on a frontage of 4,000 yards. Pressure is being maintained by the enemy. Hostile landings attempted on east coast of Bataan accompanied by 75mm fire from barges during the night. Enemy boats forced to withdraw at 1:00 AM by our artillery fire.[28]

CHAPTER TWENTY-THREE

Saturday, April 4

"I AM UTTERLY OPPOSED, UNDER ANY CIRCUMSTANCES OR CONDI-tions, to the ultimate capitulation of this command," MacArthur radioed Washington on April 1st. "If it is to be destroyed it should be on the actual field of battle taking full toll from the enemy."[1] MacArthur then outlined a plan for Luzon Force if food or ammunition failed; he called for an artillery preparation and a feint in I Corps combined with a sudden surprise attack by II Corps, using full tank and artillery strength. The language describing the attack was astonishing and totally unrealistic when compared to the plight of the men expected to execute it. MacArthur expected II Corps to seize the Dinalupihan-Olongapo Road and "thrust with all speed and force due west taking the enemy's Subic Bay positions in reverse simultaneously with a frontal attack by the I Corps." MacArthur, no doubt impressed by the audacity of his plan, had not yet passed it to Wainwright, for he feared that the plan might shake Wainwright's morale and determination.

Why MacArthur considered this plan feasible now when he did not try it himself in February when conditions were more propitious cannot easily be explained. His own message of January 23 to Marshall stated that with his occupation of the Orion-Bagac Line, "all maneuvering possibilities will cease."[2] MacArthur's remoteness from the suffering of Bataan's soldiers may have dimmed his awareness of their true physical condition, but it does not excuse what he did next. In an incredible slap at Wainwright, MacArthur, believing more food existed than Wainwright mentioned, told Washington. "It is of course possible that with my departure the rigor of application of conservation may have relaxed."[3] Maybe Mac-

487

Arthur realized his plan would fail, and maybe he raised it solely to prevent surrender and, in his words, "take full toll from the enemy."

On April 4 MacArthur sent his plan to Wainwright. The operation was to be executed only when food and ammunition stocks were exhausted. He told Wainwright that if the operation were successful, the supplies Wainwright might seize at Olongapo could solve the food situation. The breakout would allow the army to operate in central Luzon where food could be obtained and where "Bataan and the northern approaches to Corregidor could be protected."[4] Finally, MacArthur flatly ordered that the command should not be surrendered. The War Department concurred with MacArthur's surrender declaration. Any action, including complete destruction, seemed preferable to surrender.

At daybreak on April 4 thirty-four low-flying twin-engine bombers concentrated on the 41st Division's front, bombing and strafing the lines, while another forty-five heavies hit Mount Orion and Mount Samat with some propaganda leaflets thrown in with the high explosive. Results of the April 3 efforts had proved so satisfactory to the Japanese that more of the same was the order of the day. Instead of adhering to their originally cautious plan, the Japanese advanced their schedule and resumed the attack with another devastating artillery barrage. The first projectiles rumbled over the 33rd Infantry and thumped with killing power into the already demoralized 42nd and 43rd infantry. During the artillery attack, and before the Japanese could come to grips with what remained of the two regiments, the Filipinos stampeded to the rear. All attempts to rally and return the men to their units proved futile. Their officers could not stop them, and the men rushed south as fast as they could. Before the Japanese infantry even stood up to advance, General Lough's Sector D lost a major portion of the force placed there to stop the anticipated breakthrough.[5]

The only 41st Division regiment still intact was the 41st Infantry, and it was in the process of trying to reoccupy its reserve line after a full night of march and countermarch. Shortly after 0930 hours, the 65th Brigade hit the front and right of the 41st Infantry and pushed the Filipinos to positions 600 yards behind their regimental reserve line. Air attacks were heavy, and in one strike bombs killed six Filipinos and wounded nine more. As casualties flowed into the aid station, the medical section working on Trail 29 was bombed and several patients and medics killed. The 41st Infantry remained here until threatened from the right rear at 1700 hours when they again retreated, this time nearly a thousand yards, and by doing so, shuffled themselves out of position to stop further Japanese advances. They were now backed into I Corps and unable to prevent the Japanese from moving down Trail 29.[6]

In the sector held by the 21st Division another heavy artillery strike hit the 1,200-man 23rd Infantry and the left of the 1,300-man 22nd Infantry. The firing started at 0630 hours and continued for two hours. "The artillery was so concentrated it was as if they were planting rice," remembers Lieutenant Avelino Battad in H Company, 23rd Infantry.[7] Tanks of the Japanese 7th Tank Regiment joined the battle at 0830 hours and bowled back the shaken 21st Infantry slashed, behind the right battalion of the 21st Infantry, and then cut behind the 23rd Infantry's main line. Spreading out, the tanks overran positions, crushed men in their trenches, and shot at everyone in sight, even the wounded. Without antitank guns or mines to bother them, and with the Filipinos so exhausted they could hardly shoot their rifles from their foxholes, the Japanese roamed freely and contemptuously through rear areas. The 21st Infantry retreated in disorder to relative safety behind the 23rd Infantry which refused its left flank with its reserve battalion.

But the 23rd Infantry would not hold for long. At 0900 hours the Japanese Left Wing—composed of the 8th Infantry (-) and tanks—crossed the Tiawir River in front of the 23rd Infantry and positioned itself for an attack scheduled for later in the day. At 1000 hours the Filipinos, threatened by tanks from the Right Wing in their rear and this strong new infantry force of the Left Wing to their front, retreated. "We were entirely routed," remembered Lieutenant Battad. "We tried to get out of the artillery beaten zone. Most of our men were out of control. We abandoned our machine guns."[8] They were soon followed by the 22nd Infantry, the last regiment to leave the main line of resistance in Sector D. "Artillery barrage continued," recalled the 22nd Infantry's commander, Lieutenant Colonel Joaquin Esperito. "Men 10 yards away could not be seen because of dust caused by barrage and bombing! Fire broke out at the battalion reserve line. Ammunition dumps were burning. Left flank fully exposed because 23rd Infantry, and other units on the left, left their positions."[9]

The attack of the Japanese 4th Division, which subsequently overran what remained of the 21st Division, was originally scheduled to start at 1200 hours, but Colonel Gempachi Sato's right flank 61st Infantry had not advanced far enough the day before and spent the morning of April 4th mopping up scattered Filipinos. When the 61st Infantry reported they could not attack at 1200 hours, the 4th Division issued orders to delay the attack one hour. But owing to heavy Filipino fires on the 4th Division's left flank, communications were out and the tactical elements did not receive the order to wait until well past 1200 hours. So they started forward a little after noon—as originally planned—and closed with the abandoned Filipino defenses at 1230 hours, just in time to be hit by their own artillery which believed the attack would start at 1300 hours. Although fired at by both sides, the Japanese suffered few casualties and were convinced they took the Filipino positions with fewer losses than if there had been no artillery.[10]

Retiring before the enemy's advance, the Filipinos retreated to reserve and switch positions facing north and northwest. The 23rd Infantry tried to extend its left flank up the slopes of Mount Samat to block the trails while 180 survivors of the twice-battered 21st Infantry tried to reform behind the 22nd Infantry. By midnight, enemy activity had cost the 22nd Infantry fifty killed and sixty wounded and had pushed them past the regimental reserve line into the trenches occupied by the battered 21st Infantry. Colonel Jacob E. Uhrig, 22nd Infantry instructor, phoned the division command post to report the retreat of his regiment. Shortly after the call, Colonel Wappenstein entered the headquarters, learned the situation, and decided to go forward to help. Colonel O'Day watched him go, wishing he could have kept Uhrig at the command post, but realizing that the battle required as many steady hands as possible on the firing line.[11]

By nightfall the 4th Division's Right Wing reached the northern foothills of Mount Samat. This penetration was very, very serious. "If we lose our CP [actually OP] on Mt. Samat we are finished," a Luzon Force artillery officer realized.[12] Only the Filipino 33rd Infantry, somewhat forgotten by the Japanese on Mount Samat's western slopes, passed April 4 in relative peace. Although Major Holmes sent out patrols to the north, east, and west, he gained little idea of the situation. He could not place much weight in information brought in by the Filipinos, for the men were exhausted and demoralized. Significant courage and stamina is needed to pick one's way over jungle trails far beyond friendly lines, and such courage was just too much to expect at this point in the battle. Radio and telephone contact with higher headquarters still existed and trucks delivered food and medical supplies, yet despite these small contacts, the plight of the regiment was bad. Sickness was beyond the point where soldiers were simply hungry and ill; they were now dying in their foxholes before any Japanese even appeared! "Morale was not so good," recalled Lieutenant Chapin. "They seemed to sense that the end was close. That night Jap flares went up on all sides of our position."[13]

On the morning of April 4 General King began committing his Luzon Force reserves. At 1000 hours, King gave II Corps part of this reserve, the American 31st Infantry. King also directed the 45th Infantry (less 1st Battalion), then in I Corps reserve, to march east to II Corps, a march that would move the regiment across the Pantingan River to Trail Junction 29 and 8. By late afternoon King ordered his reserve 57th Infantry to move at night into the now-empty 31st Infantry bivouac near the Lamao River for easier subsequent movement into II Corps. "Hope we all come back," wrote an officer in his diary.[14] The Scouts were still a cohesive fighting force, men who never complained. They had built an excellent reputation by destroying the landings along the west coast, and they strutted around proudly and could even trade their 57th Infantry insignia to other soldiers for food. But now, on April 4, their American officers could see the unspoken question in their eyes, "What in the world have you done to us?"[15]

As early as 1900 hours on the first day of battle on April 3 the 31st Infantry had been alerted and ready to move. II Corps had already warned the Americans that in case they were released by Luzon Force to the Corps, the regiment was to move after dark to a bivouac at Trail Junction 2 and 10. Luzon Force released them for the march, but they were not to be committed without Luzon Force's permission. Under the concealment of darkness the American regiment bused to the vicinity of Trails 2 and 10 from where it could move to almost any spot in II Corps's line. But the infantrymen were in bad shape, weakened by malaria and starvation. On the morning of April 4, after King had released the regiment to II Corps, General Parker released the Americans to General Lough in Sector D where the Japanese threat was the gravest. At 1600 hours the regiment received orders to march north that night to the San Vicente River. A regimental staff officer assured the men that if they could hold the enemy for ten days, they would be evacuated to Australia. He promised that massive help was on the way including air and tank support. Not easily convinced, the soldiers asked instead for a good meal, but all they received was rice flavored with brown mule-and-horse-meat gravy. Then the men collected their gear.[16]

In preparation for the move each company screened its men and culled those who could not march. The soldiers heard that a fever of 104 degrees was required before anyone was excused. Approximately twenty men were removed from each company, about one-fifth of the regiment's rifle strength. The men left behind included the 2nd Battalion's commander, Lieutenant Colonel Cyril Q. Marron. Then, in the deepening gloom of evening, an ominous, sporadic banging, M-1 rifle fire, floated up from the hills and ravines occupied by the Americans. Three men from A Company shot themselves to avoid going north. In the 2nd Battalion, Captain Hibbs and his medical detachment heard some isolated shots. They quickly learned that they had a minor epidemic of self-inflicted wounds. Medics in the 3rd Battalion treated two self-inflicted wounds. As Private Snyder recalled, "These men had just been through so much that I'm surprised we had only two cases in the entire 3rd Battalion."[17]

After the riflemen each drew six extra bandoleers of M-1 rifle ammunition, they shouldered their gear—full packs, blanket rolls, gas masks—and, at 2000 hours, treked north away from Trail Junction 2 and 8. One of the men left behind was Private Garleb. Lying on a stretcher, he heard the noise of men lifting their equipment and the subdued rattle of infantrymen on the march, but the sounds had no significance to Garleb; he had a high temperature, and he was not interested. Even after screening the men before starting, the regiment stopped frequently and removed those men who could not keep up. Buddies propped them against trees, handed them their rifles, and marched on. Those who continued could not figure where they found the strength. As the regiment snaked along Trail 2 toward the San Vicente River, they found the trail nearly blocked by a mass of wounded, weaponless, barefoot Filipinos. When several Americans asked the Filipinos where they were going, the answers were unintelligible. Efforts to turn them northward were fruitless.[18]

The trail over which the Americans walked was narrow, rough, and walled in on both sides by heavy brush. In nearly zero visibility the tired men shuffled and stumbled over the uneven ground as intermittent rain showers pelted the dusty, caked khakis worn so long without replacement. A garish lightning and thunderstorm over the South China Sea started a rumor that a naval engagement was in progress. The regiment finally stopped just before midnight at an abandoned bivouac and remained there until the next afternoon. Ever after stopping, sleep was not sound; single and twin-engine Japanese planes were experimenting with night nuisance raids. The pilots were normally blinded by searchlights and dropped their bombs at random, but the noise kept the men from sleeping soundly.[19]

The situation at the close of April 4 was glum. In II Corps the destruction of the 41st Division opened the terrain west of Mount Samat to the Japanese. The 21st Division had lost one full battalion, two regiments were crippled, and everyone was at or behind the deepest reserve line. One day ahead of schedule the Japanese were in position to assault their main objective, Mount Samat, and Wainwright was starting to lose control of the battle. In his report of the day's activities, he claimed the Japanese had failed to gain any ground.[20]

CHAPTER TWENTY-FOUR

Easter Sunday, April 5

DURING THE NIGHT THE JAPANESE REGROUPED AND RESUPPLIED their men. When General Taniguchi took his tanks and an infantry battalion from the 61st Infantry and repositioned them farther east with the Left Wing, the weight of the Japanese effort shifted to the left. The Left Wing thereby became the main striking force for the 4th Division. The reserve regiment of the 4th Division, the 37th Infantry, assembled behind the Left Wing's 8th Infantry, and everyone spent the early morning hours of April 5 preparing to push down Trail 4. Morale was good.[1]

The Filipinos and Americans were less sanguine. "Sunday, April 5th, 1942, Easter Sunday, and I'm a sick child," wrote Lieutenant Montgomery in his diary. "My head is splitting and I've been running all night with dysentary [sic]. Mostly I'm just exhausted mentally and physically. . . . I'm jumpy as a cat. . . . I'm going to try to get some rest in the next couple of days. I can't go on this way. I'll crack up. The whole situation is very bad and the boys are leaving by squads."[2]

"Easter, and a very discouraging one," wrote Colonel Quintard as he reviewed the status of his artillery regiment. Until April 3, defending artillery had suffered surprisingly few losses. Despite bombing, artillery fire, and aerial reconnaissance as low as 200 feet, and despite aerial adjustment of Japanese fires and fragments that scarred every cannon on Bataan, the guns continued to fire. But now the defenders were starting to lose terrain on which the artillerymen depended for observation. Quintard's men had abandoned their observation post on Mount Samat the evening of April 4 and had lost all their equipment. D Battery was moving and unable to shoot, and the telephone line to C Battery was broken. "We have only two batteries which can shoot and both of them have been shelled and bombed heavily several times."[3]

Forward of Colonel Quintard's 155mm cannon the morning dawned with a serious atmosphere for the men of the 21st Division. They lay directly in the path of the recently reinforced Japanese Left Wing, and worse yet, the Filipinos were starting the morning without reserves. The proposed counterattack of the American 31st Infantry set for the next day held some hope, but the question remained, could the 21st Division hold until the arrival of the Polar Bears. The question was on the mind of the division staff, but no one voiced it. In an attempt to hedge their bets, the division clearing station, quartermaster dumps, and extra equipment began an early move toward Trail 8.[4]

At first light, Japanese artillery fired a pre-assault barrage, catching some soldiers attending Easter services. Japanese fire direction procedures had been smoothed and improved over the past two days, and the gunners and forward observers had gained valuable experience. Fifty-six light bombers savaged Filipinos around Mount Samat, and eighty-one heavies swamped Mount Orion and Mount Samat with strings of bombs. Results of Sunday's fire were not disappointing. At 1000 hours the Japanese Left Wing moved to the attack. The infantrymen, too, had gained experience over the previous two days, and the Japanese were confident because there had been so few losses and little determined resistance. Unexpectedly, and to the surprise of both Japanese and Filipinos, the morning attack floundered. The 21st Division's right flank, bolstered by two battalions of the 41st Artillery firing from Mount Samat's southern slopes, offered strong resistance. Filipino artillerymen stood fast and battered the Japanese. Gunners opened box after box of ammunition and sent round after round of 75mm and 2.95-inch whistling at the enemy. The impacting artillery repeatedly broke up enemy concentrations, including a 25-tank and infantry force on the Pilar-Bagac Road, disorganized the assault formations, and pinned the Japanese far short of their objective on Trail 4. Additional Filipino artillery fires rolled in from pieces shooting from Mount Capot and Mount Orion, fires so effective that Colonel Hiromi Oishi described Filipino efforts here as "the fiercest combat of the second Bataan campaign."[5] Dodging exploding shells, Japanese leaders urged their men forward in the belief that the loss of Mount Samat would collapse Filipino resistance.

They were correct. The Japanese of the less-harassed Right Wing were not to be denied. They started a steady, exhausting climb up Mount Samat and threatened the hard-firing artillery. Few Filipino infantrymen opposed them, for the 41st Division had disintegrated two days earlier, and efforts to throw a line in front of Mount Samat with 21st Division soldiers had failed. All too soon, Captain Jones of the 41st Artillery reported one of his batteries was under attack, and he begged the 21st Division for help. Before General Capinpin's men could organize a relief effort, firing increased around the artillerymen and the Japanese shot up a truck and killed the driver. A platoon of the 21st Division atop Mount Samat reported the Japanese were rushing their position. Then communications with the artillery were lost. The cannon, laboriously hauled yard by yard into position over rough trails or pulled up creeks and ravines by carabao, could not be saved. Some batteries continued to fire until charged and captured. In other units, artillerymen pushed their cannon over cliffs, destroyed equipment, and tried to make their way south. After the 4th Division's Right Wing secured the top of the mountain, they made remaining artillery positions untenable, and by 1630 hours the 1st and 2nd battalions, 41st Artillery, were in full flight. Filipino fires that had been holding the Japanese in check and encouraging Filipino infantry stuttered to a halt. The loss of the mountain alarmed the 21st Division headquarters, and the men quietly gathered their equipment in case a quick move became necessary. The Division headquarters organized patrols and sent them up Mount Samat on a reconnaissance and as a screen for the command post.[6]

Relieved of the galling Filipino artillery fire, the Japanese Left Wing resumed its advance and forced the faltering 21st Division to retreat. The Right Wing, after pausing to savor their accomplishment and the tremendous view from atop Mount Samat, continued down the southern slopes and at 1630 hours fell upon the 21st Division's command post, completely surprising the occupants and routing the Filipinos. Captain Sequiyo, commanding the 21st Division Signal Company, was on a telephone when the Japanese burst into the area, firing at his hut. Sequiyo fought back, killed six Japanese, and escaped down Trail 429. General Capinpin evaded the Japanese in the first few minutes and met Colonel O'Day in the thick jungle. O'Day wanted to keep out of sight and work west toward Trail 6. "I slipped into the stream bed which paralleled the trail [64] and the group followed me. . . . At the abandoned 41st Engineer campsite, an eerie sight, the General said, 'I don't like this; let's go south through the woods.' "[7]

But O'Day disagreed, he wanted to stay near telephone wire and keep in touch with Sector headquarters while setting up a new command post. O'Day moved onto a road, tapped into the telephone wire, and told Sector D that the 21st Division would try to set the command post at the Junction of Trails 6 and 64. During the subsequent move to the new location General Capinpin disappeared. He was in poor physical condition and was captured during the march. Later, harassed soldiers of the

21st Division heard the Japanese call out, "You might as well give up, since we've got your general."[8] Reestablished a half hour later, the command post was again forced to decamp at the approach of more Japanese. Attempts to rally or locate units of the division proved futile. Men flowed to the rear, claiming they were looking for the hospital or for their companies. When the last intact battalion of the 41st Artillery supporting the 21st Division fled and left their guns to the enemy, the 21st Division ceased to exist.

Having routed the 21st Division, the Japanese now turned their attention to the left flank of General Bluemel's Sector C. Japanese planes bombed the 51st Combat Team's command post six times, killed the operations officer, blew down bamboo huts, and disrupted communications. The shaken Filipino infantry then heard tanks in the direction of the Pilar-Bagac Road. When the first of four tanks pushed out of the underbrush and up the edge of the road, an old M1916 37mm antitank gun just east of Trail 2 fired and hit the tank, damaged it, and forced it back under cover. Firing from concealment, Japanese tanks retaliated with a dozen rounds and wounded two American gunners. A second American gun shifted position to join the fight, but the enemy tanks were gone by the time it arrived.[9]

As the noon hour passed, units to the left of Bluemel continued to withdraw and dissolve. Twice, Bluemel phoned II Corps and requested permission to form a new line on the east bank of the San Vicente River, but II Corps withheld permission. Instead, II Corps told Bluemel to withdraw only the left of the 51st Combat Team while maintaining contact with the shattered 21st Division. The job of moving the Filipinos through the dense jungle while retaining control proved an almost impossible task, but by late afternoon the 51st Combat Team was behind the Pilar River just west of Trail 2.[10]

When Bluemel received a telephone call at 1500 hours from General Lough commanding Sector D, he heard only bad news. Lough told Bluemel that he had lost contact with the 33rd Infantry and that both the 21st and 41st divisions were "practically gone."[11] Realizing the futility of maintaining contact with the nonexistent 21st Division, Bluemel once again asked to withdraw to the San Vicente River, and once again II Corps denied permission. After this call, Colonel Jasper Brady, commanding the American 31st Infantry, visited Bluemel's headquarters and explained that his regiment would attack at 0600 hours the next day to restore the 21st Division's regimental reserve line. Bluemel assured Brady that when the Americans drew abreast of the 51st Combat Team, the Filipinos would also advance and reoccupy their old positions. The two officers made arrangements for Bluemel's artillery to fire at 0545 hours the next morning to support the Americans. Two 21st Artillery battalions left their beach defenses to backstop the right of the Corps line, and the 2nd Battalion, 88th Artillery, began a march out of I Corps into II Corps to support Bluemel.

On this day Wainwright decided to take a firsthand look at the Bataan situation. Along with his aide, Major Dooley, Wainwright crossed the strip of water separating Bataan from Corregidor, landed at Cabcaben, and caught a jeep for the drive to Luzon Force headquarters. He talked first to General King to see what chances MacArthur's last-ditch attack would have. King wanted to accompany Wainwright to II Corps, but Wainwright asked him to stay where he was and keep an eye on both corps. King, realizing a maximum effort was needed to stave off defeat, ordered the ration doubled for combat units as of that afternoon. Then Wainwright drove to II Corps. "[Major] Dooley drove me on like a wild man, but time was indeed precious," recalled Wainwright.[12] Arriving at Parker's headquarters near Limay, Wainwright climbed a wooded hill to the command post and discussed plans for a counterattack to be launched the next day. Wainwright approved the plan shown him by Parker, but his approval was hedged "with misgivings as to the outcome." Major Dooley drove back to Cabcaben so fast he broke the jeep's axle.

Operational details of the counterattack were developed at Sector D by General Lough's G3, Colonel Robert J. Hoffman—promoted to full colonel just the day before—one of the sharpest, keenest, most intelligent thinkers in the US Army. Hoffman, a 1917 Military Academy Graduate, had served in Vladivostok from 1918 to 1920 as aide-de-camp to Major General William S. Graves, commander of the American Expeditionary Forces in Siberia. Then Hoffman served in Tokyo as Assistant Military Attache from 1923 to 1927. Eventually he ended up in the Philippines in various staff jobs in the Philippine Department. In his plan, Sector D's effort was to start at 0600 hours on April 6 and four major formations were to attack north on three trails. On the right the American 31st Infantry was to move to the base of Trail 4 and attack north to the regimental reserve line of the 21st Division. The 21st Division, still believed by II Corps and Sector D to have some strength, was to attack northwest up the slopes of Mount Samat between Trails 4 and 429. The 33rd Infantry was ordered to attack north down Trail 6, and the shattered 42nd and 43rd infantry were to follow the 33rd—if they could. At the western edge of the counterattack the 41st Infantry was ordered back across the Pantingan River to Trail 29 to which the Scouts of the 45th Infantry (less 1st Battalion) with a company of tanks would advance. In reserve was the 57th Infantry, then moving to the San Vicente River but not yet in place.[13]

When Wainwright returned to Corregidor he sent a message to MacArthur outlining his plans. Theoretically, nine regiments would participate in the counterattack. Wainwright told MacArthur he had been planning such an operation for a considerable time and was now ready to adopt it.

> The troops have been on half rations for three months and are now on less than that amount which results in much loss of physical vigor and sickness. Nevertheless before allowing a capitulation the operation you suggest will be adopted. I hope however that supplies will arrive in good time. Enemy has been very active on front of Second Corps for past two days with resultant loss of a little ground on our part. Situation still serious if not alarming. I counter attack tomorrow.[14]

Wainwright, however, was too optimistic. The 33rd Infantry was dead on its feet, and the 42nd and 43rd infantry hardly existed. At the center of his counterattack was the nonexistent 21st Division, and without their participation a major portion of the attack force would be missing.

As night descended on the scattered men of the 21st Division, those not quick enough on their feet were captured or killed. By midnight some of the survivors were surrounded. "A conference of all American advisors and all Regimental Commanders of the 21st Division was held at once to decide on a coordinated plan of action to get out of this encirclement," recalled the Filipino commander of the 21st Infantry. "A decision was reached to go through the enemy cordon by night cross-country march."[15] The move started at 0200 hours in a completely black jungle. Firing was in progress all around the men as they felt their way south. Running into Japanese, some soldiers cut their way through to the safety of the American 31st Infantry, but Colonel Wappenstein, senior instructor to the 21st Infantry, and Captain William L. Dixon and Lieutenant James W. Grothers from the 23rd Infantry were killed by machine gun fire. Colonel Wappenstein's fate was unknown until 1953 when a farmer uncovered his remains in a field near Mount Samat. His death can well mark the total destruction of the 21st Division.

As American and Filipinos of the 21st Division slipped in blind exhaustion through enemy lines, other Americans sailing low-decked China River gunboats off Bataan's east coast were in slightly better circumstances. The U.S.S. *Mindanao* and *Oahu* were patrolling the waters of Manila Bay nine miles east of Orion. At 0200 hours the gunboats spotted eleven craft silhouetted against a low moon. "We decided to let them keep coming," remembered Lieutenant David Nash, executive officer of the *Mindanao*, "and we'd continue north as though we had not seen them. Then we headed southwest to cut them off."[16]

At 0301 hours the *Mindanao* commenced fire with star shells, and the *Oahu* used the light to fire high explosives. The Japanese—soldiers from the 21st Independent Engineer Regiment sailing ersatz gunboats and launches—returned a vigorous fire and their bullets snapped into the *Mindanao.* "We were just getting warmed up when we saw smoke and fire from under the port side of our bridge," remembers Nash.[17] The *Mindanao* pulled out to assess the damage. A Japanese tracer round had set fire to a box of pyrotechnics, and Yeoman Third Class Donald T. Purling threw the burning box overboard while other crewmen quickly extinguished a fire near the 3-inch ready ammunition locker. Then the two gunboats started looking for the now-invisible enemy. After several fruitless patrols the gunboats headed southwest, spotted the Japanese, and once more opened fire. The *Mindanao*'s 3-inch star shells again lit the barges for the *Oahu,* which shelled, set afire, and sank a steam launch and another boat. Then two more Japanese craft foundered under the 3-inch storm. Along Bataan's eastern shore Filamerican beach defenders watched the action with lively interest. Colonel Mallonee recalled they were "spectators to some very vivid exchanges of bursting shells, machine-gun tracers, and a regular Fourth of July barrage of skyrockets."[18] The American sailors broke off the action and headed south for Corregidor when Bataan artillery started shooting indiscriminately into the area.

CHAPTER TWENTY-FIVE

Monday, April 6

ON APRIL 6 THE AMERICANS AND FILIPINOS STAGED A LAST-DITCH counterattack only to run into the renewed Japanese offensive, and the results of the battle decided the campaign. The Filamerican effort can best be described by examining the forces involved from left to right, west to east.

Three hundred men from Colonel Wetherby's 41st Infantry pushed eastward early that morning to establish a line across Trail 29 to which the 45th Infantry could advance. Hoping to surprise the enemy, the 41st Infantry decided against using an artillery preparation; it would be a sneak attack. It is amazing the Filipinos could still be called upon for an offensive operation and, more amazing still, it was a night attack, one of the most difficult and hazardous of military maneuvers. Because the 41st Infantry still had to protect about a mile and a half of I Corps's right flank, Wetherby was ordered to use only 300 of his 650 effectives—a provisional battalion of three 100-man companies commanded by Filipino Major Zobel. After Colonel Fortier gave them their orders about 1600 hours on April 5, American and Filipino officers organized their men for the effort and put them into motion. Leaving the west bank of the Pantingan River just after midnight, the 41st Infantry slithered down the three-hundred-foot-tall banks, crossed the boulder-strewn brush-cloaked river, and slowly scaled the steep wooded cliffs of the opposite side. After catching their breath on the east bank the Filipinos crept cautiously into their old kitchen area. Straining to see in the dark, they found a small number of Japanese asleep in the rear-area shelters and huts the 41st Infantry had recently evacuated. These Japanese were old enemies, their Abucay and Trail 2 opponents, men of Nara's 65th Brigade.

About two hours after climbing into and out of the river valley the Filipinos stole across darkened terrain, bayoneted and knifed several sleeping
enemy, and pushed ahead to their objective, Trail 29 just below Trail
429, reaching it at dawn.[1]

But Japanese who escaped from the kitchen area sounded the alarm,
and before noon the Japanese counterattacked with forces equalling a
reinforced battalion and pushed the Filipinos off Trail 29 into a defensive
position on a small ridge paralleling the Pantingan River. Here the 41st
Infantry held, listening to firing coming up from the south, and hoping
for relief from the 45th Infantry. Drawing on their experiences at Abucay and Trail 2, the hardened survivors of four months of war dug in. In
the next thirty-six hours the Filipinos, backed against the Pantingan and
armed only with rifles and machine guns, suffered 30 percent casualties,
one hundred men killed or wounded while defending their little ridge.
The Filipinos' failure to hold a line across Trail 29 was not as serious as it
could have been. The 45th Infantry was having great difficulty reaching
that line.[2]

In concert with the 41st Infantry's effort, Scouts of Colonel Doyle's
45th Infantry (less the 1st Battalion) and tanks of C Company, 194th
Tank Battalion, received orders late in the afternoon of April 5 to march
north up Trail 29 and join Colonel Wetherby's Filipinos. Once they
reached the 41st Infantry, hopefully by 0600 hours on April 6, the Scouts
would attack with the old regimental reserve line of the 41st Infantry as
their objective, occupation of which would plug Trail 29. Unfortunately
the Scouts had to start alone because the armor did not arrive until after
daybreak. Even worse than the delay in the armor, the removal of the
regiment's 1st Battalion to guard I Corps's right flank significantly reduced the strength and tactical balance of the regiment. It also showed
that the Americans still had not learned the futility of piecemeal commitment of troops. After receiving their orders, 3rd Battalion officers drove
north along Trail 29 on a reconnaissance. They found Japanese much
sooner than expected—about 3,500 yards farther south than anticipated
—and so great was the surprise to both Japanese and Americans that no
one was hurt despite heavy rifle fire. The Americans turned their three
vehicles around and sped south.[3]

After eating, the 45th Infantry, 3rd Battalion in the lead, began its
march north up Trail 29 two hours after midnight. It was a cautious move
made so by the very dark night, the unsettled situation, and by frequent
contact with bedraggled remnants of the 41st Division fleeing the Japanese. When American officers in the 45th Infantry asked these men
where they were going, they answered that they were going to Mariveles
to look for rice.[4]

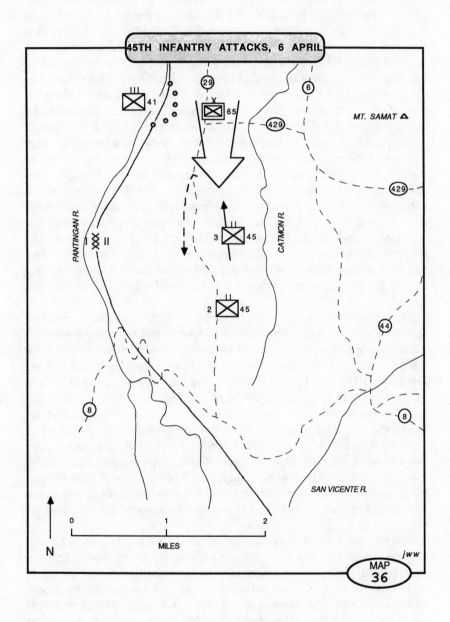

45TH INFANTRY ATTACKS, 6 APRIL

41

29

65

6

MT. SAMAT △

429

429

3 45

2 45

44

PANTINGAN R.

CATMON R.

8

8

SAN VICENTE R.

0   1   2

MILES

N

jww

MAP
36

The two Scout battalions began deploying at 0400 hours when they reached their line of departure, 3rd Battalion on the left of Trail 29 and 2nd Battalion on the right. Both battalions started north shortly after daylight. The Scouts advanced rapidly through the thick vegetation, and at 1030 hours F Company surprised some Japanese. The Japanese fled, but they tried to fight a delay while doing so. Japanese bugles sounded in the distance as the outposts of Nara's 65th Brigade fell back on the main body. Japanese resistance grew, but E Company, on higher ground to the right, supported F Company by firing down and across F Company's front. At 1300 hours E Company ran into some Japanese who were trying to flank the 2nd Battalion. The reserve G Company moved to the right to protect the battalion's flank. On the left the 3rd Battalion also advanced steadily but at 1500 hours, after advancing 2,500 yards, the Scouts stalled on heavy resistance. The tanks of C Company, although now present, were of little use because they were confined to the trail and surrounded by dense vegetation. Colonel Doyle, at 61 years old probably the oldest regimental commander on Bataan and easily identified by his snow-white hair, and the tank commander, Colonel Miller, waited for the situation to develop before pushing the tanks into the fight.[5]

The Scouts had found themselves under effective enemy mortar fire following first contact with Japanese outposts, and because of his own limited supply of 81mm mortar ammunition—only ten rounds—Doyle was reluctant to return the enemy's fire. He now decided to use half his supply, and Doyle and Miller agreed the tanks would attack after the mortars fired. Mortarmen removed safety pins from fuses, slipped one precious round after another into the tube, and sent five projectiles on their lofty way. The Japanese hastily fled their roadblock under the surprisingly effective fire, and Scout infantry charged into the enemy position ahead of the tanks, catching and killing some laggard Japanese. A sharp-eyed Scout infantryman found the trail heavily seeded with pie-pan mines and stopped Colonel Miller's tanks before any damage was done. Not only was the trail mined, but so was every opening or turn-off on which a tank could possibly move.[6]

Despite this small success, Doyle decided to halt. Although he dispatched patrols to the west to contact I Corps and to the east to find the 33rd Infantry, the patrols either failed to return or found only Japanese. As one patrol after another walked west and did not return, the Scouts realized the fate that awaited them. "As each succeeding group was called up to receive instructions and orders for patrol duty, every last man took his orders with no trace of reluctance or fear whatsoever," remembered Colonel Miller who watched them. "There was only ex-

plicit obedience in the job they had to perform. They knew the seriousness of the situation which confronted them, and I marveled at their
soldierly qualities. They knew that death undoubtedly awaited them, but
the last patrol went just as eagerly as the first."[7] Worried over his open
flanks and the onset of darkness, and now wounded in the left forearm,
Doyle ordered his men to dig in and wait out the night. Food was
brought up at 1700 hours, and the men were fed. Returning to his command post, Doyle telephoned his Sector commander, General Lough,
and reported his situation. At 1600 hours Lough confirmed the decision
to halt, but he ordered Doyle to prepare for another attack the next
morning, this time east with one battalion along Trail 8 where more
trouble was brewing.

As a third prong in the Army's April 6 counterattack, II Corps ordered
the Philippine 33rd Infantry—waiting to the right of the Scout 45th
Infantry—to attack north along Trail 6. The remnants of the 42nd and
43rd infantry would follow the 33rd. In support of the 33rd Infantry's
counterattack efforts here, Filipino 155mm artillery fired their planned
concentrations, but their effectiveness was questionable. As Colonel
Quintard recorded in his diary, "Started concentrations at 6:30 with a
badly cut regiment. 'A' has all guns in but is jittery from heavy shelling
and bombing. 'B' the same with one gun out, 'C' has one gun in, 'D' two
and B, 86 [th Artillery] can only get an elevation of 430 [mils]."[8] At the
same time Quintard's artillery was firing, the bulk of General Nara's
brigade was marching cross-country along both sides of Trail 6 in an
effort to seize Trail Junction 6-8. As the 350 spiritless survivors of the
twice-dispersed 42nd and 43rd infantry waited just north of Trail Junction 6-8, the Japanese, marching south, ran into them. The 65th Brigade
attacked when they saw the ragged collection of Filipinos, and for the
third time since the battle began, the Filipinos stampeded into the jungle.
All attempts to rally them failed.

The two-battalion 33rd Infantry was not aware of the fate overtaking
the two 41st Division regiments behind them. The day before, General
Lough had told Major Holmes that the army would counterattack the
next day. Holmes would join in when friendly troops reached him. So
the regiment sat in place waiting for help to arrive and listened anxiously
for the artillery preparation that was to signal the attack and link-up by
friendly troops. Spasmodic firing of what appeared to be only three batteries was not what the Filipinos had expected, but they were happy to
hear their own guns once again. Just before daylight they heard rifle and
machine gun fire to the southwest, and as the firing gradually came closer
and increased in volume, 31-year-old Major Holmes, selected from the
ranks in 1930 to attend West Point, made plans to sortie. But the sortie

never left. At 0900 hours, when only a thousand yards away, the noise of battle faltered and fell away to the west. Then Major Holmes's last communications link with II Corps failed. II Corps, unable to contact the 33rd Infantry, presumed them routed and destroyed. One of the five American counterattack prongs thus was totally disrupted without affecting the course of the battle in the least.[9]

The rout of the 42nd and 43rd infantry and containment of the 33rd Infantry allowed significant freedom of movement for Nara's 65th Brigade, and they continued their unopposed advance south along Trail 6 until making contact about noon with Scouts of the 1st Battalion, 57th Infantry. After some stiff fighting the Japanese slowed, but not before they seized Trail Junction 6 and 8, one of the most critical intersections in the defensive network. The 65th Brigade's arrival here split Sector D and isolated the sector commander, General Lough, west of his troops. In an effort to recover the junction, Major Scholes—the most aggressive battalion commander in the 57th Infantry—sent part of his 1st Battalion in a wide swing against Trail Junction 6 and 44, just north of 6 and 8 and to the left rear of the Japanese. Amazingly, the small Scout force grabbed the junction and held it for an hour, but when the Japanese recovered from their surprise, they drove the Scouts back to their start point. Although Granberry's 2nd Battalion then arrived, simultaneous arrival of more Japanese prevented Colonel Lilly's 57th Infantry (-) from recovering the junction.[10]

As the fourth part of the April 6 counterattack, II Corps ordered the 800-man 31st Infantry (US) to attack north to the abandoned regimental reserve line of the 21st Division. The Americans were at the intersection of Trail 2 and the San Vicente River when they received the orders for the counterattack on April 5. Lieutenant Colonel Jasper E. Brady, commanding the regiment since March 2 when Colonel Steel became II Corps's chief of staff, issued his own orders at 1600 hours. Barely were orders distributed before Brady learned that the junction of Trails 4 and 429, his line of departure, now lay in Japanese hands; the junction would have to be captured before Brady could attack northward, an attack scheduled to start at 0600 hours. Shortly after sunset Brady assembled his officers and, before issuing updated orders, had the regiment's chaplain, Captain Robert P. Taylor, lead them in a short prayer. Then Brady talked to his officers. Cooks served a hot supper and gave three C-ration meals to each infantryman, rations which had been carried on kitchen trucks throughout the campaign as an emergency issue. "We got three cans of dry and three cans of wet rations," recalls Private Rutledge. "We were so hungry some of us sat down and ate all six cans."[11]

With little time for planning and none for reconnaissance, the ex-

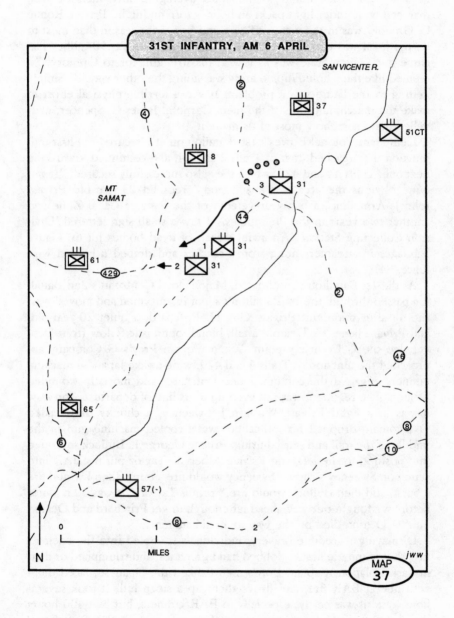

31ST INFANTRY, AM 6 APRIL

SAN VICENTE R.

MT
SAMAT

MAP
37

jww

N

MILES

0   1   2

hausted American infantry, companies averaging fifty men or less, marched west under light packs an hour before midnight. Private Romie C. Gregory was in the weary column and had more reason than most to be tired; he was carrying the heavy barrel to his unit's .50-caliber machine gun. His morale was as low as his strength, for to Gregory, "it seemed like the whole Filipino army was going the other way."[12] Simply getting to the battle was a problem. It was a terrible physical effort to make the march, and one of the men, Corporal James C. Spencer, marvelled that "somehow most of us made it."[13]

Lieutenant Colonel Bowes's 1st Battalion quietly secured the first trail junction they reached, that of Trails 2 and 44, and continued toward the next one, Trails 44 and 429, which they also successfully secured. "It was quite obvious the area was abandoned," recalled 23-year-old Private John J. Armellino, a two-year veteran of the Panama Canal Zone and another two years in the Philippines. "I saw a small sign lettered 'Division Collecting Station.' An awful stench of dead bodies hit us. Gauze bandages in streamers hung from branches and draped a barbed wire fence."[14]

As the 1st Battalion consolidated, Major Lloyd C. Moffitt's 2nd Battalion passed through the 1st Battalion's silent infantrymen and moved west shortly after midnight. Private Guy H. Pritchard, a quiet 20-year-old, and Private James G. Deaton, a tall, blond, optimistic fellow from Denver, led the G Company point. When Captain Pray's G Company approached the junction of Trails 4 and 429, wide-awake Japanese machine gunners engaged the column, killed Pritchard, and mortally wounded Deaton. The regiment was not even up to its line of departure, and now it was in a fight! Private Wilburn J. Sweeney, a chunky, red-headed Oklahoman, dropped his .30-caliber water-cooled machine gun in the middle of the trail and started firing. Private George L. Bullock squirmed into position to the left, and Private Albert L. Taylor put his BAR into action on Sweeney's right. "Sweeney would fire a burst, then I would fire a burst, and then Bullock would fire," recalls Taylor. "It was 30 minutes before we fought our way ahead far enough to get Pritchard and Deaton out."[15] Deaton died on the way to an aid station.

Displaying incredible bravery, individuals stumbled into the enemy's fire, shot at muzzle flashes, lobbed hand grenades, and triumphed or died in dark isolation. Captain Pray's men flanked the Japanese, laced them with liberal BAR fire, and drove them up a steep hill. It took several hours, and it was costly, especially in BAR gunners, but by 0400 hours the 2nd Battalion cleared the enemy from most of Trail 429 and prepared to advance again. At 0530 F Company replaced the shot-up G Company as the battalion's point, but as F Company resumed the advance and marched down the trail into the light of dawn, "the 4th of July broke loose," recalled Private Rutledge. "They let us by and then tried to separate us from the main body."[16] Some Americans were hit, but before deploying to fight the Japanese, famished F Company men rifled the packs of their wounded and dead buddies, looking for cans of food. The Japanese also hit the tail of the 2nd Battalion column and forced the men into a hasty defense. "Our casualties were severe and it was difficult to evacuate them," remembered the battalion's surgeon, Captain Denton Rees, "but we managed this with the aid of the walking wounded."[17]

Just to the east of the 2nd Battalion's troubles, at the regiment's 1st Battalion which was protecting Trail Junction 44 and 429, Private Armellino and another man had just crawled to a listening post 100 yards in front of their A Company when the Japanese struck. "We fixed bayonets and listened carefully," Armellino remembered. "We had hardly settled in when pandemonium erupted behind and below us!"[18] Rifle fire, machine guns, and mortars roared through the jungle, and excited shouting was clearly audible to Armellino as he waited in his listening post. After an hour's battle, A Company repulsed the enemy. When Armellino returned to friendly lines, he found the company's breakfast riddled and splattered across the ground, and milk cans holding precious water were likewise holed and drained.

When stragglers and survivors of the broken 21st Division filtered into the stalled American regiment, their stories convinced Colonel Brady that he was in great danger; the situation was not as had been explained to him by his superiors. Brady knew that II Corps expected the 21st to play an important role in the counterattack, yet here they were in complete rout. When Colonel Uhrig and two Filipino colonels from the 21st Division arrived at Brady's command post at 0445 hours and told him of their division's disintegration, Brady knew he could not continue with his original mission; it was obvious that there was a strong Japanese force on Trail 4. Unable to reach Sector D headquarters by telephone, Brady sent his operations officer and the 21st Division colonels to General Lough's command post to tell Lough there was little chance of the attack succeeding.[19]

As these officers departed, Brady's 2nd Battalion spotted what appeared to be an enemy regiment advancing on them from Mount Samat. "We opened up with mortars at them and had a gay time for a while," remembered Captain Hibbs. "Then one of theirs went off almost in my hip pocket. It blew me up in the air, but when I got up, there wasn't any blood. One fellow took a fragment across his trachea, almost severing it. We applied pressure and kept the blood from running into his lungs."[20] Evacuating this man and others like him was hazardous. If the wound was above the hips, Hibbs's medics would bandage them, point them in the right direction, and tell them to keep walking until they found an aid station. The wounded were reluctant to ride in ambulances because Japanese planes invariably chased them, so medics advised the walking wounded to move south through the jungle. Medics tied blankets to poles and strapped more seriously wounded men to the litters, then healthy soldiers lifted the front end and labored south, the back end of the litter dragging in the dirt.

Still on the telephone, Colonel Brady got through to General Bluemel in Sector C at 0700 hours and asked Bluemel to confirm his action, that of suspending the counterattack and deploying defensively. But Bluemel refused; his Sector artillery had fired its 0545 hour preparation as arranged the day before, and Bluemel told Brady that the 51st Combat Team was waiting to accompany the advance of the Americans. Brady answered that he had only 800 men and even if he attacked up Trail 4 and regained the 21st Division's reserve line, he could not hold it. Bluemel again refused to confirm Brady's desire to decline the counterattack order and advised Brady to counterattack immediately. Bluemel told Brady that if he still refused to attack, he should call General Lough. When Brady said he was not able to contact Sector D, Bluemel told him to call II Corps. Although uncompromising now, Bluemel soon found that even he was arguing against impossible orders.[21]

Rebuffed by Bluemel, Colonel Brady continued his telephonic efforts to reach General Lough and finally contacted Sector D's headquarters. He explained his situation to the operations officer who ordered Brady's mission changed from an offensive to a defensive one. Five minutes later the regiment's operations officer returned to the command post with confirmation of these orders. Brady immediately switched his 1st and 2nd battalions to a defensive stance, sent contact patrols to the 51st Combat Team to his right, and positioned his 3rd Battalion as the regiment's reserve. In order for the right flank 1st Battalion to assume its position, it had to secure some steep hills to its front, and the battalion commander arranged with some nearby artillery for a preparation to smooth the way. The 1st Battalion went on line with the men about fifteen feet apart. "On schedule," remembered Private Armellino in A company, "four 75mm cannon spoke up and laid a pattern before us on the slope. In quick time, heavy enemy guns replied. Three 75mm's fired, then two, and finally the pitiful whimper of the fourth ceased."[22]

Using the concealment offered by scattered growth, A Company quickly climbed the slope. No enemy small arms hindered them, but Japanese shells exploding in the tall bamboo slowed the advancing Americans. An "endless" barrage of mortar fire bounced the Americans back and forth. Swollen, stinking dead lay scattered about the hills, and one man remembered the stench being so bad that he was almost thankful he had nothing to eat. When once more able to advance, A Company's right flank platoon trotted forward into a scattering of abandoned Filipino foxholes, this time under enemy rifle fire. "Their fire was heavy," remembered Armellino, "and we replied carefully as we had limited ammo with no prospects of a fresh supply. I had one hand grenade, the only one in the group, and my corporal came for it."[23] Of the fifteen men who started the advance, only nine remained to hold the small hummock, and one after another, Japanese fire thinned the group to eight and then to seven.

Late in the morning, Bluemel reported the failure of the 31st Infantry's counterattack to II Corps and asked for permission to withdraw to the east bank of the San Vicente River. From his many terrain walks in February and March, Bluemel knew his sector and he knew the bluffs on the east side of the San Vicente offered the best fields of fire in the entire area. But II Corps refused permission and instead ordered him to place his men on the second ridgeline west of the river, the line of departure for the 31st Infantry's attack. II Corps's decision to stand on that line was made after looking at a map, but because of the vegetation and the ground, the new line did not offer any fields of fire. Nor had any ground reconnaissance been made or any entrenchments started.[24]

By now the 31st Infantry was facing the main body of the Japanese 4th Division. Attacks against Major Moffitt's 2nd Battalion on the left of the American line holding Trail Junction 44 and 429 increased to the point where, at 1400 hours, Brady sent two of the regiment's three reserve rifle companies to help. At the 3rd Battalion's meeting discussing this commitment, Captain Thompson was receiving orders from Major O'Donovan when Japanese artillery slammed into the area. Thompson was next to a tree that shattered under the fire and peppered him with pieces of tree and shell. He was evacuated to a hospital, not because of fragmentation wounds, but because the shell landed so close he lost his hearing. Sitting nearby, Private Snyder was watching the meeting when he saw the shell hit right among the officers. "It temporarily shellshocked me," Snyder recalled. "I ran to a foxhole, and after the shelling, the men had a hard time getting me out."[25]

Successful in holding to their positions until sometime after 1500 hours, the 31st Infantry, with permission from General Lough to withdraw to the San Vicente if necessary, did so. Two companies of the reserve battalion, L and K, recently attached to the left flank 2nd Battalion, fought a rear-guard action using some of their remaining 81mm rounds to disengage. Even so, the withdrawal was difficult. The Japanese were hardly one hill behind the Americans, so close that the Americans could watch the pursuit. The Americans were in such poor shape they could march for only ten minutes before having to rest, and without food or sleep the men simply could not carry the heavier weapons. One machine gunner opened the bolt of his machine gun, placed a hand grenade on it, and trotted away as it blew apart; enough discipline remained to insure abandoned weapons would be inoperable when found by the Japanese. When a 2nd Battalion machine gun squad ran out of both energy and hope during the retreat, its sergeant cried in despair, "this is as far as we go, the war ends here for me."[26] His crew positioned their gun on a knoll, laid out ammunition, and camouflaged the weapon. They fired for an hour, covering the battalion until several large explosions signalled the end of their gallant effort.

The 1st Battalion's A Company was closely engaged with the enemy and suffered when it tried to break free. After the few men with Private Armellino gathered together, the first man dashed downhill through enemy fire and reached safety. But the second man had a head wound, and he froze and would not budge until someone slapped him. Then he tried to run toward the Japanese. Although his buddies tried to grab him, he broke away, threw down his rifle, and ran at the Japanese. The men he left behind were now badly shaken. When Armellino's turn came, he ran madly down the hill through popping bullets and into a group of men trying to assemble in some dead space just short of a trail. Then more Americans carrying water-cooled machine guns and tripods staggered into the shouting, confused collection of anxious soldiers. More men leaped out of the jungle up to the trail, only to find a five-foot tall barbed wire fence between them and the route of their withdrawal. Close by, other 1st Battalion men tried to rally, one man yelling "C Company here, C Company here."[27] The roar of enemy small arms fire pressed closer and closer.

Suddenly a flood of dazed Americans ran up the trail flayed by Japanese rifle and machine gun fire. "We were trapped, penned with the fence at our rear," Armellino recalls. "It was a massacre. I hit the ground. A sergeant with me threw down his weapon, tore off his pack, and ran screaming into the hail of fire." Lieutenants Lee and Hutchinson from A Company, shouting "every man for himself," fired their pistols at the enemy and tried to hold open a low point in the fence as the men climbed over it. As the infantrymen clawed through the fence, Japanese planes dove at the packed road, strafing and dropping bombs. "Suddenly, the worst most unbelievable thing happened; blind panic and sheer terror seized the packed mad running mass of men. Machine guns, mounts, ammo boxes, BARs were being flung aside and into the road. The men had finally broken completely, screaming and yelling and running for their lives in all directions."[28]

Throughout the morning of April 6, II Corps headquarters and Luzon Force headquarters, with which II Corps was now collocated, were receiving disquieting reports about the morning's efforts to restore the main line. At a mid-morning conference General King asked his officers what percentage of the army was effective. When one man asked for a definition of "effective," King said that an effective soldier was anyone who can walk 100 yards carrying his weapon without stopping to rest and who could still shoot. King's officers answered that 15 percent of the men in units which were still cohesive met that criteria. The officers then started looking for a new line to which to retreat. They chose the San Vicente River.[29]

On the other side of the line, General Kitano of the Japanese 4th Division decided to commit his reserve, the 37th Infantry (less one battalion), to crown what had so far proved to be astonishing victories. Reinforced by tanks, artillery, and engineers, the 37th Infantry moved east from the northeast foothills of Mount Samat and, at 1030 hours, hit the Filipino 51st Combat Team just north of Trail 2. When six Japanese tanks appeared on the Pilar-Bagac Road, three antitank guns from the 31st Infantry (US) opened fire. The left two new model M-3 guns fired as fast as possible, each shooting over forty rounds. They hit one tank and, as the crew tried to escape out the turret, the gunners hit the tank again and blew the hatch off. The Americans switched to another target, hit a second tank in its tracks, and stopped it. Some time during this fighting, Colonel Sonoda, commander of the 7th Tank Regiment and an ex-member of the Japanese Tank Research Committee of the Army Ministry, was fatally wounded. By now the Japanese tanks spotted two of the three American guns, fired and destroyed them both.[30]

Forty-five-year-old First Sergeant Emanuel Hamburger from Seattle, the only first sergeant the 31st Infantry's Anti-Tank Company ever had, and a veteran of nine years service in China and eight years in the Philippines, went into the fight with an old 37mm gun, but no sooner did the crew ready it for action than enemy artillery smothered it. With no targets in sight, the crew removed the breech block, piled into a small dugout, and waited for a lull in the fire. When the Japanese infantry approached the Americans drove them to cover with rifle and pistol fire. Taking advantage of the temporary disappearance of the Japanese, three Americans left the dugout and scrambled to safety, but as Hamburger and two others tried to do the same, enemy bullets forced them back inside. Private James E. Mines turned to Hamburger and said, "Sergeant, let's surrender."[31]

Hamburger tied a white handkerchief to a twig and handed it to Mines. "OK, if you want to surrender so bad, take this white flag and go out."

"Oh, no," replied Mines, "you're the sergeant, you go first." Without any better ideas, Hamburger led his two men out and surrendered. Equally unhappy was the outcome in the 51st Combat Team's area that faced west behind the Pilar River, lying almost due north of the American 31st Infantry, part of the line the antitank guns were protecting. The Japanese 37th Infantry overran the 51st Engineers and forced the entire line out of position and into the jungle.

Finally, at 1600 hours, II Corps directed the defending forces to fall back to the east bank of the San Vicente. The decision was a direct result of the loss of Trail Junction 6 and 8 and the 57th Infantry's failure to recapture it. II Corps's withdrawal order came too late in the day to allow a worthwhile reconnaissance, but somehow a few officers succeeded in making a cursory check before moving into position. II Corps told Bluemel the American 31st Infantry was now under his command and that a battalion of the 57th Infantry would also be sent to him. With luck, combat teams might coalesce around small pockets of tanks, self-propelled mounts, and artillery. All across Bataan, rear-echelon units and General King's meager reserves were marching north toward the San Vicente River, which as a water obstacle was not significant but which, with its steep slopes, might give the Japanese trouble.[32]

Bluemel ordered his units to their new positions. He passed word through wire lines for everyone to form on the southeast side of the San Vicente. Bluemel's headquarters personnel moved to an alternate command post where wire communications proved fairly steady. The 32nd Infantry marched almost due east and crossed the San Vicente without trouble. Elements of the 51st Combat Team were to tie in with the 32nd Infantry. Then the 31st Division's engineer battalion, a provisional company, and an anti-sniper company were to link together. The American 31st Infantry would extend southwest and link with the southernmost element of Bluemel's line, the 3rd Battalion, 57th Infantry. Now that the 31st Infantry was assigned to him, General Bluemel went looking for the regiment. He found a few elements, but the men were exhausted, demoralized, and disorganized. Realizing they were all he had, Bluemel went among the Americans, explaining the situation and ordering them into a new line. He found Captain Pray with his thirty-five-man G Company and told him to outpost the line. Pray, about as far from his alma mater of Ripon College as he ever would be, was not sure if his soldiers would respond, but when he called, "Alright men, follow me," they shouldered their equipment and went forward. One of these men, Private Taylor, remembered that "we just threw up hasty positions using natural cover if possible."[33] But attempts to establish a new line along the San Vicente proved extremely difficult. When darkness finally intervened, further organization was impossible.

Finishing his efforts with the Americans, Bluemel headed northeast, collecting some 51st Combat Team stragglers, and herded them forward until he joined Major Edmund W. Wilkes who was placing elements of that unit astride Trail 2. The 51st Combat Team was badly disorganized. Enlisted men refused to identify their organization, and Filipino officers refused to step forward when officers were called for. Major Wilkes, a West Pointer class of 1934, who had commanded B Company of the American 31st Infantry before the war, and Private John E. Bowler, an American who spoke the Bicol dialect fluently, restored order in the exhausted and frightened Filipinos and spent the entire night putting the 51st Combat Team into position. Bluemel next found his 31st Engineer Battalion bivouaced close to the river on Trail 2. Because their original position covering the trail was already occupied by the 51st Combat Team, Bluemel ordered the engineers to the left of the American 31st Infantry.[34]

Continuing his travels, Bluemel found the 31st Infantry's command post and told Colonel Brady of the engineers' new position. Hiking up the trail to his command post, Bluemel met Colonel Lilly of the 57th Infantry. Lilly explained that II Corps had ordered one battalion of his regiment to support Bluemel. Bluemel told the recently promoted Lieutenant Colonel Harold K. Johnson, commander of the 3rd Battalion, 57th Infantry, where he was to place his men, and a staff officer guided the Scouts into the line. When M Company picked its way forward to the line companies after dark, it somehow passed through the riflemen into enemy territory. "The trail was narrow and we had to feel each step," recalled Captain Saalman. "I stumbled and fell over a dead body. Groping around, we found about a dozen bodies, nearly all very bloated. We were wondering if they were Japanese, American, or Filipino. Lieutenant Fleetwood found a canteen and a helmet and by the feel of them we determined they were Japanese."[35] Very quietly, the men turned around and slipped back through friendly lines without further incident. This march was the last significant movement of troops for the evening along Bluemel's line.

Almost lost in the confusion of the past several days were numerous small clearing stations that fed their patients to the two big hospitals on the southern limits of the peninsula. On the night of April 2 the Luzon Force Medical Office began evacuating sick and wounded from front-line stations and collecting centers to base hospitals in the rear. Using the

12th Medical Battalion and convoys of seventy-five buses each, 7,000 casualties lying in makeshift shelters were collected and moved out of the path of the Japanese. Sick and wounded who would normally have been handled as litter cases were required to make an all-night ride sitting in regular passenger buses. Although there were many close calls, everyone was safe by the morning of April 6. A similar evacuation took place in I Corps the nights of April 5, 6, and 7. The success of this patient evacuation was unimportant in terms of resisting the Japanese, but it was a miracle of dedication on the part of the medical personnel.[36]

The Japanese were triumphant as April 6 closed. General Homma's army had destroyed two divisions, the 21st and 41st, and one regiment, the 51st. Homma had also cut off two more regiments from the main area of interest, the 41st and 45th infantry, and isolated Sector D headquarters from its troops. The soldiers manning the San Vicente Line were disorganized and demoralized. Mentally, they were already defeated and only waiting for the event to be confirmed. The left flank of II Corps was smashed, the two corps split apart, Mount Samat lost, defending artillery all but neutralized, and the rear of Parker's II Corps invitingly open to Japanese exploitation. The chaos in II Corps was so bad that General Parker's headquarters did not fully understand the situation. When a Corps staff officer, Major Fuller, reached the 31st Infantry on the San Vicente River this night, he realized that II Corps headquarters knew nothing about the status of the withdrawal to the river.[37]

In hopes of bringing enough combat power to bear on the Japanese from both sides of Trail Junction 6 and 8, General Lough ordered the 45th Infantry to move east and link with the 57th Infantry near the critical trail junction. But the orders received by Colonel Doyle were nearly impossible to execute. After moving north at 0200 hours that morning, and after making the only significant gain of the day, Doyle's 45th Infantry was now expected to retrace its steps, march east along Trail 8, reduce the Japanese holding Trail Junction 6 and 8, and link with the 57th Infantry. Although impossible, the Scouts would try; *petay si la,* they shall die. The order was sent to Colonel Doyle by telephone from General Lough's command post and just as the officers finished talking, a voice in perfect English cut in saying, "Curtains for you, Mr. Doyle!" Colonel Miller, who was listening and heard the voice, knew that the Japanese had tapped telephone lines before, "but it was not very comforting to have them tell you about it."[38]

Three engineer battalions were ordered to the front and told to report to Colonel Lilly's 57th Infantry. That night General King ordered one of his last reserves, the 26th Cavalry, out of I Corps to Trail 2 and 10 in II Corps. The move began at 1930 hours under the concealment of darkness in organic transportation augmented by civilian buses supplied by I Corps. Colonel Lee C. Vance—a wagon corporal in 1915 with the 7th Cavalry and a sergeant in the 1916 pursuit of Pancho Villa—stopped at I Corps headquarters to pick up the troop that guarded that installation. General Jones shook hands with Vance and wished him luck.[39]

Attempts to get extra food to the Bataan garrison were bungled. Luzon Force's G4 requested three days' class C-rations be issued to the three Philippine Division regiments and the 26th Cavalry, a total of 7,219 rations. There were 100,000 C-rations in Bataan reserve stored for safety on Corregidor and were not in any respect a part of Corregidor's stock, but when the request was received at Corregidor, Wainwright's G4 recommended disapproval pending a better reason for the request. When Wainwright, sincerely concerned over rations for the Bataan garrison, saw the request and the G4's recommendation, he wrote, "The issue of class C rations to the troops listed is approved and will be issued *tonight*."[40] On the night of April 6, supply men shipped forty tons of C-rations from Fort Mills to Bataan, but distribution once on the peninsula proved impossible.

CHAPTER TWENTY-SIX

Tuesday, April 7

APRIL 7 DAWNED POORLY FOR SERGEANT DON INGLE OF THE AMERI-
can 31st Infantry. On Tuesday morning he was released from his regiment to General Hospital Number 1 with a fever of 105 degrees. As he
lined up with others awaiting admittance, he saw row after row of
stretchers lying in the raw jungle. Scattered about were a few sheetmetal
buildings, but some wards were little more than canvas tarps strung over
cleared pieces of ground where patients sprawled on the bare earth. A
red-cross flag flew below the Stars and Stripes, and white crosses fabricated from sheets stretched over several open spots. As Ingle waited to
be processed, more sick and wounded staggered in for help. The hospital
had a capacity of 2,500 patients, yet there were 4,340 men clogging
every available space and another 450 waiting with Ingle for admission.
Seven percent of King's army lay exhausted and dying in this one hospital while another 4,500 were being treated at Hospital Number 2.[1]

An officer, an American colonel, walked up to the men standing with
Sergeant Ingle. "We need volunteers to return to the front," the colonel
said. "The next 48 hours will tell the tale. We will either get reinforcements, or," he shrugged, "we will be lost."[2] That admission shocked
Ingle. Even though Ingle knew they were losing, this was the first officer
who had described how desperate the situation was. Stunned silence
greeted the colonel's request; to be so close to safety and then be asked
to return to the agony they had just escaped was almost to choose between life and death. After a pause, a single man stepped forward. Simultaneously, Ingle thought to himself, "Why the hell not?" and joined the
volunteers. Soldiers with malaria, dysentery, and sores covering their
bodies picked themselves off the ground and prepared to fight. About

seventy-five men, all eligible to occupy hospital beds, joined the colonel. A *Life* magazine photographer saw the assembly and pushed forward with his camera. "No time for pictures," ordered the colonel, and he guided the men toward buses.

This effort to recruit soldiers from the hospital, while heroic, was futile. Flying low over the drama came a formation of 62nd Air regiment Mitsubishi twin-engine Betties. At 1015 hours, as the sick men stumbled toward waiting buses, the planes dropped their bombs. Ingle and the other men looked up, saw the sun flashing off the falling bombs, and scattered as the world blew up in a reddish-orange flash. As Ingle dove for cover, he felt a burning sensation in his thigh and shoulder, fragmentation from a bomb which split open a Filipino a few feet away.[3]

Private William Garleb, a machine gunner suffering from a high fever, was just leaving a truck and starting a slow weave on unsteady feet toward the hospital when he heard the approaching planes. As bombs tumbled from the Betties, he watched carefully, judged their direction, and correctly predicted they would fall safely to his front. So he continued toward the hospital as others "ran helter skelter in terror, diving into ditches or just running straight ahead as fast as they could go."[4] Some ran so fast and in the wrong direction, they sprinted into bomb bursts. Garleb was not at all concerned with the attack. He was only interested in finding a bed and falling into it.

One man in the hospital had a special problem. Deafened by enemy artillery the day before, Captain Donald G. Thompson watched a friend scramble for cover, so Thompson did the same. He could see the planes and the dust and debris, but he felt terribly helpless because he could not hear. Another patient, Lieutenant William Montgomery, was sheltering under his bunk fifty yards away when the bombs flattened Ward 5. "The concussion was terrific," he remembered. "There were some two hundred patients in tiered bunks in the area hit. . . . I carried wounded and dead all day. I passed out water and cigarettes. We had over fifty killed including many Americans. I helped hold one man's leg while they amputated. The carnage was sickening."[5] Doctor Dan Golenternek, a warm, humorous, gentle officer and a favorite of his patients, was in the ward holding wounded Japanese. When the bombs screamed in, several Japanese threw themselves on Golenternek and shielded him with their bodies.

At least ten bombs hit the hospital. When he heard the bombs, Doctor Alvin Poweleit dropped to the ground. The explosion in his ward created a crater thirty-five feet across and seventeen feet deep. Although Poweleit was about forty feet from the edge of the crafter, he got a small splinter in his left eye. Scattered around him were arms, legs, and headless bodies. Poweleit, two nurses, and a sergeant tied tourniquets and pressed bandages into wounds. They worked alone until others gathered their wits and started helping. Nurses, one of whom was bleeding badly from a neck wound and growing paler by the second, walked among the wounded giving injections of morphine from large syringes. Survivors pulled nineteen dead Filipinos from a shelter rigged from a large piece of metal pipe; concussion from a bomb exploding close to the entrance killed each man without drawing a drop of blood.[6]

As order was restored, the count of dead soared to seventy-three. Another 117 soldiers lay wounded or re-wounded, and sixteen of those would soon die. Bombs had hit the pharmacy and destroyed most of the drugs. Hospital records mixed with broken utensils lay strewn across the ground. With ward records destroyed, many dead could not be identified. Pieces of bodies and scraps of bedding hung in a large tree. It took hours to clear the bodies and newly wounded from the devastated part of the hospital. Trucks carried the scores of dead to a military cemetery at Mariveles where quartermaster personnel used bulldozers to bury the casualties in common graves.[7]

Wainwright reported the bombing to Washington and stated he believed the attacks were deliberate. With thunder, blood, and death, April 7 opened for personnel in rear areas. Further forward, equally catastrophic events unfolded.

An early morning, two-pronged Scout attack was scheduled to retake Trail Junction 6 and 8 and reunite I and II corps. The 45th Infantry was scheduled to attack eastward along Trail 8, the 57th Infantry was to attack westward, and the two Scout regiments were to link at the trail junction and contain the Japanese. At 1600 hours on the sixth General Lough called Colonel Doyle at Doyle's command post and gave him his mission. "See if you can get through to relieve the pressure on the 31st Infantry and the 57th Infantry at the San Vicente River," he ordered, "and let me know so I can get back into II Corps."[8] The plan made sense and might have succeeded a month earlier, but the poor physical condition of the men now guaranteed failure. Doyle's regiment pulled south along Trail 29 and reached a bivouac by 2200 hours, and plans were made to attack east with one battalion.

Twenty-eight-year-old Major Andrew B. Zwaska, promoted to major just five days earlier, had assumed command of the 2nd Battalion, 45th Infantry, when Lieutenant Colonel Smith went to the hospital on March 30. Zwaska was new to the battalion, joining on March 18 after leaving the 2nd Constabulary. For the attack eastward, Zwaska built an advance guard for his battalion around two tanks and a platoon of F Company Scouts. The Scouts were to reconnoiter the road and find hidden enemy before the enemy found the battalion. Zwaska's Scouts took to the road at 0100 hours in a column of companies—F, E, H, G, battalion headquarters, regimental headquarters—while the 3rd Battalion and some tanks remained at Trail Junction 8-29 to prevent Japanese from cutting behind the eastward push; once more the regiment was entering battle piecemeal. The Scouts marched for fifty minutes, halted for a rest, then marched until the next ten-minute break. To their left was a sharp drop into a deep, rocky ravine and to the right rose a thickly forested mountain. Just as the point stopped for a break, two Scouts leading the tanks saw shadowy forms and heard a voice say, "Here comes Doyle and his gang!" The two Scouts turned and ran back yelling, "Japs, Japs."[9]

The moment the men yelled, other Scouts dropped to the ground for cover. Lieutenant Frank E. Riley in the point tank saw the Scouts drop, so he immediately tried to back his tank to cover. But a Japanese antitank gun drilled an armor-piercing round through the turret of the lead tank, just missing Riley's head. Machine guns joined the antitank gun, which penetrated Riley's tank four more times. Fragments slashed the driver's eyes, and explosions severely concussed Riley, burst his left eardrum, and injured his foot. The crew bailed out after getting off one burst at the Japanese. The second tank was in defilade, yet several shells glanced off its turret. The driver backed away under heavy covering fire from the Scout infantry. "[The heavy Scout fire] is the only thing that saved us," insisted Colonel Miller who accompanied the tanks. "Their actions that night would have been more than a credit to the best trained and bravest soldiers in the world."[10]

The first burst of firing badly scattered the point element; Major Zwaska and his E Company commander, Captain Louis F. Murphy were both wounded as they jumped out of the jeep. Their driver tried to turn the vehicle around, but an antitank round hit the right front tire and killed the driver. As isolated groups of Scouts tried to maneuver against the Japanese, Lieutenant Colonel Edgar Wright, Jr., the regiment's 34-year-old executive officer, considered the "brains" of the regiment, became separated from the battalion with fifteen Scouts. Despite efforts to rejoin the main body, they were forced to escape to the southeast. H Company commander Captain William B. Davis and regimental communications officer Captain Jerry G. Toth were killed, and Lieutenant James W. Daley was wounded and carried to the rear. With so many leaders out of action, the attack faltered.[11]

With the men badly disorganized, Lieutenant James C. Hase and his H Company Scouts unloaded their heavy weapons from carriers and emplaced the machine guns. Hase rallied his men while Captain Ralph Amato, Jr., put parts of E and F companies into line. With all of H

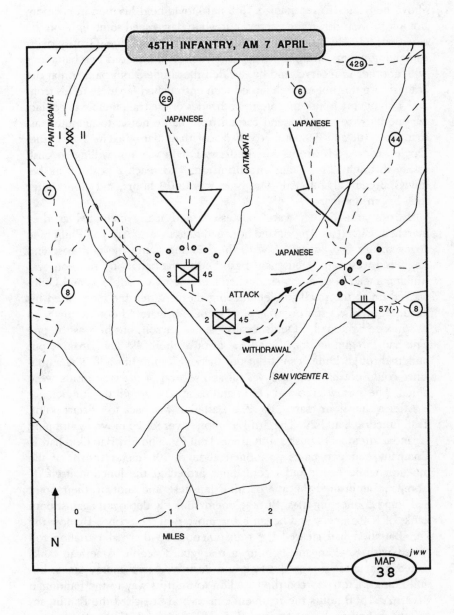

45TH INFANTRY, AM 7 APRIL

MAP
38

Company's machine guns firing, the Japanese fire dropped off enough to allow the Scouts to reorganize. Colonel Doyle held his men in position, hoping to wear down the enemy, but when dawn shed some light on the situation, he realized he could not force the Japanese line. Grossly overestimating enemy strength here, Doyle believed he faced two battalions with another in reserve, and he decided the single Scout battalion at the ambush site was not enough. Faced with entrenched Japanese to his front and with enemy infiltrating along both sides of the trail, unable to contact anyone by wire or radio, and certain from battle noises to his southeast that the 57th and 31st infantry had lost their San Vicente River line, Doyle ordered his Scouts to withdraw. Doyle was not willing to push rashly through "fire, hades and brimstone" to reach a position he believed already abandoned. The time was 0600 hours, five hours after they began the march.[12]

By now the Scouts were exhausted, and many collapsed as they marched. But all an American officer had to ask was, "Are you Philippine Army or are you Scout?"[13] With this stinging taunt, the men rose and staggered westward. Lieutenant Basil Dulin, the battalion's surgeon, was walking ahead of an ambulance when he came to a roadblock, and Dulin walked up to the small soldier sleeping there. When the man raised his head, Dulin saw a star on his cap, a Japanese private. "I don't know who was more frightened," Dulin recalls, "he or myself, but he was the one who had the gun and not I, and I got out of there!"[14] The Japanese put bullets through Dulin's shirt but not through Dulin himself. The ambulance could not back up and was hit and several of the men inside were killed. The survivors joined Dulin and escaped through the jungle.

After a four-hour march, the 2nd Battalion was back to its start point, Trail Junction 8 and 29. The 3rd Battalion covered the move by stopping Japanese attempts to push south along Trail 29. The 3rd Battalion had K Company and two tanks positioned about 1,000 meters north of the junction while L, M, and I companies protected the junction itself. K Company ambushed the approaching Japanese and shot up their point and some connecting files. But the enemy quickly deployed against both flanks of K Company and began firing mortars at the Scouts. By now the 2nd Battalion had cleared the trail junction, so the 3rd Battalion followed with K Company fighting a rear guard action. American tanks halted a Japanese armored attack and destroyed two enemy tanks, but infiltrating infantry forced the battalion to fight its way to the Pantingan River. At 1500 hours the regiment's main body reached the Pantingan, crossed it, and took up positions along the west bank. Three hours later the last of the rear guard forded the river. "Japanese bombing was intense here," recalled Major Van Oosten. "They dropped many thousands of small anti-personnel bombs all over the jungle. It sounded like rain coming down hard."[15]

The effort on the 57th Infantry's side of the penetration, the eastern side, never got off the ground. Constant enemy pressure against the two battalions of that regiment and the ultimate turning of its open western flank prevented offensive action. But the real disaster occurred on the northeast flank of the 57th Infantry. As dawn broke, the Japanese found a gaping hole in the San Vicente line north of the 57th Infantry, and elements of the 61st Japanese Infantry pushed into it. This portion of the line should have been filled by the Philippine Army 201st and 202nd engineer battalions, units organized from untrained rag-tag troops officered by American civilian mining engineers commissioned at the outbreak of war. The engineers had spent their three months on Bataan maintaining roads and trails, building bridges and dummy artillery positions, constructing field fortifications and obstacles, destroying unexploded bombs and shells, and serving as a II Corps engineer asset. A more accurate description of both units would have been "labor" battalions. They received a one-week class on jungle warfare, scouting, patrolling, interior guard, and field sanitation, but the classes were taught in January, and no other training occurred.[16]

On the evening of April 6, II Corps had ordered the engineers to move to the front. Both units were attached to, and ordered to the right of, Colonel Lilly's 57th Infantry (-). Because Sector D headquarters was unable to direct the battle at Trail 6, General Lough put Lilly in charge of all Sector D Forces east of Trail 6. On Tuesday, April 7, Lilly's 57th Infantry was scheduled to attack west toward the 45th Infantry. Because the engineers were untrained in infantry work, they would simply fill the gap between the attacking 57th Infantry and the static 3rd Battalion of that regiment a mile to the northeast. No one expected the engineers to engage in offensive operations, they would merely hold a piece of ground and let the more experienced Scouts carry the fight to the enemy.[17]

After leaving their sick in a bivouac they were preparing for the rainy season, Major Harry O. Fisher's 201st Engineer Battalion pulled up to its detrucking point early in the morning. Each man carried an Enfield rifle, but few of the engineers had ever fired one. There were no machine guns, no automatic rifles, and no hand grenades. At the dismount point, ex-Constabulary men, promoted to sergeant, spent their time getting the 340 engineers ready to move. The men were confused, spoke a variety of dialects, and were very unmilitary. They were also starving. The last issue of food to each company consisted of a small bag of rice and seven jars of mustard. Morale was very low.[18]

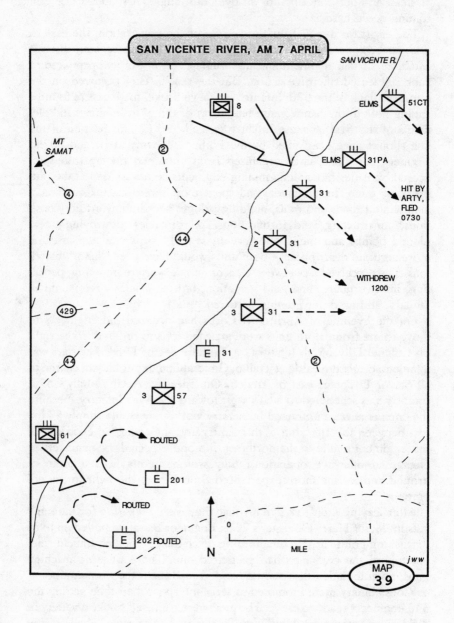

SAN VICENTE RIVER, AM 7 APRIL

SAN VICENTE R.

ELMS 51CT

8

MT
SAMAT

2

ELMS 31PA

4

1 31

HIT BY
ARTY,
FLED
0730

44

2 31

WITHDREW
1200

429

3 31

44

E 31

2

3 57

61

ROUTED

E 201

ROUTED

E 202 ROUTED

N

0   1

MILE

jww

MAP
39

Finally prepared, the point started forward to go into line to the right of Colonel Lilly's Scouts. Advancing for two miles in a single file covering several hundred yards, they stopped on a small ridge and waited for stragglers to cross a stream. Then the Japanese struck. The Filipinos crossing the stream were badly hit, and men fell, fled, or froze. Within seconds, the unengaged men broke and ran. Japanese mortars crashed down on the platoon guarding the unit's trucks at the dismount point, killing the American officer there. Those engineers who did not run at the first burst gathered their wits and returned the enemy's fire. By now the battalion was under fire from the right and rear, and Japanese were yelling commands from heavy jungle just to the front. Then bursting mortar projectiles walked back and forth chasing survivors from the rear engineer company across a ridge into the jungle. Remnants of the headquarters company, numbering twenty-five men, drove off a Japanese probe. Commanded by two American officers, these men remained relatively calm. Heavy firing could be heard to the northeast. Unknown to the Filipinos, it was Captain Mitchell Major's 250-man 202nd Engineer Battalion in the process of dying. The Japanese were all over the area assigned to the engineers.[19]

The officers decided to move what remained of the battalion south, for it was apparent they had overrun whatever front line there was. The American officers tried to organize a point with the Filipinos, but the men could not understand the English commands. The officers formed the point themselves. Of the 340 men who climbed off trucks that morning, only 100 were still together to begin the retreat. As they started back, the engineers took different paths, wandered off, or changed into civilian clothes after discarding weapons and equipment. Frequent clashes with small groups of Japanese further fragmented the battalion. By evening only a few bands numbered more than ten engineers, and the 201st Engineer Battalion was no longer a tactical entity. Because of running into units such as these engineers, the Japanese 4th Division concluded "the enemy troops had no fighting spirit."[20] The Japanese were not bothered in the least by their skirmishes here. Neither of the two battalions reached their assigned positions along the San Vicente River. When the fifty surviving engineers found Colonel Lilly's regiment, they joined the Scouts. "The Scouts began moving out about dark," recalled Lieutenant Eugene P. Boyt, "down the road in perfect formation, beautiful to see as compared to our untrained troops."[21]

Farther to the northeast, above the two engineer battalions, General Bluemel worked frantically to stem a rout and set the remains of his 31st Division and attached elements into the San Vicente Line. Just after midnight on the morning of the seventh, he walked up to his front lines. His first stop was at the 32nd Infantry's command post where the regimental commander told Bluemel his men were in position. Then Bluemel and two Filipino staff officers walked up Trail 2 toward the San Vicente. When less than a mile from the river, they met large groups of the 51st Combat Team shuffling to the rear. When Bluemel asked them where they were going, the Filipinos said they were going to Lamao. Bluemel told them there was no food in Lamao, and he and his two staff officers herded them north. Major Wilkes of the 51st Combat Team took charge of the stragglers and put them back into the line.[22]

Bluemel then checked the American 31st Infantry, three battalions on line with the right of the regiment on Trail 2. Bluemel told the regiment's executive officer, Lieutenant Colonel Leo C. Paquet, to insure his flanks connected with the units on his left and right. The 31st Engineer Battalion would be on his left, and on the left of the engineers would be the 3rd Battalion, 57th Infantry. Looking around, Bluemel saw empty and half empty trucks driving aimlessly around the front lines, blocking trails and ruining what little concealment the brush and vegetation offered. But it was still dark, and the Japanese were not able to take advantage of the confusion. Bluemel finished his inspection and walked back to his headquarters where he fell asleep.[23]

Destruction of Bluemel's right flank commenced at daybreak with another heavy Japanese artillery barrage and air attack. The fire hit the 51st Combat Team especially hard. Even though Japanese infantry were not yet in sight, the Filipinos, huddling in shallow entrenchments, began to break. The first Japanese soldiers from the 3,277-man 62nd Infantry, 21st Division—from the Nagano Detachment—waded the San Vicente at 0730 hours in front of the 32nd Infantry where the river takes a sharp turn to the southwest. Trench mortars hit Filipino lines, the battle cry of attacking Japanese carried all the way to the American Air Corps Regiment, and the 1st Battalion, 32nd Infantry scattered. The soldiers disappeared only to be replaced by "civilians" intent in hurrying south. The American regimental commander disappeared in his command car and was not seen again until after the surrender. Watching the Filipinos collapse, Captain Theodore C. Bigger withdrew his 48th Materiel Squadron's outposts and swung two platoons to face west. He stayed close to his field telephone and kept his battalion informed of the growing threat, but the little Bigger could do did not prevent the Air Corps's left flank from being turned. After crossing the main line of the Filipino 32nd Infantry, Japanese tanks and infantry continued toward the airmen of Lieutenant Colonel John W. Sewall's 2nd Battalion, the Air Corps regiment's left flank.[24]

The airmen were eating a breakfast of moldy rice when the morning artillery landed. Artillery fire was routine, but this morning it shifted farther south than usual. The men gulped their burnt rice coffee and ran to their positions. They dove into spider holes and dugouts to wait out the enemy fire. But the Japanese had more in mind this morning than simple harassment. The outpost line was hit and some of the Americans killed. Second Battalion headquarters tried to call regiment and ask what was happening, but phone lines were out, cut by artillery. The battalion adjutant, Lieutenant George Kane, encoded a message and sent it by radio. Then three Americans came in and told the airmen that Japanese were on the road leading south.[25]

Next, Captain Wohlfeld received orders from regiment to withdraw the 2nd Battalion to Limay. Everything had fallen apart to the west and south, and unless the airmen could pull out in the next few hours, they would be trapped. Captain Wohlfeld picked up his phone, contacted each squadron commander, and explained the order of march: first an advance guard, then the 17th Bomb, 2nd Observation, 27th Group Headquarters, 91st Bomb, and 48th Materiel. The order to pull out shocked everyone into realizing the long fight was almost over. Only the most optimistic could hope for a successful conclusion. Men filled their canteens and changed from flight coveralls to pants and shirts. Officers formed an ad hoc combat patrol, using the most experienced men to spearhead the withdrawal. At 0800 hours, after burning ammunition and unit records that could not be moved, the battalion picked its way south, five companies with a small advance and rear guard.[26]

Either by mistake or in fright, some men received orders to head for Mariveles and cross the channel to Corregidor. So even as the battalion abandoned its lines, it started losing men in pairs and driblets. Hitching rides or hiking off toward terrain offering easier travel, these airmen headed south for Cabcaben and Mariveles. The 91st Bomb, in particular, seemed to disintegrate early. The men vividly recall being told it was every man for himself. "The word came to evacuate," recalled Sergeant Sam Moody. "We didn't know where. We couldn't even tell if the order had come from an appointed source."[27] The men pushed along a narrow trail through miles of bamboo thickets in choking heat. The thick vegetation gave the airmen concealment from enemy air. Everyone had started with more gear than could be comfortably carried, and the route was soon littered with discarded bedding, clothing, and equipment of all kinds. The rear guard, elements of the 48th Materiel, engaged pursuing Japanese with rifle fire, but the fight was not serious. The Japanese kept the Americans moving, nothing more. If the airmen stopped or slowed for too long, the Japanese fired some rounds to encourage them.

To the west, they heard the roar of tank engines intermixed with heavy concussions. Whenever visibility allowed, the men saw Japanese foot soldiers moving parallel to their line of march. To the east, tanks hit their sister 1st Battalion. As the sound of firing reverberated back and forth across the jungle, men became apprehensive and increased the pace. Thick smoke from burning bamboo and the stink of high explosives swept over the column. There was concern as to whether or not the small amount of water in the few canteens would carry the men through to the next stream. Leaders watched their men for the first signs of panic. At noon the advance guard ran into Japanese, but the airmen reduced the roadblock. As they marched through the early afternoon, they found and turned around a platoon of unarmed Filipinos going north with surrender leaflets. In the late afternoon the thirsty men refilled canteens from some wells, then resumed the march and walked into the night. Planes flew over and dropped flares, bathing them in a dangerous glare. Farther south, searchlights illuminated the enemy planes, but no antiaircraft fire was seen. The column finally reached Trail 2 and passed to the relative safety of the Alangan River.[28]

In the Air Corps Regiment's 1st Battalion, the men had time to move to their reserve line, a ridge covered by thick woods. From concealed posts, scouts saw "waves" of Japanese infantry advancing across rice paddies lying to their front. Using field glasses, Captain John S. Coleman and Colonel Maverick watched the enemy and saw "thousands of Japanese" covering a front of about a half mile. At a fast walk the Japanese crossed the empty main line. Runners came in from the left, reporting the airmen there were under attack, then reports arrived telling of Japanese to the left rear.[29]

By now the airmen were shooting at Japanese advancing over the old main line. Filipino civilians ran into the rear of the airmen, yelling "tanks, tanks," and the sound of vehicle engines roared in from the left, confirming the cries of the Filipinos. But a creek bed slowed the tanks, and the airmen still had some time. They could not see any tanks but could hear their engines and machine gun fire. Coleman, acting under the freedom given him by his battalion commander, sent runners to the squadrons in contact with a hastily written message, "Come out on the double to the right."[30] Waiting for the men to react to his order, Coleman watched the Japanese cross rice paddies to his front. "Our troops had begun to fire on them, making them run a little way and then hit the ground; then others would come up running, while we were getting lots of rifle fire from the front." The 27th Materiel Squadron was cut off and could not retreat with the rest of the men.

The 1st Battalion broke contact, moved parallel to a dirt road, and slipped east away from the tanks. After marching two miles the airmen set up on a scrub- and brush-covered ridge, hoping and praying the tanks would not follow. But soon the roar of tank engines grew louder, and clouds of dust rose from the brush to their front. Before the Japanese could close with the defenders, a runner from the regimental commander arrived with a note that told them to continue south where he would meet them. The battalion executed its third move of the morning. Colonel Maverick and Captain Coleman met Colonel Doane, the regimental commander, under a large blown-down tree. Maverick was enraged at having been left in the lurch, unable to contact anyone from regiment. Doane had been at II Corps headquarters trying to find out where to take his regiment. "They had some hard words," Coleman recalled. "I was given a map and told where to march for the next defensive position. I told him if we were not flanked by the Japanese, [we] would be there by about 3:30 the next morning."[31]

To the right of the Provisional Air Corps Regiment was Colonel John W. Irwin's Filipino 31st Infantry. They too were retreating toward new positions. Near the Filipinos, American light tanks back-stopped Sector A, and a radio-equipped half-track kept headquarters farther to the rear appraised of the situation. Into the confusion of Sector A came Lieutenant Theodore I. Spaulding, a II Corps liaison officer, with a message for Colonel Irwin. Traveling by jeep, Spaulding started coming upon larger and larger groups of leaderless Filipinos walking south. As he tried to cross a river, his jeep bogged down and drew the attention of Japanese planes. Taking cover, Spaulding watched as they wrecked his jeep. He continued on foot until he found an abandoned automobile, but he went only a short distance before it ran out of gas. Back on foot, he found and commandeered a motorcycle. As he approached Irwin's front lines, Spaulding saw some American tanks, remnants of A and D companies, 194th Tank Battalion, shifting position to secure better fields of fire. The Filipino 31st Infantry also saw the tanks and, being utterly unfamiliar with the sight of friendly tanks, panicked. Large numbers of men dissolved in flight, yet not a single Japanese soldier was in sight. Colonel Mallonee also saw the tanks as they moved north against the Japanese. "One by one I saw these units leave the beach road and go up the trails to the certain destruction which they knew awaited them. None came back."[32]

Toward the center of the San Vicente line, General Bluemel awoke shortly after daybreak from another hour's nap. He tried to call his Sector artillery, but communications were out. Realizing personal contact was now the only means of controlling his men, he hiked back up Trail 2 where he once again met parts of the 51st Combat Team leaving their lines. Bluemel stopped them and sent them north. Then a truck roared down the trail and almost hit Bluemel when he tried to stop it. A minute later a truck column appeared. A man in the front seat identified the column as the American 31st Infantry and yelled that the San Vicente line had broken. At the same time, great numbers of Filipinos poured down the road. Bluemel tried to reform the Filipinos along a small ridge running perpendicular to the road, but Japanese artillery fell on the line, and the men scattered. "This terminated the existence of the 51st Combat Team," recalled Bluemel.[33] The 51st Team's commander could not rally his men, and Colonel Young remembers that "whenever a stand of any kind was made, low flying airplanes bombed or fired on the troops."[34] The men had suffered enough, and they were concerned now only with survival.

Unable to stop the panic along Trail 2, Bluemel walked back to his headquarters. He again tried to use his telephone but still could not reach II Corps, so he sent Lieutenant Colonel Allan E. Smith, his artillery officer, to II Corps with the news of the collapse of the San Vicente line. Bluemel might well have wondered why he was the only general officer along II Corps's entire front. Then he ordered the 31st Division command post closed and directed that the division's trains move toward Mariveles. Concluding these administrative matters, Bluemel headed northwest along Trail 2 in his Bantam car. He hoped to rally the demoralized men and wanted to find a unit or two with which to fight a delaying action. But most of his men had, by this time, thrown away their arms and equipment. They were hungry, sick, and spiritless. Dismounting from his car and hiding it in some brush, Bluemel walked west under intermittent Japanese shell fire. When artillery impacted nearby, Bluemel's driver roared south and was never seen again. The commander of the most critical sector of Bataan's defenses was without transportation.[35]

Attempting to reform the American 31st Infantry, Bluemel directed the 1st Battalion up a small trail to the north side of a ridge and the men of the 3rd Battalion south along the same ridge. They were mixed with scores of plodding Filipinos, and Bluemel pulled the Americans from the confusion. "He was grabbing men, trying to thrust them back into the line," remembers Private Wilburn Snyder. "This thing was hopeless. He tried to stop the officers. One officer all but hit Bluemel trying to move him out of the way and reason with him, trying to tell him we had orders to go to Lamao."[36] Most of the Americans retained their equipment, but they were haggard and listless. They realized that when the San Vicente was breached, the battle was over, and their instincts told them there was no way to stop the Japanese.

But Bluemel tried. He ordered the men to lie down along the small trail and organize by companies. Only four officers from the regiment were present to assist him. But artillery straddled the trail on which the American B Company was reforming. "What sounded like a runaway freight train hit us," remembered Private Kerchum. An officer and two men were killed and several others wounded. "Then sheer panic ensued. Everybody took off up the hill."[37] On the south side of the ridge the 3rd Battalion picked its way along the trail in full view of enemy artillery firing point-blank into the column of men. "We moved along quite rapidly, throwing ourselves down when the guns fired, but we lost a great number of men," recalled Private Snyder. "Men were knocked down with every shot. A man close by hollered 'aid man.' I went over there and his arm had been blown off all but a piece of skin and part of the muscle. I took out my bayonet and removed that arm. I bandaged it with a tourniquet."[38] Snyder put a tag on an officer killed in action. In his haste, Snyder thought the man was dead, but the officer gave the tag back to Snyder the next morning.

Major Howard C. Crawford's 1st Battalion, 33rd Infantry—Bluemel's Sector reserve—was in an assembly area nearby, and Bluemel ordered them to a low ridge to the right, north, of the 31st Infantry. Japanese artillery hit the newly arrived Filipino battalion, and when the explosions stopped, that unit had vanished. Bluemel and his division staff were all that remained of his 31st Division. Bluemel now realized it was impossible to expect or force further service from his Filipinos. Trails were jammed with stragglers, and mixed with them were Americans as unenthusiastic about facing the Japanese as the Filipinos. Americans wounded by artillery were placed on shelter halves, carried to the last 31st Division bus, and driven to the rear. Two hours later rifle fire erupted to the right rear of the American-held ridge. If the men stayed in place, the enemy would cut their only means of retreat, so Bluemel ordered the Americans to withdraw.[39]

With his division staff dispersed in patrol formation on Trail 2 and the battalions of the 31st Infantry, each numbering about 175 men, marching alongside, Bluemel walked slowly down the trail. Everything went well for a time, but then the Americans made an abrupt and unexpected turn and disappeared into the thick underbrush. Filipino officers tried to find them, but the Americans were nowhere to be seen. Bluemel repeatedly called "31st Infantry, 31st Infantry," but he received no reply. Bluemel was now left with his five staff officers to face the pursuing Japanese. Chief of Staff Colonel Pastor Martelino, G1 Lieutenant Colonel Jose Andrada, G2 the fiery Major Salvador T. Villa, G3 Major Pedro Deang, and G4 Major Napoleon D. Valleriano—a 1939 graduate of the U. S. Cavalry School—all stayed with Bluemel. Continuing south, Bluemel bumped into ten Americans as they emerged from the brush. Bluemel grabbed them and walked south for 500 yards where he met a major who advised Bluemel not to continue along the road but instead cut cross-country. Bluemel pulled out his map and studied the terrain. When he looked up, the major and ten Americans were gone. Bluemel and his staff were alone again.[40]

All across the wreckage of the San Vicente line, units struggled toward new positions. As the 3rd Battalion, 31st Infantry, tried to withdraw down Trail 2, it met with a horrible experience from Japanese dive bombers and strafers. "We were caught on the road," remembers Private Snyder. "Tanks came up to try to assist us in the wide open daylight. But it was futile. They were bombed. I saw tanks turned upside down, blasted, and burned. There was just no way we could evacuate our wounded—nothing could get to us, no buses, no trucks."[41] Most units moved cross-country because the Japanese held the important trails. Forcing their starved bodies over broken terrain, men melted from their organizations, soldiers straggled, and, as one company commander remembered, it was almost every man for himself. The fighting before Mount Samat and the uncontrolled retreat decimated units. Winging over the frightened men came light bombers from the 16th Air Regiment, a total of seventy-eight sorties this day.[42]

A 1st Battalion medic, Corporal James C. Spencer, was one of the Polar Bears struggling through the jungle after separating from Bluemel. Food and water were scarce, and this battalion's withdrawal in broad daylight through a wide valley was frightful. "We were bombed by an airplane which was constantly buzzing us, and we were exposed to sniper fire in the woods," Spencer recalled.[43] It proved difficult to evacuate the casualties. Seriously wounded men were helped by the walking wounded. "This was not an orderly retreat as the others had been," observed Captain Denton Rees, medical officer to the 2nd Battalion. "If casualties could not walk, we had to leave them as we had no means to transport them."[44] The 2nd Battalion lost many officers and men, Major Lloyd Moffitt, the battalion commander, among them. The remnants were exhausted and confused. The Japanese added to the difficulties of the retreat. In one disaster, a large Japanese shell landed in the middle of M Company. Half the men, thirty or more, were killed, wounded, or badly concussed.

When the American 31st Infantry left the San Vicente line, the 3rd Battalion, 57th Infantry, southwest of the Americans and now sitting in "splendid isolation," was forced to conform. Even before withdrawal orders were issued, the battalion came under sporadic small arms fire. The Scouts established a hasty defense around their vehicles and returned a blind fire. Patrols discovered Japanese to the battalion's left and rear. When Lieutenant Colonel Johnson tried to find Colonel Brady, he found instead that the Americans were gone. Johnson called his company commanders together. Because enemy forces were behind him, and because Japanese command of the air made daylight moves of large bodies of troops dangerous, Johnson decided to send each company separately to a rendezvous. There they would take up defensive positions. "I gave them a compass bearing and a trail to reach," Johnson recalled. "We would assemble there. I never saw any of those companies again. I was using a school solution, and it didn't work. It was the wrong solution."[45] The terrain, physical exhaustion, and tropic heat broke the battalion into scattered chips of its former glory. Colonel Johnson, placed in command only the day before, reached friendly lines with ten men.

One of Johnson's companies, Lieutenant Stempin's K Company, lost contact with the rest of the battalion at 1600 hours. "I tried to figure out where in the hell we were," Stempin recalls. "I knew where we were supposed to meet."[46] Stempin's attempts to find and join friendly troops failed. Soon he found numerous signs indicating his men were on the wrong side of the front lines. K Company discovered Japanese mess kits with warm rice in them, and the jungle was unnaturally quiet. After dark the Scouts tried to make their way south, but an attached heavy weapons platoon slowed the movement of the more lightly armed infantrymen. Machine gun tripods, the water-cooled guns themselves, and heavy ammunition boxes sapped the strength of the weapons crewmen. Horsing the unyielding lumps of metal up and down steep hills and across ravines made the men wonder if it was worth the effort. Several sergeants urged Lieutenant Stempin to lighten the load by abandoning a few of the weapons, but Stempin refused. Instead, he allowed frequent rest halts during which time he made compass checks and map studies. At daybreak the men ran into small arms fire. The Scouts tried to identify themselves, but they were answered in Japanese. "That was when all hell broke loose," remembered Stempin.[47] Two Scouts were hit in the first burst. "My Scouts began to return the fire, and we spread out as machine gun fire came from all directions. Before I knew it, they were on both of my flanks and up in the front. We had quite a battle there." The company could not reduce the enemy, and the men scattered. Other 3rd Battalion companies met similar fates and were destroyed or dispersed before reaching the rendezvous.

Trying to stay behind the relative safety of the front line were artillery organizations, and simply keeping the guns away from the advancing Japanese often proved impossible. "Terrible complication regarding transportation both for men, supplies and ammunition not to mention

prime movers," wrote Colonel Quintard in his diary. "[I] am supposed
to get some 32 trucks about dark."[48] At 1800 hours Quintard received
orders to pull his regiment out. The next day he reviewed the status of
his guns. "The 4 ton trucks never got to 'A' and the 2-1/2 ton trucks
[could not] pull the guns out of their emplacements in most instances."
In A Battery, Captain Willard A. Smith found himself short both prime
movers and gasoline, and he and his executive officer had to dynamite
two of their 155mm's when they found it impossible to move the guns.
Half the battery personnel retreated on foot while half rode with the
remaining two guns. B Battery blew three of its guns after they could not
be extracted. The Japanese caught C Battery on a trail and heavily
bombed it. Lieutenant Rich got one gun out, but the other three were
lost. D Battery lost two cannon. F Battery, 86th Artillery blew two
155mm's, and D Battery, 86th lost two more.

As disaster manifested itself in every form, more and more American
officers began drifting from their units. Not all the men who ran were
frightened, inexperienced recruits. Some were professionals. Even field
grade officers found one excuse or another to leave their duties and head
south. In their own minds there's little doubt they could justify, even in
terms of military necessity, the desertion of their units for more hospitable climes. There were, however, still some soldiers on the front lines,
under control, facing the Japanese. And with them was General Bluemel.
However alone he felt at this moment with just five staff officers, aid was
coming. The 26th Cavalry was entering II Corps on its way toward the
fighting. Completing a night march in buses, the two cavalry squadrons
pulled into II Corps at 0430 hours on April 7. There was little overhead
cover or concealment, and the cloak of darkness soon disappeared. Enemy bombing and shelling began at 0700 hours and continued through
the long morning.[49]

Colonel Lee C. Vance and his operations officer, Major Chandler, got
out of their command car at a very quiet Luzon Force headquarters where
they found General Funk and Colonel Collier sitting at the situation map.
Although Collier briefed the two cavalrymen on the deteriorating situation, neither Funk nor Collier could give Vance a very detailed briefing.
As Major Chandler listened, he realized Luzon Force knew "practically
nothing" about front-line conditions, and the information they did pos-
sess was not hopeful. The breakdown in the army's communications had
left the headquarters nearly blind. General Funk told Vance that General
King was asleep, so after Funk and Vance discussed the situation, Funk
directed Vance to move the regiment to the junctions of Trails 2 and 10.
Funk also told Vance to check in with II Corps headquarters. As Chandler

and Vance left, Chandler realized that the fight—although no one actually said it—was just about over.[50]

Major Paul M. Jones, the regiment's communications officer, drove a scout car to II Corps to receive any orders General Parker might have, but when Jones arrived, II Corps headquarters was gone, leaving a lonely lieutenant manning a single telephone. When Jones telephoned II Corps, that headquarters ordered the 26th Cavalry to report to Bluemel north of Trail 10 on Trail 2. Getting to Bluemel was a problem. Smashed and burning vehicles jammed the East Road, Japanese aircraft pounced on moving vehicles, and artillery worked its destructive way up and down the road. At 1130 hours, after receiving orders to move north, Colonel Vance and Major Chandler boarded their command car and led the regiment, now in approach march formation, up the road, leaving personal gear, regimental trains, and their Bren gun carriers behind. Lieutenant Ramsey and a platoon from G Troop preceded the regimental headquarters, and behind Colonel Vance came the remainder of the 2nd Squadron, G Troop and composite Troop E-F, and A and B troops of the 1st Squadron. The regiment soon reached Trail Junction 10 and 2.[51]

Overhead a Japanese plane spotted Vance's vehicle around which Vance, his executive officer, and his operations officer were discussing the situation. The whine of the bomb drove everyone to a nearby trench. The bomb narrowly missed, and after the plane left, Vance sent two scout cars north to find Bluemel. Major Chandler took one of the vehicles and threaded past bombed and burning trucks. He finally found Bluemel moving slowly and reluctantly south and told him the 26th Cavalry was at the junction of Trails 2 and 10. When Bluemel heard the regiment was to work for him, he cheered up a bit. "Bluemel was exhausted and discouraged," recalled Chandler, "I'm not sure how much he knew about us or our record, but he was sure glad to see me and hear he again had one organized unit."[52] The cavalrymen, Chandler told Bluemel, awaited his orders.

"Tell Colonel Vance to hold the 26th Cavalry in its present position until I arrive," Bluemel told Chandler.[53] Then Bluemel found the two lost 31st Infantry battalions and sent them toward the trail junction held by the cavalrymen. A few minutes later Bluemel came upon a ten-foot-deep bomb crater blocking a light tank, two scout cars, three trucks, and several other vehicles. An overturned tank lay by the side of the crater. The cavalrymen were just 100 yards south on some high ground about one kilometer north of Trail Junction 2 and 10. Colonel Vance deployed Captain Joseph R. Barker's G Troop just north of the crater, rounded up as many fleeing Filipinos as his Scouts could grab, and put them to work filling the crater. Vance was determined to get his two scout cars to safety, but a fight developed when pursuing Japanese foot soldiers arrived. As Vance added more and more of his men to the line, the shooting increased and the Japanese slowly worked around the right flank of G Troop. Captain Wheeler's Troop E-F moved to the right of G Troop and stopped the advance. When some bullets impacted around the Filipinos filling the crater, the men dropped their shovels and fled. Irate Scouts grabbed a few Filipinos but not enough to finish the job. Vance reluctantly ordered the scout cars destroyed, and he withdrew his men to the high ground south of the crater.

As the cavalrymen moved into position, they prepared to execute another delaying action, a maneuver with which they were quite familiar. Gunners emplaced machine guns, riflemen searched for cover and fields of fire, and drivers backed vehicles into defilade. The 1st Squadron moved into position to protect the 2nd Squadron's route of withdrawal. Standing on a small ridge with advance elements of the Scouts, Bluemel received a message from II Corps directing that he occupy a position now well behind Japanese lines. Bluemel had only the cavalry regiment for the mission, so even if he could launch an attack, the Scouts would end up isolated. Bluemel decided to hold the ridge he then owned and disregard the attack order.[54]

The Japanese of Colonel Haruji Morita's 8th Infantry were closely following the American 31st Infantry as it filtered through the Scouts, and Morita's men hit the 2nd Squadron, its two troops barely numbering 159 officers and men. The battle was short but lively, and when the Japanese paused for breath, they were astonished to find the Scouts still in place. But rather than take unnecessary casualties in a frontal attack, the Japanese started another flanking movement, a maneuver which quickly proved dangerous to the Scouts. The 2nd Squadron's commander, Major Blanning, issued orders to withdraw, left to right, G Troop first and then Troop E-F. Enemy fire, both small arms and artillery, made breaking off the action very difficult, but the squadron withdrew in good order protected by a rear guard of two squads.[55]

The 1st Squadron now faced the Japanese from hasty emplacements just northeast of Trail Junction 2 and 10. The ground here was open, rolling, and sparsely vegetated with low bushes and a few large mango groves, not the sort of terrain to offer much concealment. Scouts found supply elements of the 14th Engineer Battalion nearby and ordered them out of the way. When the Japanese ran into the 1st Squadron, they once again sent flanking parties around both sides of the defenders. At the same time, Japanese dive bombers fell on the cavalrymen at the junction, wounding Captain Wheeler commanding Troop E-F and practically wiping out the 2nd Squadron's two-squad rear guard. Under threat of encirclement, the 1st Squadron withdrew through the most severe bombing and shelling the regiment had ever experienced. The men had to cross the danger area by short rushes in small groups, and casualties were heavy. Captain Spies' B Troop was especially hard hit—his men never reached the rendezvous—and an ambulance and two Bren gun carriers were also lost. Bluemel had foreseen the impossibility of stopping the enemy at the junction and had issued orders to reassemble at the nearby Mamala River.[56]

The 26th Cavalry, 31st Infantry, and trucks from the 14th Engineers all jammed the road where it dropped toward the Mamala River, and the narrow, steep-sided, one-way Trail 12 overflowed with traffic. Demoralized Filipinos, flushed by the Japanese, further choked the route. Circling overhead, Japanese pilots could hardly miss seeing the target. In an easy coordination of hand and feet, pilots from the 16th Air Regiment pitched their planes earthward and delivered the most awe-inspiring bombing the soldiers had ever seen. Scout engineers had just loaded a truck with ammunition and machine guns when four planes roared in destroying the truck and wounding the Scouts. Another bomb hit a cavalry ammunition truck in the narrowest part of the trail. The truck caught fire, set nearby trees ablaze, blocked the trail, and peppered men and vehicles with fragments. The air attack smashed communications trucks, ambulances, and every sort of rolling conveyance. Three scout cars had to be destroyed after the trail proved impassable. Colonel Vance ran his rear guard past the burning trucks and separated his veteran cavalrymen from the mob surrounding him. He regained control, issued orders, and straddled Trail 12 on the south bank of the Mamala River. By 1830 hours Bluemel had another line, but it was a line without transportation. Nearly all his vehicles lay burning on Trails 2 and 12.[57]

At the end of April 7 the 33rd Infantry (-), the only unit still surviving west of Mount Samat, was destroyed. The situation in this regiment was similar to other regiments for which records do not exist yet different enough to make their action unusual, that some time will be spent on their seemingly insignificant portion of the battle. The 33rd Infantry had moved into position northwest of Mount Samat on Trail 6 the early morning of April 4. At daylight the regiment sent patrols north, east, and west, hoping to contact friendlies and determine the whereabouts of the enemy. Patrols to the west looked for Constabulary, those to the north searched for the enemy, and those sent to the east tried to find the 21st Division. But each patrol returned with the same report, no Japanese, no friendlies, nothing. On April 5 more patrols returned with the same report, but this time they collected twelve stragglers from the 21st Division, unarmed, in civilian clothes, trying to make their way to refugee camps farther south. "I advised them that they were forthwith attached to the 33rd Infantry," recalled Lieutenant Chapin who commanded the 3rd Battalion, "issued them hand grenades, and had them posted in the Catmon River on our left flank as a precaution against attacks from that quarter."[58] When a man went to check on the new arrivals an hour later, they were gone.

Finally, a patrol did spot some Japanese, but they were south of the regiment, between the Filipinos and their only route of withdrawal. The American officers knew the situation was bad but they took every precaution to keep the bad news from their men. They explained the presence of the Japanese on Trail 6 as a passing patrol. The officers watched closely for the first signs of panic or hysteria. Some of Chapin's men were beyond hysteria, for they were dying from starvation. Because the presence of dead and dying soldiers in the foxhole line badly demoralized the remaining men, stronger men made an effort to bury the dead and move the critically ill men out of sight.

On April 6 the situation deteriorated. Ration trucks failed to arrive, and the regiment's single radio could not send or receive. The regiment's officers discussed whether or not the two battalions should attack west and link with elements of I Corps. The idea was logical but Major Holmes, a 31-year-old Pennsylvanian, West Point class of '34, did not feel free to abandon the mission given him by II Corps. He sent several runners south in hopes of receiving further orders, but none of the runners returned. So Major Holmes held his men in position. Finally, in a haphazard sequence, the regiment's untouched condition changed. A four-man Filipino patrol, investigating footprints, was surprised and captured by some Japanese. The Japanese disarmed and tied the Filipinos, but one captive dashed off toward the outpost line. When his comrades saw him running in, tied, they fired to cover his escape and, in the confusion, the other three Filipinos also escaped. An hour later Japanese artillery came in on the regiment, but losses were light. When the artillery lifted, small arms and machine gun fire laced the single company on the outpost line, caused severe casualties, and forced the company to request relief. At dark another company relieved them.

After dark, Major Holmes called a conference. He learned that the 2nd Battalion's outpost company had suffered 30 percent losses. In the rest of the battalion, ten men had died during the day from sickness and another 20 percent were too tired to move. All were jittery, exhausted, and demoralized. The situation did not differ significantly in the 3rd Battalion where fifty-five men had been killed or wounded over the last three days and thirty more had died of disease. The survivors were in such bad shape they would not be very effective if attacked. Major

Holmes tried to put a better face on these reports, but he too knew the situation was desperate. "All of us Americans could see the hand writing on the wall," recalled Lieutenant Chapin. "We knew we were completely isolated and could expect no relief. We knew that we could not sustain a prolonged attack in force." The only reason the men were still in position was the physical presence of the American officers. Even so, there were growing signs of panic. When someone surfaced the question of withdrawal, Major Holmes told his officers to hold as long as humanly possible, then withdraw south on Trail 6 using rear-guard tactics. The 2nd Battalion would cover the withdrawal of the 3rd, and the 3rd would then cover the withdrawal of the 2nd. Throughout the night the 33rd Infantry received almost constant artillery fire from two enemy batteries.

At 0500 hours on April 7 Japanese artillery ceased, and mortar fire intensified. An hour later two companies of Japanese attacked the outpost line and spent ninety minutes evicting the Filipinos. As the Japanese advanced along Trail 6, their supporting automatic weapons hit the foxholes of the 3rd Battalion. Only when the Japanese arrived at a point 200 yards from the front lines did they enter an area covered by Filipino machine guns and come to a halt. But as their thrust slowed, they placed additional fires on the Filipinos from high ground off to both flanks. There were no mad, suicidal banzai charges, only the professional application of fire and maneuver. Then a 37mm cannon fired into the foxhole line. The 3rd Battalion had by now sustained heavy casualties, and the men were scared and wild-eyed. Major Holmes came down to talk to Lieutenant Chapin, and after a brief conversation Holmes promised some help from the 2nd Battalion. No sooner did Holmes leave than every machine gun in the 3rd Battalion opened a furious fire—Japanese tanks were attacking. Chapin's only antitank weapon was a .50-caliber machine gun, and it was shooting at the tanks without apparent effect. Then Chapin learned his K Company was withdrawing. Chapin yelled over the phone to stay put and promised he was on his way to help. As he ran down the slope, he bumped into K Company scrambling up the hill.

"I was nearly at the end of my string by that time," Chapin remembered. "I was groggy from loss of sleep and physical exhaustion. Something inside me snapped when I saw those men running away. They had that fear-crazed look on their faces that knows no reasoning. I kicked them, clubbed and cursed them down into position. I shot at two who wouldn't stop and finally got the company where they could fire over the heads of the rest of the Battalion into the Japs. I told them that I would shoot the first one who even looked like he was going to retreat. Of course, they didn't understand me. Hardly any of them spoke English."

Down in the draw up which the Japanese were advancing, the tanks were having more trouble getting around trees felled by engineers than fighting the Filipinos. Machine gun bullets rained onto the tanks, but they simply bounced off. As Chapin yelled into the phone trying to contact Major Holmes, he heard a shout and saw the remains of his battalion, mostly unarmed, pounding around a bend in the trail. Chapin jumped into the middle of the trail and fired twice, low enough over their heads to get their attention, but they did not even waver. Chapin had to jump off the trail to keep from being trampled. A moment later the lead Japanese tank nosed into sight. Then firing broke out to Chapin's rear, and he saw Japanese infantry run down the hill and across Trail 6. Completely cut off, Chapin looked for his men, but other than his three-man staff, not one Filipino was in sight. Chapin and his staff jumped down a steep, 100-foot incline in a heart-thumping escape. The survivors of the 33rd Infantry tried to make their way to friendly lines, but they were largely unsuccessful.

As the broken 33rd Infantry struggled south, Wainwright was ordering General King to launch an attack with I Corps's 11th Division. Wainwright, unaware the Mamala River line was already in the process of evacuation, hoped to thrust east across the Pantingan River and reunite I and II corps along the Mamala River. But even if the 11th Division could, by some miracle, reach the Mamala, it would find the Japanese holding it. Concerned over Wainwright's perception of events on Bataan, General King decided to send his chief of staff, General Funk, to Corregidor to tell Wainwright the situation was critical and surrender imminent. Wainwright realized further resistance was futile, but his orders, received from both Roosevelt and MacArthur, sternly forbade surrender. MacArthur's message of April 4 ordered Wainwright to attack if his food gave out. He was not to surrender. President Roosevelt also refused permission to surrender so long as any possibility of resistance remained. So Wainwright had little choice in the matter.[59]

General Funk arrived on Corregidor after a short trip by launch, entered the bomb-proof tunnels of Fort Mills under Malinta Hill, and walked to Wainwright's lateral. Funk had a single mission; he was to explain the military situation without reservation. King had told Funk to acquaint Wainwright in detail with the situation and give him such first-hand information as he desired. Funk had just completed a personal inspection of the Bataan front and was familiar with the worsening conditions. Standing before Wainwright and his chief of staff, Funk described the Japanese breakthrough, the sick and wounded soldiers, and the lack of food. He told Wainwright that II Corps had disintegrated, that there was nothing but confusion at the front, and that because of the physical condition of I Corps, the fall of Bataan was imminent. Despite this briefing, Wainwright had no options. On his desk was MacArthur's order to attack.[60]

In his characteristically slow drawl, Wainwright answered, "General, you go back and tell General King he will not surrender. Tell him he will attack. Those are my orders."[61]

Funk made one last effort and asked, "General, you know, of course, what the situation is over there. You know what the outcome will be."

"I do," replied Wainwright. He stood up and shook Funk's hand. "I understand the situation. God help you all over there. I have done all I can."[62] No questions remained as Funk wearily departed. He crossed the North Channel and reported to King at 1600 hours that Wainwright wanted I Corps to attack east across the Pantingan, across the north face of Mount Mariveles, and strike the Japanese in the flank.

After Funk left Corregidor, Wainwright sent a detailed report to MacArthur.

> On Bataan front near right center fierce fighting has been in progress today. Fresh reserves had been assembled permitting enemy to mass superior forces and he then attacked vigorously accompanied by heavy artillery fire and tanks. Enemy bombers and dive bombers have assisted in the attack by repeatedly dropping bombs and strafing front line troops. Superior forces have been successful in driving a wedge into Bataan position but ground is being gained slowly. Again at eleven oclock today Base Hospital Number One on Bataan was bombed by three successive flights. Numerous casualties resulting. When enemy planes bombed this hospital a few days ago, High Command of Japanese forces tendered apology in Manila broadcast. Another attack on the same hospital coming only a few days after first indicates strongly that today's bombing was intentional. . . . Enemy with aid of terrific air and artillery bombardment has penetrated to Trail Eight which is seven thousand yards south of original main line of resistance. Mount Samat now well within enemy area pocket created by separated First and Second Corps. Under pressure of terrific pounding administered by hostile artillery and dive bombers, Forty First, Twenty First, and most of Thirty First Divisions have dispersed as other units did in previous attacks. Have been forced to use all Philippine Division and other available resources in efforts to halt the attack. Hostile advance appears at this time to have been halted. I am attacking to east with elements of First Corps in an effort to strike the enemy right flank and restore communications on original front.[63]

On Bataan, General King was then in the process of placing everything he could find along the Mamala River. King gambled that the Japanese would not launch any amphibious operations and ordered the withdrawal of the 1st and 4th constabulary regiments from beach defense for commitment to battle. If the Japanese now staged an amphibious

attack along the Manila Bay coast, no infantry would contest their landing. Both regiments were ordered to move thirty minutes after dark. The
4th Constabulary started up to Limay, a point from which they would
continue north to the fight. In haste, and without reconnaissance, the
regiment's lead elements crossed the Mamala River and unexpectedly
ran into Japanese. In the ensuing melee the regiment's supply officer, his
assistant, and a considerable number of men were killed. The 4th Constabulary recoiled in confusion.[64]

With the reinforcement effort at the Mamala River in chaos, Colonel
Collier left Luzon Force Headquarters at 1600 hours carrying the attack
order to General Jones in I Corps. But Jones, then in the process of
withdrawing his entire corps to conform to II Corps's new dispositions,
said his men were too weak for the effort and success impossible. He
would, of course, do all in his power to carry out the attack, but he had to
state the mission was impossible of accomplishment. The soldiers were in
such poor physical condition that they could not even cross the Pantingan
River gorge in time for the attack to achieve its purpose. The obstacle
posed by the river was such to task fresh troops under resolute leadership. Cliffs dropped for several hundred feet and made passage of vehicles out of the question. Without vehicles to carry heavy weapons, ammunition, and food, the fighting front could not be sustained. Nor did
necessary communications equipment—radio or wire—exist to direct and
control such an attack. It would take over eighteen hours, at the very
minimum, to pull the 11th Division out of the line and turn it east.[65]

The argument was actually academic. The line to which the 11th Division was to attack was already deserted. Wainwright had left the decision
whether or not to attack to General King's discretion, so King, after
talking with Corregidor, withdrew the order. Having made the decision
to withdraw the I Corps attack order, King now told I Corps to continue
its withdrawal to the line of the Binuangan River, a distance of about five
miles. The move would accomplish two things, reduce the length of
beach requiring protection along I Corps's left flank, and cover I Corps's
right flank by tying it into the difficult terrain of Mariveles Mountain.
The corps would be ready to fight at any time during its withdrawal.
After passing this order to I Corps, King was free to turn his attention
back to II Corps.[66]

As night fell on April 7 Bluemel continued his hopeless task of building a line to stop the Japanese. When he arrived at the Mamala River he
found orders from II Corps directing him to form a line there. These
orders were part of the plan that sent the 4th Constabulary into the
middle of the retreat and which tried to send the 11th Division across the
Pantingan. But Bluemel realized he could not defend the Mamala. Japa-

nese were already on the north bank of the proposed line, and high ground and steep bluffs on the north side of the small river overlooked the lower south bank, the side he was told to occupy. The Japanese could look down the throats of anyone trying to move and fight. And at the moment the only troops at the river were Scouts of the 26th Cavalry. Bluemel learned that several units were a mile and a half south of the Mamala. While walking toward them to see if there was better terrain there on which to make a stand, he came under fire along Trail 20. Realizing the 26th Cavalry might get cut off, Bluemel ordered them out of the Mamala position. At an assembly point designated earlier in the day, Bluemel found the commanders of the 31st Infantry, 57th Infantry, 14th Engineer Battalion, and parts of the 803rd Aviation Engineer Battalion. None of the men had eaten since breakfast the day before, the strength of each unit was low, and the soldiers were without heavy machine guns, mortars, and transportation.[67]

At 2000 hours Bluemel decided to continue south to the Alangan River in hopes of breaking contact with the Japanese and finding time to set up a new line. He sent one of his two remaining vehicles with an officer-messenger to II Corps with his plan. He then dispatched his last truck with his commanders and staffs to reconnoiter the Alangan River, agree to boundaries, and guide their men into position. Without much choice, II Corps approved Bluemel's plan and ordered the remnants of Colonel Irwin's Sectors A and B to form to Bluemel's right. II Corps hoped that Irwin could prevent the Japanese from pushing down the open terrain bordering the East Road. Around midnight Colonel Mallonee, in charge of Colonel Irwin's guns, learned of the move to the Alangan. "I directed that the CP be moved at once to some location near Cabcaben," he recalled. "It didn't make any difference where it was located, since there was no phone wire and no possibility of an organized setup—I merely wanted to get it and its collection of pleasant young men the hell out of the way."[68] It was not until well past daylight the next day that the last gun shuttled to safety behind the Alangan.

In Bluemel's sector, from right to left, C Company, 803rd Engineers, was to take up position on the right (east), next the 31st Infantry, then the 57th Infantry (minus the 3rd Battalion), and finally the 26th Cavalry stretching to the west. Bluemel ordered the 14th Engineer Battalion into line just to the west of Trail 20. At 2100 hours Bluemel collected his units and swung into another withdrawal. Because elements of the 803rd Engineers were familiar with the trail, they led the march and posted guides at all trail junctions and turns. Following the engineers came the main body. "The night was one of the darkest I've ever seen," recalled Corporal Milton, "and we marched holding on to the man ahead."[69]

Visibility extended no farther than from tree to tree, and communications during the march were nonexistent. Philippine Army soldiers mixed with Scouts, Americans, and civilians. Stalled vehicles reduced progress to a crawl while a battery of broken-down 155mm guns blocked traffic and delayed the 57th Infantry's vehicles for more than an hour. North of the jammed trail at the junction of Trails 2 and 18, the 2nd Squadron, 26th Cavalry, positioned all its men, 106 Scouts, to cover Bluemel's withdrawal. At 0120 hours the last of the main body departed. Japanese patrols were nearby and fired intermittently, but Scout fire discipline held; no return fire outlined their positions. At 0220 hours the 2nd Squadron slipped quietly from their rear guard positions and headed south.

Farther east, closer to Manila Bay, the 1st Battalion, Air Corps Regiment, reached new positions at 0330 hours on April 8. The exhausted men sank to the ground while the regimental commander used a flashlight to check his map. He decided that this was not the correct place; it was back up the road a mile. Captain Coleman dreaded the thought of telling his men they had to move once more, but he got them up and the battalion backtracked to the spot designated by the colonel. But no sooner did Coleman's men arrive there than a runner brought the news that this was not the correct place either, it was back where they just came from. Unbelieving, the men backtracked again.[70]

Finally at the proper spot, Captain Coleman and Colonel Maverick set off on a reconnaissance. On a high, steep hill half a mile to their front they met Lieutenant Colonel Brady reconnoitering the area for his 31st Infantry. The officers discussed the large hill that completely dominated the line they were supposed to occupy. "It would be suicide to take up this position," Brady said.[71] The three officers decided to move their men forward of the planned line and deploy on the hill instead of below it. By this chance early morning encounter, Bluemel's Alangan River Line tied tentatively into the remnants of Colonel Irwin's Sectors A and B. Without any rest, the airmen moved to the hill, hoping to entrench before enemy planes arrived.

North of this line scattered groups of isolated Americans were still making their way south. Private Leland Sims was in the rear of a small column of twenty airmen. They had bumped into a Japanese tank earlier in the day but survived because they were so close the tank could not depress its guns enough to shoot. Now it was dark, and they were walking along a narrow trail. Private Sims heard whispers as a message passed from man to man, "Japanese, just keep walking."[72] Sims found himself picking his way through a bivouac of sleeping Japanese. To his left he saw white shirts of sleeping Japanese officers, and to his right slept the enlisted men. He pulled pins from two hand grenades and held them ready. If anyone had coughed, there would have been a fight. A fight would have been disastrous, for Sims later discovered his hand grenades did not have powder in them.

By the early morning hours of April 8 all reserves of II Corps, Luzon Force, and I Corps were committed. There was nothing left with which anyone could influence the battle. The entire Bataan army was decisively engaged. The situation had passed the critical stage and was now terminal —it was only a question of how long the death throes would last. II Corps headquarters moved that night from the Lamao River valley near Rodriguez Park to Kilometer Post 167-1/2 on the East Road. II Corps artillery displaced its remaining guns to the rear. Hospital Number 2 admitted 700 patients the evening and night of the 7th. Orderlies scattered them through the packed wards, on the ground, or on a blanket if the patient owned one. When possible, doctors administered medication. The operating room was jammed. The army's supply organizations folded. Transportation units, without orders, abandoned their motor pools and headed west and south. During the night Corregidor started shipping what would total 2,845 gallons of gasoline to Bataan. Before dawn 329 five-gallon cans and twenty-four fifty-gallon drums were unloaded on Bataan's docks. This was the first installment of 10,000 gallons headed for King's army, but by now it was too late.[73]

The Japanese decision to continue their push without delay is not surprising. They accomplished in five days what they expected would take a month, and losses were extremely light. The 4th Division spearheaded the assault and suffered 150 men killed and 250 wounded, about half a battalion. The 65th Brigade counted 77 dead and 152 wounded. The Nagano Detachment reported no casualties at all! The Japanese figures are not in serious doubt, for the defense offered by the Filamerican force was feeble. Still believing the American reserve line lay near the Mamala River, the Japanese were pleasantly surprised when they forced its evacuation without a fight. "This was beyond our expectation," remembered General Homma.[74] Instead of taking a break at the Mamala, as originally planned, the Japanese designated Cabcaben on the southeast tip of the peninsula as the next objective.

CHAPTER TWENTY-SEVEN

Wednesday, April 8

ON APRIL 8 WAINWRIGHT REPORTED HIS SITUATION TO WASHINGton.

> Continued heavy enemy pressure, constant bombing, strafing, and shelling of the front line units forced all elements of the right half of our line in Bataan to fall back. A new defensive position is forming on the high ground south of the Alangan River extending to the west. The left half of our line due to an exposed flank withdrew on orders and is taking up a defensive position south of the Binuangan River. Fighting is intense, casualties on both sides heavy. Heavy bombing in rear of peninsula was carried out by hostile aircraft.[1]

During the early morning hours of April 8, fragments of II Corps occupied the Alangan River Line. Men dropped on the river bank, pushed their faces into the water, and drank their fill—water, mud, and sand. The south bank of the river, covered with dry cogan grass two to six feet tall mixed with clumps of bamboo and a few trees, sloped steeply into the water, but the stream itself was not a significant military obstacle. Gasoline, seeping from wrecked vehicles awash in the river, tainted the water. Occupation of the Alangan was difficult, and there was great confusion on the line. Americans of Captain Robert J. Chandler's C Company, 803rd Engineers missed their position in the dark and continued south after crossing the river. The 300-man American 31st Infantry and the 500-man Scout 57th Infantry unwittingly crossed each other during the night march and took up the wrong positions. Upon learning their mistake, Colonels Brady and Lilly agreed to keep the terrain they already held; to physically move the two regiments into their planned positions was out of the question.[2]

Straddling Trail 20 on the left of the line, about 450 Scouts of the 14th Engineer Battalion covered a road block in heavily wooded terrain and refused the left flank of Bluemel's line. Lieutenant Colonel Frederick G. Saint's engineers overturned a big civilian truck in the middle of Trail 20, worked heavy rocks around the truck, and dropped large trees next to it. These engineers were the freshest, least disorganized of the soldiers along the Alangan, and they tied in with the 26th Cavalry to their right. The 26th Cavalry's rearguard arrived about 0745 hours. Both squadrons went on line covering 350 yards of the Alangan Ridge. The 173 troopers used bolos and bayonets to scratch small foxholes, and they entrenched without being seen by the Japanese. In contrast to the relatively fresh engineers, the cavalrymen had snatched but one hour's sleep in the past fifty-four hours and consumed but a single canteen of water in the past thirty hours. They were so tired that the only way to stay awake was to stand. Between the cavalry and the Americans to their right was about 600 yards of unoccupied, open, cogan grass-covered ridge. Then Colonel Brady, with slightly more than 200 Americans remaining from the 1,600 which fought at Layac on January 6, occupied a narrow piece of ground with no contact to either flank. Off to Brady's right, about 400 yards away, stood two reduced battalions of the Scout 57th Infantry guarding a front of 500 yards. Although the Scout infantry found their right flank empty because of the absence of the 803rd Engineers, they did tie in unexpectedly with two small companies, about 125 men in all, of the American 31st Infantry, men separated from the rest of the regiment. Five-foot-tall cogan grass severely limited observation here, so contact patrols would try to cover the gap between the Scouts and Americans.[3]

To the right of Bluemel's Alangan River force, parts of the Provisional Air Corps Regiment deployed without finding friendly forces on either flank. The ground was hard, and the weakened men could not entrench. The 2nd Battalion set up their two air-cooled .50-caliber machine guns, laid out ammunition belts, and waited in the growing, enervating heat. No communications existed except for messengers taking hours to make a single trip. No one knew where other elements were, and if someone did learn the location of another unit, it was normally gone before a communications team could string telephone wire to it. The dense underbrush along the river made it extremely difficult to gain or maintain contact.[4]

Bluemel, in a state of mental anguish and near physical collapse, commanded the Alangan River Line, and with him were but two Filipino staff officers. Still without sleep, food, or reinforcements, Bluemel worked to form a line from his broken units. He tapped into a telephone line along Trail 20, contacted the II Corps operations officer, and described the hole to his right, to the right of the 57th Infantry. Actually, this gap was partially plugged by two small American rifle companies, but Bluemel did not know this, so he urged that beach defense troops be sent forward immediately.

"Troops will be sent up after dark," replied Colonel Howard D. Johnston.[5]

"That'll be too late. You can be damned sure the enemy will find that big gap before dark and rush through." Then to Bluemel's surprise, II Corps told him he was now in charge of the entire corps line. Colonel Johnston offered him assistance; what would he need?

"I need four staff officers, communication personnel and equipment from II Corps."

"Use your own staff," Johnston replied, for Johnston assumed Bluemel still had his 31st Division staff with him.

"I have only two Filipino staff officers," Bluemel answered. "Like me, they've been without food since breakfast of 6 April and have had about one and a half hours' sleep a night. I have no communication personnel or equipment. The 31st Signal Company disappeared."

"Well, you'll have to take staff officers from the troops with you. Use their communication equipment and personnel."

These answers were not helping Bluemel at all. "Since you're not sending me any troops until after dark to fill the gap, I can't possibly hold the line. What line do you want me to hold next? This time I'd like to send out officers from every unit to make a daylight reconnaissance."

"Hold your present line," was the insistent reply.

"Damn it" Bluemel exploded, "I told you it was impossible. Not unless the gap is filled immediately."

"Hold that line." It was sounding like a football chant. Bluemel banged down the phone. He knew there were about thirty American officers at II Corps headquarters who were "eating and sleeping regularly," and the assertion that none could be spared for the fighting line enraged him.

Because the 26th Cavalry was nearby, Bluemel continued to use the staff of that regiment in place of the officers he requested from II Corps. But he could do nothing about the inadequate communications situation, and because of this, Bluemel effectively controlled just the 14th Engineers and the 26th Cavalry; the 31st and 57th infantry were on their own. Trying to fill the gap between the cavalry and the 31st Infantry, Bluemel assembled a sixty-man provisional company from the 31st Division trains and placed it to the right of the cavalry. Then Bluemel's officers collected stragglers and deserters, formed those with rifles into teams of ten to twenty men, and added them to the provisional company. Not surprisingly, many deserted between the time they were assembled and the time they reached the gap, and others slipped away when the officers were not looking. Few had any stomach to fight to the death among strangers.[6]

During the morning Lieutenant Colonel Joseph Ganahl arrived and asked if his battalion of 75mm self-propelled mounts could be of assistance. Although II Corps would, before noon, detail three Scout artillery battalions to support Bluemel, he did not have anything at this time, so he told Ganahl he would accept anything he had. Ganahl reconnoitered the area and promised to send two guns as soon as he reached his battalion. Ganahl soon returned with the guns and put them into position near the cavalrymen. The cannon covered the high ground north of the river, guarded the only road on which tanks could advance, and greatly cheered the spirits of the cavalrymen.[7]

Unfortunately, Japanese reconnaissance planes spotted all this activity. At 1100 hours aircraft from the 16th Air Regiment found both the 57th and the 31st Infantry as they organized their positions. Not all the strikes were as accurate as the Japanese desired. Because of the rapid advance, pilots seldom knew where their own front lines were. Between briefings at their airfield and arrival over Bataan, their information became outdated. From the air the pilots had trouble deciding if the dusty soldiers below were friends or foes. The Americans found grim amusement listening to screams coming from Japanese lines when air attacks fell short. In this case, however, the light bombers were utterly unopposed by any antiaircraft fire and accurately dropped incendiaries. Fierce grass fires drove the two American companies east of the 57th Infantry out of position. The infantrymen took refuge in some woods just south of their line, waited until the fires died, and then reoccupied their burned foxholes. Without food, out of touch with their regiment, and commanded by just three officers, their staunch refusal to flee speaks highly of their training, discipline, and esprit. The Americans, feeling themselves as good as the Scouts to their left, were determined to hold as long as the 57th Infantry.[8]

At 1400 hours advance elements of the Japanese 8th Infantry appeared before the 57th Infantry. A half hour later, as the Japanese felt their way along the line, the first of several strong probes hit the Scouts. The Japanese found both open flanks, but this did not automatically mean success. The Scout 2nd Battalion stood doggedly firm and destroyed a fourteen-man enemy patrol deep in their rear. At 1530 hours a busload of Filipinos drove north up Trail 20 where Bluemel stopped the bus and asked the men their organization. Upon learning they were a platoon from G Company, 4th Constabulary, Bluemel asked them their destination. When they said they were going to report to General Bluemel, and when Bluemel identified himself, there was a marked silence. He finally got them out of the bus carrying their combat gear and ordered them under some trees. Colonel Smyth, executive officer to the Tank Group, arrived while the Constabulary organized and asked if tanks could be used, so Bluemel and Smyth made a reconnaissance to locate positions. Returning to the trail, Bluemel was about to order the Constabulary into the line when Japanese rifle fire pattered through the area. The platoon broke and ran at the first shot. It was impossible to stop them, and Bluemel never saw them again. After watching the Filipinos run away, Colonel Smyth turned to Bluemel and promised to send him three tanks immediately. The tanks never arrived.[9]

On the far right of Bluemel's line enemy pressure increased against the two American companies fighting from sooty, blackened grasslands. With hardly four clips of rifle ammunition per man, prolonged resistance was impossible. At 1630 hours, after slowing the Japanese for ninety minutes, the Americans, under the control of their officers, withdrew to the Paalungan River, just south of the Alangan.[10]

Then the center of Bluemel's line buckled. After Japanese artillery shelled out a platoon from A Company, 31st Infantry, the company commander, Lieutenant Alfred E. Lee, ordered a six-man squad into the hole. Corporal Glenn Milton ran up with two of his men and signaled the remaining three to come forward. "I was so tired that I couldn't make my mind operate," Milton remembers. "I saw one Jap, I knew something was wrong, and until he stopped about 15 yards away and his chin strap swung in the breeze, I just couldn't coordinate my mind and body. When the strap swung, I reacted."[11] Milton dropped the man with a shot from his M-1 rifle. A moment later a mortar round burst next to Milton's left foot. Surprised to find himself alive, but sporting a piece of steel in his arm and holes in his leg, a dazed Milton watched Lieutenant Lee run up to him. "Get back to the aid station," Lee ordered, "Get back as soon as you can because we are moving out." A 57th Infantry medic helped Milton and three others to the aid station where medics cut off his trousers and shoe top, wrapped a bandage around the leg, and stopped the bleeding. Then the wounded men were abandoned as Milton's company withdrew. With some rations and cigarettes, Milton awaited the Japanese. He did not think he could walk, but when a column of Japanese passed nearby, he grabbed a bamboo pole and limped south.

As Bluemel's two-company right flank was about to withdraw, as his center 31st Infantry was being pressured, and as the 57th Infantry was repulsing probes from nearly all sides, his far left entered the fight. Three companies of Lieutenant Colonel "Freddie" Saint's 14th Engineers covered Trail 20 where the trail ran through Bluemel's lines. Saint, a 33-year-old West Point engineer, a capable, hard-working, conscientious officer from Illinois, had graduated from advanced education at Princeton in 1934 after his 1931 West Point schooling. He then taught engineering at West Point from 1936 to 1940. He was just one of many American officers who started the war as a captain and soared two grades by April, his last promotion coming on April 7. His unit, which on December 8 suffered the first casualties in the Philippine Division from Japanese bombs dropped short of the intended target, was now to suffer some of the last casualties. At 1400 hours sporadic firing in front of Saint's men announced the approach of Japanese. An hour later Captain Homer L. Jones's B Company was heavily engaged as it clung to Trail 20, yet the combat engineers held firm and feigned disinterest as Japanese bullets sizzled by. The Scouts had a good commander to emulate, for Jones was a big, hearty Pennsylvanian who could work and work and work, a man who left the hospital early in the war despite a broken leg which had not completely healed just to be with his men.[12]

As one of Jones's men, Private Mar G. Arradaza, scurried from tree to tree to deliver a message, he heard tractor engines across the river. "I thought it was our company bulldozers moving out of the area," recalled the 19-year-old demolition specialist, "but some of our men were shouting 'tanks.'"[13] A little after 1600 hours six Japanese tanks from the 7th Tank Regiment rolled into sight on the north side of the river and blindly fired cannon and machine guns at the south bank. Japanese infantry dismounted and started two wide flanking movements. After softening up suspected Filipino positions, the six tanks churned through the rocky river bed, climbed the narrow trail south of the Alangan, and ran into the rock-and-truck roadblock established earlier that day by Saint's engineers. The narrow trail, steep slopes, and virgin jungle flanking the obstacle prevented the Japanese from turning around, so they sat there firing machine guns and 47mm tank cannons. The tanks had no infantry immediately available (they were probing Bluemel's line) and were relatively unprotected, but the engineers, without antitank guns, could not hurt the tanks. For a time it was a standoff. Then more Japanese from the 8th Infantry, following the tanks in trucks, and already pressuring the 31st and 57th infantry, dismounted, deployed, and hit the 26th Cavalry.

One hundred seventy-five cavalrymen were dug into the Alangan Ridge running off the higher ground farther west. North and west of the cavalry intermittent woods extended from the Alangan River up to the Scout line, and the Japanese 8th Infantry used the sparse concealment to

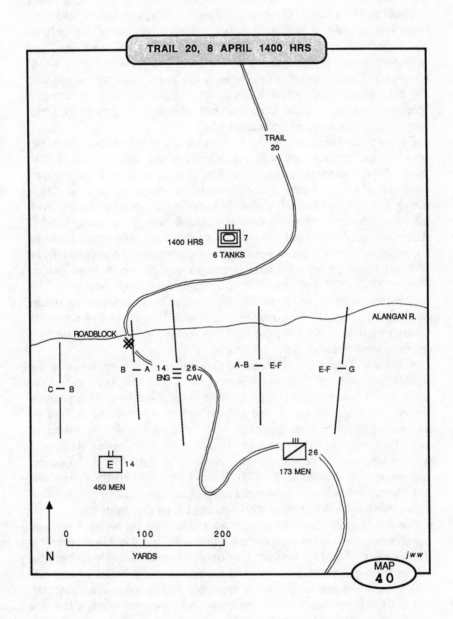

TRAIL 20, 8 APRIL 1400 HRS

TRAIL 20

1400 HRS

7

6 TANKS

ALANGAN R.

ROADBLOCK

B — A 14 ═ 26
ENG ═ CAV

A-B — E-F

E-F — G

C — B

E 14

450 MEN

26

173 MEN

N

0   100   200

YARDS

jww

MAP
40

approach the thin line of horsemen. Despite tank rounds bursting in the bamboo and small arms fire cutting along the line, the Scouts held their ridge and refused to budge. But their tenacity was costly, for only an hour after the fight started nine of the veteran Scouts were dead and seventeen wounded. The battery of American self-propelled guns, which when placed there earlier in the day gave the Scouts hope they could stop the enemy, received orders to hurry to the East Road to intercept a column of Japanese tanks, tanks that turned out to be American. Once more the Scouts were without artillery.[14]

By 1630 hours Bluemel's line was crumbling almost everywhere. Because he had contact only with the engineers and cavalry holding Trail 20, he did not know the status of the 31st or 57th infantry. He knew they were east of him along the Alangan, but he did not know how they were faring. Luckily for Bluemel, Colonel Brady, in the center of the line with his 31st Infantry, realized a critical situation was developing. Brady's Americans could not hold their ground any longer, but Brady knew he could not withdraw without warning the elements to his right and left. So at 1700 hours he wrote several messages one of which went east to Colonel Lilly's 57th Infantry, dispatched them by runners, and pulled his broken regiment toward Trail 20. A half hour later an American officer protected by two riflemen reached Colonel Lilly's command post with Brady's message. Lilly read the first two sentences, "Am being hit by a strong enemy column. Am withdrawing."[15]

"This was no news to us," recalled Colonel Lilly. "We were having the same experience."[16] Lilly knew from patrols that the Americans were under attack, but the news that they were withdrawing was an unpleasant surprise. Brady's message urged Lilly to withdraw southwest to Trail 20 and added that the 14th Engineers and the 26th Cavalry would try to hold Trail 20 until Lilly's men reached it. Lilly told Captain Anders to write withdrawal orders to Major Scholes, 1st Battalion, and Colonel Granberry, 2nd Battalion. At 1750 hours Lilly initialled the orders and sent them forward by officer-messenger. The Scouts immediately withdrew, leaving small covering forces to hold for thirty minutes.

Captain Mills received the covering force mission for his 1st Battalion. Considering the condition of the men, the trails, and the almost complete impossibility of finding his battalion once it departed, Mills realized he was in for a bad night. He deployed his Scouts in a thin line of outposts with orders to force the Japanese to deploy and thereby delay any pursuit. "2000 hours came," Mills recalled, "and we were not hit. It was a damn dark night and shortly after we pulled out, one of my men went completely off his rocker and began firing his M-1 in all directions. All hell broke loose and everyone started firing. It was one hell of a mess.

Order was finally restored. I will never know how many of my men shot each other."[17] Finding it impossible to move as a unit, Mills ordered his men to split into small groups under the control of sergeants and try to join friendly lines. The Scouts stumbled off into the dark, and the company dissolved.

Shortly before dark Bluemel learned from an officer patrol that both the 31st and 57th infantry had withdrawn. With heavy pressure on the 14th Engineers and the 26th Cavalry, there was nothing left for Bluemel to do but order the engineers and cavalry to withdraw. II Corps had refused to furnish enough troops to hold the line, failed or was not able to provide communications, and failed to designate another position upon which a subsequent stand might be made. Bluemel realized that it was impossible to hold the Alangan River Line. Further resistance appeared hopeless. Bluemel left the roadblock in the hands of Colonel Saint and his engineers, and then he headed south to find the 31st and 57th infantry.[18]

At 1830 hours Major Blanning, commanding the 2nd Squadron, received a written message from Bluemel, signed by Colonel Vance, to withdraw south down Trail 20. To delay pursuit, the Scouts placed a broken bus and a car across the trail. The cavalrymen pulled out from right to left, G Troop, Troop E-F, then the 1st Squadron's A Troop. As the cavalrymen neared the trail they found a stock of canned rations, and each man picked up a few cans. The rearguard G Troop erroneously believed that enemy tanks had cut between them and the main body, so Major Blanning moved the men off the trail and into the jungle. After floundering around without any visible progress, Blanning halted to wait for daylight. Despite their precarious position, Blanning was proud of his men. They had been in action for forty-eight hours without any sleep, yet they had not lost or abandoned a single weapon. The Scouts even carried the empty ammunition boxes. Morale remained excellent and discipline unbroken. Although each soldier carried extra food, the men ate only what was authorized despite the temptation of eating more.[19]

Earlier in the day remnants of three regiments stood to the right of Bluemel along the Alangan where it flowed into Manila Bay. The Provisional Air Corps Regiment, the Philippine Army 31st Infantry, and bits and pieces of the 4th Constabulary huddled behind the river. Backed by 75mm guns from the 21st Artillery, by three big 155mm's, and by three Scout artillery battalions, Colonel John W. Irwin's men occupied a front of some 2,500 yards. Irwin had the mission of holding the East Road. The Japanese, of course, had the mission of crossing the river, and they started with air attacks. On Irwin's left, planes worked over the 2nd Battalion, Provisional Air Corps Regiment, and prevented them from

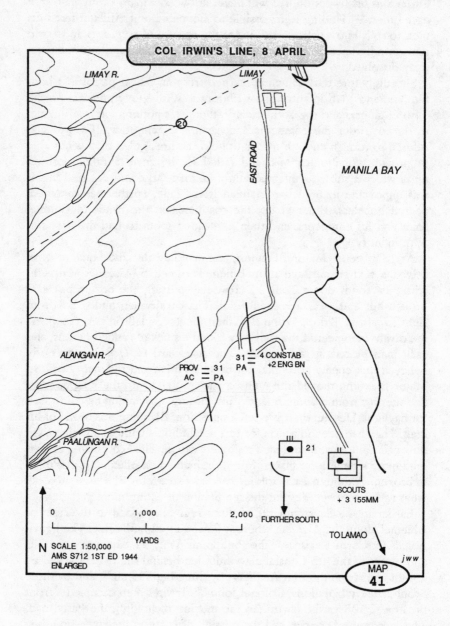

COL IRWIN'S LINE, 8 APRIL

LIMAY R.

LIMAY

②⑥

EAST ROAD

MANILA BAY

ALANGAN R.

PROV — 31
AC ≡ PA

31 ≡ 4 CONSTAB
PA +2 ENG BN

PAALUNGAN R.

21

SCOUTS
+ 3 155MM

N

0   1,000   2,000

YARDS

FURTHER SOUTH

TO LAMAO

SCALE 1:50,000
AMS S712 1ST ED 1944
ENLARGED

jww

MAP
41

moving around and getting organized. The pilots knew where the Americans were, for the widest miss by a bomb was just 200 yards from the unit. Breakfast consisted of one tablespoon of condensed milk and three tablespoons of rice per man. Lunch found every five airmen sharing one can of tomatoes and one can of corned beef, a meal eaten as artillery impacted on a hill just above them. Next, Japanese infantry placed long-range small arms fire on the airmen and drove them to cover. The Americans returned the fire, but they could not see their foe.[20]

The 1st Battalion, Provisional Air Corps Regiment, was nearby on a rocky, brush-covered hill when a platoon of Japanese infantry approached. Atop a steep hill was Captain Coleman, and he watched the Japanese. Coleman, fighting a fever of 102 degrees, moved from man to man briefing them on when to fire. On command, the battalion opened up, hitting many of the enemy and driving the survivors to cover. The airmen continued shooting as the Japanese looked about in confusion, unable to determine the direction of the fire. The airmen took heart from knowing they were not alone, for they could hear the banging of M-1s from the 31st Infantry off to their left. Too soon a Japanese artillery unit unlimbered less than a mile away, three planes plummeted from the sky dropping bombs and incendiaries, and the moderate luck of the 1st Battalion vanished. Coleman was looking through his binoculars at the artillery moving into position when he spotted the dive bombers drop out of the sun. He scrambled into a pile of leaves and squirmed until his head, shoulders, and chest were below ground level. Flying rocks and fragmentation killed and wounded many of his men. Next, Japanese artillery fired at the hill, which shook like an earthquake and caught fire. Coleman received a wound in his left leg and some phosphorous on his left hand. He pulled the fragment out of his leg with his bare hand and blistered his fingers on the hot metal, then he washed the smoking phosphorous off with water.[21]

"Several of our men were killed," remembered Sergeant Alfred C. Schrieber, a mechanic turned infantry squad leader who shared the hill with Captain Coleman. "One was badly wounded. The bombs set the woods on fire and soon the entire ridge was ablaze."[22] Sergeant Schrieber did not think his exhausted squad could fight both the Japanese and the fire, and neither did Captain Coleman. Coleman issued orders and pulled his men off the hill. Carrying their wounded on litters improvised from wood and blankets, the airmen hurried down the south side of the hill through a brush fire where the litters caught fire. Even when stretcher bearers dragged the litters on the ground to smother the flames, the wounded did not cry out or complain. Not all of Coleman's 1st Battalion received the withdrawal order. Sergeant Schrieber and six men from the 7th Materiel Squadron still occupied the burning ridge, but when they saw the Japanese advancing and noted the absence of friendly rifle fire, they decided to leave. Stumbling across a wounded airman, they loaded him onto a stretcher and dodged between burning trees. Safely off the hill, they met and joined elements of the 2nd Battalion. The 2nd Battalion was also under heavy air attack, and while crossing a straw-covered field, Captain Bigger heard the whine of diving aircraft. Bigger recognized the bombs as incendiaries, shouted a warning, and scrambled for cover. The bombs exploded and splashed flames around the airman, killing two men and severely burning two more.

To the right of the Air Corps Regiment and in the center of Colonel Irwin's "three-regiment" line stood the Philippine Army 31st Infantry. Irwin's physical appearance aided him in keeping his soldiers on the line. He carried two of everything, two compasses, two wristwatches, two knives, and with an unlit cigar poking from his mouth, he looked mean. The 1,200-man regiment had occupied the position in good order early that morning, 1st Battalion, 3rd, Provisional, and 2nd from left to right, the right flank resting on the East Road. But as the Filipinos laboriously dug in to protect the East Road, Japanese planes swept by and sent them scrambling for cover. After leaders collected the men, steadied them, and returned them to duty, Japanese planes struck again, a little before noon. The men broke, and although about 800 came back, officers had to wave their pistols to encourage the fainthearted. When Japanese planes attacked for the third time, the 400 Filipinos still on the line scattered, and this time the officers could not reform them. Although no more than seventy-five men were wounded and very few killed in all these bombings, by 1500 hours the lines to be held by Colonel Irwin's 31st Infantry and 4th Constabulary were deserted. Irwin told II Corps he was suffering so many casualties and desertions from air attack that he did not have a prayer of stopping the lightest enemy attack. Wounded were abandoned where they fell because no one knew where to take them. Dead, wounded, and exhausted men choked ditches along roads leading south.[23]

Despite confusion in Filipino lines, several units fought at isolated points and delayed, and sometimes stopped, the Japanese, but never for very long. On the right of Colonel Irwin's line, portions of the 4th Constabulary, reinforced by the 2nd Engineer Battalion, held tenaciously to their sector of the Alangan River right, east, of the East Road. Their move to the Alangan had been costly. Dive bombers hit their marching column, delaying and disorganizing it. Nor was Constabulary morale helped by the sight of the entire Philippine Army going the other way. Most of the 4th Constabulary fled when the Filipino 31st Infantry collapsed. Major McClellan, the American senior instructor to the Constabulary's 2nd Battalion, put his battalion behind the Alangan the morning of April 8. There had not been any contact, so McClellan got everyone digging. Then, because he had not slept for forty-eight hours, he laid down at his CP for a nap. When he awoke at 1400 hours the entire battalion was gone. He walked the length of what had been his line, but no one was there, neither Filipinos nor Japanese. The very few who remained from other battalions were soon in contact with the enemy. Small arms ammunition ran low, so two Constabulary officers crawled across the line gathering rifle rounds from dead Filipinos. With this tiny resupply, resistance sputtered into the afternoon.[24]

Behind this thin line, a torrent of vehicles and men coursed south along the East Road. Describing the rout even now taxes the vocabulary of the survivors. Vehicles jammed three abreast along almost the entire road. Filipinos and Americans streamed south in total confusion. American tanks and self-propelled artillery tried to stop the Japanese, but without infantry support, with little gasoline, with no communications, and experiencing great difficulty maneuvering through the tangle of fleeing men, they too were swept up by the flood. One tanker watching the army roll south was Sergeant Forrest Knox. He watched the Filipinos coming south and watched big antiaircraft searchlights and generator trailers roll past. Knox also noted that it seemed that only his tanks were headed north, toward the Japanese. The panic and mindless desire to go south was contagious. At 1700 hours Colonel Quintard heard that Japanese were crossing the Lamao River only three kilometers north of his 301st Artillery. He verified the report from stragglers on the highway, which was now crowded with traffic of all kinds moving south. Quintard decided to move the regiment—or what was left of it—to KP169 and passed the order to the batteries. Giving the order proved fatal. The minute the men heard the Japanese were coming, they panicked. They jumped onto trucks or climbed onto passing vehicles. Before Colonel Quintard knew what was happening, half his men and trucks were gone.[25]

During the afternoon General King's headquarters notified Corregidor that if they needed any Bataan troops for the defense of that island, the troops should be withdrawn at once. The time resistance could continue on Bataan "was decidedly problematical."[26] Corregidor replied that Bataan must hold, but that all or any part of the Philippine Division could be used. King decided he could spare the 45th Infantry, then in I Corps and still cohesive. He issued orders for the regiment to move by motor thirty minutes after dark for shipment from Mariveles to Corregidor. At 1600 hours the Motor Transport Service scraped together enough vehicles for the march and sent them toward I Corps with orders to carry the Scouts to Mariveles.

On Corregidor, Wainwright sent a message to MacArthur in Australia.

It is with deep regret that I am forced to report that the troops on Bataan are fast folding up. The 21st, 31st and 41st Divisions Philippine Army have disintegrated. The Second Corps has been forced south of Limay. The First Corps, to protect its right has withdrawn to the line of the Binuangan River. The troops are so weak from malnutrition that they have no power of resistance.[27]

When the Japanese broke the inland flank of the Alangan River Line the afternoon of April 8, General Bluemel undertook one more withdrawal. The night march to the Lamao River broke up some of the surviving units. All the soldiers were completely exhausted and mentally drained; they literally fell asleep on their feet and crumpled to the ground. In the hot evening a terrible lethargy stole over the soldiers, and senses became so dulled few cared what happened to them. "After the months of being beaten and battered at every turn in the road, it seemed that being killed in action wasn't so bad," recalled Captain Hibbs. "I thought a bayonet job would be a little clumsy. I didn't want to be done in by some ignorant Jap. If he had a Ph.D., I'd have felt a little more comfortable about the event."[28] Broken sedans and command cars marked the retreat of Bluemel's force. Because the trail up the south slope of the Lamao River was steep and slippery, almost every vehicle had to be pulled up by shop trucks and wreckers. Colonel Lilly assembled what was left of his regiment near the crossing of the Lamao River by Trail 20, but there was not much left.

General Bluemel arrived, waded into the middle of the Lamao, and sat down on a large, flat rock. Bluemel was exhausted and looked like death; his shirt and trousers hung on him like a gunny sack, and his decrepit boots drooped below his calves and bunched at his ankles. Bluemel found the 57th Infantry's intelligence officer on the rock, and the two men talked briefly as they soaked their feet. Captain Anders realized people needed to know of Bluemel's presence, so he hiked to II Corps's old CP location. There, Captain Arthur Christensen told Anders that II Corps wanted Bluemel on the telephone. When Bluemel heard that General Parker wanted him, he quietly exploded. "Captain," Bluemel told Anders, "you go back and tell them if General Parker wants to talk to me he can bloody well run a wire line right here to me. Those God-damned bastards back there have been sitting on their damned fat asses for months, eating three squares a day before retiring to their comfy beds for a good night's sleep. They've had their heads in the sand like a covey of ostriches. They haven't known what is going on, what has happened, and they haven't listened. And now it's all down the drain. I can't pull their dead asses out of the fire, and I don't know of anyone else who can except the Good Lord, but I can't see Him taking the trouble."[29]

Anders and Christensen carried some wire to Bluemel and ran a line from a nearby phone into the river to Bluemel's rock. Bluemel found the II Corps operations officer on the phone, and Colonel Johnston ordered Bluemel to form a line at the Lamao, a river that offered steep densely wooded slopes as potential obstacles to the enemy. When Bluemel asked where the Lamao was, Johnston said it was the stream near the phone Bluemel was using. He was soaking his feet in its chill waters. Bluemel erupted with some pointed questions. It was now dark and no reconnaissance of the proposed line could be made. He mentioned II Corps's refusal earlier that day to designate the next position so a daylight reconnaissance could be made. Why had not any of the thirty American officers at II Corps made a reconnaissance? Why were they not prepared to guide the men into their new positions? Why was not anyone from II Corps present to advise on the occupation? When Colonel Johnston said that he had not know how Bluemel wanted to put in the troops, Bluemel said he was willing to put them in any way at all just so long as they got in. Bluemel again asked for four American staff officers to come immediately to the Lamao to help him, but the request was refused. Bluemel then asked for 1,600 C rations and small arms ammunition.[30]

Barely a half hour before midnight, Bluemel waded to the south bank, and by using some officers, found two companies of the 57th Infantry—A from the 1st Battalion and F from the 2nd with some antitank and headquarters personnel. Then he found some 31st Infantrymen. "We just laid out there on the ground," remembered one of them, Private Snyder. "Most of the men were out of ammunition. Those that weren't, didn't have enough to count."[31] Cavalry and Scout engineers rounded out Bluemel's force. Bluemel collected the officers and asked if anyone was familiar with the ground. No one was, so at 2345 hours he sent the officers into the night to look at the terrain. After a check in the pitch black, Bluemel decided occupation of the Lamao was not feasible. The jungle was too thick to occupy and organize the ground at night, and fields of fire were nonexistent. Automatic weapons would have to be positioned totally by guess, nor could the men, without food, physically entrench. No artillery support existed, and even if some had been available, there was not enough telephone wire to run to the guns.

Bluemel moved his telephone line up the ridge from the river and called General Parker. When Colonel Johnston answered and said Parker was not available, Bluemel demanded that he be made available forthwith. Parker came on and repeated the order to form along the Lamao. Bluemel was exhausted, but he tightened his grip, lay back against a tree, and cradled the phone against his ear. He had been awake—marching, fighting, and trying to rally troops—for five days, and his effectiveness had declined dramatically. With a low hollow voice, he ripped into Parker in a devastating monotone, never once raising his voice, but putting a world of force and bitterness into it. "General Parker, I cannot comply with such an order. I have some 250 men who have had no food, or water, or rest, for at least three days during which time they have fought at least two delaying actions and three other actions as well as marched and countermarched some 15 miles. I have no machine guns, no mortars, no AT guns, nothing to stop or even slow a tank. I have six or seven automatic rifles and perhaps 200 M-1 rifles. I have no ammunition, no hand grenades, no dynamite. I may have 30 or 40 entrenching tools. In the dark, no effective reconnaissance of the terrain can be made. And you order me to occupy and defend a position under these conditions?"[32]

Parker talked for a few moments, and then Bluemel interrupted. "Now hold it, Parker, just you hold it!" Bluemel repeated his profane yet picturesque attack against II Corps and its staff officers. He asked where Parker's surveyed delay lines were, asked where the necessary guides were, asked where the military police straggler lines were, and asked where food and ammunition was located. Bluemel did not talk for long, but "he covered the waterfront."[33]

Finally, Bluemel demanded to talk to General King at Luzon Force headquarters. Even without Bluemel's call, King's headquarters had a good idea of II Corps's collapse. Officer patrols reported in with reports of the fighting, and radios of the tanks and self-propelled artillery carried the grim news to King's headquarters. The Tank Group even moved a radio truck into the headquarters to provide a direct link to the front. Bluemel's talk with King did not last long, for King switched him to Wainwright on Corregidor. Wainwright, hunched over a phone in Malinta Tunnel, straining to hear Bluemel's voice, told him to use his own judgment. Wainwright promised to confirm any action Bluemel took and promised to order staff officers be sent to him. Talking again to Parker, Bluemel outlined his supply needs: rifle and machine gun ammunition, loaded BAR magazines, hand grenades, C rations, and 250 gallons of potable water. Although they were near a stream, drinking the polluted water would be dangerous. "All right," Bluemel finally told Parker, "I'll form your line, but it won't hold."[34]

Bluemel talked with his regimental commanders, Colonels Brady, Lilly, and Vance, about the next position to be occupied. They decided to march south in hopes of finding a place to set the men, but they agreed to let everyone rest in place until food and ammunition arrived. A single 1/2-ton weapons carrier arrived at 0230 hours, carrying five cases of .30-caliber rifle ammunition in five-round clips unsuitable for M-1 rifles; each round had to be stripped from the Springfield slips and loaded into the eight-round M-1 clips. This paltry resupply drove Bluemel back to the phone, but before he could protest, Parker told him the Lamao need only be held until daylight.[35]

"What's going to happen then?" Bluemel asked.[36]

"A car carrying a white flag will go through the lines on the east road at daylight."

"Do you mean we're surrendering?"

"Yes. There must be no firing after the car passes through the lines."

Bluemel collected his officers and told them of Parker's orders. The men agreed to surrender. Further resistance was obviously futile. Colonel Vance polled the sergents of his much-reduced 26th Cavalry—now a phantom of its prewar organization, retaining a single section of scout cars and a few troopers from regimental headquarters. The 1st Squadron clung to remnants of A Troop while the 2nd Squadron had only the survivors of Troop E-F. The regiment had lost half the officers and 80 percent of its enlisted men killed, wounded, and missing. Vance gathered as many of the sergeants as he could, told them the situation, and asked them to make a decision whether to fight or surrender. In less than fifteen minutes, the sergeant major returned and told Vance they would surrender. Then Colonel Vance offered his officers a chance to escape to the hills. They could leave, and Vance promised that no charges would be made against them for disobeying the surrender order.[37]

Bluemel considered the Lamao River unsatisfactory as both a rest area and a place to surrender, so he disconnected the telephone to II Corps, assembled his men on Trail 20, and started the column south. Colonel Brady and sixty Americans from the 31st Infantry formed a rear guard in case the Japanese pursued. During the march the column met a supply truck. After two more hours of marching, Bluemel ordered a halt when he reached Trail Junction 20 and 26, and Bluemel and his officers decided to move west on Trail 26 for 600 yards, rest, and eat. An American captain assured Bluemel there was a deep, well-concealed gully nearby where the men could rest, but upon reaching the spot, Bluemel blew his top. The well-concealed gully was an open, recently bombed, bivouac site belonging to an antiaircraft unit. Vowing to skin the hide from the officer who picked this spot, Bluemel dispersed his force as best he could. From their supply truck, the men lifted two cases of hand grenades, eight bags of rice, half a case of canned sardines, some canned peaches, tinned tomatoes, and one case of C rations. It was dawn now, so Bluemel ordered fires lit to cook the rice. To hell with the war, it was time to eat.[38]

An hour before midnight General King, a man of high ideals and great personal integrity, held "a weighty, never to be forgotten conference" at his Luzon Force headquarters to review the situation and discuss all possible lines of action.[39] Present were his chief of staff, General Funk, and his operations officer, Colonel Collier. The question was, would the Japanese seize the southern portion of Bataan and the high ground there as quickly if they were resisted as they would if unopposed? Would resistance be of any value whatsoever? The officers concluded that the Japanese would be in Mariveles within twenty-four hours, by the evening of April 9, whether or not the Filamerican army fought. King then decided to open negotiations with the Japanese.

After King decided to surrender, he called the remainder of his staff into his tent to explain his decision. "I did not ask you here to get your opinion or your advice," he told them. "I do not want any one of you saddled with any part of the responsibility for the ignominious decision I feel forced to make. I have not communicated with General Wainwright because I do not want him to be compelled to assume any part of the responsibility. I am sending forward a flag of truce at daybreak to ask for terms of surrender. I feel that further resistance would only uselessly waste life. Already, our hospital, which is filled to capacity and directly in the line of hostile approach, is in the range of enemy light artillery. We have no further means of organized resistance."[40] Although King's decision to surrender was no surprise, it was still an awful blow, and even though everyone was expecting it, the realization that the time had come, despite all the work and sacrifice, was terrible. When King left his tent, "there was not a dry eye present."

When Lieutenant Spaulding from the Tank Group had reported earlier than evening to King's headquarters, the staff invited him to join them in a scanty meal of rice and then told him to wait for further instructions. Spaulding was too tired to be impressed with the importance of what was happening and immediately went to sleep. But he was soon awakened with orders. He became one of several officers tasked to deliver the information of pending capitulation to the front-line units. His motorcycle became particularly valuable at this moment, because no other kind of vehicle could have snaked its way through the chaotic roads.[41]

Only a half hour after King decided to surrender, and with Wainwright still ignorant of the decision, Wainwright directed King to attack with I Corps toward Olongapo, well north of the lines held in January. Far from being able to attack, I Corps was moving south in the first phase of their withdrawal to the Binuangan River where they hoped to tie into the left flank of II Corps. The physical condition of General Jones's men precluded even an unopposed advance of more than five kilometers, and an attack was out of the question. Although realizing the hopelessness of the situation, and having already set surrender plans in motion, King called Jones. After listening to Jones explain the situation of his corps, King agreed that an attack was impossible and accepted the responsibility for not transmitting Wainwright's order. Even Wainwright knew his plan was impossible to execute, but orders from MacArthur left him no choice but to try.[42]

As the hours passed, Wainwright's staff, not knowing King had not passed the order to I Corps, awaited word that I Corps had, in fact, launched, or was preparing to launch, the attack against Olongapo. Impatient over the delay and lack of information, Wainwright ordered his chief of staff to call I Corps and see if the order had been received. When General Beebe contacted I Corps and asked about the attack, Jones said he had not received any such order. At 0300 hours, when King heard of Corregidor's call to a unit subordinate to him, he phoned Corregidor to talk to Wainwright. Wainwright could not hear well because of a bad connection, so he gave the phone to Beebe, and King asked Beebe if I Corps had been removed from his command. "I want a definite answer," King declared, "as to whether or not General Jones will be left in my command regardless of what action I may take."[43] Wainwright instructed Beebe to tell King that I Corps was still his as were all the forces on Bataan. There was no further discussion of the attack order.

By midnight of that last hopeless evening the only II Corps units holding any sort of line were elements of the Provisional Artillery Brigade, and two New Mexico National Guard antiaircraft regiments, the 200th and 515th artillery. Deployment of the gunners started at 1745 hours when the 200th Artillery's operations officer reported that Japanese were nearing the Lamao River. He telephoned Luzon Force, but some doubt existed as to the report's accuracy; no one else had seen these Japanese. Luzon Force ordered another reconnaissance to confirm the sighting, so Captain Anthony R. George went out again. At 1855 hours Japanese fired at him. He reported his experience to his artillery headquarters, and they passed the report to Luzon Force.[44]

At 1900 hours King had ordered Colonel Charles G. Sage to destroy all antiaircraft equipment not practical for use as infantry weapons and assemble his men to fight as infantry. King also ordered the 1st Philippine Constabulary moved from I Corps to II Corps, but that unit never arrived. Colonel Sage directed his 515th Artillery to form near Cabcaben airfield within two hours. The 200th Artillery formed on the right of the road and linked with the 515th on the left. The artillerymen deployed along the south edge of the strip and extended their lines as far west as possible. They were in place by 0030 hours and had a single 37mm gun in support. The artillerymen were not a cohesive force. Many men were missing, either swept up in the retreat or lost somewhere in the hills. F Battery had a man killed and a gun and three trucks damaged by bombing on April 6, it lost four 37mm guns, four trucks, and three men on April 7, and it lost its fifth gun on April 8.[45]

North of the artillerymen on the Cabcaben Line, remnants of the 2nd Battalion, Provisional Air Corps Regiment, tried to withdraw cross-country, but the men lost contact with one another, hitched rides on passing trucks, or simply walked south without knowing where they were going. It was every man for himself that night. Along the East Road the route was jammed with soldiers, arms thrown away. "They were like a mass of sheep, and to clear the road, strange as it may seem, was an impossible task," recalled Colonel Collier. "Thousands poured out of the jungle like small spring freshets pouring into creeks which in turn poured into a river."[46] Through the moonless dark, trucks, tanks, and smaller vehicles crawled toward Mariveles. The MP's were utterly unable to control the traffic or the masses of soldiers and civilians. General McBride sent two American colonels into the mess to open a route, but the road was so packed with one-way traffic that the officers had to proceed on foot. "I hope never to see a broken army again," recalled Colonel Fry, one of the two officers sent on the traffic mission. "It was a terrible sight! We worked until about 4 AM and made no impression."[47] Even the smaller trails were thick with men and machines. The night was pitch black, and frightened cries and curses in all the dialects of the polyglot army mingled with those of the Americans. Adding an unearthly bass to the noise of the retreat were huge shells rolling overhead from Corregidor. The big 12-inch rifles of Batteries Hearn and Smith each fired eight rounds an hour through most of the long night. Men glanced into the black sky as freight-train sounds rumbled over them, and a rumor spread that the shells were covering a landing by reinforcements from the United States.

Deep in Bataan's woods the 1st Battalion, Provisional Air Corps Regiment, was now only a caravan of litter bearers with an advance and rear guard. Carrying the litters over a trail only wide enough for one man at a time, the litter bearers's rough handling of their charges aggravated injuries, and the wounded were dying. It was so dark that men could not see their hands before their eyes. Nor could they see the trail, and only when they heard leaves and sticks breaking under their feet did they know they were off the trail. Frequent rests were necessary. Litter bearers laid dead men along the side of the trail and left them. When the Japanese, still following closely, found the bodies, they yelled like Comanches. The

American rear guard fired at the noise, and the Japanese fired back. It was a hellish night. Brownell H. Cole and two other Americans were with their trucks when these airmen appeared out of the dark. The rear guard warned Cole the Japanese were right behind them, so he and the other drivers tossed hand grenades into their vehicles. Ducking small groups of Japanese, they joined some Spanish-speaking artillerymen from the 200th Artillery. They caught a ride atop a 1-1/2-ton truck on the East Road and headed for Mariveles.[48]

Private Eagle, a 200th Artilleryman, was hiking south and had reached the end of his strength. He had walked for miles and was about to lie down and quit when an old civilian truck converted to burning charcoal came alongside and stopped. The Filipino driver told Eagle to hop aboard; they needed him, an armed American, to keep stragglers from overloading the truck. Before they had gone a few miles, they were loaded with American soldiers who still had their weapons. "We didn't stop for any who had abandoned their equipment," Cole recalled. "I choked up when the Filipinos got off and started walking so that more Americans could come aboard. They left us with a friendly smile and a hand salute, and a 'Give 'em hell, Joe!' "[49]

In a tank outfit supply men passed out C rations, and the medical personnel issued cans of malted chocolate powder kept for emergency issue to men in shock. They spent the night eating C rations and drinking hot chocolate. Other small groups of men wandered through rear areas looking for food and were surprised to find rations neatly stacked and guarded by quartermaster guards. As Sergeant Jack D. Bradley recalled, "The guard told us not to take any, but we were starving by then. He had a gun, but we had guns too, so we helped ourselves."[50]

Not everyone was willing to stay put and accept the upcoming surrender. A platoon of B Company, 192nd Tank Battalion, tried to escape to Corregidor. Sergeant Zenon Bardowski led his three tanks and one half-track toward Mariveles, for he was sure Corregidor could use his tanks. Bardowski found Mariveles packed with hysterical civilians and demoralized soldiers. He talked to one of the barge captains, a Navy chief petty officer, and tried to convince him that Corregidor could use his three tanks. But the sailor said he had orders not to bring any equipment whatsoever over, no vehicles. Bardowski retraced his steps to his blocked platoon, determined to destroy the tanks, but this was dangerous because the area was solid wall-to-wall people. The tankers dropped hand grenades into engine and crew compartments, shattering the less sturdy parts. Nothing more could be done without hurting the mass of humanity pushing past the tanks. After Bardowski marched his seventeen men back to the barge, the Navy chief stated his orders to evacuate personnel did not include tankers. "Well," Bardowski said, by now rather irked with the Navy, "there have to be some exceptions to the rules," and he shifted him Tommy gun to a more prominent position.[51] The petty officer hastily agreed. Had he not taken the platoon, Bardowski probably would have shot him—he was tired of playing games.

At 2130 hours nature joined the orgy of destruction. Not content with the man-made explosions marching across Bataan, an earthquake rolled through the peninsula. Trees swayed as if in a strong tide, men pitched to the ground, and monkeys screamed in terror. Men tried to run but stumbled and fell and made progress only by crawling. Beds in Hospital Number 2 bounced across the wards. To the exhausted soldiers, it was the last straw; it seemed the world was coming to an end. On Corregidor, Malinta Tunnel weaved and wobbled, threatening a total collapse. The quake was so violent it shook the Philippine Islands as far south as the Visayas.[52]

The U.S.S. *Snapper*, a submarine cruising on the surface 100 miles south of Bataan felt the tremor. The calm sea instantly developed a chop, and a wind from the north shook the boat. The submariners thought they had run aground. On land, the first shock woke the 17th Pursuit Squadron. Some men, upset by the event, needed to urinate, but when they tried, another shock sent them sprawling. Before they could shut off the flow, they wet themselves fairly liberally.[53]

Colonel Miller was sitting in his jeep, waiting for a traffic jam to clear, and he told his driver to turn off the engine to save gas. When the driver said the engine was off, Miller climbed out of the shaking jeep and felt a vibration through his feet. The shaking increased until it became quite rough. Miller had to hold on to his jeep to remain standing. Private William N. Kinler was in his tank firing a machine gun at infiltrating Japanese when the quake struck. Suddenly there were no targets for Kinler. His tank was rolling backwards off a knoll and out of the fight. Sergeant Thomas Gage was awakened when a large tree began to fall in his direction. The arboreal giant roared and crashed its way to earth, and the very tip of the big tree slapped to rest on his cot. An artilleryman, Lieutenant William Miller, was sitting on the running board of his personal car. The men in his battery were finished, and although they had discussed the possibility of making a break for the hills, they were now so tired they forgot about escaping. Miller sat with his head in his hands, trying to block out the noise of exploding ammunition dumps and the firing of Japanese infiltrators. When the ground started tossing, Miller could only think, "Everything else, and now this too?"[54]

The quake created a momentary pause in activity along the East Road, but after recovering, the army resumed its trek toward Mariveles past

General Hospital Number 1. As Captain Julien M. Goodman, a doctor at the hospital, recalled, "It was the realistic enactment of mob terror and wild abandon in the flight of retreat, such as one often sees in a motion picture. It was a horrible yet awe-inspiring sound."[55] This evening more than 5,000 soldiers jammed the hospital's limited facilities. Sheets and clothing blown into the trees by the April 7 bombing still waved eerily in the branches. There was no refuge to which the wounded could be moved, so they had to await the arrival of the enemy. Orderlies passed out food and cigarettes, and wounded soldiers and doctors sat together in the dust-filled night munching a few candy bars and smoking cigarettes. Every man there was reminded of stateside 4th of July celebrations.

April 8 saw the last active service from Major Chandler. An infiltrating Japanese shot Chandler in the back as he worked with his cavalrymen at the Alangan River. His Scouts bundled him into a car and sent him south. The driver almost dropped him off at Hospital Number 2, but Chandler knew it was the closest one to the advancing Japanese, and Chandler knew he did not want to go there. He told the driver to go to Hospital Number 1. The ride was a long one, and when Chandler reached the hospital, he was losing consciousness. Lieutenant Montgomery, a patient himself, saw Chandler carried in on a litter, and he lifted Chandler off the litter and put him on a shelter half on the floor. All the beds were in use. Chandler had on a pair of canvas leggings that had not, it appeared, been off for weeks. Montgomery tried to unlace the leggings but could not find the strings. Finally, Montgomery got a pair of surgical shears and cut them off along with his trousers. Montgomery saw another man he knew now badly cut up by fragments. He helped carry him into the operating ward, and after the doctor finished, helped carry him back under some trees. When the man began bleeding badly, Montgomery took him back to the doctor. The doctor, so tired he and his surgical teammates gave each other shots of caffeine sodium benzoid to stay awake, looked at the wounded sergeant, shook his head, and directed a nurse to give him a shot of morphine to make him comfortable. The next time Montgomery walked by, the man was dead.[56]

A similar situation existed in Hospital Number 2 where doctors saw their patient load soar from 2,500 to 6,000 in six days. A steady stream of patients flowed in suffering from malaria, dysentery, fatigue, and malnutrition. Hospital personnel were reduced to eating Red Macon Rice, a rice normally fed to pigs. For supper that evening the hospital issued each man a half canteen cup of rice soup. So many patients arrived the night of the eighth that they were placed first on bare mattress springs, then on mattresses on the ground, and finally on the bare ground. All across

Bataan there were 24,000 sick and wounded soldiers in clearing stations, aid stations, or hospitals.[57]

A little after 2000 hours the American and Filipino nurses at both hospitals were ordered to pack and leave for Corregidor. Using a bus and gasoline truck, nurses from Hospital Number 1 threaded between exploding ammunition dumps toward Mariveles. By dawn the nurses from Hospital Number 1 were safely on Corregidor, but those from Hospital Number 2 were delayed by the TNT explosions. The ride, which normally took an hour, lasted seven, and at 0500 hours they finally entered Mariveles, arriving at the docks only minutes after the boat departed. The chief nurse, Lieutenant Josie Nesbitt, made a call to Corregidor asking for help. It was only through the personal intervention of General Funk that a boat was sent to pick up the nurses. The launch made quick dashes to the jetty, picked up a few nurses on each pass, then headed for open water to dodge bombs. Finally, all were aboard. The launch scarcely left the dock before a plane spotted it and gave chase. The pilot dropped several small bombs and then strafed the boat, but both bombs and bullets missed.[58]

Around 1300 hours on April 8 Luzon Force send couriers to gather commanders or representatives at Luzon Force headquarters. Then in the next several hours General King gave orders to depot commanders and warehouse personnel to prepare to destroy their installations at midnight. Even though King had not yet made a formal surrender decision, he was preparing for the inevitable. Then at 2000 hours King called General McBride, commanding Bataan's Service Command, and told him the Bataan army would surrender at 0600 hours the next day. So McBride ordered his men to start destroying their remaining stocks. Demolition teams prepared the corrugated metal storage houses—bodegas—for destruction. Destruction of equipment started earlier than midnight in some places. After receiving a telephone call that Bataan was falling, Major Arnold A. Boettcher at the Bataan Engineer Depot gathered some civilian mining engineers—four officers and eight enlisted men—and sent them into his depot. His men poured as much gasoline as possible on their few remaining supplies and set them on fire. But Boetcher could only destroy part of the dynamite because it was stored near a highway and explosions would deny use of the road to the retreating army. His men drained the oil from their vehicles and ran them until the engines, making a horrible moaning noise, froze.[59]

Luzon Force's general ammunition dumps were located in a congested area encompassing Hospital Number 2, Philippine Department Headquarters, Luzon Force Headquarters, the Ordnance Depot, Quartermaster Depot, and sundry engineer installations. In the dump near Luzon

Force headquarters were 1,600 rounds of Navy 8-inch and Army 155mm projectiles stores with a large amount of 75mm rounds. Adjacent to this ammunition was Hospital Number 2. But because there was neither the time nor the means to move the ammunition to a safer place for destruction, medics shifted those patients closest to the dump to safer locations, then demolition men lit powder trains leading to the ammunition. The first of many ear-splitting blasts signalled the start of the destruction of the carefully hoarded ammunition. The forest and sky lit up "like an exploding inferno with all the colors of the rainbow shooting through the trees into the heavens."[60] Small arms and large artillery rounds erupted, and explosions piled one atop the other until it seemed "the whole world was about to explode." The night lightened fitfully with the bright glare of burning storage buildings and the brilliant flash of exploding munitions. Tremors shook the peninsula as demolition men touched off the larger dumps. The last refuge of the infantryman, the good earth, now seemed to shake loose from its foundations. "It was like the crack of doom," remembered awestruck Sergeant Stephen N. Kramerich. "It was so loud and violent it practically tore the soul out of our body."[61] Besides providing a tremendous visual display, the 5,554 tons of ammunition that included 1,500 tons of bombs began flinging fragments all over Bataan.

At 2230 hours the Navy started destroying its materiel and munitions by blowing the tunnels at Mariveles. *Dewey Drydock* sank after the crew detonated six 155mm scuttling charges. Minesweeper *Bittern* went under. The faithful *Canopus* backed into deeper water, fifteen fathoms, under her own power, and sailors dropped her anchors so as to block Lilimbon Cove. Crewmen opened the torpedo warhead locker and forward magazine and the flood valves forward and main injection valve. The *Canopus* began a slow list and settled. The next morning the *Taiping*, loaded with bombs, blew up. All American naval personnel were ordered to Corregidor for beach defense. During the night the Navy moved 80,000 gallons of fuel oil, 130 tons of diesel, over a million rounds of .30-caliber ammunition, and forty-five tons of food to Corregidor.[62]

On the orders of the acting Ordnance Officer, Major Maxwell, the first of the Army's TNT warehouses thundered into oblivion around 0200 hours with a tremendous roar. General Jones in I Corps called King to inquire about the noise.

"For crying out loud, Ned," Jones complained, "what's going on?"[63]

"The ammunition dump is blowing up," answered King.

"Hell, I can feel the ground shaking all the way up here. It must be an earthquake."

"I hate to tell you this, Honus," King answered, "but I'm surrendering at 6:00 A.M. They're shelling the hospital. Parker's Corps is gone.

There's nothing else I can do. Put white flags all along your line. You'll have to destroy your artillery and machine guns and stand by for further orders."

Jones was in agreement. "I don't see what else you can do. I'll spike the artillery, but I'm saving the machine guns. At the last moment we can throw the bolts in the jungle."

"Use your judgment, Honus," King concluded. As the connection was broken, new blasts echoed through Bataan's hills. Luzon Force headquarters was especially hard hit by the TNT explosions. Captain Tisdelle was in the command post, 800 yards distant, when everything blew. He had never heard such loud explosions before this night. Some shells, after being tossed from their storage places, burst high in the sky. But the most violent explosions were yet to come. As Tisdelle left the bamboo and tarpaper building, a particularly violent blast knocked him flat on his face, and a terrific heat rolled over him. When he got up, he saw that the long, low tarpaper building had vanished. Tisdelle could not even find pieces of tarpaper on the ground. Captain Tisdelle was not alone during this blast. Major Hurt was also in the command post, and while he was talking on the phone, a terrific explosion occurred. As Hurt tried to get out the door, a tremendous explosion shook the ground. The building fell apart before Hurt could get out the door, but he, like Tisdelle, survived.[64]

As the morning of April 9 rolled into its third hour, Colonel Alexander was one more witness to the chaos. To Alexander, "It seemed to me the whole earth blew up. The explosion was so breathtaking, the shaking of the earth so violent, that I could not go on. Throwing myself flat with my head between the roots of, and close against, a big tree, I waited, for I did not know what, as a rain of steel splattered through the leaves. Several hot pieces fell on my legs, forcing me to scramble until I shook them off. One explosion followed another, each of them shaking the trees much more violently than the earthquake had, as I wondered if a large piece of steel might not be following the small pieces and hunt me out."[65]

The submarine U.S.S. *Seadragon,* having left Cebu on April 5 for Corregidor, had just unloaded seven tons of provisions at Corregidor when she was ordered to clear the area before unloading the remaining twenty-three tons of 100-pound sacks of rice and flour. The submarine departed the mine field at 2130 hours, carrying the last of the island's codebreakers, seventeen men plus another lucky six with other jobs. Hours later, while running submerged, the submariners felt the shock of the exploding TNT warehouses.[66]

The Army Air Corps ran its last operation just before dark. An emergency call reported that a powerful Japanese force was breaking through the front lines only two miles north of Bataan field. Armorers loaded one old, patched, and thoroughly bedraggled P-40 with six 30-pound fragmentation bombs. Major Dyess grabbed an eager-beaver pilot, Lieutenant I. V. Jack Donalson, and told him to take off, find, and hit the enemy. Dyess told Donalson that if the mission proved to be a false alarm, to come back in and land. But if the Japanese were as close as reported, he was to buzz the field, rock his wings, and head for Cebu. Donalson climbed into "old kibosh" and roared into the air. Fifteen minutes later his plane was back over the field with empty bomb racks. Donalson "rocked the plane like all hell and kept going."[67] One of his hydraulic lines was shot away during his attack, but he survived a wheels up landing at Cebu.

Evacuation of a few pilots with the one remaining P-40 and two P-35's now began. At 2130 hours Captain Joseph H. Moore lifted his composite "P-40 Something" from Cabcaben Field. One after the other two P-35's climbed into the air from Bataan Field by the light of exploding ammunition dumps. In the first plane Captain O. L. Lunde carried another pilot doubled up in the baggage compartment. Captain Henry G. Thorne lifted the second P-35 off the ground with two pilots in the baggage compartment, and as a last note of defiance, dropped fragmentation bombs on the Japanese. The major fighting arm with which the United States had hoped to insure effective defense of the Philippines ended its forlorn battle.[68]

At 1600 hours Colonel Carlos Romulo received orders to report to Wainwright. "Colonel Romulo, I'm ordering you out of Corregidor," Wainwright told him. "Bataan is hopeless. At seven tonight take the little launch to Bataan. Go to the Bataan airfield. From there you will take off for Mindanao, where you will report to General Roxas and General Sharp."[69]

"Good-by, sir," Romulo said.

Then Wainwright thawed. He took Romulo's hand and shook it warmly. "God bless you, my boy. Tell President Quezon and General MacArthur I will do my best to the end."

Romulo arrived at Bataan Field just in time to see its last P-35 climb into the night. An officer told him he would have to go to Cabcaben Field, back the tortuous route they had just driven. Some airmen were still there working on their project of the past few days, a Navy amphibian salvaged from Manila Bay. This plane was one of three J2F4 Grumman Ducks, Navy single-engine, three-seat biplanes sunk off Mariveles in December. Two were completely submerged, but the third settled high enough so the engine remained dry. Mechanics repaired it and, with three other rickety aircraft, it completed thirty-four round trips between Bataan and Mindanao. On the night of April 6 the Duck blew a cylinder and barely staggered back to Cabcaben Field where mechanics tried to fix the engine, using a cylinder from another wrecked navy plane. "I sat in my car," Romulo recalled, "and crossed my fingers and prayed while the boys spun the propeller. There was a popping noise—sparks flew. I thought for a moment that the plane had exploded. The motor choked and snarled, snorted, started. It went pup-pup-pup for a moment and then settled down to a fairly even hum."[70] Romulo was so excited he jumped from his car and put his foot squarely in a big can of oil. Major Dyess loaded Romulo and five pilots into the Duck.

A little after 0100 hours on April 9 everyone was aboard. The pilot, Captain Roland J. Barnek, had never flown this type aircraft before. Using a flashlight to check what few instruments remained, Barnek hit the power, bumped down the runway, and waddled into the air after barely clearing several obstructions. Only seventy-five feet above the water of Manila Bay, all excess gear went out the door, helmets, sidearms, baggage, even the parachutes. The passengers ripped floorboards from the plane's hull and tossed them out. With fifty feet more under her wings, the plane passed safely to the south. At the empty airfields, ground crews destroyed the remaining stores of gasoline, smashed radios, and pulled out the antiaircraft guns. Ordnance men primed and blew the remaining stock of bombs, then joined the chaotic stream of men and vehicles headed south.[71]

In compliance with orders, and as the last act of an army not yet under terms, soldiers destroyed motor vehicles, both military and civilian. Supplies, except for food and certain vehicles saved to move the defeated army to prison camps, were ordered destroyed. The Bataan Quartermaster Depot exhausted its supply dumps by issuing all the remaining food, including 45,000 C rations, but few of the rations reached the men. In all the Bataan supply dumps a single half ration remained. Small arms and artillery ammunition remained in sufficient quantities to cover the current rates of expenditure for another month, but even though it was available, it could not be distributed to the forward units; no one knew where the forward units were.[72]

Artillerymen destroyed most of the army's cannon pursuant to orders. One officer, Major Fitch, received word shortly after midnight to report to General Stevens of the 91st Division. Stevens, a tall, skinny officer with a pearl-handled revolver drooping at his side, welcomed Fitch with a real treat, a cup of coffee. Fitch had not seen coffee for months. "Well, major," General Stevens said as he blew his nose a few times, "General King has gone to Japanese headquarters to surrender the Bataan forces.

The terms are not yet known. Be prepared to complete the destruction of your guns and materiel before 6 a.m. I will telephone further instructions to you at your C.P."[73] Major Fitch returned to his men feeling deeply depressed. Some guns suffered the ignominy of capture. Telephone lines were out, commanders had only the vaguest idea where their units were, and messengers could not reach their destinations. Where discipline collapsed, gunners simply abandoned their pieces. In one of Major Fitch's batteries the gunners put an armed shell, point first, into the muzzle and fired a round up the tube. But they forgot to remove the centripetal interrupter from the long fuse, and the guns survived. Two of the 86th Artillery's work-horse 155mm's fell to the Japanese in the midst of a mortar barrage. The gunners could not blow the guns without killing scores of leaderless men jammed in to the area, so the guns were lost, intact.

In I Corps the withdrawal General King had ordered on the afternoon of April 7 was well under way. On the morning of the 8, I Corps executed the first phase and stopped at the Tiis River. A written order continuing the withdrawal was issued late in the morning. The Right Subsector would move at dusk, leaving a covering force sufficient to protect the main body. Equipment that could not be evacuated would be destroyed, and this included the 8-inch gun battery and searchlights sited along the west coast. Two attempts to wreck the 8-inch cannon with TNT failed. The crew then loaded the gun with a round, filled the chamber with 1-1/2 the normal powder charge, and drained the oil from the recoil cylinders. They stuffed dirt and gravel into the barrel and fired the gun from a safe distance. Inspection revealed complete destruction. Gunners set searchlights and other battery equipment on fire before heading south.[74]

In Captain Robert J. Lawlor's 155mm B Battery, 92nd Coast Artillery, crews smashed sights and pushed special high-power charges into gun barrels. The thirty-year-old Lawlor was a smiling Irishman, a consummate realist, yet invariably cheerful. This day, however, was a test to his spirit. One of his officers, Lieutenant Kalbfleish set charges on the guns, the first to blow at 0510 hours. The first two guns were destroyed, and after the third gun blew, Kalbfleish went around touching off the powder trains leading to nearly a thousand shells and powder increments. He then "ran like hell to get around a bend in the road."[75] I Corps headquarters also ordered maximum use of demolitions and obstacles, with priority from east to west and north to south. Engineers felled large trees and blasted side-hill cuts. Fourteen buses worked their way forward and pulled out the sick and wounded.

I Corps' Right Sub-sector's 11th Division started its withdrawal after the sun set. With the 12th Infantry deployed as rear guard, the 11th Infantry began its march at 2000 hours in the order of Headquarters Battalion, 1st, and 3rd Battalion. They headed for Trail 7 and 9 where additional delay positions were to be organized. Because a real threat existed from the broken II Corps flank, these positions also covered the northeast approaches of Trail 7. The 2nd Philippine Constabulary joined the 11th Infantry after a disorganized march out of the main line. Then the rear guard 12th Infantry withdrew. "As we moved south," remembered Captain Liles who was with the rear guard, "I began to see half-tracks, ammunition carriers and artillery pieces burning. I thought this rather strange since there had been no action in our sector during the night."[76] When the 12th Infantry reached its destination, it went on line facing the Pantingan River. Officers collected stragglers from both corps, organized them into provisional squads and platoons, and placed them here to extend the 11th Division's line westward. Patrols searched in vain for the 1st Division, which should have been to the west.

In I Corps' Left Sub–sector, the 1st Division received the same withdrawal orders as the 11th Division. Four rifle companies deployed as a covering shell, one protecting each front-line battalion. But once night fell and the men prepared to depart, the division received orders to delay in the first phase position pending an offer of surrender to be made by General King. So, outside of artillery and support forces, the bulk of the 1st Division remained well north of the 11th Division's left flank. The 91st Division, farther west and the most distant from the fighting, withdrew unmolested.[77]

After hearing from General King, General Jones telephoned General Brougher and ordered him to prepare to surrender his 11th Division, to assemble his men in bivouacs, put up white flags, and wait for the Japanese to arrive and receive the surrender. For Brougher, the news came as a staggering blow and as a terrible shock to his men. Because his men had worked unstintingly for two months building their defenses, they felt they could hold the Japanese indefinitely. He argued vehemently and even phoned General Beebe at Corregidor, telling him that he did not want to surrender the division, that Brougher would give it to anyone who wanted it. Beebe would not send a replacement, and Brougher had to obey his orders.[78]

I Corps did order two units to Corregidor, one of which was the 45th Infantry. Wainwright had sent two officers to King's headquarters with orders to pull the 45th Infantry out of the line and ship it to Corregidor. King passed the order to I Corps which, in turn, told the regiment to break contact and make its way to Mariveles where transportation officers were collecting craft to ferry the Scouts to Corregidor. Early in the campaign MacArthur had planned to pull out the entire Philippine Division if Bataan fell, but now only the 45th Infantry was ordered to Corregidor. Shipping included the coastal steamers *Elcano, Bohol II,* the Army minelayer *Colonel George E. Harrison,* two harbor boats, ten launches, and two Navy boats. But the regiment was in the Pantingan River valley when it received orders at 1800 hours, and chances of reaching Mariveles were slim. Colonel Lilly set the order of march as 3rd, 2nd, and 1st battalions. Sixty civilian buses trickled forward, and the lead vehicles picked up the first company at 2200 hours. The Scout rifle companies each owned several 1-1/2 ton trucks, but the trucks were at supply points near the rear and not immediately available. The weapons companies had some trucks too, but these men and vehicles were acting as rear guard and could not break loose.[79]

During their withdrawal out of the Pantingan River valley, the 45th Infantry was covered by a battalion of the 1st Infantry. The Filipinos assumed the old Scout positions and tried to stop the Japanese. Neither the Japanese nor the Filipinos knew a surrender was imminent, and the Filipinos opened fire at the Japanese crossing the Pantingan River. The Japanese pushed the battalion west. Putting up a glorious fight for their reduced size, the battalion was destroyed, its two American advisors killed. Few men survived. Their sacrifice was for naught. The marching Scouts were caught on jammed roads, and confusion mounted as the regiment mixed with stragglers and other formations. The lead company progressed as far as Signal Hill before the Corps Ordnance Officer stopped it because of exploding ammunition dumps. The remainder of the vehicles assigned to meet the regiment linked with the main body at daybreak on April 9. But by then it was too late.[80]

The 45th Infantry was not alone in receiving orders to head for Corregidor. The 2nd Battalion, 60th Artillery, was also ordered to the island. But the unit's guns and searchlights were scattered across the mountains of southern Bataan, and worse, it had taken days to set them in place. The four 3-inch guns of G Battery, for instance, had been winched up a steep hill, dug in, and sand-bagged. To move everything at a moment's notice was impossible. Receiving orders at 2015 hours to retreat through Mariveles to Corregidor, G Battery destroyed its 3-inch guns with dynamite, but Captain Aaron A. Abston succeeded in transporting his fire control equipment to the docks. "The traffic was one way, one line of vehicles headed for Mariveles harbor," remembered Private Svrcek from G Battery. "Vehicles were bumper to bumper and any space not occupied by vehicles was jammed with Filipino civilians and goats, cows, and horses led by civilians. Filipinos rode bumpers and hung on sides of trucks whenever they could."[81] G Battery crawled down the hills leading to Mariveles, through an unnatural layer of clouds that reflected a ghastly glow, and past caves belching smoke from exploded ammunition. "The cloud was suspended over the valley and hung about a hundred feet above the ground," Svrcek recalls. "It gave me a very eerie, spooky, disconcerting feeling of apprehension as we started our descent into this man-made cloud of fire, destruction, and smoke."[82] The 60th Artillery's other unit on Bataan, E Battery, dynamited their large radar and two vans, then headed for Mariveles. The drive south was slow and dangerous. Each truck had to weave its way around and between stalled buses and cars while suffering periodic showers of debris from exploding ammunition dumps.

Leading these two batteries into Mariveles was Major Massello, and when he reached the town, he found complete pandemonium. Naval installations and supplies were burning, munitions were exploding in nearby hills, and long-range Japanese artillery dropped random shells throughout the area. Mariveles itself was absolutely flat, bombed out of existence. "Babel, hassle, and confusion reigned supreme at the docks," remembers Private Svrcek. "How our officers located us and got us grouped together I to this day don't know. M.P.'s and soldiers several ranks deep had the docks cordoned off. There was shouting, firing, pushing and shoving all around us. Apparently the dock commander had orders to clear G Battery through this babel. Magically, the cordoned ranks opened and an M.P. escort shoved us through this 'sesame' door."[83] Major Massello found some military police who directed him where to put his equipment and assemble his men. One group departed immediately for Corregidor on the interisland steamer *Elcano* while Massello continued to collect his scattered people. B Battery, 515th Artillery, had earlier been ordered to give their 3-inch guns to the 60th Artillery for transfer to Corregidor, and Abston picked up two guns and 650 rounds. Massello and Captain Abston from G Battery then secured a minelayer and a barge and manhandled Abston's two guns, a prime mover, a 5-ton truck, and the range finder and other fire control equipment into the vessels.

Not until well after daylight were men and gear loaded, and only then did the boat and barge start a very slow passage toward Corregidor. The occupants had to push swimmers away to keep them from swamping the boat. When a Navy ammunition tunnel exploded, huge pieces of rock showered the departing boats, sinking one launch, and then Japanese artillery near-missed the minelayer. But G Battery's craft finally reached the island. C Battery, 91st Artillery, attached to the 60th, destroyed its guns the night of the eighth, climbed off Tagumpay (victory) Hill, and walked to Mariveles. Finding the rest of the battalion gone, Captain John Gulick obtained a barge and sailed his men to Corregidor.[84]

On the evening of April 8 Luzon Force headquarters signed off the radio net linking General King to Corregidor, and although Corregidor kept a radio on the mute frequency in case of emergency traffic, nothing more was heard. But Bataan could be seen. Its southern face looked like "a huge conflagration which resembled more than anything else a volcano in violent eruption . . . white hot pieces of metal from exploded shells and bombs shot skyward by the thousands in every conceivable direction."[85]

At Fort Mills on Corregidor plans for an evacuation of troops to the island were nearing completion. Wainwright felt he could absorb 12,000 of Bataan's soldiers into the harbor defenses, and he wanted all the Philippine Scouts he could get. He also agreed to accept all American Navy personnel and their boats, food, and fuel. In a memorandum written for Wainwright's chief of staff, General Drake listed the Army assets available to carry men out of Bataan. Using powered vessels exclusively, the Army Transport Service could collect twenty-one ships capable of carrying 3,260 men. If barges were towed behind the powered vessels, space for another 2,300 men could be found. This capacity meant men only, no supplies or heavy equipment, so any transport of equipment or stores would mean a decrease in men. Dock space at Mariveles and Cabcaben would allow the loading of four scows every four hours, so at best, eight could be loaded from dusk to dawn. More scows could be unloaded at Corregidor than could be loaded at Bataan.[86]

By using everything afloat, and by loading from every available dock and beach, 7,600 troops with individual equipment could be shuttled to Corregidor each night. "Without knowledge of the total number of troops to be loaded and the material to be moved," concluded General Drake in his memorandum, "loading tables cannot be prepared to accompany this plan."[87] As it turned out, more lift capacity existed than could be used. If substantial numbers of soldiers did ferry to Corregidor, it was doubtful Corregidor's food could accommodate them. It was very likely that with reinforcements, Corregidor would fall from starvation before the Japanese could capture it by force.

No evacuation took place.

CHAPTER TWENTY-EIGHT

Thursday, April 9
Surrender

GENERAL KING DECIDED TO SURRENDER JUST BEFORE MIDNIGHT ON
April 8. His conference at 2300 hours confirmed his views on the situation. He had a choice of launching a counterattack as ordered by Wainwright and seeing his men slaughtered, or he could, against orders, surrender. At 0600 hours Wainwright learned of King's decision when
Lieutenant Colonel Jesse T. Traywick, assistant operations officer on Corregidor, told him that King had sent an officer to the Japanese to arrange
for cessation of hostilities. Wainwright could not recall any conversation
with King that might have led King to believe he had authority or permission to surrender. Nor had King mentioned the possibility to Wainwright. Shocked by the news, Wainwright told Traywick, "Go back and
tell him not to do it."[1] But it was too late. Nor would receipt of such an
order have changed King's mind. Wainwright courageously fulfilled his
orders by refusing Luzon Force permission to surrender. Equally courageously, King disobeyed. Wainwright radioed the bad news to MacArthur.

> At 6 o'clock this morning General King commanding Luzon Force with-
> out my knowledge or approval sent a flag of truce to Japanese commander.
> The minute I heard of it I disapproved of his action and directed that there
> would be no surrender. I was informed it was too late to make any change,
> that the action had already been taken. Enemy on east had enveloped both
> flanks of the small groups of what was left of the Second Corps and was
> firing with artillery into the hospital area which undoubtedly prompted
> King's action. In order to relieve the pressure on the right, last night I

ordered the First Corps to attack to the north with its ultimate objective
Olongapo but the attack did not get off. Physical exhaustion and sickness
due to a long period of insufficient food is the real cause of this terrible
disaster. When I get word what terms have been arranged I will advise
you. Fearing just what happened, I endeavored last night to withdraw some
of the Philippine Division and other regular units but only succeeded in
getting out some scattered mixture of individuals. I will endeavor to hold
Corregidor.[2]

Wainwright realized the surrender could not have been avoided. He
wrote much later that he had no criticism of King for surrendering, and
he realized that it was a decision requiring great courage and mental
fortitude. As a matter of interest, Washington sent a message to MacArthur which reached him the morning of the ninth. In the message, President Roosevelt modified his earlier no-surrender stance. There was concern in Washington that Wainwright might carry his harsh orders to an
extreme, so this new guidance left to Wainwright's "best judgment any
decision affecting the future of the Bataan garrison. I have," the President wrote Wainwright, "nothing but admiration for your soldierly conduct and your performance of your most difficult mission and have every
confidence that whatever decision you may sooner or later be forced to
make will be dictated only by the best interests of the country and of your
magnificent troops."[3] Because this message reached MacArthur, who was
given permission to decide if it should continue on to Wainwright, and
because it reached him at the same time as Wainwright's surrender message, MacArthur did not forward it to Corregidor. A copy of this message did reach Wainwright directly from Washington but only after the
surrender was concluded.

At King's headquarters Colonel Everett C. Williams and Major Marshall H. Hurt, King's chief of artillery and assistant operations officer,
both bachelors, volunteered to make first contact with the Japanese. King
gave Colonel Williams a piece of paper requesting a meeting with the
Japanese officer commanding the Bataan army and gave Williams authority to negotiate if the Japanese declined to see King. Williams and Hurt
decided to leave while it was still dark and arrive at the front lines at
daybreak when destruction of equipment would be nearing completion.
They started forward at 0330 hours in a Tank Group reconnaissance car
with a motorcycle escort. But because of the jammed roads, they abandoned the car and split up. Colonel Williams climbed onto the back of a
motorcycle. Major Hurt continued forward on foot. Williams and Hurt
soon rejoined and acquired a jeep and driver in which they continued
their journey. The trio then reached the Lamao river and met an American delay force with a few tanks and two self-propelled 75mm guns.

Curious artillerymen watched the jeep approach. Colonel Williams told the artillerymen why he was there. At 0530 hours, Lieutenant Colonel Ganahl's delay force rumbled south, an hour and a half before the first Japanese reached the river. When the sky brightened, the three men drove north into Japanese territory.[4]

Without warning, thirty Japanese with leveled bayonets rushed the jeep. The two Americans each frantically waved a bed sheet from a bamboo pole and stepped out with raised hands. A Japanese sergeant arrived at this dangerous moment, and Colonel Williams showed him his letter of instruction and conveyed his desire to see the sergeant's commanding officer. Getting back into the jeep with the Japanese sergeant, they drove north for three miles until they met General Kameichiro Nagano. A very poor Japanese interpreter read Colonel Williams's letter and, after a brief discussion, General Nagano agreed to meet with General King near the front lines at the experimental farm station near Lamao. Nagano sent Major Hurt back to Luzon Force headquarters to bring King to the meeting. The Japanese required Colonel Williams to remain with them. Williams, now relieved of the possibility of having to negotiate in the absence of General King, was worried the Japanese might find King's letter authorizing him to do just that. Williams, hand in pocket, slowly shredded the letter.[5]

A few minutes after nine, immediately after Major Hurt arrived with the news, King and his party, Colonel Collier, Major Wade R. Cothran, Captain Tisdelle, and Major Hurt headed north. Just before leaving, Captain Tisdelle cut a bedsheet into halves and his orderly tied them to two separate bamboo poles. They then drove up the road in two jeeps with the white flags prominently displayed. King felt like General Lee who surrendered to General Grant the same day, April 9, seventy-seven years earlier. King believed that were he to survive the war, he would be court-martialed for surrendering the largest force the United States had ever lost.[6]

As the jeeps turned onto the East Road, a flight of Japanese planes spotted them and dove in for an attack. "We were not amatures [sic] at that game," recalled Colonel Collier. "We were displaying a white flag but this in no way dampened or hampered the zest of the chase for the next three kilometers."[7] The road was one curve after another with steep cuts in the mountain, and it offered some protection. After each attack the planes made wide circles and flew out of sight. The officers then jumped into the jeeps and sped forward until the planes appeared again as they banked to parallel the road. Collier and Hurt jumped out of their vehicle, signalled King in the next jeep to do the same, and everyone scrambled for cover. After the planes passed or were in a position they

could see the jeeps but not shoot, Collier and Tisdelle ran from the
ditches, stood in the middle of the road, and vigorously waved their
bedsheets in hopes the Japanese would stop their attacks. But the pilots
did not recognize the flags or chose to ignore them, because the strafing
continued.

Not seeing any results from his work, one pilot dropped out of formation and came in unseen after the regular run. He lined up on a curve
and fired just as Collier's jeep rounded the bend. The noise of impacting
bullets warned driver Private Burns, and he pulled sharply to the left and
jammed against the embankment. Machine gun bullets swept over the
men, missing them by inches. After an hour of this deadly game a Japanese reconnaissance plane lazed in at a right angle to the road, dipped its
wings, and the pilot waved. When the pilot leveled his plane and waved,
King's party knew the chase was finally over. The aircraft kept other
planes away, and the Americans proceeded safely and entered Japanese
lines. King's last clean uniform, coated by the brown Philippine dust so
similar to the red dust of Georgia, was now as wrinkled and dirty as the
one he left behind. The Japanese received the Americans courteously at
the Lamao River bridge, allowed them to keep their pistols, and escorted
King's party to a house at the experimental farm station in front of which
sat General Nagano and Colonel Williams. Nagano motioned for King
to take a seat. Through an interpreter, Nagano explained that he commanded an infantry division but that he himself had no authority to
arrange terms. A representative from 14th Army would soon arrive.
Nagano communicated this information on a piece of paper because the
interpreter spoke English very poorly.[8]

A few minutes later, at 1100 hours, Colonel Motoo Nakayama, senior
operations officer for the 14th Army, arrived in a commandeered Cadil-
lac with his interpreter, a captain. Captain Tisdelle, a 32-year-old Chicagoan, a lieutenant of cavalry before the war, recognized the car as
belonging to a friend of his, Juan Elizalde. General King rose, but resumed his seat after Nakayama ignored him. Nakayama took a seat at a
long table just outside the front door of the house facing the Americans;
no salutes were exchanged, nor did anyone shake hands. Nakayama sat
sideways, facing his interpreter at the far end of the table, ignoring King.
King sat erect with his hands clasped in front of him on the table. Tisdelle wrote later, "I never saw him look more like a soldier than in this
hour of defeat."[9] Colonel Williams and Major Cothran stood near the
table with Japanese staff officers and curious onlookers.

Nakayama had arrived without instructions as to terms. The Japanese
captain, Nakayama's aide, spoke a few words to Nakayama and then
spoke crisply to King, "You are General Wainwright!"[10]

"No. I am General King, commander of all forces on Bataan."[11]

When the Japanese told King he must get Wainwright, King explained he did not command all the forces in the Philippines, but rather only the forces on Bataan. He could not get Wainwright because he had no means of contacting him. The Japanese did not like this arrangement. They wanted to avoid a piecemeal surrender. They wanted all the Philippines. After further discussion, the aide turned to King and asked why he had come.[12]

King answered he had come to secure terms for his Bataan army. Another discussion between the aide and Nakayama resulted in the same demand, but phrased differently. "You'll have to get General Wainwright. The Japanese cannot accept surrender without him."[13]

King then rephrased his answer. He asked that he be allowed to send couriers to tell his forward elements of the collapse. He asked that the Japanese remain in their present positions to prevent further loss of life. King explained that his army was badly disorganized and incapable of resistance, that his men were sick, starving, and exhausted. He asked for an armistice and an end to aerial bombardment. King concluded by saying he had saved sufficient vehicles to evacuate his army to any point on Luzon designated by the Japanese. He asked to be allowed to make this move under his American officers. This was a point King and his staff had discussed earlier, and they had saved specific vehicles and fuel to move the men. Nakayama rejected both the armistice and the request for a cessation of aerial activity. He explained the pilots had missions until 1200 hours. They could not be halted until then. "Surrender must be unconditional," the aide stated.[14]

King then asked if he surrendered unconditionally, would they accept the following terms: He requested his troops be allowed to march out under their own officers, using the trucks and 13,000 gallons of gasoline saved expressly for that purpose. He asked that he be allowed to notify his forward elements of the end of hostilities. He repeatedly requested assurance that his men, both Americans and Filipinos, would be treated according to the Geneva Convention.[15]

To all these requests, Nakayama refused comment except to say he could accept only the surrender of all forces in the Philippines. "I am prepared," Nakayama answered, "to consider negotiations for the cessation of hostilities if the surrender of the entire American Philippine forces in the Philippines is included. However, it is absolutely impossible for me to consider negotiations for the cessation of hostilities in any limited area. If only the American Philippine Forces in the Bataan Area desire to surrender, then each individual or each unit should immediately surrender voluntarily and unconditionally to the Japanese Army confronting him or it. In such an event, the Japanese Army would treat them as Prisoners of War in accordance with international law."[16]

Failing to get agreement on any point, King knew additional delay would only result in more of his men dying. Again King asked if the Filipinos and Americans would be treated well. The aide answered, "We are not barbarians."[17] Those were the only terms King could arrange. After some talk, the aide turned back to King and asked how many guns King had. King answered that he did not have any guns, that he had ordered them destroyed. A question about tanks brought the same reply.

Thinking Colonel Nakayama's comment meant he would accept the unconditional surrender of the Luzon Force, King agreed to surrender at 1230 hours. To the Japanese demand, "You will surrender," King nodded his head.[18] Upon being ordered to turn over his sword, King explained he had left it in Manila. After some excited discussion among the Japanese, King interrupted and persuaded them to accept his pistol. The four American officers placed their side arms on the table and passed into captivity. At no time did Colonel Nakayama look at King. Nakayama stood up, and King rose. Without saying anything more, Nakayama and his aide walked off to their car.

No surrender document was prepared or signed, nor was an effort made to formalize the surrender. King believed he had surrendered his entire command, whereas the Japanese concluded the negotiations had failed. "The surrender of the American Philippine Forces in the Bataan Peninsula," wrote Nakayama later, "was accomplished by the voluntary and unconditional surrender of each individual or each unit. The negotiations for the cessation of hostilities failed."[19]

After Nakayama departed, the Japanese allowed Colonel Collier and Major Hurt to return to American lines to deliver the surrender order. The Japanese drove King and the other officers by jeep to Balanga where cameramen took numerous photographs of the American. Across the road the Japanese prepared the Balanga Elementary School for additional questioning. Colonel Nakayama was again present. King sat on a wooden chair, Colonel Williams to his right and Major Cothran and Captain Tisdelle to his left. The first question concerned the number of Japanese prisoners held by the Americans. When King said there were about sixty, the Japanese seemed surprised there were not more. "When a force is withdrawing, as our did, it does not have an opportunity to take many prisoners," King answered.[20]

Questions as to the number of guns and tanks received King's reply, "We have none."

Then the questions changed to Corregidor. "How many troops are there on Corregidor?"

"I don't know," King answered.

"How many guns are there on Corregidor?"

"I don't know."

The Japanese brought out a map and set it on the small table. "General King. Show me here where the tunnel leads from Mariveles to Corregidor."

"There is no such tunnel," King answered.

"There must be a tunnel," the Japanese insisted. King and Tisdelle finally convinced them there was not.

"Where is the cavern and tunnels where are stored all the large reserves of artillery?" King said there were no such caverns.

"There are such caverns," the interpreter insisted. He pointed to the Manila Bay side of Mariveles on the map. "There are caverns here where artillery is stored. Do not lie! You must have much artillery. It has been destroyed many times and you bring out additional artillery."

When King pointed out that he had saved trucks to move his army out of Bataan, and when he asked where the men should go, no one answered. The Japanese walked away and shouted for guards to lock up King's party in a nearby hut.

For the more than 75,000 soldiers affected by King's decision, the last day of resistance on Bataan was about to begin. Early in the morning the Luzon Force Signal Officer phoned Corregidor and told Colonel Teague at Fort Mills that their conversation would shortly be interrupted; the Bataan side was about to cut the submarine telephone cable linking the peninsula to Corregidor. Breaking into the call, the Luzon Force telephone officer ended the conversation just before a work detail cut through the bulky cable. Signalmen on Corregidor severed their end of the cable, dragged it out of the water, and sealed it.[21]

Two Philippine Army Q-boats and two motor boats, defying orders to sail from Mariveles to Ft. Mills, threaded their way through the mine fields and broke for the open sea. Corregidor fired a few shots across their bows in an attempt to turn them, but the intimidation failed. One Q-boat returned after being chased back by a Japanese destroyer. In Mariveles Harbor, planes from the 62nd Air Regiment bombed the British S.S. *Suisang*, which exploded with a tremendous blast. A piece of steel flung hundreds of yards from the ship landed directly on the center of a man's helmet, killing him. The *Hyde* and *Bohol II*, anchored off Bataan, were scuttled. Tug *Napa*, en route to her scuttling site with a 12-man skeleton crew, was caught by a Japanese dive bomber. A single bomb penetrated the engine room and opened the hull to Manila Bay. Despite major flooding, the *Napa* was reluctant to die and she took a long time to sink. The Water Transport Service closed its navigation head at the port-village of Cabcaben, and the men drove to Mariveles. Sailors of the U.S.S. *Canopus* scrambled into the ship's boats and made for Corregidor, but not before Bataan made a last attempt at them. Engineers had dynamited a nearby tunnel entrance, and gasoline drums inside ruptured. A gigantic bomb formed as fumes filled the air spaces. When the fumes ignited, the blast hurled huge boulders as far as half a mile into the bay. Shock waves whipped the calm waters into a vicious chop. A large rock ripped the stern off one boat and sent three men splashing into the water. More rocks crashed through a second boat's canopy, killing four sailors and injuring nine more.[22]

On land, destruction of equipment continued. The evening of April 8 General Weaver sent a message to his tank commanders telling them to make plans to destroy all tanks and combat vehicles, arms, ammunition, gas, and radios. The tankers were to keep enough trucks to move to the rear. When they received orders to execute the plan, one tank battalion demolished its trucks by firing armor-piercing shells into their engines. Other men poured sand into gas tanks and carburetors. Radio message books, personnel rosters, and even money were placed into piles, sprinkled with gasoline, and lit. The order to destroy gear and surrender came as a surprise to Private William A. Hauser's reconnaissance platoon. "We all thought that with full fuel tanks and full ammunition belts we would try to break out," Hauser recalled. "We had no idea, even remote, that the Commanding General would surrender. I for one was more scared of surrendering than trying to fight in a break out."[23]

Other tankers agreed. They felt they should make one last attack, punish the Japanese one last time. There was nothing more to lose, and it was time to earn their pay. Only the threat of court-martial drove the men to destroy their equipment. Private Hauser went to work on his half-track. He poured dirt into the gas tank. The men drained oil from engines and raced them until they froze. Tankers rendered their machine guns and side arms inoperable by throwing bolts and other pieces into the jungle. Garbled orders were received not to burn anything because of the terms of the surrender. Two tanks from headquarters company were left intact after removing the 37mm breech blocks, breaking the .30-caliber machine guns, and fouling the gas tanks. A Company, 192nd Tank Battalion, drove their tanks into the jungle and spread out in a small fan-shape formation. Drivers opened engine compartments, cut gas lines, and tossed in matches. Sergeant Knox left his tank before it caught fire; he could not bring himself to watch. Private Abel E. Ortega took a hammer and began banging on his half-track's radio. "It was kind of tough," he remembers. "They built them pretty good. I broke it open and smashed everything in it."[24]

Part of the 194th Tank Battalion laagered together that last night, and they received the order to destroy equipment at 0700 hours the next morning. A Company broke off tank gas valves, flooded the interiors with gas, and set them afire. The men field-stripped small arms and machine guns, threw the pieces into the blazing vehicles, and bent gun barrels around trees. In the 17th Ordnance Company, mechanics placed hand grenades around vehicle engines and detonated them. Tanks under repair were likewise immobilized. Men resorted to sledge hammers to smash radios and arc-welding gear. Weapons were broken and buried. The company commander, Captain Richard Kadel, offered his men the chance to escape to Central Luzon. Nine men climbed the slopes of Mount Mariveles and walked out of Bataan. Despite all these destruction efforts, eleven American tanks were repairable or found intact by the Japanese, and at least one took part in the Japanese landing on Corregidor.[25]

In the self-propelled artillery battalions, the 75mm guns mounted on half-tracks were rigged for destruction. Gunners removed piston-rod coupler keys, loaded the guns, and closed the breeches. They attached long lanyards, and when they fired the guns, both the gun and the half-track were completely wrecked. In an antiaircraft unit a captain cut a radio height-finder to pieces. He then poured gasoline over the remains and touched them off with a match. Headquarters personnel leafed through files and burned anything having possible value to the Japanese. Field glasses, cameras, and other items went into a pile and were destroyed. The men ate what was left of the reserve ration. Sergeant Gilewitch witnessed an agonizing sight. He was looking for his company when he came to a stretch in the road strewn with ruptured C ration cans where heavy trucks were driving over the cans to crush them. Men were starving all across the peninsula, yet these precious rations were being destroyed to prevent their use by the Japanese. Having accomplished this heartbreaking task, the drivers dismounted and pushed their trucks over the edge of a deep ravine.[26]

In infantry units machine gunners destroyed their .30-caliber water-cooled guns by firing pistol rounds into the water jackets. They then disassembled the rest of the gun, buried the parts or tossed them into the jungle. They buried small arms ammunition in foxholes with weapons and accoutrements. Corporal Wynn from the 31st Infantry kept his .45-caliber pistol with one bullet. He intended to shoot himself rather than surrender. But when the moment of truth arrived, he chickened out. Wynn took his pistol apart and threw the pieces into the jungle. The 45th Infantry's main body received the surrender order at 0800 hours, and the Scouts were told to move to concealed bivouacs and not to fire unless attacked. When they heard of the surrender, they broke down and cried. They still had fight in them, and their martial pride rebelled against the order. Many wanted to fight it out, come what may. The only men of the regiment to reach Corregidor were the commander, his adjutant, and the chaplain.[27]

When an American mortar platoon heard of the surrender, they emplaced their 81mm mortar, set the range and charge for maximum, and fired their last round at the Japanese. They then disassembled all their weapons and trudged south, throwing the pieces into the vegetation. As word of the imminent surrender filtered down to the men, vehicle drivers removed distributors from engines, removed the working parts from weapons, and broke up their smaller weapons. Later in the morning, medic Harold E. VanAlstyne was sleeping under a small bush when someone pounded him in the side, yelling that they were here. Trying to wake up, VanAlstyne wondered who was here. Then he saw a road where a Japanese pack artillery unit—mountain guns—a couple of wheels on one mule, a gun tube on another, a chassis on a third, a whole chain of men and animals plodded south. The artillerymen were big, burly, and tough looking. A Japanese sergeant ran yelling into the tanker's bivouac, waving a big Navy Colt pistol in one hand and a sword in the other, followed closely by six soldiers. The Americans stood up, walked to the road, and thereby satisfied the Japanese.[28]

Vehicles fleeing the Japanese were crammed to overflowing with exhausted, listless troops. Passengers in trucks waved big white sheets. Drivers carried sticks with small while flags fluttering from the end. Men raised white flags on hilltops, around bivouacs, and in other prominent places. Troops marching on roads and trails waved whatever white items they could find. The 17th Pursuit Squadron destroyed their gas masks, dumped their light and heavy machine guns into the sea and, with a little effort, toppled a heavy antiaircraft searchlight off a rocky point. Some men clowned around a little, breaking everything they could find. Several hours later someone reported the surrender order had been countermanded. There would be no quarter, no prisoners, no safety for those who surrendered. "Well, Jesus," Corporal Vogler remembered, "We went down diving in the water, trying to come up with bolts and putting guns back together and getting ammunition. It was a hell of a mess."[29] Later, they heard they could surrender after all. Sergeant Wright picked up a cookie jar, put his camera, light meter, and a tablecloth into it and buried it at the base of a tree. Lieutenant Conners, the highest ranking officer with the squadron, told the airmen to stick together. For a second time they threw away their weapons, divided the remaining food, and marched south to meet their fate. "We picked up some white sheets or whatever we had and went over a pretty defeated looking bunch of people," said Vogler. "We were absolutely whipped. We were starved to death. We were just absolutely beat down."[30] Although many men rendered their weapons inoperable, there were literally thousands strewn about still in working order. The early Filipino resistance helped arm itself by sending men and carabao with A-frames into Bataan to scavenge rifles, pistols, and machine guns. A bolt here, a stock there, a trigger housing group, all added up.

In another Air Corps unit the men of the 34th Pursuit were warned not to tell the Japanese about their service at Quinauan Point. The officers feared reprisals for the devastating defeat inflicted upon the Japanese during the west coast battles. One airman was very willing not to anger the enemy. "I don't know about you guys," he told his friends, "but if a Jap tells me to kiss his foot, I'm going to kiss his foot."[31] One man found a new pair of shoes and several new socks, and he put them on in preparation for whatever might happen. The airmen destroyed their equipment, burned their weapons, and hiked to the main road. A few men grumbled about the surrender, but no one knew which way to go to escape. When they reached the main road, the airmen had their first encounter with the Japanese. "One of the Japanese soldiers pointed to his wrist asking in Japanese what time it was," recalled Larry H. Cohen. "Foolishly I answered, and that was the last time I saw my wrist watch."[32]

Some men were extremely reluctant to lay down their arms. After leaving the surrender negotiations, Colonel Collier drove up to what was left of a battalion of the 4th Constabulary. They were under cover and in no mood to surrender. Twenty-five Japanese tanks stood 150 yards away with their cannon trained on an irrigation ditch over which poked the muzzles of Filipino rifles. Just off the road a Japanese officer was talking with great difficulty to a Filipino major. The major stood four feet from the tank commander, covering him with a .45-caliber pistol. "Colonel," the major told Collier, his voice trembling with emotion, "this SOB demands my surrender and I am not going to surrender and if he makes a move to give a command I'm going to shoot him in two."[33] Collier felt the Japanese would die if he did not intervene. He stepped between the two men, grabbed the pistol, removed the magazine, cleared the chamber, and tossed the weapon to the ground. He told the major about the surrender. The major, tears in his eyes, asked Collier to tell his men and then walked into the nearby wood.

The choice whether or not to escape was not as easy as it sounded. Captain Paul H. Krauss, commanding the 45th Infantry's antitank company, reported to his division commander, General Lough, and asked if they had to surrender. Lough said yes, explaining if there were large-scale attempts to escape, the Japanese might make hostages of those who surrendered, thereby ruining chances for a bloodless surrender. Any attempt to escape, Lough told Krauss, would be regarded as desertion. At Lough's headquarters were a lot of division records, the colors of all the regiments, and the service records of the men. The men set to work, dug big holes, and buried everything.[34]

At General Pierce's 71st Division headquarters, Lieutenant Stephen Crosby approached Pierce after hearing of the surrender and requested permission to leave the unit and try to escape. "Well, lieutenant," Pierce answered, "if General King, who is our commanding general, says that we are to surrender, then I think we ought to surrender."[35] So Crosby stayed. In the time before the Japanese arrived, Pierce told Crosby to destroy three-quarters of a million dollars in pesos, the payroll for the 71st Division. Crosby counted the money, put it in ammunition cans, and buried it in a deep foxhole.

Major Allan M. Cory decided to stay with his unit, the 51st Combat Team. He was a battalion commander and felt he had to stay until he was relieved from that duty. Many others felt the same way, being disinclined to desert their Filipino enlisted men. But men without responsibilities tried to get away. A grounded navigator from a B-17 and several Americans found a boat at Mariveles and started rowing to Corregidor. A motor launch picked them up part way across and landed them on the island just in time to be bombed by twenty-seven Japanese aircraft. Fifteen Americans from the 21st Division secured some boats and paddled to Corregidor, but one man was killed in a strafing attack. A soldier from the 194th Tank Battalion's reconnaissance platoon found little difficulty in avoiding capture. He was a Filipino who, while in the United States, was drafted and sent back to the Philippines with the tank battalion. He now merged with the civilian refugees.[36]

Most Americans were very nervous about surrendering. Throughout the battle the feeling was to hold out as long as possible and then hope for the best when it came time to surrender. The time to surrender was now here, but no one looked forward to the experience. There were rumors about the Japanese not taking prisoners. Knowledge about Japanese activities in China, and especially Nanking, did little to settle the worried soldiers. Stories of Bataan atrocities were revived and lost nothing passing from one man to the next. If the men had known of the suffering and death that awaited them at the hands of their captors, and if they could have seen how few would survive prison camp, they would have fought a last ditch fight to annihilation. As it stood, there was considerable grumbling about the surrender. Few men were offered the chance of every man for himself.

As General Bluemel was about to retrace his steps north along Trail 26 toward Trail 20 with the remnants of his Alangan River force, Scouts from the 57th Infantry spotted a large Japanese force with an armored car. Captain Anders, scouting forward of the 57th Infantry, heard grunts, looked behind him, and found two Japanese with long bayonets poised periously close to the seat of his trousers. Concurrent with Anders's capture, the Scouts turned back up Trail 26, and Bluemel tried to lead them past the enemy by a different route. He found a foot trail, and at 1100 hours Bluemel came under rifle and machine-gun fire from across a wide open field. Colonel Vance moved to the point of his cavalrymen and discussed the situation with his A Troop commander. Vance found a Japanese force of unknown strength occupying the northern side of a glade, while A Troop was on the southern edge. Vance sent flank patrols to the right and left, then organized the 1st Squadron on the left of the trail and the 2nd Squadron on the right. The cavalrymen started firing, and the fight was on.[37]

It was now nearly noon and several officers reminded Bluemel that Luzon Force headquarters had surrendered that morning. No other units were still fighting and there was no haven into which Bluemel's men could fight. Luzon Force orders forbade further fighting. Even if Bluemel fought his way out of this jam, he would have to surrender somewhere else. There was simply no place to go, and many casualties would be suffered for no reason. Bluemel believed his men would have attacked and fought to the finish. But he also realized the futility of continuing, so he gave orders to stop. "General Bluemel said we would surrender," recalled Colonel Vance. "I then stopped our firing and the Japanese firing soon ceased. While I was tying my dirty handkerchief to a small bamboo cane, one of my fine captains by the name of Cramer came up and volunteered to walk with me. I thanked him and said I needed all the moral support I could get. As we started across the glade, I realized how General King must have felt as he set forth on the same task that very morning. Moving across the glade to meet us were a couple of Japanese . . . the war in Bataan was over."[38]

The 57th Infantry, behind the cavalrymen, soon thereafter received orders "ostensibly" from Bluemel's staff to come out to the trail and surrender. Colonel Lilly thought this order might be a Japanese ruse, so he checked and found it authentic. When he ordered his men to comply, Japanese soldiers emerged from concealment and began stripping everyone of wallets, cigarettes, money, and unit and rank insignia. The Japanese were angry and ready to shoot. Japanese officers watched and did not intervene when one Scout was shot while leaning over to retrieve a family snapshot.[39]

Up to the very last moment rumors held some faint hope. The last rumor to die in the American 31st Infantry was that ships were waiting at Mariveles to evacuate them to Australia. But it was not to be. The regimental commander, Colonel Brady, gave whoever wanted it a chance to take off. The 3rd Battalion, separated from the regiment's main body, tried to make a break for Mariveles. The regimental service company, numbering twenty-five men, formed a screen to delay the Japanese and actually repulsed a few small probes. Four automatic riflemen formed the backbone of their limited firepower. One of the men in the screen was Corporal Knight. Earlier he had dropped off some wounded men from his command car and continued down the road until stopped by 27-year-old Captain Clarence R. Bess, a Missourian commanding the service company. Bess added Knight to his small force forming in a draw. Bess was just getting his Americans organized and briefed when tank engines were heard. Three Japanese tanks rolled up to Bess's men, shocking the Americans into immobility. A Japanese officer ordered them to drop their weapons and come out to the road. The Americans stood there for a heart-pounding eternity before anyone moved. Then a man pulled a white towel out of his knapsack and walked out toward the tanks. Captain Bess's screen dissolved.[40]

One incredible incident involved tankers from the 192nd Tank Battalion. Some men were thinking about escape, but as the first Japanese rode into the area they told the Americans to go to Mariveles where they would be trucked to Manila and put on a ship to be exchanged for Japanese in America. No soldier in his right mind would believe such a story, but these men were no longer completely rational. They wanted to believe the story so badly that most stopped thinking about escape. Some men tried to escape by sea. Lieutenant George A. Reed, executive officer to a battalion of self-propelled mounts, slipped from Mariveles in an outrigger canoe. The next day, April 10, a Japanese subchaser caught him. Another man, Captain Matt Dobrinic, found himself sitting on a hillside watching a long column of Japanese enter Mariveles. That night Dobrinic and a small group of men found a boat and paddled to Corregidor.[41]

Lieutenant Hummel, a tank officer, was with one of his sergeants as the Japanese started collecting prisoners. Watching from a distance, Hummel did not like what he saw. He headed for Manila Bay. Waiting until dark, Hummel and his sergeant waded into the water and swam toward Corregidor. The water was warm and the swimming easy. For a time, Corregidor was straight ahead, then it drifted off to the south. Then it was dead ahead again. The tide was sweeping the swimmers back and forth. Their trip was shortened when an American tug passed by, picked them up, and landed them on Corregidor.[42]

On Bataan, Japanese from the 4th Division entered General Parker's II Corps headquarters more intent on looting than fighting. As more and more Japanese arrived, they searched the Americans, took what they wanted, and beat anyone who hesitated or refused their demands. General Parker's units surrendered piecemeal where found by the Japanese. General Kitano's diary for the 4th Division's activities carried the happy entry: "Front line advancing westward on the Cabcaben-Mariveles road. Command post at Ano River Valley. Number of surrenders countless. Great success."[43] A tall Japanese officer collected some of the captives after Corporal Spencer waved a white medical towel. As if receiving an all-clear, a horde of Japanese came his way. "OK boys," the officer told them in English, "it's all over."[44] Corporal Gerald Wade was surprised by the appearance of the Japanese. Many had malaria and dysentery, and healthy men pushed the sick men forward.

Next, the Japanese made an appearance at Luzon Force headquarters. When Captain Gary Anloff heard a call from one of his guards, he ran up to the guard and into a Japanese tank. After a moment's hesitation, Anloff walked up to a Japanese captain standing in the turret, saluted, and asked, "What may I do for you sir?"[45]

"What is up this road?" the Japanese asked in perfect English.

"About a hundred yards up is the auto park for the Luzon Force headquarters. About a hundred yards further than that is the headquarters itself. You can drive your tank into the park but you'll have the walk the last hundred yards." The tank rattled into the vehicle park, the Japanese officer dismounted, and the two men walked to the headquarters. When the Japanese officer saw the large handmade maps in the operations room, he asked, "You use this? I have better," and displayed a beautiful four-color Coast and Geodetic Survey map so up-to-date it included recently completed trails on the American side of the front lines. By now, senior officers learned of the Japanese officer's arrival and shunted Anloff, "a mere captain," aside.

On the morning of April 9 a column of Japanese tanks approached Hospital Number 1. The lead tank sported a Japanese flag. An interpreter told Colonel James W. Duckworth, "This is the general of the tank unit." Duckworth, commander of the 12th Medical Regiment before the war, saluted and replied, "I am the commander of this hospital. It is my duty to surrender it to you."[46] A Japanese delegation inspected the hospital, and the Americans watched with interest mixed with concern. Japanese machine guns swung menacingly back and forth, and Dr.

Jack Gordon felt sure this would be his last day. Sloppily dressed, the Japanese soldiers' trousers were "truly of that universal military size, either too big or too small."[47] The Japanese were polite but firm.

Occupation of the facility went smoothly. The delegation saw the thirty-three wounded Japanese. The Japanese were housed in an intact room, the linen was clean, showers and latrines worked, and they had candy and cigarettes. American medical personnel lined up the wounded Japanese prisoners who, with their shaved heads and their Army gray pajamas, were so unmilitary looking the Japanese officer did not recognize them. When the prisoners identified themselves, the officer almost had a fit. Although he was pleased with American treatment of the wounded Japanese, he was outraged to find so many had surrendered. He lined them up and furiously rebuked them. During the harangue, several of the newly arrived Japanese left their tanks and asked the American doctors for treatment for gonorrhea. In the hospital Lieutenant (j.g.) Claud M. Fraleigh had a bad moment when a grinning Japanese soldier jumped out of the lead tank and ran up to him. The soldier had been a bellhop in the Grand Hotel in Tokyo which Fraleigh and his wife visited before the war. The Japanese remembered the large tip he received from the two Americans as they left the hotel.[48]

At 1700 hours a Japanese lieutenant and twenty men entered Hospital Number 2. The lieutenant wanted to meet the hospital commander, but he seemed most interested in the telephone and wanted to phone Corregidor. Other Japanese were more troublesome. They went from bed to bed looking at charts. If the medical records indicated a patient could walk, they pulled him out of bed and made him join the other prisoners marching out of Bataan. Any patient who refused to get up was pulled from the bed and beaten.[49]

As late as the afternoon of April 9 information about the surrender had not reached all of General King's units, especially those in I Corps. Rumors floated around concerning an all-out offensive. Officers talked about taking troops forward against the Japanese line if the surrender did come and attack north until they reached northeastern Luzon. But since the officers were good soldiers and used to obeying orders, they waited to hear what their commanders had to say. Some officers and men were enthusiastic about attacking. An offense offered more hope than sitting and waiting to be overrun, and they could then continue the fight as guerrillas. I Corps had not suffered the serious losses and disorganization that destroyed II Corps. When the I Corps quartermaster issued several days' rations at one time, the men were overjoyed. A few soldiers thought the long-awaited relief convoy had finally arrived.[50]

Trouble started the afternoon and evening of April 9. Large numbers of II Corps soldiery were fleeing the Japanese and crossed behind the front lines of General Jones's I Corps. Pursuing Japanese from the 65th Brigade ran into the exposed right flank of I Corps and, expecting resistance, fired as they advanced. General Jones knew he had to surrender, but to do so at night would be difficult and dangerous especially since the Japanese seemed unwilling to accept any surrender. At 1530 hours Japanese soldiers approached the Pantingan River. The Americans and Filipinos could see Japanese infantry and tanks moving into position, and when a nervous rifleman fired a shot, the battle was on. The Japanese hit the 11th Infantry's 1st Battalion where it guarded the north sector of Trails 7 and 9. The fighting spread to the 100-man 3rd Battalion northeast of the junction. Colonel Townsend pushed two Filipino reserve companies from the recently arrived 2nd Battalion into the thin line. By 1700 hours Japanese tanks forded the Pantingan and attacked down Trail 7.[51]

Amazingly, the Filipinos stood their ground and laced the enemy with heavy fire. The 11th Infantry fired its last 81mm rounds to harass the Japanese as they slipped and clawed their way up the steep slopes. Reports came into the 11th Infantry's headquarters that an entire regiment of Japanese infantry was coming west along Trail 8. Although the Filipinos held their ground, the situation rapidly turned desperate. No food or ammunition had reached the 11th Infantry for two days, and food supplies were now completely exhausted. The regiment's reserve rifle ammunition had been used to supply attached units, and reports now arrived reporting shortages all along the line. Urgent requests to the rear for resupply brought no response. At 1830 hours, news of the surrender finally reached the 11th Infantry. The Filipinos were still heavily engaged with the Japanese climbing the steep slopes of the Pantingan. Officers moved along the 11th Infantry's line with orders to stop firing, break contact, and head west along Trail 9 to bivouac areas. The officers told the men to destroy the crew-served weapons but warned them to keep their rifles until further notice. The Japanese continued to fire at the now unoccupied ridge but showed little desire to launch an assault. Finally, receiving no return fire, the Japanese slowed their own. The firing died.[52]

When the surrender order reached the division's engineer battalion, the men were heartbroken. "It was a very sad day for all of us," remembered Major Bautista. "Many a seasoned soldier wept unashamed. So this was to be the end! The humiliation of defeat and the added possibility of cruel treatment from the savage foe."[53] The engineers burned or destroyed all important papers, maps, and documents. In the 12th Infantry, Captain Liles was crushed by the surrender order. "I was tired, dejected and disgusted. Here I had put in four of the hardest months of my life trying to hold some territory until reinforcements could arrive. Our government, the strongest in the world, was unable to send help. I looked and felt like I had lost my last friend." When one of his Filipinos told him, "Cheer up Joe, it ain't all that bad," Liles felt like crying.[54]

General Brougher's two regimental commanders requested permission to make their way north through Japanese lines, head for the mountains, and organize guerrilla resistance. Although contrary to General Jones's orders, Brougher released the two officers, and although neither man survived the war, they helped lay the foundation for the 20,000-man guerrilla army that paved the way for MacArthur's return. Another who preferred guerrilla existence to capture was Major Volckmann, since April 1 the division's intelligence officer. Cornering Brougher on April 6, Volckmann presented his plan. "Sir, I'm still in pretty good physical shape—I have a lot of fight left in me. Would you give me permission to try and work my way north to [Colonel John P.] Horan if and when we are ordered to surrender?" Brougher thought for a moment. "Sure thing, I'll report you missing in action on a patrol. If you try, the best of luck to you."[55] Volckmann's decision cost the Japanese dearly, for he became active in the resistance. He ultimately commanded the North Luzon guerrillas, the most effective and powerful of the many groups that sprang up after Bataan's surrender.

Brougher also wanted to escape, but he felt a responsibility as division commander and believed he must remain and surrender with his men. He collected and addressed his officers, telling them he had never had a harder order to carry out. He reviewed the division's history. "We were the first to contact the enemy in the North and the last in the South. You have done a magnificent job. It is with regret that I surrender you to the Japanese."[56] Lieutenant Colonel Moses gave the assembled officers a last piece of advice. "Remember that even though you are surrendered to the Japs you are still officers in the United States Army. Conduct yourselves accordingly."[57]

Even after the fighting stopped after the Filipino withdrawal from the Pantingan River, the Japanese acted as if they did not know of the surrender. That evening they entered the 11th Division area firing machine guns despite large bonfires and white flags. They shot into unarmed soldiers and scattered them down Trail 7 toward Mariveles. When the Japanese burst into the weaponless 11th Division, Major Volckmann and Captain Blackburn, the division signal officer, slipped into a dry stream bed and crawled away from danger. They were without food and medicine and chances were greatly against them, but they ultimately reached the relative safety of central Luzon. After some quick debate, General

Brougher and his staff decided to escape south with their men before the Japanese killed them where they stood. "I knew nothing of the terms of the surrender," recalls Brougher, "and with machine gun bullets whistling around, we all got the impression the Japanese were giving no quarter and that we would all be slaughtered if we remained where we were."[58] American and Filipinos vied with one another as they streamed away in panic. Brougher assembled most of his division the next day, and the Japanese peacefully accepted its surrender.

The 1st Division also had trouble throwing in the towel. The division was spread over a large piece of ground, part on the first delay position as a covering force, one battalion near the Pantingan River, and another battalion with the division command post. The 1st Division received word of the surrender the afternoon of April 9, and the headquarters passed the information to all elements. But the four rifle companies acting as a covering force north of the main body were hit by the advancing Japanese. Either through ignorance of the surrender or on purpose, the Japanese continued their attack. The Filipinos had complied with the terms of surrender, had stacked arms, and were flying white flags. Unable to offer resistance, they suffered severe casualties. The three American officers with them were killed.[59]

Later in the afternoon heavy firing at the trail junction between the Japanese and the 11th Division had 1st Division officers worried. They had orders to surrender, yet what sounded like a medium-size battle was edging their way. Patrols tried to find out what was happening, but they were not successful. Firing drew closer that evening when the Japanese burst into the bivouacs of the 11th Division. As midnight approached, and as the Japanese neared the 1st Division's main body, Colonel Berry placed his engineer battalion and an infantry battalion astride Trail 9 near the command post. The two units were in position by 0200 hours on April 10. Luckily, when contact was made with the Japanese, fighting stopped and there were no casualties. Maybe the experience of shooting up the 11th Division without opposition convinced the Japanese the battle was finally over.[60]

The Japanese facing most of I Corps's front, in contrast to those coming in from the flank, seemed to know of the surrender. As they advanced, they took the surrender of each unit they encountered. They were courteous in their treatment of the Filipinos and simply ordered them north to Bagac or south to Mariveles. "Our captors were not too bad to us," recalled Ed Betts. "The Japanese tank commander could speak English. He asked for our C.O. and then asked Lieutenant Markham how long it had been since we had anything to eat. The lieutenant told him three days. A Japanese warrant officer had 12 cases of our field rations. He lined us up and we each received six cans of meat and beans."[61] It was not until April 10 that a Japanese officer arrived at I Corps headquarters. He told the Americans to sit tight. The next morning, the eleventh, General Jones was able to surrender.

Three hundred men from the American 31st Infantry reached Corregidor. Captain George A. Sensep burned the regiment's colors on April 9. Three weeks later Captain Earl R. Short and two men buried the treasured Shanghai Bowl in Corregidor's rocky soil. They coated the bowl and each cup with cosmoline, then packed everything in sawdust in an iron box, then in a larger wooden box. The box went into a trench. About 2,300 sailors, soldiers, and civilians escaped to Corregidor, most by swimming or by raft, small boat, or bamboo pole. The majority were so badly demoralized by their Bataan experiences, they proved of little value to the island's defense. They were physically broken down and unable to perform even light work. Corregidor doubled the ration for two days to the kitchens feeding the Bataan evacuees. Several noncombat units crossed without authorization. Despite orders as to who should cross, the 680th and 681st ordnance companies, a graves registration unit, some Constabulary, Navy, and miscellaneous troops fled to the island.[62]

"The most unforgettable sight of all," recalled Lieutenant Commander Morrill watching from the minesweeper U.S.S. *Quail,* "was the groups of men standing in the South Bataan shore in the early half light of the morning, beckoning and signalling with flashlights for help."[63] Prowling the waters off Mariveles was a launch from the 580-ton gunboat *Mindanao.* The launch picked up swimmers and men from small boats until packed with sixty refugees. The skipper, Commander Alan McCraken, outfitted the escapees in khakis and set them ashore on Corregidor.

As the sweepings of General King's Luzon Force were collected by whatever means existed, Wainwright turned his energies to informing Washington of the situation.

> Shortly after a flag of truce passed through the front lines this morning, hostilities ceased, for the most part, in Bataan. At about ten oclock this morning General King was sent for to confer with the Japanese commander. He has not returned as of seven PM nor has the result of the conference been disclosed. Japanese forces are now in control of the southern end of the Bataan peninsula and have already placed batteries in position to fire on Corregidor. One battery is located in the vicinity of Cabcaben and others are located further to the west. I do not at present feel at liberty to return the fire of these batteries as I would be firing into areas occupied by my own troops.[64]

After ninety-three days of siege the defense of Bataan ended. General King enacted a scene that had not been seen since 1865 and that has not been seen since, the surrender of an American army. Into the hands of the Japanese passed 75,000 Americans and Filipinos. Into history passed America's principal imperial possession, the Philippines.

The battle for Bataan was over. The battle for Corregidor was about to begin.

Epilogue

BECAUSE OF THE COMPLETE BREAKDOWN IN THE ARMY'S ORGAN-
ization, the losses suffered by the defenders in the final week of fighting
will never be known. The Luzon Force personnel officer's returns for
April 3 carried 78,100 Filipinos and Americans on the rolls. About 3,000
men escaped to Corregidor. There were about 45,000 Filipinos and
9,300 Americans in Camp O'Donnell prison camp between April 10 and
June 4. The difference in the two figures, 75,100 and 54,300, is due to
fighting, the Death March, and most significant, disease and starvation in
the prison camp itself. Within two months of the surrender, more than
21,000 men disappeared.

The Japanese, conversely, sustained only light losses in the final seven
days of the campaign. The 65th Brigade reported no more than 50 men
killed and 179 wounded. The Japanese 4th Division suffered only 400
killed or wounded despite carrying the brunt of the fighting.

In Australia, General MacArthur read a statement to reporters.

> The Bataan Force went out as it would have wished, fighting to the end
> its flickering, forlorn hope. No army has done so much with so little, and
> nothing became it more than its last hour of trial and agony. To the weep-
> ing mothers of its dead, I can only say that the sacrifice and halo of Jesus of
> Nazareth has descended upon their sons, and that God will take them unto
> Himself.[1]

Notes

Culo Bridge

[1] Colonel Richard C. Mallonee, *Bataan Diary,* 2 vols., vol. 1: "The Defense at the Beach, The Withdrawal to Bataan," and vol. 2: Defense of Bataan, 1:40; Russell W. Volckmann, *We Remained: Three Years Behind the Enemy Lines in the Philippines* (New York: W. W. Norton & Company, Inc., 1954), p. 21, hereafter referred to as Volckmann, *We Remained;* and Malcolm V. Fortier, "Brief History of the 41st Div From Initial Mobilization Sept. 1, 1941 to Dec. 24, 1941," p. 32, in Malcolm V. Fortier, *Notes on 41st Div.,* hereafter referred to as Fortier, *Brief Hist 41 Div.*

[2] Zenon R. Bardowski to author, (tape), 6 March 1977.

[3] James V. Collier, *Notebooks,* 4 vols., 2:69–72.

[4] Franklin O. Anders to author, 10 January 1986.

[5] Lee C. Vance to author, 27 March 1979.

[6] Theodore I. Spaulding to author, (tape), 28 October 1975; Volckmann, *We Remained,* p. 24; and Ray M. O'Day, "History of the 21st Division," 2 parts, 2:20, hereafter referred to as O'Day, "Hist of 21 Div."

[7] Duane Schultz, *Hero of Bataan: The Story of General Jonathan M. Wainwright* (New York: St. Martin's Press, 1981), p. 39, hereafter referred to as Schultz, *Hero of Bataan;* The Adjutant Generals Office, *Official Army Register January 1, 1943.* (Washington, D.C.: United States Government Printing Office, 1943), p. 816, hereafter referred to as *Army Register 1943;* Lieutenant General Richard K. Sutherland (Retired), 12 November 1946, interview by Dr. Louis Morton, p. 14; Louis Charles Beebe, BG, AUS, "Personal Experience Sketches," p. 13, in the Louis C. Beebe Papers; The Adjutant General's Office, *Official Army Register January 1, 1941* (Washington, D.C.: United States Government Printing Office,

1941), p. 607, hereafter referred to as *Army Register 1941;* and Louis Morton, *The Fall of the Philippines. United States Army in World War II. The War in the Pacific* (Washington, D.C.: Office of the Chief of Military History, United States Army, U.S. Government Printing Office, 1953), p. 225, hereafter referred to as Morton, *Fall.*

[8] O'Day, "Hist of 21 Div.," 2:20.

[9] Mallonee, "Bataan Diary," 1:138; Morton, *Fall,* p. 225; and USAFFE "Signal Operating Instructions, Astronomical Data #3," 5 January 1942.

[10] Harry A. Skerry to Chief of Staff, North Luzon Force, 1 August 1942, Subject: Organization and Operations of the North Luzon Force Engineers between Dec 8, 1941 and Jan 6, 1942, p. 12, hereafter referred to as Skerry, "Operations NLF Engineers;" and Mallonee, "Bataan Diary," 1:138.

[11] O'Day, *Hist. of 21 Div.,* 2:2 and 20; and Harry A. Skerry to Major General Orlando Ward, 16 January 1952, "Comments on *The Fall of the Philippines.*"

[12] O'Day, "Hist of 21 Div.," 2:21; William E. Chandler, *Colonel Clinton A. Pierce,* p. 3; Beebe, "Personal Experience Sketches," pp. 12–13. Two cavalry officers, neither present at this argument, doubt it took place. I have accepted O'Day's version because he was there.

[13] Interview with Avelino J. Battad, Manila, Republic of the Philippines, 6 June 1979.

[14] Forrest Knox to author, 6 April 1977.

[15] O'Day, "Hist of 21 Div," 2:21–22; and *Army Register 1941,* p. 638.

[16] Annex X: Report of Operations of the Provisional Tank Group, in Jonathan M. Wainwright, Report of Operations of USAFFE and USFIP in the Philippine Islands, 1941–1942, with eighteen annexes: Data for USAFFE-USEIP reports rendered by the separate force cdrs. after the war; official notes and extracts taken from the G-3 journals which were forwarded from the Philippines while the campaign was still in progress; notes made by officers assembled at Ft. Sam Houston, Texas by War Department orders to draw up the historical report of the Philippine Campaign, p. 16, hereafter referred to as Annex X, while the body will be referred to as Wainwright, Rpt Ops USAFFE-USFIP.

[17] Knox to author, 6 April 1977.

[18] Harry A. Skerry to Lieutenant Colonel George A. Meidling, 4 August 1947, "Comments on *Engineers in Theater Operations.*"

[19] George A. Meidling, ed. *Engineers of the Southwest Pacific 1941–1945 Vol I: Engineers in Theater Operations—United States Army Forces in the Far East, Southwest Pacific Area, Army Forces, Pacific* (Tokyo, Japan: Office of the Chief Engineer, General Headquarters Army Forces, Pacific, 1947), p. 15, hereafter referred to as Meidling, *Engrs in Theater Ops;* Skerry, "Operations NLF Engineers," pp. 5 and 11; and "Comments on the draft Engineer Reports," anonymous.

[20] John Toland, *But Not in Shame* (New York: Random House, 1961),

p. 159; Bardowski to author, (tape), 6 March 1977; and Schultz, *Hero of Bataan,* pp. 2, 21 and 65.

[21] Morton, *Fall,* p. 225.

[22] Dwight D. Eisenhower, *Crusade in Europe* (Garden City, New York: Doubleday and Co., 1948), pp. 16–17, hereafter referred to as Eisenhower, *Crusade.* It is interesting to note that even as late as 1948 Eisenhower believed that the Philippine garrison totalled only 30,000 men.

[23] *Ibid.,* p. 18. Subsequent quotes are from pages 17–22.

[24] Brigadier General Leonard T. Gerow, Memorandum for [Army] Chief of Staff, 3 January 1942, Subject: Relief of the Philippines, p. 9.

[25] Radio, Marshall to MacArthur, 3 January 1942.

[26] *Ibid.*

[27] *Ibid.* The War Department message to MacArthur received a week earlier on December 28 read, "Fifty-two dive bombers originally scheduled for the Philippines, forty-eight pursuit pilots, eighteen pursuit airplanes, the 7th Bombardment Group less flying echelon are now in Brisbane. Two pursuit groups complete with 160 airplanes, the remainder of the 35th Pursuit Group consisting of combat headquarters squadron and one combat squadron, 235 additional pursuit planes with 180 combat crews, 10 observation airplanes with combat crews and mobile air depot are either on the water now or departing first week of January for Australia. Eighty heavy airplanes are being ferried through Africa at the rate of three or more a day." (Radio, from Adams to Merle-Smith, 28 December 1941 in "Aid the Philippines," in Willoughby Papers.) Despite extensive efforts to prepare the planes then in Brisbane, the planes were not ready for another six weeks.

Mobilization

[1] A. V. H. Hartendorp, *The Japanese Occupation of the Philippines* (Manila: Makati, Rizal, MDB Printing, 1967), p. 101, hereafter referred to as Hartendorp, *Japanese Occupation;* Allison Ind, *Bataan: The Judgment Seat. The Saga of the Philippine Command of the United States Army Air Force May 1941 to May 1942* (New York: The Macmillan Co., 1944), p. 250., hereafter referred to as Ind, *Judgment Seat;* Courtney Whitney, *MacArthur: His Rendezvous with History* (New York: Alfred A. Knopf, 1956), p. 21; Karl C. Dod, *United States Army in World War II, the Technical Services, the Corps of Engineers: The War Against Japan* (Washington, D.C.: United States Government Printing Office, 1960), p. 85, hereafter referred to as Dod, *Engineers Against Japan;* John Hersey, *Men on Bataan* (New York: Alfred A. Knopf, 1942), p. 78; Morton, *Fall,* p. 245; John E. Olson, with Frank O. Anders, "Anywhere-Anytime: History of the 57th Infantry (PS)," *Bulletin American Historical Collection.* American Association of the Philippines, vol. XV, no. 3(60)(July–September 1987), 1:18, hereafter

referred to as Olson, "Anywhere-Anytime;" Charles C. Drake to Major General Orlando Ward, 12 February 1952; Walter H. Waterous, *Reminiscences of Dr. W. H. Waterous Pertinent to World War II in the Philippines* (Philippine Islands: By the author, 1953), p. 23., hereafter referred to as Waterous, *Reminiscences;* Manuel E. Buenafe, *Wartime Philippines* (Manila: Philippine Education Foundation Inc., 1950), p. 91; and Collier, "Notebooks," 3:21.

² Morton, *Fall,* p. 245.

³ *Ibid.,* p. 598; Olson, "Anywhere-Anytime," 1:19–20; and Louis Morton, *United States Army in World War II. The War in the Pacific. Strategy and Command. The First Two Years* (Washington, D.C.: Office of the Chief of Military History, United States Army, U.S. Government Printing Office, 1962), p. 181, hereafter referred to as Morton, *Strategy and Command.*

⁴ Morton, *Fall,* p. 61.

⁵ *Ibid.,* pp. 61–64; and Dod, *Engineers Against Japan,* p. 55.

⁶ Morton, *Fall,* pp. 9, 17 and 19; Sutherland, interview 12 November 1946 by Morton, p. 1; Collier, "Notebooks," 1:13; Jonathan M. Wainwright, Robert Considine, ed. *General Wainwright's Story: The Account of Four Years of Humiliating Defeat, Surrender, and Captivity* (New York: Modern Literary Editions Publishing Company, 1945), pp. 12–13, all reference is to the paperback issue, hereafter referred to as Wainwright, *Story;* and Annex V, Report of Operations of South Luzon Force, Bataan Defense Force and II Philippine Corps in the Defense of South Luzon and Bataan from 8 December 1941–9 April 1942, p. 6, in Wainwright, Rpt Ops USAFFE-USFIP, hereafter referred to as Annex V.

⁷ Morton, *Fall,* p. 67; and MacArthur to George C. Marshall, 28 October 1941, cited in John Jacob Beck, *MacArthur and Wainwright: Sacrifice of the Philippines* (Albuquerque: University of New Mexico Press, 1974), p. 5, hereafter referred to as Beck, *Sacrifice.*

⁸ Morton, *Fall,* pp. 67–69.

⁹ The Army War College, "Studies of Overseas Departments and Alaska, Group No. 2, Philippine Department Reference Data, April 1, 1940 to April 10, 1940," p. 7, produced for War Plans Course No. 13, 1939–1940, hereafter referred to as The Army War College, "Studies;" Collier, "Notebooks," 1:23; and Morton, *Fall,* p. 26.

¹⁰ USAFFE General Order #46, 18 December 1941.

¹¹ Wainwright, *Story,* p. 16; Morton, *Fall,* pp. 26–27; and Wainwright, Rpt Ops USAFFE-USFIP, p. 22.

¹² Annex XIII, Report of Operations Quartermaster Corps, United States Army in the Philippine Campaign, 1941–1942, p. 19, in Wainwright, Rpt Ops USAFFE-USFIP, hereafter referred to as Annex XIII; Teodoro A. Agoncillo, *The Fateful Years. Japan's Adventure in the Philippines, 1941–1945,* 2 vols. (Quezon City, Philippines: R. P. Garcia Publishing Company, 1965), 1:73, hereafter referred to as Agoncillo, *Fateful*

Years; Wainwright, Rpt Ops USAFFE-USFIP, pp. 4 and 7; Annex V, pp. 2–3; Dod, *Engineers Against Japan,* p. 80; and Wainwright, *Story,* p. 16.

13 Clifford Bluemel, "Oral Reminiscenses of Brigadier General Clifford Bluemel," Yardley, Pennsylvania, July 8 1971, p. 5, by Dr. D. Clayton James, hereafter referred to as Bluemel, "Oral Reminiscenses;" and Wainwright, Rpt Ops USAFFE-USFIP, p. 3. Fort Leavenworth's courses underwent several name changes. In 1922 the School of the Line became the Command and General Staff School, a one-year course. It became a two-year course from 1928 to 1935. In 1946 the course was changed to the Command and Staff College, and in 1947 to the Command and General Staff College. Data is from the US Army Command and General Staff College catalog, academic year 1983–84.

14 Charles C. Underwood, "The Defense of Luzon and Bataan, 7 Dec. 41–9 April 42," p. 10, hereafter referred to as Underwood, "Defense of Bataan;" and Clyde A. Selleck, "Notes 71st Division, Report of 71st Div in compliance with official request, August 1942," p. 43, hereafter referred to as Selleck, "Notes 71 Div."

15 Appendix B to Annex XIII, *Report of Army Transport Service Activities in the Philippine Islands from 8 December 1941 to 6 May 1942,* p. 1.

16 Dod, *Engineers Against Japan,* p. 68; and Meidling, *Engrs. in Theater Ops.,* p. 2. In mid-November 1941, an engineer general service regiment, the 47th, was being readied in the United States for deployment to the Philippines, and equipment for two aviation engineer battalions was en route. Data from Dod, *Engineers Against Japan,* p. 70.

17 Amado N. Bautista, "Operations Report 11th Engr Bn 11 Div. from 29 Aug 41 to 10 Apr 42," pp. 1–3, hereafter referred to as Bautista, "11 Engr Bn"; Meidling, *Engrs in Theater Ops,* p. 9; Beck, *Sacrifice,* p. 13; and Dod, *Engineers Against Japan,* p. 68.

18 Annex XIII, p. 11; Morton, *Fall,* p. 34; Forrest C. Pogue, *George C. Marshall,* vol. 2: *Ordeal and Hope 1939–1942* (New York: The Viking Press, 1965), pp. 188–189, hereafter referred to as Pogue, *Ordeal and Hope;* and Richard M. Leighton and Robert W. Coakley, *United States Army in World War II. Global Logistics and Strategy 1940–1943* (Washington, D.C.: Office of the Chief of Military History, United States Army, U.S. Government Printing Office, 1955), p. 125, hereafter referred to as Leighton, *Global Logistics.*

19 *Reports of General MacArthur. Japanese Operations in the Southwest Pacific Area,* 2 vols. (Washington, D.C.: United States Government Printing Office, 1966), prepared by his General Staff, 1:2, hereafter referred to as *Reports of MacArthur.*

20 Pogue, *Ordeal and Hope,* p. 193; and "Interrogation of Japanese Officials on World War II," 3 vols., General Headquarters Far East Command, MI Section, Historical Division, 1:100. Although Japanese concern over MacArthur's preparations was real, there were an equal

number of prominent Japanese who claim a better-prepared Philippines would not have affected the decision for war.

²¹ Wesley F. Craven and James Lea Cate, *The Army Air Forces in World War II. Vol. One, Plans and Early Operations, January 1939 to August 1942* (Chicago, Illinois: Office of Air Force History, The University of Chicago Press, 1948), pp. 151 and 176, hereafter referred to as Craven and Cate, *Plans and Early Operations.* Brigadier General Carl Spaatz, Chief of the Air Staff, recognized that the one company of air warning personnel in the Philippines was entirely inadequate and pressed for enlargement of the unit to composite battalion size. In a November 13, 1941, memorandum, he estimated the necessary personnel would leave San Francisco on December 10. MacArthur requested dispatch to the Philippines of three semimobile and two mobile antiaircraft regiments. Data comes from a memorandum for the Chief of Staff, Subject: Equipment for Philippine Aircraft Warning Service, 13 Nov 41, and Memorandum for Chief of Staff, Subject: Antiaircraft Artillery Personnel for the Philippines, 29 November 1941.

²² Steve Mellnik, *Philippine Diary* (New York: Van Nostrand Reinhold Co., 1969), p. 23; Wainwright, *Story,* p. 15; and Beck, *Sacrifice,* p. 9.

²³ Radio, Marshall to MacArthur, 27 November 1941. Rainbow Five concerned the Pacific War Plan. It had a worldwide provision and conformed to arrangements made with the British. It assumed a war with more than one enemy and recognized Germany as the main enemy.

²⁴ Radio, MacArthur to Chief of Staff, 28 November 1941; Annex V, p. 10; and Clifford Bluemel, "Report of Brigadier General Clifford Bluemel, U.S. Army on 31st Division, Philippine Army Sub-Sector "C" Mt. Samat Line, Bataan, P.I. and the Special Force Covering the Period 18 Nov. 1941–9 April 1942," p. 4, hereafter referred to as Bluemel, "31 Div."

²⁵ Morton, *Fall,* pp. 21–22; Harold K. Johnson, "Defense Along the Abucay Line," *Military Review* vol. XXVIII, no. 11 (February 1949), p. 45, hereafter referred to as H. K. Johnson, "Defense Along Abucay;" Ernest L. Brown, "The Operations of the 57th Infantry (P.S.) (Philippine Div) Abucay, January 1942 (Personal Experience of a Company Commander)," p. 3, monograph written for Infantry Officer Advance Course, hereafter referred to as Brown, "Ops 57 Inf;" and Anders to author, 15 March 1986.

²⁶ Annex XI, Report of Operations of the Visayan-Mindanao Force, p. 5, in Wainwright, Rpt Ops USAFFE-USFIP, hereafter referred to as Annex XI; Morton, *Fall,* p. 34; interview with General Harold K. Johnson, 6 February 1972, by Colonel Richard Jensen, pp. 32 and 34, US Army Military History Institute Debriefing Program, hereafter referred to as Jensen, interview with H. K. Johnson; and interview with Harold K. Johnson, 16 December 1975, Washington D.C.

²⁷ Marshall to MacArthur,—December 1941, not sent; Annex II, Plan

of Induction of Philippine Army and Arrival of U.S. Units for United States Forces in the Philippines, p. 1, in Wainwright, Rpt Ops USAFFE-USFIP, hereafter referred to as Annex II; Morton, *Fall,* pp. 34–35 and 48; interview with John E. Olson, Lake Quivira, Kansas, 1 December 1974; and MacArthur to Marshall, 28 October 1941.

[28] Radio, MacArthur to Marshall, 7 September 1941; Morton, *Fall,* p. 32; and Pogue, *Ordeal and Hope,* p. 188.

[29] Lida Mayo, *United States Army in World War II. The Technical Services. The Ordnance Department: On Beachhead and Battlefront* (Washington, D.C.: Office of the Chief of Military History, United States Army, 1968), p. 48, hereafter referred to as Mayo, *Beachhead and Battlefront;* Morton, *Fall,* pp. 146–147; and Robert L. Underbrink, *Destination Corregidor* (Annapolis, Maryland: United States Naval Institute, 1971), p. 41.

[30] Wainwright, Rpt. Ops. USAFFE-USFIP, pp. 17–18; Everett V. Mead, "The Operations and Movements of the 31st Infantry Regiment (Philippine Division) 7 December 1941–9 April 1942 (Philippine Island Campaign) (Personal Experience of a Regimental S-4)," p. 4, monograph written for Infantry Officer Advance Course #2, 1947–48, hereafter referred to as Mead, "Ops 31st Inf"; and Eugene B. Conrad to author, 19 January 1975.

[31] Raymond Knight to author, 27 March 1975; interview with Raymond Knight, Clearwater, Florida, 8 May 1975; Abie Abraham to author, 23 July 1975; and interview with William W. Wynn, Clearwater, Florida, 8 May 1975.

[32] Ind, *Judgment Seat,* pp. 12–13; Schultz, *Hero of Bataan,* pp. 43 and 52; interview with Burton Ellis, Clearwater, Florida, 9 May 1975; Olson, "Anywhere-Anytime," 1:17; interview with Leon O. Beck, Fremont, California, 29 December 1975; Spaulding to author (tape), 28 October 1975; and "News Letter—57th Infantry (PS)," 7 November 1941.

[33] Field Manual 7–5, Infantry Field Manual Organization and Tactics of Infantry, The Rifle Battalion, prepared under direction of the Chief of Infantry, United States Government Printing Office, Washington: 1940, para 15b, hereafter referred to as FM 7–5; Olson, "Anywhere-Anytime," 1:25–26; Annex XII, Report of Operations of the Philippine Division, pp. 5–6, in Wainwright, Rpt Ops USAFFE-USFIP, hereafter referred to as Annex XII; Eugene B. Conrad, "The Operations of the 31st Infantry (Philippine Div.) Defense of Bataan, 8 December 41–9 April 42 (Philippine Island Campaign)," p. 4, monograph written for Infantry Officer Advance Course, hereafter referred to as Conrad, "Ops 31 Inf;" Michael Gilewitch to author, 24 September 1975; and Harry C. Thomson and Lida Mayo, *United States Army in World War II. The Technical Services. The Ordnance Department: Procurement and Supply* (Washington, D.C.: Office of the Chief of Military History, Department of the Army, 1960), p. 156, hereafter referred to as Thomson, *Procurement and Supply.*

[34] Mead, "Ops 31st Inf," pp. 4 and 6–7.

[35] Wainwright, Rpt Ops USAFFE-USFIP, p. 16; interview with H. K. Johnson, 16 December 1975; Jensen, interview with H. K. Johnson, 6 February 1972, p. 30; and William E. Chandler, "Colonel Clinton A. Pierce," pp. 1–2.

[36] Adrianus J. Van Oosten to author, 19 June 1974; Mellnik, *Philippine Diary*, p. 12; Clifton A. Croom, "History and approximate diary of the 3rd Battalion, 45th Infantry (P.S.) during the Philippine campaign (December 8, 1941 to April 9, 1942)," p. 1, in Chunn, "Notebook," hereafter referred to as Croom, "3rd–45th;" Louis Besbeck, "The Operations of the 3rd Battalion 45th Infantry (Philippine Scouts) at the Hacienda at Mount Natib, Luzon, 15–25 January 1942 (The Bataan Campaign) (Personal Experience of a Battalion Executive Officer), pp. 7–8, monograph written for Infantry Officer Advance Course 1946–1947, hereafter referred to as Besbeck, "3rd, 45th Inf;" and Henry J. Pierce, "The Operations of Company L, 45th Infantry (P.S.)(Philippine Division) on the Abucay Hacienda Line Bataan, P.I., 15–25 January 1942 (Philippine Island Campaign) (Personal experience of the Company Commander)," p. 4, monograph written for Infantry Officer Advance Course #2, 1949–1950, hereafter referred to as Pierce, "Ops L, 45 Inf."

[37] Anders to author, 9 February 1984; Mellnik, *Philippine Diary*, p. 12; Olson, "Anywhere-Anytime," 1:26; and interview with Olson, 1 December 1974.

[38] Jensen, interview with H. K. Johnson, 6 February 1972, p. 30; Wainwright, Rpt Ops USAFFE-USFIP, p. 16; and interview with Adrianus J. Van Oosten, Denver, Colorado, 8 December 1974.

[39] William E. Brougher, memorandum entitled "Apalit."

[40] Ernest B. Miller, *Bataan Uncensored* (Long Prairie, Minn: The Hart Publications, Inc., February 1949), p. 145; and William E. Brougher, "To Command a Combat Division," p. 3.

[41] Mellnik, *Philippine Diary*, p. 25; Wilbur J. Lage, "The Operations of the 3rd Battalion, 11th Infantry (11th Division PA) at Zaragosa, P.I. 28 December–29 December 1941 (Personal Experience of a Regimental Machine Gun Officer and Commander of the Covering Force in the Withdrawal)," p. 3, monograph written for Infantry Officer Advance Course #2, 1947–1948, hereafter referred to as Lage, "Ops 3d, 11 Inf;" James V. Collier, "Oral Reminiscences of James V. Collier," Santa Barbara, California, 30 August 1971, p. 25, by D. Clayton James; and Brougher, "To Command a Combat Division," p. 7.

[42] John W. Fisher to wife, 28 October 1941.

[43] *Ibid.*, 29 November and 20 and 23 October 1941; and Irvin E. Alexander, "Personal Recollections of Bataan & Later," p. 87, hereafter referred to as Alexander, "Recollections."

[44] Bluemel, "31 Div," p. 4.

[45] Bluemel, "Oral Reminiscences," p. 12; the Army War College,

"Studies," p. 8; and Clifford Bluemel, interview, 14 April 1948 by Louis Morton and George Groce, p. 4.

46 Matt Dobrinic to author, 21 March 1975.

47 D. Clayton James, *The Years of MacArthur, 1880–1941,* 3 vols. (Boston: Houghton Mifflin Company, 1970–85), 1 (1970):609.

48 Van Oosten to author, 1 August 1974; Brevet-Major-General George W. Cullum, *Biographical Register of the Officers and Graduates of the U.S. Military Academy at West Point, New York Since Its Establishment in 1802,* vol. VII, 1920–1930, edited by CPT Wm. H. Donaldson, pp. 860–861, vol. VI-B, 1910–1920, edited by Col Wirt Robinson, p. 1,463, and vol. IX, 1940–1950, edited by Colonel Charles N. Branhan, p. 137, hereafter referred to as Cullum, *Register.*

49 Van Oosten to author, 1 August 1974; Toland, *But Not in Shame,* p. 184; and Dobrinic to author, 21 March 1975.

50 Dod, *Engineers Against Japan,* pp. 61–62; Bluemel, "31 Div," pp. 1–3; and Wainwright, Rpt Ops USAFFE-USFIP, p. 14.

51 Bluemel, "31 Div." p. 3; Mallonee, "Bataan Diary," 1:27; and Bluemel, "Oral Reminiscences," pp. 5 and 14.

52 Bluemel, "31 Div," pp. 2–3; and Wainwright, Rpt Ops USAFFE-USFIP, p. 8.

53 Thomson, *Procurement and Supply,* p. 156; Leighton, *Global Logistics,* p. 33; Malcolm V. Fortier to Louis Morton, 10 January 1952; and Bluemel, "31 Div.," p. 3.

54 Appendix A to Annex XIII, Report of Operations Tarlac Advance Quartermaster Depot, p. 1, hereafter referred to as Appendix A to Annex XIII; Annex XIII, pp. 18–19 and 90; Appendix 2 to Annex V: Report of Operations of South Luzon Force, Bataan Defense Force and II Philippine Corps in the Defense of South Luzon and Bataan from 8 December 1941–9 April 1942, p. 4, from Albert M. Jones, "Diary," hereafter referred to as Jones, "Diary"; and Bluemel, "31 Div.," p. 2.

55 Collier, "Oral Reminiscences," p. 14; Fortier to Morton, 10 January 1952, p. 4; Morton, *Fall,* pp. 28–29; Jones, "Diary," p. 4; Fortier, "Brief Hist 41 Div," p. 32; and Annex V, p. 6.

56 Bluemel, "31 Div," p. 3.

57 Mallonee, "Bataan Diary," 1:24, and subsequent quote is from 1:23; and Morton, *Fall,* p. 26.

58 Morton, *Fall,* p. 26; Bluemel, "31 Div," pp. 3–4; and Mallonee, "Bataan Diary," 1:2.

59 Jensen interview with H. K. Johnson, 6 February 1972, p. 5; Annex XI, p. 4; and Wainwright, Rpt Ops USAFFE-USFIP, p. 13.

60 "News Letter—57th Infantry (PS)," 7 November 1941, p. 2; Fisher to wife, 5 October 1941; and Alva R. Fitch, US Army Military History Institute, Senior Officers Oral History Program, Project 84-7, Volume I, interviewed by Harold R. Kough, 1981, 1:40, hereafter referred to as Fitch, "Oral History."

[61] Fisher to wife, 29 October 1941.

[62] *Ibid.,* 26 November 1941.

[63] The Army War College, "Studies," p. 9; Morton, *Fall,* pp. 12–13; Fortier to Morton, 10 January 1952, p. 2; Glen R. Townsend, "The 11th Infantry Regiment Philippine Army, September 1, 1941–April 9 1942, Part One—Mobilization and Training," p. 7, hereafter referred to as Townsend, "11 Inf Mob and Tng;" Fitch, "Oral History," p. 42; and Mallonee, "Bataan Diary," 1:8.

[64] Mallonee, "Bataan Diary," 1:4; and Wade H. Haislip, Memorandums to the [Army] Chief of Staff, 15 and 19 August 1941.

[65] John W. Fisher to author, 7 April 1975.

[66] Interview with John J. Martin, Dothan, Alabama, 14 February 1976.

[67] Clifford Bluemel to Orlando Ward, 17 January 1952; Bluemel, "31 Div," p. 3; and Bluemel, "Oral Reminiscences," p. 21.

[68] Collier, "Notebooks," 1:23.

The Scramble into Bataan

[1] Morton, *Fall,* pp. 125 and 142.

[2] *Ibid.,* p. 166; Anders to author, 21 January 1982; Walter D. Edmonds, *They Fought with What They Had* (Boston: Little Brown and Company, 1951), p. 38, hereafter referred to as Edmonds, *They Fought;* Dod, *Engineers Against Japan,* p. 71; and Jesse K. White to author, 29 September 1976.

[3] John J. Armellino to author, 30 January 1979; Meidling, *Engrs in Theater Ops,* p. 19; and Dod, *Engineers Against Japan,* p. 65.

[4] William Montgomery, "I Hired Out to Fight," p. 37; Meidling, *Engrs. in Theater Ops.,* p. 19; and Armellino to author, 30 January 1979.

[5] Ind, *Judgment Seat,* p. 220; Gene Gurney, *The War in the Air* (New York: Bonanza Books, 1962), p. 344; Armellino to author, 30 January 1979; Martin Cadin, *The Ragged, Rugged Warriors* (New York: Bantam Books, Inc., 1979), p. 187, hereafter referred to as Cadin, *Warriors;* and William R. Wright to author, 12 September 1974.

[6] Ind, *Judgment Seat,* pp. 216–219; Mellnik, *Philippine Diary,* p. 8; and John E. Lester, "Air Corps in the War."

[7] Morton, *Fall,* p. 156; and Edmonds, *They Fought,* pp. 193–195. In June of 1941, the term Army Air Forces replaced Army Air Corps. However, the term Air Corps will be used in this book because it was the term used by the Americans on Bataan.

[8] Maurice G. Hughett to author, 26 December 1981.

[9] John S. Coleman Jr., *Bataan and Beyond: Memories of an American POW* (College Station and London: Texas A. & M. University Press, 1978), pp. 14–15, hereafter referred to as Coleman, *Bataan and Beyond.*

[10] Edmonds, *They Fought,* p. 212.

11 *Ibid.*, pp. 212–218; and Ronald C. Dickson, untitled article in *The Quan* vol. 36, no. 2 (August 1981), p. 5.

12 Millard Hileman, "698th Ordinance [sic]," *The Quan* vol. 36, no. 3 (November 1981), p. 15.

13 Collier, "Notebooks," 2:74–75; and Ind, *Judgment Seat,* p. 181.

14 Richard C. Mallonee II, ed., *The Naked Flagpole* (San Rafael: Presidio Press, 1980), p. 21.

15 Wayne C. Liles to wife, 26 August 1945.

16 Annex XIII, p. 64; and Morton, *Fall,* p. 208.

17 Clarence R. Bess, "Operations of Service Company, 31st Infantry (Philippine Division) 5 January 1942–9 April 1942 (Philippine Island Campaign) (Personal Experience of a Service Company Commander)," p. 10, monograph written for Infantry Officer Advance Course #2, 1947–1948, hereafter referred to as Bess, "Ops Svc Co;" interview with Ellis, 9 May 1975; Thompson to author, 3 March 1975; Cullum, *Register,* VII, p. 1286; and Edmonds, *They Fought,* p. 234.

18 Charles C. Drake, "No Uncle Sam. The Story of a Hopeless Effort to Supply the Starving Army of Bataan & Corregidor," pp. 2–3, hereafter referred to as Drake, "No Uncle Sam;" Annex XIII, pp. 21–22, 28, and 30; and Alvin P. Stauffer, *The Quartermaster Corps: Operations in the War Against Japan. United States Army in World War II. The Technical Services* (Washington, D.C.: United States Government Printing Office, 1956), p. 34, hereafter referred to as Stauffer, *QM Corps.*

19 Collier, "Notebooks," 3:2–3; Morton, *Fall,* pp. 166, 179, and 188; Appendix A to Annex XIII, pp. 76, 77, and 130; and Irvin Alexander to Major General Orlando Ward, 25 December 1951, "Comments on the Fall of the Philippines."

20 Alexander to Ward, "Comments on the Fall of the Philippines;" Appendix A to Annex XIII, p. 78; *Japanese Monograph No. 11, Philippine Air Operations Record, Phase 1, December 1941–May 1942* Military History Section, Hq, Army Forces Far East, p. 31, hereafter referred to as *Japanese Monograph No. 11;* and Edmonds, *They Fought,* pp. 228–230.

21 Annex XIII, pp. 19–20 and 83; Morton, *Fall,* pp. 179 and 256; Appendix A to Annex XIII, pp. 111–112; and Charles S. Lawrence, "Notebook, Operations Report II Philippine Corps Apr 2–9, 1942," pp. 81–84, hereafter referred to as Lawrence, "Notebook."

22 Allen C. McBride, "Notes on the Fall of Bataan, 14 April 1942," p. 102, hereafter referred to as McBride, "Notes on the Fall;" Collier, "Notebooks," 3:3–4; Annex XIII, pp. 15, 23 and 66; Appendix E to Annex XIII, p. 197; and Edmonds, *They Fought,* p. 206.

23 Dean B. Smith to author, 23 March 1981; Arnold A. Boettcher to author, 31 December 1978; Cullum, *Register,* VII, p. 963; Annex XIII, pp. 21, and 29–30; Morton *Fall,* p. 255; and Drake, "No Uncle Sam," pp. 5–6.

24 Annex XIII, p. 31; Appendix A to Annex XIII, p. 113; Appendix B

to Annex XIII, p. 139; Appendix E to Annex XIII, p. 199; and Morton, *Fall,* p. 255.

²⁵ Cullum, *Register,* VIII, p. 1186; and Edmonds, *They Fought,* pp. 219–227.

²⁶ Drake, "No Uncle Sam," pp. 7–8; Annex XIII, p. 31; Stauffer, *QM Corps,* pp. 13–15; McBride, "Notes on the Fall," pp. 103–104; Morton, *Fall,* p. 256; and C. H. M. Roberts, Letter to Commanding General, Frankford Arsenal, Philippines, 4 October 1948, Subject: Philippine Records-Ammunition Reports, p. 3. It is interesting to note that the Army had tested dehydrated foods in the Philippines in 1940 and found them to be very desirable, highly nutritious and balanced. But they were low on the list of priorities and never made it to the Philippines, Annex XIII, p. 69.

²⁷ Drake, "No Uncle Sam," p. 8; Annex XIII, p. 21; and Morton, *Fall,* p. 254.

²⁸ Gary Anloff to author, (tape), 1 August 1976; Annex XIII, p. 4; Appendix A to Annex XIII, pp. 85–86; Morton, *Fall,* p. 258; Drake, "No Uncle Sam," p. 4; and Collier, "Notebooks," 3:3.

²⁹ Morton, *Fall,* p. 225; Colonel Hugh J. Casey to Chief of Staff, 2 January 1942, Subject: Congestion in Bataan Area; Anloff to author, (tape), 1 August 1976; and Brawner, G-4 HPD To: Dept A.G., 14 January 1942.

Buying Time, the Guagua Porac-Line

¹ Morton, *Fall,* p. 216.

² *Ibid;* USAFFE G-2 Information Bulletin #15, 5 January, 1942; and *Reports of MacArthur,* p. 81.

³ General Headquarters, Far East Command, Military Intelligence Section, Historical Division, "Statements of Japanese Officials on World War II, (English Translations)," interview with Masami Maeda, Chief of Staff 14th Army, 2:396, hereafter referred to as "Statements."

⁴ *Ibid.,* 2:395.

⁵ *Domei,* 2 January, 1943; Skerry, "Operations NLF Engineers," p. 5; and Morton, *Fall,* pp. 216–218.

⁶ Mateo Capinpin, "History of the 21st Division (PA)," p. 2, hereafter referred to as Capinpin, "Hist 21 Div;" and Mallonee, "Bataan Diary," 1:9–10 and 73.

⁷ O'Day, "Hist of 21 Div," 1:5; Mallonee, "Bataan Diary," 1:115–116. Catalan had never commanded any unit in his military service, not even a battery. William E. Chandler, "26th Cavalry (PS) Battles To Glory," *Armored Cavalry Journal,* in three parts, vol. LVI, no. 2 (March–August 1947), no. 3 (May–June 1947), no. 4 (July–August 1947), 2:13, hereafter referred to as Chandler, "Battles To Glory;" W. N. Foster,

"22nd Inf. (PA)," p. 12, in Chunn, "Notebook;" Morton, *Fall*, p. 218; and John C. Ellis, "History of the 23rd Infantry (PA)," p. 13, in Chunn, "Notebook."

[8] O'Day, "Hist of 21 Div," 1:3–4.

[9] *Reports of MacArthur*, p. 99; and Morton, *Fall*, p. 216. Morton, *Fall*, spells the colonel's name as Uejima, p. 127.

[10] Mallonee, "Bataan Diary," 1:116–117; and O'Day, "Hist of 21 Div," 2:16.

[11] Mallonee, "Bataan Diary," 1:118; Mallonee, *Naked Flagpole*, p. 67; Anders to author, 9 April 1986; *Army Register 1941*, p. 535; Morton, *Fall*, p. 219; and O'Day, "Hist of 21 Div," 2:17.

[12] O'Day, "Hist of 21 Div," 2:16; and Mallonee, "Bataan Diary," 2:41.

[13] Mallonee, "Bataan Diary," 1:119.

[14] Joaquin Esperitu, "A Brief History of the 22nd Infantry," p. 4, hereafter referred to as Esperitu, "Hist 22 Inf;" Grover C. Richards, "Outline of Steps to a POW Camp," p. 10; hereafter referred to as Richards, "Steps;" O'Day, "Hist of 21 Div," 2:17; and Mallonee, "Bataan Diary," 1:120.

[15] Richards, "Steps," p. 9.

[16] Mallonee, "Bataan Diary," 1:120, 9, 11, 15, 22, 25 and 118–119; Mallonee, *Naked Flagpole*, pp. 9–12; and O'Day, "Hist of 21 Div," 1:3.

[17] Mallonee, "Bataan Diary," 1:119–120 and 125; Mallonee, *Naked Flagpole*, p. 68; and USAFFE G2 Information Bulletin #15, 5 January 1942.

[18] Mallonee, "Bataan Diary," 1:121–122.

[19] Capinpin, "Hist 21 Div," p. 27.

[20] Mallonee, "Bataan Diary," 1:124; Capinpin, "Hist 21 Div," p. 28; and USAFFE G2 Information Bulletin #15, 5 January, 1942.

[21] Mallonee, "Bataan Diary," 1:135 and 130–131.

[22] Mallonee, *Naked Flagpole*, pp. 74–75.

[23] Lage, "Ops 3d, 11 Inf," pp. 6 and 10; Volckmann, *We Remained*, p. 21; and Fortier "Brief History," p. 32.

[24] Lage, "Ops 3d, 11 Inf," p. 7; Glen R. Townsend, "The 11th Infantry Regiment Philippine Army September 1, 1941–April 9, 1942, Part Two. Beach Defense and Delaying Action, December 8, 1941–January 5, 1942," p. 15, hereafter referred to as Townsend, "11 Inf Beach Defense;" William E. Brougher, "Equipment of the 11th Infantry;" and Morton, *Fall*, p. 102.

[25] Volckmann, *We Remained*, pp. 3, 6, and 21; Cullum, *Register*, IX, 813; Russell W. Volckmann, "Report of Combat and Guerrilla Activities in the Philippines (Rough Draft)," p. 7, hereafter referred to as Volckmann, "Combat and Guerrilla;" Russell W. Volckmann, "Colonel Russell William Volckmann;" and Townsend, "11 Inf Mob and Tng," p. 2.

[26] Townsend, "11 Inf Mob and Tng," pp. 3 and 6.

[27] Townsend, "11 Inf Beach Defense," p. 17; and Townsend, "Defense of Phil," pp. 3 and 5.

[28] Lage, "Ops 3d, 11 Inf," p. 3; and Townsend, "Defense of Phil," pp. 5–6.

[29] Volckmann, *We Remained,* pp. 22–23.

[30] Townsend, "11 Inf Beach Defense," pp. 22–23; James O. Rooks, "11th Infantry (PA)," p. 8, in Chunn, "Notebook;" Liles to wife, 16 September 1945; Townsend, "Defense of the Philippines," p. 12; and Morton, *Fall,* p. 221.

[31] Morton, *Fall,* pp. 216 and 221.

[32] *Ibid.,* p. 221; Captain L. E. Johnson, "Reports of S3, 194th Tank Battalion, 1/4/42," in diary of Ernest B. Miller; and Townsend, "11 Inf Beach Defense," p. 17.

[33] Annex X, pp. 15–16; Morton, *Fall,* pp. 221–223; Thomas Dooley, "The First United States Tank Action in World War II," p. 14, monograph written for Advanced Officers Course #1, 1 May 1948, hereafter referred to as Dooley, "First Tank Action;" and Captain F. G. Spoor, "Report of Battalion S2 at Lubao, 1/5/42."

[34] Volckmann, *We Remained,* p. 23; Morton, *Fall,* p. 222; Townsend, "11 Inf Beach Defense," pp. 23–24; and Glen R. Townsend to Chief of Military History, 8 January 1952.

[35] Morton, *Fall,* p. 222; and Alvin C. Poweleit, *USAFFE A Saga of Atrocities Perpetrated During the Fall of the Philippines, the Bataan Death March, and Japanese Imprisonment and Survival* (By the author, 1975), p. 29.

[36] Miller, *Bataan Uncensored,* pp. 129–130; USAFFE Signal Operating Instructions, Astronomical Data #3, 5 January 1942; and Provisional Tank Group General Order #10, 14 February 1942.

[37] William N. Kinler to author, 4 May and 15 September 1978; and Miller, *Bataan Uncensored,* p. 131.

[38] Liles to wife, 19 September 1945; Liles to author, 4 October 1978; and Morton, *Fall,* p. 222.

[39] Liles to wife, 19 September 1945; and Morton, *Fall,* p. 223.

[40] O'Day, "Hist of 21 Div," 2:19; and Morton, *Fall,* p. 224.

[41] Townsend, "Defense of Phil," pp. 12–13; O'Day, "Hist of 21 Div," 2:22; and Mallonee, "Bataan Diary," 2:3 and 8.

[42] Glen R. Townsend, "The 11th Infantry Regiment Philippine Army, Part III, The Tuol Pocket Jan 5–Feb 17, 1942," pp. 1–2, hereafter referred to as Townsend, "Tuol Pocket."

[43] Douglas MacArthur, *Reminiscences* (New York: McGraw-Hill Book Company, 1964), p. 126.

Delaying Action at Layac

[1] USAFFE General Order #54, 27 December 1941 designated the Army on Bataan as the "Bataan Force," yet almost every other document calls it the "Bataan Defense Force;" Field Manual 100-5, Field Service Regulations, Operations, prepared under direction of the Chief of Staff, United States Government Printing Office, Washington: 1941, para 618, hereafter referred to as FM 100-5; Collier, "Notebooks," 3:11; Morton, *Fall,* pp. 225–227; Annex V, p. 24; Annex IV: Report of Operations of North Luzon Force and I Philippine Corps in the Defense of Luzon and Bataan, 8 December 1941–9 April 1942, p. 15, in Wainwright, Rpt Ops USAFFE-USFIP, hereafter referred to as Annex IV; and Wainwright, Rpt Ops USAFFE-USFIP, p. 41.

[2] Morton, *Fall,* p. 226; *Army Register 1943,* p. 796; Collier, "Notebooks," 3:11; War Department, Public Information Office Biography on Brigadier General Clyde A. Selleck, p. 1; Cullum, *Register,* VIB, p. 1481; *Army Register 1941,* p. 761; Clyde A. Selleck, "Statement to Board of Officers, Subject: Prepared Statement for Consideration with Reference to My Reduction from Temporary Rank of Brigadier General and Request for Reinstatement in That Rank," 1 February 1946, pp. 1–5, hereafter referred to as Selleck, "Statement"; and Selleck, "Notes 71 Div," p. 20.

[3] Underwood, "Defense of Bataan," pp. 12–13; Selleck, "Notes 71 Div," pp. 3, 17, and 46; Manuel T. Flores, "An Analytical Study of the Defense of Bataan," 31 March 1949, written for the Command and General Staff Course; Fisher to author, 23 October 1978; Carlos P. Romulo, *I Saw the Fall of the Philippines* (Garden City, NY: Doubleday, Doran & Co., Inc., 1942), pp. 105 and 148.

[4] Selleck, "Notes 71 Div," pp. 7–8, 14, and 24; *Army Register 1943,* p. 87; Collier, "Notebooks," 3:11; personal observation by the author; *Army Register 1941,* p. 81; and Roy E. Doran to author, (tape), 6 August 1980.

[5] Selleck, "Notes 71 Div," pp. 7–9, and 24–27; and Fisher to author, 31 March 1975.

[6] Selleck, "Notes 71 Div," pp. 28, 8–10, and 26; and FM 100–5, para 620.

[7] Selleck, "Notes 71 Div," p. 22; Walter S. Strong, "History of 31st Inf. (US)," p. 2, in Chunn, "Notebook," hereafter referred to as Strong, "History 31st;" Donald G. Thompson, "Operations of Company "L", 31st Infantry Regiment (Philippine Division) in the Battle of Layac Junction, Bataan, P.I., 6–7 January 1942 (Philippine Islands Campaign) (Personal Experience of a Company Commander)," p. 6, monograph written for Infantry Officer Advance Course #2, 1947–1948, hereafter referred

to as Thompson, "Ops L, 31 Inf;" Annex V, p. 25; *Army Register 1941,* p. 806; Abraham to author, 23 July 1975; John I. Pray, "The Action of Company "G" 31st Infantry (Philippine Div.) Abucay Hacienda, 15–25 January 1942 (The Struggle for the Philippines) (Personal experience of a Company Commander)," p. 3, monograph written for Infantry Officer Advance Course #2, 1946–1947, hereafter referred to as Pray, "Action G, 31st"; and Thompson to author, 12 November 1974. Another figure given for 31st Infantry strength is 1,400 from Annex XII.

[8] Selleck, "Notes 71 Div," p. 23; Morton, *Fall,* p. 227; Annex V, p. 25; Chandler, "Colonel Clinton A. Pierce," p. 3; T. J. H. Trapnell, "The Operations of the 26th Cavalry (P.S.) Personal Experience of a Squadron Commander," p. 14, monograph written for the Command and General Staff College Regular Course, 1946–1947, hereafter referred to as Trapnell, "Ops 26 Cav;" Chandler, "Battles To Glory," 3:14; and Vance to author, 7 May 1979.

[9] Morton, *Fall,* p. 226; Selleck, "Notes 71 Div," p. 8; Annex XI, p. 11; James A. Sawicki, *Field Artillery Battalions of the U.S. Army* (Virginia: Centaur Publication, 1977), 2 vols, 1:47 and 137, hereafter referred to as Sawicki, *Field Artillery;* Annex V, p. 26; Arthur L. Shreve, "Transcription, Diary of Arthur L. Shreve, Lt. Col. (FA)," p. 13, hereafter referred to as Shreve, "Diary;" *Army Register 1941,* p. 761; and Selleck, PIO Biography, p. 1.

[10] Shreve, "Diary," pp. 20–21; Mellnik, *Philippine Diary,* p. 42; Bluemel, "31 Div," p. 7; Morton, *Fall,* pp. 197–198; and Arthur G. Christensen to author, 2 June 1984.

[11] James R. Weaver, "Memo to COL Selleck, 2-1-43, Subject: Actions Provisional Tank Group, in Connection with the Lyac [sic] Delaying Position," pp. 35–36, in Selleck, "Notes 71 Div;" Cullum, *Register,* IX, p. 151, and VIB, p. 1546; James R. Weaver, "Comments of Draft The Fall of the Philippines," cmts 28 and 29; and Annex X, pp. 2 and 15.

[12] Ivan W. Weikel to author, 8 August and 11 October 1979; Morton, *Fall,* p. 226; Selleck, "Notes 71 Div," p. 25; and David S. Babcock, "The SPMs," p. 1.

[13] Selleck, "Notes 71 Div," pp. 17 and 21; Annex V, p. 25; Morton, *Fall,* p. 226; and Skerry, "Operations NLF Engineers."

[14] Collier, "Notebooks," 3:11; Achille C. Tisdelle, "Bataan Diary of Major Achille C. Tisdelle," *Military Affairs* vol. XI, no. 3 (Fall 1947) editor, Louis Morton, 21 March 1942 entry, hereafter referred to as Tisdelle, "Diary;" Morton, *Fall,* p. 227; Tisdelle, "Diary," 21 March 1942; Mellnik, *Philippine Diary,* p. 18; and Selleck, "Notes 71 Div," pp. 25–26.

[15] Selleck, "Notes 71 Div," p. 25; and Annex V, p. 25.

[16] Selleck, "Notes 71 Div," p. 22; Thompson, "Ops L, 31 Inf," p. 8; Earl F. Walk to author, 3 November 1978; and George Uzelac to author, 28 February 1982.

17 Paul Kerchum to author, 11 March and 1 April 1980.

18 William Miller to author, 4 October 1978.

19 Fisher to author, 23 May 1977; Morton, *Fall,* pp. 121 and 227; USAFFE Signal Operation Instructions, 5 January 1942, Astronomical Data #3; Christensen to author, 8 March 1984; Selleck, "Notes 71 Div," p. 21; and Charles A. Willoughby, Memorandum for G3 USAFFE 2 Jan 41 [sic], G2 Estimate of the Enemy Situation.

20 Collier, "Notebooks," 3:12–13; Annex IV, p. 43; John Scofield, "The Jap War Machine," *Infantry Journal* vol. L, no. 2 (February 1942), pp. 23–24; and Morton, *Fall,* p. 228.

21 Interview with William Miller, San Antonio, Texas, 23 August 1977; W. Miller to author, 4 October 1978; Charles L. Steel, "Account of Action 31st Inf at Layac," p. 29, in Selleck, "Notes 71 Div;" Mellnik, *Philippine Diary,* p. 42; and Collier, "Notebooks," 3:13. Portee artillery consists of cannon carried on the back of trucks, not towed.

22 Interview with W. Miller, 23 August 1977; Morton, *Fall,* p. 228; and W. Miller to author, 4 October 1978.

23 Collier, "Notebooks," 3:13: Lee C. Vance, "Account of Action at Layac," p. 32, in Selleck, "Notes 71 Div;" Chandler, "Battles To Glory," 3:14; Selleck, "Notes 71 Div," pp. 17 and 29; Halstead C. Fowler to Louis Morton, 30 April 1949; and Selleck, "Statement," p. 10.

24 J. C. Relosa to Clyde A. Selleck, 3 August 1948; Headquarters, Philippine Army, General Order #12, 17 July 1947; Selleck, "Notes 71 Div," p. 27; Fowler to Morton, 11 March and 30 April 1949; Mallonee, "Bataan Diary," 2:35; and Selleck, "Statement," p. 11.

25 Interview with W. Miller, 22 August 1977; W. Miller to author, 4 October 1978; and USAFFE General Order #23, 4 February 1942.

26 W. Miller to author, 4 October 1978; and Fitch, "Oral History," 1:36.

27 John G. Lally to author, (tape), 13 January 1979.

28 Interview with W. Miller, 22 August 1977; Annex V, p. 26; Thompson, "Ops L, 31 Inf," pp. 9–10; Headquarters, Philippine Army, General Order #4, 6 October 1947; and USAFFE General Order #28, 19 February 1942. Calugas's act occurred before a later medal-winning act, but Calugas received his medal after the second man.

29 William Garleb to author, (tape), 6 January 1979; and William J. Priestley, Extract from Notebook #1-Diary of Major Wm. J. Priestley, "3rd Battalion, 31st Infantry," p. 2, hereafter referred to as Priestley, "3 Bn, 31 Inf;" Walk to author, 3 November 1978; and Paul C. Gilmore to author, 17 March 1981.

30 James C. Spencer to author, (tape), 12 November 1978; John I. Pray to author, 17 October 1980 and 22 February 1982; and Anders to author, 20 January 1982.

31 Harold J. Garrett to author, (tape), 7 August 1980; Thompson, "Ops L, 31 Inf," p. 7; Annex V, p. 26; and Morton, *Fall,* p. 228.

[32] Kerchum to author, 11 March and 1 April 1980; and Milton G. Alexander to author, 22 September 1980.

[33] Morton, *Fall,* p. 228; Garrett to author, (tape), 7 August 1980; Uzelac to author, 28 February 1982; Strong, "History 31st," p. 2, in Chunn, "Notebooks;" Collier, "Notebooks," 3:15; *Army Register 1943,* p. 92; and Selleck, "Notes 71 Div," p. 30.

[34] Thompson, "Ops L, 31 Inf," pp. 10–11; Priestley, "3 Bn, 31 Inf," p. 2; and *Army Register 1943,* p. 97.

[35] Thompson, "Ops L, 31 Inf," pp. 11–12; and Priestley, "3 Bn, 31 Inf," p. 2.

[36] Thompson, "Ops L, 31 Inf," pp. 12–13; and Thompson to author, 5 August 1980.

[37] Floyd R. Wade to author, (tape), 28 April 1976; Thompson, "Ops L, 31 Inf," p. 13; and Priestley, "3 Bn, 31 Inf," pp. 2–3.

[38] Grant Workman to author, 19 January 1976; and Priestley, "3 Bn, 31 Inf," p. 5. The sergeant who ordered the withdrawal was killed by artillery.

[39] Wilburn L. Snyder to author, (tape), 17 November 1978; Thompson, "Ops L, 31 Inf," p. 14; and Wade to author, (tape), 28 April 1976.

[40] Mondell White to author, (tape), 3 December 1980; Donald G. Thompson to author, 5 June 1975, 12 February 1979, and 9 September 1980; Thompson, "Ops L, 31 Inf," p. 14; and Priestley, "3 Bn, 31 Inf," p. 4.

[41] Selleck, "Notes 71 Div," pp. 31 and 39; and Wainwright, Rpt Ops USAFFE-USFIP, p. 41.

[42] Selleck, "Notes 71 Div," p. 31; Collier, "Notebooks," 3:16–17; Shreve, "Diary," p. 21; Annex IV, p. 43; Annex V, p. 27; Annex X, p. 17; and Weaver, "Comments of Draft Manuscript Fall of the Philippines."

[43] Gilmore to author, 17 March 1981; Thompson, "Ops L, 31 Inf," p. 15; Priestley, "3 Bn, 31 Inf," p. 4; USAFFE Signal Operation Instructions, 5 January 1942, Astronomical Data #3; Tillman J. Rutledge to author, (tape), 4 January 1980; Morton, *Fall,* p. 229; and Pray to author, 17 October 1980.

[44] Doran to author, (tape), 6 August 1980; and Selleck, "Notes 71 Div," p. 31.

[45] Chandler, "Battles To Glory," 3:14; Trapnell, "Ops 26 Cav," p. 14; Lee C. Vance, "Account of Action at Layac," pp. 32–33, in Selleck, "Notes 71 Div;" Major H. J. Fleeger, "Brief Regimental History 26th Cavalry World War II-Bataan," *The Cavalry Journal* vol. LIV, no. 6 (November–December 1945), p. 8, taken from the diaries of Major Fleeger; Hersey, *Men on Bataan,* p. 238; and Vance to author, 27 March 1979.

[46] Collier, "Notebooks," 3:17; Alexander to author, (tape), 22 September 1980; Lieutenant Colonel Jasper E. Brady Jr. and Major Marshall Hurt, Adjutant 31st Infantry and other Officers of 31st Infantry, "His-

tory of 31st Infantry, Rosters of Companies, Disposition of Personnel, Dates of Death, Death Reports with Place of Burial in Some Cases, Company Fund Reports," p. 59, hereafter referred to as Brady/Hurt, "History of 31st;" and Steel, "Account of Action 31st at Layac," p. 31, in Selleck, "Notes 71 Div."

[47] FM 100-5, para 621; and Shreve, "Diary," p. 13.

[48] Collier, "Notebooks," 3:10; and Morton, *Fall,* p. 242.

II Philippine Corps

[1] Morton, *Fall,* pp. 247–248 and 290; and Johnson, "Defense Along Abucay," p. 44. The rear line carried three names: rear line, rear battle position, and reserve battle position.

[2] Morton, *Fall,* pp. 247, 248, and 251; Christensen to author, 2 June 1984; War Department, Public Information Biography, George Marshall Parker, Jr., p. 1; *Army Register 1943,* p. 685; Moore, "Diary," p. 4; Annex V, pp. 16 and 29; USAFFE GO #3, 6 January and GO #4, 7 January 1942; Wainwright, Rpt Ops USAFFE-USFIP, p. 33; Shreve, "Diary," p. 5; interview, Louis Morton with Richard J. Marshall, 7 April 1948, p. 3; and Clifford Bluemel to George C. Groce, 15 June 1948. The II Corps command post was established on the high ridge north of the Mamala River in the north west acute angle formed by Trails 2 and 10, Anders to author, 24 August 1986.

[3] Sixty-Fifth Brigade, Headquarters, "Natib Mountain Area Detailed Combat Report," p. 1, captured by American forces on Cape Gloucester, 8 February 1944, hereafter referred to as "65 Bde, Natib;" and Morton, *Fall,* p. 245.

[4] Morton, *Fall,* p. 252; Mallonee, "Bataan Diary," 2:17; and Johnson, "Defense Along Abucay," p. 47.

[5] Fortier to Morton, 10 January 1952; Morton, *Fall,* p. 251; and Fortier, "Notes by Col M. V. Fortier," pp. 85–86.

[6] Interview with Martin, 14 February 1976; Romulo, *I Saw the Fall,* p. 267; and Fortier, "Brief Hist 41 Div," p. 35.

[7] Fortier, "Brief Hist 41 Div," pp. 28–34; Annex V, p. 8; Fortier to Morton, 10 January 1952, p. 3; William E. Webb, "The Operations of the 41st Infantry Regiment (Philippine Army) of the 41st Infantry Division in the Defense of the Abucay Line, Bataan, Philippine Islands, 10–18 January 1942 (Philippine Island Campaign)(Personal Experience of an American Instructor with the Philippine Army)," p. 10, monograph written for Infantry Officer Advance Course #2, 1949–1950, hereafter referred to as Webb, "Ops 41 Inf;" and Fortier, "Notes by Col M. V. Fortier," p. 86.

[8] Malcolm V. Fortier to Headquarters, Fourth Army, 14 May 1946,

"Operations of the 41st Div (PA)," p. 1, hereafter referred to as Fortier, "Ops 41 Div;" and Annex V, p. 19.

[9] Webb, "Ops 41 Inf," pp. 1 and 7; Anders to author, 7 April 1977; E. C. Atkinson, "Actions of 42d Infantry-Dec. 25 1941 to Jan. 23, 1942," p. 5, in Fortier, "Notes on 41 Div," hereafter referred to as Atkinson, "Actions 42 Inf;" and Fortier, "Brief Hist 41 Div," pp. 53–54.

[10] Annex V, p. 20; Fortier, "Ops 41 Div," p. 1; Fortier, "Narrative Report," pp. 105–106; and Anders to author, 24 August 1986.

[11] Dod, *Engineers Against Japan,* p. 88; and Bautista, "11 Engr Bn," p. 34.

[12] Brougher, "The Battle of Bataan," p. 3; Fortier to Morton, 10 January 1952, p. 4; and Dod, *Engineers Against Japan,* p. 92.

[13] Dod, *Engineers Against Japan,* p. 72; Meidling, *Engrs in Theater Ops,* pp. 8 and 19; Morton, *Fall,* p. 249; and Jensen interview with H. K. Johnson, 7 February 1972, p. 4.

[14] Webb, "Ops 41 Inf," pp. 8–9; and USAFFE Organization History 1941–1942, History of 41st FA.

[15] Jones, "Diary," pp. 4 and 17; Annex V, pp. 19 and 21; Stuart C. MacDonald, "Important Dates - SLF," p. 15; Morton, *Fall,* p. 251; and William L. Osborne, "Lessons and Trends," no. 15, p. 2, an Infantry School publication.

[16] Morton, *Fall,* p. 251; Annex V, pp. 5 and 21; Dobrinic to author, 21 March 1975; and Jones, "Diary," p. 3.

[17] Romualdo C. Din to author, 20 May 1981; Dobrinic to author, 21 March 1975; Jones, "Diary," p. 2; and Annex V, p. 5.

[18] Jones, "Diary," p. 2; Annex V, p. 5; and Osborne, "Lessons and Trends," no. 15, p. 1.

[19] O'Day, "Hist of 21 Div," 1:7.

[20] Morton, *Fall,* p. 102; Annex IV, pp. 3–5; Ambrosio P. Pena, "History of the 11th Div (PA)," p. 1; and Philip Harkins, *Blackburn's Headhunters* (New York: W. W. Norton and Company, 1955), pp. 4–6.

[21] Brougher, "To Command a Combat Division," pp. 1–2; *Army Register 1943,* p. 108; and O'Day, "Hist of 21 Div," 2:8.

[22] D. Clayton James, ed. *South to Bataan, North to Mukden: The Prison Diary of Brigadier General W. W. Brougher* (Athens, Georgia: University of Georgia Press, 1971), p. 9, hereafter referred to as James, *South to Bataan;* and Underwood, "Defense of Bataan," p. 4.

[23] James, *South to Bataan,* p. 14.

[24] 11th Division General Order #3, 8 January 1942.

[25] Townsend, "Tuol Pocket," p. 3b.

[26] Volckmann, *We Remained,* p. 24; Townsend, "Tuol Pocket," p. 3a; and Bautista, "11 Engr Bn," p. 32.

[27] Morton, *Fall,* p. 92; Annex IX: Report of Operations of Provisional Coast Artillery Brigade in the Philippine Campaign, p. 1, in Wainwright, Rpt Ops USAFFE-USFIP, hereafter referred to as Annex IX; Annex IV,

p. 27; Robert N. Amy to author, 9 June and 1 July 1976; and Henry M. Miller, "A Short History of the 200th Coast Artillery," p. 10.

[28] Amy to author, 1 July 1976.

[29] Annex X, p. 3.

[30] Bardowski to author, (tape), 13 February 1977; and John P. Cahill to author, 24 July 1975.

[31] John Minier to author, 24 February 1975; "PRECIS: Movements to Theater and Organization, The Provisional Tank Group. United States Forces in the Far East," pp. 1–2, in Annex X, hereafter referred to as "PRECIS: Tank Group;" William A. Hauser to author, 12 March 1975; Cahill to author, 21 June 1975; Poweleit, *USAFFE*, p. 8; and Bardowski to author, (tape), 13 February 1977.

[32] "PRECIS: Tank Group," pp. 1–2; Annex X, pp. 4–5; Spaulding to author, (tape), 28 October 1975; and "Armor on Luzon," A Research Report Prepared by the Armor School Ft Knox, Kentucky, by Committe 9, Officer Advance Course, 1949–1950, May 1950, pp. 16–19, hereafter referred to as "Armor on Luzon."

[33] "Armor on Luzon," p. 28; Annex X, p. 17; interview with John J. Hummel, Clearwater, Florida, 9 May 1975; and Morton, *Fall,* p. 177.

[34] Dooley, "First Tank Action," p. 15; John A. Crago to author, 6 July 1975; and Annex X, p. 17.

[35] Morton, *Fall,* p. 33; Emory A. Dunham, *The Army Ground Forces. Tank Destroyer History - Study No. 29,* (Historical Section -Army Ground Forces, 1946), pp. 2–9; Annex IX, p. 1; George A. Reed to author, 5 February 1975; Babcock, "The SPMs," pp. 2 and 8; and Collier, "Notebooks," 2:21.

[36] Annex XIII, p. 16; "Armor on Luzon," p. 23; Brigadier General Brehon Somervell, paper, Subject: Acquisition of Certain Canadian Supplies for the Far Eastern Command in the Philippines; Appendix C to Annex XIII, p. 164; and Collier, "Notebooks," 2:31.

I Philippine Corps

[1] Schultz, *Hero of Bataan,* p. 13; and Wainwright, *Story,* p. 194.

[2] Wainwright, *Story,* p. 15; Schultz, *Hero of Bataan,* pp. 6, 12, and 27; and Beck, *MacArthur and Wainwright,* p. 175.

[3] Annex IV, p. 2; Morton, *Fall,* p. 124; and *Reports of MacArthur,* p. 14.

[4] Morton, *Fall,* pp. 166–168.

[5] Casey, *Engrs in Theater Ops,* p. 10; and Morton, *Fall,* p. 216.

[6] Morton, *Fall,* p. 230.

[7] *Ibid.,* pp. 247 and 250; and USAFFE General Orders #3, 6 January 1942 and # 4, 7 January 1942.

[8] Chandler, "Colonel Clinton A. Pierce;" Chandler, "Battles To

Glory," 2:11 and 3:15; Wainwright, Rpt Ops USAFFE-USFIP, pp. 16–17; and Morton, *Fall*, p. 226.

[9] Wainwright, *Story*, pp. 39–40.

[10] Beck, *MacArthur and Wainwright*, p. 67; Wainwright, *Story*, p. 40; and Schultz, *Hero of Bataan*, p. 136.

[11] Wainwright, *Story*, p. 40; and Schultz, *Hero of Bataan*, pp. 136–137.

[12] Alfredo M. Santos, "The 1st Regular Division in the Battle of the Philippines," p. 29, a paper prepared for the Command and General Staff College, Fort Leavenworth, 7 June 1947, hereafter referred to as Santos, "1st Reg Div in Phil;" Morton, *Fall*, p. 246; Ambrosio P. Pena, "History of the 1st Regular Division," pp. 1–2; Ambrosio P. Pena, *Bataan's Own* (Manila: 2nd Regular Division Association, Munoz Press, Inc., 1967), p. 88; Bluemel, "31st Div," p. 7; and Kearie L. Berry, "History of the 3rd Infantry Regiment, 1st Regular Division (PA), During the War With Japan, 19 December 1941 to 9 April 1942," p. 1, hereafter referred to as Berry, "History 3rd Inf."

[13] MacDonald, "Important Dates-SLF," p. 11; *Army Register 1943*, p. 547; Wainwright, Rpt Ops USAFFE-USFIP, p. 35; Morton, *Fall*, p. 194; Annex IV, p. 18; and Bluemel, "31 Div," p. 7.

[14] Selleck, "Notes 71 Div," pp. 46–47.

[15] Selleck, "Notes 71 Div," pp. 3, 6–7, 45, and 47; and Fisher to author, 7 April 1975.

[16] Fisher to wife, 20 October 1941; and Fisher to author, 5 December 1974.

[17] Fisher to author, 31 March 1975.

[18] *Ibid.*, 5 December 1974; and Selleck, "Notes 71 Div," pp. 43–44.

[19] Selleck, "Notes 71 Div," pp. 18–19, and 57.

[20] Anders to Olson, 24 May 1981.

[21] Beverly N. Skardon, "The Operations of Company A, 92d Infantry, Philippine Army, 3 January 1942, 24 March 1942 (Personal Experience of a Company Commander)," pp. 3–4, and 9, monograph written for Infantry Officer Advance Course 1946–1947, hereafter referred to as Skardon, "Ops A, 92d;" John H. Rodman to Major General Orlando Ward, 1 February 1952, "Comments on the Fall of the Philippines," p. 1; and Wainwright, Rpt Ops USAFFE-USFIP, p. 15.

[22] Skardon, "Ops A, 92d," pp. 4–6; Rodman to Ward, 1 February 1952, p. 1; and Fowler to Morton, 11 March 1949.

[23] Bluemel, "31 Div," p. 7.

Philippine Scouts at Mabatang

[1] John E. Olson, "The Operations of the 57th Infantry (P.S.) Regimental Combat Team (Philippine Division) at Abucay, Bataan, P. I., 10 January–23 January 1942, (Bataan Campaign) (Personal Experience of a Reg-

imental Adjutant)", p. 9, monograph prepared for Infantry Officer Advance Course #2, 1947–1948, hereafter referred to as Olson, "Ops 57 Inf;" Jensen interview with H. K. Johnson, 6 February 1972, p. 37; John E. Olson to author, 28 August 1976; and D. Clayton James, "Oral Reminiscences of General Harold K. Johnson," Valley Forge, Pennsylvania, 7 July 1971, p. 2, hereafter referred to as James, "Johnson Oral Reminiscences." Formed in 1917 in Texas, the 57th Infantry's colors were shipped to the Philippines in 1920 where the regiment was created from men from the Second Philippine Infantry (Provisional) and officers from the 57th.

2 Edmund J. Lilly, "Report of Operations, 57th Infantry (PS), 8 December 1941 to 9 April 1942," p. 1, hereafter referred to as Lilly, "Report of Ops 57 Inf;" and Brown, "Ops 57 Inf," p. 4.

3 Olson, "Ops 57 Inf," pp. 5–6; Annex XI, p. 6; H. K. Johnson, "Defense Along Abucay," p. 46; Lilly to author, 28 September 1974; Lilly, "Report of Ops 57 Inf," p. 1; Anders to author, 9 January 1978 and 13 July 1983; and Royal Reynolds to author, 31 December 1976.

4 Collier, "Notebooks," 3:20; Anders to author, 4 May 1976 and 22 October 1986; Olson, "Ops 57 Inf," p. 9; and "65 Bde, Natib," p. 5. The American 31st Infantry had spent December 24 to 28 constructing positions vicinity Mabatang before moving north. Some of these works were occupied by the Scouts and improved.

5 Reynolds to author, 19 November 1974; *Army Register 1943*, p. 742; *Army Register 1941*, p. 709; Cullum, *Register*, VIII, p. 1033; interview with John E. Olson, Springfield, Virginia, 8 May 1988; and Anders to author, 1 April 1977.

6 Loyd Mills to author, 23 October 1974; Edmund J. Lilly to author, 28 September 1974; Reynolds to author, 19 November 1974; and interview with Carroll R. Hines, Clearwater, Florida, 8 May 1975.

7 Anders to author, 9 January 1978; Olson, "Ops 57 Inf," p. 7; Reynolds to author, 19 November 1974; Brown, "Ops 57 Inf," p. 8; and John E. Olson, "Preparing the Abucay Line: History of the 57th Regiment (PS) (III)," *Bulletin American Historical Collection*, American Association of the Philippines, vol. XV, no. 4 (60)(October–December 1987), p. 62, hereafter referred to as Olson, "Preparing the Abucay Line."

8 Brown, "Ops 57 Inf," p. 8; Anders to author, 9 January 1978; and "65 Bde, Natib," p. 19.

9 Philip T. Fry, "The Philip T. Fry Papers," notebook with numerous reports including, "A Short History of My Experiences in the Philippines During the Second World War, 1941–1942," p. 8, hereafter referred to as Fry, "A Short History;" Anders to author, 26 September 1976, 9 June 1977, and 9 August 1984; and Olson to Anders, undated, under cover letter Anders to author 17 May 1981; *Army Register 1941*, p. 295; and H. K. Johnson, "Defense Along Abucay," p. 47.

10 Fry, "A Short History," p. 20; H. K. Johnson, "Defense Along

Abucay," p. 48; Brown, "Ops 57 Inf," p. 8; Olson, "Ops 57 Inf," p. 7; and Anders to author, 9 January 1978 and 22 October 1986.

[11] Brown, "Ops 57 Inf," pp. 8–9; Olson, "Ops 57 Inf," pp. 11–12; Anders to author, 26 September 1976; Olson, "Preparing the Abucay Line," p. 64; Annex V, p. 29; Lilly, "Report of Ops 57 Inf," p. 2; Charles E. N. Howard Jr., Letter to the Adjutant General US Army, Subject: Unit History 2nd Battalion, 88th Field Artillery (Philippine Scouts) for the period 7 December 1941 to 9 April 1942 incl—in the Philippine Islands, written May–June 1946, pp. 6 and 9, hereafter referred to as Howard, "Unit History;" interview with Olson, 8 May 1988; and Dod, *Engineers Against Japan,* pp. 87 and 89.

[12] Morton, *Fall,* pp. 190, 198, and 252; Sawicki, *Field Artillery,* 1:133 and 2:1242; Diary of Colonel Alexander S. Quintard, 301st FA (PA), 30 December 1941, hereafter referred to as Quintard, "Diary;" Wainwright, Rpt Ops USAFFE-USFIP, p. 8; Alexander S. Quintard, "Copy of parts of Narrative of A S Quintard Col FA," pp. 1–2; and Captain Willard A. Smith to Louis Morton, 23 May 1949. The 155mm had been designed by a French officer, Colonel Filloux, before WWI, data from Morton, *Fall,* p. 190. In 1939, twenty-four 155mm guns and seven 8-inch railway guns arrived in the Philippines and were stored pending placement in coast defense positions, Mellnik, *Philippine Diary,* p. 17.

[13] Harold K. Johnson, "Abucay," p. 7, monograph written for the Command and General Staff Course, 6 July 1948, hereafter referred to as H. K. Johnson, "Abucay;" Anders to author, 4 May 1976 and 9 and 28 February 1984; and Lilly, "Report of Ops 57 Inf," pp. 1–2.

[14] Morton, *Fall,* pp. 269–270; Olson to author, 14 September 1976; Anders to author, 9 January 1978; H. K. Johnson, "Defense Along Abucay," p. 47; Jensen interview with H. K. Johnson, 7 February 1972, p. 3; and Brown, "Ops 57 Inf," p. 9.

[15] Manuel L. Quezon, *The Good Fight* (New York: D. Appleton-Century, Inc., 1946), p. 244; D. Clayton James, *The Years of MacArthur 1941–1945* vol. 2 (Boston: Houghton Mifflin Company, 1975):52.

[16] Radio, MacArthur to the AG, 9 January 1942.

[17] Jack D. Gordon to author, (tape), 21 August 1980; Beck, *MacArthur and Wainwright,* p. 66; Morton interview with Sutherland, 12 November 1946; James, *The Years of MacArthur,* 1:565–566 and 2:52; *Army Register 1943,* p. 864; McBride, "Notes on the Fall," p. 107; and William Manchester, *American Caesar Douglas MacArthur 1880–1964* (Boston: Little, Brown and Company, 1978), p. 235.

[18] Interview with H. K. Johnson, 17 December 1975; Anders to author, 9 November 1974 and 4 May 1976; and Edward R. Wernitznig, "Diary."

[19] Reynolds to author, 6 April 1977.

[20] Far East Command General Headquarters, letter from G-2, 16 August 1949 to Chief, Historical Division, DA, Washington, DC, "Informa-

tion Regarding Strength and Composition of Japanese Forces, Philippine Islands Dec 41–Mar 42," Encl 1, hereafter referred to as "Information Regarding Strength;" Toland, *Rising Sun*, p. 325; Toland, *But Not in Shame*, p. 160; Morton, *Fall*, p. 262; and "65 Bde, Natib," p. 3.

[21] "65 Bde, Natib," p. 2; *Reports of MacArthur*, p. 104; and Toland, *But Not in Shame*, p. 160.

[22] "65 Bde, Natib," p. 40.

[23] *Reports of MacArthur*, p. 83; Schultz, *Hero of Bataan*, p. 61; and "Statements," interrogation of Lieutenant General Masami Maeda, 1:507.

[24] "Statements," Lieutenant General Nara, 3:663; and "65 Bde, Natib," p. 74.

[25] "65 Bde, Natib," pp. 10–11 and 74; and Morton, *Fall*, pp. 262–263.

[26] Morton, *Fall*, p. 261; and *Reports of MacArthur*, pp. 14 and 62.

[27] *Reports of MacArthur*, pp. 86 and 104; *Japanese Monograph No. 11*, p. 42; General Headquarters Far East Command Military History Section, Special Staff, Appendix to Comments of Former Japanese Officers Regarding *The Fall of the Philippines;* and Morton, *Fall*, p. 261.

[28] Stanley L. Falk "Folio," p. 61; and Morton, *Fall*, p. 264.

[29] "Statements," Lieutenant General Nara, 3:663; Toland, *But Not in Shame*, p. 162; and "65 Bde, Natib," pp. 2 and 6.

[30] Morton, *Fall*, pp. 262–263.

[31] *Ibid.*, and p. 139; Toland, *But Not in Shame*, p. 163; and "65 Bde, Natib," pp. 2–3.

[32] "65 Bde, Natib," pp. 14 and 44.

[33] *Ibid.*, pp. 5 and 21. The 65th Brigade Engineer Company was organized in April 1941 and drew its men from the Hiroshima military district. Its organization and equipment was set at a level just sufficient for guard duty, and the company was inferior to engineer companies in the field divisions, from Comments of Former Japanese Officers regarding *The Fall of the Philippines,* in letter, Lieutenant Colonel James M. Miller to Major General Orlando Ward, 19 April 1952; and Anders to author, 24 August 1986.

[34] "65 Bde, Natib," pp. 45–46; and Morton, *Fall*, pp. 265–266.

[35] Morton, *Fall*, pp. 125 and 266; and "65 Bde, Natib," pp. 15 and 46.

[36] "65 Bde, Natib," p. 15; The figure of seventy cannon is an estimate based on those probably available minus those probably not used or out of range; and Mellnik, *Philippine Diary*, p. 74.

[37] FM 100-5, para 631; Shreve, "Diary," p. 13; Annex V, p. 22; Mellnik, *Philippine Diary*, pp. 42–43; Anders to author, 21 March 1984; Miller, *Bataan Uncensored*, p. 150; and "65 Bde, Natib," p. 16. Filipino and Scout 155mm cannon developed into the mainstay of Bataan's artillery. Because the Japanese soon established effective daylight aerial observation over the battlefield, Japanese fire was most effective during the day. Conversely, defending guns developed an expertise at night firing so as to avoid enemy air and counterbattery fire.

[38] "65 Bde, Natib," p. 11.

[39] *Ibid.*, pp. 16 and 19; and Anders to author, 23 April 1978.

[40] "65 Bde, Natib," pp. 6, 16, and 49.

[41] *Ibid.*, pp. 4 and 16–17.

[42] H. K. Johnson, "Defense Along Abucay," p. 48; and Anders to author, 14 March 1978.

[43] Eliseo Prado to author, 5 April 1978; Harry J. Stempin, "The Operations of Company G, 57th Infantry (P.S.)(Philippine Division) on Luzon, 7 December 1941–30 January 1942 (Philippine Island Campaign)(Personal Experience of a Company Commander)," monograph written for Infantry Officer Advance Course 1946–1947, p. 10, hereafter referred to as Stempin, "Ops G, 57;" and Harry J. Stempin to author, 14 November 1974.

[44] Anders to author, 14 March 1978.

[45] *Ibid.*, 7 July 1977.

[46] *Ibid.*, 14 March 1978.

[47] "65 Bde, Natib," p. 16; and Shreve "Diary," p. 22.

[48] Sutherland to Morton, 29 May 1951; and Anders to author, 26 July 1983.

[49] *Army Register 1941*, p. 440; Cullum, *Register*, VIII, p. 1024; Anders to author, 21 March 1984; H. K. Johnson, "Abucay," p. 8; interview with Harry J. Stempin, San Antonio, Texas, 24 August 1977; and Stempin to author, 14 November 1974.

[50] Brown, "Ops 57 Inf," p. 10; Olson, "Anywhere-Anytime," p. 23; Anders to author, 9 February 1984; *Army Register 1941*, p. 154; interview with H. K. Johnson 16 December 1975; and interview with Harold K. Johnson, Alexandria, Virginia, 30 November 1980.

[51] Interview with H. K. Johnson, 17 December 1975.

[52] "65 Bde, Natib," p. 18; Anders to author, 26 July 1983; and Reynolds to author, 19 November 1974.

[53] "65 Bde, Natib," pp. 15–16; and Anders to author, 9 June 1977.

[54] Anders to Olson, 12 December 1977; USAFFE Signal Operation Instructions, 5 January 1942, Astronomical Data #3; and Annex V, p. 29.

[55] Brown, "Ops 57 Inf," pp. 9–10; Olson, "Ops 57 Inf," p. 14; and Fry, "A Short History," p. 22.

[56] Anders to author, 26 July 1983; Olson, "Preparing the Abucay Line," p. 64; Brown, "Ops 57 Inf," p. 11; and USAFFE General Order #23, 11 February 1942.

[57] Brown, "Ops 57 Inf," p. 10; Brown's comment about moonlit ground is not substantiated by other sources, the moon actually rose at 1:24 a.m.; Anders to author, 9 June 1977; and Reynolds to author, 19 November 1974.

[58] Anders to author, 4 May 1976; and Fry, "A Short History," p. 30.

[59] Brown, "Ops 57 Inf," p. 15; Hersey, *Men on Bataan*, p. 271;

USAFFE General Order #29, 20 February 1942; and Anders to author, 4 May 1976.

[60] Brown, "Ops 57 Inf," p. 11; Fry, "A Short History," pp. 23–24; and Anders to author, 9 June 1977.

[61] Anders to author, 9 June 1977; USAFFE General Order #14, 26 January 1942; and Anders to Olson, 12 December 1977.

[62] Interview with H. K. Johnson, 30 November 1980; and Anders to author, 4 May 1976 and 22 October 1986.

[63] Anders to author, 9 November 1974 and 9 January 1978; and Collier, "Notebooks," 3:37.

[64] Anders to author, 13 June 1976, 9 November 1974, and 9 June 1977.

[65] Ibid., 9 June 1977 and 4 May 1976.

[66] Ibid., 4 May 1976.

[67] Ibid., 23 April 1978, and 1 April and 9 June 1977.

[68] Ibid., 9 June and 1 April 1977, and 4 May 1976; and USAFFE General Order #14, 26 January 1942.

[69] Ernest L. Brown, "Counter Attack by Co. L. 57th Inf at Abucay," p. 94, in "The Philip T. Fry Papers," hereafter referred to as Brown, "Counter Attack;" Toland, But Not in Shame, p. 165; and Anders to author, 9 June 1977 and 22 October 1986.

[70] USAFFE General Order #18, 31 January 1942; and Anders to author, 9 June and 7 July 1977, 4 May 1976, and 22 October 1986.

[71] Anders to author, 9 June 1977 and 25 March 1978; and interview with Olson, 8 May 1988.

[72] Anders to author, 9 June 1977.

[73] "65 Bde, Natib," p. 22; Anders to author, 9 June 1977; and H. K. Johnson, "Defense Along Abucay," pp. 50–51.

[74] Brown, "Ops 57 Inf," p. 11; "65 Bde, Natib," p. 25; and Anders to author, 23 April 1978.

[75] Brown, "Counter Attack," p. 95; Toland, But Not in Shame, p. 165; Anders to author, 9 June and 1 April 1977; Brown, "Ops 57 Inf," p. 14; and Olson to author, 28 August 1976.

[76] Morton, Fall, p. 270; Anders to author, 9 June 1977 and 22 October 1986; and interview with H. K. Johnson, 30 November 1980.

[77] Anders to author, 9 June 1977 and 4 May 1976.

[78] Olson to Anders, 24 August and 15 July 1977; Cullum, Register, IX, p. 1112; US Military Academy pamphlet, "Alexander Ramsey Nininger, Jr. 1918–1942, September 1986;" Reynolds to author, 19 November 1974; interview with Olson, 1 December 1974; Toland, But Not in Shame, p. 166; and Anders to author, 1 April and 9 June 1977.

[79] Reynolds to author, 22 June 1977; and Anders to author, 4 May 1976.

[80] Anders to author, 9 June 1977.

[81] "65 Bde, Natib," p. 51.

[82] Olson to Anders, undated, in Anders to author, 1 April 1977; *Army Register 1943*, pp. 830 and 864; USAFFE Field Order #4, 11 January 1942; and Anders to author, 4 May and 13 June 1976.

[83] Anders to author, 4 May 1976; and Morton, *Fall*, pp. 271–272.

[84] O'Day "Ops 21 Div," 1:2; interview with H. K. Johnson, 30 November 1980; Anders to author, 25 March 1978 and 4 May 1976; and Richards, "Steps," p. 14.

[85] "65 Bde, Natib," p. 52.

[86] Olson, "Ops 57 Inf," p. 15; Webb, "Ops 41 Inf," p. 14; Brown, "Ops 57 Inf," p. 12; Anders to author, 22 October 1986; and Harold K. Johnson, "Diary," p. 10.

[87] Lilly to author, 23 October 1974; and Otis E. Saalman to author, 25 March 1976.

[88] Anders to author, 13 June 1976, 1 April and 7 July 1977, and 22 October 1986; J. W. Rawlston to Olson, —September 1983, in Anders to author, 9 August 1984; James M. Sullivan, "Hospital Number "2," Bataan, PI," p. 1; Annex XIV, pp. 6–7; Thomas W. Houston, "Diary, December 1941 to February 1942, Book 1," pp. 13–14, hereafter referred to as Houston, "Diary;" Daniel N. Weitzner to author, (tape), 27 June 1981; and Alfred A. Weinstein, *Barbed Wire Surgeon* (New York: Lancer Book, Inc., This edition published by arrangement with the Macmillan Company, 1947), pp. 10–11.

[89] Weitzner to author, (tape), 27 June and 16 September 1981; Houston, "Diary," p. 15; and untitled USAAC File #999-2-60.

[90] Anders to author, 4 May 1976 and 1 April 1977; and USAFFE Signal Operation Instructions, 5 January 1942, Astronomical Data #3.

[91] "65 Bde, Natib," pp. 21, 22, and 27; Morton, *Fall*, p. 272; Anders to author, 4 May 1976 and 22 October 1986; and diary of an unidentified American officer who died at Cabanatuan, entitled, "86 FA Bn."

[92] Anders to author, 22 October 1986; O'Day, "Ops 21 Div," 1:1; Cullum, *Register*, IX, p. 1939; *Army Register 1941*, p. 665; *The Howitzer 1939*, p. 260; and interview with Olson, 8 May 1988.

[93] Richards, "Steps," p. 15; Morton, *Fall*, p. 272; and interview with Stempin, 24 August 1977.

[94] Olson, "Ops 57 Inf," p. 15; General Headquarters, Far East Command General Order #74, 19 February 1947; Respicio to author, 18 July 1980; USAFFE General Order #16, 28 January 1942; and Anders to author, 31 March 1978 and 1 April 1977.

[95] H. K. Johnson, "Diary," p. 7; Wainwright, Rpt Ops USAFFE-USFIP, p. 46; *Army Register 1943*, p. 312; War Department, Public Information Office Biography, Arnold J. Funk, p. 1; interview with Olson, 8 May 1988; Mellnik, *Philippine Diary*, p. 23; Arnold J. Funk, "Comments on Fall of the Philippines," 12 January 1952, p. 1; Dennis M. Moore, "Diary," p. 5; Annex V, p. 29; Mellnik, *Philippine Diary*, p. 21; and Anders to author, 9 November 1974 and 22 October 1986. Funk was

promoted to brigadier general on 24 January, five weeks after being promoted to colonel. He was reassigned to II Corps as Chief of Staff on January 22.

[96] Esperitu, "Hist 22 Inf," pp. 5–6; Olson, "Ops 57 Inf," p. 18; O'Day, "Ops 21 Div," 2:24; Annex V, p. 29; and Anders to author, 14 March 1978.

[97] 14 Army Headquarters, "Tactical Situation Report," in Translation of Japanese Documents, Vol II, General Headquarters, Far East Command Military Intelligence Section, Historical Division, p. 3.

[98] Radio, MacArthur to the AG, 14 January 1942.

The Center

[1] Cullum, *Register*, VIB, p. 1707 and VIII, p. 282; Wainwright, *Story*, p. 48; Kary C. Emerson to author, 17 April 1975; Fortier to Morton, 10 January 1952; Appendix 2 to Annex V, p. 1; and Fortier, "Notes of Fortier," p. 70.

[2] Fortier, "Ops 41 Div," p. 1; Calvin E. Chunn, "42nd Infantry," p. 28, and "43d Infantry (PA)," p. 29, both in Chunn, "Notebook;" and Annex V, p. 5.

[3] Webb, "Ops 41 Inf," p. 8; and II Corps Engineer Map, 14 January 1942.

[4] Atkinson, "Actions 42 Inf," p. 5, in Fortier, "Notes on 41 Div;" Loren A. Wetherby, "The Mabatang-Abucay Fight of the 41st Inf (PA) Jan 8th 1942 to Jan 30th 1942," pp. 121–122, in Fortier, "Notes on 41 Div," hereafter referred to as Wetherby, "Mabatang-Abucay;" and Chunn, "43d Infantry (PA)," p. 30, in Chunn, "Notebook."

[5] Fortier to Morton, 10 January 1952, p. 3; Arthur P. Moore, "Actions of the 41st FA (PA) Senior Inst 41 FA," pp. 26–26A, in Fortier, "Notes on 41 Div," hereafter referred to as Moore, "41st FA;" Fortier, "Brief Hist 41 Div," p. 38; Shoemake, "History of 41st F.A. (P.A.)," p. 31, in Chunn, "Notebook;" untitled article, *The Quan*, vol. 37, no. 1, (June 1982), p. 13; *Army Register 1943*, p. 631; and *Army Register 1941*, p. 602.

[6] Morton, *Fall*, p. 252; W. Miller to author, 10 November 1975; John Morrett to author, 25 January 1976; and Collier, "Notebooks," 2:24–25.

[7] Webb, "Ops 41 Inf," pp. 10–11; and Atkinson, "Actions 42 Inf," p. 6.

[8] Interview with J. Martin, 14 February 1976.

[9] *Ibid;* and Wetherby, "Mabatang-Abucay," p. 123.

[10] Wetherby, "Mabatang-Abucay," p. 124; and USAFFE General Order #40, 13 March 1942.

[11] Loren A. Wetherby to Louis Morton, 23 October 1950; Webb, "Ops

41 Inf," p. 15; Wetherby, "Mabatang-Abucay," p. 125; and *Army Register 1941,* p. 902.

12 Wetherby to Morton, 23 October 1950; and Webb, "Ops 41 Inf," pp. 17–18.

13 II Corps Engineer Map; Chunn, "43d Infantry (PA)," p. 29, in Chunn, "Notebook;" Fortier to Morton, 10 January 1952; and Fortier, "Notes of Fortier," p. 86.

14 Chunn, "43d Infantry (PA)," p. 30, in Chunn, "Notebook;" Fortier, "Ops 41 Div," p. 2; and Fortier to Morton, 10 January 1952.

15 Atkinson, "Actions 42 Inf," p. 7; Fortier, "Notes of Fortier," p. 74; and Malcolm V. Fortier, "42d Infantry. January 11th to January 18th," p. 17, in Fortier, "Notes on 41 Div," hereafter referred to as Fortier, "42 Inf."

16 Shreve "Diary," p. 22; Wetherby, "Mabatang-Abucay," p. 126; Quintard, "Diary," 18 January 1942; and Quintard, "Copy of parts of Narrative of A S Quintard Col FA," pp. 1–2.

17 14 Army Headquarters, "Tactical Situation Report," 1:88.

18 "65 Bde, Natib," p. 19; *Japanese Monograph No. 1, Philippine Operations Record Phase 1, 6 November 1941–30 June 1942* (Military History Section, Hq, USAFFE) published by the Office of the Chief of Military History, pp. 95–96, hereafter referred to as *Japanese Monograph No. 1;* and Mallonee, "Bataan Diary," 2:61.

19 "65 Bde, Natib," p. 17; and *Japanese Monograph No. 1,* p. 90.

20 "65 Bde, Natib," pp. 20, 26, and 27.

21 *Ibid.,* pp. 20–21 and 51; and Morton, *Fall,* p. 271.

22 Atkinson, "Actions 42 Inf," p. 4; Anders to author, 24 August 1986; Moore, "Actions 41 FA," p. 26A; *Army Register 1941,* p. 175; and Virgil N. Cordero, *My Experiences during the War with Japan* (Zerrelis, Nurberg: VN Cordero & Co), pp. 9 and 20–21, hereafter referred to as Cordero, *Experiences.*

23 Cordero, *Experiences,* p. 21; Albert M. Jones, "Chronological Order of Events, 51st Div (PA) from Dec 29, 41 to Jan 26, 42," p. 2, hereafter referred to as Jones, "Order of Events;" Brice J. Martin to author, 1 April 1975; and Brice J. Martin, "Regimental History, 51st Infantry, Philippine Army," p. 3, hereafter referred to as Martin, "51st Inf."

24 Jones, "Order of Events," pp. 2–3; and Colonel Stuart C. MacDonald to Major General A. M. Jones, 6 November 1950.

25 O'Day, "Hist of 21 Div," 1:1 and 2:24.

26 Morton, *Fall,* p. 272; "65 Bde, Natib," pp. 23 and 53; and *Japanese Monograph No. 1,* p. 90.

27 Atkinson, "Actions 42 Inf," p. 7; Ellis, "History of the 23rd Infantry (PA)," p. 14, in Chunn, "Notebook;" and Fortier, "Ops 41 Div," p. 2.

28 Bluemel, "31 Div," pp. 8–9; and interview with Nicanor T. Jimenez, Seoul, Korea, 6 April 1983.

29 Bluemel, "Oral Reminiscences," p. 16.

30 *Ibid.*

31 Bluemel, "31 Div," p. 9.

32 *Ibid;* Harold A. Morey, "32nd Inf. (PA)," p. 22, in Chunn, "Notebook;" *Army Register 1941,* p. 440; "Col Edwin Johnson," *The Quan,* vol. 31, no. 1 (June 1976), p. 4; interview with Jimenez, 6 April 1983; and Annex V, pp. 30 and 35.

33 Fortier, "Notes of Col M V Fortier," p. 178; Annex V, p. 40; and Bluemel, "31 Div," p. 9.

34 MacDonald, "Important Dates-SLF," p. 16; and "65 Bde, Natib," p. 23.

35 O'Day, "Hist of 21 Div," 2:25; and Skerry, "Operations NLF Engineers," pp. 2–3.

36 Beck, *MacArthur and Wainwright,* p. 69.

37 Manchester, *American Caesar,* pp. 240–241.

38 Radio, MacArthur to AG, 15 January 1942.

39 Brigadier General Richard J. Marshall, Memorandum To: Chief of Staff, USAFFE, January 13, 1942; Morton, *Fall,* pp. 273–274; and James, *Years of MacArthur,* 1:566–567.

40 Annex V, p. 32; and Morton, *Fall,* p. 274.

41 Albert M. Jones, "Notes on 51st Div (PA) 31 Dec 41–26 Jan 42, both incl," p. 3, hereafter referred to as Jones, "Notes on 51st Div;" Jones, "Order of Events," p. 3; and Jones, "Diary," p. 18.

42 Jones, "Order of Events," p. 3; War Department, Public Information Office Biography, Albert M. Jones, p. 1; *Army Register 1941,* pp. 443–444; Tisdelle, "Diary," 21 March 1942; Fortier, "Notes of Fortier," pp. 78 and 80; Morton, *Fall,* p. 274; and Richards, "Steps," p. 18.

43 Jones, "Diary," p. 3; "65 Bde, Natib," p. 24; and Morton, *Fall,* p. 275.

44 Din to author, 6 July 1981; Jones, "Order of Events," p. 3; Morton, *Fall,* p. 275; and MacDonald to Jones, 6 November 1950.

45 Morton, *Fall,* p. 275; and Atkinson, "Actions 42 Inf," p. 8.

46 "65 Bde, Natib," pp. 25 and 28; and Toland, *Rising Sun,* p. 264.

47 Fortier, "Notes of Col M V Fortier," p. 179; Annex V, pp. 30–31 and 35–36; and *Army Register 1941,* p. 505.

48 Quintard, "Diary," 16 January 1942; W. Miller to author, 10 November 1975; Morrett to author, 25 January 1976; and M. H. Rosen to author, (tape), 14 March 1976.

49 *Army Register 1941,* p. 77; *Army Register 1943,* pp. 82 and 551; and MacDonald to Jones, 6 November 1950.

50 "65 Bde, Natib," p. 25; and Richards, "Steps," p. 18.

51 MacDonald to Jones, 6 November 1950; Colonel John R. Boatwright to Dr. Groce, 22 March 1949 with paper, "52d Inf PA;" and William M. Cummings, "53d Inf. (PA)," p. 38, in Chunn, "Notebook."

52 Jones, "Order of Events," p. 4; Toland, *But Not in Shame,* p. 171; and USAFFE Organizational History 1941–1942, History of 41st FA.

53 O'Day, "Hist of 21 Div," 2:25–26; and Jones, "Order of Events," p. 4.

54 "65 Bde, Natib," pp. 23 and 52; Loren A. Wetherby to Major General Orlando Ward, 4 March 1952; Wetherby, "Mabatang-Abucay," p. 127; and Webb, "Ops 41 Inf," pp. 19–20.

55 Wetherby, "Mabatang-Abucay," pp. 128–130; Webb, "Ops 41 Inf," p. 21; and Fortier, "Narrative Report," p. 110.

56 Wetherby, "Mabatang-Abucay," p. 129; Fortier, "Narrative Report," p. 111; and Morey, "32nd Inf. (PA)," p. 22, in Chunn, "Notebook."

57 Morey, "32nd Inf. (PA)," p. 23, in Chunn, "Notebook;" Wetherby, "Mabatang-Abucay," pp. 130–131; and Wetherby to Morton, 23 October 1950.

58 Wetherby, "Mabatang-Abucay," pp. 131–132; and Fortier to Morton, 10 January 1952.

59 Fortier to Morton, 10 January 1952; Atkinson, "Actions 42 Inf," p. 8; and Webb, "Ops 41 Inf," p. 25.

60 Wetherby, "Mabatang-Abucay," p. 134; Webb, "Ops 41 Inf," pp. 21–25; and USAFFE, General Order #29, 20 February 1942.

61 "65 Bde, Natib," p. 26; Webb, "Ops 41 Inf," pp. 21–25; Wetherby, "Mabatang-Abucay," pp. 134–135; and Annex V, p. 30.

62 "65 Bde, Natib," pp. 26 and 7.

63 *Ibid.,* pp. 25; and Collier, "Notebooks," 3:28–30.

64 Radio, MacArthur to AG, 17 January 1942.

The Philippine Division Attacks

1 Annex V, p. 32; George M. Parker to Louis Morton, 14 February 1948; and FM 100-5, para 651.

2 Morton, *Fall,* p. 277; *Army Register 1943,* p. 542; *Army Register 1941,* p. 517; USAFFE Signal Operation Instructions, 5 January 1942, Astronomical Data #3; and Albert M. Jones, "Organization Day, Twenty-Fifth Anniversary, Thirty-First U.S. Infantry," p. 5.

3 Pray, "Action G, 31st," p. 6; Conrad, "Ops 31 Inf," pp. 9 and 12; Rutledge to author, (tape), 26 November 1979; Gilmore to author, 17 March 1981; Gordon to author, 23 February 1975; and interview with Ellis, 9 May 1975.

4 Pray, "Action G, 31st," pp. 6–7; and Pray to author, 20 December 1980.

5 Rutledge to author, (tape), 26 November 1979 and letter, 15 October 1978; Extract of Brady diary, p. 4; Pray, "Action G, 31st," pp. 6–7; Dr. Ronald E. Marcello, interview with Mr. Louis B. Read, 3 November 1972, Dallas, Texas, North Texas State University Oral History Collec-

tion, p. 42, hereafter referred to as Read, "Comments;" Mallonee, "Bataan Diary," 2:27–28; and Thompson to author, 26 November 1974.

[6] Pray, "Action G, 31st," p. 7; Wynn to author, 5 April 1975; FM 7-5, para 24b; Gilmore to author, 17 March 1981; and Albert L. Taylor to author, 1 July 1980.

[7] Conrad, "Ops 31 Inf," p. 13; Pray, "Action G, 31st," p. 7; USAFFE Signal Operation Instructions, 5 January 1942, Astronomical Data #3; Taylor to author, 1 July 1980; and Hibbs to author, (tape), 22 March 1978.

[8] Chunn, "43d Infantry (PA)," pp. 30–31, in Chunn, "Notebook;" Thompson to author, 3 March 1975; Pray, "Action G, 31st," pp. 7–8; and Pray to author, 20 December 1980.

[9] Fortier to Morton, 10 January 1952, Comments on Fall, p. 3; USAFFE Signal Operation Instructions, 5 January 1942, Astronomical Data #3; and Pray, "Action G, 31st," p. 8.

[10] Lally to author, (tape), 13 January 1979; Thompson to author, 26 November 1974; *Army Register 1943,* p. 97; Rees to author, 13 February 1976; and Pray, "Action G, 31st," p. 8.

[11] Pray, "Action G, 31st," p. 8; Rutledge to author, (tape), 27 February 1980; and Richard M. Gordon to author, 23 February 1975.

[12] Kerchum to author, 1 April and 29 February 1980; Cullum, *Register,* VII, p. 1476, VIII, p. 433, and IX, p. 319; Wynn to author, 5 April 1975; and Pray, "Action G, 31st," p. 8.

[13] USFIP [sic] Field Order #1, 6 January 1942; *Army Register 1941,* p. 233; Croom, "3rd–45th," pp. 3–4, in Chunn, "Notebook;" Besbeck "3d, 45 Inf," pp. 9 and 27; and Anthony M. Ulrich, "Bataan Diary," p. 32.

[14] Van Oosten to author, 7 August 1978; Besbeck, "3d, 45 Inf," pp. 10–11 and 28; Ulrich to author, (tape), 5 August 1981; and Pierce, "Ops L, 45 Inf," pp. 7 and 11.

[15] Ulrich, "Bataan Diary," pp. 35–36; and Basil Dulin to author, (tape), 12 April 1976.

[16] Kerchum to author, 1 April 1980; interview with James Laird, Fort Campbell, Kentucky, 30 December 1973; Milton to author, 2 October 1974; and Alexander to author, (tape), 20 October 1980.

[17] Garrett to author, (tape), 7 August 1980 and undated letter.

[18] Kerchum to author, 1 April 1980; Spencer to author, 29 July 1975; and Hibbs to author, (tape), 22 March 1978.

[19] FM 7-5, para 22c; interview with Wynn, 8 May 1975; and Gilewitch to author, 24 September and 13 October 1975.

[20] Glenn Milton to author, 2 October 1974; and interview with Wynn, 8 May 1975.

[21] Pray, "Action G, 31st," pp. 8–9.

[22] Pray, "Action G, 31st," pp. 3–4 and 9; Rutledge to author, (tape), 26 November 1979; and Gilmore to author, 17 March 1981.

[23] Taylor to author, 1 July 1980; and Pray, "Action G, 31st," p. 9.

[24] Hibbs to author, (tape), 22 March 1978.

[25] Garleb to author, (tape), 16 January 1976; and Pray, "Action G, 31st," pp. 9–10.

[26] Garleb to author, (tape), 16 January 1976.

[27] Walk to author, 19 June 1975 and 3 November 1978; and Pray, "Action G, 31st," p. 10.

[28] Walk to author, 8 July 1975.

[29] Pray, "Action G, 31st," p. 10.

[30] *Ibid.,* p. 21.

[31] Kerchum to author, 1 April 1980; and Pray, "Action G, 31st," p. 13.

[32] Van Oosten to author, 11 July 1974; Edward W. Stewart to author, 27 October 1975; Pierce, "Ops L, 45 Inf," p. 7; Adrianus J. Van Oosten, "History of First Battalion, 45th Inf. (PS)," p. 1, in Chunn, "Notebook," hereafter referred to as Van Oosten, "Hist 1st, 45th;" and Besbeck, "3d, 45 Inf," pp. 13–15.

[33] Besbeck, "3d, 45 Inf," p. 14; Morton, *Fall,* p. 286; and Fortier, "Brief Hist 41 Div," p. 115.

[34] Ulrich, "Bataan Diary," pp. 37–38; Morton, *Fall,* p. 286; Brown, "Ops 57 Inf," p. 7; and Pierce, "Ops L, 45 Inf," p. 9.

[35] Croom, "3rd–45th," p. 5, in Chunn, "Notebook;" Besbeck, "3d, 45 Inf," p. 16; Pierce, "Ops L, 45 Inf," p. 9; and Ulrich, "Bataan Diary," p. 40.

[36] Ulrich, "Bataan Diary," p. 42; Besbeck, "3d, 45 Inf," pp. 4 and 16; Ind, *Judgment Seat,* pp. 262–263; George Groce, interview with Charles E. N. Howard, 14 June 1948; *The Howitzer 1927,* p. 284; Ulrich to author, (tape), 5 August 1981; and Cullum, *Register,* VII, p. 2072, VIII, p. 724, and IX, p. 553.

[37] Besbeck, "3d, 45 Inf," p. 17; and Pierce, "Ops L, 45 Inf," pp. 10–11.

[38] Pierce, "Ops L, 45 Inf," p. 11; and Croom, "3rd–45th," p. 5, in Chunn, "Notebook."

[39] Besbeck, "3d, 45 Inf," p. 17; and Pierce, "Ops L, 45th Inf," p. 13.

[40] Besbeck, "3d, 45 Inf," p. 19; and Pierce, "Ops L, 45 Inf," pp. 12–13.

[41] "65 Bde, Natib," p. 11.

[42] Pray, "Ops L, 45 Inf," p. 13; and Van Oosten to author, 11 July 1974.

[43] Annex XIV, p. 40; and Dulin to author, (tape), 12 April 1976.

[44] Stewart to author, 30 March 1975; and Arthur C. Biedenstein to author, 25 July 1976.

[45] John W. Whitman, "US Army Doctrinal Effectiveness on Bataan, 1942: The First Battle," pp. 88–89, Master of Military Art and Science

thesis, 1984, US Army Command and General Staff College, Fort Leavenworth, Kansas; Olson, "Ops 57 Inf," p. 25; and Annex V, P. 30.

[46] USAFFE General Order #40, 13 March 1942.

[47] "65 Bde, Natib," p. 26; and *Japanese Monograph No. 1,* p. 99.

[48] Garleb to author, (tape), 16 January 1976; Quintard, "Diary," p. 8; and Pray, "Action G, 31st," p. 14.

[49] Conrad, "Ops 31 Inf," p. 14; Pray, "Action G, 31st," pp. 14–16; and Garleb to author, (tape), 16 January 1976.

[50] Collier, "Notebooks," 3:30; Ind, *Judgment Seat,* p. 236; and Cadin, *Warriors,* p. 188.

[51] USAFFE General Order #23, 11 February 1942; Gilewitch to author, 15 April 1975; Lally to author, (tape), 13 January 1979; and USAFFE Field Order #1, 6 January 1942, G2 Technical Data.

[52] Steward to author, 30 March 1975; and Dulin to author, (tape), 12 April 1976.

[53] Priestley, "3 Bn, 31 Inf," p. 6; Pray, "Action G, 31st," pp. 16–17; and interview with Ellis, 9 May 1975.

[54] Priestley, "3 Bn, 31 Inf," pp. 6–7; and John J. Brennan to Winter General Hospital, 22 October 1945.

[55] Taylor to author, 1 July 1980; Pray, "Action G, 31st," pp. 16–17; and USAFFE General Order #23, 11 February 1942.

[56] Kerchum to author, 1 April 1980; Ingle to author, 11 October 1975; Howard, "Unit History," p. 8; and Ulrich, "Bataan Diary," pp. 51–54.

[57] Radio, MacArthur to AG 21 January 1942.

[58] Snyder to author, (tape), 7 January 1979; Conrad, "Ops 31 Inf," p. 15; interview with Forrest F. Dreger, Clearwater, Florida, 7 May 1975; Garleb to author (tape), 16 January 1976; and Miller, *Bataan Uncensored,* p. 153.

[59] Workman to author, 9 January 1976; interviw with Dreger, 7 May 1975; and Wynn to author, 26 April 1975.

[60] "65 Bde, Natib," p. 29.

[61] Besbeck, "3d, 45 Inf," p. 20; Annex XIII, p. 70; "65 Bde, Natib," pp. 4 and 31; and paper, "9th Infantry, Bataan." The Scout 26th Cavalry had traversed similar terrain on 7 to 9 January after being cut off at Layac. Their account is amazingly like that of the Japanese. "It took until 2:00 P.M. to get the last animal across [a single] gorge, a day of herculean labor for exhausted men and animals. Zigzag trails in the precipitous slopes of the ravine had to be cut by hand, undergrowth had to be cleared away with bolos and in some cases animals had to be drawn over the worst places by ropes. On several occasions animals that lost their footing near the top rolled almost to the bottom before being stopped by the tangle of brush on the sides of the ravine. Every man and animal and every piece of equipment, including two mule-killing pack radio sets,

finally reached the top, however, and collapsed in utter exhaustion." From Chandler, "Battles To Glory," 3:15.

[62] O'Day, "Hist of 21 Div," 2:27.

[63] *Ibid.*, 2:27–28.

[64] Clifford Bluemel to Mrs. Elsie Bluemel (wife), 7 February 1942; and O'Day, "Hist of 21 Div," 2:27.

[65] Kerchum to author, 1 April 1980; Morton, *Fall,* p. 288; interview with Laird, 30 December 1973; and Pierce, "Ops L, 45 Inf," p. 13.

[66] Anders to author, 13 June 1976; Besbeck, "3d, 45 Inf," pp. 21–22; Croom, "3rd–45th," p. 6, in Chunn, "Notebook;" and Kerchum to author, 1 April 1980.

[67] James Steed to author, (tape), 10 June 1977; and Read, "Comments," p. 42.

[68] Jones, "Order of Events," p. 5; Anders to author, 13 June 1976; and Walk to author, 8 July 1975.

[69] Annex V, p. 39; and Morton, *Fall,* p. 289.

[70] "65 Bde, Natib," p. 29.

Attack on I Corps

[1] Morton, *Fall,* p. 279.

[2] Ibid., pp. 279–281; and Republic of the Philippines, *The Story of the 1st Regular Division* (Camp Murphy, Quezon City, Manila: Armed Forces of the Philippines, Bureau of Printing, 1953), 1:75, hereafter referred to as *Story 1st Div.*

[3] R. J. Marshall, Memorandum to Chief of Staff, USAFFE, January 13, 1942; Colonel Hugh J. Casey to Chief of Staff, 2 January 1942, Subject: Defense of Bataan; and Morton, *Fall,* pp. 249, 278, and 280.

[4] Morton, *Fall,* pp. 248–249; D. Clayton James, *The Years of MacArthur,* 1:568; *Army Register 1941,* p. 780; Allison L. Hartman, "Diary and Miscellaneous Notes, Captain A. L. Hartman," hereafter referred to as Hartman, "Diary;" Skerry, "NLF Engineers," p. 1; Annex XIV, Medical Department Activities in the Philippines from 1941 to 6 May 1942, and Including Medical Activities in Japanese Prisoner of War Camps, pp. 26–27, in Wainwright, Rpt Ops USAFFE-USFIP, hereafter referred to as Annex XIV; and *Story 1st Div,* 1:71.

[5] *Story 1st Div,* 1:71; Annex XIV, p. 26; and Morton, *Fall,* p. 248.

[6] Dod, *Engineers Against Japan,* p. 88.

[7] Chandler, "Battles To Glory," 3:15; John M. Fowler to author, 8 July 1976; and Chandler, "Clinton A. Pierce," p. 4.

[8] Berry, "History 3rd Inf," p. 2; and Annex IV, p. 17.

[9] Roland C. McNaughton, "31st FA (PA)," p. 21, in Chunn, "Notebook;" Morton, *Fall,* p. 278; Bluemel, "31 Div," p. 7; USAFFE letter, Subject: Plans for Counterattack, 11 January 1942; Schultz, *Hero of Ba-*

taan, pp. 137–138; Romulo, *I Saw the Fall,* p. 63; Annex IV, p. 16; Dr. George C. Groce interview with Clifford Bluemel, 14 April 1948, p. 3; and Bluemel to Ward, 17 January 1952.

[10] Fowler to Morton, 11 March 1949, pp. 1–2; and Fitch, "Siege," p. 7.

[11] Morton, *Fall,* p. 280; *Story 1st Div,* 1:77; R. J. Marshall, Memorandum to Chief of Staff, USAFFE, January 13, 1942; Fowler to Morton, 11 March 1949, p. 3; Wainwright, *Story,* p. 40; and Annex X, p. 18. Troop E-F had replaced G Troop on January 15.

[12] John Wheeler, "Rearguard in Luzon," *The Cavalry Journal* vol. LII, no. 2 (March–April 1943), p. 6; USAFFE General Order #14, 26 January 1942; Arthur K. Whitehead, "Mounted Attack In West Bataan-1942," *The Cavalry Journal* vol. LIV, no. 1 (January–February 1945), p. 51; Cullum, *Register,* VII, pp. 1251–1252, VIII, p. 350, and IX, p. 245; Alva R. Fitch, "The Siege of Bataan from the Bottom of a Foxhole," 22 April 1943, pp. 7–8, hereafter referred to as Fitch, "Siege;" *Army Register 1941,* p. 760; *Story 1st Div,* 1:78; and Fowler to Morton, 11 March 1949, p. 3.

[13] Wheeler, "Rearguard in Luzon," p. 6; and Chandler, "Battles To Glory," 3:15.

[14] Alva R. Fitch to author, 10 January 1977 and 17 February 1981; Fitch, "Siege," pp. 7–8; and Fitch, "Oral History," p. 39.

[15] Fitch, "Siege," pp. 7–8; and Annex IV, p. 19.

[16] Annex IV, p. 20; Chandler, "Battles To Glory," 4:15; *Story 1st Div,* 1:79; and Harry A. Skerry to George A. Meidling, 4 June 1949.

[17] Annex IV, p. 20; *Army Register 1941,* p. 64; and Fitch, "Siege," p. 8.

[18] Annex IV, p. 20; and Fitch to author, 17 February 1981.

[19] Fitch, "Siege," p. 9; and Morton, *Fall,* p. 281.

[20] Edwin Kalbfleish Jr., to author, 11 August 1978; Fitch, "Siege," p. 10; and Berry, "History 3rd Inf," p. 3.

[21] Fitch, "Siege," p. 10.

[22] R. J. Marshall, Memorandum to Chief of Staff, USAFFE, January 13, 1942; Fitch, "Siege," p. 7; *Army Register 1943,* p. 433; Morey, "32nd Inf. (PA)," pp. 21–22, in Chunn, "Notebook;" Cullum, *Register,* VIII, p. 933 and IX, p. 707; and Houston P. Houser to Louis Morton, 9 and 18 March 1949.

[23] *Story 1st Div,* 1:84; John H. Rodman, "Engagement of 91st Division on Moron-Bagac Road From KP 164 to 168," in letter to Louis Morton, 31 March 1949, p. 1, hereafter referred to as Rodman, "91 Div;" and Houser to Morton, 9 and 18 March 1949.

[24] Morton, *Fall,* pp. 280 and 282; Wainwright, Rpt Ops USAFFE-USFIP, p. 47; Annex IV, p. 20; Fitch to author, 17 February 1981; *Army Register 1941,* p. 287; Cullum, *Register,* VII, p. 1583, VIII, p. 467, and IX, p. 348; Fitch, "Siege," p. 11; *Story 1st Div,* 1:84–85; and Berry, "History 3rd Inf," p. 4.

[25] Rodman, "91 Div," p. 2; Schultz, *Hero of Bataan,* pp. 144–145; and Morton, *Fall,* p. 282.

[26] Rodman, "91 Div," pp. 2–3.

[27] Miller, *Bataan Uncensored,* p. 148; Rodman, "91 Div," p. 3; Annex X, p. 18; and James E. Frost to author, 15 March 1979.

[28] Fitch, "Siege," pp. 11–12; Fitch to author, 7 June 1979; Cullum, *Register,* VII, p. 1583; and Alexander, "Recollections," p. 80.

[29] Rodman, "91 Div," p. 3; and Wills to author, (tape), 21 December 1975.

[30] Pena, *Bataan's Own,* pp. 98–100.

[31] Rodman, "91 Div," p. 5.

[32] H. C. Fowler to Morton, 11 March 1949, p. 4; and Berry, "History 3rd Inf," p. 4.

[33] Fitch, "Siege," p. 12.

[34] Morton, *Fall,* p. 283; and Rodman to Ward, 1 February 1952.

[35] Rodman, "91 Div," p. 5.

[36] Santos, "1st Reg Div in Phil," p. 38; Fitch, "Siege," p. 13; Fitch to author, 7 June 1979; Morton, *Fall,* p. 284; and USAFFE Field Order #9, 22 January 1942.

[37] *Story 1st Div,* 1:89–90; and Berry, "History 3rd Inf," pp. 4–5.

[38] H. C. Fowler to Morton, 11 March 1949, p. 4; Fitch, "Siege," p. 14; Groce interview with Howard, 14 June 1948; Babcock, "The SPMs," p. 9; Collier, "Notebooks," 3:36; Fitch to author, 16 February 1977; USAFFE General Order #40, 13 March 1942; and Berry, "History 3rd Inf," p. 5.

[39] Fitch, "Siege," p. 14; and Alexander, "Recollections," p. 80.

[40] Victor J. Sevilla, *The Bataan Odyssey* (1960), p. 18, hereafter referred to as Sevilla, *Odyssey.*

[41] Vance to author, 27 March 1979; and Santos, "1st Reg Div in Phil," p. 38.

[42] Sevilla, *Odyssey,* pp. 21–22; Toland, *But Not in Shame,* p. 182; and Wainwright, *Story,* p. 41.

[43] Toland, *But Not in Shame,* p. 182; and Beebe, "Personal Experience Sketches," p. 13.

[44] Chandler, "Battles To Glory," 4:17; Vance to author, 27 March and 7 May 1979; and Rodman, "91 Div," pp. 6–7.

[45] Fitch, "Siege," p. 15; and Collier, "Notebooks," 3:37.

II Corps Retreats

[1] Annex V, p. 37; and Wainwright, Rpt Ops USAFFE-USFIP, p. 48.

[2] USAFFE Field Order #9, 22 January 1942; Wainwright, Rpt Ops USAFFE-USFIP, p. 48; Collier to Morton, 2 May 1951; and Morton, *Fall,* pp. 290–291.

[3] Parker to Morton, 14 February 1948; Beck, *MacArthur and Wainwright,* p. 259; Annex IV, p. 18; Annex V, p. 22; and Dod, *Engineers Against Japan,* pp. 89–90. The 301st Combat Engineer Regiment soon disbanded and formed the 201st and 202nd engineer battalions (PA).

[4] Skerry to Meidling, 4 June 1949; USAFFE Field Order #9, 22 January 1942; Morton, *Fall,* pp. 247 and 291; and Dod, *Engineers Against Japan,* p. 90.

[5] Radio, MacArthur to Marshall, 23 January 1942.

[6] *Ibid;* USAFFE Field Order #9, 22 January 1942; and Morton, *Fall,* p. 291.

[7] Annex XII, pp. 14–15; Quintard, "Diary," 22–24 January 1942; Quintard, "Copy of Parts of Narrative of A S Quintard Col FA," p. 1; Annex V, p. 38; Morton, *Fall,* p. 293; and USAFFE Field Order #9, 22 January 1942.

[8] Annex XIII, p. 114; Lawrence, "Notebook," p. 72; USAFFE letter, 23 January 1942 to Asst C/S G4, Subject: Quartermaster Plan of Supply; Sullivan, "Hospital Number "2," Bataan, PI," p. 15; Houston, "Diary," pp. 38 and 42; and Weinstein, *Barbed Wire Surgeon,* p. 24.

[9] Annex V, p. 38; Annex XII, pp. 14–15; USAFFE Field Order #9, 22 January 1942; Spaulding to author, (tape), 28 October 1975; and Quintard, "Diary," 22–24 January 1942.

[10] Annex XII, pp. 14–15.

[11] *Ibid.,* p. 14.

[12] Wainwright, Rpt Ops USAFFE-USFIP, p. 49; Morton, *Fall,* p. 293; Fortier, "Ops 41 Div," p. 3; Strong, "History of 31st. (US)," p. 2, in Chunn, "Notebook;" William R. Nealson, "The Operations of a Provisional Battalion, 41st Infantry, (PA), at Abucay Hacienda (Bataan) 15–25 January 1942 (Struggle for the Philippines)(Personal Experience of a Battalion Commander)," p. 18, monograph written for Infantry Officer Advance Course #2, 1947–1948, hereafter referred to as Nealson, "Provisional Battalion;" and USAFFE Signal Operation Instructions, 5 January 1942, Astronomical Data #3.

[13] Fortier, "Notes of Fortier," pp. 55–56; Atkinson, "42nd Infantry Notes," p. 194; Shoemake, "History 41st FA," p. 31, in Chunn, "Notebook;" Fortier, "Ops 41 Div," p. 3; and Toland, *But Not in Shame,* p. 181.

[14] Interview with Martin, 14 February 1976.

[15] Donald F. Ingle to author, 16 September and 11 October 1975; and Spencer to author, 29 July 1975.

[16] E. R. Fendall, "Diary," p. 9; and Fortier, "Ops 41 Div," p. 3.

[17] Spaulding to author, (tape), 28 October 1975; Fortier, "Notes of Fortier," p. 57; and Fortier to Morton, 10 January 1952.

[18] Kary C. Emerson, "The Operations of The II Philippine Corps on Bataan, 10 January–8 April 1942 (Philippine Islands Campaign) (Personal Experience of a Staff Officer)," p. 19, monograph written for Infan-

try Officer Advance Course #2, 1949–1950, hereafter referred to as Emerson, "Ops II Corps." One officer reported eight rounds hit Balanga, killing over forty soldiers, Wernitznig, "Diary;" Fortier, "Ops 41 Div," p. 3; Sixty-Fifth Brigade, "Detailed Report of Combat in the Vicinity of Mount Samat, 26 Jan to 24 Feb 42," p. 1, captured by American forces on Cape Gloucester, 8 February 1944, hereafter referred to as "65 Bde, Samat;" and "65 Bde, Natib," p. 30.

19 Wetherby, "Mabatang-Abucay," p. 138; Fortier, "Notes of Fortier," pp. 56–58; and Fortier, "Ops 41 Div," p. 3.

20 Thomas W. Doyle, "Lecture," 30 July 1942, p. 1; *Army Register 1941,* p. 285; Fortier to Morton, 10 January 1952; and Fortier, "Notes of Fortier," pp. 57–58.

21 Miller, *Bataan Uncensored,* p. 156.

22 Hibbs to author, (tape), 22 March 1978; and Lilly to author, 23 October 1974.

23 Thompson to author, 26 November 1974; and USAFFE Signal Operation Instructions, 5 January 1942, Astronomical Data #3.

24 Workman to author, 19 January 1976; and Pierce, "Ops L, 45 Inf," p. 15.

25 Milton to author, 2 October 1974; Wynn to author, 26 April 1975; Kerchum to author, 8 June 1980; and Thompson to author, 26 November 1974.

26 Milton to author, 2 October 1974 and 9 May 1975; and USAFFE General Order #23, 11 February 1942.

27 Thompson to author, 12 November 1974.

28 *Ibid.,* and 28 January 1979.

29 Snyder to author, (tape), 7 January 1979; Moore, "41st FA," p. 26A; Ulrich, "Bataan Diary," p. 69; Thompson to author, 12 November 1974; and Besbeck, "3d, 45 Inf," p. 26.

30 Thompson to author, 3 March 1975; and USAFFE General Order #39, 12 March 1942.

31 Taylor to author, 9 August 1980; Garleb to author, (tape), 16 January 1976; Ulrich, "Bataan Diary," p. 69; and Pray, "Action G, 31st," p. 18.

32 Pierce, "Ops L, 45 Inf," pp. 15–16; Besbeck, "3d, 45 Inf," p. 26; Ulrich, "Bataan Diary," p. 70; and Pray, "Action G, 31st," p. 19.

33 Knox to author, 19 June 1977; and Pierce, "Ops L, 45 Inf," p. 16.

34 Mead, "Ops 31st Inf," p. 21; and Bess, "Ops Svc Co," p. 27.

35 USAFFE Signal Operation Instructions, 5 January 1942, Astronomical Data #3; Miller, *Bataan Uncensored,* p. 158; Pray, "Action G, 31st," p. 19; and Toland, *But Not in Shame,* p. 181.

36 Amato/Murphy, "History, 2d-45th," pp. 7–8.

37 "65 Bde, Natib," p. 32; and "65 Bde, Samat," p. 1.

38 Prado to author, 5 April 1978; and Thompson to author, 26 November 1974.

[39] Henry G. Lee, *Nothing But Praise* (Culver City, California: Murray and Gee, Inc., 1948), p. 25.

[40] Anloff to author, (tape), 1 August 1976; Morton, *Fall,* p. 86; Charles G. Sage, "Report of Operations of the Philippine Prov Coast Artillery Bde AA in the Philippine Campaign," p. 3, included as Annex IX to Wainwright, Rpt Ops USAFFE-USFIP, hereafter referred to as Annex IX; and Mellnik, *Philippine Diary,* p. 91.

[41] Mark Wohlfeld to author, 26 February 1975; "PRECIS: Tank Group," pp. 1–2; Annex X, p. 19; and "65 Bde, Natib," p. 32.

[42] Gilewitch to author, 24 September 1975; and Townsend, "Tuol Pocket," p. 4.

[43] Weikel to author, 14 September 1979; Schultz, *Hero,* p. 130; "65 Bde, Samat," pp. 1, 38, and 39; and Cullum, *Register,* VII, p. 2061.

[44] "65 Bde, Samat," pp. 1–2; and "65 Bde, Natib," p. 32.

[45] Fry, "A Short History," p. 39; Morton, *Fall,* p. 291; and Anders to author, 13 June 1976.

[46] "65 Bde, Samat," p. 2; Annex X, p. 20; and "Armor on Luzon," p. 33.

[47] Annex X, p. 19.

[48] Spaulding to author, (tape), 28 October 1975; Miller, *Bataan Uncensored,* p. 167; and Ernest B. Miller, "Notes of Lieutenant Colonel Miller," p. 4.

[49] Annex X, p. 20; Miller, *Bataan Uncensored,* p. 167; "65 Bde, Samat," p. 7; and Spaulding to author, (tape), 28 October 1975.

[50] Radio, MacArthur to Marshall, 25 January 1942.

[51] Radio, MacArthur to Marshall, 27 January 1942.

[52] Dod, *Engineers Against Japan,* p. 70; and McBride, "Notes on the Fall."

[53] Dod, *Engineers Against Japan,* p. 70; and Anders to author, 21 January 1986.

[54] Fortier, "Ops 41 Div," p. 3; Loren A. Wetherby, "S-4 and Transportation," p. 184, in Fortier, "Notes on 41 Div;" and Fortier, "Notes of Fortier," p. 60.

[55] Fortier, "Notes of Fortier," p. 64; and Quintard, "Diary," 30 January 1942.

[56] Ind, *Judgment Seat,* pp. 251–256; and Craven and Cate, *Plans and Early Operations,* p. 405.

Longoskawayan Point

[1] Shoji Ohta, "Statement No 518, Subject: Bataan Operations, 18 March 1952," in Comments of Japanese Officers Regarding the Fall of the Philippines, hereafter referred to as Ohta, "Comments;" and Morton, *Fall,* p. 300.

[2] The Mauban mentioned here should not be confused with Mauban on Bataan's west coast; Ohta, "Comments;" Morton, *Fall,* p. 300; "65 Bde, Natib," p. 75; *Reports of MacArthur,* p. 95; and Clinton A. Pierce to Walter D. Edmonds, 3 March 1947.

[3] Morton, *Fall,* p. 247; McBride, "Notes on the Fall," p. 106; and Pena, *Bataan's Own,* p. 89. The 2nd Regular Division was activated on January 7 by USAFFE General Order #6, 7 January 1942.

[4] Arnold J. Funk, Memorandum for G3 USAFFE, 8 January 1942; Annex XIII, Appendix A, Narrative of Quinauan Point Landing, p. 1; Morton, *Fall,* p. 298; and Alexander, "Recollections," pp. 53 and 55.

[5] Morton, *Fall,* p. 299; Alexander, "Recollections," p. 54; Selleck, "Notes 71 Div," p. 56; and Pena, *Bataan's Own,* p. 102 and map 9.

[6] Morton, *Fall,* p. 300; Linus B. Marlow to author, 6 February 1984; and C. A. Pierce to Edmonds, 3 March 1947.

[7] John D. Bulkeley, "Report of Action of U.S.S. PT-34 on the Night of January 22–23, 1942," 27 February 1942, hereafter referred to as Bulkeley, "Report of PT-34;" *Reports of MacArthur.* p. 107; and Pena, *Bataan's Own,* p. 104.

[8] Bulkeley, "Report of PT-34."

[9] *Ibid;* W. L. White, *They Were Expendable* (New York: Harcourt, Brace & Company, 1972), pp. 78–83; and John D. Bulkeley to Louis Morton, 5 March 1948.

[10] Morton, *Fall,* p. 301; Pena, *Bataan's Own,* p. 105; and Francis J. Bridget to Commandant, Sixteenth Naval District, "Action of Longoskawayan Point against Japanese Forces," 9 February 1942, p. 2, hereafter referred to as Bridget, "Longoskawayan Point."

[11] William Massello Jr., to author, 15 April 1978. E Battery (searchlight) and G Battery (3-inch guns) 60th Artillery, provided an outer air defense ring for Corregidor; Joe Karr to author, (tape), 10 February and 17 March 1983; Olson to author, 8 December 1987; and R. Edward Friese to author (tape), 6 April 1977.

[12] Massello to author, (tape), 7 January 1977 as are subsequent conversations that include Massello; Gwinn U. Porter, "Antiaircraft Defense of Corregidor," monograph written for the Command and General Staff College, Fort Leavenworth, Kansas, 1946–1947, p. 4; Karr to author, (tape), 17 March 1983; and Dean Schedler, "Corregidor's AA. Keep 'Em Frying," *Coast Artillery Journal* vol. LXXXV, no. 3 (May–June, 1942), pp. 64–66.

[13] Bridget, "Longoskawayan Point," p. 2; "Landing Operations in the Philippines 1941;" and William F. Prickett, "Naval Battalion at Mariveles," *The Marine Corps Gazette* vol. 34, no. 6 (June 1950), pp. 41–43. There are many accounts of Japanese stashing equipment at Longoskawayan years before the war and of Japanese troops occupying hiding places weeks before they were discovered. Such accounts are incorrect.

[14] Prickett, "Naval Battalion at Mariveles," p. 40.

[15] Earl L. Sackett, "The History of the U.S.S. Canopus," *United States Naval Institute Proceedings* (January 1943), p. 13, hereafter referred to as Sackett, "History Canopus;" F. W. Rockwell, Memorandum for Captain Dessez, U.S.N. 9 January 1942; Morton, *Fall,* pp. 299 and 301; Frank O. Hough, Verle E. Ludwig, and Henry I. Shaw, *Pearl Harbor to Guadalcanal: History of U. S. Marine Corps Operations in World War II* vol. 1 (Historical Branch, G-3 Division, Headquarters, US Marine Corps), p. 175, hereafter referred to as Hough, *Pearl Harbor to Guadalcanal;* Donald Knox, *Death March. The Survivors of Bataan* (New York: Harcourt Brace Jovanovich, 1981), p. 57; Ralph C. Poness to author, 1 September 1988; and Bridget, "Longoskawayan Point," p. 3.

[16] Prickett, "Naval Battalion at Mariveles," p. 41; Massello to author, 15 April 1978 with certificate; Olson to author, 8 December 1987; and "Landing Operations in the Philippines."

[17] Joseph M. Glessner to author, 24 June 1974; and Morton, *Fall,* p. 302.

[18] Prickett, "Naval Battalion at Mariveles," p. 42; Hough *Pearl Harbor to Guadalcanal,* p. 177; Morton, *Fall,* p. 302; Massello to author, 15 April 1978; and Orville D. Roland to author, 8 September 1980.

[19] Woodrow McBride to author, 12 November 1976; Morton, *Fall,* p. 302; interview with George Koury, 27 April 1972, by Dr. Ronald E. Marcello, North Texas State University Oral History Collection, p. 21; Robert D. Rosendahl to author, 22 January 1979; Collier, "Notebooks," 3:40; and Bridget, "Longoskawayan Point," pp. 3, 4, and 7.

[20] Prickett, "Naval Battalion at Mariveles," pp. 41–42; and USAFFE Training Memorandum #10, 1 February 1942.

[21] Prickett, "Naval Battalion at Mariveles," p. 42; and Massello to author, 5 March 1977.

[22] Interview with Karl A. Bugbee, Dallas Texas, 8 December 1971, by Dr. Ronald E. Marcello, North Texas State University Oral History Collection, p. 13; and Prickett, "Naval Battalion at Mariveles," p. 42.

[23] Bridget, "Longoskawayan Point," p. 4; Prickett, "Naval Battalion at Mariveles," pp. 42–43; and Morton, *Fall,* p. 306.

[24] Radio, Marshall to MacArthur, 14 January 1942.

[25] Paul D. Bunker, "Diary," 25 January 1942; Morton, *Fall,* p. 306; and James D. Ellis, "Notebook," p. 29.

[26] Bunker, "Diary," 25 January 1942; and Annex VIII, p. 30.

[27] Roland to author, 18 August 1980.

[28] Annex VIII, p. 31, from G2 Information Bulletin, 2 February 1942; and Rosendahl to author, 22 January 1979.

[29] Bunker, "Diary," 27 and 28 January 1942; Bridget, "Longoskawayan Point," p. 4; and Morton, *Fall,* p. 305.

[30] Bridget, "Longoskawayan Point," p. 5; and Anders to author, 8 December 1980 and 24 February 1981.

[31] Bridget, "Longoskawayan Point," p. 5; Morton, *Fall,* p. 305; Mc-

Bride, "Notes on the Fall," p. 108; Anders to author, 17 March 1981; Groce, memorandum for H. H. Galbett, Subject: 57th Infantry (PS), 19 May 1948; William C. Anderson, "History of the 57th Infantry (PS)," p. 5, in Chunn, "Notebook;" and Fry, "A Short History," p. 41.

[32] *The Howitzer 1923,* p. 144; Cullum, *Register,* VII, p. 1800, VIII, p. 558, and IX, p. 423; Emerson to author, 17 April 1975; Annex V, p. 2; Stempin to author, (tape), 24 August 1977; and Anders to author, 24 February, 17 March 1981 and 13 June 1976.

[33] William F. Hogaboom, "Action Report: Bataan," *The Marine Corps Gazette* vol. 30, no. 4 (April 1946), pp. 30–31; and subsequent quote is from Prickett, "Naval Battalion at Mariveles," p. 43.

[34] Anders to author, 24 February, 17 March, and 23 April 1981; Allison L. Hartman, Diary and Miscellaneous Notes, notes on Captain Chilcote, hereafter referred to as Hartman, "Diary."

[35] Anderson, "History of the 57th Infantry (PS)," p. 5, in Chunn, "Notebook;" and Howard, "Unit History," p. 10.

[36] Mellnik, *Philippine Diary,* p. 84; Anderson, "History of the 57th Infantry (PS)," p. 5, in Chunn, "Notebook;" John Morrill to Commandant, 16th Naval District, 30 January 1942, "Action at Longoskawayan Point, 29 Jan 42;" and Bridget, "Longoskawayan Point," p. 5.

[37] Anderson, "History of the 57th Infantry (PS)," pp. 5–6, in Chunn, "Notebook;" USAFFE General Order #40, 13 March 1942; C. A. Pierce to Edmonds, 3 March 1947; Stewart Wood to Louis Morton, 23 March 1948; Morton, *Fall,* p. 307; and Anders to author, 24 February 1981.

[38] Anders to author, 8 December 1980; Bridget, "Longoskawayan Point," p. 6; and Anderson, "History of the 57th Infantry (PS)," p. 6, in Chunn, "Notebook."

[39] Bridget, "Longoskawayan Point," p. 6; Wood to Morton, 23 March 1948; Hogaboom, "Action Report: Bataan," p. 30; and Morton, *Fall,* p. 308.

[40] Morton, *Fall,* p. 308; Anderson, "History of 57th Infantry (PS)," p. 6, in Chunn, "Notebook;" and Anders to author, 8 December 1980.

[41] John D. Bulkeley, "Operations of U.S.S. PT-41 Night of January 24, 1942," dtd 26 January 1942.

Quinauan Point

[1] Charles A. Willoughby to Orlando Ward, 17 May 1951; Annex XIII, Appendix A, Narrative of Quinauan Point Landing, p. 1; USAFFE Signal Operation Instructions, 5 January 1942, Astronomical Data #3; and Pena, *Bataan's Own,* p. 104.

[2] Annex XIII, Appendix A, Narrative of Quinauan Point Landing, p.

1; Wright to author, 12 September 1974; and Marlow to author, 6 February 1984.

[3] Larry H. Cohen to author, (tape), 14 November 1978; Poweleit, *USAFFE*, p. 35; and personal observation of the author.

[4] George C. Groce interview with Clyde A. Selleck, 2 April 1948; Morton, *Fall*, p. 303; Selleck, "Statement," p. 12; Pena, *Bataan's Own*, p. 110; Collier, "Notebooks," 3:43; Annex XIII, Appendix A, Supply Operations Fort Stotsenburg, p. 1; personal observation of author; and Annex XIII, Appendix A, Narrative of Quinauan Point Landing, p. 1.

[5] Loren G. Pierce to author, 10 January 1976; and Henry S. Winslow to author, (tape), 5 February 1980.

[6] L. G. Pierce to author, 10 January 1976; E. D. Oestreich to author, 4 March and 11 February 1981. Until he changed it, Oestreich had the last name of Davis on Bataan, the name of his stepfather; Thomas E. Gage to author, 2 June 1977; and Winslow to author, (tape), 5 February 1980.

[7] Oestreich to author, 11 February 1981.

[8] L. G. Pierce to author, 10 January 1976; Gage to author, 2 June 1977; interview with James O. Bass, San Antonio, Texas, 22 August 1977; Bass to author, 30 January 1979; and USAFFE General Order #40, 13 March 1942.

[9] L. G. Pierce to author, 10 January 1976 and 17 July 1978.

[10] Gage to author, 2 June 1977; interview with Bass, 22 August 1977; *Reports of MacArthur*, p. 107; William E. Dyess, *The Dyess Story: The Eye-Witness Account of the DEATH MARCH FROM BATAAN and the Narrative of Experiences in Japanese Prison Camps and of Eventual Escape* (New York: G. P. Putnam's Sons, 1944), p. 41, hereafter referred to as Dyess, *The Dyess Story;* p. 41; and Annex XIII, Appendix A, Narrative of Quinauan Point Landing, p. 2.

[11] Pena, *Bataan's Own*, pp. 109–110; Annex XIII, Appendix A, Narrative of Quinauan Point Landing, p. 2; Ramon D. Naguiat Jr., to author, 7 February and 2 March 1983; Alexander, "Recollections," p. 52; and interview with Robert L. Miller, Alexandria, Virginia, 28 April 1981.

[12] Alexander, "Recollections," pp. 59–60; Naguiat to author, 7 February and 2 March 1983; Pena, *Bataan's Own*, pp. 110–112; and Annex XIII, Appendix A, Narrative of Quinauan Point Landing, p. 2.

[13] Clyde A. Selleck, "Memo to Gen McBride re my Command Period in the West Sector Bataan," pp. 12–13, hereafter referred to as Selleck, "Memorandum to McBride;" Selleck, "Statement," pp. 12–13; James, *The Years of MacArthur*, 1:566–567 and 2:78; Annex XIII, Appendix A, Narrative of Quinauan Point Landing, p. 2; Alexander, "Recollections," p. 62; Morton, *Fall*, pp. 304–305; and interview, Louis Morton with Richard J. Marshall, 7 April 1948.

[14] Interview, Morton with Marshall, 7 April 1948, p. 2; George C. Groce to Louis Morton, 28 May 1950 with comments by Halstead C. Fowler, p. 1; Clark Lee, *They Call It Pacific: An Eye-Witness Story of Our*

War Against Japan from Bataan to the Solomons (New York: The Viking Press, 1943), p. 223, hereafter referred to as Lee, *They Call It Pacific;* Chandler, "Colonel Clinton A. Pierce," pp. 2–3; *Army Register 1943,* p. 706; War Department, Public Information Office Biography, Clinton A. Pierce, p. 1; Clinton A. Pierce to Orlando Ward, 5 January 1952, "Comments on Chapter XVII," p. 1; C. A. Pierce to Edmonds, 3 March 1947; Lawrence Perry, North American Newspaper Alliance, account dtd 20 September 1945 from interview with Clinton A. Pierce, in undated answer to Louis Morton's letter of 12 March 1951; and Schultz, *Hero of Bataan,* p. 168.

[15] Perry account, 20 September 1945. Malin Craig was Army Chief of Staff from 1935 to 1939.

[16] Clinton A. Pierce to Louis Morton, undated, answering Morton's letter of 12 March 1951; Pierce to Ward, 5 January 1952, p. 1; and Clinton A. Pierce to the Secretary of War's Personnel Board, 11 March 1946.

[17] Pierce to Ward, 5 January 1952, p. 1; Pena, *Bataan's Own,* p. 113; James, *The Years of MacArthur,* 2:79; Morton, *Fall,* p. 305; *Army Register 1943,* p. 965; Alexander, "Recollections," p. 68; Naguiat to author, 2 March 1983; and C. A. Pierce to Ward, 5 January 1952, p. 1.

[18] Dyess, *The Dyess Story,* p. 39; Omar L. McGuire to author, 11 February 1983; and Omar L. McGuire, "Our Defense of Bataan," p. 12.

[19] McGuire, "Our Defense of Bataan," p. 12.

[20] Ray C. Hunt Jr., to author, 19 March 1977; *Reports of MacArthur,* p. 107; and Dyess, *The Dyess Story,* p. 41.

[21] Alexander, "Recollections," pp. 66–67; and C. A. Pierce to Ward, 5 January 1952, p. 1.

[22] Naguiat to author, 8 February 1983; Gage to author, 2 June 1977; Dr. Ronald E. Marcello, interview with Tom Blaylock, Dallas, Texas, 12 March 1971, North Texas State University Oral History Collection, p. 27, hereafter referred to as Blaylock, "Comments;" Edmund P. Zbikowski was a first lieutenant until promoted on 23 February by USAFFE Special Order #51; and Pena, *Bataan's Own,* p. 114.

[23] C. A. Pierce Ward, 5 January 1952, p. 1.

[24] Alexander, "Recollections," pp. 69–72.

[25] Radio, MacArthur to the AG, 24 January 1942.

[26] Pena, *Bataan's Own,* p. 115; and Liles to wife, 19 September 1945.

[27] Blaylock, "Comments," p. 30; and USAFFE General Order #23, 11 February 1942.

[28] James L. Leggett, "Brief History-Company "A"-803d. ENGR. BN. (AVN) (SEP);" Dod, *Engineers Against Japan,* p. 96; John J. Mackowski to author, 18 February 1982; Gilbert B. Soifer to author, (tape), 16 December 1977; and Floyd T. Niday to author, (tape), 6 September 1978.

[29] Niday to author, (tape), 6 September 1978; and Soifer to author, (tape), 16 December 1977.

[30] Soifer to author, (tape), 16 December 1977.

[31] Ibid; and John J. Denehy Jr., "Captain Edmond [sic] Peter Zbikowski," in *The Quan* vol. 35, no. 5 (March 1981), p. 12.

[32] Soifer to author, (tape), 16 December 1977; Mackowski to author, 18 February and 20 March 1982; Niday to author, (tape), 6 September 1978; and Alexander, "Recollections," p. 93.

[33] Mackowski to author, 18 February and 20 March 1982; and Soifer to author, (tape), 16 December 1977.

[34] Wayne C. Liles to author, 15 April 1975.

[35] Pena, *Bataan's Own*, p. 116; and Morton, *Fall*, p. 305.

[36] Morton, *Fall*, p. 308; Hunt to author, 19 March 1977.

[37] Pena, *Bataan's Own*, p. 117.

[38] Ulrich, "Bataan Diary," p. 77; and Croom, "3d-45th," p. 8, in Chunn, "Notebook."

[39] Pena, *Bataan's Own*, p. 118; and Croom, "3d-45th," p. 9, in Chunn, "Notebook."

[40] Croom, "3d-45th," pp. 9–10, in Chunn, "Notebook;" Ulrich, "Bataan Diary," pp. 85–86; Morton, *Fall*, pp. 303, 308, and 309; Lilly, "Report of Ops 57 Inf," p. 4; and Howard, "Unit History," p. 11.

[41] USAFFE draft G2 bulletin, noon Feb 3 to noon Feb 4, 1942, from intercepted Japanese message; and Falk, "Folio," p. 88.

[42] Ind, *Bataan: The Judgment Seat*, p. 265; and Ulrich, "Bataan Diary," pp. 89–94.

[43] Ulrich, "Bataan Diary," pp. 89–94; and Croom, "3d-45th," p. 11, in Chunn, "Notebook."

[44] Ulrich, "Bataan Diary," p. 96; C. A. Pierce to Edmonds, 3 March 1947; and Lee, *They Call It Pacific*, p. 223.

[45] Ulrich, "Bataan Diary," p. 96; Croom, "3d-45th," p. 11, in Chunn, "Notebook;" and Besbeck, "3d, 45 Inf," p. 15.

[46] Ulrich, "Bataan Diary," p. 96; Ulrich to author, (tape), 5 August 1981; Cullum, *Register,* VII, p. 2072 and VIII, p. 724; and Croom, "3d-45th," pp. 11–12, in Chunn, "Notebook."

[47] Ulrich, "Bataan Diary," pp. 101–102; Morton, *Fall*, p. 309; and Croom, "3d-45th," p. 12, in Chunn, "Notebook."

[48] Croom, "3d-45th," p. 12, in Chunn, "Notebook;" Morton, *Fall*, p. 310; and Weaver, Comments to the draft manuscript, Fall of the Philippines.

[49] Ulrich, "Bataan Diary," pp. 104–105.

[50] *Ibid.,* pp. 106–108.

[51] Dyess, *The Dyess Story*, p. 43; Croom, "3d-45th," pp. 12–13, in Chunn, "Notebook;" Cecil Ammons to author, 15 July 1977; Ind, *Judgment Seat,* p. 298; and Ulrich, "Bataan Diary," p. 118.

[52] Interview with R. L. Miller, 28 April 1981; Croom, "3d-45th," p. 13, in Chunn, "Notebook;" Morton, *Fall*, p. 310; interview with J. W. Bohner, San Antonio, Texas, 24 August 1977; Poweleit, *USAFFE*, p. 35;

R. L. Miller to author, 30 March 1981; and Lee, *They Call It Pacific,* p. 227.

[53] Interview with R. L. Miller, 28 April 1981; Hunt to author, 19 March 1977; and R. L. Miller to author, 30 March 1981.

[54] Interview with Bohner, 24 August 1977; and Lawrence W. Parcher, "History of the 21st Pursuit Squadron," p. 51, in Chunn, "Notebook."

[55] Interview with Bohner, 24 August 1977.

[56] Croom, "3d-45th," p. 13, in Chunn, "Notebook;" Ulrich, "Bataan Diary," p. 119; Liles to author, 8 June 1978; and Lee, *They Call It Pacific,* p. 227.

[57] Dyess, *The Dyess Story,* pp. 43–44; Morton, *Fall,* p. 311; and interview with R. L. Miller, 28 April 1981.

[58] Hunt to author, 19 March 1977.

[59] Croom, "3d-45th," p. 13, in Chunn, "Notebook;" Skerry to Meidling, 4 June 1949; Morton, *Fall,* p. 311; Wainwright, *Story,* p. 44; Collier, "Notebooks," 3:47; interview with R. L. Miller, 28 April 1981; and Skerry, Comments to *Engineers in the South West Pacific.*

[60] Henry W. Goodall to Dr. George Groce, 17 August 1948.

[61] *Ibid;* Dyess, *The Dyess Story,* p. 44; and interview with R. L. Miller, 28 April 1981.

[62] Ammons to author, 15 July 1977; R. L. Miller to author, 30 March 1981; Dyess, *The Dyess Story,* pp. 44–45; and interview with Roger Taylor, San Antonio, Texas, 22 August 1977.

[63] Goodall to Groce, 17 August 1948; Sackett, "History Canopus," p. 16; and USFIP General Order #20, 9 April 1942.

[64] Morton, *Fall,* p. 312; and Wainwright, *Story,* p. 45.

[65] Morton, *Fall,* p. 312; Annex XIII, Appendix A, Narrative of Quinauan Point Landing, p. 2; Croom, "3d-45th," p. 14, in Chunn, "Notebook;" Ulrich, "Bataan Diary," p. 124; and Skerry to Ward, 16 January 1952, "Comments on Draft Manuscript" which includes letter, 20 July 1949 to GHQ, FEC, Subject: Rough Draft of Volume VIII on Engineer Critique, Philippine Defense.

Anyasan-Silaiim

[1] Morton, *Fall,* pp. 312–313.

[2] Falk, "Folio," pp. 76 and 88; Pena, *Bataan's Own,* p. 118; Morton, *Fall,* pp. 312–313; USAFFE Signal Operation Instructions, 5 January 1942, Astronomical Data #3; and 14 Army Headquarters, "Tactical Situation Report," p. 108. The terrain between the Silaiim and Anyasan Rivers was similar to that found at Quinauan, very thick underbrush and towering trees. The Japanese landing at Silaiim Point brought into use several similar river and point names. The confusion felt by everyone can be summed up in the answer of a wire crewman on a telephone pole

when asked where he was. "For Christ's sake, sir, I don't know. I am somewhere between asinine and quinine points," from Tisdelle, "Diary," 6 February 1942.

[3] Annex IV, p. 25; Pena, *Bataan's Own*, p. 122; Morton, *Fall*, p. 314; Robert J. Vogler Jr., to author, (tape), 6 October 1975; and Wright to author, 12 September 1974.

[4] Interview with Stephen H. Crosby Jr., San Antonio, Texas, 23 August 1977; Marlow to author, 6 February 1984; and Vogler to author, (tape), 6 October 1975.

[5] Stephen H. Crosby Jr., to author, 27 June 1975 and 28 February 1977; Stephen H. Crosby Jr., "History of 17th Pursuit Squadron," pp. 48–49, in Chunn, "Notebook;" Knox, *Death March*, p. 75; Morton, *Fall*, p. 314; and interview with Crosby, 23 August 1977.

[6] Vogler to author, (tape), 6 October 1975, and subsequent quote is from the same source; Crosby, "History of 17th Pursuit Squadron," p. 49, in Chunn, "Notebook;" and Morton, *Fall*, p. 315.

[7] Interview with Crosby, 23 August 1977; and Morton, *Fall*, p. 315.

[8] Vogler to author, (tape), 6 October 1975; and Marlow to author, 6 February 1984.

[9] Crosby to author, 28 February 1977; Morton, *Fall*, pp. 314–315; Gilmer M. Bell, "Quinauan Point;" Pena, *Bataan's Own*, pp. 123–124; Crosby, "History of 17th Pursuit Squadron," p. 49, in Chunn, "Notebook;" Marlow to author, 6 February 1984; and interview with Crosby, 23 August 1977.

[10] Wainwright to MacArthur, memorandum dated 27 January 1942 in Beck, *MacArthur and Wainwright*, p. 77; and Schultz, *Hero of Bataan*, p. 153.

[11] Morton interview with Sutherland, 12 November 1946, p. 15.

[12] MacArthur to Wainwright, memorandum, 28 January 1942, in Beck, *MacArthur and Wainwright*, pp. 78–79.

[13] Vogler to author, (tape), 6 October 1975; and Morton, *Fall*, p. 315.

[14] Vogler to author, (tape), 12 June 1978; Morton, *Fall*, p. 315; Pena, *Bataan's Own*, p. 124; Robert E. Conn Jr., "War Diary of Capt. Robt E. Conn Jr," hereafter referred to as Conn, "War Diary;" Crosby to author, 28 February 1977; and Marlow to author, 6 February 1984.

[15] Crosby to author, 28 February 1977; and Morton, *Fall*, p. 315.

[16] Interview with Crosby, 23 August 1977; Ralph Amato Jr., and Louis F. Murphy, "History Second Battalion 45th Infantry (P.S.) December 8, 1941–April 9, 1942," p. 10, hereafter referred to as Amato/Murphy, "History, 2d-45th," in Chunn, "Notebook;" and Harold K. Johnson, "Defense of the Philippine Islands. Anyasen [sic] and Silaiim Points Bataan (Personal Experience of a Regimental S3) 57th Infantry (PS)," p. 6, monograph written for the Command and Staff Course 1946–1947, hereafter referred to as H. K. Johnson, "Anyasan-Silaiim."

[17] Interview with H. K. Johnson, 16 December 1975 and 30 November 1980.

[18] H. K. Johnson, "Anyasan-Silaiim," p. 11 and 5–7; H. K. Johnson, "Diary," p. 11; Amato/Murphy, "History, 2d-45th," pp. 9–10; and Morton, *Fall*, p. 316.

[19] Morton, *Fall*, p. 317; and Pena, *Bataan's Own*, p. 125.

[20] Bluemel to Groce, 15 June 1948; Collier, "Notebooks," 3:44; and Cecil M. Sanders, "The Operations of the 57th Infantry (PS)(Philippine Division) at Anyasan and Silaiim Points, Bataan, P. I., 2 February–13 February 1942 (Philippine Islands Campaign)(Personal Experience of a Regimental Staff Officer)," p. 10, monograph written for Infantry Officer Advance Course #2, 1949–1950, hereafter referred to as Sanders, "Anyasan-Silaiim."

[21] Blaylock, "Comments," p. 34; Morton, *Fall*, p. 318; Croom, "3rd-45th," p. 12, in Chunn, "Notebook;" and Amato/Murphy, "History, 2nd-45th," p. 10, in Chunn, "Notebook."

[22] White to author, 4 August 1976 and 14 March 1980; Armellino to author, 30 January 1979; and Collier, "Notebooks," 3:44.

[23] Winslow to author, (tape), 5 February 1980; Schultz, *Hero of Bataan*, p. 172; USAFFE Signal Operation Instructions, 5 January 1942, Astronomical Data #3; Morton, *Fall*, p. 318; Chandler, "Battles To Glory," 4:17; Knox, *Death March*, p. 77; Gurney, *The War in the Air*, p. 344; and Collier, "Notebooks," 3:45.

[24] Morton, *Fall*, p. 318; Dulin to author, 14 June 1980; Samuel Eliot Morison, *History of United States Naval Operations in World War II*, vol. 3: *Rising Sun in the Pacific 1931–April 1942* (Boston: Little, Brown and Company, 1948), p. 201; Liles to wife, 24 September 1945; White to author, 20 May 1976 and 14 March 1980; Collier, "Notebooks," 3:45; Knox, *Death March*, p. 77; and USAFFE General Order #21, 7 February 1942.

[25] Liles to wife, 24 September 1945; Morton, *Fall*, p. 318; and Liles to author, 8 June 1978.

[26] Vogler to author, (tape), 6 October 1975; and Marlow to author, 6 February 1984.

[27] Ulrich, "Bataan Diary," pp. 112–115; and Croom, "3rd-45th," pp. 11–12, in Chunn, "Notebook."

[28] E. G. DeLong, Commander Motor Torpedo Boat Division Nine, to Commandant, 16th Naval District, Subject: Attack of U.S.S. PT-32 on Enemy Cruiser During Night of February 1, 1942, February 3, 1942; and Robert J. Bulkley Jr., *At Close Quarters. PT Boats in the United States Navy* (Washington, D.C.: US Government Printing Office, 1962), pp. 12–14.

[29] Edmund J. Lilly to Clinton A. Pierce, 27 February 1946; and Morton, *Fall*, p. 319.

[30] Liles to wife, 24 September 1945; and Silas C. Wolf to author, 20 October 1980.

[31] H. K. Johnson, "Diary," p. 12; Howard, "Unit History," p. 12; Lilly, "Report of Ops 57 Inf," p. 4; Olson, "Anywhere-Anytime," pp. 10 and 13; and interview with H. K. Johnson, 30 November 1980.

[32] Lilly, "Report of Ops 57 Inf," p. 5; Morton, *Fall,* p. 319; *Army Register 1941,* p. 508; Lilly to author, 6 August 1974; and interview with Olson, 8 May 1988.

[33] Sanders, "Anyasan-Silaiim," pp. 12–13; Lilly, "Report of Ops 57 Inf," p. 4; and H. K. Johnson, "Anyasan-Silaiim," pp. 6–8.

[34] Interview with H. K. Johnson, 16 December 1975; Mills to author, 27 November 1974; and H. K. Johnson, "Anyasan-Silaiim," p. 6.

[35] Lilly, "Report of Ops 57 Inf," p. 5; H. K. Johnson, "Anyasan-Silaiim," p. 8; Claude N. Kline to author, (tape), 16 January 1980; and Sanders, "Anyasan-Silaiim," p. 15.

[36] Sanders, "Anyasan-Silaiim," pp. 15–16.

[37] *Ibid.,* pp. 17–19; H. K. Johnson, "Anyasan-Silaiim," p. 9; and Gordon to author, (tape), 21 August 1980. Dr. Gordon recalls that many men were wounded here, but all but ten were back to duty in two weeks. Waterous, *Reminiscences,* p. 31; and Reynolds to author, 13 March 1977.

[38] Mills to author, 11 July 1978 and 27 November 1974.

[39] H. K. Johnson, "Anyasan-Silaiim," p. 12.

[40] Knox to author, 14 May 1978; Poweleit, *USAFFE,* p. 22; Morton, *Fall,* p. 319; and Sanders, "Anyasan-Silaiim," p. 25.

[41] Kline to author, (tape), 14 December 1979; Pena, *Bataan's Own,* pp. 127–128; H. K. Johnson, "Anyasan-Silaiim," p. 9; and Poweleit, *USAFFE,* p. 35.

[42] Kline to author, (tape), 14 December 1979; and H. K. Johnson, "Anyasan-Silaiim," p. 9.

[43] Knox to author, 6 April 1977 and 14 May 1978.

[44] Knox to author, 14 May 1978; and H. K. Johnson, "Anyasan-Silaiim," p. 9.

[45] Mills to author, 11 July 1978; Saalman to author, 25 March and 6 June 1976; H. K. Johnson, "Anyasan-Silaiim," p. 11; and Sanders, "Anyasan-Silaiim," p. 26.

[46] Morton, *Fall,* p. 303 and 320; Howard, "Unit History," p. 12. One exception to the problems in using artillery was the support rendered to the 1st Battalion, 57th Infantry. Company commanders observed the fall of shells and called corrections over telephones. The resulting support was excellent; and Sanders, "Anyasan-Silaiim," p. 25.

[47] Anders to author, 9 June 1977; and Pena, *Bataan's Own,* p. 128.

[48] Pena, *Bataan's Own,* p. 129; and Leo Arhutick, "Diary," p. 3. Pena's battalion was short its C Company but had attached the 3rd Battalion's I Company.

[49] Sanders, "Anyasan-Silaiim," pp. 29–32; H. K. Johnson, "Anyasan-Silaiim," p. 12; and Annex XIV, p. 46.

[50] Knox to author, 6 April 1977.

[51] 14 Army Headquarters, "Tactical Situation Report," p. 4; and Morton, *Fall,* p. 322.

[52] Morton, *Fall,* p. 322; and Falk, "Folio," p. 84.

[53] Arhutick, "Diary," p. 3.

[54] Marlow to author, 6 February 1984; Gage to author, 2 June 1977; Arhutick, "Diary," p. 3; USAFFE International News Summary #47, Press Release Section; *Reports of MacArthur,* p. 108; *Japanese Monograph No. 1,* p. 105; and Morton, *Fall,* p. 322.

[55] H. K. Johnson, "Anyasan-Silaiim," pp. 13–14; and Reynolds to author, 13 March 1977.

[56] Pena, *Bataan's Own,* pp. 130–131; and USAFFE General Order #39, 12 March 1942.

[57] Pena, *Bataan's Own,* pp. 132–133; Morton, *Fall,* p. 322; Sanders, "Anyasan-Silaiim," p. 34; H. K. Johnson, "Anyasan-Silaiim," p. 13; and Collier, "Notebooks," 3:46.

[58] Pena, *Bataan's Own,* p. 131; and USAFFE General Order #40, 13 March 1942.

[59] Vogler to author, 12 June 1978; Mills to author, 27 November 1974; and Pena, *Bataan's Own,* pp. 131–132.

[60] Amato/Murphy, "History, 2d-45th," pp. 11–12 and 12 supplement, in Chunn, "Notebook;" Morton, *Fall,* p. 323; Marlow to author, 6 February 1984; and James O. Hase to The Adjutant General, 18 May 1944, in Chunn, "Notebook."

[61] Morton, *Fall,* p. 323; Amato/Murphy, "History, 2d-45th," pp. 11–12, in Chunn, "Notebook;" Conn, "War Diary;" Crosby, "History of 17th Pursuit Squadron," p. 49, in Chunn, "Notebook;" and H. K. Johnson, "Diary," p. 17.

[62] Saalman to author, 6 June and 25 March 1976.

[63] Amato/Murphy, "History, 2d-45th," p. 12, in Chunn, "Notebook;" and USAFFE General Order #39, 12 March 1942.

[64] Kline to author, (tape), 14 December 1979; Anders to author, 23 April and 11 September 1981 and 22 October 1986; and Saalman to author, 6 June 1976.

[65] Vogler to author, 12 June 1978; Amato/Murphy, "History, 2d-45th," p. 12, in Chunn, "Notebook;" and Saalman to author, 6 June 1976.

[66] Knox to author, 14 May 1978; Annex XIII, p. 182; Amato/Murphy, "History, 2d-45th," p. 12, in Chunn, "Notebook;" H. K. Johnson, "Diary," p. 17; and Vogler to author, 6 October 1975.

[67] Morton, *Fall,* p. 324; Headquarters, Philippine Army General Order #375, 6 October 1947; J. C. Blanning, "War Diary," pp. 11–12; and Chandler, "Battles To Glory," 2:12.

[68] Blanning, "War Diary," pp. 13–15.

[69] Morton, *Fall,* p. 324.

[70] Stempin to author, 11 February 1975; and Bardowski to author, (tape), 27 August 1976.

[71] Radio, MacArthur to AG, 15 February 1942.

[72] War Department General Order #14, 9 March 1942.

Trail 2

[1] Morton, *Fall,* p. 325; Toland, *But Not in Shame,* p. 185; and "65 Bde, Samat," p. 2.

[2] "65 Bde, Samat," p. 3.

[3] *Ibid.,* pp. 2, 8, 9, and 83.

[4] Morton, *Fall,* pp. 325 and 328; James V. Collier to Louis Morton, 2 May 1951, p. 1; and Constant L. Irwin to Orlando Ward, 13 June 1951, p. 1.

[5] Collier to Morton, 2 May 1951, p. 1.

[6] Morton, *Fall,* pp. 328–329; Annex V, p. 39; and James V. Collier to author, 30 May 1975.

[7] Morton, *Fall,* p. 329; Annex V, p. 39; and Anders to author, 13 June 1976.

[8] Bluemel, "31 Div," p. 11.

[9] *Ibid.,* p. 12; and Emerson to author, 17 April 1975.

[10] Bluemel, "31 Div," p. 12.

[11] *Ibid.*

[12] Din to author, 27 August 1981; Bluemel, "31 Div," p. 12; Stuart C. MacDonald, "Notes on Left Subsector, I Philippine Corps," p. 1, in supplement to Jones, "Diary," hereafter referred to as MacDonald, "Left Subsector;" *Army Register 1941,* p. 943; and MacDonald, "Important Dates-SLF," pp. 10–11.

[13] Mallonee, "Bataan Diary," 2:34.

[14] Toland, *But Not in Shame,* p. 184.

[15] Bluemel, "Oral Reminiscences," p. 20; and Bluemel, "31 Div," p. 13.

[16] Bluemel, "Oral Reminiscences," p. 25.

[17] Toland, *But Not in Shame,* p. 184; and Bluemel, "31 Div," p. 13.

[18] Bluemel, "Oral Reminiscences," p. 20; Bluemel, "31 Div," p. 13; and Annex V, p. 39.

[19] Bluemel, "31 Div," p. 13; Annex V, p. 39; and Morton, *Fall,* p. 331.

[20] Annex V, p. 39; Wetherby, "Mabatang-Abucay," pp. 141 and 145; Bluemel, "31 Div," p. 14; Fortier, "Notes of Fortier," p. 61; and Fortier, "Ops 41 Div," p. 3.

[21] Wetherby, "Mabatang-Abucay," pp. 140–144; and O'Day, "Hist of 21 Div," 2:31.

[22] "65 Bde, Samat," p. 4; and Morton, *Fall,* p. 330.

[23] "65 Bde, Samat," pp. 7–8.

[24] *Ibid.,* p. 1.

[25] *Ibid.,* pp. 8–9; and Morton, *Fall,* p. 332.

[26] "65 Bde, Samat," p. 9.

[27] *Ibid.,* pp. 9–10; and Morton, *Fall,* p. 332.

[28] O'Day, "Hist of 21 Div," 2:31; "65 Bde, Samat," pp. 9 and 40; and Morton, *Fall,* p. 332.

[29] Martin, "51st Inf," p. 5; and "65 Bde, Samat," p. 10.

[30] "65 Bde, Samat," pp. 2 and 5; and *Japanese Monograph No. 2,* pp. 110–111.

[31] "65 Bde, Samat," pp. 2, 4, and 6.

[32] Annex V, p. 43; Morton, *Fall,* p. 332; Wetherby, "Mabatang-Abucay," pp. 145–146; and Bluemel, "31 Div," p. 14.

[33] "65 Bde, Samat," pp. 10, 11, and 44.

[34] Mallonee, "Bataan Diary," 2:56; *Japanese Monograph No. 2,* p. 110; Falk, "Folio," pp. 81 and 84; "65 Bde, Samat," pp. 11 and 45; and Quintard, "Diary," 29 January 1942.

[35] Morton, *Fall,* p. 334.

[36] Bluemel, "31 Div," p. 15; Bluemel to Ward, 17 January 1952; Falk, "Folio," p. 81; Loren A. Wetherby, "Actions of 41st Inf fr Jan 28 1942–April-1942," pp. 146–147, copied by Fortier in his "Notes on 41st Div," hereafter referred to as Wetherby, "41st Inf Jan–April;" and Quintard, "Diary," 29 January 1942.

[37] Bluemel, "Oral Reminiscences," p. 26; Wetherby, "41st Inf Jan–April," p. 146; Bluemel, "31 Div," p. 15; and Emerson, "Ops II Corps," p. 20.

[38] "65 Bde, Samat," p. 12; and Bluemel, "31 Div," p. 15.

[39] George C. Groce to Clifford Bluemel, 24 June 1948; and "65 Bde, Samat," pp. 12–14.

[40] "9th Inf. Bataan;" and "65 Bde, Samat," pp. 47 and 85.

[41] "65 Bde, Samat," p. 14; Wetherby, "41st Inf Jan–April," p. 148; and Bluemel, "31 Div," p. 16.

[42] "65 Bde, Samat," pp. 14–15; Bluemel, "31 Div," p. 16; and Annex V, p. 44.

[43] "65 Bde, Samat," pp. 14, 16, and 47; and Morton, *Fall,* p. 335.

[44] Annex V, p. 44; Wetherby, "41st Inf Jan–April," p. 148; Bluemel, "31 Div," p. 16; and Restituto Chanco to author, 5 February 1988.

[45] "65 Bde, Samat," p. 17.

[46] *Japanese Monograph No. 1,* p. 42; Wetherby, "41st Inf Jan–April," p. 149; "65 Bde, Samat," pp. 19 and 23; and Bluemel, "31 Div," p. 17.

[47] Charles A. Willoughby, "G2 Estimate, February 3rd 1942 to February 5th 1942;" Bluemel, "31 Div," p. 16; Bluemel to Groce, 15 June

1948; "Statements," 3:93; "65 Bde, Samat," pp. 20 and 35; and *Reports of MacArthur,* p. 110.

[48] "65 Bde, Samat," p. 21.

The Pockets

[1] MacDonald, "Left Subsector," p. 9; and Rodman, "91 Div.," p. 6.

[2] William E. Brougher, "The Battle of Bataan," 21 April 1942, p. 3, hereafter referred to as Brougher, "Battle of Bataan."

[3] Volckmann, *We Remained,* p. 25; Cullum, *Register,* IX, p. 813; and Leslie T. Lathrop, "The Tuol Pocket," p. 1, hereafter referred to as Lathrop, "Tuol Pocket."

[4] 11th Division General Order #15, 27 January 1942.

[5] Annex IV, p. 22.

[6] Dod, *Engineers Against Japan,* p. 91; Lathrop, "Tuol Pocket," p. 1; Stuart C. MacDonald, "Pocket Fights," p. 1, supplement to Jones, "Diary;" Berry, "History 3rd Inf," p. 5; MacDonald, "Left Subsector," p. 1; and Fitch, "Siege," p. 17.

[7] Toland, *But Not in Shame,* p. 192; MacDonald "Left Subsector," p. 2; and MacDonald, "Pocket Fights," p. 1.

[8] Morton, *Fall,* pp. 338–339.

[9] Townsend, "Tuol Pocket," p. 6; and MacDonald, "Left Subsector," pp. 2–3.

[10] Lathrop, "Tuol Pocket," pp. 1–2; James, "11th Infantry (PA)," pp. 8–9, in Chunn, "Notebook;" and Townsend, "Tuol Pocket," pp. 6–7.

[11] Lathrop, "Tuol Pocket," p. 2; and Townsend, "Tuol Pocket," pp. 7–8.

[12] *Ibid.*

[13] Adrianus J. Van Oosten, "The Operations of the 1st Battalion, 45th Infantry (PS)(Philippine Division) in the Battle of the Tuol Pocket, Bataan, 29 January–19 February 1942 (Philippine Island Campaign)(Personal Experience of a Battalion Executive Officer)," p. 6, a monograph written for Infantry Officer Advanced Course #2, 1947–1948, hereafter referred to as Van Oosten, "1st, 45 Inf;" Lathrop, "Tuol Pocket," p. 2; and Archie L. McMasters, "Memoirs of the Tuol Pocket," 18 October 1947, p. 2, hereafter referred to as McMasters, "Memoirs Tuol."

[14] Van Oosten, "1st, 45 Inf," pp. 6–8 and 10; Van Oosten to author, 1 August 1974; *Army Register 1941,* p. 492; and Stewart to author, 14 July 1975.

[15] Van Oosten, "1st, 45 Inf," pp. 8–9 and 11; Stewart to author, 18 June 1975; Lathrop, "Tuol Pocket," p. 2; and Townsend, "Tuol Pocket," p. 10.

[16] McMasters, "Memoirs Tuol," p. 2; and Townsend, "Tuol Pocket," p. 10.

[17] McMaster, "Memoirs Tuol," p. 2.

[18] Stewart to author, 18 June 1975, and subsequent quotations are from the same source; and Stewart to Van Oosten, 7 October 1947.

[19] Van Oosten to author, 1 August 1974; Townsend, "Tuol Pocket," p. 10; Lathrop, "Tuol Pocket," p. 3; Cullum, *Register,* IX, p. 626; and Van Oosten, "1st, 45 Inf," p. 12.

[20] Lathrop, "Tuol Pocket," p. 3; Paul A. Krauss, "Anti-Tank Company 45th Inf. (PS)," p. 2, in Chunn, "Notebook;" and Stewart to Van Oosten, 7 October 1947.

[21] Interview with Daniel N. Stoudt, Bethel, Pennsylvania, 6 August 1977; Lathrop, "Tuol Pocket," p. 4; Townsend, "Tuol Pocket," p. 12; and Knox to author, 6 April 1977.

[22] McMasters, "Memoirs Tuol," pp. 3–4.

[23] Cahill to author, 24 July 1975.

[24] USAFFE General Order #35, 4 March 1942; and Van Oosten, "1st, 45 Inf," p. 15.

[25] Van Oosten to author, 1 and 17 August 1974; Van Oosten, "1st, 45 Inf," p. 15; and Townsend, "Tuol Pocket," p. 13.

[26] McMaster, "Memoirs Tuol," p. 4; Lathrop, "Tuol Pocket," p. 5; and Van Oosten, "1st, 45 Inf," p. 15.

[27] Wainwright, "Story," p. 47; and USAFFE General Order #39, 12 March 1942.

[28] Bardowski to author, (tapes), 9 July 1976 and 13 February 1977; and Wainwright, *Story,* p. 47.

[29] Van S. Merle-Smith to Asst. Chief of Staff, G-2, War Department, 27 January 1942, Subject: Arrival of hospital ship from Philippines, p. 3; and Bardowski to author, (tape), 13 February 1977 and 9 July 1976.

[30] Bardowski to author, (tape), 9 July 1976; and Poweleit, *USAFFE,* p. 16.

[31] Wildish to author, 10 November 1977; and Van Oosten, "1st, 45 Inf," p. 16.

[32] Wildish to author, 9 January 1978; and Townsend, "Tuol Pocket," p. 11.

[33] McMaster, "Memoirs Tuol," pp. 4–5; Bardowski to author, (tape), 26 August 1976; and Volckmann, "Colonel Russell William Volckmann."

[34] Stewart to author, 14 July 1975; and Van Oosten, "1st, 45 Inf," p. 28.

[35] Weinstein, *Barbed Wire Surgeon,* p. 32; Skardon, "Ops A, 92d," pp. 11–12; and Stewart to author, 14 July 1975.

[36] Bardowski to author, (tape), 27 August 1976; Provisional Tank Group General Order #10, 14 February 1942; and Poweleit, *USAFFE,* p. 36.

[37] McMasters, "Memoirs Tuol," p. 5; and Volckmann, "Colonel Russell William Volckmann."

[38] McMasters, "Memoirs Tuol," p. 5; and Van Oosten, "1st, 45 Inf," p. 17.

[39] Lathrop, "Tuol Pocket," p. 5; and Townsend, "Tuol Pocket," p. 15.

[40] Lee, *Pacific,* p. 236; MacDonald, "Left Subsector," p. 7; Philippine Army General Order #201, 16 September 1947; and Berry, "History 3rd Inf," p. 6.

[41] Townsend, "Tuol Pocket," p. 15.

[42] Toland, *But Not in Shame,* p. 195; MacDonald, "Left Subsector," pp. 4 and 8; Schultz, *Hero of Bataan,* p. 176; MacDonald, "Pocket Fights," p. 2; Annex IV, p. 27; Townsend, "Tuol Pocket," p. 14; and Morton, *Fall,* p. 342.

[43] James, *South to Bataan,* comments of Colonel Townsend, pp. 25–26; and MacDonald, "Pocket Fights," p. 2.

[44] MacDonald, "Left Subsector," pp. 5–7; USAFFE General Order #27, 16 February 1942; and MacDonald, "Pocket Fights," p. 2.

[45] MacDonald, "Left Subsector," p. 8; Van Oosten, "1st, 45 Inf," p. 19; Townsend, "Toul Pocket," p. 18; and Lathrop, "Tuol Pocket," p. 6.

[46] MacDonald, "Left Subsector," pp. 7–8; and Van Oosten, "1st, 45 Inf," p. 19.

[47] McMasters, "Memoirs Tuol," p. 5; Edward Stewart to Adrianus J. Van Oosten, 7 October 1947; Stewart to author, 14 July 1975; and MacDonald, "Left Subsector," p. 8.

[48] Falk, "Folio," pp. 88–90; Morton, *Fall,* pp. 347–348; Wood to Morton, 23 March 1948; and *Japanese Monograph No. 1,* p. 116.

[49] Sevilla, *Odyssey,* pp. 31–32; and McMasters, "Memoirs Tuol," pp. 6–7.

[50] James, *South to Bataan,* pp. 22–25; and Lathrop, "Tuol Pocket," p. 5.

[51] Lathrop, "Tuol Pocket," p. 5; Headquarters, 11th Division, "Supplemental Report to Accompany G-2 Report, 11th Division, on February 19, 1942;" Van Oosten, "1st, 45 Inf," p. 29; and Townsend, "Tuol Pocket," p. 18.

[52] Townsend, "Tuol Pocket," p. 16; and Pena, *Bataan's Own,* p. 147.

[53] Pena, *Bataan's Own,* p. 149; Townsend, "Tuol Pocket," p. 17; and Lathrop, "Tuol Pocket," p. 6.

[54] USAFFE General Order #40, 13 March 1942; Pena, *Bataan's Own,* p. 162; and Lathrop, "Tuol Pocket," p. 6.

[55] Townsend, "Tuol Pocket," p. 16; and James, *South to Bataan,* p. 25.

[56] Morton, *Fall,* p. 345; and Lathrop, "Tuol Pocket," p. 6.

[57] I Corps General Order #16, 28 February 1942.

[58] MacDonald, "Left Subsector," pp. 9–10.

The Japanese Retreat

[1] Radio, MacArthur to the AG, 26 February 1942; Toland, *But Not in Shame,* p. 197; and Morton, *Fall,* p. 347.

[2] Toland, *But Not in Shame,* pp. 197–198.

[3] Morton, *Fall,* p. 347.

[4] Ibid; Toland, *But Not In Shame,* p. 198; and Armed Forces of the Philippines, "The Japanese Plan of Maneuver in the Final Battle of Bataan," 1963, Military History Branch, hereafter referred to as Armed Forces Philippines, "Plan of Maneuver."

[5] Morton, *Fall,* p. 347; Schultz, *Hero of Bataan,* p. 61; and Agoncillo, *Fateful Years,* 1:158–159.

[6] Morton, *Fall,* p. 347; and "65 Bde, Samat," p. 86.

[7] Raymond Rudorff, *War to the Death. The Sieges of Saragossa, 1808–1809* (New York: Macmillan Publishing Co., Inc., 1974), p. 251; and Toland, *But Not in Shame,* pp. 198–199.

[8] Radio, MacArthur to the AG, 7 March 1942; and Morton, *Fall,* p. 350.

[9] Morton, *Fall,* p. 488; Wainwright, Rpt Ops USAFFE-USFIP, p. 54; and William M. Belote, interview with Colonel Jesus A. Villamor, 29 July 1963, West Hyattville, Maryland, p. 1, in Belote Research Papers, USAMHI.

[10] William N. Hess, *Pacific Sweep. The 5th and 13th Fighter Commands in World War II* (Garden City, New York: Doubleday & Company, Inc., 1974) p. 14, hereafter referred to as Hess, *Pacific Sweep;* Hersey, *Men on Bataan,* p. 218; Belote interview with Villamor, pp. 1–3; Ind, *Judgment Seat,* p. 288; and Beck, *MacArthur and Wainwright,* p. 33.

[11] J. White to author, 4 August 1976; and Ind, *Judgment Seat,* p. 290.

[12] Ind, *Judgment Seat,* pp. 291–292; Hess, *Pacific Sweep,* pp. 14–15; and J. White to author, 4 August 1976.

[13] *Reports of MacArthur,* p. 1.

[14] *Japanese Monograph No. 2, Philippine Operations Record Phase 1, (November 1941–10 April 1942),* Historical Section, G2, GHQ, FEC, supplemental chart 11, hereafter referred to as *Japanese Monograph No. 2;* Morton, *Fall,* pp. 349–350; and Louis Morton, "Estimated Japanese Ground Force Strength (Effective) On the Eve of the April Offensive," hereafter referred to as Morton, "Japanese Ground Strength."

[15] "65 Bde, Natib," pp. 33 and 38; and "65 Bde, Samat," p. 34.

[16] Morton, *Fall,* pp. 345 and 350.

[17] Quintard, "Diary," 15 February 1942; William Montgomery, "Diary," p. 21; and "65 Bde, Samat," pp. 26, 56, 86, and 87.

[18] Quintard, "Diary," 17 February 1942; and "65 Bde, Samat," pp. 26–27.

[19] "65 Bde, Samat," p. 28; Montgomery, "Diary," p. 20; and Morton, *Fall*, p. 348.

[20] Montgomery, "Diary," p. 24; and Fortier, "Notes of Fortier," p. 69.

[21] Quintard, "Diary," 24 February 1942; and USAFFE G2 Bulletin #28, February 19–24, 1942.

[22] Morton, *Fall*, pp. 350–351; and Nicoll F. Galbraith, memorandum to G4, USAFFE, 10 February 1942.

[23] Radio, MacArthur to the AG, 28 January 1942; and subsequent quote is from the same message.

[24] Radio, MacArthur to Marshall, 8 February 1942, and radio to the AG, 28 January 1942.

[25] Radio, MacArthur to Marshall, 8 February 1942.

[26] Radio, Roosevelt to Quezon, 11 February 1942.

[27] Radio, Roosevelt to MacArthur, 9 February 1942; Quezon, *The Good Fight*, pp. 270–274; and Beck, *MacArthur and Wainwright*, pp. 102–104.

[28] Radio, Roosevelt to MacArthur, 9 February 1942.

[29] Quezon, *The Good Fight*, p. 275; and Beck, *MacArthur and Wainwright*, pp. 104–105. Quezon was so upset he resigned the presidency and read his resignation to his cabinet. Obviously he reconsidered, see Beck, *MacArthur and Wainwright*, p. 107.

[30] Radio, MacArthur to Roosevelt, 11 February 1942; and Morton, *Fall*, p. 390.

[31] Bluemel, "31 Div," p. 18; USAFFE G2 Bulletin #30, February 25–26; Fortier, "Notes of Fortier," p. 69; and Morton, *Fall*, p. 351. Japanese outposts facing II Corps lay along the Balanga-Guitol Trail, Bluemel, "31 Div," p. 17.

[32] USAFFE International News Summary #65, 28 February 1942, Press Release Section.

[33] Morton, *Fall*, p. 351, a paraphrase of the actual message.

[34] Achille C. Tisdelle, "Diary," 23 February 1942; and Message from Commander Sixteenth Naval District, February 11, 1942, 110550Z from DIO for Director of Naval Intelligence.

[35] Juan B. Hernandez, *Not the Sword* (New York: Greenwich Book Publishers, 1959), pp. 46–47; and Waterous, *Reminiscences*, p. 50.

[36] *Japanese Monograph No. 2*, p. 17; Agoncillo, *Fateful Years*, 1:160–161; and Hernandez, *Not the Sword*, pp. 44–46.

[37] Hersey, *Men on Bataan* p. 98, and subsequent quotes are from the same source.

[38] Hanson Baldwin, *Battles Lost and Won: Great Campaigns of World War II* (New York: Harper & Row, 1966), pp. 1–3.

[39] Montgomery, "Diary," p. 26; Workman to author, 19 June 1976; and Waterous, *Reminiscences*, p. 19.

[40] Mallonee to Ward, 8 January 1952, p. 2; and Morton, *Fall*, p. 352.

[41] Montgomery, "I Hired Out to Fight," pp. 38–39.

[42] *Ibid.,* p. 40.

[43] Interview with Laird, 30 December 1973; Walter Bell to author, (tape), 7 July 1976; and Annex XII, pp. 22–23.

[44] Workman to author, 19 January 1976; Annex XII, p. 22; and Doyle, Lecture, 30 July 1942, p. 8.

[45] James, *South to Bataan,* p. 26; Roscoe Bonham, "Engineer Supply Luzon Campaign 41–42;" and Annex XVII: Report of Operations, Signal Corps, United States Army, 8 December 1941–6 May 1942, in four phases, 4:3, in Wainwright, Rpt Ops USAFFE-USFIP, hereafter referred to as Annex XVII.

[46] Mellnik, *Philippine Diary,* p. 32; and Gilewitch to author, 15 April 1975.

[47] Interview with J. Martin, 14 February 1976; and Montgomery, "Diary," p. 25.

[48] Skerry to Ward, 16 January 1952, from Skerry, "Operations NLF Engineers;" and E. Q. Bringas, Letter to Surgeon, Sub-Sector "D", II Corps, 14 March 1942, Subject: Medical Service of the 21st Division from Jan. 26, 1942 to Feb. 28, 1942, hereafter referred to as Bringas, "Medical Service of 21 Div."

[49] Dod, *Engineers Against Japan,* pp. 68, 90–91; and Skerry to Meidling, 4 August 1947.

[50] Clinton A Pierce to Arnold J. Funk, 16 April 1946; Morton, *Fall,* p. 411; Meidling, *Engrs in Theater Ops,* p. 21; Annex IV, p. 29; and Dod, *Engineers Against Japan,* p. 97.

[51] 11th Division General Order #15, 27 January 1942; and Brougher, "Battle of Bataan," p. 3.

[52] Brougher, "Cmd Cbt Div," pp. 1–6.

[53] Townsend, "The Final Phase," p. 1; Brougher, "Cmd Cbt Div," p. 6; and James, *South to Bataan,* p. 27.

[54] Dod, *Engineers Against Japan,* p. 97; and O'Oay, "Hist of 21 Div," 2:38–39.

[55] Annex XIV, p. 27; and O'Day, "Hist of 21 Div," 2:32.

[56] Walter H. Waterous, "Statement of Experiences and Observations Concerning the Bataan Campaign and Subsequent Imprisonment," p. 51, hereafter referred to as Waterous, "Statement;" and Annex XIV, pp. 28–32.

[57] H. W. Glattly, Memorandum to: The Surgeons, 21st and 41st Divisions, 6 March 1942; Annex XIV, p. 35; Annex VI, p. 1; and Philip R. Parish to author, 13 May 1977.

[58] Waterous, *Reminiscences,* pp. 20–23; Sullivan, "Hospital Number "2", Bataan, PI," p. 15; and Hartendorp, *Japanese Occupation,* p. 178.

[59] Alvin L. Fry to author, 26 April and 16 September 1978; and Hartendorp, *Japanese Occupation,* p. 179.

[60] Waterous, *Reminiscences,* p. 41; Weinstein, *Barbed Wire Surgeon,* p. 25; Annex XIII, p. 206; Annex XIV, p. 25; Juanita Redmond, *I Served on*

Bataan (Philadelphia & New York: J. B. Lippincott Company, 1943), pp. 44 and 56–57; Weitzner to author, (tape), 27 July 1981; and McBride, "Notes on the Fall," p. 109.

[61] USAFFE General Order #39, 12 March 1942; and O'Day, "Hist of 21 Div," 2:32–33.

[62] Montgomery, "Diary," p. 27; and Montgomery, "I Hired Out To Fight," p. 48.

[63] Montgomery, "I Hired Out to Fight," pp. 47–48; and O'Day, "Hist of 21 Div," 2:32.

[64] O'Day, "Hist of 21 Div," 2:38; and Quintard, "Diary," 27 February and 8 March 1942.

[65] Romulo, *I Saw the Fall,* pp. 200–201; Wainwright, *Story,* p. 49; Sutherland to Morton, 29 May 1951; interview with Laird, 30 December 1973; and Montgomery, "I Hired Out to Fight," p. 57.

[66] Montgomery, "I Hired Out to Fight," p. 47; and James J. Rubard to author, 4 February 1977.

[67] Stewart H. Holbrook, *None More Courageous. American War Heroes of Today* (New York: The Macmillan Company, 1942), p. 11; Mellnik, *Philippine Diary,* p. 96; and Agoncillo, *Fateful Years* p. 147.

[68] Montgomery, "I Hired Out to Fight," p. 47.

[69] USAFFE General Order #31, 22 February 1942; and Collier, "Notebooks," 2:8.

[70] Koury, "Comments," p. 23; and Conrad, "Ops 31 Inf," p. 27.

[71] Whitney, *MacArthur: His Rendezvous With History,* p. 35.

[72] Fortier, "Notes of Fortier," p. 69.

[73] Morton, *Fall,* p. 390; and radio, MacArthur to Marshall, 17 January 1942.

[74] Morton, *Fall,* pp. 391–392.

[75] Annex XIII, p. 39; Charles S. Lawrence, "Notebook, Record of Events December 27, 1941 to April 9, 1942 Bataan," p. 73, hereafter referred to as Lawrence, "Record of Events;" and Morton, *Fall,* pp. 392–393.

[76] Vincente W. Labrador, "The Ship That Died Hard," *The Quan* vol. 35, no. 4 (January 1981); Edwin P. Hoyt, *The Lonely Ships. The Life and Death of the U.S. Asiatic Fleet* (New York: David McKay Company, Inc., 1976), p. 236; radio, MG George H. Brett to MacArthur, 13 March 1942; "Blockade Running to the Philippines," pp. 31–33, all Brett radios are in Willoughby, "Aid the Philippines;" radio, Brett to AG War, 25 March 1942; and Annex XIII, pp. 39 and 147.

[77] Radio, MacArthur to Marshall, 22 February 1942, cited in Beck, *MacArthur and Wainwright,* p. 119; radio, Brett to War Department, 11 March 1942; Felix Riesenberg Jr., *Sea War. The Story of the U. S. Merchant Marine in World War II* (New York: Rinehart & Company, Inc., 1956), p. 47; and "Blockade Running to the Philippines," p. 33.

[78] "Blockade Running to the Philippines," p. 31; Drake, "No Uncle

Sam," p. 18; Annex XIII, p. 39; and Office of the Chief of Military History, "Resume of Philippine Relief Operations," p. 3, hereafter referred to as OCMH, "Resume."

79 "Aid the Philippines, Dec 41–Feb 42," extracted from Medical Diary, Hq, USASOS SW Pacific Area, Office of the Chief Surgeon, December 41 to June 42, a paper in the Charles A. Willoughby Papers; OCMH, "Resume," p. 3; and "Blockade Running to the Philippines," p. 33.

80 Drake, "No Uncle Sam," p. 14; and Annex XIII, p. 37.

81 Quezon, *The Good Fight,* p. 252; and Drake, "No Uncle Sam," p. 14.

82 Quezon, *The Good Fight,* pp. 252–253; Annex XIII, p. 37; and Drake, "No Uncle Sam," p. 14.

83 Annex XIII, pp. 38–39; and Charles C. Drake to Orlando Ward, 12 February 1952.

84 Drake, "No Uncle Sam," p. 16; and Annex XIII, pp. 38 and 69.

85 Annex XIII, p. 39.

86 "Blockade Running to the Philippines," pp. 34–36.

87 *Ibid.,* pp. 35–36.

88 *Ibid.,* p. 36.

89 Clay Blair Jr., *Silent Victory. The U.S. Submarine War Against Japan* (New York: Bantam Books, 1975), p. 172, hereafter referred to as Blair, *Silent Victory;* although Morton's *Fall,* pp. 399–400 claims fifty-three tons unloaded, that includes a complete unloading of the *Snapper's* forty-six tons, but Blair's *Silent Victory* records only twenty tons unloaded, thus the difference between the figures. I elected to use Blair's figure; and "Blockade Running to the Philippines," p. 37.

90 Blair, *Silent Victory,* pp. 206–207.

91 *Ibid.,* pp. 173, 174, and 193.

92 Dyess, *The Dyess Story,* pp. 47–48; Morton, *Fall,* p. 400; and Underbrink, *Destination Corregidor,* pp. 183–185.

93 Annex XIII, pp. 34–36 and 68.

94 Drake, "No Uncle Sam," p. 11; and Annex XIII, pp. 35–36.

95 Drake, "No Uncle Sam," p. 10; Annex XIII, p. 35; Frank Brezina, "Report, QM Philippine Department to QM USAFFE, 27 February 1942;" and Read, "Comments," pp. 47–48.

96 Read, "Comments," p. 44; Morton, *Fall,* p. 254; McBride, "Notes on the Fall," p. 110; Buenafe, *Wartime Philippines,* p. 99; Waterous, *Reminiscences,* pp. 25 and 48; Hartendorp, *Japanese Occupation,* p. 121; and USAFFE G2 Bulletin #23, February 13–14, 1942.

97 Fortier, "Brief Hist 41 Div," p. 66; and Fortier, "Ops 41 Div," p. 4.

98 Bluemel to Ward, 17 January 1952; Annex XIII, p. 36; and Charles C. Drake, Office of the Quartermaster, USFIP to the G4, 29 March 1942. Another man reported that a widely-held but erroneous belief that a few healthy maggots in fresh meat rendered it unfit resulted in the destruction of some meat which could have been eaten, from Lawrence, "Notebook," p. 19.

[99] Nicoll F. Galbraith, note to G4, USAFFE, 10 February 1942; and Morton, *Fall,* p. 371.

[100] Townsend, "Defense of Philippines," p. 14.

[101] Morton, *Fall,* p. 370; Read, "Comments," p. 47; and Quintard, "Diary," 22 and 30 March 1942.

[102] Walter King and Welbourn Kelley, *Battle Report. Pearl Harbor to Coral Sea* (New York: Farrar and Rinehart, Inc., 1944), p. 305, hereafter referred to as King and Kelley, *Battle Report;* and Sackett, "History Canopus."

[103] Sackett, "History Canopus;" and King and Kelley, *Battle Report,* pp. 305–308.

[104] Kelley, *Battle Report,* p. 308.

[105] Sackett, "History Canopus," p. 18.

[106] Mills to author, 27 November 1974; and Montgomery, "I Hired Out To Fight," p. 53.

[107] Radio, MacArthur to Marshall, 2 February 1942.

[108] Radio, Marshall to MacArthur, 2 February 1942.

[109] Blair, *Silent Victory,* p. 174; and Quezon, *The Good Fight,* p. 276.

[110] Radio, Marshall to MacArthur, 4 February 1942.

[111] *Ibid;* and MacArthur, *Reminiscences,* p. 140.

[112] Radio, Marshall to MacArthur, 22 February 1942.

[113] Radio, MacArthur to Marshall, 24 February 1942; and Morton, *Fall,* p. 357.

[114] Wainwright, *Story,* pp. 8 and 49, and subsequent conversations which include Wainwright come from *Story,* pp. 9–10.

[115] Edgar D. Whitcomb, *Escape from Corregidor* (Chicago: Henry Regnery Company, 1958), p. 40; and Wainwright, *Story,* p. 11.

[116] Toland, *But Not in Shame,* p. 301.

[117] Poweleit, *USAFFE,* p. 41.

[118] Mallonee, "Bataan Diary," 2:68; and Romulo, *I Saw the Fall,* p. 220.

[119] Morton, *Fall,* pp. 361, 362 and 365; and Arnold J. Funk, "Comments on Fall of the Philippines," 12 January 1952.

[120] Beck, *MacArthur and Wainwright,* pp. 176–177; and Morton, *Fall,* p. 362.

[121] Radio, Marshall to Wainwright, 17 March 1942.

[122] USFIP General Order #1, 21 March 1942.

[123] Beck, *MacArthur and Wainwright,* p. 177, taken from the diary of Lieutenant Colonel John R. Pugh, 15 March 1942; and Morton, *Fall,* p. 365.

Japanese Reinforcements

[1] Morton, *Fall,* p. 57.

[2] Ibid., pp. 412–413; Translations of Japanese Documents, Vol VI, "Information Regarding Strength and Composition of Japanese Forces, Philippine Islands Dec 41–May 42," 15 August 1949, p. 5, hereafter referred to as "Translations;" and *Reports of MacArthur,* p. 111.

[3] Armed Forces of the Philippines, "Plan of Maneuver," p. 5; Morton, *Fall,* p. 413; and *Reports of MacArthur,* p. 110.

[4] Morton, *Fall,* p. 413; *Reports of MacArthur,* p. 5; and Saburo Hayashi, *KOGUN. The Japanese Army in the Pacific War* (Baltimore, Maryland: Monumental Printing Co., 1959), p. 38.

[5] Morton, *Fall,* pp. 413–414; and *Reports of MacArthur,* p. 5.

[6] Morton, *Fall,* p. 414; *Reports of MacArthur,* p. 111; and Stanley L. Falk, "Folio," p. 93.

[7] Morton, *Fall,* pp. 414 and 493; and *Japanese Monograph No. 11,* p. 43.

[8] *Reports of MacArthur,* p. 112; "Statements," 4:547; and Japanese newspaper, *Maininchi,* 3 April 1943.

[9] "65 Bde, Samat," pp. 98 and 104.

[10] *Ibid.,* p. 99.

[11] *Ibid.,* p. 100.

[12] *Ibid.,* pp. 100–101.

[13] *Ibid.,* pp. 99–102.

[14] *Ibid.,* p. 110.

[15] *Ibid.,* pp. 103–104.

[16] *Mainichi,* 3 April 1943.

[17] "65 Bde, Samat," pp. 105–106.

[18] *Ibid.,* pp. 108 and 112.

[19] "Translations," 2:4; and "Interrogations," 1:3.

[20] *Japanese Monograph No. 2,* p. 17; and *Reports of MacArthur,* p. 114.

[21] "Interrogations," 1:4.

[22] Tisdelle, "Diary," 16 February 1942; and Bautista, "11 Engr Bn," p. 35.

[23] "Statements," 1:276; Morton, *Fall,* p. 412; and Homma Testimony, War Crimes Trial, pp. 2677–78, 2848–49, 3021, and 3122, hereafter referred to as Homma, "Testimony."

[24] Stanley L. Falk, *Bataan: The March of Death* (New York: Modern Literary Editions Publishing Company, 1962), p. 58; and Morton, *Fall,* p. 412.

Preparation

[1] Ind, *Judgment Seat*, pp. 306–307.

[2] *Ibid.*, p. 307.

[3] *Ibid.*, p. 308; Annex XIII, p. 143; Collier "Notebooks," 3:53; Dyess, *The Dyess Story*, p. 52; interview with R. Miller, 28 April 1981; and *Army Register 1942*, p. 243.

[4] Dyess, *The Dyess Story*, pp. 52–53.

[5] *Ibid.*, pp. 53–54.

[6] *Ibid.*, p. 55; and Ind, *Judgment Seat*, pp. 312–313.

[7] Dyess, *The Dyess Story*, pp. 55–58.

[8] Ind, *Judgment Seat*, pp. 316–317; and Dyess, *The Dyess Story*, p. 59.

[9] Dyess, *The Dyess Story*, p. 59.

[10] Dyess, *The Dyess Story*, p. 60; Ind, *Judgment Seat*, pp. 319 and 322; and Whitney, *MacArthur: His Rendezvous With History*, p. 35.

[11] "Aid the Philippines;" and Alfred D. Chandler, Jr., ed., *The Papers of Dwight David Eisenhower. The War Years* 5 vols. (Baltimore: The John Hopkins Press, 1970), 1:90.

[12] Radio, MacArthur to the AG, 4 March 1942; and Ind, *Judgment Seat*, pp. 323–324.

[13] Radio, Hq AAF #3/58, 4 March 1942 sent 5 March.

[14] Brice J. Martin, "Operations of Company F, 51st Infantry Regiment (51st. Division)(Philippine Army) In Vicinity of Mt. Samat, Bataan, 1 March 1942 (Philippine Defense Campaign)(Personal Experience of a Company Commander)," p. 9, monograph written for Infantry Officer Advanced Course #2, 1947–48, hereafter referred to as Martin, "Co F, 51st Inf."

[15] *Ibid.*

[16] *Ibid.*, p. 10.

[17] *Ibid.*, pp. 10–11.

[18] O'Day, "Hist 21 Div," 2:34.

[19] Mallonee, "Bataan Diary," 2:56; Tisdelle, "Diary," 6 March 1942; and Halstead C. Fowler to Louis Morton, 22 March 1949.

[20] Fitch, "Siege," p. 25.

[21] USAFFE Training Memorandum #15, 26 February 1942, pp. 1–2.

[22] 11th Division Training Memorandum, 18 March 1942, supplement to Training Memorandum, 4 March; and Morton, *Fall*, p. 409.

[23] Annex X, p. 5; and "Armor on Luzon," p. 20.

[24] Annex V, p. 46; 11th Division Training Memorandum, 4 March 1942, pp. 1–2; and Robert W. Levering, *Horror Trek. A True Story of Bataan, The Death March And Three And One-Half Years in Japanese Camps* (Dayton, Ohio: The Horstman Printing Co., 1948), p. 52.

[25] Dod, *Engineers Against Japan,* pp. 97–98; Fortier, "Notes of Fortier," p. 70; and USAFFE Training Memorandum #14, 25 February 1942.

[26] 11th Division Training Memorandum, 4 March 1942, p. 2.

[27] Montgomery, "I Hired Out To Fight," p. 45.

[28] USAFFE Training Memorandum #14, 25 February 1942, p. 1; and Dod, *Engineers Against Japan,* p. 98.

[29] Hugh J. Casey to Commanding General, USAFFE, 8 March 1942, Subject: Inspection of MLR, Bataan, p. 4.

[30] *Ibid.,* pp. 4–5.

[31] Dod, *Engineers Against Japan,* p. 99.

[32] Skerry to Meidling, 4 August 1947 and 4 June 1949.

[33] Collier, "Notebooks," 3:57–58; and Tisdelle, "Diary," 22 March 1942.

[34] Lewis Beebe, Memorandum For: The Deputy Chief of Staff, Advance Echelon, USAFFE, 7 February 1942; Annex VI, Report of G-4, p. 2; Fortier, "Ops 41 Div," p. 4; and Annex XIII, p. 22.

[35] McBride, "Notes on the Fall;" USFIP General Order #42, 14 March 1942; and Annex XIII, pp. 47–48.

[36] Annex XIII, pp. 47 and 168–170; and Collier, "Notebooks," 2:25.

[37] Paul Ashton to Lieutenant Colonel Glattly, Surgeon, Bataan Force, 1 April 1942; Annex VI, Report of G-4, p. 2; and Fortier, "Ops 41 Div," p. 4.

[38] Annex VI, Report of G-4, p. 2; "Armor on Luzon," p. 35; Howard, "Unit History;" and Mallonee, "Bataan Diary," 2:57.

[39] Anloff to author, (tape), 1 August 1976; Annex VI, Report of G-4, p. 2; and Annex XIII, p. 48.

[40] Regis M. Theriac to author, (tape), 14 March 1977; Richard C. Kadel to Louis Morton, 5 May 1950; and Glen R. Townsend, "The 11th Infantry Regiment Philippine Army, Part IV, Bataan: The Final Phase February 18–April 9, 1942," p. 3, hereafter referred to as Townsend, "The Final Phase."

[41] H. W. Glattly to The Commanding General, Luzon Force, 23 March 1942, Subject: Present Malarial Situation; and Waterous, *Reminiscences,* p. 25.

[42] Read, "Comments," p. 46; "What Is The Condition Of My Troops?" paper written for or by Louis Morton during his research for *The Fall of the Philippines,* p. 18, hereafter referred to as Morton, "Condition of My Troops;" "Aid the Philippines," p. 7; and Waterous, *Reminiscences,* p. 24.

[43] Hibbs to author, (tape), 7 February 1980.

[44] Poweleit, *USAFFE,* p. 42.

[45] Weinstein, *Barbed Wire Surgeon,* p. 32; and Poweleit, *USAFFE,* p. 42.

[46] Morton, "Condition of My Troops," pp. 19 and 21.

[47] Dyess, *The Dyess's Story,* pp. 61–62. Although Dyess' account sounds too noble to be true, the voluntary cut in rations is confirmed by Omar L.

McGuire, a member of the 21st Pursuit, in his paper, "Our Defense of Bataan."

[48] Annex XIV, p. 45; Bluemel, "31 Div," p. 17; and Bringas, "Medical Service of 21 Div."

[49] Montgomery, "Diary," 17 March 1942.

[50] Joe F. Svrcek to author, 28 March 1979.

[51] Annex IV, p. 29; Annex XIII, p. 36; Annex IX, p. 5; and Dod, *Engineers Against Japan,* p. 100.

[52] Annex VI, p. 1; Annex XIII, Appendix A, Narrative Report of The Supply Problems, p. 6; and Waterous, *Reminiscences,* p. 41.

[53] William J. Kerins to author, 28 November 1977; and Annex XIII, Appendix A, p. 6.

[54] Morton, "Condition of My Troops," pp. 2–4; Annex XIII, Appendix F, p. 4; Annex XIII, p. 38; and Drake, "No Uncle Sam," p. 34.

[55] Bautista, "11 Engr Bn," p. 35.

The Orion-Bagac Line

[1] Jensen interview with H. K. Johnson, 7 February 1942, p. 6; War Department, Public Information Office Biography, Edward P. King, Jr., p. 1; *Army Register 1941,* p. 469; Annex VI, Report of Operations of Luzon Force, 22 [sic] March–9 April 1942, Report of G-1, pp. 1–3, in Wainwright, Rpt Ops USAFFE-USFIP; Morton, *Fall,* pp. 366 and 405; and Fortier, "Notes of Fortier," pp. 74–75.

[2] USAFFE letter, Subject: American Officers with Combat Troop Units, To: Corps, Sub-Sector and Division Commanders, February 3, 1942; and Morton, *Fall,* p. 326–327.

[3] Morton, *Fall,* pp. 327 and 406.

[4] Seldon H. Mendelson, "Operations of the Provisional Air Corps Regiment in the Defense of Bataan Peninsula, P. I., 8 January–10 April 1942 (Philippine Island Campaign)(Personal experience of a Platoon Leader)," pp. 9–19, monograph written for Infantry Officer Advance Course 1946–47, hereafter referred to a Mendelson, "Air Corps Regiment;" Statistical Report, Third Section, The Provisional Air Corps Regiment, 31 March 1942; Morton, *Fall,* p. 327; and Jack D. Bradley to author, 6 November 1977.

[5] Samuel B. Moody to author, 14 March 1974; Coleman, *Bataan and Beyond,* p. 19; and William Marrocco to author, 1 June 1976.

[6] Bradley to author, 6 November 1977; Marrocco to author, 1 June 1976; and Coleman, *Bataan and Beyond,* p. 29.

[7] Bradley to author, (tape), 14 November 1978; Mendelson, "Air Corps Regiment," pp. 10–19; Theodore C. Bigger to author, 23 January 1976; and Mark Wohlfeld, "Two-Seven! Here We Go."

[8] George Kane to author, 17 December 1976; Mendelson, "Air Corps

Regiment," pp. 10–19; Marrocco to author, 1 June 1976; and LTC Charles H. Morhouse To: The Surgeon General, War Department, Washington, D.C. Through the Surgeon USASOS, Subject: Medical Service in the Philippines, 20 January 1943.

9 Morton, *Fall*, pp. 327 and 406; Annex V, p. 50; and Fowler to Morton, 22 March 1949.

10 Morton, *Fall*, p. 327; and Fortier, "Notes of Fortier," p. 84.

11 O'Day, "Hist of 21 Div," 2:40.

12 Annex VI, Report of G-3, pp. 1 and 6; Morton, *Fall*, pp. 406–407; Fitch, "Siege," p. 23; Annex XII, p. 22; and Annex IV, p. 7.

13 Annex VI, p. 7; USFIP Extract, Ammunition Report ending 2 April 1942; Morton, *Fall*, p. 406; Annex XII, pp. 22 and 26; and Collier, "Notebooks," 3:60.

14 Annex VI, p. 3; Collier, "Notebooks," 3:44 and 64; Morton, *Fall*, p. 411; Annex IV, p. 29; and Annex V, pp. 46–47.

15 Cordero, *Experiences,* p. 25; and Morton, *Fall*, pp. 327 and 406.

16 Morton, *Fall*, pp. 328 and 411; Annex VI, p. 6; 11th Division Training Memorandum, 4 March 1942 with appended Brougher comment; and Townsend, "The Final Phase," pp. 1–4.

17 Annex VI, p. 6; and Fitch, "Siege," p. 23.

18 Annex V, p. 47; Morton, *Fall*, p. 417; and Annex VI, Report of G-2, pp. 1–2.

19 Fowler to Morton, 22 March 1949, p. 1; Bluemel, "31 Div," pp. 18–19; Collier, "Notebooks," 3:59; interview with Beck, 29 December 1975; and O'Day, "Hist of 21 Div," 2:35.

20 Radio, Wainwright to AG War, 21 March 1942; and Annex V, p. 54.

21 Copy of document furnished the author by John E. Olson. There are numerous variations on this document; and Morton, *Fall*, p. 418.

22 Achille C. Tisdelle, "Story of Bataan Collapse, 9 Apr 42;" and Wainwright to AG, 22 March 1942.

23 Mongtomery, "Diary," 22 March 1942.

24 Annex V, p. 52; Armed Forces Philippines, "Plan of Maneuver;" Morton, *Fall*, pp. 414 and 419; Mallonee, "Bataan Diary," 2:57; and Annex VI, p. 7.

25 Bluemel to Ward, 17 January 1952.

26 Mellnik, *Philippine Diary,* p. 88; Bardowski to author, (tape), 27 August 1976; and Svrcek to author, 1 May 1979.

27 Annex V, p. 47; Annex VI, p. 2; and Townsend, "The Final Phase," p. 4.

28 Quintard, "Diary," 28 March 1942; Annex VI, Report of G-2, p. 2; Morton, *Fall*, p. 494; and Annex V, p. 52.

29 Montgomery, "Diary," 25–26 March 1942.

30 *Japanese Monograph No. 1,* p. 47; Mallonee, "Bataan Diary," 2:80; and Bluemel, "31 Div," p. 18.

[31] Svrcek to author, 28 March 1979; and Morris L. Shoss to William H. Bartsch, 7 August 1978 in *The Quan* vol. 33, (November 1978) pp. 4–6.

[32] Svrcek to author, 28 March 1979.

[33] Morton, *Fall,* p. 407; and personal observation of the author.

[34] *Japanese Monograph No. 2,* p. 16; and Morton, *Fall,* pp. 414–415.

[35] Armed Forces Philippines, "Plan of Maneuver," pp. 10–11.

[36] Morton, *Fall,* pp. 414 and 417.

[37] Ibid., pp. 416–417; and Louis Morton, "Estimated Japanese Ground Force Strength (Effective) on The Eve of the April Offensive."

[38] Morton, *Fall,* pp. 416–417.

[39] *Ibid.,* p. 416.

[40] Falk, "Folio," p. 106.

[41] *Japanese Monograph No. 2,* p. 17.

[42] Annex V, p. 47; Annex VI, Report of G-2, p. 2; Emerson, "Ops II Corps," pp. 21–22; and Fowler to Morton, 22 March 1949, p. 2.

[43] Annex VI, Report of G-2, p. 2; Tisdelle, "Diary," 27 March 1942; and Van Oosten to author, 12 June 1974.

[44] Morton, *Fall,* p. 401; radio, Wainwright to the AG, 26 March 1942; radio, Wainwright to MacArthur, 27 march 1942, in Beck, *MacArthur and Wainwright,* p. 180; Dod, *Engineers Against Japan,* p. 100; Sullivan, "Hospital Number '2,' Bataan, PI," p. 22; and Waterous, "Reminiscences," p. 50.

[45] Radio, Wainwright to Marshall, 30 March 1942; and radio, Marshall to Wainwright, 27 March 1942.

[46] Memorandum for [Army] Chief of Staff, 3 January 1942, Subject: Relief of the Philippines; and Morton, *Fall,* p. 401.

[47] Dobrinic to author, 21 March 1975.

[48] Montgomery, "Diary," 8 February 1942; Bluemel, interview 14 April 1948 by Morton, p. 2; and Mallonee, "Bataan Diary," 2:69.

[49] Morton, *Fall,* pp. 417–418; *Japanese Monograph No. 1,* p. 51; Weinstein, *Barbed Wire Surgeon,* p. 41; and William J. Kennard, "Observations on Bataan," p. 3.

[50] Poweleit, *USAFFE,* p. 43; Weinstein, *Barbed Wire Surgeon,* pp. 42–43; and Redmond, *I Served on Bataan,* pp. 94–95.

[51] Redmond, *I Served on Bataan,* pp. 109–110; Poweleit, *USAFFE,* p. 43; Annex XIV, Appendix C, p. 56; and Hartendorp, *Japanese Occupation,* p. 180.

[52] Radio, Wainwright to AG War, 30 March 1942. Not everyone agreed with Wainwright that the bombing was deliberate. See discussion in footnote for Chapter 26.

[53] Shreve, "Diary," p. 27; radio, Wainwright to AG War, 31 March 1942; and USFIP G3 Journal, 19 March–19 April 1942.

[54] Radio, Wainwright to AG War, 29 March 1942; Collier, "Notebooks," 3:69; Annex VI, p. 2; Annex XII, p. 23; Fortier, "42 Inf," p. 22; and E. C. Atkinson, "42nd Infantry Notes of Activities Following With-

drawal From Abucay Position," in Fortier, "Notes on 41 Div," pp. 203–204, hereafter referred to as Atkinson, "42nd Infantry Notes."

[55] Radio, Wainwright to AG War, 31 March 1942.

[56] Tisdelle, "Diary," 31 March and 2 April 1942; *Japanese Monograph No. 11,* p. 54; Fortier, "Ops 41 Div," p. 5; Capinpin, "Hist 21 Div," p. 44; and Collier, "Notebooks," 3:69.

[57] Montgomery, "Diary," 2 April 1942; Wetherby, "41st Inf Jan–April," p. 161; *Japanese Monograph No. 11,* p. 54; Annex V, p. 49; and Loren A. Wetherby to Louis Morton, 22 May 1951, "Activities of 41st Infantry, Philippine Army 1 to 9 April 1942," p. 1, hereafter referred to as Wetherby, "Activities of 41st Inf."

[58] Malcolm V. Fortier, "Notes of Col. M. V. Fortier (Apr 2–9)," p. 11 in Fortier, "Notes on 41 Div."

Good Friday, April 3

[1] Morton, *Fall,* pp. 416, 421, and 422; Toland, *But Not In Shame,* p. 304; and Far East Command General Headquarters, Letter from G-2, 16 August 1949 to Chief, Historical Division, DA, Headquarters, Washington, DC, "Information Regarding Strength and Composition of Japanese Forces, Philippine Islands Dec 41–May 42," hereafter referred to as "Information Regarding Strength."

[2] Fortier, "Notes of Fortier," pp. 70–71; Morton, *Fall,* pp. 421–422; Toland, *But Not In Shame,* p. 304; Shoemake, "History of 41st FA," p. 32, in Chunn, "Notebook;" and "Information Regarding Strength."

[3] Morton, *Fall,* p. 421; Collier, "Notebooks," 3:71; Roy Oster and Grover C. Richards Jr., "History of the 21st Infantry (PA)," p. 10, in Chunn, "Notebook," hereafter referred to as Oster/Richards, "History of 21st Infantry (PA);" and Annex VI, p. 3.

[4] Fortier, "Ops 41 Div," p. 5; Fortier, "Notes of Col. M. V. Fortier (Apr 2–9)," p. 12; Ellis, "History of the 23rd Infantry (PA)," p. 14, in Chunn, "Notebook;" Wetherby, "Activities of 41st Inf," pp. 1–2; Mallonee, "Bataan Diary," 2:81; and *Japanese Monograph No. 2,* p. 33.

[5] Morton, *Fall,* pp. 414 and 422; *Japanese Monograph No. 11,* pp. 55, 57, and 62; Mallonee, *The Naked Flagpole,* p. 120; Fowler to Morton, 22 March 1949; Bluemel, "31 Div," p. 20; and Fortier, "Ops 41 Div," p. 5.

[6] Quintard, "Diary," 3 April 1942; Oster/Richards, "History of 21st Infantry (PA)," p. 10; Mallonee, "Bataan Diary," 2:61; and Shoemake, "History 41st FA," p. 32, in Chunn, "Notebook."

[7] Montgomery, "I Hired Out To Fight," pp. 62–63, and subsequent quote is from the same source, p. 63; Fortier, "Notes of Col. M. V. Fortier (Apr 2–9)," p. 12; Annex XIV, p. 45; and Loren A. Wetherby, "Operations of 41st Inf PA fr 2 Apr to 10 Apr 42," pp. 164–165, in

Fortier, "Notes on 41 Div," hereafter referred to as Wetherby, "Operations of 41st Inf."

[8] Fortier, "Ops 41 Div," p. 6; Toland, *But Not in Shame,* p. 304; and Fortier to Morton, 10 January 1952.

[9] Read, "Comments," p. 41; Collier, "Notebooks," 3:71; Shoemake, "History 41st FA," p. 32; Morton, *Fall,* p. 422; Mallonee, "Bataan Diary," 2:80, 82–83; Fortier, "Notes of Col. M. V. Fortier (Apr 2–9)," p. 12; Fortier, "Ops 41 Div," p. 5; and Wetherby, "Operations of 41st Inf," p. 165.

[10] Buenafe, *Wartime Philippines,* p. 106; and USAFFE Organizational History 1941–1942, History of 41st FA.

[11] Morton, *Fall,* p. 424; and Chunn, "42nd Infantry," p. 28, in Chunn, "Notebook."

[12] Fortier, "Notes of Col. M. V. Fortier (Apr 2–9)" p. 12; Morton, *Fall,* p. 424; Atkinson, "42nd Infantry Notes," p. 204; Wetherby, "Activities of 41st Inf," pp. 1–2; and Shoemake, "History 41st FA," pp. 32–33, in Chunn, "Notebook."

[13] Morton, *Fall,* pp. 416 and 424; Fortier, "Ops 41 Div," p. 6; and Fortier, "Notes of Col. M. V. Fortier (Apr 2–9)," p. 13.

[14] Fortier, "Notes of Col. M. V. Fortier (Apr 2–9)," pp. 12–13; O'Day, "Hist of 21 Div," 1:5 and 2:40; interview with Beck, 29 December 1975; Chunn, "43d Inf," p. 30, in Chunn, "Notebook;" and Fortier, "Ops 41 Div," p. 6.

[15] Fortier, "Ops 41 Div," p. 6; and Wetherby, "Activities of 41st Infantry," p. 2.

[16] Wetherby, "Operations of 41st Inf," p. 165; Wetherby, "Activities of 41st Inf," p. 2; and Fortier, "Ops 41 Div," p. 6.

[17] Wetherby, "Activities of 41st Inf," pp. 2–3; Wetherby, "Operations of 41st Inf," p. 166–168; and Montgomery, "I Hired Out To Fight," p. 64.

[18] Montgomery, "I Hired Out To Fight," p. 64; and William H. Montgomery to author, 4 December 1978.

[19] Montgomery to author, 4 December 1978; Morton, *Fall,* p. 425; Wetherby, "Operations of 41st Inf PA fr 2 Apr 42 to 10 Apr 42," pp. 168–169; and Fortier to Morton, 10 January 1952.

[20] O'Day, "Hist of 21 Div," 1:6 and 2:39–40; Melanio Velasco to The Adjutant General, Subject: Operations of the 21st Infantry Regiment, 21st Division, USAFFE, 7 December 1941–9 April 1942, 30 December 1945, p. 5, hereafter referred to as Velasco, "Ops 21st Inf;" Morton, *Fall,* p. 425; and Anders to author, 30 December 1981.

[21] Velasco, "Ops 21st Inf," p. 5; Anders to author, 30 December 1981; Colonel Charles Steel, "Report of Operations, II Philippine Corps, 2 to 9 April, 1942;" and Morton, *Fall,* p. 425.

[22] Annex VI, pp. 1–2; and Morton, *Fall,* p. 424.

[23] Robert M. Chapin, "History of the 33rd Inf (PA), less 1st Bn, 3–9

April 1942," pp. 2–4, hereafter referred to as Chapin, "Hist of 33 Inf;" Morton, *Fall*, pp. 425 and 427; Annex V, p. 51; Annex VI, p. 3; Fortier to Morton, 10 January 1952; and obituary prepared for *Assembly* by James D. Wilmeth, in Welmeth to author, 18 November 1981, pp. 2–3.

[24] O'Day, "Hist of 21 Div," 2:40–41; Fortier to Morton, 10 January 1952; and Fortier, "Ops 41 Div," p. 6.

[25] William E. Farrell, "Diary," p. 1.

[26] *Reports of MacArthur,* 1:115.

[27] Radio, Wainwright to AG War, 3 April 1942.

[28] *Ibid.,* 4 April 1942.

Saturday, April 4

[1] Radio, MacArthur to Marshall, 1 April 1942, in Beck, *MacArthur and Wainwright,* p. 184; and subsequent quote is from the same source.

[2] *Ibid.,* 23 January 1942.

[3] *Ibid.,* 1 April 1942, cited in Beck, *MacArthur and Wainwright,* p. 184.

[4] Radio, MacArthur to Wainwright, 4 April 1942; and Beck, *MacArthur and Wainwright,* p. 186.

[5] *Japanese Monograph No. 11,* p. 59; Chapin, "Hist of 33 Inf," p. 6; Morton, *Fall,* pp. 426–427; and Fortier, "Ops 41 Div," p. 6.

[6] Wetherby, "Operations of 41st Inf," pp. 169–170; Wetherby, "Activities of 41st Inf," p. 3; and Morton, *Fall,* p. 427.

[7] Interview with Battad, 6 June 1979; O'Day, "Hist of 21 Div," 1:6 and 2:40–41; Morton, *Fall,* p. 427; and Charles A. McLaughlin to Louis Morton, 14 June 1949 with inclosure, "History of the 23rd Inf Reg, 21st Div PA USAFFE," hereafter referred to as McLaughlin, "Hist 23rd Inf."

[8] Interview with Battad, 6 June 1979; Morton, *Fall,* p. 428; and Oster/Richards, "History of the 21st Infantry (PA)," p. 10, in Chunn, "Notebook."

[9] Esperitu, "Hist 22 Inf," p. 8.

[10] "Statements," 8:114.

[11] O'Day, "Hist of 21 Div," 2:41; Oster/Richards, "History of the 21st Infantry (PA)," p. 10, in Chunn, "Notebook;" and Esperitu, "Hist 22 Inf," p. 8.

[12] Tisdelle, "Diary," 4 April 1942.

[13] Chapin, "Hist of 33 Inf," p. 6; and Morton, *Fall,* p. 428.

[14] Wernitznig, "Diary;" and Wainwright, Rpt Ops USAFFE-USFIP, pp. 58–59; Morton, *Fall,* p. 431; Doyle to Ward, 8 January 1952; and Anders to author, 8 December 1980.

[15] Jensen interview with H. K. Johnson, 6 February 1972, p. 43.

[16] Rutledge to author, (tape), 4 January 1980; Annex V, pp. 51–52; William E. Farrell, "Diary," pp. 1–2; Annex VI, p. 4; Strong, "History 31st," p. 3, in Chunn, "Notebook;" Morton, *Fall,* pp. 431–432; William

E. Farrell, "Regimental History Notes April 3–9/42," pp. 17–18, in Brady Papers; and Armellino to author, 11 December 1978 and 4 January 1980.

[17] Snyder to author, (tape), 6 February 1979; Armellino to author, 11 December 1978; Pray to author, 16 September 1981; and Hibbs to author, (tape), 7 February 1980.

[18] Armellino to author, 11 December 1978; Morton, *Fall*, p. 432; Conrad, "Ops 31 Inf," pp. 20–21 and 23; Garleb to author, (tape), 23 February 1976; Rutledge to author, (tape), 4 January 1980; and Pray to author, 31 August 1981.

[19] Thompson to author, 30 January 1975; and Kerchum to author, 8 June 1980.

[20] Morton, *Fall*, p. 429; and Radio, Wainwright to AG War, 5 April 1942.

Easter Sunday, April 5

[1] Morton, *Fall*, p. 429.

[2] Montgomery, "Diary," 5 April 1942.

[3] Quintard, "Diary," 5 April 1942; and Mallonee, "Bataan Diary," 2:23.

[4] O'Day, "Hist of 21 Div," 2:41–42.

[5] "Statements," 8:114; Morton, *Fall*, pp. 429–430; O'Day, "Hist of 21 Div," 2:41; *Japanese Monograph No. 11*, p. 59; and Chunn, "41st Division (PA)," p. 28, in Chunn, "Notebook."

[6] O'Day, "Hist of 21 Div," 2:42; Annex V, p. 56; Annex XII, p. 25; Andrew D. Shoemake, "History of the 41st F.A. (P.A.)," pp. 32–33, hereafter referred to as Shoemake, "History of 41st FA," in Chunn, "Notebook;" Mallonee, "Bataan Diary," 2:83; and USAFFE Organization History 1941–1942, History of 41st FA.

[7] O'Day, "Hist of 21 Div," 2:42 and 47; and Morton, *Fall*, p. 430.

[8] O'Day, "Hist of 21 Div," 2:48; and Annex VI, p. 4.

[9] Bluemel, "31 Div," p. 21; and Robert A. Barker, "A.T. 31st 4/2–4/7/42," p. 13, in Brady Papers.

[10] Annex V, p. 53; and Bluemel, "31 Div," p. 21.

[11] Bluemel, "31 Div," p. 21; Howard, "Unit History," p. 14; and Mallonee, *The Naked Flagpole*, p. 126.

[12] Wainwright, *Story*, p. 58; and Lawrence, "Notebook," p. 73.

[13] USFIP Special Order #13, 4 April 1942; Anders to author, 28 May 1981; *Army Register 1941*, p. 400; Cullum, *Register*, VIB, p. 1961, VII, p. 1275, VIII, p. 358, and IX, p. 251; Annex V, pp. 53–54; Morton, *Fall*, p. 432; and Wetherby, "Operations of 41st Infantry," p. 171.

[14] Radio, Wainwright to MacArthur, 5 April 1942.

[15]Velasco, "Ops 21st Inf," p. 6; McLaughlin, "Hist 23rd Inf;" and O'Day, "Hist of 21 Div," 1:6.

[16] David Nash to author, (tape), 29 August 1979.

[17] *Ibid;* and Falk, "Folio," p. 116.

[18] Mallonee, "Bataan Diary," 2:87; Donald T. Purling to author, 15 February 1982; and Nash to author, (tape), 20 August, 1979.

Monday, April 6

[1] Morton, *Fall,* pp. 433–435; Wetherby, "Operations of 41st Inf," pp. 171–172; and Wetherby, "Activities of 41st Inf," p. 4.

[2] Morton, *Fall,* pp. 435–436; Wetherby, "Operations of 41st Inf," p. 172; and Wetherby, "Activities of 41st Inf," p. 5.

[3] Annex X, p. 23; Anders to author, 28 May 1981; Doyle to Ward, 8 January 1952; Morton, *Fall,* p. 436; and Croom, "3rd-45th," p. 15, in Chunn, "Notebook."

[4] Croom, "3rd-45th," p. 15, in Chunn, "Notebook;" Amato/Murphy, "History, 2d-45th," p. 14, in Chunn, "Notebook;" Morton, *Fall,* p. 436; and Calvin Ellsworth Chunn, *Of Rice and Men* (Los Angeles: Veteran's Publishing Company, 1946), p. 2.

[5] Amato/Murphy, "History, 2d-45th," p. 14, in Chunn, "Notebook;" Croom, "3rd-45th," p. 15, in Chunn, "Notebook;" *Army Register 1941,* p. 233; Morton, *Fall,* p. 436; Ulrich to author, (tape), 5 August 1981; and Miller, *Bataan Uncensored,* pp. 200–201.

[6] Miller, *Bataan Uncensored,* p. 201; and Morton, *Fall,* p. 436.

[7] Miller, *Bataan Uncensored,* p. 201; Doyle to Ward, 8 January 1952; Amato/Murphy, "History, 2d-45th," p. 15, in Chunn, "Notebook;" Annex XII, p. 26; and Morton, *Fall,* pp. 436–437.

[8] Quintard, "Diary," 6 April 1942; Morton, *Fall,* p. 436; Chunn, "42nd Infantry," p. 29, in Chunn, "Notebook;" and Fortier to Morton, 10 January 1952.

[9] Stanley Holmes, "History of the 33rd INF. (PA)," p. 27A, hereafter referred to as Holmes, "History of 33rd Inf," in Chunn, "Notebook;" Chapin, "History of 33 Inf," pp. 11–12; and Morton, *Fall,* p. 437.

[10] Morton, *Fall,* p. 437; and Anders to author, 17 May 1980.

[11] Rutledge to author, (tape), 4 January 1980; Bluemel, "31 Div," p. 22; Morton, *Fall,* p. 434; Farrell, "Regimental History Notes April 3–9, 42," p. 19; Annex V, p. 54; Billy Keith, *Days of Anguish, Days of Hope* (New York: Doubleday & Company, Inc., 1972), p. 51; Mead, "Ops 31st Inf," p. 26; and Armellino to author, 11 December 1978.

[12] Romie C. Gregory to author, 21 July 1977; Conrad, "Ops 31 Inf," p. 24; and Armellino to author, 11 December 1978.

[13] Spencer to author, 7 September 1975.

[14] Armellino to author, 10 October and 11 December 1978; and Morton, *Fall,* p. 434.

[15] A. Taylor to author, 5 September and 28 November 1980; Annex V, p. 54; and Brady/Hurt, "History of 31st," p. 83.

[16] Rutledge to author, (tape), 4 January 1980; Pray to author, 31 August 1981; and Conrad, "Ops 31 Inf," p. 21.

[17] Denton J. Rees to author, 24 January 1976; and Rutledge to author, (tape), 4 January 1980.

[18] Armellino to author, 11 December 1978.

[19] Annex V, p. 54; Farrell, "Regimental History Notes April 3–9, 42," pp. 19–20; Conrad, "Ops 31 Inf," p. 22; Morton, *Fall,* p. 435; and Brady, "Location 31 Inf," p. 5.

[20] Hibbs to author, (tape), 7 February 1980 and 22 May 1978; and Farrell, "Regimental History Notes April 3–9, 42," p. 20.

[21] Bluemel, "31 Div," p. 22.

[22] Armellino to author, 11 December 1978; Annex V, p. 54; Farrell, "Diary," p. 3; and Farrell, "Regimental History Notes April 3–9, 42," p. 20.

[23] Armellino to author, 11 December 1978; and Milton to author, 16 February 1975.

[24] Bluemel, "31 Div," p. 22.

[25] Snyder to author, (tape), 6 February 1979; Morton, *Fall,* p. 439; Farrell, "Regimental History Notes April 3–9, 42," p. 20; Farrell, "Diary," p. 3; and Thompson to author, 30 June 1975.

[26] Hibbs to author, (tape), 7 February and 2 August 1980; Rutledge to author, (tape), 4 January 1980; Brady, "Location 31 Inf," p. 5; Farrell, "Diary," p. 3; Morton, *Fall,* p. 439; Farrell, "Regimental History Notes April 3–9, 42," pp. 20–21; Conrad, "Ops 31 Inf," p. 24; and Wade to author, (tape), 28 April 1976.

[27] Armellino to author, 11 December 1978.

[28] *Ibid.*

[29] Mallonee, *The Naked Flagpole*, p. 128.

[30] Morton, *Fall,* p. 438; Bluemel, "31 Div," p. 22; Barker, "A.T. 31st 4/2–4/7/42," pp. 13–14, in Brady Papers; and "Japanese Armor on Corregidor," *The Quan,* vol. 37, no. 3 (November 82), p. 9.

[31] Emanuel Hamburger to author, 21 May 1975; and Brady/Hurt, "History of 31st," p. 49.

[32] Annex V, p. 56; Morton, *Fall,* p. 439; Bluemel, "31 Div," pp. 22–23; and Anders to author, 24 February 1981.

[33] Taylor to author, 5 September 1980; Farrell, "Diary," p. 3; Dobrinic to author, 22 May 1975; Bluemel, "31 Div," p. 23; and Pray to author, 31 August 1981 and 22 February 1982.

[34] Bluemel, "31 Div," p. 23.

[35] Saalman to author, 25 March 1976; and Bluemel, "31 Div," pp. 23–24.

[36] Annex XIV, pp. 34, 36, and 44.

[37] Morton, *Fall*, p. 440; and Farrell, "Diary," p. 3.

[38] Miller, *Bataan Uncensored*, p. 203; Morton, *Fall*, pp. 437–438; and Doyle to Ward, 8 January 1952.

[39] Vance to author, 19 September 1978 and 1 February 1981; Steel, "Report of Operations, II Philippine Corps, 2 to 9 April, 1942;" Chandler, "Battles To Glory," 4:20; and *Army Register 1941*, p. 866.

[40] Wainwright comment on note of G4 to Chief of Staff, 6 April 1942; and A. C. McBride, "Notes on the Fall."

Tuesday, April 7

[1] Ingle to author, 5 November 1975; Thompson to author, 29 March 1979; and Annex XIII, pp. 56 and 72.

[2] Ingle to author, 5 November 1975; and Garleb to author, (tape), 28 February 1976.

[3] Ingle to author, 24 May 1978; and Gilmore to author, 17 March 1981.

[4] Garleb to author, 15 March 1976.

[5] Montgomery, "Diary," p. 39; Thompson to author, 8 March 1979; and J. Gordon to author, (tape), 21 August 1980.

[6] Poweleit, *USAFFE*, p. 43; Morton, *Fall*, p. 444; Gilmore to author, 17 March 1981; J. Gordon to author, (tape), 21 August 1980; and Montgomery, "Diary," p. 39.

[7] Annex XIII, p. 56; Morton, *Fall*, p. 444; Fred Miller to author, 24 June 1976; and Bardowski to author, (tape), 13 February 1977. The author believes the bombing to have been unintentional. The well-marked hospital at Limay was never bombed, and although enemy planes made dummy runs against the buildings there, they did not shoot. Numerous military targets were clustered near Hospital Number 1, while engineer warehouses were on one side and ordnance warehouses on the other side. Hospital Number 2 was well-marked and was not attacked.

[8] Doyle to Ward, 8 January 1952, p. 6; Annex XII, p. 26; and Amato/ Murphy, "History, 2d-45th," p. 15, in Chunn, "Notebook."

[9] Miller, *Bataan Uncensored*, p. 205; *Army Register 1941*, p. 949; Amato/ Murphy, "History, 2d-45th," pp. 13–15, in Chunn, "Notebook;" Walter Engstrom, "2nd Constabulary," p. 39, in Chunn, "Notebook;" and Doyle to Ward, 8 January 1952.

[10] Miller, *Bataan Uncensored*, p. 204; Amato/Murphy, "History, 2d-45th," pp. 15–16, in Chunn, "Notebook;" and Altman, "194th Tank Battalion (U.S.)," p. 47, in Chunn, "Notebook."

[11] Amato/Murphy, "History, 2d-45th," pp. 15–16, in Chunn, "Notebook;" Ulrich to author, (tape), 5 August 1981; Doyle to Ward, 8 January 1952, p. 3; and Conn, "War Diary."

[12] Amato/Murphy, "History, 2d-45th," p. 16, in Chunn, "Notebook;" Ralph Amato, Jr., to The Adjutant General, Washington, D.C., Subject: Award of Decoration, 21 March 1944; and Doyle to Ward, 8 January 1952, pp. 4–6.

[13] Miller, *Bataan Uncensored,* p. 205.

[14] Dulin to author, (tape), 12 April 1976.

[15] Van Oosten to author, 12 June 1974; Doyle to Ward, 8 January 1952, p. 6; Croom, "3rd-45th," p. 16, in Chunn, "Notebook;" Miller, *Bataan Uncensored,* p. 205; and Morton, *Fall,* p. 443.

[16] Morton, *Fall,* p. 443; Eugene P. Boyt to author, 8 April 1975; and P. V. Cardenas, "History and Composition 301st Engineers."

[17] Morton, *Fall,* p. 439.

[18] Boyt to author, 1 August 1975.

[19] *Ibid.*

[20] "Statements," 3:113; and Boyt to author, 1 August 1975.

[21] Boyt to author, 1 August 1975; and Morton, *Fall,* p. 443.

[22] Bluemel, "31 Div," p. 24. South of Bluemel's line, officers who tried to collect some of the scattered 21st Division met with little success. Those collected were sick, unarmed, and principally from service units. The entire 21st Infantry had but fifty-two men and six rifles after two days of straggler collection. Everyone was dejected, and because no one believed the men could ever be assembled in time to rejoin the fight, even senior American officers went about their duties in a half-hearted manner. O'Day, "Hist of 21 Div," 2:47.

[23] Bluemel, "31 Div," p. 24; and Farrell, "Regimental History Notes April 3–9, 42," p. 21.

[24] Morton, *Fall,* p. 445; "Estimated Japanese Ground Force Strength (Effective) On the Eve of the April Offensive," Encl 1; Bodine to author, (tape), 23 February 1978; Morey, "32nd Inf. (PA)," p. 23, in Chunn, "Notebook;" and Bigger to author, (tape), 23 January 1976.

[25] Kane to author, 17 December 1976.

[26] Ibid; Wohlfeld to author, 16 March 1975; Charles R. Barnes to author, (tape), 25 March 1976; and interview with Leland W. Sims, San Antonio, Texas, 23 August 1977.

[27] Samuel B. Moody and Maury Allen, *Reprieve from Hell* (Germany: copyright by Samuel B. Moody and Maury Allen, 1961), p. 69; Jackson Whisenant to author, 23 March 1976; John Wansack to author, (tape), 27 April 1976; Edward Smack to author, 25 August 1976; and Bigger to author, (tape), 23 January 1976.

[28] Wohlfeld to author, 16 March 1975; and Bigger to author, (tape), 23 January 1976.

[29] Alfred C. Schreiber to author, 29 April and 1 June 1976; and Coleman, *Bataan and Beyond,* p. 45.

[30] John S. Coleman to author, 28 July and 10 September 1975; Coleman, *Bataan and Beyond,* p. 46.

[31] Coleman to author, 28 July 1975.

[32] Mallonee, "Bataan Diary," 2:83; and Spaulding to author, (tape), 1 January 1976.

[33] Bluemel, "31 Div," p. 24.

[34] Morton, *Fall,* p. 445.

[35] Bluemel, "31 Div," pp. 24–25.

[36] Snyder to author, (tape), 6 February 1979; and Bluemel, "31 Div," p. 25.

[37] Kerchum to author, 8 June 1980; and Bluemel, "31 Div," p. 25.

[38] Snyder to author, (tape), 6 February 1979.

[39] Bluemel, "31 Div," p. 25.

[40] *Ibid.,* pp. 25–26.

[41] Snyder to author, (tape), 6 February 1979.

[42] Conrad, "Ops 31 Inf," p. 25; and *Japanese Monograph No. 11,* p. 59.

[43] Spencer to author, 7 September 1975.

[44] Rees to author, 24 January 1976; and Wade to author, (tape), 28 April 1976.

[45] Interview with H. K. Johnson, 16 December 1975; Saalman to author, 25 March 1976; and Jensen interview with H. K. Johnson, 6 February 1972, p. 44.

[46] Interview with Stempin, 24 August 1977.

[47] Stempin to author, 11 February 1975; and subsequent quote is from interview with Stempin, 24 August 1977.

[48] Quintard, "Diary," 7–8 April 1942; Smith to Morton, 23 May 1949; and Alexander S. Quintard, "The 301st Field Artillery (PA)," p. 6.

[49] Blanning, "War Diary," p. 4.

[50] Vance to author, 19 September 1978; Vance to Ward, 18 December 1951; Collier, "Notebooks," 3:76; William E. Chandler to author, 12 September 1978; Chandler, "Battles To Glory," 4:20; and Blanning, "War Diary," p. 4.

[51] Chandler, "Battles To Glory," 4:20; D. H. Wills to author, (tape), 21 December 1975; and Blanning, "War Diary," p. 4.

[52] Chandler to author, 12 September 1978; Chandler, "Battles To Glory," 4:20; and Vance to author, 19 September 1978.

[53] Bluemel, "31 Div," pp. 26–27; and Blanning, "War Diary," p. 4.

[54] Blanning, "War Diary," p. 4; and Bluemel, "31 Div," p. 27.

[55] Blanning, "War Diary," pp. 4 and 10.

[56] Ibid., pp. 4–5; Chandler, "Battles To Glory," 4:20–21; and Bluemel, "31 Div," p. 27.

[57] Mar G. Arradaza to author, 15 September 1981; Anders to author, 10 April 1980; Bluemel, "31 Div," p. 27; Chandler, "Battles To Glory," 4:21; and Blanning, "War Diary," p. 5.

[58] Chapin, "Hist of 33 Inf," p. 8; and subsequent quotes and data about this action are from pages 10–19.

[59] Morton, *Fall,* p. 447.

[60] Beck, *MacArthur and Wainwright,* p. 188; Funk, "Comments on Fall of the Philippines," 12 January 1952, p. 16; and Wainwright, *Story,* p. 59.

[61] Wainwright, *Story,* p. 59; and subsequent quote is from same source, p. 60.

[62] Beck, *MacArthur and Wainwright,* p. 188; and Funk, "Comments on Fall of The Philippines," 12 January 1952, p. 16.

[63] Radio, Wainwright to MacArthur, 7 April 1942.

[64] Annex VI, p. 5; Collier, "Notebooks," 3:76; and Pena, *Bataan's Own,* p. 185.

[65] Wainwright, Rpt Ops USAFFE-USFIP, p. 60; Collier, "Notebooks," 3:77; and Morton, *Fall,* p. 447.

[66] *Ibid.*

[67] Bluemel, "31 Div," p. 28; Mallonee, "Bataan Diary," 2:92; and Morton, *Fall,* p. 447.

[68] Mallonee, *The Naked Flagpole,* p. 131; Farrell, "Diary," p. 4; and Morton, *Fall,* p. 447.

[69] Milton to author, 16 February 1975; Bluemel, "31 Div," p. 28; Anders to author, 7 July 1980; and Blanning, "War Diary," p. 5.

[70] Coleman, *Bataan and Beyond,* p. 49; and Coleman to author, 28 July 1975.

[71] Coleman to author 28 July 1975.

[72] Interview with Sims, 23 August 1977.

[73] Annex VI, p. 5; Wainwright, Rpt Ops USAFFE-USFIP, p. 60; Annex V, p. 62; Waterous, "Reminiscences," p. 52; McBride, "Notebook," p. 91; and G4, USFIP to G4, Luzon Force, 8 April 1942, Subject: Shipment of Motor Fuel.

[74] Morton, *Fall,* p. 448.

Wednesday, April 8

[1] Radio, Wainwright to AG War, 8 April 1942.

[2] Arradaza to author, 15 September 1981; Bluemel, "31 Div," p. 29; Spencer to author, 18 June 1980; Lilly, "Report of Ops 57 Inf," p. 6; Farrell, "Diary," p. 5; Morton, *Fall,* p. 449; and Lilly to author, 28 June 1975.

[3] Anders to author, 28 April, 6 June, and 7 July 1980; *Army Register 1943,* p. 774; Cullum, *Register,* IX, p. 666; L. W. Cramer, "26th Cavalry (PS)," p. 6, in Chunn, "Notebook;" Bess, "Ops Svc Co," p. 35; Chandler, "Battles To Glory," 4:21; Blanning, "War Diary," pp. 5 and 10; and Lilly to author, 28 June 1975. Strength figures and frontages vary wildly between sources. My figures are the result of much deliberation and discussion with the participants.

[4] Wohlfeld to author, 25 April 1975; Chandler, "Battles To Glory," 4:21; and Bess, "Ops Svc Co," p. 35.

[5] Bluemel, "31 Div," pp. 29–30; Wainwright, Rpt Ops USAFFE-USFIP, p. 60; and Toland, *But Not in Shame,* pp. 316–317. Subsequent quotations come from Toland.

[6] Bluemel, "31 Div," p. 30; and Blanning, "War Diary," p. 6.

[7] Bluemel, "31 Div," p. 30; Mallonee, "Bataan Diary," 2:99; and Chandler, "Battles To Glory," 4:21.

[8] Bluemel, "31 Div," p. 31; Milton to author, 16 February 1975; and Anders to author, 28 April 1980.

[9] Lilly, "Report of Ops 57 Inf," p. 6; Anders to author, 28 April 1980; and Bluemel, "31 Div," p. 31.

[10] Anders to author, 28 April 1980.

[11] Milton to author, 30 October 1974 and 28 May 1978.

[12] Hartman, "Diary;" Cullum, *Register,* IX, p. 666 and VIII, p. 877; Annex XI, p. 7; and Arradaza to author, 15 September 1981.

[13] Arradaza to author, 15 September 1981; Blanning, "War Diary," p. 6; Anders to author, 13 August 1980 and 20 January 1982; L. W. Cramer, "26th Cavalry (PS)," p. 6, in Chunn, "Notebook;" and Bluemel, "31 Div," pp. 31–32.

[14] Blanning, "War Diary," pp. 6 and 10; and Chandler, "Battles To Glory," 4:22. The figure of 175 cavalrymen differs from the 173 mentioned earlier because two missing men rejoined the regiment.

[15] Lilly, "Report of Ops 57 Inf," p. 6; and Anders to author, 6 June 1980.

[16] Lilly to author, 28 June 1975; and Anders to author, 4 April and 6 June 1980.

[17] Mills to author, 27 November 1974.

[18] Bluemel, "31 Div," pp. 31–32.

[19] Blanning, "War Diary," pp. 6–8.

[20] Mallonee, "Bataan Diary," 2:98–99; Morton, *Fall,* p. 449; Kane to author, 17 December 1976; Coleman, *Bataan and Beyond,* p. 51; and Wohlfeld to author, 16 March 1975.

[21] Coleman, *Bataan and Beyond,* p. 52; and Coleman to author, 28 July 1975.

[22] Schreiber to author, 29 April 1976; Coleman, *Bataan and Beyond,* p. 54; Coleman to author, 28 July 1975; and Bigger to author, (tape), 23 January 1976.

[23] Interview with Marion R. Lawton, Arlington, Virginia, 3 August 1980; McKee to Mallonee in Mallonee, "Bataan Diary," 2:101; Baver and Gregory, "31st Infantry (PA)," pp. 20–21, in Chunn, "Notebook;" Bluemel, "31 Div," p. 31; Morton, *Fall,* p. 450; Tisdelle, "Diary," 8 April 1942; and Chandler, "Battles To Glory," 4:21.

[24] Pena, *Bataan's Own,* pp. 166 and 188; Morton, *Fall,* p. 450; and Mallonee, "Bataan Diary," 2:102–103.

[25] H. K. Johnson, "Diary," p. 20; Morton, *Fall,* p. 451; Knox to author, 19 June 1977; and Quintard, "Diary," 7–8 April 1942.

[26] Collier, "Notebooks," 3:81; and Annex XIII, Appendix C, p. 4.

[27] Radio, Wainwright to MacArthur, 8 April 1942.

[28] Hibbs to author, (tape), 12 February 1980; Blanning, "War Diary," p. 5; Bess, "Ops Svc Co," p. 36; and Lilly to author, 28 June 1975.

[29] Anders to author, 31 December 1979 and 21 March 1982.

[30] Anders to author, 21 March 1982; Morton, *Fall,* p. 408; and Bluemel, "31 Div," p. 32.

[31] Snyder to author, (tape), 6 February 1979; Anders to author, 31 December 1979; and interview with Olson, 1 December 1974.

[32] Anders to author, 31 December 1979; and interview with Olson, 1 December 1974.

[33] Anders to author, 31 December 1979.

[34] Interview with Olson, 1 December 1974; Annex X, p. 30; Wainwright, *Story,* p. 61; Bluemel, "31 Div," pp. 32–33; and Anders to author, 31 December 1979.

[35] Bluemel, "31 Div," p. 33; and Anders to author, 2 September 1980.

[36] Toland, *But Not in Shame,* p. 324; and subsequent quotes are from the same source.

[37] Vance to author, 20 October 1978; and Fleeger, "Diary," p. 7.

[38] Bluemel, "31 Div," p. 33; Anders to author, 14 March 1978, 8 December 1980, and 11 February 1981; and Olson to Anders, 17 May 1981.

[39] Collier, "Notebooks," 4:2; Shreve, "Diary," p. 17; and Morton, *Fall,* p. 457.

[40] Collier, "Notebooks," 4:2–4, and subsequent quote is from the same source.

[41] Spaulding to author, (tape), 1 January 1976.

[42] Collier, "Notebooks," 4:2–3; radio, Wainwright to MacArthur, 5 May 1942; Annex VI, p. 6; and Morton, *Fall,* pp. 452–453.

[43] Alexander, "Recollections," pp. 123–124; Morton, *Fall,* p. 453; and radio, Wainwright to MacArthur, 5 May 1942.

[44] Annex IX, pp. 7–8.

[45] Collier, "Notebooks," 3:80; Annex IX, p. 5; and Steel, "Report of Operations, II Philippine Corps, 2 to 9 April, 1942."

[46] Collier, "Notebooks," 4:2; Barnes to author, (tape), 25 March 1976; and Bigger to author, 23 January 1976.

[47] Fry, "A Short History," p. 46; McBride, "Notes on the Fall;" Annex VIII, pp. 50 and 82; Bunker, "Diary," 8 April 1942; interview with Knight, 8 May 1975; and Hartendorp, *Japanese Occupation,* p. 181.

[48] Coleman, *Bataan and Beyond,* p. 56; Coleman to author, 28 July 1975; and Brownell Cole to author, (tape), 22 September 1976.

[49] Edwin J. Eagle to author, 12 September 1975.

[50] Bradley to author, (tape), 14 November 1978; and interview with Harold E. VanAlstyne, Clearwater, Florida, 9 May 1975.

[51] Bardowski to author, (tape), 27 August and 9 July 1976.

[52] Morton, *Fall,* p. 459; Stephen N. Kramerich to author, 8 January 1979; Snyder to author, (tape), 6 February 1979; Frost to author, 10 February 1979; and Underbrink, *Destination Corregidor,* p. 166.

[53] Blair, *Silent Victory,* p. 195; Underbrink, *Destination Corregidor,* p. 166; and Vogler to author, (tape), 2 November 1975.

[54] W. Miller to author, 9 March 1976; Miller, *Bataan Uncensored,* p. 208; Kinler to author, 1 June 1978; and Gage to author, 2 June 1977.

[55] Dr. Julien M. Goodman, *MD POW* (New York: Exposition Press, Inc., 1972), pp. 16–17; and Montgomery, "I Hired Out to Fight," p. 69.

[56] Interview with William E. Chandler, San Francisco, California, 30 December 1975; Montgomery, "I Hired Out to Fight," p. 68; and Weitzner to author, (tape), 27 June 1981.

[57] Annex XIV, pp. 10 and 37; Bernard T. Treharn to author, 30 May 1976; and Clara L. Mueller, "Diary," p. 7.

[58] Mueller, "Diary," pp. 9–10; Toland, *But Not in Shame,* p. 324; James H. Belote and William H. Belote, *Corregidor: The Saga of a Fortress* (New York: Harper & Row, 1967), pp. 105–106; Redmond, *I Served on Bataan,* pp. 123–128; and Collier, "Notebooks," 4:7.

[59] Lieutenant J. C. Bateman interview with Major Achille Carlisle Tisdelle, Cavalry who was senior aide to General King on Bataan during the fighting in 1941–42, 22 January 1946, pp. 4–5; McBride, "Notes on the Fall;" and Boettcher to author, 19 August 1978 and 26 January 1979.

[60] Whitcomb, *Escape from Corregidor,* p. 61; and Bateman interview with Tisdelle, p. 6.

[61] Kramerich to author, 28 July 1978; McBride, "Notes on the Fall;" and Morton, *Fall,* p. 460.

[62] Beck, *MacArthur and Wainwright,* p. 191; Morton, *Fall,* pp. 459–460; Dyens W. Knoll, Intelligence Report to Vice Chief of Staff, Sixteenth Naval District, during the period March 12 to May 3, 1942; Hoyt, *The Lonely Ships,* p. 294; Annex VIII, p. 51; and Commander Sixteenth Naval District to Commander, Southwest Pacific Force, 8 April 1942.

[63] Toland, *But Not in Shame,* pp. 324–325; and subsequent quotes are from the same source. Honus is the Spanish version of Jones.

[64] Tisdelle, "Story of Bataan Collapse, 9 Apr 42;" and Chunn, *Of Rice and Men,* p. 5.

[65] Alexander, "Recollections," p. 125.

[66] Underbrink, *Destination Corregidor,* p. 166.

[67] Dyess, *The Dyess Story,* p. 63.

[68] *Ibid.,* p. 64; and Southwest Pacific Area Headquarters General Order #26, 26 August 1942.

[69] Romulo, *I Saw the Fall,* pp. 272–273.

[70] *Ibid.,* pp. 286–291; and Dyess, *The Dyess Story,* p. 65.

[71] Romulo, *I Saw the Fall,* pp. 291–294.

[72] Annex VI, pp. 7 and 20–21; Annex XIII, pp. 52–53; and McBride, "Notes on the Fall."

[73] Fitch, "Siege," p. 26; Fitch to author, 3 April 1978; Doran to author, (tape), 7 October 1980; and Diary of an unidentified American officer who died at Cabanatuan, entitled "86 FA Bn."

[74] Berry, "History 3rd Inf," p. 7; I Corps Field Order #14, 8 April 1942; and Alfred J. D'Arezzo to William F. Marquat, Subject: Eight (8″) Inch Gun Battery, Saysain Point, Bataan, P.I., 27 September 1945.

[75] *Golden Anniversary, Class of 1933,* n.a., United States Military Academy, West Point, New York, 1983, p. 165; Kalbfleish to author, 23 November 1979; and I Corps Field Order #14, 8 April 1942.

[76] Liles to author, 23 May 1978; Glen R. Townsend to CG, Luzon Force, "Reports, Subject: Narrative of Events, 11th Inf. (P.A.), April 2–9, 1942," written in Tarlac Prison Camp 30 May 1942; and Townsend, "The Final Phase," p. 6.

[77] Santos, "1st Reg Div in Phil," p. 122; and Berry, "History 3rd Inf," p. 7.

[78] William E. Brougher, "When the 11th Division PA 'Tried To' Surrender," pp. 1–3.

[79] Wainwright, Rpt Ops USAFFE-USFIP, p. 61; Wainwright, *Story,* p. 60; Annex XII, p. 27; Annex VIII, p. 33; Annex XIII, p. 53; Stewart to author, 30 September 1975; and Van Oosten to author, 19 June 1974.

[80] Santos, "1st Reg Div in Phil," p. 125; Berry, "History 3rd Inf," p. 8; Annex XII, p. 27; Van Oosten to author, 26 September 1974; and Croom, "3rd–45th," p. 17, in Chunn, "Notebook."

[81] Svrcek to author, 28 March 1979; Unit Histories, 60th Coastal Artillery (AA), "Bataan (December 2 1941 to April 9 1942)," p. 65; Annex VIII, p. 50; and A. A. Abston to Commanding Officer, 60th CA (AA) Subject: Battery History—June 1, 1941—May 6, 1942, 12-17-42, Battery "G" Sixtieth Coast Artillery (AA), pp. 115 and 118; hereafter referred to as Abston, "Battery History."

[82] Svrcek to author, 28 March 1979; and Unit Histories, 60th Coastal Artillery (AA), "Bataan (December 2 1941 to April 9 1942)," p. 66.

[83] Svrcek to author, 28 March 1979; Massello to author, (tape), 7 January and 5 March 1977; Unit Histories, 60th Coastal Artillery (AA), "Bataan (December 2 1941 to April 9 1942)," p. 66; Read, "Comments," p. 57; and Abston, "Battery History," p. 116.

[84] Abston, "Battery History," p. 116; Svrcek to author, 28 March 1979; and William Massello Jr. to The Adjutant General, Subject: Recommendation for Award, 3 January 1946.

[85] T. C. Parker, "The Epic of Corregidor-Bataan, December 24, 1941–May 4, 1942," *US Naval Institute Proceedings,* (January 1943), p. 18; and Annex XVII, Fifth Phase, p. 11.

[86] Commander Knoll to Vice Chief of Staff, Intelligence Report Sixteenth Naval District during period March 12 to May 3, 1942, p. 15; and Charles C. Drake, memorandum to Chief of Staff, USFIP, 8 April 1942.

[87] Drake, memorandum to Chief of Staff, USFIP, 8 April 1942; and Annex XIII, Appendix B, p. 141.

Thursday, April 9, Surrender

[1] Wainwright, *Story,* p. 62; and Wainwright, Rpt Ops USAFFE-USPIP, p. 62.

[2] Radio, Wainwright to MacArthur, 9 April 1942.

[3] Radio, Marshall to MacArthur, 8 April 1942; Wainwright, *Story,* pp. 62–63; Beck, *MacArthur and Wainwright,* pp. 193–195; and Schultz, *Hero of Bataan,* pp. 245–246.

[4] MAJ M. H. Hurt Jr., "The Surrender," pp. 2–3, extract of Hurt Diary; Weikel to author, 8 August 1979; and Falk, "Folio," p. 122.

[5] Hurt, "The Surrender," pp. 4–5; and Toland, *But Not in Shame,* p. 327.

[6] Achille C. Tisdelle testimony in the war crimes trial of General Homma, Vol XVIII, pp. 2302–2303, hereafter referred to as Tisdelle, "Testimony;" and Louis Morton, interview with James V. Collier, 20 November 1946.

[7] Collier, "Notebooks," 4:8–9; and Tisdelle, "Testimony," p. 2303.

[8] Collier, "Notebooks," 4:9–11; Tisdelle, "Story of Bataan Collapse, 9 Apr 42;" Morton, *Fall,* p. 461; Toland, *But Not in Shame,* p. 328; affidavit by General King in Tisdelle, "Testimony," pp. 3286–3287; and Tisdelle, "Testimony," p. 2304.

[9] Tisdelle, "Diary," 9 April 1942; and Tisdelle, "Story of Bataan Collapse, 9 Apr 42."

[10] Tisdelle, "Testimony," p. 2305.

[11] Toland, *But Not in Shame,* p. 328.

[12] Tisdelle, "Testimony," pp. 2305–2306.

[13] Toland, *But Not in Shame,* p. 328.

[14] Tisdelle, "Testimony," p. 2306; Falk, *Bataan: The March of Death,* pp. 20–21; and Morton, *Fall,* p. 466.

[15] Annex XIII, p. 54; and Morton, *Fall,* p. 466.

[16] Motoo Nakayama, "Details of Negotiations with General King Concerning Terms for the Surrender of Bataan Peninsula," 26 August 1949, hereafter referred to as Nakayama, "Details of Negotiations."

[17] Tisdelle, "Testimony," p. 2308.

[18] *Ibid.,* Tisdelle, "Diary," 9 April 1942; and Morton, *Fall,* p. 466.

[19] Nakayama, "Details of Negotiations."

[20] Tisdelle, "Testimony," p. 2312, and subsequent quotations are from

the same source pp. 3212–3214; and Achille C. Tisdelle to Joe O'Connel, 28 December 1961.

[21] Annex XVII, Fifth Phase, p. 11.

[22] Bunker, "Diary," 9 April 1942; Hartendorp, *Japanese Occupation,* p. 187; Carl L. Allen to author 4 August 1980 and 24 April and 17 May 1981; Drake, "No Uncle Sam," p. 24; and Sackett, "History Canopus," p. 22.

[23] Hauser to author, 12 March 1975; Annex X, p. 25; Falk, *Bataan: The March of Death,* p. 191; and Crago to author, (tape), 14 March 1977.

[24] Interview with Abel F. Ortega, San Antonio, Texas, 24 August 1977; Knox to author, 19 June and 9 December 1977; Joe O'Connel to author, 13 January 1980; and Hauser to author, 12 March 1975.

[25] Kinler to author, 8 March 1978; Robert L. Baltzer to author, 19 August 1975; Crago to author, 21 August 1975 and 14 March 1977; and Diary of an unidentified American officer who died at Cabanatuan entitled "86 FA Bn."

[26] USAFFE letter, Subject: Destruction of Materiel and Equipment, 7 February 1942; and Gilewitch to author, 29 February 1976.

[27] Abraham to author, 2 September 1975; Wynn to author, 8 May 1975; Stewart to author, 30 September 1975; and Annex VIII, p. 51.

[28] Walk to author, 8 July 1975; and interview with VanAlstyne, 9 May 1975.

[29] Vogler to author, (tape), 2 November 1975; and Whitcomb, *Escape from Corregidor,* p. 62.

[30] Vogler to author, (tape), 2 November 1975; Wright to author, 12 September 1974; and Beck to author, (tape), 29 December 1975.

[31] Blaylock, "Comments," p. 36.

[32] Cohen to author, 1 December 1978.

[33] Collier, "Notebooks," 4:13.

[34] Falk, *Bataan: The March of Death,* p. 71; and Read, "Comments," p. 55.

[35] Interview with Crosby, 23 August 1977.

[36] Falk, *Bataan: The March of Death,* p. 74; Whitcomb, Escape from Corregidor, p. 68; and Spaulding to author, 1 June 1976.

[37] Anders to author, 8 December 1980 and 11 February 1981; and Vance to author, 20 October 1978.

[38] Vance to author, 19 September 1978; Bluemel, "31 Div," p. 34; Lilly, "Report of Ops 57 Inf," p. 6; and Bluemel to Ward, 17 January 1952.

[39] Lilly to author, 28 June 1975.

[40] Interview with Knight, 8 May 1975; interview with Laird, 30 December 1973; Bess, "Ops Svc Co," p. 38; and Cullum, *Register,* VIII, p. 1286.

[41] Knox to author, 19 June 1977; Reed to author, 5 February 1975; and Dobrinic to author, 22 May 1975.

[42] Interview with Hummel, 9 May 1975.

[43] "Translations," 4:4; and Falk, *Bataan: The March of Death,* pp. 71–72.

[44] Spencer to author, 7 September 1975; and Wade to author, 27 March 1979.

[45] Anloff to author, (tape), 1 August 1976, and subsequent quotes are from the same source.

[46] Weinstein, *Barbed Wire Surgeon,* p. 61.

[47] Montgomery, "I Hired Out To Fight," p. 70; and J. Gordon to author, (tape), 21 August 1980.

[48] Weinstein, *Barbed Wire Surgeon,* p. 61; J. Gordon to author, (tape), 21 August 1980; Weitzner to author, (tape), 27 June 1981; and Goodman, *MD POW,* p. 26.

[49] Bodine to author, (tape), 28 February 1978; and Frost to author, 10 February 1979.

[50] Annex IV, p. 30; and Liles to author, 23 May 1978.

[51] Liles to author, 15 April 1975; Falk, *Bataan: The March of Death,* pp. 76–77; and Townsend, "The Final Phase," p. 7.

[52] Townsend, "The Final Phase," pp. 7–8.

[53] Bautista, "11 Engr Bn," p. 36.

[54] Liles to author, 15 April 1975.

[55] Volckmann, *We Remained,* p. 41.

[56] Liles to author, 15 April 1975; and James, *South to Bataan,* p. 37.

[57] Liles to wife, 27 September 1945.

[58] Brougher, "When the 11th Division PA 'Tried to' Surrender," p. 4; Wetherby, "Activities of 41st Inf," p. 174; and Volckmann, *We Remained,* p. 43.

[59] Berry, "History 3rd Inf," pp. 7–8.

[60] *Ibid.,* p. 8.

[61] Ed Betts to author, 14 November 1978 with extract of his article in the *Lompoc Elks Tale* (1975); and Falk, *Bataan: The March of Death,* pp. 78–79.

[62] Howard J. Linn to author, 1 May 1975; Wainwright, *Story,* pp. 65–66; Annex XIII, pp. 184 and 207; Annex VIII, p. 51; and Bill Johnson, "Silver Bowl Center of Reunion Shanghai Bowl Hidden from Japanese in Bataan in WWII," *The Quan* vol. 42, no. 1, (July 1987), p. 11.

[63] John Morrill and Pete Martin, *South From Corregidor* (New York: Simon and Schuster, 1943), p. 4; Belote, *Corregidor: The Saga of a Fortress,* p. 106; and Nash to author, (tape), 29 August 1979.

[64] Radio, Wainwright to AG War, 9 April 1942.

[65] John Toland, *The Rising Sun. The Decline and Fall of the Japanese Empire 1936–1945* (New York: Random House, 1970), p. 293; and Annex VI, p. 7.

Bibliography

Bibliographic Essay

The source material for the Bataan campaign is severely constrained by the loss of official records when the army surrendered and from the death of officers and enlisted men in Japanese prison camps. Although some documents were buried before surrender or smuggled between prison camps, few survived the four years of war. The standard documents from which European and post-Bataan Pacific actions are analyzed do not exist for Bataan, and the researcher must look elsewhere for his data.

Paradoxically, the fact that the Americans were defeated on Bataan encouraged a larger-than normal outpouring of personal recollections. The officers and men who served there wanted to justify their actions and therefore probably produced more data per person than their more fortunate military comrades in Europe and elsewhere. And because of the absence of standard research data, research into the Bataan campaign uncovers a wealth of "non-standard" source material.

Official records, orders, and reports: The number of these reports is small because of presurrender destruction of files and records. Additionally, Filipino units lacked clerks and did not have the institutional memory standard to American and Scout units. However, some records were shipped out of the Philippines before the surrender, others were buried and recovered after the war, while prisoners carried a few items through three years of prison-camp experiences. These records are especially valuable because they are not time-perishable; they have not changed with the passage of time as have memories. They are valuable for confirming names, dates, ranks, units, etc. Postwar compilation of official records centered on General Wainwright's "Report of Operations of USAFFE and USFIP in the Philippine Islands,

693

1941–1942," with eighteen annexes. This report forms the basis for Dr. Louis Morton's Army official history *The Fall of the Philippines.* Wainwright's report was compiled from various major commanders, from official notes and extracts taken from the Army's G-3 journals which were shipped out of the Philippines before the fall of Corregidor, and from notes made by officers assembled after the war with orders to write a report of the Philippine campaign. Before publication of *The Fall of the Philippines* numerous comments about the draft manuscript were solicited and provide useful detail on the campaign. When asked about certain subjects, several veterans wrote extremely detailed studies covering unit activities. Most of this resides in the Morton Collection at Carlisle Barracks, Pennsylvania.

Postwar books, magazine articles, Army service school monographs, Army branch histories, unit histories written by participants, and diaries, letters, and recollections provided useful data. Monographs and small histories written by participants have been valuable, in particular the papers written by students attending the Infantry Officer Advance Course at Ft. Benning. They were written relatively soon after the war, normally before 1950. Other officers wrote large histories describing the part their units played. Postwar interrogation of Japanese officers proved less revealing than one would suspect. Only a few Japanese unit histories survived the war, the most useful being the 65th Brigade history. Several American postwar books were valuable in that they pulled together official reports, messages, and orders and presented them in a convenient format. Other postwar books are often apologias or undisguised attacks on senior officers.

Data that I have collected or seen from Bataan veterans includes interviews, letters, and cassette tapes. These veterans provided an incredible wealth of material. Because these men had been vanquished on Bataan, they seemed to be very interested in explaining the terrible conditions under which they waged war. Surprisingly, only a few tried to exaggerate their own contributions to the war. The vast majority provided sober, oftentimes personally unflattering accounts, of their part in the campaign. Several oral history collections afforded a welcome source that current research could never recreate.

Three War Department Field Manuals provided the basis from which doctrinal norms were drawn: FM 100-5, Operations, 1941; FM 7-5, Infantry Field Manual, Organization and Tactics Infantry, The Rifle Battalion, 1940; and FM 6-20, Field Artillery Field Manual, Tactics and Technique, 1940. I was struck by how timeless much of this material is.

Maps were always a problem. In most cases I reproduced portions of a post-Bataan 1:50,000 military map, enlarged them, and then drew boundaries, trails, etc.

List of Abbreviations

AP	Author's Possession
CARL	Combat Arms Research Library, Fort Leavenworth, Kansas
MC	Morton Collection at the US Army Military History Institute, Carlisle Barracks, Pennsylvania
NTSU	North Texas State University, Denton, Texas
PNL	Philippine National Library, Manila
TISL	The Infantry School Library, Fort Benning, Georgia
TPL	The Pentagon Library, Washington, D.C.
USAAC	US Army Administrative Center, St. Louis, Missouri
USAMHI	US Army Military History Institute, Carlisle Barracks, Pennsylvania
WEBC	William E. Brougher Collection, Mississippi State University

A

Abraham, Abie. Letters to author, AP.

Abston, A. A. Diary, USAAC, 999-2-53.

———. Letter to Commanding Officer, 60th CA (AA) Subject: Battery History—June 1, 1941—May 6, 1942, 12-17-42, Battery "G" Sixtieth Coast Artillery (AA), USAAC, 500-5-1.

Adjutant Generals Office, The. *Official Army Register January 1, 1941.* Washington, D.C.: United States Government Printing Office, 1941.

———. *Official Army Register, January 1, 1943.* Washington, D.C.: United States Government Printing Office, 1943.

Agar, Pius R. Letters to author, AP.

Agoncillo, Theodoro A. *The Fateful Years. Japan's Adventure in the Philippines, 1941–1945,* 2 vols. Quezon City, Philippines: R. P. Garcia Publishing Company, 1965.

"Aid the Philippines, Dec 41–Feb 42," extracted from Medical Diary, Hq, USASOS SW Pacific Area, Office of the Chief Surgeon December 41 to June 42, in the Charles A. Willoughby papers, MC.

Akiyama, Monjiro. Interrogation of Colonel Monjiro, in "Interrogations," vol. 1.

Alexander, Irvin E. "Personal Recollections of Bataan & Later," MC, Box 2.

———. Letter to Major General Orlando Ward, 25 December 1951, with "Comments on the Fall of the Philippines," MC, Box 1.

———. "Narrative of Quinauan Point Landing," in Annex XIII to Wainwright, Rpt Ops USAFFE-USFIP, MC.

Alexander, Milton G. Letters and tapes to author, AP.

Allen, Carl L. Letters to author, AP.

Altman. "194th Tank Battalion (U.S.)," in Chunn, "Notebook," MC, Box 2.

Amato, Ralph Jr. Letter To: The Adjutant General, Washington, D.C., Subject: Award of Decoration, 21 March 1944, in Chunn, "Notebook," MC, Box 2.

Amato, Ralph Jr., and Murphy, Louis F. "History Second Battalion 45th Infantry (P.S.) December 8, 1941–April 9, 1942," in Chunn, "Notebook," MC, Box 2.

Ammons, Cecil. Letters to author, AP.

Amy, Robert N. Letters to author, AP.

Anders, Franklin O. Letters to author, AP.

———. Letters to John E. Olson, 12 December 1977 and 24 May 1981, AP.

Anderson, William C. "History of the 57th Infantry (PS)," in Chunn, "Notebook," MC, Box 2.

Anloff, Gary. Letters and tapes to author, AP.

Arhutick, Leo. Diary, USAAC, 999-2-141.

Armed Forces of the Philippines, "Japanese Plan of Maneuver in The Final Battle of Bataan," Military History Branch, TI&E, 1963, PIO, Philippine National Library.

Armellino, John J. Letters to author, AP.

Armored School, The. Fort Knox, Kentucky, "Armor on Luzon," A Research Report Prepared by Committee 9, Officer Advance Course, 1949–1950, May 1950, TISL.

Army War College, The. "Studies of Overseas Departments and Alaska. Group No. 2. Philippine Department Reference Data. April 1, 1940 to April 10, 1940," produced for War Plans Course No. 13, 1939–1940, CARL, N-4630.

Arradaza, Mar G. Letters to author, AP.

Ashton, Paul. Letter to Lieutenant Colonel Glattly, Surgeon, Bataan Force, 1 April 1942, MC, Box 9.

Atkinson, E. C. "Actions of 42d Infantry. Dec 25 1941 to Jan 23, 1942," in Fortier, "Notes on 41 Div," received by Fortier 2/23/51, MC.

———. "42nd Infantry Notes of Activities Following Withdrawal From Abucay Position," in Fortier, "Notes on 41 Div," MC, Box 3.

B

Babcock, David S. "The SPMs," USAAC, 500-4.

Baldwin, Hanson. *Battles Lost and Won: Great Campaigns of World War II.* New York: Harper & Row, 1966.

Baltzer, Robert L. Letters to author, AP.

Bardowski, Zenon R. Letters and tapes to author, AP.

Barker, Robert A. "A.T. 31st 4/2–4/7/42," in Brady Papers, MC, Box 15.

Barnes, Charles R. Letters and tapes to author, AP.

Bass, James O. San Antonio, Texas. Interview, 22 August 1977, AP.

————. Letters to author, AP.

Bateman, J. C. Philippine Campaign 1941–42 Reference Data (Compiled for the Use of the Combat History Division, G-1, Hq AFWESPAC), MC, Box 1.

————. Interview with Major Achille Carlisle Tisdelle, 22 January 1946, MC.

Battad, Avelino J. Manila, Republic of the Philippines. Interview, 6 June 1979, AP.

Bautista, Amado N. "Operations Report 11th Engr Bn 11 Div from 29 Aug 41 to 10 Apr 42," WEBC.

Beck, Leon O. Fremont, California. Interview, 29 December 1975, AP.

Beck, John Jacob. *MacArthur and Wainwright: Sacrifice of the Philippines.* Albuquerque: University of New Mexico Press, 1974.

Beebe, Lewis Charles. "Personal Experience Sketches," 3 October 1945, The Lewis C. Beebe Papers, USAMHI.

————. Memorandum For: The Deputy Chief of Staff, Advance Echelon, USAFFE, 7 February 1942, MC, Box 9.

————. War Department, Public Information Office Biography, Lewis C. Beebe, MC, Box 9.

Bell, Gilmer M. "Anyasan-Silaiim," MC, Box 14.

————. "Longoskaiyan [sic] Point," MC, Box 14.

————. "Quinauan Point," MC, Box 14.

Bell, Walter. Letters and tapes to author, AP.

Belote, James H. and William M. *Corregidor: The Saga of a Fortress.* New York: Harper & Row, 1967.

————. Belote Research Papers that includes the William M. Belote interview with Colonel Jesus A. Villamor, West Hyattsville, Maryland, 29 July 1963, USAMHI.

Berry, Kearie L. "History of the 3rd Infantry Regiment, 1st Regular Division (PA), During the War with Japan, 19 December 1941 to 9 April 1942," MC, Box 17.

Besbeck, Louis. "The Operations of the 3rd Battalion 45th Infantry (Philippine Scouts) at the Hacienda at MT. Natib, Luzon, 15–25 January 1942 (The Bataan Campaign)(Personal Experience of a Battalion Executive Officer)," monograph written for Infantry Officer Advance Course 1946–1947, TISL, 491.

Bess, Clarence R. "Operations of Service Company, 31st Infantry (Philippine Division) 5 January 1942–9 April 1942 (Philippine Island Campaign)(Personal Experience of a Service Company Commander)," monograph written for Infantry Officer Advance Course #2, 1947–1948, MC, Box 15.

Betts, Ed. Letter to author, 14 November 1978 with extract of his article from the *Lompoc Elks Tales* (1975), AP.

Biedenstein, Arthur C. Letters to author, AP.

Bigger, Theodore C. Letters to author, AP.

Blair, Clay Jr. *Silent Victory. The U. S. Submarine War Against Japan.* New York: Bantam Books, 1975.

Blanning, J. C. "War Diary," MC, Box 16.

Blaylock, Tom. Dallas, Texas. Interview, 12 March 1971 by Dr. Ronald E. Marcello, North Texas State University Oral History Program, NTSU.

"Blockade Running to the Philippines," anon, MC, Box 9.

Bluemel, Clifford. Letter to Dr. George C. Groce, 15 June 1948, MC, Box 1.

———. Interview, 14 April 1948 by Dr. George C. Groce, MC, Box 1.

———. Letter to Dr. George C. Groce, 16 July 1948, MC, Box 1.

———. Letter to Louis Morton, 21 April 1948, MC, Box 1.

———. Letter to Mrs. Elsie Bluemel, 7 February 1942, MC, Box 17.

———. Letter to Major General Orlando Ward, 17 January 1952, with "Comments by Brigadier General Clifford Bluemel US Army Retired," MC, Box 1.

———. "Oral Reminiscences of Brigadier General Clifford Bluemel, Yardley, Pennsylvania, July 8, 1971," by D. Clayton James, WEBC.

———. "Report of Brigadier General Clifford Bluemel, U.S. Army on 31st Division, Philippine Army Sub-Sector "C" Mt. Samat Line, Bataan, P.I. and Special Force Covering the Period 18 Nov. 1941–9 April 1942," MC, Box 17.

———. War Department, Public Information Office Biography, Clifford Bluemel, MC, Box 9.

Boatwright, John R. Letter to Dr. Groce, 22 March 1949 with paper, "53d Inf PA," MC, Box 17.

Bodine, Roy L. Letters and tapes to author, AP.

Boettcher, Arnold A. Letters to author, AP.

Bohner, J. W. San Antonio, Texas. Interview, 24 August 1977, AP.

Bonham, Roscoe. "Engineer Supply Luzon Campaign 41–42," copied in prison camp by Colonel Clyde A. Selleck, MC, Box 9.

Bowes, Ed H. "Notes on initial movements of 1st Bn. 31st Inf.," in Brady Papers, MC, Box 15.

Boyt, Eugene P. Letters to author, AP.

Bradley, Jack D. Letters to author, AP.

Brady, Jasper E. Jr. Brady Papers, MC, Box 15, which include:

———. "Location of the 31st Infantry Dec. 8, 1941–April 9, 1942."

———. "Notes for History," by Major Marshall Hurt.

————. "Notes on Initial Movements of 1st Battalion 31st Infantry," by Lieutenant Colonel Ed H. Bowes.

————. "Air Corps. Prov. Regt.," anon.

————. "A.T. 31st 4/2–4/7/42," by Captain Robert A. Barker.

————. "Signal Communications," by Thane Hooker.

————. "Regimental and Battalion Staff changes 31st Infantry. Dec. 8, 1941–Apr. 9, 1942," anon.

————. "Regimental History Notes April 3–9, 42," by Captain Wilson Farrell.

————. and Hurt, Marshall, Adjutant 31st Infantry and other officers of 31st Infantry, "History of 31st Infantry, Rosters of Companies, Disposition of Personnel, Dates of Death, Death Reports with Place of Burial in Some Cases, Company Fund Reports," USAAC, 500-12.

Brawner. G-4, HPD Memo TO: Dept. A.G., 14 January 1942.

Brennan, John J. Letter to Winter General Hospital, 22 October 1945, with Lally file, AP.

Brett, George H. Radio to MacArthur, 13 March 1942; to AG War, 25 March 1942; and to War Department, 11 March 1942, all in Willoughby, Aid the Philippines.

Brezina, Frank. "Report, QM Philippine Department to QM USAFFE, 27 February 1942," MC.

Bridget, Francis J. Letter to Commandant, Sixteenth Naval District, "Action of Longoskawayan Point against Japanese Forces," 9 February 1942, MC, Box 14.

"Brief History—Company "A"—803d. ENGR. BN. (AVN.)(SEP)," anon, USAAC, 999-2-149.

Bringas, E. Q. Letter to Surgeon, Sub-sector "D", II Corps, In the Field, 14 March 1942, Subject: Medical Service of the 21st Division from Jan. 26, 1942 to Feb. 28, 1942, MC, Box 9.

Brougher, William E. Memorandum entitled "Apalit," WEBC.

————. "Equipment of 11th Infantry (PA) on hand Dec 8 (approximate)," MC, Box 17.

————. "To Command a Combat Division," MC, Box 2.

————. "The Battle of Bataan," 21 April 1942, MC, Box 2.

————. "When the 11th Division PA 'Tried To' Surrender," MC, Box 17.

————. War Department, Public Information Office Biography, William Edward Brougher, MC, Box 9.

Brown, Ernest L. "The Operations of the 57th Infantry (P.S.)(Philippine Div.) Abucay, January 1942 (Personal experience of a Company Commander)," monograph prepared for Infantry Officer Advance Course 1946–47, TISL, 492.

————. "Counter Attack by Co. L. 57th Inf at Abucay," p. 94, in Fry's Notebook, MC.

Buenafe, Manuel E. *Wartime Philippines*. Manila: Philippine Education Foundation Inc., 1950.

Bugbee, Karl A. Dallas, Texas. Interview, 8 December 1971 by Dr. Ronald E. Marcello, North Texas State University Oral History Program, NTSU.

Bulkeley, John D. Letter to Commandant, Sixteenth Naval District, Subject: Operations of U.S.S. PT-41 Night of January 24, 1942, 26 January 1942, MC, Box 8.

———. Letter to Commandant, Sixteenth Naval District, Subject: Report of Action of U.S.S. PT-34 on the night of January 22–23, 1942, 27 February 1942, MC, Box 8.

———. Letter to Louis Morton, 5 March 1948, MC, Box 1.

Bulkley, Robert J. Jr. *At Close Quarters. PT Boats in the United States Navy.* Washington, D.C.: US Government Printing Office, 1962.

Bunker, Paul D. Diary.

C

C, F. F. Letter, G4 USFIP to G4, Luzon Force, 8 April 1942, Subject: Shipment of Motor Fuel, MC, Box 9.

Cahill, John P. Letters to author, AP.

Caidin, Martin. *The Ragged, Rugged Warriors.* New York: Bantam Books, Inc., 1979.

Capinpin, Mateo M. "History of the 21st Division (PA)(Lightning Division)," MC, Box 17.

Cardenas, P. V. "History and Composition 301st Engineers," MC, Box 15.

Carter, James D. "Oral Reminiscences of Colonel James D. Carter, Kentfield, California, August 23, 1971," by D. Clayton James, WEBC.

———. Kentfield, California. Interview, 27 July 1975, by George W. Whitman, AP.

———. Letters to author, AP.

Casey, Hugh J. Letter to Chief of Staff, 2 January 1942, Subject: Congestion in Bataan Area, MC, Box 9.

———. Letter to Chief of Staff, 2 January 1942, Subject: Defense of Bataan, MC.

———. Letter to Commanding General, USAFFE, 8 March 1942, Subject: Inspection of MLR, Bataan, MC, Box 12.

———. Memorandum to Chief of Staff, USAFFE, 13 January 1942, MC, Box 12.

———. War Department, Public Information Office Biography, Hugh John Casey, MC, Box 12.

Catalan, Nemisio. "Narrative of the 1st BN, 21ST FA Participation in the Philippine Campaign," MC, Box 13.

Chamberlain, Peter, and Gander, Terry. *Anti-Tank Weapons.* New York: Arco Publishing Company Inc., 1974, TPL.

Chanco, Restituto. Letters to author, AP.

Chandler, Alfred D. Jr., ed. *The Papers of Dwight David Eisenhower. The War Years* 5 vols. Baltimore: The Johns Hopkins Press, 1970.

Chandler, William E. "26th Cavalry (PS) Battles To Glory," *Armored Cavalry Journal,* in three parts, vol. LVI, no. 2–4 (March–August 1947), CARL.

———. "An Outline History of the Twenty-Sixth Cavalry (PS) From December 8, 1941 to April 8, 1942," MC, Box 16.

———. "Colonel Clinton A. Pierce," AP.

———. San Francisco, California. Interview, 30 December 1975, AP.

———. Letters to author, AP.

Chapin, Robert M. "History of the 33rd Inf (PA), less 1st Bn, 3–9 April 1942," MC, Box 17.

Christensen, Arthur G. Letters to author, AP.

Chunn, Calvin Ellsworth. *Of Rice and Men: The Story of Americans Under the Rising Sun.* Los Angeles: Veteran's Publishing Company, 1946.

———. "Notebook," MC, Box 2. This is a collection of accounts either written by Chunn from personal experience, as told to Chunn by a soldier, or as written by a soldier, in MC, Box 2.

Chunn. "31st Infantry (U.S.)," pp. 1–2.

Strong, Walter S. "History of 31st Inf. (US)(1st Lt. Walter S. Strong)," pp. 2–3.

Anderson, William C, Capt. "History of the 57th Infantry (PS)," pp. 3–7.

Oster, Roy, and Richards, Grover C. Jr., Captains. "History of the 21st Infantry (PA)," pp. 7–11.

Chunn. "1st Bn. 21st Inf," pp. 11–12.

Foster, W. N. Capt. "22nd Inf. (PA)," pp. 12–13.

Ellis, John C. "History of the 23rd Infantry (PA)," pp. 13–14.

Hendry, Rod K. Capt. "21st FA (PA)," pp. 14–15.

Chunn. "71st Division," pp. 15–19.

Chunn. "Order of Battle, names," pp. 19–23.

Chunn. "North Luzon Force," pp. 23–26.

Chunn. "91st Division," pp. 1–2.

Cramer, L. W. Capt. "26th Cavalry (PS)," pp. 2–7.

James, 2d Lt. "11th Infantry (PA)," pp. 7–10.

Liles, Wayne C. Capt. "12th Infantry (PA)," pp. 10–13.

Chunn. "13th Inf. (PA)," pp. 14–16.

Porter, Wm. C. Capt. "71st Inf," p. 17.

Baver, Maj. and Gregory, Lt. "31st Infantry (PA)," pp. 20–21.

Chunn. "31st FA (PA)," p. 21.

Morey, Harold A. 1st Lt. "32nd Inf. (PA)," pp. 21–24.

Holmes, Maj. "History of the 33rd Inf. (PA)," pp. 24–27B.

Chunn. "41st Division (PA)," pp. 27–31.

Shoemake, Andrew D. Capt. "History of the 41st F.A. (P.A.)," pp. 31–33.

Harris, Henry. Lt. "History of the 41st Engineer Bn. (PA)," pp. 33–37.

Cummings, Wm. M. Capt. "53rd Inf. (PA)," pp. 37–39.

Chunn. "1st Regt. Philippine Constabulary," p. 39.

Engstrom, Walter, 2d Lt. "2nd Constabulary," pp. 39–41.

Rothrock, Arthur S. Maj. "4th PC," p. 41.

McBride, Lt. "1st Regular Division (PA)," pp. 41–42.

Chunn. "1st Inf. History," pp. 42–43.

Chunn. "5th Interceptor Command Combat Unit 1," pp. 43–44.

Holland, Lt. "192nd Tank Battalion (U.S.)," pp. 44–45.

Altman, Capt. "194th Tank Battalion (U.S.)," pp. 45–47.

Ellis. Lt. "History of 3rd Pursuit Squadron," pp. 47–48.

Crosby, Lt. "History of the 17th Pursuit Squadron," pp. 48–49.

Fulks, Lt. "20th Pursuit Squadron," pp. 49–50.

Parcher, Lt. "History of the 21st Pursuit Squadron," pp. 50–51.

Paulger, Lt. "History of the 34th Pursuit Squadron," pp. 51–52.

Chunn. "Provisional Air Corps Regt.," pp. 52–53.

Chunn. "81st Infantry," p. 53.

Maguire, Lt. Col. "101st Div.," p. 53.

Van Oostin [sic], Adrianus J. Maj. "History of First Battalion, 45th Inf. (PS)," pp. 1–3.

Amato, Ralph Jr. and Murphy, Louis F. Capts. "History, Second Battalion 45th Infantry (P.S.), December 8, 1941—April 9, 1942," pp. 1–18.

USAFFE Special Orders 106, 24 December 1941.

Croom, Clifton A. Capt. "History and approximate diary of the 3rd Battalion, 45th Infantry (P.S.) during the Philippine campaign (December 8, 1941 to April 9, 1942)," pp. 1–21.

Krauss, Paul A. Capt. "Anti-Tank Company 45th Inf. (PS)," pp. 1–2.

Amato, Ralph Jr. Letter To: The Adjutant General, Washington, D.C., Subject: Award of Decoration, 21 March 1944, pp. 1–2.

Chunn. Letter To: The Adjutant General, Washington, D.C., Subject: Award of Decoration, 8 October 1942, pp. 1–2.

Hase, James O. Letter To: The Adjutant General, Washington, D.C., Subject: Award of Decoration, 18 May 1944.

Cohen, Larry H. Letters and tapes to author, AP.

Cole, Brownell H. Letters and tapes to author, AP.

Coleman, John S. Jr. *Bataan and Beyond: Memories of an American POW*. College Station and London: Texas A. & M. University Press, 1978.
———. Letters to author, AP.

Collier, James V. "Notebooks," 4 vols, MC, Box 2.
———. Letters to author, AP.

————. "Oral Reminiscences of James V. Collier," Santa Barbara, California, August 30, 1971, by D. Clayton James, WEBC.

————. Letter to Louis Morton, 2 May 1951, MC, Box 1.

————. Interview, 20 November 1946, by Louis Morton, MC, Box 1.

"Comments on the draft Engineer Reports," anon, MC.

"Comments of Former Japanese Officers Regarding *The Fall of the Philippines*", in Lieutenant Colonel James M. Miller to General Orlando Ward, 19 April 1952, MC, Box 8a.

————. Appendix to the above. General Headquarters Far East Command Military History Section, Special Staff.

Confer, Russell W. Letters to author, AP.

Conn, Robert E. Jr. "War Diary of Capt. Robt. E. Conn Jr," MC, Box 16.

Conrad, Eugene B. "The Operations of the 31st Infantry (Philippine Div.) Defense of Bataan, 8 December 41–9 April 42 (Philippine Island Campaign) (Personal Experience of a Company Commander)," monograph written for the Infantry Officer Advance Course 1946–1947, TISL, 494.

————. Letters to author, AP.

Cordero, Virgil N. *My Experiences during the War with Japan.* Zerreiss & Co, Nuremberg: VN Cordero & Co.

Crago, John A. Letters to author, AP.

Cramer, L. W. "26th Cavalry," in Chunn, "Notebook," MC, Box 2.

Craven, Wesley F., and Cate, James E. *The Army Air Forces in World War II Vol I Plans and Early Operations. January 1939 to August 1942* Chicago: The University of Chicago Press, 1948.

Croom, Clifton A. "History and approximate diary of the 3rd battalion, 45th Infantry (P.S.) during the Philippine campaign (December 8, 1941 to April 9, 1942)," in Chunn, "Notebook," MC, Box 2.

Crosby, Stephen H. Jr. San Antonio, Texas. Interview, 23 August 1977.

————. Letters to author, AP.

————. "History of 17th Pursuit Squadron," in Chunn, "Notebook," MC, Box 2.

Croxton, Warner W. Jr. "Ground Communications by An Air Unit," *Infantry Journal,* vol. LII, no. 5 (May 1943), TISL.

Cullum, George W. Brevet-Major-General. *Biographical Register of the Officers and Graduates of the U.S. Military Academy at West Point, New York Since Its Establishment in 1802,* with Supplement, vol VI-B 1910–1920, edited by Col Wirt Robinson, Seemann & Peters, Prinks, Saginaw, Michigan 1920; Supplement, vol VII, 1920–1930, edited by CPT Wm. H. Donaldson, R.R. Donnelley & Sons Company, The Lakeside Press, Chicago, 1930; vol VIII, 1930–1940, edited by Lieutenant Colonel E. E. Farman, R. R. Donnelley & Sons Company, The Lakeside Press, Chicago, 1940; Supplement, vol VIII, edited by Colonel Charles N. Branham, By The Association of Graduates US Military Academy, 1950; Supplement, vol IX, 1940–1950, edited by

Colonel Charles N. Branham, By The Association of Graduates US Military Academy, 1950.

D

D'Arezzo, Alfred J. Letter to William F. Marquat, Subject: Eight (8″) Inch Gun Battery, Saysain Point, Bataan, P.I., 27 September 1945, MC, Box 1.

DeLong, E. G. Report, Commander, Motor Torpedo Boat Division Nine, Letter to Commandant, 16th Naval District, Subject: Attack of U.S.S. PT-32 on Enemy Cruiser During Night of February 1, 1942, February 3, 1942, MC, Box 8.

Denehy, John J. Jr. "Captain Edmond [sic] Peter Zbikowski," *The Quan* vol. 35, no. 5 (March 1981), AP.

Denson, Lee A. Jr. "Memorandum For The Assistant Chief of Staff, G-4, with Tabs A-D and Chart, 'US Army Garrison—Philippines: Present and Projected 20 November,' " 27 November 1941, CARL, R11638.

Diary of an unidentified American officer who died at Cabanatuan, entitled, "86 FA Bn," TISL, file # from USAAC 999-2-60.

Dickson, Ronald C. Untitled article in *The Quan* vol. 36, no. 2 (August 1981), AP.

Diez, Fernando B. Letters and tapes to author, AP.

Din, Romualdo C. Letters to author, AP.

Dobrinic, Matt. Letters to author, AP.

Dod, Karl C. *United States Army in World War II, The Technical Services, The Corps of Engineers: The War Against Japan.* Washington, D.C.: United States Government Printing Office, 1960.

Domei, January 2, 1943.

Dooley, Thomas. "The First United States Tank Action in World War II," monograph written for the Advance Officers Course #1, 1 May 1948, AP.

Doran, Roy E. Letters and tapes to author, AP.

Doyle, Thomas W. Letter to Orlando Ward, 8 January 1952, MC, Box 11.

———. Interview, 29 July 1942, by Perry G. F. Miller, MC, Box 16.

———. Lecture given 30 July 1942, MC, Box 16.

———. "Recent Combat Conditions in Bataan and Matters of Interest to the Quartermaster Corps," 25 July 1942, Washington, D.C., MC, Box 16.

Drake, Charles C. Memorandum to Chief of Staff, USFIP, Subject: QM Plan, Evacuation of Bataan, 8 April 1942, MC, Box 10.

———. Letter, Office of the Quartermaster, USFIP, to the G4, 29 March 1942, MC, Box 9.

———. Letter to Orlando Ward, 12 February 1952, with "Comments on The Fall of the Philippines," MC, Box 1.

———. "No Uncle Sam. The Story of a Hopeless Effort to Supply the Starving Army of Bataan & Corregidor," MC.

Dreger, Forrest F. Clearwater, Florida. Interview, 7 May 1975, AP.

Dulin, Basil. Letters and tapes to author, AP.

Dunham, Emory A., *The Army Ground Forces. Tank Destroyer History— Study No. 29.* Historical Section, Army Ground Forces, 1946, TPL.

Dyess, William E. *The Dyess Story: The Eye-Witness Account of the DEATH MARCH FROM BATAAN and the Narrative of Experiences in Japanese Prison Camps and of Eventual Escape.* New York: G. P. Putnam's Sons, 1944.

E

Eagle, Edwin J. Letters to author, AP.

Edmonds, Walter D. *They Fought with What They Had.* Boston: Little, Brown and Company, 1951.

Eisenhower, Dwight D. *Crusade in Europe.* Garden City, NY: Doubleday and Co., 1948.

Eleventh Division. Equipment of the., WEBC.

———. General Order #3, 8 January 1942, MC, Box 17.

———. General Order #15, 27 January 1942, MC, Box 17.

———. "Supplemental Report to Accompany G-2 Report, 11th Division, on February 19, 1942," MC, Box 13.

———. Training Memorandum, 4 March 1942 with appended Brougher comment, "Defensive Warfare in the Jungle," MC, Box 17.

———. Training Memorandum, 18 March 1942, supplement to TM, 4 March, MC, Box 17.

Ellis, Burton. Clearwater, Florida. Interview, 9 May 1975, AP.

Ellis, James D. "Notebook," USAAC, 999-2-37.

Ellis, John C. "History of the 23rd Infantry (PA)," in Chunn, "Notebook," MC, Box 2.

Emerson, Kary C. "The Operations of The II Philippine Corps on Bataan, 10 January–8 April 1942 (Philippine Islands Campaign)(Personal Experience of a Staff Officer)," monograph written for Infantry Officer Advance Course #2, 1949–1950, TISL.

———. Letters to author, AP.

Engstrom, Walter. "2nd Constabulary," in Chunn, "Notebook," MC, Box 2.

Esperitu, Joaquin. "A Brief History of the 22nd Infantry," MC, Box 17.

F

Fairfield, William A. "Diary," loaned to the author by William Montgomery, in the possession of William Montgomery.

Falk, Stanley L. "Folio," USAAC.

———. *Bataan: The March of Death.* New York: Modern Literary Editions Publishing Company, 1962.

Far East Command, General Headquarters. General Order #74, 19 February 1947, AP.

Farrell, William E. Diary, MC, Box 15.

———. "Regimental History Notes April 3–9/42," in Brady Papers, MC, Box 15.

Fendall, E. R. Diary, USAAC, 999-2-46.

Field Manual 6-20, Field Artillery Field Manual Tactics and Technique. Prepared under direction of the Chief of Field Artillery. United States Government Printing Office, Washington: 1940, CARL.

Field Manual 7-5, Infantry Field Manual Organization and Tactics of Infantry, The Rifle Battalion. Prepared under direction of the Chief of Infantry. United States Government Printing Office, Washington: 1940, CARL.

Field Manual 100-5, Field Service Regulations, Operations. Prepared under direction of the Chief of Staff. United States Government Printing Office, Washington: 1941, CARL.

"Fifty-Seventh [57th] Infantry, News Letter," 7 November 1941, AP.

"First [1st] PC Regiment, 2nd Reg. Div.," anon, MC, Box 17.

Fisher, John W. Letters to author, AP.

———. Letter to wife, 28 October 1941, AP.

Fitch, Alva R. "The Siege of Bataan from the Bottom of a Foxhole," 22 April 1943, in the Alva R. Fitch Papers, USAMHI.

———. Interview, 1984, US Army Military History Institute, Senior Officers Oral History Program, Project 84-7, vol. 1, by Harold R. Kough, USAMHI.

———. Letters to author, AP.

Fite, James T. Letters and tapes to author, AP.

Fleeger, H. J. "Brief Regimental History 26th Cavalry World War II-Bataan," *The Cavalry Journal* vol. LIV, no. 6 (November—December 1945), TISL.

Flores, Manuel T. "An Analytical Study of the Defense of Bataan," 31 March 1949, written for the Command and General Staff Course, CARL, N-2253-195.

Fortier, Malcolm V. Letter to Headquarters, Fourth Army, 14 May 1946, "Operations of the 41st Div (PA)," MC, Box 17.

———. "41st Division Notes PA," MC, Box 3, which contains:

"Actions of 42d Infantry-Dec. 25 1941 to Jan. 23, 1942," by Colonel E. C. Atkinson, pp. 1–10.

"Notes of Col. M. V. Fortier (Apr 2–9)," pp. 11–16.

"42nd Infantry. January 11th to January 18th," unsigned, pp. 17–23.

"Battle of 43d Inf PA on Tiawir River Jan 29-1942," pp. 24–25, by Fortier.

"Actions of the 41st F.A. (PA) on the Abucay-Hacienda Front from Dec. 25, 1941 to Jan. 24th 1942, Senior Inst 41 FA," pp. 26–27.

"Brief History of the 41st Div from initial Mobilization Sept 1 1941 to Dec 24 1941," pp. 29–54.

"Notes of Col M. V. Fortier from Jan 24th to Jan 24th [sic]," pp. 55–84.

"Notes by Col M. V. Fortier," pp. 85–92.

"Narrative Report," pp. 93–120.

"The Mabatang-Abucay fight of 41st Inf. (P.A.) Jan 8th 1942 to Jan 30th 1942," by Col Wetherby, pp. 121–141.

"Report of Col L. A. Wetherby Actions of 41st Inf fr Jan 28 1942-April-1942," pp. 142–163.

"Operations of 41st Inf PA fr 2 Apr 42 to 10 Apr 42," Loren A. Wetherby-Col, Sr Inst, Tarlac 24 May 42, pp. 164–177.

"Notes of Col M V Fortier," pp. 178–181.

"S-4 and Transportation," by Wetherby, pp. 182–190.

"untitled comments re Abucay withdrawal," pp. 191–193.

"42nd Infantry Notes of Activities Following Withdrawal from Abucay Position," Atkinson, pp. 194–204.

———. Letter to Louis Morton, 10 January 1952, MC, Box 17.

Foster, W. N. "22nd Inf. (PA)," in Chunn, "Notebook," MC, Box 2.

Fourteenth Army, Headquarters. "Tactical Situation Report," in Translation of Japanese Documents, vol. II General Headquarters, Far East Command Military Intelligence Section, Historical Division.

Fourteenth Engineers, "War Department AGO Form No. 73, 31 December 1941," USAAC.

———. "Brief War History of the 14th Engrs," anon, MC, Box 16.

Fowler, Halstead C. Letter to Louis Morton, 22 March 1949, MC, Box 12.

———. Letter to Louis Morton, 11 March, 1949, MC, Box 12.

———. Letter to Louis Morton, 30 April 1949, MC, Box 12.

———. Letter to George W. Stewart, 10 March 1950, MC, Box 1.

Fowler, John M. Letters to author, AP.

Friese, R. Edward. Letters and tapes to author, AP.

Frost, James E. Letters to author, AP.

Fry, Alvin L. Letters to author, AP.

Fry, Philip T. "The Philip T. Fry Papers," USAMHI, which contains:
"A Short History of My Experiences in the Philippines During the Second World War, 1941-1942," pp. 1–47.

"Recommendation For Distinguished Service Cross," p. 48.

"Operations of Luzon Force. Report of MAJ. GEN. KING," pp. 49–52.

"Report of G-1, Luzon Force," pp. 53–55.

"Report of G-2, Luzon Force," pp. 57–61.

"BATAAN Supply Situation Mar 21–April 9-42," pp. 62–63.

"Operations of North Luzon Force," pp. 64–76.

"Copy of a Letter from General Wavell to General Percival," pp. 76–77.

"Malaya," p. 78.

"Extracts From The History of the Philippine Division December 8-41 April 9-42," pp. 79–82.

"Roster of Officers of the 57th INF (PS)," pp. 83–86.

"Copy of a Letter Dropped in a Knickerbocker Beer Can from a Japanese Airplane over Southern Bataan Near the Luzon Force," p. 87.

no entries pp. 88–90.

"Recommendation for the Award of the Congressional Medal of Honor," pp. 91–92.

"Recommendation for the Award of the Distinguished Service Cross," pp. 92–93, and 56.

"Counter Attack by Co. L. 57th Inf at Abucay. By Captain Ernest L. Brown," pp. 94–95.

"Pay Data," p. 96.

"General Information," p. 97.

"Map," p. 98.

"Fly Leaf," p. 99.

Funk, Arnold J. "Comments on Fall of the Philippines," 12 January 1952, MC, Box 1.

———. Memorandum for G3 USAFFE, 8 January, 1942, MC.

———. War Department, Public Information Office Biography, Arnold J. Funk, MC, Box 9.

G

Gage, Thomas E. Letters to author, AP.

Galbraith, Nicoll F. Memorandum to G4, USAFFE, 10 February 1942, MC, Box 9.

———. Memorandum to C/S, 6 April 1942, reference C rations, MC, Box 9.

Garleb, William. Letters and tapes to author, AP.

Garrett, Harold J. Letters and tapes to author, AP.

Gerow, Leonard T. Memorandum for [Army] Chief of Staff, 3 January 1942, Subject: Relief of the Philippines.

Gilewitch, Michael. Letters to author, AP.

Gilmore, Paul C. Letters to author, AP.

Glattly, Harold W. Memorandum To: The Surgeons, 21st and 41st Divisions, 6 March 1942, MC, Box 9.

———. Letter to The Commanding General, Luzon Force, In the Field, 23 March 1942, Subject: Present Malarial Situation, MC, Box 9.

Glessner, Joseph M. Letters to author, AP.

Golden Anniversary, Class of 1933 West Point, New York: United States Military Academy, West Point, New York, 1983.

Goodall, Henry W. Letter to Dr. George Groce, 17 August 1948, MC, Box 8.

Goodman, Julien M. Dr. *MD POW.* New York: Exposition Press, Inc., 1972.

Gordon, Jack D. Letters and tapes to author, AP.

Gordon, Richard M. Letters to author, AP.

Gregory, Romie C. Letters to author, AP.

Groce, George C. Letter to Clifford Bluemel, 24 June 1948, MC, Box 11.

———. Memorandum For: Col H. H. Galbrett, Subject: 57th Infantry (PS), 19 May 1948, MC, Box 16.

———. Letter to MG K. L. Berry, 23 January 1950, MC, Box 1.

———. Letter to Louis Morton, 28 May 1950, with comments from Holstead C. Fowler, MC, Box 1.

Guyton, Benson. Letters to author, AP.

H

Haislip, Wade H. Memorandum for the [Army] Chief of Staff, 15 August, 1941, MC.

———. Memorandum for the [Army] Chief of Staff, 19 August, 1941, MC.

Hamburger, Emanuel. Letters to author, AP.

Harkins, Philip. *Blackburn's Headhunters.* New York: W. W. Norton & Company, 1955.

Hartendorp, A. V. H. *The Japanese Occupation of the Philippines.* Manila: Makati, Rizal, MDB Printing, 1967.

Hartman, Allison L. Diary and Miscellandeous Notes, Captain A. L. Hartman, USAAC, 999-2-205.

Hase, James O. Letter to The Adjutant General, 18 May 1944, Subject: Award of Decoration, in Chunn, "Notebook," MC, Box 2.

Hashimoto, Hiromitsu. Statement Concerning Artillery for the Philippine Operations, in "Statements," vol. 1.

Hauser, William A. Letters to author, AP.

Hayashi, Saburo. *KOGUN. The Japanese Army in the Pacific War.* Baltimore, Maryland: Monumental Printing Co., 1959.

Hendry, Rod K. "21st FA (PA)," in Chunn, "Notebook," MC, Box 2.

Hernandez, Juan B. *Not the Sword.* New York: Greenwich Book Publishers, 1959.

Herrera, Carlos J. "The Philippine Constabulary in the Battle of the Philippines," paper prepared for the Command and General Staff Course 1946–1947, Fort Leavenworth, MC, Box 9.

Hersey, John. *Men on Bataan.* New York: Alfred A. Knopf, 1942.

Hess, William N. *Pacific Sweep. The 5th and 13th Fighter Commands in World War II.* Garden City, New York: Doubleday & Company, Inc., 1974.

Hewlett, Frank. Interview, 31 August 1942, "Effect of MacArthur's departure on morale," by George C. Groce, MC, Box 9.

Hibbs, Ralph. Letters and tapes to author, AP.

Hileman, Millard. "698th Ordinance [sic]," *The Quan* vol. 36, no. 3 (November 1981), AP.

———. Letters to author, AP.

Hilton, R. C. Memorandum to G4, USFIP, 3 April 1942, Box 9.

Hines, Carroll R. Clearwater, Florida. Interview, 8 May 1975, AP.

Hogaboom, William F. "Action Report: Bataan," *The Marine Corps Gazette* vol. 30, no. 4 (April 1946).

Holbrook, Stewart H. *None More Courageous. American War Heroes of Today.* New York: The Macmillan Company, 1942.

Holmes, Stanley. "History of the 33rd INF. (PA)," in Chunn, "Notebook," MC, Box 2.

Homma, Masaharu. Testimony, War Crimes Trial.

———. Interview, March 1946, by Walter E. Buchly, MC, Box 8a.

Hough, Frank O., Ludwig, Verle E., and Shaw, Henry I. *Pearl Harbor to Guadalcanal: History of U. S. Marine Corps Operations in World War II.* vol. 1: Historical Branch, G-3 Division, Headquarters, U. S. Marine Corps.

Houser, Houston P. Letters to Louis Morton, 9 and 18 March 1949, MC, Box 12.

Houston, Thomas W. Diary, December 1941 to February 1942, Book 1, USAAC, 999-?-60.

Howard, Charles E. N. Jr. Letter To The Adjutant General US Army, Subject: Unit History, 2nd Battalion, 88th Field Artillery (Philippine Scouts) for the period 7 December 1941, to 9 April 1942 incl. in the Philippine Islands, written May–June 1946, MC, Box 15.

———. Interview, 14 June 1948, by George C. Groce, MC, Box 1.

Howitzer, The. No publishing data printed in the book.

Hoyt, Edwin P. *The Lonely Ships. The Life and Death of the U.S. Asiatic Fleet.* New York: David McKay Company, Inc., 1976.

Hughett, Maurice G. Letters to author, AP.

Hummel, John J. Clearwater, Florida. Interview, 9 May 1975.

Hunt, Ray C. Jr. Letters to author, AP.

Hurt, Marshall H. Jr. Major. "The Surrender," extract of Hurt Diary, MC, Box 4.

———. "Notes for History," in Brady, "Location of the 31st Infantry," MC, Box 15.

I

I Corps Field Order #14, 8 April 1942, MC, Box 12.

———. General Order #16, 28 February 1942, MC, Box 17.

Ind, Allison. *Bataan: The Judgment Seat. The Saga of the Philippine Command of the United States Army Air Force May 1941 to May 1942.* New York: The Macmillan Co., 1944.

"Information Regarding Strength and Composition of Japanese Forces, Philippine Islands Dec 41–May 42," to 3d Ind, Letter from G-2, General Headquarters, Far East Command, 16 Aug 49 to Chief, Historical Division, DA, Wash, D.C., AP.

Ingle, Donald F. Letters to author, AP.

"Intelligence Bulletins, October 1942, September 1942, and January 1943," Military Intelligence Service, War Department, Washington, D.C.

"Interrogations of Japanese Officials on World War II," 3 vols. General Headquarters Far East Command, MI Section, Historical Divisions.

Irwin, Constant L. Letter to MG Orlando Ward, 13 June 1951, MC, Box 1.

———. Interview, Walter Reed Hospital, 7 August 1942, by Captain Perry G. E. Miller, MC, Box 1.

J

Jacoby, Melville. "Corregidor Cable No. 79," *The Field Artillery Journal* vol. 32, no. 4 (April 1942).

James, D. Clayton. *South to Bataan, North to Mukden: The Prison Diary of Brigadier General W. E. Brougher.* Athens, Georgia: University of Georgia Press, 1971.

———. *The Years of MacArthur* 3 vols. Boston: Houghton Mifflin Company, 1970–1985.

James, unknown first name. "11th Infantry (PA)," in Chunn, "Notebook," MC, Box 2.

"Japanese Armor on Corregidor," *The Quan* vol. 37, no. 3 (November 1982).

Japanese Monograph No. 1, Philippine Operations Record, Phase 1, 6 November

1941–30 June 1942. Military History Section, Hq, USAFFE, published by the Office of the Chief of Military History.

Japanese Monograph No. 2, Philippine Operations Record, Phase 1, November 1941–10 April 1942. Historical Section, G2, GHQ, FEC.

Japanese Monograph No. 11, Philippine Air Operations Record, Phase 1, December 1941–May 1942. Military History Section, Hq, Army Forces Far East.

"Japanese Operations: Bataan, West Coast," anon, MC, Box 8a.

"The Japanese Plan of Maneuver in the Final Battle of Bataan," Military History Branch, Armed Forces of the Philippines, 1963, National Library, Republic of the Philippines.

"Japs and Quinine," extract from US vs. Homma, MC, Box 8a.

Jimenez, Nicanor J. Seoul, Republic of Korea. Interview, 6 April 1983.

Johnson, Bill. "Silver Bowl Center of Reunion. Shanghai Bowl Hidden from Japanese in Bataan in WWII," *The Quan* vol. 42, no. 1 (July 1987), AP.

Johnson, Edwin COL. Obituary in *The Quan* vol. 31, no. 1 (June 1976), AP.

Johnson, Harold K. "Abucay," monograph written for the Command and General Staff Course, 6 July 1947, CARL.

———. "Defense Along the Abucay Line," *Military Review* vol. XXVIII, no. 11 (February 1949), CARL.

———. "Defense of the Philippine Islands Anyasen [sic] and Silaiim Points Bataan (Personal experience of a Regimental S-3) 57th Infantry (PS)," monograph written for the Command and General Staff Course 1946–1947, MC, Box 14.

———. Diary, USAMHI.

———. Carlisle Barracks, Pennsylvania. Interview by Colonel Richard Jensen, 6–7 February 1972, US Army Military History Institute Oral History Debriefing Program, USAMHI.

———. Interviews, Washington, D.C. . 16–17 December 1975 and Alexandria, Virginia, 30 November 1980, AP.

———. Letters to author, AP.

———. Letter to Edmund J. Lilly, 30 March 1946, MC, Box 3.

———. "Oral Reminiscences of General Harold K. Johnson, Valley Forge, Pennsylvania, July 7, 1971," by D. Clayton James, WEBC.

Johnson, L. E. "Reports of S3, 194th Tank Battalion, 1/4/42," in diary of LTC E. B. Miller, MC, Box 12.

———. "S-3 Report, 194th Tank Bn., (Less "C" Co.) 4/4–7/42 Incl," USAAC, 999-2-202.

Jones, Albert M. "Chronological Order of Events, 51st Div (PA) from Dec 29, 41 to Jan 26, 42," MC, Box 17.

———. Diary, reproduced as Appendix 2 to Annex V: Report of Operations of South Luzon Force, Bataan Defense Force and II

Philippine Corps in the Defense of South Luzon and Bataan from 8 December 1941–9 April 1942, CARL.

———. "Notes on 51st Div (PA) 31 Dec 41–26 Jan 42, both incl," MC, Box 14.

———. "Pocket Battles," MC, Box 13.

———. "Pocket Fights," written by Stuart C. MacDonald, supplement to Jones, Diary, MC, Box 13.

———. "Organization Day, Twenty-Fifth Anniversary, Thirty First U. S. Infantry," AP.

———. Letter to John R. Boatwright, 1 November 1950, MC, Box 1.

———. War Department, Public Information Office Biography, Albert M. Jones, MC, Box 9.

K

Kadel, Richard C. Letter to Louis Morton, 5 May 1950, MC, Box 12.

Kalbfleish, Edwin Jr. Letters to author, AP.

Kane, George. Letters to author, AP.

Karr, Joe. Letters to author, AP.

Keith, Billy. *Days of Anguish, Days of Hope.* New York: Doubleday & Company, Inc., 1972.

Kennard, William J. "Observations on Bataan," MC, Box 15.

———. Manuscript, "History-Medical Department," MC, Box 15.

Kerchum, Paul. Letters to author, AP.

Kerins, William J. Letters to author, AP.

King, Edward P. Affidavit in Tisdelle "Testimony."

———. Memo. of Instructions For: Col. E. C. Williams, FA Chief of FA, April 8, 1942, MC, Box 10.

———. War Department, Public Information Office Biography, Edward P. King Jr., MC, Box 9.

King, Walter, and Kelley, Welbourn. *Battle Report Pearl Harbor to Coral Sea.* New York: Farrar and Rinehart, Inc., 1944.

Kinler, William N. Letters to author, AP.

Kitano, Kenzo. Diary, 1 Jan–24 Jul 1942, extracts in "Translations," vol. IV.

Kleber, Brooks E., and Birdsell, Dale. *United States Army in World War II. The Technical Services. The Chemical Warfare Service: Chemicals in Combat.* Washington, D.C.: Office of the Chief of Military History, United States Army, U.S. Government Printing Office, 1966.

Knight, Raymond. Letters to author, AP.

———. Clearwater, Florida. Interview, 8 May 1975, AP.

Knoll, Dyens W. Letter to Vice Chief of Naval Operations, Subject: Intelligence Report to Vice Chief of Staff, Sixteenth Naval District, during the period March 12 to May 3, 1942, MC, Box 8.

Knox, Donald. *Death March. The Survivors of Bataan.* New York: Harcourt Brace Jovanovich, 1981.

Knox, Forrest K. Letters to author, AP.

Koury, George. Dallas, Texas. Interview, 27 April 1972 by Dr. Ronald E. Marcello, North Texas State University Oral History Collection, NTSU.

Kramerich, Stephen N. Letters to author, AP.

Krauss, Paul H. "Anti-Tank Company 45th Inf. (PS)," in Chunn, "Notebook," MC, Box 2.

L

Labrador, Vincente W. "The Ship That Died Hard," *The Quan* no. 35 (January 1981), AP.

Lage, Wilbur J. "The Operations of the 3d Battalion, 11th Infantry (11th Division P.A.), at Zaragosa, P. I. 28 December–29 December 1941 (Personal Experience of a Regimental Machine Gun Officer and Commander of the Covering Force in the Withdrawal)," monograph written for the Infantry Officer Advance Course #2, 1947–48, TISL.

Laird, James. Fort Campbell, Kentucky. Interview, 30 December 1973, AP.

Lally, John G. Letters and tapes to author, AP.

"Landing Operations in the Philippines 1941," anon, MC, Box 11.

Larrabee, Eric. *Commander In Chief, Franklin Delano Roosevelt, His Lieutenants, and Their War.* New York: Harper & Row, 1987.

Lathrop, Leslie T. "Tuol Pocket," MC, Box 13.

———. "The Tuol Pocket," AP.

———. Letter to Adrianus J. Van Oosten, 15 October 1947, MC, Box 13.

Lawrence, Charles S. "Notebook, Record of Events December 27, 1941 to April 9, 1942 Bataan," The Charles S. Lawrence Papers, USAMHI.

———. "Notebook, Operations Report II Philippine Corps Apr 2–9, 1942," in the Charles S. Lawrence Papers, USAMHI.

Lawton, Marion R. Arlington, Virginia. Interview, 3 August 1980, AP.

Lee, Clark. *They Call It Pacific: An Eye-Witness Story of Our War Against Japan from Bataan to the Solomons.* New York: The Viking Press, 1943.

Lee, Henry G. *Nothing But Praise.* Culver City, California: Murray and Gee, Inc., 1948.

Leggett, James L. "Records of 803rd Engineer Battalion Separate," USAAC, 999-2-149.

———. "Brief History-Company "A"-803d. ENGR. BN. (AVN)(SEP)," USAAC, 999-2-149.

Leighton, Richard M., and Coakley, Robert W. *United States Army in World War II. Global Logistics and Strategy, 1940–1943.* Washington,

D.C.: Office of the Chief of Military History, United States Army, U. S. Government Printing Office, 1955.

Lester, John E. "Air Corps in the War," MC, Box 8.

Levering, Robert W. *Horror Trek. A True Story of Bataan, The Death March And Three And One-Half Years in Japanese Camps.* Dayton, Ohio: The Horstman Printing Co., 1948.

Liles, Wayne C. Letters to author, AP.

———. Letter to wife, 26 August 1945, AP.

———. "12th Infantry (PA)," in Chunn, "Notebook," MC, Box 2.

Lilly, Edmund J. "Report of Operations, 57th Infantry (PS) 8 December 1941 to 9 April 1942," MC, Box 16.

———. Letter to Clinton A. Pierce, 27 February 1946, MC.

———. Letters to author, AP.

Linn, Howard J. Letter to author, AP.

M

MacArthur, Douglas. *Reminiscences.* New York: McGraw-Hill Book Company, 1964.

———. Letter to George C. Marshall, 28 October 1941, cited in Morton, *Fall.*

———. Memorandum to Wainwright, 28 January 1942, cited in Beck, *MacArthur and Wainwright.*

———. Message from General MacArthur To: All Unit Commanders, January 15th, 1942, AP.

MacDonald, Stuart C. "Pocket Fights," supplement to Jones, Diary, AP.

———. "Important Dates-SLF," with numerous sub titles, MC, Box 14.

———. "Notes on Left Subsector, I Philippine Corps," in supplement to Jones, Diary, MC, Box 13.

———. "Notes on 51st Div (PA)(31 Dec 41–26 Jan 42, both incl)," MC, Box 17.

———. Letter to Major General A. M. Jones, 6 November 1950, MC, Box 17.

Mackowski, John J. Letters to author, AP.

Maeda, Masami. Comments in "Statements," vol. II.

Mainichi, 3 April 1943.

Mallonee, Richard C. II, ed., *The Naked Flagpole.* San Rafael: Presidio Press, 1980.

Mallonee, Richard C. "Bataan Diary," 2 vols., vol. 1, "The defense at the beach, The Withdrawal to Bataan;" vol. 2, "The Defense of Bataan," in The Richard C. Mallonee Papers, USAMHI.

———. Letter to Orlando Ward, 8 January 1952, MC, Box 12.

Manchester, William. *American Caesar Douglas MacArthur 1880–1964.* Boston: Little, Brown and Company, 1978.

"Map, II Corps Engineer, 14 January 1942," AP.

Marlow, Linus B. Letters to author, AP.

Marrocco, William. Letters to author, AP.

Marshall, George C. Letter to MacArthur, —Dec 41, not sent.

Marshall, Richard J. Memorandum To: Chief of Staff, USAFFE, January 13, 1942, MC, Box 12.

———. Virginia Military Institute. Interview, 7 April 1948, by Louis Morton, MC, Box 11.

Martin, Brice J. "Operations of Company F, 51st. Infantry Regiment (51st. Division)(Philippine Army) In Vicinity of Mt. Samat, Bataan, 1 March 1942 (Philippine Defense Campaign)(Personal Experience of a Company Commander)," monograph written for Infantry Officer Advance Course #2, 1947–48, TISL, 504.

———. "Regimental History, 51st. Infantry, Philippine Army," MC, Box 17.

———. Letters to author, AP.

Martin, John J. Dothan, Alabama. Interview, 14 February 1976, AP.

Massello, William Jr. Letters to author, AP.

———. Letter to The Adjutant General, Subject: Recommendation for Award, 3 January 1946, AP.

Mayo, Lida. *United States Army in World War II The Technical Services The Ordnance Department: On Beachhead and Battlefront.* Washington, D.C.: Office of the Chief of Military History, United States Army, 1981.

McBride, Allan C. "Notes on the Fall of Bataan, 14 April 1942," MC, Box 14.

McBride, Woodrow. Letters to author, AP.

McCarthy, Carlton. *Detailed Minutiae of Soldier Life in the Army of Northern Virginia 1861–1865.* Richmond: Carlton McCarthy and Company, 1882.

McGlothlin, Frank Emile. *Barksdale To Bataan. History of the 48th Materiel Squadron, October 1940–April 1942.* By the Author, 1984.

McGuire, Omar L. Letters to author, with paper, "Our Defense of Bataan," AP.

McLaughlin, Charles A. Letter to Louis Morton, 14 June 1949 with inclosure, "History of the 23rd Inf Reg, 21st Div PA USAFFE," MC, Box 17.

McLaughlin, William. Letters to author, AP.

McMasters, Archie L. "Memoirs of the Tuol Pocket," 18 October 1947, MC, Box 13.

McNaughton, Roland C. "31st FA (PA)," in Chunn, "Notebook," MC, Box 2.

Mead, Everett V. "The Operations and Movements of the 31st Infantry Regiment (Philippine Division) 7 December 1941–9 April 1942 (Philippine Island Campaign)(Personal Experience of a Regimental

S-4)," monograph written for Infantry Officer Advance Course #2, 1947–48, MC, Box 15.

Meidling, George A. ed. *Engineers of the Southwest Pacific 1941–1945 Vol I: Engineers in Theater Operations—United States Army Forces in the Far East, Southwest Pacific Area, Army Forces, Pacific.* Tokyo, Japan: Office of the Chief Engineer, General Headquarters Army Forces, Pacific, 1947.

———. *Engineers of the Southwest Pacific 1941–1945 Vol III: Engineer Intelligence—United States Army Forces in the Far East, Southwest Pacific Area, Army Forces, Pacific.* Washington, D.C.: Office of the Chief Engineer, General Headquarters Army Forces, Pacific, United States Government Printing Office, 1950.

———. *Engineers of the Southwest Pacific 1941–1945 Vol VII: Engineer Supply—United States Army Forces in the Far East, Southwest Pacific Area, Army Forces, Pacific.* Tokyo, Japan: Office of the Chief Engineer, General Headquarters Army Forces, Pacific, 1947, United States Government Printing Office, Washington, 1949.

Mellnik, Steve. *Philippine Diary: 1939–1945.* New York: Van Nostrand Reinhold Co., 1969.

Memorandum for [Army] Chief of Staff, Subject: Relief of the Philippines, 3 Jan 42, MC.

Mendelson, Sheldon H. "Operations of the Provisional Air Corps Regiment in the Defense of Bataan Peninsula, P. I., 8 January–10 April 1942 (Philippine Islands Campaign)(Personal experience of a Platoon Leader)," monograph written for the Infantry Officer Advance Course, 1946–47, TISL.

Miller, Ernest B. *Bataan Uncensored.* Long Prairie, Minn: The Hart Publications, Inc., February 1949.

———. Diary which includes, CPT L. E. Johnson, Reports of S-3, 194th Tank Bn 1/4/42, dtd 14/43 [sic], and CPT F. G. Spoor, Report of Bn S-2 at Lubao on 1/5/42, MC, Box 12.

———. Letter to Orlando Ward, 31 December 1951, MC, Box 1.

———. "Notes of Lieutenant Colonel Miller," in USAAC, 999-2-202.

Miller, Fred. Letters to author, AP.

Miller, Henry M. "A Short History of the 200th Coast Artillery," USAAC, 500-4.

Miller, James M. Letter to Major General Orlando Ward, 19 April 1952 with "Comments of former Japanese Officers regarding *The Fall of the Philippines,*" MC, Box 8a.

Miller, Robert L. Alexandria, Virginia. Interview, 28 April 1981, AP.

———. Letters to author, AP.

Miller, William. Letters to author, AP.

———. San Antonio, Texas. Interview, 22 August 1977, AP.

Mills, Loyd, Letters to author, AP.

Milton, Glenn. Letters to author, AP.

Minier, John. Letters to author, AP.

Moffitt, Lloyd C. Diary, AP.

Montgomery, William H. "Diary and Notes of William H. Montgomery written as letters to his wife while on Bataan and in Prisoner of War Camps in the Philippine Islands Under the Control of the Japanese Imperial Army-December 8, 1941 to February 4, 1945," The Mark M. Wohlfeld Collection, USAMHI.

————. "I Hired Out To Fight," possession of Montgomery.

————. Letters to author, AP.

Moody, Samuel B., and Allen, Maury. *Reprieve from Hell.* Germany: copywright by Samuel B. Moody and Maury Allen, 1961.

Moody, Samuel B. Letters to author, AP.

Moore, Arthur P. "Actions of the 41st FA (PA) Senior Inst 41 FA," in Fortier, "Notes on 41st Div."

Moore, Dennis M. "The Dennis M. Moore Papers," MC, Box 14.

————. "Diary, Lt. Col. D. M. Moore," MC, Box 3.

Morey, Harold A. "32nd Inf. (PA)," in Chunn, "Notebook," MC, Box 2.

Morhouse, Charles H. Letter to The Surgeon General, War Department, Washington, D.C. Through the Surgeon USASOS. Subject: Medical Service in the Philippines, 20 January 1943, MC, Box 9.

Morison, Samuel Eliot. *History of United States Naval Operations in World War II. Vol. III The Rising Sun in the Pacific 1931–April 1942.* Boston: Little, Brown and Company, 1948.

Morrett, John. Letters to author, AP.

Morrill, John., and Martin, Pete. *South From Corregidor.* New York: Simon and Schuster, 1943.

Morrill, John. Letter to Commandant, 16th Naval District, 30 January 1942, Subject: Report of Action at Longoskawayan Point, morning of January 29th, 1942, MC, Box 8.

Morton, Louis. *United States Army in World War II The War in the Pacific The Fall of the Philippines.* Washington, D.C.: Office of the Chief of Military History, United States Army, US Government Printing Office, 1953.

————. *United States Army in World War II The War in the Pacific Strategy and Command. The First Two Years.* Washington, D. C.: Office of the Chief of Military History, United States Army, US Government Printing Office, 1962.

————. "What Is The Condition Of My Troops?" paper written for Louis Morton in his research for *The Fall of the Philippines,* MC, Box 9.

————. ed. "Bataan Diary of Major Achille Tisdelle," *Military Affairs* vol. XI, no. 3 (Fall 1947).

————. "Estimated Japanese Ground Force Strength (Effective) On the Eve of the April Offensive," MC, Box 3.

————. Interview with Richard J. Marshall, 7 April 1948, MC.

————. Letter to Samuel E. Morison, 6 October 1949, MC, Box 1.

————. Letters to Clinton A. Pierce, 23 March 1948 and 12 March 1951, MC, Box 1.
Mueller, Clara L. Diary, USAAC, 999-2-84.

N

Naguiat, Ramon D., Jr. Letters to author, AP.
Nakayama, Motoo. "Details of Negotiations with Maj Gen King Concerning Terms for the Surrender of Bataan Peninsula," 26 August 1949, MC, Box 10.
Nara, Akira. Interrogation of General Nara, in "Statements," vol III.
Nash, David. Letters and tapes to author, AP.
Nealson, William R. "The Operations of a Provisional Battalion, 41st Infantry, (PA), at Abucay Hacienda (Bataan), 15–25 January 1942 (The Struggle for the Philippines)(Personal Experience of a Battalion Commander)," monograph written for Infantry Officer Advance Course #2, 1947–1948, TISL, 490.
Niday, Floyd T. Letters and tapes to author, AP.
"Ninth [9th] Infantry, Bataan," anon, MC, Box 8a.
Noyer, William L. *Mactan: Ship of Destiny.* Fresno: Rainbow Press, 1979.

O

O'Connel, Joe. Letters to author, AP.
O'Day, Ray M. "History of the 21st Division," in two parts, MC, Box 17.
Oestreich, E. D. Letters to author, AP.
Office of the Chief of Military History. "Resume of Philippine Relief Operations," MC.
Ohta, Shoji. "Statement No 518, Subject: Bataan Operations, 18 March 1952," in "Comments."
Oishi, Hiromi. Comments in "Statements," Vol. III.
Olson, John E. Papers, John E. Olson's possession.
————. Letters to author, AP.
————. Letter to Louis Morton, 10 January 1952, MC, Box 1.
————. Lake Quivira, Kansas. Interview, 1 December 1974, AP.
————. Springfield, Virginia. Interview, 8 May 1988, AP.
————. Undated notes with Anders letter to author, 1 April 1977, AP.
————. Letters to Franklin O. Anders, 15 July, 24 August 1977, and 17 March 1981, AP.
————. "The Operations of the 57th Infantry (P.S.) Regimental Combat Team (Philippine Division) at Abucay, P.I., 10 January–23 January 1942, (Bataan Campaign)(Personal Experience of a Regimental

Adjutant)," monograph written for Infantry Officer Advance Course #2, 1947–1948, TISL, 506.

Olson, John E, and Anders, Franklin O. "Anywhere-Anytime: History of the Fifty-Seventh Infantry (PS)," *Bulletin American Historical Collection, American Association of the Philippines* vol. XV, no. 3(60) (July–September 1987), AP.

———. "Preparing the Abucay Line: History of the 57th Regiment (PS)," *Bulletin American Historical Collection, American Association of the Philippines* vol. XV, no. 4(60) (October–December 1987), AP.

Onuma, Kiyoshi. Comments in "Statements," Vol. III.

Ortega, Abel F. San Antonio, Texas. Interview, 24 August 1977, AP.

Osborne, William L. Untitled article in *Lessons and Trends* (January 28, 1943), Infantry School Publication, no. 15, TISL.

Oster, Roy, and Richards, Grover C. Jr. "History of the 21st Infantry (PA)," in Chunn, "Notebook," MC, Box 2.

P

"PA Operations in Bataan during the First Philippine Campaign," in Letter To The Adjutant General, HPA, anon, MC, Box 17.

Parcher, Lawrence W. "History of the 21st Pursuit Squadron," in Chunn, "Notebook," MC, Box 2.

Parish, Philip R. Letters to author, AP.

Parker, George M. Letter to Louis Morton, 14 February 1948, MC, Box 1.

———. War Department, Public Information Office Biography, George Marshall Parker Jr., MC, Box 9.

Parker, T. C. "The Epic of Corregidor-Bataan, December 24, 1941–May 4, 1942," *US Naval Institute Proceedings* (January 1943).

Pena, Ambrosio P. *Bataan's Own.* Manila: 2nd Regular Division Association, Munoz Press, Inc., 1967.

———. *Bataan In Retrospect.* Intramuros, Manila: National Media Production Center.

———. "History of the 11th Div (PA)," WEBC.

———. "History of the 1st Regular Division," WEBC.

Perry, Lawrence, North American Newspaper Alliance, account dated 20 September 1945 from interview with Clinton A. Pierce, in undated answer to Louis Morton's letter of 12 March 1951, in Clinton A. Pierce's papers.

Philippine Army, Headquarters, General Order #201, 16 September 1947.

———. General Order #4, 6 October 1947.

———. General Order #375, 6 October 1947.

———. General Order #12, 17 July 1947.

————. Notes on the Philippine Army, 1941–1942, anon, MC, Box 16.

Pierce, Clinton A. Papers. USAMHI, which include:

Lilly to Pierce, 27 February 1946.

Pierce to The Secretary of War's Personnel Board, 11 March 1946.

Pierce to The Adjutant General of the Army, 30 November 1945.

Pierce to Awards and Decorations Board, Hq, 4th Army, 10 April 1946.

Pierce to Arnold J. Funk, 16 April 1946.

Pierce to CO, 12 Inf Div, 18 June 1946.

Pierce to Walter D. Edmonds, 3 March and 13 March 1947.

————. Letter to MG Orlando Ward, 5 January 1952, "Comments on Chapter XVII," MC, Box 1.

————. Letter to Louis Morton, 31 March 1948, MC, Box 1.

————. War Department, Public Information Office Biography, Clinton A. Pierce, MC, Box 9.

Pierce, Henry J. "The Operations of Company L, 45th Infantry (P.S.)(Philippine Division) on the Abucay Hacienda Line, Bataan, P.I., 15–25 January 1942 (Philippine Islands Campaign)(Personal Experience of the Company Commander)," monograph written for Infantry Officer Advance Course #2, 1949–1950, TISL, 507.

Pierce, Loren G. Letters to author, AP.

Pogue, Forrest C. *George C. Marshall. Vol. 2: Ordeal and Hope 1939–1942.* New York: The Viking Press, 1965.

Pones, Ralph C. Letters to author, AP.

Porter, Gwinn U. "Antiaircraft Defense of Corregidor," monograph written for the Command and General Staff College, Fort Leavenworth, Kansas, 1946–1947, MC, Box 15.

Poweleit, Alvin C. *USAFFE A Saga of Atrocities Perpetrated During the Fall of the Philippines, the Bataan Death March, and Japanese Imprisonment and Survival.* By the Author, 1975.

————. *Kentucky's Fighting 192nd Light G.H.Q. Tank Battalion. A Saga of Kentucky's Part in the Defense of The Philippines.* Newport, Kentucky: Quality Lithographing Company, 1981.

Prado, Eliseo. Letters to author, AP.

Pray, John I. "The Action of Company "G" 31st Infantry (Philippine Div.) Abucay Hacienda, 15–25 January 1942 (The Struggle for the Philippines)(Personal experience of a Company Commander)," monograph written for Infantry Officer Advance Course, 1946–1947, TISL, 507.

————. Letters to author, AP.

Prickett, William F. "Naval Battalion At Mariveles," *The Marine Corps Gazette* vol. 34, no. 6 (June 1950).

Priestley, William J. "3rd Battalion-31st Infantry," "71ST INFANTRY (PA)," and "2nd Battalion, 24th Field Artillery (P.S.)," all extracts from Priestley's Notebook #1, MC, Boxes 15, 16, and 17.

————. "History of NLF–I Corps," MC, Box 14.

Provisional Air Corps Regiment. "Statistical Report, Third Section, the Provisional Air Corps Regiment, 31 March 1942," USAAC.

Pugh, John R. Diary, cited in Beck, *Sacrifice.*

Purling, Donald T. Letters to author, AP.

Q

Quail, U.S.S. Memorandum, CO of Quail to CPT Dessez, 9 January 1942, reference Naval Battalion, MC, Box 3.

————. Letter, CO of Quail to Commandant, 16th Naval District, 30 January 1942, Subject: Action at Longoskawayan Point, 27 January 1942, MC, Box 3.

Quezon, Manuel L. *The Good Fight.* New York: D. Appleton-Century Company, Inc., 1946.

Quintard, Alexander S. Diary of Colonel A. S. Quintard, 301st FA (PA), MC, Box 15.

————. "Copy of parts of Narrative of A S Quintard Col FA," MC, Box 15.

————. "The 301st Field Artillery (PA)," MC, Box 15.

R

Radio messages.

Army Air Force, HQ. #3/58, 4 Mar 42.

Roosevelt to MacArthur: 9 Feb 42.

Roosevelt to MacArthur: 11 Feb 42.

Roosevelt to Quezon: 11 Feb 42.

MacArthur to Marshall: 7 Sep 41, 28 Oct, 28 Nov; 23 Jan 42, 25 Jan, 27 Jan, 2 Feb, 8 Feb, 22 Feb, 24 Feb, and 1 Apr.

MacArthur to The Adjutant General: 7 Jan 42, 8 Jan, 9 Jan, 14 Jan, 15 Jan, 17 Jan, 21 Jan, 24 Jan, 28 Jan, 15 Feb, 4 Mar, 7 Mar.

MacArthur to Roosevelt: 11 Feb.

MacArthur to Wainwright: 4 Apr.

Marshall to MacArthur: 27 Nov 41; 3 Jan 42, 14 Jan, 2 Feb, 4 Feb, 22 Feb.

Marshall to Wainwright: 17 Mar 42.

Wainwright to MacArthur: 27 Mar 42, 5 Apr, 8 Apr, 9 Apr.

Wainwright to The Adjutant General: 29 Mar 42, 30 Mar, 5 Apr, 8 Apr, 9 Apr.

Rawlston, J. W. Letter to John E. Olson, —September 1983, in Franklin O. Anders to author, 9 August 1984, AP.

Read, Louis B. Dallas, Texas. Interview, 3 November 1972, by Dr.

Ronald E. Marcello, North Texas State University Oral History Research Collection, NTSU.

Redmond, Juanita. *I Served on Bataan.* Philadelphia & New York: J. B. Lippincott Company, 1943.

Reed, George A. Letters to author, AP.

Reports of General MacArthur Japanese Operations in the Southwest Pacific Area. Washington, D.C.: United States Government Printing Office, January 1966, prepared by MacArthur's General Staff.

Rees, Denton J. Letters to author, AP.

"Relief Operations, Resume of Philippine." Office of the Chief of Military History, MC.

Relosa, J. C. Letter to Clyde A. Selleck, 3 August 1948, MC, Box 17.

Republic of the Philippines. *Story of the 1st Regular Division, The After Action Report.* vol. 1, Camp Murphy, Quezon City, Manila: Armed Forces of the Philippines, Bureau of Printing, 1953.

Respicio, Francisco T. Letters to author, AP.

Reynolds, Royal. Letters to author, AP.

Richards, Grover C. "Outline of Steps to a POW Camp," MC, Box 17.

Riesenberg, Felix. Jr. *Sea War The Story of the U.S. Merchant Marine in World War II.* New York: Rinehart & Company, Inc., 1956.

Roberts, C. H. M. Letter to Commanding General, Frankford Arsenal, 4 October 1948, Subject: Philippine Records-Ammunition Reports, MC, Box 1.

Robledo, Luis T. Letters to author, AP.

Rockwell, Francis W. Memorandum for Captain Dessez, U.S.N., 9 January 1942, MC, Box 8.

Rodman, John H. "Engagement of 91st Division on Moron-Bagac Road From KP 164 to 168," in letter to Louis Morton, 31 March 1949, MC, Box 17.

———. Letter to Major General Orlando Ward, 1 February 1952, "Comments, Information, and Suggestive Changes of Chapter VIII to Chapter XIX of the Proposed History of the Fall of the Philippines," MC, Box 1.

Roland, Orville D. Letters to author, AP.

Romulo, Carlos P. *I Saw the Fall of the Philippines.* Garden City, NY: Doubleday, Doran & Co., Inc., 1942.

Rooks, James O. "11th Infantry (PA)," in Chunn, "Notebook."

Rosen, M. H. Letters and tapes to author, AP.

Rosendahl, Robert D. Letters to author, AP.

Rubard, James J. Letters to author, AP.

Rudorff, Raymond. *War to the Death. The Sieges of Saragossa, 1808–1809.* New York: Macmillan Publishing Co., Inc., 1974.

Rutherford, Ward. *Fall of the Philippines.* New York: Ballantine Books Inc., 1971.

Rutledge, Tillman J. Letters and tapes to author, AP.

S

Saalman, Otis E. Letters to author, AP.

Sackett, E. L. "The History of the U.S.S. Canopus," *US Naval Institute Proceedings* (January 1943).

Sage, Charles G. "Report of Operations of the Philippine Prov Coast Artillery Bde AA in the Philippine Campaign," MC, Box 15.

Sanders, Cecil M. "The Operations of the 57th Infantry (PS)(Philippine Division) at Anyasan and Silaiim Points, Bataan, P.I., 2 February–13 February 1942 (Philippine Islands Campaign)(Personal Experience of a Regiment Staff Officer)," monograph written for Infantry Officer Advance Course #2, 1949–1950, TISL, 509.

Santos, Alfredo M. "The 1st Regular Division in the Battle of the Philippines," paper prepared for the Command and General Staff Course, Fort Leavenworth, 7 June 1947, MC, Box 17.

Sawicki, James A. *Field Artillery Battalions of the U.S. Army* 2 vols. Virginia: Centaur Publication, 1977.

Schedler, Dean. "Corregidor's AA Keep 'Em Frying," *Coast Artillery Journal* vo. LXXXV, no. 3 (May–June, 1942).

Schreiber, Alfred C. Letters to author, AP.

Schultz, Duane. *Hero of Bataan: The Story of General Jonathan M. Wainwright.* New York: St. Martin's Press, 1981.

Scofield, John. "The Jap War Machine," *Infantry Journal* vol. L, no. 2 (February 1942).

Selleck, Clyde A. Statement to Board of Officers, Subject: Prepared Statement for Consideration with Reference to my Reduction From Temporary Rank of Brigadier General and Request for Reinstatement in that Rank. 1 February 1946, MC, Box 17.

———. Interview, 2 April 1948, by George C. Groce, MC, Box 1.

———. Memorandum to Gen McBride re my Command Period in the West Sector Bataan, MC, Box 14.

———. "Notes 71st Division, Report of 71st Div in compliance with official request, August 1942," MC, Box 17.

———. War Department, Public Information Office Biography, Clyde A. Selleck, MC, Box 9.

Sevilla, Victor J. *The Bataan Odyssey.* (1960).

Shoemake, Andrew D. "History of the 41st F.A. (P.A.)," in Chunn, "Notebook," MC, Box 2.

Shoss, Morris L. Letter to William H. Bartsch, 7 August 1978 in *The Quan* no. 33 (November 1978), AP.

Shreve, Arthur L. "Transcription, Diary of Arthur L. Shreve, Lt. Col. (FA), GSC," MC, Box 3.

Sims, Leland. San Antonio, Texas. Interview, 23 August 1977.

Sixteenth Naval District. Commander, Letter to Commander, Southwest Pacific Force, 8 April 1942, MC, Box 3.

————. Message 110550Z, February 11, 1942 from DIO for Director of Naval Intelligence.

Sixtieth Coastal Artillery (AA). Unit Histories, 60th Coastal Artillery (AA), Bataan (December 2 1942 to April 9 1942), USAAC, 500-5-1.

Sixty-Fifth Brigade. "Natib Mountain Area Detailed Combat Report," captured by American forces on Cape Gloucester, 8 February 1944, AP.

————. "Detailed Report of Combat in the Vicinity of Mount Samat, 26 Jan to 24 Feb 42," captured by American forces on Cape Gloucester, 8 February 1944, AP.

Skardon, Beverly N. "The Operations of Company A, 92d Infantry Philippine Army; 3 January 1942, 24 March 1942 (Personal Experience of a Company Commander)," monograph written for Infantry Officer Advance Course 1946–1947, TISL, 510.

Skerry, Harry A. Letter to LTC George A. Meidling, 4 August 1947, MC, Box 1, with two enclosures:
1: Order of CG NLF 1 Aug 42 directing submission of rpts.
2: Memorandum to Chief of Staff, North Luzon Force, Subject: Organization and Operations of the North Luzon Force Engineers between Dec 8, 1941 and Jan 6, 1942 by Col. Harry A. Skerry, CE, the Force Engineer submitted in accordance with Incl 1, 1 Aug 1942.

————. Letter to LTC George A. Meidling, 4 June 1949, "Comments on *Engineers in Theater Operations,*" MC, Box 1, with 23 enclosures:
1–21: Comments 1–20 incl.
22: Comment 11 1/2.
23: Rough draft of Chap II (Combat Engineering in the Philippine Defense)(not included).

————. Letter to Major General Orlando Ward, 16 January 1952, "Comments of *The Fall of the Philippines,*" MC, Box 1, with two enclosures:
1: Ltr 30 June 49 to GHQ, FEC, with 17 comments, Subject: Rough Draft of Volume II on Engineer Organization, Philippine Divisions.
2: Ltr 20 July 1949 to GHQ, FEC, Subject: Rough Draft of Volume VIII on Engineer Critique, Philippine Defense.

Smack, Edward. Letters to author, AP.

Smith, Dean B. Letters to author, AP.

Smith, Merle-, Van S. Letter to Asst. Chief of Staff, G-2, War Department, 27 January 1942, Subject: Arrival of hospital ship from Philippines, MC, Box 1.

Smith, Willard A. Letter to Louis Morton, 23 May 1949, MC, Box 12.

Snyder, Wilburn L. Letters and tapes to author, AP.

Soifer, Gilbert B. Letters and tapes to author, AP.

Somervell, Brehon. Paper, Subject: Acquisition of Certain Canadian Supplies for the Far Eastern Command in the Philippines, MC, Box 12.

Southwest Pacific Area Headquarters. General Order #26, 26 August 1942.

Spaatz, Carl. Memorandum for the Chief of Staff, 13 November 1941, Subject: Equipment for Philippine Aircraft Warning Service, MC, Box 12.

―――. Memorandum for the Chief of Staff, 29 November 1941, Subject: Antiaircraft Artillery Personnel for the Philippines, MC, Box. 9.

Spaulding, Theodore I. Letters and tapes to author, AP.

Spencer, Cornelia. *Romulo Voice of Freedom*. New York: The John Day Company, 1953.

Spencer, James C. Letters to author, AP.

Spoor, F. G. "Report of Battalion S2 at Lubao, 1/5/42," MC, Box 12.

"Statements of Japanese Officials on World War II, (English Translations)," General Headquarters, Far East Command, Military Intelligence Section, Historical Division, vols. I, II, and III.

Stauffer, Alvin P. *The Quartermaster Corps: Operations in the War Against Japan. United States Army in World War II. The Technical Services.* Washington, D.C.: United States Government Printing Office, 1956.

Steed, James. Letters and tapes to author, AP.

Steel, Charles L. "Account of Action 31st Inf at Layac," in Selleck, "Notes 71 Div," MC, Box 17.

―――. "Report of Operations, II Philippine Corps, 2 to 9 Apr, 1942," MC, Box 14.

Stempin, Harry J. "The Operations of Company G, 57th Infantry (P.S.)(Philippine Division) on Luzon, 7 December 1941–30 January 1942 (Philippine Island Campaign)(Personal experience of a Company Commander)," monograph written for Infantry Officer Advance Course, 1946–1947, TISL, 511.

―――. Letters to author, AP.

―――. San Antonio, Texas. Interview, 24 August 1977, AP.

Stewart, Edward W. Letters to author, AP.

―――. Letter to Adrianus J. Van Oosten, 7 October 1947, MC, Box 13.

Stoudt, Daniel N. Bethel, Pennsylvania. Interview, 6 August 1977, AP.

Strong, Walter S. "History of 31st Inf. (US)," in Chunn, "Notebook," MC, Box 2.

Sullivan, James M. "Hospital Number "2," Bataan, PI," USAAC, 500-8-1.

Sutherland, Richard K. Interview by Dr. Louis Morton, 12 November 1946, MC, Box 1.

―――. Letter to Louis Morton, 29 May 1951, MC, Box 1.

Svrcek, Joe F. Letters to author, AP.

T

Tank Group, Provisional. General Order #10, 14 February 1942, MC, Box 12.

———. "PRECIS: Movements to Theater and Organization, The Provisional Tank Group. United States Forces in the Far East," 14 January 1957, in Annex X to Rpt Ops USAFFE-USFIP, CARL.

Taylor, Albert L. Letters to author, AP.

Taylor, Roger. San Antonio, Texas. Interview, 22 August 1977, AP.

Theriac, Regis M. Letters and tapes to author, AP.

Thirty-First Infantry. "Miscellaneous information on the history of the Thirty-First Infantry," AP.

———. "Thirty-First Infantry Resumes Shanghai Bowl Rites," *Army Times* 11 September 1954.

Thompson, Donald G. "Operations of Company "L," 31st Infantry Regiment (Philippine Division) in the Battle of Layac Junction, Bataan, P.I., 6–7 January 1942 (Philippine Island Campaign)(Personal Experience of a Company Commander)," monograph written for Infantry Officer Advance Course #2, 1947–1948, TISL, 512.

———. Letters to author, AP.

Thompson, Harry C., and Mayo, Lida. *United States Army in World War II. The Technical Services. The Ordnance Department: Procurement and Supply.* Washington, D.C.: Office of the Chief of Military History, Department of the Army, 1960.

Tisdelle, Achille C. "Bataan Diary of Major Achille C. Tisdelle," *Military Affairs* vol. XI, no. 3 (Fall 1947) editor, Louis Morton.

———. "Journal Artillery Section, USAFFE December 1941," MC, Box 4.

———. "Story of Bataan Collapse, 9 April 1942," MC, Box 4.

———. Letter to Joe O'Connel, 28 December 1961, in O'Connel to author, 13 January 1980, AP.

———. "Interview with Major Achille Carlisle Tisdelle Cavalry who was senior aide to General King on Bataan during the fighting in 1941–42," by Lieutenant J. C. Bateman, 22 January 1946, MC, Box 4.

———. Testimony in the war crimes trial of General Homma, vol. XVIII, MC, Box 10.

Toland, John. *The Rising Sun: The Decline and Fall of the Japanese Empire 1936–1945.* New York: Random House, 1970.

———. *But Not in Shame: The Six Months After Pearl Harbor.* New York: Random House, 1961.

Towatari, Masayoshi. Comments in "Statements," vol. IV.

Townsend, Glen R. "The 11th Infantry Regiment Philippine Army, September 1, 1941–April 9, 1942," in four parts, "Part One-

Mobilization and Training," "Part Two. Beach Defense and Delaying Action, December 8, 1941–January 5, 1942," "Part III, The Tuol Pocket Jan 5–Feb 17, 1942," and "Part IV, Bataan: The Final Phase February 18–April 9, 1942," MC, Box 13.

———. Letter to CG, Luzon Force, "Reports, Subject: Narrative of Events, 11th Inf. (P.A.), April 2–9, 1942," written in Tarlac Prison Camp 30 May 1942, MC, Box 11.

———. "Defense of the Philippines," part 2 of a 2-part lecture delivered in Missouri in 1946, MC, Box 9.

———. Comments in D. Clayton James, *South to Bataan.*

———. Letter to Chief of Military History, 8 January 1952, MC, Box 1.

Translations of Japanese Documents. Six vols, vol. 6 "Information Regarding Strength and Composition of Japanese Forces, Philippine Islands Dec 41–May 42," 15 August 1949.

Trapnell, Thomas J. H. "The Operations of the 26th Cavalry (P.S.) Personal Experience of a Squadron Commander," monograph written for the Command and General Staff College Regular Course, 1946–1947, MC, Box 16.

Treharn, Bernard T. Letters to author, AP.

Twenty-Sixth Cavalry. "Statistical Report, Third Section, 26th Cavalry, In The Field, 31 March 1942," USAAC, 999-28-1.

U

Ulrich, Anthony M. "Bataan Diary," Ulrich's possession.

———. Letters to author, AP.

Underbrink, Robert L. *Destination Corregidor.* Annapolis, Maryland: United States Naval Institute, 1971.

Underwood, Charles C. "The Defense of Luzon & Bataan, 7 Dec 41–9 April 42," monograph written for Infantry Officer Advance Course, TISL.

USAFFE Field Orders #1, 6 January 1942, Technical Data; #3, 9 Jan; #4, 11 Jan; #9, 22 Jan; and #22, 16 Feb, MC, Box 12.

———. General Orders #46, 18 Dec 41; #54, 27 Dec; #1, 6 Jan 42; #3, 6 Jan; #5, 7 Jan; #6, 7 Jan; #7, 9 Jan; #11, 18 Jan; #12, 21 Jan; #14, 26 Jan; #16, 28 Jan; #18, 31 Jan; #21, 7 Feb; #23, 11 Feb; #27, 16 Feb; #28, 19 Feb; #29, 20 Feb; #31, 22 Feb; #32, 23 Feb; #35, 4 Mar; #36, 5 Mar; #37, 6 Mar; #39, 12 Mar; and #40, 13 Mar, MC, Boxes 9 and 12.

———. Special Orders #106, 24 Dec 41; #21, 23 Jan; #39, 10 Feb; and #53, 25 Feb, MC, Box 12.

———. Draft G2 bulletin, noon Feb 3 to noon Feb 4, 1942, from an intercepted Japanese message, MC.

———. G2 Information Bulletin #15, 5 January 1942; #23, February 13–14, 1942; #28, February 19–24; and #30, February 25–26, MC.

———. International News Summary #65, 28 February 1942, Press Release 1942, MC.

———. Letter, Subject: American Officers with Combat Troop Units, To: Corps, Sub-Sector and Division Commanders, Feb 3, 1942, MC, Box 12.

———. Letter, Subject: Destruction of Material and Equipment, 7 February 1942, MC, Box 12.

———. Letter, Subject: Plans for Counterattack, 11 January 1942, MC.

———. Letter, Subject: Quartermaster Plan of Supply, To: Asst C/S G4, 23 January 1942, MC.

———. USAFFE Organization History 1941–42, World War II, MC, Box 13.

———. Training Memorandums #4, 12 January 1942; #10, 1 February; and #14, 25 February; and #15, 26 February, MC, Box 12.

———. Signal Operation Instructions, 5 January 1942, Astronomical Data #3, AP.

US Army Command and General Staff College. Catalog, academic year 1983–84, AP.

US Military Academy pamphlet, "Alexander Ramsey Nininger, Jr. 1918–1942," West Point, New York, September 1986, AP.

USFIP. Ammunition Report, Extract, ending 2 April 1942, MC, Box 9.

———. Field Order #14, 8 Apr 42, MC, Box 12.

———. G3 Journal, 19 Mar–19 Apr 1942, MC, Box 13.

———. G4 Journal, 14 Jan–8 Apr 1942, MC, Box 9.

———. General Orders #42 [sic], 14 Mar 42; #1, 21 Mar; #19, 8 Apr; and #20, 9 Apr 42, MC, Box 13.

———. Special Orders #11, 2 Apr 42; #12, 3 Apr; #13, 4 Apr; and #16, 7 Apr, MC, Box 13.

———. Letter, USFIP G4 to G4, Luzon Force, 8 April 1942, Subject: Shipment of Motor Fuel, MC.

Uzelac, George. Letters to author, AP.

V

VanAlstyne, Harold E. Clearwater, Florida. Interview, 9 May 1975, AP.

Vance, Lee C. "Account of Action at Layac," in Selleck, "Notes 71 Div," AP.

———. Letters to author, AP.

———. Letter to Major General Orlando Ward, 18 December 1951, MC, Box 12.

Van Oosten, Adrianus J. "The Operations of the 1st Battalion, 45th Infantry (PS)(Philippine Division) in the Battle of the Tuol Pocket,

Bataan, 29 January–19 February 1942 (Philippine Island Campaign)(Personal Experience of a Battalion Executive Officer)," monograph written for Infantry Officer Advance Course #2, 1947–1948, TISL, 513.

———. "History of First Battalion, 45th Inf. (PS)," in Chunn, "Notebook," MC, Box 2.

———. "Tuol River Pocket," sent to Van Oosten by Chunn 13 October 1947, written by Van Oosten at Cabanatuan, MC, Box 13.

———. Letters to author, 19 June 1975, AP.

———. Denver, Colorado. Interview, 8 December 1974, AP.

Velasco, Melanio. Letter to The Adjutant General, Subject: Operations of the 21st Infantry Regiment, 21st Division, USAFFE, 7 December 1941–9 April 1942, 30 December 1945, MC, Box 17.

Villamor, Jesus A. West Hyattsville, Maryland. Interview, 29 July 1963, by William M. Belote during research for *Corregidor: The Saga of a Fortress,* Belote Collection, USAMHI.

Vogler, Robert J. Jr. Letters and tapes to author, AP.

Volckmann, Russell W. "Colonel Russell William Volckmann," MC, Box 17.

———. "Report of Combat and Guerrilla Activities in the Philippines (Rough Draft)," MC.

———. *We Remained: Three Years Behind the Enemy Lines in the Philippines.* New York: W. W. Norton & Company, Inc., 1954.

W

Wade, Floyd R. Letters and tapes to author, AP.

Wade, Gerald. Letters to author, AP.

Waeda, Masami. "Interrogations of Japanese Officials on World War II," vol. 1.

Wainwright, Jonathan M. Memorandum to MacArthur, 27 January 1942, cited in Beck, *MacArthur and Wainwright.*

———. Robert Considine, ed. *General Wainwright's Story: The Account of Four Years of Humiliating Defeat, Surrender, and Captivity.* New York: Modern Literary Editions Publishing Company, 1945.

———. Report of Operations of USAFFE and USFIP in the Philippine Islands, 1941–1942, with eighteen annexes: Data for USAFFE-USFIP from reports rendered by the separate force cdrs after the war; official notes & extracts taken from the G-3 journals which were forwarded from the Phil while the campaign was still in progress; notes made by officers assembled at Ft. Sam Houston, Texas by War Department orders to draw up the historical report of the Phil Cam, CARL.

I USAFFE Staff.

II Data Sheet: Showing Plan of mobilization of Philippine Army units and units expected to arrive from the states.

III HPD Staff

IV Report of Operations of North Luzon Force and I Philippine Corps in the Defense of Luzon and Bataan, 8 December 1941–9 April 1942.

V Report of Operations of South Luzon Force, Bataan Defense Force and II Philippine Corps in the Defense of South Luzon and Bataan from 8 December 1941–9 April 1942, with two appendices, Appendix No. 1, Citations, one page, and Appendix No. 2, Operations of the South Luzon Force from 24 Dec 41 to 1 Jan 42 Both Dates Inclusive (by Brigadier A.M. Jones, Commanding), 26 pages.

VI Report of Operations of Luzon Force, 22 [sic] March–9 April 1942, with Report of Operations of Luzon Force, March 12, 1942–April 9, 1942, eight pages by E. P. King, with five annexes, Annex Number One, Map; Annex Number Two, Report of G-1, three pages, Floyd Marshall; Annex Number Three, Report of G-2, three pages, Frank L. Holland; Annex Number Four, Report of G-3, two pages, J. W. Collier; and Annex Number Five, Report of G-4, three pages, Roy C. Hilton.

VII USFIP Staff

VIII Report of Philippine Coast Artillery Command and the Harbor Defenses of Manila and Subic Bays, 14 February 1941–6 May 1942.

IX Report of Operations of Provisional Coast Artillery Brigade in the Philippine Campaign.

X Report of Operations of the Provisional Tank Group, 1941–1942.

XI Report of Operations of the Visayan-Mindanao Force.

XII Report of Operations of the Philippine Division.

XIII Report of Operations Quartermaster Corps, United States Army in the Philippine Campaign, 1941–1942.

XIV Medical Report.

XV Finance Report.

XVI Data showing Units of U.S. Forces stationed in the Philippines on 7 December 1941.

XVII Report of Operations, Signal Corps, United States Army, 8 December 1941–6 May 1942, in four phases.

XVIII Citations.

———. Comment on note of G4 to Chief of Staff, 6 April 1942, MC.

———. War Department, Public Information Office Biography, Jonathan Mayhew Wainwright, MC, Box 9.

Walk, Earl F. Letters to author, AP.

Wansack, John. Letters and tapes to author, AP.

War Department General Order #11, 5 March 1942; and #14, 9 March 1942, MC, Box 9.

———. Intelligence Bulletin, October 1942, September 1942, and January 1943. Military Intelligence Service, War Department, Washington, D.C.

Waterous, Walter H. *Reminiscences of Dr. W. H. Waterous Pertinent to World War II in the Philippines.* Philippine Islands: By the author, 1953.

———. Statement of Experiences and Observations Concerning the Bataan Campaign and Subsequent Imprisonment, MC.

Weaver, James R. N. Comments of Draft Manuscript Fall of the Philippines, MC, Box 1.

———. Letter, —November 1949, "The Provisional Tank Group, United States Army Forces in the Far East (41–42)–Specific Information Requested from Armored School," MC, Box 12.

———. Memo to COL Selleck, 2-1-43, Subject: Actions Provisional Tank Group, USAFFE, in connection with the Lyac [sic] Delaying Position, in Selleck, "Notes 71 Div," MC, Box 12.

———. "Operations of the Provisional Tank Group United States Army Forces in the Far East," MC, Box 12.

———. War Department, Public Information Office Biography, James Ray Newman Weaver, MC, Box 9.

Webb, William E. "The Operations of the 41st Infantry Regiment (Philippine Army) of the 41st Infantry Division in the Defense of the Abucay Line, Bataan, Philippine Islands, 10–18 January 1942 (Philippine Campaign)(Personal Experience of an American Instructor with the Philippine Army)," monograph written for Infantry Officer Advance Course #2, 1949–1950, TISL, 513.

Weikel, Ivan W. Letters to author, AP.

Weinstein, Alfred A. *Barbed Wire Surgeon.* New York: Lancer Book Inc., This edition published by agreement with the Macmillan Company, 1947.

Weissblatt, Franz. Statement re COL H. C. Fowler, MC, Box 16.

Weitzner, Daniel N. Letters and tapes to author, AP.

Wernitznig, Edward R. Diary, USAAC, 999-2-32.

Wetherby, Loren A. "The Mabatang-Abucay Fight of the 41st Inf (PA) Jan 8th 1942 to Jan 30th 1942," in Fortier, "Notes on 41st Div," MC.

———. "Operations of 41st Inf PA fr 2 Apr 42 to 10 Apr 42," dated 29 May 1942, in Fortier, "Notes on 41st Div," MC.

———. "Actions of 41st Inf fr Jan 28 1942–April-1942," in Fortier, "Notes on 41st Div," MC, Box 3.

———. Letter to Louis Morton, 22 May 1951, with "Activities of 41st Infantry, Philippine Army 1 to 9 April 1942," MC, Box 17.

———. Letter to Louis Morton, 23 October 1950, MC, Box 12.

———. Letter to Orlando Ward, 4 March 1952, MC, Box 1.

Wheeler, John. "Rearguard in Luzon," *The Cavalry Journal* vol. LII, no. 2 (March–April 1943).

Whisenant, Jackson. Letters to author, AP.

Whitcomb, Edgar D. *Escape from Corregidor.* Chicago: Henry Regnery Company, 1958.

White, Jesse K. Letters to author, AP.

White, Mondell. Letters and tapes to author, AP.

White, W. L. *They Were Expendable.* New York: Harcourt, Brace & Company, 1942.

Whitehead, Arthur K. "Mounted Attack In West Bataan-1942," *The Cavalry Journal* vol. LIV, no. 1 (January–February, 1945).

Whitman, John W. "US Army Doctrinal Effectiveness on Bataan, 1942: The First Battle," Master of Military Art and Science, a thesis presented to the faculty of the U.S. Army Command and General Staff College, Fort Leavenworth, Kansas, 1984, CARL.

Whitney, Courtney. *MacArthur: His Rendezvous With History.* New York: Alfred A. Knopf, 1956.

Wildish, Myron F. Letters and tapes to author, AP.

Williamson, Lee B. Letters to author, AP.

Willoughby, Charles A. Papers, MC.

G-2 Estimates and Information in SWPA Dec 41–Jan 46.

Aid The Philippines, Dec 41–Feb 42.

G-2 Information Bulletins 24 Dec 41–9 Mar 42.

Press Releases 2 Feb–10 Mar.

———. Letter to Major General Orlando Ward, 17 May 1951, MC, Box 14.

———. "G2 Estimate, February 3rd 1942 to February 5th 1942."

———. Memorandum for G3 USAFFE 2 Jan 41 [sic], G2 Estimate of the Enemy Situation, MC.

Wills, D. H. Letters and tapes to author, AP.

Wilmeth, James D. Letters to author, AP.

Winslow, Henry S. Letters to author, AP.

Wohlfeld, Mark. Papers, The Mark Wohlfeld Collection, USAMHI.

———. "Addendum 'Two-Seven! Here We Go,'" 12 September 1977, Wohlfeld Collection, USAMHI.

———. Letters to author, AP.

Wolf, Silas C. Letters to author, AP.

Wood, Stewart. Letter to Louis Morton, 23 March 1948, MC, Box 1.

———. Staff Study. Subject: Use of U.S. Submarines to Transport Vital Supplies From Cebu City, P.I., to Corregidor through the Japanese Naval Blockade of Manila Bay, 20 March 1942, MC, Box 9.

Workman, Grant. Letters to author, AP.

Wright, William R. Letters to author, AP.

Wynn, William W. Letters to author, AP.

———. Clearwater, Florida. Interview, 8 May 1975, AP.

XYZ

Yoshida, Motoshiko. Comments in "Statements," vol. IV.

Index